ACCOUNT CLASSIFICATION AND PRESENTATION

Account Title	Classification	Financial Statement	Normal Balance
A			
Accounts Payable	Current Liability	Balance Sheet	Credit
Accounts Receivable	Current Asset	Balance Sheet	Debit
Accumulated Depreciation—Buildings	Plant Asset—Contra	Balance Sheet	Credit
Accumulated Depreciation—Equipment	Plant Asset—Contra	Balance Sheet	Credit
Administrative Expenses	Operating Expense	Income Statement	Debit
Allowance for Doubtful Accounts	Current Asset—Contra	Balance Sheet	Credit
Amortization Expense	Operating Expense	Income Statement	Debit
B			
Bad Debt Expense	Operating Expense	Income Statement	Debit
Bonds Payable	Long-Term Liability	Balance Sheet	Credit
Buildings	Plant Assets	Balance Sheet	Debit
C			
Cash	Current Asset	Balance Sheet	Debit
Common Stock	Stockholder's Equity	Balance Sheet	Credit
Copyrights	Intangible Asset	Balance Sheet	Debit
Cost of Goods Sold	Cost of Goods Sold	Income Statement	Debit
D			
Debt Investments	Current Asset/ Long-Term Investment	Balance Sheet	Debit
Depreciation Expense	Operating Expense	Income Statement	Debit
Discount on Bonds Payable	Long-Term Liability—Contra	Balance Sheet	Debit
Dividend Revenue	Other Income	Income Statement	Credit
Dividends	Temporary account closed to Retained Earnings	Retained Earnings Statement	Debit
Dividends Payable	Current Liability	Balance Sheet	Credit
E			
Equipment	Plant Asset	Balance Sheet	Debit
F			
Freight-Out	Operating Expense	Income Statement	Debit
G			
Gain on Disposal of Plant Assets	Other Income	Income Statement	Credit
Goodwill	Intangible Asset	Balance Sheet	Debit
I			
Income Summary	Temporary account closed to Retained Earnings	Not Applicable	(1)
Income Tax Expense	Income Tax Expense	Income Statement	Debit
Income Taxes Payable	Current Liability	Balance Sheet	Credit
Insurance Expense	Operating Expense	Income Statement	Debit
Interest Expense	Other Expense	Income Statement	Debit
Interest Payable	Current Liability	Balance Sheet	Credit
Interest Receivable	Current Asset	Balance Sheet	Debit
Interest Revenue	Other Income	Income Statement	Credit
Inventory	Current Asset	Balance Sheet (2)	Debit

Account Title	Classification	Financial Statement	Normal Balance
L			
Land	Plant Asset	Balance Sheet	Debit
Loss on Disposal of Plant Assets	Other Expense	Income Statement	Debit
M			
Maintenance and Repairs Expense	Operating Expense	Income Statement	Debit
Mortgage Payable	Long-Term Liability	Balance Sheet	Credit
N			
Notes Payable	Current Liability/ Long-Term Liability	Balance Sheet	Credit
P			
Patents	Intangible Asset	Balance Sheet	Debit
Paid-in Capital in Excess of Par Value—Common Stock	Stockholders' Equity	Balance Sheet	Credit
Paid-in Capital in Excess of Par Value—Preferred Stock	Stockholders' Equity	Balance Sheet	Credit
Preferred Stock	Stockholders' Equity	Balance Sheet	Credit
Premium on Bonds Payable	Long-Term Liability—Contra	Balance Sheet	Credit
Prepaid Insurance	Current Asset	Balance Sheet	Debit
Prepaid Rent	Current Asset	Balance Sheet	Debit
R			
Rent Expense	Operating Expense	Income Statement	Debit
Retained Earnings	Stockholders' Equity	Balance Sheet and Retained Earnings Statement	Credit
S			
Salaries and Wages Expense	Operating Expense	Income Statement	Debit
Salaries and Wages Payable	Current Liability	Balance Sheet	Credit
Sales Discounts	Revenue—Contra	Income Statement	Debit
Sales Returns and Allowances	Revenue—Contra	Income Statement	Debit
Sales Revenue	Revenue	Income Statement	Credit
Selling Expenses	Operating Expense	Income Statement	Debit
Service Revenue	Revenue	Income Statement	Credit
Stock Investments	Current Asset/Long-Term Investment	Balance Sheet	Debit
Supplies	Current Asset	Balance Sheet	Debit
Supplies Expense	Operating Expense	Income Statement	Debit
T			
Treasury Stock	Stockholders' Equity	Balance Sheet	Debit
U			
Unearned Service Revenue	Current Liability	Balance Sheet	Credit
Utilities Expense	Operating Expense	Income Statement	Debit

(1) The normal balance for Income Summary will be credit when there is a net income, debit when there is a net loss. The Income Summary account does not appear on any financial statement.

(2) If a periodic system is used, Inventory also appears on the income statement in the calculation of cost of goods sold.

The following is a sample chart of accounts. It does not represent a comprehensive chart of all the accounts used in this textbook but rather those accounts that are commonly used. This sample chart of accounts is for a company that generates both service revenue as well as sales revenue. It uses the perpetual approach to inventory. If a periodic system was used, the following temporary accounts would be needed to record inventory purchases: Purchases; Freight-in; Purchase Returns and Allowances; and Purchase Discounts.

CHART OF ACCOUNTS

Assets	Liabilities	Stockholders' Equity	Revenues	Expenses
Cash	Notes Payable	Common Stock	Service Revenue	Administrative Expenses
Accounts Receivable	Accounts Payable	Paid-in Capital in Excess of Par Value—Common Stock	Sales Revenue	Amortization Expense
Allowance for Doubtful Accounts	Unearned Service Revenue		Sales Discounts	Bad Debt Expense
	Salaries and Wages Payable	Preferred Stock	Sales Returns and Allowances	Cost of Goods Sold
Interest Receivable	Interest Payable	Paid-in Capital in Excess of Par Value—Preferred Stock	Interest Revenue	Depreciation Expense
Inventory	Dividends Payable		Gain on Disposal of Plant Assets	Freight-Out
Supplies	Income Taxes Payable	Treasury Stock		Income Tax Expense
Prepaid Insurance		Retained Earnings		
	Bonds Payable			Insurance Expense
Prepaid Rent		Dividends		Interest Expense
Land	Discount on Bonds Payable	Income Summary		
Equipment	Premium on Bonds Payable			Loss on Disposal of Plant Assets
Accumulated Depreciation—Equipment	Mortgage Payable			Maintenance and Repairs Expense
Buildings				Rent Expense
Accumulated Depreciation—Buildings				Salaries and Wages Expense
Copyrights				Selling Expenses
Goodwill				Supplies Expense
Patents				Utilities Expense

FINANCIAL ACCOUNTING 7e

Tools for Business Decision Making

International Student Version

WILEY

Paul D. Kimmel PhD, CPA
University of Wisconsin—Milwaukee
Milwaukee, Wisconsin

Jerry J. Weygandt PhD, CPA
University of Wisconsin—Madison
Madison, Wisconsin

Donald E. Kieso PhD, CPA
Northern Illinois University
DeKalb, Illinois

Dedicated to
*the **Wiley sales representatives***
who sell our books and service
our adopters in a professional
and ethical manner, and to
Enid, Merlynn, and Donna

Author Commitment

Jerry Weygandt

Jerry J. Weygandt, PhD, CPA, is Arthur Andersen Alumni Emeritus Professor of Accounting at the University of Wisconsin—Madison. He holds a Ph.D. in accounting from the University of Illinois. Articles by Professor Weygandt have appeared in the *Accounting Review*, *Journal of Accounting Research*, *Accounting Horizons*, *Journal of Accountancy*, and other academic and professional journals. These articles have examined such financial reporting issues as accounting for price-level adjustments, pensions, convertible securities, stock option contracts, and interim reports. Professor Weygandt is author of other accounting and financial reporting books and is a member of the American Accounting Association, the American Institute of Certified Public Accountants, and the Wisconsin Society of Certified Public Accountants. He has served on numerous committees of the American Accounting Association and as a member of the editorial board of the Accounting Review; he also has served as President and Secretary-Treasurer of the American Accounting Association. In addition, he has been actively involved with the American Institute of Certified Public Accountants and has been a member of the Accounting Standards Executive Committee (AcSEC) of that organization. He has served on the FASB task force that examined the reporting issues related to accounting for income taxes and served as a trustee of the Financial Accounting Foundation. Professor Weygandt has received the Chancellor's Award for Excellence in Teaching and the Beta Gamma Sigma Dean's Teaching Award. He is on the board of directors of M & I Bank of Southern Wisconsin. He is the recipient of the Wisconsin Institute of CPA's Outstanding Educator's Award and the Lifetime Achievement Award. In 2001 he received the American Accounting Association's Outstanding Educator Award.

Paul Kimmel

Paul D. Kimmel, PhD, CPA, received his bachelor's degree from the University of Minnesota and his doctorate in accounting from the University of Wisconsin. He is an Associate Professor at the University of Wisconsin—Milwaukee, and has public accounting experience with Deloitte & Touche (Minneapolis). He was the recipient of the UWM School of Business Advisory Council Teaching Award, the Reggie Taite Excellence in Teaching Award and a three-time winner of the Outstanding Teaching Assistant Award at the University of Wisconsin. He is also a recipient of the Elijah Watts Sells Award for Honorary Distinction for his results on the CPA exam. He is a member of the American Accounting Association and the Institute of Management Accountants and has published articles in *Accounting Review*, *Accounting Horizons*, *Advances in Management Accounting*, *Managerial Finance*, *Issues in Accounting Education*, *Journal of Accounting Education*, as well as other journals. His research interests include accounting for financial instruments and innovation in accounting education. He has published papers and given numerous talks on incorporating critical thinking into accounting education, and helped prepare a catalog of critical thinking resources for the Federated Schools of Accountancy.

Don Kieso

Donald E. Kieso, PhD, CPA, received his bachelor's degree from Aurora University and his doctorate in accounting from the University of Illinois. He has served as chairman of the Department of Accountancy and is currently the KPMG Emeritus Professor of Accountancy at Northern Illinois University. He has public accounting experience with Price Waterhouse & Co. (San Francisco and Chicago) and Arthur Andersen & Co. (Chicago) and research experience with the Research Division of the American Institute of Certified Public Accountants (New York). He has done post doctorate work as a Visiting Scholar at the University of California at Berkeley and is a recipient of NIU's Teaching Excellence Award and four Golden Apple Teaching Awards. Professor Kieso is the author of other accounting and business books and is a member of the American Accounting Association, the American Institute of Certified Public Accountants, and the Illinois CPA Society. He has served as a member of the Board of Directors of the Illinois CPA Society, then AACSB's Accounting Accreditation Committees, the State of Illinois Comptroller's Commission, as Secretary-Treasurer of the Federation of Schools of Accountancy, and as Secretary-Treasurer of the American Accounting Association. Professor Kieso is currently serving on the Board of Trustees and Executive Committee of Aurora University, as a member of the Board of Directors of Kishwaukee Community Hospital, and as Treasurer and Director of Valley West Community Hospital. From 1989 to 1993 he served as a charter member of the national Accounting Education Change Commission. He is the recipient of the Outstanding Accounting Educator Award from the Illinois CPA Society, the FSA's Joseph A. Silvoso Award of Merit, the NIU Foundation's Humanitarian Award for Service to Higher Education, a Distinguished Service Award from the Illinois CPA Society, and in 2003 an honorary doctorate from Aurora University.

What's New?

The Seventh Edition expands our emphasis on student learning and improves upon a teaching and learning package that instructors and students have rated the highest in customer satisfaction in the following ways:

Continued Emphasis on Helping Students Learn Accounting Concepts

Especially with this edition of the textbook, we have carefully scrutinized all chapter material to help students learn accounting concepts. We revised existing explanations and illustrations as well as added more explanations, examples, and illustrations. For example, we have added T-accounts in the margin to illustrate the effect of accounting procedures as well as discussed how tight credit policies nearly prevented Apple from fulfilling its first sale.

Corporate Social Responsibility

Today's companies are evaluating not just their profitability but also their corporate social responsibility. In this edition, we have profiled some of these companies in the new People, Planet, and Profit Insight boxes, such as PepsiCo, to highlight their sustainable business practices. We have also added a new *Broadening Your Perspective* problem, Considering People, Planet, and Profit, which offers students the opportunity to analyze current business practices.

Student-Friendly Companies

One of the goals of the financial accounting course is to orient students to the application of accounting principles and techniques in practice. Accordingly, we have expanded our practice of using numerous examples from real companies throughout the textbook to add more high-interest enterprises that we hope will increase student engagement, such as Clif Bar, Groupon, REI, and Skechers.

Enhanced Homework Material

In each chapter, we have updated Self-Test Questions, Questions, Brief Exercises, Do it! Review, Exercises, Problems, and Research Cases. Financial analysis and reporting problems have been updated in accordance with the new Tootsie Roll and Hershey financial statements. Finally, new Considering People, Planet, and Profit problems are included to offer students experience in evaluating corporate social responsibility.

Comprehensive Revision

This edition was also subject to an overall, comprehensive revision to ensure that it is technically accurate, relevant, and up-to-date. A chapter-by-chapter summary of content changes is provided in the chart on the next two pages.

Content Changes by Chapter

Chapter 1: Introduction to Financial Statements
- New Feature Story, on Clif Bar and its ESOP and open-book management program.
- New discussion of LLCs and S corporations, to reflect more current business practices.
- New People, Planet, and Profit Insight, on evaluating companies on social practices as well as on financial results.
- New Research Case on possible expanding role of auditors.

Chapter 2: A Further Look at Financial Statements
- Updated to reflect new conceptual framework terminology.

Chapter 3: The Accounting Information System
- Heavily revised Feature Story, now on MF Global's failure to segregate company accounts from customer accounts.
- New Ethics Insight, on Credit Suisse Group's failure to properly write down value of its securities.
- New Research Case based on Green Bay Packers' annual report publication.

Chapter 4: Accrual Accounting Concepts
- New Feature Story, on Groupon and complexity of accounting for its revenues.
- New People, Planet, and Profit Insight, on costs of disposing discarded, possibly toxic, materials.

Chapter 5: Merchandising Operations and the Multiple-Step Income Statement
- New Feature Story, on REI and its unique business model.
- New use of recent REI and Dick's Sporting Goods financial statement information.
- Revised Ethics Insight box on improving company clarity of financial disclosures by citing recent eBay's sale of Skype.
- New People, Planet, and Profit Insight, about whether PepsiCo should market green.

Chapter 6: Reporting and Analyzing Inventory
- Added new illustration, to show increase of inventory levels during a recession.
- Revised the Accounting Across the Organization box on JIT inventory, to illustrate how common events like snowstorms can seriously disrupt inventory levels.
- Added new Accounting Across the Organization box, on Sony's inventory management practices.
- New Research Case, on U.S. companies use of LIFO.
- New Considering People, Planet, and Profit Insight, about Caterpillar's annual Sustainability Report.

Chapter 7: Fraud, Internal Control, and Cash
- New People, Planet and Profit Insight, about the need for an effective system of internal controls for sustainability reporting.
- Updated chapter throughout to include use of more recent technology, such as point-of-sale terminals instead of cash registers.
- New Interpreting Financial Statements problem, based on recent Ernst & Young global survey on fraud.

Chapter 8: Reporting and Analyzing Receivables
- New Feature Story, about Nike, its products, and its receivables management.
- Featured companies in chapter are now Nike and Skechers, to increase student engagement.
- Two new illustrations, showing real-company note disclosures about receivables management.
- New example of Apple's first sale, to demonstrate importance of extending credit.
- In "Accelerating Cash Receipts" section, now discuss sale of receivables to a factor before national credit card sales.

Chapter 9: Reporting and Analyzing Long-Lived Assets
- Revised Feature Story and in-chapter examples, to focus on JetBlue as well as include more recent information about the airline industry.

- Added numerous real-world examples, to increase student engagement and understanding.
- New People, Planet, and Profit Insight, about Billiton's sustainability report.
- New Research Cases, about goodwill and Best Buy's profitability.

Chapter 10: Reporting and Analyzing Liabilities
- Expanded EOC material: 2 new Questions, 3 new Brief Exercises, 2 new Exercises, new Real-World Focus problem, new Interpreting Financial Statements problem, new Considering People, Planet, and Profit problem, and new All About You problem.

Chapter 11: Reporting and Analyzing Stockholders' Equity
- New Feature Story, about why Mark Zuckerberg delayed taking Facebook public.
- Used Facebook as example company throughout chapter to increase student engagement.
- New People, Planet, and Profit Insight, about rising level of support for shareholder proposals requesting action related to social and environmental issues.
- New Accounting Across the Organization, about how the recent financial crisis affected companies' dividend payouts.

- New Research Case, new Considering People, Planet, and Profit problem, and new IFRS Concepts and Application problem.

Chapter 12: Statement of Cash Flows
- Revamped Feature Story, to include more recent information about Apple's cash flow status.
- New Accounting Across the Organization box, about Kodak's need to sell plant assets to raise cash.
- New Investor Insight, about how 42% of companies going public had audit opinions warning about the companies' risk of failure.
- New Research Case.

Chapter 13: Financial Analysis: The Big Picture
- Revised Feature Story, to include more recent information about Warren Buffett as well as to improve readability.
- New Investor Insight, about how recently some companies have altered their pension-plan accounting to avoid prior-year events to distort current-year results.
- New Do it! box on ratio analysis.
- New Do it! Review question and Research Case.

Active Teaching and Learning Supplementary Material

For Instructors

In addition to the support instructors receive from *WileyPLUS* and the Wiley Faculty Network, we offer the following useful supplements.

Textbook Companion Website. On this website, instructors will find the Solutions Manual, Test Bank, Instructor's Manual, Computerized Test Bank, and other resources.

Solutions Manual. The Solutions Manual contains detailed solutions to all questions, brief exercises, exercises, and problems in the textbook, as well as suggested answers to the questions and cases. The estimated time to complete exercises, problems, and cases is provided.

Instructor's Manual. Included in each chapter are lecture outlines with teaching tips, chapter reviews, and review quizzes.

Test Bank and Computerized Test Bank. The test bank and computerized test bank allow instructors to tailor examinations according to study objectives and learning outcomes, including AACSB, AICPA, and IMA professional standards. Achievement tests, comprehensive examinations, and a final exam are included.

PowerPoint™. The PowerPoint™ presentations contain a combination of key concepts, images, and problems from the textbook. They are a useful, animated tool for classroom lectures.

For Students

Textbook Companion Website. On this website, students will find support materials that will help them develop their conceptual understanding of class material and increase their ability to solve problems. In addition to other resources, students will find:

- *Challenge Exercises*
- *Problems: Set B*
- *Continuing Cookie Chronicle Problem*
- *Do it!*

Study Guide. A useful tool for review, the Study Guide provides an opportunity for practice through problems and multiple-choice exercises. Demonstration problems, multiple-choice questions, true/false, matching, and other exercises are also included.

Working Papers. The working papers are partially completed accounting forms (templates) that can help students correctly format their textbook accounting solutions. Working paper templates are available for all end-of-chapter brief exercises, exercises, problems, and cases. Excel working papers are available in *WileyPLUS*.

Excel Primer: Using Excel in Accounting. The online Excel primer and accompanying Excel templates allow students to complete select end-of-chapter exercises and problems identified by a spreadsheet icon in the margin of the textbook.

Mobile Applications. Quizzing and reviewing content is available for download on iTunes.

Quantum Tutors. Adaptive learning and assessment software that will help students master the core accounting topics and skills necessary to be successful in this course. Rated as "most helpful" by students, Quantum Tutors is proven to accelerate learning and increase test scores.

Acknowledgments

Financial Accounting has benefitted greatly from the input of focus group participants, manuscript reviewers, those who have sent comments by letter or e-mail, ancillary authors, and proofers. We greatly appreciate the constructive suggestions and innovative ideas of reviewers and the creativity and accuracy of the ancillary authors and checkers.

Prior Editions

Thanks to the following reviewers and focus group participants of prior editions of Financial Accounting:

Dawn Addington, *Central New Mexico Community College;* Gilda Agacer, *Monmouth University;* Solochidi Ahiarah, *Buffalo State College;* C. Richard Aldridge, *Western Kentucky University;* Sylvia Allen, *Los Angeles Valley College;* Sheila Ammons, *Austin Community College;* Juanita Ardavany, *Los Angeles Valley College;* Thomas G. Amyot, *College of Santa Rose;* Brian Baick, *Montgomery College;* Cheryl Bartlett, *Central New Mexico Community College;* Timothy Baker, *California State University—Fresno;* and Benjamin Bean, *Utah Valley State College.*

Victoria Beard, *University of North Dakota;* Angela H. Bell, *Jacksonville State University;* Charles Bokemeier, *Michigan State University;* John A. Booker, *Tennessee Technological University;* Robert L. Braun, *Southeastern Louisiana University;* Daniel Brickner, *Eastern Michigan University;* Evangelie Brodie, *North Carolina State University;* Sarah Ruth Brown, *University of North Alabama;* Charles Bunn, *Wake Technical Community College;* Thane Butt, *Champlain College;* James Byrne, *Oregon State University;* and Sandra Byrd, *Missouri State University.*

Judy Cadle, *Tarleton State University;* Julia Camp, *University of Massachusetts—Boston;* David Carr, *Austin Community College;* Jack Cathey, *University of North Carolina—Charlotte;* Andy Chen, *Northeast Illinois University;* Jim Christianson, *Austin Community College;* Siu Chung, *Los Angeles Valley College;* Laura Claus, *Louisiana State University;* Leslie A. Cohen, *University of Arizona;* Teresa L. Conover, *University of North Texas;* Rita Kingery Cook, *University of Delaware;* Samantha Cox, *Wake Technical Community College;* Janet Courts, *San Bernardino Valley College;* Cheryl Crespi, *Central Connecticut State University;* Sue Counte, *St. Louis Community College—Meramec;* Dori Danko, *Grand Valley State University;* Brent W. Darwin, *Allan Hancock College;* Helen Davis, *Johnson and Wales University;* Michael Deschamps, *Mira Costa College;* Cheryl Dickerson, *Western Washington University;* Gadis Dillon, *Oakland University;* George M. Dow, *Valencia Community College—West;* Kathy J. Dow, *Salem State College;* and Lola Dudley, *Eastern Illinois University.*

Mary Emery, *St. Olaf College;* Martin L. Epstein, *Central New Mexico Community College;* Larry R. Falcetto, *Emporia State University;* Alan Falcon, *Loyola Marymount University;* Scott Fargason, *Louisiana State University;* Janet Farler, *Pima Community College;* Lance Fisher, *Oklahoma State University;* Sheila D. Foster, *The Citadel;* Jessica J. Frazier, *Eastern Kentucky University;* Roger Gee, *San Diego Mesa College;* Lisa Gillespie, *Loyola University—Chicago;* Norman H. Godwin, *Auburn University;* David Gotlob, *Indiana University—Purdue University—Fort Wayne;* Lisa Gray, *Seminole State College and Valencia Community College;* Emmett Griner, *Georgia State University;* Leon J. Hanouille, *Syracuse University;* Hassan Hefzi, *California State PolyTech University—Pomona;* Kenneth M. Hiltebeitel, *Villanova University;* Harry Hooper, *Santa Fe Community College;* Judith A. Hora, *University of San Diego;* Carol Olson Houston, *San Diego State University;* Ryan Huldah, *Iona College;* and Sam Isley, *Wake Technical Community College.*

Norma Jacobs, *Austin Community College;* Marianne L. James, *California State University—Los Angeles;* Stanley Jenne, *University of Montana;* Christopher Jones, *George Washington University;* Jane Kaplan, *Drexel University;* John E. Karayan, *California State University—Pomona;* Susan Kattelus, *Eastern Michigan University;* Ann Kelly, *Providence College;* Dawn Kelly, *Texas Tech University;* Cindi Khanlarian, *University of North Carolina—Greensboro;* Robert Kiddoo, *California State University—Northridge;* Robert J. Kirsch, *Southern Connecticut State University;* Frank Korman, *Mountain View College;* and Jerry G. Kreuze, *Western Michigan University.*

John Lacey, *California State University—Long Beach;* Doug Laufer, *Metropolitan State College of Denver;* Doulas Larson, *Salem State College;* Keith Leeseberg, *Manatee Community College;* Glenda Levendowski, *Arizona State University;* Seth Levine, *DeVry University;* Lihon Liang, *Syracuse University;* James Lukawitz, *University of Memphis;* Noel McKeon, *Florida Community College;* P. Merle Maddocks, *University of Alabama—Huntsville;* Janice Mardon, *Green River Community College;* Sal Marino, *Westchester Community College;* John Marts, *University of North Carolina—Wilmington;* Alan Mayer-Sommer, *Georgetown University;* Noel McKeon, *Florida Community College at Jacksonville;* Sara Melendy, *Gonzaga University;* Barbara Merino, *University of North Texas;* Paul Mihalek, *Central Connecticut State University;* Jeanne Miller, *Cypress College;* Robert Miller, *California State University—Fullerton;* Elizabeth Minbiole, *Northwood University;* Sherry Mirbod, *Montgomery College;* Andrew Morgret, *University of Memphis;* Michelle Moshier, *SUNY Albany;* Marguerite Muise, *Santa Ana College;* William J. Nealon, *Schenectady County Community College;* James Neurath, *Central Michigan University;* Gale E. Newell, *Western Michigan University;* Jim Neurath, *Central Michigan University;* Garth Novack, *Utah State University;* and Rosemary Nurre, *San Mateo Community College.*

Suzanne Ogilby, *Sacramento State University;* Sarah N. Palmer, *University of North Carolina—Charlotte;* Patricia Parker, *Columbus State Community College;* Terry Patton, *Midwestern State University;* Charles Pier, *Appalachian State University;* Ronald Pierno, *Florida State University;* Meg Pollard, *American River College;* Franklin J. Plewa, *Idaho State University;* John Purisky, *Salem State College;* Donald J. Raux, *Siena College;* Ray Reisig, *Pace University, Pleasantville;* Judith Resnick, *Borough of Manhattan Community College;* Mary Ann Reynolds, *Western Washington University;* Carla Rich, *Pensacola Junior College;* Rod Ridenour, *Montana State University—Bozeman;* Ray Rigoli, *Ramapo College of New Jersey;* Larry Rittenberg, *University of Wisconsin;* Jeff Ritter, *St. Norbert College;* Cecile M. Roberti, *Community College of Rhode Island;* Brandi Roberts, *Southeastern Louisiana University;* Patricia A. Robinson, *Johnson and Wales University;* Nancy Rochman, *University of Arizona;* Lawrence Roman, *Cuyahoga Community College;* Marc A. Rubin, *Miami University;* John A. Rude, *Bloomsburg University;* and Robert Russ, *Northern Kentucky University.*

Alfredo Salas, *El Paso Community College;* Christine Schalow, *California State University—San Bernardino;* Michael Schoderbek, *Rutgers University;* Richard Schroeder, *University of North Carolina—Charlotte;* Bill N. Schwartz, *Stevens Institute of Technology;* Jerry Searfoss, *University of Utah;* Cindy Seipel, *New Mexico State University;* Anne E. Selk, *University of Wisconsin—Green Bay;* William Seltz, *University of Massachusetts;* Suzanne Sevalstad, *University of Nevada;* Mary Alice Seville, *Oregon State University;* Donald Smillie, *Southwest Missouri State University;* Aileen Smith, *Stephen F. Austin State University;* Gerald Smith, *University of Northern Iowa;* Talitha Smith, *Auburn University;* Pam Smith, *Northern Illinois University;* William E. Smith, *Xavier University;* Will Snyder, *San Diego State University;* Chris Solomon, *Trident Technical College;* Teresa A. Speck, *St. Mary's University of Minnesota;* Charles Stanley, *Baylor University;* Vic Stanton, *University of California, Berkeley;* Ron Stone, *California State University—Northridge;* Gary Stout, *California State University—Northridge;* Gracelyn Stuart, *Palm Beach Community College;* and Ellen L. Sweatt, *Georgia Perimeter College.*

William Talbot, *Montgomery College;* Diane Tanner, *University of North Florida;* Pamadda Tantral, *Fairleigh Dickinson University;* Steve Teeter, *Utah Valley State College;* Michael Tydlaska, *Mountain View College;* Joan Van Hise, *Fairfield University;* Richard Van Ness, *Schenectady County Community College;* Barbara Warschawski, *Schenectady County Community College;* Andrea B. Weickgenannt, *Northern Kentucky University;* David P. Weiner, *University of San Francisco;* Frederick Weis, *Claremont McKenna College;* T. Sterling Wetzel, *Oklahoma State University;* Wendy Wilson, *Southern Methodist University;* Allan Young, *DeVry University;* Michael F. van Breda, *Texas Christian University;* Linda G. Wade, *Tarleton State University;* Stuart K. Webster, *University of Wyoming;* V. Joyce Yearley, *New Mexico State University;* and Joan Van Hise, *Fairfield University.*

Seventh Edition

Thanks to the following reviewers, focus group participants, and others who provided suggestions for the Seventh Edition:

Duane Brandon	*Auburn University*
Gary Braun	*University of Texas—El Paso*
Jerold K. Braun	*Daytona State College*
Robert Braun	*Southeastern Louisiana University*
Sandra Byrd	*Missouri State University*
Cheryl Corke	*Genesee Community College*
Paquita Davis-Friday	*Baruch College*
Ann Escaro	*McHenry County College*
Hubert Glover	*Drexel University*
Siriyama Kanthi Herath	*Georgia Institute of Technology*
Robert Kenny	*The College of New Jersey*
Marinilka Kimbro	*Gonzaga University*
Joseph Larkin	*Saint Joseph's University*
Nancy Lynch	*West Virginia University*
Florence McGovern	*Bergen Community College*
Kathy Munter	*Pima Community College*
Janice Pitera	*Broome Community College*
Ruthie G. Reynolds	*Howard University*
Pam Smith	*Northern Illinois University*
Naomi Soderstrom	*University of Colorado—Boulder*
Paul Swanson	*Illinois Central College*
Joan Van Hise	*Fairfield University*
Christopher Wallace	*California State University—Sacramento*
Kathryn Yarbrough	*University of North Carolina—Charlotte*
Judith Zander	*Grossmont College*

Advisory Board Participants

Sandra Byrd	*Missouri State University*
Lisa Cappozoli	*College of DuPage*
Marcye Hampton	*University of Central Florida*
Randy Johnston	*University of Colorado—Boulder*
Tony Kurek	*Eastern Michigan University*
Sal Marino	*Westchester Community College*

Ancillary Authors, Contributors, Proofers, and Accuracy Checkers

We sincerely thank the following individuals for their hard work in preparing the content that accompanies this textbook:

LuAnn Bean	*Florida Institute of Technology*
Jack Borke	*University of Wisconsin—Platteville*
Richard Campbell	*University of Rio Grande*
Sandra Cohen	*Columbia College—Chicago*
Terry Elliott	*Morehead State University*
James M. Emig	*Villanova University*
Larry R. Falcetto	*Emporia State University*
Cecelia M. Fewox	*College of Charleston*
Coby Harmon	*University of California, Santa Barbara*
Harry Howe	*State University of New York—Geneseo*
Kirk Lynch	*Sandhills Community College*
Laura McNally	*Black Hills State College*
Kevin McNelis	*New Mexico State University*
Barb Muller	*Arizona State University*
Yvonne Phang	*Borough of Manhattan Community College*
John Plouffe	*California State University—Los Angeles*
Laura Prosser	*Black Hills State University*
Rex Schildhouse	*San Diego Community College*
Eileen M. Shifflett	*James Madison University*
Sheila Viel	*University of Wisconsin—Milwaukee*
Dick D. Wasson	*Southwestern College*
Alice Sineath	*Forsyth Technical Community College*
Teresa Speck	*Saint Mary's University of Minnesota*
Lynn Stallworth	*Appalachian State University*
Andrea Weickgenannt	*Xavier University*
Bernie Weinrich	*Lindenwood University*
Melanie Yon	

We appreciate the exemplary support and commitment given to us by associate publisher Chris DeJohn, marketing manager Karolina Zarychta Honsa, operations manager Yana Mermel, content editor Ed Brislin, development editors Terry Ann Tatro and Margaret Thompson, lead product designer Allie Morris, product designer Greg Chaput, vice president of content management Sesha Bolisetty, senior content editor Dorothy Sinclair, senior production editor Erin Bascom, designers Maureen Eide and Kristine Carney, illustration editor Anna Melhorn, photo editor Mary Ann Price, project editor Jeanine Furino of Furino Production, Denise Showers at Aptara, Cyndy Taylor, project manager Matt Gauthier at Integra, and Katie Trotta at ANSR. All of these professionals provided innumerable services that helped the textbook take shape.

Finally, our thanks to Amy Scholz, Susan Elbe, George Hoffman, Tim Stookesberry, Joe Heider, and Steve Smith for their support and leadership in Wiley's College Division. We will appreciate suggestions and comments from users—instructors and students alike. You can send your thoughts and ideas about the textbook to us via email at **accountingauthors@yahoo.com**.

Paul D. Kimmel
Milwaukee, Wisconsin

Jerry J. Weygandt
Madison, Wisconsin

Donald E. Kieso
DeKalb, Illinois

Contents

Chapter 1

Introduction to Financial Statements 2

Knowing the Numbers 3
Forms of Business Organization 4
Users and Uses of Financial Information 5
  Internal Users 5
  External Users 6
  Ethics in Financial Reporting 7
Business Activities 8
  Financing Activities 9
  Investing Activities 9
  Operating Activities 9
Communicating with Users 10
  Income Statement 11
  Retained Earnings Statement 12
  Balance Sheet 13
  Statement of Cash Flows 14
  Interrelationships of Statements 15
  Other Elements of an Annual Report 17
A Look at IFRS 36

Chapter 2

A Further Look at Financial Statements 40

Just Fooling Around? 41
The Classified Balance Sheet 42
  Current Assets 43
  Long-Term Investments 44
  Property, Plant, and Equipment 45
  Intangible Assets 45
  Current Liabilities 46
  Long-Term Liabilities 46
  Stockholders' Equity 46
Using the Financial Statements 47
  Ratio Analysis 47
  Using the Income Statement 47
  Using the Statement of Stockholders' Equity 49
  Using a Classified Balance Sheet 50
Keeping an Eye on Cash 54
Financial Reporting Concepts 55
  The Standard-Setting Environment 55
  Qualities of Useful Information 56
  Assumptions in Financial Reporting 57
  Principles in Financial Reporting 58
  Cost Constraint 58
A Look at IFRS 78

Chapter 3

The Accounting Information System 82

Accidents Happen 83
The Accounting Information System 84
  Accounting Transactions 84
  Analyzing Transactions 85
  Summary of Transactions 91
The Account 92
  Debits and Credits 93
  Debit and Credit Procedures 93
  Stockholders' Equity Relationships 97
  Summary of Debit/Credit Rules 97
Steps in the Recording Process 98
  The Journal 98
  The Ledger 100
  Chart of Accounts 100
  Posting 101
  The Recording Process Illustrated 101
  Summary Illustration of Journalizing and Posting 108
The Trial Balance 109
  Limitations of a Trial Balance 110
Keeping an Eye on Cash 110
A Look at IFRS 132

Chapter 4

Accrual Accounting Concepts 134

Keeping Track of Groupons 135
Timing Issues 136
  The Revenue Recognition Principle 136
  The Expense Recognition Principle 137
  Accrual versus Cash Basis of Accounting 138
The Basics of Adjusting Entries 139
  Types of Adjusting Entries 140
  Adjusting Entries for Deferrals 141
  Adjusting Entries for Accruals 147
  Summary of Basic Relationships 152
The Adjusted Trial Balance and Financial Statements 154
  Preparing the Adjusted Trial Balance 154
  Preparing Financial Statements 155
  Quality of Earnings 156
Closing the Books 158
  Preparing Closing Entries 158
  Preparing a Post-Closing Trial Balance 159
  Summary of the Accounting Cycle 160

Keeping an Eye on Cash 161
APPENDIX 4A: **Adjusting Entries in an Automated World—Using a Worksheet** 165
A Look at IFRS 187

Chapter 5

Merchandising Operations and the Multiple-Step Income Statement 190

Buy Now, Vote Later 191
Merchandising Operations 192
    Operating Cycles 193
    Flow of Costs 193
Recording Purchases of Merchandise 195
    Freight Costs 196
    Purchase Returns and Allowances 197
    Purchase Discounts 198
    Summary of Purchasing Transactions 199
Recording Sales of Merchandise 199
    Sales Returns and Allowances 200
    Sales Discounts 202
Income Statement Presentation 203
    Sales Revenues 204
    Gross Profit 204
    Operating Expenses 205
    Nonoperating Activities 205
    Determining Cost of Goods Sold Under a Periodic System 206
Evaluating Profitability 208
    Gross Profit Rate 208
    Profit Margin 209
Keeping an Eye on Cash 211
APPENDIX 5A: **Periodic Inventory System 214**
    Recording Merchandise Transactions 214
    Recording Purchases of Merchandise 214
    Freight Costs 214
    Recording Sales of Merchandise 215
    Comparison of Entries—Perpetual vs. Periodic 216
A Look at IFRS 233

Chapter 6

Reporting and Analyzing Inventory 236

"Where Is That Spare Bulldozer Blade?" 237
Classifying and Determining Inventory 238
    Classifying Inventory 238
    Determining Inventory Quantities 240
Inventory Costing 242
    Specific Identification 242
    Cost Flow Assumptions 243
    Financial Statement and Tax Effects of Cost Flow Methods 247

Keeping an Eye on Cash 250
    Using Inventory Cost Flow Methods Consistently 251
    Lower-of-Cost-or-Market 251
Analysis of Inventory 252
    Inventory Turnover 252
    Analysts' Adjustments for LIFO Reserve 254
APPENDIX 6A: **Inventory Cost Flow Methods in Perpetual Inventory Systems 257**
    First-In, First-Out (FIFO) 258
    Last-In, First-Out (LIFO) 258
    Average-Cost 259
APPENDIX 6B: **Inventory Errors 260**
    Income Statement Effects 260
    Balance Sheet Effects 261
A Look at IFRS 279

Chapter 7

Fraud, Internal Control, and Cash 282

Minding the Money in Moose Jaw 283
Fraud and Internal Control 284
    Fraud 284
    The Sarbanes-Oxley Act 285
    Internal Control 285
    Principles of Internal Control Activities 286
    Limitations of Internal Control 293
Cash Controls 294
    Cash Receipts Controls 294
    Cash Disbursements Controls 297
Control Features: Use of a Bank 299
    Bank Statements 300
    Reconciling the Bank Account 301
Reporting Cash 306
    Cash Equivalents 306
    Restricted Cash 306
Managing and Monitoring Cash 307
    Basic Principles of Cash Management 308
Keeping an Eye on Cash 309
APPENDIX 7A: **Operation of the Petty Cash Fund 314**
    Establishing the Petty Cash Fund 314
    Making Payments from Petty Cash 314
    Replenishing the Petty Cash Fund 314
A Look at IFRS 334

Chapter 8

Reporting and Analyzing Receivables 338

What's Cooking? 339
Types of Receivables 340
Accounts Receivable 341
    Recognizing Accounts Receivable 341
    Valuing Accounts Receivable 342

Notes Receivable 349
    Determining the Maturity Date 350
    Computing Interest 350
    Recognizing Notes Receivable 350
    Valuing Notes Receivable 351
    Disposing of Notes Receivable 351
**Financial Statement Presentation
of Receivables 353**
Managing Receivables 353
    Extending Credit 354
    Establishing a Payment Period 355
    Monitoring Collections 355
    Evaluating Liquidity of Receivables 356
    Accelerating Cash Receipts 358
Keeping an Eye on Cash 361
A Look at IFRS 379

Chapter 9

Reporting and Analyzing Long-Lived Assets 382

A Tale of Two Airlines 383
Plant Assets 384
    Determining the Cost of Plant Assets 385
    To Buy or Lease? 388
Accounting for Plant Assets 389
    Depreciation 389
    Factors in Computing Depreciation 390
    Depreciation Methods 390
    Revising Periodic Depreciation 394
    Expenditures During Useful Life 395
    Impairments 396
    Plant Asset Disposals 397
Analyzing Plant Assets 398
    Return on Assets 399
    Asset Turnover 400
    Profit Margin Revisited 400
Intangible Assets 402
    Accounting for Intangible Assets 403
    Types of Intangible Assets 404
**Financial Statement Presentation
of Long-Lived Assets 406**
Keeping an Eye on Cash 407
**APPENDIX 9A: Calculation of Depreciation Using
Other Methods 410**
    Declining-Balance 410
    Units-of-Activity 411
A Look at IFRS 429

Chapter 10

Reporting and Analyzing Liabilities 434

And Then There Were Two 435

Current Liabilities 436
    What Is a Current Liability? 436
    Notes Payable 437
    Sales Taxes Payable 437
    Unearned Revenues 438
    Current Maturities of Long-Term Debt 439
    Payroll and Payroll Taxes Payable 439
Bonds: Long-Term Liabilities 441
    Types of Bonds 442
    Issuing Procedures 442
    Determining the Market Price of Bonds 443
Accounting for Bond Issues 444
    Issuing Bonds at Face Value 444
    Discount or Premium on Bonds 445
    Issuing Bonds at a Discount 446
    Issuing Bonds at a Premium 447
Accounting for Bond Redemptions 449
    Redeeming Bonds at Maturity 449
    Redeeming Bonds before Maturity 449
**Financial Statement Presentation
and Analysis 450**
    Balance Sheet Presentation 450
Keeping an Eye on Cash 450
    Analysis 451
    Off-Balance-Sheet Financing 454
APPENDIX 10A: Straight-Line Amortization 459
    Amortizing Bond Discount 459
    Amortizing Bond Premium 460
APPENDIX 10B: Effective-Interest Amortization 461
    Amortizing Bond Discount 462
    Amortizing Bond Premium 464
**APPENDIX 10C: Accounting for Long-Term
Notes Payable 465**
A Look at IFRS 487

Chapter 11

Reporting and Analyzing Stockholders' Equity 492

Oh Well, I Guess I'll Get Rich 493
The Corporate Form of Organization 494
    Characteristics of a Corporation 495
    Forming a Corporation 498
    Stockholder Rights 498
Stock Issue Considerations 499
    Authorized Stock 500
    Issuance of Stock 500
    Par and No-Par Value Stocks 501
    Accounting for Issues of Common Stock 501
Accounting for Treasury Stock 503
    Purchase of Treasury Stock 503
Preferred Stock 504
    Dividend Preferences 505
    Liquidation Preference 506

Dividends 506
    Cash Dividends 506
    Stock Dividends 509
    Stock Splits 510
Retained Earnings 512
    Retained Earnings Restrictions 512
**Financial Statement Presentation of
Stockholders' Equity 513**
    Balance Sheet Presentation 513
Keeping an Eye on Cash 514
Measuring Corporate Performance 515
    Dividend Record 515
    Earnings Performance 516
    Debt versus Equity Decision 516
APPENDIX 11A: **Entries for Stock Dividends 520**
A Look at IFRS 537

Chapter 12

Statement of Cash Flows 540

Got Cash? 541
**The Statement of Cash Flows: Usefulness
and Format 542**
    Usefulness of the Statement of Cash Flows 542
    Classification of Cash Flows 543
    Significant Noncash Activities 544
    Format of the Statement of Cash Flows 545
    The Corporate Life Cycle 546
    Preparing the Statement of Cash Flows 547
    Indirect and Direct Methods 548
**Preparation of the Statement of Cash
Flows–Indirect Method 549**
    Step 1: Operating Activities 550
    Summary of Conversion to Net Cash Provided by
        Operating Activities–Indirect Method 554
    Step 2: Investing and Financing Activities 555
    Step 3: Net Change in Cash 556
Using Cash Flows to Evaluate a Company 557
    Free Cash Flow 557
Keeping an Eye on Cash 558
    Assessing Liquidity and Solvency Using
        Cash Flows 558
APPENDIX 12A: **Statement of Cash Flows–Direct
Method 563**
    Step 1: Operating Activities 565
    Step 2: Investing and Financing Activities 569
    Step 3: Net Change in Cash 570
APPENDIX 12B: **Statement of Cash Flows—T-Account
Approach 570**
A Look at IFRS 591

Chapter 13

Financial Analysis: The Big Picture 594

It Pays to Be Patient 595
Sustainable Income 596
    Irregular Items 597

    Changes in Accounting Principle 600
    Comprehensive Income 601
    Concluding Remarks 602
Comparative Analysis 603
    Horizontal Analysis 603
    Vertical Analysis 606
Ratio Analysis 608
    Liquidity Ratios 609
    Solvency Ratios 609
    Profitability Ratios 610
Quality of Earnings 610
    Alternative Accounting Methods 611
    Pro Forma Income 611
    Improper Recognition 611
    Price-Earnings Ratio 612
APPENDIX 13A: **Comprehensive Illustration
of Ratio Analysis 616**
    Liquidity Ratios 618
    Solvency Ratios 620
    Profitability Ratios 623
A Look at IFRS 646

Appendix A

Specimen Financial Statements: Tootsie Roll Industries, Inc. A-1

The Annual Report A-1
Letter to the Stockholders A-2
Management Discussion and Analysis A-6
**Financial Statements and Accompanying
Notes A-14**
Auditor's Report A-28
Financial Highlights A-31

Appendix B

Specimen Financial Statements: The Hershey Company B-1

Appendix C

Specimen Financial Statements: Zetar plc C-1

Appendix D

Time Value of Money D-1

Nature of Interest D-1
    Simple Interest D-1
    Compound Interest D-2
Future Value Concepts D-2
    Future Value of a Single Amount D-2
    Future Value of an Annuity D-4
Present Value Concepts D-7
    Present Value Variables D-7

Present Value of a Single Amount D-7
Present Value of an Annuity D-9
Time Periods and Discounting D-11
Computing the Present Value of a Long-Term
    Note or Bond D-11
Using Financial Calculators D-14
Present Value of a Single Sum D-14
Present Value of an Annuity D-15
Useful Applications of the Financial
    Calculator D-15

Appendix E

Reporting and Analyzing Investments E-1

Why Corporations Invest E-1
Accounting for Debt Investments E-2
Recording Acquisition of Bonds E-2
Recording Bond Interest E-3
Recording Sale of Bonds E-3
Accounting for Stock Investments E-4
Holdings of Less Than 20% E-4
Holdings Between 20% and 50% E-5
Holdings of More Than 50% E-7
Valuing and Reporting Investments E-7
Categories of Securities E-8
Balance Sheet Presentation E-10
Presentation of Realized and
Unrealized Gain or Loss E-12
Statement of Cash Flows Presentation E-12

Company Index I-1

Subject Index I-5

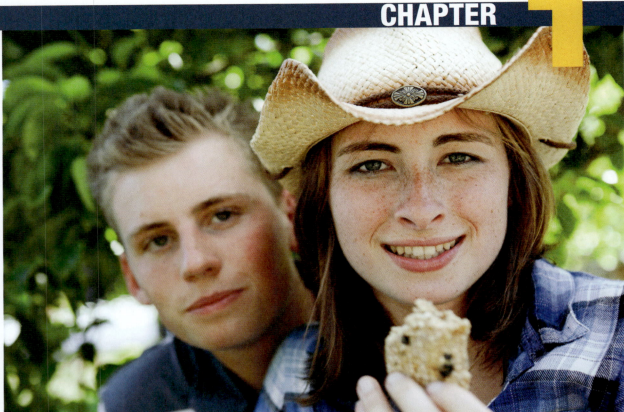

INTRODUCTION TO FINANCIAL STATEMENTS

LEARNING OBJECTIVES

After studying this chapter, you should be able to:

1 Describe the primary forms of business organization.

2 Identify the users and uses of accounting information.

3 Explain the three principal types of business activity.

4 Describe the content and purpose of each of the financial statements.

5 Explain the meaning of assets, liabilities, and stockholders' equity, and state the basic accounting equation.

6 Describe the components that supplement the financial statements in an annual report.

Many students who take this course do not plan to be accountants. If you are in that group, you might be thinking, "If I'm not going to be an accountant, why do I need to know accounting?" Well, consider this quote from Harold Geneen, the former chairman of IT&T: "To be good at your business, you have to know the numbers—cold." In business, accounting and financial statements are the means for communicating the numbers. If you don't know how to read financial statements, you can't really know your business.

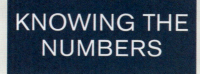

KNOWING THE NUMBERS

Many businesses agree with this view. They see the value of their employees being able to read financial statements and understand how their actions affect the company's financial results. For example, consider Clif Bar & Company. The original Clif Bar® energy bar was created in 1990 after six months of experimentation by Gary Erickson and his mother in her kitchen. Today, the company has almost 300 employees and is considered one of the leading Landor's Breakaway Brands®.

Clif Bar is guided by what it calls its Five Aspirations—Sustaining Our Business, Our Brands, Our People, Our Community, and the Planet. Its website documents its efforts and accomplishments in these five areas. Just a few examples include the company's use of organic products to protect soil, water, and biodiversity; the "smart" solar array (the largest in North America), which provides nearly all the electrical needs

for its 115,000-square-foot building; and the incentives Clif Bar provides to employees to reduce their personal environmental impact, such as $6,500 toward the purchase of an efficient car or $1,000 per year for eco-friendly improvements toward their homes.

One of the company's proudest moments was the creation of an employee stock ownership plan (ESOP) in 2010. This plan gives its employees 20% ownership of the company (Gary and his wife Kit own the other 80%). The ESOP also resulted in Clif Bar enacting an open-book management program, including the commitment to educate all employee-owners about its finances. Armed with this basic financial knowledge, employees are more aware of the financial impact of their actions, which leads to better decisions.

Even in companies that do not practice open-book management, today's employers generally assume that managers in all areas of the company are "financially literate." To help prepare you for that, in this textbook you will learn how to read and prepare financial statements, and how to use basic tools to evaluate financial results. In this first chapter, we will introduce you to the financial statements of a real company whose products you are probably familiar with—Tootsie Roll. Tootsie Roll's presentation of its financial results is complete, yet also relatively easy to understand.

INSIDE CHAPTER 1 . . .

- **The Scoop on Accounting**
- **Spinning the Career Wheel**
- **The Numbers Behind Not-for-Profit Organizations**
- **Beyond Financial Statements**

How do you start a business? How do you determine whether your business is making or losing money? How should you finance expansion—should you borrow, should you issue stock, should you use your own funds? How do you convince banks to lend you money or investors to buy your stock? Success in business requires making countless decisions, and decisions require financial information.

The purpose of this chapter is to show you what role accounting plays in providing financial information. The content and organization of the chapter are as follows.

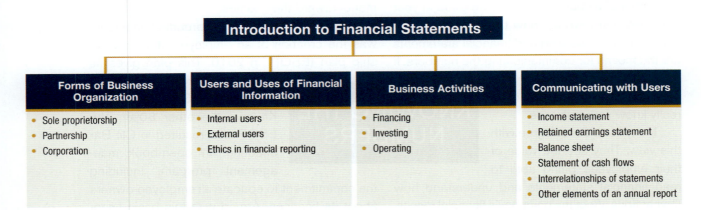

Introduction to Financial Statements

Forms of Business Organization	Users and Uses of Financial Information	Business Activities	Communicating with Users
• Sole proprietorship • Partnership • Corporation	• Internal users • External users • Ethics in financial reporting	• Financing • Investing • Operating	• Income statement • Retained earnings statement • Balance sheet • Statement of cash flows • Interrelationships of statements • Other elements of an annual report

---

Describe the primary forms of business organization.

Sole Proprietorship
-Simple to establish
-Owner controlled
-Tax advantages

Partnership
-Simple to establish
-Shared control
-Broader skills and resources
-Tax advantages

Corporation
-Easier to transfer ownership
-Easier to raise funds
-No personal liability

Forms of Business Organization

Suppose you graduate with a business degree and decide you want to start your own business. But what kind of business? You enjoy working with people, especially teaching them new skills. You also spend most of your free time outdoors, kayaking, backpacking, skiing, rock climbing, and mountain biking. You think you might be successful in opening an outdoor guide service where you grew up, in the Sierra Nevada mountains.

Your next decision is to determine the organizational form of your business. You have three choices—sole proprietorship, partnership, or corporation.

You might choose the sole proprietorship form for your outdoor guide service. A business owned by one person is a **sole proprietorship**. It is **simple to set up** and **gives you control** over the business. Small owner-operated businesses such as barber shops, law offices, and auto repair shops are often sole proprietorships, as are farms and small retail stores.

Another possibility is for you to join forces with other individuals to form a partnership. A business owned by two or more persons associated as partners is a **partnership**. Partnerships often are formed because one individual does not have **enough economic resources** to initiate or expand the business. Sometimes **partners bring unique skills or resources** to the partnership. You and your partners should formalize your duties and contributions in a written partnership agreement. Retail and service-type businesses, including professional practices (lawyers, doctors, architects, and certified public accountants), often organize as partnerships.

As a third alternative, you might organize as a corporation. A business organized as a separate legal entity owned by stockholders is a **corporation**. Investors in a corporation receive shares of stock to indicate their ownership claim. Buying stock in a corporation is often more attractive than investing in a partnership because shares of stock are **easy to sell** (transfer ownership). Selling a proprietorship or partnership interest is much more involved. Also, individuals can become, **stockholders**, or **shareholders**, by investing relatively small amounts of money. Therefore, it is **easier for corporations to raise funds**. Successful corporations often have thousands of stockholders, and their stock is traded on organized stock exchanges like the New York Stock Exchange. Many businesses start as sole proprietorships or partnerships and eventually incorporate. For example, in 1896 Leo Hirshfield started Tootsie Roll as a sole proprietorship, and by 1919 the company had incorporated.

Other factors to consider in deciding which organizational form to choose are **taxes and legal liability**. If you choose a sole proprietorship or partnership, you generally receive more favorable tax treatment than a corporation. However, proprietors and partners are personally liable for all debts and legal obligations of the business; corporate stockholders are not. In other words, corporate stockholders generally pay higher taxes but have no personal legal liability. We will discuss these issues in more depth in a later chapter.

Finally, while sole proprietorships, partnerships, and corporations represent the main types of business organizations, hybrid forms are now allowed in all states. These hybrid business forms combine the tax advantages of partnerships with the limited liability of corporations. Probably the most common among these hybrids types are limited liability companies (LLCs) and subchapter S corporations. These forms are discussed extensively in business law classes.

The combined number of proprietorships and partnerships in the United States is more than five times the number of corporations. However, the revenue produced by corporations is eight times greater. Most of the largest businesses in the United States—for example, Coca-Cola, ExxonMobil, General Motors, Citigroup, and Microsoft—are corporations. Because the majority of U.S. business is done by corporations, the emphasis in this textbook is on the corporate form of organization.

Users and Uses of Financial Information

The purpose of financial information is to provide inputs for decision-making. Accounting is the information system that identifies, records, and communicates the economic events of an organization to interested users. **Users** of accounting information can be divided broadly into two groups: internal users and external users.

LEARNING OBJECTIVE 2
Identify the users and uses of accounting information.

INTERNAL USERS

Internal users of accounting information are managers who plan, organize, and run a business. These include **marketing managers**, **production supervisors**, **finance directors**, **and company officers**. In running a business, managers must answer many important questions, as shown in Illustration 1-1.

Illustration 1-1 Questions that internal users ask

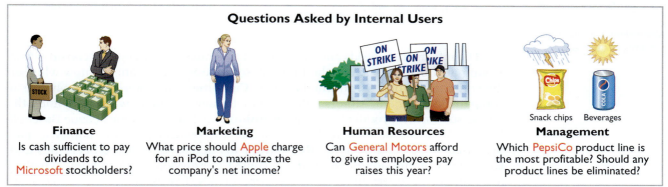

Questions Asked by Internal Users

Finance
Is cash sufficient to pay dividends to Microsoft stockholders?

Marketing
What price should Apple charge for an iPod to maximize the company's net income?

Human Resources
Can General Motors afford to give its employees pay raises this year?

Management
Which PepsiCo product line is the most profitable? Should any product lines be eliminated?

Snack chips   Beverages

To answer these and other questions, you need detailed information on a timely basis. For internal users, accounting provides internal reports, such as financial comparisons of operating alternatives, projections of income from new sales campaigns, and forecasts of cash needs for the next year. In addition, companies present summarized financial information in the form of financial statements.

Accounting Across the Organization
The Scoop on Accounting

Accounting can serve as a useful recruiting tool even for the human resources department. Rhino Foods, located in Burlington, Vermont, is a manufacturer of specialty ice cream. Its corporate website includes the following:

"Wouldn't it be great to work where you were part of a team? Where your input and hard work made a difference? Where you weren't kept in the dark about what management was thinking? . . . Well—it's not a dream! It's the way we do business . . . Rhino Foods believes in family, honesty and open communication—we really care about and appreciate our employees—and it shows. Operating results are posted and monthly group meetings inform all employees about what's happening in the Company. Employees also share in the Company's profits, in addition to having an excellent comprehensive *benefits* package."

Source: www.rhinofoods.com/workforus/workforus.html.

? What are the benefits to the company and to the employees of making the financial statements available to all employees? (Answers in *Broadening Your Perspective*.)

EXTERNAL USERS

There are several types of **external users** of accounting information. **Investors** (owners) use accounting information to make decisions to buy, hold, or sell stock. **Creditors** such as suppliers and bankers use accounting information to evaluate the risks of selling on credit or lending money. Some questions that investors and creditors may ask about a company are shown in Illustration 1-2.

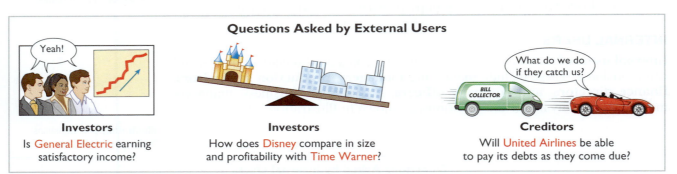

Illustration 1-2 Questions that external users ask

The information needs and questions of other external users vary considerably. **Taxing authorities**, such as the Internal Revenue Service, want to know whether the company complies with the tax laws. **Customers** are interested in whether a company like General Motors will continue to honor product warranties and otherwise support its product lines. **Labor unions**, such as the Major League Baseball Players Association, want to know whether the owners have the ability to pay increased wages and benefits. **Regulatory agencies**, such as the Securities and Exchange Commission or the Federal Trade Commission, want to know whether the company is operating within prescribed rules. For example, Enron, Dynegy,

Duke Energy, and other big energy-trading companies reported record profits at the same time as California was paying extremely high prices for energy and suffering from blackouts. This disparity caused regulators to investigate the energy traders to make sure that the profits were earned by legitimate and fair practices.

Accounting Across the Organization
Spinning the Career Wheel

How will the study of accounting help you? A working knowledge of accounting is desirable for virtually every field of business. Some examples of how accounting is used in business careers include:

General management: Managers of Ford Motors, Massachusetts General Hospital, California State University–Fullerton, a McDonald's franchise, and a Trek bike shop all need to understand accounting data in order to make wise business decisions.

Marketing: A marketing specialist at Procter & Gamble must be sensitive to costs and benefits, which accounting helps them quantify and understand. Making a sale is meaningless unless it is a profitable sale.

Finance: Do you want to be a banker for Citicorp, an investment analyst for Goldman Sachs, or a stock broker for Merrill Lynch? These fields rely heavily on accounting knowledge to analyze financial statements. In fact, it is difficult to get a good job in a finance function without two or three courses in accounting.

Real estate: Are you interested in being a real estate broker for Prudential Real Estate? Because a third party—the bank—is almost always involved in financing a real estate transaction, brokers must understand the numbers involved: Can the buyer afford to make the payments to the bank? Does the cash flow from an industrial property justify the purchase price? What are the tax benefits of the purchase?

? How might accounting help you? (Answers in *Broadening Your Perspective*.)

ETHICS IN FINANCIAL REPORTING

People won't gamble in a casino if they think it is "rigged." Similarly, people won't "play" the stock market if they think stock prices are rigged. At one time, the financial press was full of articles about financial scandals at Enron, WorldCom, HealthSouth, and AIG. As more scandals came to light, a mistrust of financial reporting in general seemed to be developing. One article in the *Wall Street Journal* noted that "repeated disclosures about questionable accounting practices have bruised investors' faith in the reliability of earnings reports, which in turn has sent stock prices tumbling."[1] Imagine trying to carry on a business or invest money if you could not depend on the financial statements to be honestly prepared. Information would have no credibility. There is no doubt that a sound, well-functioning economy depends on accurate and dependable financial reporting.

United States regulators and lawmakers were very concerned that the economy would suffer if investors lost confidence in corporate accounting because of unethical financial reporting. Congress passed the **Sarbanes-Oxley Act (SOX)** to reduce unethical corporate behavior and decrease the likelihood of future corporate scandals. As a result of SOX, top management must now certify the accuracy of financial information. In addition, penalties for fraudulent financial activity are much more severe. Also, SOX increased the independence of

---

[1]"U.S. Share Prices Slump," *Wall Street Journal* (February 21, 2002).

the outside auditors who review the accuracy of corporate financial statements, and increased the oversight role of boards of directors.

Effective financial reporting depends on sound ethical behavior. To sensitize you to ethical situations and to give you practice at solving ethical dilemmas, we address ethics in a number of ways in this textbook. (1) A number of the *Feature Stories* and other parts of the text discuss the central importance of ethical behavior to financial reporting. (2) *Ethics Insight boxes* and marginal *Ethics Notes* highlight ethics situations and issues in actual business settings. (3) Many of the *People, Planet, and Profit Insight boxes* focus on ethical issues that companies face in measuring and reporting social and environmental issues. (4) At the end of the chapter, an *Ethics Case* simulates a business situation and asks you to put yourself in the position of a decision-maker in that case.

When analyzing these various ethics cases and your own ethical experiences, you should apply the three steps outlined in Illustration 1-3.

Solving an Ethical Dilemma

1. Recognize an ethical situation and the ethical issues involved.	**2. Identify and analyze the principal elements in the situation.**	**3. Identify the alternatives, and weigh the impact of each alternative on various stakeholders.**
Use your personal ethics to identify ethical situations and issues. Some businesses and professional organizations provide written codes of ethics for guidance in some business situations.	Identify the **stakeholders**—persons or groups who may be harmed or benefited. Ask the question: What are the responsibilities and obligations of the parties involved?	Select the most ethical alternative, considering all the consequences. Sometimes there will be one right answer. Other situations involve more than one right solution; these situations require you to evaluate each alternative and select the best one.

Illustration 1-3 Steps in analyzing ethics cases

Ethics Insight

The Numbers Behind Not-for-Profit Organizations

Accounting plays an important role for a wide range of business organizations worldwide. Just as the integrity of the numbers matters for business, it matters at least as much at not-for-profit organizations. Proper control and reporting help ensure that money is used the way donors intended. Donors are less inclined to give to an organization if they think the organization is subject to waste or theft. The accounting challenges of some large international not-for-profits rival those of the world's largest businesses. For example, after the Haitian earthquake, the Haitian-born musician Wyclef Jean was criticized for the poor accounting controls in a relief fund that he founded. In response, he hired a new accountant and improved the transparency regarding funds raised and spent.

? What benefits does a sound accounting system provide to a not-for-profit organization? (Answers in *Broadening Your Perspective.*)

Business Activities

All businesses are involved in three types of activity—financing, investing, and operating. For example, Leo Hirshfield, the founder of Tootsie Roll, obtained cash through financing to start and grow his business. Some of this **financing** came from personal savings, and some likely came from outside sources like banks. Hirshfield then **invested** the cash in equipment to run the business, such as mixing equipment and delivery vehicles. Once this equipment was in place, he could begin the **operating** activities of making and selling candy.

The **accounting information system** keeps track of the results of each of the various business activities—financing, investing, and operating. Let's look at each type of business activity in more detail.

FINANCING ACTIVITIES

It takes money to make money. The two primary sources of outside funds for corporations are borrowing money (debt financing) and issuing (selling) shares of stock in exchange for cash (equity financing).

Tootsie Roll may borrow money in a variety of ways. For example, it can take out a loan at a bank or borrow directly from investors by issuing debt securities called bonds. Persons or entities to whom Tootsie Roll owes money are its **creditors**. Amounts owed to creditors—in the form of debt and other obligations—are called **liabilities**. Specific names are given to different types of liabilities, depending on their source. Tootsie Roll may have a **note payable** to a bank for the money borrowed to purchase delivery trucks. Debt securities sold to investors that must be repaid at a particular date some years in the future are **bonds payable**.

Corporations also obtain funds by selling shares of stock to investors. **Common stock** is the term used to describe the total amount paid in by stock-holders for the shares they purchase.

The claims of creditors differ from those of stockholders. If you loan money to a company, you are one of its creditors. In lending money, you specify a payment schedule (e.g., payment at the end of three months). As a creditor, you have a legal right to be paid at the agreed time. In the event of nonpayment, you may legally force the company to sell property to pay its debts. In the case of financial difficulty, creditor claims must be paid before stockholders' claims.

Stockholders, on the other hand, have no claim to corporate cash until the claims of creditors are satisfied. Suppose you buy a company's stock instead of loaning it money. You have no legal right to expect any payments from your stock ownership until all of the company's creditors are paid. However, many corporations make payments to stockholders on a regular basis as long as there is sufficient cash to cover required payments to creditors. These cash payments to stockholders are called **dividends**.

INVESTING ACTIVITIES

Once the company has raised cash through financing activities, it uses that cash in investing activities. Investing activities involve the purchase of the resources a company needs in order to operate. A growing company purchases many resources, such as computers, delivery trucks, furniture, and buildings. Resources owned by a business are called **assets**. Different types of assets are given different names. For example, Tootsie Roll's mixing equipment is a type of asset referred to as **property**, **plant**, **and equipment**, or **fixed assets**.

Cash is one of the more important assets owned by Tootsie Roll or any other business. If a company has excess cash that it does not need for a while, it might choose to invest in securities (stocks or bonds) of other corporations. **Investments** are another example of an investing activity.

OPERATING ACTIVITIES

Once a business has the assets it needs to get started, it begins operations. Tootsie Roll is in the business of selling all things that taste, look, or smell like candy. It sells Tootsie Rolls, Tootsie Pops, Blow Pops, Caramel Apple Pops, Mason Dots, Mason

Crows, Sugar Daddy, and Sugar Babies. We call amounts earned on the sale of these products **revenues**. Revenue is the increase in assets or decrease in liabilities resulting from the sale of goods or the performance of services in the normal course of business. For example, Tootsie Roll records revenue when it sells a candy product.

Revenues arise from different sources and are identified by various names depending on the nature of the business. For instance, Tootsie Roll's primary source of revenue is the sale of candy products. However, it also generates interest revenue on debt securities held as investments. Sources of revenue common to many businesses are **sales revenue**, **service revenue**, and **interest revenue**.

The company purchases its longer-lived assets through investing activities as described earlier. Other assets with shorter lives, however, result from operating activities. For example, **supplies** are assets used in day-to-day operations. Goods available for future sales to customers are assets called **inventory**. Also, if Tootsie Roll sells goods to a customer and does not receive cash immediately, then the company has a right to expect payment from that customer in the near future. This right to receive money in the future is called an **account receivable**.

Before Tootsie Roll can sell a single Tootsie Roll, Tootsie Pop, or Blow Pop, it must purchase sugar, corn syrup, and other ingredients, mix these ingredients, process the mix, and wrap and ship the finished product. It also incurs costs like salaries, rents, and utilities. All of these costs, referred to as **expenses**, are necessary to produce and sell the product. In accounting language, expenses are the cost of assets consumed or services used in the process of generating revenues.

Expenses take many forms and are identified by various names depending on the type of asset consumed or service used. For example, Tootsie Roll keeps track of these types of expenses: **cost of goods sold** (such as the cost of ingredients); **selling expenses** (such as the cost of salespersons' salaries); **marketing expenses** (such as the cost of advertising); **administrative expenses** (such as the salaries of administrative staff, and telephone and heating costs incurred at the corporate office); **interest expense** (amounts of interest paid on various debts); and **income taxes** (corporate taxes paid to the government).

Tootsie Roll may also have liabilities arising from these expenses. For example, it may purchase goods on credit from suppliers. The obligations to pay for these goods are called **accounts payable**. Additionally, Tootsie Roll may have **interest payable** on the outstanding amounts owed to the bank. It may also have **wages payable** to its employees and **sales taxes payable**, **property taxes payable**, and **income taxes payable** to the government.

Tootsie Roll compares the revenues of a period with the expenses of that period to determine whether it earned a profit. When revenues exceed expenses, net income results. When expenses exceed revenues, a net loss results.

Communicating with Users

Assets, liabilities, expenses, and revenues are of interest to users of accounting information. This information is arranged in the format of four different **financial statements**, which form the backbone of financial accounting:

- To show how successfully your business performed during a period of time, you report its revenues and expenses in an **income statement**.
- To indicate how much of previous income was distributed to you and the other owners of your business in the form of dividends, and how much was retained in the business to allow for future growth, you present a **retained earnings statement**.
- To present a picture at a point in time of what your business owns (its assets) and what it owes (its liabilities), you prepare a **balance sheet**.

- To show where your business obtained cash during a period of time and how that cash was used, you present a **statement of cash flows**.

To introduce you to these statements, we have prepared the financial statements for your outdoor guide service, Sierra Corporation, after your first month of operations. To summarize, you officially started your business in Truckee, California, on October 1, 2014. Sierra provides guide services in the Lake Tahoe area of the Sierra Nevada mountains. Its promotional materials describe outdoor day trips, such as rafting, snowshoeing, and hiking, as well as multi-day backcountry experiences. To minimize your initial investment, at this point the company has limited outdoor equipment for customer use. Instead, your customers either bring their own equipment or rent equipment through local outfitters. The financial statements for Sierra's first month of business are provided in the following pages.

INCOME STATEMENT

The income statement reports a company's revenues and expenses and resulting net income or loss for a period of time. To indicate that its income statement reports the results of operations for a **specific period of time**, Sierra dates the income statement "For the Month Ended October 31, 2014." The income statement lists the company's revenues followed by its expenses. Finally, Sierra determines the net income (or net loss) by deducting expenses from revenues. Sierra Corporation's income statement is shown in Illustration 1-4. Congratulations, you are already showing a profit!

Illustration 1-4 Sierra Corporation's income statement

SIERRA CORPORATION		
Income Statement		
For the Month Ended October 31, 2014		
Revenues		
Service revenue		$10,600
Expenses		
Salaries and wages expense	$5,200	
Rent expense	900	
Supplies expense	1,500	
Depreciation expense	40	
Interest expense	50	
Insurance expense	50	
Total expenses		7,740
Net income		$ 2,860

Why are financial statement users interested in net income? **Investors are interested in a company's past net income because it provides useful information for predicting future net income**. Investors buy and sell stock based on their beliefs about a company's future performance. If investors believe that Sierra will be successful in the future and that this will result in a higher stock price, they will buy its stock. Creditors also use the income statement to predict future earnings. When a bank loans money to a company, it believes that it will be repaid in the future. If it didn't think it would be repaid, it wouldn't loan the money. Therefore, prior to making the loan the bank loan officer uses the income statement as a source of information to predict whether the company will be profitable enough to repay its loan. Thus, reporting a strong profit will make it easier for Sierra to raise additional cash either by issuing shares of stock or borrowing.

Amounts received from issuing stock are not revenues, and amounts paid out as dividends are not expenses. As a result, they are not reported on the income statement. For example, Sierra Corporation does not treat as revenue the $10,000 of cash received from issuing new stock (see Illustration 1-7), nor does it regard as a business expense the $500 of dividends paid (see Illustration 1-5).

DECISION TOOLKIT

DECISION CHECKPOINTS	INFO NEEDED FOR DECISION	TOOL TO USE FOR DECISION	HOW TO EVALUATE RESULTS
Are the company's operations profitable?	Income statement	The income statement reports a company's revenues and expenses and resulting net income or loss for a period of time.	If the company's revenue exceeds its expenses, it will report net income; otherwise, it will report a net loss.

RETAINED EARNINGS STATEMENT

If Sierra is profitable, at the end of each period it must decide what portion of profits to pay to shareholders in dividends. In theory, it could pay all of its current-period profits, but few companies do this. Why? Because they want to retain part of the profits to allow for further expansion. High-growth companies, such as Google and Facebook, often pay no dividends. **Retained earnings** is the net income retained in the corporation.

The **retained earnings statement** shows the amounts and causes of changes in retained earnings for a specific time period. The time period is the same as that covered by the income statement. The beginning retained earnings amount appears on the first line of the statement. Then, the company adds net income and deducts dividends to determine the retained earnings at the end of the period. If a company has a net loss, it deducts (rather than adds) that amount in the retained earnings statement. Illustration 1-5 presents Sierra Corporation's retained earnings statement.

Illustration 1-5 Sierra Corporation's retained earnings statement

SIERRA CORPORATION
Retained Earnings Statement
For the Month Ended October 31, 2014

Retained earnings, October 1	$ 0
Add: Net income	2,860
	2,860
Less: Dividends	500
Retained earnings, October 31	$2,360

By monitoring the retained earnings statement, financial statement users can evaluate dividend payment practices. Some investors seek companies, such as Dow Chemical, that have a history of paying high dividends. Other investors seek companies, such as Amazon.com, that reinvest earnings to increase the company's growth instead of paying dividends. Lenders monitor their corporate customers' dividend payments because any money paid in dividends reduces a company's ability to repay its debts.

DECISION TOOLKIT

DECISION CHECKPOINTS	INFO NEEDED FOR DECISION	TOOL TO USE FOR DECISION	HOW TO EVALUATE RESULTS
What is the company's policy toward dividends and growth?	Retained earnings statement	How much of this year's income did the company pay out in dividends to shareholders?	A company striving for rapid growth will pay a low (or no) dividend.

BALANCE SHEET

The **balance sheet** reports assets and claims to assets at a specific **point** in time. Claims to assets are subdivided into two categories: claims of creditors and claims of owners. As noted earlier, claims of creditors are called **liabilities** or **debt**. The owners' claim to assets is called **stockholders' equity**.

Illustration 1-6 shows the relationship among the categories on the balance sheet in equation form. This equation is referred to as the **basic accounting equation**.

LEARNING OBJECTIVE 5
Explain the meaning of assets, liabilities, and stockholders' equity, and state the basic accounting equation.

$$\textbf{Assets = Liabilities + Stockholders' Equity}$$

Illustration 1-6 Basic accounting equation

This relationship is where the name "balance sheet" comes from. Assets must balance with the claims to assets.

As you can see from looking at Sierra's balance sheet in Illustration 1-7, the balance sheet presents the company's financial position as of a specific date—in this case, October 31, 2014. It lists assets first, followed by liabilities and stockholders' equity. Stockholders' equity is comprised of two parts: (1) common stock and (2) retained earnings. As noted earlier, common stock results when the company sells new shares of stock; retained earnings is the net income retained in the corporation. Sierra has common stock of $10,000 and retained earnings of $2,360, for total stockholders' equity of $12,360.

Illustration 1-7 Sierra Corporation's balance sheet

SIERRA CORPORATION
Balance Sheet
October 31, 2014

Assets

Cash	$15,200
Accounts receivable	200
Supplies	1,000
Prepaid insurance	550
Equipment, net	4,960
Total assets	$21,910

Liabilities and Stockholders' Equity

Liabilities		
Notes payable	$ 5,000	
Accounts payable	2,500	
Unearned service revenue	800	
Salaries and wages payable	1,200	
Interest payable	50	
Total liabilities		$ 9,550
Stockholders' equity		
Common stock	10,000	
Retained earnings	2,360	
Total stockholders' equity		12,360
Total liabilities and stockholders' equity		$21,910

Creditors analyze a company's balance sheet to determine the likelihood that they will be repaid. They carefully evaluate the nature of the company's assets and liabilities. In operating the Sierra Corporation guide service, the balance sheet will be used to determine whether cash on hand is sufficient for immediate cash needs. The balance sheet will also be used to evaluate the relationship between debt and stockholders' equity to determine whether the company has a satisfactory proportion of debt and common stock financing.

DECISION TOOLKIT

DECISION CHECKPOINTS	INFO NEEDED FOR DECISION	TOOL TO USE FOR DECISION	HOW TO EVALUATE RESULTS
Does the company rely primarily on debt or stockholders' equity to finance its assets?	Balance sheet	The balance sheet reports the company's resources and claims to those resources. There are two types of claims: liabilities and stockholders' equity.	Compare the amount of debt versus the amount of stockholders' equity to determine whether the company relies more on creditors or owners for its financing.

STATEMENT OF CASH FLOWS

The primary purpose of a **statement of cash flows** is to provide financial information about the cash receipts and cash payments of a business for a specific period of time. To help investors, creditors, and others in their analysis of a company's cash position, the statement of cash flows reports the cash effects of a company's **operating**, **investing**, and **financing** activities. In addition, the statement shows the net increase or decrease in cash during the period, and the amount of cash at the end of the period.

Users are interested in the statement of cash flows because they want to know what is happening to a company's most important resource. The statement of cash flows provides answers to these simple but important questions:

- Where did cash come from during the period?
- How was cash used during the period?
- What was the change in the cash balance during the period?

The statement of cash flows for Sierra, in Illustration 1-8, shows that cash increased $15,200 during the month. This increase resulted because operating

Illustration 1-8 Sierra Corporation's statement of cash flows

SIERRA CORPORATION
Statement of Cash Flows
For the Month Ended October 31, 2014

Cash flows from operating activities		
Cash receipts from operating activities	$11,200	
Cash payments for operating activities	(5,500)	
Net cash provided by operating activities		$ 5,700
Cash flows from investing activities		
Purchased office equipment	(5,000)	
Net cash used by investing activities		(5,000)
Cash flows from financing activities		
Issuance of common stock	10,000	
Issuance of note payable	5,000	
Payment of dividend	(500)	
Net cash provided by financing activities		14,500
Net increase in cash		15,200
Cash at beginning of period		0
Cash at end of period		$15,200

activities (services to clients) increased cash $5,700, and financing activities increased cash $14,500. Investing activities used $5,000 of cash for the purchase of equipment.

People, Planet, and Profit Insight
Beyond Financial Statements

Should we expand our corporate reports beyond the income statement, retained earnings statement, balance sheet, and statement of cash flows? Some believe we should take into account ecological and social performance, in addition to financial results, in evaluating a company. The argument is that a company's responsibility lies with anyone who is influenced by its actions. In other words, a company should be interested in benefiting many different parties, instead of only maximizing stockholders' interests.

A socially responsible business does not exploit or endanger any group of individuals. It follows fair trade practices, provides safe environments for workers, and bears responsibility for environmental damage. Granted, measurement of these factors is difficult. How to report this information is also controversial. But many interesting and useful efforts are underway. Throughout this textbook, we provide additional insights into how companies are attempting to meet the challenge of measuring and reporting their contributions to society, as well as their financial results, to stockholders.

? Why might a company's stockholders be interested in its environmental and social performance? (Answers in *Broadening Your Perspective*.)

DECISION TOOLKIT

DECISION CHECKPOINTS	INFO NEEDED FOR DECISION	TOOL TO USE FOR DECISION	HOW TO EVALUATE RESULTS
Does the company generate sufficient cash from operations to fund its investing activities?	Statement of cash flows	The statement of cash flows shows the amount of cash provided or used by operating activities, investing activities, and financing activities.	Compare the amount of cash provided by operating activities with the amount of cash used by investing activities. Any deficiency in cash from operating activities must be made up with cash from financing activities.

INTERRELATIONSHIPS OF STATEMENTS

Illustration 1-9 shows simplified financial statements of Tootsie Roll Industries, Inc. (We have simplified the financial statements to assist your learning.) Tootsie Roll's **actual financial statements** are presented in **Appendix A**, at the end of the textbook. Note that the numbers in Tootsie Roll's statements are presented in thousands—that is, the last three 000s are omitted. Thus, Tootsie Roll's net income in 2011 is $43,938,000, not $43,938. Because the results on some financial statements become inputs to other statements, the statements are interrelated. These interrelationships can be seen in Tootsie Roll's financial statements, as follows.

1. The retained earnings statement uses the results of the income statement. Tootsie Roll reported net income of $43,938,000 for the period. Net income is added to the beginning amount of retained earnings to determine ending retained earnings.

Illustration 1-9 Tootsie Roll's financial statements

TOOTSIE ROLL INDUSTRIES, INC.
Income Statement
For the Year Ended December 31, 2011 (in thousands)

Revenues		$532,505
Expenses		
Cost of goods sold	$365,225	
Selling, marketing, and administrative expense and other	106,368	
Income tax expense	16,974	
Total expenses		488,567
Net income		$ 43,938

TOOTSIE ROLL INDUSTRIES, INC.
Retained Earnings Statement
For the Year Ended December 31, 2011 (in thousands)

Retained earnings, January 1, 2011	$135,866
Add: Net income	43,938
	179,804
Less: Dividends and other (net)	65,535
Retained earnings, December 31, 2011	$114,269

TOOTSIE ROLL INDUSTRIES, INC.
Balance Sheet
December 31, 2011 (in thousands)

Assets

Cash		$ 78,612
Investments		10,895
Accounts receivable		41,895
Inventories		71,760
Prepaid expenses		5,070
Property, plant and equipment, net		212,162
Other assets		437,462
Total assets		$857,856

Liabilities and Stockholders' Equity

Liabilities		
Accounts payable	$ 10,683	
Dividends payable	4,603	
Accrued liabilities	43,069	
Deferred income taxes payable	43,521	
Bonds payable	7,500	
Employee benefits payable and other	82,545	$191,921
Stockholders' equity		
Common stock	551,666	
Retained earnings	114,269	665,935
Total liabilities and stockholders' equity		$857,856

TOOTSIE ROLL INDUSTRIES, INC.
Statement of Cash Flows
For the Year Ended December 31, 2011 (in thousands)

Cash flows from operating activities		
Cash receipts from operating activities	$528,004	
Cash payments for operating activities	(477,614)	
Net cash provided by operating activities		$ 50,390
Cash flows from investing activities		
Capital expenditures and acquisitions	(16,351)	
Net purchases/sales of investment securities and other	(34,806)	
Net cash used by investing activities		(51,157)
Cash flows from financing activities		
Repurchase of common stock	(18,190)	
Dividends paid in cash	(18,407)	
Net cash used by financing activities		(36,597)
Net increase (decrease) in cash		(37,364)
Cash at beginning of year		115,976
Cash at end of year		$ 78,612

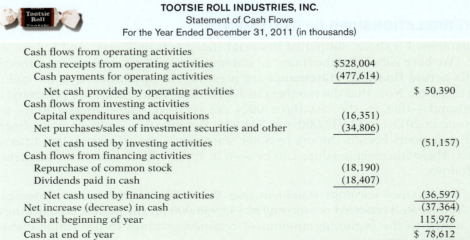

2. The balance sheet and retained earnings statement are also interrelated. Tootsie Roll reports the ending amount of $114,269,000 on the retained earnings statement as the retained earnings amount on the balance sheet.

3. Finally, the statement of cash flows relates to information on the balance sheet. The statement of cash flows shows how the Cash account changed during the period. It shows the amount of cash at the beginning of the period, the sources and uses of cash during the period, and the $78,612,000 of cash at the end of the period. The ending amount of cash shown on the statement of cash flows must agree with the amount of cash on the balance sheet.

Study these interrelationships carefully. **To prepare financial statements, you must understand the sequence in which these amounts are determined and how each statement impacts the next.**

OTHER ELEMENTS OF AN ANNUAL REPORT

Publicly traded U.S. companies must provide shareholders with an **annual report**. The annual report always includes the financial statements introduced in this chapter. The annual report also includes other important information such as a management discussion and analysis section, notes to the financial statements, and an independent auditor's report. No analysis of a company's financial situation and performance is complete without a review of these items.

Management Discussion and Analysis

The **management discussion and analysis (MD&A)** section presents management's views on the company's **ability to pay near-term obligations, its ability to fund operations and expansion, and its results of operations**. Management must highlight favorable or unfavorable trends and identify significant events and uncertainties that affect these three factors. This discussion obviously involves a number of subjective estimates and opinions. A brief excerpt from the MD&A section of Tootsie Roll's annual report is presented in Illustration 1-10.

TOOTSIE ROLL INDUSTRIES, INC.
Management's Discussion and Analysis of
Financial Condition and Results of Operations

The Company has a relatively straightforward financial structure and has historically maintained a conservative financial position. Except for an immaterial amount of operating leases, the Company has no special financing arrangements or "off-balance sheet" special purpose entities. Cash flows from operations plus maturities of short-term investments are expected to be adequate to meet the Company's overall financing needs, including capital expenditures, in 2012.

Illustration 1-10 Tootsie Roll's management discussion and analysis

Notes to the Financial Statements

Explanatory notes and supporting schedules accompany every set of financial statements and are an integral part of the statements. The **notes to the financial statements** clarify the financial statements, and provide additional detail. Information in the notes does not have to be quantifiable (numeric). Examples of notes are descriptions of the significant accounting policies and methods used in preparing the statements, explanations of uncertainties and contingencies, and various statistics and details too voluminous to be included in the statements. The notes are essential to understanding a company's operating performance and financial position.

Illustration 1-11 is an excerpt from the notes to Tootsie Roll's financial statements. It describes the methods that Tootsie Roll uses to account for revenues.

Illustration 1-11 Notes to Tootsie Roll's financial statements

TOOTSIE ROLL INDUSTRIES, INC.
Notes to Financial Statements

Revenue recognition

Revenue, net of applicable provisions for discounts, returns, allowances, and certain advertising and promotional costs, is recognized when products are delivered to customers based on a customer purchase order, and collectibility is reasonably assured.

Auditor's Report

An **auditor's report** is prepared by an independent outside auditor. It states the auditor's opinion as to the fairness of the presentation of the financial position and results of operations and their conformance with generally accepted accounting principles.

An **auditor** is an accounting professional who conducts an independent examination of a company's financial statements. Only accountants who meet certain criteria and thereby attain the designation **certified public accountant (CPA)** may perform audits. If the auditor is satisfied that the financial statements provide a fair representation of the company's financial position and results of operations in accordance with generally accepted accounting principles, then the auditor expresses an **unqualified opinion**. If the auditor expresses anything other than an unqualified opinion, then readers should only use the financial statements with caution. That is, without an unqualified opinion, we cannot have complete confidence that the financial statements give an accurate picture of the company's financial health. For example, recently Blockbuster, Inc.'s auditor stated that its financial situation raised "substantial doubt about the Company's ability to continue as a going concern."

Illustration 1-12 is an excerpt from the auditor's report from Tootsie Roll's 2011 annual report. Tootsie Roll received an unqualified opinion from its auditor, PricewaterhouseCoopers.

Illustration 1-12 Excerpt from auditor's report on Tootsie Roll's financial statements

TOOTSIE ROLL INDUSTRIES, INC.
Excerpt from Auditor's Report

To the Board of Directors and Shareholders of Tootsie Roll Industries, Inc.

In our opinion, the accompanying consolidated statements of financial position and the related consolidated statements of earnings, comprehensive earnings and retained earnings, and of cash flows present fairly, in all material respects, the financial position of Tootsie Roll Industries, Inc. and its subsidiaries at December 31, 2011 and December 31, 2010, and the results of their operations and their cash flows for each of the three years in the period ended December 31, 2011 in conformity with accounting principles generally accepted in the United States of America. Also in our opinion, the Company maintained, in all material respects, effective internal control over financial reporting as of December 31, 2011, based on criteria established in *Internal Control—Integrated Framework* issued by the Committee of Sponsoring Organizations of the Treadway Commission (COSO).

USING THE DECISION TOOLKIT

The Hershey Company, located in Hershey, Pennsylvania, is the leading North American manufacturer of chocolate. Its products include Hershey's Kisses, Reese's Peanut Butter Cups, Kit Kat, and Take 5 bars. Imagine that you are considering the purchase of shares of Hershey's common stock.

Instructions

Answer these questions related to your decision whether to invest.
(a) What financial statements should you evaluate?
(b) What should these financial statements tell you?
(c) Do you care if the financial statements have been audited? Explain.
(d) Appendix B at the end of this textbook contains financial statements for Hershey. What comparisons can you make between Tootsie Roll and Hershey in terms of their respective results from operations and financial position?

Solution

(a) Before you invest, you should evaluate the income statement, retained earnings statement, balance sheet, and statement of cash flows.
(b) You would probably be most interested in the income statement because it tells about past performance and thus gives an indication of future performance. The retained earnings statement provides a record of the company's dividend history. The balance sheet reveals the relationship between assets and liabilities. The statement of cash flows reveals where the company is getting and spending its cash. This is especially important for a company that wants to grow.
(c) You would want audited financial statements. These statements indicate that a CPA (certified public accountant) has examined and expressed an opinion that the statements present fairly the financial position and results of operations of the company. Investors and creditors should not make decisions without studying audited financial statements.
(d) Many interesting comparisons can be made between the two companies. Tootsie Roll is smaller, with total assets of $857,856,000 versus $4,412,199,000 for Hershey, and it has lower revenue—$532,505,000 versus $6,080,788,000 for Hershey. In addition, Tootsie Roll's cash provided by operating activities of $50,390,000 is less than Hershey's $580,867,000.

While useful, these basic measures are not enough to determine whether one company is a better investment than the other. In later chapters, you will learn of tools that will allow you to compare the relative profitability and financial health of these and other companies.

Summary of Learning Objectives

1 **Describe the primary forms of business organization.** A sole proprietorship is a business owned by one person. A partnership is a business owned by two or more people associated as partners. A corporation is a separate legal entity for which evidence of ownership is provided by shares of stock.

2 **Identify the users and uses of accounting information.** Internal users are managers who need accounting information to plan, organize, and run business operations. The primary external users are investors and creditors. Investors (stockholders) use accounting information to help them decide whether to buy, hold, or sell shares of a company's stock. Creditors (suppliers and bankers) use accounting information to assess the risk of granting credit or loaning money to a business. Other groups who have an indirect interest in a business are taxing authorities, customers, labor unions, and regulatory agencies.

3 **Explain the three principal types of business activity.** Financing activities involve collecting the necessary funds to support the business. Investing activities involve acquiring the resources necessary to run the business.

Operating activities involve putting the resources of the business into action to generate a profit.

4 **Describe the content and purpose of each of the financial statements.** An income statement presents the revenues and expenses of a company for a specific period of time. A retained earnings statement summarizes the changes in retained earnings that have occurred for a specific period of time. A balance sheet reports the assets, liabilities, and stockholders' equity of a business at a specific date. A statement of cash flows summarizes information concerning the cash inflows (receipts) and outflows (payments) for a specific period of time.

5 **Explain the meaning of assets, liabilities, and stockholders' equity, and state the basic accounting equation.** Assets are resources owned by a business. Liabilities are the debts and obligations of the business.

Liabilities represent claims of creditors on the assets of the business. Stockholders' equity represents the claims of owners on the assets of the business. Stockholders' equity is subdivided into two parts: common stock and retained earnings. The basic accounting equation is Assets = Liabilities + Stockholders' Equity.

6 **Describe the components that supplement the financial statements in an annual report.** The management discussion and analysis provides management's interpretation of the company's results and financial position as well as a discussion of plans for the future. Notes to the financial statements provide additional explanation or detail to make the financial statements more informative. The auditor's report expresses an opinion as to whether the financial statements present fairly the company's results of operations and financial position.

🧰 DECISION TOOLKIT *A SUMMARY*

DECISION CHECKPOINTS	INFO NEEDED FOR DECISION	TOOL TO USE FOR DECISION	HOW TO EVALUATE RESULTS
Are the company's operations profitable?	Income statement	The income statement reports a company's revenues and expenses and resulting net income or loss for a period of time.	If the company's revenue exceeds its expenses, it will report net income; otherwise, it will report a net loss.
What is the company's policy toward dividends and growth?	Retained earnings statement	How much of this year's income did the company pay out in dividends to shareholders?	A company striving for rapid growth will pay a low (or no) dividend.
Does the company rely primarily on debt or stockholders' equity to finance its assets?	Balance sheet	The balance sheet reports the company's resources and claims to those resources. There are two types of claims: liabilities and stockholders' equity.	Compare the amount of debt versus the amount of stockholders' equity to determine whether the company relies more on creditors or owners for its financing.
Does the company generate sufficient cash from operations to fund its investing activities?	Statement of cash flows	The statement of cash flows shows the amount of cash provided or used by operating activities, investing activities, and financing activities.	Compare the amount of cash provided by operating activities with the amount of cash used by investing activities. Any deficiency in cash from operating activities must be made up with cash from financing activities.

Glossary

Terms are highlighted in **blue** throughout the chapter.

Accounting The information system that identifies, records, and communicates the economic events of an organization to interested users.

Annual report A report prepared by corporate management that presents financial information including financial

statements, a management discussion and analysis section, notes, and an independent auditor's report.

Assets Resources owned by a business.

Auditor's report A report prepared by an independent outside auditor stating the auditor's opinion as to the fairness of the presentation of the financial position and results of operations and their conformance with generally accepted accounting principles.

Balance sheet A financial statement that reports the assets and claims to those assets at a specific point in time.

Basic accounting equation Assets = Liabilities + Stockholders' Equity.

Certified public accountant (CPA) An individual who has met certain criteria and is thus allowed to perform audits of corporations.

Common stock Term used to describe the total amount paid in by stockholders for the shares they purchase.

Corporation A business organized as a separate legal entity owned by stockholders.

Dividends Payments of cash from a corporation to its stockholders.

Expenses The cost of assets consumed or services used in the process of generating revenues.

Income statement A financial statement that reports a company's revenues and expenses and resulting net income or net loss for a specific period of time.

Liabilities Amounts owed to creditors in the form of debts and other obligations.

Management discussion and analysis (MD&A) A section of the annual report that presents management's views on the company's ability to pay near-term obligations, its ability to fund operations and expansion, and its results of operations.

Net income The amount by which revenues exceed expenses.

Net loss The amount by which expenses exceed revenues.

Notes to the financial statements Notes clarify information presented in the financial statements and provide additional detail.

Partnership A business owned by two or more persons associated as partners.

Retained earnings The amount of net income retained in the corporation.

Retained earnings statement A financial statement that summarizes the amounts and causes of changes in retained earnings for a specific time period.

Revenue The increase in assets or decrease in liabilities resulting from the sale of goods or the performance of services in the normal course of business.

Sarbanes-Oxley Act (SOX) Regulations passed by Congress to reduce unethical corporate behavior.

Sole proprietorship A business owned by one person.

Statement of cash flows A financial statement that provides financial information about the cash receipts and cash payments of a business for a specific period of time.

Stockholders' equity The owners' claim to assets.

WILEY PLUS

Self-Test, Brief Exercises, Exercises, Problem Set A, and many more resources are available for practice in WileyPLUS.

Self-Test Questions

(Answers in *Broadening Your Perspective*.)

(LO 1) **1.** Which is **not** one of the three forms of business organization?
(a) Sole proprietorship.
(b) Creditorship.
(c) Partnership.
(d) Corporation.

(LO 1) **2.** Which is an advantage of corporations relative to partnerships and sole proprietorships?
(a) Lower taxes.
(b) Harder to transfer ownership.
(c) Reduced legal liability for investors.
(d) Most common form of organization.

(LO 2) **3.** Which statement about users of accounting information is **incorrect**?
(a) Management is considered an internal user.
(b) Taxing authorities are considered external users.
(c) Present creditors are considered external users.
(d) Regulatory authorities are considered internal users.

(LO 2) **4.** Which of the following did **not** result from the Sarbanes-Oxley Act?
(a) Top management must now certify the accuracy of financial information.
(b) Penalties for fraudulent activity increased.

(c) Independence of auditors increased.
(d) Tax rates on corporations increased.

5. Which is **not** one of the three primary business (LO 3) activities?
(a) Financing.
(b) Operating.
(c) Advertising.
(d) Investing.

6. Which of the following is an example of a financing (LO 3) activity?
(a) Issuing shares of common stock.
(b) Selling goods on account.
(c) Buying delivery equipment.
(d) Buying inventory.

7. Net income will result during a time period when: (LO 4)
(a) assets exceed liabilities.
(b) assets exceed revenues.
(c) expenses exceed revenues.
(d) revenues exceed expenses.

8. The financial statements for Joseph Corporation (LO 4) contained the following information.

Accounts receivable	$ 5,000
Sales revenue	75,000
Cash	15,000

Salaries and wages expense   20,000
Rent expense   10,000

What was Joseph Corporation's net income?
(a) $60,000.   (c) $65,000.
(b) $15,000.   (d) $45,000.

(LO 4, 5) **9.** ⚙️ What section of a statement of cash flows indicates the cash spent on new equipment during the past accounting period?
(a) The investing activities section.
(b) The operating activities section.
(c) The financing activities section.
(d) The statement of cash flows does not give this information.

(LO 4, 5) **10.** Which statement presents information as of a specific point in time?
(a) Income statement.
(b) Balance sheet.
(c) Statement of cash flows.
(d) Retained earnings statement.

(LO 5) **11.** Which financial statement reports assets, liabilities, and stockholders' equity?
(a) Income statement.
(b) Retained earnings statement.
(c) Balance sheet.
(d) Statement of cash flows.

(LO 5) **12.** Stockholders' equity represents:
(a) claims of creditors.
(b) claims of employees.

(c) the difference between revenues and expenses.
(d) claims of owners.

13. As of December 31, 2014, Stoneland Corporation has (LO 5) assets of $3,500 and stockholders' equity of $1,500. What are the liabilities for Stoneland Corporation as of December 31, 2014?
(a) $1,500.   (c) $2,500.
(b) $1,000.   (d) $2,000.

14. The element of a corporation's annual report that (LO 6) describes the corporation's accounting methods is/are the:
(a) notes to the financial statements.
(b) management discussion and analysis.
(c) auditor's report.
(d) income statement.

15. The element of the annual report that presents an (LO 6) opinion regarding the fairness of the presentation of the financial position and results of operations is/are the:
(a) income statement.
(b) auditor's opinion.
(c) balance sheet.
(d) comparative statements.

Go to the book's companion website, **www.wiley.com/college/kimmel**, to access additional Self-Test Questions.

Questions

1. 🠔 What are the three basic forms of business organizations?

2. What are the advantages to a business of being formed as a corporation? What are the disadvantages?

3. What are the advantages to a business of being formed as a partnership or sole proprietorship? What are the disadvantages?

4. "Accounting is ingrained in our society and is vital to our economic system." Do you agree? Explain.

5. 🠔 Who are the internal users of accounting data? How does accounting provide relevant data to the internal users?

6. Who are the external users of accounting data? Give examples.

7. What are the three main types of business activity? Give examples of each activity.

8. Listed here are some items found in the financial statements of Finzelberg. Indicate in which financial statement(s) each item would appear.
(a) Service revenue.   (d) Accounts receivable.
(b) Equipment.   (e) Common stock.
(c) Advertising expense.   (f) Interest payable.

9. 🠔 ⚙️ Why would a bank want to monitor the dividend payment practices of the corporations to which it lends money?

10. "A company's net income appears directly on the income statement and the retained earnings statement, and it is included indirectly in the company's balance sheet." Do you agree? Explain.

11. ⚙️ What is the primary purpose of the statement of cash flows?

12. What are the three main categories of the statement of cash flows? Why do you think these categories were chosen?

13. What is retained earnings? What items increase the balance in retained earnings? What items decrease the balance in retained earnings?

14. What is the basic accounting equation?

15. (a) Define the terms assets, liabilities, and stockholders' equity.
(b) What items affect stockholders' equity?

16. Which of these items are liabilities of White Glove Cleaning Service?
(a) Cash.   (f) Equipment.
(b) Accounts payable.   (g) Salaries and wages
(c) Dividends.   payable.
(d) Accounts receivable. (h) Service revenue.
(e) Supplies.   (i) Rent expense.

17. How are each of the following financial statements interrelated? (a) Retained earnings statement and income statement. (b) Retained earnings statement and balance sheet. (c) Balance sheet and statement of cash flows.

18. ⚒ What is the purpose of the management discussion and analysis section (MD&A)?

19. ⚒ Why is it important for financial statements to receive an unqualified auditor's opinion?

20. ⚒ What types of information are presented in the notes to the financial statements?

21. ✏️ The accounting equation is Assets = Liabilities + Stockholders' Equity. Appendix A, at the end of this textbook, reproduces Tootsie Roll's financial statements. Replacing words in the equation with dollar amounts, what is Tootsie Roll's accounting equation at December 31, 2011?

The tool icon ⚒ indicates that an activity employs one of the decision tools presented in the chapter. The ➡️ indicates that an activity relates to a business function beyond accounting. The pencil icon ✏️ indicates that an activity requires written communication.

Brief Exercises

BE1-1 Match each of the following forms of business organization with a set of characteristics: sole proprietorship (SP), partnership (P), corporation (C).

(a) _____ Shared control, tax advantages, increased skills and resources.
(b) _____ Simple to set up and maintains control with owner.
(c) _____ Easier to transfer ownership and raise funds, no personal liability.

Describe forms of business organization.
(LO 1), K

BE1-2 Match each of the following types of evaluation with one of the listed users of accounting information.

1. Trying to determine whether the company complied with tax laws.
2. Trying to determine whether the company can pay its obligations.
3. Trying to determine whether an advertising proposal will be cost-effective.
4. Trying to determine whether the company's net income will result in a stock price increase.
5. Trying to determine whether the company should employ debt or equity financing.

(a) _____ Investors in common stock.
(b) _____ Marketing managers.
(c) _____ Creditors.
(d) _____ Chief Financial Officer.
(e) _____ Internal Revenue Service.

Identify users of accounting information.
(LO 2), K

BE1-3 Indicate in which part of the statement of cash flows each item would appear: operating activities (O), investing activities (I), or financing activities (F).

(a) _____ Cash received from customers.
(b) _____ Cash paid to stockholders (dividends).
(c) _____ Cash received from issuing new common stock.
(d) _____ Cash paid to suppliers.
(e) _____ Cash paid to purchase a new office building.

Classify items by activity.
(LO 3), K

BE1-4 Presented below are a number of transactions. Determine whether each transaction affects common stock (C), dividends (D), revenue (R), expense (E), or does not affect stockholders' equity (NSE). Provide titles for the revenues and expenses.

(a) Costs incurred for advertising.
(b) Assets received for services performed.
(c) Costs incurred for insurance.
(d) Amounts paid to employees.
(e) Cash distributed to stockholders.
(f) Assets received in exchange for allowing the use of the company's building.
(g) Costs incurred for utilities used.
(h) Cash purchase of equipment.
(i) Cash received from investors.

Determine effect of transactions on stockholders' equity.
(LO 4), C

BE1-5 In alphabetical order below are balance sheet items for Burnett Company at December 31, 2014. Prepare a balance sheet following the format of Illustration 1-7.

Prepare a balance sheet.
(LO 4, 5), AP

Accounts payable	$65,000
Accounts receivable	71,000
Cash	22,000
Common stock	18,000
Retained earnings	10,000

Determine where items appear on financial statements.
(LO 4, 5), K

BE1-6 Eskimo Pie Corporation markets a broad range of frozen treats, including its famous Eskimo Pie ice cream bars. The following items were taken from a recent income statement and balance sheet. In each case, identify whether the item would appear on the balance sheet (BS) or income statement (IS).

(a) _____ Income tax expense.   (f) _____ Sales revenue.
(b) _____ Inventory.   (g) _____ Cost of goods sold.
(c) _____ Accounts payable.   (h) _____ Common stock.
(d) _____ Retained earnings.   (i) _____ Accounts receivable.
(e) _____ Equipment.   (j) _____ Interest expense.

Determine proper financial statement.
(LO 4), K

BE1-7 Indicate which statement you would examine to find each of the following items: income statement (IS), balance sheet (BS), retained earnings statement (RES), or statement of cash flows (SCF).
(a) Revenue during the period.
(b) Supplies on hand at the end of the year.
(c) Cash received from issuing new bonds during the period.
(d) Total debts outstanding at the end of the period.

Use basic accounting equation.
(LO 5), AP

BE1-8 Use the basic accounting equation to answer these questions.
(a) The liabilities of Jantz Company are $90,000 and the stockholders' equity is $230,000. What is the amount of Jantz Company's total assets?
(b) The total assets of Foley Company are $170,000 and its stockholders' equity is $80,000. What is the amount of its total liabilities?
(c) The total assets of Sundberg Co. are $800,000 and its liabilities are equal to one-fourth of its total assets. What is the amount of Sundberg Co.'s stockholders' equity?

Use basic accounting equation.
(LO 5), AP

BE1-9 At the beginning of the year, Goren Company had total assets of $800,000 and total liabilities of $500,000. (Treat each item independently.)
(a) If total assets increased $150,000 during the year and total liabilities decreased $80,000, what is the amount of stockholders' equity at the end of the year?
(b) During the year, total liabilities increased $100,000 and stockholders' equity decreased $70,000. What is the amount of total assets at the end of the year?
(c) If total assets decreased $80,000 and stockholders' equity increased $110,000 during the year, what is the amount of total liabilities at the end of the year?

Identify assets, liabilities, and stockholders' equity.
(LO 5), K

BE1-10 Indicate whether each of these items is an asset (A), a liability (L), or part of stockholders' equity (SE).
(a) Accounts receivable.   (d) Supplies.
(b) Salaries and wages payable.   (e) Common stock.
(c) Equipment.   (f) Notes payable.

Determine required parts of annual report.
(LO 6), K

BE1-11 Which is **not** a required part of an annual report of a publicly traded company?
(a) Statement of cash flows.
(b) Notes to the financial statements.
(c) Management discussion and analysis.
(d) All of these are required.

Exercises

E1-1 Here is a list of words or phrases discussed in this chapter:

1. Corporation   4. Partnership   7. Accounts payable
2. Creditor   5. Stockholder   8. Auditor's opinion
3. Accounts receivable 6. Common stock

Match items with descriptions.
(LO 1, 2, 4, 6), K

Instructions

Match each word or phrase with the best description of it.
_____ (a) An expression about whether financial statements conform with generally accepted accounting principles.
_____ (b) A business that raises money by issuing shares of stock.
_____ (c) The portion of stockholders' equity that results from receiving cash from investors.

_____ (d) Obligations to suppliers of goods.
_____ (e) Amounts due from customers.
_____ (f) A party to whom a business owes money.
_____ (g) A party that invests in common stock.
_____ (h) A business that is owned jointly by two or more individuals but does not issue stock.

E1-2 All businesses are involved in three types of activities—financing, investing, and operating. Listed below are the names and descriptions of companies in several different industries.

Identify business activities.
(LO 3), **C**

     Abitibi Consolidated Inc.—manufacturer and marketer of newsprint
     Cal State–Northridge Stdt Union—university student union
     Oracle Corporation—computer software developer and retailer
     Sportsco Investments—owner of the Vancouver Canucks hockey club
     Grant Thornton LLP—professional accounting and business advisory firm
     Southwest Airlines—discount airline

Instructions
(a) For each of the above companies, provide examples of (1) a financing activity, (2) an investing activity, and (3) an operating activity that the company likely engages in.
(b) Which of the activities that you identified in (a) are common to most businesses? Which activities are not?

E1-3 The Clear View Golf & Country Club details the following accounts in its financial statements.

Classify accounts.
(LO 3, 4), **C**

	(a)	**(b)**
Accounts payable	_____	_____
Accounts receivable	_____	_____
Equipment	_____	_____
Sales revenue	_____	_____
Service revenue	_____	_____
Inventory	_____	_____
Mortgage payable	_____	_____
Supplies expense	_____	_____
Rent expense	_____	_____
Salaries and wages expense	_____	_____

Instructions
(a) Classify each of the above accounts as an asset (A), liability (L), stockholders' equity (SE), revenue (R), or expense (E) item.
(b) Classify each of the above accounts as a financing activity (F), investing activity (I), or operating activity (O). If you believe a particular account doesn't fit in any of these activities, explain why.

E1-4 This information relates to Molina Co. for the year 2014.

Prepare income statement and retained earnings statement.
(LO 4), **AP**

Retained earnings, January 1, 2014	$67,000
Advertising expense	1,800
Dividends	6,000
Rent expense	10,400
Service revenue	58,000
Utilities expense	2,400
Salaries and wages expense	30,000

Instructions
After analyzing the data, prepare an income statement and a retained earnings statement for the year ending December 31, 2014.

E1-5 Suppose the following information was taken from the 2014 financial statements of pharmaceutical giant Merck and Co. (All dollar amounts are in millions.)

Prepare income statement and retained earnings statement.
(LO 4), **AP**

Retained earnings, January 1, 2014	$43,698.8
Cost of goods sold	9,018.9
Selling and administrative expenses	8,543.2

Dividends	3,597.7
Sales revenue	38,576.0
Research and development expense	5,845.0
Income tax expense	2,267.6

Instructions

(a) After analyzing the data, prepare an income statement and a retained earnings statement for the year ending December 31, 2014.
(b) Suppose that Merck decided to reduce its research and development expense by 50%. What would be the short-term implications? What would be the long-term implications? How do you think the stock market would react?

Prepare a retained earnings statement.
(LO 4), AP

E1-6 Presented here is information for DeVito Inc. for 2014.

Retained earnings, January 1	$130,000
Service revenue	400,000
Total expenses	175,000
Dividends	65,000

Instructions

Prepare the 2014 retained earnings statement for DeVito Inc.

Interpret financial facts.
(LO 4), AP

E1-7 Consider each of the following independent situations.

(a) The retained earnings statement of Grant Corporation shows dividends of $68,000, while net income for the year was $75,000.
(b) The statement of cash flows for Remington Corporation shows that cash provided by operating activities was $10,000, cash used in investing activities was $110,000, and cash provided by financing activities was $130,000.

Instructions

Identify financial statement components and prepare income statement.
(LO 4, 5), C

For each company, provide a brief discussion interpreting these financial facts. For example, you might discuss the company's financial health or its apparent growth philosophy.

E1-8 The following items and amounts were taken from Motte Inc.'s 2014 income statement and balance sheet.

_____	Cash	$ 84,700	_____ Accounts receivable	$ 88,419
_____	Retained earnings	123,192	_____ Sales revenue	584,951
_____	Cost of goods sold	438,458	_____ Notes payable	6,499
_____	Salaries and wages expense	115,131	_____ Accounts payable	49,384
_____	Prepaid insurance	7,818	_____ Service revenue	4,806
_____	Inventory	64,618	_____ Interest expense	1,882

Instructions

(a) In each, case, identify on the blank line whether the item is an asset (A), liability (L), stockholder's equity (SE), revenue (R), or expense (E) item.
(b) Prepare an income statement for Motte Inc. for the year ended December 31, 2014.

Calculate missing amounts.
(LO 4, 5), AP

E1-9 Here are incomplete financial statements for Riedy, Inc.

RIEDY, INC.
Balance Sheet

Assets		Liabilities and Stockholders' Equity	
Cash	$ 7,000	Liabilities	
Inventory	10,000	Accounts payable	$ 5,000
Buildings	45,000	Stockholders' equity	
Total assets	$62,000	Common stock	(a)
		Retained earnings	(b)
		Total liabilities and stockholders' equity	$62,000

Income Statement

Revenues	$85,000
Cost of goods sold	(c)
Salaries and wages expense	10,000
Net income	$ (d)

Retained Earnings Statement

Beginning retained earnings	$12,000
Add: Net income	(e)
Less: Dividends	5,000
Ending retained earnings	$27,000

Instructions

Calculate the missing amounts.

E1-10 Flint Hills Park is a private camping ground near the Lathom Peak Recreation Area. It has compiled the following financial information as of December 31, 2014.

Compute net income and prepare a balance sheet.
(LO 4, 5), AP

Service revenue (from camping fees)	$132,000	Dividends	$ 9,000
Sales revenue (from general store)	25,000	Notes payable	50,000
Accounts payable	11,000	Expenses during 2014	126,000
Cash	8,500	Supplies	5,500
Equipment	114,000	Common stock	40,000
		Retained earnings (1/1/2014)	5,000

Instructions
(a) Determine Flint Hills Park's net income for 2014.
(b) Prepare a retained earnings statement and a balance sheet for Flint Hills Park as of December 31, 2014.
(c) Upon seeing this income statement, Joe Winsor, the campground manager, immediately concluded, "The general store is more trouble than it is worth—let's get rid of it." The marketing director isn't so sure this is a good idea. What do you think?

E1-11 Kellogg Company is the world's leading producer of ready-to-eat cereal and a leading producer of grain-based convenience foods such as frozen waffles and cereal bars. Suppose the following items were taken from its 2014 income statement and balance sheet. (All dollars are in millions.)

Identify financial statement components and prepare an income statement.
(LO 4, 5), AP

___ Retained earnings	$5,481		___ Bonds payable	$ 4,835
___ Cost of goods sold	7,184		___ Inventory	910
___ Selling and			___ Sales revenue	12,575
administrative expenses	3,390		___ Accounts payable	1,077
___ Cash	334		___ Common stock	105
___ Notes payable	44		___ Income tax expense	498
___ Interest expense	295			

Instructions

Perform each of the following.
(a) In each case, identify whether the item is an asset (A), liability (L), stockholders' equity (SE), revenue (R), or expense (E).
(b) Prepare an income statement for Kellogg Company for the year ended December 31, 2014.

E1-12 This information is for Dyckman Corporation for the year ended December 31, 2014.

Prepare a statement of cash flows.
(LO 5), AP

Cash received from lenders	$20,000
Cash received from customers	50,000
Cash paid for new equipment	28,000
Cash dividends paid	8,000
Cash paid to suppliers	16,000
Cash balance 1/1/14	12,000

Prepare a statement of cash flows.

(LO 5), AP

Instructions

(a) Prepare the 2014 statement of cash flows for Dyckman Corporation.

(b) Suppose you are one of Dyckman's creditors. Referring to the statement of cash flows, evaluate Dyckman's ability to repay its creditors.

E1-13 Suppose the following data are derived from the 2014 financial statements of Southwest Airlines. (All dollars are in millions.) Southwest has a December 31 year-end.

Cash balance, January 1, 2014	$1,390
Cash paid for repayment of debt	122
Cash received from issuance of common stock	144
Cash received from issuance of long-term debt	500
Cash received from customers	9,823
Cash paid for property and equipment	1,529
Cash paid for dividends	14
Cash paid for repurchase of common stock	1,001
Cash paid for goods and services	6,978

Instructions

(a) After analyzing the data, prepare a statement of cash flows for Southwest Airlines for the year ended December 31, 2014.

(b) Discuss whether the company's net cash provided by operating activities was sufficient to finance its investing activities. If it was not, how did the company finance its investing activities?

Correct an incorrectly prepared balance sheet.

(LO 5), AP

E1-14 Edward Waltz is the bookkeeper for Edminson Company. Edward has been trying to get the balance sheet of Edminson Company to balance. It finally balanced, but now he's not sure it is correct.

EDMINSON COMPANY
Balance Sheet
December 31, 2014

Assets		Liabilities and Stockholders' Equity	
Cash	$18,000	Accounts payable	$16,000
Supplies	9,500	Accounts receivable	(12,000)
Equipment	40,000	Common stock	40,000
Dividends	8,000	Retained earnings	31,500
Total assets	$75,500	Total liabilities and stockholders' equity	$75,500

Instructions

Prepare a correct balance sheet.

Classify items as assets, liabilities, and stockholders' equity and prepare accounting equation.

(LO 5), AP

E1-15 Suppose the following items were taken from the balance sheet of Nike, Inc. (All dollars are in millions.)

1. Cash	$2,291.1	7. Inventory	$2,357.0
2. Accounts receivable	2,883.9	8. Income taxes payable	86.3
3. Common stock	2,874.2	9. Equipment	1,957.7
4. Notes payable	342.9	10. Retained earnings	5,818.9
5. Buildings	3,759.9	11. Accounts payable	2,815.8
6. Mortgage payable	1,311.5		

Instructions

Perform each of the following.

(a) Classify each of these items as an asset, liability, or stockholders' equity and determine the total dollar amount for each classification.

(b) Determine Nike's accounting equation by calculating the value of total assets, total liabilities, and total stockholders' equity.

(c) To what extent does Nike rely on debt versus equity financing?

Use financial statement relationships to determine missing amounts.

(LO 5), AP

E1-16 The summaries of data from the balance sheet, income statement, and retained earnings statement for two corporations, Colaw Corporation and Hunter Enterprises, are presented on the next page for 2014.

	Colaw Corporation	Hunter Enterprises
Beginning of year		
Total assets	$110,000	$150,000
Total liabilities	70,000	(d)
Total stockholders' equity	(a)	70,000
End of year		
Total assets	(b)	180,000
Total liabilities	120,000	55,000
Total stockholders' equity	60,000	(e)
Changes during year in retained earnings		
Dividends	(c)	5,000
Total revenues	215,000	(f)
Total expenses	165,000	80,000

Instructions

Determine the missing amounts. Assume all changes in stockholders' equity are due to changes in retained earnings.

E1-17 The annual report provides financial information in a variety of formats, including the following.

Classify various items in an annual report.

(LO 6), **K**

    Management discussion and analysis (MD&A)
    Financial statements
    Notes to the financial statements
    Auditor's opinion

Instructions

For each of the following, state in what area of the annual report the item would be presented. If the item would probably not be found in an annual report, state "Not disclosed."
(a) The total cumulative amount received from stockholders in exchange for common stock.
(b) An independent assessment concerning whether the financial statements present a fair depiction of the company's results and financial position.
(c) The interest rate that the company is being charged on all outstanding debts.
(d) Total revenue from operating activities.
(e) Management's assessment of the company's results.
(f) The names and positions of all employees hired in the last year.

Challenge Exercises

Visit the book's companion website, at **www.wiley.com/college/kimmel**, and choose the Student Companion site to access Challenge Exercises.

Problems: Set A

P1-1A Presented below are five independent situations.
(a) Three physics professors at MIT have formed a business to improve the speed of information transfer over the Internet for stock exchange transactions. Each has contributed an equal amount of cash and knowledge to the venture. Although their approach looks promising, they are concerned about the legal liabilities that their business might confront.
(b) Al Bolt, a college student looking for summer employment, opened a bait shop in a small shed at a local marina.
(c) Rita Benedict and Joe Freeze each owned separate shoe manufacturing businesses. They have decided to combine their businesses. They expect that within the coming year they will need significant funds to expand their operations.

Determine forms of business organization.

(LO 1), **C**

(d) Andrea, Diane, and Steve recently graduated with marketing degrees. They have been friends since childhood. They have decided to start a consulting business focused on marketing sporting goods over the Internet.

(e) Jack Yaeger has developed a low-cost GPS device that can be implanted into pets so that they can be easily located when lost. He would like to build a small manufacturing facility to make the devices and then sell them to veterinarians across the country. Jack has no savings or personal assets. He wants to maintain control over the business.

Instructions

In each case, explain what form of organization the business is likely to take—sole proprietorship, partnership, or corporation. Give reasons for your choice.

Identify users and uses of financial statements.

(LO 2, 4, 5), **K**

P1-2A Financial decisions often place heavier emphasis on one type of financial statement over the others. Consider each of the following hypothetical situations independently.

(a) The North Face is considering extending credit to a new customer. The terms of the credit would require the customer to pay within 30 days of receipt of goods.

(b) An investor is considering purchasing common stock of Amazon.com. The investor plans to hold the investment for at least 5 years.

(c) JPMorgan Chase Bank is considering extending a loan to a small company. The company would be required to make interest payments at the end of each year for 5 years, and to repay the loan at the end of the fifth year.

(d) The president of Campbell Soup is trying to determine whether the company is generating enough cash to increase the amount of dividends paid to investors in this and future years, and still have enough cash to buy equipment as it is needed.

Instructions

In each situation, state whether the decision-maker would be most likely to place primary emphasis on information provided by the income statement, balance sheet, or statement of cash flows. In each case provide a brief justification for your choice. Choose only one financial statement in each case.

Prepare an income statement, retained earnings statement, and balance sheet; discuss results.

(LO 4, 5), **AP**

P1-3A On June 1, Hightower Service Co. was started with an initial investment in the company of $22,100 cash. Here are the assets, liabilities, and common stock of the company at June 30, and the revenues and expenses for the month of June, its first month of operations:

Cash	$ 4,600	Notes payable	$12,000
Accounts receivable	4,000	Accounts payable	500
Service revenue	7,500	Supplies expense	1,000
Supplies	2,400	Maintenance and repairs expense	600
Advertising expense	400	Utilities expense	300
Equipment	26,000	Salaries and wages expense	1,400
Common stock	22,100		

In June, the company issued no additional stock but paid dividends of $1,400.

Instructions

(a) Prepare an income statement and a retained earnings statement for the month of June and a balance sheet at June 30, 2014.

(b) Briefly discuss whether the company's first month of operations was a success.

(c) Discuss the company's decision to distribute a dividend.

(a) Net income $ 3,800
Ret. earnings $ 2,400
Tot. assets $37,000

Determine items included in a statement of cash flows, prepare the statement, and comment.

(LO 5), **AP**

P1-4A Presented below is selected financial information for Wenger Corporation for December 31, 2014.

Inventory	$ 25,000	Cash paid to purchase equipment	$ 12,000
Cash paid to suppliers	104,000	Equipment	40,000
Buildings	200,000	Service revenue	100,000
Common stock	50,000	Cash received from customers	132,000
Cash dividends paid	7,000	Cash received from issuing	
Cash at beginning of period	9,000	common stock	22,000

Instructions

(a) Determine which items should be included in a statement of cash flows and then prepare the statement for Wenger Corporation.

(b) Comment on the adequacy of net cash provided by operating activities to fund the company's investing activities and dividend payments.

(a) Net increase $31,000

P1-5A Merando Corporation was formed on January 1, 2014. At December 31, 2014, Bill Jensen, the president and sole stockholder, decided to prepare a balance sheet, which appeared as follows.

Comment on proper accounting treatment and prepare a corrected balance sheet.
(LO 5), **AP**

MERANDO CORPORATION
Balance Sheet
December 31, 2014

Assets		Liabilities and Stockholders' Equity	
Cash	$20,000	Accounts payable	$30,000
Accounts receivable	50,000	Notes payable	15,000
Inventory	36,000	Boat loan	22,000
Boat	24,000	Stockholders' equity	64,000

Bill willingly admits that he is not an accountant by training. He is concerned that his balance sheet might not be correct. He has provided you with the following additional information.

1. The boat actually belongs to Jensen, not to Merando Corporation. However, because he thinks he might take customers out on the boat occasionally, he decided to list it as an asset of the company. To be consistent, he also listed as a liability of the corporation his personal loan that he took out at the bank to buy the boat.
2. The inventory was originally purchased for $25,000, but due to a surge in demand Bill now thinks he could sell it for $36,000. He thought it would be best to record it at $36,000.
3. Included in the accounts receivable balance is $10,000 that Bill loaned to his brother 5 years ago. Bill included this in the receivables of Merando Corporation so he wouldn't forget that his brother owes him money.

Instructions
(a) Comment on the proper accounting treatment of the three items above.
(b) Provide a corrected balance sheet for Merando Corporation. (*Hint:* To get the balance sheet to balance, adjust stockholders' equity.)

(b) Tot. assets $85,000

Problems: Set B

Visit the book's companion website, at **www.wiley.com/college/kimmel**, and choose the Student Companion site to access Problem Set B.

Broadening Your Perspective

Financial Reporting and Analysis

FINANCIAL REPORTING PROBLEM: *Tootsie Roll Industries, Inc.*

BYP1-1 The 2011 financial statements of Tootsie Roll Industries, Inc. are provided in Appendix A.

Instructions
Refer to Tootsie Roll's financial statements to answer the following questions.
(a) What were Tootsie Roll's total assets at December 31, 2011? At December 31, 2010?
(b) How much cash did Tootsie Roll have on December 31, 2011?
(c) What amount of accounts payable did Tootsie Roll report on December 31, 2011? On December 31, 2010?
(d) What were Tootsie Roll's total revenues in 2011? In 2010?
(e) What is the amount of the change in Tootsie Roll's net income from 2010 to 2011?

COMPARATIVE ANALYSIS PROBLEM: *Tootsie Roll vs. Hershey*

BYP1-2 Tootsie Roll's financial statements are presented in Appendix A. The financial statements of The Hershey Company are presented in Appendix B.

Instructions

(a) Based on the information in these financial statements, determine the following for each company.
  (1) Total assets at December 31, 2011.
  (2) Net property, plant, and equipment at December 31, 2011.
  (3) Total revenue for 2011.
  (4) Net income for 2011.
(b) What conclusions concerning the two companies can you draw from these data?

RESEARCH CASE

BYP1-3 The June 22, 2011, issue of the *Wall Street Journal Online* includes an article by Michael Rapoport entitled "Auditors Urged to Tell More." It provides an interesting discussion of the possible expanding role of CPAs.

Instructions

Read the article and answer the following questions.

(a) What are some of the ideas that the Public Company Accounting Oversight Board proposed for expanding the role of auditors in "passing judgment on more of what a company does and says?"
(b) How might the financial crisis influence the public's opinion regarding the need for more information from auditors?
(c) Describe the proposed "Auditor's Discussion and Analysis."
(d) Discuss whether you think that auditors will view these proposals positively or negatively.

INTERPRETING FINANCIAL STATEMENTS

BYP1-4 Xerox was not having a particularly pleasant year. The company's stock price had already fallen in the previous year from $60 per share to $30. Just when it seemed things couldn't get worse, Xerox's stock fell to $4 per share. The data below were taken from the statement of cash flows of Xerox. (All dollars are in millions.)

Cash used in operating activities		$ (663)
Cash used in investing activities		(644)
Financing activities		
Dividends paid	$ (587)	
Net cash received from issuing debt	3,498	
Cash provided by financing activities		2,911

Instructions

Analyze the information, and then answer the following questions.

(a) If you were a creditor of Xerox, what reaction might you have to the above information?
(b) If you were an investor in Xerox, what reaction might you have to the above information?
(c) If you were evaluating the company as either a creditor or a stockholder, what other information would you be interested in seeing?
(d) Xerox decided to pay a cash dividend. This dividend was approximately equal to the amount paid in the previous year. Discuss the issues that were probably considered in making this decision.

REAL-WORLD FOCUS

BYP1-5 *Purpose:* Identify summary information about companies. This information includes basic descriptions of the company's location, activities, industry, financial health, and financial performance.

Address: **http://biz.yahoo.com/i**, or go to **www.wiley.com/college/kimmel**

Steps
1. Type in a company name, or use the index to find company name.
2. Choose **Quote**, then choose **Profile**, then choose **Income Statement**. Perform instructions (a) and (b) below.
3. Choose **Industry** to identify others in this industry. Perform instructions (c)–(e) below.

Instructions
Answer the following questions.
(a) What is the company's net income? Over what period was this measured?
(b) What is the company's total sales? Over what period was this measured?
(c) What is the company's industry?
(d) What are the names of four companies in this industry?
(e) Choose one of the competitors. What is this competitor's name? What is its total sales? What is its net income?

Critical Thinking

DECISION-MAKING ACROSS THE ORGANIZATION

BYP1-6 Sue Hartley recently accepted a job in the production department at Tootsie Roll. Before she starts work, she decides to review the company's annual report to better understand its operations.

Instructions
Use the annual report provided in Appendix A to answer the following questions.
(a) What CPA firm performed the audit of Tootsie Roll's financial statements?
(b) What was the amount of Tootsie Roll's earnings per share in 2011?
(c) What are the company's net sales in foreign countries in 2011?
(d) What did management suggest as the cause of the decrease in the earnings from operations in 2011?
(e) What were net sales in 2007?
(f) How many shares of Class B common stock have been authorized?
(g) How much cash was spent on capital expenditures in 2011?
(h) Over what life does the company depreciate its buildings?
(i) What was the value of raw material and supplies inventory in 2010?

COMMUNICATION ACTIVITY

BYP1-7 Lori Milner is the bookkeeper for Philco Company, Inc. Lori has been trying to get the company's balance sheet to balance. She finally got it to balance, but she still isn't sure that it is correct.

PHILCO COMPANY, INC.
Balance Sheet
For the Month Ended December 31, 2014

Assets		Liabilities and Stockholders' Equity	
Equipment	$18,000	Common stock	$12,000
Cash	9,000	Accounts receivable	(6,000)
Supplies	1,000	Dividends	(2,000)
Accounts payable	(4,000)	Notes payable	10,000
Total assets	$24,000	Retained earnings	10,000
		Total liabilities and stockholders' equity	$24,000

Instructions
Explain to Lori Milner in a memo (a) the purpose of a balance sheet, and (b) why this balance sheet is incorrect and what she should do to correct it.

ETHICS CASE

BYP1-8 Rules governing the investment practices of individual certified public accountants prohibit them from investing in the stock of a company that their firm audits. The Securities and Exchange Commission (SEC) became concerned that some accountants were violating this rule. In response to an SEC investigation, PricewaterhouseCoopers fired 10 people and spent $25 million educating employees about the investment rules and installing an investment tracking system.

Instructions
Answer the following questions.
(a) Why do you think rules exist that restrict auditors from investing in companies that are audited by their firms?
(b) Some accountants argue that they should be allowed to invest in a company's stock as long as they themselves aren't involved in working on the company's audit or consulting. What do you think of this idea?
(c) Today, a very high percentage of publicly traded companies are audited by only four very large public accounting firms. These firms also do a high percentage of the consulting work that is done for publicly traded companies. How does this fact complicate the decision regarding whether CPAs should be allowed to invest in companies audited by their firm?
(d) Suppose you were a CPA and you had invested in IBM when IBM was not one of your firm's clients. Two years later, after IBM's stock price had fallen considerably, your firm won the IBM audit contract. You will be involved in working with the IBM audit. You know that your firm's rules require that you sell your shares immediately. If you do sell immediately, you will sustain a large loss. Do you think this is fair? What would you do?
(e) Why do you think PricewaterhouseCoopers took such extreme steps in response to the SEC investigation?

ALL ABOUT YOU

BYP1-9 Some people are tempted to make their finances look worse to get financial aid. Companies sometimes also manage their financial numbers in order to accomplish certain goals. Earnings management is the planned timing of revenues, expenses, gains, and losses to smooth out bumps in net income. In managing earnings, companies' actions vary from being within the range of ethical activity, to being both unethical and illegal attempts to mislead investors and creditors.

Instructions
Provide responses for each of the following questions.
(a) Discuss whether you think each of the following actions (adapted from **www.finaid.org/fafsa/maximize.phtml**) to increase the chances of receiving financial aid is ethical.
  (i) Spend down the student's assets and income first, before spending parents' assets and income.
  (ii) Accelerate necessary expenses to reduce available cash. For example, if you need a new car, buy it before applying for financial aid.
  (iii) State that a truly financially dependent child is independent.
  (iv) Have a parent take an unpaid leave of absence for long enough to get below the "threshold" level of income.
(b) What are some reasons why a **company** might want to overstate its earnings?
(c) What are some reasons why a **company** might want to understate its earnings?
(d) Under what circumstances might an otherwise ethical person decide to illegally overstate or understate earnings?

FASB CODIFICATION ACTIVITY

BYP1-10 The FASB has developed the Financial Accounting Standards Board Accounting Standards Codification (or more simply "the Codification"). The FASB's primary goal in developing the Codification is to provide in one place all the authoritative literature related to a particular topic. To provide easy access to the Codification, the FASB also developed the Financial Accounting Standards Board Codification Research System (CRS). CRS is an online, real-time database that provides easy access to the Codification. The Codification and the related CRS provide a topically organized structure, subdivided into topic, subtopics, sections, and paragraphs, using a numerical index system.

You may find this system useful in your present and future studies, and so we have provided an opportunity to use this online system as part of the *Broadening Your Perspective* section.

Instructions

Academic access to the FASB Codification is available through university subscriptions, obtained from the American Accounting Association (at **http://aaahq.org/FASB/Access.cfm**), for an annual fee of $150. This subscription covers an unlimited number of students within a single institution. Once this access has been obtained by your school, you should log in (at **http://aaahq.org/ascLogin.cfm**) and familiarize yourself with the resources that are accessible at the FASB Codification site.

CONSIDERING PEOPLE, PLANET, AND PROFIT

BYP1-11   This chapter's Feature Story discusses the fact that although Clif Bar & Company is not a public company, it does share its financial information with its employees as part of its open-book management approach. Further, although it does not publicly share its financial information, it does provide a different form of an annual report to external users. In this report, the company provides information regarding its sustainability efforts.

Address: **www.clifbar.com/uploads/default/ClifBar_AA2010.pdf**

Instructions

Access the 2010 annual report of Clif Bar & Company at the site shown above and then answer the following questions.
(a) What are the Five Aspirations?
(b) How does this annual report differ from the annual report discussed in Illustration 1-9? Are there any similarities?
(c) What are the four key goals of the company's sustainability efforts related to the planet? Give one example of a recent initiative, and a measurable outcome for that initiative, that the company has taken related to each goal.

Answers to Insight and Accounting Across the Organization Questions

p. 6 The Scoop on Accounting Q: What are the benefits to the company and to the employees of making the financial statements available to all employees? **A:** If employees can read and use financial reports, a company will benefit in the following ways. The **marketing department** will make better decisions about products to offer and prices to charge. The **finance department** will make better decisions about debt and equity financing and how much to distribute in dividends. The **production department** will make better decisions about when to buy new equipment and how much inventory to produce. The **human resources department** will be better able to determine whether employees can be given raises. Finally, **all employees** will be better informed about the basis on which they are evaluated, which will increase employee morale.

p. 7 Spinning the Career Wheel Q: How might accounting help you? **A:** You will need to understand financial reports in any business with which you are associated. Whether you become a manager, a doctor, a lawyer, a social worker, a teacher, an engineer, an architect, or an entrepreneur, a working knowledge of accounting is relevant.

p. 8 The Numbers Behind Not-for-Profit Organizations Q: What benefits does a sound accounting system provide to a not-for-profit organization? **A:** Accounting provides at least two benefits to not-for-profit organizations. First, it helps to ensure that money is used in the way that donors intended. Second, it assures donors that their money is not going to waste and thus increases the likelihood of future donations.

p. 15 Beyond Financial Statements Q: Why might a company's stockholders be interested in its environmental and social performance? **A:** Many companies now recognize that being a socially responsible organization is not only the right thing to do, but it also is good for business. Many investment professionals understand, for example, that environmental, social, and proper corporate governance of companies affects the performance of their investment portfolios. For example, British Petroleum's oil spill disaster is a classic example of the problems that can occur for a company and its stockholders. BP's stock price was slashed, its dividend reduced, its executives replaced, and its reputation badly damaged. It is interesting that socially responsible investment funds are now gaining momentum in the marketplace such that companies now recognize this segment as an important investment group.

Answers to Self-Test Questions

1. b **2.** c **3.** d **4.** d **5.** c **6.** a **7.** d **8.** d **9.** a **10.** b **11.** c **12.** d **13.** d **14.** a **15.** b

A Look at IFRS

Many people feel that there is a need for one set of international accounting standards. Here is why:

Multinational corporations. Today's companies view the entire world as their market. For example, Coca-Cola, Intel, and McDonald's generate more than 50% of their sales outside the United States, and many foreign companies, such as Toyota, Nestlé, and Sony, find their largest market to be the United States.

Mergers and acquisitions. The mergers between Fiat/Chrysler and Vodafone/Mannesmann suggest that we will see even more such business combinations in the future.

Information technology. As communication barriers continue to topple through advances in technology, companies and individuals in different countries and markets are becoming more comfortable buying and selling goods and services from one another.

Financial markets. Financial markets are of international significance today. Whether it is currency, equity securities (stocks), bonds, or derivatives, there are active markets throughout the world trading these types of instruments.

KEY POINTS

- International standards are referred to as **International Financial Reporting Standards (IFRS)**, developed by the International Accounting Standards Board (IASB). Over 115 countries require or permit use of IFRS.

- Recent events in the global capital markets underscore the importance of financial disclosure and transparency not only in the United States but in markets around the world. As a result, many are examining which accounting and financial disclosure rules should be followed.

- U.S standards, referred to as generally accepted accounting principles (GAAP), are developed by the Financial Accounting Standards Board (FASB). The fact that there are differences between what is in this textbook (which is based on U.S. standards) and IFRS should not be surprising because the FASB and IASB have responded to different user needs. In some countries, the primary users of financial statements are private investors. In others, the primary users are tax authorities or central government planners. It appears that the United States and the international standard-setting environment are primarily driven by meeting the needs of investors and creditors.

- The internal control standards applicable to Sarbanes-Oxley (SOX) apply only to large public companies listed on U.S. exchanges. There is a continuing debate as to whether non-U.S. companies should have to comply with this extra layer of regulation. Debate about international companies (non-U.S.) adopting SOX-type standards centers on whether the benefits exceed the costs. The concern is that the higher costs of SOX compliance are making the U.S. securities markets less competitive.

- The textbook mentions a number of ethics violations, such as Enron, WorldCom, and AIG. These problems have also occurred internationally, for example, at Satyam Computer Services (India), Parmalat (Italy), and Royal Ahold (the Netherlands).

- IFRS tends to be simpler in its accounting and disclosure requirements; some people say it is more "principles-based." GAAP is more detailed; some people say it is more "rules-based." This difference in approach has resulted in a debate about the merits of "principles-based" versus "rules-based" standards.

- U.S. regulators have recently eliminated the need for foreign companies that trade shares in U.S. markets to reconcile their accounting with GAAP.

- The three most common forms of business organization, proprietorships, partnerships, and corporations, are also found in countries that use IFRS. Because the choice of business organization is influenced by factors such as legal environment, tax rates and regulations, and degree of entrepreneurism, the relative use of each form will vary across countries.

- The conceptual framework that underlies IFRS is very similar to that used to develop GAAP. The basic definitions provided in this textbook for the key elements of financial statements, that is, assets, liabilities, equity, revenues, and expenses, are simplified versions of the official definitions provided by the FASB. The more substantive definitions, using the IASB definitional structure, are as follows.

Assets. A resource controlled by the entity as a result of past events and from which future economic benefits are expected to flow to the entity.

Liabilities. A present obligation of the entity arising from past events, the settlement of which is expected to result in an outflow from the entity of resources embodying economic benefits. Liabilities may be legally enforceable via a contract or law, but need not be; i.e., they can arise due to normal business practice or customs.

Equity. A residual interest in the assets of the entity after deducting all its liabilities.

Income. Increases in economic benefits that result in increases in equity (other than those related to contributions from shareholders). Income includes both revenues (resulting from ordinary activities) and gains.

Expenses. Decreases in economic benefits that result in decreases in equity (other than those related to distributions to shareholders). Expenses includes losses that are not the result of ordinary activities.

LOOKING TO THE FUTURE

Both the IASB and the FASB are hard at work developing standards that will lead to the elimination of major differences in the way certain transactions are accounted for and reported. In fact, at one time the IASB stated that no new major standards would be issued for a period of time. The reason for this policy was to provide companies the time to translate and implement IFRS into practice, as much had happened in a very short period of time. Consider, for example, that as a result of a joint project on the conceptual framework, the definitions of the most fundamental elements (assets, liabilities, equity, revenues, and expenses) may actually change. However, whether the IASB adopts internal control provisions similar to those in SOX remains to be seen.

IFRS PRACTICE

IFRS SELF-TEST QUESTIONS

1. Which of the following is **not** a reason why a single set of high-quality international accounting standards would be beneficial?
   (a) Mergers and acquisition activity.
   (b) Financial markets.
   (c) Multinational corporations.
   (d) GAAP is widely considered to be a superior reporting system.
2. The Sarbanes-Oxley Act determines:
   (a) international tax regulations.
   (b) internal control standards as enforced by the IASB.
   (c) internal control standards of U.S. publicly traded companies.
   (d) U.S. tax regulations.
3. IFRS is considered to be more:
   (a) principles-based and less rules-based than GAAP.
   (b) rules-based and less principles-based than GAAP.
   (c) detailed than GAAP.
   (d) None of the above.
4. Which of the following statements is **false**?
   (a) IFRS is based on a conceptual framework that is similar to that used to develop GAAP.
   (b) Assets are defined by the IASB as resources controlled by the entity as a result of past events and from which future economic benefits are expected to flow to the entity.
   (c) Non-U.S. companies that trade shares in U.S. markets must reconcile their accounting with GAAP.
   (d) Proprietorships, partnerships, and corporations are also found in countries that use IFRS.
5. Which of the following statements is **true**?
   (a) Under IFRS, the term *income* refers to what would be called revenues and gains under GAAP.
   (b) The term *income* is not used under IFRS.
   (c) The term *income* refers only to gains on investments.
   (d) Under IFRS, expenses include distributions to owners.

IFRS CONCEPTS AND APPLICATION

IFRS1-1 Who are the two key international players in the development of international accounting standards? Explain their role.

IFRS1-2 What might explain the fact that different accounting standard-setters have developed accounting standards that are sometimes quite different in nature?

IFRS1-3 What is the benefit of a single set of high-quality accounting standards?

IFRS1-4 Discuss the potential advantages and disadvantages that countries outside the United States should consider before adopting regulations, such as those in the Sarbanes-Oxley Act, that increase corporate internal control requirements.

INTERNATIONAL FINANCIAL REPORTING PROBLEM: *Zetar plc*

IFRS1-5 The financial statements of Zetar plc are presented in Appendix C. The company's complete annual report, including the notes to its financial statements, is available in the Investors section at **www.zetarplc.com**.

Instructions
Visit Zetar's corporate website and answer the following questions from Zetar's 2011 annual report.
  (a) What accounting firm performed the audit of Zetar's financial statements?
  (b) Over what life does the company depreciate its buildings?
  (c) What is the address of the company's corporate headquarters?
  (d) What is the company's reporting currency?
  (e) What two segments does the company operate in, and what were the sales for each segment in the year ended April 30, 2011?

Answers to IFRS Self-Test Questions

1. d **2.** c **3.** a **4.** c **5.** a

A FURTHER LOOK AT FINANCIAL STATEMENTS

LEARNING OBJECTIVES

After studying this chapter, you should be able to:

1 Identify the sections of a classified balance sheet.

2 Identify tools for analyzing financial statements and ratios for computing a company's profitability.

3 Explain the relationship between a retained earnings statement and a statement of stockholders' equity.

4 Identify and compute ratios for analyzing a company's liquidity and solvency using a balance sheet.

5 Use the statement of cash flows to evaluate solvency.

6 Explain the meaning of generally accepted accounting principles.

7 Discuss financial reporting concepts.

Few people could have predicted how dramatically the Internet would change the investment world. One of the most interesting results is how it has changed the way ordinary people invest their savings. More and more people are striking out on their own, making their own investment decisions.

Two early pioneers in providing investment information to the masses were Tom and David Gardner, brothers who created an online investor website called The Motley Fool. The name comes from Shakespeare's *As You Like It*. The fool in Shakespeare's plays was the only one

JUST FOOLING AROUND?

who could speak unpleasant truths to kings and queens without being killed. Tom and David view themselves as 21st-century "fools," revealing the "truths" of Wall Street to the small investor, who they feel has been taken advantage of by Wall Street insiders. The Motley Fool's online bulletin board enables investors to exchange information and insights about companies.

Critics of these bulletin boards contend that they are simply high-tech rumor mills that cause investors to bid up stock prices to unreasonable levels. For example, the stock of PairGain Technologies jumped 32 percent in a single day as a result of a bogus takeover rumor on an investment bulletin board. Some observers are concerned that small investors—ironically, the very people the

Gardner brothers are trying to help—will be hurt the most by misinformation and intentional scams.

To show how these bulletin boards work, suppose that in a recent year you had $10,000 to invest. You were considering Best Buy Company, the largest seller of electronics equipment in the United States. You scanned the Internet investment bulletin boards and found messages posted by two different investors. Here are excerpts from actual postings during the same year:

TMPVenus: "Where are the prospects for positive movement for this company? Poor margins, poor management, astronomical P/E!"

broachman: "I believe that this is a LONG TERM winner, and presently at a good price."

One says sell, and one says buy. Whom should you believe? If you had taken "broachman's" advice and purchased the stock, the $10,000 you invested would have been worth over $300,000 five years later. Best Buy was one of America's best-performing stocks during that period of time.

Rather than getting swept away by rumors, investors must sort out the good information from the bad. One thing is certain—as information services such as The Motley Fool increase in number, gathering information will become even easier. Evaluating it will be the harder task.

INSIDE CHAPTER 2 . . .

- **Can a Company Be Too Liquid?**
- **When Debt Is Good**
- **The Korean Discount**
- **What Do These Companies Have in Common?**

PREVIEW OF CHAPTER 2

If you are thinking of purchasing Best Buy stock, or any stock, how can you decide what the stock is worth? If you manage J. Crew's credit department, how should you determine whether to extend credit to a new customer? If you are a financial executive of IBM, how do you decide whether your company is generating adequate cash to expand operations without borrowing? Your decision in each of these situations will be influenced by a variety of considerations. One of them should be your careful analysis of a company's financial statements. The reason: Financial statements offer relevant and reliable information, which will help you in your decision-making.

In this chapter, we take a closer look at the balance sheet and introduce some useful ways for evaluating the information provided by the financial statements. We also examine the financial reporting concepts underlying the financial statements. We begin by introducing the classified balance sheet.

A Further Look at Financial Statements

The Classified Balance Sheet	Using the Financial Statements	Financial Reporting Concepts
• Current assets • Long-term investments • Property, plant, and equipment • Intangible assets • Current liabilities • Long-term liabilities • Stockholders' equity	• Ratio analysis • Using the income statement • Using the statement of stockholders' equity • Using a classified balance sheet • Using the statement of cash flows	• The standard-setting environment • Qualities of useful information • Assumptions • Principles • Cost constraint

The Classified Balance Sheet

LEARNING OBJECTIVE 1

Identify the sections of a classified balance sheet.

In Chapter 1, you learned that a balance sheet presents a snapshot of a company's financial position at a point in time. It lists individual asset, liability, and stockholders' equity items. However, to improve users' understanding of a company's financial position, companies often use a **classified** balance sheet instead. A **classified balance sheet** groups together similar assets and similar liabilities, using a number of standard classifications and sections. This is useful because items within a group have similar economic characteristics. A classified balance sheet generally contains the standard classifications listed in Illustration 2-1.

Illustration 2-1 Standard balance sheet classifications

Assets	Liabilities and Stockholders' Equity
Current assets	Current liabilities
Long-term investments	Long-term liabilities
Property, plant, and equipment	Stockholders' equity
Intangible assets	

These groupings help financial statement readers determine such things as (1) whether the company has enough assets to pay its debts as they come due, and (2) the claims of short- and long-term creditors on the company's total assets. Many of these groupings can be seen in the balance sheet of Franklin Corporation shown in Illustration 2-2. In the sections that follow, we explain each of these groupings.

CURRENT ASSETS

Current assets are assets that a company expects to convert to cash or use up within one year or its operating cycle, whichever is longer. In Illustration 2-2, Franklin Corporation had current assets of $22,100. For most businesses, the cutoff for classification as current assets is one year from the balance sheet date. For example, accounts receivable are current assets because the company will

Illustration 2-2 Classified balance sheet

FRANKLIN CORPORATION
Balance Sheet
October 31, 2014

Assets

Current assets			
Cash		$ 6,600	
Debt investments		2,000	
Accounts receivable		7,000	
Notes receivable		1,000	
Inventory		3,000	
Supplies		2,100	
Prepaid insurance		400	
Total current assets			$22,100
Long-term investments			
Stock investments		5,200	
Investment in real estate		2,000	7,200
Property, plant, and equipment			
Land		10,000	
Equipment	$24,000		
Less: Accumulated depreciation—equipment	5,000	19,000	29,000
Intangible assets			
Patents			3,100
Total assets			$61,400

Liabilities and Stockholders' Equity

Current liabilities		
Notes payable	$11,000	
Accounts payable	2,100	
Unearned sales revenue	900	
Salaries and wages payable	1,600	
Interest payable	450	
Total current liabilities		$16,050
Long-term liabilities		
Mortgage payable	10,000	
Notes payable	1,300	
Total long-term liabilities		11,300
Total liabilities		27,350
Stockholders' equity		
Common stock	14,000	
Retained earnings	20,050	
Total stockholders' equity		34,050
Total liabilities and stockholders' equity		$61,400

collect them and convert them to cash within one year. Supplies is a current asset because the company expects to use the supplies in operations within one year.

Some companies use a period longer than one year to classify assets and liabilities as current because they have an operating cycle longer than one year. The **operating cycle** of a company is the average time required to go from cash to cash in producing revenue—to purchase inventory, sell it on account, and then collect cash from customers. For most businesses, this cycle takes less than a year, so they use a one-year cutoff. But for some businesses, such as vineyards or airplane manufacturers, this period may be longer than a year. **Except where noted, we will assume that companies use one year to determine whether an asset or liability is current or long-term.**

Common types of current assets are (1) cash, (2) investments (such as short-term U.S. government securities), (3) receivables (accounts receivable, notes receivable, and interest receivable), (4) inventories, and (5) prepaid expenses (insurance and supplies). **Companies list current assets in the order in which they expect to convert them into cash**. *Follow this rule when doing your homework.*

Illustration 2-3 presents the current assets of Southwest Airlines Co. in a recent year.

Illustration 2-3 Current assets section

SOUTHWEST AIRLINES CO. Balance Sheet (partial) (in millions)	
Current assets	
Cash and cash equivalents	$1,390
Short-term investments	369
Accounts receivable	241
Inventories	181
Prepaid expenses and other current assets	420
Total current assets	$2,601

As explained later in the chapter, a company's current assets are important in assessing its short-term debt-paying ability.

LONG-TERM INVESTMENTS

Long-term investments are generally: (1) investments in stocks and bonds of other corporations that are held for more than one year, (2) long-term assets such as land or buildings that a company is not currently using in its operating activities, and (3) long-term notes receivable. In Illustration 2-2, Franklin Corporation reported total long-term investments of $7,200 on its balance sheet.

Yahoo! Inc. reported long-term investments on its balance sheet in a recent year as shown in Illustration 2-4.

Illustration 2-4 Long-term investments section

YAHOO! INC. Balance Sheet (partial) (in thousands)	
Long-term investments	
Investments in securities	$90,266

PROPERTY, PLANT, AND EQUIPMENT

Property, plant, and equipment are assets with relatively long useful lives that are currently used in operating the business. This category includes land, buildings, equipment, delivery vehicles, and furniture. In Illustration 2-2, Franklin Corporation reported property, plant, and equipment of $29,000.

Depreciation is the allocation of the cost of an asset to a number of years. Companies do this by systematically assigning a portion of an asset's cost as an expense each year (rather than expensing the full purchase price in the year of purchase). The assets that the company depreciates are reported on the balance sheet at cost less accumulated depreciation. The **accumulated depreciation** account shows the total amount of depreciation that the company has expensed thus far in the asset's life. In Illustration 2-2, Franklin Corporation reported accumulated depreciation of $5,000.

Illustration 2-5 presents the property, plant, and equipment of Cooper Tire & Rubber Company in a recent year.

Alternative Terminology
Property, plant, and equipment is sometimes called *fixed assets* or *plant assets*.

COOPER TIRE & RUBBER COMPANY
Balance Sheet (partial)
(in thousands)

Property, plant, and equipment		
Land and land improvements	$ 41,553	
Buildings	298,706	
Machinery and equipment	1,636,091	
Molds, cores, and rings	268,158	$2,244,508
Less: Accumulated depreciation		1,252,692
		$ 991,816

Illustration 2-5 Property, plant, and equipment section

INTANGIBLE ASSETS

Many companies have assets that do not have physical substance and yet often are very valuable. We call these assets **intangible assets**. One common intangible is goodwill. Others include patents, copyrights, and trademarks or trade names that give the company **exclusive right** of use for a specified period of time. Franklin Corporation reported intangible assets of $3,100.

Illustration 2-6 shows the intangible assets of media giant Time Warner, Inc. in a recent year.

TIME WARNER, INC.
Balance Sheet (partial)
(in millions)

Intangible assets	
Goodwill	$40,953
Film library	2,690
Customer lists	2,540
Cable television franchises	38,048
Sports franchises	262
Brands, trademarks, and other intangible assets	8,313
	$92,806

Illustration 2-6 Intangible assets section

CURRENT LIABILITIES

In the liabilities and stockholders' equity section of the balance sheet, the first grouping is current liabilities. **Current liabilities** are obligations that the company is to pay within the next year or operating cycle, whichever is longer. Common examples are accounts payable, salaries and wages payable, notes payable, interest payable, and income taxes payable. Also included as current liabilities are current maturities of long-term obligations—payments to be made within the next year on long-term obligations. In Illustration 2-2, Franklin Corporation reported five different types of current liabilities, for a total of $16,050.

Illustration 2-7 shows the current liabilities section adapted from the balance sheet of Marcus Corporation in a recent year.

Illustration 2-7 Current liabilities section

MARCUS CORPORATION	
Balance Sheet (partial)	
(in thousands)	
Current liabilities	
Notes payable	$ 239
Accounts payable	24,242
Current maturities of long-term debt	57,250
Other current liabilities	27,477
Income taxes payable	11,215
Salary and wages payable	6,720
Total current liabilities	$127,143

LONG-TERM LIABILITIES

Long-term liabilities (**long-term debt**) are obligations that a company expects to pay **after** one year. Liabilities in this category include bonds payable, mortgages payable, long-term notes payable, lease liabilities, and pension liabilities. Many companies report long-term debt maturing after one year as a single amount in the balance sheet and show the details of the debt in notes that accompany the financial statements. Others list the various types of long-term liabilities. In Illustration 2-2, Franklin Corporation reported long-term liabilities of $11,300.

Illustration 2-8 shows the long-term liabilities that The Procter & Gamble Company reported in its balance sheet in a recent year.

Illustration 2-8 Long-term liabilities section

THE PROCTER & GAMBLE COMPANY	
Balance Sheet (partial)	
(in millions)	
Long-term liabilities	
Long-term debt	$23,375
Deferred income taxes	12,015
Other noncurrent liabilities	5,147
Total long-term liabilities	$40,537

STOCKHOLDERS' EQUITY

Stockholders' equity consists of two parts: common or capital stock and retained earnings. Companies record as **common stock** the investments of assets into the business by the stockholders. They record as **retained earnings** the income retained for use in the business. These two parts, combined, make up **stockholders' equity** on the balance sheet. In Illustration 2-2, Franklin reported common stock of $14,000 and retained earnings of $20,050.

Using the Financial Statements

In Chapter 1, we introduced the four financial statements. We discussed how these statements provide information about a company's performance and financial position. In this chapter, we extend this discussion by showing you specific tools that you can use to analyze financial statements in order to make a more meaningful evaluation of a company.

RATIO ANALYSIS

Ratio analysis expresses the relationship among selected items of financial statement data. A **ratio** expresses the mathematical relationship between one quantity and another. For analysis of the primary financial statements, we classify ratios as follows.

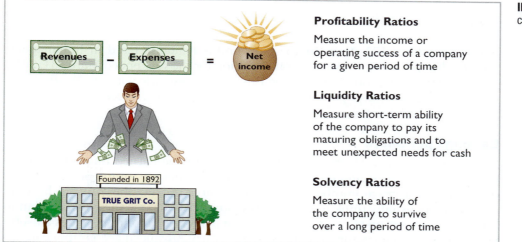

Profitability Ratios

Measure the income or operating success of a company for a given period of time

Liquidity Ratios

Measure short-term ability of the company to pay its maturing obligations and to meet unexpected needs for cash

Solvency Ratios

Measure the ability of the company to survive over a long period of time

Illustration 2-9 Financial ratio classifications

A single ratio by itself is not very meaningful. Accordingly, in this and the following chapters, we will use various comparisons to shed light on company performance:

1. **Intracompany comparisons** covering two years for the same company.
2. **Industry-average comparisons** based on average ratios for particular industries.
3. **Intercompany comparisons** based on comparisons with a competitor in the same industry.

Next, we'll use some ratios and comparisons to analyze the financial statements of Best Buy Company.

USING THE INCOME STATEMENT

Best Buy Company generates profits for its stockholders by selling electronics. The income statement reports how successful it is at generating a profit from its sales. The income statement reports the amount earned during the period (revenues) and the costs incurred during the period (expenses). Illustration 2-10 shows a simplified income statement for Best Buy.

From this income statement, we can see that Best Buy's sales increased but net income decreased during the period. Net income decreased from $1,317 million to $1,277 million. A much smaller competitor of Best Buy is hhgregg.

Illustration 2-10 Best Buy's income statement

	BEST BUY CO., INC. Income Statements For the Years Ended February 26, 2011, and February 27, 2010 (in millions)		
Real World		**2011**	**2010**
Revenues			
Net sales and other revenue		$50,325	$49,749
Expenses			
Cost of goods sold		37,635	37,534
Selling, general, and administrative expenses and other		10,699	10,096
Income tax expense		714	802
Total expenses		49,048	48,432
Net income		$ 1,277	$ 1,317

hhgregg operates 173 stores in 15 states and is headquartered in Indianapolis, Indiana. It reported net income of $48.2 million for the year ended March 31, 2011.

To evaluate the profitability of Best Buy, we will use ratio analysis. **Profitability ratios**, such as earnings per share, measure the operating success of a company for a given period of time.

Earnings per Share

Earnings per share (EPS) measures the net income earned on each share of common stock. We compute EPS by dividing net income minus preferred dividends by the average number of common shares outstanding during the year. Stockholders usually think in terms of the number of shares they own or plan to buy or sell, so stating net income earned as a per share amount provides a useful perspective for determining the investment return. Advanced accounting courses present more refined techniques for calculating earnings per share.

For now, a basic approach for calculating earnings per share is to divide earnings available to common stockholders by average common shares outstanding during the year. What is "earnings available to common stockholders"? It is an earnings amount calculated as net income less dividends paid on another type of stock, called preferred stock (Net income − Preferred dividends).

By comparing earnings per share of **a single company over time**, we can evaluate its relative earnings performance from the perspective of a stockholder—that is, on a per share basis. It is very important to note that comparisons of earnings per share across companies are **not meaningful** because of the wide variations in the numbers of shares of outstanding stock among companies.

Illustration 2-11 shows the earnings per share calculation for Best Buy in 2011 and 2010, based on the information presented below. (Note that to simplify our calculations, we assumed that any change in the number of shares for Best Buy occurred in the middle of the year.)

(in millions)	2011	2010
Net income	$1,277	$1,317
Preferred dividends	–0–	–0–
Shares outstanding at beginning of year	419	414
Shares outstanding at end of year	393	419

Illustration 2-11 Best Buy's earnings per share

Earnings per Share	$= \dfrac{\text{Net Income} - \text{Preferred Dividends}}{\text{Average Common Shares Outstanding}}$	
($ and shares in millions)	2011	2010
Earnings per share	$\dfrac{\$1,277 - \$0}{(393 + 419)/2} = \$3.14$	$\dfrac{\$1,317 - \$0}{(419 + 414)/2} = \$3.16$

DECISION TOOLKIT

DECISION CHECKPOINTS	INFO NEEDED FOR DECISION	TOOL TO USE FOR DECISION	HOW TO EVALUATE RESULTS
How does the company's earnings performance compare with that of previous years?	Net income available to common stockholders and average common shares outstanding	$\dfrac{\text{Earnings}}{\text{per share}} = \dfrac{\text{Net income} - \text{Preferred dividends}}{\text{Average common shares outstanding}}$	A higher measure suggests improved performance, although the number is subject to manipulation. Values should not be compared across companies.

USING THE STATEMENT OF STOCKHOLDERS' EQUITY

As discussed in Chapter 1, the retained earnings statement describes the changes in retained earnings during the year. This statement adds net income to beginning retained earnings and then subtracts dividends to arrive at ending retained earnings.

Stockholders' equity is comprised of two parts: retained earnings and common stock. Therefore, the stockholders' equity of most companies is affected by factors other than just changes in retained earnings. For example, the company may issue or retire shares of common stock. Most companies, therefore, use what is called a **statement of stockholders' equity** rather than a retained earnings statement. This statement presents the causes of changes to stockholders' equity during the period, including those that caused retained earnings to change. Illustration 2-12 is a simplified statement of stockholders' equity for Best Buy.

LEARNING OBJECTIVE 3
Explain the relationship between a retained earnings statement and a statement of stockholders' equity.

Illustration 2-12 Best Buy's statement of stockholders' equity

BEST BUY CO., INC.
Statement of Stockholders' Equity
(in millions)

	Common Stock	Retained Earnings
Balances at February 28, 2009	$ 246	$4,397
Issuance of common stock	237	
Net income		1,317
Dividends		(234)
Other adjustments		1,001
Balances at February 27, 2010	483	6,481
Issuance of common stock	303	
Repurchase of common stock	(729)	
Net income		1,277
Dividends		(238)
Other adjustments		(285)
Balances at February 26, 2011	$ 57	$7,235

We can observe from this financial statement that Best Buy's common stock increased in the first year as the result of an issuance of shares. However, Best Buy's common stock decreased during the second year. Even though it had an issuance of common stock, that increase was much smaller than the decrease caused by a stock repurchase. Another observation from this financial statement is that Best Buy paid dividends each year. This is a relatively recent practice for Best Buy. For many years, it did not pay dividends, even though it was profitable and could do so. You might wonder why Best Buy paid no dividends during years when it was profitable. In fact, in a prior year, two Best Buy stockholders discussed this question about the company's dividend policy on an investor bulletin board. Here are excerpts:

> *Katwoman:* "Best Buy has a nice price increase. Earnings are on the way up. But why no dividends?"

> *AngryCandy:* "I guess they feel they can make better use of the money by investing back in the business. They still view Best Buy as a rapidly growing company and would prefer to invest in expanding the infrastructure (building new stores, advertising, etc.) than in paying out dividends. . . . If Best Buy gets to the stage of 'stable, big company' with little room for expansion, then I'm sure you'll see them elect to pay out a dividend."

AngryCandy's response is an excellent explanation of the thought process that management goes through in deciding whether to pay a dividend. Management must evaluate what its cash needs are. If it has uses for cash that will increase the value of the company (for example, building a new warehouse), then it should retain cash in the company. However, if it has more cash than it has valuable opportunities, it should distribute its excess cash as a dividend.

LEARNING OBJECTIVE	4

Identify and compute ratios for analyzing a company's liquidity and solvency using a balance sheet.

USING A CLASSIFIED BALANCE SHEET

You can learn a lot about a company's financial health by also evaluating the relationship between its various assets and liabilities. Illustration 2-13 provides a simplified balance sheet for Best Buy.

Illustration 2-13 Best Buy's balance sheet

Real World	BEST BUY CO., INC. Balance Sheets (in millions)		
Assets		**February 26, 2011**	**February 27, 2010**
Current assets			
Cash and cash equivalents		$ 1,103	$ 1,826
Short-term investments		22	90
Receivables		2,348	2,020
Merchandise inventories		5,897	5,486
Other current assets		1,103	1,144
Total current assets		10,473	10,566
Property and equipment		7,905	7,453
Less: Accumulated depreciation		4,082	3,383
Net property and equipment		3,823	4,070
Other assets		3,553	3,666
Total assets		$17,849	$18,302

(continued)

Illustration 2-13 (continued)

Liabilities and Stockholders' Equity		
Current liabilities		
Accounts payable	$ 4,894	$ 5,276
Accrued liabilities	1,471	1,681
Accrued income taxes	256	316
Accrued compensation payable	570	544
Other current liabilities	1,472	1,161
Total current liabilities	8,663	8,978
Long-term liabilities		
Long-term debt	711	1,104
Other long-term liabilities	1,183	1,256
Total long-term liabilities	1,894	2,360
Total liabilities	10,557	11,338
Stockholders' equity		
Common stock	57	483
Retained earnings	7,235	6,481
Total stockholders' equity	7,292	6,964
Total liabilities and stockholders' equity	$17,849	$18,302

Liquidity

Suppose you are a banker at CitiGroup considering lending money to Best Buy, or you are a sales manager at Hewlett-Packard interested in selling computers to Best Buy on credit. You would be concerned about Best Buy's **liquidity**—its ability to pay obligations expected to become due within the next year or operating cycle. You would look closely at the relationship of its current assets to current liabilities.

WORKING CAPITAL. One measure of liquidity is **working capital**, which is the difference between the amounts of current assets and current liabilities:

Working Capital = Current Assets − Current Liabilities

Illustration 2-14 Working capital

When current assets exceed current liabilities, working capital is positive. When this occurs, there is greater likelihood that the company will pay its liabilities. When working capital is negative, a company might not be able to pay short-term creditors, and the company might ultimately be forced into bankruptcy. Best Buy had working capital in 2011 of $1,810 million ($10,473 million − $8,663 million).

CURRENT RATIO. **Liquidity ratios** measure the short-term ability of the company to pay its maturing obligations and to meet unexpected needs for cash. One liquidity ratio is the **current ratio**, computed as current assets divided by current liabilities.

The current ratio is a more dependable indicator of liquidity than working capital. Two companies with the same amount of working capital may have significantly different current ratios. Illustration 2-15 shows the 2011 and 2010 current ratios for Best Buy and for hhgregg, along with the 2011 industry average.

What does the ratio actually mean? Best Buy's 2011 current ratio of 1.21:1 means that for every dollar of current liabilities, Best Buy has $1.21 of current assets. Best Buy's current ratio increased in 2011. When compared to the industry average of 1.5:1, Best Buy's liquidity seems low. It is also less than hhgregg's.

Illustration 2-15 Current ratio

Current Ratio $= \dfrac{\text{Current Assets}}{\text{Current Liabilities}}$			
Best Buy ($ in millions)		**hhgregg**	**Industry Average**
2011	2010	2011	2011
$\dfrac{\$10,473}{\$8,663} = 1.21:1$	1.18:1	2.00:1	1.50:1

One potential weakness of the current ratio is that it does not take into account the **composition** of the current assets. For example, a satisfactory current ratio does not disclose whether a portion of the current assets is tied up in slow-moving inventory. The composition of the current assets matters because a dollar of cash is more readily available to pay the bills than is a dollar of inventory. For example, suppose a company's cash balance declined while its merchandise inventory increased substantially. If inventory increased because the company is having difficulty selling its products, then the current ratio might not fully reflect the reduction in the company's liquidity.

Accounting Across the Organization

Can a Company Be Too Liquid?

There actually is a point where a company can be too liquid—that is, it can have too much working capital. While it is important to be liquid enough to be able to pay short-term bills as they come due, a company does not want to tie up its cash in extra inventory or receivables that are not earning the company money.

By one estimate from the REL Consultancy Group, the thousand largest U.S. companies had cumulative excess working capital of $1.017 trillion in a recent year. This was an 18% increase, which REL said represented a "deterioration in the management of operations." Given that managers throughout a company are interested in improving profitability, it is clear that they should have an eye toward managing working capital. They need to aim for a "Goldilocks solution"—not too much, not too little, but just right.

Source: Maxwell Murphy, "The Big Number," *Wall Street Journal* (November 9, 2011).

? What can various company managers do to ensure that working capital is managed efficiently to maximize net income? (Answers in *Broadening Your Perspective*.)

Solvency

Now suppose that instead of being a short-term creditor, you are interested in either buying Best Buy's stock or extending the company a long-term loan. Long-term creditors and stockholders are interested in a company's **solvency**—its ability to pay interest as it comes due and to repay the balance of a debt due at its maturity. **Solvency ratios** measure the ability of the company to survive over a long period of time.

DEBT TO ASSETS RATIO. The **debt to assets ratio** is one measure of solvency. It is calculated by dividing total liabilities (both current and long-term) by total assets. It measures the percentage of total financing provided by creditors rather than stockholders. Debt financing is more risky than equity financing because debt must be repaid at specific points in time, whether the company is performing well or not. Thus, the higher the percentage of debt financing, the riskier the company.

The higher the percentage of total liabilities (debt) to total assets, the greater the risk that the company may be unable to pay its debts as they come due. Illustration 2-16 shows the debt to assets ratios for Best Buy and hhgregg, along with the 2011 industry average.

Debt to Assets Ratio $=\dfrac{\text{Total Liabilities}}{\text{Total Assets}}$			
Best Buy ($ in millions)		**hhgregg**	**Industry Average**
2011	2010	2011	2011
$\dfrac{\$10{,}557}{\$17{,}849}=59\%$	62%	42%	57%

Illustration 2-16 Debt to assets ratio

The 2011 ratio of 59% means that every dollar of assets was financed by 59 cents of debt. Best Buy's ratio exceeds the industry average of 57% and is significantly higher than hhgregg's ratio of 42%. The higher the ratio, the more reliant the company is on debt financing. This means the company has a lower equity "buffer" available to creditors if the company becomes insolvent. Thus, from the creditors' point of view, a high ratio of debt to assets is undesirable. Best Buy's solvency appears lower than hhgregg's and lower than the average company in the industry.

The adequacy of this ratio is often judged in the light of the company's earnings. Generally, companies with relatively stable earnings, such as public utilities, can support higher debt to assets ratios than can cyclical companies with widely fluctuating earnings, such as many high-tech companies. In later chapters, you will learn additional ways to evaluate solvency.

Investor Insight

When Debt Is Good

Debt financing differs greatly across industries and companies. Here are some debt to assets ratios for selected companies in a recent year:

	Debt to Assets Ratio
American Pharmaceutical Partners	19%
Callaway Golf Company	20%
Microsoft	21%
Sears Holdings Corporation	73%
Eastman Kodak Company	78%
General Motors Corporation	94%

? Discuss the difference in the debt to assets ratio of Microsoft and General Motors. (Answers in *Broadening Your Perspective*.)

DECISION TOOLKIT

DECISION CHECKPOINTS	INFO NEEDED FOR DECISION	TOOL TO USE FOR DECISION	HOW TO EVALUATE RESULTS
Can the company meet its near-term obligations?	Current assets and current liabilities	$\text{Current ratio} = \dfrac{\text{Current assets}}{\text{Current liabilities}}$	Higher ratio suggests favorable liquidity.
Can the company meet its long-term obligations?	Total liabilities and total assets	$\dfrac{\text{Debt to}}{\text{assets ratio}} = \dfrac{\text{Total liabilities}}{\text{Total assets}}$	Lower value suggests favorable solvency.

KEEPING AN EYE ON CASH

LEARNING OBJECTIVE 5

Use the statement of cash flows to evaluate solvency.

In the statement of cash flows, net cash provided by operating activities is intended to indicate the cash-generating capability of the company. Analysts have noted, however, that **net cash provided by operating activities fails to take into account that a company must invest in new property, plant, and equipment** (capital expenditures) just to maintain its current level of operations. Companies also must at least **maintain dividends at current levels** to satisfy investors. A measurement to provide additional insight regarding a company's cash-generating ability is free cash flow. **Free cash flow** describes the net cash provided by operating activities after adjusting for capital expenditures and dividends paid.

Consider the following example. Suppose that MPC produced and sold 10,000 personal computers this year. It reported $100,000 net cash provided by operating activities. In order to maintain production at 10,000 computers, MPC invested $15,000 in equipment. It chose to pay $5,000 in dividends. Its free cash flow was $80,000 ($100,000 − $15,000 − $5,000). The company could use this $80,000 to purchase new assets to expand the business, pay off debts, or increase its dividend distribution. In practice, analysts often calculate free cash flow with the formula shown below. (Alternative definitions also exist.)

$$\begin{array}{c} \text{Free Cash} \\ \text{Flow} \end{array} = \begin{array}{c} \text{Net Cash Provided} \\ \text{by Operating Activities} \end{array} - \begin{array}{c} \text{Capital} \\ \text{Expenditures} \end{array} - \begin{array}{c} \text{Cash} \\ \text{Dividends} \end{array}$$

We can calculate Best Buy's 2011 free cash flow as follows (dollars in millions).

Net cash provided by operating activities	$1,190
Less: Expenditures on property, plant, and equipment	744
Dividends paid	237
Free cash flow	$ 209

Best Buy generated free cash flow of $209 million which is available for the acquisition of new assets, the retirement of stock or debt, or the payment of additional dividends. Long-term creditors consider a high free cash flow amount an indication of solvency. hhgregg's free cash flow for 2011 is a negative $0.9 million. Given that hhgregg is considerably smaller than Best Buy, we would expect its free cash flow to be much lower. But, negative free cash flow could be cause for concern.

DECISION TOOLKIT

DECISION CHECKPOINTS	INFO NEEDED FOR DECISION	TOOL TO USE FOR DECISION	HOW TO EVALUATE RESULTS
How much cash did the company generate to expand operations, pay off debts, or distribute dividends?	Net cash provided by operating activities, cash spent on fixed assets, and cash dividends	$\dfrac{\text{Free}}{\text{cash flow}} = \begin{array}{c}\text{Net cash} \\ \text{provided by} \\ \text{operating} \\ \text{activities}\end{array} - \begin{array}{c}\text{Capital} \\ \text{expenditures}\end{array} - \begin{array}{c}\text{Cash} \\ \text{dividends}\end{array}$	Significant free cash flow indicates greater potential to finance new investment and pay additional dividends.

Financial Reporting Concepts

You have now learned about the four financial statements and some basic ways to interpret those statements. In this last section, we will discuss concepts that underlie these financial statements. It would be unwise to make business decisions based on financial statements without understanding the implications of these concepts.

LEARNING OBJECTIVE 6
Explain the meaning of generally accepted accounting principles.

THE STANDARD-SETTING ENVIRONMENT

How does Best Buy decide on the type of financial information to disclose? What format should it use? How should it measure assets, liabilities, revenues, and expenses? Accounting professionals at Best Buy and all other U.S. companies get guidance from a set of accounting standards that have authoritative support, referred to as **generally accepted accounting principles (GAAP)**. Standard-setting bodies, in consultation with the accounting profession and the business community, determine these accounting standards.

The **Securities and Exchange Commission (SEC)** is the agency of the U.S. government that oversees U.S. financial markets and accounting standard-setting bodies. The **Financial Accounting Standards Board (FASB)** is the primary accounting standard-setting body in the United States. The **International Accounting Standards Board (IASB)** issues standards called **International Financial Reporting Standards (IFRS)**, which have been adopted by many countries outside of the United States. Today, the FASB and IASB are working closely together to minimize the differences in their standards. Recently, the SEC announced that foreign companies that wish to have their shares traded on U.S stock exchanges no longer have to prepare reports that conform with GAAP, as long as their reports conform with IFRS. The SEC is currently evaluating whether the United States should eventually adopt IFRS as the required set of standards for U.S. publicly traded companies. Another relatively recent change to the financial reporting environment was that, as a result of the Sarbanes-Oxley Act, the **Public Company Accounting Oversight Board (PCAOB)** was created. Its job is to determine auditing standards and review the performance of auditing firms. If the United States adopts IFRS for its accounting standards, it will also have to coordinate its auditing regulations with those of other countries.

International Insight

The Korean Discount

If you think that accounting standards don't matter, consider recent events in South Korea. For many years, international investors complained that the financial reports of South Korean companies were inadequate and inaccurate. Accounting practices there often resulted in huge differences between stated revenues and actual revenues. Because investors did not have faith in the accuracy of the numbers, they were unwilling to pay as much for the shares of these companies relative to shares of comparable companies in different countries. This difference in share price was often referred to as the "Korean discount."

In response, Korean regulators decided that, beginning in 2011, companies would have to comply with international accounting standards. This change was motivated by a desire to "make the country's businesses more transparent" in order to build investor confidence and spur economic growth. Many other Asian countries, including China, India, Japan, and Hong Kong, have also decided either to adopt international standards or to create standards that are based on the international standards.

Source: Evan Ramstad, "End to 'Korea Discount'?" *Wall Street Journal* (March 16, 2007).

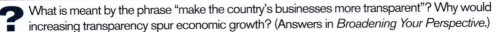

What is meant by the phrase "make the country's businesses more transparent"? Why would increasing transparency spur economic growth? (Answers in *Broadening Your Perspective*.)

QUALITIES OF USEFUL INFORMATION

Recently, the FASB and IASB completed the first phase of a joint project in which they developed a conceptual framework to serve as the basis for future accounting standards. The framework begins by stating that the primary objective of financial reporting is to provide financial information that is **useful** to investors and creditors for making decisions about providing capital. According to the FASB, useful information should possess two fundamental qualities, relevance and faithful representation, as shown in Illustration 2-17.

Illustration 2-17 Fundamental qualities of useful information

Tell me what I need to know.

BIG SHOT

Relevance Accounting information has relevance if it would make a difference in a business decision. Information is considered relevant if it provides information that has **predictive value**, that is, helps provide accurate expectations about the future, and has **confirmatory value**, that is, confirms or corrects prior expectations. Materiality is a company-specific aspect of relevance. An item is material when its **size** makes it likely to influence the decision of an investor or creditor.

Faithful Representation Faithful representation means that information accurately depicts what really happened. To provide a faithful representation, information must be **complete** (nothing important has been omitted), **neutral** (is not biased toward one position or another), and **free from error**.

Enhancing Qualities

In addition to the two fundamental qualities, the FASB and IASB also describe a number of enhancing qualities of useful information. These include **comparability, consistency, verifiability, timeliness,** and **understandability**.

Accounting Across the Organization

What Do These Companies Have in Common?

Another issue related to comparability is the accounting time period. An accounting period that is one-year long is called a **fiscal year**. But a fiscal year need not match the calendar year. For example, a company could end its fiscal year on April 30, rather than December 31.

Why do companies choose the particular year-ends that they do? For example, why doesn't every company use December 31 as the accounting year-end? Many companies choose to end their accounting year when inventory or operations are at a low point. This is advantageous because compiling accounting information requires much time and effort by managers, so they would rather do it when they aren't as busy operating the business. Also, inventory is easier and less costly to count when its volume is low.

Some companies whose year-ends differ from December 31 are Delta Air Lines, June 30; Walt Disney Productions, September 30; and Dunkin' Donuts, Inc., October 31. In the notes to its financial statements, Best Buy states that its accounting year-end is the Saturday nearest the end of February.

? What problems might Best Buy's year-end create for analysts? (Answers in *Broadening Your Perspective*.)

In accounting, **comparability** results when different companies use the same accounting principles. Another characteristic that enhances comparability is consistency. **Consistency** means that a company uses the same accounting principles and methods from year to year. Information is **verifiable** if independent observers, using the same methods, obtain similar results. As noted in Chapter 1, certified public accountants (CPAs) perform audits of financial statements to verify their accuracy. For accounting information to have relevance, it must be **timely**. That is, it must be available to decision-makers before it loses its capacity to influence decisions. The SEC requires that public companies provide their annual reports to investors within 60 days of their year-end. Information has the quality of **understandability** if it is presented in a clear and concise fashion, so that reasonably informed users of that information can interpret it and comprehend its meaning.

ASSUMPTIONS IN FINANCIAL REPORTING

To develop accounting standards, the FASB relies on some key assumptions, as shown in Illustration 2-18. These include assumptions about the monetary unit, economic entity, periodicity, and going concern.

Monetary Unit Assumption   The **monetary unit assumption** requires that only those things that can be expressed in money are included in the accounting records. This means that certain important information needed by investors, creditors, and managers, such as customer satisfaction, is not reported in the financial statements.

Illustration 2-18 Key assumptions in financial reporting

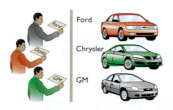

Economic Entity Assumption   The **economic entity assumption** states that every economic entity can be separately identified and accounted for. In order to assess a company's performance and financial position accurately, it is important to not blur company transactions with personal transactions (especially those of its managers) or transactions of other companies.

Margin Note The importance of the economic entity assumption is illustrated by scandals involving Adelphia. In this case, senior company employees entered into transactions that blurred the line between the employees' financial interests and those of the company. For example, Adelphia guaranteed over $2 billion of loans to the founding family.

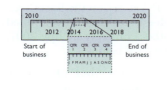

Periodicity Assumption   Notice that the income statement, retained earnings statement, and statement of cash flows all cover periods of one year, and the balance sheet is prepared at the end of each year. The **periodicity assumption** states that the life of a business can be divided into artificial time periods and that useful reports covering those periods can be prepared for the business.

Going Concern Assumption   The **going concern assumption** states that the business will remain in operation for the foreseeable future. Of course, many businesses do fail, but in general, it is reasonable to assume that the business will continue operating.

PRINCIPLES IN FINANCIAL REPORTING

Measurement Principles

GAAP generally uses one of two measurement principles, the historical cost principle or the fair value principle. Selection of which principle to follow generally relates to trade-offs between relevance and faithful representation.

HISTORICAL COST PRINCIPLE. The **historical cost principle** (or cost principle) dictates that companies record assets at their cost. This is true not only at the time the asset is purchased but also over the time the asset is held. For example, if land that was purchased for $30,000 increases in value to $40,000, it continues to be reported at $30,000.

FAIR VALUE PRINCIPLE. The **fair value principle** indicates that assets and liabilities should be reported at fair value (the price received to sell an asset or settle a liability). Fair value information may be more useful than historical cost for certain types of assets and liabilities. For example, certain investment securities are reported at fair value because market price information is often readily available for these types of assets. In choosing between cost and fair value, the FASB uses two qualities that make accounting information useful for decision-making—relevance and faithful representation. In determining which measurement principle to use, the FASB weighs the factual nature of cost figures versus the relevance of fair value. In general, the FASB indicates that most assets must follow the historical cost principle because market values may not be representationally faithful. Only in situations where assets are actively traded, such as investment securities, is the fair value principle applied.

Full Disclosure Principle

The **full disclosure principle** requires that companies disclose all circumstances and events that would make a difference to financial statement users. If an important item cannot reasonably be reported directly in one of the four types of financial statements, then it should be discussed in notes that accompany the statements.

COST CONSTRAINT

Providing information is costly. In deciding whether companies should be required to provide a certain type of information, accounting standard-setters consider the **cost constraint**. It weighs the cost that companies will incur to provide the information against the benefit that financial statement users will gain from having the information available.

 USING THE **DECISION TOOLKIT**

In this chapter, we evaluated a home electronics giant, Best Buy. Tweeter Home Entertainment sold consumer electronics products from 154 stores on the East Coast under various names. It specialized in products with high-end features. Tweeter filed for bankruptcy in June 2007 and was acquired by another company in July 2007. Financial data for Tweeter, prior to its bankruptcy, are provided below.

	September 30	
(amounts in millions)	2006	2005
Current assets	$146.4	$158.2
Total assets	258.6	284.0
Current liabilities	107.1	119.0
Total liabilities	190.4	201.1
Total common stockholders' equity	68.2	82.9
Net income (loss)	(16.5)	(74.4)
Net cash provided (used) by operating activities	15.6	(26.7)

Capital expenditures (net)	17.4	22.2
Dividends paid	0	0
Average shares of common stock (millions)	25.2	24.6

Instructions

Using the data provided, answer the following questions and discuss how these results might have provided an indication of Tweeter's financial troubles.

1. Calculate the current ratio for Tweeter for 2006 and 2005 and discuss its liquidity position.
2. Calculate the debt to assets ratio and free cash flow for Tweeter for 2006 and 2005 and discuss its solvency.
3. Calculate the earnings per share for Tweeter for 2006 and 2005, and discuss its change in profitability.
4. Best Buy's accounting year-end was February 28, 2007; Tweeter's was September 30, 2006. How does this difference affect your ability to compare their profitability?

Solution

1. Current ratio:

   2006: $146.4 ÷ $107.1 = 1.37:1   *2005:* $158.2 ÷ $119.0 = 1.33:1

   Tweeter's liquidity improved slightly from 2005 to 2006, but in both years it would most likely have been considered inadequate. In 2006, Tweeter had only $1.37 in current assets for every dollar of current liabilities. Sometimes larger companies, such as Best Buy, can function with lower current ratios because they have alternative sources of working capital. But a company of Tweeter's size would normally want a higher ratio.

2. Debt to assets:

   2006: $190.4 ÷ $258.6 = 73.6%   *2005:* $201.1 ÷ $284.0 = 70.8%

   Tweeter's solvency, as measured by its debt to assets ratio, declined from 2005 to 2006. Its ratio of 73.6% meant that every dollar of assets was financed by 73.6 cents of debt. For a retailer, this is extremely high reliance on debt. This low solvency suggests Tweeter's ability to meet its debt payments was questionable.

   Free cash flow:

   2006: $15.6 − $17.4 − $0 = −$1.8 million
   2005:   −$26.7 − $22.2 − $0 = −$48.9 million

   Tweeter's free cash flow was negative in both years. The company did not generate enough net cash provided by operating activities even to cover its capital expenditures, and it was not paying a dividend. While this is not unusual for new companies in their early years, it is also not sustainable for very long. Part of the reason that its debt to assets ratio, discussed above, was so high was that it had to borrow money to make up for its deficient free cash flow.

3. Loss per share:

   2006:   −$16.5 ÷ 25.2 = −$0.65 per share
   2005:   −$74.4 ÷ 24.6 = −$3.02 per share

   Tweeter's loss per share declined substantially. However, this was little consolation for its shareholders, who experienced losses in previous years as well. The company's lack of profitability, combined with its poor liquidity and solvency, increased the likelihood that it would eventually file for bankruptcy.

4. Tweeter's income statement covers 7 months not covered by Best Buy's. Suppose that the economy changed dramatically during this 7-month period, either improving or declining. This change in the economy would be reflected in Tweeter's income statement but would not be reflected in Best Buy's income statement until the following March, thus reducing the usefulness of a comparison of the income statements of the two companies.

Summary of Learning Objectives

1 **Identify the sections of a classified balance sheet.** In a classified balance sheet, companies classify assets as current assets; long-term investments; property, plant, and equipment; and intangibles. They classify liabilities as either current or long-term. A stockholders' equity section shows common stock and retained earnings.

2 **Identify tools for analyzing financial statements and ratios for computing a company's profitability.** Ratio analysis expresses the relationship among selected items of financial statement data. Profitability ratios, such as earnings per share (EPS), measure aspects of the operating success of a company for a given period of time.

3 **Explain the relationship between a retained earnings statement and a statement of stockholders' equity.** The retained earnings statement presents the factors that changed the retained earnings balance during the period. A statement of stockholders' equity presents the factors that changed stockholders' equity during the period, including those that changed retained earnings. Thus, a statement of stockholders' equity is more inclusive.

4 **Identify and compute ratios for analyzing a company's liquidity and solvency using a balance sheet.** Liquidity ratios, such as the current ratio, measure the short-term ability of a company to pay its maturing obligations and to meet unexpected needs for cash. Solvency ratios, such as the debt to assets ratio, measure the ability of a company to survive over a long period.

5 **Use the statement of cash flows to evaluate solvency.** Free cash flow indicates a company's ability to generate net cash provided by operating activities that is sufficient to pay debts, acquire assets, and distribute dividends.

6 **Explain the meaning of generally accepted accounting principles.** Generally accepted accounting principles are a set of rules and practices recognized as a general guide for financial reporting purposes. The basic objective of financial reporting is to provide information that is useful for decision-making.

7 **Discuss financial reporting concepts.** To be judged useful, information should have the primary characteristics of relevance and faithful representation. In addition, useful information is comparable, consistent, verifiable, timely, and understandable.

The **monetary unit assumption** requires that companies include in the accounting records only transaction data that can be expressed in terms of money. The **economic entity assumption** states that economic events can be identified with a particular unit of accountability. The **periodicity assumption** states that the economic life of a business can be divided into artificial time periods and that meaningful accounting reports can be prepared for each period. The **going concern assumption** states that the company will continue in operation long enough to carry out its existing objectives and commitments.

The **historical cost principle** states that companies should record assets at their cost. The **fair value principle** indicates that assets and liabilities should be reported at fair value. The **full disclosure principle** requires that companies disclose circumstances and events that matter to financial statement users.

The **cost constraint** weighs the cost that companies incur to provide a type of information against its benefit to financial statement users.

DECISION TOOLKIT *A SUMMARY*

DECISION CHECKPOINTS	INFO NEEDED FOR DECISION	TOOL TO USE FOR DECISION	HOW TO EVALUATE RESULTS
How does the company's earnings performance compare with that of previous years?	Net income available to common stockholders and average common shares outstanding	Earnings per share $=\dfrac{\text{Net income} - \text{Preferred dividends}}{\text{Average common shares outstanding}}$	A higher measure suggests improved performance, although the number is subject to manipulation. Values should not be compared across companies.
Can the company meet its near-term obligations?	Current assets and current liabilities	Current ratio $=\dfrac{\text{Current assets}}{\text{Current liabilities}}$	Higher ratio suggests favorable liquidity.
Can the company meet its long-term obligations?	Total liabilities and total assets	Debt to assets ratio $=\dfrac{\text{Total liabilities}}{\text{Total assets}}$	Lower value suggests favorable solvency.
How much cash did the company generate to expand operations, pay off debts, or distribute dividends?	Net cash provided by operating activities, cash spent on fixed assets, and cash dividends	Free cash flow $=$ Net cash provided by operating activities $-$ Capital expenditures $-$ Cash dividends	Significant free cash flow indicates greater potential to finance new investment and pay additional dividends.

Glossary

Terms are highlighted in blue throughout the chapter.

Classified balance sheet A balance sheet that groups together similar assets and similar liabilities, using a number of standard classifications and sections.

Comparability Ability to compare the accounting information of different companies because they use the same accounting principles.

Consistency Use of the same accounting principles and methods from year to year within a company.

Cost constraint Constraint that weighs the cost that companies will incur to provide the information against the benefit that financial statement users will gain from having the information available.

Current assets Assets that companies expect to convert to cash or use up within one year or the operating cycle, whichever is longer.

Current liabilities Obligations that a company expects to pay within the next year or operating cycle, whichever is longer.

Current ratio A measure of liquidity computed as current assets divided by current liabilities.

Debt to assets ratio A measure of solvency calculated as total liabilities divided by total assets. It measures the percentage of total financing provided by creditors.

Earnings per share (EPS) A measure of the net income earned on each share of common stock; computed as net income minus preferred dividends divided by the average number of common shares outstanding during the year.

Economic entity assumption An assumption that every economic entity can be separately identified and accounted for.

Fair value principle Assets and liabilities should be reported at fair value (the price received to sell an asset or settle a liability).

Faithful representation Information that is complete, neutral, and free from error.

Financial Accounting Standards Board (FASB) The primary accounting standard-setting body in the United States.

Free cash flow Net cash provided by operating activities after adjusting for capital expenditures and cash dividends paid.

Full disclosure principle Accounting principle that dictates that companies disclose circumstances and events that make a difference to financial statement users.

Generally accepted accounting principles (GAAP) A set of accounting standards that have substantial authoritative support, that guide accounting professionals.

Going concern assumption The assumption that the company will continue in operation for the foreseeable future.

Historical cost principle An accounting principle that states that companies should record assets at their cost.

Intangible assets Assets that do not have physical substance.

International Accounting Standards Board (IASB) An accounting standard-setting body that issues standards adopted by many countries outside of the United States.

International Financial Reporting Standards (IFRS) Accounting standards, issued by the IASB, that have been adopted by many countries outside of the United States.

Liquidity The ability of a company to pay obligations that are expected to become due within the next year or operating cycle.

Liquidity ratios Measures of the short-term ability of the company to pay its maturing obligations and to meet unexpected needs for cash.

Long-term investments Generally, (1) investments in stocks and bonds of other corporations that companies hold for more than one year; (2) long-term assets, such as land and buildings, not currently being used in the company's operations; and (3) long-term notes receivable.

Long-term liabilities (long-term debt) Obligations that a company expects to pay after one year.

Materiality Whether an item is large enough to likely influence the decision of an investor or creditor.

Monetary unit assumption An assumption that requires that only those things that can be expressed in money are included in the accounting records.

Operating cycle The average time required to purchase inventory, sell it on account, and then collect cash from customers—that is, go from cash to cash.

Periodicity assumption An assumption that the life of a business can be divided into artificial time periods and that useful reports covering those periods can be prepared for the business.

Profitability ratios Measures of the operating success of a company for a given period of time.

Property, plant, and equipment Assets with relatively long useful lives that are currently used in operating the business.

Public Company Accounting Oversight Board (PCAOB) The group charged with determining auditing standards and reviewing the performance of auditing firms.

Ratio An expression of the mathematical relationship between one quantity and another.

Ratio analysis A technique that expresses the relationship among selected items of financial statement data.

Relevance The quality of information that indicates the information makes a difference in a decision.

Securities and Exchange Commission (SEC) The agency of the U.S. government that oversees U.S. financial markets and accounting standard-setting bodies.

Solvency The ability of a company to pay interest as it comes due and to repay the balance of debt due at its maturity.

Solvency ratios Measures of the ability of the company to survive over a long period of time.

Statement of stockholders' equity A financial statement that presents the causes of changes to stockholders' equity during the period, including those that caused retained earnings to change.

Timely Information that is available to decision-makers before it loses its capacity to influence decisions.

Understandability Information presented in a clear and concise fashion so that users can interpret it and comprehend its meaning.

Verifiable The quality of information that occurs when independent observers, using the same methods, obtain similar results.

Working capital The difference between the amounts of current assets and current liabilities.

 Self-Test, Brief Exercises, Exercises, Problem Set A, and many more resources are available for practice in WileyPLUS.

Self-Test Questions

(Answers in *Broadening Your Perspective*.)

(LO 1) **1.** In a classified balance sheet, assets are usually classified as:
  (a) current assets; long-term assets; property, plant, and equipment; and intangible assets.
  (b) current assets; long-term investments; property, plant, and equipment; and common stock.
  (c) current assets; long-term investments; tangible assets; and intangible assets.
  (d) current assets; long-term investments; property, plant, and equipment; and intangible assets.

(LO 1) **2.** Current assets are listed:
  (a) by order of expected conversion to cash.
  (b) by importance.
  (c) by longevity.
  (d) alphabetically.

(LO 1) **3.** The correct order of presentation in a classified balance sheet for the following current assets is:
  (a) accounts receivable, cash, prepaid insurance, inventory.
  (b) cash, inventory, accounts receivable, prepaid insurance.
  (c) cash, accounts receivable, inventory, prepaid insurance.
  (d) inventory, cash, accounts receivable, prepaid insurance.

(LO 1) **4.** A company has purchased a tract of land. It expects to build a production plant on the land in approximately 5 years. During the 5 years before construction, the land will be idle. The land should be reported as:
  (a) property, plant, and equipment.
  (b) land expense.
  (c) a long-term investment.
  (d) an intangible asset.

(LO 2) **5.** Which is an indicator of profitability?
  (a) Current ratio.
  (b) Earnings per share.
  (c) Debt to assets ratio.
  (d) Free cash flow.

(LO 2) **6.** For 2014, Ganos Corporation reported net income $26,000; net sales $400,000; and average shares outstanding 4,000. There were preferred dividends of $2,000. What was the 2014 earnings per share?
  (a) $6.00.   (c) $99.50.
  (b) $6.50.   (d) $100.00.

7. The balance in retained earnings is **not** affected by: (LO 3)
  (a) net income.
  (b) net loss.
  (c) issuance of common stock.
  (d) dividends.

8. Which of these measures is an evaluation of (LO 4)
a company's ability to pay current liabilities?
  (a) Earnings per share.
  (b) Current ratio.
  (c) Both (a) and (b).
  (d) None of the above.

9. The following ratios are available for Bachus Inc. and (LO 2, 4)
Newton Inc.

	Current Ratio	Debt to Assets Ratio	Earnings per Share
Bachus Inc.	2:1	75%	$3.50
Newton Inc.	1.5:1	40%	$2.75

Compared to Newton Inc., Bachus Inc. has:
  (a) higher liquidity, higher solvency, and higher profitability.
  (b) lower liquidity, higher solvency, and higher profitability.
  (c) higher liquidity, lower solvency, and higher profitability.
  (d) higher liquidity and lower solvency, but profitability cannot be compared based on information provided.

10. Companies can use free cash flow to: (LO 5)
  (a) pay additional dividends.
  (b) acquire property, plant, and equipment.
  (c) pay off debts.
  (d) All of the above.

(LO 6) **11.** Generally accepted accounting principles are:
    (a) a set of standards and rules that are recognized as a general guide for financial reporting.
    (b) usually established by the Internal Revenue Service.
    (c) the guidelines used to resolve ethical dilemmas.
    (d) fundamental truths that can be derived from the laws of nature.

(LO 6) **12.** What organization issues U.S. accounting standards?
    (a) Financial Accounting Standards Board.
    (b) International Accounting Standards Committee.
    (c) International Auditing Standards Committee.
    (d) None of the above.

(LO 7) **13.** What is the primary criterion by which accounting information can be judged?
    (a) Consistency.
    (b) Predictive value.
    (c) Usefulness for decision-making.
    (d) Comparability.

14. Neutrality is an ingredient of: (LO 7)

	Faithful representation	Relevance
(a)	Yes	Yes
(b)	No	No
(c)	Yes	No
(d)	No	Yes

15. The characteristic of information that evaluates (LO 7) whether it is large enough to impact a decision.
    (a) Comparability.   (c) Cost.
    (b) Materiality.   (d) Consistency.

Go to the book's companion website, **www.wiley.com/college/kimmel**, to access additional Self-Test Questions.

Questions

1. What is meant by the term operating cycle?

2. Define current assets. What basis is used for ordering individual items within the current assets section?

3. Distinguish between long-term investments and property, plant, and equipment.

4. How do current liabilities differ from long-term liabilities?

5. Identify the two parts of stockholders' equity in a corporation and indicate the purpose of each.

6.
    (a) Lorie Power believes that the analysis of financial statements is directed at two characteristics of a company: liquidity and profitability. Is Lorie correct? Explain.
    (b) Are short-term creditors, long-term creditors, and stockholders primarily interested in the same characteristics of a company? Explain.

7. Name ratios useful in assessing (a) liquidity, (b) solvency, and (c) profitability.

8. Tim Sands, the founder of Waterboots Inc., needs to raise $500,000 to expand his company's operations. He has been told that raising the money through debt will increase the riskiness of his company much more than issuing stock. He doesn't understand why this is true. Explain it to him.

9. What do these classes of ratios measure?
    (a) Liquidity ratios.
    (b) Profitability ratios.
    (c) Solvency ratios.

10. Holding all other factors constant, indicate whether each of the following signals generally good or bad news about a company.
    (a) Increase in earnings per share.
    (b) Increase in the current ratio.
    (c) Increase in the debt to assets ratio.
    (d) Decrease in free cash flow.

11. Which ratio or ratios from this chapter do you think should be of greatest interest to:
    (a) a pension fund considering investing in a corporation's 20-year bonds?
    (b) a bank contemplating a short-term loan?
    (c) an investor in common stock?

12. (a) What are generally accepted accounting principles (GAAP)?
    (b) What body provides authoritative support for GAAP?

13. (a) What is the primary objective of financial reporting?
    (b) Identify the characteristics of useful accounting information.

14. Joe Merando, the president of Lane Company, is pleased. Lane substantially increased its net income in 2014 while keeping its unit inventory relatively the same. Donald Jantz, chief accountant, cautions Joe, however. Jantz says that since Lane changed its method of inventory valuation, there is a consistency problem and it is difficult to determine whether Lane is better off. Is Jantz correct? Why or why not?

15. What is the distinction between comparability and consistency?

16. Describe the constraint inherent in the presentation of accounting information.

17. Your roommate believes that accounting standards are uniform throughout the world. Is your roommate correct? Explain.

18. Glenda Wine is president of Better Books. She has no accounting background. Wine cannot understand why fair value is not used as the basis for all accounting measurement and reporting. Discuss.

19. What is the economic entity assumption? Give an example of its violation.

20. What was Tootsie Roll's largest current asset, largest current liability, and largest item under "Other assets" at December 31, 2011?

Brief Exercises

Classify accounts on balance sheet.
(LO 1), **K**

BE2-1 The following are the major balance sheet classifications:

Current assets (CA)	Current liabilities (CL)
Long-term investments (LTI)	Long-term liabilities (LTL)
Property, plant, and equipment (PPE)	Common stock (CS)
Intangible assets (IA)	Retained earnings (RE)

Match each of the following accounts to its proper balance sheet classification.

_____ Accounts payable   _____ Income taxes payable
_____ Accounts receivable   _____ Investment in long-term bonds
_____ Accumulated depreciation _____ Land
_____ Buildings   _____ Inventory
_____ Cash   _____ Patent
_____ Goodwill   _____ Supplies

Prepare the current assets section of a balance sheet.
(LO 1), **AP**

BE2-2 A list of financial statement items for Morales Company includes the following: accounts receivable $14,000; prepaid insurance $2,600; cash $10,400; supplies $3,800; and debt investments (short-term) $8,200. Prepare the current assets section of the balance sheet listing the items in the proper sequence.

Compute earnings per share.
(LO 2), **AP**

BE2-3 The following information (in millions of dollars) is available for Limited Brands for a recent year: sales revenue $9,043; net income $220; preferred dividend $0; and average shares outstanding 333 million. Compute the earnings per share for Limited Brands.

Identify items affecting stockholders' equity.
(LO 3), **K**

BE2-4 For each of the following events affecting the stockholders' equity of Noland, indicate whether the event would: increase retained earnings (IRE), decrease retained earnings (DRE), increase common stock (ICS), or decrease common stock (DCS).
_____ (a) Issued new shares of common stock.
_____ (b) Paid a cash dividend.
_____ (c) Reported net income of $75,000.
_____ (d) Reported a net loss of $20,000.

Calculate liquidity ratios.
(LO 4), **AP**

BE2-5 These selected condensed data are taken from a recent balance sheet of Bob Evans Farms (in millions of dollars).

Cash	$ 29.3
Accounts receivable	20.5
Inventory	28.7
Other current assets	24.0
Total current assets	$102.5
Total current liabilities	$201.2

Compute working capital and the current ratio.

Calculate liquidity and solvency ratios.
(LO 4, 5), **AP**

BE2-6 Gray's Books & Music Inc. reported the following selected information at March 31.

	2014
Total current assets	$262,787
Total assets	439,832
Total current liabilities	293,625
Total liabilities	376,002
Net cash provided by operating activities	62,300

Calculate (a) the current ratio, (b) the debt to assets ratio, and (c) free cash flow for March 31, 2014. The company paid dividends of $12,000 and spent $24,787 on capital expenditures.

Recognize generally accepted accounting principles.
(LO 6), **K**

BE2-7 Indicate whether each statement is true or false.
(a) GAAP is a set of rules and practices established by accounting standard-setting bodies to serve as a general guide for financial reporting purposes.
(b) Substantial authoritative support for GAAP usually comes from two standards-setting bodies: the FASB and the IRS.

Identify characteristics of useful information.
(LO 7), **K**

BE2-8 The accompanying chart shows the qualitative characteristics of useful accounting information. Fill in the blanks.

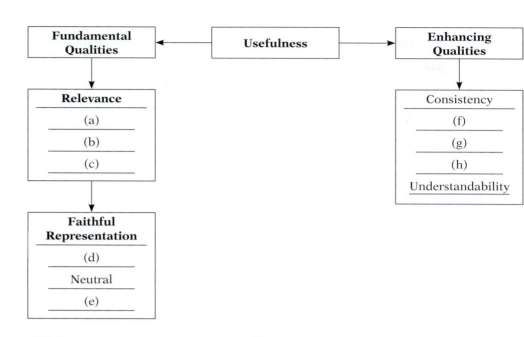

BE2-9 Given the characteristics of useful accounting information, complete each of the following statements.

(a) For information to be _____, it should have predictive and confirmatory value.

(b) _____ means that information accurately depicts what really happened.

(c) _____ means using the same accounting principles and methods from year to year within a company.

Identify characteristics of useful information.

(LO 7), K

BE2-10 Here are some qualitative characteristics of useful accounting information:

1. Predictive value   3. Verifiable
2. Neutral   4. Timely

Match each qualitative characteristic to one of the following statements.

_____ (a) Accounting information should help provide accurate expectations about future events.

_____ (b) Accounting information cannot be selected, prepared, or presented to favor one set of interested users over another.

_____ (c) The quality of information that occurs when independent observers, using the same methods, obtain similar results.

_____ (d) Accounting information must be available to decision-makers before it loses its capacity to influence their decisions.

Identify characteristics of useful information.

(LO 7), K

BE2-11 The full disclosure principle dictates that:

(a) financial statements should disclose all assets at their cost.

(b) financial statements should disclose only those events that can be measured in dollars.

(c) financial statements should disclose all events and circumstances that would matter to users of financial statements.

(d) financial statements should not be relied on unless an auditor has expressed an unqualified opinion on them.

Define full disclosure principle.

(LO 7), K

Exercises

E2-1 The following are the major balance sheet classifications.

Current assets (CA)
Long-term investments (LTI)
Property, plant, and equipment (PPE)
Intangible assets (IA)

Current liabilities (CL)
Long-term liabilities (LTL)
Stockholders' equity (SE)

Classify accounts on balance sheet.

(LO 1), AP

Instructions

Classify each of the following financial statement items taken from Mordica Corporation's balance sheet.

___ Accounts payable   ___ Income taxes payable
___ Accounts receivable   ___ Inventory
___ Accumulated depreciation—   ___ Stock investments (to be sold in 7 months)
     equipment   ___ Land (in use)
___ Buildings   ___ Mortgage payable
___ Cash   ___ Supplies
___ Interest payable   ___ Equipment
___ Goodwill   ___ Prepaid rent

Classify financial statement items by balance sheet classification.

(LO 1), **AP**

E2-2 The major balance sheet classifications are listed in E2-1.

Instructions

Classify each of the following financial statement items based upon the major balance sheet classifications listed in E2-1.

___ Prepaid advertising   ___ Patents
___ Equipment   ___ Bonds payable
___ Trademarks   ___ Common stock
___ Salaries and wages payable   ___ Accumulated depreciation—
___ Income taxes payable   equipment
___ Retained earnings   ___ Unearned sales revenue
___ Accounts receivable   ___ Inventory
___ Land (held for future use)

Classify items as current or noncurrent, and prepare assets section of balance sheet.

(LO 1), **AP**

E2-3 Suppose the following items were taken from the December 31, 2014, assets section of the Boeing Company balance sheet. (All dollars are in millions.)

Inventory	$16,933	Patents	$12,528
Notes receivable—due after		Buildings	21,579
December 31, 2015	5,466	Cash	9,215
Notes receivable—due before		Accounts receivable	5,785
December 31, 2015	368	Debt investments (short-term)	2,008
Accumulated depreciation—buildings	12,795		

Instructions

Prepare the assets section of a classified balance sheet, listing the current assets in order of their liquidity.

Prepare assets section of a classified balance sheet.

(LO 1), **AP**

E2-4 Suppose the following information (in thousands of dollars) is available for H.J. Heinz Company—famous for ketchup and other fine food products—for the year ended April 30, 2014.

Prepaid insurance	$ 125,765	Buildings	$4,033,369
Land	76,193	Cash	373,145
Goodwill	3,982,954	Accounts receivable	1,171,797
Trademarks	757,907	Accumulated depreciation—	
Inventory	1,237,613	buildings	2,131,260

Instructions

Prepare the assets section of a classified balance sheet, listing the items in proper sequence and including a statement heading.

Prepare a classified balance sheet.

(LO 1), **AP**

E2-5 These items are taken from the financial statements of Donavan Co. at December 31, 2014.

Buildings	$105,800
Accounts receivable	12,600
Prepaid insurance	3,200
Cash	11,840
Equipment	82,400
Land	61,200
Insurance expense	780

Depreciation expense	5,300
Interest expense	2,600
Common stock	60,000
Retained earnings (January 1, 2014)	40,000
Accumulated depreciation—buildings	45,600
Accounts payable	9,500
Notes payable	93,600
Accumulated depreciation—equipment	18,720
Interest payable	3,600
Service revenue	14,700

Instructions

Prepare a classified balance sheet. Assume that $13,600 of the note payable will be paid in 2015.

E2-6 Suppose the following items were taken from the 2014 financial statements of Texas Instruments, Inc. (All dollars are in millions.)

Prepare a classified balance sheet.

(LO 1), AP

Common stock	$2,826	Accumulated depreciation—	
Prepaid rent	164	equipment	$3,547
Equipment	6,705	Accounts payable	1,459
Stock investments (long-term)	637	Patents	2,210
Debt investments (short-term)	1,743	Notes payable (long-term)	810
Income taxes payable	128	Retained earnings	6,896
Cash	1,182	Accounts receivable	1,823
		Inventory	1,202

Instructions

Prepare a classified balance sheet in good form as of December 31, 2014.

E2-7 Suppose the following information is available for Callaway Golf Company for the years 2014 and 2013. (Dollars are in thousands, except share information.)

Compute and interpret profitability ratio.

(LO 2), AP

	2014	2013
Net sales	$1,117,204	$1,124,591
Net income (loss)	66,176	54,587
Total assets	855,338	838,078
Share information		
Shares outstanding at year-end	64,507,000	66,282,000
Preferred dividends	–0–	–0–

There were 73,139,000 shares outstanding at the end of 2012.

Instructions

(a) What was the company's earnings per share for each year?
(b) Based on your findings above, how did the company's profitability change from 2013 to 2014?
(c) Suppose the company had paid dividends on preferred stock and on common stock during the year. How would this affect your calculation in part (a)?

E2-8 These financial statement items are for Barfield Corporation at year-end, July 31, 2014.

Prepare financial statements.

(LO 1, 3, 4), AP

Salaries and wages payable	$ 2,080
Salaries and wages expense	57,500
Supplies expense	15,600
Equipment	18,500
Accounts payable	4,100
Service revenue	66,100
Rent revenue	8,500
Notes payable (due in 2017)	1,800
Common stock	16,000
Cash	29,200

Accounts receivable	9,780
Accumulated depreciation—equipment	6,000
Dividends	4,000
Depreciation expense	4,000
Retained earnings (beginning of the year)	34,000

Instructions

(a) Prepare an income statement and a retained earnings statement for the year. Barfield Corporation did not issue any new stock during the year.

(b) Prepare a classified balance sheet at July 31.

(c) Compute the current ratio and debt to assets ratio.

(d) Suppose that you are the president of Crescent Equipment. Your sales manager has approached you with a proposal to sell $20,000 of equipment to Barfield. He would like to provide a loan to Barfield in the form of a 10%, 5-year note payable. Evaluate how this loan would change Barfield's current ratio and debt to assets ratio, and discuss whether you would make the sale.

Compute liquidity ratios and compare results.

(LO 4), **AP**

E2-9 Nordstrom, Inc. operates department stores in numerous states. Selected financial statement data (in millions of dollars) for a recent year follow.

	End of Year	Beginning of Year
Cash and cash equivalents	$ 72	$ 358
Receivables (net)	1,942	1,788
Merchandise inventory	900	956
Other current assets	303	259
Total current assets	$3,217	$3,361
Total current liabilities	$1,601	$1,635

Instructions

(a) Compute working capital and the current ratio at the beginning of the year and at the end of the year.

(b) Did Nordstrom's liquidity improve or worsen during the year?

(c) Using the data in the chapter, compare Nordstrom's liquidity with Best Buy's (see Illustration 2-13).

Compute liquidity measures and discuss findings.

(LO 4), **AP**

E2-10 The chief financial officer (CFO) of Grienke Corporation requested that the accounting department prepare a preliminary balance sheet on December 30, 2014, so that the CFO could get an idea of how the company stood. He knows that certain debt agreements with its creditors require the company to maintain a current ratio of at least 2:1. The preliminary balance sheet is as follows.

GRIENKE CORP.

Balance Sheet

December 30, 2014

Current assets			Current liabilities		
Cash	$25,000		Accounts payable	$ 20,000	
Accounts receivable	30,000		Salaries and wages payable	10,000	$ 30,000
Prepaid insurance	5,000	$ 60,000	Long-term liabilities		
Equipment (net)		200,000	Notes payable		80,000
Total assets		$260,000	Total liabilities		110,000
			Stockholders' equity		
			Common stock	100,000	
			Retained earnings	50,000	150,000
			Total liabilities and stockholders' equity		$260,000

Instructions

(a) Calculate the current ratio and working capital based on the preliminary balance sheet.

(b) Based on the results in (a), the CFO requested that $20,000 of cash be used to pay off the balance of the accounts payable account on December 31, 2014. Calculate the new current ratio and working capital after the company takes these actions.

(c) Discuss the pros and cons of the current ratio and working capital as measures of liquidity.

(d) Was it unethical for the CFO to take these steps?

E2-11 Suppose the following data were taken from the 2014 and 2013 financial statements of American Eagle Outfitters. (All dollars are in thousands.)

Compute and interpret solvency ratios.

(LO 4, 5), AP

	2014	2013
Current assets	$ 925,359	$1,020,834
Total assets	1,963,676	1,867,680
Current liabilities	401,763	376,178
Total liabilities	554,645	527,216
Net income	179,061	400,019
Net cash provided by operating activities	302,193	464,270
Capital expenditures	265,335	250,407
Dividends paid on common stock	82,394	80,796
Weighted-average shares outstanding	205,169	216,119

Instructions

Perform each of the following.

(a) Calculate the current ratio for each year.

(b) Calculate earnings per share for each year.

(c) Calculate the debt to assets ratio for each year.

(d) Calculate the free cash flow for each year.

(e) Discuss American Eagle's solvency in 2014 versus 2013.

(f) Discuss American Eagle's ability to finance its investment activities with net cash provided by operating activities, and how any deficiency would be met.

E2-12 Presented below are the assumptions and principles discussed in this chapter.

Identify accounting assumptions and principles.

(LO 7), K

1. Full disclosure principle.
2. Going concern assumption.
3. Monetary unit assumption.
4. Periodicity assumption.
5. Historical cost principle.
6. Economic entity assumption.

Instructions

Identify by number the accounting assumption or principle that is described below. Do not use a number more than once.

_____ (a) Is the rationale for why plant assets are not reported at liquidation value. (*Note:* Do not use the historical cost principle.)

_____ (b) Indicates that personal and business record-keeping should be separately maintained.

_____ (c) Assumes that the dollar is the "measuring stick" used to report on financial performance.

_____ (d) Separates financial information into time periods for reporting purposes.

_____ (e) Measurement basis used when a reliable estimate of fair value is not available.

_____ (f) Dictates that companies should disclose all circumstances and events that make a difference to financial statement users.

E2-13 Garcia Co. had three major business transactions during 2014.

Identify the assumption or principle that has been violated.

(LO 7), C

(a) Reported at its fair value of $260,000 merchandise inventory with a cost of $208,000.

(b) The president of Garcia Co., Sal Garcia, purchased a truck for personal use and charged it to his expense account.

(c) Garcia Co. wanted to make its 2014 income look better, so it added 2 more weeks to the year (a 54-week year). Previous years were 52 weeks.

Instructions

In each situation, identify the assumption or principle that has been violated, if any, and discuss what the company should have done.

Challenge Exercises

Visit the book's companion website, at **www.wiley.com/college/kimmel**, and choose the Student Companion site to access Challenge Exercises.

Problems: Set A

Prepare a classified balance sheet.
(LO 1), **AP**

P2-1A Suppose the following items are taken from the 2014 balance sheet of Yahoo! Inc. (All dollars are in millions.)

Goodwill	$3,927
Common stock	6,283
Equipment	1,737
Accounts payable	152
Patents	234
Stock investments (long-term)	3,247
Accounts receivable	1,061
Prepaid rent	233
Debt investments (short-term)	1,160
Retained earnings	6,108
Cash	2,292
Notes payable (long-term)	734
Unearned sales revenue	413
Accumulated depreciation—equipment	201

Tot. current assets $4,746
Tot. assets $13,690

Instructions

Prepare a classified balance sheet for Yahoo! Inc. as of December 31, 2014.

Prepare financial statements.
(LO 1, 3), **AP**

P2-2A These items are taken from the financial statements of Tresh Corporation for 2014.

Retained earnings (beginning of year)	$31,000
Utilities expense	2,000
Equipment	66,000
Accounts payable	18,300
Cash	10,100
Salaries and wages payable	3,000
Common stock	12,000
Dividends	12,000
Service revenue	68,000
Prepaid insurance	3,500
Maintenance and repairs expense	1,800
Depreciation expense	3,600
Accounts receivable	11,700
Insurance expense	2,200
Salaries and wages expense	37,000
Accumulated depreciation—equipment	17,600

Net income $21,400
Tot. assets $73,700

Instructions

Prepare an income statement, a retained earnings statement, and a classified balance sheet as of December 31, 2014.

Prepare financial statements.
(LO 1, 3), **AP**

P2-3A You are provided with the following information for Ramirez Enterprises, effective as of its April 30, 2014, year-end.

Accounts payable	$ 834
Accounts receivable	810
Accumulated depreciation—equipment	670
Cash	1,270
Common stock	900
Cost of goods sold	1,060
Depreciation expense	335
Dividends	325
Equipment	2,420
Income tax expense	165
Income taxes payable	135
Insurance expense	210
Interest expense	400
Inventory	967
Land	3,100
Mortgage payable	3,500
Notes payable	61

Prepaid insurance	$ 60
Retained earnings (beginning)	1,600
Salaries and wages expense	700
Salaries and wages payable	222
Sales revenue	5,100
Stock investments (short-term)	1,200

Instructions

(a) Prepare an income statement and a retained earnings statement for Ramirez Enterprises for the year ended April 30, 2014.

(b) Prepare a classified balance sheet for Ramirez Enterprises as of April 30, 2014.

(a) Net income $2,230

(b) Tot. current assets $4,307

     Tot. assets $9,157

P2-4A Comparative financial statement data for Bosch Corporation and Fielder Corporation, two competitors, appear below. All balance sheet data are as of December 31, 2014.

Compute ratios; comment on relative profitability, liquidity, and solvency.

(LO 2, 4, 5), **AN**

	Bosch Corporation 2014	Fielder Corporation 2014
Net sales	$1,800,000	$620,000
Cost of goods sold	1,175,000	340,000
Operating expenses	283,000	98,000
Interest expense	9,000	3,800
Income tax expense	85,000	36,000
Current assets	407,200	190,336
Plant assets (net)	532,000	139,728
Current liabilities	66,325	33,716
Long-term liabilities	108,500	40,684
Net cash provided by operating activities	138,000	36,000
Capital expenditures	90,000	20,000
Dividends paid on common stock	36,000	15,000
Average number of shares outstanding	80,000	50,000

Instructions

(a) Comment on the relative profitability of the companies by computing the net income and earnings per share for each company for 2014.

(b) Comment on the relative liquidity of the companies by computing working capital and the current ratio for each company for 2014.

(c) Comment on the relative solvency of the companies by computing the debt to assets ratio and the free cash flow for each company for 2014.

P2-5A Following are the financial statements of Ogleby Company.

Compute and interpret liquidity, solvency, and profitability ratios.

(LO 2, 4, 5), **AP**

OGLEBY COMPANY
Income Statement
For the Year Ended December 31, 2014

Net sales	$2,218,500
Cost of goods sold	1,012,400
Selling and administrative expenses	906,000
Interest expense	78,000
Income tax expense	69,000
Net income	$ 153,100

OGLEBY COMPANY
Balance Sheet
December 31, 2014

Assets

Current assets

Cash	$ 60,100
Debt investments	84,000
Accounts receivable (net)	169,800
Inventory	145,000
Total current assets	458,900
Plant assets (net)	575,300
Total assets	$1,034,200

Liabilities and Stockholders' Equity

Current liabilities	
Accounts payable	$ 160,000
Income taxes payable	35,500
Total current liabilities	195,500
Bonds payable	200,000
Total liabilities	395,500
Stockholders' equity	
Common stock	350,000
Retained earnings	288,700
Total stockholders' equity	638,700
Total liabilities and stockholders' equity	$1,034,200

Additional information: The net cash provided by operating activities for 2014 was $190,800. The cash used for capital expenditures was $92,000. The cash used for dividends was $31,000. The average number of shares outstanding during the year was 50,000.

Instructions
(a) Compute the following values and ratios for 2014. (We provide the results from 2013 for comparative purposes.)
   (i) Working capital. (2013: $160,500)
   (ii) Current ratio. (2013: 1.65:1)
   (iii) Free cash flow. (2013: $48,700)
   (iv) Debt to assets ratio. (2013: 31%)
   (v) Earnings per share. (2013: $3.15)
(b) Using your calculations from part (a), discuss changes from 2013 in liquidity, solvency, and profitability.

Compute and interpret liquidity, solvency, and profitability ratios.

(LO 2, 4, 5), **AP**

P2-6A Condensed balance sheet and income statement data for Sadecki Corporation are presented here and on the next page.

SADECKI CORPORATION
Balance Sheets
December 31

Assets	2014	2013
Cash	$ 28,000	$ 20,000
Receivables (net)	70,000	62,000
Other current assets	90,000	73,000
Long-term investments	62,000	60,000
Property, plant, and equipment (net)	510,000	470,000
Total assets	$760,000	$685,000
Liabilities and Stockholders' Equity		
Current liabilities	$ 75,000	$ 70,000
Long-term liabilities	80,000	90,000
Common stock	330,000	300,000
Retained earnings	275,000	225,000
Total liabilities and stockholders' equity	$760,000	$685,000

SADECKI CORPORATION
Income Statements
For the Years Ended December 31

	2014	2013
Sales revenue	$750,000	$680,000
Cost of goods sold	440,000	400,000
Operating expenses (including income taxes)	240,000	220,000
Net income	$ 70,000	$ 60,000

Additional information:

Net cash provided by operating activities	$82,000	$56,000
Cash used for capital expenditures	$45,000	$38,000
Dividends paid	$20,000	$15,000
Average number of shares outstanding	33,000	30,000

Instructions

Compute these values and ratios for 2013 and 2014.

(a) Earnings per share.

(b) Working capital.

(c) Current ratio.

(d) Debt to assets ratio.

(e) Free cash flow.

(f) ▰▰▰▶Based on the ratios calculated, discuss briefly the improvement or lack thereof in financial position and operating results from 2013 to 2014 of Sadecki Corporation.

P2-7A Selected financial data of two competitors, Target and Wal-Mart, are presented here. (All dollars are in millions.) Suppose the data were taken from the 2014 financial statements of each company.

Compute ratios and compare liquidity, solvency, and profitability for two companies.

(LO 2, 4, 5), **AP**

	Target (1/31/14)	Wal-Mart (1/31/14)
Income Statement Data for Year		
Net sales	$64,948	$401,244
Cost of goods sold	44,157	306,158
Selling and administrative expenses	16,389	76,651
Interest expense	894	2,103
Other income	28	4,213
Income taxes	1,322	7,145
Net income	$ 2,214	$ 13,400

	Target	Wal-Mart
Balance Sheet Data (End of Year)		
Current assets	$17,488	$ 48,949
Noncurrent assets	26,618	114,480
Total assets	$44,106	$163,429
Current liabilities	$10,512	$ 55,390
Long-term liabilities	19,882	42,754
Total stockholders' equity	13,712	65,285
Total liabilities and stockholders' equity	$44,106	$163,429
Net cash provided by operating activities	$4,430	$23,147
Cash paid for capital expenditures	$3,547	$11,499
Dividends declared and paid on common stock	$465	$3,746
Average shares outstanding (millions)	774	3,951

Instructions

For each company, compute these values and ratios.

(a) Working capital.

(b) Current ratio.

(c) Debt to assets ratio.

(d) Free cash flow.

(e) Earnings per share.

(f) Compare the liquidity and solvency of the two companies.

P2-8A A friend of yours, Sue Yaeger, recently completed an undergraduate degree in science and has just started working with a biotechnology company. Sue tells you that the owners of the business are trying to secure new sources of financing which are needed in order for the company to proceed with development of a new health care product.

Comment on the objectives and qualitative characteristics of financial reporting.

(LO 6, 7), **E**

Sue said that her boss told her that the company must put together a report to present to potential investors.

Sue thought that the company should include in this package the detailed scientific findings related to the Phase I clinical trials for this product. She said, "I know that the biotech industry sometimes has only a 10% success rate with new products, but if we report all the scientific findings, everyone will see what a sure success this is going to be! The president was talking about the importance of following some set of accounting principles. Why do we need to look at some accounting rules? What they need to realize is that we have scientific results that are quite encouraging, some of the most talented employees around, and the start of some really great customer relationships. We haven't made any sales yet, but we will. We just need the funds to get through all the clinical testing and get government approval for our product. Then these investors will be quite happy that they bought in to our company early!"

Instructions

(a) What is accounting information? Explain to Sue what is meant by generally accepted accounting principles.

(b) Comment on how Sue's suggestions for what should be reported to prospective investors conforms to the qualitative characteristics of accounting information. Do you think that the things that Sue wants to include in the information for investors will conform to financial reporting guidelines?

Problems: Set B

Visit the book's companion website, at **www.wiley.com/college/kimmel**, and choose the Student Companion site to access Problem Set B.

Broadening Your Perspective

Financial Reporting and Analysis

FINANCIAL REPORTING PROBLEM: *Tootsie Roll Industries, Inc.*

BYP2-1   The financial statements of Tootsie Roll Industries, Inc., appear in Appendix A at the end of this textbook.

Instructions

Answer the following questions using the financial statements and the notes to the financial statements.

(a) What were Tootsie Roll's total current assets at December 31, 2011, and December 31, 2010?

(b) Are the assets included in current assets listed in the proper order? Explain.

(c) How are Tootsie Roll's assets classified?

(d) What were Tootsie Roll's current liabilities at December 31, 2011, and December 31, 2010?

COMPARATIVE ANALYSIS PROBLEM: *Tootsie Roll vs. Hershey*

BYP2-2   The financial statements of The Hershey Company appear in Appendix B, following the financial statements for Tootsie Roll in Appendix A. Assume Hershey's average number of shares outstanding was 227,514,000, and Tootsie Roll's was 56,997,000.

Instructions

(a) For each company calculate the following values for 2011.

    (1) Working capital.   (4) Free cash flow.

    (2) Current ratio.   (5) Earnings per share.

    (3) Debt to assets ratio.

    (*Hint:* When calculating free cash flow, **do not** consider business acquisitions to be part of capital expenditures.)

(b) Based on your findings above, discuss the relative liquidity and solvency of the two companies.

RESEARCH CASE

BYP2-3 The July 6, 2011, edition of the *Wall Street Journal Online* includes an article by Michael Rapoport entitled "U.S. Firms Clash Over Accounting Rules." The article discusses why some U.S. companies favored adoption of International Financial Reporting Standards (IFRS) while other companies opposed it.

Instructions

Read the article and answer the following questions.
(a) The articles says that the switch to IFRS tends to be favored by "larger companies, big accounting firms, and rule makers." What reasons are given for favoring the switch?
(b) What two reasons are given by many smaller companies that oppose the switch?
(c) What criticism of IFRS is raised with regard to regulated companies?
(d) Explain what is meant by "condorsement."

INTERPRETING FINANCIAL STATEMENTS

BYP2-4 The following information was reported by Gap, Inc. in its 2010 annual report.

	2010	**2009**	**2008**	**2007**	**2006**
Total assets (millions)	$7,065	$7,985	$7,564	$7,838	$8,544
Working capital	$1,831	$2,533	$1,847	$1,653	$2,757
Current ratio	1.87:1	2.19:1	1.86:1	1.68:1	2.21:1
Debt to assets ratio	.42:1	.39:1	.42:1	.45:1	.39:1
Earnings per share	$1.89	$1.59	$1.35	$1.05	$0.94

(a) Determine the overall percentage decrease in Gap's total assets from 2006 to 2010. What was the average decrease per year?
(b) Comment on the change in Gap's liquidity. Does working capital or the current ratio appear to provide a better indication of Gap's liquidity? What might explain the change in Gap's liquidity during this period?
(c) Comment on the change in Gap's solvency during this period.
(d) Comment on the change in Gap's profitability during this period. How might this affect your prediction about Gap's future profitability?

REAL-WORLD FOCUS

BYP2-5 *Purpose:* Identify summary liquidity, solvency, and profitability information about companies, and compare this information across companies in the same industry.

Address: **http://biz.yahoo.com/i**, or go to **www.wiley.com/college/kimmel**

Steps
1. Type in a company name, or use the index to find a company name. Choose **Profile**. Choose **Key Statistics**. Perform instruction (a) below.
2. Go back to **Profile**. Click on the company's particular industry behind the heading "Industry." Perform instructions (b), (c), and (d).

Instructions

Answer the following questions.
(a) What is the company's name? What was the company's current ratio and debt to equity ratio (a variation of the debt to assets ratio)?
(b) What is the company's industry?
(c) What is the name of a competitor? What is the competitor's current ratio and its debt to equity ratio?
(d) Based on these measures, which company is more liquid? Which company is more solvent?

BYP2-6 The Feature Story described the dramatic effect that investment bulletin boards are having on the investment world. This exercise will allow you to evaluate a bulletin board discussing a company of your choice.

Address: **http://biz.yahoo.com/i**, or go to **www.wiley.com/college/kimmel**

Steps
1. Type in a company name, or use the index to find a company name.
2. Choose **Msgs** or **Message Board**. (for messages).
3. Read the 10 most recent messages.

Instructions

Answer the following questions.

(a) State the nature of each of these messages (e.g., offering advice, criticizing company, predicting future results, ridiculing other people who have posted messages).

(b) For those messages that expressed an opinion about the company, was evidence provided to support the opinion?

(c) What effect do you think it would have on bulletin board discussions if the participants provided their actual names? Do you think this would be a good policy?

Critical Thinking

DECISION-MAKING ACROSS THE ORGANIZATION

BYP2-7 As a financial analyst in the planning department for Shonrock Industries, Inc., you have been requested to develop some key ratios from the comparative financial statements. This information is to be used to convince creditors that Shonrock Industries, Inc. is liquid, solvent, and profitable, and that it deserves their continued support. Lenders are particularly concerned about the company's ability to continue as a going concern.

Here are the data requested and the computations developed from the financial statements:

	2014	2013
Current ratio	3.1	2.1
Working capital	Up 22%	Down 7%
Free cash flow	Up 25%	Up 18%
Debt to assets ratio	0.60	0.70
Net income	Up 32%	Down 8%
Earnings per share	$2.40	$1.15

Instructions

Shonrock Industries, Inc. asks you to prepare brief comments stating how each of these items supports the argument that its financial health is improving. The company wishes to use these comments to support presentation of data to its creditors. With the class divided into groups, prepare the comments as requested, giving the implications and the limitations of each item regarding Shonrock's financial well-being.

COMMUNICATION ACTIVITY

BYP2-8 F. P. Fernetti is the chief executive officer of Tomorrow's Products. Fernetti is an expert engineer but a novice in accounting.

Instructions

Write a letter to F. P. Fernetti that explains (a) the three main types of ratios; (b) examples of each, how they are calculated, and what they measure; and (c) the bases for comparison in analyzing Tomorrow's Products' financial statements.

ETHICS CASE

BYP2-9 At one time, Boeing closed a giant deal to acquire another manufacturer, McDonnell Douglas. Boeing paid for the acquisition by issuing shares of its own stock to the stockholders of McDonnell Douglas. In order for the deal not to be revoked, the value of Boeing's stock could not decline below a certain level for a number of months after the deal.

During the first half of the year, Boeing suffered significant cost overruns because of inefficiencies in its production methods. Had these problems been disclosed in the quarterly financial statements during the first and second quarters of the year, the company's stock most likely would have plummeted, and the deal would have been revoked. Company managers spent considerable time debating when the bad news should be disclosed. One public relations manager suggested that the company's problems be revealed on the date of either Princess Diana's or Mother Teresa's funeral, in the hope that it would be lost among those big stories that day. Instead, the company waited until October 22 of that year to announce a $2.6 billion write-off due to cost overruns. Within one week, the company's stock price had fallen 20%, but by this time the McDonnell Douglas deal could not be reversed.

Instructions
Answer the following questions.
(a) Who are the stakeholders in this situation?
(b) What are the ethical issues?
(c) What assumptions or principles of accounting are relevant to this case?
(d) Do you think it is ethical to try to "time" the release of a story so as to diminish its effect?
(e) What would you have done if you were the chief executive officer of Boeing?
(f) Boeing's top management maintains that it did not have an obligation to reveal its problems during the first half of the year. What implications does this have for investors and analysts who follow Boeing's stock?

ALL ABOUT YOU

BYP2-10   Every company needs to plan in order to move forward. Its top management must consider where it wants the company to be in three to five years. Like a company, you need to think about where you want to be three to five years from now, and you need to start taking steps now in order to get there.

Instructions
Provide responses to each of the following items.
(a) Where would you like to be working in three to five years? Describe your plan for getting there by identifying between five and 10 specific steps that you need to take in order to get there.
(b) In order to get the job you want, you will need a résumé. Your résumé is the equivalent of a company's annual report. It needs to provide relevant and reliable information about your past accomplishments so that employers can decide whether to "invest" in you. Do a search on the Internet to find a good résumé format. What are the basic elements of a résumé?
(c) A company's annual report provides information about a company's accomplishments. In order for investors to use the annual report, the information must be reliable; that is, users must have faith that the information is accurate and believable. How can you provide assurance that the information on your résumé is reliable?
(d) Prepare a résumé assuming that you have accomplished the five to 10 specific steps you identified in part (a). Also, provide evidence that would give assurance that the information is reliable.

FASB CODIFICATION ACTIVITY

BYP2-11   If your school has a subscription to the FASB Codification, go to **http://aaahq.org/ ascLogin.cfm** to log in and prepare responses to the following.

Instructions
(a) Access the glossary ("Master Glossary") at the FASB Codification website to answer the following.
   (1) What is the definition of current assets?
   (2) What is the definition of current liabilities?
(b) A company wants to offset its accounts payable against its cash account and show a cash amount net of accounts payable on its balance sheet. Identify the criteria (found in the FASB Codification) under which a company has the right of set off. Does the company have the right to offset accounts payable against the cash account?

CONSIDERING PEOPLE, PLANET, AND PROFIT

BYP2-12   Auditors provide a type of certification of corporate financial statements. Certification is used in many other aspects of business as well. For example, it plays a critical role in the sustainability movement. The February 7, 2012, issue of the *New York Times* contained an article by S. Amanda Caudill entitled "Better Lives in Better Coffee," which discusses the role of certification in the coffee business.

Address: **http://scientistatwork.blogs.nytimes.com/2012/02/07/better-lives-in-better-coffee/**

Instructions
Read the article and answer the following questions.
(a) The article mentions three different certification types that coffee growers can obtain from three different certification bodies. Using financial reporting as an example, what potential problems might the existence of multiple certification types present to coffee purchasers?
(b) According to the author, which certification is most common among coffee growers? What are the possible reasons for this?
(c) What social and environmental benefits are coffee certifications trying to achieve? Are there also potential financial benefits to the parties involved?

Answers to Insight and Accounting Across the Organization Questions

p. 52 Can a Company Be Too Liquid? Q: What can various company managers do to ensure that working capital is managed efficiently to maximize net income? **A:** Marketing and sales managers must understand that by extending generous repayment terms, they are expanding the company's receivables balance and slowing the company's cash flow. Production managers must strive to minimize the amount of excess inventory on hand. Managers must coordinate efforts to speed up the collection of receivables, while also ensuring that the company pays its payables on time but never too early.

p. 53 When Debt Is Good Q: Discuss the difference in the debt to assets ratio of Microsoft and General Motors. **A:** Microsoft has a very low debt to assets ratio. The company is in a rapidly changing industry and thus should try to minimize the risk associated with increased debt. Also, because Microsoft generates significant amounts of cash and has minimal needs for large investments in plant assets, it does not need to borrow a lot of cash. General Motors needs to make huge investments in plant assets, and it has a very large credit operation. Thus, it has large borrowing needs.

p. 55 The Korean Discount Q: What is meant by the phrase "make the country's businesses more transparent"? Why would increasing transparency spur economic growth? **A:** Transparency refers to the extent to which outsiders have knowledge regarding a company's financial performance and financial position. If a company lacks transparency, its financial reports do not adequately inform investors of critical information that is needed to make investment decisions. If corporate transparency is increased, investors will be more willing to supply the financial capital that businesses need in order to grow, which would spur the country's economic growth.

p. 56 What Do These Companies Have in Common? Q: What problems might Best Buy's year-end create for analysts? **A:** First, if Best Buy's competitors use a different year-end, then when you compare their financial results, you are not comparing performance over the same period of time or financial position at the same point in time. Also, by not picking a particular date, the number of weeks in Best Buy's fiscal year will change. For example, fiscal years 2008 and 2009 had 52 weeks, but fiscal year 2007 had 53 weeks.

Answers to Self-Test Questions

1. d **2.** a **3.** c **4.** c **5.** b **6.** a ($26,000 − $4,000) **7.** c **8.** b **9.** d **10.** d **11.** a **12.** a **13.** c **14.** c **15.** b

A Look at IFRS

The classified balance sheet, although generally required internationally, contains certain variations in format when reporting under IFRS.

LEARNING OBJECTIVE 8

Compare the classified balance sheet format under GAAP and IFRS.

KEY POINTS

- IFRS recommends but does not require the use of the title "statement of financial position" rather than balance sheet.
- The format of statement of financial position information is often presented differently under IFRS. Although no specific format is required, most companies that follow IFRS present statement of financial position information in this order:
  - Noncurrent assets
  - Current assets
  - Equity
  - Noncurrent liabilities
  - Current liabilities
- IFRS requires a classified statement of financial position except in very limited situations. IFRS follows the same guidelines as this textbook for distinguishing between current and noncurrent assets and liabilities.

- Under IFRS, current assets are usually listed in the reverse order of liquidity. For example, under GAAP cash is listed first, but under IFRS it is listed last.
- Some companies report the subtotal **net assets**, which equals total assets minus total liabilities. See, for example, the statement of financial position of Zetar in Appendix C.
- IFRS has many differences in terminology that you will notice in this textbook. For example, in the sample statement of financial position illustrated below, notice in the investment category that stock is called shares, and in the equity section common stock is called share capital—ordinary.
- Both IFRS and GAAP require disclosures about (1) accounting policies followed, (2) judgments that management has made in the process of applying the entity's accounting policies, and (3) the key assumptions and estimation uncertainty that could result in a material adjustment to the carrying amounts of assets and liabilities within the next financial year.
- Comparative prior period information must be presented and financial statements must be prepared annually.
- Both GAAP and IFRS are increasing the use of fair value to report assets. However, at this point IFRS has adopted it more broadly. As examples, under IFRS companies can apply fair value to property, plant, and equipment; natural resources; and in some cases intangible assets.

FRANKLIN CORPORATION
Statement of Financial Position
October 31, 2014

Assets

Intangible assets			
Patents			$ 3,100
Property, plant, and equipment			
Land		$10,000	
Equipment	$24,000		
Less: Accumulated depreciation—equipment	5,000	19,000	29,000
Long-term investments			
Share investments		5,200	
Investment in real estate		2,000	7,200
Current assets			
Prepaid insurance		400	
Supplies		2,100	
Inventory		3,000	
Notes receivable		1,000	
Accounts receivable		7,000	
Debt investments		2,000	
Cash		6,600	22,100
Total assets			$61,400

Equity and Liabilities

Equity		
Share capital—ordinary	$20,000	
Retained earnings	14,050	$34,050
Non-current liabilities		
Mortgage payable	10,000	
Notes payable	1,300	11,300
Current liabilities		
Notes payable	11,000	
Accounts payable	2,100	
Salaries and wages payable	1,600	
Unearned sales revenue	900	
Interest payable	450	16,050
Total equity and liabilities		$61,400

- Recently, the IASB and FASB completed the first phase of a jointly created conceptual framework. In this first phase, they agreed on the objective of financial reporting and a common set of desired qualitative characteristics. These were presented in the Chapter 2 discussion.
- The monetary unit assumption is part of each framework. However, the unit of measure will vary depending on the currency used in the country in which the company is incorporated (e.g., Chinese yuan, Japanese yen, and British pound).
- The economic entity assumption is also part of each framework, although some cultural differences result in differences in its application. For example, in Japan many companies have formed alliances that are so strong that they act similar to related corporate divisions, although they are not actually part of the same company.

LOOKING TO THE FUTURE

The IASB and the FASB are working on a project to converge their standards related to financial statement presentation. A key feature of the proposed framework is that each of the statements will be organized in the same format, to separate an entity's financing activities from its operating and investing activities and, further, to separate financing activities into transactions with owners and creditors. Thus, the same classifications used in the statement of financial position would also be used in the income statement and the statement of cash flows. The project has three phases. You can follow the joint financial presentation project at the following link: **http://www.fasb.org/project/financial_statement_presentation.shtml**.

The IASB and the FASB face a difficult task in attempting to update, modify, and complete a converged conceptual framework. For example, how do companies choose between information that is highly relevant but difficult to verify versus information that is less relevant but easy to verify? How do companies define control when developing a definition of an asset? Is a liability the future sacrifice itself or the obligation to make the sacrifice? Should a single measurement method, such as historical cost or fair value, be used, or does it depend on whether it is an asset or liability that is being measured? It appears that the new document will be a significant improvement over its predecessors and will lead to principle-based standards, which will help financial statement users make better decisions.

IFRS PRACTICE

IFRS SELF-TEST QUESTIONS

1. Which of the following statements is **false**?
   (a) The monetary unit assumption is used under IFRS.
   (b) Under IFRS, companies sometimes net liabilities against assets to report "net assets."
   (c) The FASB and IASB are working on a joint conceptual framework project.
   (d) Under IFRS, the statement of financial position is usually referred to as the statement of assets and equity.
2. A company has purchased a tract of land and expects to build a production plant on the land in approximately 5 years. During the 5 years before construction, the land will be idle. Under IFRS, the land should be reported as:
   (a) land expense.
   (b) property, plant, and equipment.
   (c) an intangible asset.
   (d) a long-term investment.
3. Current assets under IFRS are listed generally:
   (a) by importance.
   (b) in the reverse order of their expected conversion to cash.
   (c) by longevity.
   (d) alphabetically.
4. Companies that use IFRS:
   (a) may report all their assets on the statement of financial position at fair value.
   (b) may offset assets against liabilities and show net assets and net liabilities on their statement of financial positions, rather than the underlying detailed line items.
   (c) may report noncurrent assets before current assets on the statement of financial position.
   (d) do not have any guidelines as to what should be reported on the statement of financial position.

5. Companies that follow IFRS to prepare a statement of financial position generally use the following order of classification:
   (a) current assets, current liabilities, noncurrent assets, noncurrent liabilities, equity.
   (b) noncurrent assets, noncurrent liabilities, current assets, current liabilities, equity.
   (c) noncurrent assets, current assets, equity, noncurrent liabilities, current liabilities.
   (d) equity, noncurrent assets, current assets, noncurrent liabilities, current liabilities.

IFRS CONCEPTS AND APPLICATION

IFRS2-1 In what ways does the format of a statement of financial of position under IFRS often differ from a balance sheet presented under GAAP?

IFRS2-2 Do the IFRS and GAAP conceptual frameworks differ in terms of the objective of financial reporting? Explain.

IFRS2-3 What terms commonly used under IFRS are synonymous with common stock and balance sheet?

IFRS2-4 The statement of financial position for Ruiz Company includes the following accounts (in British pounds): Accounts Receivable £12,500; Prepaid Insurance £3,600; Cash £15,400; Supplies £5,200; and Debt Investments (short-term) £6,700. Prepare the current assets section of the statement of financial position, listing the accounts in proper sequence.

IFRS2-5 Widmer Company recently received the following information related to the company's December 31, 2014, statement of financial position (in Swiss francs).

Inventory	CHF 2,900	Debt investments (short-term)	CHF 120
Cash	13,400	Accumulated depreciation—	
Equipment	21,700	equipment	5,700
Share investments		Accounts receivable	4,300
(long-term)	6,500		

Prepare the assets section of the company's classified statement of financial position.

IFRS2-6 The following information is available for Cole Bowling Alley at December 31, 2014.

Buildings	$128,800	Share Capital—Ordinary	$100,000
Accounts Receivable	14,520	Retained Earnings	15,000
Prepaid Insurance	4,680	Accumulated Depreciation—Buildings	42,600
Cash	18,040	Accounts Payable	12,300
Equipment	62,400	Notes Payable	97,780
Land	64,000	Accumulated Depreciation—Equipment	18,720
Insurance Expense	780	Interest Payable	2,600
Depreciation Expense	7,360	Service Revenue	14,180
Interest Expense	2,600		

Prepare a classified statement of financial position; assume that $13,900 of the notes payable will be paid in 2015.

IFRS2-7 Steve Trevino is interested in comparing the liquidity and solvency of a U.S. software company with a Chinese competitor. Is this possible if the two companies report using different currencies?

INTERNATIONAL COMPARATIVE ANALYSIS PROBLEM: *Tootsie Roll vs. Zetar plc*

IFRS2-8 The financial statements of Zetar plc are presented in Appendix C. The company's complete annual report, including the notes to its financial statements, is available in the Investors section at **www.zetarplc.com**.

Instructions
Identify five differences in the format of the statement of financial position used by Zetar compared to a company, such as Tootsie Roll, that follows GAAP. (Tootsie Roll's financial statements are available in Appendix A.)

Answers to IFRS Self-Test Questions
1. d **2.** d **3.** b **4.** c **5.** c

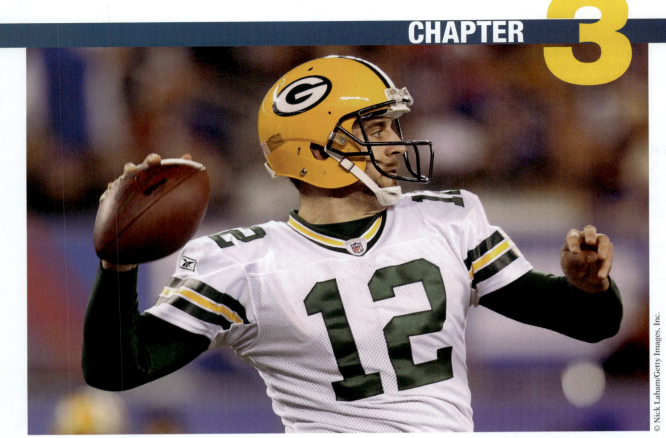

CHAPTER 3

© Nick Laham/Getty Images, Inc.

THE ACCOUNTING INFORMATION SYSTEM

LEARNING OBJECTIVES

After studying this chapter, you should be able to:

1 Analyze the effect of business transactions on the basic accounting equation.

2 Explain what an account is and how it helps in the recording process.

3 Define debits and credits and explain how they are used to record business transactions.

4 Identify the basic steps in the recording process.

5 Explain what a journal is and how it helps in the recording process.

6 Explain what a ledger is and how it helps in the recording process.

7 Explain what posting is and how it helps in the recording process.

8 Explain the purposes of a trial balance.

9 Classify cash activities as operating, investing, or financing.

How organized are you financially? Take a short quiz. Answer yes or no to each question:

- Does your wallet contain so many cash machine receipts that you've been declared a walking fire hazard?

- Is your wallet such a mess that it is often faster to fish for money in the crack of your car seat than to dig around in your wallet?

- Was Aaron Rodgers (the quarterback for the Green Bay Packers) playing high school football the last time you verified the accuracy of your bank account?

ACCIDENTS HAPPEN

If you think it is hard to keep track of the many transactions that make up *your* life, imagine how difficult it is for a big corporation to do so. Not only that, but now consider how important it is for a big company to have good accounting records, especially if it has control of *your* life savings. MF Global Holdings Ltd is such a company. As a large investment broker, it held billions of dollars of investments for clients. If you had your life savings invested at MF Global, you might be slightly displeased if you heard this from one of its representatives: "You know, I kind of remember an account for someone with a name like yours—now what did we do with that?"

Unfortunately, that is almost exactly what happened to MF Global's clients shortly before it recently filed for bankruptcy. During the days immediately following the bankruptcy filing, regulators and auditors struggled to piece things together. In the words of one regulator, "Their books are a disaster . . . we're trying to figure out what numbers are real numbers." One company that considered buying an interest in MF Global walked away from the deal because it "couldn't get a sense of what was on the balance sheet." That company said the information that should have been instantly available instead took days to produce.

It now appears that MF Global did not properly segregate customer accounts from company accounts. And, because of its sloppy record-keeping, customers were not protected when the company had financial troubles. Total customer losses were approximately $1 billion. As you can see, accounting matters!

Source: S. Patterson and A. Lucchetti, "Inside the Hunt for MF Global Cash," *Wall Street Journal Online* (November 11, 2011).

INSIDE CHAPTER 3 . . .

- **Why Accuracy Matters**
- **Keeping Score**
- **Boosting Microsoft's Profits**
- **A Convenient Overstatement**

As indicated in the Feature Story, a reliable information system is a necessity for any company. The purpose of this chapter is to explain and illustrate the features of an accounting information system. The organization and content of the chapter are as follows.

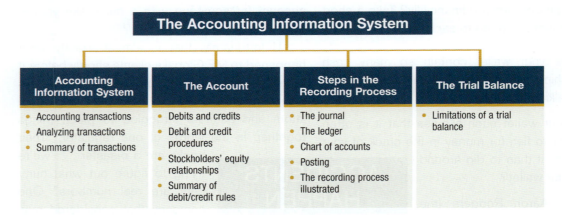

The Accounting Information System

LEARNING OBJECTIVE 1

Analyze the effect of business transactions on the basic accounting equation.

The system of collecting and processing transaction data and communicating financial information to decision-makers is known as the **accounting information system**. Factors that shape an accounting information system include the nature of the company's business, the types of transactions, the size of the company, the volume of data, and the information demands of management and others.

Most businesses use computerized accounting systems—sometimes referred to as electronic data processing (EDP) systems. These systems handle all the steps involved in the recording process, from initial data entry to preparation of the financial statements. In order to remain competitive, companies continually improve their accounting systems to provide accurate and timely data for decision-making. For example, in a recent annual report, Tootsie Roll states, "We also invested in additional processing and data storage hardware during the year. We view information technology as a key strategic tool, and are committed to deploying leading edge technology in this area." In addition, many companies have upgraded their accounting information systems in response to the requirements of Sarbanes-Oxley.

In this chapter, in order to emphasize the underlying concepts and principles, we focus on a manual accounting system. The accounting concepts and principles do not change whether a system is computerized or manual.

ACCOUNTING TRANSACTIONS

To use an accounting information system, you need to know which economic events to recognize (record). Not all events are recorded and reported in the financial statements. For example, suppose General Motors hired a new employee and purchased a new computer. Are these events entered in its accounting records? The first event would not be recorded, but the second event would. We call economic events that require recording in the financial statements **accounting transactions**.

An accounting transaction occurs when assets, liabilities, or stockholders' equity items change as a result of some economic event. The purchase of a computer by General Motors, the payment of rent by Microsoft, and the sale of a multi-day guided trip by Sierra Corporation are examples of events that change a company's assets, liabilities, or stockholders' equity. Illustration 3-1 summarizes the decision process companies use to decide whether or not to record economic events.

Illustration 3-1 Transaction identification process

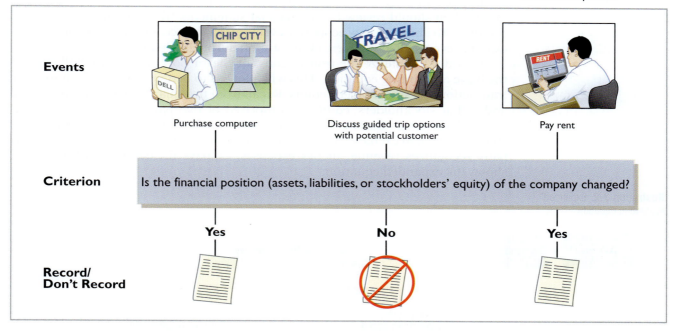

Events — Purchase computer — Discuss guided trip options with potential customer — Pay rent

Criterion — Is the financial position (assets, liabilities, or stockholders' equity) of the company changed?

Yes — No — Yes

Record/ Don't Record

ANALYZING TRANSACTIONS

In Chapter 1, you learned the basic accounting equation:

Assets = Liabilities + Stockholders' Equity

In this chapter, you will learn how to analyze transactions in terms of their effect on assets, liabilities, and stockholders' equity. **Transaction analysis** is the process of identifying the specific effects of economic events on the accounting equation.

The accounting equation must always balance. Each transaction has a dual (double-sided) effect on the equation. For example, if an individual asset is increased, there must be a corresponding:

Decrease in another asset, *or*

Increase in a specific liability, *or*

Increase in stockholders' equity.

Two or more items could be affected when an asset is increased. For example, if a company purchases a computer for $10,000 by paying $6,000 in cash and signing a note for $4,000, one asset (equipment) increases $10,000, another asset (cash) decreases $6,000, and a liability (notes payable) increases $4,000.

The result is that the accounting equation remains in balance—assets increased by a net $4,000 and liabilities increased by $4,000, as shown below.

Assets	=	Liabilities	+	Stockholders' Equity
+$10,000		+$4,000		
− 6,000				
$ 4,000	=	$4,000		

Chapter 1 presented the financial statements for Sierra Corporation for its first month. You should review those financial statements (Illustrations 1-4 to 1-8) at this time. To illustrate how economic events affect the accounting equation, we will examine events affecting Sierra Corporation during its first month.

In order to analyze the transactions for Sierra Corporation, we will expand the basic accounting equation. This will allow us to better illustrate the impact of transactions on stockholders' equity. Recall from the balance sheets in Chapters 1 and 2 that stockholders' equity is comprised of two parts: common stock and retained earnings. Common stock is affected when the company issues new shares of stock in exchange for cash. Retained earnings is affected when the company recognizes revenue, incurs expenses, or pays dividends. Illustration 3-2 shows the expanded equation.

Illustration 3-2 Expanded accounting equation

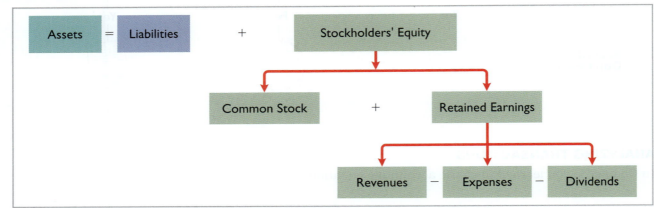

If you are tempted to skip ahead after you've read a few of the following transaction analyses, don't do it. Each has something unique to teach, something you'll need later. (We assure you that we've kept them to the minimum needed!)

EVENT (1). INVESTMENT OF CASH BY STOCKHOLDERS. On October 1, cash of $10,000 is invested in the business by investors (primarily your friends and family) in exchange for $10,000 of common stock. This event is an accounting transaction because it results in an increase in both assets and stockholders' equity.

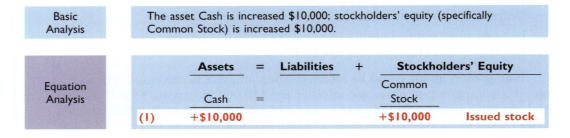

The equation is in balance after the issuance of common stock. Keeping track of the source of each change in stockholders' equity is essential for later accounting activities. In particular, items recorded in the revenue and expense columns are used for the calculation of net income.

EVENT (2). NOTE ISSUED IN EXCHANGE FOR CASH. On October 1, Sierra borrowed $5,000 from Castle Bank by signing a 3-month, 12%, $5,000 note payable. This transaction results in an equal increase in assets and liabilities. The specific effect of this transaction and the cumulative effect of the first two transactions are:

Basic Analysis	The asset Cash is increased $5,000; the liability Notes Payable is increased $5,000.

Equation Analysis

	Assets	**=**	**Liabilities**	**+**	**Stockholders' Equity**
			Notes		Common
	Cash	=	Payable	+	Stock
	$10,000				$10,000
(2)	+5,000		+$5,000		
	$15,000	=	$5,000	+	$10,000
				$15,000	

Total assets are now $15,000, and liabilities plus stockholders' equity also total $15,000.

EVENT (3). PURCHASE OF OFFICE EQUIPMENT FOR CASH. On October 2, Sierra purchased equipment by paying $5,000 cash to Superior Equipment Sales Co. This event is a transaction because an equal increase and decrease in Sierra's assets occur.

Basic Analysis	The asset Equipment is increased $5,000; the asset Cash is decreased $5,000.

Equation Analysis

	Assets			**=**	**Liabilities**	**+**	**Stockholders' Equity**
					Notes		Common
	Cash	+	Equipment	=	Payable	+	Stock
	$15,000				$5,000		$10,000
(3)	−5,000		+$5,000				
	$10,000	+	$5,000	=	$5,000	+	$10,000
		$15,000				$15,000	

The total assets are now $15,000, and liabilities plus stockholders' equity also total $15,000.

EVENT (4). RECEIPT OF CASH IN ADVANCE FROM CUSTOMER. On October 2, Sierra received a $1,200 cash advance from R. Knox, a client. This event is a transaction because Sierra received cash (an asset) for guide services for multi-day trips that are expected to be completed by Sierra in the future. Although Sierra received cash, **it does not record revenue until it has performed the work**. In some industries, such as the magazine and airline industries, customers are expected to prepay. These companies have a liability to the customer until they deliver the magazines or provide the flight. When the company eventually provides the product or service, it records the revenue.

Since Sierra received cash prior to performance of the service, Sierra has a liability for the work due.

Basic Analysis	The asset Cash is increased $1,200; the liability Unearned Service Revenue is increased $1,200 because the service has not been performed yet. That is, when an advance payment is received, an unearned revenue (a liability) should be recorded in order to recognize the obligation that exists.

Equation Analysis

	Assets			=	Liabilities			+	Stockholders' Equity
	Cash	+	Equip-ment	=	Notes Payable	+	Unearned Service Revenue	+	Common Stock
	$10,000		$5,000		$5,000				$10,000
(4)	+1,200						+$1,200		
	$11,200	+	$5,000	=	$5,000	+	$1,200	+	$10,000
		$16,200					$16,200		

EVENT (5). SERVICES PERFORMED FOR CASH. On October 3, Sierra received $10,000 in cash from Copa Company for guide services performed for a corporate event. This event is a transaction because Sierra received an asset (cash) in exchange for services.

Guide service is the principal revenue-producing activity of Sierra. **Revenue increases stockholders' equity.** This transaction, then, increases both assets and stockholders' equity.

Basic Analysis	The asset Cash is increased $10,000; the revenue Service Revenue is increased $10,000.

Equation Analysis

	Assets			=	Liabilities			+	Stockholders' Equity						
											Retained Earnings				
	Cash	+	Equip-ment	=	Notes Pay.	+	Unearned Serv. Rev.	+	Common Stock	+	Rev.	−	Exp.	−	Div.
	$11,200		$5,000		$5,000		$1,200		$10,000						
(5)	+10,000										+$10,000				Service Revenue
	$21,200	+	$5,000	=	$5,000	+	$1,200	+	$10,000	+	$10,000				
		$26,200							$26,200						

Often companies perform services "on account." That is, they perform services for which they are paid at a later date. Revenue, however, is recorded when services are performed. Therefore, revenues would increase when services are performed, even though cash has not been received. Instead of receiving cash, the company receives a different type of asset, an **account receivable**. Accounts receivable represent the right to receive payment at a later date. Suppose that Sierra had provided these services on account rather than for cash. This event would be reported using the accounting equation as:

Assets	=	**Liabilities**	+	**Stockholders' Equity**
Accounts Receivable	=			Revenues
+$10,000				+$10,000 **Service Revenue**

Later, when Sierra collects the $10,000 from the customer, Accounts Receivable decreases by $10,000, and Cash increases by $10,000.

	Assets		=	Liabilities	+	Stockholders' Equity
	Cash	Accounts Receivable				
	+$10,000	−$10,000				

Note that in this case, revenues are not affected by the collection of cash. Instead we record an exchange of one asset (Accounts Receivable) for a different asset (Cash).

EVENT (6). PAYMENT OF RENT. On October 3, Sierra Corporation paid its office rent for the month of October in cash, $900. This rent payment is a transaction because it results in a decrease in an asset, cash.

Rent is a cost incurred by Sierra Corporation in its effort to generate revenues. It is treated as an expense because it pertains only to the current month. **Expenses decrease stockholders' equity.** Sierra records the rent payment by decreasing cash and increasing expenses to maintain the balance of the accounting equation.

Basic Analysis	The expense account Rent Expense is increased $900 because the payment pertains only to the current month; the asset Cash is decreased $900.

Equation Analysis

	Assets			=	Liabilities			+	Stockholders' Equity					
	Cash	+	Equipment	=	Notes Pay.	+	Unearned Serv. Rev.	+	Common Stock	+	Rev.	−	Exp.	−	Div.
												Retained Earnings		
	$21,200		$5,000		$5,000		$1,200		$10,000		$10,000			
(6)	−900												−$900			Rent Expense
	$20,300	+	$5,000	=	$5,000	+	$1,200	+	$10,000	+	$10,000	−	$900	
		$25,300								$25,300				

EVENT (7). PURCHASE OF INSURANCE POLICY FOR CASH. On October 4, Sierra paid $600 for a one-year insurance policy that will expire next year on September 30. Payments of expenses that will benefit more than one accounting period are identified as assets called prepaid expenses or prepayments.

Basic Analysis	The asset Cash is decreased $600; the asset Prepaid Insurance is increased $600.

Equation Analysis

	Assets					=	Liabilities			+	Stockholders' Equity				
	Cash	+	Prepaid Insurance	+	Equipment	=	Notes Pay.	+	Unearned Serv. Rev.	+	Common Stock	+	Rev.	−	Exp.	−	Div.
													Retained Earnings		
	$20,300				$5,000		$5,000		$1,200		$10,000		$10,000		$900	
(7)	−600		+$600												
	$19,700	+	$600	+	$5,000	=	$5,000	+	$1,200	+	$10,000	+	$10,000	−	$900	
			$25,300								$25,300				

The balance in total assets did not change; one asset account decreased by the same amount that another increased.

EVENT (8). PURCHASE OF SUPPLIES ON ACCOUNT. On October 5, Sierra purchased an estimated three months of supplies on account from Aero Supply for $2,500. In this case, "on account" means that the company receives goods or services that it will pay for at a later date.

| Basic Analysis | The asset Supplies is increased $2,500; the liability Accounts Payable is increased $2,500. |

Equation Analysis

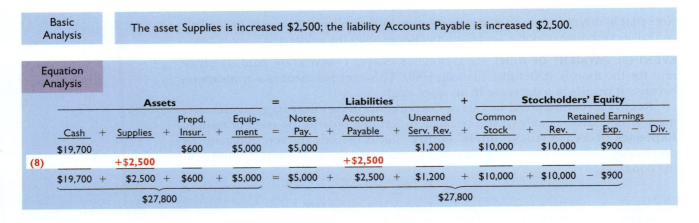

	Assets				=	Liabilities			+	Stockholders' Equity			
			Prepd.	Equip-		Notes	Accounts	Unearned		Common		Retained Earnings	
Cash	+ Supplies	+	Insur. +	ment	= Pay.	+	Payable	+ Serv. Rev.	+	Stock	+ Rev.	− Exp.	− Div.
$19,700			$600	$5,000	$5,000			$1,200		$10,000	$10,000	$900	
(8)	**+$2,500**						**+$2,500**						
$19,700 +	$2,500 +	$600	+ $5,000	= $5,000 +		$2,500 +	$1,200	+	$10,000	+ $10,000	− $900	
		$27,800							$27,800				

EVENT (9). HIRING OF NEW EMPLOYEES. On October 9, Sierra hired four new employees to begin work on October 15. Each employee will receive a weekly salary of $500 for a five-day work week, payable every two weeks. Employees will receive their first paychecks on October 26. On the date Sierra hires the employees, there is no effect on the accounting equation because the assets, liabilities, and stockholders' equity of the company have not changed.

| Basic Analysis | An accounting transaction has not occurred. There is only an agreement that the employees will begin work on October 15. (See Event (11) for the first payment.) |

EVENT (10). PAYMENT OF DIVIDEND. On October 20, Sierra paid a $500 dividend. **Dividends** are a reduction of stockholders' equity but not an expense. Dividends are not included in the calculation of net income. Instead, a dividend is a distribution of the company's assets to its stockholders.

| Basic Analysis | The dividends account is increased $500; the asset Cash is decreased $500. |

Equation Analysis

	Assets				=	Liabilities			+	Stockholders' Equity			
	Sup-		Prepd.	Equip-		Notes	Accts.	Unearned		Common		Retained Earnings	
Cash	+ plies	+	Insur. +	ment	= Pay.	+	Pay.	+ Serv. Rev.	+	Stock	+ Rev.	− Exp.	− Div.
$19,700	$2,500		$600	$5,000	$5,000		$2,500	$1,200		$10,000	$10,000	$900	
(10)	**−500**												**− $500**
$19,200 +	$2,500 +	$600	+ $5,000	= $5,000 +		$2,500 +	$1,200	+	$10,000	+ $10,000	− $900	− $500
		$27,300							$27,300				

EVENT (11). PAYMENT OF CASH FOR EMPLOYEE SALARIES. Employees have worked two weeks, earning $4,000 in salaries, which were paid on October 26.

Salaries and Wages Expense is an expense that reduces stockholders' equity. This event is a transaction because assets and stockholders' equity are affected.

Basic Analysis	The asset Cash is decreased $4,000; the expense account Salaries and Wages Expense is increased $4,000.

Equation Analysis

	Assets				=	Liabilities			+	Stockholders' Equity				
	Cash	Sup-plies	Prepd. Insur.	Equip-ment		Notes Pay.	Accts. Pay.	Unearned Serv. Rev.		Common Stock	Rev.	Exp.	Div.	
	$19,200	$2,500	$600	$5,000		$5,000	$2,500	$1,200		$10,000	$10,000	$ 900	$500	
(11)	−4,000											− 4,000		Sal./Wages Expense
	$15,200 +	$2,500 +	$600 +	$5,000 =		$5,000 +	$2,500 +	$1,200	+	$10,000 +	$10,000 −	$4,900 −	$500	

$23,300 $23,300

Investor Insight

Why Accuracy Matters

While most companies record transactions very carefully, the reality is that mistakes still happen. For example, bank regulators fined Bank One Corporation (now JPMorgan Chase) $1.8 million because they felt that the unreliability of the bank's accounting system caused it to violate regulatory requirements.

Also, in recent years Fannie Mae, the government-chartered mortgage association, announced a series of large accounting errors. These announcements caused alarm among investors, regulators, and politicians because they fear that the errors may suggest larger, undetected problems. This is important because the home-mortgage market depends on Fannie Mae to buy hundreds of billions of dollars of mortgages each year from banks, thus enabling the banks to issue new mortgages.

Finally, before a major overhaul of its accounting system, the financial records of Waste Management Company were in such disarray that of the company's 57,000 employees, 10,000 were receiving pay slips that were in error.

The Sarbanes-Oxley Act was created to minimize the occurrence of errors like these by increasing every employee's responsibility for accurate financial reporting.

? In order for these companies to prepare and issue financial statements, their accounting equations (debits and credits) must have been in balance at year-end. How could these errors or misstatements have occurred? (Answers in *Broadening Your Perspective.*)

SUMMARY OF TRANSACTIONS

Illustration 3-3 summarizes the transactions of Sierra Corporation to show their cumulative effect on the basic accounting equation. It includes the transaction number in the first column on the left. The right-most column shows the specific effect of any transaction that affects stockholders' equity. Remember that Event (9) did not result in a transaction, so no entry is included for that event. The illustration demonstrates three important points:

1. Each transaction is analyzed in terms of its effect on assets, liabilities, and stockholders' equity.

2. The two sides of the equation must always be equal.

3. The cause of each change in stockholders' equity must be indicated.

Illustration 3-3 Summary of transactions

	Cash	+	Sup- plies	+	Prepd. Insur.	+	Equip- ment	=	Notes Pay.	+	Accts. Pay.	+	Unearned Serv. Rev.	+	Common Stock	+	Rev.	–	Exp.	–	Div.	
(1)	+$10,000							=							+$10,000							Issued stock
(2)	+5,000								+$5,000													
(3)	–5,000						+$5,000															
(4)	+1,200												+$1,200									
(5)	+10,000																+$10,000					Service Revenue
(6)	–900																		–$ 900			Rent Expense
(7)	–600					+$600																
(8)			+$2,500								+ $2,500											
(10)	–500																				–$500	Dividends
(11)	–4,000																		–4,000			Sal./Wages Expense
	$15,200	+	$2,500	+	$600	+	$5,000	=	$5,000	+	$2,500	+	$1,200	+	$10,000	+	$10,000	–	$4,900	–	$500	
			$23,300													$23,300					

DECISION TOOLKIT

DECISION CHECKPOINTS	INFO NEEDED FOR DECISION	TOOL TO USE FOR DECISION	HOW TO EVALUATE RESULTS
Has an accounting transaction occurred?	Details of the event	Accounting equation	If the event affected assets, liabilities, or stockholders' equity, then record as a transaction.

The Account

LEARNING OBJECTIVE 2

Explain what an account is and how it helps in the recording process.

Rather than using a tabular summary like the one in Illustration 3-3 for Sierra Corporation, an accounting information system uses accounts. An **account** is an individual accounting record of increases and decreases in a specific asset, liability, stockholders' equity, revenue, or expense item. For example, Sierra Corporation has separate accounts for Cash, Accounts Receivable, Accounts Payable, Service Revenue, Salaries and Wages Expense, and so on. (Note that whenever we are referring to a specific account, we capitalize the name.)

In its simplest form, an account consists of three parts: (1) the title of the account, (2) a left or debit side, and (3) a right or credit side. Because the alignment of these parts of an account resembles the letter T, it is referred to as a **T-account**. The basic form of an account is shown in Illustration 3-4.

Illustration 3-4 Basic form of account

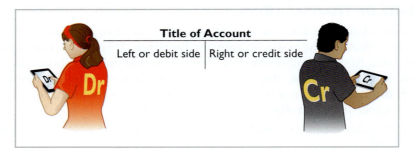

We use this form of account often throughout this book to explain basic accounting relationships.

DEBITS AND CREDITS

The term **debit** indicates the left side of an account, and **credit** indicates the right side. They are commonly abbreviated as **Dr.** for debit and **Cr.** for credit. They **do not** mean increase or decrease, as is commonly thought. We use the terms debit and credit repeatedly in the recording process to describe **where** entries are made in accounts. For example, the act of entering an amount on the left side of an account is called **debiting** the account. Making an entry on the right side is **crediting** the account.

When comparing the totals of the two sides, an account shows a **debit balance** if the total of the debit amounts exceeds the credits. An account shows a **credit balance** if the credit amounts exceed the debits. Note the position of the debit side and credit side in Illustration 3-4.

The procedure of recording debits and credits in an account is shown in Illustration 3-5 for the transactions affecting the Cash account of Sierra Corporation. The data are taken from the Cash column of the tabular summary in Illustration 3-3.

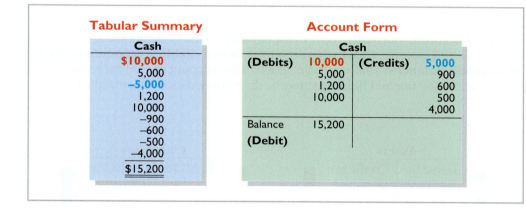

Illustration 3-5 Tabular summary and account form for Sierra Corporation's Cash account

Every positive item in the tabular summary represents a receipt of cash; every negative amount represents a payment of cash. **Notice that in the account form we record the increases in cash as debits, and the decreases in cash as credits.** For example, the $10,000 receipt of cash (in red) is debited to Cash, and the −$5,000 payment of cash (in blue) is credited to Cash.

Having increases on one side and decreases on the other reduces recording errors and helps in determining the totals of each side of the account as well as the account balance. The balance is determined by netting the two sides (subtracting one amount from the other). The account balance, a debit of $15,200, indicates that Sierra had $15,200 more increases than decreases in cash. That is, since it started with a balance of zero, it has $15,200 in its Cash account.

DEBIT AND CREDIT PROCEDURES

Each transaction must affect two or more accounts to keep the basic accounting equation in balance. In other words, **for each transaction, debits must equal credits**. The equality of debits and credits provides the basis for the double-entry accounting system.

Under the **double-entry system**, the two-sided effect of each transaction is recorded in appropriate accounts. This system provides a logical method for recording transactions. The double-entry system also helps to ensure the accuracy of the recorded amounts and helps to detect errors such as those at MF Global as discussed in the Feature Story. If every transaction is recorded with equal debits and credits, then the sum of all the debits to the accounts must equal the sum of all the credits. The double-entry system for determining the equality of the accounting equation is much more efficient than the plus/minus procedure used earlier.

Dr./Cr. Procedures for Assets and Liabilities

In Illustration 3-5 for Sierra Corporation, increases in Cash—an asset—were entered on the left side, and decreases in Cash were entered on the right side. We know that both sides of the basic equation (Assets = Liabilities + Stockholders' Equity) must be equal. It therefore follows that increases and decreases in liabilities will have to be recorded **opposite from** increases and decreases in assets. Thus, increases in liabilities must be entered on the right or credit side, and decreases in liabilities must be entered on the left or debit side. The effects that debits and credits have on assets and liabilities are summarized in Illustration 3-6.

Illustration 3-6 Debit and credit effects–assets and liabilities

Debits	Credits
Increase assets	Decrease assets
Decrease liabilities	Increase liabilities

Asset accounts normally show debit balances. That is, debits to a specific asset account should exceed credits to that account. Likewise, **liability accounts normally show credit balances**. That is, credits to a liability account should exceed debits to that account. The **normal balances** may be diagrammed as in Illustration 3-7.

Illustration 3-7 Normal balances–assets and liabilities

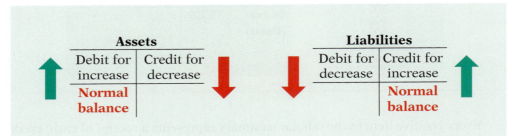

Knowing which is the normal balance in an account may help when you are trying to identify errors. For example, a credit balance in an asset account, such as Land, or a debit balance in a liability account, such as Salaries and Wages Payable, usually indicates errors in recording. Occasionally, however, an abnormal balance may be correct. The Cash account, for example, will have a credit balance when a company has overdrawn its bank balance (written a check that "bounced"). In automated accounting systems, the computer is programmed to flag violations of the normal balance and to print out error or exception reports. In manual systems, careful visual inspection of the accounts is required to detect normal balance problems.

Dr./Cr. Procedures for Stockholders' Equity

In Chapter 1, we indicated that stockholders' equity is comprised of two parts: common stock and retained earnings. In the transaction events earlier in this chapter, you saw that revenues, expenses, and the payment of dividends affect retained earnings. Therefore, the subdivisions of stockholders' equity are common stock, retained earnings, dividends, revenues, and expenses.

COMMON STOCK. Common stock is issued to investors in exchange for the stockholders' investment. The Common Stock account is increased by credits and decreased by debits. For example, when cash is invested in the business,

Cash is debited and Common Stock is credited. The effects of debits and credits on the Common Stock account are shown in Illustration 3-8.

Debits	Credits
Decrease Common Stock	Increase Common Stock

Illustration 3-8 Debit and credit effects–Common Stock

The normal balance in the Common Stock account may be diagrammed as in Illustration 3-9.

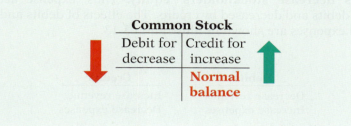

Illustration 3-9 Normal balance–Common Stock

RETAINED EARNINGS. Retained earnings is net income that is retained in the business. It represents the portion of stockholders' equity that has been accumulated through the profitable operation of the company. Retained Earnings is increased by credits (for example, by net income) and decreased by debits (for example, by a net loss), as shown in Illustration 3-10.

Debits	Credits
Decrease Retained Earnings	Increase Retained Earnings

Illustration 3-10 Debit and credit effects–Retained Earnings

The normal balance for Retained Earnings may be diagrammed as in Illustration 3-11.

Retained Earnings

Debit for decrease	Credit for increase
	Normal balance

Illustration 3-11 Normal balance–Retained Earnings

DIVIDENDS. A dividend is a distribution by a corporation to its stockholders. The most common form of distribution is a cash dividend. Dividends result in a reduction of the stockholders' claims on retained earnings. Because dividends reduce stockholders' equity, increases in the Dividends account are recorded with debits. As shown in Illustration 3-12, the Dividends account normally has a debit balance.

Illustration 3-12 Normal balance–Dividends

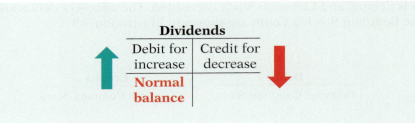

REVENUES AND EXPENSES. When a company recognizes revenues, stockholders' equity is increased. Revenue accounts are increased by credits and decreased by debits.

Expenses decrease stockholders' equity. Thus, expense accounts are increased by debits and decreased by credits. The effects of debits and credits on revenues and expenses are shown in Illustration 3-13.

Illustration 3-13 Debit and credit effects–revenues and expenses

Debits	Credits
Decrease revenue	Increase revenue
Increase expenses	Decrease expenses

Credits to revenue accounts should exceed debits; debits to expense accounts should exceed credits. Thus, **revenue accounts normally show credit balances, and expense accounts normally show debit balances**. The normal balances may be diagrammed as in Illustration 3-14.

Illustration 3-14 Normal balances–revenues and expenses

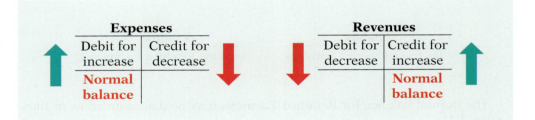

Investor Insight

Keeping Score

The Chicago Cubs baseball team has these major revenue and expense accounts:

Revenues	Expenses
Admissions (ticket sales)	Players' salaries
Concessions	Administrative salaries
Television and radio	Travel
Advertising	Ballpark maintenance

? Do you think that the Chicago Bears football team would be likely to have the same major revenue and expense accounts as the Cubs? (Answers in *Broadening Your Perspective*.)

STOCKHOLDERS' EQUITY RELATIONSHIPS

Companies report the subdivisions of stockholders' equity in various places in the financial statements:

- Common stock and retained earnings: in the stockholders' equity section of the balance sheet.
- Dividends: on the retained earnings statement.
- Revenues and expenses: on the income statement.

Dividends, revenues, and expenses are eventually transferred to retained earnings at the end of the period. As a result, a change in any one of these three items affects stockholders' equity. Illustration 3-15 shows the relationships of the accounts affecting stockholders' equity.

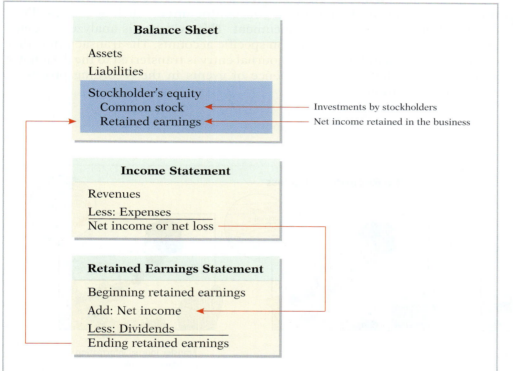

Illustration 3-15
Stockholders' equity relationships

SUMMARY OF DEBIT/CREDIT RULES

Illustration 3-16 summarizes the debit/credit rules and effects on each type of account. **Study this diagram carefully.** It will help you understand the fundamentals

Illustration 3-16 Summary of debit/credit rules

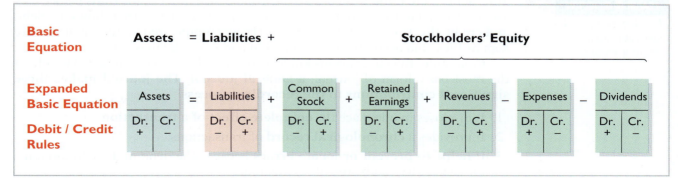

of the double-entry system. No matter what the transaction, total debits must equal total credits in order to keep the accounting equation in balance.

Steps in the Recording Process

LEARNING OBJECTIVE 4
Identify the basic steps in the recording process.

Although it is possible to enter transaction information directly into the accounts, few businesses do so. Practically every business uses these basic steps in the recording process:

1. Analyze each transaction in terms of its effect on the accounts.
2. Enter the transaction information in a journal.
3. Transfer the journal information to the appropriate accounts in the ledger.

The actual sequence of events begins with the transaction. Evidence of the transaction comes in the form of a **source document**, such as a sales slip, a check, a bill, or a cash register document. This evidence is analyzed to determine the effect of the transaction on specific accounts. The transaction is then entered in the **journal**. Finally, the journal entry is transferred to the designated accounts in the **ledger**. The sequence of events in the recording process is shown in Illustration 3-17.

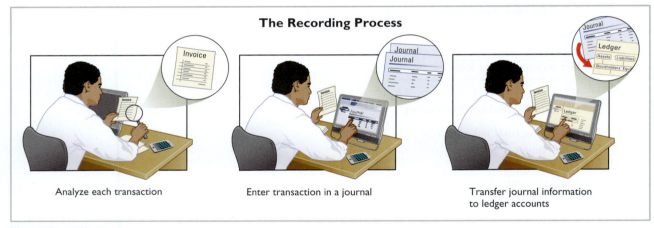

The Recording Process

Analyze each transaction | Enter transaction in a journal | Transfer journal information to ledger accounts

Illustration 3-17 The recording process

THE JOURNAL

LEARNING OBJECTIVE 5
Explain what a journal is and how it helps in the recording process.

Transactions are initially recorded in chronological order in journals before they are transferred to the accounts. For each transaction, the journal shows the debit and credit effects on specific accounts. (In a computerized system, journals are kept as files, and accounts are recorded in computer databases.)

Companies may use various kinds of journals, but every company has at least the most basic form of journal, a **general journal**. **The journal makes three significant contributions to the recording process:**

1. It discloses in one place the **complete effect of a transaction**.
2. It provides a **chronological record** of transactions.
3. It **helps to prevent or locate errors** because the debit and credit amounts for each entry can be readily compared.

Entering transaction data in the journal is known as **journalizing**. To illustrate the technique of journalizing, let's look at the first three transactions of Sierra Corporation in equation form.

On October 1, Sierra issued common stock in exchange for $10,000 cash:

Assets	=	Liabilities	+	Stockholders' Equity
				Common
Cash	=			Stock
+$10,000				+$10,000 Issued stock

On October 1, Sierra borrowed $5,000 by signing a note:

Assets	=	Liabilities	+	Stockholders' Equity
		Notes		
Cash	=	Payable		
+$5,000		+$5,000		

On October 2, Sierra purchased equipment for $5,000:

Assets		=	Liabilities	+	Stockholders' Equity
Cash	Equipment				
−$5,000	+$5,000				

Sierra makes separate journal entries for each transaction. A complete entry consists of: (1) the date of the transaction, (2) the accounts and amounts to be debited and credited, and (3) a brief explanation of the transaction. These transactions are journalized in Illustration 3-18.

Illustration 3-18 Recording transactions in journal form

GENERAL JOURNAL

Date		Account Titles and Explanation	Debit	Credit
2014				
Oct.	1	Cash	10,000	
		Common Stock		10,000
		(Issued stock for cash)		
	1	Cash	5,000	
		Notes Payable		5,000
		(Issued 3-month, 12% note payable for cash)		
	2	Equipment	5,000	
		Cash		5,000
		(Purchased equipment for cash)		

Note the following features of the journal entries.

1. The date of the transaction is entered in the Date column.
2. The account to be debited is entered first at the left. The account to be credited is then entered on the next line, indented under the line above. The indentation differentiates debits from credits and decreases the possibility of switching the debit and credit amounts.

3. The amounts for the debits are recorded in the Debit (left) column, and the amounts for the credits are recorded in the Credit (right) column.

4. A brief explanation of the transaction is given.

It is important to use correct and specific account titles in journalizing. Erroneous account titles lead to incorrect financial statements. Some flexibility exists initially in selecting account titles. The main criterion is that each title must appropriately describe the content of the account. For example, a company could use any of these account titles for recording the cost of delivery trucks: Equipment, Delivery Equipment, Delivery Trucks, or Trucks. Once the company chooses the specific title to use, however, it should record under that account title all subsequent transactions involving the account.

Accounting Across the Organization

Boosting Microsoft's Profits

At one time, Microsoft's Home and Entertainment Division lost over $4 billion, mostly due to losses on the original Xbox videogame console. With the Xbox 360 videogame console, the division's head of finance, Bryan Lee, hoped the division would become profitable. He set strict goals for sales, revenue, and profit. "A manager seeking to spend more on a feature such as a disk drive has to find allies in the group to cut spending elsewhere, or identify new revenue to offset the increase," he explained.

For example, Microsoft originally designed the Xbox 360 to have 256 megabytes of memory. But the design department said that amount of memory wouldn't support the best special effects. The purchasing department said that adding more memory would cost $30—which was 10% of the estimated selling price of $300. The marketing department, however, "determined that adding the memory would let Microsoft reduce marketing costs and attract more game developers, boosting royalty revenue. It would also extend the life of the console, generating more sales." As a result, Microsoft doubled the memory to 512 megabytes. Today, the division enjoys great success.

Source: Robert A. Guth, "New Xbox Aim for Microsoft: Profitability," *Wall Street Journal* (May 24, 2005), p. C1.

? In what ways is this Microsoft division using accounting to assist in its effort to become more profitable? (Answers in *Broadening Your Perspective*.)

THE LEDGER

The entire group of accounts maintained by a company is referred to collectively as the **ledger**. The ledger provides the balance in each of the accounts as well as keeps track of changes in these balances.

Companies may use various kinds of ledgers, but every company has a general ledger. A **general ledger** contains all the assets, liabilities, stockholders' equity, revenue, and expense accounts, as shown in Illustration 3-19. Whenever we use the term **ledger** in this textbook without additional specification, it will mean the general ledger.

CHART OF ACCOUNTS

The number and type of accounts used differ for each company, depending on the size, complexity, and type of business. For example, the number of accounts depends on the amount of detail desired by management. The management of one company may want one single account for all types of utility expense. Another may keep separate expense accounts for each type of utility

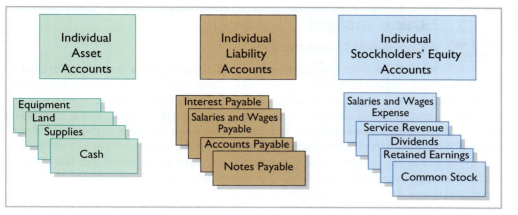

Illustration 3-19 The general ledger

expenditure, such as gas, electricity, and water. A small corporation like Sierra Corporation will not have many accounts compared with a corporate giant like Ford Motor Company. Sierra may be able to manage and report its activities in 20 to 30 accounts, whereas Ford requires thousands of accounts to keep track of its worldwide activities.

Most companies list the accounts in a **chart of accounts**. They may create new accounts as needed during the life of the business. Illustration 3-20 shows the chart of accounts for Sierra Corporation in the order that they are typically listed (assets, liabilities, stockholders' equity, revenues, and expenses). **Accounts shown in red are used in this chapter**; accounts shown in black are explained in later chapters.

Illustration 3-20 Chart of accounts for Sierra Corporation

SIERRA CORPORATION—CHART OF ACCOUNTS

Assets	Liabilities	Stockholders' Equity	Revenues	Expenses
Cash	Notes Payable	Common Stock	Service Revenue	Salaries and Wages Expense
Accounts Receivable	Accounts Payable	Retained Earnings		
Supplies	Interest Payable	Dividends		Supplies Expense
Prepaid Insurance	Unearned	Income Summary		Rent Expense
Equipment	Service Revenue			Insurance Expense
Accumulated Depreciation—	Salaries and Wages			Interest Expense
Equipment	Payable			Depreciation Expense

POSTING

The procedure of transferring journal entry amounts to ledger accounts is called **posting**. **This phase of the recording process accumulates the effects of journalized transactions in the individual accounts.** Posting involves these steps:

LEARNING OBJECTIVE **7**

Explain what posting is and how it helps in the recording process.

1. In the ledger, enter in the appropriate columns of the debited account(s) the date and debit amount shown in the journal.

2. In the ledger, enter in the appropriate columns of the credited account(s) the date and credit amount shown in the journal.

THE RECORDING PROCESS ILLUSTRATED

Illustrations 3-21 through 3-31 on the following pages show the basic steps in the recording process using the October transactions of Sierra Corporation. Sierra's accounting period is a month. A basic analysis and a debit–credit analysis pre-

Ethics Insight

A Convenient Overstatement

Sometimes a company's investment securities suffer a permanent decline in value below their original cost. When this occurs, the company is supposed to reduce the recorded value of the securities on its balance sheet ("write-them down" in common financial lingo) and record a loss. It appears, however, that during the financial crisis, employees at some financial institutions chose to look the other way as the value of their investments skidded. A number of Wall Street traders that worked for the investment bank Credit Suisse Group were charged with intentionally overstating the value of securities that had suffered declines of approximately $2.85 billion. One reason that they may have been reluctant to record the losses is out of fear that the company's shareholders and clients would panic if they saw the magnitude of the losses. However, personal self-interest might have been equally to blame—the bonuses of the traders were tied to the value of the investment securities.

Source: S. Pulliam, J. Eaglesham, and M. Siconolfi, "U.S. Plans Changes on Bond Fraud," *Wall Street Journal Online* (February 1, 2012).

? What incentives might employees have had to overstate the value of these investment securities on the company's financial statements? (Answers in *Broadening Your Perspective.*)

cede the journalizing and posting of each transaction. Study these transaction analyses carefully. **The purpose of transaction analysis is first to identify the type of account involved and then to determine whether a debit or a credit to the account is required.** You should always perform this type of analysis before preparing a journal entry. Doing so will help you understand the journal entries discussed in this chapter as well as more complex journal entries to be described in later chapters.

Illustration 3-21 Investment of cash by stockholders

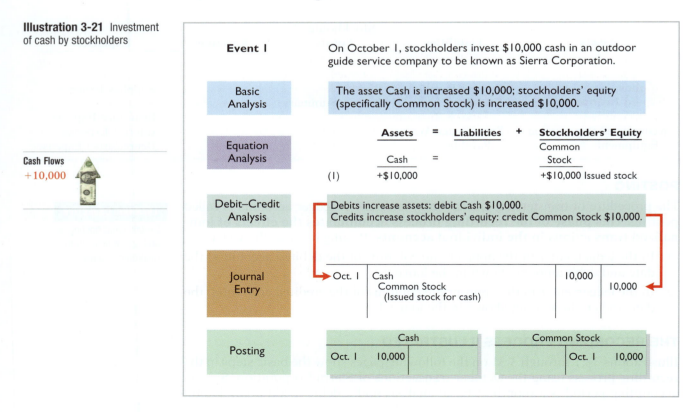

Illustration 3-22 Issue of note payable

Event 2	On October 1, Sierra borrows cash of $5,000 by signing a 3-month, 12%, $5,000 note payable.
Basic Analysis	The asset Cash is increased $5,000; the liability Notes Payable is increased $5,000.

Equation Analysis

	Assets	=	Liabilities	+	Stockholders' Equity
	Cash	=	Notes Payable		
(2)	+$5,000		+$5,000		

Cash Flows
+5,000

Debit–Credit Analysis

Debits increase assets: debit Cash $5,000.
Credits increase liabilities: credit Notes Payable $5,000.

Journal Entry

Oct. 1	Cash	5,000	
	Notes Payable		5,000
	(Issued 3-month, 12% note payable for cash)		

Posting

Cash		Notes Payable	
Oct. 1 10,000			Oct. 1 5,000
1 5,000			

Illustration 3-23 Purchase of equipment

Event 3	On October 2, Sierra used $5,000 cash to purchase equipment.
Basic Analysis	The asset Equipment is increased $5,000; the asset Cash is decreased $5,000.

Equation Analysis

	Assets			=	Liabilities	+	Stockholders' Equity
	Cash	+	Equipment	=			
(3)	–$5,000		+$5,000				

Cash Flows
−5,000

Debit–Credit Analysis

Debits increase assets: debit Equipment $5,000.
Credits decrease assets: credit Cash $5,000.

Journal Entry

Oct. 2	Equipment	5,000	
	Cash		5,000
	(Purchased equipment for cash)		

Posting

Cash			Equipment	
Oct. 1 10,000	Oct. 2 5,000		Oct. 2 5,000	
1 5,000				

Illustration 3-24 Receipt of cash in advance from customer

Cash Flows
+1,200

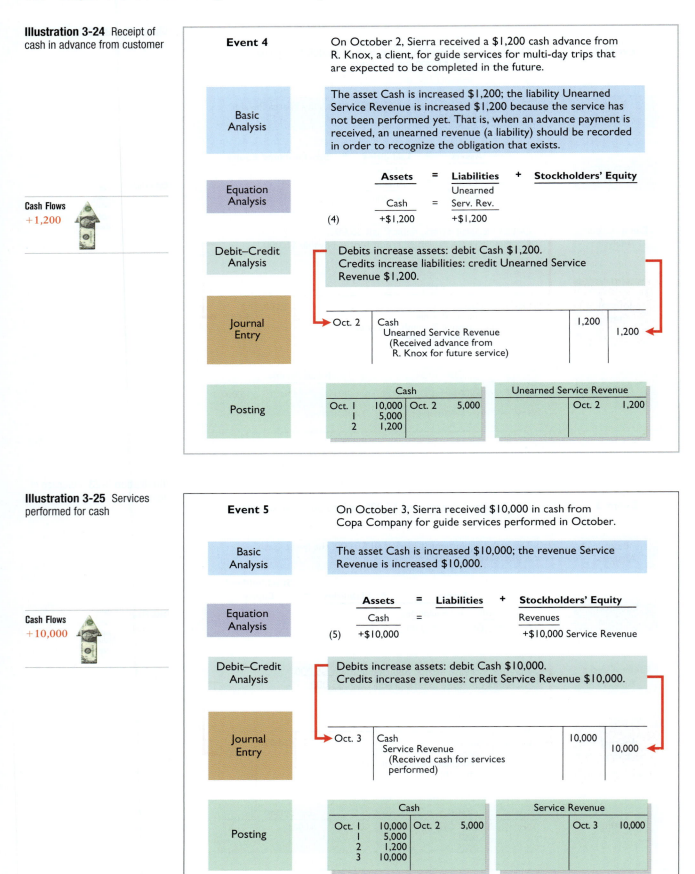

Event 4	On October 2, Sierra received a $1,200 cash advance from R. Knox, a client, for guide services for multi-day trips that are expected to be completed in the future.
Basic Analysis	The asset Cash is increased $1,200; the liability Unearned Service Revenue is increased $1,200 because the service has not been performed yet. That is, when an advance payment is received, an unearned revenue (a liability) should be recorded in order to recognize the obligation that exists.

	Assets	**=**	**Liabilities**	**+**	**Stockholders' Equity**
	Cash	=	Unearned Serv. Rev.		
(4)	+$1,200		+$1,200		

Equation Analysis

Debit–Credit Analysis

Debits increase assets: debit Cash $1,200.
Credits increase liabilities: credit Unearned Service Revenue $1,200.

Journal Entry

Oct. 2	Cash	1,200	
	Unearned Service Revenue		1,200
	(Received advance from R. Knox for future service)		

Posting

Cash				
Oct. 1	10,000	Oct. 2	5,000
1	5,000		
2	1,200		

Unearned Service Revenue		
	Oct. 2	1,200

Illustration 3-25 Services performed for cash

Cash Flows
+10,000

Event 5	On October 3, Sierra received $10,000 in cash from Copa Company for guide services performed in October.
Basic Analysis	The asset Cash is increased $10,000; the revenue Service Revenue is increased $10,000.

	Assets	**=**	**Liabilities**	**+**	**Stockholders' Equity**
	Cash	=			Revenues
(5)	+$10,000				+$10,000 Service Revenue

Equation Analysis

Debit–Credit Analysis

Debits increase assets: debit Cash $10,000.
Credits increase revenues: credit Service Revenue $10,000.

Journal Entry

Oct. 3	Cash	10,000	
	Service Revenue		10,000
	(Received cash for services performed)		

Posting

Cash				
Oct. 1	10,000	Oct. 2	5,000
1	5,000		
2	1,200		
3	10,000		

Service Revenue		
	Oct. 3	10,000

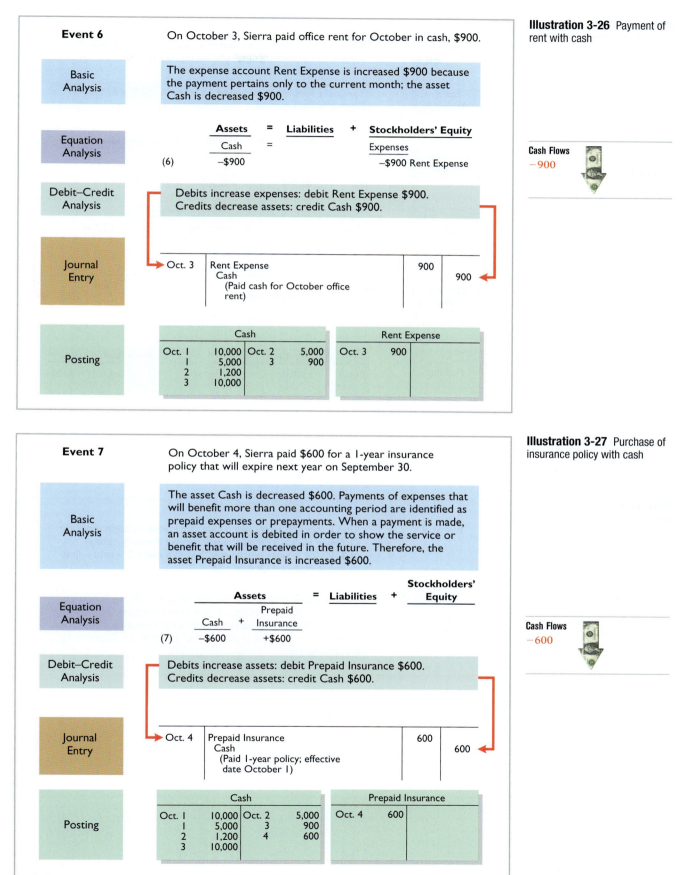

Event 6

On October 3, Sierra paid office rent for October in cash, $900.

Illustration 3-26 Payment of rent with cash

Basic Analysis

The expense account Rent Expense is increased $900 because the payment pertains only to the current month; the asset Cash is decreased $900.

Equation Analysis

	Assets	=	Liabilities	+	Stockholders' Equity
	Cash	=			Expenses
(6)	−$900				−$900 Rent Expense

Cash Flows
−900

Debit–Credit Analysis

Debits increase expenses: debit Rent Expense $900.
Credits decrease assets: credit Cash $900.

Journal Entry

Oct. 3	Rent Expense	900	
	Cash		900
	(Paid cash for October office rent)		

Posting

Cash					Rent Expense	
Oct. 1	10,000	Oct. 2	5,000	Oct. 3	900	
1	5,000	3	900			
2	1,200					
3	10,000					

Event 7

On October 4, Sierra paid $600 for a 1-year insurance policy that will expire next year on September 30.

Illustration 3-27 Purchase of insurance policy with cash

Basic Analysis

The asset Cash is decreased $600. Payments of expenses that will benefit more than one accounting period are identified as prepaid expenses or prepayments. When a payment is made, an asset account is debited in order to show the service or benefit that will be received in the future. Therefore, the asset Prepaid Insurance is increased $600.

Equation Analysis

	Assets			=	Liabilities	+	Stockholders' Equity
	Cash	+	Prepaid Insurance				
(7)	−$600		+$600				

Cash Flows
−600

Debit–Credit Analysis

Debits increase assets: debit Prepaid Insurance $600.
Credits decrease assets: credit Cash $600.

Journal Entry

Oct. 4	Prepaid Insurance	600	
	Cash		600
	(Paid 1-year policy; effective date October 1)		

Posting

Cash					Prepaid Insurance	
Oct. 1	10,000	Oct. 2	5,000	Oct. 4	600	
1	5,000	3	900			
2	1,200	4	600			
3	10,000					

Illustration 3-28 Purchase of supplies on account

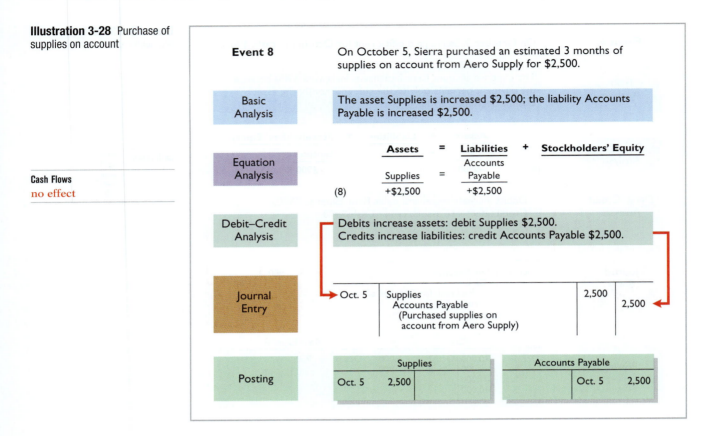

Event 8

On October 5, Sierra purchased an estimated 3 months of supplies on account from Aero Supply for $2,500.

Basic Analysis

The asset Supplies is increased $2,500; the liability Accounts Payable is increased $2,500.

Equation Analysis

	Assets	=	Liabilities	+	Stockholders' Equity
	Supplies	=	Accounts Payable		
(8)	+$2,500		+$2,500		

Debit–Credit Analysis

Debits increase assets: debit Supplies $2,500.
Credits increase liabilities: credit Accounts Payable $2,500.

Journal Entry

Oct. 5	Supplies	2,500	
	Accounts Payable		2,500
	(Purchased supplies on account from Aero Supply)		

Posting

Supplies		Accounts Payable	
Oct. 5 2,500			Oct. 5 2,500

Cash Flows
no effect

Illustration 3-29 Hiring of new employees

Event 9

On October 9, Sierra hired four employees to begin work on October 15. Each employee will receive a weekly salary of $500 for a 5-day work week, payable every 2 weeks—first payment made on October 26.

Basic Analysis

An accounting transaction has not occurred. There is only an agreement that the employees will begin work on October 15. Thus, a debit–credit analysis is not needed because there is no accounting entry. (See transaction of October 26 (Event 11) for first payment.)

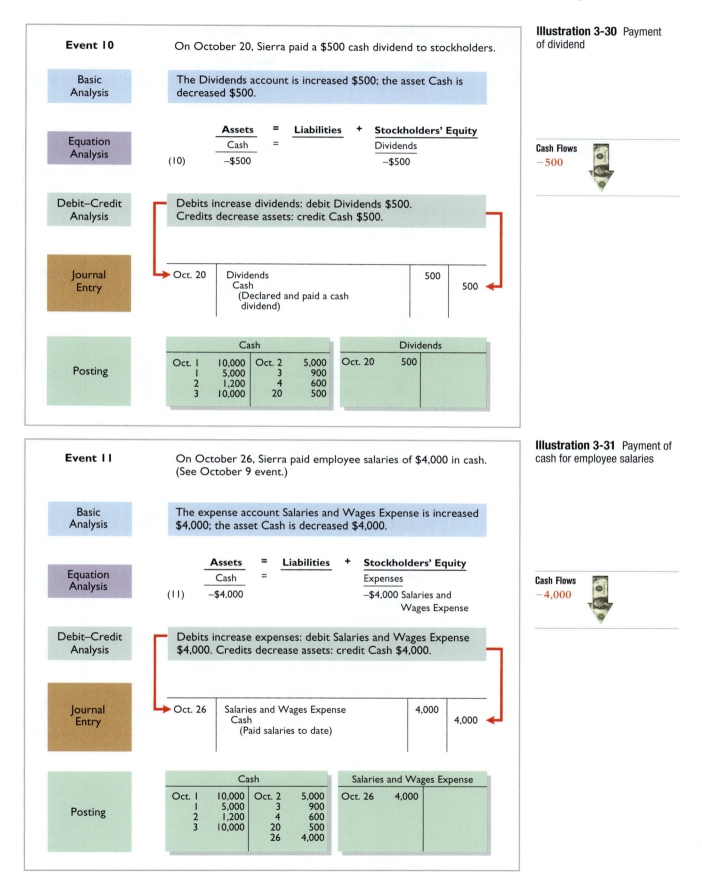

Illustration 3-30 Payment of dividend

Event 10   On October 20, Sierra paid a $500 cash dividend to stockholders.

Basic Analysis   The Dividends account is increased $500; the asset Cash is decreased $500.

Equation Analysis

	Assets	**=**	**Liabilities**	**+**	**Stockholders' Equity**
	Cash	=			Dividends
(10)	−$500				−$500

Cash Flows
−500

Debit–Credit Analysis   Debits increase dividends: debit Dividends $500. Credits decrease assets: credit Cash $500.

Journal Entry

Oct. 20	Dividends	500	
	Cash		500
	(Declared and paid a cash dividend)		

Posting

Cash				Dividends	
Oct. 1	10,000	Oct. 2	5,000	Oct. 20	500
1	5,000	3	900		
2	1,200	4	600		
3	10,000	20	500		

Illustration 3-31 Payment of cash for employee salaries

Event 11   On October 26, Sierra paid employee salaries of $4,000 in cash. (See October 9 event.)

Basic Analysis   The expense account Salaries and Wages Expense is increased $4,000; the asset Cash is decreased $4,000.

Equation Analysis

	Assets	**=**	**Liabilities**	**+**	**Stockholders' Equity**
	Cash	=			Expenses
(11)	−$4,000				−$4,000 Salaries and Wages Expense

Cash Flows
−4,000

Debit–Credit Analysis   Debits increase expenses: debit Salaries and Wages Expense $4,000. Credits decrease assets: credit Cash $4,000.

Journal Entry

Oct. 26	Salaries and Wages Expense	4,000	
	Cash		4,000
	(Paid salaries to date)		

Posting

Cash				Salaries and Wages Expense	
Oct. 1	10,000	Oct. 2	5,000	Oct. 26	4,000
1	5,000	3	900		
2	1,200	4	600		
3	10,000	20	500		
		26	4,000		

SUMMARY ILLUSTRATION OF JOURNALIZING AND POSTING

The journal for Sierra Corporation for the month of October is summarized in Illustration 3-32. The ledger is shown in Illustration 3-33 with all balances highlighted in red.

Illustration 3-32 General journal for Sierra Corporation

GENERAL JOURNAL

Date		Account Titles and Explanation	Debit	Credit
2014				
Oct.	1	Cash	10,000	
		Common Stock		10,000
		(Issued stock for cash)		
	1	Cash	5,000	
		Notes Payable		5,000
		(Issued 3-month, 12% note payable for cash)		
	2	Equipment	5,000	
		Cash		5,000
		(Purchased equipment for cash)		
	2	Cash	1,200	
		Unearned Service Revenue		1,200
		(Received advance from R. Knox for future service)		
	3	Cash	10,000	
		Service Revenue		10,000
		(Received cash for services performed)		
	3	Rent Expense	900	
		Cash		900
		(Paid cash for October office rent)		
	4	Prepaid Insurance	600	
		Cash		600
		(Paid 1-year policy; effective date October 1)		
	5	Supplies	2,500	
		Accounts Payable		2,500
		(Purchased supplies on account from Aero Supply)		
	20	Dividends	500	
		Cash		500
		(Declared and paid a cash dividend)		
	26	Salaries and Wages Expense	4,000	
		Cash		4,000
		(Paid salaries to date)		

Illustration 3-33 General
ledger for Sierra Corporation

GENERAL LEDGER

Cash
Oct.	1	10,000	Oct.	2	5,000
	1	5,000		3	900
	2	1,200		4	600
	3	10,000		20	500
				26	4,000
Bal.		**15,200**			

Supplies
Oct.	5	2,500
Bal.		**2,500**

Prepaid Insurance
Oct.	4	600
Bal.		**600**

Equipment
Oct.	2	5,000
Bal.		**5,000**

Notes Payable
			Oct.	1	5,000
			Bal.		**5,000**

Accounts Payable
			Oct.	5	2,500
			Bal.		**2,500**

Unearned Service Revenue
			Oct.	2	1,200
			Bal.		**1,200**

Common Stock
			Oct.	1	10,000
			Bal.		**10,000**

Dividends
Oct.	20	500
Bal.		**500**

Service Revenue
			Oct.	3	10,000
			Bal.		**10,000**

Salaries and Wages Expense
Oct.	26	4,000
Bal.		**4,000**

Rent Expense
Oct.	3	900
Bal.		**900**

The Trial Balance

A **trial balance** lists accounts and their balances at a given time. A company usually prepares a trial balance at the end of an accounting period. The accounts are listed in the order in which they appear in the ledger. Debit balances are listed in the left column and credit balances in the right column. The totals of the two columns must be equal.

LEARNING OBJECTIVE 8
Explain the purposes of a trial balance.

The trial balance proves the mathematical equality of debits and credits after posting. Under the double-entry system, this equality occurs when the sum of the debit account balances equals the sum of the credit account balances. **A trial balance may also uncover errors in journalizing and posting.** For example, a trial balance may well have detected the error at MF Global discussed in the Feature Story. **In addition, a trial balance is useful in the preparation of financial statements.**

These are the procedures for preparing a trial balance:

1. List the account titles and their balances.
2. Total the debit column and total the credit column.
3. Verify the equality of the two columns.

Illustration 3-34 presents the trial balance prepared from the ledger of Sierra Corporation. Note that the total debits, $28,700, equal the total credits, $28,700.

Illustration 3-34 Sierra Corporation trial balance

SIERRA CORPORATION
Trial Balance
October 31, 2014

	Debit	Credit
Cash	$ 15,200	
Supplies	2,500	
Prepaid Insurance	600	
Equipment	5,000	
Notes Payable		$ 5,000
Accounts Payable		2,500
Unearned Service Revenue		1,200
Common Stock		10,000
Dividends	500	
Service Revenue		10,000
Salaries and Wages Expense	4,000	
Rent Expense	900	
	$28,700	**$28,700**

Margin Note Note that the order of presentation in the trial balance is:

Assets
Liabilities
Stockholders' equity
Revenues
Expenses

Ethics Note An **error** is the result of an unintentional mistake. It is neither ethical nor unethical. An **irregularity** is an intentional misstatement, which is viewed as unethical.

LIMITATIONS OF A TRIAL BALANCE

A trial balance does not prove that all transactions have been recorded or that the ledger is correct. Numerous errors may exist even though the trial balance column totals agree. For example, the trial balance may balance even when any of the following occurs: (1) a transaction is not journalized, (2) a correct journal entry is not posted, (3) a journal entry is posted twice, (4) incorrect accounts are used in journalizing or posting, or (5) offsetting errors are made in recording the amount of a transaction. In other words, as long as equal debits and credits are posted, even to the wrong account or in the wrong amount, the total debits will equal the total credits. Nevertheless, despite these limitations, the trial balance is a useful screen for finding errors and is frequently used in practice.

🧰 DECISION TOOLKIT

DECISION CHECKPOINTS	INFO NEEDED FOR DECISION	TOOL TO USE FOR DECISION	HOW TO EVALUATE RESULTS
How do you determine that debits equal credits?	All account balances	Trial balance	List the account titles and their balances; total the debit and credit columns; verify equality.

KEEPING AN EYE ON CASH

LEARNING OBJECTIVE 9

Classify cash activities as operating, investing, or financing.

The Cash account shown below reflects all of the inflows and outflows of cash that occurred during October for Sierra Corporation (see Illustrations 3-21 to 3-31). We have also provided a description of each transaction that affected the Cash account.

1. Oct. 1 Issued stock for $10,000 cash.
2. Oct. 1 Issued note payable for $5,000 cash.
3. Oct. 2 Purchased equipment for $5,000 cash.
4. Oct. 2 Received $1,200 cash in advance from customer.
5. Oct. 3 Received $10,000 cash for services performed.
6. Oct. 3 Paid $900 cash for October rent.
7. Oct. 4 Paid $600 cash for one-year insurance policy.

8. Oct. 20 Paid $500 cash dividend to stockholders.
9. Oct. 26 Paid $4,000 cash salaries.

The Cash account and the related cash transactions indicate why cash changed during October. However, to make this information useful for analysis, it is summarized in a statement of cash flows. The statement of cash flows classifies each transaction as an operating activity, an investing activity, or a financing activity. A user of this statement can then determine the amount of net cash provided by operating activities, the amount of cash used for investing purposes, and the amount of cash provided by financing activities.

Operating activities are the types of activities the company performs to generate profits. Sierra Corporation is an outdoor guide business, so its operating activities involve providing guide services. Activities 4, 5, 6, 7, and 9 relate to cash received or spent to directly support its guide services.

Investing activities include the purchase or sale of long-lived assets used in operating the business, or the purchase or sale of investment securities (stocks and bonds of companies other than Sierra). Activity 3, the purchase of equipment, is an investment activity.

The primary types of **financing activities** are borrowing money, issuing shares of stock, and paying dividends. The financing activities of Sierra Corporation are Activities 1, 2, and 8.

Cash				
Oct.	1	10,000	Oct. 2	5,000
	1	5,000	3	900
	2	1,200	4	600
	3	10,000	20	500
			26	4,000
Bal.		**15,200**		

USING THE DECISION TOOLKIT

The Kansas Farmers' Vertically Integrated Cooperative, Inc. (K-VIC) was formed by over 200 northeast Kansas farmers in the late 1980s. Its purpose is to use raw materials, primarily grain and meat products grown by K-VIC's members, to process this material into end-user food products, and to distribute the products nationally. Profits not needed for expansion or investment are returned to the members annually, on a pro rata basis, according to the fair value of the grain and meat products received from each farmer.

Assume that the following trial balance was prepared for K-VIC.

KANSAS FARMERS' VERTICALLY INTEGRATED COOPERATIVE, INC.
Trial Balance
December 31, 2014
(in thousands)

	Debit	Credit
Accounts Receivable	$ 712,000	
Accounts Payable		$ 673,000
Buildings	365,000	
Cash	32,000	
Cost of Goods Sold	2,384,000	
Notes Payable (due in 2015)		12,000
Inventory	1,291,000	
Land	110,000	
Mortgage Payable		873,000
Equipment	63,000	
Retained Earnings		822,000
Sales Revenue		3,741,000
Salaries and Wages Payable		62,000
Salaries and Wages Expense	651,000	
Maintenance and Repairs Expense	500,000	
	$6,108,000	$6,183,000

Because the trial balance is not in balance, you have checked with various people responsible for entering accounting data and have discovered the following.

1. The purchase of 35 new trucks, costing $7 million and paid for with cash, was not recorded.

2. A data entry clerk accidentally deleted the account name for an account with a credit balance of $472 million, so the amount was added to the Mortgage Payable account in the trial balance.

3. December cash sales revenue of $75 million was credited to the Sales Revenue account, but the other half of the entry was not made.

4. $50 million of salaries expense were mistakenly charged to Maintenance and Repairs Expense.

Instructions

Answer these questions.

(a) Which mistake(s) have caused the trial balance to be out of balance?

(b) Should all of the items be corrected? Explain.

(c) What is the name of the account the data entry clerk deleted?

(d) Make the necessary corrections and prepare a correct trial balance with accounts listed in proper order.

(e) On your trial balance, write BAL beside the accounts that go on the balance sheet and INC beside those that go on the income statement.

Solution

(a) Only mistake #3 has caused the trial balance to be out of balance.

(b) All of the items should be corrected. The misclassification error (mistake #4) on the salaries expense would not affect bottom-line net income, but it does affect the amounts reported in the two expense accounts.

(c) There is no Common Stock account, so that must be the account that was deleted by the data entry clerk.

(d) and (e):

KANSAS FARMERS' VERTICALLY INTEGRATED COOPERATIVE, INC.
Trial Balance
December 31, 2014
(in thousands)

	Debit	Credit	
Cash ($32,000 − $7,000 + $75,000)	$ 100,000		BAL
Accounts Receivable	712,000		BAL
Inventory	1,291,000		BAL
Land	110,000		BAL
Buildings	365,000		BAL
Equipment ($63,000 + $7,000)	70,000		BAL
Accounts Payable		$ 673,000	BAL
Salaries and Wages Payable		62,000	BAL
Notes Payable (due in 2015)		12,000	BAL
Mortgage Payable ($873,000 − $472,000)		401,000	BAL
Common Stock		472,000	BAL
Retained Earnings		822,000	BAL
Sales Revenue		3,741,000	INC
Cost of Goods Sold	2,384,000		INC
Salaries and Wages Expense	701,000		INC
($651,000 + $50,000)			
Maintenance and Repairs Expense	450,000		INC
($500,000 − $50,000)			
	$6,183,000	$6,183,000	

Summary of Learning Objectives

1 **Analyze the effect of business transactions on the basic accounting equation.** Each business transaction must have a dual effect on the accounting equation. For example, if an individual asset is increased, there must be a corresponding (a) decrease in another asset, or (b) increase in a specific liability, or (c) increase in stockholders' equity.

2 **Explain what an account is and how it helps in the recording process.** An account is an individual accounting record of increases and decreases in specific asset, liability, and stockholders' equity items.

3 **Define debits and credits and explain how they are used to record business transactions.** The terms debit and credit are synonymous with left and right. Assets, dividends, and expenses are increased by debits and decreased by credits. Liabilities, common stock, retained earnings, and revenues are increased by credits and decreased by debits.

4 **Identify the basic steps in the recording process.** The basic steps in the recording process are (a) analyze each transaction in terms of its effect on the accounts, (b) enter the transaction information in a journal, and (c) transfer the journal information to the appropriate accounts in the ledger.

5 **Explain what a journal is and how it helps in the recording process.** The initial accounting record of a transaction is entered in a journal before the data are entered in the accounts. A journal (a) discloses in one place the complete effect of a transaction, (b) provides a chronological record of transactions, and (c) prevents or locates errors because the debit and credit amounts for each entry can be readily compared.

6 **Explain what a ledger is and how it helps in the recording process.** The entire group of accounts maintained by a company is referred to collectively as a ledger. The ledger provides the balance in each of the accounts as well as keeps track of changes in these balances.

7 **Explain what posting is and how it helps in the recording process.** Posting is the procedure of transferring journal entries to the ledger accounts. This phase of the recording process accumulates the effects of journalized transactions in the individual accounts.

8 **Explain the purposes of a trial balance.** A trial balance is a list of accounts and their balances at a given time. The primary purpose of the trial balance is to prove the mathematical equality of debits and credits after posting. A trial balance also uncovers errors in journalizing and posting and is useful in preparing financial statements.

9 **Classify cash activities as operating, investing, or financing.** Operating activities are the types of activities the company performs to generate profits. Investing activities relate to the purchase or sale of long-lived assets used in operating the business, or to the purchase or sale of investment securities (stock and bonds of other companies). Financing activities are borrowing money, issuing shares of stock, and paying dividends.

DECISION TOOLKIT *A SUMMARY*

DECISION CHECKPOINTS	INFO NEEDED FOR DECISION	TOOL TO USE FOR DECISION	HOW TO EVALUATE RESULTS
Has an accounting transaction occurred?	Details of the event	Accounting equation	If the event affected assets, liabilities, or stockholders' equity, then record as a transaction.
How do you determine that debits equal credits?	All account balances	Trial balance	List the account titles and their balances; total the debit and credit columns; verify equality.

Glossary

Terms are highlighted in **blue** throughout the chapter.

Account An individual accounting record of increases and decreases in specific asset, liability, stockholders' equity, revenue or expense items.

Accounting information system The system of collecting and processing transaction data and communicating financial information to decision-makers.

Accounting transactions Events that require recording in the financial statements because they affect assets, liabilities, or stockholders' equity.

Chart of accounts A list of a company's accounts.

Credit The right side of an account.

Debit The left side of an account.

Double-entry system A system that records the two-sided effect of each transaction in appropriate accounts.

General journal The most basic form of journal.

General ledger A ledger that contains all asset, liability, stockholders' equity, revenue, and expense accounts.

Journal An accounting record in which transactions are initially recorded in chronological order.

Journalizing The procedure of entering transaction data in the journal.

Ledger The group of accounts maintained by a company.

Posting The procedure of transferring journal entry amounts to the ledger accounts.

T-account The basic form of an account.

Trial balance A list of accounts and their balances at a given time.

Self-Test, Brief Exercises, Exercises, Problem Set A, and many more resources are available for practice in WileyPLUS.

Self-Test Questions

(Answers in *Broadening Your Perspective*.)

(LO 1) **1.** The effects on the basic accounting equation of performing services for cash are to:
(a) increase assets and decrease stockholders' equity.
(b) increase assets and increase stockholders' equity.
(c) increase assets and increase liabilities.
(d) increase liabilities and increase stockholders' equity.

(LO 1) **2.** Genesis Company buys a $900 machine on credit. This transaction will affect the:
(a) income statement only.
(b) balance sheet only.
(c) income statement and retained earnings statement only.
(d) income statement, retained earnings statement, and balance sheet.

(LO 1) **3.** Which of the following events is **not** recorded in the accounting records?
(a) Equipment is purchased on account.
(b) An employee is terminated.
(c) A cash investment is made into the business.
(d) Company pays dividend to stockholders.

(LO 1) **4.** During 2014, Gibson Company assets decreased $50,000 and its liabilities decreased $90,000. Its stockholders' equity therefore:
(a) increased $40,000.
(b) decreased $140,000.
(c) decreased $40,000.
(d) increased $140,000.

(LO 2) **5.** Which statement about an account is **true**?
(a) In its simplest form, an account consists of two parts.
(b) An account is an individual accounting record of increases and decreases in specific asset, liability, and stockholders' equity items.
(c) There are separate accounts for specific assets and liabilities but only one account for stockholders' equity items.
(d) The left side of an account is the credit or decrease side.

(LO 3) **6.** Debits:
(a) increase both assets and liabilities.
(b) decrease both assets and liabilities.
(c) increase assets and decrease liabilities.
(d) decrease assets and increase liabilities.

(LO 3) **7.** A revenue account:
(a) is increased by debits.
(b) is decreased by credits.
(c) has a normal balance of a debit.
(d) is increased by credits.

(LO 3) **8.** Which accounts normally have debit balances?
(a) Assets, expenses, and revenues.
(b) Assets, expenses, and retained earnings.
(c) Assets, liabilities, and dividends.
(d) Assets, dividends, and expenses.

(LO 3) **9.** Paying an account payable with cash affects the components of the accounting equation in the following way:
(a) Decreases stockholders' equity and decreases liabilities.
(b) Increases assets and decreases liabilities.
(c) Decreases assets and increases stockholders' equity.
(d) Decreases assets and decreases liabilities.

10. Which is **not** part of the recording process?
(a) Analyzing transactions. (LO 4)
(b) Preparing a trial balance.
(c) Entering transactions in a journal.
(d) Posting transactions.

11. Which of these statements about a journal is **false**?
(a) It contains only revenue and expense accounts. (LO 5)
(b) It provides a chronological record of transactions.
(c) It helps to locate errors because the debit and credit amounts for each entry can be readily compared.
(d) It discloses in one place the complete effect of a transaction.

12. A ledger:
(a) contains only asset and liability accounts.
(b) should show accounts in alphabetical order.
(c) is a collection of the entire group of accounts maintained by a company. (LO 6)
(d) provides a chronological record of transactions.

13. Posting:

    (a) normally occurs before journalizing.

    (b) transfers ledger transaction data to the journal.

(LO 7)   (c) is an optional step in the recording process.

    (d) transfers journal entries to ledger accounts.

14. A trial balance:

    (a) is a list of accounts with their balances at a given time.

    (b) proves that proper account titles were used.

(LO 8)   (c) will not balance if a correct journal entry is posted twice.

    (d) proves that all transactions have been recorded.

15. A trial balance will **not** balance if: (LO 8)

    (a) a correct journal entry is posted twice.

    (b) the purchase of supplies on account is debited to Supplies and credited to Cash.

    (c) a $100 cash dividend is debited to Dividends for $1,000 and credited to Cash for $100.

    (d) a $450 payment on account is debited to Accounts Payable for $45 and credited to Cash for $45.

Go to the book's companion website, **www.wiley.com/college/kimmel**, to access additional Self-Test Questions.

Questions

1. Describe the accounting information system.

2. Can a business enter into a transaction that affects only the left side of the basic accounting equation? If so, give an example.

3. Are the following events recorded in the accounting records? Explain your answer in each case.

    (a) A major stockholder of the company dies.

    (b) Supplies are purchased on account.

    (c) An employee is fired.

    (d) The company pays a cash dividend to its stockholders.

4. Indicate how each business transaction affects the basic accounting equation.

    (a) Paid cash for janitorial services.

    (b) Purchased equipment for cash.

    (c) Issued common stock to investors in exchange for cash.

    (d) Paid an account payable in full.

5. Why is an account referred to as a T-account?

6. The terms debit and credit mean "increase" and "decrease," respectively. Do you agree? Explain.

7. Terry Rabas, a fellow student, contends that the double-entry system means each transaction must be recorded twice. Is Terry correct? Explain.

8. Misty Reno, a beginning accounting student, believes debit balances are favorable and credit balances are unfavorable. Is Misty correct? Discuss.

9. State the rules of debit and credit as applied to (a) asset accounts, (b) liability accounts, and (c) the Common Stock account.

10. What is the normal balance for each of these accounts?

    (a) Accounts Receivable.

    (b) Cash.

    (c) Dividends.

    (d) Accounts Payable.

    (e) Service Revenue.

    (f) Salaries and Wages Expense.

    (g) Common Stock.

11. Indicate whether each account is an asset, a liability, or a stockholders' equity account, and whether it would have a normal debit or credit balance.

    (a) Accounts Receivable.   (d) Dividends.

    (b) Accounts Payable.   (e) Supplies.

    (c) Equipment.

12. For the following transactions, indicate the account debited and the account credited.

    (a) Supplies are purchased on account.

    (b) Cash is received on signing a note payable.

    (c) Employees are paid salaries in cash.

13. For each account listed here, indicate whether it generally will have debit entries only, credit entries only, or both debit and credit entries.

    (a) Cash.

    (b) Accounts Receivable.

    (c) Dividends.

    (d) Accounts Payable.

    (e) Salaries and Wages Expense.

    (f) Service Revenue.

14. What are the normal balances for the following accounts of Tootsie Roll Industries? (a) Accounts Receivable, (b) Income Taxes Payable, (c) Sales, and (d) Selling, Marketing, and Administrative Expenses.

15. What are the basic steps in the recording process?

16. (a) When entering a transaction in the journal, should the debit or credit be written first?

    (b) Which should be indented, the debit or the credit?

17. (a) Should accounting transaction debits and credits be recorded directly in the ledger accounts?

    (b) What are the advantages of first recording transactions in the journal and then posting to the ledger?

18. Journalize these accounting transactions.
    (a) Stockholders invested $12,000 in the business in exchange for common stock.
    (b) Insurance of $800 is paid for the year.
    (c) Supplies of $1,800 are purchased on account.
    (d) Cash of $7,500 is received for services rendered.

19. (a) What is a ledger?
    (b) Why is a chart of accounts important?

20. What is a trial balance and what are its purposes?

21. Tyler Bazil is confused about how accounting information flows through the accounting system. He believes information flows in this order:
    (a) Debits and credits are posted to the ledger.
    (b) Accounting transaction occurs.
    (c) Information is entered in the journal.
    (d) Financial statements are prepared.
    (e) Trial balance is prepared.

    Indicate to Tyler the proper flow of the information.

22. Two students are discussing the use of a trial balance. They wonder whether the following errors, each considered separately, would prevent the trial balance from balancing. What would you tell them?
    (a) The bookkeeper debited Cash for $600 and credited Salaries and Wages Expense for $600 for payment of wages.
    (b) Cash collected on account was debited to Cash for $800, and Service Revenue was credited for $80.

Brief Exercises

Determine effect of transactions on basic accounting equation.

(LO 1), C

BE3-1 Presented below are three economic events. On a sheet of paper, list the letters (a), (b), and (c) with columns for assets, liabilities, and stockholders' equity. In each column, indicate whether the event increased (+), decreased (−), or had no effect (NE) on assets, liabilities, and stockholders' equity.
(a) Purchased supplies on account.
(b) Received cash for providing a service.
(c) Expenses paid in cash.

Determine effect of transactions on basic accounting equation.

(LO 1), AP

BE3-2 During 2014, Damon Corp. entered into the following transactions.
1. Borrowed $60,000 by issuing bonds.
2. Paid $9,000 cash dividend to stockholders.
3. Received $13,000 cash from a previously billed customer for services performed.
4. Purchased supplies on account for $3,100.

Using the following tabular analysis, show the effect of each transaction on the accounting equation. Put explanations for changes to Stockholders' Equity in the right-hand margin. For Retained Earnings, use separate columns for Revenues, Expenses, and Dividends if necessary. Use Illustration 3-3 as a model.

Assets			=	Liabilities		+	Stockholders' Equity	
	Accounts			Accounts	Bonds		Common	Retained
Cash +	Receivable +	Supplies	=	Payable +	Payable +		Stock +	Earnings

Determine effect of transactions on basic accounting equation.

(LO 1), AP

BE3-3 During 2014, Comstock Company entered into the following transactions.
1. Purchased equipment for $286,176 cash.
2. Issued common stock to investors for $137,590 cash.
3. Purchased inventory of $68,480 on account.

Using the following tabular analysis, show the effect of each transaction on the accounting equation. Put explanations for changes to Stockholders' Equity in the right-hand margin. For Retained Earnings, use separate columns for Revenues, Expenses, and Dividends if necessary. Use Illustration 3-3 as a model.

Assets			=	Liabilities	+	Stockholders' Equity	
				Accounts		Common	Retained
Cash +	Inventory +	Equipment	=	Payable	+	Stock +	Earnings

Indicate debit and credit effects.

(LO 3), K

BE3-4 For each of the following accounts, indicate the effect of a debit or a credit on the account and the normal balance.
(a) Accounts Payable.
(b) Advertising Expense.
(c) Service Revenue.
(d) Accounts Receivable.
(e) Retained Earnings.
(f) Dividends.

BE3-5 Transactions for Grover Company for the month of June are presented below. Identify the accounts to be debited and credited for each transaction.

Identify accounts to be debited and credited.
(LO 3), **C**

June 1 Issues common stock to investors in exchange for $5,000 cash.
2 Buys equipment on account for $1,100.
3 Pays $740 to landlord for June rent.
12 Bills Matt Wilfer $700 for welding work done.

BE3-6 Use the data in BE3-5 and journalize the transactions. (You may omit explanations.)

Journalize transactions.
(LO 5), **AP**

BE3-7 Rachelle Mohling, a fellow student, is unclear about the basic steps in the recording process. Identify and briefly explain the steps in the order in which they occur.

Identify steps in the recording process.
(LO 4), **C**

BE3-8 Upton Corporation has the following transactions during August of the current year. Indicate (a) the basic analysis and (b) the debit–credit analysis demonstrated in Illustrations 3-21 to 3-31.

Indicate basic debit–credit analysis.
(LO 4), **C**

Aug. 1 Issues shares of common stock to investors in exchange for $10,000.
4 Pays insurance in advance for 3 months, $1,500.
16 Receives $900 from clients for services rendered.
27 Pays the secretary $620 salary.

BE3-9 Use the data in BE3-8 and journalize the transactions. (You may omit explanations.)

Journalize transactions.
(LO 5), **AP**

BE3-10 Selected transactions for Perez Company are presented below in journal form (without explanations). Post the transactions to T-accounts.

Post journal entries to T-accounts.
(LO 7), **AP**

Date	Account Title	Debit	Credit
May 5	Accounts Receivable	3,800	
	Service Revenue		3,800
12	Cash	1,600	
	Accounts Receivable		1,600
15	Cash	2,000	
	Service Revenue		2,000

BE3-11 From the ledger balances below, prepare a trial balance for Yeager Company at June 30, 2014. All account balances are normal.

Prepare a trial balance.
(LO 8), **AP**

Accounts Payable	$ 1,000	Service Revenue	$8,600
Cash	5,400	Accounts Receivable	3,000
Common Stock	18,000	Salaries and Wages Expense	4,000
Dividends	1,200	Rent Expense	1,000
Equipment	13,000		

BE3-12 An inexperienced bookkeeper prepared the following trial balance that does not balance. Prepare a correct trial balance, assuming all account balances are normal.

Prepare a corrected trial balance.
(LO 8), **AP**

CINELLI COMPANY
Trial Balance
December 31, 2014

	Debit	Credit
Cash	$20,800	
Prepaid Insurance		$ 3,500
Accounts Payable		2,500
Unearned Service Revenue	1,800	
Common Stock		10,000
Retained Earnings		6,600
Dividends		5,000
Service Revenue		25,600
Salaries and Wages Expense	14,600	
Rent Expense		2,600
	$37,200	$55,800

Exercises

Analyze the effect of transactions.

(LO 1), **C**

E3-1 Selected transactions for Warner Advertising Company, Inc., are listed here.

1. Issued common stock to investors in exchange for cash received from investors.
2. Paid monthly rent.
3. Received cash from customers when service was performed.
4. Billed customers for services performed.
5. Paid dividend to stockholders.
6. Incurred advertising expense on account.
7. Received cash from customers billed in (4).
8. Purchased additional equipment for cash.
9. Purchased equipment on account.

Instructions

Describe the effect of each transaction on assets, liabilities, and stockholders' equity. For example, the first answer is (1) Increase in assets and increase in stockholders' equity.

Analyze the effect of transactions on assets, liabilities, and stockholders' equity.

(LO 1), **AP**

E3-2 Manning Company entered into these transactions during May 2014, its first month of operations.

1. Stockholders invested $40,000 in the business in exchange for common stock of the company.
2. Purchased computers for office use for $30,000 from Dell on account.
3. Paid $4,000 cash for May rent on storage space.
4. Performed computer services worth $19,000 on account.
5. Performed computer services to Lawton Construction Company for $5,000 cash.
6. Paid Southern States Power Co. $8,000 cash for energy usage in May.
7. Paid Dell for the computers purchased in (2).
8. Incurred advertising expense for May of $1,300 on account.
9. Received $12,000 cash from customers for contracts billed in (4).

Instructions

Using the following tabular analysis, show the effect of each transaction on the accounting equation. Put explanations for changes to Stockholders' Equity in the right-hand margin. Use Illustration 3-3 as a model.

Assets			=	Liabilities	+	Stockholders' Equity				
	Accounts			Accounts		Common		Retained Earnings		
Cash	+ Receivable	+ Equipment	=	Payable	+	Stock	+ Revenues	− Expenses	− Dividends	

Determine effect of transactions on basic accounting equation.

(LO 1), **AP**

E3-3 During 2014, its first year of operations as a delivery service, Persinger Corp. entered into the following transactions.

1. Issued shares of common stock to investors in exchange for $100,000 in cash.
2. Borrowed $45,000 by issuing bonds.
3. Purchased delivery trucks for $60,000 cash.
4. Received $16,000 from customers for services performed.
5. Purchased supplies for $4,700 on account.
6. Paid rent of $5,200.
7. Performed services on account for $10,000.
8. Paid salaries of $28,000.
9. Paid a dividend of $11,000 to shareholders.

Instructions

Using the following tabular analysis, show the effect of each transaction on the accounting equation. Put explanations for changes to Stockholders' Equity in the right-hand margin. Use Illustration 3-3 as a model.

Assets				=	Liabilities		+	Stockholders' Equity				
	Accounts		Equip-		Accounts	Bonds		Common		Retained Earnings		
Cash	+ Receivable	+ Supplies	+ ment	=	Payable	+ Payable	+	Stock	+ Revenues	− Expenses	− Dividends	

E3-4   A tabular analysis of the transactions made during August 2014 by Colaw Company during its first month of operations is shown below. Each increase and decrease in stockholders' equity is explained.

Analyze transactions and compute net income.
(LO 1), **AP**

	Assets				=	Liabilities	+			Stockholders' Equity				
						Accounts		Common			Retained Earnings			
Cash	+ A/R	+ Supp.	+ Equip.	=	Payable	+	Stock	+	Rev.	− Exp.	− Div.			
1. +$20,000							+$20,000							Com. Stock
2. −1,000			+$5,000		+$4,000									
3. −750		+$750												
4. +4,100	+$5,400								+$9,500					Serv. Rev.
5. −1,500					−1,500									
6. −2,000											−$2,000			Div.
7. −800										−$ 800				Rent Exp.
8. +450	−450													
9. −3,000										−3,000				Salar. Exp.
10.					+300					−300				Util. Exp.

Instructions
(a) Describe each transaction.
(b) Determine how much stockholders' equity increased for the month.
(c) Compute the net income for the month.

E3-5   The tabular analysis of transactions for Colaw Company is presented in E3-4.

Prepare an income statement, retained earnings statement, and balance sheet.
(LO 1), **AP**

Instructions

Prepare an income statement and a retained earnings statement for August and a classified balance sheet at August 31, 2014.

E3-6   Selected transactions for Home Place, an interior decorator corporation, in its first month of business, are as follows.

Identify debits, credits, and normal balances and journalize transactions.
(LO 3, 5), **AP**

 1. Issued stock to investors for $15,000 in cash.
 2. Purchased used car for $10,000 cash for use in business.
 3. Purchased supplies on account for $300.
 4. Billed customers $3,700 for services performed.
 5. Paid $200 cash for advertising start of the business.
 6. Received $1,100 cash from customers billed in transaction (4).
 7. Paid creditor $300 cash on account.
 8. Paid dividends of $400 cash to stockholders.

Instructions
(a) For each transaction indicate (a) the basic type of account debited and credited (asset, liability, stockholders' equity); (b) the specific account debited and credited (Cash, Rent Expense, Service Revenue, etc.); (c) whether the specific account is increased or decreased; and (d) the normal balance of the specific account. Use the following format in which transaction 1 is given as an example.

	Account Debited				Account Credited			
	(a)	**(b)**	**(c)**	**(d)**	**(a)**	**(b)**	**(c)**	**(d)**
Trans-action	Basic Type	Specific Account	Effect	Normal Balance	Basic Type	Specific Account	Effect	Normal Balance
1	Asset	Cash	Increase	Debit	Stock-holders' equity	Common Stock	Increase	Credit

(b) Journalize the transactions. Do not provide explanations.

Analyze transactions and determine their effect on accounts.

(LO 3), **C**

E3-7 This information relates to Crofoot Real Estate Agency.

Oct. 1 Stockholders invest $30,000 in exchange for common stock of the corporation.
2 Hires an administrative assistant at an annual salary of $36,000.
3 Buys office furniture for $3,800, on account.
6 Sells a house and lot for M.E. Graves; commissions due from Graves, $10,800 (not paid by Graves at this time).
10 Receives cash of $140 as commission for acting as rental agent renting an apartment.
27 Pays $700 on account for the office furniture purchased on October 3.
30 Pays the administrative assistant $3,000 in salary for October.

Instructions
Prepare the debit–credit analysis for each transaction, as demonstrated in Illustrations 3-21 to 3-31.

Journalize transactions.

(LO 5), **AP**

E3-8 Transaction data for Crofoot Real Estate Agency are presented in E3-7.

Instructions

Journalize the transactions. Do not provide explanations.

Journalize a series of transactions.

(LO 4, 5), **AP**

E3-9 The May transactions of Hanschu Corporation were as follows.

May 4 Paid $700 due for supplies previously purchased on account.
7 Performed advisory services on account for $6,800.
8 Purchased supplies for $850 on account.
9 Purchased equipment for $1,000 in cash.
17 Paid employees $530 in cash.
22 Received bill for equipment repairs of $900.
29 Paid $1,200 for 12 months of insurance policy. Coverage begins June 1.

Instructions
Journalize the transactions. Do not provide explanations.

Post journal entries and prepare a trial balance.

(LO 7, 8), **AP**

E3-10 Transaction data and journal entries for Crofoot Real Estate Agency are presented in E3-7 and E3-8.

Instructions
(a) Post the transactions to T-accounts.
(b) Prepare a trial balance at October 31, 2014.

Analyze transactions, prepare journal entries, and post transactions to T-accounts.

(LO 1, 5, 7), **AP**

E3-11 Selected transactions for Protheroe Corporation during its first month in business are presented below.

Sept. 1 Issued common stock in exchange for $20,000 cash received from investors.
5 Purchased equipment for $9,000, paying $3,000 in cash and the balance on account.
8 Performed services on account for $18,000.
14 Paid salaries of $1,200.
25 Paid $4,000 cash on balance owed for equipment.
30 Paid $500 cash dividend.

Protheroe's chart of accounts shows Cash, Accounts Receivable, Equipment, Accounts Payable, Common Stock, Dividends, Service Revenue, and Salaries and Wages Expense.

Instructions
(a) Prepare a tabular analysis of the September transactions. The column headings should be Cash + Accounts Receivable + Equipment = Accounts Payable + Stockholders' Equity. For transactions affecting stockholders' equity, provide explanations in the right margin, as shown in Illustration 3-3.
(b) Journalize the transactions. Do not provide explanations.
(c) Post the transactions to T-accounts.

E3-12 The T-accounts below summarize the ledger of Wheeling Gardening Company, Inc. at the end of the first month of operations.

Journalize transactions from T-accounts and prepare a trial balance.

(LO 5, 8), **AP**

	Cash			
Apr.	1	15,000	Apr. 15	800
	12	700	25	3,500
	29	800		
	30	900		

	Unearned Service Revenue		
		Apr. 30	900

	Accounts Receivable			
Apr.	7	3,400	Apr. 29	800

	Common Stock		
		Apr. 1	15,000

	Supplies	
Apr.	4	5,200

	Service Revenue		
		Apr. 7	3,400
		12	700

	Accounts Payable			
Apr.	25	3,500	Apr. 4	5,200

	Salaries and Wages Expense	
Apr.	15	800

Instructions

(a) Prepare the journal entries (including explanations) that resulted in the amounts posted to the accounts. Present them in the order they occurred.

(b) Prepare a trial balance at April 30, 2014. (*Hint:* Compute ending balances of T-accounts first.)

E3-13 Selected transactions from the journal of Eberle Inc. during its first month of operations are presented here.

Post journal entries and prepare a trial balance.

(LO 7, 8), **AP**

Date		Account Titles	Debit	Credit
Aug.	1	Cash	8,000	
		Common Stock		8,000
	10	Cash	1,700	
		Service Revenue		1,700
	12	Equipment	6,200	
		Cash		1,200
		Notes Payable		5,000
	25	Accounts Receivable	3,400	
		Service Revenue		3,400
	31	Cash	600	
		Accounts Receivable		600

Instructions

(a) Post the transactions to T-accounts.

(b) Prepare a trial balance at August 31, 2014.

E3-14 Here is the ledger for Keisler Co.

Journalize transactions from T-accounts and prepare a trial balance.

(LO 5, 8), **AP**

	Cash			
Oct.	1	7,000	Oct. 4	400
	10	980	12	1,500
	10	8,000	15	250
	20	700	30	300
	25	2,000	31	500

	Common Stock		
		Oct. 1	7,000
		25	2,000

	Accounts Receivable			
Oct.	6	800	Oct. 20	700
	20	920		

	Dividends	
Oct.	30	300

	Supplies			
Oct.	4	400	Oct. 31	180

	Service Revenue		
		Oct. 6	800
		10	980
		20	920

Equipment				Salaries and Wages Expense		
Oct.	3	3,000		Oct.	31	500

Notes Payable				Supplies Expense		
	Oct.	10	8,000	Oct.	31	180

Accounts Payable					Rent Expense		
Oct.	12	1,500	Oct.	3	3,000	Oct. 15	250

Instructions

(a) Reproduce the journal entries for only the transactions that **occurred on October 1, 10, and 20,** and provide explanations for each.

(b) Prepare a trial balance at October 31, 2014. (*Hint:* Compute ending balances of T-accounts first.)

Analyze errors and their effects on trial balance.

(LO 8), **AN**

E3-15 The bookkeeper for Willingham Corporation made these errors in journalizing and posting.

1. A credit posting of $400 to Accounts Receivable was omitted.
2. A debit posting of $750 for Prepaid Insurance was debited to Insurance Expense.
3. A collection on account of $100 was journalized and posted as a debit to Cash $100 and a credit to Accounts Payable $100.
4. A credit posting of $300 to Income Taxes Payable was made twice.
5. A cash purchase of supplies for $250 was journalized and posted as a debit to Supplies $25 and a credit to Cash $25.
6. A debit of $395 to Advertising Expense was posted as $359.

Instructions

For each error, indicate (a) whether the trial balance will balance; if the trial balance will not balance, indicate (b) the amount of the difference and (c) the trial balance column that will have the larger total. Consider each error separately. Use the following form, in which error 1 is given as an example.

	(a)	(b)	(c)
Error	In Balance	Difference	Larger Column
1	No	$400	Debit

Prepare a trial balance and financial statements.

(LO 8), **AP**

E3-16 The accounts in the ledger of Bastin Delivery Service contain the following balances on July 31, 2014.

Accounts Receivable	$13,400	Prepaid Insurance	$ 2,200
Accounts Payable	8,400	Service Revenue	15,500
Cash	?	Dividends	700
Equipment	59,360	Common Stock	40,000
Maintenance and		Salaries and Wages Expense	7,428
Repairs Expense	1,958	Salaries and Wages Payable	820
Insurance Expense	900	Retained Earnings	5,200
Notes Payable (due 2017)	28,450	(July 1, 2014)	

Instructions

(a) Prepare a trial balance with the accounts arranged as illustrated in the chapter, and fill in the missing amount for Cash.

(b) Prepare an income statement, a retained earnings statement, and a classified balance sheet for the month of July 2014.

Identify normal account balance and corresponding financial statement.

(LO 3), **K**

E3-17 The following accounts, in alphabetical order, were selected from recent financial statements of Krispy Kreme Doughnuts, Inc.

Accounts payable	Interest income
Accounts receivable	Inventories
Common stock	Prepaid expenses
Depreciation expense	Property and equipment
Interest expense	Revenues

Instructions

For each account, indicate (a) whether the normal balance is a debit or a credit, and (b) the financial statement—balance sheet or income statement—where the account should be presented.

E3-18   Review the transactions listed in E3-1 for Warner Advertising Company and classify each transaction as either an operating activity, investing activity, or financing activity, or if no cash is exchanged, as a noncash event.

Classify transactions as cash-flow activities.
(LO 9), **AP**

E3-19   Review the transactions listed in E3-3 for Persinger Corp. and classify each transaction as either an operating activity, investing activity, or financing activity, or if no cash is exchanged, as a noncash event.

Classify transactions as cash-flow activities.
(LO 9), **AP**

Challenge Exercises

Visit the book's companion website, at **www.wiley.com/college/kimmel**, and choose the Student Companion site to access Challenge Exercises.

Problems: Set A

P3-1A   On April 1, DeDonder Travel Agency Inc. was established. These transactions were completed during the month.
1. Stockholders invested $30,000 cash in the company in exchange for common stock.
2. Paid $900 cash for April office rent.
3. Purchased office equipment for $3,400 cash.
4. Purchased $200 of advertising in the *Chicago Tribune*, on account.
5. Paid $500 cash for office supplies.
6. Performed services worth $12,000. Cash of $3,000 is received from customers, and the balance of $9,000 is billed to customers on account.
7. Paid $400 cash dividends.
8. Paid *Chicago Tribune* amount due in transaction (4).
9. Paid employees' salaries $1,800.
10. Received $9,000 in cash from customers billed previously in transaction (6).

Analyze transactions and compute net income.
(LO 1), **AP**

Instructions
(a) Prepare a tabular analysis of the transactions using these column headings: Cash, Accounts Receivable, Supplies, Equipment, Accounts Payable, Common Stock, and Retained Earnings (with separate columns for Revenues, Expenses, and Dividends). Include margin explanations for any changes in Retained Earnings.
(b) From an analysis of the Retained Earnings columns, compute the net income or net loss for April.

(a) Cash $34,800
    Total assets $38,700

P3-2A   Nina Finzelberg started her own consulting firm, Finzelberg Consulting Inc., on May 1, 2014. The following transactions occurred during the month of May.

Analyze transactions and prepare financial statements.
(LO 1), **AP**

May	1	Stockholders invested $15,000 cash in the business in exchange for common stock.
	2	Paid $600 for office rent for the month.
	3	Purchased $500 of supplies on account.
	5	Paid $150 to advertise in the *County News*.
	9	Received $1,400 cash for services performed.
	12	Paid $200 cash dividend.
	15	Performed $4,200 of services on account.
	17	Paid $2,500 for employee salaries.
	20	Paid for the supplies purchased on account on May 3.
	23	Received a cash payment of $1,200 for services performed on account on May 15.
	26	Borrowed $5,000 from the bank on a note payable.
	29	Purchased office equipment for $2,000 paying $200 in cash and the balance on account.
	30	Paid $180 for utilities.

Instructions
(a) Show the effects of the previous transactions on the accounting equation using the following format. Assume the note payable is to be repaid within the year.

(a) Cash $18,270
    Total assets $23,770

	Assets			=	Liabilities		+	Stockholders' Equity			
		Accounts				Notes	Accounts	Common		Retained Earnings	
Date	Cash +	Receivable +	Supplies + Equipment =	Payable +	Payable +	Stock	+ Revenues − Expenses − Dividends

Include margin explanations for any changes in Retained Earnings.

(b) Prepare an income statement for the month of May 2014.

(c) Prepare a classified balance sheet at May 31, 2014.

(b) Net income $2,170

Analyze transactions and prepare an income statement, retained earnings statement, and balance sheet.

(LO 1), AP

GLS XLS

P3-3A Cindy Braun created a corporation providing legal services, Cindy Braun Inc., on July 1, 2014. On July 31 the balance sheet showed Cash $4,000; Accounts Receivable $2,500; Supplies $500; Equipment $5,000; Accounts Payable $4,200; Common Stock $6,200; and Retained Earnings $1,600. During August, the following transactions occurred.

Aug. 1 Collected $1,100 of accounts receivable due from customers.
4 Paid $2,700 cash for accounts payable due.
9 Performed services worth $5,400, of which $3,600 is collected in cash and the balance is due in September.
15 Purchased additional office equipment for $4,000, paying $700 in cash and the balance on account.
19 Paid salaries $1,400, rent for August $700, and advertising expenses $350.
23 Paid a cash dividend of $700.
26 Borrowed $5,000 from Standard Federal Bank; the money was borrowed on a 4-month note payable.
31 Incurred utility expenses for the month on account $380.

Instructions

(a) Cash $7,150

(a) Prepare a tabular analysis of the August transactions beginning with July 31 balances. The column heading should be Cash + Accounts Receivable + Supplies + Equipment = Notes Payable + Accounts Payable + Common Stock + Retained Earnings + Revenues − Expenses − Dividends. Include margin explanations for any changes in Retained Earnings.

(b) Net income $2,570
Ret. earnings $3,470

(b) Prepare an income statement for August, a retained earnings statement for August, and a classified balance sheet at August 31.

Journalize a series of transactions.

(LO 4, 5), AP

GLS

P3-4A Friendley's Miniature Golf and Driving Range Inc. was opened on March 1 by Dean Barley. These selected events and transactions occurred during March.

Mar. 1 Stockholders invested $50,000 cash in the business in exchange for common stock of the corporation.
3 Purchased Arnie's Golf Land for $38,000 cash. The price consists of land $23,000, building $9,000, and equipment $6,000. (Record this in a single entry.)
5 Advertised the opening of the driving range and miniature golf course, paying advertising expenses of $1,200 cash.
6 Paid cash $2,400 for a 1-year insurance policy.
10 Purchased golf clubs and other equipment for $5,500 from Golden Bear Company, payable in 30 days.
18 Received golf fees of $1,600 in cash from customers for golf services performed.
19 Sold 100 coupon books for $25 each in cash. Each book contains 10 coupons that enable the holder to play one round of miniature golf or to hit one bucket of golf balls. (*Hint:* The revenue should not be recognized until the customers use the coupons.)
25 Paid a $500 cash dividend.
30 Paid salaries of $800.
30 Paid Golden Bear Company in full for equipment purchased on March 10.
31 Received $900 in cash from customers for golf services performed.

The company uses these accounts: Cash, Prepaid Insurance, Land, Buildings, Equipment, Accounts Payable, Unearned Service Revenue, Common Stock, Retained Earnings, Dividends, Service Revenue, Advertising Expense, and Salaries and Wages Expense.

Instructions

Journalize the March transactions, including explanations. Friendley's records golf fees as service revenue.

P3-5A Foyle Architects incorporated as licensed architects on April 1, 2014. During the first month of the operation of the business, these events and transactions occurred:

Journalize transactions, post, and prepare a trial balance.

(LO 5, 6, 7, 8), **AP**

Apr.	1	Stockholders invested $18,000 cash in exchange for common stock of the corporation.
	1	Hired a secretary-receptionist at a salary of $375 per week, payable monthly.
	2	Paid office rent for the month $900.
	3	Purchased architectural supplies on account from Burlington Company $1,300.
	10	Completed blueprints on a carport and billed client $1,900 for services.
	11	Received $700 cash advance from J. Madison to design a new home.
	20	Received $2,800 cash for services completed and delivered to M. Svetlana.
	30	Paid secretary-receptionist for the month $1,500.
	30	Paid $300 to Burlington Company for accounts payable due.

The company uses these accounts: Cash, Accounts Receivable, Supplies, Accounts Payable, Unearned Service Revenue, Common Stock, Service Revenue, Salaries and Wages Expense, and Rent Expense.

Instructions

(a) Journalize the transactions, including explanations.
(b) Post to the ledger T-accounts.
(c) Prepare a trial balance on April 30, 2014.

(c) Cash $18,800
    Tot. trial balance $24,400

P3-6A This is the trial balance of Solis Company on September 30.

Journalize transactions, post, and prepare a trial balance.

(LO 5, 6, 7, 8), **AP**

SOLIS COMPANY
Trial Balance
September 30, 2014

	Debit	Credit
Cash	$19,200	
Accounts Receivable	2,600	
Supplies	2,100	
Equipment	8,000	
Accounts Payable		$ 4,800
Unearned Service Revenue		1,100
Common Stock		15,000
Retained Earnings		11,000
	$31,900	$31,900

The October transactions were as follows.

Oct.	5	Received $1,300 in cash from customers for accounts receivable due.
	10	Billed customers for services performed $5,100.
	15	Paid employee salaries $1,200.
	17	Performed $600 of services in exchange for cash.
	20	Paid $1,900 to creditors for accounts payable due.
	29	Paid a $300 cash dividend.
	31	Paid utilities $400.

Instructions

(a) Prepare a general ledger using T-accounts. Enter the opening balances in the ledger accounts as of October 1. Provision should be made for these additional accounts: Dividends, Service Revenue, Salaries and Wages Expense, and Utilities Expense.
(b) Journalize the transactions, including explanations.
(c) Post to the ledger accounts.
(d) Prepare a trial balance on October 31, 2014.

(d) Cash $17,300
    Tot. trial balance $35,700

Prepare a correct trial balance.

(LO 8), **AN**

P3-7A This trial balance of Swisher Co. does not balance.

SWISHER CO.
Trial Balance
June 30, 2014

	Debit	Credit
Cash		$ 3,090
Accounts Receivable	$ 3,190	
Supplies	800	
Equipment	3,000	
Accounts Payable		3,686
Unearned Service Revenue	1,200	
Common Stock		9,000
Dividends	800	
Service Revenue		3,480
Salaries and Wages Expense	3,600	
Utilities Expense	910	
	$13,500	$19,256

Each of the listed accounts has a normal balance per the general ledger. An examination of the ledger and journal reveals the following errors:

1. Cash received from a customer on account was debited for $780, and Accounts Receivable was credited for the same amount. The actual collection was for $870.
2. The purchase of a printer on account for $340 was recorded as a debit to Supplies for $340 and a credit to Accounts Payable for $340.
3. Services were performed on account for a client for $900. Accounts Receivable was debited for $90 and Service Revenue was credited for $900.
4. A debit posting to Salaries and Wages Expense of $700 was omitted.
5. A payment on account for $206 was credited to Cash for $206 and credited to Accounts Payable for $260.
6. Payment of a $600 cash dividend to Swisher's stockholders was debited to Salaries and Wages Expense for $600 and credited to Cash for $600.

Tot. trial balance $16,900

Instructions
Prepare the correct trial balance. (*Hint:* All accounts have normal balances.)

Journalize transactions, post, and prepare a trial balance.

(LO 5, 6, 7, 8), **AP**

P3-8A The Sequel Theater Inc. was recently formed. It began operations in March 2014. The Sequel is unique in that it will show only triple features of sequential theme movies. On March 1, the ledger of The Sequel showed Cash $16,000; Land $38,000; Buildings (concession stand, projection room, ticket booth, and screen) $22,000; Equipment $16,000; Accounts Payable $12,000; and Common Stock $80,000. During the month of March, the following events and transactions occurred.

Mar. 2   Rented the three *Star Wars* movies (*Star Wars®*, *The Empire Strikes Back*, and *The Return of the Jedi*) to be shown for the first three weeks of March. The film rental was $10,000; $2,000 was paid in cash and $8,000 will be paid on March 10.

3   Ordered the first three *Star Trek* movies to be shown the last 10 days of March. It will cost $500 per night.

9   Received $9,900 cash from admissions.

10   Paid balance due on *Star Wars* movies' rental and $2,900 on March 1 accounts payable.

11   The Sequel Theater contracted with J. Russo to operate the concession stand. Russo agrees to pay The Sequel 15% of gross receipts, payable monthly, for the rental of the concession stand.

12   Paid advertising expenses $500.
20   Received $8,300 cash from customers for admissions.
20   Received the *Star Trek* movies and paid rental fee of $5,000.
31   Paid salaries of $3,800.
31   Received statement from J. Russo showing gross receipts from concessions of $10,000 and the balance due to The Sequel of $1,500 ($10,000 × .15) for March. Russo paid half the balance due and will remit the remainder on April 5.
31   Received $20,000 cash from customers for admissions.

In addition to the accounts identified above, the chart of accounts includes Accounts Receivable, Service Revenue, Rent Revenue, Advertising Expense, Rent Expense, and Salaries and Wages Expense.

Instructions

(a) Using T-accounts, enter the beginning balances to the ledger.
(b) Journalize the March transactions, including explanations. The Sequel records admission revenue as service revenue, concession revenue as sales revenue, and film rental expense as rent expense.
(c) Post the March journal entries to the ledger.
(d) Prepare a trial balance on March 31, 2014.

(d) Cash   *$ 32,750*
Tot. trial balance   *$128,800*

P3-9A The bookkeeper for Ginger's dance studio made the following errors in journalizing and posting.

Analyze errors and their effects on the trial balance.
(LO 8), AN

1. A credit to Supplies of $600 was omitted.
2. A debit posting of $300 to Accounts Payable was inadvertently debited to Accounts Receivable.
3. A purchase of supplies on account of $450 was debited to Supplies for $540 and credited to Accounts Payable for $540.
4. A credit posting of $680 to Interest Payable was posted twice.
5. A debit posting to Income Taxes Payable for $250 and a credit posting to Cash for $250 were made twice.
6. A debit posting for $1,200 of Dividends was inadvertently posted to Salaries and Wages Expense instead.
7. A credit to Service Revenue for $450 was inadvertently posted as a debit to Service Revenue.
8. A credit to Accounts Receivable of $250 was credited to Accounts Payable.

Instructions

For each error, indicate (a) whether the trial balance will balance; (b) the amount of the difference if the trial balance will not balance; and (c) the trial balance column that will have the larger total. Consider each error separately. Use the following form, in which error 1 is given as an example.

Error	(a) In Balance	(b) Difference	(c) Larger Column
1.	No	$600	Debit

Problems: Set B

Visit the book's companion website, at **www.wiley.com/college/kimmel**, and choose the Student Companion site to access Problem Set B.

Broadening Your Perspective

Financial Reporting and Analysis

FINANCIAL REPORTING PROBLEM: *Tootsie Roll Industries Inc.*

BYP3-1   The financial statements of Tootsie Roll in Appendix A at the back of this textbook contain the following selected accounts, all in thousands of dollars.

Common Stock	$ 25,040
Accounts Payable	9,791
Accounts Receivable	37,394
Selling, Marketing, and Administrative Expenses	106,316
Prepaid Expenses	6,499
Net Property, Plant, and Equipment	215,492
Net Product Sales	517,149

Instructions
(a) What is the increase and decrease side for each account? What is the normal balance for each account?
(b) Identify the probable other account in the transaction and the effect on that account when:
   (1) Accounts Receivable is decreased.
   (2) Accounts Payable is decreased.
   (3) Prepaid Expenses is increased.
(c) Identify the other account(s) that ordinarily would be involved when:
   (1) Interest Expense is increased.
   (2) Property, Plant, and Equipment is increased.

COMPARATIVE ANALYSIS PROBLEM: *Tootsie Roll vs. Hershey*

BYP3-2   The financial statements of The Hershey Company appear in Appendix B, following the financial statements for Tootsie Roll in Appendix A.

Instructions
(a) Based on the information contained in these financial statements, determine the normal balance for:

Tootsie Roll Industries	**The Hershey Company**
(1) Accounts Receivable	(1) Inventories
(2) Net Property, Plant, and Equipment	(2) Provision for Income Taxes
(3) Accounts Payable	(3) Accrued Liabilities
(4) Retained Earnings	(4) Common Stock
(5) Net Product Sales	(5) Interest Expense

(b) Identify the other account ordinarily involved when:
   (1) Accounts Receivable is increased.
   (2) Notes Payable is decreased.
   (3) Machinery is increased.
   (4) Interest Revenue is increased.

RESEARCH CASE

BYP3-3   The January 27, 2011, edition of the *New York Times* contains an article by Richard Sandomir entitled "N.F.L. Finances, as Seen Through Packers' Records." The article discusses the fact that the Green Bay Packers are the only NFL team that publicly publishes its annual report.

Instructions

Read the article and answer the following questions.
(a) Why are the Green Bay Packers the only professional football team to publish and distribute an annual report?
(b) Why is the football players' labor union particularly interested in the Packers' annual report?

(c) In addition to the players' labor union, what other outside party might be interested in the annual report?

(d) Even though the Packer's revenue increased in recent years, the company's operating profit fell significantly. How does the article explain this decline?

INTERPRETING FINANCIAL STATEMENTS

BYP3-4 Chieftain International, Inc., is an oil and natural gas exploration and production company. A recent balance sheet reported $208 million in assets with only $4.6 million in liabilities, all of which were short-term accounts payable.

During the year, Chieftain expanded its holdings of oil and gas rights, drilled 37 new wells, and invested in expensive 3-D seismic technology. The company generated $19 million cash from operating activities and paid no dividends. It had a cash balance of $102 million at the end of the year.

Instructions

(a) Name at least two advantages to Chieftain from having no long-term debt. Can you think of disadvantages?

(b) What are some of the advantages to Chieftain from having this large a cash balance? What is a disadvantage?

(c) Why do you suppose Chieftain has the $4.6 million balance in accounts payable, since it appears that it could have made all its purchases for cash?

REAL-WORLD FOCUS

BYP3-5 *Purpose:* This activity provides information about career opportunities for CPAs.

Address: **www.startheregoplaces.com/why-accounting**, or go to **www.wiley.com/college/kimmel**

Steps

1. Go to the address shown above and click on **Students/Educators**.
2. Click on **High School**, then **CPA101** for parts (a), (b), and (c).
3. Click **College** to answer part (d).

Instructions

Answer the following questions.

(a) Where do CPAs work?

(b) What skills does a CPA need?

(c) What is the salary range for a CPA at a large firm during the first three years? What is the salary range for chief financial officers and treasurers at large corporations?

Critical Thinking

DECISION-MAKING ACROSS THE ORGANIZATION

BYP3-6 Sally Saia operates Double S Riding Academy, Inc. The academy's primary sources of revenue are riding fees and lesson fees, which are provided on a cash basis. Sally also boards horses for owners, who are billed monthly for boarding fees. In a few cases, boarders pay in advance of expected use. For its revenue transactions, the academy maintains these accounts: Cash, Accounts Receivable, Unearned Service Revenue, and Service Revenue.

The academy owns 10 horses, a stable, a riding corral, riding equipment, and office equipment. These assets are accounted for in the following accounts: Horses, Buildings, and Equipment.

The academy employs stable helpers and an office employee, who receive weekly salaries. At the end of each month, the mail usually brings bills for advertising, utilities, and veterinary service. Other expenses include feed for the horses and insurance. For its expenses, the academy maintains the following accounts: Supplies, Prepaid Insurance, Accounts Payable, Salaries and Wages Expense, Advertising Expense, Utilities Expense, Maintenance and Repairs Expense, Supplies Expense, and Insurance Expense.

Sally Saia's sole source of personal income is dividends from the academy. Thus, the corporation declares and pays periodic dividends. To account for stockholders' equity in the business and dividends, two accounts are maintained: Common Stock and Dividends.

During the first month of operations an inexperienced bookkeeper was employed. Sally Saia asks you to review the following eight entries of the 50 entries made during the month. In each case, the explanation for the entry is correct.

May 1	Cash		15,000	
	Unearned Service Revenue			15,000
	(Issued common stock in exchange for $15,000 cash)			
5	Cash		250	
	Service Revenue			250
	(Received $250 cash for lesson fees)			
7	Cash		500	
	Service Revenue			500
	(Received $500 for boarding of horses beginning June 1)			
9	Supplies Expense		1,500	
	Cash			1,500
	(Purchased estimated 5 months' supply of feed and hay for $1,500 on account)			
14	Equipment		80	
	Cash			800
	(Purchased desk and other office equipment for $800 cash)			
15	Salaries and Wages Expense		400	
	Cash			400
	(Issued check to Sally Saia for personal use)			
20	Cash		145	
	Service Revenue			154
	(Received $154 cash for riding fees)			
31	Maintenance and Repairs Expense		75	
	Accounts Receivable			75
	(Received bill of $75 from carpenter for repair services performed)			

Instructions

With the class divided into groups, answer the following.
(a) For each journal entry that is correct, so state. For each journal entry that is incorrect, prepare the entry that should have been made by the bookkeeper.
(b) Which of the incorrect entries would prevent the trial balance from balancing?
(c) What was the correct net income for May, assuming the bookkeeper originally reported net income of $4,500 after posting all 50 entries?
(d) What was the correct cash balance at May 31, assuming the bookkeeper reported a balance of $12,475 after posting all 50 entries?

COMMUNICATION ACTIVITY

BYP3-7 Clean Sweep Company offers home cleaning service. Two recurring transactions for the company are billing customers for services performed and paying employee salaries. For example, on March 15 bills totaling $6,000 were sent to customers, and $2,000 was paid in salaries to employees.

Instructions

Write a memorandum to your instructor that explains and illustrates the steps in the recording process for each of the March 15 transactions. Use the format illustrated in the textbook under the heading "The Recording Process Illustrated" (pp. 121–126).

ETHICS CASES

BYP3-8 Jennifer VanPelt is the assistant chief accountant at BIT Company, a manufacturer of computer chips and cellular phones. The company presently has total sales of $20 million. It is the end of the first quarter and Jennifer is hurriedly trying to prepare a trial balance so that quarterly financial statements can be prepared and released to management and the regulatory agencies. The total credits on the trial balance exceed the debits by $1,000.

In order to meet the 4 P.M. deadline, Jennifer decides to force the debits and credits into balance by adding the amount of the difference to the Equipment account. She chose Equipment because it is one of the larger account balances; percentage-wise it will be the least misstated. Jennifer plugs the difference! She believes that the difference is quite small and will not affect anyone's decisions. She wishes that she had another few days to find the error but realizes that the financial statements are already late.

Instructions
(a) Who are the stakeholders in this situation?
(b) What ethical issues are involved?
(c) What are Jennifer's alternatives?

BYP3-9 The July 28, 2007, issue of the *Wall Street Journal* includes an article by Kathryn Kranhold entitled "GE's Accounting Draws Fresh Focus on News of Improper Sales Bookings."

Instructions

Read the article and answer the following questions.
(a) What improper activity did the employees at GE engage in?
(b) Why might the employees have engaged in this activity?
(c) What were the implications for the employees who engaged in this activity?
(d) What does it mean to "restate" financial results? Why didn't GE restate its results to correct for the improperly reported locomotive sales?

ALL ABOUT YOU

BYP3-10 In their annual reports to stockholders, companies must report or disclose information about all liabilities, including potential liabilities related to environmental clean-up. There are many situations in which you will be asked to provide personal financial information about your assets, liabilities, revenue, and expenses. Sometimes you will face difficult decisions regarding what to disclose and how to disclose it.

Instructions

Suppose that you are putting together a loan application to purchase a home. Based on your income and assets, you qualify for the mortgage loan, but just barely. How would you address each of the following situations in reporting your financial position for the loan application? Provide responses for each of the following questions.
(a) You signed a guarantee for a bank loan that a friend took out for $20,000. If your friend doesn't pay, you will have to pay. Your friend has made all of the payments so far, and it appears he will be able to pay in the future.
(b) You were involved in an auto accident in which you were at fault. There is the possibility that you may have to pay as much as $50,000 as part of a settlement. The issue will not be resolved before the bank processes your mortgage request.
(c) The company at which you work isn't doing very well, and it has recently laid off employees. You are still employed, but it is quite possible that you will lose your job in the next few months.

Answers to Insight and Accounting Across the Organization Questions

p. 91 Why Accuracy Matters Q: In order for these companies to prepare and issue financial statements, their accounting equations (debit and credits) must have been in balance at year-end. How could these errors or misstatements have occurred? **A:** A company's accounting equation (its books) can be in balance yet its financial statements have errors or misstatements because of the following: entire transactions were not recorded; transactions were recorded at wrong amounts; transactions were recorded in the wrong accounts; transactions were recorded in the wrong accounting period. Audits of financial statements uncover some, but obviously not all, errors or misstatements.

p. 96 Keeping Score Q: Do you think that the Chicago Bears football team would be likely to have the same major revenue and expense accounts as the Cubs? **A:** Because their businesses are similar—professional sports—many of the revenue and expense accounts for the baseball and football teams might be similar.

p. 100 Boosting Microsoft's Profits Q: In what ways is this Microsoft division using accounting to assist in is effort to become more profitable? **A:** The division has used accounting to set very strict sales, revenue, and profit goals. In addition, the managers in this division use accounting to keep a tight rein on product costs. Also, accounting serves as the basis of communication so that the marketing managers and product designers can work with production managers, engineers, and accountants to create an exciting product within specified cost constraints.

p. 108 Convenient Overstatement Q: What incentives might employees have had to overstate of these investment securities on the company's financial statements? **A:** One reason that they may have been reluctant to record the losses is out of fear that the company's shareholders clients would panic if they saw the magnitude of the losses. However, personal self-interest might have been equally to blame—the bonuses of the traders were tied to the value of the investment securities.

Answers to Self-Test Questions

1. b   **2.** b   **3.** b   **4.** a ($-\$50,000 = -\$90,000 + \$40,000$)   **5.** b   **6.** c   **7.** d   **8.** d   **9.** d   **10.** b
11. a   **12.** c   **13.** d   **14.** a   **15.** c

A Look at IFRS

LEARNING OBJECTIVE	10
Compare the procedures for the recording process under GAAP and IFRS.	

International companies use the same set of procedures and records to keep track of transaction data. Thus, the material in Chapter 3 dealing with the account, general rules of debit and credit, and steps in the recording process—the journal, ledger, and chart of accounts—is the same under both GAAP and IFRS.

KEY POINTS

- Transaction analysis is the same under IFRS and GAAP but, as you will see in later chapters, different standards sometimes impact how transactions are recorded.
- Rules for accounting for specific events sometimes differ across countries. For example, European companies rely less on historical cost and more on fair value than U.S. companies. Despite the differences, the double-entry accounting system is the basis of accounting systems worldwide.
- Both the IASB and FASB go beyond the basic definitions provided in this textbook for the key elements of financial statements, that is, assets, liabilities, equity, revenues, and expenses. The more substantive definitions, using the IASB definitional structure, are provided in the Chapter 1 *A Look at IFRS* discussion.
- A trial balance under IFRS follows the same format as shown in the textbook.
- As shown in the textbook, dollar signs are typically used only in the trial balance and the financial statements. The same practice is followed under IFRS, using the currency of the country in which the reporting company is headquartered.
- The SEC has expressed a desire to continue working toward a single set of high-quality standards. In deciding whether the United States should adopt IFRS, some of the issues the SEC stated should be considered are:
  - Whether IFRS is sufficiently developed and consistent in application.
  - Whether the IASB is sufficiently independent.
  - Whether IFRS is established for the benefit of investors.
  - The issues involved in educating investors about IFRS.
  - The impact of a switch to IFRS on U.S. laws and regulations.
  - The impact on companies including changes to their accounting systems, contractual arrangements, corporate governance, and litigation.
  - The issues involved in educating accountants, so they can prepare statements under IFRS.

LOOKING TO THE FUTURE

The basic recording process shown in this textbook is followed by companies across the globe. It is unlikely to change in the future. The definitional structure of assets, liabilities, equity, revenues, and expenses may change over time as the IASB and FASB evaluate their overall conceptual framework for establishing accounting standards.

IFRS PRACTICE

IFRS SELF-TEST QUESTIONS

1. Which statement is **correct** regarding IFRS?
   (a) IFRS reverses the rules of debits and credits; that is, debits are on the right and credits are on the left.
   (b) IFRS uses the same process for recording transactions as GAAP.
   (c) The chart of accounts under IFRS is different because revenues follow assets.
   (d) None of the above statements are correct.
2. The expanded accounting equation under IFRS is as follows:
   (a) Assets = Liabilities + Share Capital + Dividends + Revenues − Expenses.
   (b) Assets + Liabilities = Share Capital + Dividends + Revenues − Expenses.
   (c) Assets = Liabilities + Share Capital − Dividends + Revenues − Expenses.
   (d) Assets = Liabilities + Share Capital + Dividends − Revenues − Expenses.
3. A trial balance:
   (a) is the same under IFRS and GAAP.
   (b) proves that transactions are recorded correctly.
   (c) proves that all transactions have been recorded.
   (d) will not balance if a correct journal entry is posted twice.
4. One difference between IFRS and GAAP is that:
   (a) GAAP uses accrual-accounting concepts and IFRS uses primarily the cash basis of accounting.
   (b) IFRS uses a different posting process than GAAP.
   (c) IFRS uses more fair value measurements than GAAP.
   (d) the limitations of a trial balance are different between IFRS and GAAP.
5. The general policy for using proper currency signs (dollar, yen, pound, etc.) is the same for both IFRS and this textbook. This policy is as follows:
   (a) Currency signs only appear in ledgers and journal entries.
   (b) Currency signs are only shown in the trial balance.
   (c) Currency signs are shown for all compound journal entries.
   (d) Currency signs are shown in trial balances and financial statements.

IFRS CONCEPTS AND APPLICATION

IFRS3-1 Describe some of the issues the SEC must consider in deciding whether the United States should adopt IFRS.

INTERNATIONAL FINANCIAL REPORTING PROBLEM: *Zetar plc*

IFRS3-2 The financial statements of Zetar plc are presented in Appendix C. The company's complete annual report, including the notes to its financial statements, is available in the Investors section at **www.zetarplc.com**.

Instructions
Describe in which statement each of the following items is reported, and the position in the statement (e.g., current asset).
   (a) Share capital.
   (b) Goodwill.
   (c) Borrowings and overdrafts.
   (d) Amortization of intangible assets.
   (e) Derivative financial asset.

Answers to IFRS Self-Test Questions

1. b **2.** c **3.** a **4.** c **5.** d

CHAPTER 4

Rudy Archuleta/Redux Pictures

ACCRUAL ACCOUNTING CONCEPTS

LEARNING OBJECTIVES

After studying this chapter, you should be able to:

1   Explain the revenue recognition principle and the expense recognition principle.

2   Differentiate between the cash basis and the accrual basis of accounting.

3   Explain why adjusting entries are needed, and identify the major types of adjusting entries.

4   Prepare adjusting entries for deferrals.

5   Prepare adjusting entries for accruals.

6   Describe the nature and purpose of the adjusted trial balance.

7   Explain the purpose of closing entries.

8   Describe the required steps in the accounting cycle.

9   Understand the causes of differences between net income and net cash provided by operating activities.

Who doesn't like buying things at a discount? That's why it's not surprising that three years after it started as a company, Groupon was estimated to be worth $16 billion. This translates into an average increase in value of almost $15 million per day.

Now consider that Groupon had previously been estimated to be worth even more than that. What happened? Well, accounting regulators and investors began to question the way that Groupon had accounted for some of its transactions. But if Groupon sells only coupons ("Groupons"), you're probably wondering how hard can it be to accurately account for that? It turns out that accounting for coupons is not as easy as you might think.

KEEPING TRACK OF GROUPONS

First, consider what happens when Groupon makes a sale. Suppose it sells a Groupon for $30 for Highrise Hamburgers. When it receives the $30 from the customer, it must turn over half of that amount ($15) to Highrise Hamburgers. So should Groupon record revenue for the full $30 or just $15? Until recently, Groupon recorded the full $30. But, in response to an SEC ruling on the issue, Groupon now records revenue of $15 instead. Groupon also had to restate its previous financial statements. This restatement reduced annual revenue by $312.9 million.

A second issue is a matter of timing. When should Groupon record this $15 revenue? Should it record the revenue when it sells the Groupon, or must it wait until the customer uses the Groupon at Highrise Hamburgers? You can find the answer to this question in the notes to Groupon's financial statements. It recognizes the revenue once "the number of customers who purchase the daily deal exceeds the predetermined threshold, the Groupon has been electronically delivered to the purchaser and a listing of Groupons sold has been made available to the merchant."

The accounting becomes even more complicated when you consider the company's loyalty programs. Groupon offers free or discounted Groupons to its subscribers for doing things such as referring new customers or participating in promotions. These Groupons are to be used for future purchases, yet the company must record the expense at the time the customer receives the Groupon. The cost of these programs is huge for Groupon, so the timing of this expense can definitely affect its reported income.

The final kicker is that Groupon, like all other companies, must rely on many estimates in its financial reporting. For example, Groupon reports that "estimates are utilized for, but not limited to, stock-based compensation, income taxes, valuation of acquired goodwill and intangible assets, customer refunds, contingent liabilities and the depreciable lives of fixed assets." It concludes by saying that "actual results could differ materially from those estimates." So, next time you use a coupon, think about what that means for the company's accountants!

INSIDE CHAPTER 4 . . .

- **Reporting Revenue Accurately**
- **Cashing In on Accrual Accounting**
- **Turning Gift Cards into Revenue**
- **Got Junk?**
- **Cooking the Books?**

As indicated in the Feature Story, making adjustments is necessary to avoid misstatement of revenues and expenses such as those at Groupon. In this chapter, we introduce you to the accrual accounting concepts that make such adjustments possible.

The organization and content of the chapter are as follows.

Accrual Accounting Concepts			
Timing Issues	**The Basics of Adjusting Entries**	**The Adjusted Trial Balance and Financial Statements**	**Closing the Books**
• Revenue recognition principle • Expense recognition principle • Accrual versus cash basis of accounting	• Types of adjusting entries • Adjusting entries for deferrals • Adjusting entries for accruals • Summary of basic relationships	• Preparing the adjusted trial balance • Preparing financial statements • Quality of earnings	• Preparing closing entries • Preparing a post-closing trial balance • Summary of the accounting cycle

Timing Issues

LEARNING OBJECTIVE 1

Explain the revenue recognition principle and the expense recognition principle.

Most businesses need immediate feedback about how well they are doing. For example, management usually wants monthly reports on financial results, most large corporations are required to present quarterly and annual financial statements to stockholders, and the Internal Revenue Service requires all businesses to file annual tax returns. **Accounting divides the economic life of a business into artificial time periods.** As indicated in Chapter 2, this is the **periodicity assumption**. **Accounting time periods are generally a month, a quarter, or a year.**

Margin Note An accounting time period that is one year long is called a **fiscal year**.

Many business transactions affect more than one of these arbitrary time periods. For example, a new building purchased by Citigroup or a new airplane purchased by Delta Air Lines will be used for many years. It doesn't make sense to expense the full cost of the building or the airplane at the time of purchase because each will be used for many subsequent periods. Instead, we determine the impact of each transaction on specific accounting periods.

Determining the amount of revenues and expenses to report in a given accounting period can be difficult. Proper reporting requires an understanding of the nature of the company's business. Two principles are used as guidelines: the revenue recognition principle and the expense recognition principle.

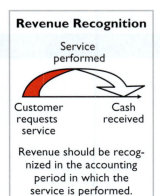

Revenue Recognition

Service performed

Customer requests service → Cash received

Revenue should be recognized in the accounting period in which the service is performed.

THE REVENUE RECOGNITION PRINCIPLE

When a company agrees to perform a service or sell a product to a customer, it has a performance obligation. The **revenue recognition principle** requires that companies recognize revenue in the accounting period **in which the performance obligation is satisfied**. To illustrate, assume Conrad Dry Cleaners cleans clothing on June 30, but customers do not claim and pay for their clothes until the first week of July. Under the revenue recognition principle, Conrad records revenue in June when it performs the service, not in July when it receives the cash. At June 30, Conrad would report a receivable on its balance sheet and revenue in its income statement for the service performed. The journal entries for June and July would be as follows.

June	Accounts Receivable	xxx	
	Service Revenue		xxx
July	Cash	xxx	
	Accounts Receivable		xxx

DECISION TOOLKIT

DECISION CHECKPOINTS	INFO NEEDED FOR DECISION	TOOL TO USE FOR DECISION	HOW TO EVALUATE RESULTS
At what point should the company record revenue?	Need to understand the nature of the company's business	Record revenue in the period in which the performance obligation is satisfied.	Recognizing revenue too early overstates current period revenue; recognizing it too late understates current period revenue.

THE EXPENSE RECOGNITION PRINCIPLE

In recognizing expenses, a simple rule is followed: "Let the expenses follow the revenues." Thus, expense recognition is tied to revenue recognition. Applied to the preceding example, this means that the salary expense Conrad incurred in performing the cleaning service on June 30 should be reported in the same period in which it recognizes the service revenue. The critical issue in expense recognition is determining when the expense makes its contribution to revenue. This may or may not be the same period in which the expense is paid. If Conrad does not pay the salary incurred on June 30 until July, it would report salaries and wages payable on its June 30 balance sheet.

The practice of expense recognition is referred to as the **expense recognition principle** (often referred to as the **matching principle**). It dictates that efforts (expenses) be matched with results (revenues). Illustration 4-1 shows these relationships.

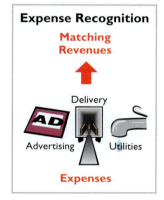

Illustration 4-1 GAAP relationships in revenue and expense recognition

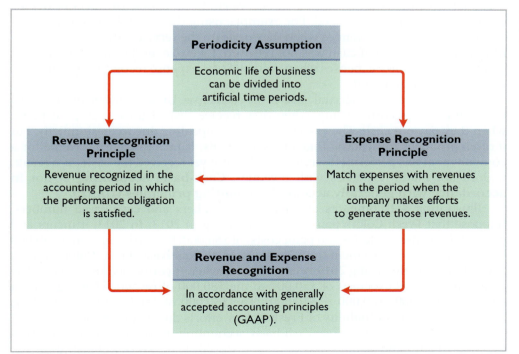

🧰 DECISION TOOLKIT

DECISION CHECKPOINTS	INFO NEEDED FOR DECISION	TOOL TO USE FOR DECISION	HOW TO EVALUATE RESULTS
At what point should the company record expenses?	Need to understand the nature of the company's business	Expenses should "follow" revenues—that is, match the effort (expense) with the result (revenue).	Recognizing expenses too early overstates current period expense; recognizing them too late understates current period expense.

Investor Insight
Reporting Revenue Accurately

Until recently, electronics manufacturer Apple was required to spread the revenues from iPhone sales over the two-year period following the sale of the phone. Accounting standards required this because it was argued that Apple was obligated to provide software updates after the phone was sold. Therefore, since Apple had service obligations after the initial date of sale, it was forced to spread the revenue over a two-year period. However, since the company received full payment upfront, the cash flows from iPhones significantly exceeded the revenue reported from iPhone sales in each accounting period. It also meant that the rapid growth of iPhone sales was not fully reflected in the revenue amounts reported in Apple's income statement. A new accounting standard now enables Apple to report nearly all of its iPhone revenue at the point of sale. It was estimated that under the new rule revenues would have been about 17% higher and earnings per share almost 50% higher.

? In the past, why was it argued that Apple should spread the recognition of iPhone revenue over a two-year period, rather than recording it upfront? (Answers in *Broadening Your Perspective.*)

ACCRUAL VERSUS CASH BASIS OF ACCOUNTING

LEARNING OBJECTIVE 2

Differentiate between the cash basis and the accrual basis of accounting.

Accrual-basis accounting means that transactions that change a company's financial statements are recorded **in the periods in which the events occur**, even if cash was not exchanged. For example, using the accrual basis means that companies recognize revenues when they perform the services (the revenue recognition principle), even if cash was not received. Likewise, under the accrual basis, companies recognize expenses when incurred (the expense recognition principle), even if cash was not paid.

An alternative to the accrual basis is the cash basis. Under **cash-basis accounting**, companies record revenue when they receive cash. They record an expense when they pay out cash. The cash basis seems appealing due to its simplicity, but it often produces misleading financial statements. It fails to record revenue for a company that has performed services but has not yet received the cash. As a result, it does not match expenses with revenues. **Cash-basis accounting is not in accordance with generally accepted accounting principles (GAAP).**

Illustration 4-2 compares accrual-based numbers and cash-based numbers. Suppose that Fresh Colors paints a large building in 2013. In 2013, it incurs and pays total expenses (salaries and paint costs) of $50,000. It bills the customer $80,000 but does not receive payment until 2014. On an accrual basis, Fresh Colors reports $80,000 of revenue during 2013 because that is when it performed the service. The company matches expenses of $50,000 to the $80,000 of revenue. Thus, 2013 net income is $30,000 ($80,000 − $50,000). The $30,000 of net income reported for 2013 indicates the profitability of Fresh Colors' efforts during that period.

If Fresh Colors were to use cash-basis accounting, it would report $50,000 of expenses in 2013 and $80,000 of revenues during 2014. As shown in Illustration 4-2,

	2013	2014
Activity	Purchased paint, painted building, paid employees	Received payment for work done in 2013
Accrual basis	Revenue $80,000 Expense 50,000 Net income $30,000	Revenue $ 0 Expense 0 Net income $ 0
Cash basis	Revenue $ 0 Expense 50,000 Net loss $(50,000)	Revenue $80,000 Expense 0 Net income $80,000

Illustration 4-2 Accrual-versus cash-basis accounting

it would report a loss of $50,000 in 2013 and would report net income of $80,000 in 2014. Clearly, the cash-basis measures are misleading because the financial performance of the company would be misstated for both 2013 and 2014.

International Insight

Cashing In on Accrual Accounting

The Chinese government, like most governments, uses cash accounting. It is therefore interesting that for about $38 billion of expenditures in a recent budget projection, the Chinese government used accrual accounting instead of cash accounting. It decided to expense the amount in the year in which it was originally allocated rather than when the payments would be made. Why did it do this? It enabled the government to keep its projected budget deficit below a 3% threshold. While it was able to keep its projected shortfall below 3%, China did suffer some criticism for its inconsistent accounting. Critics charge that this inconsistent treatment reduces the transparency of China's accounting information. That is, it is not easy for outsiders to accurately evaluate what is really going on.

Source: Andrew Batson, "China Altered Budget Accounting to Reduce Deficit Figure," *Wall Street Journal Online* (March 15, 2010).

? Accrual accounting is often considered superior to cash accounting. Why, then, were some people critical of China's use of accrual accounting in this instance? (Answers in *Broadening Your Perspective*.)

The Basics of Adjusting Entries

In order for revenues to be recorded in the period in which the performance obligations are satisfied, and for expenses to be recognized in the period in which they are incurred, companies make adjusting entries. **Adjusting entries** ensure that the revenue recognition and expense recognition principles are followed.

LEARNING OBJECTIVE 3

Explain why adjusting entries are needed, and identify the major types of adjusting entries.

Adjusting entries are necessary because the **trial balance**—the first pulling together of the transaction data—may not contain up-to-date and complete data. This is true for several reasons:

1. Some events are not recorded daily because it is not efficient to do so. Examples are the use of supplies and the earning of wages by employees.
2. Some costs are not recorded during the accounting period because these costs expire with the passage of time rather than as a result of recurring daily transactions. Examples are charges related to the use of buildings and equipment, rent, and insurance.
3. Some items may be unrecorded. An example is a utility service bill that will not be received until the next accounting period.

Adjusting entries are required every time a company prepares financial statements. The company analyzes each account in the trial balance to determine whether it is complete and up-to-date for financial statement purposes. **Every adjusting entry will include one income statement account and one balance sheet account.**

TYPES OF ADJUSTING ENTRIES

Adjusting entries are classified as either deferrals or accruals. As Illustration 4-3 shows, each of these classes has two subcategories.

Illustration 4-3 Categories of adjusting entries

Deferrals:

1. Prepaid expenses: Expenses paid in cash before they are used or consumed.
2. Unearned revenues: Cash received before services are performed.

Accruals:

1. Accrued revenues: Revenues for services performed but not yet received in cash or recorded.
2. Accrued expenses: Expenses incurred but not yet paid in cash or recorded.

Subsequent sections give examples of each type of adjustment. Each example is based on the October 31 trial balance of Sierra Corporation from Chapter 3. It is reproduced in Illustration 4-4. Note that Retained Earnings has been added to this trial balance with a zero balance. We will explain its use later.

Illustration 4-4 Trial balance

SIERRA CORPORATION
Trial Balance
October 31, 2014

	Debit	Credit
Cash	$15,200	
Supplies	2,500	
Prepaid Insurance	600	
Equipment	5,000	
Notes Payable		$ 5,000
Accounts Payable		2,500
Unearned Service Revenue		1,200
Common Stock		10,000
Retained Earnings		0
Dividends	500	
Service Revenue		10,000
Salaries and Wages Expense	4,000	
Rent Expense	900	
	$28,700	$28,700

We assume that Sierra Corporation uses an accounting period of one month. Thus, monthly adjusting entries are made. The entries are dated October 31.

ADJUSTING ENTRIES FOR DEFERRALS

LEARNING OBJECTIVE   **4**
Prepare adjusting entries for deferrals.

To defer means to postpone or delay. Deferrals are costs or revenues that are recognized at a date later than the point when cash was originally exchanged. Companies make adjusting entries for deferred expenses to record the portion that was incurred during the period. Companies also make adjusting entries for deferred revenues to record services performed during the period. The two types of deferrals are prepaid expenses and unearned revenues.

Prepaid Expenses

Companies record payments of expenses that will benefit more than one accounting period as assets. These **prepaid expenses** or **prepayments** are expenses paid in cash before they are used or consumed. When expenses are prepaid, an asset account is increased (debited) to show the service or benefit that the company will receive in the future. Examples of common prepayments are insurance, supplies, advertising, and rent. In addition, companies make prepayments when they purchase buildings and equipment.

Prepaid expenses are costs that expire either with the passage of time (e.g., rent and insurance) **or through use** (e.g., supplies). The expiration of these costs does not require daily entries, which would be impractical and unnecessary. Accordingly, companies postpone the recognition of such cost expirations until they prepare financial statements. At each statement date, they make adjusting entries to record the expenses applicable to the current accounting period and to show the remaining amounts in the asset accounts.

Prior to adjustment, assets are overstated and expenses are understated. Therefore, as shown in Illustration 4-5, **an adjusting entry for prepaid expenses results in an increase (a debit) to an expense account and a decrease (a credit) to an asset account**.

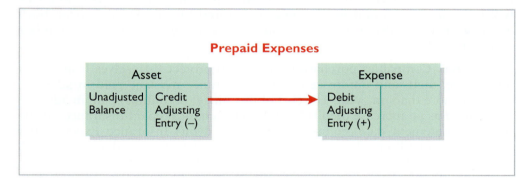

Illustration 4-5 Adjusting entries for prepaid expenses

Let's look in more detail at some specific types of prepaid expenses, beginning with supplies.

SUPPLIES. The purchase of supplies, such as paper and envelopes, results in an increase (a debit) to an asset account. During the accounting period, the company uses supplies. Rather than record supplies expense as the supplies are used, companies recognize supplies expense at the **end** of the accounting period. At the end of the accounting period, the company counts the remaining supplies. The difference between the unadjusted balance in the Supplies (asset) account and the actual cost of supplies on hand represents the supplies used (an expense) for that period.

Recall from Chapter 3 that Sierra Corporation purchased supplies costing $2,500 on October 5. Sierra recorded the purchase by increasing (debiting) the asset Supplies. This account shows a balance of $2,500 in the October 31 trial

Supplies

Oct. 5

Supplies purchased; record asset

Oct. 31
Supplies used; record supplies expense

balance. A physical count of the inventory at the close of business on October 31 reveals that $1,000 of supplies are still on hand. Thus, the cost of supplies used is $1,500 ($2,500 − $1,000). This use of supplies decreases an asset, Supplies. It also decreases stockholders' equity by increasing an expense account, Supplies Expense. This is shown in Illustration 4-6.

Illustration 4-6
Adjustment for supplies

Margin Note Due to their nature, adjusting entries have **no effect** on cash flows. As a result, we do not show the cash flow effects as we did in Chapter 3.

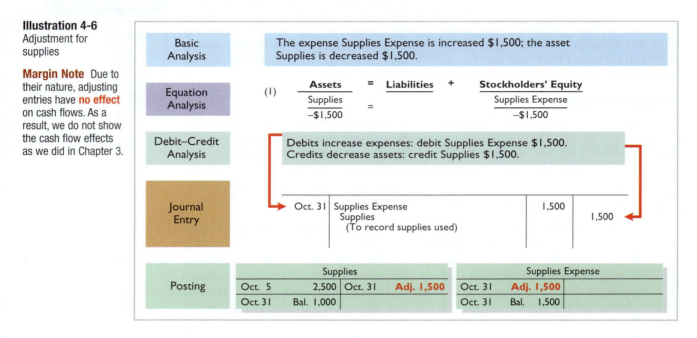

After adjustment, the asset account Supplies shows a balance of $1,000, which is equal to the cost of supplies on hand at the statement date. In addition, Supplies Expense shows a balance of $1,500, which equals the cost of supplies used in October. **If Sierra does not make the adjusting entry, October expenses will be understated and net income overstated by $1,500. Moreover, both assets and stockholders' equity will be overstated by $1,500 on the October 31 balance sheet.**

INSURANCE. Companies purchase insurance to protect themselves from losses due to fire, theft, and unforeseen events. Insurance must be paid in advance, often for more than one year. The cost of insurance (premiums) paid in advance is recorded as an increase (debit) in the asset account Prepaid Insurance. At the financial statement date, companies increase (debit) Insurance Expense and decrease (credit) Prepaid Insurance for the cost of insurance that has expired during the period.

On October 4, Sierra Corporation paid $600 for a one-year fire insurance policy. Coverage began on October 1. Sierra recorded the payment by increasing (debiting) Prepaid Insurance. This account shows a balance of $600 in the October 31 trial balance. Insurance of $50 ($600 ÷ 12) expires each month. The expiration of prepaid insurance decreases an asset, Prepaid Insurance. It also decreases stockholders' equity by increasing an expense account, Insurance Expense.

As shown in Illustration 4-7, the asset Prepaid Insurance shows a balance of $550, which represents the unexpired cost for the remaining 11 months of coverage. At the same time, the balance in Insurance Expense equals the insurance cost that expired in October. If Sierra does not make this adjustment, October expenses are understated by $50 and net income is overstated by $50. Moreover, as the accounting equation shows, both assets and stockholders' equity will be overstated by $50 on the October 31 balance sheet.

Insurance

Oct. 4

Insurance purchased; record asset

Insurance Policy			
Oct	Nov	Dec	Jan
$50	$50	$50	$50
Feb	March	April	May
$50	$50	$50	$50
June	July	Aug	Sept
$50	$50	$50	$50
1 YEAR $600			

Oct. 31
  Insurance expired; record insurance expense

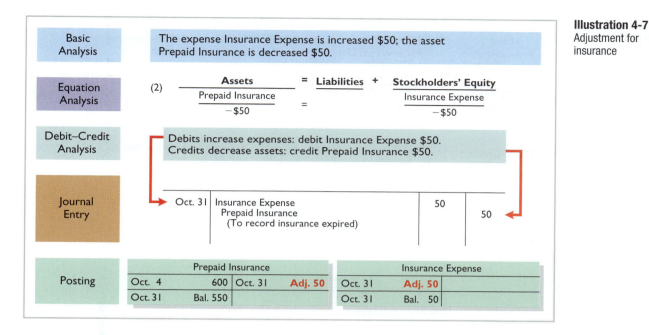

Illustration 4-7
Adjustment for insurance

| Basic Analysis | The expense Insurance Expense is increased $50; the asset Prepaid Insurance is decreased $50. |

Equation Analysis

(2)

Assets	= Liabilities +	Stockholders' Equity
Prepaid Insurance		Insurance Expense
−$50	=	−$50

Debit–Credit Analysis

Debits increase expenses: debit Insurance Expense $50.
Credits decrease assets: credit Prepaid Insurance $50.

Journal Entry

Oct. 31	Insurance Expense	50	
	Prepaid Insurance		50
	(To record insurance expired)		

Posting

Prepaid Insurance			
Oct. 4	600	Oct. 31	**Adj. 50**
Oct. 31	Bal. 550		

Insurance Expense		
Oct. 31	**Adj. 50**	
Oct. 31	Bal. 50	

DEPRECIATION. A company typically owns a variety of assets that have long lives, such as buildings, equipment, and motor vehicles. The period of service is referred to as the **useful life** of the asset. Because a building is expected to provide service for many years, it is recorded as an asset, rather than an expense, on the date it is acquired. As explained in Chapter 2, companies record such assets **at cost**, as required by the historical cost principle. To follow the expense recognition principle, companies allocate a portion of this cost as an expense during each period of the asset's useful life. **Depreciation** is the process of allocating the cost of an asset to expense over its useful life.

Need for adjustment. The acquisition of long-lived assets is essentially a long-term prepayment for the use of an asset. An adjusting entry for depreciation is needed to recognize the cost that has been used (an expense) during the period and to report the unused cost (an asset) at the end of the period. One very important point to understand: **Depreciation is an allocation concept, not a valuation concept.** That is, depreciation **allocates an asset's cost to the periods in which it is used. Depreciation does not attempt to report the actual change in the value of the asset.**

For Sierra Corporation, assume that depreciation on the equipment is $480 a year, or $40 per month. As shown in Illustration 4-8, rather than decrease (credit) the asset account directly, Sierra instead credits Accumulated Depreciation—Equipment. Accumulated Depreciation is called a **contra asset account**. Such an account is offset against an asset account on the balance sheet. Thus, the Accumulated Depreciation—Equipment account offsets the asset Equipment. This account keeps track of the total amount of depreciation expense taken over the life of the asset. To keep the accounting equation in balance, Sierra decreases stockholders' equity by increasing an expense account, Depreciation Expense.

The balance in the Accumulated Depreciation—Equipment account will increase $40 each month, and the balance in Equipment remains $5,000.

Statement presentation. As noted above, Accumulated Depreciation—Equipment is a contra asset account. It is offset against Equipment on the balance sheet. The normal balance of a contra asset account is a credit. A theoretical alternative to using a contra asset account would be to decrease (credit) the asset account by the amount of depreciation each period. But using the contra account

Depreciation

Oct. 2

Equipment purchased; record asset

Equipment			
Oct	Nov	Dec	Jan
$40	$40	$40	$40
Feb	March	April	May
$40	$40	$40	$40
June	July	Aug	Sept
$40	$40	$40	$40
Depreciation = $480/year			

Oct. 31
Depreciation recognized; record depreciation expense

Illustration 4-8
Adjustment for
depreciation

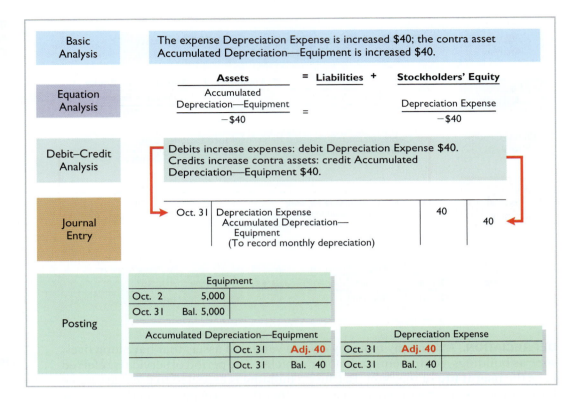

is preferable for a simple reason: It discloses both the original cost of the equipment and the total cost that has expired to date. Thus, in the balance sheet, Sierra deducts Accumulated Depreciation—Equipment from the related asset account, as shown in Illustration 4-9.

Illustration 4-9 Balance sheet presentation of accumulated depreciation

Equipment	$ 5,000
Less: Accumulated depreciation—equipment	40
	$4,960

Alternative Terminology Book value is also referred to as *carrying value*.

Book value is the difference between the cost of any depreciable asset and its related accumulated depreciation. In Illustration 4-9, the book value of the equipment at the balance sheet date is $4,960. The book value and the fair value of the asset are generally two different values. As noted earlier, **the purpose of depreciation is not valuation but a means of cost allocation**.

Depreciation expense identifies the portion of an asset's cost that expired during the period (in this case, in October). The accounting equation shows that without this adjusting entry, total assets, total stockholders' equity, and net income are overstated by $40 and depreciation expense is understated by $40.

Illustration 4-10 summarizes the accounting for prepaid expenses.

Illustration 4-10 Accounting for prepaid expenses

	ACCOUNTING FOR PREPAID EXPENSES		
Examples	Reason for Adjustment	Accounts Before Adjustment	Adjusting Entry
Insurance, supplies, advertising, rent, depreciation	Prepaid expenses recorded in asset accounts have been used.	Assets overstated. Expenses understated.	Dr. Expenses Cr. Assets or Contra Assets

Unearned Revenues

Companies record cash received before services are performed by increasing (crediting) a liability account called **unearned revenues**. In other words, the company has a performance obligation to transfer a service to one of its customers. Items like rent, magazine subscriptions, and customer deposits for future service may result in unearned revenues. Airlines such as United, American, and Delta, for instance, treat receipts from the sale of tickets as unearned revenue until the flight service is provided.

Unearned revenues are the opposite of prepaid expenses. Indeed, unearned revenue on the books of one company is likely to be a prepaid expense on the books of the company that has made the advance payment. For example, if identical accounting periods are assumed, a landlord will have unearned rent revenue when a tenant has prepaid rent.

When a company receives payment for services to be performed in a future accounting period, it increases (credits) an unearned revenue account. Unearned revenue is a liability account used to recognize the obligation that exists. The company subsequently recognizes revenues when it performs the service. During the accounting period, it is not practical to make daily entries as the company performs services. Instead, the company delays recognition of revenue until the adjustment process. The company then makes an adjusting entry to record the revenue for services performed during the period and to show the liability that remains at the end of the accounting period. Prior to adjustment, liabilities are typically overstated and revenues are understated. Therefore, as shown in Illustration 4-11, **the adjusting entry for unearned revenues results in a decrease (a debit) to a liability account and an increase (a credit) to a revenue account**.

Unearned Revenues

Oct. 2

Cash is received in advance; liability is recorded

Oct. 31
Some service has been performed; some revenue is recorded

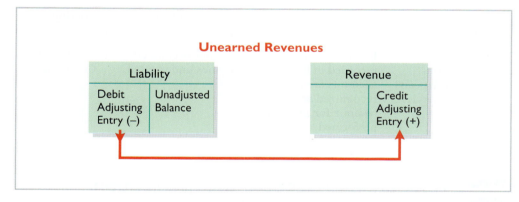

Illustration 4-11 Adjusting entries for unearned revenues

Sierra Corporation received $1,200 on October 2 from R. Knox for guide services for multi-day trips expected to be completed by December 31. Sierra credited the payment to Unearned Service Revenue. This liability account shows a balance of $1,200 in the October 31 trial balance. From an evaluation of the service Sierra performed for Knox during October, the company determines that it should recognize $400 of revenue in October. The liability (Unearned Service Revenue) is therefore decreased and stockholders' equity (Service Revenue) is increased.

As shown in Illustration 4-12, the liability Unearned Service Revenue now shows a balance of $800. That amount represents the remaining guide services expected to be performed in the future. Service Revenue shows total revenue for October of $10,400. **Without this adjustment, revenues and net income are understated by $400 in the income statement. Moreover, liabilities are overstated and stockholders' equity is understated by $400 on the October 31 balance sheet.**

Illustration 4-12
Service revenue
accounts after
adjustment

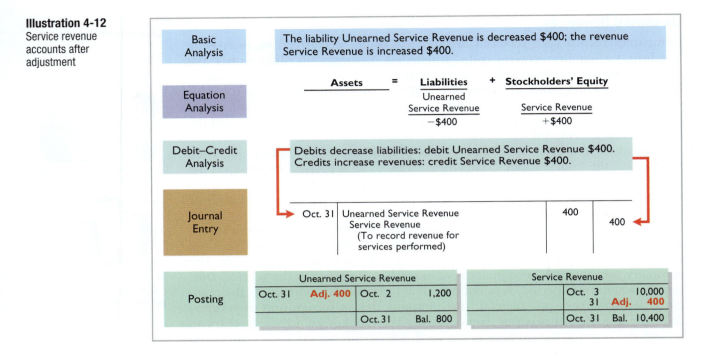

| Basic Analysis | The liability Unearned Service Revenue is decreased $400; the revenue Service Revenue is increased $400. |

Equation Analysis

Assets	=	Liabilities	+	Stockholders' Equity
		Unearned Service Revenue		Service Revenue
		−$400		+$400

Debit–Credit Analysis

Debits decrease liabilities: debit Unearned Service Revenue $400.
Credits increase revenues: credit Service Revenue $400.

Journal Entry

Oct. 31	Unearned Service Revenue	400	
	Service Revenue		400
	(To record revenue for services performed)		

Posting

Unearned Service Revenue				Service Revenue		
Oct. 31	Adj. 400	Oct. 2	1,200			Oct. 3	10,000
						31	Adj. 400
		Oct. 31	Bal. 800			Oct. 31	Bal. 10,400

Illustration 4-13 summarizes the accounting for unearned revenues.

Illustration 4-13 Accounting
for unearned revenues

ACCOUNTING FOR UNEARNED REVENUES

Examples	Reason for Adjustment	Accounts Before Adjustment	Adjusting Entry
Rent, magazine subscriptions, customer deposits for future service	Unearned revenues recorded in liability accounts are now recognized as revenue for services performed.	Liabilities overstated. Revenues understated.	Dr. Liabilities Cr. Revenues

Accounting Across the Organization

Turning Gift Cards into Revenue

Those of you who are marketing majors (and even most of you who are not) know that gift cards are among the hottest marketing tools in merchandising today. Customers purchase gift cards and give them to someone for later use. In a recent year, gift-card sales topped $95 billion.

Although these programs are popular with marketing executives, they create accounting questions. Should revenue be recorded at the time the gift card is sold, or when it is exercised? How should expired gift cards be accounted for? In a recent balance sheet, Best Buy reported unearned revenue related to gift cards of $479 million.

Source: Robert Berner, "Gift Cards: No Gift to Investors," *BusinessWeek* (March 14, 2005), p. 86.

 Suppose that Robert Jones purchases a $100 gift card at Best Buy on December 24, 2013, and gives it to his wife, Mary Jones, on December 25, 2013. On January 3, 2014, Mary uses the card to purchase $100 worth of CDs. When do you think Best Buy should recognize revenue and why? (Answers in *Broadening Your Perspective.*)

ADJUSTING ENTRIES FOR ACCRUALS

The second category of adjusting entries is **accruals**. Prior to an accrual adjustment, the revenue account (and the related asset account) or the expense account (and the related liability account) are understated. Thus, the adjusting entry for accruals will **increase both a balance sheet and an income statement account**.

LEARNING OBJECTIVE 5
Prepare adjusting entries for accruals.

Accrued Revenues

Revenues for services performed but not yet recorded at the statement date are accrued revenues. Accrued revenues may accumulate (accrue) with the passing of time, as in the case of interest revenue. These are unrecorded because the earning of interest does not involve daily transactions. Companies do not record interest revenue on a daily basis because it is often impractical to do so. Accrued revenues also may result from services that have been performed but not yet billed nor collected, as in the case of commissions and fees. These may be unrecorded because only a portion of the total service has been performed and the clients won't be billed until the service has been completed.

Accrued Revenues

Revenue and receivable are recorded for unbilled services

Nov. 10

Cash is received; receivable is reduced

An adjusting entry records the receivable that exists at the balance sheet date and the revenue for the services performed during the period. Prior to adjustment, both assets and revenues are understated. As shown in Illustration 4-14, **an adjusting entry for accrued revenues results in an increase (a debit) to an asset account and an increase (a credit) to a revenue account**.

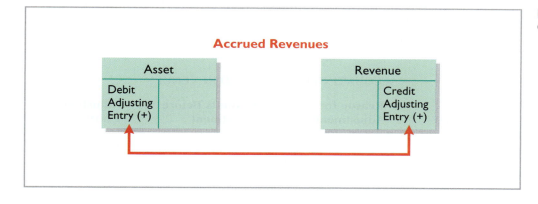

Illustration 4-14 Adjusting entries for accrued revenues

In October, Sierra Corporation performed guide services worth $200 that were not billed to clients on or before October 31. Because these services are not billed, they are not recorded. The accrual of unrecorded service revenue increases an asset account, Accounts Receivable. It also increases stockholders' equity by increasing a revenue account, Service Revenue, as shown in Illustration 4-15.

The asset Accounts Receivable shows that clients owe Sierra $200 at the balance sheet date. The balance of $10,600 in Service Revenue represents the total revenue for services Sierra performed during the month ($10,000 + $400 + $200). **Without the adjusting entry, assets and stockholders' equity on the balance sheet and revenues and net income on the income statement are understated.**

On November 10, Sierra receives cash of $200 for the services performed in October and makes the following entry.

A	=	L	+	SE
+200				
−200				

Cash Flows
+200

Nov. 10	Cash	200	
	Accounts Receivable		200
	(To record cash collected on account)		

Illustration 4-15
Adjustment for
accrued revenue

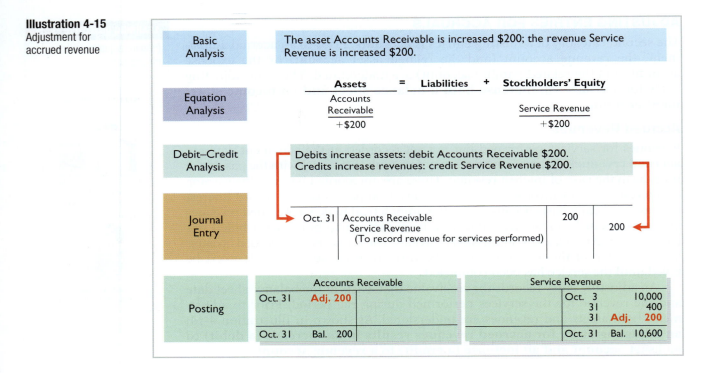

The company records the collection of the receivables by a debit (increase) to Cash and a credit (decrease) to Accounts Receivable.

Illustration 4-16 summarizes the accounting for accrued revenues.

Illustration 4-16
Accounting for accrued
revenues

	ACCOUNTING FOR ACCRUED REVENUES		
Examples	**Reason for Adjustment**	**Accounts Before Adjustment**	**Adjusting Entry**
Interest, rent, services	Services performed but not yet received in cash or recorded.	Assets understated. Revenues understated.	Dr. Assets Cr. Revenues

Accrued Expenses

Expenses incurred but not yet paid or recorded at the statement date are called **accrued expenses**. Interest, taxes, utilities, and salaries are common examples of accrued expenses.

Companies make adjustments for accrued expenses to record the obligations that exist at the balance sheet date and to recognize the expenses that apply to the current accounting period. Prior to adjustment, both liabilities and expenses are understated. Therefore, **an adjusting entry for accrued expenses results in an increase (a debit) to an expense account and an increase (a credit) to a liability account**.

Let's look in more detail at some specific types of accrued expenses, beginning with accrued interest.

ACCRUED INTEREST. Sierra Corporation signed a three-month note payable in the amount of $5,000 on October 1. The note requires Sierra to pay interest at an annual rate of 12%.

The amount of the interest recorded is determined by three factors: (1) the face value of the note; (2) the interest rate, which is always expressed as an annual rate;

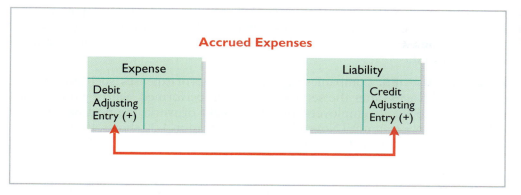

Illustration 4-17
Adjusting entries for accrued expenses

and (3) the length of time the note is outstanding. For Sierra, the total interest due on the $5,000 note at its maturity date three months in the future is $150 ($5,000 × 12% × $\frac{3}{12}$), or $50 for one month. Illustration 4-18 shows the formula for computing interest and its application to Sierra Corporation for the month of October.

Face Value of Note	×	Annual Interest Rate	×	Time in Terms of One Year	=	Interest
$5,000	×	12%	×	$\frac{1}{12}$	=	$50

Illustration 4-18 Formula for computing interest

As Illustration 4-19 shows, the accrual of interest at October 31 increases a liability account, Interest Payable. It also decreases stockholders' equity by increasing an expense account, Interest Expense.

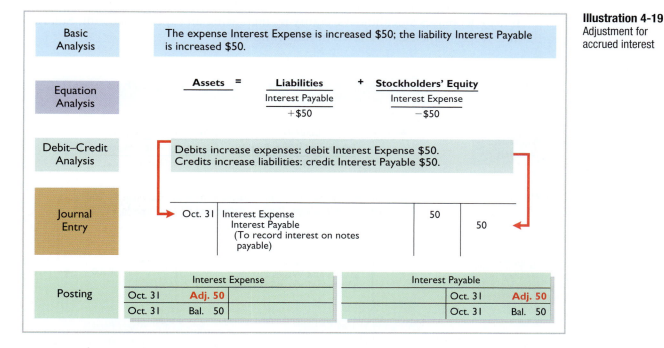

Illustration 4-19
Adjustment for accrued interest

Interest Expense shows the interest charges for the month of October. Interest Payable shows the amount of interest the company owes at the statement date. Sierra will not pay the interest until the note comes due at the end of three months. Companies use the Interest Payable account, instead of crediting Notes

Payable, to disclose the two different types of obligations—interest and principal—in the accounts and statements. **Without this adjusting entry, liabilities and interest expense are understated, and net income and stockholders' equity are overstated.**

ACCRUED SALARIES. Companies pay for some types of expenses, such as employee salaries and wages, after the services have been performed. Sierra paid salaries on October 26 for its employees' first two weeks of work; the next payment of salaries will not occur until November 9. As Illustration 4-20 shows, three working days remain in October (October 29–31).

Illustration 4-20 Calendar showing Sierra Corporation's pay periods

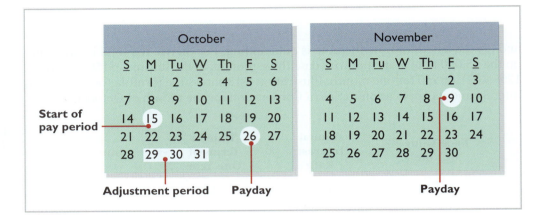

At October 31, the salaries for these three days represent an accrued expense and a related liability to Sierra. The employees receive total salaries of $2,000 for a five-day work week, or $400 per day. Thus, accrued salaries at October 31 are $1,200 ($400 × 3). This accrual increases a liability, Salaries and Wages Payable. It also decreases stockholders' equity by increasing an expense account, Salaries and Wages Expense, as shown in Illustration 4-21.

Illustration 4-21 Adjustment for accrued salaries

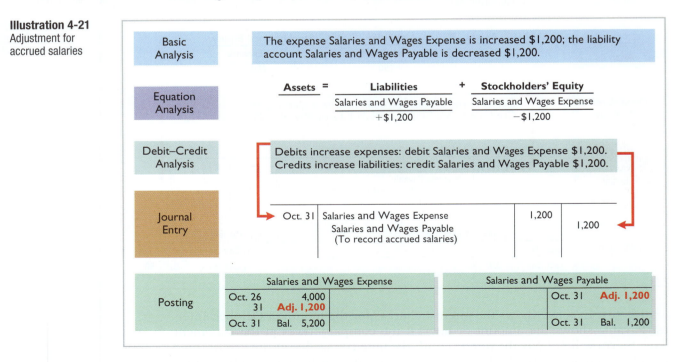

After this adjustment, the balance in Salaries and Wages Expense of $5,200 (13 days × $400) is the actual salary expense for October. (The employees worked 13 days in October after being hired on October 15.) The balance in Salaries and Wages Payable of $1,200 is the amount of the liability for salaries Sierra owes as of October 31. **Without the $1,200 adjustment for salaries, Sierra's expenses are understated $1,200 and its liabilities are understated $1,200.**

Sierra Corporation pays salaries every two weeks. Consequently, the next payday is November 9, when the company will again pay total salaries of $4,000. The payment consists of $1,200 of salaries and wages payable at October 31 plus $2,800 of salaries and wages expense for November (7 working days, as shown in the November calendar × $400). Therefore, Sierra makes the following entry on November 9.

Nov. 9	Salaries and Wages Payable	1,200	
	Salaries and Wages Expense	2,800	
	Cash		4,000
	(To record November 9 payroll)		

This entry eliminates the liability for Salaries and Wages Payable that Sierra recorded in the October 31 adjusting entry, and it records the proper amount of Salaries and Wages Expense for the period between November 1 and November 9.

Illustration 4-22 summarizes the accounting for accrued expenses.

ACCOUNTING FOR ACCRUED EXPENSES

Examples	Reason for Adjustment	Accounts Before Adjustment	Adjusting Entry
Interest, rent, salaries	Expenses have been incurred but not yet paid in cash or recorded.	Expenses understated. Liabilities understated.	Dr. Expenses Cr. Liabilities

Illustration 4-22
Accounting for accrued expenses

People, Planet, and Profit Insight

Got Junk?

Do you have an old computer or two in your garage? How about an old TV that needs replacing? Many people do. Approximately 163,000 computers and televisions become obsolete **each day**. Yet, in a recent year, only 11% of computers were recycled. It is estimated that 75% of all computers ever sold are sitting in storage somewhere, waiting to be disposed of. Each of these old TVs and computers is loaded with lead, cadmium, mercury, and other toxic chemicals. If you have one of these electronic gadgets, you have a responsibility, and a probable cost, for disposing of it. Companies have the same problem, but their discarded materials may include lead paint, asbestos, and other toxic chemicals.

? What accounting issue might this cause for companies? (Answers in *Broadening Your Perspective*.)

SUMMARY OF BASIC RELATIONSHIPS

Illustration 4-23 summarizes the four basic types of adjusting entries. Take some time to study and analyze the adjusting entries. Be sure to note that **each adjusting entry affects one balance sheet account and one income statement account**.

Illustration 4-23
Summary of adjusting entries

Type of Adjustment	Accounts Before Adjustment	Adjusting Entry
Prepaid expenses	Assets overstated. Expenses understated.	Dr. Expenses Cr. Assets or Contra Assets
Unearned revenues	Liabilities overstated. Revenues understated.	Dr. Liabilities Cr. Revenues
Accrued revenues	Assets understated. Revenues understated.	Dr. Assets Cr. Revenues
Accrued expenses	Expenses understated. Liabilities understated.	Dr. Expenses Cr. Liabilities

Illustrations 4-24 and 4-25 show the journalizing and posting of adjusting entries for Sierra Corporation on October 31. When reviewing the general ledger in Illustration 4-25, note that for learning purposes we have highlighted the adjustments in color.

Illustration 4-24 General journal showing adjusting entries

GENERAL JOURNAL

Date	Account Titles and Explanation	Debit	Credit
2014	*Adjusting Entries*		
Oct. 31	Supplies Expense	1,500	
	Supplies		1,500
	(To record supplies used)		
31	Insurance Expense	50	
	Prepaid Insurance		50
	(To record insurance expired)		
31	Depreciation Expense	40	
	Accumulated Depreciation—Equipment		40
	(To record monthly depreciation)		
31	Unearned Service Revenue	400	
	Service Revenue		400
	(To record revenue for services performed)		
31	Accounts Receivable	200	
	Service Revenue		200
	(To record revenue for services performed)		
31	Interest Expense	50	
	Interest Payable		50
	(To record interest on notes payable)		
31	Salaries and Wages Expense	1,200	
	Salaries and Wages Payable		1,200
	(To record accrued salaries)		

Illustration 4-25 General ledger after adjustments

GENERAL LEDGER

Cash

Oct. 1	10,000	Oct. 2	5,000
1	5,000	3	900
2	1,200	4	600
3	10,000	20	500
		26	4,000

Oct. 31 Bal. 15,200

Accounts Receivable

Oct. 31	**200**		

Oct. 31 Bal. 200

Supplies

Oct. 5	2,500	Oct. 31	**1,500**

Oct. 31 Bal. 1,000

Prepaid Insurance

Oct. 4	600	Oct. 31	**50**

Oct. 31 Bal. 550

Equipment

Oct. 2	5,000		

Oct. 31 Bal. 5,000

Accumulated Depreciation—Equipment

		Oct. 31	**40**
		Oct. 31	Bal. 40

Notes Payable

		Oct. 1	5,000
		Oct. 31	Bal. 5,000

Accounts Payable

		Oct. 5	2,500
		Oct. 31	Bal. 2,500

Interest Payable

		Oct. 31	**50**
		Oct. 31	Bal. 50

Unearned Service Revenue

Oct. 31	**400**	Oct. 2	1,200
		Oct. 31	Bal. 800

Salaries and Wages Payable

		Oct. 31	**1,200**
		Oct. 31	Bal. 1,200

Common Stock

		Oct. 1	10,000
		Oct. 31	Bal. 10,000

Retained Earnings

		Oct. 31	Bal. 0

Dividends

Oct. 20	500		

Oct. 31 Bal. 500

Service Revenue

		Oct. 3	10,000
		31	**400**
		31	**200**
		Oct. 31	Bal. 10,600

Salaries and Wages Expense

Oct. 26	4,000		
31	**1,200**		

Oct. 31 Bal. 5,200

Supplies Expense

Oct. 31	**1,500**		

Oct. 31 Bal. 1,500

Rent Expense

Oct. 3	900		

Oct. 31 Bal. 900

Insurance Expense

Oct. 31	**50**		

Oct. 31 Bal. 50

Interest Expense

Oct. 31	**50**		

Oct. 31 Bal. 50

Depreciation Expense

Oct. 31	**40**		

Oct. 31 Bal. 40

The Adjusted Trial Balance and Financial Statements

LEARNING OBJECTIVE 6

Describe the nature and purpose of the adjusted trial balance.

After a company has journalized and posted all adjusting entries, it prepares another trial balance from the ledger accounts. This trial balance is called an **adjusted trial balance**. It shows the balances of all accounts, including those adjusted, at the end of the accounting period. The purpose of an adjusted trial balance is to **prove the equality** of the total debit balances and the total credit balances in the ledger after all adjustments. Because the accounts contain all data needed for financial statements, the adjusted trial balance is the **primary basis for the preparation of financial statements**.

PREPARING THE ADJUSTED TRIAL BALANCE

Illustration 4-26 presents the adjusted trial balance for Sierra Corporation prepared from the ledger accounts in Illustration 4-25. The amounts affected by the adjusting entries are highlighted in color.

Illustration 4-26
Adjusted trial balance

SIERRA CORPORATION
Adjusted Trial Balance
October 31, 2014

	Dr.	Cr.
Cash	$ 15,200	
Accounts Receivable	200	
Supplies	1,000	
Prepaid Insurance	550	
Equipment	5,000	
Accumulated Depreciation—Equipment		$ 40
Notes Payable		5,000
Accounts Payable		2,500
Interest Payable		50
Unearned Service Revenue		800
Salaries and Wages Payable		1,200
Common Stock		10,000
Retained Earnings		0
Dividends	500	
Service Revenue		10,600
Salaries and Wages Expense	5,200	
Supplies Expense	1,500	
Rent Expense	900	
Insurance Expense	50	
Interest Expense	50	
Depreciation Expense	40	
	$30,190	$30,190

PREPARING FINANCIAL STATEMENTS

Companies can prepare financial statements directly from an adjusted trial balance. Illustrations 4-27 and 4-28 present the relationships between the data in the adjusted trial balance of Sierra Corporation and the corresponding financial statements. As Illustration 4-27 shows, companies prepare the income statement from the revenue and expense accounts. Similarly, they derive the retained earnings statement from the Retained Earnings account, Dividends account, and the net income (or net loss) shown in the income statement. As Illustration 4-28 shows, companies then prepare the balance sheet from the asset, liability, and stockholders' equity accounts. They obtain the amount reported for retained earnings on the balance sheet from the ending balance in the retained earnings statement.

Illustration 4-27
Preparation of the income statement and retained earnings statement from the adjusted trial balance

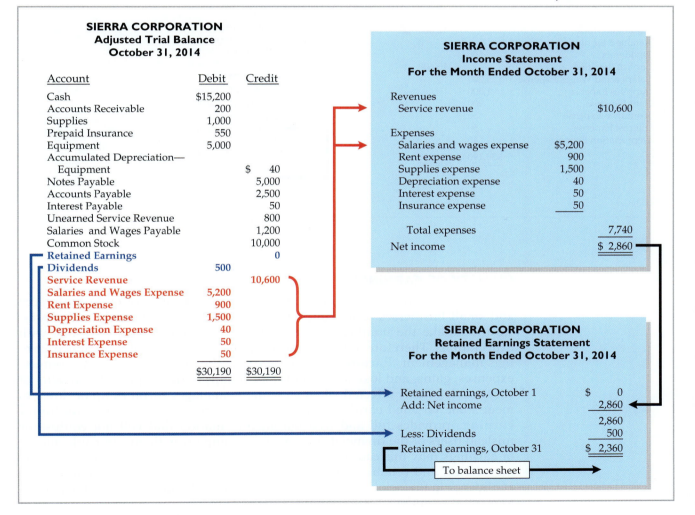

Illustration 4-28
Preparation of the balance
sheet from the adjusted
trial balance

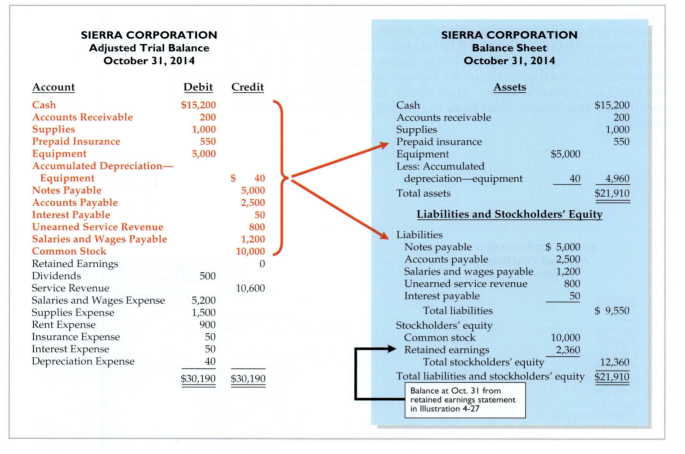

QUALITY OF EARNINGS

"Did you make your numbers today?" is a question asked often in both large and small businesses. Companies and employees are continually under pressure to "make the numbers"—that is, to have earnings that are in line with expectations. Therefore, it is not surprising that many companies practice earnings management. **Earnings management** is the planned timing of revenues, expenses, gains, and losses to smooth out bumps in net income. The quality of earnings is greatly affected when a company manages earnings up or down to meet some targeted earnings number. A company that has a high **quality of earnings** provides full and transparent information that will not confuse or mislead users of the financial statements. A company with questionable quality of earnings may mislead investors and creditors, who believe they are relying on relevant and reliable information. As a result, investors and creditors lose confidence in financial reporting, and it becomes difficult for our capital markets to work efficiently.

Companies manage earnings in a variety of ways. One way is through the use of **one-time items** to prop up earnings numbers. For example, ConAgra Foods recorded a nonrecurring gain from the sale of Pilgrim's Pride stock for $186 million to help meet an earnings projection for the quarter.

Another way is to **inflate revenue** numbers in the short-run to the detriment of the long-run. For example, Bristol-Myers Squibb provided sales incentives to its wholesalers to encourage them to buy products at the end of the quarter (often referred to as channel-stuffing). As a result Bristol-Myers was able to meet its sales projections. The problem was that the wholesalers could not sell that amount of merchandise and ended up returning it to Bristol-Myers. The result was that Bristol-Myers had to restate its income numbers.

Ethics Insight

Cooking the Books?

Allegations of abuse of the revenue recognition principle have become all too common in recent years. For example, it was alleged that Krispy Kreme sometimes doubled the number of doughnuts shipped to wholesale customers at the end of a quarter to boost quarterly results. The customers shipped the unsold doughnuts back after the beginning of the next quarter for a refund. Conversely, Computer Associates International was accused of backdating sales—that is, reporting a sale in one quarter that did not actually occur until the beginning of the following quarter in order to achieve the previous quarter's sales targets.

? What motivates sales executives and finance and accounting executives to participate in activities that result in inaccurate reporting of revenues? (Answers in *Broadening Your Perspective*.)

Companies also manage earnings through **improper adjusting entries**. Regulators investigated Xerox for accusations that it was booking too much revenue upfront on multi-year contract sales. Financial executives at Office Max resigned amid accusations that the company was recognizing rebates from its vendors too early and therefore overstating revenue. Finally, WorldCom's abuse of adjusting entries to meet its net income targets is unsurpassed. It used adjusting entries to increase net income by reclassifying liabilities as revenue and reclassifying expenses as assets. Investigations of the company's books after it went bankrupt revealed adjusting entries of more than a billion dollars that had no supporting documentation.

The good news is that, as a result of investor pressure as well as the **Sarbanes-Oxley Act**, many companies are trying to improve the quality of their financial reporting. For example, hotel operator Marriott is now providing detailed information on the write-offs it has on loan guarantees it gives hotels. General Electric has decided to provide more detail on its revenues and operating profits for individual businesses it owns. IBM is attempting to provide a better breakdown of its earnings. At the same time, regulators are taking a tough stand on the issue of quality of earnings. For example, one regulator noted that companies may be required to restate their financials every single time that they account for any transaction that had no legitimate purpose but was done solely for an accounting purpose, such as to smooth net income.

Closing the Books

In previous chapters, you learned that revenue and expense accounts and the Dividends account are subdivisions of retained earnings, which is reported in the stockholders' equity section of the balance sheet. Because revenues, expenses, and dividends relate only to a given accounting period, they are considered **temporary accounts**. In contrast, all balance sheet accounts are considered **permanent accounts** because their balances are carried forward into future accounting periods. Illustration 4-29 identifies the accounts in each category.

Illustration 4-29
Temporary versus permanent accounts

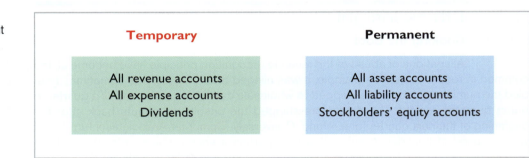

Temporary	Permanent
All revenue accounts	All asset accounts
All expense accounts	All liability accounts
Dividends	Stockholders' equity accounts

PREPARING CLOSING ENTRIES

At the end of the accounting period, companies transfer the temporary account balances to the permanent stockholders' equity account—Retained Earnings—through the preparation of closing entries. **Closing entries** transfer net income (or net loss) and dividends to Retained Earnings, so the balance in Retained Earnings agrees with the retained earnings statement. For example, in the adjusted trial balance in Illustration 4-24, Retained Earnings has a balance of zero. Prior to the closing entries, the balance in Retained Earnings is its beginning-of-the-period balance. (For Sierra, this is zero because it is Sierra's first month of operations.)

In addition to updating Retained Earnings to its correct ending balance, closing entries produce a **zero balance in each temporary, or nominal, account**. As a result, these accounts are ready to accumulate data about revenues, expenses, and dividends that occur in the next accounting period. **Permanent, or real, accounts are not closed.**

When companies prepare closing entries, they could close each income statement account directly to Retained Earnings. However, to do so would result in excessive detail in the Retained Earnings account. Instead, companies close the revenue and expense accounts to another temporary account, **Income Summary**. The balance in Income Summary is the net income or loss for the year. Income Summary is then closed, which transfers the net income or net loss from this account to Retained Earnings. Illustration 4-30 depicts the closing process. While it still takes the average large company seven days to close, some companies such as Cisco employ technology that allows them to do a so-called "virtual close" almost instantaneously any time during the year. Besides dramatically reducing the cost of closing, the virtual close provides companies with accurate data for decision-making whenever they desire it.

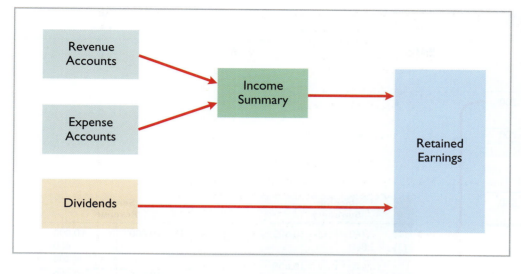

Illustration 4-30 The closing process

Illustration 4-31 shows the closing entries for Sierra Corporation. Illustration 4-32 diagrams the posting process for Sierra Corporation's closing entries.

Illustration 4-31 Closing entries journalized

GENERAL JOURNAL			
Date	Account Titles and Explanation	Debit	Credit
	Closing Entries		
2014	(1)		
Oct. 31	Service Revenue	10,600	
	Income Summary		10,600
	(To close revenue account)		
	(2)		
31	Income Summary	7,740	
	Salaries and Wages Expense		5,200
	Supplies Expense		1,500
	Rent Expense		900
	Insurance Expense		50
	Interest Expense		50
	Depreciation Expense		40
	(To close expense accounts)		
	(3)		
31	Income Summary	2,860	
	Retained Earnings		2,860
	(To close net income to retained earnings)		
	(4)		
31	Retained Earnings	500	
	Dividends		500
	(To close dividends to retained earnings)		

PREPARING A POST-CLOSING TRIAL BALANCE

After a company journalizes and posts all closing entries, it prepares another trial balance, called a **post-closing trial balance**, from the ledger. A post-closing trial balance is a list of all permanent accounts and their balances after

Illustration 4-32 Posting of closing entries

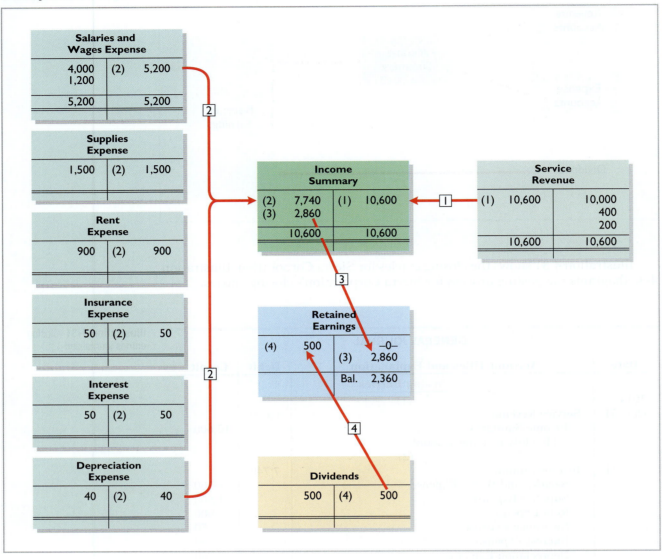

closing entries are journalized and posted. **The purpose of this trial balance is to prove the equality of the total debit balances and total credit balances of the permanent account balances that the company carries forward into the next accounting period.** Since all temporary accounts will have zero balances, **the post-closing trial balance will contain only permanent—balance sheet—accounts**.

SUMMARY OF THE ACCOUNTING CYCLE

LEARNING OBJECTIVE 8

Describe the required steps in the accounting cycle.

Illustration 4-33 shows the required steps in the accounting cycle. You can see that the cycle begins with the analysis of business transactions and ends with the preparation of a post-closing trial balance. Companies perform the steps in the cycle in sequence and repeat them in each accounting period.

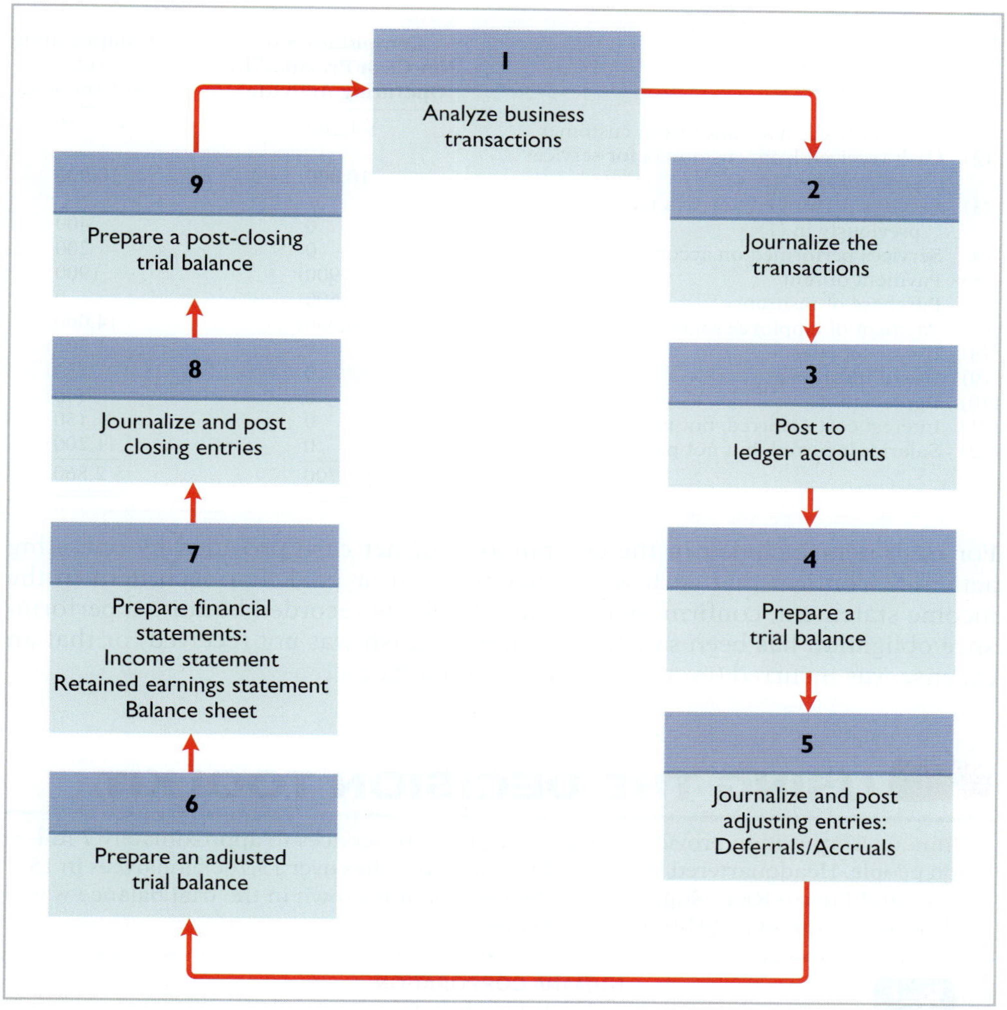

Illustration 4-33
Required steps in the
accounting cycle

Steps 1–3 may occur daily during the accounting period, as explained in Chapter 3. Companies perform Steps 4–7 on a periodic basis, such as monthly, quarterly, or annually. Steps 8 and 9, closing entries and a post-closing trial balance, usually take place only at the end of a company's **annual** accounting period.

Margin Note Some companies reverse certain adjusting entries at the beginning of a new accounting period. The company makes a **reversing entry** at the beginning of the next accounting period. This entry is the exact opposite of the adjusting entry made in the previous period.

In this chapter, you learned that adjusting entries are used to adjust numbers that would otherwise be stated on a cash basis. Sierra Corporation's income statement (Illustration 4-27) shows net income of $2,860. The statement of cash flows reports a form of cash-basis income referred to as "Net cash provided by operating activities." For example, Illustration 1-8, which shows a statement of cash flows, reports net cash provided by operating activities of $5,700 for Sierra. Net income and net cash provided by operating activities often differ. The difference for Sierra is $2,840 ($5,700 − $2,860). The following summary shows the causes of this difference of $2,840.

**KEEPING AN EYE
ON CASH**

LEARNING OBJECTIVE 9

Understand the causes of differences between net income and net cash provided by operating activities.

	Computation of Net Cash Provided by Operating Activities	Computation of Net Income
(1) Cash received in advance from customer	$ 1,200	$ 0
(2) Cash received from customers for services performed	10,000	10,000
(3) Services performed for cash received previously in (1)	0	400
(4) Services performed on account	0	200
(5) Payment of rent	(900)	(900)
(6) Purchase of insurance	(600)	0
(7) Payment of employee salaries	(4,000)	(4,000)
(8) Use of supplies	0	(1,500)
(9) Use of insurance	0	(50)
(10) Depreciation	0	(40)
(11) Interest cost incurred, but not paid	0	(50)
(12) Salaries incurred, but not paid	0	(1,200)
	$ 5,700	$ 2,860

For each item included in the computation of net cash provided by operating activities, confirm that cash was either received or paid. For each item in the income statement, confirm that revenue should be recorded because a performance obligation has been satisfied (even when cash was not received) or that an expense was incurred (even when cash was not paid).

USING THE DECISION TOOLKIT

Humana Corporation provides managed health care services to approximately 7 million people. Headquartered in Louisville, Kentucky, it has over 13,700 employees in 15 states and Puerto Rico. Suppose that the information shown in the trial balance was taken from Humana's 2014 financial records.

Real World

HUMANA CORPORATION
Adjusted Trial Balance
December 31, 2014
(in millions)

Account	Dr.	Cr.
Cash	$ 1,613	
Debt Investments (current)	6,190	
Accounts Receivable	824	
Other Current Assets	626	
Equipment	2,402	
Accumulated Depreciation—Equipment		$ 1,723
Stock Investments (noncurrent)	1,307	
Goodwill	1,993	
Other Long-Term Assets	921	
Benefits Payable		3,222
Accounts Payable		1,308
Other Current Liabilities		730
Notes Payable (noncurrent)		3,117
Common Stock		1,690
Dividends	0	
Retained Earnings		3,046
Revenues		30,960
Medical Cost Expense	24,775	
Selling and Administrative Expenses	4,227	
Depreciation Expense	250	
Interest Expense	106	
Income Tax Expense	562	
	$45,796	$45,796

Instructions

From the trial balance, prepare an income statement, retained earnings statement, and classified balance sheet. **Be sure to prepare them in that order since each statement depends on information determined in the preceding statement.**

Solution

Real World

HUMANA CORPORATION
Income Statement
For the Year Ended December 31, 2014
(in millions)

Revenues		$30,960
Medical cost expense	$24,775	
Selling and administrative expenses	4,227	
Depreciation expense	250	
Interest expense	106	
Income tax expense	562	29,920
Net income		$ 1,040

Real World

HUMANA CORPORATION
Retained Earnings Statement
For the Year Ended December 31, 2014
(in millions)

Beginning retained earnings	$3,046
Add: Net income	1,040
Less: Dividends	0
Ending retained earnings	$4,086

Real World

HUMANA CORPORATION
Balance Sheet
December 31, 2014
(in millions)

Assets

Current assets		
Cash	$1,613	
Debt investments	6,190	
Accounts receivable	824	
Other current assets	626	
Total current assets		$ 9,253
Long-term investments		
Stock investments		1,307
Property, plant, and equipment		
Equipment	2,402	
Accumulated depreciation—equipment	1,723	679
Intangible assets		
Goodwill		1,993
Other long-term assets		921
Total assets		$14,153

Liabilities and Stockholders' Equity

Liabilities		
Current liabilities		
Accounts payable	$1,308	
Benefits payable	3,222	
Other current liabilities	730	
Total current liabilities		$ 5,260
Long-term liabilities		
Notes payable		3,117
Total liabilities		8,377
Stockholders' equity		
Common stock	1,690	
Retained earnings	4,086	
Total stockholders' equity		5,776
Total liabilities and stockholders' equity		$14,153

Summary of Learning Objectives

1 **Explain the revenue recognition principle and the expense recognition principle.** The revenue recognition principle dictates that companies recognize revenue when a performance obligation has been satisfied. The expense recognition principle dictates that companies recognize expenses in the period when the company makes efforts to generate those revenues.

2 **Differentiate between the cash basis and the accrual basis of accounting.** Under the cash basis, companies record events only in the periods in which the company receives or pays cash. Accrual-based accounting means that companies record, in the periods in which the events occur, events that change a company's financial statements even if cash has not been exchanged.

3 **Explain why adjusting entries are needed, and identify the major types of adjusting entries.** Companies make adjusting entries at the end of an accounting period. These entries ensure that companies record revenues in the period in which the performance obligation is satisfied and that companies recognize expenses in the period in which they are incurred. The major types of adjusting entries are prepaid expenses, unearned revenues, accrued revenues, and accrued expenses.

4 **Prepare adjusting entries for deferrals.** Deferrals are either prepaid expenses or unearned revenues. Companies make adjusting entries for deferrals at the statement date to record the portion of the deferred item that represents the expense incurred or the revenue for services performed in the current accounting period.

5 **Prepare adjusting entries for accruals.** Accruals are either accrued revenues or accrued expenses. Adjusting entries for accruals record revenues for services performed and expenses incurred in the current accounting period that have not been recognized through daily entries.

6 **Describe the nature and purpose of the adjusted trial balance.** An adjusted trial balance is a trial balance that shows the balances of all accounts, including those that have been adjusted, at the end of an accounting period. The purpose of an adjusted trial balance is to show the effects of all financial events that have occurred during the accounting period.

7 **Explain the purpose of closing entries.** One purpose of closing entries is to transfer net income or net loss for the period to Retained Earnings. A second purpose is to "zero-out" all temporary accounts (revenue accounts, expense accounts, and Dividends) so that they start each new period with a zero balance. To accomplish this, companies "close" all temporary accounts at the end of an accounting period. They make separate entries to close revenues and expenses to Income Summary, Income Summary to Retained Earnings, and Dividends to Retained Earnings. Only temporary accounts are closed.

8 **Describe the required steps in the accounting cycle.** The required steps in the accounting cycle are (a) analyze business transactions, (b) journalize the transactions, (c) post to ledger accounts, (d) prepare a trial balance, (e) journalize and post adjusting entries, (f) prepare an adjusted trial balance, (g) prepare financial statements, (h) journalize and post closing entries, and (i) prepare a post-closing trial balance.

9 **Understand the causes of differences between net income and net cash provided by operating activities.** Net income is based on accrual accounting, which relies on the adjustment process. Net cash provided by operating activities is determined by adding cash received from operating the business and subtracting cash expended during operations.

DECISION TOOLKIT *A SUMMARY*

DECISION CHECKPOINTS	INFO NEEDED FOR DECISION	TOOL TO USE FOR DECISION	HOW TO EVALUATE RESULTS
At what point should the company record revenue?	Need to understand the nature of the company's business	Record revenue in the period in which the performance obligation is satisfied.	Recognizing revenue too early overstates current period revenue; recognizing it too late understates current period revenue.
At what point should the company record expenses?	Need to understand the nature of the company's business	Expenses should "follow" revenues—that is, match the effort (expense) with the result (revenue).	Recognizing expenses too early overstates current period expense; recognizing them too late understates current period expense.

Appendix 4A

Adjusting Entries in an Automated World—Using a Worksheet

In the previous discussion, we used T-accounts and trial balances to arrive at the amounts used to prepare financial statements. Accountants frequently use a device known as a worksheet to determine these amounts. A **worksheet** is a multiple-column form that may be used in the adjustment process and in preparing financial statements. Accountants can prepare worksheets manually, but today most use computer spreadsheets.

> **LEARNING OBJECTIVE** **10**
> Describe the purpose and the basic form of a worksheet.

As its name suggests, the worksheet is a working tool for the accountant. **A worksheet is not a permanent accounting record**; it is neither a journal nor a part of the general ledger. The worksheet is merely a supplemental device used to make it easier to prepare adjusting entries and the financial statements. Small companies with relatively few accounts and adjustments may not need a worksheet. In large companies with numerous accounts and many adjustments, a worksheet is almost indispensable.

Illustration 4A-1 shows the basic form and procedures for preparing a worksheet. Note the headings: The worksheet starts with two columns for the Trial Balance. The next two columns record all Adjustments. Next is the Adjusted Trial Balance. The last two sets of columns correspond to the Income Statement and the Balance Sheet. All items listed in the Adjusted Trial Balance columns are included in either the Income Statement or the Balance Sheet columns.

Summary of Learning Objective for Appendix 4A

10 **Describe the purpose and the basic form of a worksheet.** The worksheet is a device to make it easier to prepare adjusting entries and the financial statements. Companies often prepare a worksheet using a computer spreadsheet. The sets of columns of the worksheet are, from left to right, the unadjusted trial balance, adjustments, adjusted trial balance, income statement, and balance sheet.

Illustration 4A-1
Form and procedure
for a worksheet

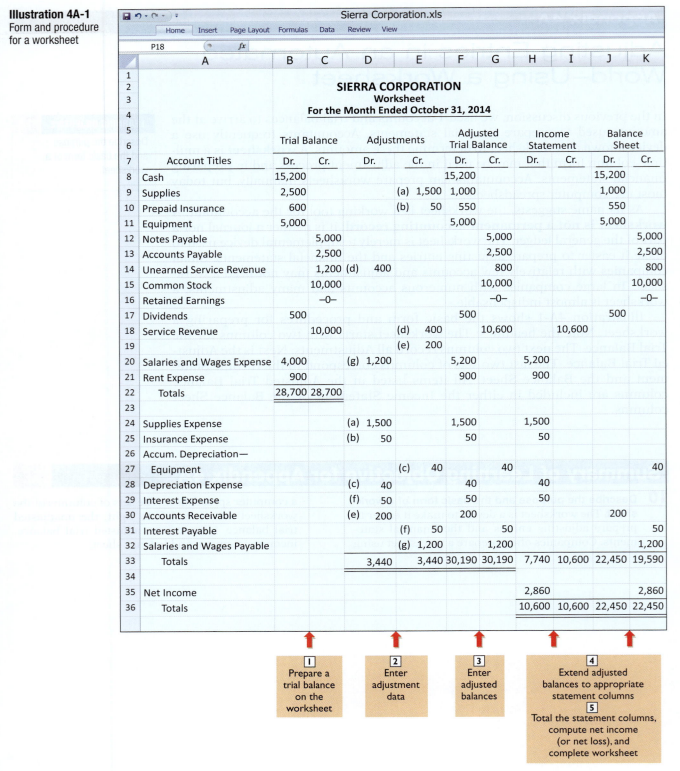

	A	B	C	D	E	F	G	H	I	J	K
2					**SIERRA CORPORATION**						
3					Worksheet						
4					For the Month Ended October 31, 2014						
5			Trial Balance		Adjustments		Adjusted Trial Balance		Income Statement		Balance Sheet	
6												
7	Account Titles	Dr.	Cr.	Dr.	Cr.	Dr.	Cr.	Dr.	Cr.	Dr.	Cr.
8	Cash	15,200				15,200				15,200	
9	Supplies	2,500			(a) 1,500	1,000				1,000	
10	Prepaid Insurance	600			(b) 50	550				550	
11	Equipment	5,000				5,000				5,000	
12	Notes Payable		5,000				5,000				5,000
13	Accounts Payable		2,500				2,500				2,500
14	Unearned Service Revenue		1,200	(d) 400			800				800
15	Common Stock		10,000				10,000				10,000
16	Retained Earnings		–0–				–0–				–0–
17	Dividends	500				500				500	
18	Service Revenue		10,000		(d) 400		10,600		10,600		
19					(e) 200						
20	Salaries and Wages Expense	4,000		(g) 1,200		5,200		5,200			
21	Rent Expense	900				900		900			
22	Totals	28,700	28,700								
23											
24	Supplies Expense			(a) 1,500		1,500		1,500			
25	Insurance Expense			(b) 50		50		50			
26	Accum. Depreciation—										
27	Equipment				(c) 40		40				40
28	Depreciation Expense			(c) 40		40		40			
29	Interest Expense			(f) 50		50		50			
30	Accounts Receivable			(e) 200		200				200	
31	Interest Payable				(f) 50		50				50
32	Salaries and Wages Payable				(g) 1,200		1,200				1,200
33	Totals			3,440	3,440	30,190	30,190	7,740	10,600	22,450	19,590
34											
35	Net Income							2,860			2,860
36	Totals							10,600	10,600	22,450	22,450

1	2	3	4
Prepare a trial balance on the worksheet	Enter adjustment data	Enter adjusted balances	Extend adjusted balances to appropriate statement columns

5
Total the statement columns, compute net income (or net loss), and complete worksheet

Glossary

Terms are highlighted in **blue** throughout the chapter.

Accrual-basis accounting Accounting basis in which companies record, in the periods in which the events occur, transactions that change a company's financial statements, even if cash was not exchanged.

Accrued expenses Expenses incurred but not yet paid in cash or recorded.

Accrued revenues Revenues for services performed but not yet received in cash or recorded.

Adjusted trial balance A list of accounts and their balances after all adjustments have been made.

Adjusting entries Entries made at the end of an accounting period to ensure that the revenue recognition and expense recognition principles are followed.

Book value The difference between the cost of a depreciable asset and its related accumulated depreciation.

Cash-basis accounting Accounting basis in which a company records revenue only when it receives cash and an expense only when it pays cash.

Closing entries Entries at the end of an accounting period to transfer the balances of temporary accounts to a permanent stockholders' equity account, Retained Earnings.

Contra asset account An account that is offset against an asset account on the balance sheet.

Depreciation The process of allocating the cost of an asset to expense over its useful life.

Earnings management The planned timing of revenues, expenses, gains, and losses to smooth out bumps in net income.

Expense recognition principle (matching principle) The principle that matches expenses with revenues in the period when the company makes efforts to generate those revenues.

Fiscal year An accounting period that is one year long.

Income Summary A temporary account used in closing revenue and expense accounts.

Periodicity assumption An assumption that the economic life of a business can be divided into artificial time periods.

Permanent accounts Balance sheet accounts whose balances are carried forward to the next accounting period.

Post-closing trial balance A list of permanent accounts and their balances after a company has journalized and posted closing entries.

Prepaid expenses (prepayments) Expenses paid in cash before they are used or consumed.

Quality of earnings Indicates the level of full and transparent information that a company provides to users of its financial statements.

Revenue recognition principle The principle that companies recognize revenue in the accounting period in which the performance obligation is satisfied.

Reversing entry An entry made at the beginning of the next accounting period; the exact opposite of the adjusting entry made in the previous period.

Temporary accounts Revenue, expense, and dividend accounts whose balances a company transfers to Retained Earnings at the end of an accounting period.

Unearned revenues Cash received and a liability recorded before services are performed.

Useful life The length of service of a productive asset.

Worksheet A multiple-column form that companies may use in the adjustment process and in preparing financial statements.

 Self-Test, Brief Exercises, Exercises, Problem Set A, and many more resources are available for practice in WileyPLUS.

Note: All Questions, Exercises, and Problems marked with an asterisk relate to material in the appendix to the chapter.

Self-Test Questions

(Answers in *Broadening Your Perspective*.)

(LO 1) **1.** What is the periodicity assumption?
  (a) Companies should recognize revenue in the accounting period in which services are performed.
  (b) Companies should match expenses with revenues.
  (c) The economic life of a business can be divided into artificial time periods.
  (d) The fiscal year should correspond with the calendar year.

2. Which principle dictates that efforts (expenses) be (LO 1) recorded with accomplishments (revenues)?
  (a) Expense recognition principle.
  (b) Historical cost principle.
  (c) Periodicity principle.
  (d) Revenue recognition principle.

(LO 2) **3.** Which one of these statements about the accrual basis of accounting is **false**?
  (a) Companies record events that change their financial statements in the period in which events occur, even if cash was not exchanged.
  (b) Companies recognize revenue in the period in which the performance obligation is satisfied.
  (c) This basis is in accord with generally accepted accounting principles.
  (d) Companies record revenue only when they receive cash, and record expense only when they pay out cash.

(LO 3) **4.** Adjusting entries are made to ensure that:
  (a) expenses are recognized in the period in which they are incurred.
  (b) revenues are recorded in the period in which the performance obligation is satisfied.
  (c) balance sheet and income statement accounts have correct balances at the end of an accounting period.
  (d) All of the above.

(LO 4, 5) **5.** Each of the following is a major type (or category) of adjusting entry **except**:
  (a) prepaid expenses.   (c) accrued expenses.
  (b) accrued revenues.   (d) unearned expenses.

(LO 4) **6.** The trial balance shows Supplies $1,350 and Supplies Expense $0. If $600 of supplies are on hand at the end of the period, the adjusting entry is:
  (a) Supplies   600
        Supplies Expense   600
  (b) Supplies   750
        Supplies Expense   750
  (c) Supplies Expense   750
        Supplies   750
  (d) Supplies Expense   600
        Supplies   600

(LO 4) **7.** Adjustments for unearned revenues:
  (a) decrease liabilities and increase revenues.
  (b) increase liabilities and increase revenues.
  (c) increase assets and increase revenues.
  (d) decrease revenues and decrease assets.

(LO 4) **8.** Adjustments for prepaid expenses:
  (a) decrease assets and increase revenues.
  (b) decrease expenses and increase assets.
  (c) decrease assets and increase expenses.
  (d) decrease revenues and increase assets.

(LO 4) **9.** Queenan Company computes depreciation on delivery equipment at $1,000 for the month of June. The adjusting entry to record this depreciation is as follows:
  (a) Depreciation Expense   1,000
        Accumulated Depreciation—
          Queenan Company   1,000
  (b) Depreciation Expense   1,000
        Equipment   1,000

  (c) Depreciation Expense   1,000
        Accumulated Depreciation—
          Equipment   1,000
  (d) Equipment Expense   1,000
        Accumulated Depreciation—
          Equipment   1,000

(LO 5) **10.** Adjustments for accrued revenues:
  (a) increase assets and increase liabilities.
  (b) increase assets and increase revenues.
  (c) decrease assets and decrease revenues.
  (d) decrease liabilities and increase revenues.

(LO 5) **11.** Colleen Mooney earned a salary of $400 for the last week of September. She will be paid on October 1. The adjusting entry for Colleen's employer at September 30 is:
  (a) No entry is required.
  (b) Salaries and Wages Expense   400
        Salaries and Wages Payable   400
  (c) Salaries and Wages Expense   400
        Cash   400
  (d) Salaries and Wages Payable   400
        Cash   400

(LO 6) **12.** Which statement is **incorrect** concerning the adjusted trial balance?
  (a) An adjusted trial balance proves the equality of the total debit balances and the total credit balances in the ledger after all adjustments are made.
  (b) The adjusted trial balance provides the primary basis for the preparation of financial statements.
  (c) The adjusted trial balance does not list temporary accounts.
  (d) The company prepares the adjusted trial balance after it has journalized and posted the adjusting entries.

(LO 7) **13.** Which account will have a zero balance after a company has journalized and posted closing entries?
  (a) Service Revenue.
  (b) Supplies.
  (c) Prepaid Insurance.
  (d) Accumulated Depreciation.

(LO 7) **14.** Which types of accounts will appear in the post-closing trial balance?
  (a) Permanent accounts.
  (b) Temporary accounts.
  (c) Expense accounts.
  (d) None of the above.

(LO 8) **15.** All of the following are required steps in the accounting cycle **except**:
  (a) journalizing and posting closing entries.
  (b) preparing an adjusted trial balance.
  (c) preparing a post-closing trial balance.
  (d) reversing entries.

Go to the book's companion website, **www.wiley.com/college/kimmel**, to access additional Self-Test Questions.

Questions

1. (a) How does the periodicity assumption affect an accountant's analysis of accounting transactions?
   (b) Explain the term fiscal year.

2. Identify and state two generally accepted accounting principles that relate to adjusting the accounts.

3. Sam Milner, a lawyer, accepts a legal engagement in March, performs the work in April, and is paid in May. If Milner's law firm prepares monthly financial statements, when should it recognize revenue from this engagement? Why?

4. In completing the engagement in Question 3, Milner pays no costs in March, $2,500 in April, and $2,200 in May (incurred in April). How much expense should the firm deduct from revenues in the month when it recognizes the revenue? Why?

5. "The historical cost principle of accounting requires adjusting entries." Do you agree? Explain.

6. Why may the financial information in an unadjusted trial balance not be up-to-date and complete?

7. Distinguish between the two categories of adjusting entries, and identify the types of adjustments applicable to each category.

8. What types of accounts does a company debit and credit in a prepaid expense adjusting entry?

9. "Depreciation is a process of valuation that results in the reporting of the fair value of the asset." Do you agree? Explain.

10. Explain the differences between depreciation expense and accumulated depreciation.

11. Remington Company purchased equipment for $15,000. By the current balance sheet date, the company had depreciated $7,000. Indicate the balance sheet presentation of the data.

12. What types of accounts are debited and credited in an unearned revenue adjusting entry?

13. Ace Technologies provides maintenance service for computers and office equipment for companies throughout the Northeast. The sales manager is elated because she closed a $300,000, three-year maintenance contract on December 29, 2013, two days before the company's year-end. "Now we will hit this year's net income target for sure," she crowed. The customer is required to pay $100,000 on December 29 (the day the deal was closed). Two more payments of $100,000 each are also required on December 29, 2014 and 2015. Discuss the effect that this event will have on the company's financial statements.

14. ValuMart, a large national retail chain, is nearing its fiscal year-end. It appears that the company is not going to hit its revenue and net income targets. The company's marketing manager, Steve Edmiston, suggests running a promotion selling $50 gift cards for $45. He believes that this would be very popular and would enable the company to meet its targets for revenue and net income. What do you think of this idea?

15. A company fails to recognize revenue for services performed but not yet received. Which of the following types of accounts are involved in the adjusting entry: (a) asset, (b) liability, (c) revenue, or (d) expense? For the accounts selected, indicate whether they would be debited or credited in the entry.

16. A company fails to recognize an expense incurred but not paid. Indicate which of the following types of accounts is debited and which is credited in the adjusting entry: (a) asset, (b) liability, (c) revenue, or (d) expense.

17. A company makes an accrued revenue adjusting entry for $780 and an accrued expense adjusting entry for $510. How much was net income understated or overstated prior to these entries? Explain.

18. On January 9, a company pays $6,200 for salaries, of which $1,100 was reported as Salaries and Wages Payable on December 31. Give the entry to record the payment.

19. For each of the following items before adjustment, indicate the type of adjusting entry—prepaid expense, unearned revenue, accrued revenue, and accrued expense—that is needed to correct the misstatement. If an item could result in more than one type of adjusting entry, indicate each of the types.
    (a) Assets are understated.
    (b) Liabilities are overstated.
    (c) Liabilities are understated.
    (d) Expenses are understated.
    (e) Assets are overstated.
    (f) Revenue is understated.

20. One-half of the adjusting entry is given below. Indicate the account title for the other half of the entry.
    (a) Salaries and Wages Expense is debited.
    (b) Depreciation Expense is debited.
    (c) Interest Payable is credited.
    (d) Supplies is credited.
    (e) Accounts Receivable is debited.
    (f) Unearned Service Revenue is debited.

21. "An adjusting entry may affect more than one balance sheet or income statement account." Do you agree? Why or why not?

22. Which balance sheet account provides evidence that Tootsie Roll records sales on an accrual basis rather than a cash basis? Explain.

23. Why is it possible to prepare financial statements directly from an adjusted trial balance?

24. ⊙━━⊙
 (a) What information do accrual-basis financial statements provide that cash-basis statements do not?
 (b) What information do cash-basis financial statements provide that accrual-basis statements do not?

25. What is the relationship, if any, between the amount shown in the adjusted trial balance column for an account and that account's ledger balance?

26. Identify the account(s) debited and credited in each of the four closing entries, assuming the company has net income for the year.

27. ◀━━ Some companies employ technologies that allow them to do a so-called "virtual close." This enables them to close their books nearly instantaneously any time during the year. What advantages does a "virtual close" provide?

28. Describe the nature of the Income Summary account, and identify the types of summary data that may be posted to this account.

29. What items are disclosed on a post-closing trial balance, and what is its purpose?

30. Which of these accounts would not appear in the post-closing trial balance? Interest Payable, Equipment, Depreciation Expense, Dividends, Unearned Service Revenue, Accumulated Depreciation— Equipment, and Service Revenue.

31. Indicate, in the sequence in which they are made, the three required steps in the accounting cycle that involve journalizing.

32. Identify, in the sequence in which they are prepared, the three trial balances that are required in the accounting cycle.

33. ◀━━ Explain the terms earnings management and quality of earnings.

34. ◀━━ Give examples of how companies manage earnings.

*35. What is the purpose of a worksheet?

*36. What is the basic form of a worksheet?

Brief Exercises

Identify impact of transactions on cash and net income.
(LO 2, 9), C

BE4-1 Transactions that affect earnings do not necessarily affect cash. Identify the effect, if any, that each of the following transactions would have upon cash and net income. The first transaction has been completed as an example.

	Cash	Net Income
(a) Purchased $100 of supplies for cash.	−$100	$ 0
(b) Recorded an adjusting entry to record use of $20 of the above supplies.		
(c) Made sales of $1,300, all on account.		
(d) Received $800 from customers in payment of their accounts.		
(e) Purchased equipment for cash, $2,500.		
(f) Recorded depreciation of building for period used, $600.		

Indicate why adjusting entries are needed.
(LO 3), C

BE4-2 The ledger of Berkman Company includes the following accounts. Explain why each account may require adjustment.
(a) Prepaid Insurance.
(b) Depreciation Expense.
(c) Unearned Service Revenue.
(d) Interest Payable.

Identify the major types of adjusting entries.
(LO 3), AN
⊙━━⊙

BE4-3 Molina Company accumulates the following adjustment data at December 31. Indicate (1) the type of adjustment (prepaid expense, accrued revenue, and so on) and (2) the status of the accounts before adjustment (overstated or understated).
(a) Supplies of $400 are on hand. Supplies account shows $1,600 balance.
(b) Services performed but unbilled total $700.
(c) Interest of $300 has accumulated on a note payable.
(d) Rent collected in advance totaling $1,100 has been earned.

Prepare adjusting entry for supplies.
(LO 4), AP

BE4-4 Foley Advertising Company's trial balance at December 31 shows Supplies $8,800 and Supplies Expense $0. On December 31, there are $1,100 of supplies on hand. Prepare the adjusting entry at December 31 and, using T-accounts, enter the balances in the accounts, post the adjusting entry, and indicate the adjusted balance in each account.

Prepare adjusting entry for depreciation.
(LO 4), AP

BE4-5 At the end of its first year, the trial balance of Boyer Company shows Equipment $22,000 and zero balances in Accumulated Depreciation—Equipment and Depreciation Expense. Depreciation for the year is estimated to be $2,750. Prepare the adjusting entry for depreciation at December 31, post the adjustments to T-accounts, and indicate the balance sheet presentation of the equipment at December 31.

BE4-6 On July 1, 2014, Seng Co. pays $12,400 to Nance Insurance Co. for a 2-year insurance contract. Both companies have fiscal years ending December 31. For Seng Co., journalize and post the entry on July 1 and the adjusting entry on December 31.

Prepare adjusting entry for prepaid expense.
(LO 4), AP

BE4-7 Using the data in BE4-6, journalize and post the entry on July 1 and the adjusting entry on December 31 for Nance Insurance Co. Nance uses the accounts Unearned Service Revenue and Service Revenue.

Prepare adjusting entry for unearned revenue.
(LO 4), AP

BE4-8 The bookkeeper for Beltran Company asks you to prepare the following accrual adjusting entries at December 31. Use these account titles: Service Revenue, Accounts Receivable, Interest Expense, Interest Payable, Salaries and Wages Expense, and Salaries and Wages Payable.
(a) Interest on notes payable of $300 is accrued.
(b) Services performed but unbilled totals $1,700.
(c) Salaries of $780 earned by employees have not been recorded.

Prepare adjusting entries for accruals.
(LO 5), AP

BE4-9 The trial balance of Goodwin Company includes the following balance sheet accounts. Identify the accounts that might require adjustment. For each account that requires adjustment, indicate (1) the type of adjusting entry (prepaid expenses, unearned revenues, accrued revenues, and accrued expenses) and (2) the related account in the adjusting entry.
(a) Accounts Receivable.
(b) Prepaid Insurance.
(c) Equipment.
(d) Accumulated Depreciation—Equipment.
(e) Notes Payable.
(f) Interest Payable.
(g) Unearned Service Revenue.

Analyze accounts in an adjusted trial balance.
(LO 6), AN

BE4-10 The adjusted trial balance of Ravine Corporation at December 31, 2014, includes the following accounts: Retained Earnings $17,200; Dividends $6,000; Service Revenue $32,000; Salaries and Wages Expense $14,000; Insurance Expense $1,800; Rent Expense $3,900; Supplies Expense $1,500; and Depreciation Expense $1,000. Prepare an income statement for the year.

Prepare an income statement from an adjusted trial balance.
(LO 6), AP

BE4-11 Partial adjusted trial balance data for Ravine Corporation are presented in BE4-10. The balance in Retained Earnings is the balance as of January 1. Prepare a retained earnings statement for the year assuming net income is $10,400.

Prepare a retained earnings statement from an adjusted trial balance.
(LO 6), AP

BE4-12 The following selected accounts appear in the adjusted trial balance for Baden Company. Indicate the financial statement on which each account would be reported.
(a) Accumulated Depreciation.
(b) Depreciation Expense.
(c) Retained Earnings (beginning).
(d) Dividends.
(e) Service Revenue.
(f) Supplies.
(g) Accounts Payable.

Identify financial statement for selected accounts.
(LO 6), K

BE4-13 Using the data in BE4-12, identify the accounts that would be included in a post-closing trial balance.

Identify post-closing trial balance accounts.
(LO 7), K

BE4-14 The income statement for the Four Oaks Golf Club Inc. for the month ended July 31 shows Service Revenue $16,000; Salaries and Wages Expense $8,400; Maintenance and Repairs Expense $2,500; and Income Tax Expense $1,000. The statement of retained earnings shows an opening balance for Retained Earnings of $20,000 and Dividends $1,300.
(a) Prepare closing journal entries.
(b) What is the ending balance in Retained Earnings?

Prepare and post closing entries.
(LO 7), AP

BE4-15 The required steps in the accounting cycle are listed in random order below. List the steps in proper sequence.
(a) Prepare a post-closing trial balance.
(b) Prepare an adjusted trial balance.
(c) Analyze business transactions.
(d) Prepare a trial balance.
(e) Journalize the transactions.
(f) Journalize and post closing entries.
(g) Prepare financial statements.
(h) Journalize and post adjusting entries.
(i) Post to ledger accounts.

List required steps in the accounting cycle sequence.
(LO 8), K

Exercises

Identify point of revenue recognition.
(LO 1), C

E4-1   The following independent situations require professional judgment for determining when to recognize revenue from the transactions.
(a) Southwest Airlines sells you an advance-purchase airline ticket in September for your flight home at Christmas.
(b) Ultimate Electronics sells you a home theater on a "no money down and full payment in three months" promotional deal.
(c) The Toronto Blue Jays sell season tickets online to games in the Skydome. Fans can purchase the tickets at any time, although the season doesn't officially begin until April. The major league baseball season runs from April through October.
(d) You borrow money in August from RBC Financial Group. The loan and the interest are repayable in full in November.
(e) In August, you order a sweater from Sears using its online catalog. The sweater arrives in September, which you charged to your Sears credit card. You receive and pay the Sears bill in October.

Instructions

Identify when revenue should be recognized in each of the above situations.

Identify accounting assumptions, principles, and constraint.
(LO 1), K

E4-2   These accounting concepts were discussed in this and previous chapters.

1. Economic entity assumption.
2. Expense recognition principle.
3. Monetary unit assumption.
4. Periodicity assumption.
5. Historical cost principle.
6. Materiality.
7. Full disclosure principle.
8. Going concern assumption.
9. Revenue recognition principle.
10. Cost constraint.

Instructions

Identify by number the accounting concept that describes each situation below. Do not use a number more than once.
_____ (a) Is the rationale for why plant assets are not reported at liquidation value. (Do not use the historical cost principle.)
_____ (b) Indicates that personal and business record-keeping should be separately maintained.
_____ (c) Ensures that all relevant financial information is reported.
_____ (d) Assumes that the dollar is the "measuring stick" used to report on financial performance.
_____ (e) Requires that accounting standards be followed for all items of **significant** size.
_____ (f) Separates financial information into time periods for reporting purposes.
_____ (g) Requires recognition of expenses in the same period as related revenues.
_____ (h) Indicates that fair value changes subsequent to purchase are not recorded in the accounts.

Identify the violated assumption, principle, or constraint.
(LO 1), C

E4-3   Here are some accounting reporting situations.
(a) Bonilla Company recognizes revenue at the end of the production cycle but before sale. The price of the product, as well as the amount that can be sold, is not certain.
(b) Barto Company is in its fifth year of operation and has yet to issue financial statements. (Do not use the full disclosure principle.)
(c) Lopez, Inc. is carrying inventory at its original cost of $100,000. Inventory has a fair value of $110,000.
(d) Ryno Hospital Supply Corporation reports only current assets and current liabilities on its balance sheet. Equipment and bonds payable are reported as current assets and current liabilities, respectively. Liquidation of the company is unlikely.
(e) Liu Company has inventory on hand that cost $400,000. Liu reports inventory on its balance sheet at its current fair value of $425,000.
(f) Sara Toney, president of Classic Music Company, bought a computer for her personal use. She paid for the computer by using company funds and debited the "Computers" account.

Instructions ▬▬▬▶

For each situation, list the assumption, principle, or constraint that has been violated, if any. (Some were presented in earlier chapters.) List only one answer for each situation.

E4-4 Your examination of the records of a company that follows the cash basis of accounting tells you that the company's reported cash-basis earnings in 2014 are $33,640. If this firm had followed accrual-basis accounting practices, it would have reported the following year-end balances.

Convert earnings from cash to accrual basis.
(LO 2, 4, 5, 9), **AP**

	2014	2013
Accounts receivable	$3,400	$2,800
Supplies on hand	1,300	1,460
Unpaid wages owed	2,000	2,400
Other unpaid expenses	1,400	1,100

Instructions

Determine the company's net earnings on an accrual basis for 2014. Show all your calculations in an orderly fashion.

E4-5 In its first year of operations, Ramirez Company recognized $28,000 in service revenue, $6,000 of which was on account and still outstanding at year-end. The remaining $22,000 was received in cash from customers.

Determine cash-basis and accrual-basis earnings.
(LO 2, 9), **AP**

The company incurred operating expenses of $15,800. Of these expenses, $12,000 were paid in cash; $3,800 was still owed on account at year-end. In addition, Ramirez prepaid $2,400 for insurance coverage that would not be used until the second year of operations.

Instructions

(a) Calculate the first year's net earnings under the cash basis of accounting, and calculate the first year's net earnings under the accrual basis of accounting.
(b) Which basis of accounting (cash or accrual) provides more useful information for decision-makers?

E4-6 Kaffen Company, a ski tuning and repair shop, opened on November 1, 2013. The company carefully kept track of all its cash receipts and cash payments. The following information is available at the end of the ski season, April 30, 2014.

Convert earnings from cash to accrual basis; prepare accrual-based financial statements.
(LO 2, 4, 5, 9), **AP**

	Cash Receipts	Cash Payments
Issuance of common shares	$20,000	
Payment to purchase repair shop equipment		$ 9,200
Rent payments		1,225
Newspaper advertising payment		375
Utility bill payments		970
Part-time helper's wage payments		2,600
Income tax payment		10,000
Cash receipts from ski and snowboard repair services	32,150	
Subtotals	52,150	24,370
Cash balance		27,780
Totals	$52,150	$52,150

The repair shop equipment was purchased on November 1 and has an estimated useful life of 4 years. The company rents space at a cost of $175 per month on a one-year lease. The lease contract requires payment of the first and last months' rent in advance, which was done. The part-time helper is owed $420 at April 30, 2014, for unpaid wages. At April 30, 2014, customers owe Kaffen Company $540 for services they have received but have not yet paid for.

Instructions

(a) Prepare an accrual-basis income statement for the 6 months ended April 30, 2014.
(b) Prepare the April 30, 2014, classified balance sheet.

E4-7 VidGam, a consulting firm, has just completed its first year of operations. The company's sales growth was explosive. To encourage clients to hire its services, VidGam

Identify differences between cash and accrual accounting.
(LO 2, 3, 9), **C**

offered 180-day financing—meaning its largest customers do not pay for nearly 6 months. Because VidGam is a new company, its equipment suppliers insist on being paid cash on delivery. Also, it had to pay up front for 2 years of insurance. At the end of the year, VidGam owed employees for one full month of salaries, but due to a cash shortfall, it promised to pay them the first week of next year.

Instructions

(a) Explain how cash and accrual accounting would differ for each of the events listed above and describe the proper accrual accounting.
(b) Assume that at the end of the year, VidGam reported a favorable net income, yet the company's management is concerned because the company is very short of cash. Explain how VidGam could have positive net income and yet run out of cash.

Identify types of adjustments and accounts before adjustment.

(LO 3, 4, 5), **AN**

E4-8 Kwun Company accumulates the following adjustment data at December 31.
(a) Services performed but unbilled totals $600.
(b) Store supplies of $160 are on hand. The supplies account shows a $1,900 balance.
(c) Utility expenses of $275 are unpaid.
(d) Services performed of $490 collected in advance.
(e) Salaries of $620 are unpaid.
(f) Prepaid insurance totaling $400 has expired.

Instructions

For each item, indicate (1) the type of adjustment (prepaid expense, unearned revenue, accrued revenue, or accrued expense) and (2) the status of the accounts before adjustment (overstated or understated).

Prepare adjusting entries from selected account data.

(LO 4, 5), **AP**

E4-9 The ledger of Beckett Rental Agency on March 31 of the current year includes the selected accounts below before adjusting entries have been prepared.

	Debit	Credit
Supplies	$ 3,000	
Prepaid Insurance	3,600	
Equipment	25,000	
Accumulated Depreciation—Equipment		$ 8,400
Notes Payable		20,000
Unearned Rent Revenue		12,400
Rent Revenue		60,000
Interest Expense	0	
Salaries and Wages Expense	14,000	

An analysis of the accounts shows the following.

1. The equipment depreciates $280 per month.
2. Half of the unearned rent revenue was earned during the quarter.
3. Interest of $400 is accrued on the notes payable.
4. Supplies on hand total $850.
5. Insurance expires at the rate of $400 per month.

Instructions

Prepare the adjusting entries at March 31, assuming that adjusting entries are made quarterly. Additional accounts are Depreciation Expense, Insurance Expense, Interest Payable, and Supplies Expense.

Prepare adjusting entries.

(LO 4, 5), **AP**

E4-10 Jim Haught, D.D.S., opened an incorporated dental practice on January 1, 2014. During the first month of operations, the following transactions occurred.

1. Performed services for patients who had dental plan insurance. At January 31, $760 of such services was completed but not yet billed to the insurance companies.
2. Utility expenses incurred but not paid prior to January 31 totaled $450.
3. Purchased dental equipment on January 1 for $80,000, paying $20,000 in cash and signing a $60,000, 3-year note payable (interest is paid each December 31). The equipment depreciates $400 per month. Interest is $500 per month.
4. Purchased a 1-year malpractice insurance policy on January 1 for $24,000.
5. Purchased $1,750 of dental supplies (recorded as increase to Supplies). On January 31, determined that $550 of supplies were on hand.

Instructions

Prepare the adjusting entries on January 31. Account titles are Accumulated Depreciation—Equipment, Depreciation Expense, Service Revenue, Accounts Receivable, Insurance Expense, Interest Expense, Interest Payable, Prepaid Insurance, Supplies, Supplies Expense, Utilities Expense, and Accounts Payable.

E4-11 The unadjusted trial balance for Sierra Corp. is shown in Illustration 4-4. Instead of the adjusting entries shown in the text at October 31, assume the following adjustment data.

Prepare adjusting entries.
(LO 4, 5), **AP**

1. Supplies on hand at October 31 total $500.
2. Expired insurance for the month is $100.
3. Depreciation for the month is $75.
4. As of October 31, services worth $800 related to the previously recorded unearned revenue had been performed.
5. Services performed but unbilled (and no receivable has been recorded) at October 31 are $280.
6. Interest expense accrued at October 31 is $70.
7. Accrued salaries at October 31 are $1,400.

Instructions

Prepare the adjusting entries for the items above.

E4-12 The income statement of Garska Co. for the month of July shows net income of $2,000 based on Service Revenue $5,500; Salaries and Wages Expense $2,100; Supplies Expense $900; and Utilities Expense $500. In reviewing the statement, you discover the following:

Prepare a correct income statement.
(LO 1, 4, 5, 6), **AP**

1. Insurance expired during July of $350 was omitted.
2. Supplies expense includes $200 of supplies that are still on hand at July 31.
3. Depreciation on equipment of $150 was omitted.
4. Accrued but unpaid wages at July 31 of $360 were not included.
5. Services performed but unrecorded totaled $700.

Instructions

Prepare a correct income statement for July 2014.

E4-13 This is a partial adjusted trial balance of Barone Company.

Analyze adjusted data.
(LO 1, 4, 5, 6), **AN**

BARONE COMPANY
Adjusted Trial Balance
January 31, 2014

	Debit	Credit
Supplies	$ 700	
Prepaid Insurance	1,560	
Salaries and Wages Payable		$1,060
Unearned Service Revenue		750
Supplies Expense	950	
Insurance Expense	520	
Salaries and Wages Expense	1,800	
Service Revenue		4,000

Instructions

Answer these questions, assuming the year begins January 1.
(a) If the amount in Supplies Expense is the January 31 adjusting entry, and $300 of supplies was purchased in January, what was the balance in Supplies on January 1?
(b) If the amount in Insurance Expense is the January 31 adjusting entry, and the original insurance premium was for 1 year, what was the total premium and when was the policy purchased?
(c) If $2,500 of salaries was paid in January, what was the balance in Salaries and Wages Payable at December 31, 2013?
(d) If $1,800 was received in January for services performed in January, what was the balance in Unearned Service Revenue at December 31, 2013?

Prepare closing entries.
(LO 7), **AP**

E4-14 A partial adjusted trial balance for Barone Company is given in E4-13.

Instructions
Prepare the closing entries at January 31, 2014.

*Journalize basic transactions
and adjusting entries.*
(LO 4, 5, 6), **AN**

E4-15 Selected accounts of Castle Company are shown here.

Supplies Expense			**Salaries and Wages Payable**		
July 31	750			July 31	1,000

Salaries and Wages Expense			**Accounts Receivable**		
July 15	1,000		July 31	500	
31	1,000				

Service Revenue			**Unearned Service Revenue**				
	July 14	3,800	July 31	900	July 1	Bal.	1,500
	31	900			20		600
	31	500					

Supplies				
July 1	Bal. 1,100	July 31	750	
10	200			

Instructions
After analyzing the accounts, journalize (a) the July transactions and (b) the adjusting entries that were made on July 31. (*Hint:* July transactions were for cash.)

*Prepare adjusting entries
from analysis of trial balance.*
(LO 4, 5, 6), **AP**

E4-16 The trial balances shown below are before and after adjustment for Bere Company at the end of its fiscal year.

BERE COMPANY
Trial Balance
August 31, 2014

	Before Adjustment		After Adjustment	
	Dr.	**Cr.**	**Dr.**	**Cr.**
Cash	$10,900		$10,900	
Accounts Receivable	8,800		9,400	
Supplies	2,500		500	
Prepaid Insurance	4,000		2,500	
Equipment	16,000		16,000	
Accumulated Depreciation—Equipment		$ 3,600		$ 4,800
Accounts Payable		5,800		5,800
Salaries and Wages Payable		0		1,100
Unearned Rent Revenue		1,800		800
Common Stock		10,000		10,000
Retained Earnings		5,500		5,500
Dividends	2,800		2,800	
Service Revenue		34,000		34,600
Rent Revenue		12,100		13,100
Salaries and Wages Expense	17,000		18,100	
Supplies Expense	0		2,000	
Rent Expense	10,800		10,800	
Insurance Expense	0		1,500	
Depreciation Expense	0		1,200	
	$72,800	$72,800	$75,700	$75,700

Instructions

Prepare the adjusting entries that were made.

E4-17 The adjusted trial balance for Bere Company is given in E4-16.

Instructions

Prepare the income and retained earnings statements for the year and the classified balance sheet at August 31.

E4-18 The adjusted trial balance for Bere Company is given in E4-16.

Instructions

Prepare the closing entries for the temporary accounts at August 31.

*Prepare financial statements
from adjusted trial balance.*
(LO 6), **AP**

Prepare closing entries.
(LO 7), **AP**

Challenge Exercises

Visit the book's companion website, at **www.wiley.com/college/kimmel**, and choose the Student Companion site to access Challenge Exercises.

Problems: Set A

P4-1A The following selected data are taken from the comparative financial statements of American Curling Club. The club prepares its financial statements using the accrual basis of accounting.

*Record transactions on
accrual basis; convert
revenue to cash receipts.*
(LO 2, 4, 9), **AP**

September 30	2014	2013
Accounts receivable for member dues	$ 15,000	$ 19,000
Unearned sales revenue	20,000	23,000
Service revenue (from member dues)	151,000	135,000

Dues are billed to members based upon their use of the club's facilities. Unearned sales revenues arise from the sale of tickets to events, such as the Skins Game.

Instructions

(*Hint:* You will find it helpful to use T-accounts to analyze the following data. You must analyze these data sequentially, as missing information must first be deduced before moving on. Post your journal entries as you progress, rather than waiting until the end.)

(a) Prepare journal entries for each of the following events that took place during 2014.

1. Dues receivable from members from 2013 were all collected during 2014.
2. During 2014, goods were provided for all of the unearned sales revenue at the end of 2013.
3. Additional tickets were sold for $44,000 cash during 2014; a portion of these were used by the purchasers during the year. The entire balance remaining in Unearned Sales Revenue relates to the upcoming Skins Game in 2014.
4. Dues for the 2013–2014 fiscal year were billed to members.
5. Dues receivable for 2014 (i.e., those billed in item (4) above) were partially collected.

(b) Determine the amount of cash received by American from the above transactions during the year ended September 30, 2014.

(b) Cash received $199,000

*Prepare adjusting entries,
post to ledger accounts, and
prepare adjusted trial
balance.*
(LO 4, 5, 6), **AP**

P4-2A Ken Lumas started his own consulting firm, Lumas Consulting, on June 1, 2014. The trial balance at June 30 is as follows.

LUMAS CONSULTING
Trial Balance
June 30, 2014

	Debit	Credit
Cash	$ 6,850	
Accounts Receivable	7,000	
Supplies	2,000	
Prepaid Insurance	2,880	
Equipment	15,000	
Accounts Payable		$ 4,230
Unearned Service Revenue		5,200
Common Stock		22,000
Service Revenue		8,300
Salaries and Wages Expense	4,000	
Rent Expense	2,000	
	$39,730	$39,730

In addition to those accounts listed on the trial balance, the chart of accounts for Lumas also contains the following accounts: Accumulated Depreciation—Equipment, Salaries and Wages Payable, Depreciation Expense, Insurance Expense, Utilities Expense, and Supplies Expense.

Other data:
1. Supplies on hand at June 30 total $720.
2. A utility bill for $180 has not been recorded and will not be paid until next month.
3. The insurance policy is for a year.
4. Services were performed for $4,100 of unearned service revenue by the end of the month.
5. Salaries of $1,250 are accrued at June 30.
6. The equipment has a 5-year life with no salvage value and is being depreciated at $250 per month for 60 months.
7. Invoices representing $3,900 of services performed during the month have not been recorded as of June 30.

Instructions
(a) Prepare the adjusting entries for the month of June.
(b) Post the adjusting entries to the ledger accounts. Enter the totals from the trial balance as beginning account balances. (Use T-accounts.)
(c) Prepare an adjusted trial balance at June 30, 2014.

(b) Service rev. $16,300

(c) Tot. trial balance $45,310

Prepare adjusting entries, adjusted trial balance, and financial statements.
(LO 4, 5, 6, 7), **AP**
GLS

P4-3A The Solo Hotel opened for business on May 1, 2014. Here is its trial balance before adjustment on May 31.

SOLO HOTEL
Trial Balance
May 31, 2014

	Debit	Credit
Cash	$ 2,500	
Supplies	2,600	
Prepaid Insurance	1,800	
Land	15,000	
Buildings	70,000	
Equipment	16,800	
Accounts Payable		$ 4,700
Unearned Rent Revenue		3,300
Mortgage Payable		36,000
Common Stock		60,000
Rent Revenue		9,000
Salaries and Wages Expense	3,000	
Utilities Expense	800	
Advertising Expense	500	
	$113,000	$113,000

Other data:

1. Insurance expires at the rate of $450 per month.
2. A count of supplies shows $1,050 of unused supplies on May 31.
3. Annual depreciation is $3,600 on the building and $3,000 on equipment.
4. The mortgage interest rate is 6%. (The mortgage was taken out on May 1.)
5. Unearned rent of $2,500 has been earned.
6. Salaries of $900 are accrued and unpaid at May 31.

Instructions
(a) Journalize the adjusting entries on May 31.
(b) Prepare a ledger using T-accounts. Enter the trial balance amounts and post the adjusting entries.
(c) Prepare an adjusted trial balance on May 31.
(d) Prepare an income statement and a retained earnings statement for the month of May and a classified balance sheet at May 31.
(e) Identify which accounts should be closed on May 31.

(c) Rent revenue $11,500
    Tot. adj. trial
        balance $114,630
(d) Net income $3,570

P4-4A   Wolf Creek Golf Inc. was organized on July 1, 2014. Quarterly financial statements are prepared. The trial balance and adjusted trial balance on September 30 are shown here.

Prepare adjusting entries and financial statements; identify accounts to be closed.

(LO 4, 5, 6, 7), **AP**

GLS

WOLF CREEK GOLF INC.
Trial Balance
September 30, 2014

	Unadjusted Dr.	Unadjusted Cr.	Adjusted Dr.	Adjusted Cr.
Cash	$ 6,700		$ 6,700	
Accounts Receivable	400		1,000	
Supplies	1,200		180	
Prepaid Rent	1,800		900	
Equipment	15,000		15,000	
Accumulated Depreciation—Equipment				$ 350
Notes Payable		$ 5,000		5,000
Accounts Payable		1,070		1,070
Salaries and Wages Payable				600
Interest Payable				50
Unearned Rent Revenue		1,000		800
Common Stock		14,000		14,000
Retained Earnings		0		0
Dividends	600		600	
Service Revenue		14,100		14,700
Rent Revenue		700		900
Salaries and Wages Expense	8,800		9,400	
Rent Expense	900		1,800	
Depreciation Expense			350	
Supplies Expense			1,020	
Utilities Expense	470		470	
Interest Expense			50	
	$35,870	$35,870	$37,470	$37,470

Instructions
(a) Journalize the adjusting entries that were made.
(b) Prepare an income statement and a retained earnings statement for the 3 months ending September 30 and a classified balance sheet at September 30.
(c) Identify which accounts should be closed on September 30.
(d) If the note bears interest at 12%, how many months has it been outstanding?

(b) Net income $2,510
    Tot. assets $23,430

P4-5A   A review of the ledger of Dempsey Company at December 31, 2014, produces these data pertaining to the preparation of annual adjusting entries.

Prepare adjusting entries.
(LO 4, 5), **AP**

1. Prepaid Insurance $15,200. The company has separate insurance policies on its buildings and its motor vehicles. Policy B4564 on the building was purchased on

July 1, 2013, for $9,600. The policy has a term of 3 years. Policy A2958 on the vehicles was purchased on January 1, 2014, for $7,200. This policy has a term of 18 months.

2. Rent revenue $84,000

2. Unearned Rent Revenue $429,000. The company began subleasing office space in its new building on November 1. At December 31, the company had the following rental contracts that are paid in full for the entire term of the lease.

Date	Term (in months)	Monthly Rent	Number of Leases
Nov. 1	9	$5,000	5
Dec. 1	6	$8,500	4

3. Notes Payable $40,000. This balance consists of a note for 6 months at an annual interest rate of 7%, dated October 1.
4. Salaries and Wages Payable $0. There are eight salaried employees. Salaries are paid every Friday for the current week. Five employees receive a salary of $600 each per week, and three employees earn $700 each per week. Assume December 31 is a Wednesday. Employees do not work weekends. All employees worked the last 3 days of December.

Instructions

Prepare the adjusting entries at December 31, 2014.

Prepare adjusting entries and a corrected income statement.

(LO 4, 5), **AN**

P4-6A Astromech Travel Court was organized on July 1, 2013, by Jessica Browning. Jessica is a good manager but a poor accountant. From the trial balance prepared by a part-time bookkeeper, Jessica prepared the following income statement for her fourth quarter, which ended June 30, 2014.

ASTROMECH TRAVEL COURT
Income Statement
For the Quarter Ended June 30, 2014

Revenues		
Rent revenue		$212,000
Operating expenses		
Advertising expense	$ 3,800	
Salaries and wages expense	80,500	
Utilities expense	900	
Depreciation expense	2,700	
Maintenance and repairs expense	4,300	
Total operating expenses		92,200
Net income		$119,800

Jessica suspected that something was wrong with the statement because net income had never exceeded $30,000 in any one quarter. Knowing that you are an experienced accountant, she asks you to review the income statement and other data.

You first look at the trial balance. In addition to the account balances reported above in the income statement, the trial balance contains the following additional selected balances at June 30, 2014.

Supplies	$ 8,200
Prepaid Insurance	14,400
Notes Payable	14,000

You then make inquiries and discover the following.
1. Travel court rental revenues include advanced rental payments received for summer occupancy, in the amount of $57,000.
2. There were $1,800 of supplies on hand at June 30.
3. Prepaid insurance resulted from the payment of a one-year policy on April 1, 2014.
4. The mail in July 2014 brought the following bills: advertising for the week of June 24, $110; repairs made June 18, $4,450; and utilities for the month of June, $215.
5. There are three employees who receive wages that total $300 per day. At June 30, four days' wages have been incurred but not paid.

6. The note payable is a 6% note dated May 1, 2014, and due on July 31, 2014.
7. Income tax of $13,400 for the quarter is due in July but has not yet been recorded.

Instructions
(a) Prepare any adjusting journal entries required at June 30, 2014.
(b) Prepare a correct income statement for the quarter ended June 30, 2014.
(c) Explain to Jessica the generally accepted accounting principles that she did not recognize in preparing her income statement and their effect on her results.

P4-7A On November 1, 2014, the following were the account balances of Rijo Equipment Repair.

(b) Net income $33,285

Journalize transactions and follow through accounting cycle to preparation of financial statements.

(LO 4, 5, 6), **AP**

GLS

	Debit		Credit
Cash	$ 2,790	Accumulated Depreciation—Equipment	$ 500
Accounts Receivable	2,910	Accounts Payable	2,300
Supplies	1,120	Unearned Service Revenue	400
Equipment	10,000	Salaries and Wages Payable	620
		Common Stock	10,000
		Retained Earnings	3,000
	$16,820		$16,820

During November, the following summary transactions were completed.

Nov. 8 Paid $1,220 for salaries due employees, of which $600 is for November and $620 is for October salaries payable.
  10 Received $1,800 cash from customers in payment of account.
  12 Received $3,700 cash for services performed in November.
  15 Purchased store equipment on account $3,600.
  17 Purchased supplies on account $1,300.
  20 Paid creditors $2,500 of accounts payable due.
  22 Paid November rent $480.
  25 Paid salaries $1,000.
  27 Performed services on account worth $900 and billed customers.
  29 Received $750 from customers for services to be provided in the future.

Adjustment data:
1. Supplies on hand are valued at $1,100.
2. Accrued salaries payable are $480.
3. Depreciation for the month is $250.
4. Services were performed to satisfy $500 of unearned service revenue.

Instructions
(a) Enter the November 1 balances in the ledger accounts. (Use T-accounts.)
(b) Journalize the November transactions.
(c) Post to the ledger accounts. Use Service Revenue, Depreciation Expense, Supplies Expense, Salaries and Wages Expense, and Rent Expense.
(d) Prepare a trial balance at November 30.
(e) Journalize and post adjusting entries.
(f) Prepare an adjusted trial balance.
(g) Prepare an income statement and a retained earnings statement for November and a classified balance sheet at November 30.

(f) Cash $3,840
   Tot. adj. trial
       balance $24,680
(g) Net income $970

Complete all steps in accounting cycle.
(LO 4, 5, 6, 7, 8), **AP**
GLS

P4-8A Mike Greenberg opened Clean Window Washing Inc. on July 1, 2014. During July, the following transactions were completed.

July 1 Issued 12,000 shares of common stock for $12,000 cash.
  1 Purchased used truck for $8,000, paying $2,000 cash and the balance on account.
  3 Purchased cleaning supplies for $900 on account.
  5 Paid $1,800 cash on a 1-year insurance policy effective July 1.
  12 Billed customers $3,700 for cleaning services.
  18 Paid $1,000 cash on amount owed on truck and $500 on amount owed on cleaning supplies.
  20 Paid $2,000 cash for employee salaries.

> 21 Collected $1,600 cash from customers billed on July 12.
>
> 25 Billed customers $2,500 for cleaning services.
>
> 31 Paid $290 for maintenance of the truck during month.
>
> 31 Declared and paid $600 cash dividend.

The chart of accounts for Clean Window Washing contains the following accounts: Cash, Accounts Receivable, Supplies, Prepaid Insurance, Equipment, Accumulated Depreciation—Equipment, Accounts Payable, Salaries and Wages Payable, Common Stock, Retained Earnings, Dividends, Income Summary, Service Revenue, Maintenance and Repairs Expense, Supplies Expense, Depreciation Expense, Insurance Expense, Salaries and Wages Expense.

Instructions

(a) Journalize the July transactions.

(b) Post to the ledger accounts. (Use T-accounts.)

(c) Prepare a trial balance at July 31.

(d) Journalize the following adjustments.

(1) Services performed but unbilled and uncollected at July 31 were $1,700.

(2) Depreciation on equipment for the month was $180.

(3) One-twelfth of the insurance expired.

(4) An inventory count shows $320 of cleaning supplies on hand at July 31.

(5) Accrued but unpaid employee salaries were $400.

(e) Post adjusting entries to the T-accounts.

(f) Cash $5,410   (f) Prepare an adjusted trial balance.

(g) Tot. assets $21,500   (g) Prepare the income statement and a retained earnings statement for July and a classified balance sheet at July 31.

(h) Journalize and post closing entries and complete the closing process.

(i) Prepare a post-closing trial balance at July 31.

Problems: Set B

Visit the book's companion website, at **www.wiley.com/college/kimmel**, and choose the Student Companion site to access Problem Set B.

Broadening Your Perspective

Financial Reporting and Analysis

FINANCIAL REPORTING PROBLEM: *Tootsie Roll Industries, Inc.*

BYP4-1 The financial statements of Tootsie Roll are presented in Appendix A at the end of this textbook.

Instructions

(a) Using the consolidated income statement and balance sheet, identify items that may result in adjusting entries for deferrals.

(b) Using the consolidated income statement, identify two items that may result in adjusting entries for accruals.

(c) What was the amount of depreciation expense for 2011 and 2010? (You will need to examine the notes to the financial statements or the statement of cash flows.) Where was accumulated depreciation reported?

(d) What was the cash paid for income taxes during 2011, reported at the bottom of the consolidated statement of cash flows? What was income tax expense (provision for income taxes) for 2011?

COMPARATIVE ANALYSIS PROBLEM: *Tootsie Roll vs. Hershey*

BYP4-2   The financial statements of The Hershey Company are presented in Appendix B, following the financial statements for Tootsie Roll in Appendix A.

Instructions
(a) Identify two accounts on Hershey's balance sheet that provide evidence that Hershey uses accrual accounting. In each case, identify the income statement account that would be affected by the adjustment process.
(b) Identify two accounts on Tootsie Roll's balance sheet that provide evidence that Tootsie Roll uses accrual accounting (different from the two you listed for Hershey). In each case, identify the income statement account that would be affected by the adjustment process.

RESEARCH CASE

BYP4-3   The February 13, 2010, issue of the *Wall Street Journal* includes an article by Scott Thurm entitled "For Some Firms, a Case of 'Quadrophobia'."

Instructions
Read the article and answer the following.
(a) What method did the study's authors use to determine that companies were "managing" their earnings per share calculation?
(b) For the average company in the study, how much would the company have to boost earnings in order to increase earnings per share by 1/10 of a cent?
(c) What examples did the authors cite of accounting adjustments that companies can make to boost net income enough that they can round up to the next highest cent? Why aren't these methods of adjustment considered illegal?
(d) What is an earnings restatement? What relationship did the authors identify about companies that restate earnings?
(e) What incentive do companies have to round up their earnings per share to the next highest cent?

INTERPRETING FINANCIAL STATEMENTS

BYP4-4   Laser Recording Systems, founded in 1981, produces disks for use in the home market. The following is an excerpt from Laser Recording Systems' financial statements (all dollars in thousands).

LASER RECORDING SYSTEMS
Management Discussion

Accrued liabilities increased to $1,642 at January 31, from $138 at the end of the previous fiscal year. Compensation and related accruals increased $195 due primarily to increases in accruals for severance, vacation, commissions, and relocation expenses. Accrued professional services increased by $137 primarily as a result of legal expenses related to several outstanding contractual disputes. Other expenses increased $35, of which $18 was for interest payable.

Instructions
(a) Can you tell from the discussion whether Laser Recording Systems has prepaid its legal expenses and is now making an adjustment to the asset account Prepaid Legal Expenses, or whether the company is handling the legal expense via an accrued expense adjustment?
(b) Identify each of the adjustments Laser Recording Systems is discussing as one of the four types of possible adjustments discussed in the chapter. How is net income ultimately affected by each of the adjustments?
(c) What journal entry did Laser Recording make to record the accrued interest?

REAL-WORLD FOCUS

BYP4-5 *Purpose:* To learn about the functions of the Securities and Exchange Commission (SEC).

Address: **www.sec.gov/about/whatwedo.shtml**, or go to **www.wiley.com/college/kimmel**

Instructions
Use the information in this site to answer the following questions.
(a) What event spurred the creation of the SEC? Why was the SEC created?
(b) What are the five divisions of the SEC? Briefly describe the purpose of each.
(c) What are the responsibilities of the chief accountant?

Critical Thinking

DECISION-MAKING ACROSS THE ORGANIZATION

BYP4-6 Lincoln Park was organized on April 1, 2013, by Judy Tercek. Judy is a good manager but a poor accountant. From the trial balance prepared by a part-time bookkeeper, Judy prepared the following income statement for the quarter that ended March 31, 2014.

LINCOLN PARK
Income Statement
For the Quarter Ended March 31, 2014

Revenues		
Rent revenue		$83,000
Operating expenses		
Advertising expense	$ 4,200	
Salaries and wages expense	27,600	
Utilities expense	1,500	
Depreciation expense	800	
Maintenance and repairs expense	2,800	
Total operating expenses		36,900
Net income		$46,100

Judy knew that something was wrong with the statement because net income had never exceeded $20,000 in any one quarter. Knowing that you are an experienced accountant, she asks you to review the income statement and other data.

You first look at the trial balance. In addition to the account balances reported in the income statement, the ledger contains these selected balances at March 31, 2014.

Supplies	$ 4,500
Prepaid Insurance	7,200
Notes Payable	20,000

You then make inquiries and discover the following.

1. Rent revenue includes advanced rentals for summer-month occupancy, $21,000.
2. There were $600 of supplies on hand at March 31.
3. Prepaid insurance resulted from the payment of a 1-year policy on January 1, 2014.
4. The mail on April 1, 2014, brought the following bills: advertising for week of March 24, $110; repairs made March 10, $1,040; and utilities $240.
5. There are four employees who receive wages totaling $290 per day. At March 31, 3 days' wages have been incurred but not paid.
6. The note payable is a 3-month, 7% note dated January 1, 2014.

Instructions
With the class divided into groups, answer the following.
(a) Prepare a correct income statement for the quarter ended March 31, 2014.
(b) Explain to Judy the generally accepted accounting principles that she did not follow in preparing her income statement and their effect on her results.

COMMUNICATION ACTIVITY

BYP4-7 On numerous occasions, proposals have surfaced to put the federal government on the accrual basis of accounting. This is no small issue because if this basis were used, it would mean that billions in unrecorded liabilities would have to be booked and the federal deficit would increase substantially.

Instructions
(a) What is the difference between accrual-basis accounting and cash-basis accounting?
(b) Comment on why politicians prefer a cash-basis accounting system over an accrual-basis system.
(c) Write a letter to your senators explaining why you think the federal government should adopt the accrual basis of accounting.

ETHICS CASE

BYP4-8 Eaton Company is a pesticide manufacturer. Its sales declined greatly this year due to the passage of legislation outlawing the sale of several of Eaton's chemical pesticides. During the coming year, Eaton will have environmentally safe and competitive replacement chemicals to replace these discontinued products. Sales in the next year are expected to greatly exceed those of any prior year. Therefore, the decline in this year's sales and profits appears to be a one-year aberration.

Even so, the company president believes that a large dip in the current year's profits could cause a significant drop in the market price of Eaton's stock and make it a takeover target. To avoid this possibility, he urges Mark Trane, controller, to accrue every possible revenue and to defer as many expenses as possible in making this period's year-end adjusting entries. The president says to Mark, "We need the revenues this year, and next year we can easily absorb expenses deferred from this year. We can't let our stock price be hammered down!" Mark didn't get around to recording the adjusting entries until January 17, but he dated the entries December 31 as if they were recorded then. Mark also made every effort to comply with the president's request.

Instructions
(a) Who are the stakeholders in this situation?
(b) What are the ethical considerations of the president's request and Mark's dating the adjusting entries December 31?
(c) Can Mark accrue revenues and defer expenses and still be ethical?

ALL ABOUT YOU

BYP4-9 Companies prepare balance sheets in order to know their financial position at a specific point in time. This enables them to make a comparison to their position at previous points in time and gives them a basis for planning for the future. In order to evaluate *your* financial position, you can prepare a personal balance sheet. Assume that you have compiled the following information regarding your finances. (*Hint:* Some of the items might not be used in your personal balance sheet.)

Amount owed on student loan balance (long-term)	$5,000
Balance in checking account	1,200
Certificate of deposit (6-month)	3,000
Annual earnings from part-time job	11,300
Automobile	7,000
Balance on automobile loan (current portion)	1,500
Balance on automobile loan (long-term portion)	4,000
Home computer	800
Amount owed to you by younger brother	300
Balance in money market account	1,800
Annual tuition	6,400
Video and stereo equipment	1,250
Balance owed on credit card (current portion)	150
Balance owed on credit card (long-term portion)	1,650

Instructions

Prepare a personal balance sheet using the format you have learned for a classified balance sheet for a company. For the equity account, use M. Y. Own, Capital.

FASB CODIFICATION ACTIVITY

BYP4-10 If your school has a subscription to the FASB Codification, go to **http://aaahq.org/ascLogin.cfm** to log in and prepare responses to the following.

Instructions

Access the glossary ("Master Glossary") to answer the following.
(a) What is the definition of revenue?
(b) What is the definition of compensation?

Answers to Insight and Accounting Across the Organization Questions

p. 138 Reporting Revenue Accurately Q: In the past, why was it argued that Apple should spread the recognition of iPhone revenue over a two-year period, rather than recording it upfront? **A:** Apple promises to provide software updates over the life of the phone's use. Because this represents an unfulfilled performance obligation, it was argued that Apple should spread its revenue recognition over a two-year estimated life of the phone.

p. 139 Cashing In on Accrual Accounting Q: Accrual accounting is often considered superior to cash accounting. Why, then, were some people critical of China's use of accrual accounting in this instance? **A:** In this case, some people were critical because, in general, China uses cash accounting. By switching to accrual accounting for this transaction, China was not being consistent in its accounting practices. Lack of consistency reduces the transparency and usefulness of accounting information.

p. 146 Turning Gift Cards into Revenue Q: Suppose that Robert Jones purchases a $100 gift card at Best Buy on December 24, 2013, and gives it to his wife, Mary Jones, on December 25, 2013. On January 3, 2014, Mary uses the card to purchase $100 worth of CDs. When do you think Best Buy should recognize revenue and why? **A:** According to the revenue recognition principle, companies should recognize revenue when the performance obligation is satisfied. In this case, revenue results when Best Buy provides the goods. Thus, when Best Buy receives cash in exchange for the gift card on December 24, 2013, it should recognize a liability, Unearned Sales Revenue, for $100. On January 3, 2014, when Mary Jones exchanges the card for merchandise, Best Buy should recognize revenue and eliminate $100 from the balance in the Unearned Sales Revenue account.

p. 151 Got Junk? Q: What accounting issue might this cause for companies? **A:** The balance sheet should provide a fair representation of what a company owns and what it owes. If significant obligations of the company are not reported on the balance sheet, the company's net worth (its equity) will be overstated. While it is true that it is not possible to estimate the **exact** amount of future environmental cleanup costs, it is becoming clear that companies will be held accountable. Therefore, it doesn't seem reasonable to not accrue for environmental costs. Recognition of these liabilities provides a more accurate picture of the company's financial position. It also has the potential to improve the environment. As companies are forced to report these amounts on their financial statements, they will start to look for more effective and efficient means to reduce toxic waste and therefore reduce their costs.

p. 157 Cooking the Books? Q: What motivates sales executives and finance and accounting executives to participate in activities that result in inaccurate reporting of revenues? **A:** Sales executives typically receive bonuses based on their ability to meet quarterly sales targets. In addition, they often face the possibility of losing their jobs if they miss those targets. Executives in accounting and finance are very aware of the earnings targets of Wall Street analysts and investors. If they fail to meet these targets, the company's stock price will fall. As a result of these pressures, executives sometimes knowingly engage in unethical efforts to misstate revenues. As a result of the Sarbanes-Oxley Act, the penalties for such behavior are now much more severe.

Answers to Self-Test Questions

1. c **2.** a **3.** d **4.** d **5.** d **6.** c ($1,350 − $600 = $750) **7.** a **8.** c **9.** c **10.** b **11.** b
12. c **13.** a **14.** a **15.** d

A Look at IFRS

It is often difficult for companies to determine in what time period they should report particular revenues and expenses. Both the IASB and FASB are working on a joint project to develop a common conceptual framework, as well as a revenue recognition project, that will enable companies to better use the same principles to record transactions consistently over time.

LEARNING OBJECTIVE   **11**

Compare the procedures for revenue recognition under GAAP and IFRS.

KEY POINTS

- In this chapter, you learned accrual-basis accounting applied under GAAP. Companies applying IFRS also use accrual-basis accounting to ensure that they record transactions that change a company's financial statements in the period in which events occur.
- Similar to GAAP, cash-basis accounting is not in accordance with IFRS.
- IFRS also divides the economic life of companies into artificial time periods. Under both GAAP and IFRS, this is referred to as the **periodicity assumption**.
- IFRS requires that companies present a complete set of financial statements, including comparative information annually.
- GAAP has more than 100 rules dealing with revenue recognition. Many of these rules are industry-specific. In contrast, revenue recognition under IFRS is determined primarily by a single standard. Despite this large disparity in the amount of detailed guidance devoted to revenue recognition, the **general** revenue recognition principles required by GAAP that are used in this textbook are similar to those under IFRS.
- Revenue recognition fraud is a major issue in U.S. financial reporting. The same situation occurs in other countries, as evidenced by revenue recognition breakdowns at Dutch software company Baan NV, Japanese electronics giant NEC, and Dutch grocer AHold NV.
- A specific standard exists for revenue recognition under IFRS *(IAS 18)*. In general, the standard is based on the **probability that the economic benefits associated with the transaction will flow to the company** selling the goods, providing the service, or receiving investment income. In addition, the revenues and costs **must be capable of being measured reliably**.
- Under IFRS, revaluation of items such as land and buildings is permitted. IFRS allows depreciation based on revaluation of assets, which is not permitted under GAAP.
- The terminology used for revenues and gains, and expenses and losses, differs somewhat between IFRS and GAAP. For example, income under IFRS is defined as:

  > Increases in economic benefits during the accounting period in the form of inflows or enhancements of assets or decreases of liabilities that result in increases in equity, other than those relating to contributions from shareholders.

  Income includes **both** revenues, which arise during the normal course of operating activities, and gains, which arise from activities outside of the normal sales of goods and services. The term **income** is not used this way under GAAP. Instead, under GAAP income refers to the net difference between revenues and expenses. Expenses under IFRS are defined as:

  > Decreases in economic benefits during the accounting period in the form of outflows or depletions of assets or incurrences of liabilities that result in decreases in equity other than those relating to distributions to shareholders.

  Note that under IFRS expenses include both those costs incurred in the normal course of operations, as well as losses that are not part of normal operations. This is in contrast to GAAP, which defines each separately.
- The procedures of the closing process are applicable to all companies whether they are using IFRS or GAAP.

LOOKING TO THE FUTURE

The IASB and FASB are now involved in a joint project on revenue recognition. The purpose of this project is to develop comprehensive guidance on when to recognize revenue. Presently, the Boards are considering an approach that focuses on changes in assets and liabilities (rather than on earned and realized) as the basis for revenue recognition. It is hoped that this approach will lead to more consistent accounting in this area. For more on this topic, see **www.fasb.org/project/ revenue_recognition.shtml**.

IFRS PRACTICE

IFRS SELF-TEST QUESTIONS

1. GAAP:
   (a) provides very detailed, industry-specific guidance on revenue recognition, compared to the general guidance provided by IFRS.
   (b) provides only general guidance on revenue recognition, compared to the detailed guidance provided by IFRS.
   (c) allows revenue to be recognized when a customer makes an order.
   (d) requires that revenue not be recognized until cash is received.
2. Which of the following statements is **false**?
   (a) IFRS employs the periodicity assumption.
   (b) IFRS employs accrual accounting.
   (c) IFRS requires that revenues and costs must be capable of being measured reliably.
   (d) IFRS uses the cash basis of accounting.
3. As a result of the revenue recognition project being undertaken by the FASB and IASB:
   (a) revenue recognition will place more emphasis on when revenue is earned.
   (b) revenue recognition will place more emphasis on when revenue is realized.
   (c) revenue recognition will place more emphasis on when changes occur in assets and liabilities.
   (d) revenue will no longer be recorded unless cash has been received.
4. Which of the following is **false**?
   (a) Under IFRS, the term **income** describes both revenues and gains.
   (b) Under IFRS, the term **expenses** includes losses.
   (c) Under IFRS, firms do not engage in the closing process.
   (d) IFRS has fewer standards than GAAP that address revenue recognition.
5. Accrual-basis accounting:
   (a) is optional under IFRS.
   (b) results in companies recording transactions that change a company's financial statements in the period in which events occur.
   (c) will likely be eliminated as a result of the IASB/FASB joint project on revenue recognition.
   (d) is not consistent with the IASB conceptual framework.

IFRS CONCEPTS AND APPLICATION

IFRS4-1 Compare and contrast the rules regarding revenue recognition under IFRS versus GAAP.

IFRS4-2 Under IFRS, do the definitions of revenues and expenses include gains and losses? Explain.

INTERNATIONAL FINANCIAL REPORTING PROBLEM: *Zetar plc*

IFRS4-3 The financial statements of Zetar plc are presented in Appendix C. The company's complete annual report, including the notes to its financial statements, is available in the Investors section at **www.zetarplc.com**. Visit Zetar's corporate website and answer the following questions from Zetar's 2011 annual report.

(a) From the notes to the financial statements, how does the company determine the amount of revenue to record at the time of a sale?

(b) From the notes to the financial statements, how does the company determine whether a sale has occurred?

(c) Using the consolidated income statement and consolidated statement of financial position, identify items that may result in adjusting entries for deferrals.

(d) Using the consolidated income statement, identify two items that may result in adjusting entries for accruals.

Answers to IFRS Self-Test Questions

1. a   **2.** d   **3.** c   **4.** c   **5.** b

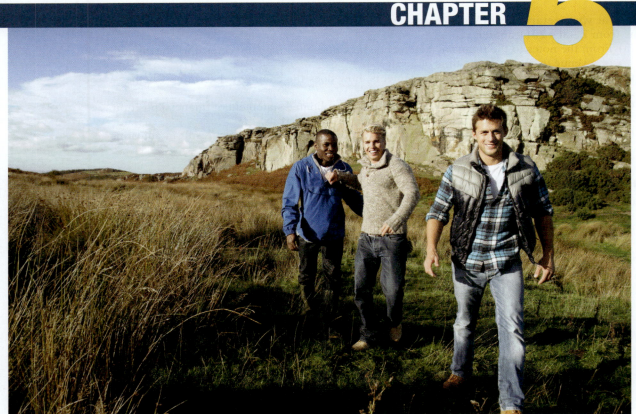

CHAPTER 5

MERCHANDISING OPERATIONS AND THE MULTIPLE-STEP INCOME STATEMENT

© omgimages/iStockphoto

LEARNING OBJECTIVES

After studying this chapter, you should be able to:

1 Identify the differences between a service company and a merchandising company.

2 Explain the recording of purchases under a perpetual inventory system.

3 Explain the recording of sales revenues under a perpetual inventory system.

4 Distinguish between a single-step and a multiple-step income statement.

5 Determine cost of goods sold under a periodic system.

6 Explain the factors affecting profitability.

7 Identify a quality of earnings indicator.

Have you ever shopped for outdoor gear at an REI (Recreational Equipment Incorporated) store? If so, you might have been surprised if a sales-clerk asked if you were a member. A member? What do you mean a member? You soon realize that REI might not be your typical store. In fact, there's a lot about REI that makes it different.

REI is a consumer cooperative, or "co-op" for short. To figure out what that means, consider this quote from the company's annual report:

> As a cooperative, the Company is owned by its members. Each member is entitled to one vote in the election of the Company's Board of Directors. Since January 1, 2008, the nonrefundable, nontransferable, one-time membership fee has been $20 dollars. As of December 31, 2010, there were approximately 10.8 million members.

Voting rights? Now that's something you don't get from shopping at Wal-Mart. REI members get other benefits as well, including sharing in the company's profits through a dividend at the end of the year, which can be used for purchases at REI stores during the next two years. The more you spend, the bigger your dividend.

Since REI is a co-op, you might wonder whether management's incentives might be a lit-tle different. For example, is management still concerned about making a profit? The answer is yes, as it ensures the long-term viability of the company. At the same time, REI's members want the company to be run efficiently, so that prices remain low. In order for its members to evaluate just how well management is doing, REI publishes an audited annual report, just like publicly traded companies do. So, while profit maximization might not be the ultimate goal for REI, the accounting and reporting issues are similar to those of a typ-ical corporation.

BUY NOW, VOTE LATER

How well is this business model working for REI? Well, it has consistently been rated as one of the best places to work in the United States. It was ranked 8th on *Fortune*'s 2012 list. Also, REI had sustainable business practices long before social responsibility became popular at other companies. The CEO's Stewardship Report states "we reduced the absolute amount of energy we use despite opening four new stores and growing our business; we grew the amount of FSC-certified paper we use to 58.4 percent of our total paper footprint—including our cash register receipt paper; we facilitated 2.2 million volunteer hours and we provided $3.7 million to more than 330 conservation and recreation nonprofits."

So, while REI, like other retailers, closely monitors its financial results, it also strives to succeed in other areas. And, with over 10 million votes at stake, REI's management knows that it has to deliver.

INSIDE CHAPTER 5 . . .

- **Morrow Snowboards Improves Its Stock Appeal**
- **Should Costco Change Its Return Policy?**
- **Disclosing More Details**
- **Selling Green**

PREVIEW OF CHAPTER 5

Merchandising is one of the largest and most influential industries in the United States. It is likely that a number of you will work for a merchandiser. Therefore, understanding the financial statements of merchandising companies is important. In this chapter, you will learn the basics about reporting merchandising transactions. In addition, you will learn how to prepare and analyze a commonly used form of the income statement—the multiple-step income statement. The content and organization of the chapter are as follows.

Merchandising Operations

Merchandising Operations	Recording Purchases of Merchandise	Recording Sales of Merchandise	Income Statement Presentation	Evaluating Profitability
• Operating cycles • Flow of costs—perpetual and periodic inventory systems	• Freight costs • Purchase returns and allowances • Purchase discounts • Summary of purchasing transactions	• Sales returns and allowances • Sales discounts	• Sales revenues • Gross profit • Operating expenses • Nonoperating activities • Determining cost of goods sold—periodic system	• Gross profit rate • Profit margin

Merchandising Operations

LEARNING OBJECTIVE 1

Identify the differences between a service company and a merchandising company.

REI, Wal-Mart, and Amazon.com are called merchandising companies because they buy and sell merchandise rather than perform services as their primary source of revenue. Merchandising companies that purchase and sell directly to consumers are called **retailers**. Merchandising companies that sell to retailers are known as **wholesalers**. For example, retailer Walgreens might buy goods from wholesaler McKesson; retailer Office Depot might buy office supplies from wholesaler United Stationers. The primary source of revenues for merchandising companies is the sale of merchandise, often referred to simply as **sales revenue** or **sales**. A merchandising company has two categories of expenses: the cost of goods sold and operating expenses.

The **cost of goods sold** is the total cost of merchandise sold during the period. This expense is directly related to the revenue recognized from the sale of goods. Illustration 5-1 shows the income measurement process for a merchandising

Illustration 5-1 Income measurement process for a merchandising company

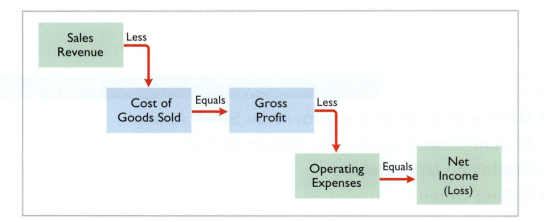

company. The items in the two blue boxes are unique to a merchandising company; they are not used by a service company.

OPERATING CYCLES

The operating cycle of a merchandising company ordinarily is longer than that of a service company. The purchase of inventory and its eventual sale lengthen the cycle. Illustration 5-2 contrasts the operating cycles of service and merchandising companies. Note that the added asset account for a merchandising company is the Inventory account.

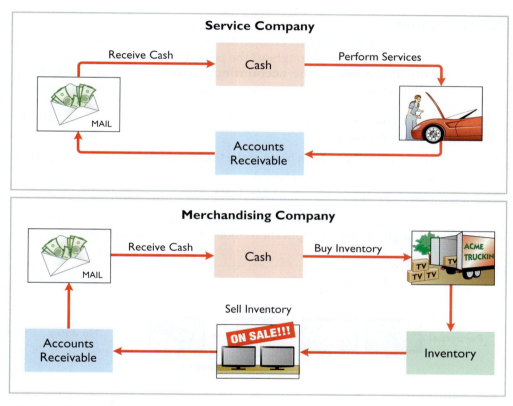

Illustration 5-2 Operating cycles for a service company and a merchandising company

FLOW OF COSTS

The flow of costs for a merchandising company is as follows. Beginning inventory plus the cost of goods purchased is the cost of goods available for sale. As goods are sold, they are assigned to cost of goods sold. Those goods that are not sold by the end of the accounting period represent ending inventory. Illustration 5-3 describes these relationships. Companies use one of two systems to account for inventory: a **perpetual inventory system** or a **periodic inventory system**.

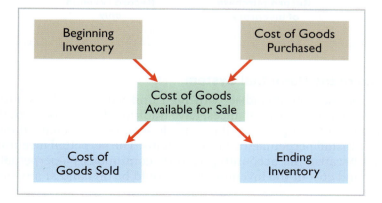

Illustration 5-3 Flow of costs

Perpetual System

In a **perpetual inventory system**, companies maintain detailed records of the cost of each inventory purchase and sale. These records continuously—perpetually—show the inventory that should be on hand for every item. For example, a Ford dealership has separate inventory records for each automobile, truck, and van on its lot and showroom floor. Similarly, a grocery store uses bar codes and optical scanners to keep a daily running record of every box of cereal and every jar of jelly that it buys and sells. Under a perpetual inventory system, a company determines the cost of goods sold **each time a sale occurs**.

Periodic System

In a **periodic inventory system**, companies do not keep detailed inventory records of the goods on hand throughout the period. They determine the cost of goods sold **only at the end of the accounting period**—that is, periodically. At that point, the company takes a physical inventory count to determine the cost of goods on hand.

To determine the cost of goods sold under a periodic inventory system, the following steps are necessary:

1. Determine the cost of goods on hand at the beginning of the accounting period.
2. Add to it the cost of goods purchased.
3. Subtract the cost of goods on hand at the end of the accounting period.

Illustration 5-4 graphically compares the sequence of activities and the timing of the cost of goods sold computation under the two inventory systems.

Illustration 5-4 Comparing perpetual and periodic inventory systems

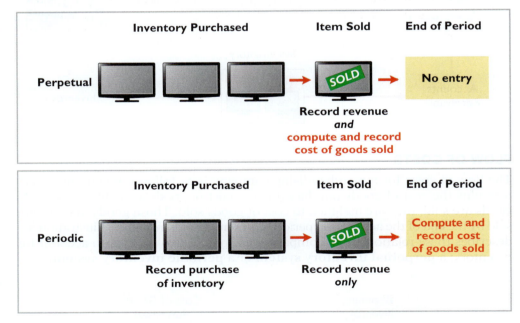

Advantages of the Perpetual System

Companies that sell merchandise with high unit values, such as automobiles, furniture, and major home appliances, have traditionally used perpetual systems. The growing use of computers and electronic scanners has enabled many more companies to install perpetual inventory systems. The perpetual inventory system is so named because the accounting records continuously—perpetually—show the quantity and cost of the inventory that should be on hand at any time.

A perpetual inventory system provides better control over inventories than a periodic system. Since the inventory records show the quantities that should be on hand, the company can count the goods at any time to see whether the amount of goods actually on hand agrees with the inventory records. If shortages are uncovered, the company can investigate immediately. Although a perpetual inventory system requires additional clerical work and additional cost to maintain inventory records, a computerized system can minimize this cost. Much of Amazon.com's success is attributed to its sophisticated inventory system.

Some businesses find it either unnecessary or uneconomical to invest in a sophisticated, computerized perpetual inventory system such as Amazon's. However, many small merchandising businesses find that basic computerized accounting packages provide some of the essential benefits of a perpetual inventory system. Yet, managers of some small businesses still find that they can control their merchandise and manage day-to-day operations using a periodic inventory system.

Because of the widespread use of the perpetual inventory system, we illustrate it in this chapter. An appendix to this chapter describes the journal entries for the periodic system.

Investor Insight

Morrow Snowboards Improves Its Stock Appeal

Investors are often eager to invest in a company that has a hot new product. However, when snowboard maker Morrow Snowboards, Inc., issued shares of stock to the public for the first time, some investors expressed reluctance to invest in Morrow because of a number of accounting control problems. To reduce investor concerns, Morrow implemented a perpetual inventory system to improve its control over inventory. In addition, it stated that it would perform a physical inventory count every quarter until it felt that the perpetual inventory system was reliable.

? If a perpetual system keeps track of inventory on a daily basis, why do companies ever need to do a physical count? (Answers in *Broadening Your Perspective*.)

Recording Purchases of Merchandise

Companies may purchase inventory for cash or on account (credit). They normally record purchases when they receive the goods from the seller. Every purchase should be supported by business documents that provide written evidence of the transaction. Each cash purchase should be supported by a canceled check or a cash register receipt indicating the items purchased and amounts paid. Companies record cash purchases by an increase (debit) in Inventory and a decrease (credit) in Cash.

Each purchase should be supported by a **purchase invoice**, which indicates the total purchase price and other relevant information. However, the purchaser does not prepare a separate purchase invoice. Instead, the purchaser uses as a purchase invoice the copy of the sales invoice sent by the seller. In Illustration 5-5, for example, Sauk Stereo (the buyer) uses as a purchase invoice the sales invoice prepared by PW Audio Supply, Inc. (the seller).

The associated entry for Sauk Stereo for the invoice from PW Audio Supply increases (debits) Inventory and increases (credits) Accounts Payable.

LEARNING OBJECTIVE	2
Explain the recording of purchases under a perpetual inventory system.	

May	4	Inventory	3,800	
		Accounts Payable		3,800
		(To record goods purchased on account		
		from PW Audio Supply)		

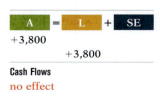

A	=	L	+	SE
+3,800				
				+3,800

Cash Flows
no effect

Illustration 5-5 Sales invoice used as purchase invoice by Sauk Stereo

Margin Note To better understand the contents of this invoice, identify these items:
1. Seller
2. Invoice date
3. Purchaser
4. Salesperson
5. Credit terms
6. Freight terms
7. Goods sold: catalog number, description, quantity, price per unit
8. Total invoice amount

INVOICE NO. 731

PW AUDIO SUPPLY, INC.
27 CIRCLE DRIVE
HARDING, MICHIGAN 48281

SOLD TO

Firm Name ___ Sauk Stereo ___

Attention of ___ James Hoover, Purchasing Agent ___

Address ___ 125 Main Street ___

Chelsea ___ Illinois ___ 60915 ___
City _____ State _____ Zip

Date 5/4/14	Salesperson Malone	Terms 2/10, n/30	FOB Shipping Point		
Catalog No.	Description		Quantity	Price	Amount
X572Y9820	Printed Circuit Board-prototype		1	2,300	$2,300
A2547Z45	Production Model Circuits		5	300	1,500
IMPORTANT: ALL RETURNS MUST BE MADE WITHIN 10 DAYS				**TOTAL**	$3,800

Under the perpetual inventory system, companies record purchases of merchandise for sale in the Inventory account. Thus, REI would increase (debit) Inventory for clothing, sporting goods, and anything else purchased for resale to customers. Not all purchases are debited to Inventory, however. Companies record purchases of assets acquired for use and not for resale, such as supplies, equipment, and similar items, as increases to specific asset accounts rather than to Inventory. For example, to record the purchase of materials used to make shelf signs or for cash register receipt paper, REI would increase (debit) Supplies.

FREIGHT COSTS

The sales agreement should indicate who—the seller or the buyer—is to pay for transporting the goods to the buyer's place of business. When a common carrier such as a railroad, trucking company, or airline transports the goods, the carrier prepares a freight bill in accord with the sales agreement.

Freight terms are expressed as either FOB shipping point or FOB destination. The letters FOB mean **free on board**. Thus, **FOB shipping point** means that the seller places the goods free on board the carrier, and the buyer pays the freight costs. Conversely, **FOB destination** means that the seller places the goods free on board to the buyer's place of business, and the seller pays the freight. For example, the sales invoice in Illustration 5-5 indicates FOB shipping point.

Thus, the buyer (Sauk Stereo) pays the freight charges. Illustration 5-6 illustrates these shipping terms.

Illustration 5-6 Shipping terms

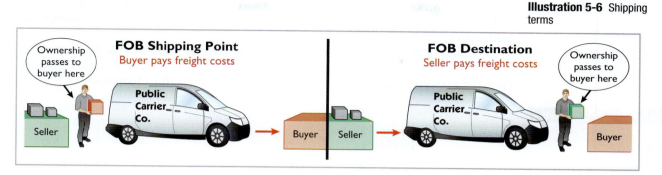

Freight Costs Incurred by Buyer

When the buyer pays the transportation costs, these costs are considered part of the cost of purchasing inventory. As a result, the account **Inventory is increased (debited)**. For example, if Sauk Stereo (the buyer) pays Public Freight Company $150 for freight charges on May 6, the entry on Sauk Stereo's books is:

May	6	Inventory	150	
		Cash		150
		(To record payment of freight on goods purchased)		

A	=	L	+	SE
+150				
−150				

Cash Flows
−150

Thus, any freight costs incurred by the buyer are part of the cost of merchandise purchased. The reason: Inventory cost should include all costs to acquire the inventory, including freight necessary to deliver the goods to the buyer. Companies recognize these costs as cost of goods sold when inventory is sold.

Freight Costs Incurred by Seller

In contrast, **freight costs incurred by the seller on outgoing merchandise are an operating expense to the seller**. These costs increase an expense account titled Freight-Out (sometimes called Delivery Expense). For example, if the freight terms on the invoice in Illustration 5-5 had required that PW Audio Supply (the seller) pay the $150 freight charges, the entry by PW Audio Supply would be:

May	4	Freight-Out	150	
		Cash		150
		(To record payment of freight on goods sold)		

A	=	L	+	SE
				−150 Exp
−150				

Cash Flows
−150

When the seller pays the freight charges, the seller will usually establish a higher invoice price for the goods, to cover the expense of shipping.

PURCHASE RETURNS AND ALLOWANCES

A purchaser may be dissatisfied with the merchandise received because the goods are damaged or defective, of inferior quality, or do not meet the purchaser's specifications. In such cases, the purchaser may return the goods to the seller for credit if the sale was made on credit, or for a cash refund if the purchase was for cash. This transaction is known as a **purchase return**. Alternatively, the purchaser may choose to keep the merchandise if the seller is willing to grant a reduction of the purchase price. This transaction is known as a **purchase allowance**.

Assume that Sauk Stereo returned goods costing $300 to PW Audio Supply on May 8. The following entry by Sauk Stereo for the returned merchandise decreases (debits) Accounts Payable and decreases (credits) Inventory.

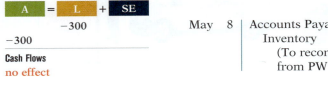

May	8	Accounts Payable	300	
		Inventory		300
		(To record return of goods purchased from PW Audio Supply)		

Because Sauk Stereo increased Inventory when the goods were received, Inventory is decreased (credited) when Sauk Stereo returns the goods.

Suppose instead that Sauk Stereo chose to keep the goods after being granted a $50 allowance (reduction in price). It would reduce (debit) Accounts Payable and reduce (credit) Inventory for $50.

PURCHASE DISCOUNTS

The credit terms of a purchase on account may permit the buyer to claim a cash discount for prompt payment. The buyer calls this cash discount a **purchase discount**. This incentive offers advantages to both parties. The purchaser saves money, and the seller is able to shorten the operating cycle by converting the accounts receivable into cash earlier.

The **credit terms** specify the amount of the cash discount and time period during which it is offered. They also indicate the length of time in which the purchaser is expected to pay the full invoice price. In the sales invoice in Illustration 5-5, credit terms are 2/10, n/30, which is read "two-ten, net thirty." This means that a 2% cash discount may be taken on the invoice price, less ("net of") any returns or allowances, if payment is made within 10 days of the invoice date (the **discount period**). Otherwise, the invoice price, less any returns or allowances, is due 30 days from the invoice date. Alternatively, the discount period may extend to a specified number of days following the month in which the sale occurs. For example, 1/10 EOM (end of month) means that a 1% discount is available if the invoice is paid within the first 10 days of the next month.

When the seller elects not to offer a cash discount for prompt payment, credit terms will specify only the maximum time period for paying the balance due. For example, the credit terms may state the time period as n/30, n/60, or n/10 EOM. This means, respectively, that the buyer must pay the net amount in 30 days, 60 days, or within the first 10 days of the next month.

When an invoice is paid within the discount period, the amount of the discount decreases Inventory. Why? Because the merchandiser records inventory at its cost and, by paying within the discount period, it has reduced that cost. To illustrate, assume Sauk Stereo pays the balance due of $3,500 (gross invoice price of $3,800 less purchase returns and allowances of $300) on May 14, the last day of the discount period. The cash discount is $70 ($3,500 × 2%), and the amount of cash Sauk Stereo paid is $3,430 ($3,500 − $70). The entry Sauk Stereo makes to record its May 14 payment decreases (debits) Accounts Payable by the amount of the gross invoice price, reduces (credits) Inventory by the $70 discount, and reduces (credits) Cash by the net amount owed.

May 14	Accounts Payable	3,500	
	Cash		3,430
	Inventory		70
	(To record payment within discount period)		

If Sauk Stereo failed to take the discount and instead made full payment of $3,500 on June 3, Sauk Stereo would reduce (debit) Accounts Payable and reduce (credit) Cash for $3,500 each.

June 3	Accounts Payable	3,500	
	Cash		3,500
	(To record payment with no discount taken)		

A merchandising company usually should take all available discounts. Passing up the discount may be viewed as **paying interest** for use of the money. For example, passing up the discount offered by PW Audio Supply would be like Sauk Stereo paying an interest rate of 2% for the use of $3,500 for 20 days. This is the equivalent of an annual interest rate of approximately 36.5% (2% $\times$ 365/20). Obviously, it would be better for Sauk Stereo to borrow at prevailing bank interest rates of 6% to 10% than to lose the discount.

SUMMARY OF PURCHASING TRANSACTIONS

The following T-account (with transaction descriptions in blue) provides a summary of the effect of the previous transactions on Inventory. Sauk Stereo originally purchased $3,800 worth of inventory for resale. It then returned $300 of goods. It paid $150 in freight charges, and finally, it received a $70 discount off the balance owed because it paid within the discount period. This results in a balance in Inventory of $3,580.

	Inventory				
Purchase	May 4	3,800	May 8	300	Purchase return
Freight-in	6	150	14	70	Purchase discount
Balance		3,580			

Recording Sales of Merchandise

In accordance with the revenue recognition principle, companies record sales revenue, like service revenue, when the performance obligation is satisfied. Typically, that performance obligation is satisfied when the goods are transferred from the seller to the buyer. At this point, the sales transaction is completed and the sales price is established.

Sales may be made on credit or for cash. Every sales transaction should be supported by a **business document** that provides written evidence of the sale. **Cash register documents** provide evidence of cash sales. A *sales invoice*, like the one that was shown in Illustration 5-5, provides support for each sale. The original copy of the invoice goes to the customer, and the seller keeps a copy for use in recording the sale. The invoice shows the date of sale, customer name, total sales price, and other relevant information.

LEARNING OBJECTIVE 3

Explain the recording of sales revenues under a perpetual inventory system.

The seller makes two entries for each sale. (1) It increases (debits) Accounts Receivable or Cash, as well as increases (credits) Sales Revenue. (2) It increases (debits) Cost of Goods Sold and decreases (credits) Inventory. As a result, the Inventory account will show at all times the amount of inventory that should be on hand.

To illustrate a credit sales transaction, PW Audio Supply records the sale of $3,800 on May 4 to Sauk Stereo (see Illustration 5-5) as follows (assume the merchandise cost PW Audio Supply $2,400).

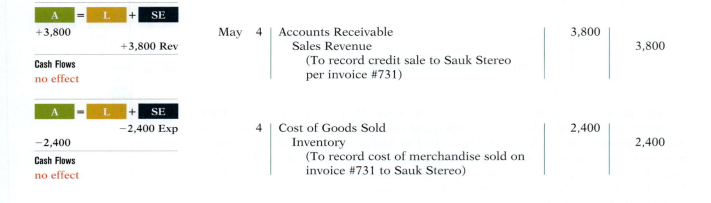

A	=	L	+	SE				
+3,800								
				+3,800 Rev	May 4	Accounts Receivable	3,800	
						Sales Revenue		3,800
Cash Flows						(To record credit sale to Sauk Stereo		
no effect						per invoice #731)		

A	=	L	+	SE				
				−2,400 Exp	4	Cost of Goods Sold	2,400	
−2,400						Inventory		2,400
Cash Flows						(To record cost of merchandise sold on		
no effect						invoice #731 to Sauk Stereo)		

For internal decision-making purposes, merchandising companies may use more than one sales account. For example, PW Audio Supply may decide to keep separate sales accounts for its sales of TVs, DVD players, and microwave ovens. REI might use separate accounts for camping gear, children's clothing, and ski equipment—or it might have even more narrowly defined accounts. By using separate sales accounts for major product lines, rather than a single combined sales account, company management can monitor sales trends more closely and respond more strategically to changes in sales patterns. For example, if TV sales are increasing while microwave oven sales are decreasing, the company might reevaluate both its advertising and pricing policies on each of these items to ensure they are optimal.

On its income statement presented to outside investors, a merchandising company would normally provide only a single sales figure—the sum of all of its individual sales accounts. This is done for two reasons. First, providing detail on all of its individual sales accounts would add considerable length to its income statement. Second, companies do not want their competitors to know the details of their operating results. However, at one time Microsoft expanded its disclosure of revenue from three to five types. The reason: The additional categories enabled financial statement users to better evaluate the growth of the company's consumer and Internet businesses.

SALES RETURNS AND ALLOWANCES

We now look at the "flip side" of purchase returns and allowances, which the seller records as **sales returns and allowances**. These are transactions where the seller either accepts goods back from a purchaser (a return) or grants a reduction in the purchase price (an allowance) so that the buyer will keep the goods. PW Audio Supply's entries to record credit for returned goods involve (1) an increase (debit) in Sales Returns and Allowances (a contra account to Sales Revenue) and a decrease (credit) in Accounts Receivable at the $300 selling price, and (2) an increase (debit) in Inventory (assume a $140 cost) and a decrease (credit) in Cost of Goods Sold, as shown below. (We assumed that the goods were

ANATOMY OF A FRAUD[1]

Holly Harmon was a cashier at a national superstore for only a short while when she began stealing merchandise using three methods. Under the first method, her husband or friends took UPC labels from cheaper items and put them on more expensive items. Holly then scanned the goods at the register. Using the second method, Holly scanned an item at the register but then voided the sale and left the merchandise in the shopping cart. A third approach was to put goods into large plastic containers. She scanned the plastic containers but not the goods within them. One day, Holly did not call in sick or show up for work. In such instances, the company reviews past surveillance tapes to look for suspicious activity by employees. This enabled the store to observe the thefts and to identify the participants.

Total take: $12,000

THE MISSING CONTROLS

Human resource controls. A background check would have revealed Holly's previous criminal record. She would not have been hired as a cashier.

Physical controls. Software can flag high numbers of voided transactions or a high number of sales of low-priced goods. Random comparisons of video records with cash register records can ensure that the goods reported as sold on the register are the same goods that are shown being purchased on the video recording. Finally, employees should be aware that they are being monitored.

Source: Adapted from Wells, *Fraud Casebook* (2007), pp. 251–259.

not defective. If they were defective, PW Audio Supply would make an entry to the Inventory account to reflect their decline in value.)

May	8	Sales Returns and Allowances	300	
		Accounts Receivable		300
		(To record credit granted to Sauk Stereo		
		for returned goods)		
	8	Inventory	140	
		Cost of Goods Sold		140
		(To record cost of goods returned)		

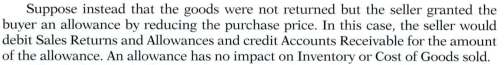

A	=	L	+	SE
				−300 Rev
−300				

Cash Flows
no effect

A	=	L	+	SE
+140				
				+140 Exp

Cash Flows
no effect

Suppose instead that the goods were not returned but the seller granted the buyer an allowance by reducing the purchase price. In this case, the seller would debit Sales Returns and Allowances and credit Accounts Receivable for the amount of the allowance. An allowance has no impact on Inventory or Cost of Goods sold.

Sales Returns and Allowances is a **contra revenue account** to Sales Revenue, which means it is offset against a revenue account on the income statement. The normal balance of Sales Returns and Allowances is a debit. Companies use a contra account, instead of debiting Sales Revenue, to disclose in the accounts and in the income statement the amount of sales returns and allowances. Disclosure of this information is important to management. Excessive returns and allowances suggest problems—inferior merchandise, inefficiencies in filling orders, errors in billing customers, or mistakes in delivery or shipment of goods. Moreover, a

---

[1]The "Anatomy of a Fraud" stories in this textbook are adapted from *Fraud Casebook: Lessons from the Bad Side of Business,* edited by Joseph T. Wells (Hoboken, NJ: John Wiley & Sons, Inc., 2007). Used by permission. The names of some of the people and organizations in the stories are fictitious, but the facts in the stories are true.

decrease (debit) recorded directly to Sales Revenue would obscure the relative importance of sales returns and allowances as a percentage of sales. It also could distort comparisons between total sales in different accounting periods.

Accounting Across the Organization

Should Costco Change Its Return Policy?

In most industries, sales returns are relatively minor. But returns of consumer electronics can really take a bite out of profits. Recently, the marketing executives at Costco Wholesale Corp. faced a difficult decision. Costco has always prided itself on its generous return policy. Most goods have had an unlimited grace period for returns. A new policy will require that certain electronics must be returned within 90 days of their purchase. The reason? The cost of returned products such as high-definition TVs, computers, and iPods cut an estimated 8¢ per share off Costco's earnings per share, which was $2.30.

Source: Kris Hudson, "Costco Tightens Policy on Returning Electronics," *Wall Street Journal* (February 27, 2007), p. B4.

? If a company expects significant returns, what are the implications for revenue recognition? (Answers in *Broadening Your Perspective.*)

SALES DISCOUNTS

As mentioned in our discussion of purchase transactions, the seller may offer the customer a cash discount—called by the seller a **sales discount**—for the prompt payment of the balance due. Like a purchase discount, a sales discount is based on the invoice price less returns and allowances, if any. The seller increases (debits) the Sales Discounts account for discounts that are taken. The entry by PW Audio Supply to record the cash receipt on May 14 from Sauk Stereo within the discount period is:

A	=	L	+	SE
+3,430				
				−70 Rev
−3,500				

Cash Flows
+3,430

May 14	Cash	3,430	
	Sales Discounts	70	
	Accounts Receivable		3,500
	(To record collection within 2/10, n/30 discount period from Sauk Stereo)		

Like Sales Returns and Allowances, Sales Discounts is a **contra revenue account** to Sales Revenue. Its normal balance is a debit. Sellers use this account, instead of debiting Sales Revenue, to disclose the amount of cash discounts taken by customers. If the customer does not take the discount, PW Audio Supply increases (debits) Cash for $3,500 and decreases (credits) Accounts Receivable for the same amount at the date of collection.

The following T-accounts summarize the three sales-related transactions and show their combined effect on net sales.

Sales Revenue	Sales Returns and Allowances	Sales Discounts
3,800	300	70

Net Sales
$3,430

Income Statement Presentation

Companies widely use two forms of the income statement. One is the **single-step income statement**. The statement is so named because only one step, subtracting total expenses from total revenues, is required in determining net income (or net loss).

In a single-step statement, all data are classified into two categories: (1) **revenues**, which include both operating revenues and nonoperating revenues and gains (for example, interest revenue and gain on sale of equipment); and (2) **expenses**, which include cost of goods sold, operating expenses, and nonoperating expenses and losses (for example, interest expense, loss on sale of equipment, or income tax expense). The single-step income statement is the form we have used thus far in the text. Illustration 5-7 shows a single-step statement for REI.

Illustration 5-7 Single-step income statements

Real World	RECREATIONAL EQUIPMENT, INC. Income Statements (in thousands)		
		For the years ended December 31	
		2010	**2009**
Revenues			
Net sales		$1,658,751	$1,455,351
Other revenues		14,190	14,010
		1,672,941	1,469,361
Expenses			
Cost of goods sold		929,787	804,834
Payroll-related expenses		331,159	281,502
Occupancy, general and administrative		282,368	268,455
Patronage refunds		79,848	67,222
Income taxes		19,549	17,541
		1,642,711	1,439,554
Net income		$ 30,230	$ 29,807

There are two primary reasons for using the single-step form. (1) A company does not realize any type of profit or income until total revenues exceed total expenses, so it makes sense to divide the statement into these two categories. (2) The form is simple and easy to read.

A second form of the income statement is the **multiple-step income statement**. The multiple-step income statement is often considered more useful because it highlights the components of net income. The REI income statement in Illustration 5-8 is an example.

The multiple-step income statement has three important line items: gross profit, income from operations, and net income. They are determined as follows.

1. Subtract cost of goods sold from net sales to determine **gross profit**.

2. Deduct operating expenses from gross profit to determine **income from operations**.

3. Add or subtract the results of activities not related to operations to determine **net income**.

Note that companies report income tax expense in a separate section of the income statement before net income. The net incomes in Illustrations 5-7 and 5-8

Illustration 5-8 Multiple-step income statements

	RECREATIONAL EQUIPMENT, INC. Income Statements (in thousands)		
		For the years ended December 31	
		2010	**2009**
Net sales		$1,658,751	$1,455,351
Cost of goods sold		929,787	804,834
Gross profit		728,964	650,517
Operating expenses			
Payroll-related expenses		331,159	281,502
Occupancy, general and administrative		282,368	268,455
Total operating expenses		613,527	549,957
Income from operations		115,437	100,560
Other revenues and gains			
Other revenues		14,190	14,010
Other expenses and losses			
Patronage refunds		79,848	67,222
Income before income taxes		49,779	47,348
Income tax expense		19,549	17,541
Net income		$ 30,230	$ 29,807

are the same. The two income statements differ in the amount of detail displayed and the order presented. The following discussion provides additional information about the components of a multiple-step income statement.

SALES REVENUES

The income statement for a merchandising company typically presents gross sales revenues for the period. The company deducts sales returns and allowances and sales discounts (both contra accounts) from sales revenue in the income statement to arrive at **net sales**. Illustration 5-9 shows the sales section of the income statement for PW Audio Supply.

Illustration 5-9 Statement presentation of sales section

PW AUDIO SUPPLY, INC. Income Statement (partial)		
Sales		
Sales revenue		$ 480,000
Less: Sales returns and allowances	$12,000	
Sales discounts	8,000	20,000
Net sales		**$460,000**

GROSS PROFIT

The excess of net sales over cost of goods sold is **gross profit, or gross margin**. It is determined by deducting **cost of goods sold** from sales revenue. As shown in Illustration 5-8, REI had a gross profit of $729 million in 2010. This computation uses **net sales**, which takes into account sales returns and allowances and sales discounts.

On the basis of the PW Audio Supply sales data presented in Illustration 5-9 (net sales of $460,000) and the cost of goods sold (assume a balance of $316,000), PW Audio Supply's gross profit is $144,000, computed as follows.

Net sales	$ 460,000
Cost of goods sold	316,000
Gross profit	**$144,000**

It is important to understand what gross profit is—and what it is not. Gross profit represents the **merchandising profit** of a company. Because operating expenses have not been deducted, it is **not a measure of the overall profit** of a company. Nevertheless, management and other interested parties closely watch the amount and trend of gross profit. Comparisons of current gross profit with past amounts and rates and with those in the industry indicate the effectiveness of a company's purchasing and pricing policies.

OPERATING EXPENSES

Operating expenses are the next component in measuring net income for a merchandising company. At REI, for example, operating expenses were $613.5 million in 2010.

At PW Audio Supply, operating expenses were $114,000. The firm determines its income from operations by subtracting operating expenses from gross profit. Thus, income from operations is $30,000, as shown below.

Gross profit	$144,000
Operating expenses	**114,000**
Income from operations	$ 30,000

NONOPERATING ACTIVITIES

Nonoperating activities consist of various revenues and expenses and gains and losses that are unrelated to the company's main line of operations. When nonoperating items are included, the label "**Income from operations**" (or "Operating income") precedes them. This label clearly identifies the results of the company's normal operations, an amount determined by subtracting cost of goods sold and operating expenses from net sales. The results of nonoperating activities are shown in the categories "**Other revenues and gains**" and "**Other expenses and losses**." Illustration 5-10 lists examples of each.

Illustration 5-10 Examples of nonoperating activities

Other Revenues and Gains
Interest revenue from notes receivable and marketable securities.
Dividend revenue from investments in capital stock.
Rent revenue from subleasing a portion of the store.
Gain from the sale of property, plant, and equipment.

Other Expenses and Losses
Interest expense on notes and loans payable.
Casualty losses from recurring causes, such as vandalism and accidents.
Loss from the sale or abandonment of property, plant, and equipment.
Loss from strikes by employees and suppliers.

Margin Note Companies manage earnings in various ways. ConAgra Foods recorded a nonrecurring gain for $186 million from the sale of Pilgrim's Pride stock to help meet an earnings projection for the quarter.

Nonoperating income is sometimes very significant. For example, in a recent quarter, Sears Holdings earned more than half of its net income from investments in derivative securities.

The distinction between operating and nonoperating activities is crucial to external users of financial data. These users view operating income as sustainable and many nonoperating activities as nonrecurring. When forecasting next year's income, analysts put the most weight on this year's operating income and less weight on this year's nonoperating activities.

Ethics Insight
Disclosing More Details

After Enron, increased investor criticism and regulator scrutiny forced many companies to improve the clarity of their financial disclosures. For example, IBM began providing more detail regarding its "Other gains and losses." It had previously included these items in its selling, general, and administrative expenses, with little disclosure.

Disclosing other gains and losses in a separate line item on the income statement will not have any effect on bottom-line income. However, analysts complained that burying these details in the selling, general, and administrative expense line reduced their ability to fully understand how well IBM was performing. For example, previously if IBM sold off one of its buildings at a gain, it would include this gain in the selling, general, and administrative expense line item, thus reducing that expense. This made it appear that the company had done a better job of controlling operating expenses than it actually had.

As another example, when eBay recently sold the remainder of its investment in Skype to Microsoft, it reported a gain in "Other revenues and gains" of $1.7 billion. Since eBay's total income from operations was $2.4 billion, it was very important that the gain from the Skype sale not be buried in operating income.

? Why have investors and analysts demanded more accuracy in isolating "Other gains and losses" from operating items? (Answers in *Broadening Your Perspective*.)

Nonoperating activities are reported in the income statement immediately after operating activities. Included among "Other revenues and gains" in Illustration 5-8 are Interest Revenue and Gain on Disposal of Plant Assets. Included in "Other expenses and losses" are Interest Expense and Casualty Loss from Vandalism.

In Illustration 5-11, we have provided the multiple-step income statement of PW Audio Supply. This statement provides more detail than that of REI and thus is useful as a guide for homework. *For homework problems, use the multiple-step form of the income statement unless the requirements state otherwise.*

DETERMINING COST OF GOODS SOLD UNDER A PERIODIC SYSTEM

LEARNING OBJECTIVE 5
Determine cost of goods sold under a periodic system.

Determining cost of goods sold is different when a periodic inventory system is used rather than a perpetual system. As you have seen, a company using a **perpetual system** makes an entry to record cost of goods sold and to reduce inventory **each time a sale is made**. A company using a **periodic system** does not determine cost of goods sold **until the end of the period.** At the end of the period, the company performs a count to determine the ending balance of inventory.

Illustration 5-11 Multiple-step income statement

PW AUDIO SUPPLY, INC.
Income Statement
For the Year Ended December 31, 2014

Sales		
Sales revenue		$480,000
Less: Sales returns and allowances	$12,000	
Sales discounts	8,000	20,000
Net sales		460,000
Cost of goods sold		316,000
Gross profit		144,000
Operating expenses		
Salaries and wages expense	64,000	
Utilities expense	17,000	
Advertising expense	16,000	
Depreciation expense	8,000	
Freight-out	7,000	
Insurance expense	2,000	
Total operating expenses		114,000
Income from operations		30,000
Other revenues and gains		
Interest revenue	3,000	
Gain on disposal of plant assets	600	3,600
Other expenses and losses		
Interest expense	1,800	
Casualty loss from vandalism	200	2,000
Income before income taxes		31,600
Income tax expense		10,100
Net income		$ 21,500

Calculation of gross profit

Calculation of income from operations

Results of activities not related to operations

It then **calculates cost of goods sold by subtracting ending inventory from the goods available for sale**. Goods available for sale is the sum of beginning inventory plus purchases, as shown in Illustration 5-12.

Illustration 5-12 Basic formula for cost of goods sold using the periodic system

Beginning Inventory
+ Cost of Goods Purchased
Cost of Goods Available for Sale
− Ending Inventory
Cost of Goods Sold

Another difference between the two approaches is that the perpetual system directly adjusts the Inventory account for any transaction that affects inventory (such as freight costs, purchase returns, and purchase discounts). The periodic system does not do this. Instead, it creates different accounts for purchases, freight costs, purchase returns, and purchase discounts. These various accounts are shown in Illustration 5-13, which presents the calculation of cost of goods sold for PW Audio Supply using the periodic approach. Note that the basic elements from Illustration 5-12 are highlighted in Illustration 5-13. You will learn more in Chapter 6 about how to determine cost of goods sold using the periodic system.

The use of the periodic inventory system does not affect the form of presentation in the balance sheet. As under the perpetual system, a company reports inventory in the current assets section.

Appendix 5A provides further detail on the use of the periodic system.

Illustration 5-13 Cost of goods sold for a merchandiser using a periodic inventory system

Margin Note The far right column identifies the primary items that make up cost of goods sold of $316,000. The middle column explains cost of goods purchased of $320,000. The left column reports contra purchase items of $17,200.

PW AUDIO SUPPLY, INC.
Cost of Goods Sold
For the Year Ended December 31, 2014

Cost of goods sold			
Inventory, January 1			**$ 36,000**
Purchases		$325,000	
Less: Purchase returns and			
allowances	$10,400		
Purchase discounts	6,800	17,200	
Net purchases		307,800	
Add: Freight-in		12,200	
Cost of goods purchased			**320,000**
Cost of goods available for sale			356,000
Inventory, December 31			**40,000**
Cost of goods sold			**$316,000**

Evaluating Profitability

GROSS PROFIT RATE

LEARNING OBJECTIVE 6
Explain the factors affecting profitability.

A company's gross profit may be expressed as a **percentage** by dividing the amount of gross profit by net sales. This is referred to as the **gross profit rate**. For PW Audio Supply, the gross profit rate is 31.3% ($144,000 ÷ $460,000).

Analysts generally consider the gross profit **rate** to be more informative than the gross profit **amount** because it expresses a more meaningful (qualitative) relationship between gross profit and net sales. For example, a gross profit amount of $1,000,000 may sound impressive. But if it was the result of sales of $100,000,000, the company's gross profit rate was only 1%. A 1% gross profit rate is acceptable in very few industries. Illustration 5-14 demonstrates that gross profit rates differ greatly across industries.

Illustration 5-14 Gross profit rate by industry

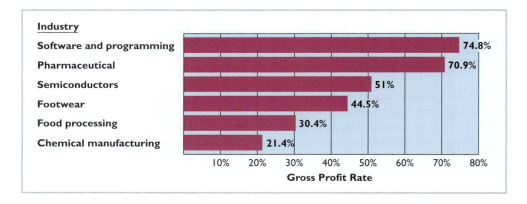

A decline in a company's gross profit rate might have several causes. The company may have begun to sell products with a lower "markup"—for example, budget blue jeans versus designer blue jeans. Increased competition may have resulted in a lower selling price. Or, the company may be forced to pay higher prices to its suppliers without being able to pass these costs on to its customers. The gross profit rates for REI and Dick's Sporting Goods, and the industry average, are presented in Illustration 5-15.

Illustration 5-15 Gross profit rate

Gross Profit Rate = $\dfrac{\text{Gross Profit}}{\text{Net Sales}}$			
REI ($ in thousands)		**Dick's Sporting Goods**	**Industry Average**
2010	2009	2010	2010
$\dfrac{\$728{,}964}{\$1{,}658{,}751} = 43.9\%$	44.7%	29.7%	34.0%

REI's gross profit rate decreased from 44.7% in 2009 to 43.9% in 2010. What might cause changes in REI's gross profit rate? When the economy slows, retailers must reduce selling prices in order to sell merchandise. This cuts into the gross profit rate. Changes in national weather patterns can also affect the amount of time people spend outdoors—and therefore impact their purchases of REI merchandise. For example, if winter provides below-average snow or extreme cold, or if summer is cooler and wetter than normal, then REI will have to discount its goods to sell them.

Why does REI's gross profit rate differ so much from that of Dick's Sporting Goods and the industry average? The gross profit rate often differs across retailers because of differences in the nature of their goods. First, REI focuses on outdoor equipment, while Dick's also sells sporting goods and hunting gear. The markup may differ significantly in these different product sectors. Also, although REI and Dick's both sell outdoor equipment, the quality of the equipment they sell differs. REI tends to sell more "high-end" goods, while Dick's tends to sell goods in a more "affordable" range. Higher-quality goods demand a higher markup. However, the retailer also sells fewer of them. In general, retailers adopt either a high-volume–low-margin approach (e.g., Wal-Mart) or a low-volume–high-margin approach (e.g., Saks Fifth Avenue). The strategic choice is often revealed in differences in the companies' gross profit rate.

🧰 DECISION TOOLKIT

DECISION CHECKPOINTS	INFO NEEDED FOR DECISION	TOOL TO USE FOR DECISION	HOW TO EVALUATE RESULTS
Is the price of goods keeping pace with changes in the cost of inventory?	Gross profit and net sales	Gross profit rate = $\dfrac{\text{Gross profit}}{\text{Net sales}}$	Higher ratio suggests the average margin between selling price and inventory cost is increasing. Too high a margin may result in lost sales.

PROFIT MARGIN

The **profit margin** measures the percentage of each dollar of sales that results in net income. We compute this ratio by dividing net income by net sales (revenue) for the period.

How do the gross profit rate and profit margin differ? The gross profit rate measures the margin by which selling price exceeds cost of goods sold.

The profit margin measures the extent by which selling price covers all expenses (including cost of goods sold). A company can improve its profit margin by either increasing its gross profit rate and/or by controlling its operating expenses and other costs. For example, at one time Radio Shack reported increased profit margins which it accomplished by closing stores and slashing costs. While its total sales have been declining, its profitability as measured by its profit margin has increased.

Profit margins vary across industries. Businesses with high turnover, such as grocery stores (Safeway and Kroger) and discount stores (Target and Wal-Mart), generally experience low profit margins. Low-turnover businesses, such as high-end jewelry stores (Tiffany and Co.) or major drug manufacturers (Merck), have high profit margins. Illustration 5-16 shows profit margins from a variety of industries.

Illustration 5-16 Profit margins by industry

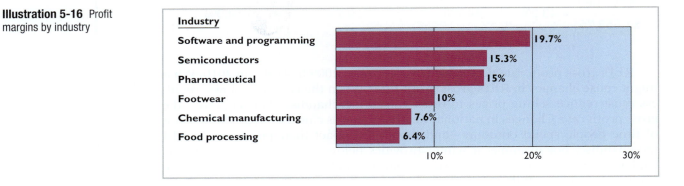

Profit margins for REI and Dick's Sporting Goods and the industry average are presented in Illustration 5-17.

Illustration 5-17 Profit margin

Profit Margin = Net Income / Net Sales			
REI ($ in thousands)		**Dick's Sporting Goods**	**Industry Average**
2010	2009	2010	2010
$\dfrac{\$30{,}230}{\$1{,}658{,}751} = 1.8\%$	2.0%	3.7%	5.1%

REI's profit margin declined from 2.0% to 1.8% between 2009 and 2010. This means that the company generated 1.8¢ of profit on each dollar of sales. This decline occurred partly because the gross profit rate decreased.

A change in the profit margin can be caused by a change in the gross profit rate, a change in the amount of operating expenses relative to sales, or a change in the amount of other items (other revenues and gains, or other expenses and losses) relative to sales. In Illustration 5-8, we can see that neither operating expenses nor other items increased significantly in proportion to sales. (That is, the percentage of these items relative to sales did not change significantly. For example, sales increased by almost 14% in 2010, but operating expenses also increased by a similar amount, so that operating expenses as a percentage of sales in 2010 was about the same as in 2009.) Therefore, in 2010, most of the decline in REI's profit margin occurred because of the decline in the gross profit rate. When the gross profit rate declines, the company has less profit available to cover its operating costs.

How does REI compare to its competitors? Its profit margin was lower than Dick's in 2010 and was less than the industry average. Thus, its profit margin does not suggest exceptional profitability.

People, Planet, and Profit Insight

Selling Green

Here is a question an executive of PepsiCo was asked: Should PepsiCo market green? The executive indicated that the company should, as he believes it's the No. 1 thing consumers all over the world care about. Here are some of his thoughts on this issue:

"Sun Chips are part of the food business I run. It's a 'healthy snack.' We decided that Sun Chips, if it's a healthy snack, should be made in facilities that have a net-zero footprint. In other words, I want off the electric grid everywhere we make Sun Chips. We did that. Sun Chips should be made in a facility that puts back more water than it uses. It does that. And we partnered with our suppliers and came out with the world's first compostable chip package.

Now, there was an issue with this package: It was louder than the New York subway, louder than jet engines taking off. What would a company that's committed to green do: walk away or stay committed? If your people are passionate, they're going to fix it for you as long as you stay committed. Six months later, the compostable bag has half the noise of our current package.

So the view today is: we should market green, we should be proud to do it . . . it has to be a 360 process, both internal and external. And if you do that, you can monetize environmental sustainability for the shareholders."

Source: "Four Problems—and Solutions," *Wall Street Journal* (March 7, 2011), p. R2.

? What is meant by "monetize environmental sustainability" for shareholders? (Answers in *Broadening Your Perspective.*)

DECISION TOOLKIT

DECISION CHECKPOINTS	INFO NEEDED FOR DECISION	TOOL TO USE FOR DECISION	HOW TO EVALUATE RESULTS
Is the company maintaining an adequate margin between sales and expenses?	Net income and net sales	$\text{Profit margin} = \dfrac{\text{Net income}}{\text{Net sales}}$	Higher value suggests favorable return on each dollar of sales.

In Chapter 4, you learned that **earnings have high quality if they provide a full and transparent depiction of how a company performed**. In order to quickly assess earnings quality, analysts sometimes employ the **quality of earnings ratio**. It is calculated as net cash provided by operating activities divided by net income.

$$\text{Quality of Earnings Ratio} = \frac{\text{Net Cash Provided by Operating Activities}}{\text{Net Income}}$$

In general, a measure significantly less than 1 suggests that a company may be using more aggressive accounting techniques in order to accelerate income recognition (record income in earlier periods). A measure significantly greater than 1 suggests that a company is using conservative accounting techniques, which cause it to delay the recognition of income.

Measures that are significantly less than 1 do not provide definitive evidence of low-quality earnings. Low measures do, however, indicate that analysts should investigate the company's earnings quality by evaluating the causes of the difference between net income and net cash provided by operating activities. Examples of factors that would cause differences are presented in Chapter 4 (Illustration 4-33).

Here are recent quality of earnings ratios for a number of well-known companies, all of which have measures in excess of 1.

Company Name ($ in millions)	Net Cash Provided by Operating Activities	÷	Net Income	=	Quality of Earnings Ratio
DuPont	$4,741		$1,769		2.7
Intel	$11,170		$4,369		2.6
Nike	$1,736		$1,487		1.2
Microsoft	$19,037		$14,569		1.3
Wal-Mart	$26,249		$14,335		1.8

USING THE DECISION TOOLKIT

Like REI, Mountain Equipment Cooperative (MEC) is a retailer of outdoor equipment organized as a cooperative (though MEC *only* sells to its members, who pay a one-time fee of $5). Also like REI, MEC has a significant commitment to sustainability. Many of its stores employ state-of-the-art building techniques to minimize energy use, and it pledges 1% of annual sales revenue to environmental causes. Since MEC is a Canadian company, it follows International Financial Reporting Standards (IFRS) rather than U.S. GAAP. The *A Look at IFRS* section at the end of each chapter of this textbook discusses some of the main accounting differences that you would need to be aware of to make a thorough comparison of REI and MEC. Here is recent data for MEC.

($ in thousands)	Year ended	
	12/26/10	12/27/09
Net income	$ 815	$ 300
Sales revenue	261,374	262,056
Cost of goods sold	174,871	175,606

Instructions

Using the basic facts in the table, evaluate the following components of MEC's profitability for the years ended December 26, 2010, and December 27, 2009.

　　Profit margin
　　Gross profit rate

How do MEC's profit margin and gross profit rate compare to those of REI and Dick's Sporting Goods for 2010?

Solution

($ in thousands)	Year ended	
	12/26/10	12/27/09
Profit margin	$\dfrac{\$815}{\$261,374} = 0.3\%$	$\dfrac{\$300}{\$262,056} = 0.1\%$
Gross profit rate	$\dfrac{\$86,503^*}{\$261,374} = 33.1\%$	$\dfrac{\$86,450^{**}}{\$262,056} = 33.0\%$

*$261,374 − $174,871   **$262,056 − $175,606

MEC's profit margin (income per dollar of sales) increased from 0.1% to 0.3%. This is well below both REI's (1.8%) and Dick's (3.7%). Thus, MEC is not as effective at turning its sales into net income as these two competitors.

MEC's gross profit rate improved from 33.0% to 33.1%. This suggests that its ability to maintain its markup above its cost of goods sold improved slightly during this period. MEC's gross profit rate of 33.1% is lower than REI's (43.9%) but higher than Dick's (29.7%). Dick's gross profit is depressed by the fact that it sells many low-margin products. REI is superior to MEC both in its ability to maintain its markup above its costs of goods sold (its gross profit rate) and in its ability to control operating costs (its profit margin).

Summary of Learning Objectives

1 **Identify the differences between a service company and a merchandising company.** Because of the presence of inventory, a merchandising company has sales revenue, cost of goods sold, and gross profit. To account for inventory, a merchandising company must choose between a perpetual inventory system and a periodic inventory system.

2 **Explain the recording of purchases under a perpetual inventory system.** The Inventory account is debited for all purchases of merchandise and for freight costs, and it is credited for purchase discounts and purchase returns and allowances.

3 **Explain the recording of sales revenues under a perpetual inventory system.** When inventory is sold, Accounts Receivable (or Cash) is debited and Sales Revenue is credited for the selling price of the merchandise. At the same time, Cost of Goods Sold is debited and Inventory is credited for the cost of inventory items sold. Separate contra revenue accounts are maintained for Sales Returns and Allowances and Sales Discounts. These accounts are debited as needed to record returns, allowances, or discounts related to the sale.

4 **Distinguish between a single-step and a multiple-step income statement.** In a single-step income statement, companies classify all data under two categories, revenues or expenses, and net income is determined in one step. A multiple-step income statement shows numerous steps in determining net income, including results of nonoperating activities.

5 **Determine cost of goods sold under a periodic system.** The periodic system uses multiple accounts to keep track of transactions that affect inventory. To determine cost of goods sold, first calculate cost of goods purchased by adjusting purchases for returns, allowances, discounts, and freight-in. Then calculate cost of goods sold by adding cost of goods purchased to beginning inventory and subtracting ending inventory.

6 **Explain the factors affecting profitability.** Profitability is affected by gross profit, as measured by the gross profit rate, and by management's ability to control costs, as measured by the profit margin.

7 **Identify a quality of earnings indicator.** Earnings have high quality if they provide a full and transparent depiction of how a company performed. An indicator of the quality of earnings is the quality of earnings ratio, which is net cash provided by operating activities divided by net income. Measures above 1 suggest the company is employing conservative accounting practices. Measures significantly below 1 might suggest the company is using aggressive accounting to accelerate the recognition of income.

DECISION TOOLKIT *A SUMMARY*

DECISION CHECKPOINTS	INFO NEEDED FOR DECISION	TOOL TO USE FOR DECISION	HOW TO EVALUATE RESULTS
Is the price of goods keeping pace with changes in the cost of inventory?	Gross profit and net sales	$\text{Gross profit rate} = \dfrac{\text{Gross profit}}{\text{Net sales}}$	Higher ratio suggests the average margin between selling price and inventory cost is increasing. Too high a margin may result in lost sales.
Is the company maintaining an adequate margin between sales and expenses?	Net income and net sales	$\text{Profit margin} = \dfrac{\text{Net income}}{\text{Net sales}}$	Higher value suggests favorable return on each dollar of sales.

Periodic Inventory System

LEARNING OBJECTIVE 8

Explain the recording of purchases and sales of inventory under a periodic inventory system.

As described in this chapter, companies may use one of two basic systems of accounting for inventories: (1) the perpetual inventory system or (2) the periodic inventory system. In the chapter, we focused on the characteristics of the perpetual inventory system. In this appendix, we discuss and illustrate the **periodic inventory system**. One key difference between the two systems is the point at which the company computes cost of goods sold. For a visual reminder of this difference, you may want to refer back to Illustration 5-4.

RECORDING MERCHANDISE TRANSACTIONS

In a **periodic inventory system**, companies record revenues from the sale of merchandise when sales are made, just as in a perpetual system. Unlike the perpetual system, however, companies **do not attempt on the date of sale to record the cost of the merchandise sold**. Instead, they take a physical inventory count at the **end of the period** to determine (1) the cost of the merchandise then on hand and (2) the cost of the goods sold during the period. And, **under a periodic system, companies record purchases of merchandise in the Purchases account rather than the Inventory account**. Also, in a periodic system, purchase returns and allowances, purchase discounts, and freight costs on purchases are recorded in separate accounts.

To illustrate the recording of merchandise transactions under a periodic inventory system, we will use purchase/sale transactions between PW Audio Supply, Inc. and Sauk Stereo, as illustrated for the perpetual inventory system in this chapter.

RECORDING PURCHASES OF MERCHANDISE

On the basis of the sales invoice (Illustration 5-5, shown) and receipt of the merchandise ordered from PW Audio Supply, Sauk Stereo records the $3,800 purchase as follows.

May	4	Purchases	3,800	
		Accounts Payable		3,800
		(To record goods purchased on account		
		from PW Audio Supply)		

Purchases is a temporary account whose normal balance is a debit.

FREIGHT COSTS

When the purchaser directly incurs the freight costs, it debits the account Freight-In (or Transportation-In). For example, if Sauk Stereo pays Public Freight Company $150 for freight charges on its purchase from PW Audio Supply on May 6, the entry on Sauk Stereo's books is:

May	6	Freight-In (Transportation-In)	150	
		Cash		150
		(To record payment of freight on		
		goods purchased)		

Like Purchases, Freight-In is a temporary account whose normal balance is a debit. **Freight-In is part of cost of goods purchased.** The reason is that cost of goods purchased should include any freight charges necessary to bring the goods to the purchaser. Freight costs are not subject to a purchase discount. Purchase discounts apply on the invoice cost of the merchandise.

Purchase Returns and Allowances

Because $300 of merchandise received from PW Audio Supply is inoperable, Sauk Stereo returns the goods and prepares the following entry to recognize the return.

May	8	Accounts Payable	300	
		Purchase Returns and Allowances		300
		(To record return of goods purchased from PW Audio Supply)		

Purchase Returns and Allowances is a temporary account whose normal balance is a credit.

Purchase Discounts

On May 14, Sauk Stereo pays the balance due on account to PW Audio Supply, taking the 2% cash discount allowed by PW Audio Supply for payment within 10 days. Sauk Stereo records the payment and discount as follows.

May	14	Accounts Payable ($3,800 − $300)	3,500	
		Purchase Discounts ($3,500 ×.02)		70
		Cash		3,430
		(To record payment within the discount period)		

Purchase Discounts is a temporary account whose normal balance is a credit.

RECORDING SALES OF MERCHANDISE

The seller, PW Audio Supply, records the sale of $3,800 of merchandise to Sauk Stereo on May 4 (sales invoice No. 731, Illustration 5-5) as follows.

May	4	Accounts Receivable	3,800	
		Sales Revenue		3,800
		(To record credit sales to Sauk Stereo per invoice #731)		

Sales Returns and Allowances

To record the returned goods received from Sauk Stereo on May 8, PW Audio Supply records the $300 sales return as follows.

May	8	Sales Returns and Allowances	300	
		Accounts Receivable		300
		(To record credit granted to Sauk Stereo for returned goods)		

Sales Discounts

On May 14, PW Audio Supply receives payment of $3,430 on account from Sauk Stereo. PW Audio Supply honors the 2% cash discount and records the payment of Sauk Stereo's account receivable in full as follows.

May	14	Cash	3,430	
		Sales Discounts ($3,500 × .02)	70	
		Accounts Receivable ($3,800 − $300)		3,500
		(To record collection within 2/10, n/30 discount period from Sauk Stereo)		

COMPARISON OF ENTRIES–PERPETUAL vs. PERIODIC

ENTRIES ON SAUK STEREO'S BOOKS

Transaction		Perpetual Inventory System			Periodic Inventory System		

May 4	Purchase of merchandise on credit.	Inventory
		  Accounts Payable
			3,800	3,800	Purchases
					  Accounts Payable
						3,800	3,800

May 6	Freight costs on purchases.	Inventory
		  Cash
			150	150	Freight-In
					  Cash
						150	150

May 8	Purchase returns and allowances.	Accounts Payable
		  Inventory
			300	300	Accounts Payable
					  Purchase Returns
					    and Allowances
						300	300

May 14	Payment on account with a discount.	Accounts Payable
		  Cash
		  Inventory
			3,500	3,430
				70
					Accounts Payable
					  Cash
					  Purchase Discounts
						3,500	3,430
							70

ENTRIES ON PW AUDIO SUPPLY'S BOOKS

Transaction		Perpetual Inventory System			Periodic Inventory System		

May 4	Sale of merchandise on credit.	Accounts Receivable
		  Sales Revenue
			3,800	3,800	Accounts Receivable
					  Sales Revenue
						3,800	3,800

		Cost of Goods Sold
		  Inventory
			2,400	2,400	No entry for cost of
					  goods sold		

May 8	Return of merchandise sold.	Sales Returns and
		Allowances
		  Accounts Receivable
			300	300	Sales Returns and
					Allowances
					  Accounts Receivable
						300	300

		Inventory Cost of Goods Sold	140	140	No entry		

May 14	Cash received on account with a discount.	Cash
		Sales Discounts
		  Accounts Receivable
			3,430
			70
				3,500	Cash
					Sales Discounts
					  Accounts Receivable
						3,430
						70
							3,500

Summary of Learning Objective for Appendix 5A

8 **Explain the recording of purchases and sales of inventory under a periodic inventory system.** To record purchases, entries are required for (a) cash and credit purchases, (b) purchase returns and allowances, (c) purchase discounts, and (d) freight costs. To record sales, entries are required for (a) cash and credit sales, (b) sales returns and allowances, and (c) sales discounts.

Glossary

Terms are highlighted in blue throughout the chapter.

Contra revenue account An account that is offset against a revenue account on the income statement.

Cost of goods sold The total cost of merchandise sold during the period.

Gross profit The excess of net sales over the cost of goods sold.

Gross profit rate Gross profit expressed as a percentage by dividing the amount of gross profit by net sales.

Net sales Sales less sales returns and allowances and sales discounts.

Periodic inventory system An inventory system in which a company does not maintain detailed records of goods on hand throughout the period and determines the cost of goods sold only at the end of an accounting period.

Perpetual inventory system A detailed inventory system in which a company maintains the cost of each inventory item, and the records continuously show the inventory that should be on hand.

Profit margin Measures the percentage of each dollar of sales that results in net income, computed by dividing net income by net sales.

Purchase allowance A deduction made to the selling price of merchandise, granted by the seller, so that the buyer will keep the merchandise.

Purchase discount A cash discount claimed by a buyer for prompt payment of a balance due.

Purchase invoice A document that provides support for each purchase.

Purchase return A return of goods from the buyer to the seller for cash or credit.

Quality of earnings ratio A measure used to indicate the extent to which a company's earnings provide a full and transparent depiction of its performance; computed as

net cash provided by operating activities divided by net income.

Sales discount A reduction given by a seller for prompt payment of a credit sale.

Sales invoice A document that provides support for each sale.

Sales returns and allowances Transactions in which the seller either accepts goods back from the purchaser (a return) or grants a reduction in the purchase price (an allowance) so that the buyer will keep the goods.

Sales revenue Primary source of revenue for a merchandising company.

WILEY PLUS Self-Test, Brief Exercises, Exercises, Problem Set A, and many more resources are available for practice in WileyPLUS.

Note: All Questions, Exercises, and Problems marked with an asterisk relate to material in the appendix to the chapter.

Self-Test Questions

(Answers in *Broadening Your Perspective.*)

(LO 1) **1.** Which of the following statements about a periodic inventory system is **true**?
(a) Companies determine cost of goods sold only at the end of the accounting period.
(b) Companies continuously maintain detailed records of the cost of each inventory purchase and sale.
(c) The periodic system provides better control over inventories than a perpetual system.
(d) The increased use of computerized systems has increased the use of the periodic system.

(LO 2) **2.** Which of the following items does **not** result in an adjustment in the Inventory account under a perpetual system?
(a) A purchase of merchandise.
(b) A return of merchandise to the supplier.
(c) Payment of freight costs for goods shipped to a customer.
(d) Payment of freight costs for goods received from a supplier.

(LO 3) **3.** Which sales accounts normally have a debit balance?
(a) Sales discounts.
(b) Sales returns and allowances.
(c) Both (a) and (b).
(d) Neither (a) nor (b).

(LO 3) **4.** A company makes a credit sale of $750 on June 13, terms 2/10, n/30, on which it grants a return of $50 on June 16. What amount is received as payment in full on June 23?
(a) $700.   (c) $685.
(b) $686.   (d) $650.

(LO 3) **5.** To record the sale of goods for cash in a perpetual inventory system:

(a) only one journal entry is necessary to record cost of goods sold and reduction of inventory.
(b) only one journal entry is necessary to record the receipt of cash and the sales revenue.
(c) two journal entries are necessary: one to record the receipt of cash and sales revenue, and one to record the cost of goods sold and reduction of inventory.
(d) two journal entries are necessary: one to record the receipt of cash and reduction of inventory, and one to record the cost of goods sold and sales revenue.

6. Gross profit will result if: (LO 4)
(a) operating expenses are less than net income.
(b) sales revenues are greater than operating expenses.
(c) sales revenues are greater than cost of goods sold.
(d) operating expenses are greater than cost of goods sold.

7. If sales revenues are $400,000, cost of goods sold is (LO 4) $310,000, and operating expenses are $60,000, what is the gross profit?
(a) $30,000.   (c) $340,000.
(b) $90,000.   (d) $400,000.

8. The multiple-step income statement for a merchan- (LO 4) dising company shows each of these features **except**:
(a) gross profit.
(b) cost of goods sold.
(c) a sales section.
(d) All of these are present.

9. If beginning inventory is $60,000, cost of goods (LO 5) purchased is $380,000, and ending inventory is $50,000, what is cost of goods sold under a periodic system?
(a) $390,000.
(b) $370,000.
(c) $330,000.
(d) $420,000.

(LO 5) **10.** Bufford Corporation had reported the following amounts at December 31, 2014: sales revenue $184,000; ending inventory $11,600; beginning inventory $17,200; purchases $60,400; purchase discounts $3,000; purchase returns and allowances $1,100; freight-in $600; freight-out $900. Calculate the cost of goods available for sale.
  (a) $69,400.
  (b) $74,100.
  (c) $56,900.
  (d) $197,700.

(LO 6) **11.** ◯▬▬◖ Which of the following would affect the gross profit rate? (Assume sales remains constant.)
  (a) An increase in advertising expense.
  (b) A decrease in depreciation expense.
  (c) An increase in cost of goods sold.
  (d) A decrease in insurance expense.

(LO 6) **12.** ◯▬▬◖ The gross profit rate is equal to:
  (a) net income divided by sales.
  (b) cost of goods sold divided by sales.
  (c) net sales minus cost of goods sold, divided by net sales.
  (d) sales minus cost of goods sold, divided by cost of goods sold.

(LO 6) **13.** During the year ended December 31, 2014, Bjornstad Corporation had the following results: sales revenue $267,000; cost of good sold $107,000; net income

$92,400; operating expenses $55,400; net cash provided by operating activities $108,950. What was the company's profit margin?
  (a) 40%.
  (b) 60%.
  (c) 20.5%.
  (d) 34.6%.

14. A quality of earnings ratio: (LO 7)
  (a) is computed as net income divided by net cash provided by operating activities.
  (b) that is less than 1 indicates that a company might be using aggressive accounting tactics.
  (c) that is greater than 1 indicates that a company might be using aggressive accounting tactics.
  (d) is computed as net cash provided by operating activities divided by total assets.

15. When goods are purchased for resale by a company (LO 8) using a periodic inventory system:
  (a) purchases on account are debited to Inventory.
  (b) purchases on account are debited to Purchases.
  (c) purchase returns are debited to Purchase Returns and Allowances.
  (d) freight costs are debited to Purchases.

Go to the book's companion website, **www.wiley.com/college/kimmel**, to access additional Self-Test Questions.

Questions

1. (a) "The steps in the accounting cycle for a merchandising company differ from the steps in the accounting cycle for a service company." Do you agree or disagree?
  (b) Is the measurement of net income in a merchandising company conceptually the same as in a service company? Explain.

2. How do the components of revenues and expenses differ between a merchandising company and a service company?

3. ◀▬ Laurie Massoth, CEO of Bargain Den Stores, is considering a recommendation made by both the company's purchasing manager and director of finance that the company should invest in a sophisticated new perpetual inventory system to replace its periodic system. Explain the primary difference between the two systems, and discuss the potential benefits of a perpetual inventory system.

4. (a) Explain the income measurement process in a merchandising company.
  (b) How does income measurement differ between a merchandising company and a service company?

5. Dillard Co. has sales revenue of $100,000, cost of goods sold of $70,000, and operating expenses of $18,000. What is its gross profit?

6. Angie Milner believes revenues from credit sales may be recorded before they are collected in cash. Do you agree? Explain.

7. (a) What is the primary source document for recording (1) cash sales and (2) credit sales?
  (b) Using XXs for amounts, give the journal entry for each of the transactions in part (a), assuming perpetual inventory.

8. A credit sale is made on July 10 for $900, terms 1/15, n/30. On July 12, the purchaser returns $100 of goods for credit. Give the journal entry on July 19 to record the receipt of the balance due within the discount period.

9. ◀▬ As the end of Petit Company's fiscal year approached, it became clear that the company had considerable excess inventory. Ronald Morel, the head of marketing and sales, ordered salespeople to "add 20% more units to each order that you ship. The customers can always ship the extra back next period if they decide they don't want it. We've got to do it to meet this year's sales goal." Discuss the accounting implications of Ronald's action.

10. ◀▬ To encourage bookstores to buy a broader range of book titles and to discourage price discounting, the publishing industry allows bookstores to return unsold books to the publisher. This results in very significant returns each year. To ensure proper recognition of revenues, how should publishing companies account for these returns?

11. Goods costing $1,900 are purchased on account on July 15 with credit terms of 2/10, n/30. On July 18, the purchaser receives a $300 credit from the supplier for damaged goods. Give the journal entry on July 24 to record payment of the balance due within the discount period.

12. ◄ Scribner Company reports net sales of $800,000, gross profit of $560,000, and net income of $230,000. What are its operating expenses?

13. ◄ Luo Company has always provided its customers with payment terms of 1/10, n/30. Members of its sale force have commented that competitors are offering customers 2/10, n/45. Explain what these terms mean, and discuss the implications to Luo of switching its payment terms to those of its competitors.

14. ◄ In its year-end earnings announcement press release, Brantley Corp. announced that its earnings increased by $15 million relative to the previous year. This represented a 20% increase. Inspection of its income statement reveals that the company reported a $20 million gain under "Other revenues and gains" from the sale of one of its factories. Discuss the implications of this gain from the perspective of a potential investor.

15. Identify the distinguishing features of an income statement for a merchandising company.

16. Why is the normal operating cycle for a merchandising company likely to be longer than for a service company?

17. What title does Tootsie Roll use for gross profit? How did it present gross profit? By how much did its total gross profit change, and in what direction, in 2011?

18. What merchandising account(s) will appear in the post-closing trial balance?

19. What types of businesses are most likely to use a perpetual inventory system?

20. Identify the accounts that are added to or deducted from purchases to determine the cost of goods purchased under a periodic system. For each account, indicate (a) whether it is added or deducted, and (b) its normal balance.

21. In the following cases, use a periodic inventory system to identify the item(s) designated by the letters X and Y.
(a) Purchases $-X-Y=$ Net purchases.
(b) Cost of goods purchased $-$ Net purchases $=X$.
(c) Beginning inventory $+X=$ Cost of goods available for sale.
(d) Cost of goods available for sale $-$ Cost of goods sold $=X$.

22. What two ratios measure factors that affect profitability?

23. What factors affect a company's gross profit rate—that is, what can cause the gross profit rate to increase and what can cause it to decrease?

24. ◄ Mark Elarton, director of marketing, wants to reduce the selling price of his company's products by 15% to increase market share. He says, "I know this will reduce our gross profit rate, but the increased number of units sold will make up for the lost margin." Before this action is taken, what other factors does the company need to consider?

25. George Mallein is considering investing in Wigginton Pet Food Company. Wigginton's net income increased considerably during the most recent year even though many other companies in the same industry reported disappointing earnings. George wants to know whether the company's earnings provide a reasonable depiction of its results. What initial step can George take to help determine whether he needs to investigate further?

*26. On July 15, a company purchases on account goods costing $1,900, with credit terms of 2/10, n/30. On July 18, the company receives a $400 credit memo from the supplier for damaged goods. Give the journal entry on July 24 to record payment of the balance due within the discount period assuming a periodic inventory system.

Brief Exercises

BE5-1 Presented here are the components in Casilla Company's income statement. Determine the missing amounts.

Compute missing amounts in determining net income. (LO 1, 4), **AP**

Sales Revenue	Cost of Goods Sold	Gross Profit	Operating Expenses	Net Income
$ 71,200	(b)	$ 30,000	(d)	$12,100
$108,000	$70,000	(c)	(e)	$29,500
(a)	$71,900	$109,600	$46,200	(f)

BE5-2 Gerish Company buys merchandise on account from Mangus Company. The selling price of the goods is $900 and the cost of the goods sold is $590. Both companies use perpetual inventory systems. Journalize the transactions on the books of both companies.

Journalize perpetual inventory entries. (LO 2, 3), **AP**

BE5-3 Prepare the journal entries to record the following transactions on Horst Company's books using a perpetual inventory system.
(a) On March 2, Horst Company sold $800,000 of merchandise to Bernadina Company, terms 2/10, n/30. The cost of the merchandise sold was $540,000.
(b) On March 6, Bernadina Company returned $140,000 of the merchandise purchased on March 2. The cost of the merchandise returned was $94,000.
(c) On March 12, Horst Company received the balance due from Bernadina Company.

Journalize sales transactions. (LO 3), **AP**

Journalize purchase transactions.
(LO 2), **AP**

BE5-4 From the information in BE5-3, prepare the journal entries to record these transactions on Bernadina Company's books under a perpetual inventory system.

Prepare sales section of income statement.
(LO 4), **AP**

BE5-5 Alvarado Company provides this information for the month ended October 31, 2014: sales on credit $300,000; cash sales $150,000; sales discounts $5,000; and sales returns and allowances $19,000. Prepare the sales section of the income statement based on this information.

Identify placement of items on a multiple-step income statement.
(LO 4), **AP**

BE5-6 Explain where each of these items would appear on a multiple-step income statement: gain on disposal of plant assets; cost of goods sold; depreciation expense; and sales returns and allowances.

Determine cost of goods sold using basic periodic formula.
(LO 5), **AP**

BE5-7 Sands Company sold goods with a total selling price of $800,000 during the year. It purchased goods for $380,000 and had beginning inventory of $67,000. A count of its ending inventory determined that goods on hand was $50,000. What was its cost of goods sold?

Compute net purchases and cost of goods purchased.
(LO 5), **AP**

BE5-8 Assume that Tracy Company uses a periodic inventory system and has these account balances: Purchases $404,000; Purchase Returns and Allowances $13,000; Purchase Discounts $9,000; and Freight-In $16,000. Determine net purchases and cost of goods purchased.

Compute cost of goods sold and gross profit.
(LO 5), **C**

BE5-9 Assume the same information as in BE5-8 and also that Tracy Company has beginning inventory of $60,000, ending inventory of $90,000, and net sales of $612,000. Determine the amounts to be reported for cost of goods sold and gross profit.

Calculate profitability ratios.
(LO 6), **AP**

BE5-10 Durbin Corporation reported net sales of $250,000, cost of goods sold of $150,000, operating expenses of $50,000, net income of $32,500, beginning total assets of $520,000, and ending total assets of $600,000. Calculate each of the following values and explain what they mean: (a) profit margin and (b) gross profit rate.

Calculate profitability ratios.
(LO 6), **AP**

BE5-11 Barten Corporation reported net sales $800,000; cost of goods sold $520,000; operating expenses $210,000; and net income $68,000. Calculate the following values and explain what they mean: (a) profit margin and (b) gross profit rate.

Evaluate quality of earnings.
(LO 7), **C**

BE5-12 Moritz Corporation reported net income of $346,000, cash of $67,800, and net cash provided by operating activities of $221,200. What does this suggest about the quality of the company's earnings? What further steps should be taken?

Journalize purchase transactions.
(LO 8), **AP**

*__BE5-13__ Prepare the journal entries to record these transactions on Kimbrel Company's books using a periodic inventory system.
(a) On March 2, Kimbrel Company purchased $800,000 of merchandise from Pineda Company, terms 2/10, n/30.
(b) On March 6, Kimbrel Company returned $95,000 of the merchandise purchased on March 2.
(c) On March 12, Kimbrel Company paid the balance due to Pineda Company.

Exercises

Journalize purchase transactions.
(LO 2), **AP**

E5-1 This information relates to Crisp Co.
1. On April 5, purchased merchandise from Frost Company for $28,000, terms 2/10, n/30.
2. On April 6, paid freight costs of $700 on merchandise purchased from Frost.
3. On April 7, purchased equipment on account for $30,000.
4. On April 8, returned $3,600 of April 5 merchandise to Frost Company.
5. On April 15, paid the amount due to Frost Company in full.

Instructions
(a) Prepare the journal entries to record the transactions listed above on Crisp Co.'s books. Crisp Co. uses a perpetual inventory system.
(b) Assume that Crisp Co. paid the balance due to Frost Company on May 4 instead of April 15. Prepare the journal entry to record this payment.

Journalize perpetual inventory entries.
(LO 2, 3), **AP**

E5-2 Assume that on September 1, Office Depot had an inventory that included a variety of calculators. The company uses a perpetual inventory system. During September, these transactions occurred.

Sept.   6   Purchased calculators from Dragoo Co. at a total cost of $1,650, terms n/30.
        9   Paid freight of $50 on calculators purchased from Dragoo Co.
       10   Returned calculators to Dragoo Co. for $66 credit because they did not meet specifications.
       12   Sold calculators costing $520 for $690 to Fryer Book Store, terms n/30.
       14   Granted credit of $45 to Fryer Book Store for the return of one calculator that was not ordered. The calculator cost $34.
       20   Sold calculators costing $570 for $760 to Heasley Card Shop, terms n/30.

Instructions
Journalize the September transactions.

E5-3   The following transactions are for Solarte Company.

1. On December 3, Solarte Company sold $500,000 of merchandise to Rooney Co., terms 1/10, n/30. The cost of the merchandise sold was $330,000.
2. On December 8, Rooney Co. was granted an allowance of $25,000 for merchandise purchased on December 3.
3. On December 13, Solarte Company received the balance due from Rooney Co.

Journalize sales transactions.
(LO 3), **AP**

Instructions
(a) Prepare the journal entries to record these transactions on the books of Solarte Company. Solarte uses a perpetual inventory system.
(b) Assume that Solarte Company received the balance due from Rooney Co. on January 2 of the following year instead of December 13. Prepare the journal entry to record the receipt of payment on January 2.

E5-4   On June 10, Purcey Company purchased $9,000 of merchandise from Guyer Company, terms 3/10, n/30. Purcey pays the freight costs of $400 on June 11. Goods totaling $600 are returned to Guyer for credit on June 12. On June 19, Purcey Company pays Guyer Company in full, less the purchase discount. Both companies use a perpetual inventory system.

Journalize perpetual inventory entries.
(LO 2, 3), **AP**

Instructions
(a) Prepare separate entries for each transaction on the books of Purcey Company.
(b) Prepare separate entries for each transaction for Guyer Company. The merchandise purchased by Purcey on June 10 cost Guyer $5,000, and the goods returned cost Guyer $310.

E5-5   The adjusted trial balance of Hodges Company shows these data pertaining to sales at the end of its fiscal year, October 31, 2014: Sales Revenue $900,000; Freight-Out $14,000; Sales Returns and Allowances $22,000; and Sales Discounts $13,500.

Prepare sales section of income statement.
(LO 4), **AP**

Instructions
Prepare the sales section of the income statement.

E5-6   Presented below is information for Zhou Co. for the month of January 2014.

Cost of goods sold	$212,000	Rent expense	$ 32,000
Freight-out	7,000	Sales discounts	8,000
Insurance expense	12,000	Sales returns and allowances	20,000
Salaries and wages expense	60,000	Sales revenue	370,000

Prepare an income statement and calculate profitability ratios.
(LO 4, 6), **AP**
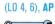

Instructions
(a) Prepare an income statement using the format presented in Illustration 5-11. Assume a 25% tax rate.
(b) Calculate the profit margin and the gross profit rate.

E5-7   Financial information is presented here for two companies.

	Yanik Company	Nunez Company
Sales revenue	$90,000	?
Sales returns and allowances	?	$ 5,000
Net sales	84,000	100,000
Cost of goods sold	58,000	?
Gross profit	?	40,000
Operating expenses	14,380	?
Net income	?	17,000

Compute missing amounts and calculate profitability ratios.
(LO 4, 6), **AP**

Instructions

(a) Fill in the missing amounts. Show all computations.
(b) Calculate the profit margin and the gross profit rate for each company.
(c) Discuss your findings in part (b).

Prepare multiple-step income statement and calculate profitability ratios.

(LO 4, 6), **AP**

E5-8 In its income statement for the year ended December 31, 2014, Gavin Company reported the following condensed data.

Salaries and wages		Loss on disposal of plant	
expense	$465,000	assets	$ 83,500
Cost of goods sold	987,000	Sales revenue	2,210,000
Interest expense	71,000	Income tax expense	25,000
Interest revenue	65,000	Sales discounts	160,000
Depreciation expense	310,000	Utilities expense	110,000

Instructions

(a) Prepare a multiple-step income statement.
(b) Calculate the profit margin and gross profit rate.
(c) In 2013, Gavin had a profit margin of 5%. Is the decline in 2014 a cause for concern? (Ignore income tax effects.)

Prepare multiple-step income statement and calculate profitability ratios.

(LO 4, 6), **C**

E5-9 Suppose in its income statement for the year ended June 30, 2014, The Clorox Company reported the following condensed data (dollars in millions).

Salaries and wages expense	$ 460	Research and	
Depreciation expense	90	development expense	$ 114
Sales revenue	5,730	Income tax expense	276
Interest expense	161	Loss on disposal of plant assets	46
Advertising expense	499	Cost of goods sold	3,104
Sales returns and		Rent expense	105
allowances	280	Utilities expense	60

Instructions

(a) Prepare a multiple-step income statement.
(b) Calculate the gross profit rate and the profit margin and explain what each means.
(c) Assume the marketing department has presented a plan to increase advertising expenses by $340 million. It expects this plan to result in an increase in both net sales and cost of goods sold of 25%. (*Hint:* Increase both sales revenue and sales returns and allowances by 25%.) Redo parts (a) and (b) and discuss whether this plan has merit. (Assume a tax rate of 34%, and round all amounts to whole dollars.)

Prepare cost of goods sold section using periodic system.

(LO 5), **AP**

E5-10 The trial balance of Sanchez Company at the end of its fiscal year, August 31, 2014, includes these accounts: Beginning Inventory $18,700; Purchases $154,000; Sales Revenue $190,000; Freight-In $8,000; Sales Returns and Allowances $3,000; Freight-Out $1,000; and Purchase Returns and Allowances $5,000. The ending inventory is $21,000.

Instructions

Prepare a cost of goods sold section (periodic system) for the year ending August 31, 2014.

Prepare cost of goods sold section using periodic system.

(LO 5), **AP**

E5-11 Below is a series of cost of goods sold sections for companies A, L, N, and R.

	A	L	N	R
Beginning inventory	$ 250	$ 120	$ 700	$ (j)
Purchases	1,500	1,080	(g)	43,590
Purchase returns and allowances	80	(d)	290	(k)
Net purchases	(a)	1,040	7,410	42,290
Freight-in	130	(e)	(h)	2,240
Cost of goods purchased	(b)	1,230	8,050	(l)
Cost of goods available for sale	1,800	1,350	(i)	49,530
Ending inventory	310	(f)	1,150	6,230
Cost of goods sold	(c)	1,230	7,600	43,300

Instructions

Fill in the lettered blanks to complete the cost of goods sold sections.

E5-12   Dorcas Corporation reported sales revenue of $257,000, net income of $45,300, cash of $9,300, and net cash provided by operating activities of $23,200. Accounts receivable have increased at three times the rate of sales during the last 3 years.

Evaluate quality of earnings.
(LO 7), **C**

Instructions
(a) Explain what is meant by high quality of earnings.
(b) Evaluate the quality of the company's earnings. Discuss your findings.
(c) What factors might have contributed to the company's quality of earnings?

*E5-13   This information relates to Woodward Co.
  1. On April 5, purchased merchandise from Cozart Company for $27,000, terms 2/10, n/30.
  2. On April 6, paid freight costs of $1,200 on merchandise purchased from Cozart Company.
  3. On April 7, purchased equipment on account for $30,000.
  4. On April 8, returned some of the April 5 merchandise to Cozart Company, which cost $3,600.
  5. On April 15, paid the amount due to Cozart Company in full.

Journalize purchase transactions.
(LO 8), **AP**

Instructions
(a) Prepare the journal entries to record these transactions on the books of Woodward Co. using a periodic inventory system.
(b) Assume that Woodward Co. paid the balance due to Cozart Company on May 4 instead of April 15. Prepare the journal entry to record this payment.

Challenge Exercises

Visit the book's companion website, at **www.wiley.com/college/kimmel**, and choose the Student Companion site to access Challenge Exercises.

Problems: Set A

P5-1A   Waters Hardware Store completed the following merchandising transactions in the month of May. At the beginning of May, Waters' ledger showed Cash of $8,000 and Common Stock of $8,000.

Journalize, post, prepare partial income statement, and calculate ratios.
(LO 2, 3, 4, 6), **AP**

May	1	Purchased merchandise on account from Hauke Wholesale Supply for $8,000, terms 1/10, n/30.
	2	Sold merchandise on account for $4,400, terms 2/10, n/30. The cost of the merchandise sold was $3,300.
	5	Received credit from Hauke Wholesale Supply for merchandise returned $200.
	9	Received collections in full, less discounts, from customers billed on May 2.
	10	Paid Hauke Wholesale Supply in full, less discount.
	11	Purchased supplies for cash $900.
	12	Purchased merchandise for cash $3,100.
	15	Received $230 refund for return of poor-quality merchandise from supplier on cash purchase.
	17	Purchased merchandise from Friedrich Distributors for $2,500, terms 2/10, n/30.
	19	Paid freight on May 17 purchase $250.
	24	Sold merchandise for cash $5,500. The cost of the merchandise sold was $4,100.
	25	Purchased merchandise from Fasteners Inc. for $800, terms 3/10, n/30.
	27	Paid Friedrich Distributors in full, less discount.
	29	Made refunds to cash customers for returned merchandise $124. The returned merchandise had cost $90.
	31	Sold merchandise on account for $1,280, terms n/30. The cost of the merchandise sold was $830.

Waters Hardware's chart of accounts includes Cash, Accounts Receivable, Inventory, Supplies, Accounts Payable, Common Stock, Sales Revenue, Sales Returns and Allowances, Sales Discounts, and Cost of Goods Sold.

Instructions
(a) Journalize the transactions using a perpetual inventory system.
(b) Post the transactions to T-accounts. Be sure to enter the beginning cash and common stock balances.

(c) Gross profit $2,828

(c) Prepare an income statement through gross profit for the month of May 2014.
(d) Calculate the profit margin and the gross profit rate. (Assume operating expenses were $1,400.)

Journalize purchase and sale transactions under a perpetual system.

(LO 2, 3), AP

P5-2A McCoy Warehouse distributes hardback books to retail stores and extends credit terms of 2/10, n/30 to all of its customers. During the month of June, the following merchandising transactions occurred.

June	1	Purchased books on account for $1,040 (including freight) from Carlin Publishers, terms 2/10, n/30.
	3	Sold books on account to the Goldschmidt bookstore for $1,200. The cost of the merchandise sold was $720.
	6	Received $40 credit for books returned to Carlin Publishers.
	9	Paid Carlin Publishers in full.
	15	Received payment in full from the Goldschmidt bookstore.
	17	Sold books on account to Town Crier for $1,200. The cost of the merchandise sold was $730.
	20	Purchased books on account for $720 from Good Book Publishers, terms 1/15, n/30.
	24	Received payment in full from Town Crier.
	26	Paid Good Book Publishers in full.
	28	Sold books on account to Emporia Bookstore for $1,300. The cost of the merchandise sold was $780.
	30	Granted Emporia Bookstore $130 credit for books returned costing $80.

Instructions
Journalize the transactions for the month of June for McCoy Warehouse, using a perpetual inventory system.

Journalize, post, and prepare trial balance and partial income statement.

(LO 2, 3, 4), AP

GLS

P5-3A At the beginning of the current season on April 1, the ledger of Flint Hills Pro Shop showed Cash $2,500; Inventory $3,500; and Common Stock $6,000. The following transactions were completed during April 2014.

Apr.	5	Purchased golf bags, clubs, and balls on account from Akers Co. $1,500, terms 3/10, n/60.
	7	Paid freight on Akers purchase $80.
	9	Received credit from Akers Co. for merchandise returned $200.
	10	Sold merchandise on account to members $1,340, terms n/30. The merchandise sold had a cost of $820.
	12	Purchased golf shoes, sweaters, and other accessories on account from Palmer Sportswear $830, terms 1/10, n/30.
	14	Paid Akers Co. in full.
	17	Received credit from Palmer Sportswear for merchandise returned $30.
	20	Made sales on account to members $810, terms n/30. The cost of the merchandise sold was $550.
	21	Paid Palmer Sportswear in full.
	27	Granted an allowance to members for clothing that did not fit properly $80.
	30	Received payments on account from members $1,220.

The chart of accounts for the pro shop includes Cash, Accounts Receivable, Inventory, Accounts Payable, Common Stock, Sales Revenue, Sales Returns and Allowances, and Cost of Goods Sold.

Instructions
(a) Journalize the April transactions using a perpetual inventory system.
(b) Using T-accounts, enter the beginning balances in the ledger accounts and post the April transactions.

(c) Tot. trial balance $8,150
(d) Gross profit $ 700

(c) Prepare a trial balance on April 30, 2014.
(d) Prepare an income statement through gross profit for the month of April 2014.

P5-4A Lambert Department Store is located in midtown Metropolis. During the past several years, net income has been declining because suburban shopping centers have been attracting business away from city areas. At the end of the company's fiscal year on November 30, 2014, these accounts appeared in its adjusted trial balance.

Prepare financial statements and calculate profitability ratios.

(LO 4, 6), **AP**

Accounts Payable	$ 26,800
Accounts Receivable	17,200
Accumulated Depreciation—Equipment	68,000
Cash	8,000
Common Stock	35,000
Cost of Goods Sold	614,300
Freight-Out	6,200
Equipment	157,000
Depreciation Expense	13,500
Dividends	12,000
Gain on Disposal of Plant Assets	2,000
Income Tax Expense	10,000
Insurance Expense	9,000
Interest Expense	5,000
Inventory	26,200
Notes Payable	43,500
Prepaid Insurance	6,000
Advertising Expense	33,500
Rent Expense	34,000
Retained Earnings	14,200
Salaries and Wages Expense	117,000
Sales Revenue	904,000
Salaries and Wages Payable	6,000
Sales Returns and Allowances	20,000
Utilities Expense	10,600

Additional data: Notes payable are due in 2018.

Instructions
(a) Prepare a multiple-step income statement, a retained earnings statement, and a classified balance sheet.
(b) Calculate the profit margin and the gross profit rate.
(c) The vice president of marketing and the director of human resources have developed a proposal whereby the company would compensate the sales force on a strictly commission basis. Given the increased incentive, they expect net sales to increase by 15%. As a result, they estimate that gross profit will increase by $40,443 and expenses by $58,600. Compute the expected new net income. (*Hint:* You do not need to prepare an income statement.) Then, compute the revised profit margin and gross profit rate. Comment on the effect that this plan would have on net income and on the ratios, and evaluate the merit of this proposal. (Ignore income tax effects.)

(a) Net income $ 32,900
    Tot. assets $146,400

P5-5A An inexperienced accountant prepared this condensed income statement for Sundberg Company, a retail firm that has been in business for a number of years.

Prepare a correct multiple-step income statement.

(LO 4), **AP**

SUNDBERG COMPANY
Income Statement
For the Year Ended December 31, 2014

Revenues	
Net sales	$850,000
Other revenues	22,000
	872,000
Cost of goods sold	555,000
Gross profit	317,000
Operating expenses	
Selling expenses	109,000
Administrative expenses	103,000
	212,000
Net earnings	$105,000

As an experienced, knowledgeable accountant, you review the statement and determine the following facts.

1. Net sales consist of sales $911,000, less freight-out on merchandise sold $33,000, and sales returns and allowances $28,000.
2. Other revenues consist of sales discounts $18,000 and rent revenue $4,000.
3. Selling expenses consist of salespersons' salaries $80,000; depreciation on equipment $10,000; advertising $13,000; and sales commissions $6,000. The commissions represent commissions paid. At December 31, $3,000 of commissions have been earned by salespersons but have not been paid. All compensation should be recorded as Salaries and Wages Expense.
4. Administrative expenses consist of office salaries $47,000; dividends $18,000; utilities $12,000; interest expense $2,000; and rent expense $24,000, which includes prepayments totaling $6,000 for the first quarter of 2015.

Instructions

Net income $67,500

Prepare a correct detailed multiple-step income statement. Assume a 25% tax rate.

Journalize, post, and prepare adjusted trial balance and financial statements.

(LO 4), **AP**

P5-6A   The trial balance of Customer Choice Wholesale Company contained the accounts shown at December 31, the end of the company's fiscal year.

CUSTOMER CHOICE WHOLESALE COMPANY
Trial Balance
December 31, 2014

	Debit	Credit
Cash	$ 31,400	
Accounts Receivable	37,600	
Inventory	70,000	
Land	92,000	
Buildings	200,000	
Accumulated Depreciation—Buildings		$ 60,000
Equipment	83,500	
Accumulated Depreciation—Equipment		40,500
Notes Payable		54,700
Accounts Payable		17,500
Common Stock		160,000
Retained Earnings		67,200
Dividends	10,000	

	Debit	Credit
Sales Revenue		$ 922,100
Sales Discounts	$ 6,000	
Cost of Goods Sold	709,900	
Salaries and Wages Expense	51,300	
Utilities Expense	11,400	
Maintenance and Repairs Expense	8,900	
Advertising Expense	5,200	
Insurance Expense	4,800	
	$1,322,000	$1,322,000

Adjustment data:

1. Depreciation is $8,000 on buildings and $7,000 on equipment. (Both are operating expenses.)
2. Interest of $4,500 is due and unpaid on notes payable at December 31.
3. Income tax due and unpaid at December 31 is $24,000.

Other data: $15,000 of the notes payable are payable next year.

Instructions

(a) Journalize the adjusting entries.
(b) Create T-accounts for all accounts used in part (a). Enter the trial balance amounts into the T-accounts and post the adjusting entries.

(c) Prepare an adjusted trial balance.
(d) Prepare a multiple-step income statement and a retained earnings statement for the year, and a classified balance sheet at December 31, 2014.

P5-7A At the end of Ermler Department Store's fiscal year on November 30, 2014, these accounts appeared in its adjusted trial balance.

Determine cost of goods sold and gross profit under a periodic system.

(LO 4, 5), **AP**

Freight-In	$ 5,060
Inventory (beginning)	41,300
Purchases	613,000
Purchase Discounts	7,000
Purchase Returns and Allowances	6,760
Sales Revenue	902,000
Sales Returns and Allowances	20,000

Additional facts:
1. Inventory on November 30, 2014, is $36,200.
2. Note that Ermler Department Store uses a periodic system.

Instructions

Prepare an income statement through gross profit for the year ended November 30, 2014.

Gross profit $272,600

P5-8A Yang Inc. operates a retail operation that purchases and sells snowmobiles, among other outdoor products. The company purchases all inventory on credit and uses a periodic inventory system. The Accounts Payable account is used for recording inventory purchases only; all other current liabilities are accrued in separate accounts. You are provided with the following selected information for the fiscal years 2012 through 2015, inclusive.

Calculate missing amounts and assess profitability.

(LO 4, 5, 6), **AN**

	2012	2013	2014	2015
Income Statement Data				
Sales revenue		$96,890	$ (e)	$82,220
Cost of goods sold		(a)	28,060	26,490
Gross profit		67,800	59,620	(i)
Operating expenses		63,640	(f)	52,870
Net income		$ (b)	$ 3,510	$ (j)
Balance Sheet Data				
Inventory	$13,000	$ (c)	$14,700	$ (k)
Accounts payable	5,800	6,500	4,600	(l)
Additional Information				
Purchases of inventory on account		$25,890	$ (g)	$24,050
Cash payments to suppliers		(d)	(h)	24,650

Instructions

(a) Calculate the missing amounts.
(b) The vice presidents of sales, marketing, production, and finance are discussing the company's results with the CEO. They note that sales declined over the 3-year fiscal period, 2013–2015. Does that mean that profitability necessarily also declined? Explain, computing the gross profit rate and the profit margin for each fiscal year to help support your answer.

*P5-9A At the beginning of the current season on April 1, the ledger of Flint Hills Pro Shop showed Cash $2,500; Inventory $3,500; and Common Stock $6,000. The following transactions occurred during April 2014.

Journalize, post, and prepare trial balance and partial income statement under a periodic system.

(LO 5, 8), **AP**

Apr.	5	Purchased golf bags, clubs, and balls on account from Akers Co. $1,500, terms 3/10, n/60.
	7	Paid freight on Akers Co. purchases $80.
	9	Received credit from Akers Co. for merchandise returned $200.
	10	Sold merchandise on account to members $1,340, terms n/30.
	12	Purchased golf shoes, sweaters, and other accessories on account from Palmer Sportswear $830, terms 1/10, n/30.
	14	Paid Akers Co. in full.
	17	Received credit from Palmer Sportswear for merchandise returned $30.

20 Made sales on account to members $810, terms n/30.
21 Paid Palmer Sportswear in full.
27 Granted credit to members for clothing that did not fit properly $80.
30 Received payments on account from members $1,220.

The chart of accounts for the pro shop includes Cash, Accounts Receivable, Inventory, Accounts Payable, Common Stock, Sales Revenue, Sales Returns and Allowances, Purchases, Purchase Returns and Allowances, Purchase Discounts, and Freight-In.

Instructions
(a) Journalize the April transactions using a periodic inventory system.
(b) Using T-accounts, enter the beginning balances in the ledger accounts and post the April transactions.
(c) Tot. trial balance $8,427   (c) Prepare a trial balance on April 30, 2014.
(d) Gross profit $ 700   (d) Prepare an income statement through gross profit, assuming inventory on hand at April 30 is $4,263.

Problems: Set B

Visit the book's companion website, at **www.wiley.com/college/kimmel**, and choose the Student Companion site to access Problem Set B.

Comprehensive Problem

CP5 On December 1, 2014, Boline Distributing Company had the following account balances.

	Debit		Credit
Cash	$ 7,200	Accumulated Depreciation—	
Accounts Receivable	4,600	Equipment	$ 2,200
Inventory	12,000	Accounts Payable	4,500
Supplies	1,200	Salaries and Wages Payable	1,000
Equipment	22,000	Common Stock	15,000
	$47,000	Retained Earnings	24,300
			$47,000

During December, the company completed the following summary transactions.

Dec. 6 Paid $1,600 for salaries due employees, of which $600 is for December and $1,000 is for November salaries payable.
8 Received $1,900 cash from customers in payment of account (no discount allowed).
10 Sold merchandise for cash $6,300. The cost of the merchandise sold was $4,100.
13 Purchased merchandise on account from Gong Co. $9,000, terms 2/10, n/30.
15 Purchased supplies for cash $2,000.
18 Sold merchandise on account $12,000, terms 3/10, n/30. The cost of the merchandise sold was $8,000.
20 Paid salaries $1,800.
23 Paid Gong Co. in full, less discount.
27 Received collections in full, less discounts, from customers billed on December 18.

Adjustment data:
1. Accrued salaries payable $800.
2. Depreciation $200 per month.
3. Supplies on hand $1,500.
4. Income tax due and unpaid at December 31 is $200.

Instructions
(a) Journalize the December transactions using a perpetual inventory system.
(b) Enter the December 1 balances in the ledger T-accounts and post the December transactions. Use Cost of Goods Sold, Depreciation Expense, Salaries and Wages Expense, Sales Revenue, Sales Discounts, Supplies Expense, Income Tax Expense, and Income Taxes Payable.
(c) Journalize and post adjusting entries.
(d) Prepare an adjusted trial balance.
(e) Prepare an income statement and a retained earnings statement for December and a classified balance sheet at December 31.

Broadening Your Perspective

Financial Reporting and Analysis

FINANCIAL REPORTING PROBLEM: *Tootsie Roll Industries, Inc.*

BYP5-1 The financial statements for Tootsie Roll Industries appear in Appendix A at the end of this textbook.

Instructions
Answer these questions using the Consolidated Income Statement.
(a) What was the percentage change in total revenue and in net income from 2010 to 2011?
(b) What was the profit margin in each of the 3 years? (Use "Total Revenue.") Comment on the trend.
(c) What was Tootsie Roll's gross profit rate in each of the 3 years? (Use "Net Product Sales" amounts.) Comment on the trend.

COMPARATIVE ANALYSIS PROBLEM: *Tootsie Roll vs. Hershey*

BYP5-2 The financial statements of The Hershey Company appear in Appendix B, following the financial statements for Tootsie Roll in Appendix A.

Instructions
(a) Based on the information contained in these financial statements, determine the following values for each company.
   (1) Profit margin for 2011. (For Tootsie Roll, use "Total Revenue.")
   (2) Gross profit for 2011. (For Tootsie Roll, use "Product" amounts.)
   (3) Gross profit rate for 2011. (For Tootsie Roll, use "Product" amounts.)
   (4) Operating income for 2011.
   (5) Percentage change in operating income from 2011 to 2010.
(b) What conclusions concerning the relative profitability of the two companies can be drawn from these data?

RESEARCH CASE

BYP5-3 The February 21, 2012, edition of the *New York Times* contains an article by Stephanie Clifford entitled "High-End Retailers Report Strong Profits, but Wal-Mart Still Struggles."

Instructions
Read the article and answer the following questions.
(a) Explain why Wal-Mart's gross profit margin fell even though its total sales revenue increased.
(b) Saks Fifth Avenue experienced an increase in its gross profit rate for the year. What factors contributed to this increase?
(c) Macy's experienced a decline in its gross profit rate. The article said that the decline could be attributed to two factors: a free-shipping promotion and markdowns on cold-weather gear. Discuss whether this explanation is consistent with what you learned in this chapter about the financial presentation of these items in the income statement.

(d) The article mentions that Home Depot experienced increases in "same store sales." What does "increase in same store sales" mean? What implications does an increase in same store sales have for the profit margin?

INTERPRETING FINANCIAL STATEMENTS

BYP5-4   Recently, it was announced that two giant French retailers, Carrefour SA and Promodes SA, would merge. A headline in the *Wall Street Journal* blared, "French Retailers Create New Wal-Mart Rival." While Wal-Mart's total sales would still exceed those of the combined company, Wal-Mart's international sales are far less than those of the combined company. This is a serious concern for Wal-Mart, since its primary opportunity for future growth lies outside of the United States.

Below are basic financial data for the combined corporation (in euros) and Wal-Mart (in U.S. dollars). Even though their results are presented in different currencies, by employing ratios we can make some basic comparisons.

	Carrefour (in millions)	Wal-Mart (in millions)
Sales revenue	€70,486	$256,329
Cost of goods sold	54,630	198,747
Net income	1,738	9,054
Total assets	39,063	104,912
Current assets	14,521	34,421
Current liabilities	13,660	37,418
Total liabilities	29,434	61,289

Instructions
Compare the two companies by answering the following.
(a) Calculate the gross profit rate for each of the companies, and discuss their relative abilities to control cost of goods sold.
(b) Calculate the profit margin, and discuss the companies' relative profitability.
(c) Calculate the current ratio and debt to assets ratios for the two companies, and discuss their relative liquidity and solvency.
(d) What concerns might you have in relying on this comparison?

REAL-WORLD FOCUS

BYP5-5   *Purpose:* No financial decision-maker should ever rely solely on the financial information reported in the annual report to make decisions. It is important to keep abreast of financial news. This activity demonstrates how to search for financial news on the Internet.

Address: **http://biz.yahoo.com/i,** or go to **www.wiley.com/college/kimmel**

Steps
1. Type in either Wal-Mart, Target Corp., or Kmart.
2. Choose **News**.
3. Select an article that sounds interesting to you and that would be relevant to an investor in these companies.

Instructions
(a) What was the source of the article (e.g., Reuters, Businesswire, Prnewswire)?
(b) Assume that you are a personal financial planner and that one of your clients owns stock in the company. Write a brief memo to your client summarizing the article and explaining the implications of the article for their investment.

Critical Thinking

DECISION-MAKING ACROSS THE ORGANIZATION

BYP5-6   Three years ago, Sue Kienholz and her brother-in-law Jeremy Reyes opened Megamart Department Store. For the first 2 years, business was good, but the following condensed income statement results for 2014 were disappointing.

MEGAMART DEPARTMENT STORE
Income Statement
For the Year Ended December 31, 2014

Net sales		$700,000
Cost of goods sold		560,000
Gross profit		140,000
Operating expenses		
Selling expenses	$100,000	
Administrative expenses	20,000	
		120,000
Net income		$ 20,000

Sue believes the problem lies in the relatively low gross profit rate of 20%. Jeremy believes the problem is that operating expenses are too high. Sue thinks the gross profit rate can be improved by making two changes. (1) Increase average selling prices by 15%; this increase is expected to lower sales volume so that total sales dollars will increase only 4%. (2) Buy merchandise in larger quantities and take all purchase discounts; these changes are expected to increase the gross profit rate from 20% to 25%. Sue does not anticipate that these changes will have any effect on operating expenses.

Jeremy thinks expenses can be cut by making these two changes. (1) Cut 2014 sales salaries of $60,000 in half and give sales personnel a commission of 2% of net sales. (2) Reduce store deliveries to one day per week rather than twice a week; this change will reduce 2014 delivery expenses of $40,000 by 40%. Jeremy feels that these changes will not have any effect on net sales.

Sue and Jeremy come to you for help in deciding the best way to improve net income.

Instructions
With the class divided into groups, answer the following.
(a) Prepare a condensed income statement for 2015 assuming (1) Sue's changes are implemented and (2) Jeremy's ideas are adopted.
(b) What is your recommendation to Sue and Jeremy?
(c) Prepare a condensed income statement for 2015 assuming both sets of proposed changes are made.
(d) Discuss the impact that other factors might have. For example, would increasing the quantity of inventory increase costs? Would a salary cut affect employee morale? Would decreased morale affect sales? Would decreased store deliveries decrease customer satisfaction? What other suggestions might be considered?

COMMUNICATION ACTIVITY

BYP5-7   The following situation is presented in chronological order.
1. Shafer decides to buy a surfboard.
2. He calls Surfing USA Co. to inquire about their surfboards.
3. Two days later, he requests Surfing USA Co. to make him a surfboard.
4. Three days later, Surfing USA Co. sends him a purchase order to fill out.
5. He sends back the purchase order.
6. Surfing USA Co. receives the completed purchase order.
7. Surfing USA Co. completes the surfboard.
8. Shafer picks up the surfboard.
9. Surfing USA Co. bills Shafer.
10. Surfing USA Co. receives payment from Shafer.

Instructions
In a memo to the president of Surfing USA Co., answer the following questions.
(a) When should Surfing USA Co. record the sale?
(b) Suppose that with his purchase order, Shafer is required to make a down payment. Would that change your answer to part (a)?

ETHICS CASE

BYP5-8   Andrea Tabares was just hired as the assistant treasurer of Northshore Stores, a specialty chain store company that has nine retail stores concentrated in one metropolitan area. Among other things, the payment of all invoices is centralized in one of the departments

Andrea will manage. Her primary responsibility is to maintain the company's high credit rating by paying all bills when due and to take advantage of all cash discounts.

William Parks, the former assistant treasurer, who has been promoted to treasurer, is training Andrea in her new duties. He instructs Andrea that she is to continue the practice of preparing all checks "net of discount" and dating the checks the last day of the discount period. "But," William continues, "we always hold the checks at least 4 days beyond the discount period before mailing them. That way we get another 4 days of interest on our money. Most of our creditors need our business and don't complain. And, if they scream about our missing the discount period, we blame it on the mail room or the post office. We've only lost one discount out of every hundred we take that way. I think everybody does it. By the way, welcome to our team!"

Instructions
(a) What are the ethical considerations in this case?
(b) What stakeholders are harmed or benefited?
(c) Should Andrea continue the practice started by William? Does she have any choice?

ALL ABOUT YOU

BYP5-9 There are many situations in business where it is difficult to determine the proper period in which to record revenue. Suppose that after graduation with a degree in finance, you take a job as a manager at a consumer electronics store called Midwest Electronics. The company has expanded rapidly in order to compete with Best Buy.

Midwest has also begun selling gift cards. The cards are available in any dollar amount and allow the holder of the card to purchase an item for up to 2 years from the time the card is purchased. If the card is not used during those 2 years, it expires.

Instructions
Answer the following questions.

At what point should the revenue from the gift cards be recognized? Should the revenue be recognized at the time the card is sold, or should it be recorded when the card is redeemed? Explain the reasoning to support your answers.

FASB CODIFICATION ACTIVITY

BYP5-10 If your school has a subscription to the FASB Codification, go to **http://aaahg.org/ascLogin.cfm** to log in and prepare responses to the following.
(a) Access the glossary ("Master Glossary") to answer the following.
   (1) What is the definition provided for inventory?
   (2) What is a customer?
(b) What guidance does the Codification provide concerning reporting inventories above cost?

Answers to Insight and Accounting Across the Organization Questions

p. 195 Morrow Snowboards Improves Its Stock Appeal Q: If a perpetual system keeps track of inventory on a daily basis, why do companies ever need to do a physical count? **A:** A perpetual system keeps track of all sales and purchases on a continuous basis. This provides a constant record of the number of units in the inventory. However, if employees make errors in recording sales or purchases, or if there is theft, the inventory value will not be correct. As a consequence, all companies do a physical count of inventory at least once a year.

p. 202 Should Costco Change Its Return Policy? Q: If a company expects significant returns, what are the implications for revenue recognition? **A:** If a company expects significant returns, it should make an adjusting entry at the end of the year to increase Sales Returns and Allowances by the estimated amount of sales returns. This is necessary so as not to overstate the amount of revenue recognized in the period.

p. 206 Disclosing More Details Q: Why have investors and analysts demanded more accuracy in isolating "Other gains and losses" from operating items? **A:** Greater accuracy in the classification of operating versus nonoperating ("Other gains and losses") items permits investors and analysts to judge the real operating margin, the results of continuing operations, and management's ability to control operating expenses.

p. 211 Selling Green Q: What is meant by "monetize environmental sustainability" for shareholders? **A:** By marketing green, not only does PepsiCo help the environment in the long run, but it also leads to long-term profitability as well. In other words, sound sustainability practices are good business and lead to sound financial results.

Answers to Self-Test Questions

1. a   **2.** c   **3.** c   **4.** b (($750 − $50) ×.98)   **5.** c   **6.** c   **7.** b ($400,000 − $310,000)   **8.** d   **9.** a ($60,000 + $380,000 − $50,000)   **10.** b ($17,200 + ($60,400 − $3,000 − $1,100 + $600))   **11.** c   **12.** c   **13.** d ($92,400 ÷ $267,000)   **14.** b   ***15.** b

A Look at IFRS

The basic accounting entries for merchandising are the same under both GAAP and IFRS. The income statement is a required statement under both sets of standards. The basic format is similar although some differences do exist.

LEARNING OBJECTIVE 9

Compare the accounting procedures for merchandising under GAAP and IFRS.

KEY POINTS

- Under both GAAP and IFRS, a company can choose to use either a perpetual or a periodic system.

- Inventories are defined by IFRS as held-for-sale in the ordinary course of business, in the process of production for such sale, or in the form of materials or supplies to be consumed in the production process or in the providing of services.

- Under GAAP, companies generally classify income statement items by function. Classification by function leads to descriptions like administration, distribution, and manufacturing. Under IFRS, companies must classify expenses by either nature or function. Classification by nature leads to descriptions such as the following: salaries, depreciation expense, and utilities expense. If a company uses the functional-expense method on the income statement, disclosure by nature is required in the notes to the financial statements.

- Presentation of the income statement under GAAP follows either a single-step or multiple-step format. IFRS does not mention a single-step or multiple-step approach.

- Under IFRS, revaluation of land, buildings, and intangible assets is permitted. The initial gains and losses resulting from this revaluation are reported as adjustments to equity, often referred to as **other comprehensive income**. The effect of this difference is that the use of IFRS results in more transactions affecting equity (other comprehensive income) but not net income.

- *IAS 1*, "Presentation of Financial Statements," provides general guidelines for the reporting of income statement information. Subsequently, a number of international standards have been issued that provide additional guidance to issues related to income statement presentation.

- Similar to GAAP, comprehensive income under IFRS includes unrealized gains and losses (such as those on certain types of investment securities) that are not included in the calculation of net income.

- IFRS requires that two years of income statement information be presented, whereas GAAP requires three years.

LOOKING TO THE FUTURE

The IASB and FASB are working on a project that would rework the structure of financial statements. Specifically, this project will address the issue of how to classify various items in the income statement. A main goal of this new approach is to provide information that better represents how businesses are run. In addition, this approach draws attention away from just one number—net income. It will adopt major groupings similar to those currently used by the statement of cash flows (operating, investing, and financing), so that numbers can be more readily traced across statements. For example, the amount of income that is generated by operations would be traceable to the assets and liabilities used to generate the income. Finally, this approach would also provide detail, beyond that currently seen in most statements (either GAAP or IFRS), by requiring that line items be presented both by function and by nature. The new financial statement format was heavily influenced by suggestions from financial statement analysts.

IFRS PRACTICE
IFRS SELF-TEST QUESTIONS

1. Which of the following would **not** be included in the definition of inventory under IFRS?
   (a) Photocopy paper held for sale by an office-supply store.
   (b) Stereo equipment held for sale by an electronics store.
   (c) Used office equipment held for sale by the human relations department of a plastics company.
   (d) All of the above would meet the definition.
2. Which of the following would **not** be a line item of a company reporting costs by nature?
   (a) Depreciation expense.
   (b) Salaries expense.
   (c) Interest expense.
   (d) Manufacturing expense.
3. Which of the following would **not** be a line item of a company reporting costs by function?
   (a) Administration.
   (b) Manufacturing.
   (c) Utilities expense.
   (d) Distribution.
4. Which of the following statements is **false**?
   (a) IFRS specifically requires use of a multiple-step income statement.
   (b) Under IFRS, companies can use either a perpetual or periodic system.
   (c) The proposed new format for financial statements was heavily influenced by the suggestions of financial statement analysts.
   (d) The new income statement format will try to de-emphasize the focus on the "net income" line item.
5. Under the new format for financial statements being proposed under a joint IASB/FASB project:
   (a) all financial statements would adopt headings similar to the current format of the balance sheet.
   (b) financial statements would be presented consistent with the way management usually run companies.
   (c) companies would be required to report income statement line items by function only.
   (d) the amount of detail shown in the income statement would decrease compared to current presentations.

IFRS CONCEPTS AND APPLICATION

IFRS5-1 Explain the difference between the "nature-of-expense" and "function-of-expense" classifications.

IFRS5-2 For each of the following income statement line items, state whether the item is a "by nature" expense item or a "by function" expense item.

_____ Cost of goods sold
_____ Depreciation expense
_____ Salaries and wages expense
_____ Selling expenses
_____ Utilities expense
_____ Delivery expense
_____ General and administrative expenses

IFRS5-3 Reinsch Company reported the following amounts (in euros) in 2014: Net income, €150,000; Unrealized gain related to revaluation of buildings, €10,000; and Unrealized loss on nontrading securities, €(35,000). Determine Reinsch's total comprehensive income for 2014.

INTERNATIONAL FINANCIAL REPORTING PROBLEM: *Zetar plc*

IFRS5-4   The financial statements of Zetar plc are presented in Appendix C. The company's complete annual report, including the notes to its financial statements, is available in the Investors section at **www.zetarplc.com**.

Instructions

Visit Zetar's corporate website and answer the following questions from Zetar's 2011 annual report.

(a) Does Zetar use a multiple-step or a single-step income statement format? Explain how you made your determination.

(b) Instead of "interest expense," what label does Zetar use for interest costs that it incurs?

(c) What is the approximate tax rate of Zetar's "Tax on profit from continuing activities"?

(d) Using the notes to the company's financial statements, explain what each of the following are:

    (1) Adjusted results.

    (2) One-off items.

Answers to IFRS Self-Test Questions

1. c   **2.** d   **3.** c   **4.** a   **5.** b

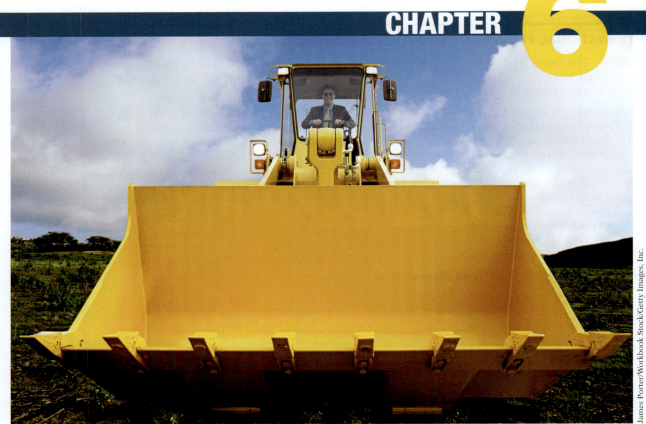

CHAPTER 6

James Porter/Workbook Stock/Getty Images, Inc.

REPORTING AND ANALYZING INVENTORY

LEARNING OBJECTIVES

After studying this chapter, you should be able to:

1 Determine how to classify inventory and inventory quantities.

2 Explain the basis of accounting for inventories and apply the inventory cost flow methods under a periodic inventory system.

3 Explain the financial statement and tax effects of each of the inventory cost flow assumptions.

4 Explain the lower-of-cost-or-market basis of accounting for inventories.

5 Compute and interpret the inventory turnover.

6 Describe the LIFO reserve and explain its importance for comparing results of different companies.

Let's talk inventory—big, bulldozer-size inventory. Caterpillar Inc. is the world's largest manufacturer of construction and mining equipment, diesel and natural gas engines, and industrial gas turbines. It sells its products in over 200 countries, making it one of the most successful U.S. exporters. More than 70% of its productive assets are located domestically, and nearly 50% of its sales are foreign.

In the past, Caterpillar's profitability suffered, but today it is very successful. A big part of this turnaround can be attributed to effective management of its inventory. Imagine what a bulldozer costs. Now imagine what it costs Caterpillar to have too many bulldozers sitting around in inventory—a situation the company definitely wants to avoid. Conversely, Caterpillar must make sure it has enough inventory to meet demand.

At one time during a 7-year period, Caterpillar's sales increased by 100%, while its inventory increased by only 50%. To achieve this dramatic reduction in the amount of resources tied up in inventory, while continuing to meet customers' needs, Caterpillar used a two-pronged approach. First, it completed a factory modernization program, which dramatically increased its production efficiency. The program reduced by 60% the amount of inventory the company processed at any one time. It also reduced by an incredible 75% the time it takes to manufacture a part.

"WHERE IS THAT SPARE BULLDOZER BLADE?"

Second, Caterpillar dramatically improved its parts distribution system. It ships more than 100,000 items daily from its 23 distribution centers strategically located around the world (10 million square feet of warehouse space—remember, we're talking bulldozers). The company can virtually guarantee that it can get any part to anywhere in the world within 24 hours.

After these changes, Caterpillar had record exports, profits, and revenues. It would have seemed that things couldn't have been better. But industry analysts, as well as the company's managers, thought otherwise. In order to maintain Caterpillar's position as the industry leader, management began another major overhaul of inventory production and inventory management processes. The goal: to cut the number of repairs in half, increase productivity by 20%, and increase inventory turnover by 40%. In short, Caterpillar's ability to manage its inventory has been a key reason for its past success, and inventory management will very likely play a huge part in its ability to succeed in the future.

INSIDE CHAPTER 6 ...

- **A Big Hiccup**
- **Falsifying Inventory to Boost Income**
- **Is LIFO Fair?**
- **Too Many TVs or Too Few?**

In the previous chapter, we discussed the accounting for merchandise inventory using a perpetual inventory system. In this chapter, we explain the methods used to calculate the cost of inventory on hand at the balance sheet date and the cost of goods sold. We conclude by illustrating methods for analyzing inventory.

The content and organization of this chapter are as follows.

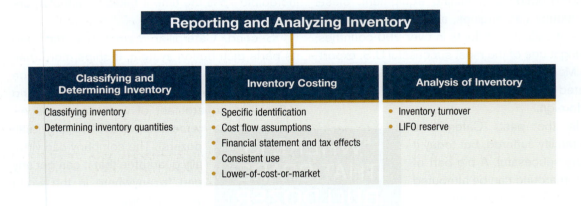

Classifying and Determining Inventory

LEARNING OBJECTIVE 1

Determine how to classify inventory and inventory quantities.

Two important steps in the reporting of inventory at the end of the accounting period are the classification of inventory based on its degree of completeness and the determination of inventory amounts.

CLASSIFYING INVENTORY

How a company classifies its inventory depends on whether the firm is a merchandiser or a manufacturer. In a **merchandising** company, such as those described in Chapter 5, inventory consists of many different items. For example, in a grocery store, canned goods, dairy products, meats, and produce are just a few of the inventory items on hand. These items have two common characteristics: (1) They are owned by the company, and (2) they are in a form ready for sale to customers in the ordinary course of business. Thus, merchandisers need only one inventory classification, **merchandise inventory**, to describe the many different items that make up the total inventory.

In a **manufacturing** company, some inventory may not yet be ready for sale. As a result, manufacturers usually classify inventory into three categories: finished goods, work in process, and raw materials. **Finished goods inventory** is manufactured items that are completed and ready for sale. **Work in process** is that portion of manufactured inventory that has begun the production process but is not yet complete. **Raw materials** are the basic goods that will be used in production but have not yet been placed into production.

For example, Caterpillar classifies earth-moving tractors completed and ready for sale as **finished goods**. It classifies the tractors on the assembly line in various stages of production as **work in process**. The steel, glass, tires, and other components that are on hand waiting to be used in the production of tractors are identified as **raw materials**. Illustration 6-1 shows an excerpt from Note 7 of Caterpillar's annual report, which shows the significant increases in each type of Caterpillar's inventory levels as the economy began to recover during this period.

Illustration 6-1 Composition of Caterpillar's inventory

(millions of dollars)	December 31		
	2011	**2010**	**2009**
Raw materials	$3,872	$2,766	$1,979
Work-in-process	2,845	1,483	656
Finished goods	7,570	5,098	3,465
Other	257	240	260
Total inventories	$14,544	$9,587	$6,360

By observing the levels and changes in the levels of these three inventory types, financial statement users can gain insight into management's production plans. For example, low levels of raw materials and high levels of finished goods suggest that management believes it has enough inventory on hand, and production will be slowing down—perhaps in anticipation of a recession. On the other hand, high levels of raw materials and low levels of finished goods probably signal that management is planning to step up production.

Many companies have significantly lowered inventory levels and costs using **just-in-time (JIT) inventory** methods. Under a just-in-time method, companies manufacture or purchase goods just in time for use. Dell is famous for having developed a system for making computers in response to individual customer requests. Even though it makes computers to meet a customer's particular specifications, Dell is able to assemble the computer and put it on a truck in less than 48 hours. The success of a JIT system depends on reliable suppliers. By integrating its information systems with those of its suppliers, Dell reduced its inventories to nearly zero. This is a huge advantage in an industry where products become obsolete nearly overnight.

The accounting concepts discussed in this chapter apply to the inventory classifications of both merchandising and manufacturing companies. Our focus throughout most of this chapter is on merchandise inventory. Additional issues specific to manufacturing companies are discussed in managerial accounting courses.

Accounting Across the Organization

A Big Hiccup

JIT can save a company a lot of money, but it isn't without risk. An unexpected disruption in the supply chain can cost a company a lot of money. Japanese automakers experienced just such a disruption when a 6.8-magnitude earthquake caused major damage to the company that produces 50% of their piston rings. The rings themselves cost only $1.50, but without them you cannot make a car. No other supplier could quickly begin producing sufficient quantities of the rings to match the desired specifications. As a result, the automakers were forced to shut down production for a few days—a loss of tens of thousands of cars.

Similarly, a major snowstorm halted production at Canadian plants of General Motors and Ford. A Ford spokesperson said, "Because the plants run with just-in-time inventory, we don't have large stockpiles of parts sitting around. When you have a somewhat significant disruption, you can pretty quickly run out of parts."

Sources: Amy Chozick, "A Key Strategy of Japan's Car Makers Backfires," *Wall Street Journal* (July 20, 2007); Kate Linebaugh, "Canada Military Evacuates Motorists Stranded by Snow," *Wall Street Journal* (December 15, 2010).

 What steps might the companies take to avoid such a serious disruption in the future? (Answers in *Broadening Your Perspective*.)

DETERMINING INVENTORY QUANTITIES

No matter whether they are using a periodic or perpetual inventory system, all companies need to determine inventory quantities at the end of the accounting period. If using a perpetual system, companies take a physical inventory for the following reasons. The first is to check the accuracy of their perpetual inventory records. The second is to determine the amount of inventory lost due to wasted raw materials, shoplifting, or employee theft.

Companies using a periodic inventory system must take a physical inventory for two different purposes: to determine the inventory on hand at the balance sheet date, and to determine the cost of goods sold for the period.

Determining inventory quantities involves two steps: (1) taking a physical inventory of goods on hand and (2) determining the ownership of goods.

Taking a Physical Inventory

Companies take the physical inventory at the end of the accounting period. Taking a physical inventory involves actually counting, weighing, or measuring each kind of inventory on hand. In many companies, taking an inventory is a formidable task. Retailers such as Target, True Value Hardware, or Home Depot have thousands of different inventory items. An inventory count is generally more accurate when a limited number of goods are being sold or received during the counting. Consequently, companies often "take inventory" when the business is closed or when business is slow. Many retailers close early on a chosen day in January—after the holiday sales and returns, when inventories are at their lowest level—to count inventory. Wal-Mart, for example, has a year-end of January 31.

Ethics Insight
Falsifying Inventory to Boost Income

Managers at women's apparel maker Leslie Fay were convicted of falsifying inventory records to boost net income—and consequently to boost management bonuses. In another case, executives at Craig Consumer Electronics were accused of defrauding lenders by manipulating inventory records. The indictment said the company classified "defective goods as new or refurbished" and claimed that it owned certain shipments "from overseas suppliers" when, in fact, Craig either did not own the shipments or the shipments did not exist.

? What effect does an overstatement of inventory have on a company's financial statements? (Answers in *Broadening Your Perspective*.)

Determining Ownership of Goods

One challenge in determining inventory quantities is making sure a company owns the inventory. To determine ownership of goods, two questions must be answered: Do all of the goods included in the count belong to the company? Does the company own any goods that were not included in the count?

GOODS IN TRANSIT. A complication in determining ownership is **goods in transit** (on board a truck, train, ship, or plane) at the end of the period. The company may have purchased goods that have not yet been received, or it may have sold goods that have not yet been delivered. To arrive at an accurate count, the company must determine ownership of these goods.

Goods in transit should be included in the inventory of the company that has legal title to the goods. Legal title is determined by the terms of the sale, as shown in Illustration 6-2.

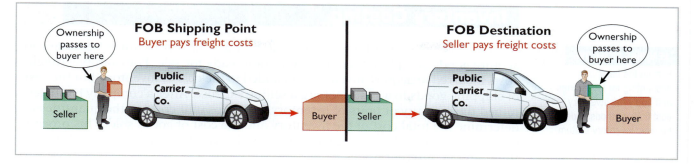

Illustration 6-2 Terms of sale

1. When the terms are **FOB (free on board) shipping point**, ownership of the goods passes to the buyer when the public carrier accepts the goods from the seller.

2. When the terms are **FOB destination**, ownership of the goods remains with the seller until the goods reach the buyer.

CONSIGNED GOODS. In some lines of business, it is common to hold the goods of other parties and try to sell the goods for them for a fee, but without taking ownership of the goods. These are called **consigned goods**.

For example, you might have a used car that you would like to sell. If you take the item to a dealer, the dealer might be willing to put the car on its lot and charge you a commission if it is sold. Under this agreement, the dealer **would not take ownership** of the car, which would still belong to you. If an inventory count were taken, the car would not be included in the dealer's inventory because the dealer does not own it.

Many car, boat, and antique dealers sell goods on consignment to keep their inventory costs down and to avoid the risk of purchasing an item that they will not be able to sell. Today, even some manufacturers are making consignment agreements with their suppliers in order to keep their inventory levels low.

ANATOMY OF A FRAUD

Ted Nickerson, CEO of clock manufacturer Dally Industries, was feared by all of his employees. Ted had expensive tastes. To support his expensive tastes, Ted took out large loans, which he collateralized with his shares of Dally Industries stock. If the price of Dally's stock fell, he was required to provide the bank with more shares of stock. To achieve target net income figures and thus maintain the stock price, Ted coerced employees in the company to alter inventory figures. Inventory quantities were manipulated by changing the amounts on inventory control tags after the year-end physical inventory count. For example, if a tag said there were 20 units of a particular item, the tag was changed to 220. Similarly, the unit costs that were used to determine the value of ending inventory were increased from, for example, $125 per unit to $1,250. Both of these fraudulent changes had the effect of increasing the amount of reported ending inventory. This reduced cost of goods sold and increased net income.

Total take: $245,000

THE MISSING CONTROL

Independent internal verification. The company should have spot-checked its inventory records periodically, verifying that the number of units in the records agreed with the amount on hand and that the unit costs agreed with vendor price sheets.

Source: Adapted from Wells, *Fraud Casebook* (2007), pp. 502–509.

Inventory Costing

LEARNING OBJECTIVE 2

Explain the basis of accounting for inventories and apply the inventory cost flow methods under a periodic inventory system.

Inventory is accounted for at cost. Cost includes all expenditures necessary to acquire goods and place them in a condition ready for sale. For example, freight costs incurred to acquire inventory are added to the cost of inventory, but the cost of shipping goods to a customer are a selling expense. After a company has determined the quantity of units of inventory, it applies unit costs to the quantities to determine the total cost of the inventory and the cost of goods sold. This process can be complicated if a company has purchased inventory items at different times and at different prices.

For example, assume that Crivitz TV Company purchases three identical 50-inch TVs on different dates at costs of $700, $750, and $800. During the year, Crivitz sold two sets at $1,200 each. These facts are summarized in Illustration 6-3.

Illustration 6-3 Data for inventory costing example

Purchases		
February 3	1 TV at	$700
March 5	1 TV at	$750
May 22	1 TV at	$800
Sales		
June 1	2 TVs for	$2,400 ($1,200 × 2)

Cost of goods sold will differ depending on which two TVs the company sold. For example, it might be $1,450 ($700 + $750), or $1,500 ($700 + $800), or $1,550 ($750 + $800). In this section, we discuss alternative costing methods available to Crivitz.

SPECIFIC IDENTIFICATION

If Crivitz can positively identify which particular units it sold and which are still in ending inventory, it can use the **specific identification method** of inventory costing. For example, if Crivitz sold the TVs it purchased on February 3 and May 22, then its cost of goods sold is $1,500 ($700 + $800), and its ending inventory is $750 (see Illustration 6-4). Using this method, companies can accurately determine ending inventory and cost of goods sold.

Illustration 6-4 Specific identification method

Ending inventory

$750

$700 SOLD

$800 SOLD

Cost of goods sold = $700 + $800 = $1,500
Ending inventory = $750

Specific identification requires that companies keep records of the original cost of each individual inventory item. Historically, specific identification was possible only when a company sold a limited variety of high-unit-cost items that could be identified clearly from the time of purchase through the time of sale. Examples of such products are cars, pianos, or expensive antiques.

Today, with bar coding, electronic product codes, and radio frequency identification, it is theoretically possible to do specific identification with nearly any type of product. The reality is, however, that this practice is still relatively rare. Instead, rather than keep track of the cost of each particular item sold, most companies make assumptions, called **cost flow assumptions**, about which units were sold.

COST FLOW ASSUMPTIONS

Because specific identification is often impractical, other cost flow methods are permitted. These differ from specific identification in that they **assume** flows of costs that may be unrelated to the actual physical flow of goods. There are three assumed cost flow methods:

1. First-in, first-out (FIFO)
2. Last-in, first-out (LIFO)
3. Average-cost

There is no accounting requirement that the cost flow assumption be consistent with the physical movement of the goods. Company management selects the appropriate cost flow method.

To demonstrate the three cost flow methods, we will use a **periodic** inventory system. We assume a periodic system because very few companies use **perpetual** LIFO, FIFO, or average-cost to cost their inventory and related cost of goods sold. Instead, companies that use perpetual systems, as shown in Chapter 5, often use an assumed cost (called a standard cost) to record cost of goods sold at the time of sale. Then, at the end of the period when they count their inventory, they **recalculate** cost of goods sold using **periodic** FIFO, LIFO, or average-cost as shown in this chapter and adjust cost of goods sold to this recalculated number.[1]

To illustrate the three inventory cost flow methods, we will use the data for Houston Electronics' Astro condensers, shown in Illustration 6-5.

HOUSTON ELECTRONICS
Astro Condensers

Date	Explanation	Units	Unit Cost	Total Cost
Jan. 1	Beginning inventory	100	$10	$ 1,000
Apr. 15	Purchase	200	11	2,200
Aug. 24	Purchase	300	12	3,600
Nov. 27	Purchase	400	13	5,200
	Total units available for sale	1,000		$12,000
	Units in ending inventory	450		
	Units sold	550		

Illustration 6-5 Data for Houston Electronics

From Chapter 5, the cost of goods sold formula in a periodic system is:

(Beginning Inventory + Purchases) − Ending Inventory = Cost of Goods Sold

---

[1]Also, some companies use a perpetual system to keep track of units, but they do not make an entry for perpetual cost of goods sold. In addition, firms that employ LIFO tend to use **dollar-value LIFO**, a method discussed in upper-level courses. FIFO periodic and FIFO perpetual give the same result. Therefore, firms should not incur the additional cost to use FIFO perpetual. Few firms use perpetual average-cost because of the added cost of record-keeping. Finally, for instructional purposes, we believe it is easier to demonstrate the cost flow assumptions under the periodic system, which makes it more pedagogically appropriate.

Houston Electronics had a total of 1,000 units available to sell during the period (beginning inventory plus purchases). The total cost of these 1,000 units is $12,000, referred to as **cost of goods available for sale**. A physical inventory taken at December 31 determined that there were 450 units in ending inventory. Therefore, Houston sold 550 units (1,000 − 450) during the period. To determine the cost of the 550 units that were sold (the cost of goods sold), we assign a cost to the ending inventory and subtract that value from the cost of goods available for sale. The value assigned to the ending inventory **will depend on which cost flow method we use**. No matter which cost flow assumption we use, though, the sum of cost of goods sold plus the cost of the ending inventory must equal the cost of goods available for sale—in this case, $12,000.

First-In, First-Out (FIFO)

The **first-in, first-out (FIFO) method** assumes that the **earliest goods** purchased are the first to be sold. FIFO often parallels the actual physical flow of merchandise because it generally is good business practice to sell the oldest units first. Under the FIFO method, therefore, the **costs** of the earliest goods purchased are the first to be recognized in determining cost of goods sold, regardless of which units were actually sold. (Note that this does not mean that the oldest units **are** sold first, but that the costs of the oldest units are **recognized** first. In a bin of picture hangers at the hardware store, for example, no one really knows, nor would it matter, which hangers are sold first.) Illustration 6-6 shows the allocation of the cost of goods available for sale at Houston Electronics under FIFO.

Illustration 6-6 Allocation of costs-FIFO method

COST OF GOODS AVAILABLE FOR SALE

Date	Explanation	Units	Unit Cost	Total Cost
Jan. 1	Beginning inventory	100	$10	$ 1,000
Apr. 15	Purchase	200	11	2,200
Aug. 24	Purchase	300	12	3,600
Nov. 27	Purchase	400	13	5,200
	Total	1,000		$12,000

STEP 1: ENDING INVENTORY   **STEP 2: COST OF GOODS SOLD**

Margin Note Another way of thinking about the calculation of FIFO **ending inventory** is the *LISH assumption*—last in still here.

Date	Units	Unit Cost	Total Cost		
Nov. 27	400	$13	$5,200	Cost of goods available for sale	$12,000
Aug. 24	50	12	600	Less: Ending inventory	5,800
Total	450		$5,800	Cost of goods sold	$ 6,200

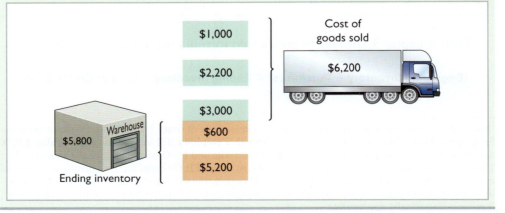

Under FIFO, since it is assumed that the first goods purchased were the first goods sold, ending inventory is based on the prices of the most recent units purchased. That is, **under FIFO, companies determine the cost of the ending inventory by taking the unit cost of the most recent purchase and working backward until all units of inventory have been costed**. In this example, Houston Electronics prices the 450 units of ending inventory using the **most recent** prices. The last purchase was 400 units at $13 on November 27. The remaining 50 units are priced using the unit cost of the second most recent purchase, $12, on August 24. Next, Houston Electronics calculates cost of goods sold by subtracting the cost of the units **not sold** (ending inventory) from the cost of all goods available for sale.

Illustration 6-7 demonstrates that companies also can calculate cost of goods sold by pricing the 550 units sold using the prices of the first 550 units acquired. Note that of the 300 units purchased on August 24, only 250 units are assumed sold. This agrees with our calculation of the cost of ending inventory, where 50 of these units were assumed unsold and thus included in ending inventory.

Date	Units	Unit Cost	Total Cost
Jan. 1	100	$10	$1,000
Apr. 15	200	11	2,200
Aug. 24	250	12	3,000
Total	550		$6,200

Illustration 6-7 Proof of cost of goods sold

Last-In, First-Out (LIFO)

The last-in, first-out (LIFO) method assumes that the **latest goods** purchased are the first to be sold. LIFO seldom coincides with the actual physical flow of inventory. (Exceptions include goods stored in piles, such as coal or hay, where goods are removed from the top of the pile as they are sold.) Under the LIFO method, the **costs** of the latest goods purchased are the first to be recognized in determining cost of goods sold. Illustration 6-8 shows the allocation of the cost of goods available for sale at Houston Electronics under LIFO.

Under LIFO, since it is assumed that the first goods sold were those that were most recently purchased, ending inventory is based on the prices of the oldest units purchased. That is, **under LIFO, companies obtain the cost of the ending inventory by taking the unit cost of the earliest goods available for sale and working forward until all units of inventory have been costed**. In this example, Houston Electronics prices the 450 units of ending inventory using the **earliest** prices. The first purchase was 100 units at $10 in the January 1 beginning inventory. Then, 200 units were purchased at $11. The remaining 150 units needed are priced at $12 per unit (August 24 purchase). Next, Houston Electronics calculates cost of goods sold by subtracting the cost of the units **not sold** (ending inventory) from the cost of all goods available for sale.

Illustration 6-9 demonstrates that we can also calculate cost of goods sold by pricing the 550 units sold using the prices of the last 550 units acquired. Note that of the 300 units purchased on August 24, only 150 units are assumed sold. This agrees with our calculation of the cost of ending inventory, where 150 of these units were assumed unsold and thus included in ending inventory.

Under a periodic inventory system, which we are using here, **all goods purchased during the period are assumed to be available for the first sale, regardless of the date of purchase**.

Illustration 6-8 Allocation of costs—LIFO method

COST OF GOODS AVAILABLE FOR SALE

Date	Explanation	Units	Unit Cost	Total Cost
Jan. 1	Beginning inventory	100	$10	$ 1,000
Apr. 15	Purchase	200	11	2,200
Aug. 24	Purchase	300	12	3,600
Nov. 27	Purchase	400	13	5,200
	Total	1,000		$12,000

STEP 1: ENDING INVENTORY

Date	Units	Unit Cost	Total Cost
Jan. 1	100	$10	$1,000
Apr. 15	200	11	2,200
Aug. 24	150	12	1,800
Total	450		$5,000

STEP 2: COST OF GOODS SOLD

Cost of goods available for sale	$12,000
Less: Ending inventory	5,000
Cost of goods sold	$ 7,000

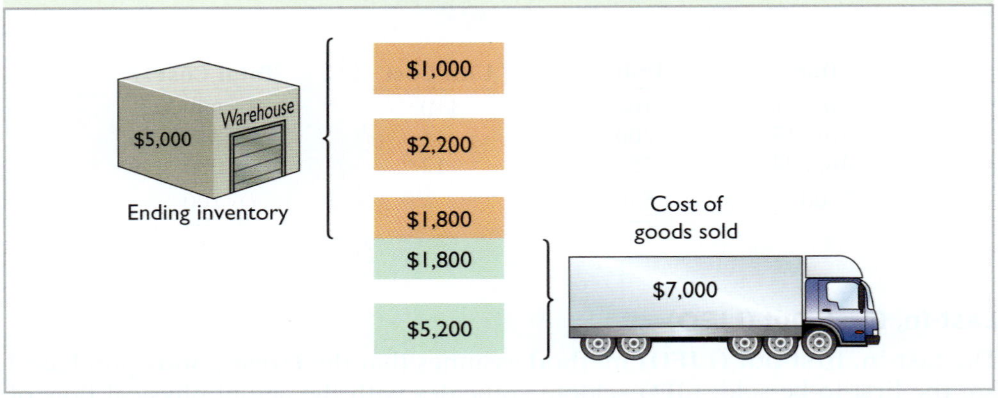

Illustration 6-9 Proof of cost of goods sold

Date	Units	Unit Cost	Total Cost
Nov. 27	400	$13	$5,200
Aug. 24	150	12	1,800
Total	550		$7,000

Average-Cost

The **average-cost method** allocates the cost of goods available for sale on the basis of the **weighted-average unit cost** incurred. Illustration 6-10 presents the formula and a sample computation of the weighted-average unit cost.

Illustration 6-10 Formula for weighted-average unit cost

Cost of Goods Available for Sale	÷	Total Units Available for Sale	=	Weighted-Average Unit Cost
$12,000	÷	1,000	=	$12.00

The company then applies the weighted-average unit cost to the units on hand to determine the cost of the ending inventory. Illustration 6-11 shows the allocation of the cost of goods available for sale at Houston Electronics using average-cost.

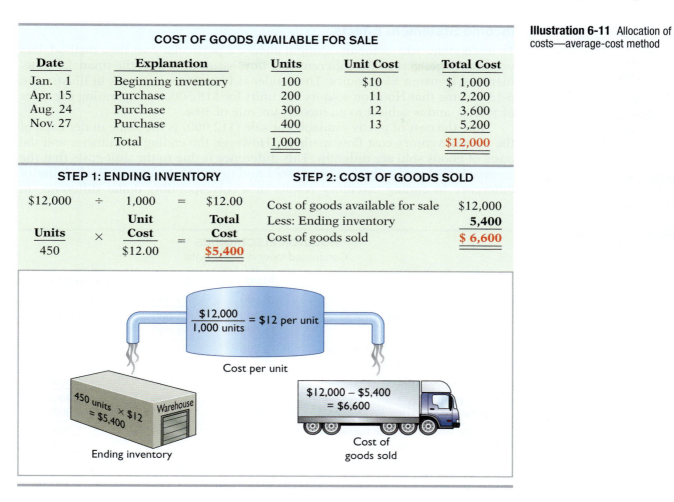

Illustration 6-11 Allocation of costs—average-cost method

COST OF GOODS AVAILABLE FOR SALE

Date	Explanation	Units	Unit Cost	Total Cost
Jan. 1	Beginning inventory	100	$10	$ 1,000
Apr. 15	Purchase	200	11	2,200
Aug. 24	Purchase	300	12	3,600
Nov. 27	Purchase	400	13	5,200
	Total	1,000		$12,000

STEP 1: ENDING INVENTORY

$12,000 ÷ 1,000 = $12.00

Units	×	Unit Cost	=	Total Cost
450	×	$12.00	=	$5,400

STEP 2: COST OF GOODS SOLD

Cost of goods available for sale	$12,000
Less: Ending inventory	5,400
Cost of goods sold	$ 6,600

$\dfrac{\$12,000}{1,000 \text{ units}} = \$12 \text{ per unit}$

Cost per unit

450 units × $12 = $5,400   Warehouse

Ending inventory

$12,000 − $5,400 = $6,600

Cost of goods sold

We can verify the cost of goods sold under this method by multiplying the units sold times the weighted-average unit cost (550 × $12 = $6,600). Note that this method does not use the simple average of the unit costs. The simple average is $11.50 ($10 + $11 + $12 + $13 = $46; $46 ÷ 4). The average-cost method instead uses the average **weighted by** the quantities purchased at each unit cost.

FINANCIAL STATEMENT AND TAX EFFECTS OF COST FLOW METHODS

LEARNING OBJECTIVE 3
Explain the financial statement and tax effects of each of the inventory cost flow assumptions.

Each of the three assumed cost flow methods is acceptable for use under GAAP. For example, Reebok International Ltd. and Wendy's International currently use the FIFO method of inventory costing. Campbell Soup Company, Kroger, and Walgreens use LIFO for part or all of their inventory. Bristol-Myers Squibb, Starbucks, and Motorola use the average-cost method. In fact, a company may also use more than one cost flow method at the same time. Stanley Black & Decker Manufacturing Company, for example, uses LIFO for domestic inventories and FIFO for foreign inventories. Illustration 6-12 shows the use of the three cost flow methods in 500 large U.S. companies.

The reasons companies adopt different inventory cost flow methods are varied, but they usually involve at least one of the following three factors:

1. Income statement effects
2. Balance sheet effects
3. Tax effects

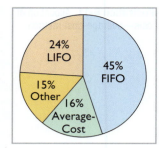

Illustration 6-12 Use of cost flow methods in major U.S. companies

Income Statement Effects

To understand why companies might choose a particular cost flow method, let's examine the effects of the different cost flow assumptions on the financial statements of Houston Electronics. The condensed income statements in Illustration 6-13 assume that Houston sold its 550 units for $18,500, had operating expenses of $9,000, and is subject to an income tax rate of 30%.

Note the cost of goods available for sale ($12,000) is the same under each of the three inventory cost flow methods. However, the ending inventories and the costs of goods sold are different. This difference is due to the unit costs that the company allocated to cost of goods sold and to ending inventory. Each dollar of difference in ending inventory results in a corresponding dollar difference in

Illustration 6-13 Comparative effects of cost flow methods

HOUSTON ELECTRONICS
Condensed Income Statements

	FIFO	LIFO	Average-Cost
Sales revenue	$18,500	$18,500	$18,500
Beginning inventory	1,000	1,000	1,000
Purchases	11,000	11,000	11,000
Cost of goods available for sale	12,000	12,000	12,000
Less: Ending inventory	5,800	5,000	5,400
Cost of goods sold	6,200	7,000	6,600
Gross profit	12,300	11,500	11,900
Operating expenses	9,000	9,000	9,000
Income before income taxes	3,300	2,500	2,900
Income tax expense (30%)	990	750	870
Net income	$ 2,310	$ 1,750	$ 2,030

income before income taxes. For Houston, an $800 difference exists between FIFO and LIFO cost of goods sold.

In periods of changing prices, the cost flow assumption can have a significant impact on income and on evaluations based on income. In most instances, prices are rising (inflation). In a period of inflation, FIFO produces a higher net income because the lower unit costs of the first units purchased are matched against revenues. In a period of rising prices (as is the case in the Houston example), FIFO reports the highest net income ($2,310) and LIFO the lowest ($1,750); average-cost falls in the middle ($2,030). If prices are falling, the results from the use of FIFO and LIFO are reversed: FIFO will report the lowest net income and LIFO the highest.

To management, higher net income is an advantage: It causes external users to view the company more favorably. In addition, management bonuses, if based on net income, will be higher. Therefore, when prices are rising (which is usually the case), companies tend to prefer FIFO because it results in higher net income.

Some argue that the use of LIFO in a period of inflation reduces the likelihood that the company will report **paper** (or **phantom**) **profit** as economic gain. To illustrate, assume that Kralik Company buys 200 units of a product at $20 per unit on January 10 and 200 more on December 31 at $24 each. During the year, Kralik sells 200 units at $30 each. Illustration 6-14 shows the results under FIFO and LIFO.

Under LIFO, Kralik Company has recovered the current replacement cost ($4,800) of the units sold. Thus, the gross profit in economic terms is real.

	FIFO		LIFO	
Sales revenue (200 × $30)	$6,000		$6,000	
Cost of goods sold	**4,000**	**(200 × $20)**	**4,800**	**(200 × $24)**
Gross profit	$2,000		$1,200	

Illustration 6-14 Income statement effects compared

However, under FIFO, the company has recovered only the January 10 cost ($4,000). To replace the units sold, it must reinvest $800 (200 × $4) of the gross profit. Thus, $800 of the gross profit is said to be phantom or illusory. As a result, reported net income is also overstated in real terms.

Balance Sheet Effects

A major advantage of the FIFO method is that in a period of inflation, the costs allocated to ending inventory will approximate their current cost. For example, for Houston Electronics, 400 of the 450 units in the ending inventory are costed under FIFO at the higher November 27 unit cost of $13.

Conversely, a major shortcoming of the LIFO method is that in a period of inflation, the costs allocated to ending inventory may be significantly understated in terms of current cost. The understatement becomes greater over prolonged periods of inflation if the inventory includes goods purchased in one or more prior accounting periods. For example, Caterpillar has used LIFO for 50 years. Its balance sheet shows ending inventory of $14.5 billion. But the inventory's actual current cost if FIFO had been used is $17.0 billion.

Tax Effects

We have seen that both inventory on the balance sheet and net income on the income statement are higher when companies use FIFO in a period of inflation. Yet, many companies use LIFO. Why? The reason is that LIFO results in the lowest income taxes (because of lower net income) during times of rising prices. For example, in Illustration 6-13 income taxes are $750 under LIFO, compared to $990 under FIFO. The tax savings of $240 makes more cash available for use in the business.

International Insight
Is LIFO Fair?

ExxonMobil Corporation, like many U.S. companies, uses LIFO to value its inventory for financial reporting and tax purposes. In one recent year, this resulted in a cost of goods sold figure that was $5.6 billion higher than under FIFO. By increasing cost of goods sold, ExxonMobil reduces net income, which reduces taxes. Critics say that LIFO provides an unfair "tax dodge." As Congress looks for more sources of tax revenue, some lawmakers favor the elimination of LIFO. Supporters of LIFO argue that the method is conceptually sound because it matches current costs with current revenues. In addition, they point out that this matching provides protection against inflation.

International accounting standards do not allow the use of LIFO. Because of this, the net income of foreign oil companies, such as BP and Royal Dutch Shell, are not directly comparable to U.S. companies, which makes analysis difficult.

Source: David Reilly, "Big Oil's Accounting Methods Fuel Criticism," *Wall Street Journal* (August 8, 2006), p. C1.

? What are the arguments for and against the use of LIFO? (Answers in *Broadening Your Perspective*.)

You have just seen that when prices are rising the use of LIFO can have a big effect on taxes. The lower taxes paid using LIFO can significantly increase cash flows. To demonstrate the effect of the cost flow assumptions on cash flow, we will calculate net cash provided by operating activities, using the data for Houston Electronics from Illustration 6-13. To simplify our example, we assume that Houston's sales and purchases are all cash transactions. We also assume that operating expenses, other than $4,600 of depreciation, are cash transactions.

	FIFO	LIFO	Average-Cost
Cash received from customers	$18,500	$18,500	$18,500
Cash purchases of goods	11,000	11,000	11,000
Cash paid for operating expenses ($9,000 − $4,600)	4,400	4,400	4,400
Cash paid for taxes	990	750	870
Net cash provided by operating activities	$ 2,110	$ 2,350	$ 2,230

LIFO has the highest net cash provided by operating activities because it results in the lowest tax payments. Since cash flow is the lifeblood of any organization, the choice of inventory method is very important.

LIFO also impacts the quality of earnings ratio. Recall that the quality of earnings ratio is net cash provided by operating activities divided by net income. Here, we calculate the quality earnings ratio under each cost flow assumption.

	FIFO	LIFO	Average-Cost
Net income (from Illustration 6-13)	$2,310	$1,750	$2,030
Quality of earnings ratio	0.91	1.34	1.1

LIFO has the highest quality of earnings ratio for two reasons: (1) It has the highest net cash provided by operating activities, which increases the ratio's numerator. (2) It reports a conservative measure of net income, which decreases the ratio's denominator. As discussed earlier, LIFO provides a conservative measure of net income because it does not include the phantom profits reported under FIFO.

DECISION TOOLKIT

DECISION CHECKPOINTS	INFO NEEDED FOR DECISION	TOOL TO USE FOR DECISION	HOW TO EVALUATE RESULTS
Which inventory costing method should be used?	Are prices increasing, or are they decreasing?	Income statement, balance sheet, and tax effects	Depends on objective. In a period of rising prices, income and inventory are higher and cash flow is lower under FIFO. LIFO provides opposite results. Average-cost can moderate the impact of changing prices.

USING INVENTORY COST FLOW METHODS CONSISTENTLY

Whatever cost flow method a company chooses, it should use that method consistently from one accounting period to another. Consistent application enhances the ability to analyze a company's financial statements over successive time periods. In contrast, using the FIFO method one year and the LIFO method the next year would make it difficult to compare the net incomes of the two years.

Although consistent application is preferred, it does not mean that a company may never change its method of inventory costing. When a company adopts a different method, it should disclose in the financial statements the change and its effects on net income. A typical disclosure is shown in Illustration 6-15, using information from recent financial statements of Quaker Oats Company.

Illustration 6-15 Disclosure of change in cost flow method

QUAKER OATS COMPANY
Notes to the Financial Statements

Note 1: Effective July 1, the Company adopted the LIFO cost flow assumption for valuing the majority of U.S. Grocery Products inventories. The Company believes that the use of the LIFO method better matches current costs with current revenues. The effect of this change on the current year was to decrease net income by $16.0 million.

LOWER-OF-COST-OR-MARKET

The value of inventory for companies selling high-technology or fashion goods can drop very quickly due to changes in technology or changes in fashions. These circumstances sometimes call for inventory valuation methods other than those presented so far. For example, in a recent year, purchasing managers at Ford decided to make a large purchase of palladium, a precious metal used in vehicle emission devices. They made this large purchase because they feared a future shortage. The shortage did not materialize, and by the end of the year the price of palladium had plummeted. Ford's inventory was then worth $1 billion less than its original cost. Do you think Ford's inventory should have been stated at cost, in accordance with the historical cost principle, or at its lower replacement cost?

> **LEARNING OBJECTIVE 4**
> Explain the lower-of-cost-or-market basis of accounting for inventories.

As you probably reasoned, this situation requires a departure from the cost basis of accounting. This is done by valuing the inventory at the **lower-of-cost-or-market (LCM)** in the period in which the price decline occurs. LCM is a basis whereby inventory is stated at the lower of either its cost or market value as determined by current replacement cost. LCM is an example of the accounting **convention of conservatism**. Conservatism means that the approach adopted among accounting alternatives is the method that is least likely to overstate assets and net income.

Companies apply LCM to the items in inventory after they have used one of the cost flow methods (specific identification, FIFO, LIFO, or average-cost) to determine cost. Under the LCM basis, market is defined as **current replacement cost**, not selling price. For a merchandising company, current replacement cost is the cost of purchasing the same goods at the present time from the usual suppliers in the usual quantities. Current replacement cost is used because a decline in the replacement cost of an item usually leads to a decline in the selling price of the item.

To illustrate the application of LCM, assume that Ken Tuckie TV has the following lines of merchandise with costs and market values as indicated. LCM produces the results shown in Illustration 6-16. Note that the amounts shown in the final column are the lower-of-cost-or-market amounts for each item.

Adherence to LCM is important. Acer Inc. recently took a charge of $150 million on personal computers, which declined in value before they could be sold. A Chinese manufacturer of silicon wafers for solar energy panels, LDK Solar Co.,

Illustration 6-16 Computation of inventory at lower-of-cost-or-market

	Cost	Market	Lower-of-Cost-or-Market
Flat-panel TVs	$60,000	$55,000	$ 55,000
Satellite radios	45,000	52,000	45,000
DVD recorders	48,000	45,000	45,000
DVDs	15,000	14,000	14,000
Total inventory			$159,000

was accused of violating LCM. When the financial press reported accusations that two-thirds of its inventory of silicon was unsuitable for processing, the company's stock price fell by 40%.

Analysis of Inventory

LEARNING OBJECTIVE   5

Compute and interpret the inventory turnover.

For companies that sell goods, managing inventory levels can be one of the most critical tasks. Having too much inventory on hand costs the company money in storage costs, interest cost (on funds tied up in inventory), and costs associated with the obsolescence of technical goods (e.g., computer chips) or shifts in fashion (e.g., clothes). But having too little inventory on hand results in lost sales. In this section, we discuss some issues related to evaluating inventory levels.

INVENTORY TURNOVER

The **inventory turnover** is calculated as cost of goods sold divided by average inventory. It indicates the liquidity of inventory by measuring the number of times the average inventory "turns over" (is sold) during the year. Inventory turnover can be divided into 365 days to compute **days in inventory**, which indicates the average number of days inventory is held.

High inventory turnover (low days in inventory) indicates the company has minimal funds tied up in inventory—that it has a minimal amount of inventory on hand at any one time. Although minimizing the funds tied up in inventory is efficient, too high an inventory turnover may indicate that the company is losing sales opportunities because of inventory shortages. For example, investment analysts at one time suggested that Office Depot had gone too far in reducing its inventory—they said they were seeing too many empty shelves. Thus, management should closely monitor this ratio to achieve the best balance between too much and too little inventory.

In Chapter 5, we discussed the increasingly competitive environment of retailers, such as Wal-Mart and Target. Wal-Mart has implemented **just-in-time inventory procedures** as well as many technological innovations to improve the efficiency of its inventory management. The following data are available for Wal-Mart.

(in millions)	2011	2010
Ending inventory	$ 36,318	$32,713
Cost of goods sold	315,287	

Illustration 6-17 presents the inventory turnovers and days in inventory for Wal-Mart and Target, using data from the financial statements of those corporations for 2011 and 2010.

The calculations in Illustration 6-17 show that Wal-Mart turns its inventory more frequently than Target and the industry average (9.1 times for Wal-Mart versus 6.2 times for Target and 8.4 for the industry). Consequently, the average time an item spends on a Wal-Mart shelf is shorter (40.1 days for Wal-Mart versus 58.9 days for Target and 43.5 days for the industry).

Ratio	Wal-Mart ($ in millions)		Target	Industry Average
	2011	2010	2011	2011
Inventory turnover	$\dfrac{\$315{,}287}{(\$36{,}318 + \$32{,}713)/2} = 9.1$ times	9.1 times	6.2 times	8.4 times
Days in inventory	$\dfrac{365\ \text{days}}{9.1} = 40.1$ days	40.1 days	58.9 days	43.5 days

$$\text{Inventory Turnover} = \frac{\text{Cost of Goods Sold}}{\text{Average Inventory}}$$

$$\text{Days in Inventory} = \frac{365}{\text{Inventory Turnover}}$$

This analysis suggests that Wal-Mart is more efficient than Target in its inventory management. Wal-Mart's sophisticated inventory tracking and distribution system allows it to keep minimum amounts of inventory on hand, while still keeping the shelves full of what customers are looking for.

Illustration 6-17 Inventory turnovers and days in inventory

Accounting Across the Organization

Too Many TVs or Too Few?

Financial analysts closely monitored the inventory management practices of companies during the recent recession. For example, some analysts following Sony expressed concern because the company built up its inventory of televisions in an attempt to sell 25 million liquid crystal display (LCD) TVs—a 60% increase over the prior year. A year earlier, Sony had cut its inventory levels so that its quarterly days in inventory was down to 38 days, compared to 61 days for the same quarter a year before that. But now, as a result of its inventory build-up, days in inventory rose to 59 days. While management was saying that it didn't think that Sony's inventory levels were now too high, analysts were concerned that the company would have to engage in very heavy discounting in order to sell off its inventory. Analysts noted that the losses from discounting can be "punishing."

Source: Daisuke Wakabayashi, "Sony Pledges to Corral Inventory," *Wall Street Journal Online* (November 2, 2010).

? For Sony, what are the advantages and disadvantages of having a low days in inventory measure? (Answers in *Broadening Your Perspective*.)

DECISION TOOLKIT

DECISION CHECKPOINTS	INFO NEEDED FOR DECISION	TOOL TO USE FOR DECISION	HOW TO EVALUATE RESULTS
How long is an item in inventory?	Cost of goods sold; beginning and ending inventory	$\text{Inventory turnover} = \dfrac{\text{Cost of goods sold}}{\text{Average inventory}}$ $\text{Days in inventory} = \dfrac{365\ \text{days}}{\text{Inventory turnover}}$	A higher inventory turnover or lower average days in inventory suggests that management is reducing the amount of inventory on hand, relative to cost of goods sold.

ANALYSTS' ADJUSTMENTS FOR LIFO RESERVE

LEARNING OBJECTIVE 6
Describe the LIFO reserve and explain its importance for comparing results of different companies.

Earlier, we noted that using LIFO rather than FIFO can result in significant differences in the results reported in the balance sheet and the income statement. With increasing prices, FIFO will result in higher income than LIFO. On the balance sheet, FIFO will result in higher reported inventory. The financial statement differences from using LIFO normally increase the longer a company uses LIFO.

Use of different inventory cost flow assumptions complicates analysts' attempts to compare companies' results. Fortunately, companies using LIFO are required to report the difference between inventory reported using LIFO and inventory using FIFO. This amount is referred to as the **LIFO reserve**. Reporting the LIFO reserve enables analysts to make adjustments to compare companies that use different cost flow methods.

Illustration 6-18 presents an excerpt from the notes to Caterpillar's 2011 financial statements that discloses and discusses Caterpillar's LIFO reserve.

Illustration 6-18 Caterpillar's LIFO reserve

Real World

CATERPILLAR INC.
Notes to the Financial Statements

Inventories: Inventories are stated at the lower of cost or market. Cost is principally determined using the last-in, first-out (LIFO) method . . . . If the FIFO (first-in, first-out) method had been in use, inventories would have been $2,422, $2,575, and $3,022 million higher than reported at December 31, 2011, 2010, and 2009, respectively.

Caterpillar has used LIFO for over 50 years. Thus, the cumulative difference between LIFO and FIFO reflected in the Inventory account is very large. In fact, the 2011 LIFO reserve of $2,422 million is nearly 17% of the 2011 LIFO inventory of $14,544 million. Such a huge difference would clearly distort any comparisons you might try to make with one of Caterpillar's competitors that used FIFO.

To adjust Caterpillar's inventory balance, we add the LIFO reserve to reported inventory, as shown in Illustration 6-19. That is, if Caterpillar had used FIFO all along, its inventory would be $16,966 million, rather than $14,544 million.

Illustration 6-19 Conversion of inventory from LIFO to FIFO

	(in millions)
2011 inventory using LIFO	$14,544
2011 LIFO reserve	2,422
2011 inventory assuming FIFO	**$16,966**

The LIFO reserve can have a significant effect on ratios that analysts commonly use. Using the LIFO reserve adjustment, Illustration 6-20 calculates the value of the current ratio (current assets ÷ current liabilities) for Caterpillar under both the LIFO and FIFO cost flow assumptions.

Illustration 6-20 Impact of LIFO reserve on ratios

($ in millions)	LIFO	FIFO
Current ratio	$\frac{\$38,128}{\$28,561} = 1.33:1$	$\frac{\$38,128 + \$2,422}{\$28,561} = 1.42:1$

As Illustration 6-20 shows, if Caterpillar used FIFO, its current ratio would be 1.42:1 rather than 1.33:1 under LIFO. Thus, Caterpillar's liquidity appears stronger if a FIFO assumption were used in valuing inventories. If a similar adjustment is made for the inventory turnover, Caterpillar's inventory turnover actually would look worse under FIFO than under LIFO, dropping from 3.6 times for LIFO to 3.0 times for FIFO.[2] The reason: LIFO reports low inventory amounts, which cause inventory turnover to be higher.

CNH Global, a competitor of Caterpillar, uses FIFO to account for its inventory. Comparing Caterpillar to CNH without converting Caterpillar's inventory to FIFO would lead to distortions and potentially erroneous decisions.

 DECISION TOOLKIT

DECISION CHECKPOINTS	INFO NEEDED FOR DECISION	TOOL TO USE FOR DECISION	HOW TO EVALUATE RESULTS
What is the impact of LIFO on the company's reported inventory?	LIFO reserve, cost of goods sold, ending inventory, current assets, current liabilities	$\dfrac{\text{LIFO}}{\text{inventory}} + \dfrac{\text{LIFO}}{\text{reserve}} = \dfrac{\text{FIFO}}{\text{inventory}}$	If these adjustments are material, they can significantly affect such measures as the current ratio and the inventory turnover.

USING THE DECISION TOOLKIT

The Manitowoc Company is located in Manitowoc, Wisconsin. In recent years, it has made a series of strategic acquisitions to grow and enhance its market-leading positions in each of its three business segments. These include: cranes and related products (crawler cranes, tower cranes, and boom trucks); food service equipment (commercial ice-cube machines, ice-beverage dispensers, and commercial refrigeration equipment); and marine operations (shipbuilding and ship-repair services). The company reported inventory of $668.7 million for 2011 and of $558.8 million for 2010. Here is the inventory note taken from the 2011 financial statements.

Real World

THE MANITOWOC COMPANY
Notes to the Financial Statements

Inventories: The components of inventories at December 31 are summarized as follows (in millions).

	2011	2010
Inventories—gross		
Raw materials	$249.7	$223.9
Work-in-process	168.1	119.8
Finished goods	357.6	326.4
Total	775.4	670.1
Less: Excess and obsolete inventory reserve	(75.3)	(80.3)
Net inventories at FIFO cost	700.1	589.8
Less: Excess of FIFO costs over LIFO value	(31.4)	(31.0)
Inventories—net (as reported on balance sheet)	$668.7	$558.8

Manitowoc carries inventory at the lower-of-cost-or-market using the first-in, first-out (FIFO) method for approximately 89% and 87% of total inventory for 2011 and 2010, respectively. The remainder of the inventory is costed using the last-in, first-out (LIFO) method.

Additional facts:

2011 Current liabilities	$1,104.6
2011 Current assets (as reported)	1,239.8
2011 Cost of goods sold	2,813.9

[2]The LIFO reserve also affects cost of goods sold although typically by a much less material amount. The cost of goods sold adjustment is discussed in more advanced financial statement analysis texts.

Instructions

Answer the following questions.
1. Why does the company report its inventory in three components?
2. Why might the company use two methods (LIFO and FIFO) to account for its inventory?
3. Perform each of the following.
    (a) Calculate the inventory turnover and days in inventory using the LIFO inventory.
    (b) Calculate the 2011 current ratio using LIFO and the current ratio using FIFO. Discuss the difference.

Solution

1. The Manitowoc Company is a manufacturer, so it purchases raw materials and makes them into finished products. At the end of each period, it has some goods that have been started but are not yet complete (work in process).

    By reporting all three components of inventory, a company reveals important information about its inventory position. For example, if amounts of raw materials have increased significantly compared to the previous year, we might assume the company is planning to step up production. On the other hand, if levels of finished goods have increased relative to last year and raw materials have declined, we might conclude that sales are slowing down—that the company has too much inventory on hand and is cutting back production.

2. Companies are free to choose different cost flow assumptions for different types of inventory. A company might choose to use FIFO for a product that is expected to decrease in price over time. One common reason for choosing a method other than LIFO is that many foreign countries do not allow LIFO; thus, the company cannot use LIFO for its foreign operations.

3. (a) $\text{Inventory turnover} = \dfrac{\text{Cost of goods sold}}{\text{Average inventory}} = \dfrac{\$2,813.9}{(\$668.7 + \$558.8)/2} = 4.6$

    $\dfrac{\text{Days in}}{\text{inventory}} = \dfrac{365}{\text{Inventory turnover}} = \dfrac{365}{4.6} = 79.3 \text{ days}$

    (b) Current ratio

	LIFO	**FIFO**

$\dfrac{\text{Current assets}}{\text{Current liabilities}} = \dfrac{\$1,239.8}{\$1,104.6} = 1.12{:}1 \qquad \dfrac{\$1,239.8 + \$31.4}{\$1,104.6} = 1.15{:}1$

This represents a 2.7% increase in the current ratio $(1.15 - 1.12)/1.12$.

Summary of Learning Objectives

1 **Determine how to classify inventory and inventory quantities.** Merchandisers need only one inventory classification, merchandise inventory, to describe the different items that make up total inventory. Manufacturers, on the other hand, usually classify inventory into three categories: finished goods, work in process, and raw materials. To determine inventory quantities, manufacturers (1) take a physical inventory of goods on hand and (2) determine the ownership of goods in transit or on consignment.

2 **Explain the basis of accounting for inventories and apply the inventory cost flow methods under a periodic inventory system.** The primary basis of accounting for inventories is cost. Cost includes all expenditures necessary to acquire goods and place them in a condition ready for sale. Cost of goods available for sale includes (a) cost of beginning inventory and (b) cost of goods purchased. The inventory cost flow methods are specific identification and three assumed cost flow methods—FIFO, LIFO, and average-cost.

3 **Explain the financial statement and tax effects of each of the inventory cost flow assumptions.** The cost of goods available for sale may be allocated to cost of goods sold and ending inventory by specific identification or by a method based on an assumed cost flow. When prices are rising, the first-in, first-out (FIFO) method results in lower cost of goods sold and higher net income than the average-cost and the last-in, first-out (LIFO) methods. The reverse is true when prices are falling. In the balance sheet, FIFO results in an ending inventory that is closest to current value, whereas the inventory under LIFO is the farthest from current value. LIFO results in the lowest income taxes (because of lower taxable income).

4 **Explain the lower-of-cost-or-market basis of accounting for inventories.** Companies use the lower-of-cost-or-market (LCM) basis when the current replacement cost (market) is less than cost. Under LCM, companies recognize the loss in the period in which the price decline occurs.

5 **Compute and interpret the inventory turnover.** Inventory turnover is calculated as cost of goods sold divided by average inventory. It can be converted to average days in inventory by dividing 365 days by the inventory turnover. A higher inventory turnover or lower average days in inventory suggests that management is trying to keep inventory levels low relative to its sales level.

6 **Describe the LIFO reserve and explain its importance for comparing results of different companies.** The LIFO reserve represents the difference between ending inventory using LIFO and ending inventory if FIFO were employed instead. For some companies this difference can be significant, and ignoring it can lead to inappropriate conclusions when using the current ratio or inventory turnover.

DECISION TOOLKIT *A SUMMARY*

DECISION CHECKPOINTS	INFO NEEDED FOR DECISION	TOOL TO USE FOR DECISION	HOW TO EVALUATE RESULTS
Which inventory costing method should be used?	Are prices increasing, or are they decreasing?	Income statement, balance sheet, and tax effects	Depends on objective. In a period of rising prices, income and inventory are higher and cash flow is lower under FIFO. LIFO provides opposite results. Average-cost can moderate the impact of changing prices.
How long is an item in inventory?	Cost of goods sold; beginning and ending inventory	$\text{Inventory turnover} = \dfrac{\text{Cost of goods sold}}{\text{Average inventory}}$ $\text{Days in inventory} = \dfrac{\text{365 days}}{\text{Inventory turnover}}$	A higher inventory turnover or lower average days in inventory suggests that management is reducing the amount of inventory on hand, relative to cost of goods sold.
What is the impact of LIFO on the company's reported inventory?	LIFO reserve, cost of goods sold, ending inventory, current assets, current liabilities	$\text{LIFO inventory} + \text{LIFO reserve} = \text{FIFO inventory}$	If these adjustments are material, they can significantly affect such measures as the current ratio and the inventory turnover.

Appendix 6A

Inventory Cost Flow Methods in Perpetual Inventory Systems

Each of the inventory cost flow methods described in the chapter for a periodic inventory system may be used in a perpetual inventory system. To illustrate the application of the three assumed cost flow methods (FIFO, LIFO, and average-cost), we will use the data shown in Illustration 6A-1 and in this chapter for Houston Electronics' Astro condensers.

LEARNING OBJECTIVE **7**

Apply the inventory cost flow methods to perpetual inventory records.

Illustration 6A-1 Inventoriable units and costs

| HOUSTON ELECTRONICS | | | | | |
| Astro Condensers | | | | | |
Date	Explanation	Units	Unit Cost	Total Cost	Balance in Units
1/1	Beginning inventory	100	$10	$ 1,000	100
4/15	Purchase	200	11	2,200	300
8/24	Purchase	300	12	3,600	600
9/10	Sale	550			50
11/27	Purchase	400	13	5,200	450
				$12,000	

FIRST-IN, FIRST-OUT (FIFO)

Under FIFO, the cost of the earliest goods on hand **prior to each sale** is charged to cost of goods sold. Therefore, the cost of goods sold on September 10 consists of the units on hand January 1 and the units purchased April 15 and August 24. Illustration 6A-2 shows the inventory under a FIFO method perpetual system.

The ending inventory in this situation is $5,800, and the cost of goods sold is $6,200 [(100 @ $10) + (200 @ $11) + (250 @ $12)].

Illustration 6A-2 Perpetual system—FIFO

Date	Purchases	Cost of Goods Sold	Balance
Jan. 1			(100 @ $10) $1,000
Apr. 15	(200 @ $11) $2,200		(100 @ $10)⎤
			(200 @ $11)⎦ $3,200
Aug. 24	(300 @ $12) $3,600		(100 @ $10)⎤
			(200 @ $11)⎬ $6,800
			(300 @ $12)⎦
Sept. 10		(100 @ $10)	
		(200 @ $11)	
		(250 @ $12)	(50 @ $12) $ 600
		$6,200	
Nov. 27	(400 @ $13) $5,200		(50 @ $12)⎤ $5,800
			(400 @ $13)⎦

The results under FIFO in a perpetual system are the **same as in a periodic system**. (See Illustration 6-6 where, similarly, the ending inventory is $5,800 and cost of goods sold is $6,200.) Regardless of the system, the first costs in are the costs assigned to cost of goods sold.

LAST-IN, FIRST-OUT (LIFO)

Under the LIFO method using a perpetual system, the cost of the most recent purchase prior to sale is allocated to the units sold. Therefore, the cost of the goods sold on September 10 consists of all the units from the August 24 and April 15 purchases plus 50 of the units in beginning inventory. The ending inventory under the LIFO method is computed in Illustration 6A-3.

The use of LIFO in a perpetual system will usually produce cost allocations that differ from use of LIFO in a periodic system. In a perpetual system, the latest units purchased **prior to each sale** are allocated to cost of goods sold. In contrast, in a periodic system, the latest units purchased **during the period** are allocated to cost of goods sold. Thus, when a purchase is made after the last sale, the LIFO periodic system will apply this purchase to the previous sale. See Illustration 6-9 where the proof shows the 400 units at $13 purchased on November 27 applied to the sale of 550 units on September 10.

Date	Purchases	Cost of Goods Sold	Balance
Jan. 1			(100 @ $10) $1,000
Apr. 15	(200 @ $11) $2,200		(100 @ $10)⎤
			(200 @ $11)⎦ $3,200
Aug. 24	(300 @ $12) $3,600		(100 @ $10)⎤
			(200 @ $11)⎬ $6,800
			(300 @ $12)⎦
Sept. 10		(300 @ $12)	
		(200 @ $11)	
		(50 @ $10)	(50 @ $10) $ 500
		$6,300	
Nov. 27	(400 @ $13) $5,200		(50 @ $10)⎤ **$5,700**
			(400 @ $13)⎦

Illustration 6A-3 Perpetual system—LIFO

As shown above, under the LIFO perpetual system the 400 units at $13 purchased on November 27 are all applied to the ending inventory.

The ending inventory in this LIFO perpetual illustration is $5,700 and cost of goods sold is $6,300. Compare this to the LIFO periodic illustration (Illustration 6-8) where the ending inventory is $5,000 and cost of goods sold is $7,000.

AVERAGE-COST

The average-cost method in a perpetual inventory system is called the **moving-average method**. Under this method, the company computes a new average **after each purchase**. The average cost is computed by dividing the cost of goods available for sale by the units on hand. The average cost is then applied to (1) the units sold, to determine the cost of goods sold, and (2) the remaining units on hand, to determine the ending inventory amount. Illustration 6A-4 shows the application of the average-cost method by Houston Electronics.

Date	Purchases	Cost of Goods Sold	Balance
Jan. 1			(100 @ $10) $1,000
Apr. 15	(200 @ $11) $2,200		(300 @ $10.667) $3,200
Aug. 24	(300 @ $12) $3,600		(600 @ $11.333) $6,800
Sept. 10		(550 @ $11.333)	(50 @ $11.333) $ 567
		$6,233	
Nov. 27	(400 @ $13) $5,200		(450 @ $12.816) **$5,767**

Illustration 6A-4 Perpetual system—average-cost method

As indicated above, the company computes **a new average each time it makes a purchase**. On April 15, after 200 units are purchased for $2,200, a total of 300 units costing $3,200 ($1,000 + $2,200) are on hand. The average unit cost is $10.667 ($3,200 ÷ 300). On August 24, after 300 units are purchased for $3,600, a total of 600 units costing $6,800 ($1,000 + $2,200 + $3,600) are on hand at an average cost per unit of $11.333 ($6,800 ÷ 600). Houston Electronics uses this unit cost of $11.333 in costing sales until another purchase is made, when the company computes a new unit cost. Accordingly, the unit cost of the 550 units sold on September 10 is $11.333, and the total cost of goods sold is $6,233. On November 27, following the purchase of 400 units for $5,200, there are 450 units on hand costing $5,767 ($567 + $5,200) with a new average cost of $12.816 ($5,767 ÷ 450).

Compare this moving-average cost under the perpetual inventory system to Illustration 6-11 showing the weighted-average method under a periodic inventory system.

Summary of Learning Objective for Appendix 6A

7 **Apply the inventory cost flow methods to perpetual inventory records.** Under FIFO, the cost of the earliest goods on hand prior to each sale is charged to cost of goods sold. Under LIFO, the cost of the most recent purchase prior to sale is charged to cost of goods sold. Under the average-cost method, a new average cost is computed after each purchase.

Appendix 6B

Inventory Errors

LEARNING OBJECTIVE **8**

Indicate the effects of inventory errors on the financial statements.

Unfortunately, errors occasionally occur in accounting for inventory. In some cases, errors are caused by failure to count or price the inventory correctly. In other cases, errors occur because companies do not properly recognize the transfer of legal title to goods that are in transit. When inventory errors occur, they affect both the income statement and the balance sheet.

INCOME STATEMENT EFFECTS

Under a periodic inventory system, both the beginning and ending inventories appear in the income statement. The ending inventory of one period automatically becomes the beginning inventory of the next period. Thus, inventory errors affect the computation of cost of goods sold and net income in two periods.

The effects on cost of goods sold can be computed by entering incorrect data in the formula in Illustration 6B-1 and then substituting the correct data.

Illustration 6B-1 Formula for cost of goods sold

Beginning Inventory	+	Cost of Goods Purchased	−	Ending Inventory	=	Cost of Goods Sold

If **beginning** inventory is understated, cost of goods sold will be understated. If **ending** inventory is understated, cost of goods sold will be overstated. Illustration 6B-2 shows the effects of inventory errors on the current year's income statement.

Illustration 6B-2 Effects of inventory errors on current year's income statement

Inventory Error	Cost of Goods Sold	Net Income
Beginning inventory understated	Understated	Overstated
Beginning inventory overstated	Overstated	Understated
Ending inventory understated	Overstated	Understated
Ending inventory overstated	Understated	Overstated

An error in the ending inventory of the current period will have a **reverse effect on net income of the next accounting period**. This is shown in Illustration 6B-3. Note that the understatement of ending inventory in 2013 results in an understatement of beginning inventory in 2014 and an overstatement of net income in 2014.

Over the two years, total net income is correct because the errors offset each other. Notice that total two-year income using incorrect data is $35,000 ($22,000 + $13,000), which is the same as the total two-year income of $35,000 ($25,000 + $10,000) using correct data. Also note in this example that an error in the beginning inventory does not result in a corresponding error in the ending inventory for that period. The correctness of the ending inventory depends entirely on the accuracy of taking and costing the inventory at the balance sheet date under the periodic inventory system.

SAMPLE COMPANY
Condensed Income Statements

	2013				2014			
	Incorrect		Correct		Incorrect		Correct	
Sales revenue		$80,000		$80,000		$90,000		$90,000
Beginning inventory	$20,000		$20,000		$12,000		$15,000	
Cost of goods purchased	40,000		40,000		68,000		68,000	
Cost of goods available for sale	60,000		60,000		80,000		83,000	
Ending inventory	12,000		15,000		23,000		23,000	
Cost of goods sold		48,000		45,000		57,000		60,000
Gross profit		32,000		35,000		33,000		30,000
Operating expenses		10,000		10,000		20,000		20,000
Net income		$22,000		$25,000		$13,000		$10,000

$(3,000)
Net income
understated

$3,000
Net income
overstated

The errors cancel. Thus, the combined total
income for the 2-year period is correct.

Illustration 6B-3 Effects of inventory errors on two years' income statements

BALANCE SHEET EFFECTS

The effect of ending inventory errors on the balance sheet can be determined by using the basic accounting equation: Assets = Liabilities + Stockholders' Equity. Errors in the ending inventory have the effects shown in Illustration 6B-4.

Ending Inventory Error	Assets	Liabilities	Stockholders' Equity
Overstated	Overstated	No effect	Overstated
Understated	Understated	No effect	Understated

Illustration 6B-4 Effects of ending inventory errors on balance sheet

The effect of an error in ending inventory on the subsequent period was shown in Illustration 6B-3. Recall that if the error is not corrected, the combined total net income for the two periods would be correct. Thus, total stockholders' equity reported on the balance sheet at the end of 2014 will also be correct.

Summary of Learning Objective for Appendix 6B

8 **Indicate the effects of inventory errors on the financial statements.** In the income statement of the current year: (1) An error in beginning inventory will have a reverse effect on net income (e.g., overstatement of inventory results in understatement of net income, and vice versa). (2) An error in ending inventory will have a similar effect on net income (e.g., overstatement of inventory effect on net income (e.g., overstatement of inventory results in overstatement of net income). If ending inventory errors are not corrected in the following period, their effect on net income for that period is reversed, and total net income for the two years will be correct.

In the balance sheet: Ending inventory errors will have the same effect on total assets and total stockholders' equity and no effect on liabilities.

Glossary

Terms are highlighted in **blue** throughout the chapter.

Average-cost method An inventory costing method that uses the weighted-average unit cost to allocate the cost of goods available for sale to ending inventory and cost of goods sold.

Consigned goods Goods held for sale by one party although ownership of the goods is retained by another party.

Current replacement cost The cost of purchasing the same goods at the present time from the usual suppliers in the usual quantities.

Days in inventory Measure of the average number of days inventory is held; calculated as 365 divided by inventory turnover.

Finished goods inventory Manufactured items that are completed and ready for sale.

First-in, first-out (FIFO) method An inventory costing method that assumes that the earliest goods purchased are the first to be sold.

FOB destination Freight terms indicating that ownership of goods remains with the seller until the goods reach the buyer.

FOB shipping point Freight terms indicating that ownership of goods passes to the buyer when the public carrier accepts the goods from the seller.

Inventory turnover A ratio that indicates the liquidity of inventory by measuring the number of times average inventory sold during the period; computed by dividing cost of goods sold by the average inventory during the period.

Just-in-time (JIT) inventory Inventory system in which companies manufacture or purchase goods just in time for use.

Last-in, first-out (LIFO) method An inventory costing method that assumes that the latest units purchased are the first to be sold.

LIFO reserve For a company using LIFO, the difference between inventory reported using LIFO and inventory using FIFO.

Lower-of-cost-or-market (LCM) A basis whereby inventory is stated at the lower of either its cost or its market value as determined by current replacement cost.

Raw materials Basic goods that will be used in production but have not yet been placed in production.

Specific identification method An actual physical-flow costing method in which particular items sold and items still in inventory are specifically costed to arrive at cost of goods sold and ending inventory.

Weighted-average unit cost Average cost that is weighted by the number of units purchased at each unit cost.

Work in process That portion of manufactured inventory that has begun the production process but is not yet complete.

WILEY PLUS **Self-Test, Brief Exercises, Exercises, Problem Set A, and many more resources are available for practice in WileyPLUS.**

Note: All Questions, Exercises, and Problems marked with an asterisk relate to material in the appendices to the chapter.

Self-Test Questions

(Answers in *Broadening Your Perspective*.)

(LO 1) **1.** When is a physical inventory usually taken?
(a) When the company has its greatest amount of inventory.
(b) When a limited number of goods are being sold or received.
(c) At the end of the company's fiscal year.
(d) Both (b) and (c).

(LO 1) **2.** Which of the following should **not** be included in the physical inventory of a company?
(a) Goods held on consignment from another company.
(b) Goods shipped on consignment to another company.

(c) Goods in transit from another company shipped FOB shipping point.
(d) All of the above should be included.

3. As a result of a thorough physical inventory, Rail- (LO 1) way Company determined that it had inventory worth $180,000 at December 31, 2014. This count did not take into consideration the following facts. Rogers Consignment store currently has goods worth $35,000 on its sales floor that belong to Railway but are being sold on consignment by Rogers. The selling price of these goods is $50,000. Railway purchased $13,000 of goods that were shipped on December 27, FOB destination, that will be

received by Railway on January 3. Determine the correct amount of inventory that Railway should report.
(a) $230,000.   (c) $228,000.
(b) $215,000.   (d) $193,000.

(LO 2) **4.** Kam Company has the following units and costs.

	Units	Unit Cost
Inventory, Jan. 1	8,000	$11
Purchase, June 19	13,000	12
Purchase, Nov. 8	5,000	13

If 9,000 units are on hand at December 31, what is the cost of the ending inventory under FIFO?
(a) $99,000.   (c) $113,000.
(b) $108,000.   (d) $117,000.

(LO 2) **5.** From the data in Question 4, what is the cost of the ending inventory under LIFO?
(a) $113,000.   (c) $99,000.
(b) $108,000.   (d) $100,000.

(LO 2) **6.** Davidson Electronics has the following:

	Units	Unit Cost
Inventory, Jan. 1	5,000	$ 8
Purchase, April 2	15,000	10
Purchase, Aug. 28	20,000	12

If Davidson has 7,000 units on hand at December 31, the cost of ending inventory under the average-cost method is:
(a) $84,000.   (c) $56,000.
(b) $70,000.   (d) $75,250.

(LO 3) **7.** In periods of rising prices, LIFO will produce:
(a) higher net income than FIFO.
(b) the same net income as FIFO.
(c) lower net income than FIFO.
(d) higher net income than average-cost.

(LO 3) **8.** Considerations that affect the selection of an inventory costing method do **not** include:
(a) tax effects.
(b) balance sheet effects.
(c) income statement effects.
(d) perpetual versus periodic inventory system.

(LO 4) **9.** The lower-of-cost-or-market rule for inventory is an example of the application of:
(a) the conservatism convention.
(b) the historical cost principle.
(c) the materiality concept.
(d) the economic entity assumption.

(LO 5) **10.** Which of these would cause inventory turnover to increase the most?
(a) Increasing the amount of inventory on hand.
(b) Keeping the amount of inventory on hand constant but increasing sales.

(c) Keeping the amount of inventory on hand constant but decreasing sales.
(d) Decreasing the amount of inventory on hand and increasing sales.

(LO 5) **11.** Carlos Company had beginning inventory of $80,000, ending inventory of $110,000, cost of goods sold of $285,000, and sales of $475,000. Carlos's days in inventory is:
(a) 73 days.   (c) 102.5 days.
(b) 121.7 days.   (d) 84.5 days.

(LO 6) **12.** The LIFO reserve is:
(a) the difference between the value of the inventory under LIFO and the value under FIFO.
(b) an amount used to adjust inventory to the lower-of-cost-or-market.
(c) the difference between the value of the inventory under LIFO and the value under average-cost.
(d) an amount used to adjust inventory to historical cost.

(LO 7) **13.** In a perpetual inventory system,
(a) LIFO cost of goods sold will be the same as in a periodic inventory system.
(b) average costs are based entirely on unit-cost simple averages.
(c) a new average is computed under the average-cost method after each sale.
(d) FIFO cost of goods sold will be the same as in a periodic inventory system.

(LO 8) **14.** Fran Company's ending inventory is understated by $4,000. The effects of this error on the current year's cost of goods sold and net income, respectively, are:
(a) understated and overstated.
(b) overstated and understated.
(c) overstated and overstated.
(d) understated and understated.

(LO 4) **15.** Harold Company overstated its inventory by $15,000 at December 31, 2014. It did not correct the error in 2014 or 2015. As a result, Harold's stockholders' equity was:
(a) overstated at December 31, 2014, and understated at December 31, 2015.
(b) overstated at December 31, 2014, and properly stated at December 31, 2015.
(c) understated at December 31, 2014, and understated at December 31, 2015.
(d) overstated at December 31, 2014, and overstated at December 31, 2015.

Go to the book's companion website, **www.wiley.com/college/kimmel**, to access additional Self-Test Questions.

Questions

1. "The key to successful business operations is effective inventory management." Do you agree? Explain.

2. An item must possess two characteristics to be classified as inventory. What are these two characteristics?

3. What is just-in-time inventory management? What are its potential advantages?

4. Your friend Jill Wurtz has been hired to help take the physical inventory in Proehl's Hardware Store. Explain to Jill what this job will entail.

5. (a) Millar Company ships merchandise to Branyan Corporation on December 30. The merchandise reaches the buyer on January 5. Indicate the terms of sale that will result in the goods being included in (1) Millar's December 31 inventory and (2) Branyan's December 31 inventory.

   (b) Under what circumstances should Millar Company include consigned goods in its inventory?

6. Nida Hat Shop received a shipment of hats for which it paid the wholesaler $2,940. The price of the hats was $3,000, but Nida was given a $60 cash discount and required to pay freight charges of $75. What amount should Nida include in inventory? Why?

7. What is the primary basis of accounting for inventories? What is the major objective in accounting for inventories?

8. Stan Koevner believes that the allocation of cost of goods available for sale should be based on the actual physical flow of the goods. Explain to Stan why this may be both impractical and inappropriate.

9. What is the major advantage and major disadvantage of the specific identification method of inventory costing?

10. "The selection of an inventory cost flow method is a decision made by accountants." Do you agree? Explain. Once a method has been selected, what accounting requirement applies?

11. Which assumed inventory cost flow method:

    (a) usually parallels the actual physical flow of merchandise?

    (b) divides cost of goods available for sale by total units available for sale to determine a unit cost?

    (c) assumes that the latest units purchased are the first to be sold?

12. In a period of rising prices, the inventory reported in Long Company's balance sheet is close to the current cost of the inventory, whereas Windsor Company's inventory is considerably below its current cost. Identify the inventory cost flow method used by each company. Which company probably has been reporting the higher gross profit?

13. Espinosa Corporation has been using the FIFO cost flow method during a prolonged period of inflation. During the same time period, Espinosa has been paying out all of its net income as dividends. What adverse effects may result from this policy?

14. George Orear, a mid-level product manager for Theresa's Shoes, thinks his company should switch from LIFO to FIFO. He says, "My bonus is based on net income. If we switch it will increase net income and increase my bonus. The company would be better off and so would I." Is he correct? Explain.

15. Discuss the impact the use of LIFO has on taxes paid, cash flows, and the quality of earnings ratio relative to the impact of FIFO when prices are increasing.

16. What inventory cost flow method does Tootsie Roll Industries use for U.S. inventories? What method does it use for foreign inventories? (*Hint:* You will need to examine the notes for Tootsie Roll's financial statements.) Why does it use a different method for foreign inventories?

17. Alison Hinck is studying for the next accounting midterm examination. What should Alison know about (a) departing from the cost basis of accounting for inventories and (b) the meaning of "market" in the lower-of-cost-or-market method?

18. Rondeli Music Center has five TVs on hand at the balance sheet date that cost $400 each. The current replacement cost is $350 per unit. Under the lower-of-cost-or-market basis of accounting for inventories, what value should Rondeli report for the TVs on the balance sheet? Why?

19. What cost flow assumption may be used under the lower-of-cost-or-market basis of accounting for inventories?

20. Why is it inappropriate for a company to include freight-out expense in the Cost of Goods Sold account?

21. Dipoto Company's balance sheet shows Inventory $162,800. What additional disclosures should be made?

22. Under what circumstances might inventory turnover be too high—that is, what possible negative consequences might occur?

23. What is the LIFO reserve? What are the consequences of ignoring a large LIFO reserve when analyzing a company?

*24. "When perpetual inventory records are kept, the results under the FIFO and LIFO methods are the same as they would be in a periodic inventory system." Do you agree? Explain.

*25. How does the average-cost method of inventory costing differ between a perpetual inventory system and a periodic inventory system?

*26. Marshall Company discovers in 2014 that its ending inventory at December 31, 2013, was $5,000 understated. What effect will this error have on (a) 2013 net income, (b) 2014 net income, and (c) the combined net income for the 2 years?

Brief Exercises

BE6-1 Tiffee Company identifies the following items for possible inclusion in the physical inventory. Indicate whether each item should be included or excluded from the inventory taking.
(a) 900 units of inventory shipped on consignment by Tiffee to another company.
(b) 3,000 units of inventory in transit from a supplier shipped FOB destination.
(c) 1,200 units of inventory sold but being held for customer pickup.
(d) 500 units of inventory held on consignment from another company.

Identify items to be included in taking a physical inventory.
(LO 1), **C**

BE6-2 In its first month of operations, Giffin Company made three purchases of merchandise in the following sequence: (1) 300 units at $6, (2) 400 units at $8, and (3) 500 units at $9. Assuming there are 200 units on hand at the end of the period, compute the cost of the ending inventory under (a) the FIFO method and (b) the LIFO method. Giffin uses a periodic inventory system.

Compute ending inventory using FIFO and LIFO.
(LO 2), **AP**

BE6-3 Data for Giffin Company are presented in BE6-2. Compute the cost of the ending inventory under the average-cost method. (Round the cost per unit to three decimal places.)

Compute the ending inventory using average-cost.
(LO 2), **AP**

BE6-4 The management of Rosenquist Corp. is considering the effects of various inventory-costing methods on its financial statements and its income tax expense. Assuming that the price the company pays for inventory is increasing, which method will:
(a) provide the highest net income?
(b) provide the highest ending inventory?
(c) result in the lowest income tax expense?
(d) result in the most stable earnings over a number of years?

Explain the financial statement effect of inventory cost flow assumptions.
(LO 3), **C**

BE6-5 In its first month of operation, Kuhlman Company purchased 100 units of inventory for $6, then 200 units for $7, and finally 140 units for $8. At the end of the month, 180 units remained. Compute the amount of phantom profit that would result if the company used FIFO rather than LIFO. Explain why this amount is referred to as phantom profit. The company uses the periodic method.

Explain the financial statement effect of inventory cost flow assumptions.
(LO 3), **AP**

BE6-6 For each of the following cases, state whether the statement is true for LIFO or for FIFO. Assume that prices are rising.
(a) Results in a higher quality of earnings ratio.
(b) Results in higher phantom profits.
(c) Results in higher net income.
(d) Results in lower taxes.
(e) Results in lower net cash provided by operating activities.

Identify the impact of LIFO versus FIFO.
(LO 3), **C**

BE6-7 Sadowski Video Center accumulates the following cost and market data at December 31.

Determine the LCM valuation.
(LO 4), **AP**

Inventory Categories	Cost Data	Market Data
Cameras	$12,500	$13,400
Camcorders	9,000	9,500
DVDs	13,000	12,200

Compute the lower-of-cost-or-market valuation for Sadowski inventory.

BE6-8 Suppose at December 31 of a recent year, the following information (in thousands) was available for sunglasses manufacturer Oakley, Inc.: ending inventory $155,377; beginning inventory $119,035; cost of goods sold $349,114; and sales revenue $761,865. Calculate the inventory turnover and days in inventory for Oakley, Inc.

Compute inventory turnover and days in inventory.
(LO 5), **AP**

BE6-9 Winnebago Industries, Inc. is a leading manufacturer of motor homes. Suppose Winnebago reported ending inventory at August 29, 2014, of $46,850,000 under the LIFO inventory method. In the notes to its financial statements, assume Winnebago reported a LIFO reserve of $30,346,000 at August 29, 2014. What would Winnebago Industries' ending inventory have been if it had used FIFO?

Determine ending inventory and cost of goods sold using LIFO reserve.
(LO 6), **C**

***BE6-10** Hogan's Department Store uses a perpetual inventory system. Data for product E2-D2 include the following purchases.

Apply cost flow methods to perpetual inventory records.
(LO 7), **AP**

Date	Number of Units	Unit Price
May 7	50	$10
July 28	30	15

On June 1, Hogan sold 25 units, and on August 27, 30 more units. Compute the cost of goods sold using (a) FIFO, (b) LIFO, and (c) average-cost. (Round the cost per unit to three decimal places.)

Determine correct financial statement amount.

(LO 8), AN

*BE6-11 Nickels Company reports net income of $92,000 in 2014. However, ending inventory was understated by $7,000. What is the correct net income for 2014? What effect, if any, will this error have on total assets as reported in the balance sheet at December 31, 2014?

Exercises

Determine the correct inventory amount.

(LO 1), AN

E6-1 Columbia Bank and Trust is considering giving Gallup Company a loan. Before doing so, it decides that further discussions with Gallup's accountant may be desirable. One area of particular concern is the Inventory account, which has a year-end balance of $275,000. Discussions with the accountant reveal the following.

1. Gallup sold goods costing $55,000 to Bazil Company FOB shipping point on December 28. The goods are not expected to reach Bazil until January 12. The goods were not included in the physical inventory because they were not in the warehouse.
2. The physical count of the inventory did not include goods costing $95,000 that were shipped to Gallup FOB destination on December 27 and were still in transit at year-end.
3. Gallup received goods costing $25,000 on January 2. The goods were shipped FOB shipping point on December 26 by Lynch Co. The goods were not included in the physical count.
4. Gallup sold goods costing $51,000 to Lamey of Canada FOB destination on December 30. The goods were received in Canada on January 8. They were not included in Gallup's physical inventory.
5. Gallup received goods costing $42,000 on January 2 that were shipped FOB destination on December 29. The shipment was a rush order that was supposed to arrive December 31. This purchase was included in the ending inventory of $275,000.

Instructions

Determine the correct inventory amount on December 31.

Determine the correct inventory amount.

(LO 1), AN

E6-2 Kevin Farley, an auditor with Koews CPAs, is performing a review of Knight Company's Inventory account. Knight did not have a good year, and top management is under pressure to boost reported income. According to its records, the inventory balance at year-end was $740,000. However, the following information was not considered when determining that amount.

1. Included in the company's count were goods with a cost of $228,000 that the company is holding on consignment. The goods belong to Mather Corporation.
2. The physical count did not include goods purchased by Knight with a cost of $40,000 that were shipped FOB shipping point on December 28 and did not arrive at Knight's warehouse until January 3.
3. Included in the Inventory account was $17,000 of office supplies that were stored in the warehouse and were to be used by the company's supervisors and managers during the coming year.
4. The company received an order on December 29 that was boxed and was sitting on the loading dock awaiting pick-up on December 31. The shipper picked up the goods on January 1 and delivered them on January 6. The shipping terms were FOB shipping point. The goods had a selling price of $40,000 and a cost of $29,000. The goods were not included in the count because they were sitting on the dock.
5. On December 29, Knight shipped goods with a selling price of $80,000 and a cost of $50,000 to Houchins Sales Corporation FOB shipping point. The goods arrived on January 3. Houchins Sales had only ordered goods with a selling price of $10,000 and a cost of $6,000. However, a sales manager at Knight had authorized the shipment and said that if Houchins wanted to ship the goods back next week, it could.

6. Included in the count was $50,000 of goods that were parts for a machine that the company no longer made. Given the high-tech nature of Knight's products, it was unlikely that these obsolete parts had any other use. However, management would prefer to keep them on the books at cost, "since that is what we paid for them, after all."

Instructions

Prepare a schedule to determine the correct inventory amount. Provide explanations for each item above, stating why you did or did not make an adjustment for each item.

E6-3 Mateo Inc. had the following inventory situations to consider at January 31, its year-end.

Identify items in inventory.
(LO 1), K

(a) Goods held on consignment for Schrader Corp. since December 12.
(b) Goods shipped on consignment to Lyman Holdings Inc. on January 5.
(c) Goods shipped to a customer, FOB destination, on January 29 that are still in transit.
(d) Goods shipped to a customer, FOB shipping point, on January 29 that are still in transit.
(e) Goods purchased FOB destination from a supplier on January 25, that are still in transit.
(f) Goods purchased FOB shipping point from a supplier on January 25, that are still in transit.
(g) Office supplies on hand at January 31.

Instructions

Identify which of the preceding items should be included in inventory. If the item should not be included in inventory, state in what account, if any, it should have been recorded.

E6-4 Delmott sells a snowboard, Xpert, that is popular with snowboard enthusiasts. Below is information relating to Delmott's purchases of Xpert snowboards during September. During the same month, 102 Xpert snowboards were sold. Delmott uses a periodic inventory system.

Compute inventory and cost of goods sold using periodic FIFO and LIFO.
(LO 2), AP

Date	Explanation	Units	Unit Cost	Total Cost
Sept. 1	Inventory	12	$100	$ 1,200
Sept. 12	Purchases	45	103	4,635
Sept. 19	Purchases	50	104	5,200
Sept. 26	Purchases	20	105	2,100
	Totals	127		$13,135

Instructions

Compute the ending inventory at September 30 and the cost of goods sold using the FIFO, LIFO, and average-cost methods. (For average-cost, round the average unit cost to three decimal places.) Prove the amount allocated to cost of goods sold under each method.

E6-5 Horne Inc. uses a periodic inventory system. Its records show the following for the month of May, in which 74 units were sold.

Calculate inventory and cost of goods sold using FIFO, average-cost, and LIFO in a periodic inventory system.
(LO 2), AP

Date	Explanation	Units	Unit Cost	Total Cost
May 1	Inventory	30	$ 9	$270
15	Purchase	25	10	250
24	Purchase	38	11	418
	Total	93		$938

Instructions

Calculate the ending inventory at May 31 using the (a) FIFO, (b) LIFO, and (c) average-cost methods. (For average-cost, round the average unit cost to three decimal places.) Prove the amount allocated to cost of goods sold under each method.

Calculate cost of goods sold using specific identification and FIFO periodic.
(LO 2, 3), AN

E6-6 On December 1, Quality Electronics has three DVD players left in stock. All are identical, all are priced to sell at $85. One of the three DVD players left in stock, with serial #1012, was purchased on June 1 at a cost of $52. Another, with serial #1045, was purchased on November 1 for $48. The last player, serial #1056, was purchased on November 30 for $40.

Instructions
(a) Calculate the cost of goods sold using the FIFO periodic inventory method, assuming that two of the three players were sold by the end of December, Quality Electronics' year-end.
(b) If Quality Electronics used the specific identification method instead of the FIFO method, how might it alter its earnings by "selectively choosing" which particular players to sell to the two customers? What would Quality's cost of goods sold be if the company wished to minimize earnings? Maximize earnings?
(c) Which inventory method, FIFO or specific identification, do you recommend that Quality use? Explain why.

Compute inventory and cost of goods sold using periodic FIFO, LIFO, and average-cost.

(LO 2, 3), **AP**

E6-7 Eggers Company reports the following for the month of June.

Date	Explanation	Units	Unit Cost	Total Cost
June 1	Inventory	120	$5	$ 600
12	Purchase	370	6	2,220
23	Purchase	200	7	1,400
30	Inventory	230		

Instructions
(a) Compute the cost of the ending inventory and the cost of goods sold under (1) FIFO, (2) LIFO, and (3) average-cost. (Round average unit cost to three decimal places).
(b) Which costing method gives the highest ending inventory? The highest cost of goods sold? Why?
(c) How do the average-cost values for ending inventory and cost of goods sold relate to ending inventory and cost of goods sold for FIFO and LIFO?
(d) Explain why the average cost is not $6.

Evaluate impact of LIFO and FIFO on cash flows and earnings quality.

(LO 3), **AP**

E6-8 The following comparative information is available for Keysor Company for 2014.

	LIFO	FIFO
Sales revenue	$86,000	$86,000
Cost of goods sold	38,000	29,000
Operating expenses (including depreciation)	27,000	27,000
Depreciation	10,000	10,000
Cash paid for inventory purchases	32,000	32,000

Instructions
(a) Determine net income under each approach. Assume a 30% tax rate.
(b) Determine net cash provided by operating activities under each approach. Assume that all sales were on a cash basis and that income taxes and operating expenses, other than depreciation, were on a cash basis.
(c) Calculate the quality of earnings ratio under each approach and explain your findings.

Determine LCM valuation.

(LO 4), **AP**

E6-9 Birk Camera Shop Inc. uses the lower-of-cost-or-market basis for its inventory. The following data are available at December 31.

	Units	Cost/Unit	Market Value/Unit
Cameras			
Minolta	5	$170	$158
Canon	7	145	152
Light Meters			
Vivitar	12	125	114
Kodak	10	120	135

Instructions
What amount should be reported on Birk Camera Shop's financial statements, assuming the lower-of-cost-or-market rule is applied?

E6-10   Suppose this information is available for PepsiCo, Inc. for 2012, 2013, and 2014.

(in millions)	2012	2013	2014
Beginning inventory	$ 1,926	$ 2,290	$ 2,522
Ending inventory	2,290	2,522	2,618
Cost of goods sold	18,038	20,351	20,099
Sales revenue	39,474	43,251	43,232

Compute inventory turnover, days in inventory, and gross profit rate.

(LO 5), **AP**

Instructions

Calculate the inventory turnover, days in inventory, and gross profit rate for PepsiCo., Inc. for 2012, 2013, and 2014. Comment on any trends.

E6-11   Deere & Company is a global manufacturer and distributor of agricultural, construction, and forestry equipment. Suppose it reported the following information in its 2014 annual report.

Compute inventory turnover and determine the effect of the LIFO reserve on current ratio.

(LO 5, 6), **AP**

(in millions)	2014	2013
Inventories (LIFO)	$ 2,397	$3,042
Current assets	30,857	
Current liabilities	12,753	
LIFO reserve	1,367	
Cost of goods sold	16,255	

Instructions

(a) Compute Deere's inventory turnover and days in inventory for 2014.
(b) Compute Deere's current ratio using the 2014 data as presented, and then again after adjusting for the LIFO reserve.
(c) Comment on how ignoring the LIFO reserve might affect your evaluation of Deere's liquidity.

*E6-12   Inventory data for Eggers Company are presented in E6-7.

Calculate inventory and cost of goods sold using three cost flow methods in a perpetual inventory system.

(LO 7), **AP**

Instructions

(a) Calculate the cost of the ending inventory and the cost of goods sold for each cost flow assumption, using a perpetual inventory system. Assume a sale of 410 units occurred on June 15 for a selling price of $8 and a sale of 50 units on June 27 for $9. (*Note:* For the moving-average method, round unit cost to three decimal places.)
(b) How do the results differ from E6-7?
(c) Why is the average unit cost not $6 [($5 + $6 + $7) ÷ 3 = $6]?

*E6-13   Information about Delmott is presented in E6-4. Additional data regarding the company's sales of Xpert snowboards are provided below. Assume that Delmott uses a perpetual inventory system.

Apply cost flow methods to perpetual records.

(LO 7), **AP**

Date		Units
Sept. 5	Sale	8
Sept. 16	Sale	48
Sept. 29	Sale	46
	Totals	102

Instructions

Compute ending inventory at September 30 using FIFO, LIFO, and moving-average. (*Note:* For moving-average, round unit cost to three decimal places.)

*E6-14   Foyle Hardware reported cost of goods sold as follows.

Determine effects of inventory errors.

(LO 8), **AN**

	2014	2013
Beginning inventory	$ 30,000	$ 20,000
Cost of goods purchased	175,000	164,000
Cost of goods available for sale	205,000	184,000
Less: Ending inventory	37,000	30,000
Cost of goods sold	$168,000	$154,000

Foyle made two errors:
 1. 2013 ending inventory was overstated by $2,000.
 2. 2014 ending inventory was understated by $5,000.

Instructions

Compute the correct cost of goods sold for each year.

Prepare correct income statements.

(LO 8), AN

*E6-15 Holcomb Company reported these income statement data for a 2-year period.

	2014	2013
Sales revenue	$250,000	$210,000
Beginning inventory	40,000	32,000
Cost of goods purchased	202,000	173,000
Cost of goods available for sale	242,000	205,000
Less: Ending inventory	55,000	40,000
Cost of goods sold	187,000	165,000
Gross profit	$ 63,000	$ 45,000

Holcomb Company uses a periodic inventory system. The inventories at January 1, 2013, and December 31, 2014, are correct. However, the ending inventory at December 31, 2013, is overstated by $8,000.

Instructions

(a) Prepare correct income statement data for the 2 years.
(b) What is the cumulative effect of the inventory error on total gross profit for the 2 years?
(c) ▬▬▶ Explain in a letter to the president of Holcomb Company what has happened—that is, the nature of the error and its effect on the financial statements.

Challenge Exercises

Visit the book's companion website, at **www.wiley.com/college/kimmel**, and choose the Student Companion site to access Challenge Exercises.

Problems: Set A

Determine items and amounts to be recorded in inventory.

(LO 1), AN

P6-1A Aber Limited is trying to determine the value of its ending inventory as of February 28, 2014, the company's year-end. The accountant counted everything that was in the warehouse, as of February 28, which resulted in an ending inventory valuation of $48,000. However, she didn't know how to treat the following transactions so she didn't record them.

(a) On February 26, Aber shipped to a customer goods costing $800. The goods were shipped FOB shipping point, and the receiving report indicates that the customer received the goods on March 2.
(b) On February 26, Landis Inc. shipped goods to Aber FOB destination. The invoice price was $350 plus $25 for freight. The receiving report indicates that the goods were received by Aber on March 2.
(c) Aber had $500 of inventory at a customer's warehouse "on approval." The customer was going to let Aber know whether it wanted the merchandise by the end of the week, March 4.
(d) Aber also had $400 of inventory at a Newten craft shop, on consignment from Aber.
(e) On February 26, Aber ordered goods costing $750. The goods were shipped FOB shipping point on February 27. Aber received the goods on March 1.
(f) On February 28, Aber packaged goods and had them ready for shipping to a customer FOB destination. The invoice price was $350 plus $25 for freight; the cost of the items was $280. The receiving report indicates that the goods were received by the customer on March 2.
(g) Aber had damaged goods set aside in the warehouse because they are no longer saleable. These goods originally cost $400 and, originally, Aber expected to sell these items for $600.

Instructions

For each of the above transactions, specify whether the item in question should be included in ending inventory, and if so, at what amount. For each item that is not included in ending inventory, indicate who owns it and what account, if any, it should have been recorded in.

P6-2A   Dunbar Distribution markets CDs of numerous performing artists. At the beginning of March, Dunbar had in beginning inventory 2,500 CDs with a unit cost of $7. During March, Dunbar made the following purchases of CDs.

Determine cost of goods sold and ending inventory using FIFO, LIFO, and average-cost with analysis.

(LO 2, 3), **AP**

| March 5 | 2,000 @ $8 | March 21 | 5,000 @ $10 |
| March 13 | 3,500 @ $9 | March 26 | 2,000 @ $11 |

During March 12,000 units were sold. Dunbar uses a periodic inventory system.

Instructions

(a) Determine the cost of goods available for sale.
(b) Determine (1) the ending inventory and (2) the cost of goods sold under each of the assumed cost flow methods (FIFO, LIFO, and average-cost). Prove the accuracy of the cost of goods sold under the FIFO and LIFO methods. (*Note:* For average-cost, round cost per unit to three decimal places.)
(c) Which cost flow method results in (1) the highest inventory amount for the balance sheet and (2) the highest cost of goods sold for the income statement?

(b) Cost of goods sold:

FIFO	$105,000
LIFO	$115,500
Average	$109,601

P6-3A   Groves Company Inc. had a beginning inventory of 100 units of Product MLN at a cost of $8 per unit. During the year, purchases were:

Determine cost of goods sold and ending inventory using FIFO, LIFO, and average-cost in a periodic inventory system and assess financial statement effects.

(LO 2, 3), **AP**

| Feb. 20 | 600 units at $ 9 | Aug. 12 | 400 units at $11 |
| May 5 | 500 units at $10 | Dec. 8 | 100 units at $12 |

Groves Company uses a periodic inventory system. Sales totaled 1,500 units.

Instructions

(a) Determine the cost of goods available for sale.
(b) Determine the ending inventory and the cost of goods sold under each of the assumed cost flow methods (FIFO, LIFO, and average-cost). Prove the accuracy of the cost of goods sold under the FIFO and LIFO methods. (Round average unit cost to three decimal places.)
(c) Which cost flow method results in the lowest inventory amount for the balance sheet? The lowest cost of goods sold for the income statement?

(b) Cost of goods sold:

FIFO	$14,500
LIFO	$15,100
Average	$14,824

P6-4A   The management of Tinker Inc. asks your help in determining the comparative effects of the FIFO and LIFO inventory cost flow methods. For 2014, the accounting records show these data.

Compute ending inventory, prepare income statements, and answer questions using FIFO and LIFO.

(LO 2, 3), **AN**

Inventory, January 1 (10,000 units)	$ 35,000
Cost of 120,000 units purchased	468,500
Selling price of 98,000 units sold	750,000
Operating expenses	124,000

Units purchased consisted of 35,000 units at $3.70 on May 10; 60,000 units at $3.90 on August 15; and 25,000 units at $4.20 on November 20. Income taxes are 28%.

Instructions

(a) Prepare comparative condensed income statements for 2014 under FIFO and LIFO. (Show computations of ending inventory.)
(b) ✏➤ Answer the following questions for management in the form of a business letter.
  (1) Which inventory cost flow method produces the inventory amount that most closely approximates the amount that would have to be paid to replace the inventory? Why?
  (2) Which inventory cost flow method produces the net income amount that is a more likely indicator of next period's net income? Why?
  (3) Which inventory cost flow method is most likely to approximate the actual physical flow of the goods? Why?
  (4) How much more cash will be available under LIFO than under FIFO? Why?
  (5) How much of the gross profit under FIFO is illusionary in comparison with the gross profit under LIFO?

(a) Gross profit:

| FIFO | $378,800 |
| LIFO | $362,900 |

Calculate ending inventory, cost of goods sold, gross profit, and gross profit rate under periodic method; compare results.

(LO 2, 3), **AP**

P6-5A You have the following information for Vincent Inc. for the month ended October 31, 2014. Vincent uses a periodic method for inventory.

Date	Description	Units	Unit Cost or Selling Price
Oct. 1	Beginning inventory	60	$24
Oct. 9	Purchase	120	26
Oct. 11	Sale	100	35
Oct. 17	Purchase	100	27
Oct. 22	Sale	60	40
Oct. 25	Purchase	70	29
Oct. 29	Sale	110	40

(a) Gross profit:

LIFO	$2,970
FIFO	$3,310
Average	$3,133

Instructions

(a) Calculate (i) ending inventory, (ii) cost of goods sold, (iii) gross profit, and (iv) gross profit rate under each of the following methods.
  (1) LIFO.
  (2) FIFO.
  (3) Average-cost. (Round cost per unit to three decimal places.)
(b) Compare results for the three cost flow assumptions.

Compare specific identification, FIFO, and LIFO under periodic method; use cost flow assumption to influence earnings.

(LO 2, 3), **AP**

P6-6A You have the following information for Wooderson Gems. Wooderson uses the periodic method of accounting for its inventory transactions. Wooderson only carries one brand and size of diamonds—all are identical. Each batch of diamonds purchased is carefully coded and marked with its purchase cost.

March 1   Beginning inventory 150 diamonds at a cost of $310 per diamond.
March 3   Purchased 200 diamonds at a cost of $350 each.
March 5   Sold 180 diamonds for $600 each.
March 10   Purchased 330 diamonds at a cost of $375 each.
March 25   Sold 390 diamonds for $650 each.

(a) Gross profit:

Maximum	$162,500
Minimum	$155,350

Instructions

(a) Assume that Wooderson Gems uses the specific identification cost flow method.
  (1) Demonstrate how Wooderson could maximize its gross profit for the month by specifically selecting which diamonds to sell on March 5 and March 25.
  (2) Demonstrate how Wooderson could minimize its gross profit for the month by selecting which diamonds to sell on March 5 and March 25.
(b) Assume that Wooderson uses the FIFO cost flow assumption. Calculate cost of goods sold. How much gross profit would Wooderson report under this cost flow assumption?
(c) Assume that Wooderson uses the LIFO cost flow assumption. Calculate cost of goods sold. How much gross profit would the company report under this cost flow assumption?
(d) Which cost flow method should Wooderson Gems select? Explain.

Compute inventory turnover and days in inventory; compute current ratio based on LIFO and after adjusting for LIFO reserve.

(LO 5, 6), **AP**

P6-7A Suppose this information (in millions) is available for the Automotive and Other Operations Divisions of General Motors Corporation for a recent year. General Motors uses the LIFO inventory method.

Beginning inventory	$ 13,921
Ending inventory	14,939
LIFO reserve	1,423
Current assets	60,135
Current liabilities	70,308
Cost of goods sold	166,259
Sales revenue	178,199

Calculate cost of goods sold, ending inventory, and gross profit for LIFO, FIFO, and moving-average under the perpetual system; compare results.

(LO 3, 7), **AP**

Instructions

(a) Calculate the inventory turnover and days in inventory.
(b) Calculate the current ratio based on inventory as reported using LIFO.
(c) Calculate the current ratio after adjusting for the LIFO reserve.
(d) Comment on any difference between parts (b) and (c).

*P6-8A** Pember Inc. is a retailer operating in Edmonton, Alberta. Pember uses the perpetual inventory method. Assume that there are no credit transactions; all amounts are settled in cash. You are provided with the following information for Pember Inc. for the month of January 2014.

Date	Description	Quantity	Unit Cost or Selling Price
Dec. 31	Ending inventory	160	$20
Jan. 2	Purchase	100	22
Jan. 6	Sale	180	40
Jan. 9	Purchase	75	24
Jan. 10	Sale	50	45
Jan. 23	Purchase	100	25
Jan. 30	Sale	130	48

Instructions

(a) For each of the following cost flow assumptions, calculate (i) cost of goods sold, (ii) ending inventory, and (iii) gross profit.
   (1) LIFO.
   (2) FIFO.
   (3) Moving-average. (Round cost per unit to three decimal places.)
(b) Compare results for the three cost flow assumptions.

(a) Gross profit:
LIFO $7,490
FIFO $7,865
Average $7,763

*P6-9A Lambert Center began operations on July 1. It uses a perpetual inventory system. During July, the company had the following purchases and sales.

Determine ending inventory under a perpetual inventory system.

(LO 3, 7), **AP**

Date	Purchases Units	Purchases Unit Cost	Sales Units
July 1	7	$62	
July 6			5
July 11	3	$66	
July 14			3
July 21	4	$71	
July 27			3

Instructions

(a) Determine the ending inventory under a perpetual inventory system using (1) FIFO, (2) moving-average (round unit cost to three decimal places), and (3) LIFO.
(b) Which costing method produces the highest ending inventory valuation?

(a) FIFO $213
Average $207
LIFO $195

Problems: Set B

Visit the book's companion website, at **www.wiley.com/college/kimmel**, and choose the Student Companion site to access Problem Set B.

Comprehensive Problem

CP6 On December 1, 2014, Harrisen Company had the account balances shown below.

	Debit		Credit
Cash	$ 4,800	Accumulated Depreciation—Equipment	$ 1,500
Accounts Receivable	3,900	Accounts Payable	3,000
Inventory	1,800*	Common Stock	10,000
Equipment	21,000	Retained Earnings	17,000
	$31,500		$31,500

*(3,000 × $0.60)

The following transactions occurred during December.

Dec. 3   Purchased 4,000 units of inventory on account at a cost of $0.72 per unit.
     5   Sold 4,400 units of inventory on account for $0.90 per unit. (It sold 3,000 of the $0.60 units and 1,400 of the $0.72 units.)

7   Granted the December 5 customer $180 credit for 200 units of inventory returned costing $150. These units were returned to inventory.

17   Purchased 2,200 units of inventory for cash at $0.80 each.

22   Sold 2,000 units of inventory on account for $0.95 per unit. (It sold 2,000 of the $0.72 units.)

Adjustment data:
1. Accrued salaries and wages payable $400.
2. Depreciation on equipment $200 per month.
3. Income tax expense was $215, to be paid next year.

Instructions
(a) Journalize the December transactions and adjusting entries, assuming Harrisen uses the perpetual inventory method.
(b) Enter the December 1 balances in the ledger T-accounts and post the December transactions. In addition to the accounts mentioned above, use the following additional accounts: Income Taxes Payable, Salaries and Wages Payable, Sales Revenue, Sales Returns and Allowances, Cost of Goods Sold, Depreciation Expense, Salaries and Wages Expense, and Income Tax Expense.
(c) Prepare an adjusted trial balance as of December 31, 2014.
(d) Prepare an income statement for December 2014 and a classified balance sheet at December 31, 2014.
(e) Compute ending inventory and cost of goods sold under FIFO, assuming Harrisen Company uses the periodic inventory system.
(f) Compute ending inventory and cost of goods sold under LIFO, assuming Harrisen Company uses the periodic inventory system.

Broadening Your Perspective

Financial Reporting and Analysis

FINANCIAL REPORTING PROBLEM: *Tootsie Roll Industries, Inc.*

BYP6-1   The notes that accompany a company's financial statements provide informative details that would clutter the amounts and descriptions presented in the statements. Refer to the financial statements of Tootsie Roll and the accompanying Notes to Consolidated Financial Statements in Appendix A.

Instructions

Answer the following questions. (Give the amounts in thousands of dollars, as shown in Tootsie Roll's annual report.)
(a) What did Tootsie Roll report for the amount of inventories in its Consolidated Balance Sheet at December 31, 2011? At December 31, 2010?
(b) Compute the dollar amount of change and the percentage change in inventories between 2010 and 2011. Compute inventory as a percentage of current assets for 2011.
(c) What are the (product) cost of goods sold reported by Tootsie Roll for 2011, 2010, and 2009? Compute the ratio of (product) cost of goods sold to net (product) sales in 2011.

COMPARATIVE ANALYSIS PROBLEM: *Tootsie Roll vs. Hershey*

BYP6-2   The financial statements of The Hershey Company appear in Appendix B, following the financial statements for Tootsie Roll in Appendix A.

Instructions
(a) Based on the information in the financial statements, compute these 2011 values for each company. (Do not adjust for the LIFO reserve.)
   (1) Inventory turnover. (Use product cost of goods sold and total inventory.)
   (2) Days in inventory.
(b) What conclusions concerning the management of the inventory can you draw from these data?

RESEARCH CASE

BYP6-3 The July 15, 2010, edition of *CFO.com* contains an article by Marie Leone entitled "Sucking the LIFO out of Inventory."

Instructions

Read the article, which can be found at **www.cfo.com/printable/article.cfm/14508745**, and answer the following questions.
(a) What type of company benefits most from the use of LIFO?
(b) What is the estimated boost in federal tax receipts over 10 years if the use of LIFO for taxes was not allowed?
(c) If the United States decides to adopt International Financial Reporting Standards (IFRS), what would be the implications for IFRS?
(d) What conceptual justification for LIFO do its proponents provide?
(e) What types of companies prefer to use FIFO?

INTERPRETING FINANCIAL STATEMENTS

BYP6-4 Suppose the following information is from the 2014 annual report of American Greetings Corporation (all dollars in thousands).

	Feb. 28, 2014	Feb. 28, 2013
Inventories		
Finished goods	$232,893	$244,379
Work in process	7,068	10,516
Raw materials and supplies	49,937	43,861
	289,898	298,756
Less: LIFO reserve	86,025	82,085
Total (as reported)	$203,873	$216,671
Cost of goods sold	$809,956	$780,771
Current assets (as reported)	$561,395	$669,340
Current liabilities	$343,405	$432,321

The notes to the company's financial statements also include the following information.

Finished products, work in process, and raw material inventories are carried at the lower-of-cost-or-market. The last-in, first-out (LIFO) cost method is used for approximately 75% of the domestic inventories in 2014 and approximately 70% in 2013. The foreign subsidiaries principally use the first-in, first-out (FIFO) method. Display material and factory supplies are carried at average-cost.

Instructions

(a) Define each of the following: finished goods, work in process, and raw materials.
(b) What might be a possible explanation for why the company uses FIFO for its nondomestic inventories?
(c) Calculate the company's inventory turnover and days in inventory for 2013 and 2014. (2012 inventory was $182,618.) Discuss the implications of any change in the ratios.
(d) What percentage of total inventory does the 2014 LIFO reserve represent? If the company used FIFO in 2014, what would be the value of its inventory? Do you consider this difference a "material" amount from the perspective of an analyst? Which value accurately represents the value of the company's inventory?
(e) Calculate the company's 2014 current ratio with the numbers as reported, then recalculate after adjusting for the LIFO reserve.

REAL-WORLD FOCUS

BYP6-5 *Purpose:* Use SEC filings to learn about a company's inventory accounting practices.

Address: **http://biz.yahoo.com/p/_capgds-bldmch.html**,
or go to **www.wiley.com/college/kimmel**

Steps

1. Go to this site and click on the name of an equipment manufacturer other than those discussed in the chapter.
2. Click on **SEC filings**.
3. Under "Recent filings" choose **Form 10K** (annual report) and click on **Full Filing at Edgar Online**.
4. Choose option "3," **Online HTML Version**.

If the 10K is not listed among the recent filings, then click on **View All Filings on EDGAR Online**.

Instructions

Review the 10K to answer the following questions.

(a) What is the name of the company?
(b) How has its inventory changed from the previous year?
(c) What is the amount of raw materials, work in process, and finished goods inventory?
(d) What inventory method does the company use?
(e) Calculate the inventory turnover and days in inventory for the current year.
(f) If the company uses LIFO, what was the amount of its LIFO reserve?

Critical Thinking

DECISION-MAKING ACROSS THE ORGANIZATION

BYP6-6 Heineken Electronics has enjoyed tremendous sales growth during the last 10 years. However, even though sales have steadily increased, the company's CEO, Beth Dains, is concerned about certain aspects of its performance. She has called a meeting with the corporate controller and the vice presidents of finance, operations, sales, and marketing to discuss the company's performance. Beth begins the meeting by making the following observations:

> We have been forced to take significant write-downs on inventory during each of the last three years because of obsolescence. In addition, inventory storage costs have soared. We rent four additional warehouses to store our increasingly diverse inventory. Five years ago inventory represented only 20% of the value of our total assets. It now exceeds 35%. Yet, even with all of this inventory, "stockouts" (measured by complaints by customers that the desired product is not available) have increased by 40% during the last three years. And worse yet, it seems that we constantly must discount merchandise that we have too much of.

Beth asks the group to review the following data and make suggestions as to how the company's performance might be improved.

(in millions)	2014	2013	2012	2011
Inventory				
Raw materials	$242	$198	$155	$128
Work in process	116	77	49	33
Finished goods	567	482	398	257
Total inventory	$925	$757	$602	$418
Current assets	$1,800	$1,423	$1,183	$841
Total assets	$2,643	$2,523	$2,408	$2,090
Current liabilities	$600	$590	$525	$420
Sales revenue	$9,428	$8,674	$7,536	$6,840
Cost of goods sold	$6,328	$5,474	$4,445	$3,557
Net income	$754	$987	$979	$958

Instructions

Using the information provided, answer the following questions.

(a) Compute the current ratio, gross profit rate, profit margin, inventory turnover, and days in inventory for 2012, 2013, and 2014.
(b) Discuss the trends and potential causes of the changes in the ratios in part (a).

(c) Discuss potential remedies to any problems discussed in part (b).
(d) What concerns might be raised by some members of management with regard to your suggestions in part (c)?

COMMUNICATION ACTIVITIES

BYP6-7   In a discussion of dramatic increases in coffee-bean prices, a *Wall Street Journal* article noted the following fact about Starbucks.

> Before this year's bean-price hike, Starbucks added several defenses that analysts say could help it maintain earnings and revenue. The company last year began accounting for its coffee-bean purchases by taking the average price of all beans in inventory.

Prior to this change, the company was using FIFO.

Instructions

Your client, the CEO of Supreme Coffee, Inc., read this article and sent you an e-mail message requesting that you explain why Starbucks might have taken this action. Your response should explain what impact this change in accounting method has on earnings, why the company might want to do this, and any possible disadvantages of such a change.

*BYP6-8   You are the controller of Fagan Inc. K. L. Howard, the president, recently mentioned to you that she found an error in the 2013 financial statements which she believes has corrected itself. She determined, in discussions with the purchasing department, that 2013 ending inventory was overstated by $1 million. K. L. says that the 2014 ending inventory is correct, and she assumes that 2014 income is correct. K. L. says to you, "What happened has happened—there's no point in worrying about it anymore."

Instructions

You conclude that K. L. is incorrect. Write a brief, tactful memo to her, clarifying the situation.

ETHICS CASE

BYP6-9   Reagen Wholesale Corp. uses the LIFO cost flow method. In the current year, profit at Reagen is running unusually high. The corporate tax rate is also high this year, but it is scheduled to decline significantly next year. In an effort to lower the current year's net income and to take advantage of the changing income tax rate, the president of Reagen Wholesale instructs the plant accountant to recommend to the purchasing department a large purchase of inventory for delivery 3 days before the end of the year. The price of the inventory to be purchased has doubled during the year, and the purchase will represent a major portion of the ending inventory value.

Instructions

(a) What is the effect of this transaction on this year's and next year's income statement and income tax expense? Why?
(b) If Reagen Wholesale had been using the FIFO method of inventory costing, would the president give the same directive?
(c) Should the plant accountant order the inventory purchase to lower income? What are the ethical implications of this order?

ALL ABOUT YOU

BYP6-10   Some of the largest business frauds ever perpetrated have involved the misstatement of inventory. Two classics were at Leslie Fay and McKesson Corporation.

Instructions

There is considerable information regarding inventory frauds available on the Internet. Search for information about one of the two cases mentioned above, or inventory fraud at any other company, and prepare a short explanation of the nature of the inventory fraud.

FASB CODIFICATION ACTIVITY

BYP6-11   If your school has a subscription to the FASB Codification, go to **http://aaahq.org/ascLogin.cfm** to log in and prepare responses to the following.
(a) The primary basis for accounting for inventories is cost. How is cost defined in the Codification?

(b) What does the Codification state regarding the use of consistency in the selection or employment of a basis for inventory?

(c) What does the Codification indicate is a justification for the use of the lower-of-cost-or-market for inventory valuation?

CONSIDERING PEOPLE, PLANET, AND PROFIT

BYP6-12 Caterpillar publishes an annual Sustainability Report to explain its position on sustainability, describe its goals, and report on its achievements. The report can be found at **http://www. caterpillar.com/sustainability/sustainability-report**.

Instructions

Access the report and answer the following questions.

(a) Page 24 of the report describes Caterpillar's efforts in the area of coke oven gas. Read this section and discuss how the company's efforts address both sustainability and profitability.

(b) Page 43 describes the company's goals for the year 2020. What are these goals?

(c) Page 44 describes the company's results relative to 2003 with regard to worker safety. Summarize the company's progress in this area.

(d) Page 48 describes the company's results regarding energy use. Explain how the company measures its progress, and comment on its results thus far.

Answers to Insight and Accounting Across the Organization Questions

p. 239 A Big Hiccup Q: What steps might the companies take to avoid such a serious disruption in the future? **A:** The manufacturer of the piston rings should spread its manufacturing facilities across a few locations that are far enough apart that they would not all be at risk at once. In addition, the automakers might consider becoming less dependent on a single supplier as well as having weather contingency plans.

p. 240 Falsifying Inventory to Boost Income Q: What effect does an overstatement of inventory have on a company's financial statements? **A:** The balance sheet looks stronger because inventory and retained earnings are overstated. The income statement looks better because cost of goods sold is understated and income is overstated.

p. 249 Is LIFO Fair? Q: What are the arguments for and against the use of LIFO? **A:** Proponents of LIFO argue that it is conceptually superior because it matches the most recent cost with the most recent selling price. Critics contend that it artificially understates the company's net income and consequently reduces tax payments. Also, because most foreign companies are not allowed to use LIFO, its use by U.S. companies reduces the ability of investors to compare U.S. companies with foreign companies.

p. 253 Too Many TVs or Too Few? Q: For Sony, what are the advantages and disadvantages of having a low days in inventory measure? **A:** If Sony has a low days in inventory, it reduces the amount of cash it has tied up in inventory. It also minimizes the risk that it will be stuck with excess inventory that could force it to provide big discounts, resulting in punishing losses. Sony also faces the risk that the TVs will become obsolete before they are sold. However, Sony increases the risk that it will encounter "stockouts," that is, it will not have adequate inventory to meet customer demand.

Answers to Self-Test Questions

1. d **2.** a **3.** b ($180,000 + $35,000) **4.** c ((5,000 × $13) + (4,000 × $12)) **5.** d ((8,000 × $11) + (1,000 × $12)) **6.** d ((5,000 × $8) + (15,000 × $10) + (20,000 × $12)) ÷ 40,000 = $10.75; $10.75 × 7,000 **7.** c **8.** d **9.** a **10.** d **11.** b ($285,000 ÷ (($80,000 + $110,000) ÷ 2) = 3; 365 ÷ 3) **12.** a ***13.** d ***14.** b ***15.** b

A Look at IFRS

The major IFRS requirements related to accounting and reporting for inventories are the same as GAAP. The major differences are that IFRS prohibits the use of the LIFO cost flow assumption and determines market in the lower-of-cost-or-market inventory valuation differently.

LEARNING OBJECTIVE 9

Compare the accounting procedures for inventories under GAAP and IFRS.

KEY POINTS

- The requirements for accounting for and reporting inventories are more principles-based under IFRS. That is, GAAP provides more detailed guidelines in inventory accounting.

- The definitions for inventory are essentially similar under IFRS and GAAP. Both define inventory as assets held-for-sale in the ordinary course of business, in the process of production for sale (work in process), or to be consumed in the production of goods or services (e.g., raw materials).

- Who owns the goods—goods in transit or consigned goods—as well as the costs to include in inventory, are accounted for the same under IFRS and GAAP.

- Both GAAP and IFRS permit specific identification where appropriate. IFRS actually requires that the specific identification method be used where the inventory items are not interchangeable (i.e., can be specifically identified). If the inventory items are not specifically identifiable, a cost flow assumption is used. GAAP does not specify situations in which specific identification must be used.

- A major difference between IFRS and GAAP relates to the LIFO cost flow assumption. GAAP permits the use of LIFO for inventory valuation. IFRS prohibits its use. FIFO and average-cost are the only two acceptable cost flow assumptions permitted under IFRS.

- IFRS requires companies to use the same cost flow assumption for all goods of a similar nature. GAAP has no specific requirement in this area.

- In the lower-of-cost-or-market test for inventory valuation, IFRS defines market as net realizable value. Net realizable value is the estimated selling price in the ordinary course of business, less the estimated costs of completion and estimated selling expenses. In other words, net realizable value is the best estimate of the net amounts that inventories are expected to realize. GAAP, on the other hand, defines market as essentially replacement cost.

- Under GAAP, if inventory is written down under the lower-of-cost-or-market valuation, the new value becomes its cost basis. As a result, the inventory may not be written back up to its original cost in a subsequent period. Under IFRS, the write-down may be reversed in a subsequent period up to the amount of the previous write-down. Both the write-down and any subsequent reversal should be reported on the income statement as an expense. An item-by-item approach is generally followed under IFRS.

- An example of the use of lower-of-cost-or-net realizable value under IFRS follows.

Mendel Company has the following four items in its ending inventory as of December 31, 2014. The company uses the lower-of-cost-or-net realizable value approach for inventory valuation following IFRS.

Item No.	Cost	Net Realizable Value
1320	$3,600	$3,400
1333	4,000	4,100
1428	2,800	2,100
1510	5,000	4,700

The computation of the ending inventory value to be reported in the financial statements at December 31, 2014, is as follows.

Item No.	Cost	Net Realizable Value	Lower-of-Cost-or-NRV
1320	$ 3,600	$ 3,400	$ 3,400
1333	4,000	4,100	4,000
1428	2,800	2,100	2,100
1510	5,000	4,700	4,700
Total	$15,400	$14,300	$14,200

- Unlike property, plant, and equipment, IFRS does not permit the option of valuing inventories at fair value. As indicated above, IFRS requires inventory to be written down, but inventory cannot be written up above its original cost.
- Similar to GAAP, certain agricultural products and mineral products can be reported at net realizable value using IFRS.
- IFRS allows companies to report inventory at standard cost if it does not differ significantly from actual cost. Standard cost is addressed in managerial accounting courses.

LOOKING TO THE FUTURE

One convergence issue that will be difficult to resolve relates to the use of the LIFO cost flow assumption. As indicated, IFRS specifically prohibits its use. Conversely, the LIFO cost flow assumption is widely used in the United States because of its favorable tax advantages. In addition, many argue that LIFO from a financial reporting point of view provides a better matching of current costs against revenue and, therefore, enables companies to compute a more realistic income.

With a new conceptual framework being developed, it is highly probable that the use of the concept of conservatism will be eliminated. Similarly, the concept of "prudence" in the IASB literature will also be eliminated. This may ultimately have implications for the application of the lower-of-cost-or-net realizable value.

IFRS PRACTICE

IFRS SELF-TEST QUESTIONS

1. Which of the following should **not** be included in the inventory of a company using IFRS?
   (a) Goods held on consignment from another company.
   (b) Goods shipped on consignment to another company.
   (c) Goods in transit from another company shipped FOB shipping point.
   (d) None of the above.

2. Which method of inventory costing is prohibited under IFRS?
   (a) Specific identification.   (c) FIFO.
   (b) LIFO.   (d) Average-cost.

3. Yang Company purchased 2,000 phones and has 400 phones in its ending inventory at a cost of $90 each and a current replacement cost of $80 each. The net realizable value of each phone in the ending inventory is $70. The ending inventory under lower-of-cost-or-net realizable value is:
   (a) $36,000.   (c) $28,000.
   (b) $32,000.   (d) None of the above.

4. Specific identification:
   (a) must be used under IFRS if the inventory items are not interchangeable.
   (b) cannot be used under IFRS.
   (c) cannot be used under GAAP.
   (d) must be used under IFRS if it would result in the most conservative net income.

5. IFRS requires the following:
   (a) Ending inventory is written up and down to net realizable value each reporting period.
   (b) Ending inventory is written down to net realizable value but cannot be written up.
   (c) Ending inventory is written down to net realizable value and may be written up in future periods to its net realizable value but not above its original cost.
   (d) Ending inventory is written down to net realizable value and may be written up in future periods to its net realizable value.

IFRS CONCEPTS AND APPLICATION

IFRS6-1   Briefly describe some of the similarities and differences between GAAP and IFRS with respect to the accounting for inventories.

IFRS6-2   LaTour Inc. is based in France and prepares its financial statements in accordance with IFRS. In 2014, it reported cost of goods sold (in euros) of €578 million and average inventory of €154 million. Briefly discuss how analysis of LaTour's inventory turnover (and comparisons to a company using GAAP) might be affected by differences in inventory accounting between IFRS and GAAP.

IFRS6-3   Franklin Company has the following four items in its ending inventory as of December 31, 2014. The company uses the lower-of-cost-or-net realizable value approach for inventory valuation following IFRS.

Item No.	Cost	Net Realizable Value
AB	$1,700	$1,400
TRX	2,200	2,300
NWA	7,800	7,100
SGH	3,000	3,700

Compute the lower-of-cost-or-net realizable value.

INTERNATIONAL FINANCIAL REPORTING PROBLEM: *Zetar plc*

IFRS6-4   The financial statements of Zetar plc are presented in Appendix C. The company's complete annual report, including the notes to its financial statements, is available in the Investors section at **www.zetarplc.com**.

Instructions
Using the notes to the company's financial statements, answer the following questions.
  (a) What cost flow assumption does the company use to value inventory?
  (b) What was the amount of expense that the company reported for inventory write-downs during 2011?
  (c) What amount of raw materials, work in process, and finished goods inventory did the company report at April 30, 2011?

Answers to IFRS Self-Test Questions
1. a **2.** b **3.** c **4.** a **5.** c

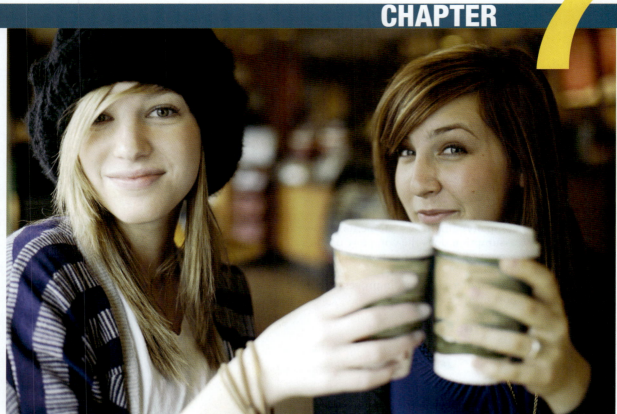

CHAPTER 7

© James Pauls/iStockphoto

FRAUD, INTERNAL CONTROL, AND CASH

LEARNING OBJECTIVES

After studying this chapter, you should be able to:

1 Define fraud and internal control.

2 Identify the principles of internal control activities.

3 Explain the applications of internal control principles to cash receipts.

4 Explain the applications of internal control principles to cash disbursements.

5 Prepare a bank reconciliation.

6 Explain the reporting of cash.

7 Discuss the basic principles of cash management.

8 Identify the primary elements of a cash budget.

If you're ever looking for a cappuccino in Moose Jaw, Saskatchewan, stop by Stephanie's Gourmet Coffee and More, located on Main Street. Staff there serve, on average, 650 cups of coffee a day, including both regular and specialty coffees, not to mention soups, Italian sandwiches, and a wide assortment of gourmet cheesecakes.

"We've got high school students who come here, and students from the community college," says owner/manager Stephanie Mintenko, who has run the place since opening it in 1995. "We have customers who are retired, and others who are working people and have only 30 minutes for lunch. We have to be pretty quick."

That means that the cashiers have to be efficient. Like most businesses where purchases are low-cost and high-volume, cash control has to be simple.

"We have an electronic cash register, but it's not the fancy new kind where you just punch in the item," explains Ms. Mintenko. "You have to punch in the prices." The machine does keep track of sales in several categories, however. Cashiers punch a button to indicate whether each item is a beverage, a meal, or other type of item. An internal tape in the machine keeps a record of all transactions; the customer receives a receipt only upon request.

There is only one cash register. "Up to three of us might operate it on any given shift, including myself," says Ms. Mintenko.

She and her staff do two "cashouts" each day—one with the shift change at 5:00 p.m. and one when the shop closes at 10:00 p.m. At each cashout, they count the cash in the register drawer. That amount, minus the cash change carried forward (the float), should match the shift total on the register tape. If there's a discrepancy, they do another count. Then, if necessary, "we go through the whole tape to find the mistake," she explains. "It usually turns out to be someone who punched in $18 instead of $1.80, or something like that."

Ms. Mintenko sends all the cash tapes and float totals to a bookkeeper, who double-checks everything and provides regular reports. "We try to keep the accounting simple, so we can concentrate on making great coffee and food."

MINDING THE MONEY IN MOOSE JAW

INSIDE CHAPTER 7 . . .

- **And the Controls Are . . .**
- **SOX Boosts the Role of Human Resources**
- **How Employees Steal**
- **Madoff's Ponzi Scheme**

As the story about recording cash sales at Stephanie's Gourmet Coffee and More indicates, control of cash is important to ensure that fraud does not occur. Companies also need controls to safeguard other types of assets. For example, Stephanie's undoubtedly has controls to prevent the theft of food and supplies, and controls to prevent the theft of tableware and dishes from its kitchen.

In this chapter, we explain the essential features of an internal control system and how it prevents fraud. We also describe how those controls apply to a specific asset—cash. The applications include some controls with which you may be already familiar, such as the use of a bank.

The content and organization of Chapter 7 are as follows.

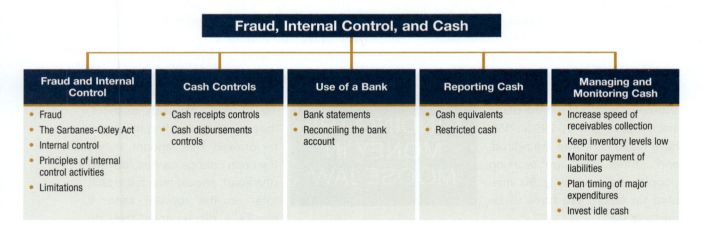

Fraud and Internal Control

LEARNING OBJECTIVE 1

Define fraud and internal control.

The Feature Story describes many of the internal control procedures used by Stephanie's Gourmet Coffee and More. These procedures are necessary to discourage employees from fraudulent activities.

FRAUD

A **fraud** is a dishonest act by an employee that results in personal benefit to the employee at a cost to the employer. Examples of fraud reported in the financial press include:

- A bookkeeper in a small company diverted $750,000 of bill payments to a personal bank account over a three-year period.
- A shipping clerk with 28 years of service shipped $125,000 of merchandise to himself.
- A computer operator embezzled $21 million from Wells Fargo Bank over a two-year period.
- A church treasurer "borrowed" $150,000 of church funds to finance a friend's business dealings.

Why does fraud occur? The three main factors that contribute to fraudulent activity are depicted by the **fraud triangle** in Illustration 7-1.

The most important element of the fraud triangle is **opportunity**. For an employee to commit fraud, the workplace environment must provide opportunities that an employee can exploit. Opportunities occur when the work-place lacks sufficient controls to deter and detect fraud. For example, inadequate monitoring of employee actions can create opportunities for theft and can embolden employees because they believe they will not be caught.

A second factor that contributes to fraud is **financial pressure**. Employees sometimes commit fraud because of personal financial problems caused by too much debt. Or they might commit fraud because they want to lead a lifestyle that they cannot afford on their current salary.

The third factor that contributes to fraud is **rationalization**. In order to justify their fraud, employees rationalize their dishonest actions. For example, employees sometimes justify fraud because they believe they are underpaid while the employer is making lots of money. These employees feel justified in stealing because they believe they deserve to be paid more.

Illustration 7-1 Fraud triangle

THE SARBANES-OXLEY ACT

What can be done to prevent or to detect fraud? After numerous corporate scandals came to light in the early 2000s, Congress addressed this issue by passing the Sarbanes-Oxley Act (SOX). Under SOX, all publicly traded U.S. corporations are required to maintain an adequate system of internal control. Corporate executives and boards of directors must ensure that these controls are reliable and effective. In addition, independent outside auditors must attest to the adequacy of the internal control system. Companies that fail to comply are subject to fines, and company officers can be imprisoned. SOX also created the Public Company Accounting Oversight Board (PCAOB) to establish auditing standards and regulate auditor activity.

One poll found that 60% of investors believe that SOX helps safeguard their stock investments. Many say they would be unlikely to invest in a company that fails to follow SOX requirements. Although some corporate executives have criticized the time and expense involved in following the SOX requirements, SOX appears to be working well. For example, the chief accounting officer of Eli Lily noted that SOX triggered a comprehensive review of how the company documents controls. This review uncovered redundancies and pointed out controls that needed to be added. In short, it added up to time and money well spent. And the finance chief at General Electric noted, "We have seen value in SOX. It helps build investors' trust and gives them more confidence."[1]

INTERNAL CONTROL

Internal control consists of all the related methods and measures adopted within an organization to safeguard assets, enhance the reliability of accounting records, increase efficiency of operations, and ensure compliance with laws and regulations. Internal control systems have five primary components as listed below.[2]

- **A control environment.** It is the responsibility of top management to make it clear that the organization values integrity and that unethical activity will not be tolerated. This component is often referred to as the "tone at the top."

[1]"Corporate Regulation Must Be Working—There's a Backlash," *Wall Street Journal* (June 16, 2004), p. C1; and Judith Burns, "Is Sarbanes-Oxley Working?" *Wall Street Journal* (June 21, 2004), pp. R8–R9.
[2]The Committee of Sponsoring Organizations of the Treadway Commission, "Internal Control—Integrated Framework," **www.coso.org/publications/executive_summary_integrated_framework.htm** (accessed March 2008).

- **Risk assessment.** Companies must identify and analyze the various factors that create risk for the business and must determine how to manage these risks.
- **Control activities.** To reduce the occurrence of fraud, management must design policies and procedures to address the specific risks faced by the company.
- **Information and communication.** The internal control system must capture and communicate all pertinent information both down and up the organization, as well as communicate information to appropriate external parties.
- **Monitoring.** Internal control systems must be monitored periodically for their adequacy. Significant deficiencies need to be reported to top management and/or the board of directors.

PEOPLE, PLANET, AND PROFIT INSIGHT
And the Controls Are . . .

Internal controls are important for an effective financial reporting system. The same is true for sustainability reporting. An effective system of internal controls for sustainability reporting will help in the following ways: (1) prevent the unauthorized use of data; (2) provide reasonable assurance that the information is accurate, valid, and complete; and (3) report information that is consistent with overall sustainability accounting policies. With these types of controls, users will have the confidence that they can use the sustainability information effectively.

Some regulators are calling for even more assurance through audits of this information. Companies that potentially can cause environmental damage through greenhouse gases are subject to reporting requirements as well as companies in the mining and extractive industries. And, as demand for more information in the sustainability area expands, the need for audits of this information will grow.

? Why is sustainability information important to investors? (Answers in *Broadening Your Perspective*.)

PRINCIPLES OF INTERNAL CONTROL ACTIVITIES

LEARNING OBJECTIVE 2
Identify the principles of internal control activities.

Each of the five components of an internal control system is important. Here, we will focus on one component, the control activities. The reason? These activities are the backbone of the company's efforts to address the risks it faces, such as fraud. The specific control activities used by a company will vary, depending on management's assessment of the risks faced. This assessment is heavily influenced by the size and nature of the company.

The six principles of control activities are as follows.

- Establishment of responsibility
- Segregation of duties
- Documentation procedures
- Physical controls
- Independent internal verification
- Human resource controls

We explain these principles in the following sections. You should recognize that they apply to most companies and are relevant to both manual and computerized accounting systems.

Establishment of Responsibility

An essential principle of internal control is to assign responsibility to specific employees. **Control is most effective when only one person is responsible for a given task.**

To illustrate, assume that the cash on hand at the end of the day in a Safeway supermarket is $10 short of the cash entered in the cash register. If only one person has operated the register, the shift manager can quickly determine responsibility for the shortage. What happens, though, if two or more individuals work the register? For example, in the Feature Story, the principle of establishing responsibility does not appear to be strictly applied by Stephanie's Gourmet Coffee and More since three people operate the cash register on any given shift. Many retailers solve this problem by having registers with multiple drawers. This makes it possible for more than one person to operate a register but still allows identification of a particular employee with a specific drawer. Only the signed-in cashier has access to his or her drawer.

Establishing responsibility often requires limiting access only to authorized personnel, and then identifying those personnel. For example, the automated systems used by many companies have mechanisms such as identifying passcodes that keep track of who made a journal entry, who entered a sale, or who went into an inventory storeroom at a particular time. Use of identifying passcodes enables the company to establish responsibility by identifying the particular employee who carried out the activity.

It's your shift now. I'm turning in my cash drawer and heading home.

Transfer of cash drawers

ANATOMY OF A FRAUD

Maureen Frugali was a training supervisor for claims processing at Colossal Healthcare. As a standard part of the claims-processing training program, Maureen created fictitious claims for use by trainees. These fictitious claims were then sent to the accounts payable department. After the training claims had been processed, she was to notify Accounts Payable of all fictitious claims, so that they would not be paid. However, she did not inform Accounts Payable about every fictitious claim. She created some fictitious claims for entities that she controlled (that is, she would receive the payment), and she let Accounts Payable pay her.

Total take: $11 million

THE MISSING CONTROL

Establishment of responsibility. The health-care company did not adequately restrict the responsibility for authorizing and approving claims transactions. The training supervisor should not have been authorized to create claims in the company's "live" system.

Source: Adapted from Wells, *Fraud Casebook* (2007), pp. 61–70.

Segregation of Duties

Segregation of duties is indispensable in an internal control system. There are two common applications of this principle:

1. Different individuals should be responsible for related activities.
2. The responsibility for record-keeping for an asset should be separate from the physical custody of that asset.

The rationale for segregation of duties is this: **The work of one employee should, without a duplication of effort, provide a reliable basis for evaluating the work of another employee.** For example, the personnel that design and program computerized systems should not be assigned duties related to day-to-day use of the system. Otherwise, they could design the system to benefit them personally and conceal the fraud through day-to-day use.

SEGREGATION OF RELATED ACTIVITIES. **Making one individual responsible for related activities increases the potential for errors and irregularities.** Instead, companies should, for example, assign related **purchasing activities** to different individuals. Related purchasing activities include ordering merchandise, order approval, receiving goods, authorizing payment, and paying for goods or services. Various frauds are possible when one person handles related purchasing activities:

- If a purchasing agent is allowed to order goods without supervisory approval, the likelihood of the agent receiving kickbacks from suppliers increases.
- If an employee who orders goods also handles receipt of the goods and invoice, as well as payment authorization, he or she might authorize payment for a fictitious invoice.

These abuses are less likely to occur when companies divide the purchasing tasks.

Similarly, companies should assign related **sales activities** to different individuals. Related selling activities include making a sale, shipping (or delivering) the goods to the customer, billing the customer, and receiving payment. Various frauds are possible when one person handles related sales activities. For example:

- If a salesperson can make a sale without obtaining supervisory approval, he or she might make sales at unauthorized prices to increase sales commissions.
- A shipping clerk who also has access to accounting records could ship goods to himself.
- A billing clerk who handles billing and cash receipts could understate the amount billed for sales made to friends and relatives.

These abuses are less likely to occur when companies divide the sales tasks: the salespeople make the sale; the shipping department ships the goods on the basis of the sales order; and the billing department prepares the sales invoice after comparing the sales order with the report of goods shipped.

ANATOMY OF A FRAUD

Lawrence Fairbanks, the assistant vice-chancellor of communications at Aesop University, was allowed to make purchases of under $2,500 for his department without external approval. Unfortunately, he also sometimes bought items for himself, such as expensive antiques and other collectibles. How did he do it? He replaced the vendor invoices he received with fake vendor invoices that he created. The fake invoices had descriptions that were more consistent with communications department purchases. He submitted these fake invoices to the accounting department as the basis for their journal entries and to the accounts payable department as the basis for payment.

Total take: $475,000

THE MISSING CONTROL

Segregation of duties. The university had not properly segregated related purchasing activities. Lawrence was ordering items, receiving the items, and receiving the invoice. By receiving the invoice, he had control over the documents that were used to account for the purchase and thus was able to substitute a fake invoice.

Source: Adapted from Wells, *Fraud Casebook* (2007), pp. 3–15.

SEGREGATION OF RECORD-KEEPING FROM PHYSICAL CUSTODY. The account-ant should have neither physical custody of the asset nor access to it. Like-wise, the custodian of the asset should not maintain or have access to the accounting records. **The custodian of the asset is not likely to convert the asset to personal use when one employee maintains the record of the asset, and a different employee has physical custody of the asset.** The separa-tion of accounting responsibility from the custody of assets is especially important for cash and inventories because these assets are very vulnerable to fraud.

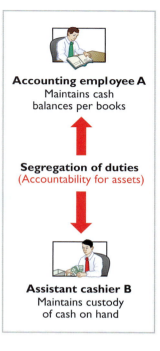

Accounting employee A
Maintains cash balances per books

Segregation of duties
(Accountability for assets)

Assistant cashier B
Maintains custody of cash on hand

ANATOMY OF A FRAUD

Angela Bauer was an accounts payable clerk for Aggasiz Construction Company. Angela prepared and issued checks to vendors and reconciled bank statements. She perpetrated a fraud in this way: She wrote checks for costs that the company had not actually incurred (e.g., fake taxes). A supervisor then approved and signed the checks. Before issuing the check, though, Angela would "white-out" the payee line on the check and change it to personal accounts that she controlled. She was able to conceal the theft because she also reconciled the bank account. That is, nobody else ever saw that the checks had been altered.

Total take: $570,000

THE MISSING CONTROL

Segregation of duties. Aggasiz Construction Company did not properly segregate record-keeping from physical custody. Angela had physical custody of the blank checks, which essentially was control of the cash. She also had record-keeping responsibility because she prepared the bank reconciliation.

Source: Adapted from Wells, *Fraud Casebook* (2007), pp. 100–107.

Documentation Procedures

Documents provide evidence that transactions and events have occurred. At Stephanie's Gourmet Coffee and More, the cash register tape is the restaurant's documentation for the sale and the amount of cash received. More sophisti-cated registers, called point-of-sale terminals, do not rely on tapes. Rather, they are networked with the company's computing and accounting records, which results in direct documentation. Similarly, a shipping document indicates that the goods have been shipped, and a sales invoice indicates that the company has billed the customer for the goods. By requiring signatures (or initials) on the documents, the company can identify the individual(s) responsible for the transaction or event. Companies should document transactions when the trans-action occurs.

Companies should establish procedures for documents. First, whenever possible, companies should use **prenumbered documents, and all docu-ments should be accounted for**. Prenumbering helps to prevent a transaction from being recorded more than once, or conversely, from not being recorded at all. Second, the control system should require that employees **promptly forward source documents for accounting entries to the accounting department. This control measure helps to ensure timely recording of the transaction** and contributes directly to the accuracy and reliability of the accounting records.

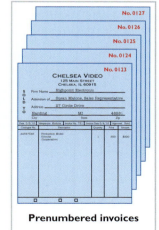

Prenumbered invoices

ANATOMY OF A FRAUD

To support their reimbursement requests for travel costs incurred, employees at Mod Fashions Corporation's design center were required to submit receipts. The receipts could include the detailed bill provided for a meal, or the credit card receipt provided when the credit card payment is made, or a copy of the employee's monthly credit card bill that listed the item. A number of the designers who frequently traveled together came up with a fraud scheme: They submitted claims for the same expenses. For example, if they had a meal together that cost $200, one person submitted the detailed meal bill, another submitted the credit card receipt, and a third submitted a monthly credit card bill showing the meal as a line item. Thus, all three received a $200 reimbursement.

Total take: $75,000

THE MISSING CONTROL

Documentation procedures. Mod Fashions should require the original, detailed receipt. It should not accept photocopies, and it should not accept credit card statements. In addition, documentation procedures could be further improved by requiring the use of a corporate credit card (rather than personal credit card) for all business expenses.

Source: Adapted from Wells, *Fraud Casebook* (2007), pp. 79–90.

Physical Controls

Use of physical controls is essential. **Physical controls** relate to the safeguarding of assets and enhance the accuracy and reliability of the accounting records. Illustration 7-2 shows examples of these controls.

ANATOMY OF A FRAUD

At Centerstone Health, a large insurance company, the mailroom each day received insurance applications from prospective customers. Mailroom employees scanned the applications into electronic documents before the applications were processed. Once the applications are scanned, they can be accessed online by authorized employees.

Insurance agents at Centerstone Health earn commissions based upon successful applications. The sales agent's name is listed on the application. However, roughly 15% of the applications are from customers who did not work with a sales agent. Two friends—Alex, an employee in record-keeping, and Parviz, a sales agent—thought up a way to perpetrate a fraud. Alex identified scanned applications that did not list a sales agent. After business hours, he entered the mailroom and found the hardcopy applications that did not show a sales agent. He wrote in Parviz's name as the sales agent and then rescanned the application for processing. Parviz received the commission, which the friends then split.

Total take: $240,000

THE MISSING CONTROL

Physical controls. Centerstone Health lacked two basic physical controls that could have prevented this fraud. First, the mailroom should have been locked during nonbusiness hours, and access during business hours should have been tightly controlled. Second, the scanned applications supposedly could be accessed only by authorized employees using their password. However, the password for each employee was the same as the employee's user ID. Since employee user ID numbers were available to all other employees, all employees knew all other employees' passwords. Thus, Alex could enter the system using another employee's password and access the scanned applications.

Source: Adapted from Wells, *Fraud Casebook* (2007), pp. 316–326.

Physical Controls

| Safes, vaults, and safety deposit boxes for cash and business papers | Locked warehouses and storage cabinets for inventories and records | Computer facilities with pass key access or fingerprint or eyeball scans | Alarms to prevent break-ins | Television monitors and garment sensors to deter theft | Time clocks for recording time worked |

Illustration 7-2 Physical controls

Independent Internal Verification

Most internal control systems provide for **independent internal verification**. This principle involves the review of data prepared by employees. To obtain maximum benefit from independent internal verification:

1. Companies should verify records periodically or on a surprise basis.
2. An employee who is independent of the personnel responsible for the information should make the verification.
3. Discrepancies and exceptions should be reported to a management level that can take appropriate corrective action.

Independent internal verification is especially useful in comparing recorded transactions with existing assets. The reconciliation of the cash register tape with the cash in the register at Stephanie's Gourmet Coffee and More is an example of this internal control principle. Another common example is the reconciliation of a company's cash balance per books with the cash balance per bank and the verification of the perpetual inventory records through a count of physical inventory. Illustration 7-3 shows the relationship between this principle and the segregation of duties principle.

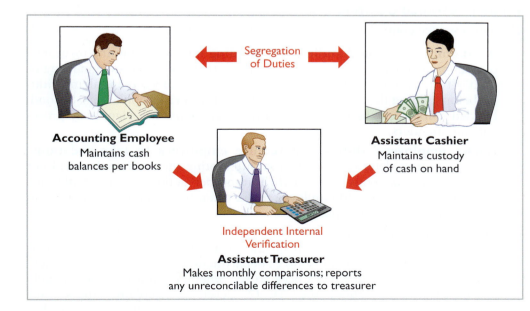

Illustration 7-3 Comparison of segregation of duties principle with independent internal verification principle

Large companies often assign independent internal verification to internal auditors. **Internal auditors** are company employees who continuously evaluate the effectiveness of the company's internal control systems. They review the activities of departments and individuals to determine whether prescribed internal controls are being followed. They also recommend improvements when needed. In fact, most fraud is discovered by the company through internal mechanisms such as existing internal controls and internal audits. For example, WorldCom was at one time the second largest U.S. telecommunications company. The fraud that caused its bankruptcy (the largest ever when it occurred) involved billions of dollars. It was uncovered by an internal auditor.

ANATOMY OF A FRAUD

Bobbi Jean Donnelly, the office manager for Mod Fashions Corporation's design center, was responsible for preparing the design center budget and reviewing expense reports submitted by design center employees. Her desire to upgrade her wardrobe got the better of her, and she enacted a fraud that involved filing expense-reimbursement requests for her own personal clothing purchases. She was able to conceal the fraud because she was responsible for reviewing all expense reports, including her own. In addition, she sometimes was given ultimate responsibility for signing off on the expense reports when her boss was "too busy." Also, because she controlled the budget, when she submitted her expenses, she coded them to budget items that she knew were running under budget, so that they would not catch anyone's attention.

Total take: $275,000

THE MISSING CONTROL

Independent internal verification. Bobbi Jean's boss should have verified her expense reports. When asked what he thought her expenses for a year were, the boss said about $10,000. At $115,000 per year, her actual expenses were more than 10 times what would have been expected. However, because he was "too busy" to verify her expense reports or to review the budget, he never noticed.

Source: Adapted from Wells, *Fraud Casebook* (2007), pp. 79–90.

Human Resource Controls

Human resource control activities include the following.

If I take a vacation they will know that I've been stealing.

1. **Bond employees who handle cash. Bonding** involves obtaining insurance protection against theft by employees. It contributes to the safeguarding of cash in two ways. First, the insurance company carefully screens all individuals before adding them to the policy and may reject risky applicants. Second, bonded employees know that the insurance company will vigorously prosecute all offenders.

2. **Rotate employees' duties and require employees to take vacations.** These measures deter employees from attempting thefts since they will not be able to permanently conceal their improper actions. Many banks, for example, have discovered employee thefts when the employee was on vacation or assigned to a new position.

3. **Conduct thorough background checks.** Many believe that the most important and inexpensive measure any business can take to reduce employee theft and fraud is for the human resources department to conduct thorough background checks. Two tips: (1) Check to see whether job applicants actually graduated from the schools they list. (2) Never use telephone numbers for previous employers provided by the applicant; always look them up yourself.

ANATOMY OF A FRAUD

Ellen Lowry was the desk manager and Josephine Rodriquez was the head of housekeeping at the Excelsior Inn, a luxury hotel. The two best friends were so dedicated to their jobs that they never took vacations, and they frequently filled in for other employees. In fact, Ms. Rodriquez, whose job as head of housekeeping did not include cleaning rooms, often cleaned rooms herself, "just to help the staff keep up." These two "dedicated" employees, working as a team, found a way to earn a little more cash. Ellen, the desk manager, provided significant discounts to guests who paid with cash. She kept the cash and did not register the guest in the hotel's computerized system. Instead, she took the room out of circulation "due to routine maintenance." Because the room did not show up as being used, it did not receive a normal housekeeping assignment. Instead, Josephine, the head of housekeeping, cleaned the rooms during the guests' stay.

Total take: $95,000

THE MISSING CONTROL

Human resource controls. Ellen, the desk manager, had been fired by a previous employer after being accused of fraud. If the Excelsior Inn had conducted a thorough background check, it would not have hired her. The hotel fraud was detected when Ellen missed work for a few days due to illness. A system of mandatory vacations and rotating days off would have increased the chances of detecting the fraud before it became so large.

Source: Adapted from Wells, *Fraud Casebook* (2007), pp. 145–155.

LIMITATIONS OF INTERNAL CONTROL

Companies generally design their systems of internal control to provide **reasonable assurance** of proper safeguarding of assets and reliability of the accounting records. The concept of reasonable assurance rests on the premise that the costs of establishing control procedures should not exceed their expected benefit.

To illustrate, consider shoplifting losses in retail stores. Stores could eliminate such losses by having a security guard stop and search customers as they leave the store. But store managers have concluded that the negative effects of such a procedure cannot be justified. Instead, they have attempted to control shoplifting losses by less costly procedures. They post signs saying, "We reserve the right to inspect all packages" and "All shoplifters will be prosecuted." They use hidden TV cameras and store detectives to monitor customer activity, and they install sensor equipment at exits.

Accounting Across the Organization
SOX Boosts the Role of Human Resources

Under SOX, a company needs to keep track of employees' degrees and certifications to ensure that employees continue to meet the specified requirements of a job. Also, to ensure proper employee supervision and proper separation of duties, companies must develop and monitor an organizational chart. When one corporation went through this exercise it found that out of 17,000 employees, there were 400 people who did not report to anyone. The corporation had 35 people who reported to each other. In addition, SOX also mandates that, if an employee complains of an unfair firing and mentions financial issues at the company, HR must refer the case to the company audit committee and possibly to its legal counsel.

? Why would unsupervised employees or employees who report to each other represent potential internal control threats? (Answers in *Broadening Your Perspective*.)

The **human element** is an important factor in every system of internal control. A good system can become ineffective as a result of employee fatigue, carelessness, or indifference. For example, a receiving clerk may not bother to count goods received and may just "fudge" the counts. Occasionally, two or more individuals work together to get around prescribed controls. Such **collusion** can significantly reduce the effectiveness of a system, eliminating the protection offered by segregation of duties. No system of internal control is perfect.

The **size of the business** also may impose limitations on internal control. Small companies often find it difficult to segregate duties or to provide for independent internal verification. A study by the Association of Certified Fraud Examiners (*2012 Report to the Nation on Occupational Fraud and Abuse*) indicates that businesses with fewer than 100 employees are most at risk for employee theft. In fact, 31.8% of frauds occurred at companies with fewer than 100 employees. The median loss at small companies was $147,000, which was higher than the median fraud at companies with more than 10,000 employees ($140,000). A $147,000 loss can threaten the very existence of a small company.

DECISION TOOLKIT

DECISION CHECKPOINTS	INFO NEEDED FOR DECISION	TOOL TO USE FOR DECISION	HOW TO EVALUATE RESULTS
Are the company's financial statements supported by adequate internal controls?	Auditor's report, management discussion and analysis, articles in financial press	The principles of internal control activities are (1) establishment of responsibility, (2) segregation of duties, (3) documentation procedures, (4) physical controls, (5) independent internal verification, and (6) human resource controls.	If any indication is given that these or other controls are lacking, use the financial statements with caution.

Cash Controls

LEARNING OBJECTIVE 3

Explain the applications of internal control principles to cash receipts.

Cash is the one asset that is readily convertible into any other type of asset. It also is easily concealed and transported, and is highly desired. Because of these characteristics, **cash is the asset most susceptible to fraudulent activities**. In addition, because of the large volume of cash transactions, numerous errors may occur in executing and recording them. To safeguard cash and to ensure the accuracy of the accounting records for cash, effective internal control over cash is critical.

CASH RECEIPTS CONTROLS

Illustration 7-4 shows how the internal control principles explained earlier apply to cash receipts transactions. As you might expect, companies vary considerably in how they apply these principles. To illustrate internal control over cash receipts, we will examine control activities for a retail store with both over-the-counter and mail receipts.

Cash Receipts Controls

Establishment of Responsibility
Only designated personnel
are authorized to handle cash
receipts (cashiers)

Segregation of Duties
Different individuals receive
cash, record cash receipts,
and hold the cash

Documentation Procedures
Use remittance advice (mail
receipts), cash register tapes or
computer records, and deposit slips

Physical Controls
Store cash in safes and bank
vaults; limit access to storage
areas; use cash registers

Independent Internal Verification
Supervisors count cash
receipts daily; assistant treasurer
compares total receipts to
bank deposits daily

Human Resource Controls
Bond personnel who handle
cash; require employees to
take vacations; conduct
background checks

Illustration 7-4 Application
of internal control principles
to cash receipts

Over-the-Counter Receipts

In retail businesses, control of over-the-counter receipts centers on cash registers
that are visible to customers. A cash sale is entered in a cash register with the
amount clearly visible to the customer. This activity prevents the cashier from
entering a lower amount and pocketing the difference. The customer receives an
itemized cash register receipt slip and is expected to count the change received.
(One weakness at Stephanie's Gourmet Coffee and More in the Feature Story is
that customers were only given a receipt if they requested it.) The cash register's
tape is locked in the register until a supervisor removes it. This tape accumulates
the daily transactions and totals. Alternatively, cash registers called point-of-sale
terminals are often networked with the company's computers for direct recording in its records.

At the end of the clerk's shift, the clerk counts the cash and sends the cash and
the count to the cashier. The cashier counts the cash, prepares a deposit slip, and
deposits the cash at the bank. The cashier also sends a duplicate of the deposit
slip to the accounting department to indicate cash received. The supervisor
removes the cash register tape and sends it to the accounting department (in a
non-point-of-sale system) as the basis for a journal entry to record the cash
received. The tape is compared to the deposit slip for any discrepancies. Illustration 7-5 summarizes this process.

This system for handling cash receipts uses an important internal control
principle—segregation of record-keeping from physical custody. The supervisor
has access to the cash register tape, but **not** to the cash. The clerk and the cashier have access to the cash, but **not** to the register tape. In addition, the cash

Illustration 7-5 Control of over-the-counter receipts

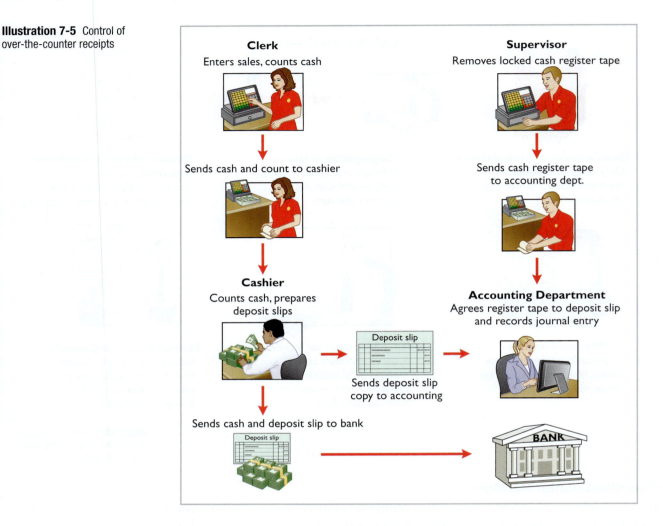

register tape provides documentation and enables independent internal verification with the deposit slip. Use of these three principles of internal control (segregation of record-keeping from physical custody, documentation, and independent internal verification) provides an effective system of internal control. Any attempt at fraudulent activity should be detected unless there is collusion among the employees.

In some instances, the amount deposited at the bank will not agree with the cash recorded in the accounting records based on the cash register tape. These differences often result because the clerk hands incorrect change back to the retail customer. In this case, the difference between the actual cash and the amount reported on the cash register tape is reported in a Cash Over and Short account. For example, suppose that the cash register tape indicated sales of $6,956.20 but the amount of cash was only $6,946.10. A cash shortfall of $10.10 exists. To account for this cash shortfall and related cash, the company makes the following entry.

A	=	L	+	SE
+6,946.10				
				−10.10
				+6,956.20

Cash Flows
+6,946.10

Cash	6,946.10	
Cash Over and Short	10.10	
Sales Revenue		6,956.20
(To record cash shortfall)		

Cash Over and Short is an income statement item. It is reported as miscellaneous expense when there is a cash shortfall, and as miscellaneous revenue when there is an overage. Clearly, the amount should be small. Any material amounts in this account should be investigated.

Mail Receipts

All mail receipts should be opened in the presence of at least two mail clerks. These receipts are generally in the form of checks. A mail clerk should endorse each check "For Deposit Only." This restrictive endorsement reduces the likelihood that someone could divert the check to personal use. Banks will not give an individual cash when presented with a check that has this type of endorsement.

The mail clerks prepare, in triplicate, a list of the checks received each day. This list shows the name of the check issuer, the purpose of the payment, and the amount of the check. Each mail clerk signs the list to establish responsibility for the data. The original copy of the list, along with the checks, is then sent to the cashier's department. A copy of the list is sent to the accounting department for recording in the accounting records. The clerks also keep a copy.

This process provides excellent internal control for the company. By employing two clerks, the chance of fraud is reduced. Each clerk knows he or she is being observed by the other clerk(s). To engage in fraud, they would have to collude. The customers who submit payments also provide control because they will contact the company with a complaint if they are not properly credited for payment. Because the cashier has access to cash but not the records, and the accounting department has access to records but not cash, neither can engage in undetected fraud.

CASH DISBURSEMENTS CONTROLS

Companies disburse cash for a variety of reasons, such as to pay expenses and liabilities or to purchase assets. **Generally, internal control over cash disbursements is more effective when companies pay by check or electronic funds transfer (EFT) rather than by cash.** One exception is **payments for incidental amounts that are paid out of petty cash.**[3]

> **LEARNING OBJECTIVE 4**
> Explain the applications of internal control principles to cash disbursements.

Companies generally issue checks only after following specified control procedures. Illustration 7-6 shows how principles of internal control apply to cash disbursements.

Voucher System Controls

Most medium and large companies use vouchers as part of their internal control over cash disbursements. A **voucher system** is a network of approvals by authorized individuals, acting independently, to ensure that all disbursements by check are proper.

The system begins with the authorization to incur a cost or expense. It ends with the issuance of a check for the liability incurred. A **voucher** is an authorization form prepared for each expenditure in a voucher system. Companies require vouchers for all types of cash disbursements except those from petty cash.

The starting point in preparing a voucher is to fill in the appropriate information about the liability on the face of the voucher. The vendor's invoice provides most of the needed information. Then, an employee in accounts payable records the voucher (in a journal called a **voucher register**) and files it according to the date on which it is to be paid. The company issues and sends a check on that date, and stamps the voucher "paid." The paid voucher is sent to the accounting department for recording (in a journal called the **check register**). A voucher system involves two journal entries, one to record the liability when the voucher is issued and a second to pay the liability that relates to the voucher.

---

[3]We explain the operation of a petty cash fund in the appendix to this chapter.

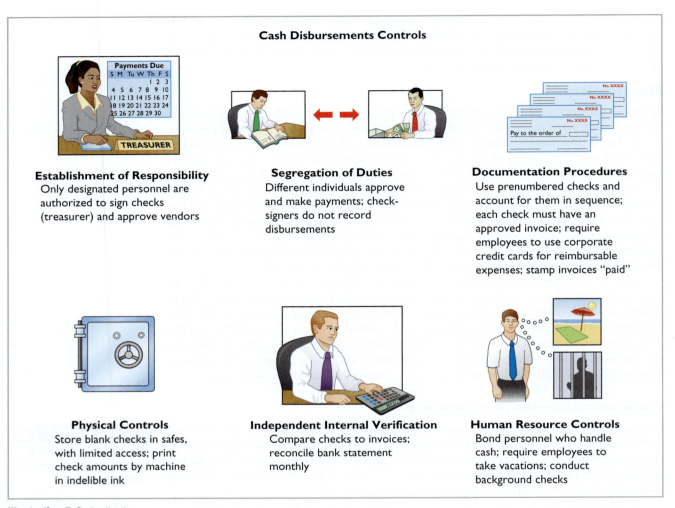

Cash Disbursements Controls

Establishment of Responsibility
Only designated personnel are authorized to sign checks (treasurer) and approve vendors

Segregation of Duties
Different individuals approve and make payments; check-signers do not record disbursements

Documentation Procedures
Use prenumbered checks and account for them in sequence; each check must have an approved invoice; require employees to use corporate credit cards for reimbursable expenses; stamp invoices "paid"

Physical Controls
Store blank checks in safes, with limited access; print check amounts by machine in indelible ink

Independent Internal Verification
Compare checks to invoices; reconcile bank statement monthly

Human Resource Controls
Bond personnel who handle cash; require employees to take vacations; conduct background checks

Illustration 7-6 Application of internal control principles to cash disbursements

The use of a voucher system, whether done manually or electronically, improves internal control over cash disbursements. First, the authorization process inherent in a voucher system establishes responsibility. Each individual has responsibility to review the underlying documentation to ensure that it is correct. In addition, the voucher system keeps track of the documents that back up each transaction. By keeping these documents in one place, a supervisor can independently verify the authenticity of each transaction. Consider, for example, the case of Aesop University presented on page 288. Aesop did not use a voucher system for transactions under $2,500. As a consequence, there was no independent verification of the documents, which enabled the employee to submit fake invoices to hide his unauthorized purchases.

Petty Cash Fund

As you learned earlier in the chapter, better internal control over cash disbursements is possible when companies make payments by check. However, using checks to pay such small amounts as those for postage due, employee working lunches, and taxi fares is both impractical and a nuisance. A common way of handling such payments, while maintaining satisfactory control, is to use a petty cash fund. A **petty cash fund** is a cash fund used to pay relatively small amounts. We explain the operation of a petty cash fund in the appendix at the end of this chapter.

Ethics Insight

How Employees Steal

A recent study by the Association of Certified Fraud Examiners found that two-thirds of all employee thefts involved a fraudulent disbursement by an employee. The most common form (24.9% of cases) was fraudulent billing schemes. In these, the employee causes the company to issue a payment to the employee by submitting a bill for nonexistent goods or services, purchases of personal goods by the employee, or inflated invoices. The graph below shows various types of fraudulent disbursements and the median loss from each.

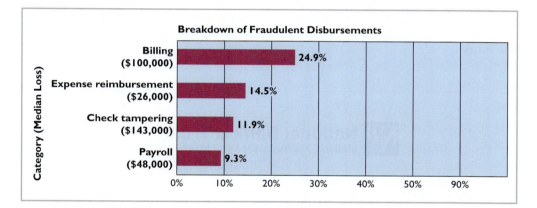

Source: 2012 Report to the Nation on Occupational Fraud and Abuse, Association of Certified Fraud Examiners, *www.acfe.com/uploadedfiles/ACFE_website/content/rttn/2012-report-to-nations.pdf,* p. 12.

? How can companies reduce the likelihood of fraudulent disbursements? (Answers in *Broadening Your Perspective.*)

Control Features: Use of a Bank

The use of a bank contributes significantly to good internal control over cash. A company can safeguard its cash by using a bank as a depository and clearinghouse for checks received and checks written. The use of a bank checking account minimizes the amount of currency that must be kept on hand. It also facilitates control of cash because a double record is maintained of all bank transactions—one by the business and the other by the bank. The asset account Cash maintained by the company is the "flip-side" of the bank's liability account for that company. A **bank reconciliation** is the process of comparing the bank's balance with the company's balance, and explaining the differences to make them agree.

Many companies have more than one bank account. For efficiency of operations and better control, national retailers like Wal-Mart and Target often have regional bank accounts. Similarly, a company such as ExxonMobil with more than 100,000 employees may have a payroll bank account as well as one or more general bank accounts. In addition, a company may maintain several bank accounts in order to have more than one source for short-term loans.

> **LEARNING OBJECTIVE 5**
>
> Prepare a bank reconciliation.

BANK STATEMENTS

Each month, the company receives from the bank a **bank statement** showing its bank transactions and balances.[4] For example, the statement for Laird Company in Illustration 7-7 shows the following: (1) checks paid and other debits (such as debit card transactions or direct withdrawals for bill payments) that reduce the balance in the depositor's account, (2) deposits and other credits that increase the balance in the depositor's account, and (3) the account balance after each day's transactions.

Remember that **bank statements are prepared from the *bank's* perspective**. For example, **every deposit the bank receives is an increase in the bank's liabilities (an account payable to the depositor)**. Therefore, in Illustration 7-7, National Bank and Trust **credits** to Laird Company every deposit it received from Laird. The reverse occurs when the bank "pays" a check issued by Laird Company on its checking account balance: Payment reduces the bank's liability and is therefore **debited** to Laird's account with the bank.

Illustration 7-7 Bank statement

National Bank & Trust
Midland, Michigan 48654   Member FDIC

ACCOUNT STATEMENT

LAIRD COMPANY
77 WEST CENTRAL AVENUE
MIDLAND, MICHIGAN 48654

Statement Date/Credit Line Closing Date

April 30, 2014

457923

ACCOUNT NUMBER

Balance Last Statement	Deposits and Credits		Checks and Debits		Balance This Statement
	No.	Total Amount	No.	Total Amount	
13,256.90	20	34,805.10	26	32,154.55	15,907.45

CHECKS AND DEBITS			DEPOSITS AND CREDITS		DAILY BALANCE	
Date	No.	Amount	Date	Amount	Date	Amount
4–2	435	644.95	4–2	4,276.85	4–2	16,888.80
4–5	436	3,260.00	4–3	2,137.50	4–3	18,249.65
4–4	437	1,185.79	4–5	1,350.47	4–4	17,063.86
4–3	438	776.65	4–7	982.46	4–5	15,154.33
4–8	439	1,781.70	4–8	1,320.28	4–7	14,648.89
4–7	440	1,487.90	4–9 CM	1,035.00	4–8	11,767.47
4–8	441	2,420.00	4–11	2,720.00	4–9	12,802.47
4–11	442	1,585.60	4–12	757.41	4–11	13,936.87
4–12	443	1,226.00	4–13	1,218.56	4–12	13,468.28
4–29	NSF	425.60	4–27	1,545.57	4–27	13,005.45
4–29	459	1,080.30	4–29	2,929.45	4–29	14,429.00
4–30	DM	30.00	4–30	2,128.60	4–30	15,907.45
4–30	461	620.15				

Symbols: **CM** Credit Memo   **EC** Error Correction   **NSF** Not Sufficient Funds
DM Debit Memo   **INT** Interest Earned   **SC** Service Charge

Reconcile Your Account Promptly

---

[4]Our presentation assumes that a company makes all adjustments at the end of the month. In practice, a company may also make journal entries during the month as it reviews information from the bank regarding its account.

The bank statement lists in numerical sequence all paid checks along with the date the check was paid and its amount. Upon paying a check, the bank stamps the check "paid"; a paid check is sometimes referred to as a **canceled** check. In addition, the bank includes with the bank statement memoranda explaining other debits and credits it made to the depositor's account.

A check that is not paid by a bank because of insufficient funds in a bank account is called an **NSF check** (not sufficient funds). The bank uses a debit memorandum when a previously deposited customer's check "bounces" because of insufficient funds. In such a case, the customer's bank marks the check NSF (not sufficient funds) and returns it to the depositor's bank. The bank then debits (decreases) the depositor's account, as shown by the symbol NSF in Illustration 7-7, and sends the NSF check and debit memorandum to the depositor as notification of the charge. The NSF check creates an account receivable for the depositor and reduces cash in the bank account.

RECONCILING THE BANK ACCOUNT

Because the bank and the company maintain independent records of the company's checking account, you might assume that the respective balances will always agree. In fact, the two balances are seldom the same at any given time, and both balances differ from the "correct or true" balance. Therefore, it is necessary to make the balance per books and the balance per bank agree with the correct or true amount—a process called **reconciling the bank account**. The need for reconciliation has two causes:

1. **Time lags** that prevent one of the parties from recording the transaction in the same period.

2. **Errors** by either party in recording transactions.

Time lags occur frequently. For example, several days may elapse between the time a company pays by check and the date the bank pays the check. Similarly, when a company uses the bank's night depository to make its deposits, there will be a difference of one day between the time the company records the receipts and the time the bank does so. A time lag also occurs whenever the bank mails a debit or credit memorandum to the company.

You might think that if a company never writes checks (for example, if a small company uses only a debit card or electronic bill payment), it does not need to reconcile its account. However, **the possibility of errors or fraud still necessitates periodic reconciliation**. The incidence of errors or fraud depends on the effectiveness of the internal controls maintained by the company and the bank. Bank errors are infrequent. However, either party could accidentally record a $450 check as $45 or $540. In addition, the bank might mistakenly charge a check drawn by C. D. Berg to the account of C. D. Burg.

Reconciliation Procedure

In reconciling the bank account, it is customary to reconcile the balance per books and balance per bank to their adjusted (correct or true) cash balances. **To obtain maximum benefit from a bank reconciliation, an employee who has no other responsibilities related to cash should prepare the reconciliation.** When companies do not follow the internal control principle of independent internal verification in preparing the reconciliation, cash embezzlements may escape unnoticed. For example, in the Anatomy of a Fraud box on page 289, a bank reconciliation by someone other than Angela Bauer might have exposed her embezzlement.

Illustration 7-8 shows the reconciliation process. The starting point in preparing the reconciliation is to enter the balance per bank statement and balance

Illustration 7-8 Bank reconciliation adjustments

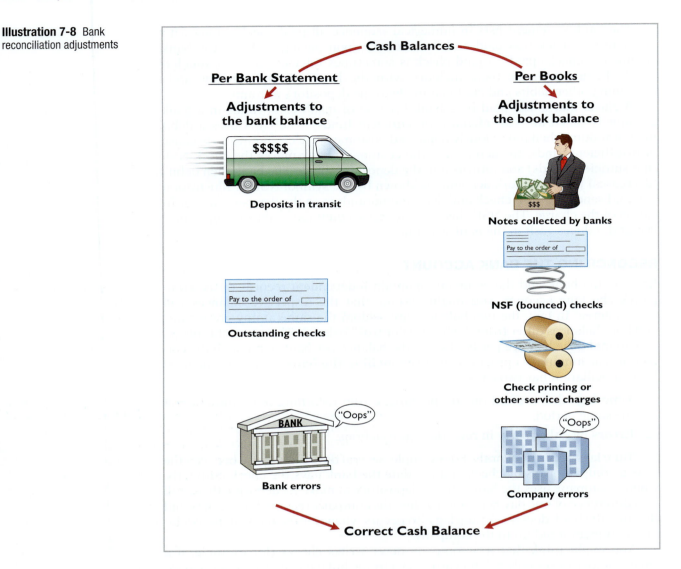

per books on a schedule. The following steps should reveal all the reconciling items that cause the difference between the two balances.

Step 1. **Deposits in transit.** Compare the individual deposits on the bank statement with the deposits in transit from the preceding bank reconciliation and with the deposits per company records or copies of duplicate deposit slips. Deposits recorded by the depositor that have not been recorded by the bank represent **deposits in transit**. Add these deposits to the balance per bank.

Step 2. **Outstanding checks.** Compare the paid checks shown on the bank statement or the paid checks returned with the bank statement with (a) checks outstanding from the preceding bank reconciliation, and (b) checks issued by the company as recorded in the cash payments journal. Issued checks recorded by the company that have not been paid by the bank represent **outstanding checks**. Deduct outstanding checks from the balance per the bank.

Step 3. **Errors.** Note any errors discovered in the previous steps and list them in the appropriate section of the reconciliation schedule. For example, if the company mistakenly recorded as $159 a paid check correctly written for $195, the company would deduct the error of $36 from the balance per books. All errors made by the depositor are reconciling items in determining the adjusted cash balance per books. In contrast, all errors made by the bank are reconciling items in determining the adjusted cash balance per the bank.

Step 4. Bank memoranda. Trace bank memoranda to the depositor's records. The company lists in the appropriate section of the reconciliation schedule any unrecorded memoranda. For example, the company would deduct from the balance per books a $5 debit memorandum for bank service charges. Similarly, it would add to the balance per books a $32 credit memorandum for interest earned.

Bank Reconciliation Illustrated

Illustration 7-7 presented the bank statement for Laird Company which the company accessed online. It shows a balance per bank of $15,907.45 on April 30, 2014. On this date the balance of cash per books is $11,589.45. From the foregoing steps, Laird determines the following reconciling items.

Step 1.	**Deposits in transit:** April 30 deposit (received by bank on May 1).	$2,201.40
Step 2.	**Outstanding checks:** No. 453, $3,000.00; No. 457, $1,401.30; No. 460, $1,502.70.	5,904.00
Step 3.	**Errors:** Check No. 443 was correctly written by Laird for $1,226.00 and was correctly paid by the bank. However, Laird recorded the check as $1,262.00.	36.00
Step 4.	**Bank memoranda:**	
	(a) Debit—NSF check from J. R. Baron for $425.60	425.60
	(b) Debit—Printing company checks charge, $30	30.00
	(c) Credit—Collection of note receivable for $1,000 plus interest earned $50, less bank collection fee $15	1,035.00

Illustration 7-9 shows Laird's bank reconciliation.

LAIRD COMPANY
Bank Reconciliation
April 30, 2014

Cash balance per bank statement		$ 15,907.45
Add: Deposits in transit		2,201.40
		18,108.85
Less: Outstanding checks		
No. 453	$3,000.00	
No. 457	1,401.30	
No. 460	1,502.70	5,904.00
Adjusted cash balance per bank		**$12,204.85**
Cash balance per books		$ 11,589.45
Add: Collection of note receivable for $1,000 plus interest earned $50, less collection fee $15	$1,035.00	
Error in recording check No. 443	36.00	1,071.00
		12,660.45
Less: NSF check	425.60	
Bank service charge	30.00	455.60
Adjusted cash balance per books		**$12,204.85**

Illustration 7-9 Bank reconciliation

Alternative Terminology The terms *adjusted cash balance*, *true cash balance*, and *correct cash balance* are used interchangeably.

Entries from Bank Reconciliation

The depositor (that is, the company) next must record each reconciling item used to determine the **adjusted cash balance per books**. If the company does not journalize and post these items, the Cash account will not show the correct balance. The adjusting entries for the Laird Company bank reconciliation on April 30 are as follows.

COLLECTION OF NOTE RECEIVABLE. This entry involves four accounts. Assuming that the interest of $50 has not been recorded and the collection fee is charged to Miscellaneous Expense, the entry is:

A	=	L	+	SE
+1,035				
				−15 Exp
−1,000				
				+50 Rev

Cash Flows
+1,035

Apr. 30	Cash	1,035	
	Miscellaneous Expense	15	
	Notes Receivable		1,000
	Interest Revenue		50
	(To record collection of note		
	receivable by bank)		

BOOK ERROR. An examination of the cash disbursements journal shows that check No. 443 was a payment on account to Andrea Company, a supplier. The correcting entry is:

A	=	L	+	SE
+36				
		+36		

Cash Flows
+36

Apr. 30	Cash	36	
	Accounts Payable—Andrea Company		36
	(To correct error in recording check		
	No. 443)		

NSF CHECK. As indicated earlier, an NSF check becomes an accounts receivable to the depositor. The entry is:

A	=	L	+	SE
+425.60				
−425.60				

Cash Flows
−425.60

Apr. 30	Accounts Receivable—J. R. Baron	425.60	
	Cash		425.60
	(To record NSF check)		

BANK SERVICE CHARGES. Companies typically debit to Miscellaneous Expense the check printing charges (DM) and other bank service charges (SC) because they are usually small in amount. Laird's entry is:

A	=	L	+	SE
				−30 Exp
−30				

Cash Flows
−30

Apr. 30	Miscellaneous Expense	30	
	Cash		30
	(To record charge for printing company		
	checks)		

The foregoing entries could also be combined into one compound entry.

After Laird posts the entries, the Cash account will appear as in Illustration 7-10. The adjusted cash balance in the ledger should agree with the adjusted cash balance per books in the bank reconciliation in Illustration 7-9.

What entries does the bank make? If the company discovers any bank errors in preparing the reconciliation, it should notify the bank so the bank can make the necessary corrections on its records. The bank does not make any entries for

Cash				
Apr. 30	Bal.	11,589.45	Apr. 30	425.60
30		1,035.00	30	30.00
30		36.00		
Apr. 30	Bal.	**12,204.85**		

Illustration 7-10
Adjusted balance in Cash account

deposits in transit or outstanding checks. Only when these items reach the bank will the bank record these items.

Electronic Funds Transfer (EFT) System

It is not surprising that companies and banks have developed approaches to transfer funds among parties without the use of paper (deposit tickets, checks, etc.). Such procedures, called **electronic funds transfers (EFTs)**, are disbursement systems that use wire, telephone, or computers to transfer cash from one location to another. Use of EFT is quite common. For example, many employees receive no formal payroll checks from their employers. Instead, employers send electronic payroll data to the appropriate banks. Also, individuals and companies now frequently make regular payments such as those for house, car, and utilities by EFT.

EFT transactions normally result in better internal control since no cash or checks are handled by company employees. This does not mean that opportunities for fraud are eliminated. In fact, the same basic principles related to internal control apply to EFT transactions. For example, without proper segregation of duties and authorizations, an employee might be able to redirect electronic payments into a personal bank account and conceal the theft with fraudulent accounting entries.

Investor Insight

Madoff's Ponzi Scheme

No recent fraud has generated more interest and rage than the one perpetrated by Bernard Madoff. Madoff was an elite New York investment fund manager who was highly regarded by securities regulators. Investors flocked to him because he delivered steady returns of between 10% and 15%, no matter whether the market was going up or going down. However, for many years, Madoff did not actually invest the cash that people gave to him. Instead, he was running a Ponzi scheme: He paid returns to existing investors using cash received from new investors. As long as the size of his investment fund continued to grow from new investments at a rate that exceeded the amounts that he needed to pay out in returns, Madoff was able to operate his fraud smoothly. To conceal his misdeeds, he fabricated false investment statements that were provided to investors. In addition, Madoff hired an auditor that never verified the accuracy of the investment records but automatically issued unqualified opinions each year. A competing fund manager warned the SEC a number of times over a nearly 10-year period that he thought Madoff was engaged in fraud. The SEC never aggressively investigated the allegations. Investors, many of which were charitable organizations, lost more than $18 billion. Madoff was sentenced to a jail term of 150 years.

 How was Madoff able to conceal such a giant fraud? (Answers in *Broadening Your Perspective*.)

Reporting Cash

Cash consists of coins, currency (paper money), checks, money orders, and money on hand or on deposit in a bank or similar depository. Checks that are dated later than the current date (post-dated checks) are not included in cash. Companies report cash in two different statements: the balance sheet and the statement of cash flows. The balance sheet reports the amount of cash available at a given point in time. The statement of cash flows shows the sources and uses of cash during a period of time. The statement of cash flows was introduced in Chapters 1 and 2 and will be discussed in much detail in Chapter 12. In this section, we discuss some important points regarding the presentation of cash in the balance sheet.

When presented in a balance sheet, cash on hand, cash in banks, and petty cash are often combined and reported simply as **Cash**. Because it is the most liquid asset owned by the company, cash is listed first in the current assets section of the balance sheet.

CASH EQUIVALENTS

Many companies use the designation "Cash and cash equivalents" in reporting cash. (See Illustration 7-11 for an example.) **Cash equivalents** are short-term, highly liquid investments that are both:

1. Readily convertible to known amounts of cash, and
2. So near their maturity that their market value is relatively insensitive to changes in interest rates.

Illustration 7-11 Balance sheet presentation of cash

Real World

DELTA AIR LINES, INC.
Balance Sheet (partial)
December 31, 2011
(in millions)

Assets	
Current assets	
Cash and cash equivalents	**$2,657**
Short-term investments	958
Restricted cash	**305**
Accounts receivable and other, net	1,563
Parts inventories	367
Prepaid expenses and other	1,879
Total current assets	$ 7,729

Examples of cash equivalents are Treasury bills, commercial paper (short-term corporate notes), and money market funds. All typically are purchased with cash that is in excess of immediate needs.

Occasionally a company will have a net negative balance in its bank account. In this case, the company should report the negative balance among current liabilities. For example, farm equipment manufacturer Ag-Chem recently reported "Checks outstanding in excess of cash balances" of $2,145,000 among its current liabilities.

RESTRICTED CASH

A company may have **restricted cash**, cash that is not available for general use but rather is restricted for a special purpose. For example, landfill companies are often required to maintain a fund of restricted cash to ensure they will have adequate resources to cover closing and clean-up costs at the end of a landfill site's useful life. McKesson Corp. recently reported restricted cash of $962 million to be paid out as the result of investor lawsuits.

Cash restricted in use should be reported separately on the balance sheet as restricted cash. If the company expects to use the restricted cash within the next year, it reports the amount as a current asset. When this is not the case, it reports the restricted funds as a noncurrent asset.

Illustration 7-11 shows restricted cash reported in the financial statements of Delta Air Lines. The company is required to maintain restricted cash as collateral to support insurance obligations related to workers' compensation claims. Delta does not have access to these funds for general use, and so it must report them separately, rather than as part of cash and cash equivalents.

🧰 DECISION TOOLKIT

DECISION CHECKPOINTS	INFO NEEDED FOR DECISION	TOOL TO USE FOR DECISION	HOW TO EVALUATE RESULTS
Is all of the company's cash available for general use?	Balance sheet and notes to financial statements	Does the company report any cash as being restricted?	A restriction on the use of cash limits management's ability to use those resources for general obligations. This might be considered when assessing liquidity.

Managing and Monitoring Cash

Many companies struggle, not because they fail to generate sales, but because they can't manage their cash. A real-life example of this is a clothing manufacturing company owned by Sharon McCollick. McCollick gave up a stable, high-paying marketing job with Intel Corporation to start her own company. Soon she had more orders from stores such as JC Penney and Dayton Hudson (now Target) than she could fill. Yet she found herself on the brink of financial disaster, owing three mortgage payments on her house and $2,000 to the IRS. Her company could generate sales, but it was not collecting cash fast enough to support its operations. The bottom line is that a business must have cash.[5]

A merchandising company's operating cycle is generally shorter than that of a manufacturing company. Illustration 7-12 shows the cash to cash operating cycle of a merchandising operation.

> **LEARNING OBJECTIVE 7**
> Discuss the basic principles of cash management.

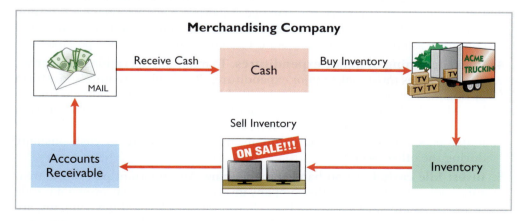

Illustration 7-12
Operating cycle of a merchandising company

---

[5]Adapted from T. Petzinger, Jr., "The Front Lines—Sharon McCollick Got Mad and Tore Down a Bank's Barriers," *Wall Street Journal* (May 19, 1995), p. B1.

To understand cash management, consider the operating cycle of Sharon McCollick's clothing manufacturing company. First, it purchases cloth. Let's assume that it purchases the cloth on credit provided by the supplier, so the company owes its supplier money. Next, employees convert the cloth to clothing. Now the company also owes its employees money. Next, it sells the clothing to retailers, on credit. McCollick's company will have no money to repay suppliers or employees until it receives payments from customers. In a manufacturing operation there may be a significant lag between the original purchase of raw materials and the ultimate receipt of cash from customers.

Managing the often-precarious balance created by the ebb and flow of cash during the operating cycle is one of a company's greatest challenges. The objective is to ensure that a company has sufficient cash to meet payments as they come due, yet minimize the amount of non-revenue-generating cash on hand.

BASIC PRINCIPLES OF CASH MANAGEMENT

Management of cash is the responsibility of the company **treasurer**. Any company can improve its chances of having adequate cash by following five basic principles of cash management.

1. **Increase the speed of receivables collection.** Money owed Sharon McCollick by her customers is money that she can't use. The more quickly customers pay her, the more quickly she can use those funds. Thus, rather than have an average collection period of 30 days, she may want an average collection period of 15 days. However, she must carefully weigh any attempt to force her customers to pay earlier against the possibility that she may anger or alienate customers. Perhaps her competitors are willing to provide a 30-day grace period. As noted in Chapter 5, one common way to encourage customers to pay more quickly is to offer cash discounts for early payment under such terms as 2/10, n/30.

2. **Keep inventory levels low.** Maintaining a large inventory of cloth and finished clothing is costly. It ties up large amounts of cash, as well as warehouse space. Increasingly, companies are using techniques to reduce the inventory on hand, thus conserving their cash. Of course, if Sharon McCollick has inadequate inventory, she will lose sales. The proper level of inventory is an important decision.

3. **Monitor payment of liabilities.** Sharon McCollick should monitor when her bills are due, so she avoids paying bills too early. Let's say her supplier allows 30 days for payment. If she pays in 10 days, she has lost the use of that cash for 20 days. Therefore, she should use the full payment period. But, she should not pay late. This could damage her credit rating (and future borrowing ability). Also, late payments to suppliers can damage important supplier relationships and may even threaten a supplier's viability. Sharon McCollick's company also should conserve cash by taking cash discounts offered by suppliers, when possible.

4. **Plan the timing of major expenditures.** To maintain operations or to grow, all companies must make major expenditures. These often require some form of outside financing. To increase the likelihood of obtaining outside financing, McCollick should carefully consider the timing of major expenditures in light of her company's operating cycle. If at all possible, she should make any major expenditure when the company normally has excess cash—usually during the off-season.

5. **Invest idle cash.** Cash on hand earns nothing. An important part of the treasurer's job is to ensure that the company invests any excess cash, even if it is only overnight. Many businesses, such as Sharon McCollick's clothing company, are seasonal. During her slow season, when she has excess cash, she should invest it.

To avoid a cash crisis, however, it is very important that investments of idle cash be highly liquid and risk-free. A **liquid investment** is one with a

Margin Note International sales complicate cash management. For example, if Nike must repay a Japanese supplier 30 days from today in Japanese yen, Nike will be concerned about how the exchange rate of U.S. dollars for yen might change during those 30 days. Often, corporate treasurers make investments known as *hedges* to lock in an exchange rate to reduce the company's exposure to exchange-rate fluctuation.

market in which someone is always willing to buy or sell the investment. A **risk-free investment** means there is no concern that the party will default on its promise to pay its principal and interest. For example, using excess cash to purchase stock in a small company because you heard that it was probably going to increase in value in the near term is totally inappropriate. First, the stock of small companies is often illiquid. Second, if the stock suddenly decreases in value, you might be forced to sell the stock at a loss in order to pay your bills as they come due. The most common form of liquid investments is interest-paying U.S. government securities.

Illustration 7-13 summarizes these five principles of cash management.

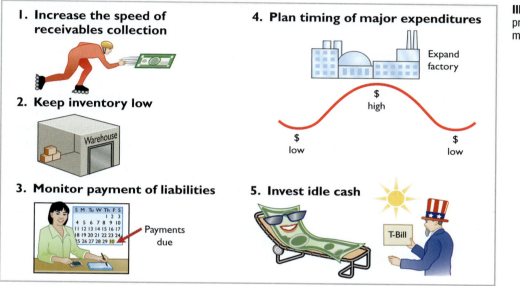

Illustration 7-13 Five principles of sound cash management

Because cash is so vital to a company, **planning the company's cash needs** is a key business activity. It enables the company to plan ahead to cover possible cash shortfalls and to make investments of idle funds. The **cash budget** shows anticipated cash flows, usually over a one- to two-year period. In this section, we introduce the basics of cash budgeting. More advanced discussion of cash budgets and budgets in general is provided in managerial accounting texts.

As shown below, the cash budget contains three sections—cash receipts, cash disbursements, and financing—and the beginning and ending cash balances.

ANY COMPANY	
Cash Budget	
Beginning cash balance	$X,XXX
Add: **Cash receipts** (itemized)	X,XXX
Total available cash	X,XXX
Less: **Cash disbursements** (itemized)	X,XXX
Excess (deficiency) of available cash over cash disbursements	X,XXX
Financing	
Add: Borrowings	X,XXX
Less: Repayments	X,XXX
Ending cash balance	$X,XXX

The **Cash receipts** section includes expected receipts from the company's principal source(s) of cash, such as cash sales and collections from customers on credit sales. This section also shows anticipated receipts of interest and dividends, and proceeds from planned sales of investments, plant assets, and the company's capital stock.

The **Cash disbursements** section shows expected payments for inventory, labor, overhead, and selling and administrative expenses. It also includes projected payments for income taxes, dividends, investments, and plant assets. Note that it does not include depreciation since depreciation expense does not use cash.

The **Financing** section shows expected borrowings and repayments of borrowed funds plus interest. Financing is needed when there is a cash deficiency or when the cash balance is less than management's minimum required balance.

Companies must prepare multi-period cash budgets in sequence because the ending cash balance of one period becomes the beginning cash balance for the next period. In practice, companies often prepare cash budgets for the next 12 months on a monthly basis.

To minimize detail, we will assume that Hayes Company prepares an annual cash budget by quarters. Preparing a cash budget requires making some assumptions. For example, Hayes makes assumptions regarding collection of accounts receivable, sales of securities, payments for materials and salaries, and purchases of property, plant, and equipment. The accuracy of the cash budget is very dependent on the accuracy of these assumptions.

Below we present the cash budget for Hayes Company. The budget indicates that the company will need $3,000 of financing in the second quarter to maintain

HAYES COMPANY
Cash Budget
For the Year Ending December 31, 2014

	Quarter			
	1	2	3	4
Beginning cash balance	$ 38,000	$ 25,500	$ 15,000	$ 19,400
Add: **Cash receipts**				
Collections from customers	168,000	198,000	228,000	258,000
Sale of securities	2,000	0	0	0
Total receipts	170,000	198,000	228,000	258,000
Total available cash	208,000	223,500	243,000	277,400
Less: **Cash disbursements**				
Inventory	23,200	27,200	31,200	35,200
Salaries	62,000	72,000	82,000	92,000
Selling and administrative expenses (excluding depreciation)	94,300	99,300	104,300	109,300
Purchase of truck	0	10,000	0	0
Income tax expense	3,000	3,000	3,000	3,000
Total disbursements	182,500	211,500	220,500	239,500
Excess (deficiency) of available cash over disbursements	25,500	12,000	22,500	37,900
Financing				
Add: Borrowings	0	3,000	0	0
Less: Repayments—plus $100 interest	0	0	3,100	0
Ending cash balance	$ 25,500	$ 15,000	$ 19,400	$ 37,900

a minimum cash balance of $15,000. Since there is an excess of available cash over disbursements of $22,500 at the end of the third quarter, Hayes will repay the borrowing, plus $100 interest, in that quarter.

A cash budget contributes to more effective cash management. For example, it can show when a company will need additional financing well before the actual need arises. Conversely, it can indicate when the company will have excess cash available for investments or other purposes.

DECISION TOOLKIT

DECISION CHECKPOINTS	INFO NEEDED FOR DECISION	TOOL TO USE FOR DECISION	HOW TO EVALUATE RESULTS
Will the company be able to meet its projected cash needs?	Cash budget (typically available only to management)	The cash budget shows projected sources and uses of cash. If cash uses exceed internal cash sources, then the company must look for outside sources.	Two issues: (1) Are management's projections reasonable? (2) If outside sources are needed, are they available?

USING THE DECISION TOOLKIT

Presented below is hypothetical financial information for Mattel Corporation. Included in this information is financial statement data from the year ended December 31, 2013, which should be used to evaluate Mattel's cash position.

Selected Financial Information
Year Ended December 31, 2013
(in millions)

Net cash provided by operating activities	$325
Capital expenditures	162
Dividends paid	80
Total expenses	680
Depreciation expense	40
Cash balance	206

Also provided on the next paragraph are projected data which are management's best estimate of its sources and uses of cash during the year ended December 31, 2014. This information should be used to prepare a cash budget for 2014.

Projected Sources and Uses of Cash
(in millions)

Beginning cash balance	$206
Cash receipts from sales of product	355
Cash receipts from sale of short-term investments	20
Cash payments for inventory	357
Cash payments for selling and administrative costs	201
Cash payments for property, plant, and equipment	45
Cash payments for taxes	17

Mattel Corporation's management believes it should maintain a balance of $200 million cash.

Instructions

(a) Using the hypothetical projected sources and uses of cash information presented above, prepare a cash budget for 2014 for Mattel Corporation.

(b) Comment on the company's cash adequacy, and discuss steps that might be taken to improve its cash position.

Solution

(a)

MATTEL CORPORATION
Cash Budget
For the Year Ending December 31, 2014
(in millions)

Beginning cash balance		$206
Add: Cash receipts		
From sales of product	$355	
From sale of short-term investments	20	375
Total available cash		581
Less: Cash disbursements		
Payments for inventory	357	
Payments for selling and administrative costs	201	
Payments for property, plant, and equipment	45	
Payments for taxes	17	
Total disbursements		620
Excess (deficiency) of available cash over disbursements		(39)
Financing		
Add: **Borrowings**		**239**
Ending cash balance		$200

(b) Using these hypothetical data, Mattel's cash position appears adequate. For 2014, Mattel is projecting a cash shortfall. This is not necessarily of concern, but it should be investigated. Its primary line of business is toys. Most toys are sold during December. We would expect Mattel's cash position to vary significantly during the course of the year. After the holiday season, once its customers have paid Mattel, it probably has a lot of excess cash. However, when it is making and selling its product but has not yet been paid, it may need to borrow to meet any temporary cash shortfalls.

If Mattel's management is concerned with its cash position, it could take the following steps: (1) Offer its customers cash discounts for early payment, such as 2/10, n/30. (2) Implement inventory management techniques to reduce the need for large inventories of such things as the plastics used to make its toys. (3) Carefully time payments to suppliers by keeping track of when payments are due, so as not to pay too early. (4) If it has plans for major expenditures, time those expenditures to coincide with its seasonal period of excess cash.

Summary of Learning Objectives

1 **Define fraud and internal control.** A fraud is a dishonest act by an employee that results in personal benefit to the employee at a cost to the employer. The fraud triangle refers to the three factors that contribute to fraudulent activity by employees: opportunity, financial pressure, and rationalization. Internal control consists of all the related methods and measures adopted within an organization to safeguard assets, enhance the reliability of accounting records, increase efficiency of operations, and ensure compliance with laws and regulations.

2 **Identify the principles of internal control activities.** The principles of internal control are establishment of responsibility; segregation of duties; documentation procedures; physical controls; independent internal verification; and human resource controls.

3 **Explain the applications of internal control principles to cash receipts.** Internal controls over cash receipts include: (a) designating only personnel such as cashiers to handle cash; (b) assigning the duties of receiving cash, recording cash, and having custody of cash to different individuals; (c) obtaining remittance advices for mail receipts, cash register tapes or computer records for over-the-counter receipts, and deposit slips for bank deposits; (d) using company safes and bank vaults to store cash with access limited to authorized personnel, and using cash registers in executing over-the-counter receipts; (e) making independent daily counts of register receipts and daily comparisons of total receipts with total deposits; and (f) conducting background checks and bonding personnel who handle cash, as well as requiring them to take vacations.

4 **Explain the applications of internal control principles to cash disbursements.** Internal controls over cash disbursements include: (a) having only specified individuals such as the treasurer authorized to sign checks; (b) assigning the duties of approving items for payment, paying the items, and recording the payment to different individuals; (c) using prenumbered checks and accounting for all checks, with each check supported by an approved invoice; after payment, stamping each approved invoice "paid"; (d) storing blank checks in a safe or vault with access restricted to authorized personnel, and using a machine with indelible ink to imprint amounts on checks; (e) comparing each check with the approved invoice before issuing the check, and making monthly reconciliations of bank and book balances; and

(f) bonding personnel who handle cash, requiring employees to take vacations, and conducting background checks.

5 **Prepare a bank reconciliation.** In reconciling the bank account, it is customary to reconcile the balance per books and the balance per bank to their adjusted balance. The steps reconciling the Cash account are to determine deposits in transit, outstanding checks, errors by the depositor or the bank, and unrecorded bank memoranda.

6 **Explain the reporting of cash.** Cash is listed first in the current assets section of the balance sheet. Companies often report cash together with cash equivalents. Cash restricted for a special purpose is reported separately as a current asset or as a noncurrent asset, depending on when the company expects to use the cash.

7 **Discuss the basic principles of cash management.** The basic principles of cash management include: (a) increase the speed of receivables collection, (b) keep inventory levels low, (c) monitor the timing of payment of liabilities, (d) plan timing of major expenditures, and (e) invest idle cash.

8 **Identify the primary elements of a cash budget.** The three main elements of a cash budget are the cash receipts section, cash disbursements section, and financing section.

DECISION TOOLKIT *A SUMMARY*

DECISION CHECKPOINTS	INFO NEEDED FOR DECISION	TOOL TO USE FOR DECISION	HOW TO EVALUATE RESULTS
Are the company's financial statements supported by adequate internal controls?	Auditor's report, management discussion and analysis, articles in financial press	The principles of internal control activities are (1) establishment of responsibility, (2) segregation of duties, (3) documentation procedures, (4) physical controls, (5) independent internal verification, and (6) human resource controls.	If any indication is given that these or other controls are lacking, use the financial statements with caution.
Is all of the company's cash available for general use?	Balance sheet and notes to financial statements	Does the company report any cash as being restricted?	A restriction on the use of cash limits management's ability to use those resources for general obligations. This might be considered when assessing liquidity.
Will the company be able to meet its projected cash needs?	Cash budget (typically available only to management)	The cash budget shows projected sources and uses of cash. If cash uses exceed internal cash sources, then the company must look for outside sources.	Two issues: (1) Are management's projections reasonable? (2) If outside sources are needed, are they available?

Operation of the Petty Cash Fund

LEARNING OBJECTIVE **9**

Explain the operation of a petty cash fund.

The operation of a petty cash fund involves (1) establishing the fund, (2) making payments from the fund, and (3) replenishing the fund.

ESTABLISHING THE PETTY CASH FUND

Two essential steps in establishing a petty cash fund are: (1) appointing a petty cash custodian who will be responsible for the fund, and (2) determining the size of the fund. Ordinarily, a company expects the amount in the fund to cover anticipated disbursements for a three- to four-week period.

When the company establishes the petty cash fund, it issues a check payable to the petty cash custodian for the stipulated amount. If Laird Company decides to establish a $100 fund on March 1, the entry in general journal form is:

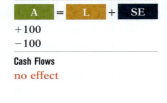

A = L + SE
+100
−100

Cash Flows
no effect

Mar. 1	Petty Cash	100	
	Cash		100
	(To establish a petty cash fund)		

The fund custodian cashes the check and places the proceeds in a locked petty cash box or drawer. Most petty cash funds are established on a fixed-amount basis. Moreover, the company will make no additional entries to the Petty Cash account unless the stipulated amount of the fund is changed. For example, if Laird Company decides on July 1 to increase the size of the fund to $250, it would debit Petty Cash $150 and credit Cash $150.

MAKING PAYMENTS FROM PETTY CASH

The custodian of the petty cash fund has the authority to make payments from the fund that conform to prescribed management policies. Usually, management limits the size of expenditures that come from petty cash and does not permit use of the fund for certain types of transactions (such as making short-term loans to employees).

Each payment from the fund must be documented on a prenumbered petty cash receipt (or petty cash voucher). The signatures of both the custodian and the individual receiving payment are required on the receipt. If other supporting documents such as a freight bill or invoice are available, they should be attached to the petty cash receipt.

The custodian keeps the receipts in the petty cash box until the fund is replenished. As a result, the sum of the petty cash receipts and money in the fund should equal the established total at all times. This means that management can make surprise counts at any time by an independent person, such as an internal auditor, to determine the correctness of the fund.

The company does not make an accounting entry to record a payment at the time it is taken from petty cash. It is considered both inexpedient and unnecessary to do so. Instead, the company recognizes the accounting effects of each payment when the fund is replenished.

REPLENISHING THE PETTY CASH FUND

When the money in the petty cash fund reaches a minimum level, the company replenishes the fund. The petty cash custodian initiates a request for reimbursement. This individual prepares a schedule (or summary) of the payments that have been made and sends the schedule, supported by petty cash receipts and other documentation, to the treasurer's office. The receipts and supporting documents are examined in the treasurer's office to verify that they were proper payments from the fund. The treasurer then approves the request, and a check is prepared to restore the fund to its established amount. At the same time, all supporting documentation is stamped "paid" so that it cannot be submitted again for payment.

To illustrate, assume that on March 15 the petty cash custodian requests a check for $87. The fund contains $13 cash and petty cash receipts for postage $44, supplies $38, and miscellaneous expenses $5. The entry, in general journal form, to record the check is:

Mar. 15	Postage Expense	44	
	Supplies	38	
	Miscellaneous Expense	5	
	Cash		87
	(To replenish petty cash fund)		

Note that the reimbursement entry does not affect the Petty Cash account. Replenishment changes the composition of the fund by replacing the petty cash receipts with cash, but it does not change the balance in the fund.

Occasionally, in replenishing a petty cash fund the company may need to recognize a cash shortage or overage. To illustrate, assume in the preceding example that the custodian had only $12 in cash in the fund plus the receipts as listed. The request for reimbursement would therefore be for $88, and the following entry would be made.

Mar. 15	Postage Expense	44	
	Supplies	38	
	Miscellaneous Expense	5	
	Cash Over and Short	1	
	Cash		88
	(To replenish petty cash fund)		

Conversely, if the custodian had $14 in cash, the reimbursement request would be for $86, and Cash Over and Short would be credited for $1. A debit balance in Cash Over and Short is reported in the income statement as miscellaneous expense; a credit balance is reported as miscellaneous revenue. The company closes Cash Over and Short to Income Summary at the end of the year.

Companies should replenish a petty cash fund **at the end of the accounting period**, **regardless of the cash in the fund**. Replenishment at this time is necessary in order to recognize the effects of the petty cash payments on the financial statements.

Internal control over a petty cash fund is strengthened by (1) having a supervisor make surprise counts of the fund to ascertain whether the paid petty cash receipts and fund cash equal the designated amount, and (2) canceling or mutilating the paid petty cash receipts so they cannot be resubmitted for reimbursement.

Summary of Learning Objective for Appendix 7A

9 **Explain the operation of a petty cash fund.** In operating a petty cash fund, a company establishes the fund by appointing a custodian and determining the size of the fund. The custodian makes payments from the fund for documented expenditures. The company replenishes the fund as needed, and at the end of each accounting period. Accounting entries to record payments are made each time the fund is replenished.

Glossary

Terms are highlighted in blue throughout the chapter.

Bank reconciliation The process of comparing the bank's account balance with the company's balance, and explaining the differences to make them agree.

Bank statement A statement received monthly from the bank that shows the depositor's bank transactions and balances.

Bonding Obtaining insurance protection against theft by employees.

Cash Resources that consist of coins, currency, checks, money orders, and money on hand or on deposit in a bank or similar depository.

Cash budget A projection of anticipated cash flows, usually over a one- to two-year period.

Cash equivalents Short-term, highly liquid investments that can be readily converted to a specific amount of cash and which are relatively insensitive to interest rate changes.

Deposits in transit Deposits recorded by the depositor that have not been recorded by the bank.

Electronic funds transfer (EFT) A disbursement system that uses wire, telephone, or computer to transfer cash from one location to another.

Fraud A dishonest act by an employee that results in personal benefit to the employee at a cost to the employer.

Fraud triangle The three factors that contribute to fraudulent activity by employees: opportunity, financial pressure, and rationalization.

Internal auditors Company employees who continuously evaluate the effectiveness of the company's internal control systems.

Internal control All the related methods and measures adopted within an organization to safeguard assets and enhance the reliability of accounting records, increase efficiency of operations, and ensure compliance with laws and regulations.

NSF check A check that is not paid by a bank because of insufficient funds in a bank account.

Outstanding checks Checks issued and recorded by a company that have not been paid by the bank.

Petty cash fund A cash fund used to pay relatively small amounts.

Restricted cash Cash that is not available for general use but instead is restricted for a particular purpose.

Sarbanes-Oxley Act (SOX) Law that requires publicly traded companies to maintain adequate systems of internal control.

Treasurer Employee responsible for the management of a company's cash.

Voucher An authorization form prepared for each expenditure in a voucher system.

Voucher system A network of approvals by authorized individuals, acting independently, to ensure that all disbursements by check are proper.

 PLUS **Self-Test, Brief Exercises, Exercises, Problem Set A, and many more resources are available for practice in WileyPLUS.**

Note: All Questions, Exercises, and Problems marked with an asterisk relate to material in the appendix to the chapter.

Self-Test Questions

(Answers in *Broadening Your Perspective*.)

(LO 1) **1.** Which of the following is **not** an element of the fraud triangle?
  (a) Rationalization.
  (b) Financial pressure.
  (c) Segregation of duties.
  (d) Opportunity.

(LO 1) **2.** Internal control is used in a business to enhance the accuracy and reliability of its accounting records and to:
  (a) safeguard its assets.
  (b) create fraud.
  (c) analyze financial statements.
  (d) determine employee bonuses.

3. The principles of internal control do **not** (LO 2) include:
  (a) establishment of responsibility.
  (b) documentation procedures.
  (c) financial performance measures.
  (d) independent internal verification.

4. Physical controls do **not** include: (LO 2)
  (a) safes and vaults to store cash.
  (b) independent bank reconciliations.
  (c) locked warehouses for inventories.
  (d) bank safety deposit boxes for important papers.

(LO 1) **5.** Which of the following was **not** a result of the Sarbanes-Oxley Act?
(a) Companies must file financial statements with the Internal Revenue Service.
(b) All publicly traded companies must maintain adequate internal controls.
(c) The Public Company Accounting Oversight Board was created to establish auditing standards and regulate auditor activity.
(d) Corporate executives and boards of directors must ensure that controls are reliable and effective, and they can be fined or imprisoned for failure to do so.

(LO 3) **6.** Permitting only designated personnel such as cashiers to handle cash receipts is an application of the principle of:
(a) documentation procedures.
(b) establishment of responsibility.
(c) independent internal verification.
(d) other controls.

(LO 4) **7.** The use of prenumbered checks in disbursing cash is an application of the principle of:
(a) establishment of responsibility.
(b) segregation of duties.
(c) physical controls.
(d) documentation procedures.

(LO 4) **8.** The control features of a bank account do **not** include:
(a) having bank auditors verify the correctness of the bank balance per books.
(b) minimizing the amount of cash that must be kept on hand.
(c) providing a double record of all bank transactions.
(d) safeguarding cash by using a bank as a depository.

(LO 2) **9.** Which of the following control activities is **not** relevant when a company uses a computerized (rather than manual) accounting system?
(a) Establishment of responsibility.
(b) Segregation of duties.
(c) Independent internal verification.
(d) All of these control activities are relevant to a computerized system.

(LO 5) **10.** In a bank reconciliation, deposits in transit are:
(a) deducted from the book balance.
(b) added to the book balance.
(c) added to the bank balance.
(d) deducted from the bank balance.

11. Which of the following items in a cash drawer at (LO 6) November 30 is **not** cash?
(a) Money orders.
(b) Coins and currency.
(c) A customer check dated December 1.
(d) A customer check dated November 28.

12. Which statement correctly describes the (LO 6) reporting of cash?
(a) Cash cannot be combined with cash equivalents.
(b) Restricted cash funds may be combined with cash.
(c) Cash is listed first in the current assets section.
(d) Restricted cash funds cannot be reported as a current asset.

13. Which of the following would **not** be an example of (LO 7) good cash management?
(a) Provide discounts to customers to encourage early payment.
(b) Invest temporary excess cash in stock of a small company.
(c) Carefully monitor payments so that payments are not made early.
(d) Employ just-in-time inventory methods to keep inventory low.

14. Which of the following is **not** one of the sec- (LO 8) tions of a cash budget?
(a) Cash receipts section.
(b) Cash disbursements section.
(c) Financing section.
(d) Cash from operations section.

***15.** A check is written to replenish a $100 petty cash fund (LO 9) when the fund contains receipts of $94 and $2 in cash. In recording the check:
(a) Cash Over and Short should be debited for $4.
(b) Petty Cash should be debited for $94.
(c) Cash should be credited for $94.
(d) Petty Cash should be credited for $4.

Go to the book's companion website, **www.wiley.com/college/kimmel**, to access additional Self-Test Questions.

Questions

1. A local bank reported that it lost $150,000 as the result of employee fraud. Fred Raburn is not clear on what is meant by "employee fraud." Explain the meaning of fraud to Fred and give an example of fraud that might occur at a bank.

2. Fraud experts often say that there are three primary factors that contribute to employee fraud. Identify the three factors and explain what is meant by each.

3. Identify the five components of a good internal control system.

4. "Internal control is concerned only with enhancing the accuracy of the accounting records." Do you agree? Explain.

5. Discuss how the Sarbanes-Oxley Act has increased the importance of internal control to top managers of a company.

6. What principles of internal control apply to most businesses?

7. In the corner grocery store, all sales clerks make change out of one cash register drawer. Is this a violation of internal control? Why?

8. Donald Bowen is reviewing the principle of segregation of duties. What are the two common applications of this principle?

9. How do documentation procedures contribute to good internal control?

10. What internal control objectives are met by physical controls?

11. (a) Explain the control principle of independent internal verification.
(b) What practices are important in applying this principle?

12. ← As the company accountant, explain the following ideas to the management of Jurgens Company.
(a) The concept of reasonable assurance in internal control.
(b) The importance of the human factor in internal control.

13. ← Discuss the human resources department's involvement in internal controls.

14. Hoskins Inc. owns the following assets at the balance sheet date.

Cash in bank—savings account	$ 8,000
Cash on hand	1,100
Cash refund due from the IRS	1,000
Checking account balance	12,000
Postdated checks	500

What amount should be reported as Cash in the balance sheet?

15. What principle(s) of internal control is (are) involved in making daily cash counts of over-the-counter receipts?

16. Assume that Kohl's Department Stores installed new cash registers in its stores. How do cash registers improve internal control over cash receipts?

17. At Solis Wholesale Company, two mail clerks open all mail receipts. How does this strengthen internal control?

18. "To have maximum effective internal control over cash disbursements, all payments should be made by check." Is this true? Explain.

19. Napoli Company's internal controls over cash disbursements provide for the treasurer to sign checks imprinted by a checkwriter after comparing the check with the approved invoice. Identify the internal control principles that are present in these controls.

20. How do these principles apply to cash disbursements?
(a) Physical controls.
(b) Human resource controls.

21. What is the essential feature of an electronic funds transfer (EFT) procedure?

22. "The use of a bank contributes significantly to good internal control over cash." Is this true? Why?

23. Chris Hite is confused about the lack of agreement between the cash balance per books and the balance per bank. Explain the causes for the lack of agreement to Chris and give an example of each cause.

24. ← Identify the basic principles of cash management.

25. Marcia Tague asks your help concerning an NSF check. Explain to Marcia (a) what an NSF check is, (b) how it is treated in a bank reconciliation, and (c) whether it will require an adjusting entry on the company's books.

26. ←
(a) Describe cash equivalents and explain how they are reported.
(b) How should restricted cash funds be reported on the balance sheet?

27. ← What was Tootsie Roll's balance in cash and cash equivalents at December 31, 2011? Did it report any restricted cash? How did Tootsie Roll define cash equivalents?

*28. (a) Identify the three activities that pertain to a petty cash fund, and indicate an internal control principle that is applicable to each activity.
(b) When are journal entries required in the operation of a petty cash fund?

Brief Exercises

Identify fraud-triangle concepts.
(LO 1), C

BE7-1 Match each situation with the fraud triangle factor (opportunity, financial pressure, or rationalization) that best describes it.
(a) An employee's monthly credit card payments are nearly 75% of their monthly earnings.
(b) An employee earns minimum wage at a firm that has reported record earnings for each of the last five years.
(c) An employee has an expensive gambling habit.
(d) An employee has check writing and signing responsibilities for a small company, and is also responsible for reconciling the bank account.

BE7-2 Beth Pitchford is the new owner of Brigham Co. She has heard about internal control but is not clear about its importance for her business. Explain to Beth the four purposes of internal control, and give her one application of each purpose for Brigham Co.

Explain the importance of internal control.
(LO 2), C

BE7-3 The internal control procedures in Edmiston Company make the following provisions. Identify the principles of internal control that are being followed in each case.
(a) Employees who have physical custody of assets do not have access to the accounting records.
(b) Each month, the assets on hand are compared to the accounting records by an internal auditor.
(c) A prenumbered shipping document is prepared for each shipment of goods to customers.

Identify internal control principles.
(LO 2), C

BE7-4 Halleran Company has the following internal control procedures over cash receipts. Identify the internal control principle that is applicable to each procedure.
(a) All over-the-counter receipts are entered in cash registers.
(b) All cashiers are bonded.
(c) Daily cash counts are made by cashier department supervisors.
(d) The duties of receiving cash, recording cash, and having custody of cash are assigned to different individuals.
(e) Only cashiers may operate cash registers.

Identify the internal control principles applicable to cash receipts.
(LO 3), C

BE7-5 While examining cash receipts information, the accounting department determined the following information: opening cash balance $150, cash on hand $1,125.74, and cash sales per register tape $988.62. Prepare the required journal entry based upon the cash count sheet.

Make journal entry using cash count sheet.
(LO 3), AP

BE7-6 Catt Company has the following internal control procedures over cash disbursements. Identify the internal control principle that is applicable to each procedure.
(a) Company checks are prenumbered.
(b) The bank statement is reconciled monthly by an internal auditor.
(c) Blank checks are stored in a safe in the treasurer's office.
(d) Only the treasurer or assistant treasurer may sign checks.
(e) Check-signers are not allowed to record cash disbursement transactions.

Identify the internal control principles applicable to cash disbursements.
(LO 4), C

BE7-7 Roy Luber is uncertain about the control features of a bank account. Explain the control benefits of (a) a checking account and (b) a bank statement.

Identify the control features of a bank account.
(LO 4), C

BE7-8 The following reconciling items are applicable to the bank reconciliation for Nuessen Co. Indicate how each item should be shown on a bank reconciliation.
(a) Outstanding checks.
(b) Bank debit memorandum for service charge.
(c) Bank credit memorandum for collecting a note for the depositor.
(d) Deposit in transit.

Indicate location of reconciling items in a bank reconciliation.
(LO 5), C

BE7-9 Using the data in BE7-8, indicate (a) the items that will result in an adjustment to the depositor's records and (b) why the other items do not require adjustment.

Identify reconciling items that require adjusting entries.
(LO 5), C

BE7-10 At July 31, Farmer Company has this bank information: cash balance per bank $7,291; outstanding checks $762; deposits in transit $1,350; and a bank service charge $40. Determine the adjusted cash balance per bank at July 31.

Prepare partial bank reconciliation.
(LO 5), AP

BE7-11 In the month of November, Halladay Company Inc. wrote checks in the amount of $9,750. In December, checks in the amount of $11,762 were written. In November, $8,800 of these checks were presented to the bank for payment, and $10,889 in December. What is the amount of outstanding checks at the end of November? At the end of December?

Analyze outstanding checks.
(LO 5), AP

BE7-12 Span Company has these cash balances: cash in bank $12,742; payroll bank account $6,000; and plant expansion fund cash $25,000. Explain how each balance should be reported on the balance sheet.

Explain the statement presentation of cash balances.
(LO 6), C

BE7-13 The following information is available for Conger Company for the month of January: expected cash receipts $59,000; expected cash disbursements $67,000; and cash balance on January 1, $12,000. Management wishes to maintain a minimum cash balance of $9,000. Prepare a basic cash budget for the month of January.

Prepare a cash budget.
(LO 8), AP

*BE7-14 On March 20, Garber's petty cash fund of $100 is replenished when the fund contains $19 in cash and receipts for postage $40, supplies $26, and travel expense $15. Prepare the journal entry to record the replenishment of the petty cash fund.

Prepare entry to replenish a petty cash fund.
(LO 9), AP

Exercises

Identify the principles of internal control.
(LO 2), **C**

E7-1   Bank employees use a system known as the "maker-checker" system. An employee will record an entry in the appropriate journal, and then a supervisor will verify and approve the entry. These days, as all of a bank's accounts are computerized, the employee first enters a batch of entries into the computer, and then the entries are posted automatically to the general ledger account after the supervisor approves them on the system.

   Access to the computer system is password-protected and task-specific, which means that the computer system will not allow the employee to approve a transaction or the supervisor to record a transaction.

Instructions
Identify the principles of internal control inherent in the "maker-checker" procedure used by banks.

Identify the principles of internal control.
(LO 2), **C**

E7-2   Rosa's Pizza operates strictly on a carryout basis. Customers pick up their orders at a counter where a clerk exchanges the pizza for cash. While at the counter, the customer can see other employees making the pizzas and the large ovens in which the pizzas are baked.

Instructions
Identify the six principles of internal control and give an example of each principle that you might observe when picking up your pizza. (*Note:* It may not be possible to observe all the principles.)

List internal control weaknesses over cash receipts and suggest improvements.
(LO 2, 3), **E**

E7-3   The following control procedures are used in Kelton Company for over-the-counter cash receipts.
  1. Each store manager is responsible for interviewing applicants for cashier jobs. They are hired if they seem honest and trustworthy.
  2. All over-the-counter receipts are registered by three clerks who share a cash register with a single cash drawer.
  3. To minimize the risk of robbery, cash in excess of $100 is stored in an unlocked attaché case in the stock room until it is deposited in the bank.
  4. At the end of each day the total receipts are counted by the cashier on duty and reconciled to the cash register total.
  5. The company accountant makes the bank deposit and then records the day's receipts.

Instructions
(a) For each procedure, explain the weakness in internal control and identify the control principle that is violated.
(b) For each weakness, suggest a change in the procedure that will result in good internal control.

List internal control weaknesses for cash disbursements and suggest improvements.
(LO 2, 4), **E**

E7-4   The following control procedures are used in Penny's Boutique Shoppe for cash disbursements.
  1. Each week, 100 company checks are left in an unmarked envelope on a shelf behind the cash register.
  2. The store manager personally approves all payments before she signs and issues checks.
  3. The store purchases used goods for resale from people that bring items to the store. Since that can occur anytime that the store is open, all employees are authorized to purchase goods for resale by issuing cash from the register. The purchase is documented by having the store employee write on a piece of paper a description of the item that was purchased and the amount that was paid. The employee then signs the paper and puts it in the register.
  4. After payment, bills are "filed" in a paid invoice folder.
  5. The company accountant prepares the bank reconciliation and reports any discrepancies to the owner.

Instructions
(a) For each procedure, explain the weakness in internal control and identify the internal control principle that is violated.
(b) For each weakness, suggest a change in the procedure that will result in good internal control.

E7-5 At Nunez Company, checks are not prenumbered because both the purchasing agent and the treasurer are authorized to issue checks. Each signer has access to unissued checks kept in an unlocked file cabinet. The purchasing agent pays all bills pertaining to goods purchased for resale. Prior to payment, the purchasing agent determines that the goods have been received and verifies the mathematical accuracy of the vendor's invoice. After payment, the invoice is filed by vendor name and the purchasing agent records the payment in the cash disbursements journal. The treasurer pays all other bills following approval by authorized employees. After payment, the treasurer stamps all bills "paid," files them by payment date, and records the checks in the cash disbursements journal. Nunez Company maintains one checking account that is reconciled by the treasurer.

Identify internal control weaknesses for cash disbursements and suggest improvements.

(LO 2, 4), **E**

Instructions
(a) List the weaknesses in internal control over cash disbursements.
(b) Identify improvements for correcting these weaknesses.

E7-6 Sally Rice is unable to reconcile the bank balance at January 31. Sally's reconciliation is shown here.

Prepare bank reconciliation and adjusting entries.

(LO 5), **AP**

Cash balance per bank	$3,677.20
Add: NSF check	450.00
Less: Bank service charge	28.00
Adjusted balance per bank	$4,099.20
Cash balance per books	$3,975.20
Less: Deposits in transit	590.00
Add: Outstanding checks	770.00
Adjusted balance per books	$4,155.20

Instructions
(a) What is the proper adjusted cash balance per bank?
(b) What is the proper adjusted cash balance per books?
(c) Prepare the adjusting journal entries necessary to determine the adjusted cash balance per books.

E7-7 At April 30, the bank reconciliation of Longacre Company shows three outstanding checks: No. 254 $650, No. 255 $700, and No. 257 $410. The May bank statement and the May cash payments journal are given here.

Determine outstanding checks.

(LO 5), **AP**

Bank Statement				**Cash Payments Journal**		
Checks Paid				**Checks Issued**		
Date	Check No.	Amount		Date	Check No.	Amount
5-4	254	$650		5-2	258	$159
5-2	257	410		5-5	259	275
5-17	258	159		5-10	260	925
5-12	259	275		5-15	261	500
5-20	260	925		5-22	262	750
5-29	263	480		5-24	263	480
5-30	262	750		5-29	264	360

Instructions
Using step 2 in the reconciliation procedure (see page 302), list the outstanding checks at May 31.

E7-8 The following information pertains to Joyce Company.
1. Cash balance per bank, July 31, $7,328.
2. July bank service charge not recorded by the depositor $38.
3. Cash balance per books, July 31, $7,364.
4. Deposits in transit, July 31, $2,700.
5. Note for $2,000 collected for Joyce Company in July by the bank, plus interest $36 less fee $20. The collection has not been recorded by Joyce Company, and no interest has been accrued.
6. Outstanding checks, July 31, $686.

Prepare bank reconciliation and adjusting entries.

(LO 5), **AP**

Prepare bank reconciliation and adjusting entries.

(LO 5), **AP**

Compute deposits in transit and outstanding checks for two bank reconciliations.

(LO 5), **AP**

Prepare bank reconciliation and adjusting entries.

(LO 5), **AP**

Instructions

(a) Prepare a bank reconciliation at July 31, 2014.

(b) Journalize the adjusting entries at July 31 on the books of Joyce Company.

E7-9 This information relates to the Cash account in the ledger of Treanor Company.

Balance September 1—$16,400; Cash deposited—$64,000
Balance September 30—$17,600; Checks written—$62,800

The September bank statement shows a balance of $16,500 at September 30 and the following memoranda.

Credits		Debits	
Collection of $1,800 note plus interest $30	$1,830	NSF check: H. Kane	$560
Interest earned on checking account	45	Safety deposit box rent	60

At September 30, deposits in transit were $4,738 and outstanding checks totaled $2,383.

Instructions

(a) Prepare the bank reconciliation at September 30, 2014.

(b) Prepare the adjusting entries at September 30, assuming (1) the NSF check was from a customer on account, and (2) no interest had been accrued on the note.

E7-10 The cash records of Downs Company show the following.

For July:

1. The June 30 bank reconciliation indicated that deposits in transit total $580. During July, the general ledger account Cash shows deposits of $16,900, but the bank statement indicates that only $15,600 in deposits were received during the month.

2. The June 30 bank reconciliation also reported outstanding checks of $940. During the month of July, Downs Company books show that $17,500 of checks were issued, yet the bank statement showed that $16,400 of checks cleared the bank in July.

For September:

3. In September, deposits per bank statement totaled $25,900, deposits per books were $26,400, and deposits in transit at September 30 were $2,200.

4. In September, cash disbursements per books were $23,500, checks clearing the bank were $24,000, and outstanding checks at September 30 were $2,100.

There were no bank debit or credit memoranda, and no errors were made by either the bank or Downs Company.

Instructions

Answer the following questions.

(a) In situation 1, what were the deposits in transit at July 31?

(b) In situation 2, what were the outstanding checks at July 31?

(c) In situation 3, what were the deposits in transit at August 31?

(d) In situation 4, what were the outstanding checks at August 31?

E7-11 Werth Inc.'s bank statement from Hometown Bank at August 31, 2014, gives the following information.

Balance, August 1	$18,400	Bank debit memorandum:		
August deposits	71,000	Safety deposit box fee	$	25
Checks cleared in August	68,678	Service charge		50
Bank credit memorandum:		Balance, August 31		20,692
Interest earned	45			

A summary of the Cash account in the ledger for August shows the following: balance, August 1, $18,700; receipts $74,000; disbursements $73,570; and balance, August 31, $19,130. Analysis reveals that the only reconciling items on the July 31 bank reconciliation were a deposit in transit for $4,800 and outstanding checks of $4,500. In addition, you determine that there was an error involving a company check drawn in August: A check for $400 to a creditor on account that cleared the bank in August was journalized and posted for $40.

Instructions
(a) Determine deposits in transit.
(b) Determine outstanding checks. (*Hint:* You need to correct disbursements for the check error.)
(c) Prepare a bank reconciliation at August 31.
(d) Journalize the adjusting entry(ies) to be made by Werth Inc. at August 31.

E7-12 A new accountant at Leftwich Inc. is trying to identify which of the amounts shown below should be reported as the current asset "Cash and cash equivalents" in the year-end balance sheet, as of April 30, 2014.

Identify reporting of cash.
(LO 6), AP

1. $60 of currency and coin in a locked box used for incidental cash transactions.
2. A $10,000 U.S. Treasury bill, due May 31, 2014.
3. $260 of April-dated checks that Leftwich has received from customers but not yet deposited.
4. An $85 check received from a customer in payment of its April account, but postdated to May 1.
5. $2,500 in the company's checking account.
6. $4,800 in its savings account.
7. $75 of prepaid postage in its postage meter.
8. A $25 IOU from the company receptionist.

Instructions
(a) What balance should Leftwich report as its "Cash and cash equivalents" balance at April 30, 2014?
(b) In what account(s) and in what financial statement(s) should the items not included in "Cash and cash equivalents" be reported?

E7-13 Canzer, Morel, and Wang, three law students who have joined together to open a law practice, are struggling to manage their cash flow. They haven't yet built up suffi-cient clientele and revenues to support their legal practice's ongoing costs. Initial costs, such as advertising, renovations to their premises, and the like, all result in outgoing cash flow at a time when little is coming in. Canzer, Morel, and Wang haven't had time to establish a billing system since most of their clients' cases haven't yet reached the courts, and the lawyers didn't think it would be right to bill them until "results were achieved."

Review cash management practices.
(LO 7), C

Unfortunately, Canzer, Morel, and Wang's suppliers don't feel the same way. Their suppliers expect them to pay their accounts payable within a few days of receiving their bills. So far, there hasn't even been enough money to pay the three lawyers, and they are not sure how long they can keep practicing law without getting some money into their pockets.

Instructions
Can you provide any suggestions for Canzer, Morel, and Wang to improve their cash man-agement practices?

Prepare a cash budget for two months.

E7-14 Enright Company expects to have a cash balance of $46,000 on January 1, 2014. These are the relevant monthly budget data for the first two months of 2014.

(LO 8), AP

1. Collections from customers: January $71,000, February $146,000.
2. Payments to suppliers: January $40,000, February $75,000.
3. Wages: January $30,000, February $40,000. Wages are paid in the month they are incurred.
4. Administrative expenses: January $21,000, February $24,000. These costs include depreciation of $1,000 per month. All other costs are paid as incurred.
5. Selling expenses: January $15,000, February $20,000. These costs are exclusive of depreciation. They are paid as incurred.
6. Sales of short-term investments in January are expected to realize $12,000 in cash. Enright has a line of credit at a local bank that enables it to borrow up to $25,000. The company wants to maintain a minimum monthly cash balance of $20,000.

Instructions
Prepare a cash budget for January and February.

Prepare journal entries for a petty cash fund.

(LO 9), AP

*E7-15 During October, Wichita Light Company experiences the following transactions in establishing a petty cash fund.

Oct. 1 A petty cash fund is established with a check for $150 issued to the petty cash custodian.

 31 A check was written to reimburse the fund and increase the fund to $200. A count of the petty cash fund disclosed the following items:

Currency		$59.00
Coins		0.70
Expenditure receipts (vouchers):		
Supplies	$26.10	
Telephone, Internet, and fax	16.40	
Postage	39.70	
Freight-out	6.80	

Instructions

Journalize the entries in October that pertain to the petty cash fund.

Journalize and post petty cash fund transactions.

(LO 9), AP

*E7-16 Lyle Company maintains a petty cash fund for small expenditures. These transactions occurred during the month of August.

Aug. 1 Established the petty cash fund by writing a check on Westown Bank for $200.

 15 Replenished the petty cash fund by writing a check for $175. On this date, the fund consisted of $25 in cash and these petty cash receipts: freight-out $74.40, entertainment expense $36, postage expense $33.70, and miscellaneous expense $27.50.

 16 Increased the amount of the petty cash fund to $400 by writing a check for $200.

 31 Replenished the petty cash fund by writing a check for $283. On this date, the fund consisted of $117 in cash and these petty cash receipts: postage expense $145, entertainment expense $90.60, and freight-out $46.40.

Instructions

(a) Journalize the petty cash transactions.

(b) Post to the Petty Cash account.

(c) What internal control features exist in a petty cash fund?

Challenge Exercises

Visit the book's companion website, at **www.wiley.com/college/kimmel**, and choose the Student Companion site to access Challenge Exercises.

Problems: Set A

Identify internal control weaknesses for cash receipts.

(LO 2, 3), C

P7-1A Granada Theater is in the Greenbelt Mall. A cashier's booth is located near the entrance to the theater. Two cashiers are employed. One works from 1:00 to 5:00 P.M., the other from 5:00 to 9:00 P.M. Each cashier is bonded. The cashiers receive cash from customers and operate a machine that ejects serially numbered tickets. The rolls of tickets are inserted and locked into the machine by the theater manager at the beginning of each cashier's shift.

After purchasing a ticket, the customer takes the ticket to a doorperson stationed at the entrance of the theater lobby some 60 feet from the cashier's booth. The doorperson tears the ticket in half, admits the customer, and returns the ticket stub to the customer. The other half of the ticket is dropped into a locked box by the doorperson.

At the end of each cashier's shift, the theater manager removes the ticket rolls from the machine and makes a cash count. The cash count sheet is initialed by the cashier. At the end of the day, the manager deposits the receipts in total in a bank night deposit vault located in the mall. In addition, the manager sends copies of the deposit slip and the initialed cash count sheets to the theater company treasurer for verification and to the company's accounting department. Receipts from the first shift are stored in a safe located in the manager's office.

Instructions

(a) Identify the internal control principles and their application to the cash receipts transactions of Granada Theater.

(b) If the doorperson and cashier decided to collaborate to misappropriate cash, what actions might they take?

P7-2A   Flint Hills Middle School wants to raise money for a new sound system for its auditorium. The primary fund-raising event is a dance at which the famous disc jockey Jay Dee will play classic and not-so-classic dance tunes. Trent Greeley, the music and theater instructor, has been given the responsibility for coordinating the fund-raising efforts. This is Trent's first experience with fund-raising. He decides to put the eighth-grade choir in charge of the event; he will be a relatively passive observer.

Identify internal control weaknesses in cash receipts and cash disbursements.
(LO 2, 3, 4), **C**

Trent had 500 unnumbered tickets printed for the dance. He left the tickets in a box on his desk and told the choir students to take as many tickets as they thought they could sell for $5 each. In order to ensure that no extra tickets would be floating around, he told them to dispose of any unsold tickets. When the students received payment for the tickets, they were to bring the cash back to Trent, and he would put it in a locked box in his desk drawer.

Some of the students were responsible for decorating the gymnasium for the dance. Trent gave each of them a key to the money box and told them that if they took money out to purchase materials, they should put a note in the box saying how much they took and what it was used for. After two weeks, the money box appeared to be getting full, so Trent asked Sandy Overbay to count the money, prepare a deposit slip, and deposit the money in a bank account Trent had opened.

The day of the dance, Trent wrote a check from the account to pay Jay Dee. The DJ said, however, that he accepted only cash and did not give receipts. So Trent took $200 out of the cash box and gave it to Jay. At the dance, Trent had Deb Younger working at the entrance to the gymnasium, collecting tickets from students and selling tickets to those who had not pre-purchased them. Trent estimated that 400 students attended the dance.

The following day, Trent closed out the bank account, which had $250 in it, and gave that amount plus the $180 in the cash box to Principal Ramirez. Principal Ramirez seemed surprised that, after generating roughly $2,000 in sales, the dance netted only $430 in cash. Trent did not know how to respond.

Instructions

Identify as many internal control weaknesses as you can in this scenario, and suggest how each could be addressed.

P7-3A   On July 31, 2014, Redeker Company had a cash balance per books of $6,140. The statement from Nashota State Bank on that date showed a balance of $7,690.80. A comparison of the bank statement with the Cash account revealed the following facts.

Prepare a bank reconciliation and adjusting entries.
(LO 5), **AP**

1. The bank service charge for July was $25.
2. The bank collected a note receivable of $1,500 for Redeker Company on July 15, plus $30 of interest. The bank made a $10 charge for the collection. Redeker has not accrued any interest on the note.
3. The July 31 receipts of $1,193.30 were not included in the bank deposits for July. These receipts were deposited by the company in a night deposit vault on July 31.
4. Company check No. 2480 issued to T. Laird, a creditor, for $384 that cleared the bank in July was incorrectly entered in the cash payments journal on July 10 for $348.
5. Checks outstanding on July 31 totaled $1,860.10.
6. On July 31, the bank statement showed an NSF charge of $575 for a check received by the company from K. Wagner, a customer, on account.

Instructions

(a) Prepare the bank reconciliation as of July 31.
(b) Prepare the necessary adjusting entries at July 31.

(a) Adjusted cash bal. $7,024.00

Prepare a bank reconciliation and adjusting entries from detailed data.
(LO 5), **AP**

P7-4A The bank portion of the bank reconciliation for LaRoche Company at October 31, 2014, is shown below.

LAROCHE COMPANY
Bank Reconciliation
October 31, 2014

Cash balance per bank			$12,367.90
Add: Deposits in transit			1,530.20
			13,898.10
Less: Outstanding checks			

Check Number	Check Amount	
2451	$1,260.40	
2470	684.20	
2471	844.50	
2472	426.80	
2474	1,050.00	4,265.90
Adjusted cash balance per bank		$ 9,632.20

The adjusted cash balance per bank agreed with the cash balance per books at October 31. The November bank statement showed the following checks and deposits.

Bank Statement

	Checks			Deposits	
Date	Number	Amount	Date		Amount
11-1	2470	$ 684.20	11-1		$ 1,530.20
11-2	2471	844.50	11-4		1,211.60
11-5	2474	1,050.00	11-8		990.10
11-4	2475	1,640.70	11-13		2,575.00
11-8	2476	2,830.00	11-18		1,472.70
11-10	2477	600.00	11-21		2,945.00
11-15	2479	1,750.00	11-25		2,567.30
11-18	2480	1,330.00	11-28		1,650.00
11-27	2481	695.40	11-30		1,186.00
11-30	2483	575.50	Total		$16,127.90
11-29	2486	940.00			
	Total	$12,940.30			

The cash records per books for November showed the following.

	Cash Payments Journal						Cash Receipts Journal	
Date	Number	Amount	Date	Number	Amount		Date	Amount
11-1	2475	$1,640.70	11-20	2483	$ 575.50		11-3	$ 1,211.60
11-2	2476	2,830.00	11-22	2484	829.50		11-7	990.10
11-2	2477	600.00	11-23	2485	974.80		11-12	2,575.00
11-4	2478	538.20	11-24	2486	940.00		11-17	1,472.70
11-8	2479	1,705.00	11-29	2487	398.00		11-20	2,954.00
11-10	2480	1,330.00	11-30	2488	800.00		11-24	2,567.30
11-15	2481	695.40	Total		$14,469.10		11-27	1,650.00
11-18	2482	612.00					11-29	1,186.00
							11-30	1,304.00
							Total	$15,910.70

The bank statement contained two bank memoranda:

1. A credit of $2,242 for the collection of a $2,100 note for LaRoche Company plus interest of $157 and less a collection fee of $15. LaRoche Company has not accrued any interest on the note.
2. A debit for the printing of additional company checks $85.

At November 30, the cash balance per books was $11,073.80 and the cash balance per bank statement was $17,712.50. The bank did not make any errors, but **LaRoche Company made two errors.**

Instructions

(a) Using the four steps in the reconciliation procedure described on page 303, prepare a bank reconciliation at November 30, 2014.

(b) Prepare the adjusting entries based on the reconciliation. (*Note:* The correction of any errors pertaining to recording checks should be made to Accounts Payable. The correction of any errors relating to recording cash receipts should be made to Accounts Receivable.)

(a) Adjusted cash bal. $13,176.80

P7-5A Zimmerman Company of Shawnee, Kansas, spreads herbicides and applies liquid fertilizer for local farmers. On May 31, 2014, the company's Cash account per its general ledger showed a balance of $6,738.90.

Prepare a bank reconciliation and adjusting entries.
(LO 5), AP

The bank statement from Shawnee State Bank on that date showed the following balance.

SHAWNEE STATE BANK

Checks and Debits	Deposits and Credits	Daily Balance
XXX	XXX	5-31 6,968.00

A comparison of the details on the bank statement with the details in the Cash account revealed the following facts.

1. The statement included a debit memo of $40 for the printing of additional company checks.
2. Cash sales of $883.15 on May 12 were deposited in the bank. The cash receipts journal entry and the deposit slip were incorrectly made for $933.15. The bank credited Zimmerman Company for the correct amount.
3. Outstanding checks at May 31 totaled $276.25, and deposits in transit were $1,880.15.
4. On May 18, the company issued check No. 1181 for $685 to M. Hartley, on account. The check, which cleared the bank in May, was incorrectly journalized and posted by Zimmerman Company for $658.
5. A $2,600 note receivable was collected by the bank for Zimmerman Company on May 31 plus $110 interest. The bank charged a collection fee of $20. No interest has been accrued on the note.
6. Included with the canceled checks was a check issued by Zinderberg Company to P. Conard for $360 that was incorrectly charged to Zimmerman Company by the bank.
7. On May 31, the bank statement showed an NSF charge of $380 for a check issued by Bev Sullivan, a customer, to Zimmerman Company on account.

Instructions

(a) Prepare the bank reconciliation at May 31, 2014.
(b) Prepare the necessary adjusting entries for Zimmerman Company at May 31, 2014.

(a) Adjusted cash bal. $8,931.90

P7-6A You are provided with the following information taken from Langerhan Inc.'s March 31, 2014, balance sheet.

Prepare a cash budget.
(LO 8), AP

Cash	$ 11,000
Accounts receivable	20,000
Inventory	36,000
Property, plant, and equipment, net of depreciation	120,000
Accounts payable	22,400
Common stock	150,000
Retained earnings	11,600

Additional information concerning Langerhan Inc. is as follows.

1. Gross profit is 25% of sales.
2. Actual and budgeted sales data:

March (actual)	$46,000	
April (budgeted)	70,000	

3. Sales are both cash and credit. Cash collections expected in April are:

March	$18,400	(40% of $46,000)
April	42,000	(60% of $70,000)
	$60,400	

4. Half of a month's purchases are paid for in the month of purchase and half in the following month. Cash disbursements expected in April are:

Purchases March	$22,400
Purchases April	28,100
	$50,500

5. Cash operating costs are anticipated to be $11,200 for the month of April.
6. Equipment costing $2,500 will be purchased for cash in April.
7. The company wishes to maintain a minimum cash balance of $9,000. An open line of credit is available at the bank. All borrowing is done at the beginning of the month, and all repayments are made at the end of the month. The interest rate is 12% per year, and interest expense is accrued at the end of the month and paid in the following month.

Instructions

Prepare a cash budget for the month of April. Determine how much cash Langerhan Inc. must borrow, or can repay, in April.

Apr. borrowings $1,800

Prepare a cash budget.

(LO 8), **AP**

P7-7A Castle Corporation prepares monthly cash budgets. Here are relevant data from operating budgets for 2014.

	January	February
Sales	$360,000	$400,000
Purchases	120,000	130,000
Salaries	84,000	81,000
Administrative expenses	72,000	75,000
Selling expenses	79,000	88,000

All sales and purchases are on account. Budgeted collections and disbursement data are given below. All other expenses are paid in the month incurred except for administrative expenses, which include $1,000 of depreciation per month.

Other data.

1. Collections from customers: January $326,000; February $378,000.
2. Payments for purchases: January $110,000; February $135,000.
3. Other receipts: January: collection of December 31, 2013, notes receivable $15,000; February: proceeds from sale of securities $4,000.
4. Other disbursements: February $10,000 cash dividend.

The company's cash balance on January 1, 2014, is expected to be $46,000. The company wants to maintain a minimum cash balance of $40,000.

Instructions

Prepare a cash budget for January and February.

Jan. 31 adjusted cash bal. $43,000

Prepare a comprehensive bank reconciliation with theft and internal control deficiencies.

(LO 2, 3, 4, 5), **E**

P7-8A Heisey Company is a very profitable small business. It has not, however, given much consideration to internal control. For example, in an attempt to keep clerical and office expenses to a minimum, the company has combined the jobs of cashier and bookkeeper. As a result, Terry Baden handles all cash receipts, keeps the accounting records, and prepares the monthly bank reconciliations.

The balance per the bank statement on October 31, 2014, was $18,380. Outstanding checks were: No. 62 for $140.75, No. 183 for $180, No. 284 for $253.25, No. 862 for

$190.71, No. 863 for $226.80, and No. 864 for $165.28. Included with the statement was a credit memorandum of $185 indicating the collection of a note receivable for Heisey Company by the bank on October 25. This memorandum has not been recorded by Heisey.

The company's ledger showed one Cash account with a balance of $21,877.72. The balance included undeposited cash on hand. Because of the lack of internal controls, Terry took for personal use all of the undeposited receipts in excess of $3,795.51. He then prepared the following bank reconciliation in an effort to conceal his theft of cash.

Cash balance per books, October 31		$21,877.72
Add: Outstanding checks		
No. 862	$190.71	
No. 863	226.80	
No. 864	165.28	482.79
		22,360.51
Less: Undeposited receipts		3,795.51
Unadjusted balance per bank, October 31		18,565.00
Less: Bank credit memorandum		185.00
Cash balance per bank statement, October 31		$18,380.00

Instructions

(a) Prepare a correct bank reconciliation. (*Hint:* Deduct the amount of the theft from the adjusted balance per books.)

(b) Indicate the three ways that Terry attempted to conceal the theft and the dollar amount involved in each method.

(c) What principles of internal control were violated in this case?

(a) Adjusted cash bal. $21,018.72

Problems: Set B

Visit the book's companion website, at **www.wiley.com/college/kimmel**, and choose the Student Companion site to access Problem Set B.

Comprehensive Problem

CP7 On December 1, 2014, Havenhill Company had the following account balances.

	Debit		Credit
Cash	$18,200	Accumulated Depreciation—	
Notes Receivable	2,000	Equipment	$ 3,000
Accounts Receivable	7,500	Accounts Payable	6,100
Inventory	16,000	Common Stock	50,000
Prepaid Insurance	1,600	Retained Earnings	14,200
Equipment	28,000		$73,300
	$73,300		

During December, the company completed the following transactions.

Dec. 7   Received $3,600 cash from customers in payment of account (no discount allowed).

12   Purchased merchandise on account from Brown Co. $12,000, terms 1/10, n/30.

17   Sold merchandise on account $16,000, terms 2/10, n/30. The cost of the merchandise sold was $10,000.

19   Paid salaries $2,200.

22   Paid Brown Co. in full, less discount.

26   Received collections in full, less discounts, from customers billed on December 17.

31   Received $2,700 cash from customers in payment of account (no discount allowed).

Adjustment data:

1. Depreciation $200 per month.
2. Insurance expired $400.
3. Income tax expense was $425. It was unpaid at December 31.

Instructions
(a) Journalize the December transactions. (Assume a perpetual inventory system.)
(b) Enter the December 1 balances in the ledger T-accounts and post the December transactions. Use Cost of Goods Sold, Depreciation Expense, Insurance Expense, Salaries and Wages Expense, Sales Revenue, Sales Discounts, Income Taxes Payable, and Income Tax Expense.
(c) The statement from Jackson County Bank on December 31 showed a balance of $25,930. A comparison of the bank statement with the Cash account revealed the following facts.
   1. The bank collected a note receivable of $2,000 for Havenhill Company on December 15.
   2. The December 31 receipts were deposited in a night deposit vault on December 31. These deposits were recorded by the bank in January.
   3. Checks outstanding on December 31 totaled $1,210.
   4. On December 31, the bank statement showed a NSF charge of $680 for a check received by the company from L. Menke, a customer, on account.

Prepare a bank reconciliation as of December 31 based on the available information. (*Hint:* The cash balance per books is $26,100. This can be proven by finding the balance in the Cash account from parts (a) and (b).)
(d) Journalize the adjusting entries resulting from the bank reconciliation and adjustment data.
(e) Post the adjusting entries to the ledger T-accounts.
(f) Prepare an adjusted trial balance.
(g) Prepare an income statement for December and a classified balance sheet at December 31.

(f) Totals $89,500
(g) Net income $ 2,455
     Total assets $73,180

Broadening Your Perspective

Financial Reporting and Analysis

FINANCIAL REPORTING PROBLEM: *Tootsie Roll Industries, Inc.*

BYP7-1 The financial statements of Tootsie Roll are presented in Appendix A of this book, together with an auditor's report—Report of Independent Auditors.

Instructions
Using the financial statements and reports, answer these questions about Tootsie Roll's internal controls and cash.
(a) What comments, if any, are made about cash in the "Report of Independent Registered Public Accounting Firm"?
(b) What data about cash and cash equivalents are shown in the consolidated balance sheet (statement of financial position)?
(c) What activities are identified in the consolidated statement of cash flows as being responsible for the changes in cash during 2011?
(d) How are cash equivalents defined in the Notes to Consolidated Financial Statements?
(e) Read the section of the report titled "Management's Report on Internal Control Over Financial Reporting." Summarize the statements made in that section of the report.

COMPARATIVE ANALYSIS PROBLEM: *Tootsie Roll vs. Hershey*

BYP7-2 The financial statements of The Hershey Company are presented in Appendix B, following the financial statements for Tootsie Roll in Appendix A.

Instructions
Answer the following questions for each company.

(a) What is the balance in cash and cash equivalents at December 31, 2011?
(b) What percentage of total assets does cash represent for each company over the last two years? Has it changed significantly for either company?
(c) How much cash was provided by operating activities during 2011?
(d) Comment on your findings in parts (a) through (c).

RESEARCH CASE

BYP7-3 The website **www.cpa2biz.com** has an article dated February 4, 2010, by Mary Schaeffer entitled "Emerging Issues: Demise of Paper Checks."

Instructions
Go to the website and do a search on the article title. Read the article and answer the following questions.
(a) How many different forms of payment types does the article list? What are the payment types?
(b) What problems does the shift away from paper checks to alternative payment options present for companies?
(c) What five controls does the article suggest incorporating, to decrease problems associated with multiple payment options?

INTERPRETING FINANCIAL STATEMENTS

BYP7-4 The international accounting firm Ernst & Young performed a global survey on fraud. The results of that survey are summarized in a report titled "Driving Ethical Growth—New Markets, New Challenges" (Ernst & Young, *11th Global Fraud Survey*). You can find this report by doing an Internet search on the title, or go to **http://www.ey.com/Publication/vwLUAssets/Driving_ ethical_growth_-_new_markets,_new_challenges:_11th_Global_Fraud_Survey/$FILE/EY_11th_ Global_Fraud_Survey.pdf**.

Instructions
Read the Executive Summary section, and then skim the remainder of the report to answer the following questions.
(a) What was the global percentage of companies that experienced fraud during the period covered by the survey, and what region of the world had the highest rate?
(b) What percentage of survey respondents performed a fraud risk assessment in the six months prior to the survey? What percentage of survey respondents have never performed a fraud risk assessment?
(c) What percentage of respondents thought members of the board of directors were either "very concerned" or "fairly concerned" about board members' personal legal liability resulting from fraud at their companies?
(d) What are the top three issues of concern to compliance officers according to the survey?

REAL-WORLD FOCUS

BYP7-5 The Financial Accounting Standards Board (FASB) is a private organization established to improve accounting standards and financial reporting. The FASB conducts extensive research before issuing a "Statement of Financial Accounting Standards," which represents an authoritative expression of generally accepted accounting principles.

Address: **www.fasb.org**, or go to **www.wiley.com/college/kimmel**

Steps
Choose **About FASB**.

Instructions
Answer the following questions.
(a) What is the mission of the FASB?
(b) How are topics added to the FASB technical agenda? (*Hint:* See Project Plans in Our Rules of Procedure.)
(c) What characteristics make the FASB's procedures an "open" decision-making process? (*Hint:* See Due Process in Our Rules of Procedure.)

BYP7-6 The Public Company Accounting Oversight Board (PCAOB) was created as a result of the Sarbanes-Oxley Act. It has oversight and enforcement responsibilities over accounting firms in the United States.

Address: **http://www.pcaobus.org/**, or go to **www.wiley.com/college/kimmel**

Instructions
Answer the following questions.
(a) What is the mission of the PCAOB?
(b) Briefly summarize its responsibilities related to inspections.
(c) Briefly summarize its responsibilities related to enforcement.

Critical Thinking

DECISION-MAKING ACROSS THE ORGANIZATION

BYP7-7 Alternative Distributor Corp., a distributor of groceries and related products, is head-quartered in Medford, Massachusetts.

During a recent audit, Alternative Distributor Corp. was advised that existing internal controls necessary for the company to develop reliable financial statements were inadequate. The audit report stated that the current system of accounting for sales, receivables, and cash receipts constituted a material weakness. Among other items, the report focused on nontimely deposit of cash receipts, exposing Alternative Distributor to potential loss or misappropriation, excessive past due accounts receivable due to lack of collection efforts, disregard of advantages offered by vendors for prompt payment of invoices, absence of appropriate segregation of duties by personnel consistent with appropriate control objectives, inadequate procedures for applying accounting principles, lack of qualified management personnel, lack of supervision by an outside board of directors, and overall poor record-keeping.

Instructions
(a) Identify the principles of internal control violated by Alternative Distributor Corporation.
(b) Explain why managers of various functional areas in the company should be concerned about internal controls.

COMMUNICATION ACTIVITY

BYP7-8 As a new auditor for the CPA firm of Good and Rich, you have been assigned to review the internal controls over mail cash receipts of Lyman Company. Your review reveals that checks are promptly endorsed "For Deposit Only," but no list of the checks is prepared by the person opening the mail. The mail is opened either by the cashier or by the employee who maintains the accounts receivable records. Mail receipts are deposited in the bank weekly by the cashier.

Instructions
Write a letter to D. A. Flynn, owner of the Lyman Company, explaining the weaknesses in internal control and your recommendations for improving the system.

ETHICS CASES

BYP7-9 Banks charge fees for "bounced" checks—that is, checks that exceed the balance in the account. It has been estimated that processing bounced checks costs a bank roughly $1.50 per check. Thus, the profit margin on bounced checks is very high. Recognizing this, some banks have started to process checks from largest to smallest. By doing this, they maximize the number of checks that bounce if a customer overdraws an account. For example, NationsBank (now Bank of America) projected a $14 million increase in fee revenue as a result of processing largest checks first. In response to criticism, banks have responded that their customers prefer to have large checks processed first, because those tend to be the most important. At the other extreme, some banks will cover their customers' bounced checks, effectively extending them an interest-free loan while their account is overdrawn.

Instructions
Answer each of the following questions.
(a) Richard Coulsen had a balance of $1,500 in his checking account at First National Bank on a day when the bank received the following five checks for processing against his account.

Check Number	Amount	Check Number	Amount
3150	$ 35	3165	$ 550
3162	400	3166	1,510
		3169	180

Assuming a $30 fee assessed by the bank for each bounced check, how much fee revenue would the bank generate if it processed checks (1) from largest to smallest, (2) from smallest to largest, and (3) in order of check number?

(b) Do you think that processing checks from largest to smallest is an ethical business practice?

(c) In addition to ethical issues, what other issues must a bank consider in deciding whether to process checks from largest to smallest?

(d) If you were managing a bank, what policy would you adopt on bounced checks?

BYP7-10 The National Fraud Information Center (NFIC) was originally established in 1992 by the National Consumers League, the oldest nonprofit consumer organization in the United States, to fight the growing menace of telemarketing fraud by improving prevention and enforcement. It maintains a website that provides many useful fraud-related resources.

Address: **www.fraud.org/scamsagainstbusinesses/bizscams.htm** or go to **www.wiley.com/college/kimmel**

Instructions
Go to the site and find an item of interest to you. Write a short summary of your findings.

ALL ABOUT YOU

BYP7-11 The print and electronic media are full of stories about potential security risks that can arise from your personal computer. It is important to keep in mind, however, that there are also many ways that your identity can be stolen other than from your computer. The federal government provides many resources to help protect you from identity thieves.

Instructions
Go to **http://onguardonline.gov/idtheft.html**, and click Games, then click ID Theft Faceoff. Complete the quiz provided there.

FASB CODIFICATION ACTIVITY

BYP7-12 If your school has a subscription to the FASB Codification, go to **http://aaahq.org/ascLogin.cfm** to log in and prepare responses to the following.

(a) How is cash defined in the Codification?

(b) How are cash equivalents defined in the Codification?

(c) What are the disclosure requirements related to cash and cash equivalents?

Answers to Insight and Accounting Across the Organization Questions

p. 286 And the Controls Are . . . Q: Why is sustainability information important to investors? **A:** Investors, customers, suppliers, and employees want more information about companies' long-term impact on society. There is a growing awareness that sustainability issues can affect a company's financial performance. Proper reporting on sustainability issues develops a solid reputation for transparency and provides confidence to shareholders.

p. 293 SOX Boosts the Role of Human Resources Q: Why would unsupervised employees or employees who report to each other represent potential internal control threats? **A:** An unsupervised employee may have a fraudulent job (or may even be a fictitious person)—e.g., a person drawing a paycheck without working. Or, if two employees supervise each other, there is no real separation of duties, and they can conspire to defraud the company.

p. 299 How Employees Steal Q: How can companies reduce the likelihood of fraudulent disbursements? **A:** To reduce the occurrence of fraudulent disbursements, a company should follow the procedures discussed in this chapter. These include having only designated personnel sign checks; having different personnel approve payments and make payments; ensuring that check-signers do not record disbursements; using prenumbered checks and matching each check to an approved invoice; storing blank checks securely; reconciling the bank statement; and stamping invoices paid.

p. 305 Madoff's Ponzi Scheme Q: How was Madoff able to conceal such a giant fraud? **A:** Madoff fabricated false investment statements that were provided to investors. In addition, his auditor never verified these investment statements even though the auditor gave him an unqualified opinion each year.

A Look at IFRS

LEARNING OBJECTIVE	10

Compare the accounting procedures for fraud, internal control, and cash under GAAP and IFRS.

Fraud can occur anywhere. And because the three main factors that contribute to fraud are universal in nature, the principles of internal control activities are used globally by companies. While Sarbanes-Oxley (SOX) does not apply to international companies, most large international companies have internal controls similar to those indicated in the chapter. IFRS and GAAP are very similar in accounting for cash. *IAS No. 1 (revised),* "Presentation of Financial Statements," is the only standard that discusses issues specifically related to cash.

KEY POINTS

- The fraud triangle discussed in this chapter is applicable to all international companies. Some of the major frauds on an international basis are Parmalat (Italy), Royal Ahold (the Netherlands), and Satyam Computer Services (India).

- Rising economic crime poses a growing threat to companies, with nearly half of all organizations worldwide being victims of fraud in a recent two-year period (*PricewaterhouseCoopers' Global Economic Crime Survey,* 2005). Specifically, 44% of Romanian companies surveyed experienced fraud in the past two years.

- Globally, the number of companies reporting fraud increased from 37% to 45% since 2003, a 22% increase. The cost to companies was an average $1.7 million in losses from "tangible frauds," that is, those that result in an immediate and direct financial loss. These include asset misappropriation, false pretenses, and counterfeiting (*PricewaterhouseCoopers' Global Economic Crime Survey*, 2005).

- Accounting scandals both in the United States and internationally have re-ignited the debate over the relative merits of GAAP, which takes a "rules-based" approach to accounting, versus IFRS, which takes a "principles-based" approach. The FASB announced that it intends to introduce more principles-based standards.

- On a lighter note, at one time the Ig Nobel Prize in Economics went to the CEOs of those companies involved in the corporate accounting scandals of that year for "adapting the mathematical concept of imaginary numbers for use in the business world." A parody of the Nobel Prizes, the Ig Nobel Prizes (read Ignoble, as not noble) are given each year in early October for 10 achievements that "first make people laugh, and then make them think." Organized by the scientific humor magazine *Annals of Improbable Research* (*AIR*), they are presented by a group that includes genuine Nobel laureates at a ceremony at Harvard University's Sanders Theater. (See **en.wikipedia.org/wiki/Ig_Nobel_Prize**.)

- Internal controls are a system of checks and balances designed to prevent and detect fraud and errors. While most companies have these systems in place, many have never completely documented them, nor had an independent auditor attest to their effectiveness. Both of these actions are required under SOX.

- Companies find that internal control review is a costly process but badly needed. One study estimates the cost of SOX compliance for U.S. companies at over $35 billion, with audit fees doubling in the first year of compliance. At the same time, examination of internal controls indicates lingering problems in the way companies operate. One study of first compliance with the internal-control testing provisions documented material weaknesses for about 13% of companies reporting in a two-year period (*PricewaterhouseCoopers' Global Economic Crime Survey*, 2005).

- The SOX internal control standards apply only to companies listed on U.S. exchanges. There is continuing debate over whether foreign issuers should have to comply with this extra layer of regulation.

- The accounting and internal control procedures related to cash are essentially the same under both IFRS and this textbook. In addition, the definition used for cash equivalents is the same.

- Most companies report cash and cash equivalents together under IFRS, as shown in this textbook. In addition, IFRS follows the same accounting policies related to the reporting of restricted cash.
- IFRS defines cash and cash equivalents as follows.
  - **Cash** is comprised of cash on hand and demand deposits.
  - **Cash equivalents** are short-term, highly liquid investments that are readily convertible to known amounts of cash and which are subject to an insignificant risk of changes in value.
- Under IFRS, cash and cash equivalents are often shown last in the statement of financial position.

LOOKING TO THE FUTURE

Ethics has become a very important aspect of reporting. Different cultures have different perspectives on bribery and other questionable activities, and consequently penalties for engaging in such activities vary considerably across countries.

High-quality international accounting requires both high-quality accounting standards and high-quality auditing. Similar to the convergence of GAAP and IFRS, there is movement to improve international auditing standards. The International Auditing and Assurance Standards Board (IAASB) functions as an independent standard-setting body. It works to establish high-quality auditing and assurance and quality-control standards throughout the world. Whether the IAASB adopts internal control provisions similar to those in SOX remains to be seen. You can follow developments in the international audit arena at **http://www.ifac.org/iaasb/**.

Under proposed new standards for financial statements, companies would not be allowed to combine cash equivalents with cash.

IFRS PRACTICE

IFRS SELF-TEST QUESTIONS

1. Non-U.S companies that follow IFRS:
   (a) do not normally use the principles of internal control activities described in this textbook.
   (b) often offset cash with accounts payable on the statement of financial position.
   (c) are not required to follow SOX.
   (d) None of the above.
2. Which of the following is the correct reporting under IFRS for cash?
   (a) Cash cannot be combined with cash equivalents.
   (b) Restricted cash funds may be reported as a current or non-current asset depending on the circumstances.
   (c) Restricted cash funds cannot be reported as a current asset.
   (d) Cash on hand is not reported on the statement of financial position as Cash.
3. The Sarbanes-Oxley Act applies to:
   (a) all U.S. companies listed on U.S. exchanges.
   (b) all companies that list shares on any securities exchange in any country.
   (c) all European companies listed on European exchanges.
   (d) Both (a) and (c).
4. High-quality international accounting requires both high-quality accounting standards and:
   (a) a reconsideration of SOX to make it less onerous.
   (b) high-quality auditing standards.
   (c) government intervention to ensure that the public interest is protected.
   (d) the development of new principles of internal control activities.
5. Cash equivalents under IFRS:
   (a) are significantly different than the cash equivalents discussed in the textbook.
   (b) are generally disclosed separately from cash.
   (c) may be required to be reported separately from cash in the future.
   (d) None of the above.

IFRS CONCEPTS AND APPLICATION

IFRS7-1 Some people argue that the internal control requirements of the Sarbanes-Oxley Act (SOX) put U.S. companies at a competitive disadvantage to companies outside the United States. Discuss the competitive implications (both pros and cons) of SOX.

IFRS7-2   State whether each of the following is true or false. For those that are false, explain why.
(a) A proposed new financial accounting standard would not allow cash equivalents to be reported in combination with cash.
(b) Perspectives on bribery and penalties for engaging in bribery are the same across all countries.
(c) Cash equivalents are comprised of cash on hand and demand deposits.
(d) SOX was created by the International Accounting Standards Board.

INTERNATIONAL FINANCIAL REPORTING PROBLEM: *Zetar plc*

IFRS7-3   The financial statements of Zetar plc are presented in Appendix C. The company's complete annual report, including the notes to its financial statements, is available in the Investors section at **www.zetarplc.com**.

Instructions

Use the company's annual report to answer the following questions.
(a) Which committee of the board of directors is responsible for considering management's reports on internal control?
(b) What are the company's key control procedures?
(c) Does the company have an internal audit department?
(d) In what section or sections does Zetar report its bank overdrafts?

Answers to IFRS Self-Test Questions

1. c   **2.** b   **3.** a   **4.** b   **5.** c

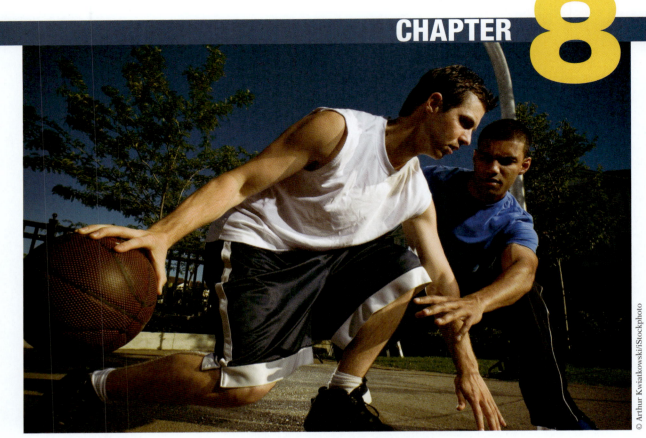

CHAPTER **8**

REPORTING AND ANALYZING RECEIVABLES

© Arthur Kwiatkowski/iStockphoto

LEARNING OBJECTIVES

After studying this chapter, you should be able to:

1 Identify the different types of receivables.

2 Explain how accounts receivable are recognized in the accounts.

3 Describe the methods used to account for bad debts.

4 Compute the interest on notes receivable.

5 Describe the entries to record the disposition of notes receivable.

6 Explain the statement presentation of receivables.

7 Describe the principles of sound accounts receivable management.

8 Identify ratios to analyze a company's receivables.

9 Describe methods to accelerate the receipt of cash from receivables.

What major U.S corporation got its start 38 years ago with a waffle iron? *Hint:* It doesn't sell food. *Another hint:* Swoosh. *Another hint:* "Just do it." That's right, Nike. In 1971, Nike co-founder Bill Bowerman put a piece of rubber into a kitchen waffle iron, and the trademark waffle sole was born. It seems fair to say that at Nike, "They don't make 'em like they used to."

Nike, was co-founded by Bowerman and Phil Knight, a member of Bowerman's University of Oregon track team. Each began in the shoe business independently during the early 1960s. Bowerman got his start by making hand-crafted running shoes for his University of Oregon track team. Knight, after completing graduate school, started a small business importing low-cost, high-quality shoes from Japan. In 1964, the two joined forces, each contributing $500, and formed Blue Ribbon Sports, a partnership that marketed Japanese shoes.

It wasn't until 1971 that the company began manufacturing its own line of shoes. With the new shoes came a new corporate name—Nike—the Greek goddess of victory. It is hard to imagine that the company that now boasts a stable full of world-class athletes as promoters at one time had part-time employees selling shoes out of car trunks at track meets on a cash-and-carry basis.

WHAT'S COOKING?

As the business grew, Nike sold its shoes to sporting good shops and department stores on a credit basis. This necessitated receivables management. Today, with sales of $20.8 billion and accounts receivable of $3.1 billion, managing accounts receivable is vitally important to Nike's success. If it makes a major mistake with its receivables, it will definitely affect the bottom line.

In recent years, Nike has expanded its product line to a diverse range of products, including performance equipment such as soccer balls and golf clubs. While this has increased sales revenue, it has also complicated Nike's receivables management efforts. Now, instead of selling shoes at a limited number of retail outlets, it sells its vast number of products to a diverse array of stores, large and small. For example, Nike golf clubs are sold at local country clubs and golf shops across the country, while soccer equipment can be sold directly to customers through Internet sales. This diversification of its customer list complicates matters because Nike has to approve each new store or customer for credit sales, monitor cash collections, and pursue slow-paying accounts. That's a lot of work. Maybe cash-and-carry wasn't so bad after all.

INSIDE CHAPTER 8 . . .

- **When Investors Ignore Warning Signs**
- **Can Fair Value Be Unfair?**
- **Bad Information Can Lead to Bad Loans**
- **eBay for Receivables**

In this chapter, we discuss some of the decisions related to reporting and analyzing receivables. As indicated in the Feature Story, receivables are a significant asset on the books of Nike. Receivables are important to companies in other industries as well because a larger portion of sales are made on credit in the United States. As a consequence, companies must pay close attention to their receivables balances and manage them carefully. In this chapter, we will look at the accounting and management of receivables at Nike and one of its competitors, Skechers USA.

The organization and content of the chapter are as follows.

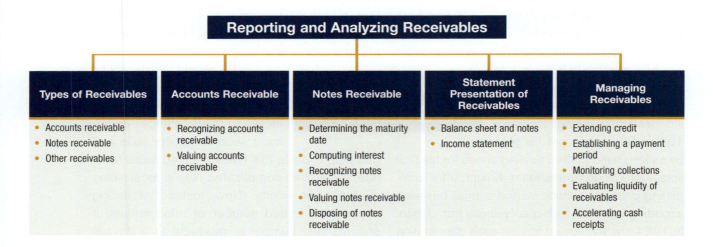

Types of Receivables

LEARNING OBJECTIVE 1

Identify the different types of receivables.

The term **receivables** refers to amounts due from individuals and companies. Receivables are claims that are expected to be collected in cash. The management of receivables is a very important activity for any company that sells goods or services on credit.

Receivables are important because they represent one of a company's most liquid assets. For many companies, receivables are also one of the largest assets. For example, receivables represent 20% of the assets of Nike. Illustration 8-1 lists receivables as a percentage of total assets for five other well-known companies in a recent year.

Illustration 8-1 Receivables as a percentage of assets

Company	Receivables as a Percentage of Total Assets
General Electric	52%
Ford Motor Company	42%
Minnesota Mining and Manufacturing Company (3M)	14%
DuPont Co.	17%
Intel Corporation	5%

The relative significance of a company's receivables as a percentage of its assets depends on various factors: its industry, the time of year, whether it extends long-term financing, and its credit policies. To reflect important differences among receivables, they are frequently classified as (1) accounts receivable, (2) notes receivable, and (3) other receivables.

Accounts receivable are amounts customers owe on account. They result from the sale of goods and services. Companies generally expect to collect accounts receivable within 30 to 60 days. They are usually the most significant type of claim held by a company.

Notes receivable are a written promise (as evidenced by a formal instrument) for amounts to be received. The note normally requires the collection of interest and extends for time periods of 60–90 days or longer. Notes and accounts receivable that result from sales transactions are often called **trade receivables**.

Other receivables include nontrade receivables such as interest receivable, loans to company officers, advances to employees, and income taxes refundable. These do not generally result from the operations of the business. Therefore, they are generally classified and reported as separate items in the balance sheet.

Accounts Receivable

Two accounting issues associated with accounts receivable are:

1. **Recognizing** accounts receivable.
2. **Valuing** accounts receivable.

A third issue, accelerating cash receipts from receivables, is discussed later in the chapter.

> **LEARNING OBJECTIVE 2**
> Explain how accounts receivable are recognized in the accounts.

RECOGNIZING ACCOUNTS RECEIVABLE

Recognizing accounts receivable is relatively straightforward. A service organization records a receivable when it performs service on account. A merchandiser records accounts receivable at the point of sale of merchandise on account. When a merchandiser sells goods, it increases (debits) Accounts Receivable and increases (credits) Sales Revenue.

The seller may offer terms that encourage early payment by providing a discount. Sales returns also reduce receivables. The buyer might find some of the goods unacceptable and choose to return the unwanted goods.

To review, assume that Jordache Co. on July 1, 2014, sells merchandise on account to Polo Company for $1,000, terms 2/10, n/30. On July 5, Polo returns merchandise worth $100 to Jordache Co. On July 11, Jordache receives payment from Polo Company for the balance due. The journal entries to record these transactions on the books of Jordache Co. are as follows. **(Cost of goods sold entries are omitted.)**

July	1	Accounts Receivable—Polo Company	1,000	
		Sales Revenue		1,000
		(To record sales on account)		
July	5	Sales Returns and Allowances	100	
		Accounts Receivable—Polo Company		100
		(To record merchandise returned)		
July	11	Cash ($900 − $18)	882	
		Sales Discounts ($900 × .02)	18	
		Accounts Receivable—Polo Company		900
		(To record collection of accounts		
		receivable)		

Some retailers issue their own credit cards. When you use a retailer's credit card (JCPenney, for example), the retailer charges interest on the balance due if not paid within a specified period (usually 25–30 days).

To illustrate, assume that you use your JCPenney Company credit card to purchase clothing with a sales price of $300 on June 1, 2014. JCPenney will increase (debit) Accounts Receivable for $300 and increase (credit) Sales Revenue for $300 (cost of goods sold entry omitted), as follows.

+300

+300 Rev

Cash Flows
no effect

June	1	Accounts Receivable		300	
		Sales Revenue			300
		(To record sales on account)			

Assuming that you owe $300 at the end of the month and JCPenney charges 1.5% per month on the balance due, the adjusting entry that JCPenney makes to record interest revenue of $4.50 ($300 × 1.5%) on June 30 is as follows.

+4.50

+4.50 Rev

Cash Flows
no effect

June	30	Accounts Receivable		4.50	
		Interest Revenue			4.50
		(To record interest on amount due)			

Interest revenue is often substantial for many retailers.

ANATOMY OF A FRAUD

Tasanee was the accounts receivable clerk for a large non-profit foundation that provided performance and exhibition space for the performing and visual arts. Her responsibilities included activities normally assigned to an accounts receivable clerk, such as recording revenues from various sources that included donations, facility rental fees, ticket revenue, and bar receipts. However, she was also responsible for handling all cash and checks from the time they were received until the time she deposited them, as well as preparing the bank reconciliation. Tasanee took advantage of her situation by falsifying bank deposits and bank reconciliations so that she could steal cash from the bar receipts. Since nobody else logged the donations or matched the donation receipts to pledges prior to Tasanee receiving them, she was able to offset the cash that was stolen against donations that she received but didn't record. Her crime was made easier by the fact that her boss, the company's controller, only did a very superficial review of the bank reconciliation and thus didn't notice that some numbers had been cut out from other documents and taped onto the bank reconciliation.

Total take: $1.5 million

THE MISSING CONTROLS

Segregation of duties. The foundation should not have allowed an accounts receivable clerk, whose job was to record receivables, to also handle cash, record cash, and make deposits, and especially prepare the bank reconciliation.

Independent internal verification. The controller was supposed to perform a thorough review of the bank reconciliation. Because he did not, he was terminated from his position.

Source: Adapted from Wells, *Fraud Casebook* (2007), pp. 183–194.

VALUING ACCOUNTS RECEIVABLE

Once companies record receivables in the accounts, the next question is: How should they report receivables in the financial statements? Companies report accounts receivable on the balance sheet as an asset. Determining the **amount** to report is sometimes difficult because some receivables will become uncollectible.

Although each customer must satisfy the credit requirements of the seller before the credit sale is approved, inevitably some accounts receivable become uncollectible. For example, a corporate customer may not be able to pay because it experienced a sales decline due to an economic downturn. Similarly, individuals may be laid off from their jobs or be faced with unexpected hospital bills. The seller records these losses that result from extending credit as **Bad Debt Expense**. Such losses are a normal and necessary risk of doing business on a credit basis.

Margin Note You will sometimes see *Bad Debt Expense* called *Uncollectible Accounts Expense*.

Recently, when U.S. home prices fell, home foreclosures rose, and the economy in general slowed, lenders experienced huge increases in their bad debt expense. For example, during a recent quarter Wachovia, a large U.S. bank now owned by Wells Fargo, increased bad debt expense from $108 million to $408 million. Similarly, American Express increased its bad debt expense by 70%.

Accounting uses two methods for uncollectible accounts: (1) the direct write-off method, and (2) the allowance method. We explain each of these methods in the following sections.

Direct Write-Off Method for Uncollectible Accounts

Under the **direct write-off method**, when a company determines receivables from a particular company to be uncollectible, it charges the loss to Bad Debt Expense. Assume, for example, that Warden Co. writes off M. E. Doran's $200 balance as uncollectible on December 12. Warden's entry is:

Dec. 12	Bad Debt Expense	200	
	Accounts Receivable—M. E. Doran		200
	(To record write-off of M. E. Doran		
	account)		

A = L + SE

−200 Exp

−200

Cash Flows
no effect

Under this method, bad debt expense will show only **actual losses** from uncollectibles. The company reports accounts receivable at its gross amount without any adjustment for estimated losses for bad debts.

Use of the direct write-off method can reduce the usefulness of both the income statement and balance sheet. Consider the following example. In 2014 Quick Buck Computer Company decided it could increase its revenues by offering computers to college students without requiring any money down, and with no credit-approval process. It went on campuses across the country and sold one million computers at a selling price of $800 each. This promotion increased Quick Buck's revenues and receivables by $800,000,000. It was a huge success: The 2014 balance sheet and income statement looked wonderful. Unfortunately, during 2015, nearly 40% of the college student customers defaulted on their loans. The 2015 income statement and balance sheet looked terrible. Illustration 8-2 shows the effect of these events on the financial statements using the direct write-off method.

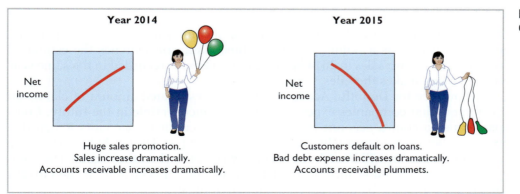

Illustration 8-2 Effects of direct write-off method

Under the direct write-off method, companies often record bad debt expense in a period different from the period in which they recorded the revenue. Thus, no attempt is made to match bad debt expense to sales revenues in the income statement. Nor does the company try to show accounts receivable in the balance sheet at the amount actually expected to be received. Consequently, unless a company expects bad debt losses to be insignificant, **the direct write-off method is not acceptable for financial reporting purposes.**

Allowance Method for Uncollectible Accounts

The **allowance method** of accounting for bad debts involves estimating uncollectible accounts at the end of each period. This provides better matching of expenses with revenues on the income statement. It also ensures that receivables are stated at their cash (net) realizable value on the balance sheet. **Cash (net) realizable value** is the net amount a company expects to receive in cash from receivables. It excludes amounts that the company estimates it will not collect. Estimated uncollectible receivables therefore reduce receivables on the balance sheet through use of the allowance method.

Companies must use the allowance method for financial reporting purposes when bad debts are material in amount. It has three essential features:

1. Companies **estimate** uncollectible accounts receivable and **match them against revenues** in the same accounting period in which the revenues are recorded.

2. Companies record estimated uncollectibles as an increase (a debit) to Bad Debt Expense and an increase (a credit) to Allowance for Doubtful Accounts through an adjusting entry at the end of each period. Allowance for Doubtful Accounts is a contra account to Accounts Receivable.

3. Companies debit actual uncollectibles to Allowance for Doubtful Accounts and credit them to Accounts Receivable at the time the specific account is written off as uncollectible.

RECORDING ESTIMATED UNCOLLECTIBLES. To illustrate the allowance method, assume that Hampson Furniture has credit sales of $1,200,000 in 2014, of which $200,000 remains uncollected at December 31. The credit manager estimates that $12,000 of these sales will prove uncollectible. The adjusting entry to record the estimated uncollectibles increases (debits) Bad Debt Expense and increases (credits) Allowance for Doubtful Accounts, as follows.

A = L + SE
                    −12,000 Exp
−12,000
Cash Flows
no effect

Dec. 31	Bad Debt Expense	12,000	
	Allowance for Doubtful Accounts		12,000
	(To record estimate of uncollectible accounts)		

Companies report Bad Debt Expense in the income statement as an operating expense (usually as a selling expense). Thus, Hampson matches the estimated uncollectibles with sales in 2014 because the expense is recorded in the same year the company makes the sales.

Allowance for Doubtful Accounts shows the estimated amount of claims on customers that companies expect will become uncollectible in the future. Companies use a contra account instead of a direct credit to Accounts Receivable because they do not know which customers will not pay. The credit balance in the allowance account will absorb the specific write-offs when they occur. The company deducts the allowance account from Accounts Receivable in the current assets section of the balance sheet, as shown in Illustration 8-3.

Illustration 8-3 Presentation of allowance for doubtful accounts

HAMPSON FURNITURE
Balance Sheet (partial)

Current assets		
Cash		$ 14,800
Accounts receivable	**$200,000**	
Less: Allowance for doubtful accounts	**12,000**	188,000
Inventory		310,000
Supplies		25,000
Total current assets		$537,800

The amount of $188,000 in Illustration 8-3 represents the expected **cash realizable value** of the accounts receivable at the statement date. **Companies do not close Allowance for Doubtful Accounts at the end of the fiscal year.**

RECORDING THE WRITE-OFF OF AN UNCOLLECTIBLE ACCOUNT. Various methods are used to collect past-due accounts. When a company exhausts all means of collecting a past-due account and collection appears unlikely, the company writes off the account. In the credit card industry, it is standard practice to write off accounts that are 210 days past due. To prevent premature or unauthorized write-offs, authorized management personnel should formally approve each write-off. **To maintain segregation of duties, the employee authorized to write off accounts should not have daily responsibilities related to cash or receivables.**

To illustrate a receivables write-off, assume that the vice president of finance of Hampson Furniture on March 1, 2015, authorizes a write-off of the $500 balance owed by R. A. Ware. The entry to record the write-off is:

Mar. 1	Allowance for Doubtful Accounts		500	
	Accounts Receivable—R. A. Ware			500
	(Write-off of R. A. Ware account)			

A = L + SE
+500
−500

Cash Flows
no effect

The company does not increase Bad Debt Expense when the write-off occurs. **Under the allowance method, a company debits every bad debt write-off to the allowance account and not to Bad Debt Expense.** A debit to Bad Debt Expense would be incorrect because the company has already recognized the expense when it made the adjusting entry for estimated bad debts. Instead, the entry to record the write-off of an uncollectible account reduces both Accounts Receivable and Allowance for Doubtful Accounts. After posting, the general ledger accounts appear as shown in Illustration 8-4.

Illustration 8-4 General ledger balances after write-off

Accounts Receivable				Allowance for Doubtful Accounts			
Jan. 1 Bal. 200,000		Mar. 1	**500**	Mar. 1	**500**	Jan. 1	Bal. 12,000
Mar. 1 Bal. 199,500						Mar. 1	Bal. 11,500

A write-off affects only balance sheet accounts. Cash realizable value in the balance sheet, therefore, remains the same before and after the write-off, as shown in Illustration 8-5.

Illustration 8-5 Cash realizable value comparison

	Before Write-Off	**After Write-Off**
Accounts receivable	$ 200,000	$ 199,500
Allowance for doubtful accounts	12,000	11,500
Cash realizable value	**$188,000**	**$188,000**

RECOVERY OF AN UNCOLLECTIBLE ACCOUNT. Occasionally, a company collects from a customer after the account has been written off as uncollectible. The company must make two entries to record the recovery of a bad debt: (1) It reverses the entry made in writing off the account. This reinstates the customer's account. (2) It journalizes the collection in the usual manner.

To illustrate, assume that on July 1, R. A. Ware pays the $500 amount that Hampson Furniture had written off on March 1. Hampson makes these entries:

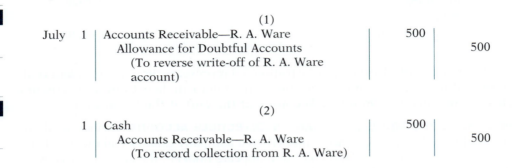

	(1)		
July 1	Accounts Receivable—R. A. Ware	500	
	Allowance for Doubtful Accounts		500
	(To reverse write-off of R. A. Ware account)		
	(2)		
1	Cash	500	
	Accounts Receivable—R. A. Ware		500
	(To record collection from R. A. Ware)		

Note that the recovery of a bad debt, like the write-off of a bad debt, affects only balance sheet accounts. The net effect of the two entries is an increase in Cash and an increase in Allowance for Doubtful Accounts for $500. Accounts Receivable and Allowance for Doubtful Accounts both increase in entry (1) for two reasons. First, the company made an error in judgment when it wrote off the account receivable. Second, R. A. Ware did pay, and therefore the Accounts Receivable account should show this reinstatement and collection for possible future credit purposes.

ESTIMATING THE ALLOWANCE. For Hampson Furniture in Illustration 8-3, the amount of the expected uncollectibles was given. However, in "real life," companies must estimate the amount of expected uncollectible accounts if they use the allowance method. Illustration 8-6 shows an excerpt from the notes to Nike's financial statements discussing its use of the allowance method.

Illustration 8-6 Nike's allowance method disclosure

> **NIKE, INC.**
> Notes to the Financial Statements
>
> ***Allowance for Uncollectible Accounts Receivable***
>
> We make ongoing estimates relating to the ability to collect our accounts receivable and maintain an allowance for estimated losses resulting from the inability of our customers to make required payments. In determining the amount of the allowance, we consider our historical level of credit losses and make judgments about the creditworthiness of significant customers based on ongoing credit evaluations. Since we cannot predict future changes in the financial stability of our customers, actual future losses from uncollectible accounts may differ from our estimates.

Frequently, companies estimate the allowance as a percentage of the outstanding receivables. Under the **percentage-of-receivables basis**, management establishes a percentage relationship between the amount of receivables and expected losses from uncollectible accounts. For example, suppose Steffen Company has an ending balance in Accounts Receivable of $200,000, and an unadjusted credit balance in Allowance for Doubtful Accounts of $1,500. It estimates that 5% of its accounts receivable will eventually be uncollectible. It should report a balance in Allowance for Doubtful Accounts of $10,000 (.05 × $200,000). To increase the balance in Allowance for Doubtful Accounts from $1,500 to $10,000, the company debits (increases) Bad Debt Expense and credits (increases) Allowance for Doubtful Accounts by $8,500 ($10,000 − $1,500).

Allowance for Doubtful Accounts

	Dec. 31 Unadj. Bal. 1,500
	Dec. 31 Adj. **8,500**
	Dec. 31 Bal. 10,000

To more accurately estimate the ending balance in the allowance account, a company often prepares a schedule, called **aging the accounts receivable**. This schedule classifies customer balances by the length of time they have been unpaid.

After the company arranges the accounts by age, it determines the expected bad debt losses by applying percentages, based on past experience, to the totals of each category. The longer a receivable is past due, the less likely it is to be collected. As a result, the estimated percentage of uncollectible debts increases as the number of days past due increases. Illustration 8-7 shows an aging schedule for Dart Company. Note the increasing uncollectible percentages from 2% to 40%.

Customer	Total	Not Yet Due	Number of Days Past Due			
			1–30	31–60	61–90	Over 90
T. E. Adert	$ 600		$ 300		$ 200	$ 100
R. C. Bortz	300	$ 300				
B. A. Carl	450		200	$ 250		
O. L. Diker	700	500			200	
T. O. Ebbet	600			300		300
Others	36,950	26,200	5,200	2,450	1,600	1,500
	$39,600	$27,000	$5,700	$3,000	$2,000	$1,900
Estimated percentage uncollectible		2%	4%	10%	20%	40%
Total estimated uncollectible accounts	**$ 2,228**	**$ 540**	**$ 228**	**$ 300**	**$ 400**	**$ 760**

Illustration 8-7 Aging schedule

Total estimated uncollectible accounts for Dart Company ($2,228) represent the existing customer claims expected to become uncollectible in the future. Thus, this amount represents the **required balance** in Allowance for Doubtful Accounts at the balance sheet date. Accordingly, **the amount of bad debt expense that should be recorded in the adjusting entry is the difference between the required balance and the existing balance in the allowance account**. The existing, unadjusted balance in Allowance for Doubtful Accounts is the net result of the beginning balance (a normal credit balance) less the write-offs of specific accounts during the year (debits to the allowance account).

For example, if the unadjusted trial balance shows Allowance for Doubtful Accounts with a credit balance of $528, then an adjusting entry for $1,700 ($2,228 − $528) is necessary:

Dec. 31	Bad Debt Expense	1,700	
	Allowance for Doubtful Accounts		1,700
	(To adjust allowance account to total estimated uncollectibles)		

A = L + SE
−1,700 Exp
−1,700
Cash Flows
no effect

After Dart posts the adjusting entry, its accounts appear as shown in Illustration 8-8.

Bad Debt Expense		**Allowance for Doubtful Accounts**	
Dec. 31 Adj. **1,700**			Dec. 31 Unadj.
			Bal. 528
			Dec. 31 Adj. **1,700**
			Dec. 31 Bal. 2,228

Illustration 8-8 Bad debt accounts after posting

An important aspect of accounts receivable management is simply maintaining a close watch on the accounts. Studies have shown that accounts more than

60 days past due lose approximately 50% of their value if no payment activity occurs within the next 30 days. For each additional 30 days that pass, the collectible value halves once again.

Occasionally, the allowance account will have a **debit balance** prior to adjustment. This occurs because the debits to the allowance account from write-offs during the year **exceeded** the beginning balance in the account which was based on previous estimates for bad debts. In such a case, the company **adds the debit balance to the required balance** when it makes the adjusting entry. Thus, if there was a $500 **debit** balance in the allowance account before adjustment, the adjusting entry would be for $2,728 ($2,228 + $500) to arrive at a credit balance of $2,228 (see T-account in margin).

The percentage-of-receivables basis provides an estimate of the cash realizable value of the receivables. It also provides a reasonable matching of expense to revenue.

Allowance for Doubtful Accounts

Dec. 31 Unadj. Bal. 500	
	Dec. 31 Adj. 2,728
	Dec. 31 Bal. 2,228

DECISION TOOLKIT

DECISION CHECKPOINTS	INFO NEEDED FOR DECISION	TOOL TO USE FOR DECISION	HOW TO EVALUATE RESULTS
Is the amount of past due accounts increasing? Which accounts require management's attention?	List of outstanding receivables and their due dates	Prepare an aging schedule showing the receivables in various stages: outstanding 0–30 days, 31–60 days, 61–90 days, and over 90 days.	Accounts in the older categories require follow-up: letters, phone calls, and possible renegotiation of terms.

The following note regarding accounts receivable comes from the annual report of the shoe company Skechers USA.

Illustration 8-9 Skechers USA's note disclosure of accounts receivable

Real World	SKECHERS USA
	Notes to the Financial Statements

Gross trade accounts receivable balance were $196.4 million and $285.8 million and the allowance for bad debts, returns, sales allowances and customer chargebacks was $20.4 million and $19.7 million, at December 31, 2011 and 2010, respectively. The Company's credit losses due to write-offs for the years ended December 31, 2011, 2010 and 2009 were $7.0 million, $4.8 million and $1.2 million, respectively.

Ethics Insight

When Investors Ignore Warning Signs

At one time, Nortel Networks announced that half of its previous year's earnings were "fake." Should investors have seen this coming? Well, there were issues in its annual report that should have caused investors to ask questions. The company had cut its allowance for doubtful accounts on all receivables from $1,253 million to $544 million even though its total balance of receivables remained relatively unchanged.

This reduction in bad debt expense was responsible for a very large part of the company's earnings that year. At the time, it was unclear whether Nortel might have set the reserves too high originally and needed to reduce them, or whether it slashed the allowance to artificially boost earnings. But one thing is certain—when a company makes an accounting change of this magnitude, investors need to ask questions.

Source: Jonathan Weil, "Outside Audit: At Nortel, Warning Signs Existed Months Ago," *Wall Street Journal* (May 18, 2004), p. C3.

? When would it be appropriate for a company to lower its allowance for doubtful accounts as a percentage of its receivables? (Answers in *Broadening Your Perspective*.)

Notes Receivable

Companies also may grant credit in exchange for a formal credit instrument known as a promissory note. A **promissory note** is a written promise to pay a specified amount of money on demand or at a definite time. Promissory notes may be used (1) when individuals and companies lend or borrow money, (2) when the amount of the transaction and the credit period exceed normal limits, and (3) in settlement of accounts receivable.

In a promissory note, the party making the promise to pay is called the **maker**. The party to whom payment is to be made is called the **payee**. The promissory note may specifically identify the payee by name or may designate the payee simply as the bearer of the note.

In the note shown in Illustration 8-10, Brent Company is the maker, and Wilma Company is the payee. To Wilma Company, the promissory note is a note receivable. To Brent Company, the note is a note payable.

LEARNING OBJECTIVE   **4**

Compute the interest on notes receivable.

Illustration 8-10
Promissory note

$1,000 ← Amount

Chicago, Illinois   May 1, 2014 ← Date of Note

2 months ← Date Due   after date   We ← ... promise to pay

to the order of ___ Wilma Company ← Payee

One Thousand and no/100 ← Amount — — — — — — — — — — dollars

for value received with annual interest at __ 8% ← Interest Rate

Maker → Brent Company

Treasurer ___ Phylis Miller

Notes receivable give the holder a stronger legal claim to assets than do accounts receivable. Like accounts receivable, notes receivable can be readily sold to another party. Promissory notes are negotiable instruments (as are checks), which means that, when sold, the seller can transfer them to another party by endorsement.

Companies frequently accept notes receivable from customers who need to extend the payment of an outstanding account receivable. Companies also often require notes from high-risk customers. In some industries (e.g., the pleasure and sport boat industry), all credit sales are supported by notes. The majority of notes, however, originate from lending transactions.

There are five issues in accounting for notes receivable:

1. **Determining** the maturity date.
2. **Computing** interest.
3. **Recognizing** notes receivable.
4. **Valuing** notes receivable.
5. **Disposing** of notes receivable.

We look at each of these issues.

DETERMINING THE MATURITY DATE

The maturity date of a promissory note may be stated in one of three ways: (1) on demand, (2) on a stated date, and (3) at the end of a stated period of time. When it is stated to be at the end of a period of time, the parties to the note will need to determine the maturity date.

When the life of a note is expressed in terms of months, you find the date when it matures by counting the months from the date of issue. For example, the maturity date of a three-month note dated May 1 is August 1. A note drawn on the last day of a month matures on the last day of a subsequent month. That is, a July 31 note due in two months matures on September 30.

When the due date is stated in terms of days, you need to count the exact number of days to determine the maturity date. In counting, **omit the date the note is issued but include the due date**.

COMPUTING INTEREST

Illustration 8-11 gives the basic formula for computing interest on an interest-bearing note.

Illustration 8-11 Formula for computing interest

$$\text{Face Value of Note} \times \text{Annual Interest Rate} \times \text{Time in Terms of One Year} = \text{Interest}$$

The interest rate specified on the note is an **annual** rate of interest. The time factor in the computation expresses the fraction of a year that the note is outstanding. When the maturity date is stated in days, the time factor is frequently the number of days divided by 360. **When counting days, omit the date the note is issued but include the due date.** When the due date is stated in months, the time factor is the number of months divided by 12. Illustration 8-12 shows computation of interest for various time periods.

Illustration 8-12
Computation of interest

Terms of Note		Interest Computation				
		Face	× Rate ×	Time	=	Interest
$ 730, 12%, 120 days		$ 730 ×	12% ×	**120/360**	=	$ 29.20
$1,000, 9%, 6 months		$1,000 ×	9% ×	**6/12**	=	$ 45.00
$2,000, 6%, 1 year		$2,000 ×	6% ×	**1/1**	=	$120.00

There are different ways to calculate interest. For example, the computation in Illustration 8-12 assumes 360 days for the year. Most financial institutions use 365 days to compute interest. *For homework problems, assume 360 days to simplify computations.*

RECOGNIZING NOTES RECEIVABLE

To illustrate the basic entry for notes receivable, we will use Brent Company's $1,000, two-month, 8% promissory note dated May 1. Assuming that Brent Company wrote the note to settle an open account, Wilma Company makes the following entry for the receipt of the note.

A	=	L	+	SE
+1,000				
−1,000				

Cash Flows
no effect

May 1	Notes Receivable		1,000	
	Accounts Receivable—Brent Company			1,000
	(To record acceptance of Brent Company note)			

The company records the note receivable at its **face value**, the value shown on the face of the note. No interest revenue is reported when the company accepts the note because the revenue recognition principle does not recognize revenue until the performance obligation is satisfied. Interest is earned (accrued) as time passes.

If a company issues cash in exchange for a note, the entry is a debit to Notes Receivable and a credit to Cash in the amount of the loan.

VALUING NOTES RECEIVABLE

Like accounts receivable, companies report short-term notes receivable at their **cash (net) realizable value**. The notes receivable allowance account is Allowance for Doubtful Accounts. Valuing short-term notes receivable is the same as valuing accounts receivable. The computations and estimations involved in determining cash realizable value and in recording the proper amount of bad debt expense and related allowance are similar.

Long-term notes receivable, however, pose additional estimation problems. As an example, we need only look at the problems large U.S. banks sometimes have in collecting their receivables. Loans to less-developed countries are particularly worrisome. Developing countries need loans for development but often find repayment difficult. In some cases, developed nations have intervened to provide financial assistance to the financially troubled borrowers so as to minimize the political and economic turmoil to the borrower and to ensure the survival of the lender.

International Insight
Can Fair Value Be Unfair?

The FASB and the International Accounting Standards Board (IASB) are considering proposals for how to account for financial instruments. The FASB has proposed that loans and receivables be accounted for at their fair value (the amount they could currently be sold for), as are most investments. The FASB believes that this would provide a more accurate view of a company's financial position. It might be especially useful as an early warning when a bank is in trouble because of poor-quality loans. But, banks argue that fair values are difficult to estimate accurately. They are also concerned that volatile fair values could cause large swings in a bank's reported net income.

Source: David Reilly, "Banks Face a Mark-to-Market Challenge," *Wall Street Journal Online* (March 15, 2010).

? What are the arguments in favor of and against fair value accounting for loans and receivables? (Answers in *Broadening Your Perspective*.)

DISPOSING OF NOTES RECEIVABLE

Notes may be held to their maturity date, at which time the face value plus accrued interest is due. In some situations, the maker of the note defaults, and the payee must make an appropriate adjustment. In other situations, similar to accounts receivable, the holder of the note speeds up the conversion to cash by selling the receivables (as described later in this chapter).

LEARNING OBJECTIVE	5

Describe the entries to record the disposition of notes receivable.

Honor of Notes Receivable

A note is **honored** when its maker pays in full at its maturity date. For each interest-bearing note, the **amount due at maturity** is the face value of the note plus interest for the length of time specified on the note.

To illustrate, assume that Wolder Co. lends Higley Inc. $10,000 on June 1, accepting a five-month, 9% interest note. In this situation, interest is $375 ($10,000 × 9% × $\frac{5}{12}$). The amount due, the **maturity value**, is $10,375 ($10,000 + $375). To obtain payment, Wolder (the payee) must present the note either to Higley Inc. (the maker) or to the maker's agent, such as a bank. If Wolder presents the note to Higley Inc. on November 1, the maturity date, Wolder's entry to record the collection is:

A = L + SE
+10,375
−10,000
            +375 Rev

Cash Flows
+10,375

Nov. 1	Cash	10,375	
	Notes Receivable		10,000
	Interest Revenue ($10,000 × 9% × $\frac{5}{12}$)		375
	(To record collection of Higley Inc. note and interest)		

Accrual of Interest Receivable

Suppose instead that Wolder Co. prepares financial statements as of September 30. The timeline in Illustration 8-13 presents this situation.

Illustration 8-13 Timeline of interest earned

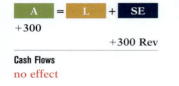

June I   4 months   **Sept. 30**   I month   **Nov. I**

Earns $300   Earns $75

Receives $375

To reflect interest earned but not yet received, Wolder must accrue interest on September 30. In this case, the adjusting entry by Wolder is for four months of interest, or $300, as shown below.

A = L + SE
+300
            +300 Rev

Cash Flows
no effect

Sept. 30	Interest Receivable ($10,000 × 9% × $\frac{4}{12}$)	300	
	Interest Revenue		300
	(To accrue 4 months' interest on Higley note)		

At the note's maturity on November 1, Wolder receives $10,375. This amount represents repayment of the $10,000 note as well as five months of interest, or $375, as shown in the following paragraph. The $375 is comprised of the $300 Interest Receivable accrued on September 30 plus $75 earned during October. Wolder's entry to record the honoring of the Higley note on November 1 is:

A = L + SE
+10,375
−10,000
−300
            +75 Rev

Cash Flows
+10,375

Nov. 1	Cash [$10,000 + ($10,000 × 9% × $\frac{5}{12}$)]	10,375	
	Notes Receivable		10,000
	Interest Receivable		300
	Interest Revenue ($10,000 × 9% × $\frac{1}{12}$)		75
	(To record collection of Higley Inc. note and interest)		

In this case, Wolder credits Interest Receivable because the receivable was established in the adjusting entry on September 30.

Dishonor of Notes Receivable

A **dishonored (defaulted) note** is a note that is not paid in full at maturity. A dishonored note receivable is no longer negotiable. However, the payee still has a claim against the maker of the note for both the note and the interest. If the lender expects that it eventually will be able to collect, the two parties negotiate new terms to make it easier for the borrower to repay the debt. If there is no hope of collection, the payee should write off the face value of the note.

Financial Statement Presentation of Receivables

Companies should identify in the balance sheet or in the notes to the financial statements each of the major types of receivables. Short-term receivables are reported in the current assets section of the balance sheet, below short-term investments. Short-term investments appear before short-term receivables because these investments are nearer to cash. Companies report both the gross amount of receivables and the allowance for doubtful accounts.

LEARNING OBJECTIVE 6
Explain the statement presentation of receivables.

Receivables represent 53% of the total assets of heavy equipment manufacturer Deere & Company. Illustration 8-14 shows a presentation of receivables for Deere & Company from its balance sheet and notes in a recent year.

DEERE & COMPANY Balance Sheet (partial) (in millions)		
Receivables		
Receivables from unconsolidated subsidiaries	$	38
Trade accounts and notes receivable		2,694
Financing receivables		15,469
Restricted financing receivables		3,108
Other receivables		864
Total receivables		22,173
Less: Allowance for doubtful trade receivables		290
Net receivables		$21,883

(Real World)

Illustration 8-14 Balance sheet presentation of receivables

In the income statement, companies report bad debt expense under "Selling expenses" in the operating expenses section. They show interest revenue under "Other revenues and gains" in the nonoperating section of the income statement.

If a company has significant risk of uncollectible accounts or other problems with its receivables, it is required to discuss this possibility in the notes to the financial statements.

Managing Receivables

Managing accounts receivable involves five steps:

LEARNING OBJECTIVE 7
Describe the principles of sound accounts receivable management.

1. Determine to whom to extend credit.
2. Establish a payment period.
3. Monitor collections.
4. Evaluate the liquidity of receivables.
5. Accelerate cash receipts from receivables when necessary.

EXTENDING CREDIT

Every entrepreneur struggles with financing issues. For example, the very first order that Apple's founders received was 50 circuit boards to a computer hobby shop. To produce the $25,000 order, Steve Jobs and Steve Wozniak needed $15,000 of parts. To purchase the parts, they borrowed $5,000 from friends but then were turned down when they applied for a bank loan for the $10,000 balance. They approached two parts suppliers in an effort to negotiate a purchase on credit, but both suppliers said no. Finally, a third supplier agreed to sell them the parts on 30-day credit after he called the computer hobby shop to confirm that it had, in fact, placed a $25,000 order to purchase goods.

A critical part of managing receivables is determining who should be extended credit and who should not. Many companies increase sales by being generous with their credit policy. However, they sometimes extend credit to risky customers who do not pay. But if your credit policy is too tight, you will lose sales. If it is too loose, you may sell to "deadbeats" who will pay either very late or not at all. One CEO noted that prior to getting his credit and collection department in order, his salespeople had 300 square feet of office space **per person**, while the people in credit and collections had six people crammed into a single 300-square-foot space. Although this focus on sales boosted sales revenue, it had very expensive consequences in bad debt expense.

Companies can take certain steps to help minimize losses due to bad debts when they decide to relax credit standards for new customers. They might require risky customers to provide letters of credit or bank guarantees. Then, if the customer does not pay, the bank that provided the guarantee will do so. Particularly risky customers might be required to pay cash on delivery. For example, at one time retailer Linens'n Things, Inc. reported that its largest suppliers were requiring cash payment before delivery. The suppliers had cut off shipments because the company had been slow in paying. Kmart's suppliers also required it to pay cash in advance when it was financially troubled.

In addition, companies should ask potential customers for references from banks and suppliers, to determine their payment history. It is important to check references of potential new customers as well as periodically to check the financial health of continuing customers. Many resources are available for investigating customers. For example, *The Dun & Bradstreet Reference Book of American Business* (**www.dnb.com**) lists millions of companies and provides credit ratings for many of them.

Accounting Across the Organization

Bad Information Can Lead to Bad Loans

Many factors contributed to the recent credit crisis. One significant factor that resulted in many bad loans was a failure by lenders to investigate loan customers sufficiently. For example, Countrywide Financial Corporation wrote many loans under its "Fast and Easy" loan program. That program allowed borrowers to provide little or no documentation for their income or their assets. Other lenders had similar programs, which earned the nickname "liars' loans." One study found that in these situations, 60% of applicants overstated their incomes by more than 50% in order to qualify for a loan. Critics of the banking industry say that because loan officers were compensated for loan volume, and because banks were selling the loans to investors rather than holding them, the lenders had little incentive to investigate the borrowers' creditworthiness.

Sources: Glenn R. Simpson and James R. Hagerty, "Countrywide Loss Focuses Attention on Underwriting," *Wall Street Journal* (April 30, 2008), p. B1; and Michael Corkery, "Fraud Seen as Driver in Wave of Foreclosures," *Wall Street Journal* (December 21, 2007), p. A1.

 What steps should the banks have taken to ensure the accuracy of financial information provided on loan applications? (Answers in *Broadening Your Perspective*.)

ESTABLISHING A PAYMENT PERIOD

Companies that extend credit should determine a required payment period and communicate that policy to their customers. It is important that the payment period is consistent with that of competitors. For example, if you require payment within 15 days but your competitors allow payment within 45 days, you may lose sales to your competitors. To match your competitors' generous terms yet still encourage prompt payment of accounts, you might allow up to 45 days to pay but offer a sales discount for people paying within 15 days.

MONITORING COLLECTIONS

We discussed preparation of the accounts receivable aging schedule earlier in the chapter. Companies should prepare an accounts receivable aging schedule at least monthly. In addition to estimating the allowance for doubtful accounts, the aging schedule has other uses. It helps managers estimate the timing of future cash inflows, which is very important to the treasurer's efforts to prepare a cash budget. It provides information about the overall collection experience of the company and identifies problem accounts. For example, management would compute and compare the percentage of receivables that are over 90 days past due. Illustration 8-15 contains an excerpt from the notes to Skechers' financial statements discussing how it monitors receivables.

Illustration 8-15 Note on monitoring Skechers' receivables

SKECHERS USA
Notes to the Financial Statements

To minimize the likelihood of uncollectibility, customers' credit-worthiness is reviewed periodically based on external credit reporting services, financial statements issued by the customer and our experience with the account, and it is adjusted accordingly. When a customer's account becomes significantly past due, we generally place a hold on the account and discontinue further shipments to that customer, minimizing further risk of loss.

The aging schedule identifies problem accounts that the company needs to pursue with phone calls, letters, and occasionally legal action. Sometimes, special arrangements must be made with problem accounts. For example, it was reported that Intel Corporation (a major manufacturer of computer chips) required that Packard Bell (at one time one of the largest U.S. sellers of personal computers) exchange its past-due account receivable for an interest-bearing note receivable. This caused concern within the investment community. The move suggested that Packard Bell was in trouble, which worried Intel investors concerned about Intel's accounts receivable.

🧰 DECISION TOOLKIT

DECISION CHECKPOINTS	INFO NEEDED FOR DECISION	TOOL TO USE FOR DECISION	HOW TO EVALUATE RESULTS
Is the company's credit risk increasing?	Customer account balances and due dates	Accounts receivable aging schedule	Compute and compare the percentage of receivables over 90 days old.

If a company has significant concentrations of credit risk, it must discuss this risk in the notes to its financial statements. A **concentration of credit risk** is a threat of nonpayment from a single large customer or class of customers that could adversely affect the financial health of the company. Illustration 8-16 shows an excerpt from the credit risk note from the 2011 annual report of Skechers.

Skechers reports that its five largest customers account for 17.8% of its net sales, and two of its customers account for 22.5% of its receivables.

Illustration 8-16 Excerpt from Skechers' note on concentration of credit risk

SKECHERS USA
Notes to the Financial Statements

We Depend Upon a Relatively Small Group of Customers for a Large Portion of Our Sales.
During 2011, 2010 and 2009, our net sales to our five largest customers accounted for approximately 17.8%, 24.9% and 25.1% of total net sales, respectively. No customer accounted for more than 10.0% of our net sales during 2011, 2010 and 2009. One customer accounted for 12.5% and another accounted for 10.0% of net trade receivables at December 31, 2011. No customer accounted for more than 10% of net trade receivables at December 31, 2010. If we lose a major customer, experience a significant decrease in sales to a major customer or are unable to collect the accounts receivable of a major customer, our business could be harmed.

This note to Skechers' financial statements indicates it has a relatively high concentration of credit risk. A default by any of these large customers could have a significant negative impact on its financial performance.

DECISION TOOLKIT

DECISION CHECKPOINTS	INFO NEEDED FOR DECISION	TOOL TO USE FOR DECISION	HOW TO EVALUATE RESULTS
Does the company have significant concentrations of credit risk?	Note to the financial statements on concentrations of credit risk	If risky credit customers are identified, the financial health of those customers should be evaluated to gain an independent assessment of the potential for a material credit loss.	If a material loss appears likely, the potential negative impact of that loss on the company should be carefully evaluated, along with the adequacy of the allowance for doubtful accounts.

EVALUATING LIQUIDITY OF RECEIVABLES

LEARNING OBJECTIVE 8
Identify ratios to analyze a company's receivables.

Investors and managers keep a watchful eye on the relationship among sales, accounts receivable, and cash collections. If sales increase, then accounts receivable are also expected to increase. But a disproportionate increase in accounts receivable might signal trouble. Perhaps the company increased its sales by loosening its credit policy, and these receivables may be difficult or impossible to collect. Such receivables are considered less liquid. Recall that liquidity is measured by how quickly certain assets can be converted to cash.

The ratio that analysts use to assess the liquidity of receivables is the **accounts receivable turnover**, computed by dividing net credit sales (net sales less cash sales) by the average net accounts receivable during the year. This ratio measures the number of times, on average, a company collects receivables during the period. Unless seasonal factors are significant, **average** accounts receivable outstanding can be computed from the beginning and ending balances of the net receivables.[1]

A popular variant of the accounts receivable turnover is the **average collection period**, which measures the average amount of time that a receivable is outstanding. This is done by dividing the accounts receivable turnover into 365 days. Companies use the average collection period to assess the effectiveness of a company's credit and collection policies. The average collection period should not greatly exceed the credit term period (i.e., the time allowed for payment).

---

[1]If seasonal factors are significant, determine the average accounts receivable balance by using monthly or quarterly amounts.

The following data (in millions) are available for Nike.

	For the year ended March 31,	
	2011	**2010**
Sales	$20,862	$19,014
Accounts receivable (net)	3,138	2,650

Illustration 8-17 shows the accounts receivable turnover and average collection period for Nike and Skechers, along with comparative industry data. These calculations assume that all sales were credit sales.

$$\text{Accounts Receivable Turnover} = \frac{\text{Net Credit Sales}}{\text{Average Net Accounts Receivable}}$$

$$\text{Average Collection Period} = \frac{365}{\text{Accounts Receivable Turnover}}$$

Ratio	Nike ($ in millions)		Skechers USA	Industry Average
	2011	2010	2011	2010
Accounts receivable turnover	$\frac{\$20,862}{(\$3,138 + \$2,650)/2} = 7.2$ times	6.9 times	7.3 times	12.2 times
Average collection period	$\frac{365 \text{ days}}{7.2} = 50.7$ days	52.9 days	50.0 days	29.9 days

Illustration 8-17 Accounts receivable turnover and average collection period

Nike's accounts receivable turnover was 7.2 times in 2011, with a corresponding average collection period of 50.7 days. This was slightly faster than its 2010 collection period. It was slower than the industry average collection period of 29.9 days and slightly higher than Skechers, which was 50 days. What this means is that Nike turned its receivables into cash more slowly than most other companies in its industry. Therefore, it was less likely to pay its current obligations than a company with a quicker accounts receivable turnover (all else equal) and is more likely to need outside financing to meet cash shortfalls.

DECISION TOOLKIT

DECISION CHECKPOINTS	INFO NEEDED FOR DECISION	TOOL TO USE FOR DECISION	HOW TO EVALUATE RESULTS
Are collections being made in a timely fashion?	Net credit sales and average net accounts receivable balance	$\text{Accounts receivable turnover} = \frac{\text{Net credit sales}}{\text{Average net accounts receivable}}$ $\text{Average collection period} = \frac{365 \text{ days}}{\text{Accounts receivable turnover}}$	Average collection period should be consistent with corporate credit policy. An increase may suggest a decline in financial health of customers.

In some cases, accounts receivable turnover may be misleading. Some large retail chains that issue their own credit cards encourage customers to use these cards for purchases. If customers pay slowly, the stores earn a healthy return on the outstanding receivables in the form of interest at rates of 18% to 22%. On the other hand, companies that sell (factor) their receivables on a consistent basis will have a faster turnover than those that do not. Thus, to interpret accounts receivable turnover, you must know how a company manages its receivables. In general, the faster the turnover, the greater the reliability of the current ratio for assessing liquidity.

ACCELERATING CASH RECEIPTS

LEARNING OBJECTIVE 9

Describe methods to accelerate the receipt of cash from receivables.

In the normal course of events, companies collect accounts receivable in cash and remove them from the books. However, as credit sales and receivables have grown in size and significance, the "normal course of events" has changed. Two common expressions apply to the collection of receivables: (1) "Time is money"—that is, waiting for the normal collection process costs money. (2) "A bird in the hand is worth two in the bush"—that is, getting the cash now is better than getting it later or not at all. Therefore, in order to accelerate the receipt of cash from receivables, companies frequently sell their receivables to another company for cash, thereby shortening the cash-to-cash operating cycle.

There are three reasons for the sale of receivables. The first is their **size**. In recent years, for competitive reasons, sellers (retailers, wholesalers, and manufacturers) often have provided financing to purchasers of their goods. For example, many major companies in the automobile, truck, industrial and farm equipment, computer, and appliance industries have created companies that accept responsibility for accounts receivable financing. Caterpillar has Caterpillar Financial Services, General Electric has GE Capital, and Ford has Ford Motor Credit Corp. (FMCC). These companies are referred to as **captive finance companies** because they are owned by the company selling the product. The purpose of captive finance companies is to encourage the sale of the company's products by assuring financing to buyers. However, the parent companies involved do not necessarily want to hold large amounts of receivables, so they may sell them.

Second, **companies may sell receivables because they may be the only reasonable source of cash**. When credit is tight, companies may not be able to borrow money in the usual credit markets. Even if credit is available, the cost of borrowing may be prohibitive.

A final reason for selling receivables is that **billing and collection are often time-consuming and costly**. As a result, it is often easier for a retailer to sell the receivables to another party that has expertise in billing and collection matters. Credit card companies such as MasterCard, Visa, American Express, and Discover specialize in billing and collecting accounts receivable.

Sale of Receivables to a Factor

A common way to accelerate receivables collection is a sale to a factor. A **factor** is a finance company or bank that buys receivables from businesses for a fee and then collects the payments directly from the customers.

Factoring was traditionally associated with the textiles, apparel, footwear, furniture, and home furnishing industries. It has now spread to other types of businesses and is a multibillion dollar industry. For example, Sears, Roebuck & Co. (now Sears Holdings) once sold $14.8 billion of customer accounts receivable. McKesson has a pre-arranged agreement allowing it to sell up to $700 million of its receivables.

Factoring arrangements vary widely, but typically the factor charges a commission. It ranges from 1% to 3% of the amount of receivables purchased. To illustrate, assume that Hendredon Furniture factors $600,000 of receivables to Federal Factors, Inc. Federal Factors assesses a service charge of 2% of the amount of receivables sold. The following journal entry records Hendredon's sale of receivables on April 2, 2014.

A = L + SE

+588,000
　　　　　　−12,000 Exp
−600,000

Cash Flows
+588,000

Apr. 2	Cash	588,000	
	Service Charge Expense (2% × $600,000)	12,000	
	Accounts Receivable		600,000
	(To record the sale of accounts		
	receivable)		

If the company usually sells its receivables, it records the service charge expense as a selling expense. If the company sells receivables infrequently, it may report this amount under "Other expenses and losses" in the income statement.

Accounting Across the Organization
eBay for Receivables

The credit crunch has hit small businesses especially hard. Because banks have been very reluctant to loan, entrepreneurs have had to look more frequently to factoring as a source of cash. This created an opportunity for a new business called The Receivables Exchange. It offers a website where small companies can anonymously display a list of their receivables that they would like to factor in exchange for cash. Parties that are interested in providing cash in exchange for the receivables can also view the receivables and bid on those they like without revealing their identity. It has been described as "eBay for receivables." Because of his continued use of the service, one experienced participant has reduced the monthly rate that he pays to The Receivables Exchange from 4% to below 3%.

Source: Simona Covel, "Getting Your Due," *Wall Street Journal Online* (May 11, 2009).

? What issues should management consider in deciding whether to factor its receivables? (Answers in *Broadening Your Perspective*.)

National Credit Card Sales

Approximately one billion credit cards were in use recently—more than three credit cards for every man, woman, and child in this country. A common type of credit card is a national credit card such as Visa and MasterCard. Three parties are involved when national credit cards are used in making retail sales: (1) the credit card issuer, who is independent of the retailer; (2) the retailer; and (3) the customer. **A retailer's acceptance of a national credit card is another form of selling—factoring—the receivable by the retailer.**

The use of national credit cards translates to more sales and zero bad debts for the retailer. Both are powerful reasons for a retailer to accept such cards. Illustration 8-18 shows the major advantages of national credit cards to the retailer. In exchange for these advantages, the retailer pays the credit card issuer a fee of 2% to 4% of the invoice price for its services.

The retailer considers sales resulting from the use of Visa and MasterCard as **cash sales**. Upon notification of a credit card charge from a retailer, the bank that issued the card immediately adds the amount to the seller's bank balance. Companies therefore record these credit card charges in the same manner as checks deposited from a cash sale.

To illustrate, Morgan Marie purchases $1,000 of compact discs for her restaurant from Sondgeroth Music Co., and she charges this amount on her Visa First Bank Card. The service fee that First Bank charges Sondgeroth Music is 3%. Sondgeroth Music's entry to record this transaction on March 22, 2014, is:

	A	=	L	+	SE
	+970				
					−30 Exp
					+1,000 Rev

Mar. 22	Cash	970	
	Service Charge Expense	30	
	Sales Revenue		1,000
	(To record Visa credit card sales)		

Cash Flows
+970

Illustration 8-18 Advantages of credit cards to the retailer

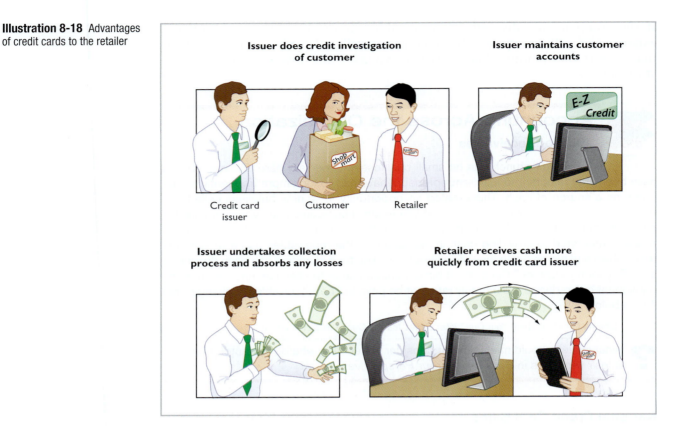

Illustration 8-19 summarizes the basic principles of managing accounts receivable.

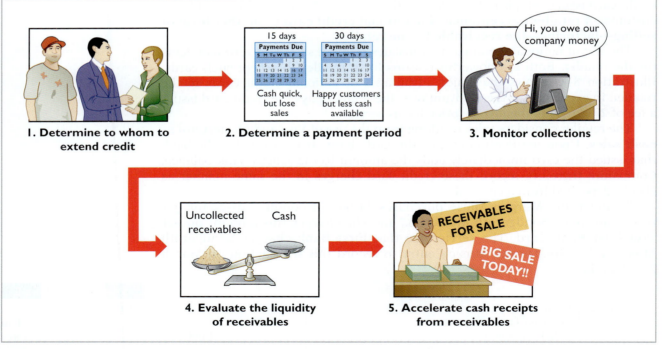

Illustration 8-19
Managing receivables

Using the Decision Toolkit **361**

A lot of companies report strong sales growth but have cash flow problems. How can this be? The reason for the difference is timing: Sales revenue is recorded when goods are delivered even if cash is not received until later. For example, Nike had sales of $20,862 million during 2011. Does that mean it received cash of $20,862 million from its customers? Most likely not. So how do we determine the amount of cash related to sales revenue that is actually received from customers? We analyze the changes that take place in Accounts Receivable.

To illustrate, suppose Bestor Corporation started the year with $10,000 in accounts receivable. During the year, it had credit sales of $100,000. At the end of the year, the balance in accounts receivable was $25,000. As a result, accounts receivable increased $15,000 during the year. How much cash did Bestor collect from customers during the year? Using the following T-account, we can determine that collections were $85,000.

Accounts Receivable

Beginning balance	10,000	85,000	Collections
Sales	100,000		
Ending balance	25,000		

As shown, the difference between sales and cash collections is explained by the change in Accounts Receivable. Accounts Receivable increased by $15,000. Therefore, since credit sales were $100,000, cash collections were only $85,000.

To illustrate another situation, let's use Nike (see data on page 357). Recall that it had credit sales of $20,862 million. Its ending receivables balance was $3,138 million, and its beginning receivables balance was $2,650 million—an increase of $488 million. Given this change, we can determine that the cash collected from customers during the year was $20,374 million ($20,862 − $488). This is shown in the following T-account.

Accounts Receivable

Beginning balance	2,650	20,374	Collections
Sales	20,862		
Ending balance	3,138		

USING THE DECISION TOOLKIT

The information below was taken from the 2011 financial statements of adidas. Similar to Nike and Skechers, adidas sells shoes as well as other products.

Instructions

Comment on adidas' accounts receivable management and liquidity relative to that of Nike, using (1) the current ratio and (2) the accounts receivable turnover and average collection period. Nike's current ratio was 2.85:1. The other ratio values for Nike were calculated earlier in the chapter (page 357).

Real World	ADIDAS AG Selected Financial Information (in millions)		
		2011	**2010**
Sales		$13,344	$11,990
Current assets			
Cash and cash equivalents		$ 906	$ 1,156
Short-term investment securities		465	233
Accounts receivable (net)		1,707	1,667
Merchandise inventories		2,482	2,119
Other		875	705
Total current assets		$ 6,435	$ 5,880
Total current liabilities		$ 4,281	$ 3,908

Solution

1. Here is the 2011 current ratio (Current assets ÷ Current liabilities) for each company.

Nike	**adidas**
2.85:1	$\frac{\$6,435}{\$4,281} = 1.50:1$

Nike's current ratio far exceeds that of adidas. In fact, Nike's might be excessive. A company of its size would not normally want to have so much capital tied up in current assets.

2. The accounts receivable turnover and average collection period for each company are:

	Nike	**adidas**
Accounts receivable turnover	7.2 times	$\frac{\$13,344}{(\$1,707 + \$1,667)/2} = 7.9$ times
Average collection period	50.7 days	$\frac{365}{7.9} = 46.2$ days

adidas' accounts receivable turnover of 7.9 compared to Nike's 7.2, and its average collection period of 46.2 days versus Nike's 50.7 days, suggest that adidas is able to collect from its customers slightly more quickly. It is important to note, however, that adidas is a German corporation. It reports under IFRS. A thorough comparison of adidas and Nike would require consideration of differences in the treatment of accounts receivable under IFRS and GAAP.

Summary of Learning Objectives

1 **Identify the different types of receivables.** Receivables are frequently classified as accounts, notes, and other. Accounts receivable are amounts customers owe on account. Notes receivable represent claims that are evidenced by formal instruments of credit. Other receivables include nontrade receivables such as interest receivable, loans to company officers, advances to employees, and income taxes refundable.

2 **Explain how accounts receivable are recognized in the accounts.** Companies record accounts receivable when they perform a service on account or at the point-of-sale of merchandise on account. Sales returns and allowances, and cash discounts reduce the amount received on accounts receivable.

3 **Describe the methods used to account for bad debts.** The two methods of accounting for uncollectible accounts are the allowance method and the direct write-off method. Under the allowance method, companies estimate uncollectible accounts as a percentage of receivables. It emphasizes the cash realizable value of the accounts receivable. An aging schedule is frequently used with this approach.

4 **Compute the interest on notes receivable.** The formula for computing interest is: Face value of note × Annual interest rate × Time in terms of one year.

5 **Describe the entries to record the disposition of notes receivable.** Notes can be held to maturity, at which time the borrower (maker) pays the face value plus accrued interest and the payee removes the note from the accounts. In many cases, however, similar to accounts receivable, the holder of the note speeds up the conversion by selling the receivable to another party. In some situations, the maker of the note dishonors the note (defaults), and the note is written off.

6 **Explain the statement presentation of receivables.** Companies should identify each major type of receivable in the balance sheet or in the notes to the financial statements. Short-term receivables are considered current assets. Companies report the gross amount of receivables and allowance for doubtful accounts. They report bad debt and service charge expenses in the income statement as operating (selling) expenses, and interest revenue as other revenues and gains in the nonoperating section of the statement.

7 **Describe the principles of sound accounts receivable management.** To properly manage receivables, management must (a) determine to whom to extend credit, (b) establish a payment period, (c) monitor collections, (d) evaluate the liquidity of receivables, and (e) accelerate cash receipts from receivables when necessary.

8 **Identify ratios to analyze a company's receivables.** The accounts receivable turnover and the average collection period both are useful in analyzing management's effectiveness in managing receivables. The accounts receivable aging schedule also provides useful information.

9 **Describe methods to accelerate the receipt of cash from receivables.** If the company needs additional cash, management can accelerate the collection of cash from receivables by selling (factoring) its receivables or by allowing customers to pay with bank credit cards.

DECISION TOOLKIT *A SUMMARY*

DECISION CHECKPOINTS	INFO NEEDED FOR DECISION	TOOL TO USE FOR DECISION	HOW TO EVALUATE RESULTS
Is the amount of past due accounts increasing? Which accounts require management's attention?	List of outstanding receivables and their due dates	Prepare an aging schedule showing the receivables in various stages: outstanding 0–30 days, 31–60 days, 61–90 days, and over 90 days.	Accounts in the older categories require follow-up: letters, phone calls, and possible renegotiation of terms.
Is the company's credit risk increasing?	Customer account balances and due dates	Accounts receivable aging schedule	Compute and compare the percentage of receivables over 90 days old.
Does the company have significant concentrations of credit risk?	Note to the financial statements on concentrations of credit risk	If risky credit customers are identified, the financial health of those customers should be evaluated to gain an independent assessment of the potential for a material credit loss.	If a material loss appears likely, the potential negative impact of that loss on the company should be carefully evaluated, along with the adequacy of the allowance for doubtful accounts.
Are collections being made in a timely fashion?	Net credit sales and average net receivables balance	$\text{Accounts receivable turnover} = \dfrac{\text{Net credit sales}}{\text{Average net accounts receivable}}$ $\text{Average collection period} = \dfrac{365 \text{ days}}{\text{Accounts receivable turnover}}$	Average collection period should be consistent with corporate credit policy. An increase may suggest a decline in financial health of customers.

Glossary

Terms are highlighted in blue throughout the chapter.

Accounts receivable Amounts customers owe on account.

Accounts receivable turnover A measure of the liquidity of accounts receivable, computed by dividing net credit sales by average net accounts receivable.

Aging the accounts receivable A schedule of customer balances classified by the length of time they have been unpaid.

Allowance method A method of accounting for bad debts that involves estimating uncollectible accounts at the end of each period.

Average collection period The average amount of time that a receivable is outstanding, calculated by dividing 365 days by the accounts receivable turnover.

Bad Debt Expense An expense account to record losses from extending credit.

Cash (net) realizable value The net amount a company expects to receive in cash from receivables.

Concentration of credit risk The threat of nonpayment from a single large customer or class of customers that could adversely affect the financial health of the company.

Direct write-off method A method of accounting for bad debts that involves charging receivable balances to Bad Debt Expense at the time receivables from a particular company are determined to be uncollectible.

Dishonored (defaulted) note A note that is not paid in full at maturity.

Factor A finance company or bank that buys receivables from businesses for a fee and then collects the payments directly from the customers.

Maker The party in a promissory note who is making the promise to pay.

Notes receivable Written promise (as evidenced by a formal instrument) for amounts to be received.

Payee The party to whom payment of a promissory note is to be made.

Percentage-of-receivables basis A method of estimating the amount of bad debt expense whereby management establishes a percentage relationship between the amount of receivables and the expected losses from uncollectible accounts.

Promissory note A written promise to pay a specified amount of money on demand or at a definite time.

Receivables Amounts due from individuals and companies that are expected to be collected in cash.

Trade receivables Notes and accounts receivable that result from sales transactions.

WILEY **PLUS**   **Self-Test, Brief Exercises, Exercises, Problem Set A, and many more resources are available for practice in WileyPLUS.**

Self-Test Questions

(Answers in *Broadening Your Perspective*.)

(LO 1) 1. A receivable that is evidenced by a formal instrument and that normally requires the payment of interest is:
  (a) an account receivable.
  (b) a trade receivable.
  (c) a note receivable.
  (d) a classified receivable.

(LO 2) 2. Kersee Company on June 15 sells merchandise on account to Soo Eng Co. for $1,000, terms 2/10, n/30. On June 20, Eng Co. returns merchandise worth $300 to Kersee Company. On June 24, payment is received from Eng Co. for the balance due. What is the amount of cash received?
  (a) $700.   (c) $686.
  (b) $680.   (d) None of the above.

(LO 3, 6) 3. Accounts and notes receivable are reported in the current assets section of the balance sheet at:
  (a) cash (net) realizable value
  (b) net book value.
  (c) lower-of-cost-or-market value.
  (d) invoice cost.

(LO 3) 4. Net credit sales for the month are $800,000. The accounts receivable balance is $160,000. The allowance is calculated as 7.5% of the receivables balance using the percentage-of-receivables basis. If Allowance for Doubtful Accounts has a credit balance of $5,000 before adjustment, what is the balance after adjustment?
  (a) $12,000.   (c) $17,000.
  (b) $7,000.   (d) $31,000.

(LO 3) 5. In 2014, Patterson Wholesale Company had net credit sales of $750,000. On January 1, 2014, Allowance for Doubtful Accounts had a credit balance of $18,000. During 2014, $30,000 of uncollectible accounts receivable were written off. Past experience indicates that the allowance should be 10% of the balance in receivables (percentage-of-receivables basis). If the accounts receivable balance at December 31 was $200,000, what is the required adjustment to Allowance for Doubtful Accounts at December 31, 2014?
  (a) $20,000.   (c) $32,000.
  (b) $75,000.   (d) $30,000.

(LO 3) 6. An analysis and aging of the accounts receivable of Raja Company at December 31 reveal these data:

Accounts receivable	$800,000
Allowance for doubtful accounts per books before adjustment (credit)	50,000
Amounts expected to become uncollectible	65,000

What is the cash realizable value of the accounts receivable at December 31, after adjustment?
  (a) $685,000.   (c) $800,000.
  (b) $750,000.   (d) $735,000.

(LO 4) 7. Which of these statements about promissory notes is **incorrect?**
 (a) The party making the promise to pay is called the maker.
 (b) The party to whom payment is to be made is called the payee.
 (c) A promissory note is not a negotiable instrument.
 (d) A promissory note is more liquid than an account receivable.

(LO 4) 8. Michael Co. accepts a $1,000, 3-month, 12% promissory note in settlement of an account with Tani Co. The entry to record this transaction is:

(a) Notes Receivable	1,030	
Accounts Receivable		1,030
(b) Notes Receivable	1,000	
Accounts Receivable		1,000
(c) Notes Receivable	1,000	
Sales Revenue		1,000
(d) Notes Receivable	1,020	
Accounts Receivable		1,020

(LO 5) 9. Schleis Co. holds Murphy Inc.'s $10,000, 120-day, 9% note. The entry made by Schleis Co. when the note is collected, assuming no interest has previously been accrued, is:

(a) Cash	10,300	
Notes Receivable		10,300
(b) Cash	10,000	
Notes Receivable		10,000
(c) Accounts Receivable	10,300	
Notes Receivable		10,000
Interest Revenue		300
(d) Cash	10,300	
Notes Receivable		10,000
Interest Revenue		300

(LO 7) 10. If a company is concerned about extending credit to a risky customer, it could do any of the following **except:**
 (a) require the customer to pay cash in advance.
 (b) require the customer to provide a letter of credit or a bank guarantee.
 (c) contact references provided by the customer, such as banks and other suppliers.
 (d) provide the customer a lengthy payment period to increase the chance of paying.

11. Eddy Corporation had net credit sales during **(LO 8)** the year of $800,000 and cost of goods sold of $500,000. The balance in receivables at the beginning of the year was $100,000 and at the end of the year was $150,000. What was the accounts receivable turnover?
 (a) 6.4 (c) 5.3
 (b) 8.0 (d) 4.0

12. Prall Corporation sells its goods on terms of **(LO 8)** 2/10, n/30. It has an accounts receivable turnover of 7. What is its average collection period (days)?
 (a) 2,555 (c) 52
 (b) 30 (d) 210

13. Which of these statements about Visa credit card **(LO 9)** sales is **incorrect?**
 (a) The credit card issuer conducts the credit investigation of the customer.
 (b) The retailer is not involved in the collection process.
 (c) The retailer must wait to receive payment from the issuer.
 (d) The retailer receives cash more quickly than it would from individual customers.

14. Good Stuff Retailers accepted $50,000 of Citibank **(LO 9)** Visa credit card charges for merchandise sold on July 1. Citibank charges 4% for its credit card use. The entry to record this transaction by Good Stuff Retailers will include a credit to Sales Revenue of $50,000 and a debit(s) to:
 (a) Cash $48,000 and Service Charge Expense $2,000.
 (b) Accounts Receivable $48,000 and Service Charge Expense $2,000.
 (c) Cash $50,000.
 (d) Accounts Receivable $50,000.

15. A company can accelerate its cash receipts by all of **(LO 9)** the following **except:**
 (a) offering discounts for early payment.
 (b) accepting national credit cards for customer purchases.
 (c) selling receivables to a factor.
 (d) writing off receivables.

Go to the book's companion website, **www.wiley.com/college/kimmel**, to access additional Self-Test Questions.

Questions

1. What is the difference between an account receivable and a note receivable?

2. What are some common types of receivables other than accounts receivable or notes receivable?

3. What are the essential features of the allowance method of accounting for bad debts?

4. Mitch Lang cannot understand why the cash realizable value does not decrease when an uncollectible account is written off under the allowance method. Clarify this point for Mitch.

5. Mendosa Company has a credit balance of $2,200 in Allowance for Doubtful Accounts before adjustment. The estimated uncollectibles under the percentage-of-receivables basis is $5,100. Prepare the adjusting entry.

6. What types of receivables does Tootsie Roll report on its balance sheet? Does it use the allowance method or the direct write-off method to account for uncollectibles?

7. How are bad debts accounted for under the direct write-off method? What are the disadvantages of this method?

8. ◄— Debbie Trevino, the vice president of sales for Tropical Pools and Spas, wants the company's credit department to be less restrictive in granting credit. "How can we sell anything when you guys won't approve anybody?" she asks. Discuss the pros and cons of "easy credit." What are the accounting implications?

9. Your roommate is uncertain about the advantages of a promissory note. Compare the advantages of a note receivable with those of an account receivable.

10. How may the maturity date of a promissory note be stated?

11. Compute the missing amounts for each of the following notes.

Principal	Annual Interest Rate	Time	Total Interest
(a)	6%	60 days	$ 270
$30,000	8%	3 years	(d)
$60,000	(b)	5 months	$2,500
$50,000	11%	(c)	$2,750

12. Carrera Company dishonors a note at maturity. What are the options available to the lender?

13. General Motors Company has accounts receivable and notes receivable. How should the receivables be reported on the balance sheet?

14. ◄— ⊙═══⊏ What are the steps to good receivables management?

15. ⊙═══⊏ How might a company monitor the risk related to its accounts receivable?

16. ⊙═══⊏ What is meant by a concentration of credit risk?

17. ⊙═══⊏ The president of Dickerson Inc. proudly announces her company's improved liquidity since its current ratio has increased substantially from one year to the next. Does an increase in the current ratio always indicate improved liquidity? What other ratio or ratios might you review to determine whether or not the increase in the current ratio is an improvement in financial health?

18. ◄— Since hiring a new sales director, Hilson Inc. has enjoyed a 50% increase in sales. The CEO has also noticed, however, that the company's average collection period has increased from 17 days to 38 days. What might be the cause of this increase? What are the implications to management of this increase?

19. ⊙═══⊏ The Coca-Cola Company's accounts receivable turnover was 9.05 in 2011, and its average amount of net receivables during the period was $3,424 million. What is the amount of its net credit sales for the period? What is the average collection period in days?

20. ◄— ⊙═══⊏ JCPenney Company accepts both its own credit cards and national credit cards. What are the advantages of accepting both types of cards?

21. ◄— ⊙═══⊏ An article in the *Wall Street Journal* indicated that companies are selling their receivables at a record rate. Why do companies sell their receivables?

22. Calico Corners decides to sell $400,000 of its accounts receivable to Quick Central Factors Inc. Quick Central Factors assesses a service charge of 3% of the amount of receivables sold. Prepare the journal entry that Calico Corners makes to record this sale.

23. Pine Corp. has experienced tremendous sales growth this year, but it is always short of cash. What is one explanation for this occurrence?

24. How can the amount of collections from customers be determined?

Brief Exercises

Identify different types of receivables.

(LO 1), C

BE8-1 Presented below are three receivables transactions. Indicate whether these receivables are reported as accounts receivable, notes receivable, or other receivables on a balance sheet.
(a) Advanced $10,000 to an employee.
(b) Received a promissory note of $34,000 for services performed.
(c) Sold merchandise on account for $60,000 to a customer.

Record basic accounts receivable transactions.

(LO 2), AP

BE8-2 Record the following transactions on the books of Cohen Co. (Omit cost of goods sold entries.)
(a) On July 1, Cohen Co. sold merchandise on account to Tracy Inc. for $23,000, terms 2/10, n/30.
(b) On July 8, Tracy Inc. returned merchandise worth $2,400 to Cohen Co.
(c) On July 11, Tracy Inc. paid for the merchandise.

Prepare entry for write-off, and determine cash realizable value.

(LO 3), AP

BE8-3 At the end of 2013, Morley Co. has accounts receivable of $700,000 and an allowance for doubtful accounts of $25,000. On January 24, 2014, it is learned that the company's

receivable from Spears Inc. is not collectible and therefore management authorizes a write-off of $4,300.
(a) Prepare the journal entry to record the write-off.
(b) What is the cash realizable value of the accounts receivable (1) before the write-off and (2) after the write-off?

BE8-4 Assume the same information as BE8-3 and that on March 4, 2014, Morley Co. receives payment of $4,300 in full from Spears Inc. Prepare the journal entries to record this transaction.

Prepare entries for collection of bad debt write-off.
(LO 3), AP

BE8-5 Hirdt Co. uses the percentage-of-receivables basis to record bad debt expense and concludes that 2% of accounts receivable will become uncollectible. Accounts receivable are $400,000 at the end of the year, and the allowance for doubtful accounts has a credit balance of $2,800.
(a) Prepare the adjusting journal entry to record bad debt expense for the year.
(b) If the allowance for doubtful accounts had a debit balance of $900 instead of a credit balance of $2,800, prepare the adjusting journal entry for bad debt expense.

Prepare entry using percentage-of-receivables method.
(LO 3), AP

BE8-6 Compute interest and find the maturity date for the following notes.

Compute interest and determine maturity dates on notes.
(LO 4), AP

Date of Note	Principal	Interest Rate (%)	Terms
(a) June 10	$80,000	6%	60 days
(b) July 14	$50,000	7%	90 days
(c) April 27	$12,000	8%	75 days

BE8-7 Presented below are data on three promissory notes. Determine the missing amounts.

Determine maturity dates and compute interest and rates on notes.
(LO 4), AP

Date of Note	Terms	Maturity Date	Principal	Annual Interest Rate	Total Interest
(a) April 1	60 days	?	$600,000	9%	?
(b) July 2	30 days	?	90,000	?	$600
(c) March 7	6 months	?	120,000	10%	?

BE8-8 On January 10, 2014, Tolleson Co. sold merchandise on account to Simmons for $8,000, terms n/30. On February 9, Simmons gave Tolleson Co. a 7% promissory note in settlement of this account. Prepare the journal entry to record the sale and the settlement of the accounts receivable. (Omit cost of goods sold entries.)

Prepare entry for note receivable exchanged for accounts receivable.
(LO 4), AP

BE8-9 During its first year of operations, Gehrig Company had credit sales of $3,000,000, of which $400,000 remained uncollected at year-end. The credit manager estimates that $18,000 of these receivables will become uncollectible.
(a) Prepare the journal entry to record the estimated uncollectibles. (Assume an unadjusted balance of zero in Allowance for Doubtful Accounts.)
(b) Prepare the current assets section of the balance sheet for Gehrig Company, assuming that in addition to the receivables it has cash of $90,000, merchandise inventory of $180,000, and supplies of $13,000.
(c) Calculate the accounts receivable turnover and average collection period. Assume that average net accounts receivable were $300,000. Explain what these measures tell us.

Prepare entry for estimated uncollectibles and classifications, and compute ratios.
(LO 3, 6, 7, 8), AP

BE8-10 Suppose the 2014 financial statements of 3M Company report net sales of $23.1 billion. Accounts receivable (net) are $3.2 billion at the beginning of the year and $3.25 billion at the end of the year. Compute 3M's accounts receivable turnover. Compute 3M's average collection period for accounts receivable in days.

Analyze accounts receivable.
(LO 8), AP

BE8-11 Consider these transactions:
(a) Draber Restaurant accepted a Visa card in payment of a $200 lunch bill. The bank charges a 3% fee. What entry should Draber make?
(b) Marin Company sold its accounts receivable of $65,000. What entry should Marin make, given a service charge of 3% on the amount of receivables sold?

Prepare entries for credit card sale and sale of accounts receivable.
(LO 9), AP

BE8-12 Richman Corp. had a beginning balance in accounts receivable of $70,000 and an ending balance of $91,000. Credit sales during the period were $598,000. Determine cash collections.

Determine cash collections.
(LO 9), AP

Exercises

Prepare entries for recognizing accounts receivable.

(LO 2), **AP**

E8-1 On January 6, Aaron Co. sells merchandise on account to Foley Inc. for $9,200, terms 1/10, n/30. On January 16, Foley pays the amount due.

Instructions

Prepare the entries on Aaron Co.'s books to record the sale and related collection. (Omit cost of goods sold entries.)

Prepare entries for recognizing accounts receivable.

(LO 2), **AP**

E8-2 On January 10, Allison Milo uses her Crawford Co. credit card to purchase merchandise from Crawford Co. for $1,700. On February 10, Milo is billed for the amount due of $1,700. On February 12, Milo pays $1,100 on the balance due. On March 10, Milo is billed for the amount due, including interest at 1% per month on the unpaid balance as of February 12.

Instructions

Prepare the entries on Crawford Co.'s books related to the transactions that occurred on January 10, February 12, and March 10. (Omit cost of goods sold entries.)

Journalize receivables transactions.

(LO 2, 3), **AP**

E8-3 At the beginning of the current period, Griffey Corp. had balances in Accounts Receivable of $200,000 and in Allowance for Doubtful Accounts of $9,000 (credit). During the period, it had net credit sales of $800,000 and collections of $763,000. It wrote off as uncollectible accounts receivable of $7,300. However, a $3,100 account previously written off as uncollectible was recovered before the end of the current period. Uncollectible accounts are estimated to total $25,000 at the end of the period. (Omit cost of goods sold entries.)

Instructions

(a) Prepare the entries to record sales and collections during the period.
(b) Prepare the entry to record the write-off of uncollectible accounts during the period.
(c) Prepare the entries to record the recovery of the uncollectible account during the period.
(d) Prepare the entry to record bad debt expense for the period.
(e) Determine the ending balances in Accounts Receivable and Allowance for Doubtful Accounts.
(f) What is the net realizable value of the receivables at the end of the period?

Prepare entries to record allowance for doubtful accounts.

(LO 3), **AP**

E8-4 The ledger of Wainwright Company at the end of the current year shows Accounts Receivable $78,000; Credit Sales $810,000; and Sales Returns and Allowances $40,000.

Instructions

(a) If Wainwright uses the direct write-off method to account for uncollectible accounts, journalize the adjusting entry at December 31, assuming Wainwright determines that Hiller's $900 balance is uncollectible.
(b) If Allowance for Doubtful Accounts has a credit balance of $1,100 in the trial balance, journalize the adjusting entry at December 31, assuming bad debts are expected to be 10% of accounts receivable.
(c) If Allowance for Doubtful Accounts has a debit balance of $500 in the trial balance, journalize the adjusting entry at December 31, assuming bad debts are expected to be 8% of accounts receivable.

Determine bad debt expense, and prepare the adjusting entry.

(LO 3), **AP**

E8-5 Stine Company has accounts receivable of $95,400 at March 31, 2014. An analysis of the accounts shows these amounts.

	Balance, March 31	
Month of Sale	**2014**	**2013**
March	$65,000	$75,000
February	12,900	8,000
December and January	10,100	2,400
November and October	7,400	1,100
	$95,400	$86,500

Credit terms are 2/10, n/30. At March 31, 2014, there is a $2,100 credit balance in Allowance for Doubtful Accounts prior to adjustment. The company uses the percentage-of-receivables basis for estimating uncollectible accounts. The company's estimates of bad debts are as shown in the following.

Age of Accounts	Estimated Percentage Uncollectible
Current	2%
1–30 days past due	5
31–90 days past due	30
Over 90 days past due	50

Instructions

(a) Determine the total estimated uncollectibles.
(b) Prepare the adjusting entry at March 31, 2014, to record bad debt expense.
(c) Discuss the implications of the changes in the aging schedule from 2013 to 2014.

E8-6 On December 31, 2013, when its Allowance for Doubtful Accounts had a debit balance of $1,400, Hunt Co. estimates that 9% of its accounts receivable balance of $90,000 will become uncollectible and records the necessary adjustment to Allowance for Doubtful Accounts. On May 11, 2014, Hunt Co. determined that J. Byrd's account was uncollectible and wrote off $1,200. On June 12, 2014, Byrd paid the amount previously written off.

Prepare entry for estimated uncollectibles, write-off, and recovery.

(LO 3), **AP**

Instructions

Prepare the journal entries on December 31, 2013, May 11, 2014, and June 12, 2014.

E8-7 Malone Supply Co. has the following transactions related to notes receivable during the last 2 months of the year. The company does not make entries to accrue interest except at December 31.

Prepare entries for notes receivable transactions.

(LO 4, 5), **AP**

Nov.	1	Loaned $60,000 cash to B. Carr on a 12-month, 7% note.
Dec.	11	Sold goods to R. P. Kiner, Inc., receiving a $3,600, 90-day, 8% note.
	16	Received a $12,000, 180-day, 9% note to settle an open account from M. Adcock.
	31	Accrued interest revenue on all notes receivable.

Instructions

Journalize the transactions for Malone Supply Co. (Omit cost of goods sold entries.)

E8-8 These transactions took place for Glavine Co.

Journalize notes receivable transactions.

(LO 4, 5), **AP**

2013

May	1	Received a $5,000, 12-month, 6% note in exchange for an outstanding account receivable from S. Rooney.
Dec.	31	Accrued interest revenue on the S. Rooney note.

2014

May	1	Received principal plus interest on the S. Rooney note. (No interest has been accrued since December 31, 2013.)

Instructions

Record the transactions in the general journal. The company does not make entries to accrue interest except at December 31.

E8-9 Shannon Corp. had the following balances in receivable accounts at October 31, 2014 (in thousands): Allowance for Doubtful Accounts $52; Accounts Receivable $2,910; Other Receivables $189; Notes Receivable $1,353.

Prepare a balance sheet presentation of receivables.

(LO 6), **AP**

Instructions

Prepare the balance sheet presentation of Shannon Corp.'s receivables in good form.

E8-10 The following is a list of activities that companies perform in relation to their receivables.

Identify the principles of receivables management.

(LO 7), **K**

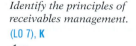

1. Selling receivables to a factor.
2. Reviewing company ratings in *The Dun and Bradstreet Reference Book of American Business*.
3. Collecting information on competitors' payment period policies.
4. Preparing monthly accounts receivable aging schedule and investigating problem accounts.
5. Calculating the accounts receivable turnover and average collection period.

Instructions

Match each of the activities listed above with a purpose of the activity listed below.
(a) Determine to whom to extend credit.
(b) Establish a payment period.
(c) Monitor collections.
(d) Evaluate the liquidity of receivables.
(e) Accelerate cash receipts from receivable when necessary.

Compute ratios to evaluate a company's receivables balance.
(LO 7, 8), **AN**

E8-11 Suppose the following information was taken from the 2014 financial statements of FedEx Corporation, a major global transportation/delivery company.

(in millions)	2014	2013
Accounts receivable (gross)	$ 3,587	$ 4,517
Accounts receivable (net)	3,391	4,359
Allowance for doubtful accounts	196	158
Sales revenue	35,497	37,953
Total current assets	7,116	7,244

Instructions

Answer each of the following questions.
(a) Calculate the accounts receivable turnover and the average collection period for 2014 for FedEx.
(b) Is accounts receivable a material component of the company's total current assets?
(c) Evaluate the balance in FedEx's allowance for doubtful accounts.

Evaluate liquidity.
(LO 7, 8, 9), **AN**

E8-12 The following ratios are available for Lin Inc.

	2014	2013
Current ratio	1.3:1	1.5:1
Accounts receivable turnover	12 times	10 times
Inventory turnover	11 times	9 times

Instructions

(a) Is Lin's short-term liquidity improving or deteriorating in 2014? Be specific in your answer, referring to relevant ratios.
(b) Do changes in turnover ratios affect profitability? Explain.
(c) Identify any steps Lin might have taken, or might wish to take, to improve its management of its accounts receivable and inventory turnovers.

Prepare entry for sale of accounts receivable.
(LO 9), **AP**

E8-13 On March 3, Beachy Appliances sells $710,000 of its receivables to National Factors Inc. National Factors Inc. assesses a service charge of 4% of the amount of receivables sold.

Instructions

Prepare the entry on Beachy Appliances' books to record the sale of the receivables.

Identify reason for sale of receivables.
(LO 9), **C**

E8-14 In a recent annual report, Office Depot, Inc. notes that the company entered into an agreement to sell all of its credit card program receivables to financial service companies.

Instructions

Explain why Office Depot, a financially stable company with positive cash flow, would choose to sell its receivables.

Prepare entry for credit card sale.
(LO 9), **AP**

E8-15 On May 10, Renn Company sold merchandise for $4,000 and accepted the customer's First Business Bank MasterCard. At the end of the day, the First Business Bank MasterCard receipts were deposited in the company's bank account. First Business Bank charges a 3.8% service charge for credit card sales.

Instructions

Prepare the entry on Renn Company's books to record the sale of merchandise.

E8-16   On July 4, Susie's Restaurant accepts a Visa card for a $250 dinner bill. Visa charges a 4% service fee.

Prepare entry for credit card sale.

(LO 9), **AP**

Instructions

Prepare the entry on Susie's books related to the transaction.

E8-17   Kimbrel Corp. significantly reduced its requirements for credit sales. As a result, sales during the current year increased dramatically. It had receivables at the beginning of the year of $38,000 and ending receivables of $191,000. Credit sales were $380,000.

Determine cash flows and evaluate quality of earnings.

(LO 9), **AN**

Instructions

(a) Determine cash collections during the period.
(b) Discuss how your findings in part (a) would affect Kimbrel Corp.'s quality of earnings ratio. (Do not compute.)
(c) What concerns might you have regarding Kimbrel's accounting?

Challenge Exercises

Visit the book's companion website, at **www.wiley.com/college/kimmel**, and choose the Student Companion site to access Challenge Exercises.

Problems: Set A

P8-1A   Reynolds.com uses the allowance method of accounting for bad debts. The company produced the following aging of the accounts receivable at year-end.

Journalize transactions related to bad debts.

(LO 2, 3), **AP**

	Total	Number of Days Outstanding				
		0–30	31–60	61–90	91–120	Over 120
Accounts receivable	$377,000	$222,000	$90,000	$38,000	$15,000	$12,000
% uncollectible		1%	4%	5%	8%	10%
Estimated bad debts						

Instructions

(a) Calculate the total estimated bad debts based on the above information.
(b) Prepare the year-end adjusting journal entry to record the bad debts using the aged uncollectible accounts receivable determined in (a). Assume the unadjusted balance in Allowance for Doubtful Accounts is a $4,000 debit.
(c) Of the above accounts, $5,000 is determined to be specifically uncollectible. Prepare the journal entry to write off the uncollectible account.
(d) The company collects $5,000 subsequently on a specific account that had previously been determined to be uncollectible in (c). Prepare the journal entry(ies) necessary to restore the account and record the cash collection.
(e) Comment on how your answers to (a)–(d) would change if Reynolds.com used 3% of total accounts receivable, rather than aging the accounts receivable. What are the advantages to the company of aging the accounts receivable rather than applying a percentage to total accounts receivable?

(a) Tot. est. bad debts $10,120

P8-2A   At December 31, 2013, Weiss Imports reported this information on its balance sheet.

Accounts receivable	$600,000
Less: Allowance for doubtful accounts	37,000

Prepare journal entries related to bad debt expense, and compute ratios.

(LO 2, 3, 8), **AP**

During 2014, the company had the following transactions related to receivables.

1. Sales on account	$2,500,000
2. Sales returns and allowances	50,000
3. Collections of accounts receivable	2,200,000
4. Write-offs of accounts receivable deemed uncollectible	41,000
5. Recovery of bad debts previously written off as uncollectible	15,000

Instructions

(a) Prepare the journal entries to record each of these five transactions. Assume that no cash discounts were taken on the collections of accounts receivable. (Omit cost of goods sold entries.)

(b) A/R bal. $809,000 (b) Enter the January 1, 2014, balances in Accounts Receivable and Allowance for Doubtful Accounts, post the entries to the two accounts (use T-accounts), and determine the balances.

(c) Prepare the journal entry to record bad debt expense for 2014, assuming that aging the accounts receivable indicates that estimated bad debts are $46,000.

(d) Compute the accounts receivable turnover and average collection period.

Journalize transactions related to bad debts.

(LO 2, 3), **AP**

P8-3A Presented below is an aging schedule for Bosworth Company.

| Customer | Total | Not Yet Due | Number of Days Past Due | | | |
			1–30	31–60	61–90	Over 90
Aneesh	$ 24,000		$ 9,000	$15,000		
Bird	30,000	$ 30,000				
Cope	50,000	5,000	5,000		$40,000	
DeSpears	38,000					$38,000
Others	120,000	72,000	35,000	13,000		
	$262,000	$107,000	$49,000	$28,000	$40,000	$38,000
Estimated percentage uncollectible			3%	7%	12%	24%	60%
Total estimated bad debts	$ 42,400	$ 3,210	$ 3,430	$ 3,360	$ 9,600	$22,800

At December 31, 2013, the unadjusted balance in Allowance for Doubtful Accounts is a credit of $8,000.

Instructions

(a) Journalize and post the adjusting entry for bad debts at December 31, 2013. (Use T-accounts.)

(b) Journalize and post to the allowance account these 2014 events and transactions:
  1. March 1, a $600 customer balance originating in 2013 is judged uncollectible.
  2. May 1, a check for $600 is received from the customer whose account was written off as uncollectible on March 1.

(c) Journalize the adjusting entry for bad debts at December 31, 2014, assuming that the unadjusted balance in Allowance for Doubtful Accounts is a debit of $1,400 and the aging schedule indicates that total estimated bad debts will be $36,700.

Compute bad debt amounts.

(LO 3), **AP**

P8-4A Here is information related to Freeman Company for 2014.

Total credit sales	$1,500,000
Accounts receivable at December 31	840,000
Bad debts written off	37,000

Instructions

(a) What amount of bad debt expense will Freeman Company report if it uses the direct write-off method of accounting for bad debts?

(b) Assume that Freeman Company decides to estimate its bad debt expense based on 4% of accounts receivable. What amount of bad debt expense will the company record if Allowance for Doubtful Accounts has a credit balance of $3,000?

(c) Assume the same facts as in part (b), except that there is a $1,000 debit balance in Allowance for Doubtful Accounts. What amount of bad debt expense will Freeman record?

(d) ━━▶ What is a weakness of the direct write-off method of reporting bad debt expense?

P8-5A At December 31, 2014, the trial balance of Sloane Company contained the following amounts before adjustment.

Journalize entries to record transactions related to bad debts.

(LO 2, 3), **AP**

	Debit	**Credit**
Accounts Receivable	$180,000	
Allowance for Doubtful Accounts		$ 1,500
Sales Revenue		875,000

Instructions

(a) Prepare the adjusting entry at December 31, 2014, to record bad debt expense, assuming that the aging schedule indicates that $10,200 of accounts receivable will be uncollectible.

(b) Repeat part (a), assuming that instead of a credit balance there is a $1,500 debit balance in Allowance for Doubtful Accounts.

(c) During the next month, January 2015, a $2,100 account receivable is written off as uncollectible. Prepare the journal entry to record the write-off.

(d) Repeat part (c), assuming that Sloane Company uses the direct write-off method instead of the allowance method in accounting for uncollectible accounts receivable.

(e) ✏️ What are the advantages of using the allowance method in accounting for uncollectible accounts as compared to the direct write-off method?

P8-6A On January 1, 2014, Oswalt Company had Accounts Receivable of $54,200 and Allowance for Doubtful Accounts of $3,700. Oswalt Company prepares financial statements annually. During the year, the following selected transactions occurred.

Journalize various receivables transactions.

(LO 2, 4, 5), **AP**

Jan.	5	Sold $4,000 of merchandise to Ross Company, terms n/30.
Feb.	2	Accepted a $4,000, 4-month, 9% promissory note from Ross Company for balance due.
	12	Sold $12,000 of merchandise to Cano Company and accepted Cano's $12,000, 2-month, 10% note for the balance due.
	26	Sold $5,200 of merchandise to Meachum Co., terms n/10.
Apr.	5	Accepted a $5,200, 3-month, 8% note from Meachum Co. for balance due.
	12	Collected Cano Company note in full.
June	2	Collected Ross Company note in full.
	15	Sold $2,000 of merchandise to Glanvile Inc. and accepted a $2,000, 6-month, 12% note for the amount due.

Instructions

Journalize the transactions. (Omit cost of goods sold entries.)

P8-7A The president of Giraldi Enterprises asks if you could indicate the impact certain transactions have on the following ratios.

Explain the impact of transactions on ratios.

(LO 8), **C**

Transaction	Current Ratio (2:1)	Accounts Receivable Turnover (10×)	Average Collection Period (36.5 days)
1. Received $5,000 on cash sale. The cost of the goods sold was $2,600.			
2. Recorded bad debt expense of $500 using allowance method.			
3. Wrote off a $100 account receivable as uncollectible (Uses allowance method.)			
4. Recorded $2,500 sales on account. The cost of the goods sold was $1,500.			

Instructions

Complete the table, indicating whether each transaction will increase (I), decrease (D), or have no effect (NE) on the specific ratios provided for Giraldi Enterprises.

Prepare entries for various credit card and notes receivable transactions.

(LO 4, 5, 6, 9), **AP**

GLS

P8-8A Kolton Company closes its books on its July 31 year-end. The company does not make entries to accrue for interest except at its year-end. On June 30, the Notes Receivable account balance is $23,800. Notes Receivable include the following.

Date	Maker	Face Value	Term	Maturity Date	Interest Rate
April 21	Booth Inc.	$ 6,000	90 days	July 20	8%
May 25	Manning Co.	7,800	60 days	July 24	10%
June 30	ANF Corp.	10,000	6 months	December 31	6%

During July, the following transactions were completed.

July   5   Made sales of $4,500 on Kolton credit cards.
      14   Made sales of $600 on Visa credit cards. The credit card service charge is 3%.
      20   Received payment in full from Booth Inc. on the amount due.
      24   Received payment in full from Manning Co. on the amount due.

Instructions

(a) Journalize the July transactions and the July 31 adjusting entry for accrued interest receivable. (Interest is computed using 360 days; omit cost of goods sold entries.)

(b) A/R bal. $ 4,500

(b) Enter the balances at July 1 in the receivable accounts and post the entries to all of the receivable accounts. (Use T-accounts.)

(c) Tot. receivables $14,550

(c) Show the balance sheet presentation of the receivable accounts at July 31.

Calculate and interpret various ratios.

(LO 7, 8), **AN**

P8-9A Suppose the amounts presented here are basic financial information (in millions) from the 2014 annual reports of Nike and adidas.

	Nike	adidas
Sales revenue	$19,176.1	$10,381
Allowance for doubtful accounts, beginning	78.4	119
Allowance for doubtful accounts, ending	110.8	124
Accounts receivable balance (gross), beginning	2,873.7	1,743
Accounts receivable balance (gross), ending	2,994.7	1,553

Instructions

Calculate the accounts receivable turnover and average collection period for both companies. Comment on the difference in their collection experiences.

Problems: Set B

Visit the book's companion website, at **www.wiley.com/college/kimmel**, and choose the Student Companion site to access Problem Set B.

Comprehensive Problem

CP8 Madson Corporation's balance sheet at December 31, 2013, is presented below.

MADSON CORPORATION
Balance Sheet
December 31, 2013

Cash	$13,100	Accounts payable	$ 8,750
Accounts receivable	19,780	Common stock	20,000
Allowance for doubtful accounts	(800)	Retained earnings	12,730
Inventory	9,400		
	$41,480		$41,480

During January 2014, the following transactions occurred. Madson uses the perpetual inventory method.

Jan.   1   Madson accepted a 4-month, 8% note from Matheny Company in payment of Matheny's $1,200 account.
       3   Madson wrote off as uncollectible the accounts of Payton Corporation ($450) and Cruz Company ($280).

8   Madson purchased $17,200 of inventory on account.
11 Madson sold for $25,000 on account inventory that cost $17,500.
15 Madson sold inventory that cost $700 to Rich Jenson for $1,000. Jenson charged this amount on his Visa First Bank card. The service fee charged Madson by First Bank is 3%.
17 Madson collected $22,900 from customers on account.
21 Madson paid $16,300 on accounts payable.
24 Madson received payment in full ($280) from Cruz Company on the account written off on January 3.
27 Madson purchased advertising supplies for $1,400 cash.
31 Madson paid other operating expenses, $3,218.

Adjustment data:

1. Interest is recorded for the month on the note from January 1.
2. Bad debts are expected to be 6% of the January 31, 2014, accounts receivable.
3. A count of advertising supplies on January 31, 2014, reveals that $560 remains unused.
4. The income tax rate is 30%. (*Hint:* Prepare the income statement up to "Income before taxes" and multiply by 30% to compute the amount; round to whole dollars.)

Instructions

(You may want to set up T-accounts to determine ending balances.)

(a) Prepare journal entries for the transactions listed above and adjusting entries. (Include entries for cost of goods sold using the perpetual inventory system.)
(b) Prepare an adjusted trial balance at January 31, 2014.
(c) Prepare an income statement and a retained earnings statement for the month ending January 31, 2014, and a classified balance sheet as of January 31, 2014.

Broadening Your Perspective

Financial Reporting and Analysis

FINANCIAL REPORTING PROBLEM: *Tootsie Roll Industries, Inc.*

BYP8-1   Refer to the financial statements of Tootsie Roll Industries and the accompanying notes to its financial statements in Appendix A.

Instructions

(a) Calculate the accounts receivable turnover and average collection period for 2011. (Use "Net Product Sales." Assume all sales were credit sales.)
(b) Did Tootsie Roll have any potentially significant credit risks in 2011? (*Hint:* Review Note 1 under Revenue recognition and Note 9 to the financial statements.)
(c) What conclusions can you draw from the information in parts (a) and (b)?

COMPARATIVE ANALYSIS PROBLEM: *Tootsie Roll vs. Hershey*

BYP8-2   The financial statements of The Hershey Company are presented in Appendix B, following the financial statements for Tootsie Roll in Appendix A.

Instructions

(a) Based on the information contained in these financial statements, compute the following 2011 values for each company.
   (1) Accounts receivable turnover. (For Tootsie Roll, use "Net product sales." Assume all sales were credit sales.)
   (2) Average collection period for accounts receivable.
(b) What conclusions concerning the management of accounts receivable can be drawn from these data?

RESEARCH CASE

BYP8-3 The August 31, 2009, issue of the *Wall Street Journal* includes an article by Serena Ng and Cari Tuna entitled "Big Firms Are Quick to Collect, Slow to Pay."

Instructions

Read the article and answer the following questions.
(a) How many days did InBev tell its suppliers that it was going to take to pay? How many days did it take previously?
(b) What steps did General Electric take to free up cash? How much cash did it free up?
(c) On average, how many days did companies with more than $5 billion take to pay suppliers, and how many days did they take to collect from their customers? How did this compare to companies with less than $500 million in sales?
(d) Are there any risks involved with being too tough in negotiating delayed payment terms with suppliers?

INTERPRETING FINANCIAL STATEMENTS

BYP8-4 Suppose the information below is from the 2014 financial statements and accompanying notes of The Scotts Company, a major manufacturer of lawn-care products.

(in millions)	2014	2013
Accounts receivable	$ 270.4	$ 259.7
Allowance for uncollectible accounts	10.6	11.4
Sales revenue	2,981.8	2,871.8
Total current assets	1,044.9	999.3

THE SCOTTS COMPANY
Notes to the Financial Statements

Note 19. Concentrations of Credit Risk

Financial instruments which potentially subject the Company to concentration of credit risk consist principally of trade accounts receivable. The Company sells its consumer products to a wide variety of retailers, including mass merchandisers, home centers, independent hardware stores, nurseries, garden outlets, warehouse clubs, food and drug stores and local and regional chains. Professional products are sold to commercial nurseries, greenhouses, landscape services and growers of specialty agriculture crops. Concentrations of accounts receivable at September 30, net of accounts receivable pledged under the terms of the New MARP Agreement whereby the purchaser has assumed the risk associated with the debtor's financial inability to pay ($146.6 million and $149.5 million for 2014 and 2013, respectively), were as follows.

	2014	2013
Due from customers geographically located in North America	53%	52%
Applicable to the consumer business	61%	54%
Applicable to Scotts LawnService®, the professional businesses (primarily distributors), Smith & Hawken® and Morning Song®	39%	46%
Top 3 customers within consumer business as a percent of total consumer accounts receivable	0%	0%

The remainder of the Company's accounts receivable at September 30, 2014 and 2013, were generated from customers located outside of North America, primary retailers, distributors, nurseries and growers in Europe. No concentrations of customers of individual customers within this group account for more than 10% of the Company's accounts receivable at either balance sheet date.

The Company's three largest customers are reported within the Global Consumer segment, and are the only customers that individually represent more than 10% of reported consolidated net sales for each of the last three fiscal years. These three customers accounted for the following percentages of consolidated net sales for the fiscal years ended September 30:

	Largest Customer	2nd Largest Customer	3rd Largest Customer
2014	21.0%	13.5%	13.4%
2013	20.2%	10.9%	10.2%
2012	21.5%	11.2%	10.5%

Instructions

Answer each of the following questions.
(a) Calculate the accounts receivable turnover and average collection period for 2014 for the company.
(b) Is accounts receivable a material component of the company's total 2014 current assets?
(c) Scotts sells seasonal products. How might this affect the accuracy of your answer to part (a)?
(d) Evaluate the credit risk of Scotts' 2014 concentrated receivables.
(e) Comment on the informational value of Scotts' Note 19 on concentrations of credit risk.

REAL-WORLD FOCUS

BYP8-5 *Purpose:* To learn more about factoring from websites that provide factoring services.

Address: **www.ccapital.net**, or go to **www.wiley.com/college/kimmel**

Instructions

Go to the website, click on **Invoice Factoring**, and answer the following questions.
(a) What are some of the benefits of factoring?
(b) What is the range of the percentages of the typical discount rate?
(c) If a company factors its receivables, what percentage of the value of the receivables can it expect to receive from the factor in the form of cash, and how quickly will it receive the cash?

Critical Thinking

DECISION-MAKING ACROSS THE ORGANIZATION

BYP8-6 Jan and Roy Falcon own Club Fab. From its inception, Club Fab has sold merchandise on either a cash or credit basis, but no credit cards have been accepted. During the past several months, the Falcons have begun to question their credit-sales policies. First, they have lost some sales because of their refusal to accept credit cards. Second, representatives of two metropolitan banks have convinced them to accept their national credit cards. One bank, City National Bank, has stated that (1) its credit card fee is 4% and (2) it pays the retailer 96 cents on each $1 of sales within 3 days of receiving the credit card billings.

The Falcons decide that they should determine the cost of carrying their own credit sales. From the accounting records of the past 3 years, they accumulate these data:

	2014	2013	2012
Net credit sales	$500,000	$600,000	$400,000
Collection agency fees for slow-paying customers	2,900	2,600	1,600
Salary of part-time accounts receivable clerk	4,400	4,400	4,400

Credit and collection expenses as a percentage of net credit sales are as follows: uncollectible accounts 1.6%, billing and mailing costs .5%, and credit investigation fee on new customers .2%.

Jan and Roy also determine that the average accounts receivable balance outstanding during the year is 5% of net credit sales. The Falcons estimate that they could earn an average of 10% annually on cash invested in other business opportunities.

Instructions

With the class divided into groups, answer the following.
(a) Prepare a tabulation for each year showing total credit and collection expenses in dollars and as a percentage of net credit sales.

(b) Determine the net credit and collection expenses in dollars and as a percentage of sales after considering the revenue not earned from other investment opportunities. (*Note:* The income lost on the cash held by the bank for 3 days is considered to be immaterial.)

(c) Discuss both the financial and nonfinancial factors that are relevant to the decision.

COMMUNICATION ACTIVITY

BYP8-7 Santana Corporation is a recently formed business selling the "World's Best Doormat." The corporation is selling doormats faster than Santana can make them. It has been selling the product on a credit basis, telling customers to "pay when they can." Oddly, even though sales are tremendous, the company is having trouble paying its bills.

Instructions

Write a memo to the president of Santana Corporation discussing these questions:

(a) What steps should be taken to improve the company's ability to pay its bills?

(b) What accounting steps should be taken to measure its success in improving collections and in recording its collection success?

(c) If the corporation is still unable to pay its bills, what additional steps can be taken with its receivables to ease its liquidity problems?

ETHICS CASE

BYP8-8 As its year-end approaches, it appears that Ortiz Corporation's net income will increase 10% this year. The president of Ortiz Corporation, nervous that the stockholders might expect the company to sustain this 10% growth rate in net income in future years, suggests that the controller increase the allowance for doubtful accounts to 4% of receivables in order to lower this year's net income. The president thinks that the lower net income, which reflects a 6% growth rate, will be a more sustainable rate of growth for Ortiz Corporation in future years. The controller of Ortiz Corporation believes that the company's yearly allowance for doubtful accounts should be 2% of receivables.

Instructions

(a) Who are the stakeholders in this case?

(b) Does the president's request pose an ethical dilemma for the controller?

(c) Should the controller be concerned with Ortiz Corporation's growth rate in estimating the allowance? Explain your answer.

ALL ABOUT YOU

BYP8-9 Credit card usage in the United States is substantial. Many startup companies use credit cards as a way to help meet short-term financial needs. The most common forms of debt for startups are use of credit cards and loans from relatives.

Suppose that you start up Spangles Sandwich Shop. You invested your savings of $20,000 and borrowed $70,000 from your relatives. Although sales in the first few months are good, you see that you may not have sufficient cash to pay expenses and maintain your inventory at acceptable levels, at least in the short term. You decide you may need to use one or more credit cards to fund the possible cash shortfall.

Instructions

(a) Go to the Internet and find two sources that provide insight into how to compare credit card terms.

(b) Develop a list, in descending order of importance, as to what features are most important to you in selecting a credit card for your business.

(c) Examine the features of your present credit card. (If you do not have a credit card, select a likely one online for this exercise.) Given your analysis above, what are the three major disadvantages of your present credit card?

FASB CODIFICATION ACTIVITY

BYP8-10 If your school has a subscription to the FASB Codification, go to **http://aaahq.org/ascLogin.cfm** to log in and prepare responses to the following.

(a) How are receivables defined in the Codification?

(b) What are the conditions under which losses from uncollectible receivables (Bad Debt Expense) should be reported?

Answers to Insight and Accounting Across the Organization Questions

p. 348 When Investors Ignore Warning Signs Q: When would it be appropriate for a company to lower its allowance for doubtful accounts as a percentage of its receivables? **A:** It would be appropriate for a company to lower its allowance for doubtful accounts as a percentage of its receivables if the company's collection experience had improved, or was expected to improve, and therefore the company expected lower defaults as a percentage of receivables.

p. 351 Can Fair Value Be Unfair? Q: What are the arguments in favor of and against fair value accounting for loans and receivables? **A:** Arguments in favor of fair value accounting for loans and receivables are that fair value would provide a more accurate view of a company's financial position. This might provide a useful early warning of when a bank or other financial institution was in trouble because its loans were of poor quality. But, banks argue that estimating fair values is very difficult to do accurately. They are also concerned that volatile fair values could cause large swings in a bank's reported net income.

p. 354 Bad Information Can Lead to Bad Loans Q: What steps should the banks have taken to ensure the accuracy of financial information provided on loan applications? **A:** At a minimum, the bank should have requested copies of recent income tax forms and contacted the supposed employer to verify income. To verify ownership and value of assets, it should have examined bank statements, investment statements, and title documents, and should have employed appraisers.

p. 359 eBay for Receivables Q: What issues should management consider in deciding whether to factor its receivables? **A:** Management must prepare a cash budget and evaluate its projected cash needs. If it projects a cash deficiency, it should first pursue traditional bank financing since it tends to be less expensive than factoring. If traditional financing is not available, management could pursue factoring. If carefully structured, a factoring arrangement can be cost-effective since it can enable the company to outsource many billing and collection activities.

Answers to Self-Test Questions

1. c **2.** c ($1,000 − $300) × (100% − 2%) **3.** a **4.** a ($160,000 × .075) **5.** c ($200,000 ×.10) + ($30,000 − $18,000) **6.** d ($800,000 − $65,000) **7.** c **8.** b **9.** d **10.** d **11.** a $800,000 ÷ (($100,000 + $150,000) ÷ 2) **12.** c (365 days ÷ 7) **13.** c **14.** a **15.** d

A Look at IFRS

The basic accounting and reporting issues related to recognition and measurement of receivables, such as the use of allowance accounts, how to record discounts, use of the allowance method to account for bad debts, and factoring, are essentially the same between IFRS and GAAP.

LEARNING OBJECTIVE 10

Compare the accounting procedures for receivables under GAAP and IFRS.

KEY POINTS

- IFRS requires that loans and receivables be accounted for at amortized cost, adjusted for allowances for doubtful accounts. IFRS sometimes refers to these allowances as **provisions**. The entry to record the allowance would be:

Bad Debt Expense	xxxxxx	
Allowance for Doubtful Accounts		xxxxxx

- Although IFRS implies that receivables with different characteristics should be reported separately, there is no standard that mandates this segregation.

- The FASB and IASB have worked to implement fair value measurement (the amount they currently could be sold for) for financial instruments. Both Boards have faced bitter opposition from various factions. As a consequence, the Boards have adopted a piecemeal approach. The first step is disclosure of fair value information in the notes. The second step is the **fair value option**, which permits, but does not require, companies to record some types of financial instruments at fair values in the financial statements.

- IFRS requires a two-tiered approach to test whether the value of loans and receivables are impaired. First, a company should look at specific loans and receivables to determine whether they are impaired. Then, the loans and receivables as a group should be evaluated for impairment. GAAP does not prescribe a similar two-tiered approach.

- IFRS and GAAP differ in the criteria used to determine how to record a factoring transaction. IFRS is a combination of an approach focused on risks and rewards and loss of control. GAAP uses loss of control as the primary criterion. In addition, IFRS permits partial derecognition of receivables; GAAP does not.

LOOKING TO THE FUTURE

It appears likely that the question of recording fair values for financial instruments will continue to be an important issue to resolve as the Boards work toward convergence. Both the IASB and the FASB have indicated that they believe that financial statements would be more transparent and understandable if companies recorded and reported all financial instruments at fair value. That said, in *IFRS 9*, which was issued in 2009, the IASB created a split model, where some financial instruments are recorded at fair value, but other financial assets, such as loans and receivables, can be accounted for at amortized cost if certain criteria are met. Critics say that this can result in two companies with identical securities accounting for those securities in different ways. A proposal by the FASB would require that nearly all financial instruments, including loans and receivables, be accounted for at fair value. It has been suggested that *IFRS 9* will likely be changed or replaced as the FASB and IASB continue to deliberate the best treatment for financial instruments. In fact, one past member of the IASB said that companies should ignore *IFRS 9* and continue to report under the old standard because in his opinion, it was extremely likely that it would be changed before 2013, the mandatory adoption date of the standard. An ongoing FASB/IASB project on financial instruments addresses a number of issues with implications for receivables.

IFRS PRACTICE

IFRS SELF-TEST QUESTIONS

1. Under IFRS, loans and receivables are to be reported on the statement of financial position at:
   (a) amortized cost.
   (b) amortized cost adjusted for estimated loss provisions.
   (c) historical cost.
   (d) replacement cost.
2. Which of the following statements is **false**?
   (a) Loans and receivables include equity securities purchased by the company.
   (b) Loans and receivables include credit card receivables.
   (c) Loans and receivables include amounts owed by employees as a result of company loans to employees.
   (d) Loans and receivables include amounts resulting from transactions with customers.
3. In recording a factoring transaction:
   (a) IFRS focuses on loss of control.
   (b) GAAP focuses on loss of control and risks and rewards.
   (c) IFRS and GAAP allow partial derecognition.
   (d) IFRS allows partial derecognition
4. Under IFRS:
   (a) the entry to record estimated uncollected accounts is the same as GAAP.
   (b) loans and receivables should only be tested for impairment as a group.
   (c) it is always acceptable to use the direct write-off method.
   (d) all financial instruments are recorded at fair value.
5. Which of the following statements is **true**?
   (a) The fair value option requires that some types of financial instruments be recorded at fair value.
   (b) The fair value option permits, but does not require, that some types of financial instruments be recorded at fair value.
   (c) The fair value option requires that all types of financial instruments be recorded at fair value.
   (d) The FASB and IASB would like to reduce the reliance on fair value accounting for financial instruments in the future.

IFRS CONCEPTS AND APPLICATION

IFRS8-1 What are some steps taken by both the FASB and IASB to move to fair value measurement for financial instruments? In what ways have some of the approaches differed?

INTERNATIONAL FINANCIAL REPORTING PROBLEM: *Zetar plc*

IFRS8-2 The financial statements of Zetar plc are presented in Appendix C. The company's complete annual report, including the notes to its financial statements, is available in the Investors section at **www.zetarplc.com**.

Instructions

Use the company's annual report to answer the following questions.
   (a) According to the Operational Review of Financial Performance, what was one reason why the balance in receivables increased relative to the previous year?
   (b) According to the notes to the financial statements, how are loans and receivables defined?
   (c) Using the notes to the financial statements, what amount of trade receivables were written off (utilised) during 2011?
   (d) Using information in the notes to the financial statements, determine what percentage the provision for impairment of receivables was as a percentage of total trade receivables for 2011 and 2010. How did the ratio change from 2010 to 2011, and what does this suggest about the company's receivables?

Answers to IFRS Self-Test Questions

1. b   **2.** a   **3.** d   **4.** a   **5.** b

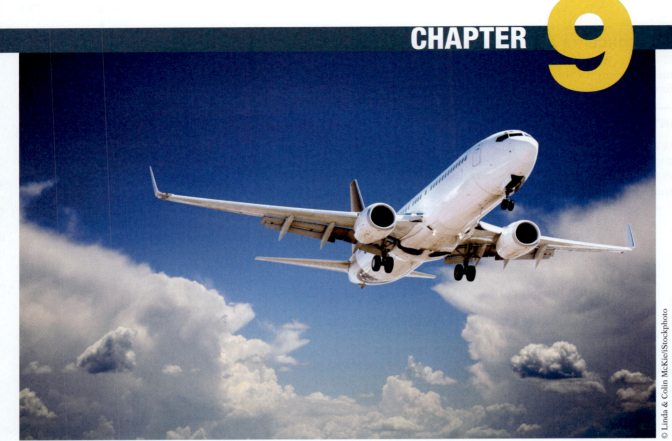

CHAPTER 9

© Linda & Colin McKie/iStockphoto

REPORTING AND ANALYZING LONG-LIVED ASSETS

LEARNING OBJECTIVES

After studying this chapter, you should be able to:

1 Describe how the historical cost principle applies to plant assets.

2 Explain the concept of depreciation.

3 Compute periodic depreciation using the straight-line method, and contrast its expense pattern with those of other methods.

4 Describe the procedure for revising periodic depreciation.

5 Explain how to account for the disposal of plant assets.

6 Describe methods for evaluating the use of plant assets.

7 Identify the basic issues related to reporting intangible assets.

8 Indicate how long-lived assets are reported in the financial statements.

So, you're interested in starting a new business. Have you thought about the airline industry? Is your only experience with airlines as a passenger? Don't let that stop you. Today, the most profitable airlines in the industry are not well-known majors like American Airlines and United. In fact, most giant, older airlines are either bankrupt or on the verge of bankruptcy. In a recent year, five major airlines representing 24% of total U.S. capacity were operating under bankruptcy protection.

Not all airlines are hurting. The growth and profitability in the airline industry today is found at relative newcomers like Southwest Airlines and, more recently, JetBlue Airways. These and other new airlines compete primarily on ticket prices. During a recent five-year period, the low-fare airline market share increased by 47%, reaching 22% of U.S. airline capacity.

Southwest was the first upstart to make it big. It did so by taking a different approach. It bought small, new, fuel-efficient planes. Also, instead of the "hub-and-spoke" approach used by the majors, it opted for direct, short hop, no frills flights. It was all about controlling costs—getting the most out of its efficient new planes.

JetBlue, founded by former employees of Southwest, was recently ranked as the number 1

A TALE OF TWO AIRLINES

airline in the United States by the airline rating company SkyTrax. Management initially attempted to differentiate JetBlue by offering amenities not found on other airlines, such as TVs in every seatback, while adopting Southwest's low-fare model. This approach was successful during JetBlue's early years, as it enjoyed both profitability and rapid growth. However, more recently the company has had to take aggressive steps to rein in costs in order to return to profitability.

In the past, upstarts such as Valujet chose a different approach. They bought planes that were 20 to 30 years old (known in the industry as *zombies*). By buying used planes, Valujet was able to add one or two planes a month to its fleet—an unheard of expansion. Valujet started with a $3.4 million investment and grew to be worth $630 million in its first three years.

But with fuel costs at record high levels, airlines are no longer in the market for old planes. In fact, the old Boeing 727, which until very recently was a mainstay of nearly every airline, is no longer used for passenger flights because it couldn't be operated efficiently. Today, success in the airline business comes from owning the newest and most efficient equipment, and knowing how to get the most out of it.

INSIDE CHAPTER 9 . . .

- **Many U.S. Firms Use Leases**
- **Marketing ROI as Profit Indicator**
- **Sustainability Report Please**
- **Should Companies Write Up Goodwill?**

For airlines and many other companies, making the right decisions regarding long-lived assets is critical because these assets represent huge investments. Management must make many ongoing decisions about long-lived assets—what assets to acquire and when, how to finance them, how to account for them, and when to dispose of them.

In this chapter, we address these and other issues surrounding long-lived assets. The discussion is in two parts: plant assets and intangible assets. **Plant assets** are the property, plant, and equipment (physical assets) that commonly come to mind when we think of what a company owns. Companies also have many important **intangible assets**. These assets, such as copyrights and patents, lack physical substance but can be extremely valuable and vital to a company's success.

The content and organization of this chapter are as follows.

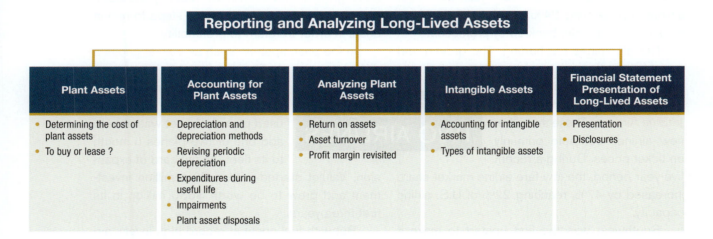

Plant Assets	Accounting for Plant Assets	Analyzing Plant Assets	Intangible Assets	Financial Statement Presentation of Long-Lived Assets
• Determining the cost of plant assets • To buy or lease ?	• Depreciation and depreciation methods • Revising periodic depreciation • Expenditures during useful life • Impairments • Plant asset disposals	• Return on assets • Asset turnover • Profit margin revisited	• Accounting for intangible assets • Types of intangible assets	• Presentation • Disclosures

Plant Assets

LEARNING OBJECTIVE 1

Describe how the historical cost principle applies to plant assets.

Plant assets are resources that have physical substance (a definite size and shape), are used in the operations of a business, and are not intended for sale to customers. They are called various names—property, plant, and equipment; plant and equipment; and fixed assets. By whatever name, these assets are expected to provide service to the company for a number of years. Except for land, plant assets decline in service potential (ability to produce revenue) over their useful lives.

Plant assets are critical to a company's success because they determine the company's capacity and therefore its ability to satisfy customers. With too few planes, for example, JetBlue Airways and Southwest Airlines would lose customers to their competitors. But with too many planes, they would be flying with empty seats. Management must constantly monitor its needs and acquire assets accordingly. Failure to do so results in lost business opportunities or inefficient use of existing assets and is likely to show up eventually in poor financial results.

It is important for a company to (1) keep assets in good operating condition, (2) replace worn-out or outdated assets, and (3) expand its productive assets as needed. The decline of rail travel in the United States can be traced in part to the failure of railroad companies to maintain and update their assets. Conversely, the growth of air travel in this country can be attributed in part to the general willingness of airline companies to follow these essential guidelines.

For many companies, investments in plant assets are substantial. Illustration 9-1 shows the percentages of plant assets in relation to total assets in various companies in a recent year.

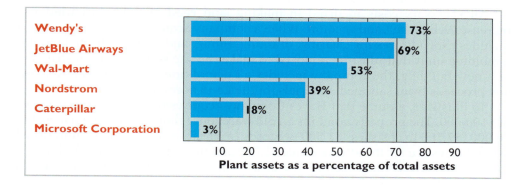

Illustration 9-1 Percentages of plant assets in relation to total assets

DETERMINING THE COST OF PLANT ASSETS

The **historical cost principle** requires that companies record plant assets at cost. Thus, JetBlue Airways and Southwest Airlines record their planes at cost. **Cost consists of all expenditures necessary to acquire an asset and make it ready for its intended use.** For example, when Boeing buys equipment, the purchase price, freight costs paid by Boeing, and installation costs are all part of the cost of the equipment.

Determining which costs to include in a plant asset account and which costs not to include is very important. If a cost is not included in a plant asset account, then it must be expensed immediately. Such costs are referred to as **revenue expenditures**. On the other hand, costs that are not expensed immediately but are instead included in a plant asset account are referred to as **capital expenditures**. JetBlue reported capital expenditures of $480 million during 2011.

This distinction is important; it has immediate, and often material, implications for the income statement. Some companies, in order to boost current income, have **improperly capitalized expenditures** that they should have expensed. For example, suppose that a company improperly capitalizes to a building account $1,000 of maintenance costs incurred at the end of the year. (That is, the costs are included in the asset account Buildings rather than being expensed immediately as Maintenance and Repairs Expense.) If the company is allocating the cost of the building as an expense (depreciating it) over a 40-year life, then the maintenance cost of $1,000 will be incorrectly spread across 40 years instead of being expensed in the current year. As a result, the company will understate current-year expenses by approximately $1,000, and will overstate current-year income by approximately $1,000. Thus, determining which costs to capitalize and which to expense is very important.

Cost is measured by the cash paid in a cash transaction or by the **cash equivalent price** paid when companies use noncash assets in payment. **The cash equivalent price is equal to the fair value of the asset given up or the fair value of the asset received, whichever is more clearly determinable.** Once cost is established, it becomes the basis of accounting for the plant asset over its useful life. Current fair value is not used to increase the recorded cost after acquisition. We explain the application of the historical cost principle to each of the major classes of plant assets in the following sections.

Land

Companies often use land as a building site for a manufacturing plant or office site. The cost of land includes (1) the cash purchase price, (2) closing costs such as title and attorney's fees, (3) real estate brokers' commissions, and (4) accrued property taxes and other liens on the land assumed by the purchaser. For example, if the cash price is $50,000 and the purchaser agrees to pay accrued taxes of $5,000, the cost of the land is $55,000.

All necessary costs incurred in making land **ready for its intended use** increase (debit) the Land account. When a company acquires vacant land, its cost includes expenditures for clearing, draining, filling, and grading. If the land has a building on it that must be removed to make the site suitable for construction of a new building, the company includes all demolition and removal costs, less any proceeds from salvaged materials, in the Land account.

To illustrate, assume that Hayes Company acquires real estate at a cash cost of $100,000. The property contains an old warehouse that is razed at a net cost of $6,000 ($7,500 in costs less $1,500 proceeds from salvaged materials). Additional expenditures are for the attorney's fee $1,000 and the real estate broker's commission $8,000. Given these factors, the cost of the land is $115,000, computed as shown in Illustration 9-2.

Illustration 9-2 Computation of cost of land

Land	
Cash price of property	$ 100,000
Net removal cost of warehouse	6,000
Attorney's fee	1,000
Real estate broker's commission	8,000
Cost of land	**$115,000**

When Hayes records the acquisition, it debits Land and credits Cash for $115,000.

Land Improvements

Land improvements are structural additions made to land, such as driveways, parking lots, fences, landscaping, and underground sprinklers. The cost of land improvements includes all expenditures necessary to make the improvements ready for their intended use. For example, the cost of a new company parking lot includes the amount paid for paving, fencing, and lighting. Thus, the company would debit the total of all of these costs to Land Improvements.

Land improvements have limited useful lives, and their maintenance and replacement are the responsibility of the company. As a result, companies expense (depreciate) the cost of land improvements over their useful lives.

Buildings

Buildings are facilities used in operations, such as stores, offices, factories, warehouses, and airplane hangars. Companies charge to the Buildings account all necessary expenditures relating to the purchase or construction of a building. When a building is **purchased**, such costs include the purchase price, closing costs (attorney's fees, title insurance, etc.), and real estate broker's commission. Costs to make the building ready for its intended use consist of expenditures for remodeling rooms and offices and replacing or repairing the roof, floors, electrical wiring, and plumbing. When a new building is **constructed**, its cost consists of the contract price plus payments made by the owner for architects' fees, building permits, and excavation costs.

In addition, companies add certain interest costs to the cost of a building. Interest costs incurred to finance a construction project are included in the cost of the asset when a significant period of time is required to get the asset ready for use. In these circumstances, interest costs are considered as necessary as materials and labor. However, the inclusion of interest costs in the cost of a constructed building is **limited to interest costs incurred during the construction period**. When construction has been completed, subsequent interest payments on funds borrowed to finance the construction are recorded as increases (debits) to Interest Expense.

Equipment

Equipment includes assets used in operations, such as store check-out counters, office furniture, factory machinery, and delivery trucks. JetBlue Airways' equipment includes aircraft, in-flight entertainment systems, and trucks for ground operations. The cost of equipment consists of the cash purchase price, sales taxes, freight charges, and insurance during transit paid by the purchaser. It also includes expenditures required in assembling, installing, and testing the unit. However, companies treat as expenses the costs of motor vehicle licenses and accident insurance on company trucks and cars. Such items are **annual recurring expenditures and do not benefit future periods**. Two criteria apply in determining the cost of equipment: (1) the frequency of the cost—one time or recurring, and (2) the benefit period—the life of the asset or one year.

To illustrate, assume that Lenard Company purchases a delivery truck at a cash price of $22,000. Related expenditures are sales taxes $1,320, painting and lettering $500, motor vehicle license $80, and a three-year accident insurance policy $1,600. The cost of the delivery truck is $23,820, computed as shown in Illustration 9-3.

Delivery Truck	
Cash price	$ 22,000
Sales taxes	1,320
Painting and lettering	500
Cost of delivery truck	**$23,820**

Illustration 9-3 Computation of cost of delivery truck

Lenard treats the cost of a motor vehicle license as an expense and the cost of an insurance policy as a prepaid asset. Thus, the company records the purchase of the truck and related expenditures as follows.

Equipment	23,820	
License Expense	80	
Prepaid Insurance	1,600	
Cash		25,500
(To record purchase of delivery truck and related expenditures)		

A	=	L	+	SE
+23,820				
				−80 Exp
+1,600				
−25,500				

Cash Flows
−25,500

For another example, assume Merten Company purchases factory machinery at a cash price of $50,000. Related expenditures are sales taxes $3,000, insurance during shipping $500, and installation and testing $1,000. The cost of the factory machinery is $54,500, computed as in Illustration 9-4.

Factory Machinery	
Cash price	$ 50,000
Sales taxes	3,000
Insurance during shipping	500
Installation and testing	1,000
Cost of factory machinery	**$54,500**

Illustration 9-4 Computation of cost of factory machinery

Thus, Merten records the purchase and related expenditures as follows.

Equipment	54,500	
Cash		54,500
(To record purchase of factory machinery and related expenditures)		

A	=	L	+	SE
+54,500				
−54,500				

Cash Flows
−54,500

TO BUY OR LEASE?

In this chapter, we focus on purchased assets, but we want to expose you briefly to an alternative—leasing. A lease is a contractual agreement in which the owner of an asset (the **lessor**) allows another party (the **lessee**) to use the asset for a period of time at an agreed price. In many industries, leasing is quite common. For example, one-third of heavy-duty commercial trucks are leased.

Some advantages of leasing an asset versus purchasing it are:

1. **Reduced risk of obsolescence.** Frequently, lease terms allow the party using the asset (the lessee) to exchange the asset for a more modern one if it becomes outdated. This is much easier than trying to sell an obsolete asset.
2. **Little or no down payment.** To purchase an asset, most companies must borrow money, which usually requires a down payment of at least 20%. Leasing an asset requires little or no down payment.
3. **Shared tax advantages.** Startup companies typically earn little or no profit in their early years, and so they have little need for the tax deductions available from owning an asset. In a lease, the lessor gets the tax advantage because it owns the asset. It often will pass these tax savings on to the lessee in the form of lower lease payments.
4. **Assets and liabilities not reported.** Many companies prefer to keep assets and especially liabilities off their books. Reporting lower assets improves the return on assets (discussed later in this chapter). Reporting fewer liabilities makes the company look less risky. Certain types of leases, called **operating leases**, allow the lessee to account for the transaction as a rental, with neither an asset nor a liability recorded.

Airlines often choose to lease many of their airplanes in long-term lease agreements. In recent financial statements, JetBlue Airways stated that it leased 60 of its 169 planes under operating leases. Because operating leases are accounted for as rentals, these 60 planes were not presented on its balance sheet.

Under another type of lease, a **capital lease**, lessees show both the asset and the liability on the balance sheet. The lessee accounts for capital lease agreements in a way that is very similar to debt-financed purchases: The lessee shows the leased item as an asset on its balance sheet, and the obligation owed to the

---

Accounting Across the Organization
Many U.S. Firms Use Leases

Leasing is big business for U.S. companies. For example, in a recent year leasing accounted for about 31% of all business investment ($218 billion).

Who does the most leasing? Interestingly, major banks such as Continental Bank, J.P. Morgan Leasing, and US Bancorp Equipment Finance are the major lessors. Also, many companies have established separate leasing companies, such as Boeing Capital Corporation, Dell Financial Services, and John Deere Capital Corporation. As an example of the magnitude of leasing, leased planes account for nearly 40% of the U.S. fleet of commercial airlines. Lease Finance Corporation in Los Angeles owns more planes than any airline in the world.

In addition, leasing is becoming increasingly common in the hotel industry. Marriott, Hilton, and InterContinental are increasingly choosing to lease hotels that are owned by someone else.

? Why might airline managers choose to lease rather than purchase their planes? (Answers in *Broadening Your Perspective*.)

lessor as a liability. The lessee depreciates the leased asset in a manner similar to purchased assets. Only four of JetBlue's aircraft were held under capital leases. We discuss leasing further in Chapter 10.

Accounting for Plant Assets

DEPRECIATION

As explained in Chapter 4, depreciation **is the process of allocating to expense the cost of a plant asset over its useful (service) life in a rational and systematic manner**. Such cost allocation is designed to properly match expenses with revenues. (See Illustration 9-5.)

LEARNING OBJECTIVE | 2
Explain the concept of depreciation.

Illustration 9-5 Depreciation as a cost allocation concept

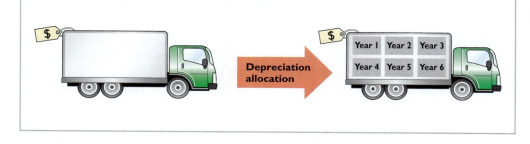

Depreciation affects the balance sheet through accumulated depreciation, which companies report as a deduction from plant assets. It affects the income statement through depreciation expense.

It is important to understand that **depreciation is a cost allocation process, not an asset valuation process**. No attempt is made to measure the change in an asset's fair value during ownership. Thus, the **book value**—cost less accumulated depreciation—of a plant asset may differ significantly from its **fair value**. In fact, if an asset is fully depreciated, it can have zero book value but still have a significant fair value.

Depreciation applies to **three classes of plant assets**: land improvements, buildings, and equipment. Each of these classes is considered to be a **depreciable asset** because the usefulness to the company and the revenue-producing ability of each class decline over the asset's useful life. Depreciation **does not apply to land** because its usefulness and revenue-producing ability generally remain intact as long as the land is owned. In fact, in many cases, the usefulness of land increases over time because of the scarcity of good sites. Thus, **land is not a depreciable asset**.

During a depreciable asset's useful life, its revenue-producing ability declines because of wear and tear. A delivery truck that has been driven 100,000 miles will be less useful to a company than one driven only 800 miles.

A decline in revenue-producing ability may also occur because of obsolescence. **Obsolescence** is the process by which an asset becomes out of date before it physically wears out. The rerouting of major airlines from Chicago's Midway Airport to Chicago-O'Hare International Airport because Midway's runways were too short for giant jets is an example. Similarly, many companies replace their computers long before they originally planned to do so because improvements in new computers make their old computers obsolete.

Recognizing depreciation for an asset does not result in the accumulation of cash for replacement of the asset. The balance in Accumulated Depreciation represents the total amount of the asset's cost that the company has charged to expense to date; **it is not a cash fund**.

FACTORS IN COMPUTING DEPRECIATION

Three factors affect the computation of depreciation, as shown in Illustration 9-6.

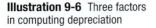

Illustration 9-6 Three factors in computing depreciation

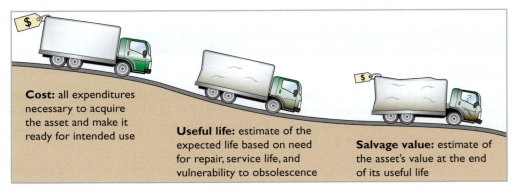

Cost: all expenditures necessary to acquire the asset and make it ready for intended use

Useful life: estimate of the expected life based on need for repair, service life, and vulnerability to obsolescence

Salvage value: estimate of the asset's value at the end of its useful life

1. **Cost.** Earlier in the chapter, we explained the considerations that affect the cost of a depreciable asset. Remember that companies record plant assets at cost, in accordance with the historical cost principle.
2. **Useful life.** Useful life is an estimate of the expected productive life, also called service life, of the asset for its owner. Useful life may be expressed in terms of time, units of activity (such as machine hours), or units of output. Useful life is an estimate. In making the estimate, management considers such factors as the intended use of the asset, repair and maintenance policies, and vulnerability of the asset to obsolescence. The company's past experience with similar assets is often helpful in deciding on expected useful life.
3. **Salvage value.** Salvage value is an estimate of the asset's value at the end of its useful life for its owner. Companies may base the value on the asset's worth as scrap or on its expected trade-in value. Like useful life, salvage value is an estimate. In making the estimate, management considers how it plans to dispose of the asset and its experience with similar assets.

DEPRECIATION METHODS

LEARNING OBJECTIVE 3

Compute periodic depreciation using the straight-line method, and contrast its expense pattern with those of other methods.

Although a number of methods exist, depreciation is generally computed using one of three methods:

1. Straight-line
2. Declining-balance
3. Units-of-activity

Like the alternative inventory methods discussed in Chapter 6, each of these depreciation methods is acceptable under generally accepted accounting principles. Management selects the method it believes best measures an asset's contribution to revenue over its useful life. Once a company chooses a method, it should apply that method consistently over the useful life of the asset. Consistency enhances the ability to analyze financial statements over multiple years.

Illustration 9-7 shows the distribution of the primary depreciation methods in a sample of the largest U.S. companies. Clearly, straight-line depreciation is the most widely used approach. In fact, because some companies use more than one method, **straight-line depreciation is used for some or all of the depreciation taken by more than 95% of U.S. companies**. For this reason, we illustrate procedures for straight-line depreciation and discuss the alternative depreciation approaches only at a conceptual level. This coverage introduces you to the basic idea of depreciation as an allocation concept without entangling you in too much procedural detail. (Also, note that many hand-held calculators are preprogrammed to perform the basic depreciation methods.) Details on the alternative approaches are presented in Appendix 9A.

Our illustration of depreciation methods, both here and in the appendix, is based on the following data relating to a small delivery truck purchased by Bill's Pizzas on January 1, 2014.

Cost	$13,000
Expected salvage value	$1,000
Estimated useful life (in years)	5
Estimated useful life (in miles)	100,000

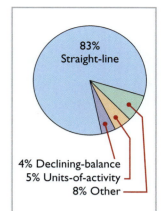

Illustration 9-7 Use of depreciation methods in major U.S. companies

Straight-Line

Under the **straight-line method**, companies expense an equal amount of depreciation each year of the asset's useful life. Management must choose the useful life of an asset based on its own expectations and experience.

To compute the annual depreciation expense, we divide depreciable cost by the estimated useful life. **Depreciable cost** represents the total amount subject to depreciation; it is calculated as the cost of the plant asset less its salvage value. Illustration 9-8 shows the computation of depreciation expense in the first year for Bill's Pizzas' delivery truck.

Illustration 9-8 Formula for straight-line method

Cost	−	**Salvage Value**	=	**Depreciable Cost**
$13,000	−	$1,000	=	$12,000

Depreciable Cost	÷	**Useful Life (in years)**	=	**Depreciation Expense**
$12,000	÷	5	=	**$2,400**

Alternatively, we can compute an annual **rate** at which the company depreciates the delivery truck. In this case, the rate is 20% (100% ÷ 5 years). When an annual rate is used under the straight-line method, the company applies the percentage rate to the depreciable cost of the asset, as shown in the **depreciation schedule** in Illustration 9-9.

Illustration 9-9 Straight-line depreciation schedule

BILL'S PIZZAS

	Computation				Annual	End of Year	
Year	Depreciable Cost	×	Depreciation Rate	=	Depreciation Expense	Accumulated Depreciation	Book Value
2014	$12,000		20%		$ 2,400	$ 2,400	$10,600*
2015	12,000		20		2,400	4,800	8,200
2016	12,000		20		2,400	7,200	5,800
2017	12,000		20		2,400	9,600	3,400
2018	12,000		20		2,400	12,000	**1,000**
				Total	**$12,000**		

*$13,000 − $2,400

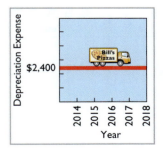

Note that the depreciation expense of $2,400 is the same each year. The book value at the end of the useful life is equal to the estimated $1,000 salvage value.

What happens when an asset is purchased **during** the year, rather than on January 1 as in our example? In that case, it is necessary to **prorate the annual depreciation** for the portion of a year used. If Bill's Pizzas had purchased the delivery truck on April 1, 2014, the company would use the truck for 9 months in 2014. The depreciation for 2014 would be $1,800 ($12,000 × 20% × $\frac{9}{12}$ of a year).

As indicated earlier, the straight-line method predominates in practice. For example, such large companies as Campbell Soup, Marriott, and General Mills use the straight-line method. It is simple to apply, and it matches expenses with revenues appropriately when the use of the asset is reasonably uniform throughout the service life. The types of assets that give equal benefits over useful life generally are those for which daily use does not affect productivity. Examples are office furniture and fixtures, buildings, warehouses, and garages for motor vehicles.

Declining-Balance

The **declining-balance method** computes depreciation expense using a constant rate applied to a declining book value. This method is called an **accelerated-depreciation method** because it results in higher depreciation in the early years of an asset's life than does the straight-line approach. However, because the total amount of depreciation (the depreciable cost) taken over an asset's life is the same **no matter what approach** is used, the declining-balance method produces a decreasing annual depreciation expense over the asset's useful life. In early years, declining-balance depreciation expense will exceed straight-line, but in later years, it will be less than straight-line. Managers might choose an accelerated approach if they think that an asset's utility will decline quickly.

Companies can apply the declining-balance approach at different rates, which result in varying speeds of depreciation. A common declining-balance rate is double the straight-line rate. Using that rate, the method is referred to as the **double-declining-balance method**.

If we apply the double-declining-balance method to Bill's Pizzas' delivery truck, assuming a five-year life, we get the pattern of depreciation shown in Illustration 9-10. **Illustration 9A-2 presents the computations behind these numbers.** Again, note that total depreciation over the life of the truck is $12,000, the depreciable cost.

Illustration 9-10 Declining-balance depreciation schedule

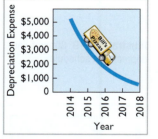

		BILL'S PIZZAS		
		Annual	**End of Year**	
	Year	**Depreciation Expense**	**Accumulated Depreciation**	**Book Value**
	2014	$ 5,200	$ 5,200	$7,800
	2015	3,120	8,320	4,680
	2016	1,872	10,192	2,808
	2017	1,123	11,315	1,685
	2018	685	12,000	1,000
	Total	$12,000		

Units-of-Activity

As indicated earlier, useful life can be expressed in ways other than a time period. Under the **units-of-activity method**, useful life is expressed in terms of the total units of production or the use expected from the asset. The units-of-activity method is ideally suited to factory machinery: Companies can measure production in terms of units of output or in terms of machine hours used in operating the machinery. It is also possible to use the method for such items as delivery equipment (miles driven) and airplanes (hours in use). The units-of-activity method is generally not suitable for such assets as buildings or furniture because activity levels are difficult to measure for these assets.

Applying the units-of-activity method to the delivery truck owned by Bill's Pizzas, we first must know some basic information. Bill's expects to be able to drive the truck a total of 100,000 miles. Illustration 9-11 shows depreciation over the five-year life based on an assumed mileage pattern. **Illustration 9A-4 presents the computations used to arrive at these results.**

BILL'S PIZZAS

Year	Units of Activity (miles)	Annual Depreciation Expense	Accumulated Depreciation	Book Value
			End of Year	
2014	15,000	$ 1,800	$ 1,800	$11,200
2015	30,000	3,600	5,400	7,600
2016	20,000	2,400	7,800	5,200
2017	25,000	3,000	10,800	2,200
2018	10,000	1,200	12,000	1,000
Total	100,000	$12,000		

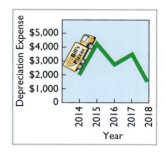

Illustration 9-11 Units-of-activity depreciation schedule

As the name implies, under units-of-activity depreciation, the amount of depreciation is proportional to the activity that took place during that period. For example, the delivery truck was driven twice as many miles in 2015 as in 2014, and depreciation was exactly twice as much in 2015 as it was in 2014.

Management's Choice: Comparison of Methods

Illustration 9-12 compares annual and total depreciation expense for Bill's Pizzas under the three methods.

Year	Straight-Line	Declining-Balance	Units-of-Activity
2014	$ 2,400	$ 5,200	$ 1,800
2015	2,400	3,120	3,600
2016	2,400	1,872	2,400
2017	2,400	1,123	3,000
2018	2,400	685	1,200
	$12,000	$12,000	$12,000

Illustration 9-12 Comparison of depreciation methods

Annual depreciation expense varies considerably among the methods, but **total depreciation expense is the same ($12,000) for the five-year period**. Each method is acceptable in accounting because each recognizes the decline in service potential of the asset in a rational and systematic manner. Illustration 9-13 graphs the depreciation expense pattern under each method.

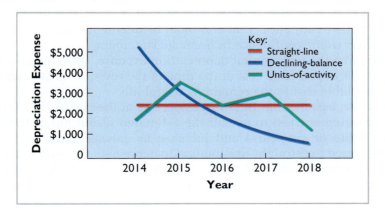

Illustration 9-13 Patterns of depreciation

Depreciation and Income Taxes

The Internal Revenue Service (IRS) allows corporate taxpayers to deduct depreciation expense when computing taxable income. However, the tax regulations of the IRS do not require the taxpayer to use the same depreciation method on the tax return that it uses in preparing financial statements.

Consequently, many large corporations use straight-line depreciation in their financial statements in order to maximize net income; at the same time, they use a special accelerated-depreciation method on their tax returns in order to minimize their income taxes. For tax purposes, taxpayers must use on their tax returns either the straight-line method or a special accelerated-depreciation method called the **Modified Accelerated Cost Recovery System** (MACRS).

Depreciation Disclosure in the Notes

Companies must disclose the choice of depreciation method in their financial statements or in related notes that accompany the statements. Illustration 9-14 shows excerpts from the "Property and equipment" notes from the financial statements of Southwest Airlines.

Illustration 9-14 Disclosure of depreciation policies

SOUTHWEST AIRLINES
Notes to the Financial Statements

Property and equipment Depreciation is provided by the straight-line method to estimated residual values over periods ranging from 20 to 25 years for flight equipment and 5 to 30 years for ground property and equipment once the asset is placed in service. Amortization of property under capital leases is on a straight-line basis over the lease term and is included in depreciation expense.

From this note, we learn that Southwest Airlines uses the straight-line method to depreciate its planes over periods of 20 to 25 years.

REVISING PERIODIC DEPRECIATION

LEARNING OBJECTIVE 4
Describe the procedure for revising periodic depreciation.

Management should periodically review annual depreciation expense. If wear and tear or obsolescence indicates that annual depreciation is either inadequate or excessive, the company should change the depreciation expense amount.

When a change in an estimate is required, the company makes the change in **current and future years but not to prior periods**. Thus, when making the change, the company (1) does not correct previously recorded depreciation expense, but (2) revises depreciation expense for current and future years. The rationale for this treatment is that continual restatement of prior periods would adversely affect users' confidence in financial statements.

To determine the new annual depreciation expense, the company first computes the asset's depreciable cost at the time of the revision. It then allocates the revised depreciable cost to the remaining useful life.

To illustrate, assume that Bill's Pizzas decides at the end of 2017 (prior to the year-end adjusting entries) to extend the estimated useful life of the truck one year (a total life of six years) and increase its salvage value to $2,200. The company has used the straight-line method to depreciate the asset to date. Depreciation per year was $2,400 (($13,000 − $1,000) ÷ 5). Accumulated depreciation after three years (2014–2016) is $7,200 ($2,400 × 3), and book value is

$5,800 ($13,000 − $7,200). The new annual depreciation is $1,200, computed on December 31, 2017, as follows.

Book value, 1/1/17	$ 5,800	
Less: New salvage value	2,200	
Depreciable cost	$ 3,600	
Remaining useful life	3 years	(2017–2019)
Revised annual depreciation ($3,600 ÷ 3)	**$1,200**	

Illustration 9-15 Revised depreciation computation

Bill's Pizzas does not make a special entry for the change in estimate. On December 31, 2017, during the preparation of adjusting entries, it records depreciation expense of $1,200.

Companies must disclose in the financial statements significant changes in estimates. Although a company may have a legitimate reason for changing an estimated life, financial statement users should be aware that some companies might change an estimate simply to achieve financial statement goals. For example, extending an asset's estimated life reduces depreciation expense and increases current period income.

In a recent year, AirTran Airways (now owned by Southwest Airlines) increased the estimated useful lives of some of its planes from 25 to 30 years and increased the estimated lives of related aircraft parts from 5 years to 30 years. It disclosed that the change in estimate decreased its net loss for the year by approximately $0.6 million, or about $0.01 per share. Whether these changes were appropriate depends on how reasonable it is to assume that planes will continue to be used for a long time. Our Feature Story suggests that although in the past many planes lasted a long time, it is also clear that because of high fuel costs, airlines are now scrapping many of their old, inefficient planes.

EXPENDITURES DURING USEFUL LIFE

During the useful life of a plant asset, a company may incur costs for ordinary repairs, additions, and improvements. **Ordinary repairs** are expenditures to maintain the operating efficiency and expected productive life of the unit. They usually are fairly small amounts that occur frequently throughout the service life. Examples are motor tune-ups and oil changes, the painting of buildings, and the replacing of worn-out gears on factory machinery. Ordinary repairs are debited to Maintenance and Repairs Expense as incurred.

In contrast, **additions and improvements** are costs incurred to **increase** the operating efficiency, productive capacity, or expected useful life of the plant asset. These expenditures are usually material in amount and occur infrequently during the period of ownership. Expenditures for additions and improvements increase the company's investment in productive facilities and are generally debited to the plant asset affected. Thus, they are **capital expenditures**. The accounting for capital expenditures varies depending on the nature of the expenditure.

Northwest Airlines at one time spent $120 million to spruce up 40 jets. The improvements were designed to extend the lives of the planes, meet stricter government noise limits, and save money. The capital expenditure was expected to extend the life of the jets by 10 to 15 years and save about $560 million compared to the cost of buying new planes. The jets were, on average, 24 years old.

ANATOMY OF A FRAUD

Bernie Ebbers was the founder and CEO of the phone company WorldCom. The company engaged in a series of increasingly large, debt-financed acquisitions of other companies. These acquisitions made the company grow quickly, which made the stock price increase dramatically. However, because the acquired companies all had different accounting systems, WorldCom's financial records were a mess. When WorldCom's performance started to flatten out, Bernie coerced WorldCom's accountants to engage in a number of fraudulent activities to make net income look better than it really was and thus prop up the stock price. One of these frauds involved treating $7 billion of line costs as capital expenditures. The line costs, which were rental fees paid to other phone companies to use their phone lines, had always been properly expensed in previous years. Capitalization delayed expense recognition to future periods and thus boosted current-period profits.

Total take: $7 billion

THE MISSING CONTROLS

Documentation procedures. The company's accounting system was a disorganized collection of non-integrated systems, which resulted from a series of corporate acquisitions. Top management took advantage of this disorganization to conceal its fraudulent activities.

Independent internal verification. A fraud of this size should have been detected by a routine comparison of the actual physical assets with the list of physical assets shown in the accounting records.

IMPAIRMENTS

As noted earlier, the book value of plant assets is rarely the same as the fair value. In instances where the value of a plant asset declines substantially, its fair value might fall materially below book value. This may happen because a machine has become obsolete, or the market for the product made by the machine has dried up or has become very competitive. A **permanent decline** in the fair value of an asset is referred to as an impairment. So as not to overstate the asset on the books, the company writes the asset down to its new fair value during the year in which the decline in value occurs. Recently, Disney recorded a $200 million write-down on its action movie *John Carter*. Disney spent more than $300 million producing the film.

In the past, some companies **improperly** delayed recording losses on impairments until a year when it was "convenient" to do so—when the impact on the company's reported results was minimized. For example, in a year when a company has record profits, it can afford to write down some of its bad assets without hurting its reported results too much. As discussed in Chapter 4, the practice of timing the recognition of gains and losses to achieve certain income results is known as **earnings management**. Earnings management reduces earnings quality. To minimize earnings management, accounting standards now require immediate loss recognition on impaired assets.

Write-downs can create problems for users of financial statements. Critics of write-downs note that after a company writes down assets, its depreciation expense will be lower in all subsequent periods. Some companies improperly inflate asset write-downs in bad years, when they are going to report poor results anyway. (This practice is referred to as "taking a big bath.") Then in subsequent years, when the company recovers, its results will look even better because of lower depreciation expense.

PLANT ASSET DISPOSALS

Companies dispose of plant assets that are no longer useful to them. Illustration 9-16 shows the three ways in which companies make plant asset disposals.

Whatever the disposal method, the company must determine the book value of the plant asset at the time of disposal in order to determine the gain or loss. Recall that the book value is the difference between the cost of the plant asset and the accumulated depreciation to date. If the disposal occurs at any time prior to the end of

LEARNING OBJECTIVE 5

Explain how to account for the disposal of plant assets.

Illustration 9-16 Methods of plant asset disposal

Sale	**Retirement**	**Exchange**
Equipment is sold to another party.	Equipment is scrapped or discarded.	Existing equipment is traded for new equipment.

the year, the company must record depreciation for the fraction of the year to the date of disposal. The company then eliminates the book value by reducing (debiting) Accumulated Depreciation for the total depreciation associated with that asset to the date of disposal and reducing (crediting) the asset account for the cost of the asset.

Sale of Plant Assets

In a disposal by sale, the company compares the book value of the asset with the proceeds received from the sale. If the proceeds from the sale **exceed** the book value of the plant asset, a **gain on disposal** occurs. If the proceeds from the sale **are less than** the book value of the plant asset sold, a **loss on disposal** occurs.

Only by coincidence will the book value and the fair value of the asset be the same at the time the asset is sold. Gains and losses on sales of plant assets are therefore quite common. As an example, Delta Air Lines reported a $94 million gain on the sale of five Boeing B-727-200 aircraft and five Lockheed L-1011-1 aircraft.

GAIN ON SALE. To illustrate a gain on sale of plant assets, assume that on July 1, 2014, Wright Company sells office furniture for $16,000 cash. The office furniture originally cost $60,000 and as of January 1, 2014, had accumulated depreciation of $41,000. Depreciation for the first six months of 2014 is $8,000. Wright records depreciation expense and updates accumulated depreciation to July 1 as follows.

July 1	Depreciation Expense		8,000	
	Accumulated Depreciation—Equipment			8,000
	(To record depreciation expense for the first 6 months of 2014)			

A = L + SE

−8,000 Exp

−8,000

Cash Flows
no effect

After the accumulated depreciation balance is updated, the company computes the gain or loss as the difference between the proceeds from sale and the book value at the date of disposal. Wright Company has a gain on disposal of $5,000, as computed in Illustration 9-17.

Cost of office furniture	$60,000
Less: Accumulated depreciation ($41,000 + $8,000)	49,000
Book value at date of disposal	11,000
Proceeds from sale	16,000
Gain on disposal of plant asset	**$ 5,000**

Illustration 9-17 Computation of gain on disposal

Wright records the sale and the gain on sale of the plant asset as follows.

A	=	L	+	SE
+16,000				
+49,000				
−60,000				
				+5,000 Rev

Cash Flows
+16,000

July	1	Cash			16,000	
		Accumulated Depreciation—Equipment			49,000	
		Equipment				60,000
		Gain on Disposal of Plant Assets				5,000
		(To record sale of office furniture				
		at a gain)				

Companies report a gain on disposal of plant assets in the "Other revenues and gains" section of the income statement. Recently, the shares of Sears Holdings Corporation rose 19% when the company announced its intention to sell 1,200 stores to raise cash.

LOSS ON SALE. Assume that instead of selling the office furniture for $16,000, Wright sells it for $9,000. In this case, Wright experiences a loss of $2,000, as computed in Illustration 9-18.

Illustration 9-18 Computation of loss on disposal

Cost of office furniture	$60,000
Less: Accumulated depreciation	49,000
Book value at date of disposal	11,000
Proceeds from sale	9,000
Loss on disposal of plant asset	**$ 2,000**

Wright records the sale and the loss on sale of the plant asset as follows.

A	=	L	+	SE
+9,000				
+49,000				
				−2,000 Exp
−60,000				

Cash Flows
+9,000

July	1	Cash			9,000	
		Accumulated Depreciation—Equipment			49,000	
		Loss on Disposal of Plant Assets			2,000	
		Equipment				60,000
		(To record sale of office furniture at				
		a loss)				

Companies report a loss on disposal of the plant asset in the "Other expenses and losses" section of the income statement.

Retirement of Plant Assets

Companies simply retire, rather than sell, some assets at the end of their useful life. For example, some productive assets used in manufacturing may have very specific uses, and they consequently have no ready market when the company no longer needs them. In such a case, the asset is simply retired.

Companies record retirement of an asset as a special case of a disposal where no cash is received. They decrease (debit) Accumulated Depreciation for the full amount of depreciation taken over the life of the asset and decrease (credit) the asset account for the original cost of the asset. The loss (a gain is not possible on a retirement) is equal to the asset's book value on the date of retirement.[1]

Analyzing Plant Assets

LEARNING OBJECTIVE **6**

Describe methods for evaluating the use of plant assets.

The presentation of financial statement information about plant assets enables decision makers to analyze the company's use of its plant assets. We will use two measures to analyze plant assets: return on assets and asset turnover. We also show how profit margin relates to both.

[1]More advanced courses discuss the accounting for exchanges, the third method of plant asset disposal.

RETURN ON ASSETS

An overall measure of profitability is the **return on assets**. This ratio is computed by dividing net income by average assets. (Average assets are commonly calculated by adding the beginning and ending values of assets and dividing by 2.) Return on assets indicates the amount of net income generated by each dollar of assets. Thus, the higher the return on assets, the more profitable the company.

Information is provided below related to JetBlue Airways.

	JetBlue (in millions)
Net income, 2011	$ 86
Total assets, 12/31/11	7,071
Total assets, 12/31/10	6,593
Net sales, 2011	4,504

Illustration 9-19 presents the 2011 and 2010 return on assets of JetBlue Airways, Southwest Airlines, and industry averages.

$$\text{Return on Assets} = \frac{\text{Net Income}}{\text{Average Total Assets}}$$

JetBlue Airways ($ in millions)		Southwest Airlines	Industry Average
2011	2010	2011	2011
$\dfrac{\$86}{(\$7{,}071 + \$6{,}593)/2} = 1.3\%$	1.5%	1.1%	4.0%

Illustration 9-19 Return on assets for JetBlue and Southwest

JetBlue's return on assets was better than that of Southwest's but significantly lower than the airline industry. The airline industry has experienced financial difficulties in recent years as it attempted to cover high labor, fuel, and security costs while offering fares low enough to attract customers. Such difficulties are reflected in the low industry average for return on assets and the very low values for JetBlue and Southwest. Recently, Southwest announced that it would not add

Accounting Across the Organization

Marketing ROI as Profit Indicator

Marketing executives use the basic finance concept underlying return on assets to determine "marketing return on investment (ROI)." They calculate *marketing ROI* as the profit generated by a marketing initiative divided by the investment in that initiative.

It can be tricky to determine what to include in the "investment" amount and how to attribute profit to a particular marketing initiative. However, many firms feel that measuring marketing ROI is worth the effort because it allows managers to evaluate the relative effectiveness of various programs. In addition, it helps quantify the benefits that marketing provides to the organization. In periods of tight budgets, the marketing ROI number can provide particularly valuable evidence to help a marketing manager avoid budget cuts.

Source: James O. Mitchel, "Marketing ROI," *LIMRA's MarketFacts Quarterly* (Summer 2004), p. 15.

 How does measuring marketing ROI support the overall efforts of the organization? (Answers in *Broadening Your Perspective*.)

additional planes beyond the 700 it already had until it met its investment-return targets. Instead, the company is adding seats to existing planes and replacing some smaller planes with larger ones.

DECISION TOOLKIT

DECISION CHECKPOINTS	INFO NEEDED FOR DECISION	TOOL TO USE FOR DECISION	HOW TO EVALUATE RESULTS
Is the company using its assets effectively?	Net income and average assets	$\text{Return on assets} = \dfrac{\text{Net income}}{\text{Average total assets}}$	Higher value suggests favorable efficiency (use of assets).

ASSET TURNOVER

Asset turnover indicates how efficiently a company uses its assets to generate sales—that is, how many dollars of sales a company generates for each dollar invested in assets. It is calculated by dividing net sales by average total assets. When we compare two companies in the same industry, the one with the higher asset turnover is operating more efficiently. It is generating more sales per dollar invested in assets. Illustration 9-20 presents the asset turnovers for JetBlue Airways and Southwest Airlines.

Illustration 9-20 Asset turnovers for JetBlue and Southwest

$$\text{Asset Turnover} = \frac{\text{Net Sales}}{\text{Average Total Assets}}$$

JetBlue Airways ($ in millions)		Southwest Airlines	Industry Average
2011		2011	2011
$\dfrac{\$4,504}{(\$7,071 + \$6,593)/2} = 0.66$ times	0.58 times	0.93 times	0.80 times

(2010 for JetBlue: 0.58 times)

These asset turnover values tell us that for each dollar of assets, JetBlue generates sales of $0.66 and Southwest $0.93. Southwest is more successful in generating sales per dollar invested in assets. The average asset turnover for the airline industry is 0.80 times. In recent years, airlines have reduced both the number of planes used and routes flown to try to pack more customers on a plane. This would increase the asset turnover.

Asset turnovers vary considerably across industries. During a recent year, the average asset turnover for electric utility companies was 0.34. The grocery industry had an average asset turnover of 2.89. Asset turnover values, therefore, are only comparable within—not between—industries.

PROFIT MARGIN REVISITED

In Chapter 5, you learned about **profit margin**. That ratio is calculated by dividing net income by net sales. It tells how effective a company is in turning its sales into income—that is, how much income each dollar of sales provides. Illustration 9-21 shows that return on assets can be computed as the product of profit margin and asset turnover.

This relationship has very important strategic implications for management. From Illustration 9-21, we can see that if a company wants to increase its return on assets, it can do so in two ways: (1) by increasing the margin it generates from

Illustration 9-21 Composition of return on assets

Profit Margin	×	Asset Turnover	=	Return on Assets
$\dfrac{\text{Net Income}}{\text{Net Sales}}$	×	$\dfrac{\text{Net Sales}}{\text{Average Total Assets}}$	=	$\dfrac{\text{Net Income}}{\text{Average Total Assets}}$

each dollar of goods that it sells (the profit margin), or (2) by increasing the volume of goods that it sells (the asset turnover). For example, most grocery stores have very low profit margins, often in the range of 1 or 2 cents for every dollar of goods sold. Grocery stores, therefore, focus on asset turnover: They rely on high turnover to increase their return on assets. Alternatively, a store selling luxury goods, such as expensive jewelry, doesn't generally have a high turnover. Consequently, a seller of luxury goods focuses on having a high profit margin. Recently, Apple decided to offer a less expensive version of its popular iPod. This new product would provide a lower margin, but higher volume, than Apple's more expensive version.

Let's evaluate the return on assets of JetBlue Airways for 2011 by evaluating its components—profit margin and asset turnover. See Illustration 9-22.

Illustration 9-22 Components of rate of return for JetBlue and Southwest

	Profit Margin	×	Asset Turnover	=	Return on Assets
JetBlue Airways	1.9%	×	0.66	=	1.3%
Southwest Airlines	1.2%	×	0.93	=	1.1%

JetBlue's return on asset of 1.3% versus Southwest's 1.1% means that JetBlue generates 1.3 cents per each dollar invested in assets, while Southwest generates 1.1 cents. Illustration 9-22 reveals that although these two airlines have similar return on asset values, they achieve this return in a slightly different fashion. First, JetBlue's profit margin of 1.9% versus Southwest's of 1.2% means that for every dollar of sales, JetBlue generates approximately 1.9 cents of net income, while Southwest generates approximately 1.2 cents. Second, JetBlue's asset turnover of 0.66 means that it generates 66 cents of sales per each dollar invested in assets, while Southwest generates 93 cents. Therefore, in 2011, Southwest was more effective at generating sales from its assets, while JetBlue was better at deriving profit from those sales.

DECISION TOOLKIT

DECISION CHECKPOINTS	INFO NEEDED FOR DECISION	TOOL TO USE FOR DECISION	HOW TO EVALUATE RESULTS
How effective is the company at generating sales from its assets?	Net sales and average total assets	$\text{Asset turnover} = \dfrac{\text{Net sales}}{\text{Average total assets}}$	Indicates the sales dollars generated per dollar of assets. A high value suggests the company is effective in using its resources to generate sales.

People, Planet, and Profit Insight

Sustainability Report Please

Sustainability reports identify how the company is meeting its corporate social responsibilities. Many companies, both large and small, are now issuing these reports. For example, companies such as Disney, Best Buy, Microsoft, Ford, and ConocoPhilips issue these reports. Presented below is an adapted section of BHP Billiton's (a global mining, oil, and gas company) sustainability report on its environmental policies. These policies are to (1) take action to address the challenges of climate change, (2) set and achieve targets that reduce pollution, and (3) enhance biodiversity by assessing and considering ecological values and land-use aspects. Here is how BHP Billiton measures the success or failure of some of these policies:

Environment	Result	Trend	Commentary	Target Date
Aggregate Group target of 6% reduction in greenhouse gas emissions per unit of production	On track	Improvement	Our greenhouse gas emissions intensity index has reduced 7% on our FY2006 baseline year	30 June 2012
Aggregate Group target of 13% reduction in carbon-based energy use per unit of production	On track	Improvement	Our energy intensity index has reduced 6% on our FY2006 baseline year	30 June 2012
Aggregate Group target of a 10% improvement in the ratio of water recycled/reused to high-quality water consumed	On track	Deterioration	Our water use index has improved 7% on our FY2007 baseline year	30 June 2012

In addition to the environment, BHP Billiton has sections in its sustainability report which discuss people, safety, health, and community.

Source: BHP Billiton, *2010 Sustainability Report.*

? Why do you believe companies issue sustainability reports? (Answers in *Broadening Your Perspective.*)

Intangible Assets

Intangible assets are rights, privileges, and competitive advantages that result from ownership of long-lived assets that do not possess physical substance. Many companies' most valuable assets are intangible. Some widely known intangibles are Microsoft's patents, McDonalds's franchises, the trade name iPod, and Nike's trademark "swoosh."

Analysts estimated that in the early 1980s, the fair value of intangible assets to total assets was close to 40%. By 2000, the percentage was over 80%—quite a difference. What has happened is that research and development (e.g., hi-tech and bio-tech) has grown substantially. At the same time, many companies (e.g., Nike and Microsoft) have developed brand power which enables them to maintain their market position.

As you will learn in this section, financial statements do report numerous intangibles. Yet, many other financially significant intangibles are not reported. To give an example, according to its financial statements in a recent year, Google had total stockholders' equity of $22.7 billion. But its market value—the total market price of all its shares on that same date—was roughly $178.5 billion. Thus, its actual market value was about $155.8 billion greater than the amount reported for stockholders' equity on the balance sheet. It is not uncommon for a company's reported book value to differ from its market value because balance sheets are reported at historical cost. But such an extreme difference seriously diminishes the usefulness of the balance sheet to decision-makers.

In the case of Google, the difference is due to unrecorded intangibles. For many high-tech or so-called intellectual-property companies, most of their value is from intangibles, many of which are not reported under current accounting rules.

Intangibles may be evidenced by contracts, licenses, and other documents. Intangibles may arise from the following sources:

1. Government grants, such as patents, copyrights, licenses, trademarks, and trade names.

2. Acquisition of another business in which the purchase price includes a payment for goodwill.

3. Private monopolistic arrangements arising from contractual agreements, such as franchises and leases.

ACCOUNTING FOR INTANGIBLE ASSETS

Companies record intangible assets at cost. Intangibles are categorized as having either a limited life or an indefinite life. If an intangible has a **limited life**, the company allocates its cost over the asset's useful life using a process similar to depreciation. The process of allocating to expense the cost of intangibles is referred to as amortization. The cost of intangible assets with **indefinite lives should not be amortized**.

To record amortization of an intangible asset, a company increases (debits) Amortization Expense, and decreases (credits) the specific intangible asset. (Unlike depreciation, no contra account, such as Accumulated Amortization, is usually used.)

Intangible assets are typically amortized on a straight-line basis. For example, the legal life of a patent is 20 years. Companies **amortize the cost of a patent over its 20-year life or its useful life, whichever is shorter**. To illustrate the computation of patent amortization, assume that National Labs purchases a patent at a cost of $60,000 on June 30. If National estimates the useful life of the patent to be eight years, the annual amortization expense is $7,500 ($60,000 ÷ 8) per year. National records $3,750 ($7,500 × $\frac{6}{12}$) of amortization for the six-month period ended December 31 as follows.

Dec. 31	Amortization Expense	3,750	
	Patent		3,750
	(To record patent amortization)		

When a company has significant intangibles, analysts should evaluate the reasonableness of the useful life estimates that the company discloses in the notes to its financial statements. In determining useful life, the company should consider obsolescence, inadequacy, and other factors. These may cause a patent or other intangible to become economically ineffective before the end of its legal life.

For example, suppose Intel obtained a patent on a new computer chip it had developed. The legal life of the patent is 20 years. From experience, however, we know that the useful life of a computer chip patent is rarely more than five years. Because new superior chips are developed so rapidly, existing chips become obsolete. Consequently, we would question the amortization expense of Intel if it amortized its patent on a computer chip for a life significantly longer than a five-year period. Amortizing an intangible over a period that is too long will understate amortization expense, overstate Intel's net income, and overstate its assets.

DECISION TOOLKIT

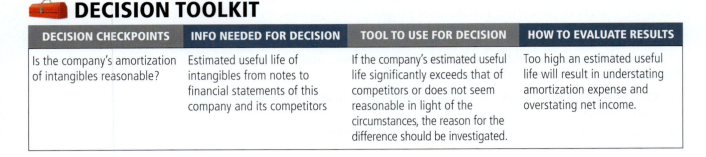

DECISION CHECKPOINTS	INFO NEEDED FOR DECISION	TOOL TO USE FOR DECISION	HOW TO EVALUATE RESULTS
Is the company's amortization of intangibles reasonable?	Estimated useful life of intangibles from notes to financial statements of this company and its competitors	If the company's estimated useful life significantly exceeds that of competitors or does not seem reasonable in light of the circumstances, the reason for the difference should be investigated.	Too high an estimated useful life will result in understating amortization expense and overstating net income.

TYPES OF INTANGIBLE ASSETS

Patents

A patent is an exclusive right issued by the U.S. Patent Office that enables the recipient to manufacture, sell, or otherwise control an invention for a period of 20 years from the date of the grant. **The initial cost of a patent is the cash or cash equivalent price paid to acquire the patent.**

The saying "A patent is only as good as the money you're prepared to spend defending it" is very true. Most patents are subject to some type of litigation by competitors. A well-known example is the patent infringement suit brought by Amazon.com against Barnes & Noble.com regarding its online shopping software. If the owner incurs legal costs in successfully defending the patent in an infringement suit, such costs are considered necessary to establish the validity of the patent. Thus, **the owner adds those costs to the Patent account and amortizes them over the remaining life of the patent**.

Research and Development Costs

Research and development costs are expenditures that may lead to patents, copyrights, new processes, and new products. Many companies spend considerable sums of money on research and development (R&D) in an ongoing effort to develop new products or processes. For example, in a recent year IBM spent over $5.1 billion on research and development. There are uncertainties in identifying the extent and timing of the future benefits of these expenditures. As a result, companies usually record research and development costs **as an expense when incurred**, whether the R&D is successful or not.

To illustrate, assume that Laser Scanner Company spent $3 million on research and development that resulted in two highly successful patents. It spent $20,000 on legal fees for the patents. It can include the legal fees in the cost of the patents but cannot include the R&D costs in the cost of the patents. Instead, Laser Scanner records the R&D costs as an expense when incurred.

Many disagree with this accounting approach. They argue that to expense these costs leads to understated assets and net income. Others argue that capitalizing these costs would lead to highly speculative assets on the balance sheet. Who is right is difficult to determine.

Copyrights

The federal government grants copyrights, which give the owner the exclusive right to reproduce and sell an artistic or published work. Copyrights last for the life of the creator plus 70 years. The cost of the copyright consists of the **cost of acquiring and defending it**. The cost may be only the small fee paid to the U.S. Copyright Office, or it may amount to a great deal more if a copyright is acquired from another party. The useful life of a copyright generally is significantly shorter than its legal life.

Trademarks and Trade Names

A **trademark** or **trade name** is a word, phrase, jingle, or symbol that distinguishes or identifies a particular enterprise or product. Trade names like Wheaties, Monopoly, Sunkist, Kleenex, Coca-Cola, Big Mac, and Jeep create immediate product identification and generally enhance the sale of the product. The creator or original user may obtain the exclusive legal right to the trademark or trade name by registering it with the U.S. Patent Office. Such registration provides 20 years' protection and may be renewed indefinitely as long as the trademark or trade name is in use.

If a company purchases the trademark or trade name, the cost is the purchase price. If the company develops the trademark or trade name itself, the cost includes attorney's fees, registration fees, design costs, successful legal defense costs, and other expenditures directly related to securing it. Because trademarks and trade names have indefinite lives, they are not amortized.

Franchises

When you purchase a RAV4 from a Toyota dealer, fill up your tank at the corner Shell station, eat lunch at Subway, or make reservations at a Marriott hotel, you are dealing with franchises. A **franchise** is a contractual arrangement under which the franchisor grants the franchisee the right to sell certain products, to perform specific services, or to use certain trademarks or trade names, usually within a designated geographic area.

Another type of franchise is a license. Licenses granted by a governmental body permit a business to use public property in performing its services. Examples are the use of city streets for a bus line or taxi service; the use of public land for telephone, electric, and cable television lines; and the use of airwaves for radio or TV broadcasting. In a recent license agreement, Fox, CBS, and NBC agreed to pay $27.9 billion for the right to broadcast NFL football games over an eight-year period.

Franchises and licenses may be granted for a definite period of time, or the time period may be indefinite or perpetual. **When a company can identify costs with the acquisition of the franchise or license, it should recognize an intangible asset.** Companies record as **operating expenses** annual payments made under a franchise agreement in the period in which they are incurred. In the case of a limited life, a company amortizes the cost of a franchise (or license) as operating expense over the useful life. If the life is indefinite or perpetual, the cost is not amortized.

Goodwill

Usually, the largest intangible asset that appears on a company's balance sheet is goodwill. **Goodwill** represents the value of all favorable attributes that relate to a company that are not attributable to any other specific asset. These include exceptional management, desirable location, good customer relations, skilled employees, high-quality products, fair pricing policies, and harmonious relations with labor unions. Goodwill is unique because unlike other assets such as investments, plant assets, and even other intangibles, which can be sold **individually** in the marketplace, goodwill can be identified only with the business **as a whole**.

If goodwill can be identified only with the business as a whole, how can it be determined? Certainly, many business enterprises have many of the factors cited above (exceptional management, desirable location, and so on). However, to determine the amount of goodwill in these situations would be difficult and very subjective. In other words, to recognize goodwill without an exchange transaction that puts a value on the goodwill would lead to subjective valuations that do not contribute to the reliability of financial statements. **Therefore, companies record goodwill only when there is an exchange transaction that involves the purchase of an entire business. When an entire business is purchased,**

goodwill is the excess of cost over the fair value of the net assets (assets less liabilities) acquired.

In recording the purchase of a business, a company debits the identifiable acquired assets and credits liabilities at their fair values, credits cash for the purchase price, and records the difference as the cost of goodwill. Goodwill is not amortized because it is considered to have an indefinite life. However, it must be written down if a company determines the value of goodwill has been permanently impaired.

International Insight

Should Companies Write Up Goodwill?

Softbank Corp. was Japan's biggest Internet company. At one time, it boosted the profit margin of its mobile-phone unit from 3.2% to 11.2% through what appeared to some as accounting tricks. What did it do? It wrote down the value of its mobile-phone-unit assets by half. This would normally result in a huge loss. But rather than take a loss, the company wrote up goodwill by the same amount. How did this move increase earnings? The assets were being depreciated over 10 years, but the company amortizes goodwill over 20 years. (Amortization of goodwill was allowed under the accounting standards it followed at that time.) While the new treatment did not break any rules, the company was criticized by investors for not providing sufficient justification or a detailed explanation for the sudden shift in policy.

Source: Andrew Morse and Yukari Iwatani Kane, "Softbank's Accounting Shift Raises Eyebrows," *Wall Street Journal* (August 28, 2007), p. C1.

? Do you think that this treatment would be allowed under U.S. GAAP? (Answers in *Broadening Your Perspective*.)

Financial Statement Presentation of Long-Lived Assets

LEARNING OBJECTIVE 8

Indicate how long-lived assets are reported in the financial statements.

Usually, companies show plant assets in the financial statements under "Property, plant, and equipment," and they show intangibles separately under "Intangible assets." Illustration 9-23 shows a typical balance sheet presentation of long-lived assets, adapted from a recent The Coca-Cola Company balance sheet.

Illustration 9-23
Presentation of property, plant, and equipment and intangible assets

THE COCA-COLA COMPANY Balance Sheet (partial) (in millions)		
Property, plant, and equipment		
Land	$	699
Buildings and improvements		3,816
Machinery and equipment		10,355
Containers and other		1,597
		16,467
Less: Accumulated depreciation		6,906
		9,561
Intangible assets		
Trademarks with indefinite lives		6,183
Goodwill		4,224
Other intangible assets		2,421
		$12,828

Intangibles do not usually use a contra asset account like the contra asset account Accumulated Depreciation used for plant assets. Instead, companies record amortization of intangibles as a direct decrease (credit) to the asset account.

Either within the balance sheet or in the notes, companies should disclose the balances of the major classes of assets, such as land, buildings, and equipment, and of accumulated depreciation by major classes or in total. In addition, they should describe the depreciation and amortization methods used and disclose the amount of depreciation and amortization expense for the period.

KEEPING AN EYE ON CASH

Depreciation and amortization expense are among the biggest causes of differences between accrual-accounting net income and net cash provided by operating activities. Depreciation and amortization reduce net income, but they do not use up any cash. Therefore, to determine net cash provided by operating activities, companies add depreciation and amortization back to net income. For example, if a company reported net income of $175,000 during the year and had depreciation expense of $40,000, net cash provided by operating activities would be $215,000 (assuming no other accrual-accounting differences). The operating activities section of Coca-Cola's statement of cash flows reports the following adjustment for depreciation and amortization.

THE COCA-COLA COMPANY
Statement of Cash Flows (partial)
(in millions)

Real World

Cash flow from operating activities

Net income	$6,906
Plus: Depreciation and amortization	1,236

The adjustment for depreciation and amortization was more than twice as big as any other adjustment required to convert net income to net cash provided by operating activities.

It is also interesting to examine the statement of cash flows to determine the amount of property, plant, and equipment a company purchased and the cash it received from property, plant, and equipment sold in a given year. For example, the investing activities section of Coca-Cola reports the following.

THE COCA-COLA COMPANY
Statement of Cash Flows (partial)
(in millions)

Real World

Cash flow from investing activities

Acquisitions and investments	$(2,452)
Purchases of property, plant, and equipment	(1,993)
Proceeds from disposals of property, plant, and equipment	104
Other	192

As indicated, Coca-Cola made significant purchases and sales of property, plant, and equipment. The level of purchases suggests that Coca-Cola believes that it can earn a reasonable rate of return on these assets.

USING THE DECISION TOOLKIT

Delta Air Lines, Inc., headquartered in Atlanta, Georgia, is one of the largest airlines in the world. It serves 342 destinations in 61 countries.

Instructions

Review the excerpts from the company's 2011 annual report that follow and then answer the following questions.

1. What method does the company use to depreciate its aircraft? Over what period is the company depreciating these aircraft?
2. What type of intangible assets does the company have, and how are they being accounted for?
3. Compute the company's return on assets ratio, asset turnover ratio, and profit margin ratio for 2011 and 2010. Comment on your results.

(in millions)	2011	2010
Net income (loss)	$ 854	$ 593
Net sales	35,115	31,755
Beginning total assets	43,188	43,539
Ending total assets	43,499	43,188

DELTA AIR LINES, INC.
Notes to the Financial Statements (Partial)

Long-Lived Assets

The following table shows our property and equipment:

(in millions, except for estimated useful life)	Estimated Useful Life	December 31, 2011	December 31, 2010
Flight equipment	21–30 years	$21,001	$20,312
Ground property and equipment	3–40 years	3,256	3,123
Flight and ground equipment under capital leases	Shorter of lease term or estimated useful life	1,127	988
Assets constructed for others	30 years	234	—
Advance payments for equipment		77	48
Less: accumulated depreciation and amortization		(5,472)	(4,164)
Total property and equipment, net		$20,223	$20,307

We record property and equipment at cost and depreciate or amortize these assets on a straight-line basis to their estimated residual values over their estimated useful lives.

Goodwill and Other Intangible Assets

Goodwill. As of December 31, 2011 and 2010, our goodwill balance was $9.8 billion. In evaluating goodwill for impairment, we estimate the fair value of our reporting unit by considering market capitalization and other factors if it is more likely than not that the fair value of our reporting unit is less than its carrying value. If the reporting unit's fair value exceeds its carrying value, no further testing is required. If, however, the reporting unit's carrying value exceeds its fair value, we then determine the amount of the impairment charge, if any. We recognize an impairment charge if the carrying value of the reporting unit's goodwill exceeds its estimated fair value.

Identifiable Intangible Assets. Our identifiable intangible assets had a net carrying amount of $4.8 billion at December 31, 2011. Indefinite-lived assets are not amortized and consist primarily of routes, slots, the Delta tradename, and assets related to SkyTeam. Definite-lived intangible assets consist primarily of marketing agreements and contracts and are amortized on a straight-line basis or under the undiscounted cash flows method over the estimated economic life of the respective agreements and contracts. Costs incurred to renew or extend the term of an intangible asset are expensed as incurred.

We perform the impairment test for indefinite-lived intangible assets by comparing the asset's fair value to its carrying value. . . . We recognize an impairment charge if the asset's carrying value exceeds its estimated fair value.

Solution

1. The company depreciates property and equipment using the straight-line approach. It depreciates aircraft over a 21–30-year life.
2. The company has a goodwill balance of $9.8 billion which it tests for impairment. It also has other identifiable intangible assets with a carrying value of $4.8 billion. These include indefinite-life assets such as routes, slots, the Delta tradename, and assets related to SkyTeam. Indefinite-life intangibles are tested for impairment. Definite-life intangibles, including marketing agreements and contracts, are amortized on a straight-line basis or using the undiscounted cash flows method.
3.

	2011	2010
Return on assets	$\dfrac{\$854}{(\$43,188 + \$43,499)/2} = 2.0\%$	$\dfrac{\$593}{(\$43,539 + \$43,188)/2} = 1.4\%$
Asset turnover	$\dfrac{\$35,115}{(\$43,188 + \$43,499)/2} = 0.81 \text{ times}$	$\dfrac{\$31,755}{(\$43,539 + \$43,188)/2} = 0.73 \text{ times}$
Profit margin	$\dfrac{\$854}{\$35,115} = 2.4\%$	$\dfrac{\$593}{\$31,755} = 1.9\%$

Delta's return on assets increased from 2011 to 2010. While its profit margin was low in both years, Delta was able to increase its asset turnover and profit margin. This suggests that its ability to generate sales from its planes and its ability to generate profits from sales both increased.

Summary of Learning Objectives

1 **Describe how the historical cost principle applies to plant assets.** The cost of plant assets includes all expenditures necessary to acquire the asset and make it ready for its intended use. Once cost is established, a company uses that amount as the basis of accounting for the plant asset over its useful life.

2 **Explain the concept of depreciation.** Depreciation is the process of allocating to expense the cost of a plant asset over its useful (service) life in a rational and systematic manner. Depreciation is not a process of valuation, and it is not a process that results in an accumulation of cash. Depreciation reflects an asset's decreasing usefulness and revenue-producing ability, resulting from wear and tear and from obsolescence.

3 **Compute periodic depreciation using the straight-line method, and contrast its expense pattern with those of other methods.** The formula for straight-line depreciation is:

$$\frac{\text{Cost} - \text{Salvage value}}{\text{Useful life (in years)}}$$

The expense patterns of the three depreciation methods are as follows.

Method	Annual Depreciation Pattern
Straight-line	Constant amount
Declining-balance	Decreasing amount
Units-of-activity	Varying amount

4 **Describe the procedure for revising periodic depreciation.** Companies make revisions of periodic depreciation in present and future periods, not retroactively.

5 **Explain how to account for the disposal of plant assets.** The procedure for accounting for the disposal of a plant asset through sale or retirement is: (a) Eliminate the book value of the plant asset at the date of disposal. (b) Record cash proceeds, if any. (c) Account for the difference between the book value and the cash proceeds as a gain or a loss on disposal.

6 **Describe methods for evaluating the use of plant assets.** Plant assets may be analyzed using return on assets and asset turnover. Return on assets consists of two components: asset turnover and profit margin.

7 **Identify the basic issues related to reporting intangible assets.** Companies report intangible assets at their cost less any amounts amortized. If an intangible asset has a limited life, its cost should be allocated (amortized) over its useful life. Intangible assets with indefinite lives should not be amortized.

8 **Indicate how long-lived assets are reported in the financial statements.** Companies usually show plant assets under "Property, plant, and equipment"; they show intangibles separately under "Intangible assets." Either within the balance sheet or in the notes, companies disclose the balances of the major classes of assets, such as land, buildings, and equipment, and accumulated depreciation by major classes or in total. They describe the depreciation and amortization methods used, and disclose the amount of depreciation and amortization expense for the period. In the statement of cash flows, depreciation and amortization expense are added back to net income to determine net cash provided by operating activities. The investing section reports cash paid or received to purchase or sell property, plant, and equipment.

DECISION TOOLKIT *A SUMMARY*

DECISION CHECKPOINTS	INFO NEEDED FOR DECISION	TOOL TO USE FOR DECISION	HOW TO EVALUATE RESULTS
Is the company using its assets effectively?	Net income and average assets	$\text{Return on assets} = \dfrac{\text{Net income}}{\text{Average total assets}}$	Higher value suggests favorable efficiency (use of assets).
How effective is the company at generating sales from its assets?	Net sales and average total assets	$\text{Asset turnover} = \dfrac{\text{Net income}}{\text{Average total assets}}$	Indicates the sales dollars generated per dollar of assets. A high value suggests the company is effective in using its resources to generate sales.
Is the company's amortization of intangibles reasonable?	Estimated useful life of intangibles from notes to financial statements of this company and its competitors	If the company's estimated useful life significantly exceeds that of competitors or does not seem reasonable in light of the circumstances, the reason for the difference should be investigated.	Too high an estimated useful life will result in understating amortization expense and overstating net income.

Appendix 9A

Calculation of Depreciation Using Other Methods

LEARNING OBJECTIVE 9

Compute periodic depreciation using the declining-balance method and the units-of-activity method.

In this appendix, we show the calculations of the depreciation expense amounts that we used in the chapter for the declining-balance and units-of-activity methods.

DECLINING-BALANCE

The **declining-balance method** produces a decreasing annual depreciation expense over the useful life of the asset. The method is so named because the computation of periodic depreciation is based on a **declining book value** (cost less accumulated depreciation) of the asset. Annual depreciation expense is computed by multiplying the book value at the beginning of the year by the declining-balance depreciation rate. **The depreciation rate remains constant from year to year, but the book value to which the rate is applied declines each year.**

Book value for the first year is the cost of the asset because the balance in accumulated depreciation at the beginning of the asset's useful life is zero. In subsequent years, book value is the difference between cost and accumulated depreciation at the beginning of the year. **Unlike other depreciation methods, the declining-balance method ignores salvage value in determining the amount to which the declining-balance rate is applied.** Salvage value, however, does limit the total depreciation that can be taken. Depreciation stops when the asset's book value equals its expected salvage value.

As noted in the chapter, a common declining-balance rate is double the straight-line rate—the **double-declining-balance method**. If Bill's Pizzas uses the double-declining-balance method, the depreciation rate is 40% (2 × the straight-line rate of 20%). Illustration 9A-1 presents the formula and computation of depreciation for the first year on the delivery truck.

Book Value at Beginning of Year	×	Declining-Balance Rate	=	Depreciation Expense
$13,000	×	40%	=	$5,200

Illustration 9A-1 Formula for declining-balance method

Illustration 9A-2 presents the depreciation schedule under this method.

BILL'S PIZZAS

	Computation			Annual	End of Year	
Year	Book Value Beginning of Year ×	Depreciation Rate =		Depreciation Expense	Accumulated Depreciation	Book Value
2014	$13,000	40%		$5,200	$ 5,200	$7,800*
2015	7,800	40		3,120	8,320	4,680
2016	4,680	40		1,872	10,192	2,808
2017	2,808	40		1,123	11,315	1,685
2018	1,685	40		685**	12,000	1,000

*$13,000 − $5,200
**Computation of $674 ($1,685 × 40%) is adjusted to $685 in order for book value to equal salvage value.

Illustration 9A-2 Double-declining-balance depreciation schedule

The delivery equipment is 69% depreciated ($8,320 ÷ $12,000) at the end of the second year. Under the straight-line method, it would be depreciated 40% ($4,800 ÷ $12,000) at that time. Because the declining-balance method produces higher depreciation expense in the early years than in the later years, it is considered an **accelerated-depreciation method**.

The declining-balance method is compatible with the expense recognition principle. It matches the higher depreciation expense in early years with the higher benefits received in these years. Conversely, it recognizes lower depreciation expense in later years when the asset's contribution to revenue is less. Also, some assets lose their usefulness rapidly because of obsolescence. In these cases, the declining-balance method provides a more appropriate depreciation amount.

When an asset is purchased during the year, it is necessary to prorate the declining-balance depreciation in the first year on a time basis. For example, if Bill's Pizzas had purchased the delivery equipment on April 1, 2014, depreciation for 2014 would be $3,900 ($13,000 × 40% × $\frac{9}{12}$). The book value for computing depreciation in 2015 then becomes $9,100 ($13,000 − $3,900), and the 2015 depreciation is $3,640 ($9,100 × 40%).

UNITS-OF-ACTIVITY

Under the **units-of-activity method**, sometimes called the *units-of-production method*, useful life is expressed in terms of the total units of production or use expected from the asset. The units-of-activity method is ideally suited to equipment whose activity can be measured in units of output, miles driven, or hours in use. The units-of-activity method is generally not suitable for assets for which depreciation is a function more of time than of use.

To use this method, a company estimates the total units of activity for the entire useful life and divides that amount into the depreciable cost to determine the depreciation cost per unit. It then multiplies the depreciation cost per unit by the units of activity during the year to find the annual depreciation for that year.

To illustrate, assume that Bill's Pizzas estimates it will drive its new delivery truck 15,000 miles in the first year. Illustration 9A-3 presents the formula and computation of depreciation expense in the first year.

Illustration 9A-3 Formula for units-of-activity method

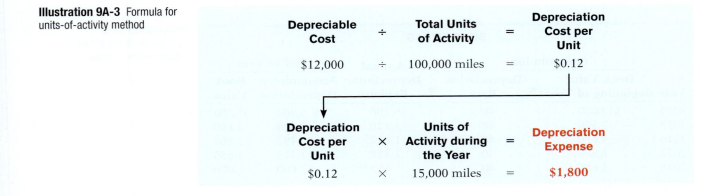

Illustration 9A-4 shows the depreciation schedule, using assumed mileage data.

Illustration 9A-4 Units-of-activity depreciation schedule

			BILL'S PIZZAS			
	Computation			**Annual**	**End of Year**	
Year	**Units of Activity**	×	**Depreciation Cost/Unit** =	**Depreciation Expense**	**Accumulated Depreciation**	**Book Value**
2014	15,000		$0.12	**$1,800**	$ 1,800	$11,200*
2015	30,000		0.12	**3,600**	5,400	7,600
2016	20,000		0.12	**2,400**	7,800	5,200
2017	25,000		0.12	**3,000**	10,800	2,200
2018	10,000		0.12	**1,200**	12,000	**1,000**

*$13,000 − $1,800

The units-of-activity method is not nearly as popular as the straight-line method, primarily because it is often difficult to make a reasonable estimate of total activity. However, this method is used by some very large companies, such as Standard Oil Company of California and Boise Cascade Corporation. When the productivity of the asset varies significantly from one period to another, the units-of-activity method results in the best matching of expenses with revenues.

This method is easy to apply when assets are purchased during the year. In such a case, companies use the productivity of the asset for the partial year in computing the depreciation.

Summary of Learning Objective for Appendix 9A

9 Compute periodic depreciation using the declining-balance method and the units-of-activity method. The depreciation expense calculation for each of these methods is:

Declining-balance:

$$\begin{array}{c} \text{Book value at} \\ \text{beginning of year} \end{array} \times \begin{array}{c} \text{Declining-balance} \\ \text{rate} \end{array} = \begin{array}{c} \text{Depreciation} \\ \text{expense} \end{array}$$

Units-of-activity:

$$\begin{array}{c} \text{Depreciable} \\ \text{cost} \end{array} \div \begin{array}{c} \text{Total units} \\ \text{of activity} \end{array} = \begin{array}{c} \text{Depreciation} \\ \text{cost per unit} \end{array}$$

$$\begin{array}{c} \text{Depreciation cost} \\ \text{per unit} \end{array} \times \begin{array}{c} \text{Units of activity} \\ \text{during year} \end{array} = \begin{array}{c} \text{Depreciation} \\ \text{expense} \end{array}$$

Glossary

Terms are highlighted in blue throughout the chapter.

Accelerated-depreciation method A depreciation method that produces higher depreciation expense in the early years than the straight-line approach.

Additions and improvements Costs incurred to increase the operating efficiency, productive capacity, or expected useful life of a plant asset.

Amortization The process of allocating to expense the cost of an intangible asset.

Asset turnover Indicates how efficiently a company uses its assets to generate sales; calculated as net sales divided by average total assets.

Capital expenditures Expenditures that increase the company's investment in plant assets.

Capital lease A contractual agreement allowing one party (the lessee) to use another party's asset (the lessor); accounted for like a debt-financed purchase by the lessee.

Cash equivalent price An amount equal to the fair value of the asset given up or the fair value of the asset received, whichever is more clearly determinable.

Copyright An exclusive right granted by the federal government allowing the owner to reproduce and sell an artistic or published work.

Declining-balance method A depreciation method that applies a constant rate to the declining book value of the asset and produces a decreasing annual depreciation expense over the asset's useful life.

Depreciable cost The cost of a plant asset less its salvage value.

Depreciation The process of allocating to expense the cost of a plant asset over its useful life in a rational and systematic manner.

Franchise A contractual arrangement under which the franchisor grants the franchisee the right to sell certain products, to perform specific services, or to use certain trademarks or trade names, usually within a designated geographic area.

Goodwill The value of all favorable attributes that relate to a company that are not attributable to any other specific asset.

Impairment A permanent decline in the fair value of an asset.

Intangible assets Rights, privileges, and competitive advantages that result from the ownership of long-lived assets that do not possess physical substance.

Lessee A party that has made contractual arrangements to use another party's asset for a period at an agreed price.

Lessor A party that has agreed contractually to let another party use its asset for a period at an agreed price.

Operating lease A contractual agreement allowing one party (the lessee) to use the asset of another party (the lessor); accounted for as a rental by the lessee.

Ordinary repairs Expenditures to maintain the operating efficiency and expected productive life of the asset.

Patent An exclusive right issued by the U.S. Patent Office that enables the recipient to manufacture, sell, or otherwise control an invention for a period of 20 years from the date of the grant.

Plant assets Resources that have physical substance, are used in the operations of the business, and are not intended for sale to customers.

Research and development costs Expenditures that may lead to patents, copyrights, new processes, and new products; must be expensed as incurred.

Return on assets A profitability measure that indicates the amount of net income generated by each dollar of assets; computed as net income divided by average assets.

Revenue expenditures Expenditures that are immediately charged against revenues as an expense.

Straight-line method A method in which companies expense an equal amount of depreciation for each year of the asset's useful life.

Trademark (trade name) A word, phrase, jingle, or symbol that distinguishes or identifies a particular enterprise or product.

Units-of-activity method A depreciation method in which useful life is expressed in terms of the total units of production or use expected from the asset.

WILEY PLUS

Self-Test, Brief Exercises, Exercises, Problem Set A, and many more resources are available for practice in WileyPLUS.

Note: All Questions, Exercises, and Problems marked with an asterisk relate to material in the appendix to the chapter.

Self-Test Questions

(Answers in *Broadening Your Perspective*.)

(LO 1) **1.** Corrieten Company purchased equipment and incurred these costs:

Cash price	$24,000
Sales taxes	1,200
Insurance during transit	200
Installation and testing	400
Total costs	$25,800

What amount should be recorded as the cost of the equipment?
(a) $24,000.   (c) $25,400.
(b) $25,200.   (d) $25,800.

(LO 1) **2.** ◎━━◎ Harrington Corporation recently leased a number of trucks from Andre Corporation. In inspecting the books of Harrington Corporation, you notice that the trucks have not been recorded as assets on its balance sheet. From this, you can conclude that Harrington is accounting for this transaction as a/an:
(a) operating lease.   (c) purchase.
(b) capital lease.   (d) None of the above.

(LO 2) **3.** Depreciation is a process of:
(a) valuation.   (c) cash accumulation.
(b) cost allocation.   (d) appraisal.

(LO 3) **4.** Cuso Company purchased equipment on January 1, 2013, at a total invoice cost of $400,000. The equipment has an estimated salvage value of $10,000 and an estimated useful life of 5 years. What is the amount of accumulated depreciation at December 31, 2014, if the straight-line method of depreciation is used?
(a) $80,000.   (c) $78,000.
(b) $160,000.   (d) $156,000.

(LO 3) **5.** ◎━━◎ A company would minimize its depreciation expense in the first year of owning an asset if it used:
(a) a high estimated life, a high salvage value, and declining-balance depreciation.
(b) a low estimated life, a high salvage value, and straight-line depreciation.
(c) a high estimated life, a high salvage value, and straight-line depreciation.
(d) a low estimated life, a low salvage value, and declining-balance depreciation.

(LO 4) **6.** When there is a change in estimated depreciation:
(a) previous depreciation should be corrected.
(b) current and future years' depreciation should be revised.
(c) only future years' depreciation should be revised.
(d) None of the above.

(LO 4) **7.** Able Towing Company purchased a tow truck for $60,000 on January 1, 2014. It was originally depreciated on a straight-line basis over 10 years with an assumed salvage value of $12,000. On December 31, 2016, before adjusting entries had been made, the company decided to change the remaining estimated life to 4 years (including 2016) and the salvage value to $2,000. What was the depreciation expense for 2016?
(a) $6,000.   (c) $15,000.
(b) $4,800.   (d) $12,100.

(LO 4) **8.** Additions to plant assets:
(a) decrease liabilities.
(b) increase a repair expense account.
(c) increase a purchases account.
(d) are capital expenditures.

(LO 5) **9.** Bennie Razor Company has decided to sell one of its old manufacturing machines on June 30, 2014. The machine was purchased for $80,000 on January 1, 2010, and was depreciated on a straight-line basis for 10 years assuming no salvage value. If the machine was sold for $26,000, what was the amount of the gain or loss recorded at the time of the sale?
(a) $18,000 loss.   (c) $22,000 gain.
(b) $54,000 loss.   (d) $46,000 gain.

(LO 6) **10.** Which of the following measures provides an indication of how efficient a company is in employing its assets?
(a) Current ratio.
(b) Profit margin.
(c) Debt to assets ratio.
(d) Asset turnover.

(LO 6) **11.** Lake Coffee Company reported net sales of $180,000, net income of $54,000, beginning total assets of $200,000, and ending total assets of $300,000. What was the company's asset turnover?
(a) 0.90   (c) 0.72
(b) 0.20   (d) 1.39

(LO 7) **12.** Pierce Company incurred $150,000 of research and development costs in its laboratory to develop a new product. It spent $20,000 in legal fees for a patent granted on January 2, 2014. On July 31, 2014, Pierce paid $15,000 for legal fees in a successful defense of the patent. What is the total amount that should be debited to Patents through July 31, 2014?
(a) $150,000.   (c) $185,000.
(b) $35,000.   (d) Some other amount.

(LO 7) **13.** Indicate which one of these statements is **true**.
(a) Since intangible assets lack physical substance, they need to be disclosed only in the notes to the financial statements.

(b) Goodwill should be reported as a contra account in the stockholders' equity section.

(c) Totals of major classes of assets can be shown in the balance sheet, with asset details disclosed in the notes to the financial statements.

(d) Intangible assets are typically combined with plant assets and inventory and then shown in the property, plant, and equipment section.

(LO 7) **14.** If a company reports goodwill as an intangible asset on its books, what is the one thing you know with certainty?

(a) The company is a valuable company worth investing in.

(b) The company has a well-established brand name.

(c) The company purchased another company.

(d) The goodwill will generate a lot of positive business for the company for many years to come.

(LO 7) **15.** Which of the following statements is **false**?

(a) If an intangible asset has a finite life, it should be amortized.

(b) The amortization period of an intangible asset can exceed 20 years.

(c) Goodwill is recorded only when a business is purchased.

(d) Research and development costs are expensed when incurred, except when the research and development expenditures result in a successful patent.

*16. Kant Enterprises purchased a truck for $11,000 on (LO 9) January 1, 2013. The truck will have an estimated salvage value of $1,000 at the end of 5 years. If you use the units-of-activity method, the balance in accumulated depreciation at December 31, 2014, can be computed by the following formula:

(a) ($11,000 ÷ Total estimated activity) × Units of activity for 2014.

(b) ($10,000 ÷ Total estimated activity) × Units of activity for 2014.

(c) ($11,000 ÷ Total estimated activity) × Units of activity for 2013 and 2014.

(d) ($10,000 ÷ Total estimated activity) × Units of activity for 2013 and 2014.

Go to the book's companion website, **www.wiley.com/college/kimmel**, to access additional Self-Test Questions.

Questions

1. Mrs. Betancourt is uncertain about how the historical cost principle applies to plant assets. Explain the principle to Mrs. Betancourt.

2. How is the cost for a plant asset measured in a cash transaction? In a noncash transaction?

3. Carington Company acquires the land and building owned by Ankiel Company. What types of costs may be incurred to make the asset ready for its intended use if Carington Company wants to use only the land? If it wants to use both the land and the building?

4. Malor Inc. needs to upgrade its diagnostic equipment. At the time of purchase, Malor had expected the equipment to last 8 years. Unfortunately, it was obsolete after only 4 years. Ronald Nolan, CFO of Malor Inc., is considering leasing new equipment rather than buying it. What are the potential benefits of leasing?

5. In a recent newspaper release, the president of Ferguson Company asserted that something has to be done about depreciation. The president said, "Depreciation does not come close to accumulating the cash needed to replace the asset at the end of its useful life." What is your response to the president?

6. Adriana is studying for the next accounting examination. She asks your help on two questions: (a) What is salvage value? (b) How is salvage value used in determining depreciable cost under the straight-line method? Answer Adriana's questions.

7. Contrast the straight-line method and the units-of-activity method in relation to (a) useful life and (b) the pattern of periodic depreciation over useful life.

8. Contrast the effects of the three depreciation methods on annual depreciation expense.

9. In the fourth year of an asset's 5-year useful life, the company decides that the asset will have a 6-year service life. How should the revision of depreciation be recorded? Why?

10. Distinguish between ordinary repairs and capital expenditures during an asset's useful life.

11. How is a gain or a loss on the sale of a plant asset computed?

12. Lakeland Corporation owns a machine that is fully depreciated but is still being used. How should Lakeland account for this asset and report it in the financial statements?

13. What does Tootsie Roll use as the estimated useful life on its buildings? On its machinery and equipment?

14. What are the similarities and differences between depreciation and amortization?

15. During a recent management meeting, David Bryce, director of marketing, proposed that the company begin capitalizing its marketing expenditures as goodwill. In his words, "Marketing expenditures create goodwill for the company which benefits the company for multiple periods. Therefore it doesn't make good sense to have to expense it as it is incurred. Besides, if we capitalize it as goodwill, we won't have to amortize it, and this will boost reported income." Discuss the merits of David's proposal.

16. Berwik Company hires an accounting intern who says that intangible assets should always be amortized over their legal lives. Is the intern correct? Explain.

17. Goodwill has been defined as the value of all favorable attributes that relate to a business enterprise. What types of attributes could result in goodwill?

18. Megan Keen, a business major, is working on a case problem for one of her classes. In this case problem, the company needs to raise cash to market a new product it developed. Jeff Denton, an engineering major, takes one look at the company's balance sheet and says, "This company has an awful lot of goodwill. Why don't you recommend that they sell some of it to raise cash?" How should Megan respond to Jeff?

19. Under what conditions is goodwill recorded? What is the proper accounting treatment for amortizing goodwill?

20. Often research and development costs provide companies with benefits that last a number of years. (For example, these costs can lead to the development of a patent that will increase the company's income for many years.) However, generally accepted accounting principles require that such costs be recorded as an expense when incurred. Why?

21. Suppose in 2014, Campbell Soup Company reported average total assets of $6,265 million, net sales of $7,586 million, and net income of $736 million. What was Campbell Soup's return on assets?

22. Diane Carey, a marketing executive for Fresh Views Inc., has proposed expanding its product line of framed graphic art by producing a line of lower-quality products. These would require less processing by the company and would provide a lower profit margin. Joe Moreb, the company's CFO, is concerned that this new product line would reduce the company's return on assets. Discuss the potential effect on return on assets that this product might have.

23. Give an example of an industry that would be characterized by (a) a high asset turnover and a low profit margin, and (b) a low asset turnover and a high profit margin.

24. Gooden Corporation and Perron Corporation operate in the same industry. Gooden uses the straight-line method to account for depreciation, whereas Perron uses an accelerated method. Explain what complications might arise in trying to compare the results of these two companies.

25. Garcia Corporation uses straight-line depreciation for financial reporting purposes but an accelerated method for tax purposes. Is it acceptable to use different methods for the two purposes? What is Garcia Corporation's motivation for doing this?

26. You are comparing two companies in the same industry. You have determined that Leslie Corp. depreciates its plant assets over a 40-year life, whereas Camby Corp. depreciates its plant assets over a 20-year life. Discuss the implications this has for comparing the results of the two companies.

27. Explain how transactions related to plant assets and intangibles are reported in the statement of cash flows.

Brief Exercises

Determine the cost of land.
(LO 1), AP

BE9-1 These expenditures were incurred by Dunston Company in purchasing land: cash price $60,000; accrued taxes $5,000; attorney's fees $2,100; real estate broker's commission $3,300; and clearing and grading $3,500. What is the cost of the land?

Determine the cost of a truck.
(LO 1), AP

BE9-2 Tolbert Company incurs these expenditures in purchasing a truck: cash price $24,000; accident insurance (during use) $2,000; sales taxes $1,080; motor vehicle license $300; and painting and lettering $1,700. What is the cost of the truck?

Compute straight-line depreciation.
(LO 3), AP

BE9-3 Howe Chemicals Company acquires a delivery truck at a cost of $31,000 on January 1, 2014. The truck is expected to have a salvage value of $4,000 at the end of its 4-year useful life. Compute annual depreciation for the first and second years using the straight-line method.

Compute depreciation and evaluate treatment.
(LO 3), AN

BE9-4 Iris Company purchased land and a building on January 1, 2014. Management's best estimate of the value of the land was $100,000 and of the building $250,000. However, management told the accounting department to record the land at $230,000 and the building at $120,000. The building is being depreciated on a straight-line basis over 20 years with no salvage value. Why do you suppose management requested this accounting treatment? Is it ethical?

Compute revised depreciation.
(LO 4), AP

BE9-5 On January 1, 2014, the Ferman Company ledger shows Equipment $36,000 and Accumulated Depreciation $13,600. The depreciation resulted from using the straight-line method with a useful life of 10 years and a salvage value of $2,000. On this date, the company concludes that the equipment has a remaining useful life of only 2 years with the same salvage value. Compute the revised annual depreciation.

BE9-6 Harmon Company had the following two transactions related to its delivery truck.
1. Paid $38 for an oil change.
2. Paid $400 to install special shelving units, which increase the operating efficiency of the truck.

Prepare Harmon's journal entries to record these two transactions.

Prepare entries for delivery truck costs.
(LO 4), **AP**

BE9-7 Prepare journal entries to record these transactions: (a) Rangel Company retires its delivery equipment, which cost $41,000. Accumulated depreciation is also $41,000 on this delivery equipment. No salvage value is received. (b) Assume the same information as in part (a), except that accumulated depreciation for the equipment is $37,200 instead of $41,000.

Journalize entries for disposal of plant assets.
(LO 5), **AP**

BE9-8 Quinn Company sells office equipment on July 31, 2014, for $21,000 cash. The office equipment originally cost $72,000 and as of January 1, 2014, had accumulated depreciation of $42,000. Depreciation for the first 7 months of 2014 is $4,600. Prepare the journal entries to (a) update depreciation to July 31, 2014, and (b) record the sale of the equipment.

Journalize entries for sale of plant assets.
(LO 5), **AP**

BE9-9 Suppose in its 2014 annual report, McDonald's Corporation reports beginning total assets of $28.46 billion; ending total assets of $30.22 billion; net sales of $22.74 billion; and net income of $4.55 billion.
(a) Compute McDonald's return on assets.
(b) Compute McDonald's asset turnover.

Compute return on assets and asset turnover.
(LO 6), **AP**

BE9-10 Downs Company purchases a patent for $156,000 on January 2, 2014. Its estimated useful life is 6 years.
(a) Prepare the journal entry to record amortization expense for the first year.
(b) Show how this patent is reported on the balance sheet at the end of the first year.

Account for intangibles— patents.
(LO 7), **AP**

BE9-11 Suppose Nike, Inc. reported the following plant assets and intangible assets for the year ended May 31, 2014 (in millions): other plant assets $965.8; land $221.6; patents and trademarks (at cost) $515.1; machinery and equipment $2,094.3; buildings $974.0; goodwill (at cost) $193.5; accumulated amortization $47.7; and accumulated depreciation $2,298.0. Prepare a partial balance sheet for Nike for these items.

Classification of long-lived assets on balance sheet.
(LO 8), **AP**

BE9-12 Gant Company reported net income of $157,000. It reported depreciation expense of $12,000 and accumulated depreciation of $47,000. Amortization expense was $8,000. Gant purchased new equipment during the year for $50,000. Show how this information would be used to determine net cash provided by operating activities.

Determine net cash provided by operating activities.
(LO 8), **AP**

*BE9-13 Depreciation information for Howe Chemicals Company is given in BE9-3. Assuming the declining-balance depreciation rate is double the straight-line rate, compute annual depreciation for the first and second years under the declining-balance method.

Compute declining-balance depreciation.
(LO 9), **AP**

*BE9-14 Speedy Taxi Service uses the units-of-activity method in computing depreciation on its taxicabs. Each cab is expected to be driven 150,000 miles. Taxi 10 cost $27,500 and is expected to have a salvage value of $500. Taxi 10 was driven 32,000 miles in 2013 and 33,000 miles in 2014. Compute the depreciation for each year.

Compute depreciation using units-of-activity method.
(LO 9), **AP**

Exercises

E9-1 The following expenditures relating to plant assets were made by Watkens Company during the first 2 months of 2014.
1. Paid $7,000 of accrued taxes at the time the plant site was acquired.
2. Paid $200 insurance to cover a possible accident loss on new factory machinery while the machinery was in transit.
3. Paid $850 sales taxes on a new delivery truck.
4. Paid $21,000 for parking lots and driveways on the new plant site.
5. Paid $250 to have the company name and slogan painted on the new delivery truck.
6. Paid $8,000 for installation of new factory machinery.
7. Paid $900 for a 1-year accident insurance policy on the new delivery truck.
8. Paid $75 motor vehicle license fee on the new truck.

Determine cost of plant acquisitions.
(LO 1), **C**

Instructions
(a) ▬▬▶ Explain the application of the historical cost principle in determining the acquisition cost of plant assets.

(b) List the numbers of the transactions, and opposite each indicate the account title to which each expenditure should be debited.

Determine property, plant, and equipment costs.
(LO 1), **C**

E9-2 Petrino Company incurred the following costs.

1. Sales tax on factory machinery purchased	$ 5,000
2. Painting of and lettering on truck immediately upon purchase	700
3. Installation and testing of factory machinery	2,000
4. Real estate broker's commission on land purchased	3,500
5. Insurance premium paid for first year's insurance on new truck	880
6. Cost of landscaping on property purchased	7,200
7. Cost of paving parking lot for new building constructed	17,900
8. Cost of clearing, draining, and filling land	13,300
9. Architect's fees on self-constructed building	10,000

Instructions

Indicate to which account Petrino would debit each of the costs.

Determine acquisition costs of land.
(LO 1), **AP**

E9-3 On March 1, 2014, Zobrist Company acquired real estate, on which it planned to construct a small office building, by paying $80,000 in cash. An old warehouse on the property was demolished at a cost of $8,200; the salvaged materials were sold for $1,700. Additional expenditures before construction began included $1,900 attorney's fee for work concerning the land purchase, $5,200 real estate broker's fee, $9,100 architect's fee, and $14,000 to put in driveways and a parking lot.

Instructions

(a) Determine the amount to be reported as the cost of the land.
(b) For each cost not used in part (a), indicate the account to be debited.

Understand depreciation concepts.
(LO 2), **C**

E9-4 Melissa Adduci has prepared the following list of statements about depreciation.

1. Depreciation is a process of asset valuation, not cost allocation.
2. Depreciation provides for the proper matching of expenses with revenues.
3. The book value of a plant asset should approximate its fair value.
4. Depreciation applies to three classes of plant assets: land, buildings, and equipment.
5. Depreciation does not apply to a building because its usefulness and revenue-producing ability generally remain intact over time.
6. The revenue-producing ability of a depreciable asset will decline due to wear and tear and to obsolescence.
7. Recognizing depreciation on an asset results in an accumulation of cash for replacement of the asset.
8. The balance in accumulated depreciation represents the total cost that has been charged to expense since placing the asset in service.
9. Depreciation expense and accumulated depreciation are reported on the income statement.
10. Four factors affect the computation of depreciation: cost, useful life, salvage value, and residual value.

Instructions

Identify each statement as true or false. If false, indicate how to correct the statement.

Determine straight-line depreciation for partial period.
(LO 3), **AP**

E9-5 Hinshaw Company purchased a new machine on October 1, 2014, at a cost of $90,000. The company estimated that the machine has a salvage value of $8,000. The machine is expected to be used for 70,000 working hours during its 8-year life.

Instructions

Compute the depreciation expense under the straight-line method for 2014 and 2015, assuming a December 31 year-end.

Compute revised annual depreciation.
(LO 3, 4), **AN**

E9-6 Danny Venable, the new controller of Seratelli Company, has reviewed the expected useful lives and salvage values of selected depreciable assets at the beginning of 2014. Here are his findings:

Type of Asset	Date Acquired	Cost	Accumulated Depreciation, Jan. 1, 2014	Useful Life (in years) Old	Useful Life (in years) Proposed	Salvage Value Old	Salvage Value Proposed
Building	Jan. 1, 2006	$700,000	$130,000	40	48	$50,000	$35,000
Warehouse	Jan. 1, 2009	120,000	23,000	25	20	5,000	3,600

All assets are depreciated by the straight-line method. Seratelli Company uses a calendar year in preparing annual financial statements. After discussion, management has agreed to accept Danny's proposed changes. (The "Proposed" useful life is total life, not remaining life.)

Instructions
(a) Compute the revised annual depreciation on each asset in 2014. (Show computations.)
(b) Prepare the entry (or entries) to record depreciation on the building in 2014.

E9-7 Wang Co. has delivery equipment that cost $50,000 and has been depreciated $24,000.

Journalize transactions related to disposals of plant assets.
(LO 5), **AP**

Instructions
Record entries for the disposal under the following assumptions.
(a) It was scrapped as having no value.
(b) It was sold for $37,000.
(c) It was sold for $20,000.

E9-8 Here are selected 2014 transactions of Cleland Corporation.

Record disposal of equipment.
(LO 5), **AP**

Jan. 1 Retired a piece of machinery that was purchased on January 1, 2004. The machine cost $62,000 and had a useful life of 10 years with no salvage value.

June 30 Sold a computer that was purchased on January 1, 2012. The computer cost $36,000 and had a useful life of 3 years with no salvage value. The computer was sold for $5,000 cash.

Dec. 31 Sold a delivery truck for $9,000 cash. The truck cost $25,000 when it was purchased on January 1, 2011, and was depreciated based on a 5-year useful life with a $4,000 salvage value.

Instructions
Journalize all entries required on the above dates, including entries to update depreciation on assets disposed of, where applicable. Cleland Corporation uses straight-line depreciation.

E9-9 The following situations are independent of one another.

Apply accounting concepts.
(LO 1, 2, 6, 7), **C**

1. An accounting student recently employed by a small company doesn't understand why the company is only depreciating its buildings and equipment, but not its land. The student prepared journal entries to depreciate all the company's property, plant, and equipment for the current year-end.
2. The same student also thinks the company's amortization policy on its intangible assets is wrong. The company is currently amortizing its patents but not its goodwill. As a result, the student added goodwill to her adjusting entry for amortization at the end of the current year. She told a fellow employee that she felt she had improved the consistency of the company's accounting policies by making these changes.
3. The same company has a building still in use that has a zero book value but a substantial fair value. The student felt that this practice didn't benefit the company's users—especially the bank—and wrote the building up to its fair value. After all, she reasoned, you can write down assets if fair values are lower. Writing them up if fair value is higher is yet another example of the improved consistency that she has brought to the company's accounting practices.

Instructions
Explain whether or not the accounting treatment in each of the above situations is in accordance with generally accepted accounting principles. Explain what accounting principle or assumption, if any, has been violated and what the appropriate accounting treatment should be.

E9-10 Suppose during 2014 that Federal Express reported the following information (in millions): net sales of $35,497 and net income of $98. Its balance sheet also showed total assets at the beginning of the year of $25,633 and total assets at the end of the year of $24,244.

Calculate asset turnover and return on assets.
(LO 6), **AP**

Instructions
Calculate the (a) asset turnover and (b) return on assets.

E9-11 Shonrock International is considering a significant expansion to its product line. The sales force is excited about the opportunities that the new products will bring. The new products are a significant step up in quality above the company's current offerings,

Calculate and interpret ratios.
(LO 6), **AP**

but offer a complementary fit to its existing product line. Richard Farley, senior production department manager, is very excited about the high-tech new equipment that will have to be acquired to produce the new products. Donna Beson, the company's CFO, has provided the following projections based on results with and without the new products.

	Without New Products	With New Products
Sales revenue	$10,000,000	$16,000,000
Net income	$500,000	$960,000
Average total assets	$5,000,000	$12,000,000

Instructions
(a) Compute the company's return on assets, profit margin, and asset turnover, both with and without the new product line.
(b) Discuss the implications that your findings in part (a) have for the company's decision.

Calculate and interpret ratios.
(LO 6), **AP**

E9-12 Bakely Company reports the following information (in millions) during a recent year: net sales, $11,408.5; net earnings, $264.8; total assets, ending, $4,312.6; and total assets, beginning, $4,254.3.

Instructions
(a) Calculate the (1) return on assets, (2) asset turnover, and (3) profit margin.
(b) Prove mathematically how the profit margin and asset turnover work together to explain return on assets, by showing the appropriate calculation.
(c) Bakely Company owns Villas (grocery), Bakely Theaters, Kurt Drugstores, and Derosa (heavy equipment), and manages commercial real estate, among other activities. Does this diversity of activities affect your ability to interpret the ratios you calculated in (a)? Explain.

Prepare adjusting entries for amortization.
(LO 7), **AN**

E9-13 These are selected 2014 transactions for Amarista Corporation:

Jan. 1   Purchased a copyright for $120,000. The copyright has a useful life of 6 years and a remaining legal life of 30 years.
Mar. 1   Purchased a patent with an estimated useful life of 4 years and a legal life of 20 years for $54,000.
Sept. 1   Purchased a small company and recorded goodwill of $150,000. Its useful life is indefinite.

Instructions
Prepare all adjusting entries at December 31 to record amortization required by the events.

Prepare entries to set up appropriate accounts for different intangibles; calculate amortization.
(LO 7), **AN**

E9-14 Haley Company, organized in 2014, has these transactions related to intangible assets in that year:

Jan. 2   Purchased a patent (5-year life) $280,000.
Apr. 1   Goodwill acquired as a result of purchased business (indefinite life) $360,000.
July 1   Acquired a 9-year franchise; expiration date July 1, 2023, $540,000.
Sept. 1   Research and development costs $185,000.

Instructions
(a) Prepare the necessary entries to record these transactions related to intangibles. All costs incurred were for cash.
(b) Make the entries as of December 31, 2014, recording any necessary amortization.
(c) Indicate what the intangible asset account balances should be on December 31, 2014.

Discuss implications of amortization period.
(LO 7), **C**

E9-15 Alliance Atlantis Communications Inc. changed its accounting policy to amortize broadcast rights over the contracted exhibition period, which is based on the estimated useful life of the program. Previously, the company amortized broadcast rights over the lesser of 2 years or the contracted exhibition period.

Instructions

Answer questions on depreciation and intangibles.
(LO 2, 7), **C**

Write a short memo to your client explaining the implications this has for the analysis of Alliance Atlantis's results.

E9-16 The following questions listed are independent of one another.

Instructions

Provide a brief answer to each question.

(a) Why should a company depreciate its buildings?

(b) How can a company have a building that has a zero reported book value but substantial fair value?

(c) What are some examples of intangibles that you might find on your college campus?

(d) Give some examples of company or product trademarks or trade names. Are trade names and trademarks reported on a company's balance sheet?

E9-17 Gonzalez Corporation reported net income of $58,000. Depreciation expense for the year was $132,000. The company calculates depreciation expense using the straight-line method, with a useful life of 10 years. Top management would like to switch to a 15-year useful life because depreciation expense would be reduced to $88,000. The CEO says, "Increasing the useful life would increase net income and net cash provided by operating activities."

Determine net cash provided by operating activities.
(LO 8), **AN**

Instructions

Provide a comparative analysis showing net income and net cash provided by operating activities (ignoring other accrual adjustments) using a 10-year and a 15-year useful life. (Ignore income taxes.) Evaluate the CEO's suggestion.

*E9-18 Jayhawk Bus Lines uses the units-of-activity method in depreciating its buses. One bus was purchased on January 1, 2014, at a cost of $100,000. Over its 4-year useful life, the bus is expected to be driven 160,000 miles. Salvage value is expected to be $8,000.

Compute depreciation under units-of-activity method.
(LO 9), **AP**

Instructions

(a) Compute the depreciation cost per unit.

(b) Prepare a depreciation schedule assuming actual mileage was: 2014, 40,000; 2015, 52,000; 2016, 41,000; and 2017, 27,000.

*E9-19 Basic information relating to a new machine purchased by Hinshaw Company is presented in E9-5.

Compute declining-balance and units-of-activity depreciation.
(LO 9), **AP**

Instructions

Using the facts presented in E9-5, compute depreciation using the following methods in the year indicated.

(a) Declining-balance using double the straight-line rate for 2014 and 2015.

(b) Units-of-activity for 2014, assuming machine usage was 3,900 hours. (Round depreciation per unit to the nearest cent.)

Challenge Exercises

Visit the book's companion website, at **www.wiley.com/college/kimmel**, and choose the Student Companion site to access Challenge Exercises.

Problems: Set A

P9-1A Seger Company was organized on January 1. During the first year of operations, the following plant asset expenditures and receipts were recorded in random order.

Determine acquisition costs of land and building.
(LO 1), **C**

	Debit
1. Cost of real estate purchased as a plant site (land $255,000 and building $25,000)	$ 280,000
2. Installation cost of fences around property	6,800
3. Cost of demolishing building to make land suitable for construction of new building	31,000
4. Excavation costs for new building	23,000
5. Accrued real estate taxes paid at time of purchase of real estate	3,170
6. Cost of parking lots and driveways	29,000
7. Architect's fees on building plans	33,000
8. Real estate taxes paid for the current year on land	6,400

9. Full payment to building contractor — 640,000

$1,052,370

Credit

10. Proceeds from salvage of demolished building — $ 12,000

Instructions

Analyze the transactions using the following table column headings. Enter the number of each transaction in the Item column, and enter the amounts in the appropriate columns. For amounts in the Other Accounts column, also indicate the account title.

Item	Land	Buildings	Other Accounts

Land $302,170

Journalize equipment transactions related to purchase, sale, retirement, and depreciation.

(LO 3, 5, 8), **AP**

P9-2A At December 31, 2014, Navaro Corporation reported the following plant assets.

Land		$ 3,000,000
Buildings	$26,500,000	
Less: Accumulated depreciation—buildings	11,925,000	14,575,000
Equipment	40,000,000	
Less: Accumulated depreciation—equipment	5,000,000	35,000,000
Total plant assets		$52,575,000

During 2015, the following selected cash transactions occurred.

Apr.	1	Purchased land for $2,200,000.
May	1	Sold equipment that cost $600,000 when purchased on January 1, 2008. The equipment was sold for $170,000.
June	1	Sold land for $1,600,000. The land cost $1,000,000.
July	1	Purchased equipment for $1,100,000.
Dec.	31	Retired equipment that cost $700,000 when purchased on December 31, 2005. No salvage value was received.

Instructions

(a) Journalize the transactions. (*Hint:* You may wish to set up T-accounts, post beginning balances, and then post 2015 transactions.) Navaro uses straight-line depreciation for buildings and equipment. The buildings are estimated to have a 40-year useful life and no salvage value; the equipment is estimated to have a 10-year useful life and no salvage value. Update depreciation on assets disposed of at the time of sale or retirement.

(b) Record adjusting entries for depreciation for 2015.

(c) Tot. plant assets $50,037,500

(c) Prepare the plant assets section of Navaro's balance sheet at December 31, 2015.

Journalize entries for disposal of plant assets.

(LO 5), **AP**

P9-3A Presented here are selected transactions for Pine Company for 2014.

Jan.	1	Retired a piece of machinery that was purchased on January 1, 2004. The machine cost $71,000 on that date and had a useful life of 10 years with no salvage value.
June	30	Sold a computer that was purchased on January 1, 2011. The computer cost $30,000 and had a useful life of 5 years with no salvage value. The computer was sold for $12,000.
Dec.	31	Discarded a delivery truck that was purchased on January 1, 2009. The truck cost $33,400 and was depreciated based on an 8-year useful life with a $3,000 salvage value.

Instructions

Journalize all entries required on the above dates, including entries to update depreciation, where applicable, on assets disposed of. Pine Company uses straight-line depreciation. (Assume depreciation is up to date as of December 31, 2013.)

Prepare entries to record transactions related to acquisition and amortization of intangibles; prepare the intangible assets section and note.

(LO 7, 8), **AP**

P9-4A The intangible assets section of Cedeno Corporation's balance sheet at December 31, 2014, is presented here.

Patents ($60,000 cost less $6,000 amortization)	$54,000
Copyrights ($36,000 cost less $25,200 amortization)	10,800
Total	$64,800

The patent was acquired in January 2014 and has a useful life of 10 years. The copyright was acquired in January 2008 and also has a useful life of 10 years. The following cash transactions may have affected intangible assets during 2015.

Jan.   2   Paid $46,800 legal costs to successfully defend the patent against infringement by another company.

Jan.–June   Developed a new product, incurring $230,000 in research and development costs. A patent was granted for the product on July 1, and its useful life is equal to its legal life. Legal and other costs for the patent were $20,000.

Sept.   1   Paid $40,000 to a quarterback to appear in commercials advertising the company's products. The commercials will air in September and October.

Oct.   1   Acquired a copyright for $200,000. The copyright has a useful life and legal life of 50 years.

Instructions
(a) Prepare journal entries to record the transactions.
(b) Prepare journal entries to record the 2015 amortization expense for intangible assets.
(c) Prepare the intangible assets section of the balance sheet at December 31, 2015.
(d) Prepare the note to the financial statements on Cedeno Corporation's intangible assets as of December 31, 2015.

(c) Tot. intangibles $315,300

P9-5A Due to rapid employee turnover in the accounting department, the following transactions involving intangible assets were improperly recorded by Eveland Corporation in 2014.

Prepare entries to correct errors in recording and amortizing intangible assets.
(LO 7), AP

1. Eveland developed a new manufacturing process, incurring research and development costs of $160,000. The company also purchased a patent for $40,000. In early January, Eveland capitalized $200,000 as the cost of the patents. Patent amortization expense of $10,000 was recorded based on a 20-year useful life.

2. On July 1, 2014, Eveland purchased a small company and as a result acquired goodwill of $80,000. Eveland recorded a half-year's amortization in 2014, based on a 20-year life ($2,000 amortization). The goodwill has an indefinite life.

Instructions
Prepare all journal entries necessary to correct any errors made during 2014. Assume the books have not yet been closed for 2014.

P9-6A Danner Corporation and London Corporation, two companies of roughly the same size, are both involved in the manufacture of shoe-tracing devices. Each company depreciates its plant assets using the straight-line approach. An investigation of their financial statements reveals the information shown below.

Calculate and comment on return on assets, profit margin, and asset turnover.
(LO 6), AN

	Danner Corp.	London Corp.
Net income	$ 240,000	$ 300,000
Sales revenue	1,150,000	1,200,000
Total assets (average)	3,200,000	3,000,000
Plant assets (average)	2,400,000	1,800,000
Intangible assets (goodwill)	300,000	0

Instructions
(a) For each company, calculate these values:
    (1) Return on assets.
    (2) Profit margin.
    (3) Asset turnover.
(b) Based on your calculations in part (a), comment on the relative effectiveness of the two companies in using their assets to generate sales. What factors complicate your ability to compare the two companies?

P9-7A In recent years, Farr Company has purchased three machines. Because of frequent employee turnover in the accounting department, a different accountant was in charge of selecting the depreciation method for each machine, and various methods have been used. Information concerning the machines is summarized in the table below.

Compute depreciation under different methods.
(LO 3, 9), AP

Machine	Acquired	Cost	Salvage Value	Useful Life (in years)	Depreciation Method
1	Jan. 1, 2012	$96,000	$12,000	8	Straight-line
2	July 1, 2013	85,000	10,000	5	Declining-balance
3	Nov. 1, 2013	66,000	6,000	6	Units-of-activity

For the declining-balance method, Farr Company uses the double-declining rate. For the units-of-activity method, total machine hours are expected to be 30,000. Actual hours of use in the first 3 years were: 2013, 800; 2014, 4,500; and 2015, 6,000.

Instructions

(a) Machine 2 $60,520

(a) Compute the amount of accumulated depreciation on each machine at December 31, 2015.

(b) If machine 2 was purchased on April 1 instead of July 1, what would be the depreciation expense for this machine in 2013? In 2014?

Compute depreciation under different methods.

(LO 3, 9), **AP**

*P9-8A Boscan Corporation purchased machinery on January 1, 2014, at a cost of $250,000. The estimated useful life of the machinery is 4 years, with an estimated salvage value at the end of that period of $30,000. The company is considering different depreciation methods that could be used for financial reporting purposes.

Instructions

(a) Double-declining-balance expense 2016 $31,250

(a) Prepare separate depreciation schedules for the machinery using the straight-line method, and the declining-balance method using double the straight-line rate. (Round to the nearest dollar.)

(b) Which method would result in the higher reported 2014 income? In the highest total reported income over the 4-year period?

(c) Which method would result in the lower reported 2014 income? In the lowest total reported income over the 4-year period?

Problems: Set B

Visit the book's companion website, at **www.wiley.com/college/kimmel**, and choose the Student Companion site to access Problem Set B.

Comprehensive Problem

CP9 Kenseth Corporation's unadjusted trial balance at December 1, 2014, is presented below.

	Debit	Credit
Cash	$ 22,000	
Accounts Receivable	36,800	
Notes Receivable	10,000	
Interest Receivable	–0–	
Inventory	36,200	
Prepaid Insurance	3,600	
Land	20,000	
Buildings	150,000	
Equipment	60,000	
Patent	9,000	
Allowance for Doubtful Accounts		$ 500
Accumulated Depreciation—Buildings		50,000
Accumulated Depreciation—Equipment		24,000
Accounts Payable		27,300
Salaries and Wages Payable		–0–
Notes Payable (due April 30, 2015)		11,000
Income Taxes Payable		–0–
Interest Payable		–0–
Notes Payable (due in 2020)		35,000
Common Stock		50,000
Retained Earnings		63,600
Dividends	12,000	
Sales Revenue		900,000
Interest Revenue		–0–
Gain on Disposal of Plant Assets		–0–

Bad Debt Expense	–0–	
Cost of Goods Sold	630,000	
Depreciation Expense	–0–	
Income Tax Expense	–0–	
Insurance Expense	–0–	
Interest Expense	–0–	
Other Operating Expenses	61,800	
Amortization Expense	–0–	
Salaries and Wages Expense	110,000	
Total	$1,161,400	$1,161,400

The following transactions occurred during December.

Dec. 2 Purchased equipment for $16,000, plus sales taxes of $800 (paid in cash).
   2 Kenseth sold for $3,500 equipment which originally cost $5,000. Accumulated depreciation on this equipment at January 1, 2014, was $1,800; 2014 depreciation prior to the sale of equipment was $825.
   15 Kenseth sold for $5,000 on account inventory that cost $3,500.
   23 Salaries and wages of $6,600 were paid.

Adjustment data:

1. Kenseth estimates that uncollectible accounts receivable at year-end are $4,000.
2. The note receivable is a one-year, 8% note dated April 1, 2014. No interest has been recorded.
3. The balance in prepaid insurance represents payment of a $3,600, 6-month premium on September 1, 2014.
4. The building is being depreciated using the straight-line method over 30 years. The salvage value is $30,000.
5. The equipment owned prior to this year is being depreciated using the straight-line method over 5 years. The salvage value is 10% of cost.
6. The equipment purchased on December 2, 2014, is being depreciated using the straight-line method over 5 years, with a salvage value of $1,800.
7. The patent was acquired on January 1, 2014, and has a useful life of 9 years from that date.
8. Unpaid salaries at December 31, 2014, total $2,200.
9. Both the short-term and long-term notes payable are dated January 1, 2014, and carry a 10% interest rate. All interest is payable in the next 12 months.
10. Income tax expense was $15,000. It was unpaid at December 31.

Instructions
(a) Prepare journal entries for the transactions listed above and adjusting entries.
(b) Prepare an adjusted trial balance at December 31, 2014.
(c) Prepare a 2014 income statement and a 2014 retained earnings statement.
(d) Prepare a December 31, 2014, balance sheet.

(b) Totals $1,205,775
(c) Net income $50,775
(d) Total assets $247,475

Broadening Your Perspective

Financial Reporting and Analysis

FINANCIAL REPORTING PROBLEM: *Tootsie Roll Industries, Inc.*

BYP9-1 Refer to the financial statements and the Notes to Consolidated Financial Statements of Tootsie Roll Industries in Appendix A.

Instructions
Answer the following questions.
(a) What were the total cost and book value of property, plant, and equipment at December 31, 2011?
(b) What method or methods of depreciation are used by Tootsie Roll for financial reporting purposes?
(c) What was the amount of depreciation expense for each of the 3 years 2009–2011? (*Hint:* Use the statement of cash flows.)

(d) Using the statement of cash flows, what are the amounts of property, plant, and equipment purchased (capital expenditures) in 2011 and 2010?

(e) Explain how Tootsie Roll accounted for its intangible assets in 2011.

COMPARATIVE ANALYSIS PROBLEM: *Tootsie Roll vs. Hershey*

BYP9-2 The financial statements of The Hershey Company are presented in Appendix B, following the financial statements for Tootsie Roll Industries in Appendix A.

Instructions

(a) Based on the information in these financial statements and the accompanying notes and schedules, compute the following values for each company in 2011.
   (1) Return on assets.
   (2) Profit margin (use "Total Revenue").
   (3) Asset turnover.

(b) What conclusions concerning the management of plant assets can be drawn from these data?

RESEARCH CASE

BYP9-3 The November 16, 2011, edition of the *Wall Street Journal Online* contains an article by Maxwell Murphy entitled "The Big Number: 51."

Instructions

Read the article and answer the following questions.

(a) What do the 51 companies referred to in the title have in common? What implications does this have regarding the fair value of a company's assets?

(b) What significance does the common trait referred to in part (a) have for a company's goodwill?

(c) How does a company get to record goodwill on its books—that is, what must have occurred for goodwill to show up on a company's books?

(d) If these companies write down their goodwill, will this reduce their cash?

INTERPRETING FINANCIAL STATEMENTS

BYP9-4 The March 29, 2012, edition of the *Wall Street Journal Online* contains an article by Miguel Bustillo entitled, "Best Buy Forced to Rethink Big Box." The article explains how the 1,100 giant stores, which enabled Best Buy to obtain its position as the largest retailer of electronics, are now reducing the company's profitability and even threatening its survival. The problem is that many customers go to Best Buy stores to see items but then buy them for less from online retailers. As a result, Best Buy recently announced that it would close 50 stores and switch to smaller stores. However, some analysts think that these changes are not big enough.

The following data were extracted from the 2011 and 2006 annual reports of Best Buy. (All amounts are in millions.)

	2011	2010	2006	2005
Total assets at year-end	$17,849	$18,302	$11,864	$10,294
Net sales	50,272		30,848	
Net income	1,277		1,140	

Instructions

Using the data above, answer the following questions.

(a) How might the return on assets and asset turnover of Best Buy differ from an online retailer?

(b) Compute the profit margin, asset turnover, and return on assets for 2011 and 2006.

(c) Present the ratios calculated in part (b) in the equation format shown in Illustration 9-21.

(d) Discuss the implications of the ratios calculated in parts (b) and (c).

REAL-WORLD FOCUS

BYP9-5 *Purpose:* Use an annual report to identify a company's plant assets and the depreciation method used.

Address: **www.annualreports.com**, or go to **www.wiley.com/college/kimmel**

Steps

1. Select a particular company.
2. Search by company name.
3. Follow instructions below.

Instructions

Answer the following questions.
(a) What is the name of the company?
(b) What is the Internet address of the annual report?
(c) At fiscal year-end, what is the net amount of its plant assets?
(d) What is the accumulated depreciation?
(e) Which method of depreciation does the company use?

Critical Thinking

DECISION-MAKING ACROSS THE ORGANIZATION

BYP9-6   Payton Furniture Corp. is nationally recognized for making high-quality products. Management is concerned that it is not fully exploiting its brand power. Payton's production managers are also concerned because their plants are not operating at anywhere near full capacity. Management is currently considering a proposal to offer a new line of affordable furniture.

Those in favor of the proposal (including the vice president of production) believe that, by offering these new products, the company could attract a clientele that it is not currently servicing. Also, it could operate its plants at full capacity, thus taking better advantage of its assets.

The vice president of marketing, however, believes that the lower-priced (and lower-margin) product would have a negative impact on the sales of existing products. The vice president believes that $10,000,000 of the sales of the new product will be from customers that would have purchased the more expensive product but switched to the lower-margin product because it was available. (This is often referred to as cannibalization of existing sales.) Top management feels, however, that even with cannibalization, the company's sales will increase and the company will be better off.

The following data are available.

(in thousands)	Current Results	Proposed Results without Cannibalization	Proposed Results with Cannibalization
Sales revenue	$45,000	$60,000	$50,000
Net income	$12,000	$13,500	$12,000
Average total assets	$100,000	$100,000	$100,000

Instructions

(a) Compute Payton's return on assets, profit margin, and asset turnover, both with and without the new product line.
(b) Discuss the implications that your findings in part (a) have for Payton's decision.
(c) Are there any other options that Payton should consider? What impact would each of these have on the above ratios?

COMMUNICATION ACTIVITY

BYP9-7   The chapter presented some concerns regarding the current accounting standards for research and development expenditures.

Instructions

Assume that you are either (a) the president of a company that is very dependent on ongoing research and development, writing a memo to the FASB complaining about the current accounting standards regarding research and development, or (b) the FASB member defending the current standards regarding research and development. Your memo should address the following questions.

1. By requiring expensing of R&D, do you think companies will spend less on R&D? Why or why not? What are the possible implications for the competitiveness of U.S. companies?
2. If a company makes a commitment to spend money for R&D, it must believe it has future benefits. Shouldn't these costs therefore be capitalized just like the purchase of any long-lived asset that you believe will have future benefits?

ETHICS CASE

BYP9-8   Fresh Air Anti-Pollution Company is suffering declining sales of its principal product, nonbiodegradable plastic cartons. The president, Tyler Weber, instructs his controller, Robin Cain, to lengthen asset lives to reduce depreciation expense. A processing line of automated plastic extruding equipment, purchased for $3.5 million in January 2014, was originally estimated to have a useful life of 8 years and a salvage value of $400,000. Depreciation has been recorded for 2 years on that basis. Tyler wants the estimated life changed to 12 years total and the straight-line method continued. Robin is hesitant to make the change, believing it is unethical to increase net income in this manner. Tyler says, "Hey, the life is only an estimate, and I've heard that our competition uses a 12-year life on their production equipment."

Instructions
(a) Who are the stakeholders in this situation?
(b) Is the proposed change in asset life unethical, or is it simply a good business practice by an astute president?
(c) What is the effect of Tyler's proposed change on income before taxes in the year of change?

ALL ABOUT YOU

BYP9-9 A company's tradename is a very important asset to the company, as it creates immediate product identification. Companies invest substantial sums to ensure that their product is well-known to the consumer. Test your knowledge of who owns some famous brands and their impact on the financial statements.

Instructions
(a) Provide an answer to the five multiple-choice questions below.
   (1) Which company owns both Taco Bell and Pizza Hut?
      (a) McDonald's.   (b) CKE.   (c) Yum Brands.   (d) Wendy's.
   (2) Dairy Queen belongs to:
      (a) Breyer.   (b) Berkshire Hathaway.   (c) GE.   (d) The Coca-Cola Company.
   (3) Phillip Morris, the cigarette maker, is owned by:
      (a) Altria.   (b) GE.   (c) Boeing.   (d) ExxonMobil.
   (4) AOL, a major Internet provider, belongs to:
      (a) Microsoft.   (b) Cisco.   (c) NBC.   (d) Time Warner.
   (5) ESPN, the sports broadcasting network, is owned by:
      (a) Procter & Gamble.   (b) Altria.   (c) Walt Disney.   (d) The Coca-Cola Company.
(b) How do you think the value of these brands is reported on the appropriate company's balance sheet?

FASB CODIFICATION ACTIVITY

BYP9-10 If your school has a subscription to the FASB Codification, go to **http://aaahq.org/ascLogin.cfm** to log in and prepare responses to the following.
(a) What does it mean to capitalize an item?
(b) What is the definition provided for an intangible asset?
(c) Your great-uncle, who is a CPA, is impressed that you are taking an accounting class. Based on his experience, he believes that depreciation is something that companies do based on past practice, not on the basis of authoritative guidance. Provide the authoritative literature to support the practice of fixed-asset depreciation.

CONSIDERING PEOPLE, PLANET, AND PROFIT

BYP9-11 The March 6, 2012, edition of the *Wall Street Journal Online* contains an article by David Kesmodel entitled "Air War: 'Winglet' Versus 'Sharklet'." This article demonstrates how a company focused on green technology has also been profitable.

Instructions
Read the article and answer the following questions.
(a) Why did Airbus file a lawsuit against Aviation Partners?
(b) What are the percentage fuel savings provided by Aviation Partners' Winglets on Boeing jetliners? How much total jet fuel did Aviation Partners say that its Winglets have provided at the time the article was written?
(c) Describe the history of the relationship between Aviation Partners and Airbus, and the development of the Airbus Sharklet.
(d) What would be the likely accounting implications if Aviation Partners were to lose the lawsuit?

Answers to Insight and Accounting Across the Organization Questions

p. 388 Many U.S. Firms Use Leases Q: Why might airline managers choose to lease rather than purchase their planes? **A:** The reasons for leasing include favorable tax treatment, better financing options, increased flexibility, reduced risk of obsolescence, and often less debt shown on the balance sheet.

p. 399 Marketing ROI as Profit Indicator Q: How does measuring marketing ROI support the overall efforts of the organization? **A:** Top management is ultimately concerned about maximizing the company's return on assets. Holding marketing managers accountable for the marketing ROI will contribute to the company's overall goal of maximizing return on assets.

p. 402 Sustainability Report Please Q: Why do you believe companies issue sustainability reports? **A:** It is important that companies clearly describe the things they value in addition to overall profitability. Most companies recognize that the health, safety, and environmental protections of their workforce and community are important components in developing strategies for continued growth and longevity. Without a strong commitment to the principles of corporate social responsibility, it is unlikely that a company will be able to maintain long-term stability and profitability. The development of a sustainability report helps companies to consider these issues and develop measures to assess whether they are meeting their goals in this area.

p. 406 Should Companies Write Up Goodwill? Q: Do you think that this treatment would be allowed under U.S. GAAP? **A:** The write-down of assets would have been allowed if it could be shown that the assets had declined in value (an impairment). However, the creation of goodwill to offset the write-down would not have been allowed. Goodwill can be recorded only when it results from the acquisition of a business. It cannot be recorded as the result of being created internally.

Answers to Self-Test Questions

1. d ($24,000 + $1,200 + $200 + $400)   **2.** a   **3.** b   **4.** d (($400,000 − $10,000) ÷ 5) × 2   **5.** c
6. b   **7.** d (($60,000 − $12,000) ÷ 10) × 2 = $9,600; ($60,000 − $9,600 − $2,000) ÷ 4   **8.** d   **9.** a
(($80,000 − 0) ÷ 10) × 4.5 = $36,000; ($26,000 − ($80,000 − $36,000))   **10.** d   **11.** c $180,000 ÷
(($200,000 + $300,000) ÷ 2)   **12.** b ($20,000 + $15,000)   **13.** c   **14.** c   **15.** d   *16. d

A Look at IFRS

LEARNING OBJECTIVE 10
Compare the accounting procedures for long-lived assets under GAAP and IFRS.

IFRS related to property, plant, and equipment is found in *IAS 16* ("Property, Plant and Equipment") and *IAS 23* ("Borrowing Costs"). IFRS follows most of the same principles as GAAP in the accounting for property, plant, and equipment. There are, however, some significant differences in the implementation. IFRS allows the use of revaluation of property, plant, and equipment, and it also requires the use of component depreciation. In addition, there are some significant differences in the accounting for both intangible assets and impairments. IFRS related to intangible assets is presented in *IAS 38* ("Intangible Assets"). IFRS related to impairments is found in *IAS 36* ("Impairment of Assets").

KEY POINTS

- The definition for plant assets for both IFRS and GAAP is essentially the same.
- Both IFRS and GAAP follow the historical cost principle when accounting for property, plant, and equipment at date of acquisition. Cost consists of all expenditures necessary to acquire the asset and make it ready for its intended use.
- Under both IFRS and GAAP, interest costs incurred during construction are capitalized. Recently, IFRS converged to GAAP requirements in this area.
- IFRS, like GAAP, capitalizes all direct costs in self-constructed assets such as raw materials and labor. IFRS does not address the capitalization of fixed overhead, although in practice these costs are generally capitalized.

- IFRS also views depreciation as an allocation of cost over an asset's useful life. IFRS permits the same depreciation methods (e.g., straight-line, accelerated, and units-of-activity) as GAAP. However, a major difference is that IFRS requires component depreciation. **Component depreciation** specifies that any significant parts of a depreciable asset that have different estimated useful lives should be separately depreciated. Component depreciation is allowed under GAAP but is seldom used.

  To illustrate, assume that Lexure Construction builds an office building for $4,000,000, not including the cost of the land. If the $4,000,000 is allocated over the 40-year useful life of the building, Lexure reports $100,000 of depreciation per year, assuming straight-line depreciation and no disposal value. However, assume that $320,000 of the cost of the building relates to personal property and $600,000 relates to land improvements. The personal property has a depreciable life of 5 years, and the land improvements have a depreciable life of 10 years. In accordance with IFRS, Lexure must use component depreciation. It must reclassify $320,000 of the cost of the building to personal property and $600,000 to the cost of land improvements. Assuming that Lexure uses straight-line depreciation, component depreciation for the first year of the office building is computed as follows.

Building cost adjusted ($4,000,000 − $320,000 − $600,000)	$3,080,000
Building cost depreciation per year ($3,080,000/40)	$ 77,000
Personal property depreciation ($320,000/5)	64,000
Land improvements depreciation ($600,000/10)	60,000
Total component depreciation in first year	$ 201,000

- IFRS uses the term **residual value**, rather than salvage value, to refer to an owner's estimate of an asset's value at the end of its useful life for that owner.
- IFRS allows companies to revalue plant assets to fair value at the reporting date. Companies that choose to use the revaluation framework must follow revaluation procedures. If revaluation is used, it must be applied to all assets within the same class. Assets that are experiencing rapid price changes must be revalued on an annual basis. Otherwise, less frequent revaluation is acceptable.

  To illustrate asset revaluation accounting, assume that Pernice Company applies revaluation to plant assets with a carrying value of $1,000,000, a useful life of 5 years, and no residual value. Pernice makes the following journal entries in year 1, assuming straight-line depreciation.

Depreciation Expense	200,000	
Accumulated Depreciation—Plant Assets		200,000
(To record depreciation expense in year 1)		

After this entry, Pernice's plant assets have a carrying amount of $800,000 ($1,000,000 − $200,000). At the end of year 1, independent appraisers determine that the assets have a fair value of $850,000. To report the plant assets at fair value, or $850,000, Pernice eliminates the Accumulated Depreciation—Plant Assets account, reduces Plant Assets to its fair value of $850,000, and records Revaluation Surplus of $50,000. The entry to record the revaluation is as follows.

Accumulated Depreciation—Plant Assets	200,000	
Plant Assets		150,000
Revaluation Surplus		50,000
(To record adjusting the plant assets to fair value)		

Thus, Pernice follows a two-step process. First, Pernice records depreciation based on the cost basis of $1,000,000. As a result, it reports depreciation expense of $200,000 on the income statement. Second, it records the revaluation. It does this by eliminating any accumulated depreciation, adjusting the recorded value of the plant assets to fair value, and debiting or crediting the Revaluation Surplus account. In this example, the revaluation surplus is $50,000, which is the difference between the fair value of $850,000 and the book value of $800,000. Revaluation surplus is an example of an item reported as other comprehensive income, as discussed in the *A Look at IFRS* section of Chapter 5. Pernice now reports the following information in its statement of financial position at the end of year 1.

Plant assets ($1,000,000 − $150,000)	$850,000
Accumulated depreciation—plant assets	0
	$850,000
Revaluation surplus (equity)	$ 50,000

As indicated, $850,000 is the new basis of the assets. Pernice reports depreciation expense of $200,000 in the income statement and $50,000 in other comprehensive income. Assuming no change in the total useful life, depreciation in year 2 will be $212,500 ($850,000 ÷ 4).

- Under both IFRS and GAAP, changes in the depreciation method used and changes in useful life are handled in current and future periods. Prior periods are not affected. GAAP recently conformed to IFRS in the accounting for changes in depreciation methods.

- The accounting for subsequent expenditures, such as ordinary repairs and additions, are essentially the same under IFRS and GAAP.

- The accounting for plant asset disposals is essentially the same under IFRS and GAAP.

- Initial costs to acquire natural resources are essentially the same under IFRS and GAAP.

- The definition of intangible assets is essentially the same under IFRS and GAAP.

- Intangibles generally arise when a company buys another company. In this case, specific criteria are needed to separate goodwill from other intangibles. Both IFRS and GAAP follow the same approach to make this separation; that is, companies recognize an intangible asset separately from goodwill if the intangible represents contractual or legal rights or is capable of being separated or divided and sold, transferred, licensed, rented, or exchanged. In addition, under both IFRS and GAAP, companies recognize acquired in-process research and development (IPR&D) as a separate intangible asset if it meets the definition of an intangible asset and its fair value can be measured reliably.

- As in GAAP, under IFRS the costs associated with research and development are segregated into the two components. Costs in the research phase are always expensed under both IFRS and GAAP. Under IFRS, however, costs in the development phase are capitalized as Development Costs once technological feasibility is achieved.

  To illustrate, assume that Laser Scanner Company spent $1 million on research and $2 million on development of new products. Of the $2 million in development costs, $500,000 was incurred prior to technological feasibility and $1,500,000 was incurred after technological feasibility had been demonstrated. The company would record these costs as follows.

Research Expense	1,000,000	
Development Expense	500,000	
Development Costs	1,500,000	
Cash		3,000,000
(To record research and development costs)		

- IFRS permits revaluation of intangible assets (except for goodwill). GAAP prohibits revaluation of intangible assets.

- IFRS requires an impairment test at each reporting date for plant assets and intangibles and records an impairment if the asset's carrying amount exceeds its recoverable amount. The recoverable amount is the higher of the asset's fair value less costs to sell or its value-in-use. **Value-in-use** is the future cash flows to be derived from the particular asset, discounted to present value. Under GAAP, impairment loss is measured as the excess of the carrying amount over the asset's fair value.

- IFRS allows reversal of impairment losses when there has been a change in economic conditions or in the expected use of the asset. Under GAAP, impairment losses cannot be reversed for assets to be held and used; the impairment loss results in a new cost basis for the asset. IFRS and GAAP are similar in the accounting for impairments of assets held for disposal.

- The accounting for exchanges of nonmonetary assets has recently converged between IFRS and GAAP. GAAP now requires that gains on exchanges of nonmonetary assets be recognized if the exchange has commercial substance. This is the same framework used in IFRS.

LOOKING TO THE FUTURE

With respect to revaluations, as part of the conceptual framework project, the Boards will examine the measurement bases used in accounting. It is too early to say whether a converged conceptual framework will recommend fair value measurement (and revaluation accounting) for plant assets and intangibles. However, this is likely to be one of the more contentious issues, given the long-standing use of historical cost as a measurement basis in GAAP.

The IASB and FASB have identified a project that would consider expanded recognition of internally generated intangible assets. IFRS permits more recognition of intangibles compared to GAAP. Thus, it will be challenging to develop converged standards for intangible assets, given the long-standing prohibition on capitalizing internally generated intangible assets and research and development costs in GAAP.

IFRS PRACTICE

IFRS SELF-TEST QUESTIONS

1. Which of the following statements is **correct**?
   (a) Both IFRS and GAAP permit revaluation of property, plant, and equipment and intangible assets (except for goodwill).
   (b) IFRS permits revaluation of property, plant, and equipment and intangible assets (except for goodwill).
   (c) Both IFRS and GAAP permit revaluation of property, plant, and equipment but not intangible assets.
   (d) GAAP permits revaluation of property, plant, and equipment but not intangible assets.

2. International Company has land that cost $450,000 but now has a fair value of $600,000. International Company decides to use the revaluation method specified in IFRS to account for the land. Which of the following statements is **correct**?
   (a) International Company must continue to report the land at $450,000.
   (b) International Company would report a net income increase of $150,000 due to an increase in the value of the land.
   (c) International Company would debit Revaluation Surplus for $150,000.
   (d) International Company would credit Revaluation Surplus by $150,000.

3. Francisco Corporation is constructing a new building at a total initial cost of $10,000,000. The building is expected to have a useful life of 50 years with no residual value. The building's finished surfaces (e.g., roof cover and floor cover) are 5% of this cost and have a useful life of 20 years. Building services systems (e.g., electric, heating, and plumbing) are 20% of the cost and have a useful life of 25 years. The depreciation in the first year using component depreciation, assuming straight-line depreciation with no residual value, is:
   (a) $200,000.   (b) $215,000.   (c) $255,000.   (d) None of the above.

4. Research and development costs are:
   (a) expensed under GAAP.
   (b) expensed under IFRS.
   (c) expensed under both GAAP and IFRS.
   (d) None of the above.

5. Under IFRS, value-in-use is defined as:
   (a) net realizable value.
   (b) fair value.
   (c) future cash flows discounted to present value.
   (d) total future undiscounted cash flows.

IFRS CONCEPTS AND APPLICATION

IFRS9-1   What is component depreciation, and when must it be used?

IFRS9-2   What is revaluation of plant assets? When should revaluation be applied?

IFRS9-3   Some product development expenditures are recorded as development expenses and others as development costs. Explain the difference between these accounts and how a company decides which classification is appropriate.

IFRS9-4   Holland Company constructed a warehouse for $280,000. Holland estimates that the warehouse has a useful life of 20 years and no residual value. Construction records indicate that $40,000 of the cost of the warehouse relates to its heating, ventilation, and air conditioning (HVAC) system, which has an estimated useful life of only 10 years. Compute the first year of depreciation expense using straight-line component depreciation.

IFRS9-5   At the end of its first year of operations, Mordica Company chose to use the revaluation framework allowed under IFRS. Mordica's ledger shows Plant Assets $480,000 and Accumulated Depreciation—Plant Assets $60,000. Prepare journal entries to record the following.
   (a) Independent appraisers determine that the plant assets have a fair value of $460,000.
   (b) Independent appraisers determine that the plant assets have a fair value of $400,000.

IFRS9-6   Parman Industries spent $300,000 on research and $600,000 on development of a new product. Of the $600,000 in development costs, $400,000 was incurred prior to technological feasibility and $200,000 after technological feasibility had been demonstrated. Prepare the journal entry to record research and development costs.

INTERNATIONAL FINANCIAL STATEMENT ANALYSIS: *Zetar plc*

IFRS9-7   The financial statements of Zetar plc are presented in Appendix C.

Instructions

Use the company's annual report, available in the Investors section at **www.zetarplc.com**, to answer the following questions.

(a) According to the notes to the financial statements, what method or methods does the company use to depreciate "plant and equipment?" What rate does it use to depreciate plant and equipment?

(b) According to the notes to the financial statements, how often is goodwill tested for impairment?

(c) Using the notes to the financial statements, as well as information from the statement of cash flows, prepare the journal entry to record the disposal of property, plant and equipment during 2011. (Round your amounts to the nearest thousand.)

Answers to IFRS Self-Test Questions

1. b   **2.** d   **3.** c (($10,000,000 × .05)/20) + (($10,000,000 × .20)/25) + (($10,000,000 × .75)/50)
4. a   **5.** c

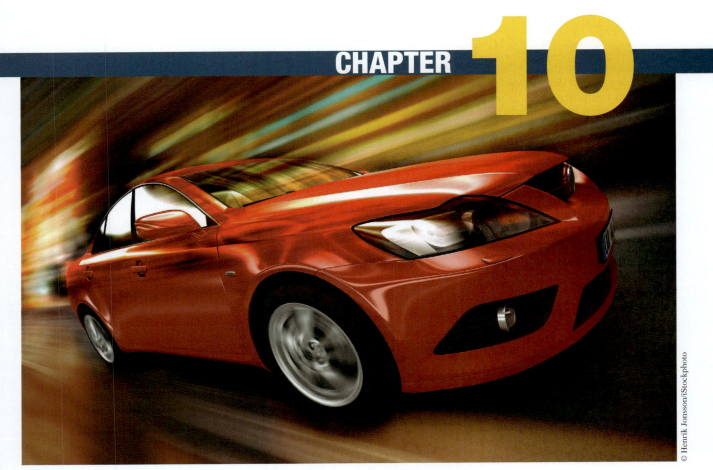

CHAPTER 10

© Henrik Jonsson/iStockphoto

REPORTING AND ANALYZING LIABILITIES

LEARNING OBJECTIVES

After studying this chapter, you should be able to:

1 Explain a current liability and identify the major types of current liabilities.

2 Describe the accounting for notes payable.

3 Explain the accounting for other current liabilities.

4 Identify the types of bonds.

5 Prepare the entries for the issuance of bonds and interest expense.

6 Describe the entries when bonds are redeemed.

7 Identify the requirements for the financial statement presentation and analysis of liabilities.

Debt can help a company acquire the things it needs to grow, but it is often the very thing that kills a company. A brief history of Maxwell Car Company illustrates the role of debt in the U.S. auto industry. In 1920, Maxwell Car Company was on the brink of financial ruin. Because it was unable to pay its bills, its creditors stepped in and took over. They hired a former General Motors (GM) executive named Walter Chrysler to reorganize the company. By 1925, he had taken over the company and renamed it Chrysler. By 1933, Chrysler was booming, with sales surpassing even those of Ford.

But the next few decades saw Chrysler make a series of blunders. By 1980, with its creditors pounding at the gates, Chrysler was again on the brink of financial ruin.

At that point, Chrysler brought in a former Ford executive named Lee Iacocca to save the company. Iacocca argued that the United States could not afford to let Chrysler fail because of the loss of jobs. He convinced the federal government to grant loan guarantees—promises that if Chrysler failed to pay its creditors, the government would pay them. Iacocca then streamlined

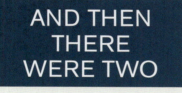

AND THEN THERE WERE TWO

operations and brought out some profitable products. Chrysler repaid all of its government-guaranteed loans by 1983, seven years ahead of the scheduled final payment.

To compete in today's global vehicle market, you must be big—really big. So in 1998, Chrysler merged with German automaker Daimler-Benz to form DaimlerChrysler. For a time, this left just two U.S.-based auto manufacturers—GM and Ford. But in 2007, DaimlerChrysler sold 81% of Chrysler to Cerberus, an investment group, to provide much-needed cash infusions to the automaker. In 2009, Daimler turned over its remaining stake to Cerberus. Three days later, Chrysler filed for bankruptcy. But by 2010, it was beginning to show signs of a turnaround.

The car companies are giants. GM and Ford typically rank among the top five U.S. firms in total assets. But GM and Ford accumulated truckloads of debt on their way to getting big. Although debt made it possible to get so big, the Chrysler story, and GM's recent bankruptcy, make it clear that debt can also threaten a company's survival.

INSIDE CHAPTER 10 . . .

- **When Convertible Bonds Don't**
- **Debt Masking**
- **"Covenant-Lite" Debt**

The Feature Story suggests that General Motors (GM) and Ford accumulated tremendous amounts of debt in their pursuit of auto industry dominance. It is unlikely that they could have grown so large without this debt, but at times the debt threatens their very existence. Given this risk, why do companies borrow money? Why do they sometimes borrow short-term and other times long-term? Besides bank borrowings, what other kinds of debts do companies incur? In this chapter, we address these issues.

The content and organization of the chapter are as follows.

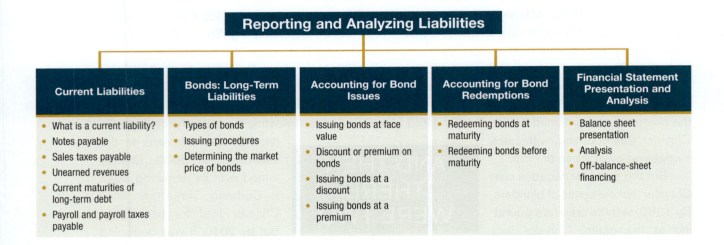

Current Liabilities

WHAT IS A CURRENT LIABILITY?

LEARNING OBJECTIVE 1

Explain a current liability and identify the major types of current liabilities.

You have learned that liabilities are defined as "creditors' claims on total assets" and as "existing debts and obligations." Companies must settle or pay these claims, debts, and obligations at some time in the future by transferring assets or services. The future date on which they are due or payable (the maturity date) is a significant feature of liabilities.

As explained in Chapter 2, a **current liability** is a debt that a company reasonably expects to pay (1) from existing current assets or through the creation of other current liabilities, and (2) within one year or the operating cycle, whichever is longer. Debts that do not meet both criteria are **long-term liabilities**.

Financial statement users want to know whether a company's obligations are current or long-term. A company that has more current liabilities than current assets often lacks liquidity, or short-term debt-paying ability. In addition, users want to know the types of liabilities a company has. If a company declares bankruptcy, a specific, predetermined order of payment to creditors exists. Thus, the amount and type of liabilities are of critical importance.

The different types of current liabilities include notes payable, accounts payable, unearned revenues, and accrued liabilities such as taxes, salaries and wages, and interest. In the sections that follow, we discuss a few of the common types of current liabilities.

NOTES PAYABLE

Companies record obligations in the form of written notes as **notes payable**. They often use notes payable instead of accounts payable because notes payable provide written documentation of the obligation in case legal remedies are needed to collect the debt. Companies frequently issue notes payable to meet short-term financing needs. Notes payable usually require the borrower to pay interest.

LEARNING OBJECTIVE 2
Describe the accounting for notes payable.

Notes are issued for varying periods of time. **Those due for payment within one year of the balance sheet date are usually classified as current liabilities.**

To illustrate the accounting for notes payable, assume that on September 1, 2014, Cole Williams Co. signs a $100,000, 12%, four-month note maturing on January 1 with First National Bank. When a company issues an interest-bearing note, the amount of assets it receives generally equals the note's face value. Cole Williams Co. therefore will receive $100,000 cash and will make the following journal entry.

Sept. 1	Cash	100,000	
	Notes Payable		100,000
	(To record issuance of 12%, 4-month		
	note to First National Bank)		

A = L + SE
+100,000
    +100,000

Cash Flows
+100,000

Interest accrues over the life of the note, and the issuer must periodically record that accrual. (You may find it helpful to review the discussion of interest computations that was provided in Chapter 8 with regard to notes receivable.) If Cole Williams Co. prepares financial statements annually, it makes an adjusting entry at December 31 to recognize four months of interest expense and interest payable of $4,000 ($100,000 $\times$ 12% $\times \frac{4}{12}$):

Dec. 31	Interest Expense	4,000	
	Interest Payable		4,000
	(To accrue interest for 4 months on		
	First National Bank note)		

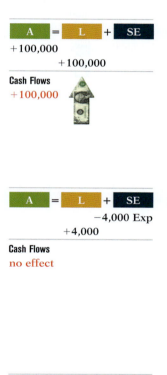

A = L + SE
    −4,000 Exp
    +4,000

Cash Flows
no effect

In the December 31 financial statements, the current liabilities section of the balance sheet will show notes payable $100,000 and interest payable $4,000. In addition, the company will report interest expense of $4,000 under "Other expenses and losses" in the income statement.

At maturity (January 1), Cole Williams Co. must pay the face value of the note ($100,000) plus $4,000 interest ($100,000 $\times$ 12% $\times \frac{4}{12}$). It records payment of the note and accrued interest as follows.

Jan. 1	Notes Payable	100,000	
	Interest Payable	4,000	
	Cash		104,000
	(To record payment of First National		
	Bank interest-bearing note and accrued		
	interest at maturity)		

A = L + SE
    −100,000
    −4,000
−104,000

Cash Flows
−104,000

Appendix 10C at the end of this chapter discusses the accounting for long-term installment notes payable.

SALES TAXES PAYABLE

Many of the products we purchase at retail stores are subject to sales taxes. Many states are now implementing sales taxes on purchases made on the Internet as well. Sales taxes are expressed as a percentage of the sales price. The selling company collects the tax from the customer when the sale occurs and periodically (usually monthly) remits the collections to the state's department of revenue. Collecting

LEARNING OBJECTIVE 3
Explain the accounting for other current liabilities.

sales taxes is important. For example, the State of New York recently sued Sprint Nextel Corporation for $300 million for its alleged failure to collect sales taxes on phone calls.

Under most state laws, the selling company must enter separately on the cash register the amount of the sale and the amount of the sales tax collected. (Gasoline sales are a major exception.) The company then uses the cash register readings to credit Sales Revenue and Sales Taxes Payable. For example, if the March 25 cash register readings for Cooley Grocery show sales of $10,000 and sales taxes of $600 (sales tax rate of 6%), the journal entry is:

A = L + SE
+10,600
+10,000 Rev
+600

Cash Flows
+10,600

Mar. 25	Cash	10,600	
	Sales Revenue		10,000
	Sales Taxes Payable		600
	(To record daily sales and sales taxes)		

When the company remits the taxes to the taxing agency, it decreases (debits) Sales Taxes Payable and decreases (credits) Cash. The company does not report sales taxes as an expense. It simply forwards to the government the amount paid by the customer. Thus, Cooley Grocery serves only as a **collection agent** for the taxing authority.

Sometimes companies do not enter sales taxes separately on the cash register. To determine the amount of sales in such cases, divide total receipts by 100% plus the sales tax percentage. For example, assume that Cooley Grocery enters total receipts of $10,600. Because the amount received from the sale is equal to the sales price (100%) plus 6% of sales, or 1.06 times the sales total, we can compute sales as follows: $10,600 ÷ 1.06 = $10,000. Thus, we can find the sales tax amount of $600 by either (1) subtracting sales from total receipts ($10,600 − $10,000) or (2) multiplying sales by the sales tax rate ($10,000 × 6%).

UNEARNED REVENUES

A magazine publisher such as Sports Illustrated collects cash when customers place orders for magazine subscriptions. An airline company such as American Airlines often receives cash when it sells tickets for future flights. Season tickets for concerts, sporting events, and theatre programs are also paid for in advance. How do companies account for unearned revenues that are received before goods are delivered or services are performed?

1. When the company receives an advance, it increases (debits) Cash and increases (credits) a current liability account identifying the source of the unearned revenue.

2. When the company recognizes revenue, it decreases (debits) the unearned revenue account and increases (credits) a revenue account.

To illustrate, assume that Superior University sells 10,000 season football tickets at $50 each for its five-game home schedule. The university makes the following entry for the sale of season tickets.

A = L + SE
+500,000
+500,000

Cash Flows
+500,000

Aug. 6	Cash	500,000	
	Unearned Ticket Revenue		500,000
	(To record sale of 10,000 season tickets)		

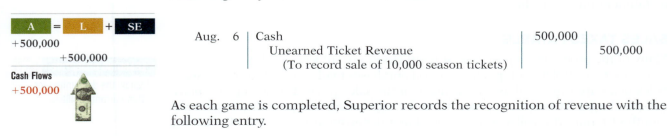

As each game is completed, Superior records the recognition of revenue with the following entry.

Sept. 7	Unearned Ticket Revenue	100,000	
	Ticket Revenue		100,000
	(To record football ticket revenues)		

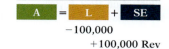

−100,000
+100,000 Rev

Cash Flows
no effect

The account Unearned Ticket Revenue represents unearned revenue, and Superior reports it as a current liability. As the school recognizes revenue, it reclassifies the amount from unearned revenue to Ticket Revenue. Unearned revenue is material for some companies. In the airline industry, tickets sold for future flights represent almost 50% of total current liabilities. At United Air Lines, unearned ticket revenue is its largest current liability, recently amounting to more than $1 billion.

Illustration 10-1 shows specific unearned revenue and revenue accounts used in selected types of businesses.

Type of Business	Account Title	
	Unearned Revenue	**Revenue**
Airline	Unearned Ticket Revenue	Ticket Revenue
Magazine publisher	Unearned Subscription Revenue	Subscription Revenue
Hotel	Unearned Rental Revenue	Rental Revenue

Illustration 10-1 Unearned revenue and revenue accounts

CURRENT MATURITIES OF LONG-TERM DEBT

Companies often have a portion of long-term debt that comes due in the current year. As an example, assume that Wendy Construction issues a five-year, interest-bearing $25,000 note on January 1, 2013. This note specifies that each January 1, starting January 1, 2014, Wendy should pay $5,000 of the note. When the company prepares financial statements on December 31, 2013, it should report $5,000 as a current liability and $20,000 as a long-term liability. (The $5,000 amount is the portion of the note that is due to be paid within the next 12 months.) Companies often identify current maturities of long-term debt on the balance sheet as **long-term debt due within one year**. In a recent year, General Motors had $724 million of such debt.

It is not necessary to prepare an adjusting entry to recognize the current maturity of long-term debt. At the balance sheet date, all obligations due within one year are classified as current, and all other obligations are long-term.

PAYROLL AND PAYROLL TAXES PAYABLE

Assume that Susan Alena works 40 hours this week for Pepitone Inc., earning a wage of $10 per hour. Will Susan receive a $400 check at the end of the week? Not likely. The reason: Pepitone is required to withhold amounts from her wages to pay various governmental authorities. For example, Pepitone will withhold amounts for Social Security taxes[1] and for federal and state income taxes. If these withholdings total $100, Susan will receive a check for only $300. Illustration 10-2 summarizes the types of payroll deductions that normally occur for most companies.

---

[1]Social Security taxes are commonly called FICA taxes. In 1937, Congress enacted the Federal Insurance Contribution Act (FICA). As can be seen in the following journal entry and the payroll tax journal entry, the employee and employer must make equal contributions to Social Security. The Social Security rate in 2012 was 7.65% for each except employees received a 2% reduction of the rate for 2012. *Our examples and homework use 7.65% for both.*

Illustration 10-2 Payroll deductions

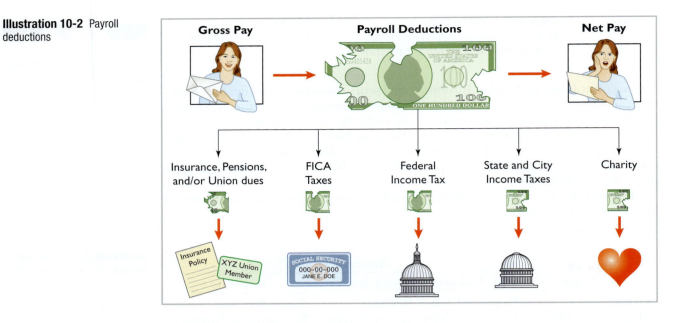

As a result of these deductions, companies withhold from employee paychecks amounts that must be paid to other parties. Pepitone therefore has incurred a liability to pay these third parties and must report this liability in its balance sheet.

As a second illustration, assume that Cargo Corporation records its payroll for the week of March 7 with the journal entry shown below.

A	=	L	+	SE
				−100,000 Exp
		+7,650		
		+21,864		
		+2,922		
		+67,564		

Cash Flows
no effect

Mar. 7	Salaries and Wages Expense	100,000	
	FICA Taxes Payable		7,650
	Federal Income Taxes Payable		21,864
	State Income Taxes Payable		2,922
	Salaries and Wages Payable		67,564
	(To record payroll and withholding taxes for the week ending March 7)		

Cargo then records payment of this payroll on March 7 as follows.

A	=	L	+	SE
		−67,564		
−67,564				

Cash Flows
−67,564

Mar. 7	Salaries and Wages Payable	67,564	
	Cash		67,564
	(To record payment of the March 7 payroll)		

In this case, Cargo reports $100,000 in salaries and wages expense. In addition, it reports liabilities for the salaries and wages payable as well as liabilities to governmental agencies. Rather than pay the employees $100,000, Cargo instead must withhold the taxes and make the tax payments directly. In summary, Cargo is essentially serving as a tax collector.

In addition to the liabilities incurred as a result of withholdings, employers also incur a second type of payroll-related liability. With every payroll, the employer incurs liabilities to pay various **payroll taxes** levied upon the employer. These payroll taxes include the **employer's share** of Social Security (FICA) taxes and state and federal unemployment taxes. Based on Cargo Corp.'s $100,000 payroll, the company would record the employer's expense and liability for these payroll taxes as follows.

Mar. 7	Payroll Tax Expense		13,850	
	FICA Taxes Payable			7,650
	Federal Unemployment Taxes Payable			800
	State Unemployment Taxes Payable			5,400
	(To record employer's payroll taxes on March 7 payroll)			

A	=	L	+	SE
				−13,850 Exp
		+7,650		
		+800		
		+5,400		

Cash Flows
no effect

Companies classify the payroll and payroll tax liability accounts as current liabilities because they must be paid to employees or remitted to taxing authorities periodically and in the near term. Taxing authorities impose substantial fines and penalties on employers if the withholding and payroll taxes are not computed correctly and paid on time.

ANATOMY OF A FRAUD

Art was a custodial supervisor for a large school district. The district was supposed to employ between 35 and 40 regular custodians, as well as 3 or 4 substitute custodians to fill in when regular custodians were missing. Instead, in addition to the regular custodians, Art "hired" 77 substitutes. In fact, almost none of these people worked for the district. Instead, Art submitted time cards for these people, collected their checks at the district office, and personally distributed the checks to the "employees." If a substitute's check was for $1,200, that person would cash the check, keep $200, and pay Art $1,000.

Total take: $150,000

THE MISSING CONTROLS

Human Resource Controls. Thorough background checks should be performed. No employees should begin work until they have been approved by the Board of Education and entered into the payroll system. No employees should be entered into the payroll system until they have been approved by a supervisor. All paychecks should be distributed directly to employees at the official school locations by designated employees.

Independent internal verification. Budgets should be reviewed monthly to identify situations where actual costs significantly exceed budgeted amounts.

Source: Adapted from Wells, *Fraud Casebook* (2007), pp. 164–171.

Bonds: Long-Term Liabilities

Long-term liabilities are obligations that a company expects to pay more than one year in the future. In this section, we explain the accounting for the principal types of obligations reported in the long-term liabilities section of the balance sheet. These obligations often are in the form of bonds or long-term notes.

Bonds are a form of interest-bearing note payable issued by corporations, universities, and governmental agencies. Bonds, like common stock, are sold in small denominations (usually $1,000 or multiples of $1,000). As a result, bonds attract many investors. When a corporation issues bonds, it is borrowing money. The person who buys the bonds (the bondholder) is investing in bonds.

LEARNING OBJECTIVE 4
Identify the types of bonds.

Convertible Bonds

Callable Bonds

TYPES OF BONDS

Bonds may have different features. In the following sections, we describe some commonly issued types of bonds.

Secured and Unsecured Bonds

Secured bonds have specific assets of the issuer pledged as collateral for the bonds. **Unsecured bonds** are issued against the general credit of the borrower. Large corporations with good credit ratings use unsecured bonds extensively. For example, at one time DuPont reported more than $2 billion of unsecured bonds outstanding.

Convertible and Callable Bonds

Bonds that can be converted into common stock at the bondholder's option are **convertible bonds**. Bonds that the issuing company can redeem (buy back) at a stated dollar amount prior to maturity are **callable bonds**. Convertible bonds have features that are attractive both to bondholders and to the issuer. The conversion feature often gives bondholders an opportunity to benefit if the market price of the common stock increases substantially. Furthermore, until conversion, the bondholder receives interest on the bond. For the issuer, the bonds sell at a higher price and pay a lower rate of interest than comparable debt securities that do not have a conversion option. Many corporations, such as USAir, United States Steel Corp., and General Motors Corporation, have issued convertible bonds.

Accounting Across the Organization
When Convertible Bonds Don't

During the boom times of the late 1990s, many rapidly growing companies issued large quantities of convertible bonds. Investors found the convertible bonds attractive because they paid regular interest but also had the upside potential of being converted to stock if the stock price increased. At the time, stock prices were increasing rapidly, so many investors viewed convertible bonds as a cheap and safe way to buy stock.

As a consequence, companies were able to pay much lower interest rates on convertible bonds than on standard bonds. When the bonds were issued, company managers assumed that the bonds would be converted. Thus, the company would never have to repay the debt with cash. It seemed too good to be true—and it was.

When stock prices plummeted in the early 2000s, investors no longer had an incentive to convert, since the market price was below the conversion price. When many of these massive bonds came due, companies were forced either to pay them off or to issue new debt at much higher rates.

? The drop in stock prices did not change the debt to assets ratios of these companies. Discuss how the perception of a high debt to assets ratio changed before and after the fall in stock prices. (Answers in *Broadening Your Perspective*.)

ISSUING PROCEDURES

A **bond certificate** is issued to the investor to provide evidence of the investor's claim against the company. As Illustration 10-3 shows, the bond certificate provides information such as the name of the company that issued the bonds, the face value of the bonds, the maturity date of the bonds, and the contractual interest rate. The **face value** is the amount of principal due at the maturity date. The **maturity date** is the date that the final payment is due to the investor from the issuing company. The **contractual interest rate** is the rate used to determine the amount of cash interest the borrower pays and the investor receives. Usually, the contractual rate is stated as an annual rate, and interest is generally paid semiannually. (We use annual payments in our examples to simplify.)

Alternative Terminology The contractual rate is often referred to as the *stated rate*.

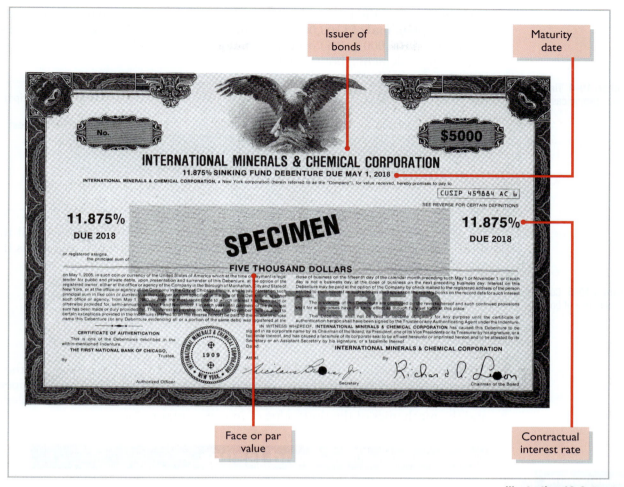

Issuer of bonds

Maturity date

Face or par value

Contractual interest rate

Illustration 10-3 Bond certificate

DETERMINING THE MARKET PRICE OF BONDS

If you were an investor wanting to purchase a bond, how would you determine how much to pay? To be more specific, assume that Coronet, Inc. issues a zero-interest (pays no interest) bond with a face value of $1,000,000 due in 20 years. For this bond, the only cash you receive is $1 million at the end of 20 years. Would you pay $1 million for this bond? We hope not because $1 million received 20 years from now is not the same as $1 million received today.

The term **time value of money** is used to indicate the relationship between time and money—that a dollar received today is worth more than a dollar promised at some time in the future. If you had $1 million today, you would invest it and earn interest so that at the end of 20 years, your investment would be worth much more than $1 million. Thus, if someone is going to pay you $1 million 20 years from now, you would want to find its equivalent today, or its **present value**. In other words, you would want to determine the value today of the amount to be received in the future after taking into account current interest rates.

Same dollars at different times are not equal.

The current market price (present value) of a bond is therefore a function of three factors: (1) the dollar amounts to be received, (2) the length of time until the amounts are received, and (3) the market interest rate. The **market interest rate** is the rate investors demand for loaning funds. The process of finding the present value is referred to as **discounting** the future amounts.

To illustrate, assume that Acropolis Company on January 1, 2014, issues $100,000 of 9% bonds, due in five years, with interest payable annually at year-end.

The purchaser of the bonds would receive the following two types of cash payments: (1) **principal** of $100,000 to be paid at maturity, and (2) five $9,000 **interest payments** ($100,000 × 9%) over the term of the bonds. Illustration 10-4 shows a time diagram depicting both cash flows.

Illustration 10-4 Time diagram depicting cash flows

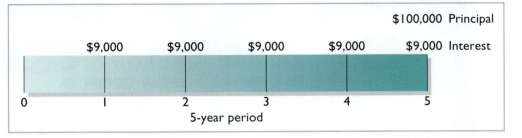

The current market price of a bond is equal to the present value of all the future cash payments promised by the bond. Illustration 10-5 lists and totals the present values of these amounts, assuming the market rate of interest is 9%.

Illustration 10-5 Computing the market price of bonds

Present value of $100,000 received in 5 years	$ 64,993
Present value of $9,000 received annually for 5 years	35,007
Market price of bonds	**$100,000**

Tables are available to provide the present value numbers to be used, or these values can be determined mathematically or with financial calculators.[2] Appendix D, near the end of the textbook, provides further discussion of the concepts and the mechanics of the time value of money computations.

Accounting for Bond Issues

LEARNING OBJECTIVE 5

Prepare the entries for the issuance of bonds and interest expense.

A corporation records bond transactions when it issues (sells) or redeems (buys back) bonds and when bondholders convert bonds into common stock. If bondholders sell their bond investments to other investors, the issuing firm receives no further money on the transaction, **nor does the issuing corporation journalize the transaction** (although it does keep records of the names of bondholders in some cases).

Bonds may be issued at face value, below face value (discount), or above face value (premium). Bond prices for both new issues and existing bonds are quoted as **a percentage of the face value of the bond. Face value is usually $1,000.** Thus, a $1,000 bond with a quoted price of 97 means that the selling price of the bond is 97% of face value, or $970.

ISSUING BONDS AT FACE VALUE

To illustrate the accounting for bonds issued at face value, assume that Devor Corporation issues 100, five-year, 10%, $1,000 bonds dated January 1, 2014, at 100 (100% of face value). The entry to record the sale is:

A = L + SE
+100,000
      +100,000

Cash Flows
+100,000

Jan.	1	Cash	100,000	
		Bonds Payable		100,000
		(To record sale of bonds at face value)		

---

[2]For those knowledgeable in the use of present value tables, the computations in this example are $100,000 × .64993 = $64,993 and $9,000 × 3.88965 = $35,007 (rounded).

Devor reports bonds payable in the long-term liabilities section of the balance sheet because the maturity date is January 1, 2019 (more than one year away).

Over the term (life) of the bonds, companies make entries to record bond interest. Interest on bonds payable is computed in the same manner as interest on notes payable, as explained earlier. If we assume that interest is payable annually on January 1 on the bonds described above, Devor accrues interest of $10,000 ($100,000 \times 10\% \times \frac{12}{12}$) on December 31. At December 31, Devor recognizes the $10,000 of interest expense incurred with the following adjusting entry.

Dec. 31	Interest Expense	10,000	
	Interest Payable		10,000
	(To accrue bond interest)		

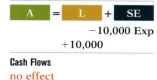

The company classifies **interest payable as a current liability** because it is scheduled for payment within the next year. When Devor pays the interest on January 1, 2015, it decreases (debits) Interest Payable and decreases (credits) Cash for $10,000. Devor records the payment on January 1 as follows.

Jan. 1	Interest Payable	10,000	
	Cash		10,000
	(To record payment of bond interest)		

DISCOUNT OR PREMIUM ON BONDS

The previous illustrations assumed that the contractual (stated) interest rate and the market (effective) interest rate paid on bonds were the same. Recall that the **contractual interest rate** is the rate applied to the face (par) value to arrive at the interest paid in a year. The **market interest rate** is the rate investors demand for loaning funds to the corporation. When the contractual interest rate and the market interest rate are the same, **bonds sell at face value**.

However, market interest rates change daily. The type of bond issued, the state of the economy, current industry conditions, and the company's individual performance all affect market interest rates. As a result, the contractual and market interest rates often differ. To make bonds salable when the two rates differ, bonds sell below or above face value.

To illustrate, suppose that a company issues 10% bonds at a time when other bonds of similar risk are paying 12%. Investors will not be interested in buying the 10% bonds, so their value will fall below their face value. When a bond is sold for less than its face value, the difference between the face value of a bond and its selling price is called a **discount**. As a result of the decline in the bonds' selling price, the actual interest rate incurred by the company increases to the level of the current market interest rate.

Conversely, if the market rate of interest is **lower than** the contractual interest rate, investors will have to pay more than face value for the bonds. That is, if the market rate of interest is 8% but the contractual interest rate on the bonds is 10%, the price on the bonds will be bid up. When a bond is sold for more than its face value, the difference between the face value and its selling price is called a **premium**. Illustration 10-6 shows these relationships graphically.

Illustration 10-6 Interest rates and bond prices

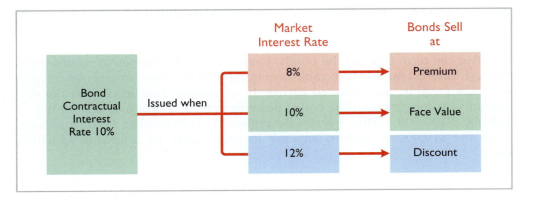

Issuance of bonds at an amount different from face value is quite common. By the time a company prints the bond certificates and markets the bonds, it will be a coincidence if the market rate and the contractual rate are the same. Thus, the issuance of bonds at a discount does not mean that the financial strength of the issuer is suspect. Conversely, the sale of bonds at a premium does not indicate that the financial strength of the issuer is exceptional.

ISSUING BONDS AT A DISCOUNT

To illustrate the issuance of bonds at a discount, assume that on January 1, 2014, Candlestick Inc. sells $100,000, five-year, 10% bonds at 98 (98% of face value) with interest payable on January 1. The entry to record the issuance is:

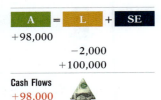

| A | = | L | + | SE |

+98,000

−2,000
+100,000

Cash Flows
+98,000

Jan.	1	Cash	98,000	
		Discount on Bonds Payable	2,000	
		Bonds Payable		100,000
		(To record sale of bonds at a discount)		

Although Discount on Bonds Payable has a debit balance, **it is not an asset**. Rather it is a **contra account**, which is **deducted from bonds payable** on the balance sheet as shown in Illustration 10-7.

Illustration 10-7 Statement presentation of discount on bonds payable

CANDLESTICK INC.
Balance Sheet (partial)

Long-term liabilities		
Bonds payable		$100,000
Less: Discount on bonds payable	2,000	$98,000

The $98,000 represents the **carrying (or book) value** of the bonds. On the date of issue, this amount equals the market price of the bonds.

The issuance of bonds below face value causes the total cost of borrowing to differ from the bond interest paid. That is, the issuing corporation not only must pay the contractual interest rate over the term of the bonds but also must pay the face value (rather than the issuance price) at maturity. Therefore, the difference between the issuance price and the face value of the bonds—the discount—is an **additional cost of borrowing**. The company records this cost as **interest expense** over the life of the bonds. The total cost of borrowing $98,000 for Candlestick Inc. is $52,000, computed as shown in Illustration 10-8.

Illustration 10-8
Computation of total cost of borrowing—bonds issued at discount

Bonds Issued at a Discount	
Annual interest payments	
($100,000 × 10% = $10,000; $10,000 × 5)	$ 50,000
Add: Bond discount ($100,000 − $98,000)	2,000
Total cost of borrowing	**$52,000**

Alternatively, we can compute the total cost of borrowing as shown in Illustration 10-9.

Illustration 10-9 Alternative computation of total cost of borrowing—bonds issued at discount

Bonds Issued at a Discount	
Principal at maturity	$100,000
Annual interest payments ($10,000 × 5)	50,000
Cash to be paid to bondholders	150,000
Cash received from bondholders	98,000
Total cost of borrowing	**$ 52,000**

To follow the expense recognition principle, companies allocate bond discount to expense in each period in which the bonds are outstanding. This is referred to as **amortizing the discount**. Amortization of the discount **increases** the amount of interest expense reported each period. That is, after the company amortizes the discount, the amount of interest expense it reports in a period will exceed the contractual amount. As shown in Illustration 10-8, for the bonds issued by Candlestick Inc., total interest expense will exceed the contractual interest by $2,000 over the life of the bonds.

As the discount is amortized, its balance declines. As a consequence, the carrying value of the bonds will increase, until at maturity the carrying value of the bonds equals their face amount. This is shown in Illustration 10-10. Appendices 10A and 10B at the end of this chapter discuss procedures for amortizing bond discount.

Illustration 10-10
Amortization of bond discount

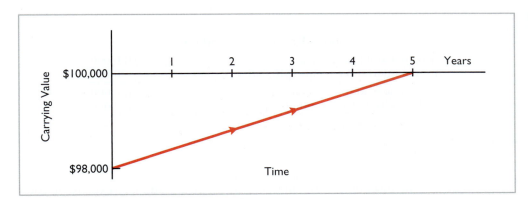

ISSUING BONDS AT A PREMIUM

We can illustrate the issuance of bonds at a premium by now assuming the Candlestick Inc. bonds described above sell at 102 (102% of face value) rather than at 98. The entry to record the sale is:

Jan.	1	Cash	102,000	
		Bonds Payable		100,000
		Premium on Bonds Payable		2,000
		(To record sale of bonds at a premium)		

A	=	L	+	SE
+102,000				
		+100,000		
		+2,000		

Cash Flows
+102,000

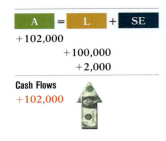

Candlestick adds the premium on bonds payable **to the bonds payable** amount on the balance sheet, as shown in Illustration 10-11.

Illustration 10-11 Statement presentation of bond premium

CANDLESTICK INC.		
Balance Sheet (partial)		
Long-term liabilities		
Bonds payable	$100,000	
Add: Premium on bonds payable	2,000	$102,000

The sale of bonds above face value causes the total cost of borrowing to be **less than the bond interest paid** because the borrower is not required to pay the bond premium at the maturity date of the bonds. Thus, the premium is considered to be **a reduction in the cost of borrowing** that reduces bond interest expense over the life of the bonds. The total cost of borrowing $102,000 for Candlestick Inc. is $48,000, computed as in Illustration 10-12.

Illustration 10-12 Computation of total cost of borrowing—bonds issued at a premium

Bonds Issued at a Premium	
Annual interest payments	
($100,000 × 10% = $10,000; $10,000 × 5)	$ 50,000
Less: Bond premium ($102,000 − $100,000)	2,000
Total cost of borrowing	**$48,000**

Alternatively, we can compute the cost of borrowing as shown in Illustration 10-13.

Illustration 10-13 Alternative computation of total cost of borrowing—bonds issued at a premium

Bonds Issued at a Premium	
Principal at maturity	$100,000
Annual interest payments ($10,000 × 5)	50,000
Cash to be paid to bondholders	150,000
Cash received from bondholders	102,000
Total cost of borrowing	**$ 48,000**

Similar to bond discount, companies allocate bond premium to expense in each period in which the bonds are outstanding. This is referred to as **amortizing the premium**. Amortization of the premium **decreases** the amount of interest expense reported each period. That is, after the company amortizes the premium, the amount of interest expense it reports in a period will be less than the contractual amount. As shown in Illustration 10-12, for the bonds issued by Candlestick Inc., contractual interest will exceed the interest expense by $2,000 over the life of the bonds.

As the premium is amortized, its balance declines. As a consequence, the carrying value of the bonds will decrease, until at maturity the carrying value of the bonds equals their face amount. This is shown in Illustration 10-14. Appendices 10A and 10B at the end of this chapter discuss procedures for amortizing bond premium.

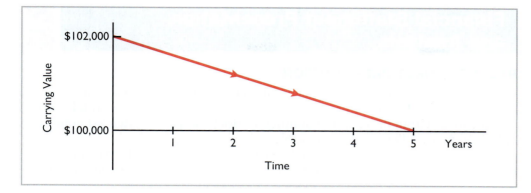

Illustration 10-14
Amortization of bond premium

Accounting for Bond Redemptions

Bonds are redeemed when the issuing corporation buys them back. The appropriate entries for these transactions are explained next.

LEARNING OBJECTIVE 6
Describe the entries when bonds are redeemed.

REDEEMING BONDS AT MATURITY

Regardless of the issue price of bonds, the book value of the bonds at maturity will equal their face value. Assuming that the company pays and records separately the interest for the last interest period, Candlestick records the redemption of its bonds at maturity as:

Bonds Payable	100,000	
Cash		100,000
(To record redemption of bonds at maturity)		

A = **L** + **SE**
−100,000
−100,000

Cash Flows
−100,000

REDEEMING BONDS BEFORE MATURITY

Bonds may be redeemed before maturity. A company may decide to redeem bonds before maturity in order to reduce interest cost and remove debt from its balance sheet. A company should redeem debt early only if it has sufficient cash resources.

When bonds are redeemed before maturity, it is necessary to (1) eliminate the carrying value of the bonds at the redemption date, (2) record the cash paid, and (3) recognize the gain or loss on redemption. The **carrying value** of the bonds is the face value of the bonds less unamortized bond discount or plus unamortized bond premium at the redemption date.

To illustrate, assume at the end of the fourth period, Candlestick Inc., having sold its bonds at a premium, redeems the $100,000 face value bonds at 103 after paying the annual interest. Assume that the carrying value of the bonds at the redemption date is $100,400 (principal $100,000 and premium $400). Candlestick records the redemption at the end of the fourth interest period (January 1, 2018) as:

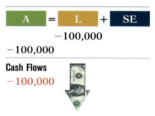

Jan. 1	Bonds Payable	100,000	
	Premium on Bonds Payable	400	
	Loss on Bond Redemption	2,600	
	Cash		103,000
	(To record redemption of bonds at 103)		

A = **L** + **SE**
−100,000
−400
−2,600 Exp
−103,000

Cash Flows
−103,000

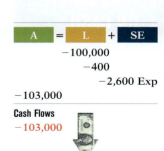

Note that the loss of $2,600 is the difference between the $103,000 cash paid and the $100,400 carrying value of the bonds.

Financial Statement Presentation and Analysis

LEARNING OBJECTIVE 7

Identify the requirements for the financial statement presentation and analysis of liabilities.

BALANCE SHEET PRESENTATION

Current liabilities are the first category under "Liabilities" on the balance sheet. Companies list each of the principal types of current liabilities separately within the category. Within the current liabilities section, companies often list notes payable first, followed by accounts payable.

Companies report long-term liabilities in a separate section of the balance sheet immediately following "Current liabilities." Illustration 10-15 shows an example.

Illustration 10-15
Balance sheet presentation of liabilities

MARAIS COMPANY
Balance Sheet (partial)

Liabilities		
Current liabilities		
Notes payable	$ 250,000	
Accounts payable	125,000	
Current maturities of long-term debt	300,000	
Accrued liabilities	75,000	
Total current liabilities		$ 750,000
Long-term liabilities		
Bonds payable	1,000,000	
Less: Discount on bonds payable	80,000	920,000
Notes payable, secured by plant assets		540,000
Lease liability		500,000
Total long-term liabilities		1,960,000
Total liabilities		$2,710,000

Disclosure of debt is very important. Failures at Enron, WorldCom, and Global Crossing have made investors very concerned about companies' debt obligations. Summary data regarding debts may be presented in the balance sheet with detailed data (such as interest rates, maturity dates, conversion privileges, and assets pledged as collateral) shown in a supporting schedule in the notes. Companies should report current maturities of long-term debt as a current liability.

KEEPING AN EYE ON CASH

The balance sheet presents the balances of a company's debts at a point in time. The statement of cash flows also presents information about a company's debts. Information regarding cash inflows and outflows during the year that resulted from the principal portion of debt transactions appears in the "Financing activities" section of the statement of cash flows. Interest expense is reported in the "Operating activities" section even though it resulted from debt transactions.

The statement of cash flows shown below presents the cash flows from financing activities for General Motors Company (Automotive Division). From this we learn that the company issued new debt of $476 million and repaid debt of $1,471 million.

GENERAL MOTORS COMPANY—Automotive Division
Statement of Cash Flows (partial)
2011
(in millions)

Real World

Cash flows from financing activities

Proceeds from issuance of stock	$ 11
Proceeds from issuance of debt	476
Payments of debt	(1,471)
Increase in short-term borrowings	131
Dividends paid	(916)
Other	(100)
Net cash provided by (used in) financing activities	$(1,869)

ANALYSIS

Careful examination of debt obligations helps you assess a company's ability to pay its current and long-term obligations. It also helps you determine whether a company can obtain debt financing in order to grow. We will use the following information from the financial statements of the nonfinancial services division (primarily the Automotive Division) of Toyota Motor Corporation to illustrate the analysis of a company's liquidity and solvency.

Illustration 10-16
Simplified balance sheets for Toyota Motor Corporation

TOYOTA MOTOR CORPORATION—Automotive Division
Balance Sheets
December 31, 2011 and 2010
(in millions)

Real World

Assets	2011	2010
Total current assets	$ 78,273	$ 88,643
Noncurrent assets	125,487	102,601
Total assets	$203,760	$191,244
Liabilities and Stockholders' Equity		
Total current liabilities	$ 60,319	$ 59,315
Noncurrent liabilities	24,713	25,506
Total liabilities	85,032	84,821
Total stockholders' equity	118,728	106,423
Total liabilities and stockholders' equity	$203,760	$191,244

Liquidity

Liquidity ratios measure the short-term ability of a company to pay its maturing obligations and to meet unexpected needs for cash. A commonly used measure of liquidity is the current ratio (presented in Chapter 2). The current ratio is calculated as current assets divided by current liabilities. Illustration 10-17 presents the current ratio for the Automotive Division of Toyota along with the industry average.

Illustration 10-17
Current ratio

Ratio	Toyota (Automotive Division) ($ in millions)		Industry Average
	2011	2010	2011
Current Ratio	$\dfrac{\$78,273}{\$60,319} = 1.30{:}1$	$\dfrac{\$88,643}{\$59,315} = 1.49{:}1$	1.00:1

Toyota's current ratio declined from 1.49:1 to 1.30:1 from 2010 to 2011. Although Toyota's ratio declined, it still exceeds the industry average current ratio for manufacturers of autos and trucks of 1.00:1.

Toyota's current ratio, like the industry average, is quite low. Many companies today minimize their liquid assets (such as accounts receivable and inventory) in order to improve profitability measures, such as return on assets. This is particularly true of large companies such as Ford, GM, and Toyota. Companies that keep fewer liquid assets on hand must rely on other sources of liquidity. One such source is a **bank line of credit**. A line of credit is a prearranged agreement between a company and a lender that permits the company, should it be necessary, to borrow up to an agreed-upon amount. For example, a recent disclosure regarding debt in Toyota's financial statements states that it has $23.5 billion of unused lines of credit. This represents a substantial amount of available cash.

 DECISION TOOLKIT

DECISION CHECKPOINTS	INFO NEEDED FOR DECISION	TOOL TO USE FOR DECISION	HOW TO EVALUATE RESULTS
Can the company obtain short-term financing when necessary?	Available lines of credit, from notes to the financial statements.	Compare available lines of credit to current liabilities. Also, evaluate liquidity ratios.	If liquidity ratios are low, then lines of credit should be high to compensate.

Solvency

Solvency ratios measure the ability of a company to survive over a long period of time. The Feature Story in this chapter mentioned that, although there once were many U.S. automobile manufacturers, only three U.S.-based companies remain today. Many of the others went bankrupt. This highlights the fact that when making a long-term loan or purchasing a company's stock, you must give consideration to a company's solvency.

To reduce the risks associated with having a large amount of debt during an economic downturn, some U.S. automobile manufacturers took two precautionary steps while they enjoyed strong profits. First, they built up large balances of cash and cash equivalents to avoid a cash crisis. Second, they were reluctant to build new plants or hire new workers to meet their production needs. Instead, they asked workers to put in overtime, or they "outsourced" work to other companies. In this way, when the economic downturn occurred, they hoped to avoid having to make debt payments on idle production plants and to minimize layoffs. As a result, when the crisis first hit, Ford had cash of $29 billion, about double the amount of cash it would expect to use over a two-year period.

In Chapter 2, you learned that one measure of a company's solvency is the debt to assets ratio. This is calculated as total liabilities (debt) divided by total assets. This ratio indicates the extent to which a company's assets are financed with debt.

Another useful solvency measure is the **times interest earned**. It provides an indication of a company's ability to meet interest payments as they come due. It is computed by dividing income before interest expense and income taxes by interest expense. It uses income before interest expense and taxes because this number best represents the amount available to pay interest.

We can use the balance sheet information presented on the previous page and the additional information below to calculate solvency ratios for the Automotive Division of Toyota.

($ in millions)	2011	2010
Net income	$2,254	$904
Interest expense	350	560
Income tax expense	2,150	455

The debt to assets ratios and times interest earned for the Automotive Division of Toyota and averages for the industry are shown in Illustration 10-18.

Toyota's debt to assets ratio was 42%. The industry average for manufacturers of autos and trucks is 62%. Thus, Toyota is less reliant on debt financing than the average firm in the auto and truck industry.

Toyota's times interest earned increased from 3.4 times in 2010 to 13.6 in 2011. This means that in 2011 Toyota had earnings before interest and taxes that were more than 13 times the amount needed to pay interest. The higher the multiple, the lower the likelihood that the company will default on interest payments. Because many of the companies in this industry were still recovering from the recent recession, the industry average was only 3.2. This suggests that while Toyota's ability to meet interest payments was high, the average company in the industry had a lower ability to meet interest payments in 2011.

$$\text{Debt to Assets Ratio} = \frac{\text{Total Liabilities}}{\text{Total Assets}}$$

$$\text{Times Interest Earned} = \frac{\text{Net Income + Interest Expense + Tax Expense}}{\text{Interest Expense}}$$

Ratio	Toyota (Automotive Division) ($ in millions) 2011	2010	Industry Average 2011
Debt to Assets Ratio	$\frac{\$85,032}{\$203,760} = 42\%$	44%	62%
Times Interest Earned	$\frac{\$2,254 + \$350 + \$2,150}{\$350} = 13.6$ times	3.4 times	3.2 times

Illustration 10-18
Solvency ratios

Investor Insight

Debt Masking

In the wake of the financial crisis, many financial institutions are wary of reporting too much debt on their financial statements, for fear that investors will consider them too risky. The Securities and Exchange Commission (SEC) is concerned that some companies engage in "debt masking" to make it appear that they use less debt than they actually do. These companies enter into transactions at the end of the accounting period that essentially remove debt from their books. Shortly after the end of the period, they reverse the transaction and the debt goes back on their books. The *Wall Street Journal* reported that 18 large banks "had consistently lowered one type of debt at the end of each of the past five quarters, reducing it on average by 42% from quarterly peaks."

Source: Tom McGinty, Kate Kelly, and Kara Scannell, "Debt 'Masking' Under Fire," *Wall Street Journal Online* (April 21, 2010).

? What implications does debt masking have for an investor that is using the debt to assets ratio to evaluate a company's solvency? (Answers in *Broadening Your Perspective*.)

DECISION TOOLKIT

DECISION CHECKPOINTS	INFO NEEDED FOR DECISION	TOOL TO USE FOR DECISION	HOW TO EVALUATE RESULTS
Can the company meet its obligations in the long term?	Interest expense and net income before interest and taxes	$$\text{Times interest earned} = \frac{\text{Net income} + \text{Interest expense} + \text{Tax expense}}{\text{Interest expense}}$$	High ratio indicates ability to meet interest payments as scheduled.

OFF-BALANCE-SHEET FINANCING

A concern for analysts when they evaluate a company's liquidity and solvency is whether that company has properly recorded all of its obligations. The bankruptcy of Enron Corporation, one of the largest bankruptcies in U.S. history, demonstrated how much damage can result when a company does not properly record or disclose all of its debts. Many would say Enron was practicing off-balance-sheet financing. **Off-balance-sheet financing** is an intentional effort by a company to structure its financing arrangements so as to avoid showing liabilities on its balance sheet. Two common types of off-balance-sheet financing result from unreported contingencies and lease transactions.

Contingencies

One reason a company's balance sheet might not fully reflect its potential obligations is due to contingencies. **Contingencies** are events with uncertain outcomes that may represent potential liabilities. A common type of contingency is lawsuits. Suppose, for example, that you were analyzing the financial statements of a cigarette manufacturer and did not consider the possible negative implications of existing unsettled lawsuits. Your analysis of the company's financial position would certainly be misleading. Other common types of contingencies are product warranties and environmental cleanup obligations. For example, in a recent year, Novartis AG began offering a money-back guarantee on its blood-pressure medications. This guarantee would necessitate an accrual for the estimated claims that will result from returns.

Accounting rules require that companies disclose contingencies in the notes. In some cases, they must accrue them as liabilities. For example, suppose that Waterbury Inc. is sued by a customer for $1 million due to an injury sustained by a defective product. If at the company's year-end the lawsuit had not yet been resolved, how should Waterbury account for this event? If the company can determine

a reasonable estimate of the expected loss and if it is **probable** it will lose the suit, then the company should accrue for the loss. It records the loss by increasing (debiting) a loss account and increasing (crediting) a liability such as Lawsuit Liability. If **both** of these conditions are not met, then the company discloses the basic facts regarding this suit in the notes to its financial statements.

Leasing

One common type of off-balance-sheet financing results from leasing. Most lessees do not like to report leases on their balance sheets because the lease increases the company's total liabilities. Recall from Chapter 9 that operating leases are treated like rentals—no asset or liabilities show on the books. Capital leases are treated like a debt-financed purchase—increasing both assets and liabilities. **As a result, many companies structure their lease agreements to avoid meeting the criteria of a capital lease.**

Recall from Chapter 9 that many U.S. airlines lease a large portion of their planes without showing any debt related to them on their balance sheets. For example, the total increase in assets and liabilities that would result if Southwest Airlines recorded on the balance sheet its off-balance-sheet "operating" leases would be approximately $2.3 billion. Illustration 10-19 presents Southwest Airlines' debt to assets ratio for a recent year using the numbers presented in its balance sheet. It also shows the ratio after adjusting for the off-balance-sheet leases. After those adjustments, Southwest has a ratio of 62% versus 67% before. This means that of every dollar of assets, 67 cents was funded by debt. This would be of interest to analysts evaluating Southwest's solvency.

	Using numbers as presented on balance sheet	Adjusted for off-balance-sheet leases
Debt to assets ratio	$\frac{\$8,803}{\$14,269} = 62\%$	$\frac{\$8,803 + \$2,371}{\$14,269 + \$2,371} = 67\%$

Illustration 10-19 Debt to assets ratio adjusted for leases

Critics of off-balance-sheet financing contend that many leases represent unavoidable obligations that meet the definition of a liability. Therefore, companies should report them as liabilities on the balance sheet. To reduce these concerns, companies are required to report their operating lease obligations for subsequent years in a note. This allows analysts and other financial statement users to adjust a company's financial statements by adding leased assets and lease liabilities if they feel that this treatment is more appropriate.

🧰 DECISION TOOLKIT

DECISION CHECKPOINTS	INFO NEEDED FOR DECISION	TOOL TO USE FOR DECISION	HOW TO EVALUATE RESULTS
Does the company have any contingent liabilities?	Knowledge of events with uncertain negative outcomes	Notes to financial statements and financial statements	If negative outcomes are possible, determine the probability, the amount of loss, and the potential impact on financial statements.
Does the company have significant off-balance-sheet financing, such as unrecorded lease obligations?	Information on unrecorded obligations, such as a schedule of minimum lease payments from the notes to the financial statements	Compare liquidity and solvency ratios with and without unrecorded obligations included	If ratios differ significantly after including unrecorded obligations, these obligations should not be ignored in analysis.

Investor Insight

"Covenant-Lite" Debt

In many corporate loans and bond issuances, the lending agreement specifies **debt covenants**. These covenants typically are specific financial measures, such as minimum levels of retained earnings, cash flows, times interest earned, or other measures that a company must maintain during the life of the loan. If the company violates a covenant, it is considered to have violated the loan agreement. The creditors can then demand immediate repayment, or they can renegotiate the loan's terms. Covenants protect lenders because they enable lenders to step in and try to get their money back before the borrower gets too deep into trouble.

During the 1990s, most traditional loans specified between three to six covenants or "triggers." In more recent years, however, when there was lots of cash available, lenders began reducing or completely eliminating covenants from loan agreements in order to be more competitive with other lenders. When the economy declined, these lenders lost big money when companies defaulted.

Source: Cynthia Koons, "Risky Business: Growth of 'Covenant-Lite' Debt," *Wall Street Journal* (June 18, 2007), p. C2.

? How can financial ratios such as those covered in this chapter provide protection for creditors? (Answers in *Broadening Your Perspective*.)

USING THE DECISION TOOLKIT

Ford Motor Company has enjoyed some tremendous successes, including its popular Taurus and Explorer vehicles. Yet observers are looking for the next big hit. Development of a new vehicle costs billions. A flop is financially devastating, and the financial effect is magnified if the company has large amounts of outstanding debt.

The following balance sheets provide financial information for the Automotive Division of Ford Motor Company as of December 31, 2011 and 2010. We have chosen to analyze only the Automotive Division rather than the total corporation, which includes Ford's giant financing division. In an actual analysis, you would want to analyze the major divisions individually as well as the combined corporation as a whole.

Instructions

1. Evaluate Ford's liquidity using appropriate ratios, and compare to those of Toyota and to industry averages.
2. Evaluate Ford's solvency using appropriate ratios, and compare to those of Toyota and to industry averages.
3. Comment on Ford's available lines of credit.

FORD MOTOR COMPANY—Automotive Division
Balance Sheets
December 31, 2011 and 2010
(in millions)

Real World

Assets	2011	2010
Current assets	$38,147	$34,368
Noncurrent assets	40,639	30,238
Total assets	$78,786	$64,606
Liabilities and Shareholders' Equity		
Current liabilities	$32,825	$34,516
Noncurrent liabilities	39,226	40,388
Total liabilities	72,051	74,904
Total shareholders' equity (deficit)	6,735	(10,298)
Total liabilities and shareholders' equity	$78,786	$64,606
Other Information		
Net income	$ 6,250	$ 4,146
Tax expense*	563	373
Interest expense	817	1,807
Available lines of credit (Automotive Division)	9,000	

*Estimated based on 2010 effective rate.

Solution

1. Ford's liquidity can be measured using the current ratio:

	2011	2010
Current ratio	$\dfrac{\$38,147}{\$32,825} = 1.16{:}1$	$\dfrac{\$34,368}{\$34,516} = 1.00{:}1$

Ford's current ratio improved from 2010 to 2011. Ford's 2011 current ratio exceeds the industry average of 1.00:1 but is somewhat less than Toyota's. These are increasingly common levels for large companies that have reduced the amount of inventory and receivables they hold. As noted earlier, these low current ratios are not necessarily cause for concern, but they do require more careful monitoring. Ford must also make sure to have other short-term financing options available, such as lines of credit.

2. Ford's solvency can be measured with the debt to assets ratio and the times interest earned:

	2011	2010
Debt to assets ratio	$\dfrac{\$72,051}{\$78,786} = 91\%$	$\dfrac{\$74,904}{\$64,606} = 116\%$
Times interest earned	$\dfrac{\$6,250 + \$817 + \$563}{\$817} = 9.4 \text{ times}$	$\dfrac{\$4,146 + \$1,807 + \$373}{\$1,807} = 3.5 \text{ times}$

The debt to assets ratio suggests that Ford relies very heavily on debt financing. The ratio decreased from 2010 to 2011, indicating that the company's solvency improved slightly. In 2010, it exceeded 100%. This is possible because we have calculated the ratio for the Automotive Division only, rather than for the whole company. The debt to assets ratio for the entire company in 2011 is 92%. This is extremely high.

The times interest earned is 9.4 times in 2011 and 3.5 times in 2010. This exceeds the industry average of 3.2 times. It is likely that the company's solvency was a concern to investors and creditors during the recession and was closely monitored. However, as Ford's income rose in 2010 and 2011, its solvency improved.

3. Ford has available lines of credit of $9 billion. These financing sources significantly improve its liquidity and help reduce the concerns of its short-term creditors.

Summary of Learning Objectives

1 **Explain a current liability and identify the major types of current liabilities.** A current liability is a debt that a company can reasonably expect to pay (a) from existing current assets or through the creation of other current liabilities, and (b) within one year or the operating cycle, whichever is longer. The major types of current liabilities are notes payable, accounts payable, sales taxes payable, unearned revenues, and accrued liabilities such as taxes, salaries and wages, and interest payable.

2 **Describe the accounting for notes payable.** When a note payable is interest-bearing, the amount of assets received upon the issuance of the note is generally equal to the face value of the note, and interest expense is accrued over the life of the note. At maturity, the amount paid is equal to the face value of the note plus accrued interest.

3 **Explain the accounting for other current liabilities.** Companies record sales taxes payable at the time the related sales occur. The company serves as a collection agent for the taxing authority. Sales taxes are not an expense to the company. Companies hold employee withholding taxes, and credit them to appropriate liability accounts, until they remit these taxes to the governmental taxing authorities. Unearned revenues are initially recorded in an unearned revenue account. As a company recognizes revenue, a transfer from unearned revenue to revenue occurs. Companies report the current maturities of long-term debt as a current liability in the balance sheet.

4 **Identify the types of bonds.** The following different types of bonds may be issued: secured and unsecured bonds, and convertible and callable bonds.

5 **Prepare the entries for the issuance of bonds and interest expense.** When companies issue bonds, they debit Cash for the cash proceeds and credit Bonds Payable for the face value of the bonds. In addition, they use the accounts Premium on Bonds Payable and Discount on Bonds Payable to show the bond premium and bond discount, respectively. Bond discount and bond premium are amortized over the life of the bond, which increases or decreases interest expense, respectively.

6 **Describe the entries when bonds are redeemed.** When companies redeem bonds at maturity, they credit Cash and debit Bonds Payable for the face value of the bonds. When companies redeem bonds before maturity, they (a) eliminate the carrying value of the bonds at the redemption date, (b) record the cash paid, and (c) recognize the gain or loss on redemption.

7 **Identify the requirements for the financial statement presentation and analysis of liabilities.** Current liabilities appear first on the balance sheet, followed by long-term liabilities. Companies should report the nature and amount of each liability in the balance sheet or in schedules in the notes accompanying the statements. They report inflows and outflows of cash related to the principal portion of long-term debt in the financing section of the statement of cash flows.

The liquidity of a company may be analyzed by computing the current ratio. The long-run solvency of a company may be analyzed by computing the debt to assets ratio and the times interest earned. Other factors to consider are contingent liabilities and lease obligations.

DECISION TOOLKIT *A SUMMARY*

DECISION CHECKPOINTS	INFO NEEDED FOR DECISION	TOOL TO USE FOR DECISION	HOW TO EVALUATE RESULTS
Can the company obtain short-term financing when necessary?	Available lines of credit, from notes to the financial statements	Compare available lines of credit to current liabilities. Also, evaluate liquidity ratios.	If liquidity ratios are low, then lines of credit should be high to compensate.
Can the company meet its obligations in the long term?	Interest expense and net income before interest and taxes	$$\text{Times interest earned} = \frac{\text{Net income} + \text{Interest expense} + \text{Tax expense}}{\text{Interest expense}}$$	High ratio indicates ability to meet interest payments as scheduled.
Does the company have any contingent liabilities?	Knowledge of events with uncertain negative outcomes	Notes to financial statements and financial statements	If negative outcomes are possible, determine the probability, the amount of loss, and the potential impact on financial statements.
Does the company have significant off-balance-sheet financing, such as unrecorded lease obligations?	Information on unrecorded obligations, such as a schedule of minimum lease payments from the notes to the financial statements	Compare liquidity and solvency ratios with and without unrecorded obligations included	If ratios differ significantly after including unrecorded obligations, these obligations should not be ignored in analysis.

Appendix 10A

Straight-Line Amortization

AMORTIZING BOND DISCOUNT

To follow the expense recognition principle, companies allocate bond discount to expense in each period in which the bonds are outstanding. The **straight-line method of amortization** allocates the same amount to interest expense in each interest period. The calculation is presented in Illustration 10A-1.

LEARNING OBJECTIVE **8**
Apply the straight-line method of amortizing bond discount and bond premium.

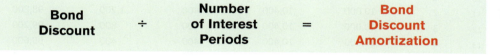

Illustration 10A-1 Formula for straight-line method of bond discount amortization

In the Candlestick Inc. example (page 446), the company sold $100,000, five-year, 10% bonds on January 1, 2014, for $98,000. This resulted in a $2,000 bond discount ($100,000 − $98,000). The bond discount amortization is $400 ($2,000 ÷ 5) for each of the five amortization periods. Candlestick records the first accrual of bond interest and the amortization of bond discount on December 31 as follows.

Dec. 31	Interest Expense	10,400	
	Discount on Bonds Payable		400
	Interest Payable		10,000
	(To record accrued bond interest and		
	amortization of bond discount)		

A	=	L	+	SE
				−10,400 Exp
				+400
				+10,000

Cash Flows
no effect

Over the term of the bonds, the balance in Discount on Bonds Payable will decrease annually by the same amount until it has a zero balance at the maturity date of the bonds. Thus, the carrying value of the bonds at maturity will be equal to the face value of the bonds.

Preparing a bond discount amortization schedule, as shown in Illustration 10A-2, is useful to determine interest expense, discount amortization, and the carrying value of the bond. As indicated, the interest expense recorded each period is $10,400. Also note that the carrying value of the bond increases $400 each period until it reaches its face value of $100,000 at the end of period 5.

Margin Note The amount in the Discount on Bonds Payable account is often referred to as *Unamortized Discount on Bonds Payable*.

Illustration 10A-2 Bond discount amortization schedule

Candlestick Inc.xls

Home Insert Page Layout Formulas Data Review View

P18   fx

	A	B	C	D	E	F
1			**CANDLESTICK, INC.**			
2			**Bond Discount Amortization Schedule**			
3			**Straight-Line Method—Annual Interest Payments**			
4			**$100,000 of 10%, 5-Year Bonds**			
5		**(A)**	**(B)**	**(C)**	**(D)**	**(E)**
6		**Interest to**	**Interest Expense**	**Discount**	**Unamortized**	**Bond**
7	**Interest**	**Be Paid**	**to Be Recorded**	**Amortization**	**Discount**	**Carrying Value**
8	**Periods**	**(10% × $100,000)**	**(A) + (C)**	**($2,000 ÷ 5)**	**(D) – (C)**	**($100,000 – D)**
9	Issue date				$2,000	$ 98,000
10	1	$10,000	$10,400	$ 400	1,600	98,400
11	2	10,000	10,400	400	1,200	98,800
12	3	10,000	10,400	400	800	99,200
13	4	10,000	10,400	400	400	99,600
14	5	10,000	10,400	400	0	100,000
15		$50,000	$52,000	$2,000		
16						
17	Column **(A)** remains constant because the face value of the bonds ($100,000) is multiplied by the annual contractual interest rate (10%) each period.					
18	Column **(B)** is computed as the interest paid (Column A) plus the discount amortization (Column C).					
19	Column **(C)** indicates the discount amortization each period.					
20	Column **(D)** decreases each period by the same amount until it reaches zero at maturity.					
21	Column **(E)** increases each period by the amount of discount amortization until it equals the face value at maturity.					

Illustration 10A-3 Formula for straight-line method of bond premium amortization

$$\text{Bond Premium} \div \text{Number of Interest Periods} = \text{Bond Premium Amortization}$$

AMORTIZING BOND PREMIUM

The amortization of bond premium parallels that of bond discount. Illustration 10A-3 presents the formula for determining bond premium amortization under the straight-line method.

Continuing our example, assume Candlestick Inc., sells the bonds described above for $102,000, rather than $98,000 (see page 448). This results in a bond premium of $2,000 ($102,000 − $100,000). The premium amortization for each interest period is $400 ($2,000 ÷ 5). Candlestick records the first accrual of interest on December 31 as follows.

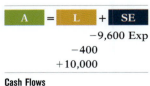

A	=	L	+	SE
				−9,600 Exp
		−400		
		+10,000		

Cash Flows
no effect

Dec. 31	Interest Expense		9,600	
	Premium on Bonds Payable		400	
	Interest Payable			10,000
	(To record accrued bond interest and amortization of bond premium)			

Over the term of the bonds, the balance in Premium on Bonds Payable will decrease annually by the same amount until it has a zero balance at maturity.

A bond premium amortization schedule, as shown in Illustration 10A-4, is useful to determine interest expense, premium amortization, and the carrying value of the bond. As indicated, the interest expense Candlestick records each period is $9,600. Note that the carrying value of the bond decreases $400 each period until it reaches its face value of $100,000 at the end of period 5.

Illustration 10A-4 Bond premium amortization schedule

	Candlestick Inc.xls				
Home Insert Page Layout Formulas Data Review View					
P18	fx				
A	**B**	**C**	**D**	**E**	**F**

	(A)	(B)	(C)	(D)	(E)
	Interest to	Interest Expense	Premium	Unamortized	Bond
Interest	**Be Paid**	**to Be Recorded**	**Amortization**	**Premium**	**Carrying Value**
Periods	**(10% × $100,000)**	**(A) – (C)**	**($2,000 ÷ 5)**	**(D) – (C)**	**($100,000 + D)**
Issue date				$2,000	$102,000
1	$ 10,000	$ 9,600	$ 400	1,600	101,600
2	10,000	9,600	400	1,200	101,200
3	10,000	9,600	400	800	100,800
4	10,000	9,600	400	400	100,400
5	10,000	9,600	400	0	100,000
	$50,000	$48,000	$2,000		

CANDLESTICK, INC.
Bond Premium Amortization Schedule
Straight-Line Method—Annual Interest Payments
$100,000 of 10%, 5-Year Bonds

Column **(A)** remains constant because the face value of the bonds ($100,000) is multiplied by the annual contractual interest rate (10%) each period.

Column **(B)** is computed as the interest paid (Column A) less the premium amortization (Column C).

Column **(C)** indicates the premium amortization each period.

Column **(D)** decreases each period by the same amount until it reaches zero at maturity.

Column **(E)** decreases each period by the amount of premium amortization until it equals the face value at maturity.

Summary of Learning Objective for Appendix 10A

8 **Apply the straight-line method of amortizing bond discount and bond premium.** The straight-line method of amortization results in a constant amount of amortization and interest expense per period.

Appendix 10B

Effective-Interest Amortization

To follow the expense recognition principle, companies allocate bond discount to expense in each period in which the bonds are outstanding. However, to completely comply with the expense recognition principle, interest expense as a percentage of carrying value should not change over the life of the bonds.

LEARNING OBJECTIVE 9

Apply the effective-interest method of amortizing bond discount and bond premium.

This percentage, referred to as the **effective-interest rate**, is established when the bonds are issued and remains constant in each interest period. Unlike the straight-line method, the effective-interest method of amortization accomplishes this result.

Under the **effective-interest method**, the amortization of bond discount or bond premium results in periodic interest expense equal to a constant percentage of the carrying value of the bonds. The effective-interest method results in **varying amounts** of amortization and interest expense per period but a **constant percentage rate.** In contrast, the straight-line method results in constant amounts of amortization and interest expense per period but a varying percentage rate.

Companies follow three steps under the effective-interest method:

1. Compute the **bond interest expense** by multiplying the carrying value of the bonds at the beginning of the interest period by the effective-interest rate.

2. Compute the **bond interest paid** (or accrued) by multiplying the face value of the bonds by the contractual interest rate.

3. Compute the **amortization amount** by determining the difference between the amounts computed in steps (1) and (2).

Illustration 10B-1 depicts these steps.

Illustration 10B-1
Computation of amortization using effective-interest method

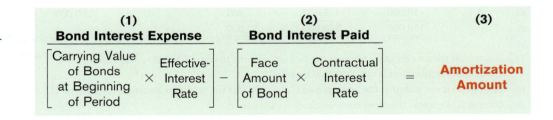

Both the straight-line and effective-interest methods of amortization result in the same total amount of interest expense over the term of the bonds. Furthermore, interest expense each interest period is generally comparable in amount. However, **when the amounts are materially different, generally accepted accounting principles (GAAP) require use of the effective-interest method**.

AMORTIZING BOND DISCOUNT

In the Candlestick Inc. example (page 446), the company sold $100,000, five-year, 10% bonds on January 1, 2014, for $98,000. This resulted in a $2,000 bond discount ($100,000 − $98,000). This discount results in an effective-interest rate of approximately 10.53%. (The effective-interest rate can be computed using the techniques shown in Appendix D at the end of this book.)

Preparing a bond discount amortization schedule as shown in Illustration 10B-2 facilitates the recording of interest expense and the discount amortization. Note that interest expense as a percentage of carrying value remains constant at 10.53%.

	A	B	C	D	E	F
			Candlestick Inc.xls			
	Home Insert Page Layout Formulas Data Review View					
	P18		fx			
1			**CANDLESTICK, INC.**			
2			**Bond Discount Amortization Schedule**			
3			**Effective-Interest Method—Annual Interest Payments**			
4			**10% Bonds Issued at 10.53%**			
5		**(A)**	**(B)**	**(C)**	**(D)**	**(E)**
6		**Interest to**	**Interest Expense to Be Recorded**	**Discount**	**Unamortized**	**Bond**
7	**Interest**	**Be Paid**	**(10.53% × Preceding**	**Amortization**	**Discount**	**Carrying Value**
8	**Periods**	**(10% × $100,000)**	**Bond Carrying Value)**	**(B) – (A)**	**(D) – (C)**	**($100,000 – D)**
9	Issue date				$2,000	$98,000
10	1	$ 10,000	$ 10,319 (10.53% × $98,000)	$ 319	1,681	98,319
11	2	10,000	10,353 (10.53% × $98,319)	353	1,328	98,672
12	3	10,000	10,390 (10.53% × $98,672)	390	938	99,062
13	4	10,000	10,431 (10.53% × $99,062)	431	507	99,493
14	5	10,000	10,507* (10.53% × $99,493)	507*	–0–	100,000
15		$50,000	$52,000	$2,000		
16						
17	Column **(A)** remains constant because the face value of the bonds ($100,000) is multiplied by the annual contractual interest rate (10%) each period.					
18	Column **(B)** is computed as the preceding bond carrying value times the annual effective-interest rate (10.53%).					
19	Column **(C)** indicates the discount amortization each period.					
20	Column **(D)** decreases each period until it reaches zero at maturity.					
21	Column **(E)** increases each period until it equals face value at maturity.					
22						
23	*Rounded to eliminate remaining discount resulting from rounding the effective rate.					

Illustration 10B-2 Bond discount amortization schedule

For the first interest period, the computations of bond interest expense and the bond discount amortization are as follows.

Bond interest expense ($98,000 × 10.53%)	$10,319
Bond interest paid ($100,000 × 10%)	10,000
Bond discount amortization	$ 319

Illustration 10B-3
Computation of bond discount amortization

As a result, Candlestick Inc. records the accrual of interest and amortization of bond discount on December 31 as follows.

Dec. 31	Interest Expense	10,319	
	Discount on Bonds Payable		319
	Interest Payable		10,000
	(To record accrued interest and amortization of bond discount)		

A	=	L	+	SE
				−10,319 Exp
		+319		
		+10,000		

Cash Flows
no effect

For the second interest period, bond interest expense will be $10,353 ($98,319 × 10.53%), and the discount amortization will be $353. At December 31, Candlestick makes the following adjusting entry.

Cash Flows
no effect

	Dec. 31	Interest Expense	10,353	
		Discount on Bonds Payable		353
		Interest Payable		10,000
		(To record accrued interest and amortization of bond discount)		

AMORTIZING BOND PREMIUM

Continuing our example, assume Candlestick Inc. sells the bonds described above for $102,000 rather than $98,000 (see page 448). This would result in a bond premium of $2,000 ($102,000 − $100,000). This premium results in an effective-interest rate of approximately 9.48%. (The effective-interest rate can be solved for using the techniques shown in Appendix D at the end of this book.) Illustration 10B-4 shows the bond premium amortization schedule.

```
Candlestick Inc.xls
Home   Insert   Page Layout   Formulas   Data   Review   View

P18        fx
```

	A	B	C	D	E	F
1			**CANDLESTICK, INC.**			
2			**Bond Premium Amortization Schedule**			
3			**Effective-Interest Method—Annual Interest Payments**			
4			**10% Bonds Issued at 9.48%**			
5		**(A)**	**(B)**	**(C)**	**(D)**	**(E)**
6		**Interest to**	**Interest Expense to Be Recorded**	**Premium**	**Unamortized**	**Bond**
7	**Interest**	**Be Paid**	**(9.48% × Preceding**	**Amortization**	**Premium**	**Carrying Value**
8	**Periods**	**(10% × $100,000)**	**Bond Carrying Value)**	**(A) − (B)**	**(D) − (C)**	**($100,000 + D)**
9	Issue date				$2,000	$102,000
10	1	**$10,000**	**$ 9,670 (9.48% × $102,000)**	**$ 330**	**1,670**	**101,670**
11	2	10,000	9,638 (9.48% × $101,670)	362	1,308	101,308
12	3	10,000	9,604 (9.48% × $101,308)	396	912	100,912
13	4	10,000	9,566 (9.48% × $100,912)	434	478	100,478
14	5	10,000	9,522* (9.48% × $100,478)	478*	−0−	100,000
15		$50,000	$48,000	$2,000		
16						
17	Column **(A)** remains constant because the face value of the bonds ($100,000) is multiplied by the contractual interest rate (10%) each period.					
18	Column **(B)** is computed as the carrying value of the bonds times the annual effective-interest rate (9.48%).					
19	Column **(C)** indicates the premium amortization each period.					
20	Column **(D)** decreases each period until it reaches zero at maturity.					
21	Column **(E)** decreases each period until it equals face value at maturity.					
22						
23	*Rounded to eliminate remaining discount resulting from rounding the effective rate.					

Illustration 10B-4 Bond premium amortization schedule

For the first interest period, the computations of bond interest expense and the bond premium amortization are:

Illustration 10B-5
Computation of bond premium amortization

Bond interest paid ($100,000 × 10%)	$10,000
Bond interest expense ($102,000 × 9.48%)	9,670
Bond premium amortization	**$ 330**

The entry Candlestick makes on December 31 is:

Dec. 31	Interest Expense	9,670	
	Premium on Bonds Payable	330	
	Interest Payable		10,000
	(To record accrued interest and		
	amortization of bond premium)		

A = L + SE
−9,670 Exp
−330
+10,000

Cash Flows
no effect

For the second interest period, interest expense will be $9,638, and the premium amortization will be $362. Note that the amount of periodic interest expense decreases over the life of the bond when companies apply the effective-interest method to bonds issued at a premium. The reason is that a constant percentage is applied to a decreasing bond carrying value to compute interest expense. The carrying value is decreasing because of the amortization of the premium.

Summary of Learning Objective for Appendix 10B

9 **Apply the effective-interest method of amortizing bond discount and bond premium.** The effective-interest method results in varying amounts of amortization and interest expense per period but a constant percentage rate of interest. When the difference between the straight-line and effective-interest method is material, GAAP requires use of the effective-interest method.

Appendix 10C

Accounting for Long-Term Notes Payable

The use of notes payable in long-term debt financing is quite common. Long-term notes payable are similar to short-term interest-bearing notes payable except that the terms of the notes exceed one year. In periods of unstable interest rates, lenders may tie the interest rate on long-term notes to changes in the market rate for comparable loans. Examples are the 8.03% adjustable rate notes issued by General Motors (GM) and the floating-rate notes issued by American Express Company.

LEARNING OBJECTIVE 10
Describe the accounting for long-term notes payable.

A long-term note may be secured by a document called a **mortgage** that pledges title to specific assets as security for a loan. Individuals widely use **mortgage notes payable** to purchase homes, as do many small and some large companies to acquire plant assets. For example, at one time approximately 18% of McDonald's long-term debt related to mortgage notes on land, buildings, and improvements.

Like other long-term notes payable, the mortgage loan terms may stipulate either a fixed or an adjustable interest rate. Typically, the terms require the borrower to make equal installment payments over the term of the loan. Each payment consists of (1) interest on the unpaid balance of the loan and (2) a reduction of loan principal. While the total amount paid remains constant, the interest decreases each period and the portion applied to the loan principal increases.

Companies initially record mortgage notes payable at face value, and subsequently make entries for each installment payment. To illustrate, assume that Porter Technology Inc. issues a $500,000, 12%, 20-year mortgage note on December 31, 2014, to obtain needed financing for the construction of a new research laboratory. The terms provide for semiannual installment payments of

$33,231 (not including real estate taxes and insurance). The installment payment schedule for the first two years is as follows.

Illustration 10C-1 Mortgage installment payment schedule

Semiannual Interest Period	(A) Cash Payment	(B) Interest Expense (D) × 6%	(C) Reduction of Principal (A) − (B)	(D) Principal Balance (D) − (C)
Issue date				$500,000
1	$33,231	$30,000	$3,231	496,769
2	33,231	29,806	3,425	493,344
3	33,231	29,601	3,630	489,714
4	33,231	29,383	3,848	485,866

Porter Technology records the mortgage loan on December 31, 2014, as follows.

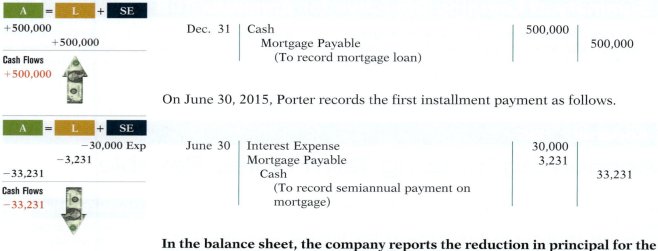

A	=	L	+	SE
+500,000				
		+500,000		

Cash Flows
+500,000

Dec. 31	Cash	500,000	
	Mortgage Payable		500,000
	(To record mortgage loan)		

On June 30, 2015, Porter records the first installment payment as follows.

A	=	L	+	SE
				−30,000 Exp
		−3,231		
−33,231				

Cash Flows
−33,231

June 30	Interest Expense	30,000	
	Mortgage Payable	3,231	
	Cash		33,231
	(To record semiannual payment on		
	mortgage)		

In the balance sheet, the company reports the reduction in principal for the next year as a current liability, and classifies the remaining unpaid principal balance as a long-term liability. At December 31, 2015 (the end of semi-annual period 2), the total liability is $493,344, of which $7,478 ($3,630 + $3,848) is current and $485,866 ($493,344 − $7,478) is long-term.

Summary of Learning Objective for Appendix 10C

10 **Describe the accounting for long-term notes payable.** Each payment consists of (1) interest on the unpaid balance of the loan, and (2) a reduction of loan principal. The interest decreases each period, while the portion applied to the loan principal increases each period.

Glossary

Terms are highlighted in **blue** throughout the chapter.

Bond certificate A legal document that indicates the name of the issuer, the face value of the bonds, and other data such as the contractual interest rate and the maturity date of the bonds.

Bonds A form of interest-bearing notes payable issued by corporations, universities, and governmental entities.

Callable bonds Bonds that the issuing company can redeem (buy back) at a stated dollar amount prior to maturity.

Capital lease A contractual agreement allowing one party (the lessee) to use the assets of another party (the lessor); accounted for like a debt-financed purchase by the lessee.

Contingencies Events with uncertain outcomes that may represent potential liabilities.

Contractual (stated) interest rate Rate used to determine the amount of interest the borrower pays and the investor receives.

Convertible bonds Bonds that can be converted into common stock at the bondholder's option.

Current liability A debt that a company reasonably expects to pay (1) from existing current assets or through the creation of other current liabilities, and (2) within one year or the operating cycle, whichever is longer.

Discount (on a bond) The difference between the face value of a bond and its selling price when a bond is sold for less than its face value.

Effective-interest method of amortization A method of amortizing bond discount or bond premium that results in periodic interest expense equal to a constant percentage of the carrying value of the bonds.

Effective-interest rate Rate established when bonds are issued that maintains a constant value for interest expense as a percentage of bond carrying value in each interest period.

Face value Amount of principal due at the maturity date of the bond.

Long-term liabilities Obligations that a company expects to pay more than one year in the future.

Market interest rate The rate investors demand for loaning funds to the corporation.

Maturity date The date on which the final payment on a bond is due from the bond issuer to the investor.

Mortgage note payable A long-term note secured by a mortgage that pledges title to specific assets as security for the loan.

Notes payable An obligation in the form of a written note.

Off-balance-sheet financing The intentional effort by a company to structure its financing arrangements so as to avoid showing liabilities on its balance sheet.

Operating lease A contractual agreement allowing one party (the lessee) to use the asset of another party (the lessor); accounted for as a rental.

Premium (on a bond) The difference between the selling price and the face value of a bond when a bond is sold for more than its face value.

Present value The value today of an amount to be received at some date in the future after taking into account current interest rates.

Secured bonds Bonds that have specific assets of the issuer pledged as collateral.

Straight-line method of amortization A method of amortizing bond discount or bond premium that allocates the same amount to interest expense in each interest period.

Times interest earned A measure of a company's solvency, calculated by dividing income before interest expense and taxes by interest expense.

Time value of money The relationship between time and money. A dollar received today is worth more than a dollar promised at some time in the future.

Unsecured bonds Bonds issued against the general credit of the borrower.

Self-Test, Brief Exercises, Exercises, Problem Set A, and many more resources are available for practice in WileyPLUS.

Note: All Questions, Exercises, and Problems marked with an asterisk relate to material in the appendices to the chapter.

Self-Test Questions

(Answers in *Broadening Your Perspective*.)

(LO 1) **1.** The time period for classifying a liability as current is one year or the operating cycle, whichever is:
  (a) longer. (c) probable.
  (b) shorter. (d) possible.

(LO 1) **2.** To be classified as a current liability, a debt must be expected to be paid:
  (a) out of existing current assets.
  (b) by creating other current liabilities.
  (c) within 2 years.
  (d) Either (a) or (b).

(LO 2) **3.** Ottman Company borrows $88,500 on September 1, 2014, from Farley State Bank by signing an $88,500,

12%, one-year note. What is the accrued interest at December 31, 2014?
  (a) $2,655. (c) $4,425.
  (b) $3,540. (d) $10,620.

(LO 2) **4.** JD Company borrowed $70,000 on December 1 on a 6-month, 12% note. At December 31:
  (a) neither the note payable nor the interest payable is a current liability.
  (b) the note payable is a current liability but the interest payable is not.
  (c) the interest payable is a current liability but the note payable is not.
  (d) both the note payable and the interest payable are current liabilities.

(LO 3) **5.** Alexis Company has total proceeds from sales of $4,515. If the proceeds include sales taxes of 5%, what is the amount to be credited to Sales Revenue?
(a) $4,000.
(b) $4,300.
(c) $4,289.25.
(d) The correct answer is not given.

(LO 3) **6.** When recording payroll:
(a) gross earnings are recorded as salaries and wages payable.
(b) net pay is recorded as salaries and wages expense.
(c) payroll deductions are recorded as liabilities.
(d) More than one of the above.

(LO 3) **7.** No Fault Insurance Company collected a premium of $18,000 for a 1-year insurance policy on April 1. What amount should No Fault report as a current liability for Unearned Insurance Premiums at December 31?
(a) $0.   (c) $13,500.
(b) $4,500.   (d) $18,000.

(LO 4) **8.** What term is used for bonds that have specific assets pledged as collateral?
(a) Callable bonds.   (c) Secured bonds.
(b) Convertible bonds.   (d) Discount bonds.

(LO 4) **9.** The market interest rate:
(a) is the contractual interest rate used to determine the amount of cash interest paid by the borrower.
(b) is listed in the bond indenture.
(c) is the rate investors demand for loaning funds.
(d) More than one of the above is true.

(LO 5) **10.** Laurel Inc. issues 10-year bonds with a maturity value of $200,000. If the bonds are issued at a premium, this indicates that:
(a) the contractual interest rate exceeds the market interest rate.
(b) the market interest rate exceeds the contractual interest rate.
(c) the contractual interest rate and the market interest rate are the same.
(d) no relationship exists between the two rates.

(LO 5) **11.** On January 1, 2014, Kelly Corp. issues $200,000, 5-year, 7% bonds at face value. The entry to record the issuance of the bonds would include a:
(a) debit to Cash for $14,000.
(b) debit to Bonds Payable for $200,000.
(c) credit to Bonds Payable for $200,000.
(d) credit to Interest Expense of $14,000.

(LO 5) **12.** Prescher Corporation issued bonds that pay interest every July 1 and January 1. The entry to accrue bond interest at December 31 includes a:
(a) debit to Interest Payable.
(b) credit to Cash.
(c) credit to Interest Expense.
(d) credit to Interest Payable.

(LO 6) **13.** Goethe Corporation redeems its $100,000 face value bonds at 105 on January 1, following the payment of interest. The carrying value of the bonds at the redemption date is $103,745. The entry to record the redemption will include a:

(a) credit of $3,745 to Loss on Bond Redemption.
(b) debit of $3,745 to Premium on Bonds Payable.
(c) credit of $1,255 to Gain on Bond Redemption.
(d) debit of $5,000 to Premium on Bonds Payable.

14. ⚙⚙ In a recent year, Derek Corporation had net (LO 7) income of $150,000, interest expense of $30,000, and income tax expense of $20,000. What was Derek Corporation's times interest earned for the year?
(a) 5.00.   (c) 6.67.
(b) 4.00.   (d) 7.50.

15. ⚙⚙ Which of the following is **not** a measure of (LO 7) liquidity?
(a) Debt to assets ratio.
(b) Working capital.
(c) Current ratio.
(d) Current cash debt coverage.

*16. On January 1, Xiang Corporation issues $500,000, (LO 8) 5-year, 12% bonds at 96 with interest payable on January 1. The entry on December 31 to record accrued bond interest and the amortization of bond discount using the straight-line method will include a:
(a) debit to Interest Expense, $57,600.
(b) debit to Interest Expense, $60,000.
(c) credit to Discount on Bonds Payable, $4,000.
(d) credit to Discount on Bonds Payable, $2,000.

*17. For the bonds issued in Question 16, what is the car- (LO 8) rying value of the bonds at the end of the third interest period?
(a) $492,000.   (c) $472,000.
(b) $488,000.   (d) $464,000.

*18. On January 1, Holly Ester Inc. issued $1,000,000, (LO 9) 10-year, 9% bonds for $938,554. The market rate of interest for these bonds is 10%. Interest is payable annually on December 31. Holly Ester uses the effective-interest method of amortizing bond discount. At the end of the first year, Holly Ester should report unamortized bond discount of:
(a) $54,900.   (c) $51,610.
(b) $57,591.   (d) $51,000.

*19. On January 1, Nicholas Corporation issued (LO 9) $1,000,000, 14%, 5-year bonds with interest payable on December 31. The bonds sold for $1,072,096. The market rate of interest for these bonds was 12%. On the first interest date, using the effective-interest method, the debit entry to Interest Expense is for:
(a) $120,000.   (c) $128,652.
(b) $125,581.   (d) $140,000.

*20. Sampson Corp. purchased a piece of equipment by (LO 10) issuing a $20,000, 6% installment note payable. Quarterly payments on the note are $1,165. What will be the reduction in the principal portion of the note payable that results from the first payment?
(a) $1,165.   (c) $865.
(b) $300.   (d) $1,200.

Go to the book's companion website, **www.wiley.com/college/kimmel**, to access additional Self-Test Questions.

Questions

1. Peggy Jantzen believes a current liability is a debt that can be expected to be paid in one year. Is Peggy correct? Explain.

2. Trayer Company obtains $20,000 in cash by signing a 9%, 6-month, $20,000 note payable to First Bank on July 1. Trayer's fiscal year ends on September 30. What information should be reported for the note payable in the annual financial statements?

3. (a) Your roommate says, "Sales taxes are reported as an expense in the income statement." Do you agree? Explain.
   (b) Amanda's Cafe has cash proceeds from sales of $8,550. This amount includes $550 of sales taxes. Give the entry to record the proceeds.

4. Dakota University sold 9,000 season football tickets at $100 each for its five-game home schedule. What entries should be made (a) when the tickets are sold and (b) after each game?

5. Identify three taxes commonly withheld by the employer from an employee's gross pay.

6. (a) Identify three taxes commonly paid by employers on employees' salaries and wages.
   (b) Where in the financial statements does the employer report taxes withheld from employees' pay?

7. Identify the liabilities classified by Tootsie Roll as current.

8. (a) What are long-term liabilities? Give two examples.
   (b) What is a bond?

9. Contrast these types of bonds:
   (a) Secured and unsecured.
   (b) Convertible and callable.

10. Explain each of these important terms in issuing bonds:
    (a) Face value.
    (b) Contractual interest rate.
    (c) Bond certificate.

11. (a) What is a convertible bond?
    (b) Discuss the advantages of a convertible bond from the standpoint of the bondholders and of the issuing corporation.

12. Describe the two major obligations incurred by a company when bonds are issued.

13. Assume that Ziegler Inc. sold bonds with a face value of $100,000 for $104,000. Was the market interest rate equal to, less than, or greater than the bonds' contractual interest rate? Explain.

14. Jack and Lance are discussing how the market price of a bond is determined. Jack believes that the market price of a bond is solely a function of the amount of the principal payment at the end of the term of a bond. Is he right? Discuss.

15. If a 6%, 10-year, $800,000 bond is issued at face value and interest is paid annually, what is the amount of the interest payment at the end of the first period?

16. If the Bonds Payable account has a balance of $700,000 and the Discount on Bonds Payable account has a balance of $36,000, what is the carrying value of the bonds?

17. Which accounts are debited and which are credited if a bond issue originally sold at a premium is redeemed before maturity at 97 immediately following the payment of interest?

18. Natalie Pendlay, the chief financial officer of Mullins Inc., is considering the options available to her for financing the company's new plant. Short-term interest rates right now are 6%, and long-term rates are 8%. The company's current ratio is 2.2:1. If she finances the new plant with short-term debt, the current ratio will fall to 1.5:1. Briefly discuss the issues that Natalie should consider.

19. (a) In general, what are the requirements for the financial statement presentation of long-term liabilities?
    (b) What ratios may be computed to evaluate a company's liquidity and solvency?

20. Samuel Engels says that liquidity and solvency are the same thing. Is he correct? If not, how do they differ?

21. The management of Hinrichs Corporation is concerned because survey data suggest that many potential customers do not buy vehicles due to quality concerns. It is considering taking the bold step of increasing the length of its warranty from the industry standard of 3 years up to an unprecedented 10 years in an effort to increase confidence in its quality. Discuss the business as well as accounting implications of this move.

22. Matt Higgins needs a few new trucks for his business. He is considering buying the trucks but is concerned that the additional debt he will need to borrow will make his liquidity and solvency ratios look bad. What options does he have other than purchasing the trucks, and how will these options affect his financial statements?

23. Norman Corporation has a current ratio of 1.1. Tim has always been told that a corporation's current ratio should exceed 2.0. The company maintains that its ratio is low because it has a minimal amount of inventory on hand so as to reduce operating costs. Norman also has significant available lines of credit. Is Tim still correct? What do some companies do to compensate for having fewer liquid assets?

24. What are the implications for analysis if a company has significant operating leases?

25. What criteria must be met before a contingency must be recorded as a liability? How should the contingency be disclosed if the criteria are not met?

*26. ⚒ Explain the straight-line method of amortizing discount and premium on bonds payable.

*27. Knobler Corporation issues $200,000 of 6%, 5-year bonds on January 1, 2014, at 103. Assuming that the straight-line method is used to amortize the premium, what is the total amount of interest expense for 2014?

*28. Glenda Hope is discussing the advantages of the effective-interest method of bond amortization with her accounting staff. What do you think Glenda is saying?

*29. Whitson Corporation issues $400,000 of 9%, 5-year bonds on January 1, 2014, at 104. If Whitson uses the effective-interest method in amortizing the premium, will the annual interest expense increase or decrease over the life of the bonds? Explain.

*30. Your friend just received a car loan. It is a 7-year installment note. He does not understand the mechanics of how the loan works. Explain the important aspects of the installment note.

*31. Roy Toth, a friend of yours, has recently purchased a home for $125,000, paying $25,000 down and the remainder financed by a 6.5%, 20-year mortgage, payable at $745.57 per month. At the end of the first month, Roy receives a statement from the bank indicating that only $203.90 of principal was paid during the month. At this rate, he calculates that it will take over 40 years to pay off the mortgage. Is he right? Discuss.

Brief Exercises

Identify whether obligations are current liabilities.
(LO 1), C

BE10-1 Linton Company has these obligations at December 31: (a) a note payable for $100,000 due in 2 years, (b) a 10-year mortgage payable of $200,000 payable in ten $20,000 annual payments, (c) interest payable of $15,000 on the mortgage, and (d) accounts payable of $60,000. For each obligation, indicate whether it should be classified as a current liability.

Prepare entries for an interest-bearing note payable.
(LO 2), AP

BE10-2 Graves Company borrows $90,000 on July 1 from the bank by signing a $90,000, 7%, 1-year note payable. Prepare the journal entries to record (a) the proceeds of the note and (b) accrued interest at December 31, assuming adjusting entries are made only at the end of the year.

Compute and record sales taxes payable.
(LO 3), AP

BE10-3 Bluestem Supply does not segregate sales and sales taxes at the time of sale. The register total for March 16 is $10,388. All sales are subject to a 6% sales tax. Compute sales taxes payable and make the entry to record sales taxes payable and sales.

Prepare entries for unearned revenues.
(LO 3), AP

BE10-4 Washburn University sells 3,500 season basketball tickets at $80 each for its 10-game home schedule. Give the entry to record (a) the sale of the season tickets and (b) the revenue recognized after playing the first home game.

Compute gross earnings and net pay.
(LO 3), AP

BE10-5 Susan Braun's regular hourly wage rate is $16, and she receives an hourly rate of $24 for work in excess of 40 hours. During a January pay period, Susan works 47 hours. Susan's federal income tax withholding is $95, and she has no voluntary deductions. Compute Susan Braun's gross earnings and net pay for the pay period. Assume that the FICA tax rate is 7.65%.

Record a payroll and the payment of wages.
(LO 3), AP

BE10-6 Data for Susan Braun are presented in BE10-5. Prepare the employer's journal entries to record (a) Susan's pay for the period and (b) the payment of Susan's wages. Use January 15 for the end of the pay period and the payment date.

Prepare entries for payroll taxes.
(LO 3), AP

BE10-7 Data for Susan Braun are presented in BE10-5. Prepare the employer's journal entry to record payroll taxes for the period. Ignore unemployment taxes.

Prepare entries for issuance of bonds.
(LO 5), AP

BE10-8 Saddle Inc. issues $300,000, 10-year, 8% bonds at 98. Prepare the journal entry to record the sale of these bonds on March 1, 2014.

Prepare entries for issuance of bonds.
(LO 5), AP

BE10-9 Range Company issues $400,000, 20-year, 7% bonds at 101. Prepare the journal entry to record the sale of these bonds on June 1, 2014.

Prepare journal entries for bonds issued at face value.
(LO 5), AP

BE10-10 Rooney Corporation issued 3,000 7%, 5-year, $1,000 bonds dated January 1, 2014, at face value. Interest is paid each January 1.
(a) Prepare the journal entry to record the sale of these bonds on January 1, 2014.
(b) Prepare the adjusting journal entry on December 31, 2014, to record interest expense.
(c) Prepare the journal entry on January 1, 2015, to record interest paid.

BE10-11 The balance sheet for Fogelberg Company reports the following information on July 1, 2014.

Prepare journal entry for redemption of bonds.
(LO 6), **AP**

FOGELBERG COMPANY
Balance Sheet (partial)

Long-term liabilities		
Bonds payable	$2,000,000	
Less: Discount on bonds payable	45,000	$1,955,000

Fogelberg decides to redeem these bonds at 102 after paying annual interest. Prepare the journal entry to record the redemption on July 1, 2014.

BE10-12 Presented here are long-term liability items for Evenson Inc. at December 31, 2014. Prepare the long-term liabilities section of the balance sheet for Evenson Inc.

Prepare statement presentation of long-term liabilities.
(LO 7), **AP**

Bonds payable (due 2018)	$700,000
Notes payable (due 2016)	80,000
Discount on bonds payable	28,000

BE10-13 Presented here are liability items for Desmond Inc. at December 31, 2014. Prepare the liabilities section of Desmond's balance sheet.

Prepare liabilities section of balance sheet.
(LO 7), **AP**

Accounts payable	$157,000	FICA taxes payable	$ 7,800
Notes payable	20,000	Interest payable	40,000
(due May 1, 2015)		Notes payable (due 2016)	80,000
Bonds payable (due 2018)	900,000	Income taxes payable	3,500
Unearned		Sales taxes payable	1,700
rent revenue	240,000		
Discount on bonds payable	41,000		

BE10-14 Suppose the 2014 adidas financial statements contain the following selected data (in millions).

Analyze solvency.
(LO 7), **AP**

Current assets	$4,485	Interest expense	$169
Total assets	8,875	Income taxes	113
Current liabilities	2,836	Net income	245
Total liabilities	5,099		
Cash	775		

Compute the following values and provide a brief interpretation of each.
(a) Working capital.   (c) Debt to assets ratio.
(b) Current ratio.   (d) Times interest earned.

BE10-15 Suppose the Canadian National Railway Company's (CN) total assets in a recent year were $24,004 million and its total liabilities were $14,180 million. That year, CN reported operating lease commitments for its locomotives, freight cars, and equipment totaling $740 million. If these assets had been recorded as capital leases, assume that assets and liabilities would have risen by approximately $740 million.

Analyze solvency.
(LO 7), **AN**

(a) Calculate CN's debt to assets ratio, first using the figures reported, and then after increasing assets and liabilities for the unrecorded operating leases.
(b) Discuss the potential effect of these operating leases on your assessment of CN's solvency.

BE10-16 Verlin Company issues $2 million, 10-year, 7% bonds at 99, with interest payable on December 31. The straight-line method is used to amortize bond discount.

Prepare journal entries for bonds issued at a discount.
(LO 8), **AP**

(a) Prepare the journal entry to record the sale of these bonds on January 1, 2014.
(b) Prepare the journal entry to record interest expense and bond discount amortization on December 31, 2014, assuming no previous accrual of interest.

BE10-17 Oxford Inc. issues $4 million, 5-year, 8% bonds at 102, with interest payable on January 1. The straight-line method is used to amortize bond premium.

Prepare journal entries for bonds issued at a premium.
(LO 8), **AP**

(a) Prepare the journal entry to record the sale of these bonds on January 1, 2014.
(b) Prepare the journal entry to record interest expense and bond premium amortization on December 31, 2014, assuming no previous accrual of interest.

Use effective-interest method of bond amortization.
(LO 9), **AP**

*BE10-18 Presented below is the partial bond discount amortization schedule for Pape Corp., which uses the effective-interest method of amortization.

Interest Periods	Interest to Be Paid	Interest Expense to Be Recorded	Discount Amortization	Unamortized Discount	Bond Carrying Value
Issue date				$38,609	$961,391
1	$45,000	$48,070	$3,070	35,539	964,461
2	45,000	48,223	3,223	32,316	967,684

Instructions
(a) Prepare the journal entry to record the payment of interest and the discount amortization at the end of period 1.
(b) ✏→ Explain why interest expense is greater than interest paid.
(c) ✏→ Explain why interest expense will increase each period.

Prepare entries for long-term notes payable.
(LO 10), **AP**

BE10-19 Leihsing Inc. issues a $600,000, 10%, 10-year mortgage note on December 31, 2013, to obtain financing for a new building. The terms provide for semiannual installment payments of $48,145. Prepare the entry to record the mortgage loan on December 31, 2013, and the first installment payment.

Exercises

Prepare entries for interest-bearing notes.
(LO 2), **AP**

E10-1 Jenny Kane and Cindy Travis borrowed $15,000 on a 7-month, 8% note from Golden State Bank to open their business, KT's Coffee House. The money was borrowed on June 1, 2014, and the note matures January 1, 2015.

Instructions
(a) Prepare the entry to record the receipt of the funds from the loan.
(b) Prepare the entry to accrue the interest on June 30.
(c) Assuming adjusting entries are made at the end of each month, determine the balance in the interest payable account at December 31, 2014.
(d) Prepare the entry required on January 1, 2015, when the loan is paid back.

Prepare entries for interest-bearing notes.
(LO 2), **AP**

E10-2 On May 15, Criqui Outback Clothiers borrowed some money on a 4-month note to provide cash during the slow season of the year. The interest rate on the note was 8%. At the time the note was due, the amount of interest owed was $480.

Instructions
(a) Determine the amount borrowed by Criqui.
(b) Assume the amount borrowed was $18,500. What was the interest rate if the amount of interest owed was $555?
(c) Prepare the entry for the initial borrowing and the repayment for the facts in part (a).

Prepare entries for interest-bearing notes.
(LO 2), **AP**

E10-3 On June 1, Fancher Company Ltd. borrows $60,000 from First Bank on a 6-month, $60,000, 8% note. The note matures on December 1.

Instructions
(a) Prepare the entry on June 1.
(b) Prepare the adjusting entry on June 30.
(c) Prepare the entry at maturity (December 1), assuming monthly adjusting entries have been made through November 30.
(d) What was the total financing cost (interest expense)?

Journalize sales and related taxes.
(LO 3), **AP**

E10-4 In providing accounting services to small businesses, you encounter the following situations pertaining to cash sales.
1. Furcal Company enters sales and sales taxes separately on its cash register. On April 10, the register totals are sales $22,000 and sales taxes $1,100.
2. Crystal Company does not segregate sales and sales taxes. Its register total for April 15 is $13,780, which includes a 6% sales tax.

Instructions
Prepare the entries to record the sales transactions and related taxes for (a) Furcal Company and (b) Crystal Company.

E10-5 During the month of March, Olinger Company's employees earned wages of $64,000. Withholdings related to these wages were $4,896 for Social Security (FICA), $7,500 for federal income tax, $3,100 for state income tax, and $400 for union dues. The company incurred no cost related to these earnings for federal unemployment tax but incurred $700 for state unemployment tax.

Journalize payroll entries.
(LO 3), **AP**

Instructions
(a) Prepare the necessary March 31 journal entry to record salaries and wages expense and salaries and wages payable. Assume that wages earned during March will be paid during April.
(b) Prepare the entry to record the company's payroll tax expense.

E10-6 Season tickets for the Wildcats are priced at $320 and include 16 games. Revenue is recognized after each game is played. When the season began, the amount credited to Unearned Ticket Revenue was $1,728,000. By the end of October, $1,188,000 of the Unearned Ticket Revenue had been recognized as revenue.

Journalize unearned revenue transactions.
(LO 3), **AP**

Instructions
(a) How many season tickets did the Wildcats sell?
(b) How many home games had the Wildcats played by the end of October?
(c) Prepare the entry for the initial recording of the Unearned Ticket Revenue.
(d) Prepare the entry to recognize the revenue after the first home game had been played.

E10-7 Valenti Company Ltd. publishes a monthly sports magazine, *Fishing Preview*. Subscriptions to the magazine cost $28 per year. During November 2014, Valenti sells 6,300 subscriptions for cash, beginning with the December issue. Valenti prepares financial statements quarterly and recognizes subscription revenue at the end of the quarter. The company uses the accounts Unearned Subscription Revenue and Subscription Revenue. The company has a December 31 year-end.

Journalize unearned subscription revenue.
(LO 3), **AP**

Instructions
(a) Prepare the entry in November for the receipt of the subscriptions.
(b) Prepare the adjusting entry at December 31, 2014, to record subscription revenue in December 2014.
(c) Prepare the adjusting entry at March 31, 2015, to record subscription revenue in the first quarter of 2015.

E10-8 On August 1, 2014, Ortega Corporation issued $600,000, 7%, 10-year bonds at face value. Interest is payable annually on August 1. Ortega's year-end is December 31.

Prepare journal entries for issuance of bonds and payment and accrual of interest.
(LO 5), **AP**

Instructions
Prepare journal entries to record the following events.
(a) The issuance of the bonds.
(b) The accrual of interest on December 31, 2014.
(c) The payment of interest on August 1, 2015.

E10-9 On January 1, Newkirk Company issued $300,000, 8%, 10-year bonds at face value. Interest is payable annually on January 1.

Prepare journal entries for issuance of bonds and payment and accrual of interest.
(LO 5), **AP**

Instructions
Prepare journal entries to record the following events.
(a) The issuance of the bonds.
(b) The accrual of interest on December 31.
(c) The payment of interest on January 1.

E10-10 Canyon Company issued $600,000, 10-year, 6% bonds at 103.

Prepare entries for issuance of bonds, balance sheet presentation, and cause of deviations from face value.
(LO 5), **AP**

Instructions
(a) Prepare the journal entry to record the sale of these bonds on January 1, 2014.
(b) Suppose the remaining Premium on Bonds Payable was $10,800 on December 31, 2017. Show the balance sheet presentation on this date.
(c) Explain why the bonds sold at a price above the face amount.

Prepare entries for issuance of bonds, balance sheet presentation, and cause of deviations from face value.
(LO 5), AP

E10-11 Riot Company issued $500,000, 15-year, 7% bonds at 96.

Instructions
(a) Prepare the journal entry to record the sale of these bonds on January 1, 2014.
(b) Suppose the remaining Discount on Bonds Payable was $12,000 on December 31, 2019. Show the balance sheet presentation on this date.
(c) Explain why the bonds sold at a price below the face amount.

Prepare entries for issue of bonds.
(LO 5), AN

E10-12 Assume that the following are independent situations recently reported in the *Wall Street Journal*.
  1. General Electric (GE) 7% bonds, maturing January 28, 2015, were issued at 111.12.
  2. Boeing 7% bonds, maturing September 24, 2029, were issued at 99.08.

Instructions
(a) Were GE and Boeing bonds issued at a premium or a discount?
(b) Explain how bonds, both paying the same contractual interest rate, could be issued at different prices.
(c) Prepare the journal entry to record the issue of each of these two bonds, assuming each company issued $800,000 of bonds in total.

Prepare journal entries to record issuance of bonds, payment of interest, and redemption at maturity.
(LO 5, 6), AP

E10-13 Romine Company issued $350,000 of 8%, 20-year bonds on January 1, 2014, at face value. Interest is payable annually on January 1.

Instructions
Prepare the journal entries to record the following events.
(a) The issuance of the bonds.
(b) The accrual of interest on December 31, 2014.
(c) The payment of interest on January 1, 2015.
(d) The redemption of the bonds at maturity, assuming interest for the last interest period has been paid and recorded.

Prepare journal entries for redemption of bonds.
(LO 6), AP

E10-14 The situations presented here are independent of each other.

Instructions
For each situation, prepare the appropriate journal entry for the redemption of the bonds.
(a) Pelfer Corporation redeemed $140,000 face value, 9% bonds on April 30, 2014, at 101. The carrying value of the bonds at the redemption date was $126,500. The bonds pay annual interest, and the interest payment due on April 30, 2014, has been made and recorded.
(b) Youngman, Inc., redeemed $170,000 face value, 12.5% bonds on June 30, 2014, at 98. The carrying value of the bonds at the redemption date was $184,000. The bonds pay annual interest, and the interest payment due on June 30, 2014, has been made and recorded.

Prepare liabilities section of balance sheet.
(LO 7), AP

E10-15 Santana, Inc. reports the following liabilities (in thousands) on its January 31, 2014, balance sheet and notes to the financial statements.

Accounts payable	$4,263.9	Mortgage payable	$6,746.7
Accrued pension liability	1,115.2	Operating leases	1,641.7
Unearned rent revenue	1,058.1	Notes payable (due in 2017)	335.6
Bonds payable	1,961.2	Salaries and wages payable	858.1
Current portion of		Notes payable (due in 2015)	2,563.6
mortgage payable	1,992.2	Unused operating line of credit	3,337.6
Income taxes payable	265.2	Warranty liability—current	1,417.3

Instructions
(a) Identify which of the above liabilities are likely current and which are likely long-term. List any items that do not fit in either category. Explain the reasoning for your selection.
(b) Prepare the liabilities section of Santana's balance sheet as at January 31, 2014.

Calculate liquidity and solvency ratios; discuss impact of unrecorded obligations on liquidity and solvency.
(LO 7), AP

E10-16 Suppose McDonald's 2014 financial statements contain the following selected data (in millions).

Current assets	$ 3,416.3	Interest expense	$ 473.2
Total assets	30,224.9	Income taxes	1,936.0
Current liabilities	2,988.7	Net income	4,551.0
Total liabilities	16,191.0		

Instructions
(a) Compute the following values and provide a brief interpretation of each.
  (1) Working capital.   (3) Debt to assets ratio.
  (2) Current ratio.   (4) Times interest earned.

(b) Suppose the notes to McDonald's financial statements show that subsequent to 2014 the company will have future minimum lease payments under operating leases of $10,717.5 million. If these assets had been purchased with debt, assets and liabilities would rise by approximately $8,800 million. Recompute the debt to assets ratio after adjusting for this. Discuss your result.

E10-17 Suppose 3M Company reported the following financial data for 2014 and 2013 (in millions).

Calculate current ratio before and after paying accounts payable.

(LO 7), **AN**

3M COMPANY		
Balance Sheet (partial)		
	2014	**2013**
Current assets		
Cash and cash equivalents	$ 3,040	$1,849
Accounts receivable, net	3,250	3,195
Inventories	2,639	3,013
Other current assets	1,866	1,541
Total current assets	$10,795	$9,598
Current liabilities	$ 4,897	$5,839

Instructions
(a) Calculate the current ratio for 3M for 2014 and 2013.
(b) Suppose that at the end of 2014, 3M management used $300 million cash to pay off $300 million of accounts payable. How would its current ratio change?

E10-18 Sedgewick Boutique reported the following financial data for 2014 and 2013.

Calculate current ratio before and after paying accounts payable.

(LO 7), **AN**

SEDGEWICK BOUTIQUE		
Balance Sheet (partial)		
September 30 (in thousands)		
	2014	**2013**
Current assets		
Cash and short-term deposits	$2,574	$1,021
Accounts receivable	2,147	1,575
Inventories	1,201	1,010
Other current assets	322	192
Total current assets	$6,244	$3,798
Current liabilities	$4,503	$2,619

Instructions
(a) Calculate the current ratio for Sedgewick Boutique for 2014 and 2013.
(b) Suppose that at the end of 2014, Sedgewick Boutique used $1.5 million cash to pay off $1.5 million of accounts payable. How would its current ratio change?
(c) At September 30, Sedgewick Boutique has an undrawn operating line of credit of $12.5 million. Would this affect any assessment that you might make of Sedgewick Boutique's short-term liquidity? Explain.

E10-19 A large retailer was sued nearly 5,000 times in a recent year—about once every two hours every day of the year. It has been sued for everything imaginable—ranging from falls on icy parking lots to injuries sustained in shoppers' stampedes to a murder with a rifle purchased at one of its stores. The company reported the following in the notes to its financial statements:

Discuss contingent liabilities.

(LO 7), **C**

The Company and its subsidiaries are involved from time to time in claims, proceedings, and litigation arising from the operation of its business. The Company does not believe that any such claim, proceeding, or litigation, either alone or in the aggregate, will have a material adverse effect on the Company's financial position or results of its operations.

Instructions

(a) Explain why the company does not have to record these contingent liabilities.

(b) Comment on any implications for analysis of the financial statements.

Prepare journal entries to record issuance of bonds, payment of interest, amortization of premium using straight-line, and redemption at maturity.

(LO 5, 6, 8), **AP**

*E10-20 Prophet Company issued $500,000, 6%, 30-year bonds on January 1, 2014, at 103. Interest is payable annually on January 1. Prophet uses straight-line amortization for bond premium or discount.

Instructions

Prepare the journal entries to record the following events.

(a) The issuance of the bonds.

(b) The accrual of interest and the premium amortization on December 31, 2014.

(c) The payment of interest on January 1, 2015.

(d) The redemption of the bonds at maturity, assuming interest for the last interest period has been paid and recorded.

Prepare journal entries to record issuance of bonds, payment of interest, amortization of discount using straight-line, and redemption at maturity.

(LO 5, 6, 8), **AP**

*E10-21 Dailey Company issued $300,000, 8%, 15-year bonds on December 31, 2013, for $288,000. Interest is payable annually on December 31. Dailey uses the straight-line method to amortize bond premium or discount.

Instructions

Prepare the journal entries to record the following events.

(a) The issuance of the bonds.

(b) The payment of interest and the discount amortization on December 31, 2014.

(c) The redemption of the bonds at maturity, assuming interest for the last interest period has been paid and recorded.

Prepare journal entries for issuance of bonds, payment of interest, and amortization of discount using effective-interest method.

(LO 5, 9), **AP**

*E10-22 Cole Corporation issued $400,000, 7%, 20-year bonds on January 1, 2014, for $360,727. This price resulted in an effective-interest rate of 8% on the bonds. Interest is payable annually on January 1. Cole uses the effective-interest method to amortize bond premium or discount.

Instructions

Prepare the journal entries to record (round to the nearest dollar):

(a) The issuance of the bonds.

(b) The accrual of interest and the discount amortization on December 31, 2014.

(c) The payment of interest on January 1, 2015.

Prepare journal entries for issuance of bonds, payment of interest, and amortization of premium using effective-interest method.

(LO 5, 9), **AP**

*E10-23 Gomez Company issued $380,000, 7%, 10-year bonds on January 1, 2014, for $407,968. This price resulted in an effective-interest rate of 6% on the bonds. Interest is payable annually on January 1. Gomez uses the effective-interest method to amortize bond premium or discount.

Instructions

Prepare the journal entries (rounded to the nearest dollar) to record:

(a) The issuance of the bonds.

(b) The accrual of interest and the premium amortization on December 31, 2014.

(c) The payment of interest on January 1, 2015.

Prepare journal entries to record mortgage note and installment payments.

(LO 10), **AP**

*E10-24 Nance Co. receives $280,000 when it issues a $280,000, 6%, mortgage note payable to finance the construction of a building at December 31, 2014. The terms provide for semiannual installment payments of $14,285 on June 30 and December 31.

Instructions

Prepare the journal entries to record the mortgage loan and the first two installment payments.

Balance sheet presentation of installment note payable.

(LO 10), **AP**

*E10-25 Goins Corporation issued a $50,000, 10%, 10-year installment note payable on January 1, 2014. Payments of $8,137 are made each January 1, beginning January 1, 2015.

Instructions

(a) What amounts should be reported under current liabilities related to the note on December 31, 2014?

(b) What should be reported under long-term liabilities?

Challenge Exercises

Visit the book's companion website, at **www.wiley.com/college/kimmel**, and choose the Student Companion site to access Challenge Exercises.

Problems: Set A

P10-1A   On January 1, 2014, the ledger of Hiatt Company contained these liability accounts.

Accounts Payable	$42,500
Sales Taxes Payable	6,600
Unearned Service Revenue	19,000

Prepare current liability entries, adjusting entries, and current liabilities section.
(LO 1, 2, 3, 7), AP

During January, the following selected transactions occurred.

Jan. 1   Borrowed $18,000 in cash from Premier Bank on a 4-month, 5%, $18,000 note.
    5   Sold merchandise for cash totaling $6,254, which includes 6% sales taxes.
    12   Performed services for customers who had made advance payments of $10,000. (Credit Service Revenue.)
    14   Paid state treasurer's department for sales taxes collected in December 2013, $6,600.
    20   Sold 500 units of a new product on credit at $48 per unit, plus 6% sales tax.

During January, the company's employees earned wages of $70,000. Withholdings related to these wages were $5,355 for Social Security (FICA), $5,000 for federal income tax, and $1,500 for state income tax. The company owed no money related to these earnings for federal or state unemployment tax. Assume that wages earned during January will be paid during February. No entry had been recorded for wages or payroll tax expense as of January 31.

Instructions
(a)   Journalize the January transactions.
(b)   Journalize the adjusting entries at January 31 for the outstanding note payable and for salaries and wages expense and payroll tax expense.
(c)   Prepare the current liabilities section of the balance sheet at January 31, 2014. Assume no change in Accounts Payable.

(c) Tot. current
liabilities $146,724

P10-2A   Ermlar Corporation sells rock-climbing products and also operates an indoor climbing facility for climbing enthusiasts. During the last part of 2014, Ermlar had the following transactions related to notes payable.

Journalize and post note transactions; show balance sheet presentation.
(LO 2, 7), AP

Sept. 1   Issued a $12,000 note to Lippert to purchase inventory. The 3-month note payable bears interest of 6% and is due December 1. (Ermlar uses a perpetual inventory system.)
Sept. 30   Recorded accrued interest for the Lippert note.
Oct. 1   Issued a $16,500, 8%, 4-month note to Shanee Bank to finance the purchase of a new climbing wall for advanced climbers. The note is due February 1.
Oct. 31   Recorded accrued interest for the Lippert note and the Shanee Bank note.
Nov. 1   Issued a $26,000 note and paid $8,000 cash to purchase a vehicle to transport clients to nearby climbing sites as part of a new series of climbing classes. This note bears interest of 6% and matures in 12 months.
Nov. 30   Recorded accrued interest for the Lippert note, the Shanee Bank note, and the vehicle note.
Dec. 1   Paid principal and interest on the Lippert note.
Dec. 31   Recorded accrued interest for the Shanee Bank note and the vehicle note.

Instructions
(a)   Prepare journal entries for the transactions noted above.
(b)   Post the above entries to the Notes Payable, Interest Payable, and Interest Expense accounts. (Use T-accounts.)
(c)   Show the balance sheet presentation of notes payable and interest payable at December 31.
(d)   How much interest expense relating to notes payable did Ermlar incur during the year?

(b) Interest
Payable $590

Prepare journal entries to record interest payments and redemption of bonds.

(LO 5, 6), **AP**

P10-3A The following section is taken from Mareska's balance sheet at December 31, 2013.

Current liabilities	
Interest payable	$ 40,000
Long-term liabilities	
Bonds payable (8%, due January 1, 2017)	500,000

Interest is payable annually on January 1. The bonds are callable on any annual interest date.

Instructions

(a) Journalize the payment of the bond interest on January 1, 2014.

(b) Loss $6,000

(b) Assume that on January 1, 2014, after paying interest, Mareska calls bonds having a face value of $200,000. The call price is 103. Record the redemption of the bonds.

(c) Prepare the adjusting entry on December 31, 2014, to accrue the interest on the remaining bonds.

Prepare journal entries to record issuance of bonds, interest, balance sheet presentation, and bond redemption.

(LO 5, 6, 7), **AP**

P10-4A On October 1, 2013, Koppa Corp. issued $700,000, 5%, 10-year bonds at face value. The bonds were dated October 1, 2013, and pay interest annually on October 1. Financial statements are prepared annually on December 31.

Instructions

(a) Prepare the journal entry to record the issuance of the bonds.

(b) Prepare the adjusting entry to record the accrual of interest on December 31, 2013.

(c) Show the balance sheet presentation of bonds payable and bond interest payable on December 31, 2013.

(d) Prepare the journal entry to record the payment of interest on October 1, 2014.

(e) Prepare the adjusting entry to record the accrual of interest on December 31, 2014.

(f) Loss $28,000

(f) Assume that on January 1, 2015, Koppa pays the accrued bond interest and calls the bonds. The call price is 104. Record the payment of interest and redemption of the bonds.

Prepare journal entries to record issuance of bonds, show balance sheet presentation, and record bond redemption.

(LO 5, 6, 7), **AP**

P10-5A Slocombe Company sold $6,000,000, 7%, 15-year bonds on January 1, 2014. The bonds were dated January 1, 2014, and pay interest on December 31. The bonds were sold at 98.

Instructions

(a) Prepare the journal entry to record the issuance of the bonds on January 1, 2014.

(b) At December 31, 2014, $8,000 of the bond discount had been amortized. Show the long-term liability balance sheet presentation of the bond liability at December 31, 2014.

(c) Loss $224,000

(c) At January 1, 2016, when the carrying value of the bonds was $5,896,000, the company redeemed the bonds at 102. Record the redemption of the bonds assuming that interest for the year had already been paid.

Calculate and comment on ratios.

(LO 7), **AN**

P10-6A Suppose you have been presented with selected information taken from the financial statements of Southwest Airlines Co., shown below.

SOUTHWEST AIRLINES CO.
Balance Sheet (partial)
December 31
(in millions)

	2014	2013
Total current assets	$ 2,893	$ 4,443
Noncurrent assets	11,415	12,329
Total assets	$14,308	$16,772
Current liabilities	$ 2,806	$ 4,836
Long-term liabilities	6,549	4,995
Total liabilities	9,355	9,831
Shareholders' equity	4,953	6,941
Total liabilities and shareholders' equity	$14,308	$16,772

Other information:

	2014	2013
Net income (loss)	$ 178	$ 645
Income tax expense	100	413
Interest expense	130	119
Cash provided by operations	(1,521)	2,845
Capital expenditures	923	1,331
Cash dividends	13	14

Note 8. Leases

The majority of the Company's terminal operations space, as well as 82 aircraft, were under operating leases at December 31, 2014. Future minimum lease payments under noncancelable operating leases are as follows: 2015, $376,000; 2016, $324,000; 2017, $249,000; 2018, $208,000; 2019, $152,000; after 2020, $728,000.

Instructions
(a) Calculate each of the following ratios for 2014 and 2013.
   (1) Current ratio.
   (2) Free cash flow.
   (3) Debt to assets ratio.
   (4) Times interest earned.
(b) Comment on the trend in ratios.
(c) Read the company's note on leases. If the operating leases had instead been accounted for like a purchase, assets and liabilities would increase by approximately $1,600 million. Recalculate the debt to assets ratio for 2014 in light of this information, and discuss the implications for analysis.

*P10-7A The following information is taken from Oler Corp.'s balance sheet at December 31, 2013.

Current liabilities		
Interest payable		$ 96,000
Long-term liabilities		
Bonds payable (4%, due January 1, 2024)	$2,400,000	
Less: Discount on bonds payable	24,000	2,376,000

Prepare journal entries to record interest payments, straight-line discount amortization, and redemption of bonds.

(LO 5, 6, 8), AP

Interest is payable annually on January 1. The bonds are callable on any annual interest date. Oler uses straight-line amortization for any bond premium or discount. From December 31, 2013, the bonds will be outstanding for an additional 10 years (120 months).

Instructions
(Round all computations to the nearest dollar.)
(a) Journalize the payment of bond interest on January 1, 2014.
(b) Prepare the entry to amortize bond discount and to accrue the interest on December 31, 2014.
(c) Assume on January 1, 2015, after paying interest, that Oler Corp. calls bonds having a face value of $400,000. The call price is 102. Record the redemption of the bonds.
(d) Prepare the adjusting entry at December 31, 2015, to amortize bond discount and to accrue interest on the remaining bonds.

(c) Loss $11,600

*P10-8A Yung Corporation sold $2,000,000, 7%, 5-year bonds on January 1, 2014. The bonds were dated January 1, 2014, and pay interest on January 1. Yung Corporation uses the straight-line method to amortize bond premium or discount.

Prepare journal entries to record issuance of bonds, interest, and straight-line amortization, and balance sheet presentation.

Instructions
(a) Prepare all the necessary journal entries to record the issuance of the bonds and bond interest expense for 2014, assuming that the bonds sold at 102.
(b) Prepare journal entries as in part (a) assuming that the bonds sold at 97.
(c) Show the balance sheet presentation for the bond issue at December 31, 2014, using (1) the 102 selling price, and then (2) the 97 selling price.

(LO 5, 7, 8), AP

Prepare journal entries to record issuance of bonds, interest, and straight-line amortization, and balance sheet presentation.
(LO 5, 7, 8), **AP**

*P10-9A Wempe Co. sold $3,000,000, 8%, 10-year bonds on January 1, 2014. The bonds were dated January 1, 2014, and pay interest on January 1. The company uses straight-line amortization on bond premiums and discounts. Financial statements are prepared annually.

Instructions
(a) Prepare the journal entries to record the issuance of the bonds assuming they sold at:
    (1) 103.
    (2) 98.

(c) (2) 12/31/14 Interest
    Expense $246,000

(b) Prepare amortization tables for both assumed sales for the first three interest payments.
(c) Prepare the journal entries to record interest expense for 2014 under both of the bond issuances assumed in part (a).
(d) Show the long-term liabilities balance sheet presentation for both of the bond issuances assumed in part (a) at December 31, 2014.

Prepare journal entries to record issuance of bonds, payment of interest, and amortization of bond discount using effective-interest method.
(LO 5, 9), **AP**

*P10-10A On January 1, 2014, Lock Corporation issued $1,800,000 face value, 5%, 10-year bonds at $1,667,518. This price resulted in an effective-interest rate of 6% on the bonds. Lock uses the effective-interest method to amortize bond premium or discount. The bonds pay annual interest January 1.

Instructions
(Round all computations to the nearest dollar.)
(a) Prepare the journal entry to record the issuance of the bonds on January 1, 2014.
(b) Prepare an amortization table through December 31, 2016 (three interest periods) for this bond issue.

(c) Interest
    Expense $100,051

(c) Prepare the journal entry to record the accrual of interest and the amortization of the discount on December 31, 2014.
(d) Prepare the journal entry to record the payment of interest on January 1, 2015.
(e) Prepare the journal entry to record the accrual of interest and the amortization of the discount on December 31, 2015.

Prepare journal entries to record issuance of bonds, payment of interest, and effective-interest amortization, and balance sheet presentation.
(LO 5, 7, 9), **AP**

*P10-11A On January 1, 2014, Jade Company issued $2,000,000 face value, 7%, 10-year bonds at $2,147,202. This price resulted in a 6% effective-interest rate on the bonds. Jade uses the effective-interest method to amortize bond premium or discount. The bonds pay annual interest on each January 1.

Instructions
(a) Prepare the journal entries to record the following transactions.
    (1) The issuance of the bonds on January 1, 2014.
    (2) Accrual of interest and amortization of the premium on December 31, 2014.
    (3) The payment of interest on January 1, 2015.

(a) (4) Interest
    Expense $128,162

    (4) Accrual of interest and amortization of the premium on December 31, 2015.
(b) Show the proper long-term liabilities balance sheet presentation for the liability for bonds payable at December 31, 2015.
(c) Provide the answers to the following questions in narrative form.
    (1) What amount of interest expense is reported for 2015?
    (2) Would the bond interest expense reported in 2015 be the same as, greater than, or less than the amount that would be reported if the straight-line method of amortization were used?

Prepare installment payments schedule, journal entries, and balance sheet presentation for a mortgage note payable.
(LO 7, 10), **AP**

*P10-12A Frevert purchased a new piece of equipment to be used in its new facility. The $370,000 piece of equipment was purchased with a $50,000 down payment and with cash received through the issuance of a $320,000, 8%, 3-year mortgage note payable issued on October 1, 2014. The terms provide for quarterly installment payments of $30,259 on December 31, March 31, June 30, and September 30.

Instructions
(Round all computations to the nearest dollar.)
(a) Prepare an installment payments schedule for the first five payments of the notes payable.
(b) Prepare the journal entry related to the notes payable for December 31, 2014.

(c) Current portion $100,304

(c) Show the balance sheet presentation for this obligation for December 31, 2014. (*Hint:* Be sure to distinguish between the current and long-term portions of the note.)

*P10-13A Grace Herron has just approached a venture capitalist for financing for her new business venture, the development of a local ski hill. On July 1, 2013, Grace was loaned $150,000 at an annual interest rate of 7%. The loan is repayable over 5 years in annual installments of $36,584, principal and interest, due each June 30. The first payment is due June 30, 2014. Grace uses the effective-interest method for amortizing debt. Her ski hill company's year-end will be June 30.

Prepare journal entries to record payments for long-term note payable, and balance sheet presentation.
(LO 7, 10), **AP**

Instructions
(a) Prepare an amortization schedule for the 5 years, 2013–2018. (Round all calculations to the nearest dollar.)
(b) Prepare all journal entries for Grace Herron for the first 2 fiscal years ended June 30, 2014, and June 30, 2015. (Round all calculations to the nearest dollar.)
(c) Show the balance sheet presentation of the note payable as of June 30, 2015. (*Hint:* Be sure to distinguish between the current and long-term portions of the note.)

(b) 6/30/14 Interest
    Expense $10,500

Problems: Set B

Visit the book's companion website, at **www.wiley.com/college/kimmel**, and choose the Student Companion site to access Problem Set B.

Comprehensive Problem

CP10 Trevor Corporation's balance sheet at December 31, 2013, is presented below.

TREVOR CORPORATION
Balance Sheet
December 31, 2013

Cash	$ 30,000	Accounts payable	$ 13,750
Inventory	30,750	Interest payable	2,500
Prepaid insurance	5,600	Bonds payable	50,000
Equipment	38,000	Common stock	25,000
	$104,350	Retained earnings	13,100
			$104,350

During 2014, the following transactions occurred.
1. Trevor paid $2,500 interest on the bonds on January 1, 2014.
2. Trevor purchased $241,100 of inventory on account.
3. Trevor sold for $480,000 cash inventory which cost $265,000. Trevor also collected $28,800 sales taxes.
4. Trevor paid $230,000 on accounts payable.
5. Trevor paid $2,500 interest on the bonds on July 1, 2014.
6. The prepaid insurance ($5,600) expired on July 31.
7. On August 1, Trevor paid $10,200 for insurance coverage from August 1, 2014, through July 31, 2015.
8. Trevor paid $17,000 sales taxes to the state.
9. Paid other operating expenses, $91,000.
10. Redeemed the bonds on December 31, 2014, by paying $48,000 plus $2,500 interest.
11. Issued $90,000 of 8% bonds on December 31, 2014, at 103. The bonds pay interest every June 30 and December 31.

Adjustment data:
1. Recorded the insurance expired from item 7.
2. The equipment was acquired on December 31, 2013, and will be depreciated on a straight-line basis over 5 years with a $3,000 salvage value.
3. The income tax rate is 30%. (*Hint:* Prepare the income statement up to income before taxes and multiply by 30% to compute the amount.)

Instructions
(You may want to set up T-accounts to determine ending balances.)
(a) Prepare journal entries for the transactions listed above and adjusting entries.
(b) Prepare an adjusted trial balance at December 31, 2014.
(c) Prepare an income statement and a retained earnings statement for the year ending December 31, 2014, and a classified balance sheet as of December 31, 2014.

(b) Totals $687,695
(c) N.I. $72,905

Broadening Your Perspective

Financial Reporting and Analysis

FINANCIAL REPORTING PROBLEM: *Tootsie Roll Industries, Inc.*

BYP10-1 Refer to the financial statements of Tootsie Roll Industries and the Notes to Consolidated Financial Statements in Appendix A.

Instructions
Answer the following questions.
(a) What were Tootsie Roll's total current liabilities at December 31, 2011? What was the increase/decrease in Tootsie Roll's total current liabilities from the prior year?
(b) How much were the accounts payable at December 31, 2011?
(c) What were the components of total current liabilities on December 31, 2011 (other than accounts payable already discussed above)?

COMPARATIVE ANALYSIS PROBLEM: *Tootsie Roll vs. Hershey*

BYP10-2 The financial statements of The Hershey Company are presented in Appendix B, following the financial statements for Tootsie Roll Industries in Appendix A.

Instructions
(a) Based on the information contained in these financial statements, compute the current ratio for 2011 for each company. What conclusions concerning the companies' liquidity can be drawn from these ratios?
(b) Based on the information contained in these financial statements, compute the following 2011 ratios for each company.
  (1) Debt to assets ratio.
  (2) Times interest earned. (Hershey's total interest expense for 2011 was $94,780,000. See Tootsie Roll's Note 6 for its interest expense.)

  What conclusions about the companies' long-run solvency can be drawn from the ratios?

RESEARCH CASE

BYP10-3 The September 1, 2009, edition of *CFO.com* contains an article by Marie Leone and Tim Reason entitled "Dirty Secrets." You can access this article at **www.cfo.com/article. cfm/14292477?f=singlepage**.

Instructions
Read the article and answer the following questions.
(a) Summarize the accounting for contingent items that is provided in this textbook.
(b) The authors of the article suggest that many companies are basically accounting for contingencies on a cash basis. Is this consistent with the approach you described in part (a)?
(c) The article suggests that many companies report one set of liability estimates to insurers and a different (lower) set of numbers in their financial statements. How is this possible, and what are the implications for investors?
(d) How do international accounting standards differ in terms of the amounts reported in these types of situations?

INTERPRETING FINANCIAL STATEMENTS

BYP10-4 Hechinger Co. and Home Depot are two home improvement retailers. Compared to Hechinger, founded in the early 1900s, Home Depot is a relative newcomer. But in recent years, while Home Depot was reporting large increases in net income, Hechinger was reporting increasingly large net losses. Finally, largely due to competition from Home Depot, Hechinger was forced to file for bankruptcy. Here are financial data for both companies (in millions).

	Hechinger	Home Depot
Cash	$ 21	$ 62
Receivables	0	469
Total current assets	1,153	4,933
Beginning total assets	1,668	11,229
Ending total assets	1,577	13,465
Beginning current liabilities	935	2,456
Ending current liabilities	938	2,857
Beginning total liabilities	1,392	4,015
Ending total liabilities	1,339	4,716
Interest expense	67	37
Income tax expense	3	1,040
Cash provided (used) by operations	(257)	1,917
Net income	(93)	1,614
Net sales	3,444	30,219

Instructions
Using the data provided, perform the following analysis.
(a) Calculate working capital and the current ratio for each company. Discuss their relative liquidity.
(b) Calculate the debt to assets ratio and times interest earned for each company. Discuss their relative solvency.
(c) Calculate the return on assets and profit margin for each company. Comment on their relative profitability.
(d) The notes to Home Depot's financial statements indicate that it leases many of its facilities using operating leases. If these assets had instead been purchased with debt, assets and liabilities would have increased by approximately $2,347 million. Calculate the company's debt to assets ratio employing this adjustment. Discuss the implications.

BYP10-5 For many years, Borders Group and Barnes and Noble were the dominant booksellers in the United States. They experienced rapid growth, and in the process they forced many small, independent bookstores out of business. Recently, Borders filed for bankruptcy. It was the victim of its inability to change with the times. It did not develop a viable business plan for dealing with digital books and online sales. Below is financial information (in millions) for the two companies, taken from the annual reports of each company one year before Borders filed for bankruptcy.

	Borders	Barnes and Noble
Current assets	$ 978.7	$1,719.5
Total assets	1,415.6	3,705.7
Current liabilities	918.1	1,724.4
Total liabilities	1,257.3	2,802.3
Net income/(loss)	(109.4)	36.7
Interest expense	24.1	28.2
Tax expense/(income tax benefit)	(31.3)	8.4

Instructions
(a) Compute the current ratio for each company.
(b) Compute the debt to assets ratio and times interest earned for each company. (*Hint:* A tax benefit means that rather than pay taxes, the company was due a refund because of its losses. For ratio purposes, a tax benefit is treated the opposite of tax expense.)
(c) Discuss the relative liquidity and solvency of each company. Did the bankruptcy of Borders seem likely?

REAL-WORLD FOCUS

BYP10-6 Bond or debt securities pay a stated rate of interest. This rate of interest is dependent on the risk associated with the investment. Also, bond prices change when the risks associated with those bonds change. Standard & Poor's provides ratings for companies that issue debt securities.

Address: **www.standardandpoors.com/ratings/definitions-and-faqs/en/us**, or go to **www.wiley.com/college/kimmel**

Instructions
Go to the website shown and answer the following questions.
(a) Explain the meaning of an "A" rating. Explain the meaning of a "C" rating.
(b) What types of things can cause a change in a company's credit rating?
(c) Explain the relationship between a company's credit rating and the merit of an investment in that company's bonds.

Critical Thinking

DECISION-MAKING ACROSS THE ORGANIZATION

BYP10-7 On January 1, 2012, Kenard Corporation issued $3,000,000, 5-year, 8% bonds at 97. The bonds pay interest annually on January 1. By January 1, 2014, the market rate of interest for bonds of risk similar to those of Kenard Corporation had risen. As a result, the market price of these bonds was $2,500,000 on January 1, 2014—below their carrying value of $2,946,000.

Mel Garner, president of the company, suggests repurchasing all of these bonds in the open market at the $2,500,000 price. But to do so the company will have to issue $2,500,000 (face value) of new 10-year, 12% bonds at par. The president asks you, as controller, "What is the feasibility of my proposed repurchase plan?"

Instructions
With the class divided into groups, answer the following.
(a) Prepare the journal entry to redeem the 5-year bonds on January 1, 2014. Prepare the journal entry to issue the new 10-year bonds.
(b) Prepare a short memo to the president in response to his request for advice. List the economic factors that you believe should be considered for his repurchase proposal.

COMMUNICATION ACTIVITY

BYP10-8 Harry Jackman, president of Weast, Inc., is considering the issuance of bonds to finance an expansion of his business. He has asked you to do the following: (1) discuss the advantages of bonds over common stock financing, (2) indicate the types of bonds he might issue, and (3) explain the issuing procedures used in bond transactions.

Instructions
Write a memorandum to the president, answering his request.

ETHICS CASES

BYP10-9 The July 1998 issue of *Inc.* magazine includes an article by Jeffrey L. Seglin entitled "Would You Lie to Save Your Company?" It recounts the following true situation:

"A Chief Executive Officer (CEO) of a $20-million company that repairs aircraft engines received notice from a number of its customers that engines that it had recently repaired had failed, and that the company's parts were to blame. The CEO had not yet determined whether his company's parts were, in fact, the cause of the problem. The Federal Aviation Administration (FAA) had been notified and was investigating the matter.

What complicated the situation was that the company was in the midst of its year-end audit. As part of the audit, the CEO was required to sign a letter saying that he was not aware of any significant outstanding circumstances that could negatively impact the company—in accounting terms, of any contingent liabilities. The auditor was not aware of the customer complaints or the FAA investigation.

The company relied heavily on short-term loans from eight banks. The CEO feared that if these lenders learned of the situation, they would pull their loans. The loss of these loans would force the company into bankruptcy, leaving hundreds of people without jobs. Prior to this problem, the company had a stellar performance record."

Instructions

Answer the following questions.

(a) Who are the stakeholders in this situation?

(b) What are the CEO's possible courses of action? What are the potential results of each course of action? (Take into account the two alternative outcomes: the FAA determines the company (1) was not at fault, and (2) was at fault.)

(c) What would you do, and why?

(d) Suppose the CEO decides to conceal the situation, and that during the next year the company is found to be at fault and is forced into bankruptcy. What losses are incurred by the stakeholders in this situation? Do you think the CEO should suffer legal consequences if he decides to conceal the situation?

BYP10-10   During the summer of 2002, the financial press reported that Citigroup was being investigated for allegations that it had arranged transactions for Enron so as to intentionally misrepresent the nature of the transactions and consequently achieve favorable balance sheet treatment. Essentially, the deals were structured to make it appear that money was coming into Enron from trading activities, rather than from loans.

A July 23, 2002, *New York Times* article by Richard Oppel and Kurt Eichenwald entitled "Citigroup Said to Mold Deal to Help Enron Skirt Rules" suggested that Citigroup intentionally kept certain parts of a secret oral agreement out of the written record for fear that it would change the accounting treatment. Critics contend that this had the effect of significantly understating Enron's liabilities, thus misleading investors and creditors. Citigroup maintains that, as a lender, it has no obligation to ensure that its clients account for transactions properly. The proper accounting, Citigroup insists, is the responsibility of the client and its auditor.

Instructions

Answer the following questions.

(a) Who are the stakeholders in this situation?

(b) Do you think that a lender, in general, in arranging so-called "structured financing" has a responsibility to ensure that its clients account for the financing in an appropriate fashion, or is this the responsibility of the client and its auditor?

(c) What effect did the fact that the written record did not disclose all characteristics of the transaction probably have on the auditor's ability to evaluate the accounting treatment of this transaction?

(d) The *New York Times* article noted that in one presentation made to sell this kind of deal to Enron and other energy companies, Citigroup stated that using such an arrangement "eliminates the need for capital markets disclosure, keeping structure mechanics private." Why might a company wish to conceal the terms of a financing arrangement from the capital markets (investors and creditors)? Is this appropriate? Do you think it is ethical for a lender to market deals in this way?

(e) Why was this deal more potentially harmful to shareholders than other off-balance-sheet transactions (for example, lease financing)?

ALL ABOUT YOU

BYP10-11   For most U.S. families, medical costs are substantial and rising. But will medical costs be your most substantial expense over your lifetime? Not likely. Will it be housing or food? Again, not likely. The answer: Taxes are likely to be your biggest expense. On average, Americans work 74 days to afford their federal taxes. Companies, too, have large tax burdens. They look very hard at tax issues in deciding where to build their plants and where to locate their administrative headquarters.

Instructions

(a) Determine what your state income taxes are if your taxable income is $60,000 and you file as a single taxpayer in the state in which you live.

(b) Assume that you own a home worth $200,000 in your community and the tax rate is 2.1%. Compute the property taxes you would pay.

(c) Assume that the total gasoline bill for your automobile is $1,200 a year (300 gallons at $4 per gallon). What are the amounts of state and federal taxes that you pay on the $1,200?

(d) Assume that your purchases for the year total $9,000. Of this amount, $5,000 was for food and prescription drugs. What is the amount of sales tax you would pay on these purchases? (*Note:* Many states do not have a sales tax for food or prescription drug purchases. Does yours?)

(e) Determine what your Social Security taxes are if your income is $60,000.

(f) Determine what your federal income taxes are if your taxable income is $60,000 and you file as a single taxpayer.

(g) Determine your total taxes paid based on the above calculations, and determine the percentage of income that you would pay in taxes based on the following formula: Total taxes paid ÷ Total income.

BYP10-12 Some employees are encouraging and setting up preventive healthcare programs. Here are the percentages for five unhealthy behaviors for individuals with some college education: current cigarette smoker (22.9%), five or more alcoholic drinks at one sitting at least once in the past year (30%), physically inactive (30%), obese (25.2%), or sleep less than 6 hours per day (30.3%).

Suppose you own a business. About a quarter of your employees smoke, and an even higher percentage are overweight. You decide to implement a mandatory health program that requires employees to quit smoking and to exercise regularly, with regular monitoring. If employees do not participate in the program, they will have to pay their own insurance premiums. Is this fair?

YES: It is the responsibility of management to try to maximize a company's profit. Employees with unhealthy habits drive up the cost of health insurance because they require more frequent and more costly medical attention.

NO: What people do on their own time is their own business. This represents an invasion of privacy, and is a form of discrimination.

Instructions
Write a response indicating your position regarding the situation. Provide support for your view.

FASB CODIFICATION ACTIVITY

BYP10-13 If your school has a subscription to the FASB Codification, go to **http://aaahq.org/asclogin.cfm** to log in and prepare responses to the following.
(a) What is the definition of current liabilities?
(b) What is the definition of long-term obligations?
(c) What guidance does the Codification provide for the disclosure of long-term obligations?

CONSIDERING PEOPLE, PLANET, AND PROFIT

BYP10-14 The December 10, 2011, edition of *The Economist* contains an article entitled "Helping the Poor to Save: Small Wonder." This article discusses how many of the world's poorest people benefit from borrowing small amounts of money.

Instructions
Read the article and answer the following questions. (The article can be accessed by doing an Internet search that includes the title of the article and magazine.)
(a) What monthly rate of interest do people pay on the loans they borrow from the microfinance organizations described in the article? What would these rates be on an annualized basis?
(b) The rates described in your answer to part (a) are very high. Explain how somebody can pay such high rates and yet still benefit from borrowing.
(c) Describe the structure of the typical village savings and loan organization.

Answers to Insight and Accounting Across the Organization Questions

p. 442 When Convertible Bonds Don't Q: The drop in stock prices did not change the debt to assets ratios of these companies. Discuss how the perception of a high debt to assets ratio changed before and after the fall in stock prices. **A:** When stock prices fell, the debt to assets of these companies was unchanged. The debt was outstanding before the fall, and it was outstanding after the fall. However, before the fall, many investors did not worry if a company had a high debt to assets ratio. They assumed that the debt would be converted to stock and so would never have to be repaid with cash. After the fall, it became clear that the debt would not be converted to stock. Suddenly, a high debt to assets ratio was a real concern.

p. 454 Debt Masking Q: What implications does debt masking have for an investor that is using the debt to assets ratio to evaluate a company's solvency? **A:** Since the debt to assets ratio is calculated using financial statement numbers from the end of the accounting period, debt masking could result in investors making incorrect assumptions about a company's solvency. By engaging in debt masking, a company is misleading investors because what it is disclosing at the end of the period does not reflect what its normal financial position was during most of the accounting period.

p. 456 "Covenant-Lite" Debt Q: How can financial ratios such as those covered in this chapter provide protection for creditors? **A:** Financial ratios such as the current ratio, debt to assets ratio, and the times interest earned provide indications of a company's liquidity and solvency. By specifying minimum levels of liquidity and solvency, as measured by these ratios, a creditor creates triggers that enable it to step in before a company's financial situation becomes too dire.

Answers to Self-Test Questions

1. a   **2.** d   **3.** b ($88,500 \times .12 \times \frac{4}{12}$)   **4.** d   **5.** b ($4,515 \div 1.05$)   **6.** c   **7.** b ($18,000 \times \frac{3}{12}$)   **8.** c
9. c   **10.** a   **11.** c   **12.** d   **13.** b ($103,745 - $100,000)   **14.** c ($150,000 + $30,000 + $20,000) \div
$30,000   **15.** a   ***16.** c (($500,000 \times .04) \div 5)   ***17.** a ($500,000 - ($20,000 - (3 \times $4,000)))
*18. b (($938,554 \times .10) - ($1,000,000 \times .09)) = $3,855; ($1,000,000 - $938,554) - $3,855
*19. c ($1,072,096 \times .12)   ***20.** c ($1,165 - ($20,000 \times .015))

A Look at IFRS

IFRS and GAAP have similar definitions of liabilities. IFRSs related to reporting and recognition of liabilities are found in *IAS 1 (revised)* ("Presentation of Financial Statements") and *IAS 37* ("Provisions, Contingent Liabilities, and Contingent Assets"). The general recording procedures for payroll are similar although differences occur depending on the types of benefits that are provided in different countries.

LEARNING OBJECTIVE 11
Compare the accounting procedures for liabilities under GAAP and IFRS.

KEY POINTS

- The basic definition of a liability under GAAP and IFRS is very similar. In a more technical way, liabilities are defined by the IASB as a present obligation of the entity arising from past events, the settlement of which is expected to result in an outflow from the entity of resources embodying economic benefits. Liabilities may be legally enforceable via a contract or law but need not be. That is, they can arise due to normal business practices or customs.

- IFRS requires that companies classify liabilities as current or non-current on the face of the statement of financial position (balance sheet) except in industries where a **presentation** based on liquidity would be considered to provide more useful information (such as financial institutions). When current liabilities (also called short-term liabilities) are presented, they are generally presented in order of liquidity.

- Under IFRS, liabilities are classified as current if they are expected to be paid within 12 months.

- Similar to GAAP, items are normally reported in order of liquidity. Companies sometimes show liabilities before assets. Also, they will sometimes show non-current (long-term) liabilities before current liabilities.

- Under both GAAP and IFRS, preferred stock that is required to be redeemed at a specific point in time in the future must be reported as debt, rather than being presented as either equity or in a "mezzanine" area between debt and equity.

- Under IFRS, companies sometimes will net current liabilities against current assets to show working capital on the face of the statement of financial position. (This is evident in the Zetar financial statements in Appendix C.)

- IFRS requires use of the effective-interest method for amortization of bond discounts and premiums. GAAP allows use of the straight-line method where the difference is not material. Under IFRS, companies do not use a premium or discount account but instead show the bond at its net amount. For example, if a $100,000 bond was issued at 97, under IFRS a company would record:

Cash	97,000	
Bonds Payable		97,000

- The accounting for convertible bonds differs across IFRS and GAAP. Unlike GAAP, IFRS splits the proceeds from the convertible bond between an equity component and a debt component. The equity conversion rights are reported in equity.

    To illustrate, assume that Harris Corp. issues convertible 7% bonds with a face value of $1,000,000 and receives $1,000,000. Comparable bonds without a conversion feature would have required a 9% rate of interest. To determine how much of the proceeds would be allocated to debt and how much to equity, the promised payments of the bond obligation would be discounted at the market rate of 9%. Suppose that this results in a present value of $850,000. The entry to record the issuance would be:

Cash	1,000,000	
Bonds Payable		850,000
Equity Conversion Rights (Equity)		150,000

- The IFRS leasing standard is *IAS 17*. Both Boards share the same objective of recording leases by lessees and lessors according to their economic substance—that is, according to the definitions of assets and liabilities. However, GAAP for leases is much more "rules-based," with specific bright-line criteria (such as the "90% of fair value" test) to determine if a lease arrangement transfers the risks and rewards of ownership. IFRS is more conceptual in its provisions. Rather than a 90% cut-off, it asks whether the agreement transfers substantially all of the risks and rewards associated with ownership.

- Under GAAP, some contingent liabilities are recorded in the financial statements, others are disclosed, and in some cases no disclosure is required. Unlike GAAP, IFRS reserves the use of the term **contingent liability** to refer only to possible obligations that are **not** recognized in the financial statements but may be disclosed if certain criteria are met. Contingent liabilities are defined in *IAS 37* as being:

    ♦ A possible obligation that arises from past events and whose existence will be confirmed only by the occurrence or non-occurrence of one or more uncertain future events not wholly within the control of the entity; or

    ♦ A present obligation that arises from past events but is not recognized because:

        ○ It is not probable that an outflow of resources embodying economic benefits will be required to settle the obligation; or

        ○ The amount of the obligation cannot be measured with sufficient reliability.

- For those items that GAAP would treat as recordable contingent liabilities, IFRS instead uses the term provisions. **Provisions** are defined as liabilities of uncertain timing or amount. Examples of provisions would be provisions for warranties, employee vacation pay, or anticipated losses. Under IFRS, the measurement of a provision related to an uncertain obligation is based on the best estimate of the expenditure required to settle the obligation.

LOOKING TO THE FUTURE

The FASB and IASB are currently involved in two projects, each of which has implications for the accounting for liabilities. One project is investigating approaches to differentiate between debt and equity instruments. The other project, the elements phase of the conceptual framework project, will evaluate the definitions of the fundamental building blocks of accounting. The results of these projects could change the classification of many debt and equity securities.

In addition to these projects, the FASB and IASB have also identified leasing as one of the most problematic areas of accounting. A joint project will initially focus primarily on lessee accounting. One of the first areas to be studied is, "What are the assets and liabilities to be recognized related to a lease contract?" Should the focus remain on the leased item or the right to use the leased item? This question is tied to the Boards' joint project on the conceptual framework—defining an "asset" and a "liability."

IFRS PRACTICE
IFRS SELF-TEST QUESTIONS

1. Which of the following is **false**?
   (a) Under IFRS, current liabilities must always be presented before non-current liabilities.
   (b) Under IFRS, an item is a current liability if it will be paid within the next 12 months.
   (c) Under IFRS, current liabilities are shown in order of liquidity.
   (d) Under IFRS, a liability is only recognized if it is a present obligation.

2. Under IFRS, a contingent liability is:
   (a) disclosed in the notes if certain criteria are met.
   (b) reported on the face of the financial statements if certain criteria are met.
   (c) the same as a provision.
   (d) not addressed by IFRS.

3. Stevens Corporation issued 5% convertible bonds with a total face value of $3,000,000 for $3,000,000. If the bonds had not had a conversion feature, they would have sold for $2,600,000. Under IFRS, the entry to record the transaction would require a credit to:
   (a) Bonds Payable for $3,000,000.
   (b) Bonds Payable for $400,000.
   (c) Equity Conversion Rights for $400,000.
   (d) Discount on Bonds Payable for $400,000.

4. Under IFRS, if preference shares (preferred stock) have a requirement to be redeemed at a specific point in time in the future, they are treated:
   (a) as a type of asset account.
   (b) as ordinary shares (common stock).
   (c) in the same fashion as other types of preference shares.
   (d) as a liability.

5. The joint projects of the FASB and IASB could potentially:
   (a) change the definition of liabilities.
   (b) change the definition of equity.
   (c) change the definition of assets.
   (d) All of the above.

IFRS CONCEPTS AND APPLICATION

IFRS10-1 Explain how IFRS defines a provision and give an example.

IFRS10-2 Explain how IFRS defines a contingent liability and give an example.

IFRS10-3 Briefly describe some of the similarities and differences between GAAP and IFRS with respect to the accounting for liabilities.

IFRS10-4 Ratzlaff Company issues €2 million, 10-year, 8% bonds at 97, with interest payable on July 1 and January 1.

Instructions
(a) Prepare the journal entry to record the sale of these bonds on January 1, 2014.
(b) Assuming instead that the above bonds sold for 104, prepare the journal entry to record the sale of these bonds on January 1, 2014.

IFRS10-5 Many multinational companies find it beneficial to have their shares listed on securities exchanges in foreign countries. In order to do this, they must comply with the securities laws of those countries. Some of these laws relate to the form of financial disclosure the company must provide, including disclosures related to contingent liabilities. This exercise investigates the Tokyo Stock Exchange, the largest securities exchange in Japan.

Address: **www.tse.or.jp/english/**, or go to **www.wiley.com/college/kimmel**

Steps

1. Choose **About TSE**.
2. Choose **History of TSE**. Answer questions (a) and (b).
3. Choose **Listed Company information**.
4. Choose **Disclosure**. Answer questions (c) and (d).
5. Answer the following questions.
   (a) When was the first securities exchange opened in Japan? How many exchanges does Japan have today?

    (b) What event caused trading to stop for a period of time in Japan?

    (c) What are four examples of decisions by corporations that must be disclosed at the time of their occurrence?

    (d) What are four examples of "occurrence of material fact" that must be disclosed at the time of their occurrence?

INTERNATIONAL FINANCIAL STATEMENT ANALYSIS: *Zetar plc*

IFRS10-6   The financial statements of Zetar plc are presented in Appendix C. The company's complete annual report, including the notes to its financial statements, is available in the Investors section at **www.zetarplc.com**.

Instructions
Use the company's annual report to answer the following questions.

    (a) According to the notes to the financial statements, what types of transactions do trade payables relate to? What was the average amount of time it took the company to pay its payables?

    (b) Note 4.2 discusses provisions that the company records for certain types of activities. What do the provisions relate to, what are the estimates based on, and what could cause those estimates to change in subsequent periods?

    (c) What was the average interest rate paid on bank loans and overdrafts?

Answers to IFRS Self-Test Questions
1. a 2. a 3. c 4. d 5. d

Facebook

REPORTING AND ANALYZING STOCKHOLDERS' EQUITY

Learning Objectives

After studying this chapter, you should be able to:

1. Identify and discuss the major characteristics of a corporation.
2. Record the issuance of common stock.
3. Explain the accounting for the purchase of treasury stock.
4. Differentiate preferred stock from common stock.
5. Prepare the entries for cash dividends and understand the effect of stock dividends and stock splits.
6. Identify the items that affect retained earnings.
7. Prepare a corporate stockholders' equity section.
8. Evaluate a corporation's dividend and earnings performance from a stockholder's perspective.

CHAPTER 11

Paul Sakuma/AP/Wide World Photos

REPORTING AND ANALYZING STOCKHOLDERS' EQUITY

LEARNING OBJECTIVES

After studying this chapter, you should be able to:

1 Identify and discuss the major characteristics of a corporation.

2 Record the issuance of common stock.

3 Explain the accounting for the purchase of treasury stock.

4 Differentiate preferred stock from common stock.

5 Prepare the entries for cash dividends and understand the effect of stock dividends and stock splits.

6 Identify the items that affect retained earnings.

7 Prepare a comprehensive stockholders' equity section.

8 Evaluate a corporation's dividend and earnings performance from a stockholder's perspective.

Suppose you started one of the fastest-growing companies in the history of business. Now suppose that by "going public"—issuing stock of your company to outside investors who are foaming at the mouth for the chance to buy its shares—you would instantly become one of the richest people in the world. Would you hesitate?

That is exactly what Mark Zuckerberg, the founder of Facebook, did. Many people who start high-tech companies go public as soon as possible to cash in on their riches. But Zuckerberg was reluctant to do so. To understand why, you need to understand the advantages and disadvantages of being a public company.

OH WELL, I GUESS I'LL GET RICH

The main motivation for issuing shares to the public is to raise money so you can grow your business. However, unlike a manufacturer or even an online retailer, Facebook doesn't need major physical resources, it doesn't have inventory, and it doesn't really need much money for marketing. So in the past, the company hasn't had much need for additional cash beyond what it was already generating on its own.

But why not go public anyway, so the company would have some extra cash on hand—and so you personally get rich? As head of a closely held, nonpublic company, Zuckerberg is subject to far fewer regulations than a public company.

Also, the chief executive officer (CEO) of a publicly traded company must respond to shareholder and board of director demands. Prior to going public, Zuckerberg could basically run the company however he wanted to.

For example, consider this recent, huge Facebook transaction. Early in 2012, the company shocked the investment community by purchasing the photo-sharing service Instagram. The purchase was startling both for its speed and price. After considering the purchase over the course of a weekend (while the rest of us were probably wasting time on our Facebook pages), Zuckerberg dropped $1 billion. He basically didn't seek anyone's approval. He thought it was a good idea, so he just did it. The structured decision-making process of a public company would make it very difficult for a public company to move that fast.

Speed is useful, but it is likely that Facebook will make even bigger acquisitions in the future. To survive among the likes of Microsoft, Google, and Apple, it needs lots of cash. To raise that amount of money, the company really needed to go public. So in 2012, Mark Zuckerberg reluctantly made Facebook a public company, thus becoming one of the richest people in the world.

INSIDE CHAPTER 11 . . .

- **The Impact of Corporate Social Responsibility**
- **How to Read Stock Quotes**
- **Up, Down, and ??**
- **A No-Split Philosophy**

Corporations like Facebook and Google have substantial resources at their disposal. In fact, the corporation is the dominant form of business organization in the United States in terms of sales, earnings, and number of employees. All of the 500 largest U.S. companies are corporations. In this chapter, we look at the essential features of a corporation and explain the accounting for a corporation's capital stock transactions.

The content and organization of the chapter are as follows.

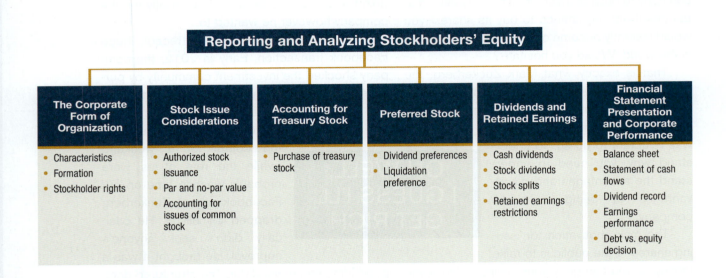

Reporting and Analyzing Stockholders' Equity

The Corporate Form of Organization	Stock Issue Considerations	Accounting for Treasury Stock	Preferred Stock	Dividends and Retained Earnings	Financial Statement Presentation and Corporate Performance
• Characteristics • Formation • Stockholder rights	• Authorized stock • Issuance • Par and no-par value • Accounting for issues of common stock	• Purchase of treasury stock	• Dividend preferences • Liquidation preference	• Cash dividends • Stock dividends • Stock splits • Retained earnings restrictions	• Balance sheet • Statement of cash flows • Dividend record • Earnings performance • Debt vs. equity decision

The Corporate Form of Organization

LEARNING OBJECTIVE 1

Identify and discuss the major characteristics of a corporation.

A corporation is created by law. As a legal entity, a **corporation** has most of the rights and privileges of a person. The major exceptions relate to privileges that can be exercised only by a living person, such as the right to vote or to hold public office. Similarly, a corporation is subject to the same duties and responsibilities as a person. For example, it must abide by the law and it must pay taxes.

We can classify corporations in a variety of ways. Two common classifications are **by purpose** and **by ownership**. A corporation may be organized for the purpose of making a profit (such as Facebook or General Motors), or it may be a nonprofit charitable, medical, or educational corporation (such as the Salvation Army or the American Cancer Society).

Classification by ownership differentiates publicly held and privately held corporations. A **publicly held corporation** may have thousands of stockholders, and its stock is traded on a national securities market such as the New York Stock Exchange. Examples are IBM, Caterpillar, and General Electric. In contrast, a **privately held corporation**, often referred to as a closely held corporation, usually has only a few stockholders and does not offer its stock for sale to the general public. Privately held companies are generally much smaller than publicly held companies although some notable exceptions exist. Before going public, Facebook was one example. Also, Cargill Inc., a private corporation that trades in grain and other commodities, is one of the largest companies in the United States. This chapter deals primarily with issues related to publicly held companies.

CHARACTERISTICS OF A CORPORATION

Many businesses start as partnerships or sole proprietorships but eventually convert to the corporate form. For example, Nike's founders formed their original organization as a partnership. In 1968, they reorganized the company as a corporation. A number of characteristics distinguish a corporation from sole proprietorships and partnerships. The most important of these characteristics are explained below.

Separate Legal Existence

As an entity separate and distinct from its owners, the corporation acts under its own name rather than in the name of its stockholders. Facebook, for example, buys, owns, and sells property, borrows money, and enters into legally binding contracts in its own name. It may also sue or be sued. It pays taxes as a separate entity.

Stockholders
Legal existence separate from owners

In a partnership, the acts of the owners (partners) bind the partnership. In contrast, the acts of corporate owners (stockholders) do not bind the corporation unless such owners are agents of the corporation. For example, if you own shares of Facebook stock, you do not have the right to purchase inventory for the company unless you are also designated as an agent of the corporation.

Limited Liability of Stockholders

Since a corporation is a separate legal entity, creditors ordinarily have recourse only to corporate assets to satisfy their claims. The liability of stockholders is normally limited to their investment in the corporation. Creditors have no legal claim on the personal assets of the stockholders unless fraud has occurred. Thus, even in the event of bankruptcy of the corporation, stockholders' losses are generally limited to the amount of capital they have invested in the corporation.

Stockholders
Limited liability of stockholders

Transferable Ownership Rights

Ownership of a corporation is held in shares of capital stock, which are transferable units. Stockholders may dispose of part or all of their interest in a corporation simply by selling their stock. The transfer of an ownership interest in a partnership requires the consent of each partner. In contrast, the transfer of stock is entirely at the discretion of the stockholder. It does not require the approval of either the corporation or other stockholders.

Transferable ownership rights

The transfer of ownership rights among stockholders normally has no effect on the operating activities of the corporation. Nor does it affect the corporation's assets, liabilities, and total stockholders' equity. The transfer of ownership rights is a transaction between individual owners. The company does not participate in the transfer of these ownership rights after the original sale of the capital stock.

Ability to Acquire Capital

It is relatively easy for a corporation to obtain capital through the issuance of stock. Buying stock in a corporation is often attractive to an investor because a stockholder has limited liability and shares of stock are readily transferable. Also, numerous individuals can become stockholders by investing small amounts of money.

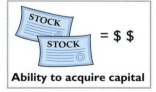

Ability to acquire capital

Continuous Life

The life of a corporation is stated in its charter. The life may be perpetual or it may be limited to a specific number of years. If it is limited, the company extends the period of existence through renewal of the charter. Since a corporation is a separate legal entity, its continuance as a going concern is not affected by the withdrawal, death, or incapacity of a stockholder, employee, or officer. As a result, a successful corporation can have a continuous and perpetual life.

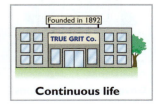

Continuous life

Corporation Management

Although stockholders legally own the corporation, they manage it indirectly through a board of directors they elect. Mark Zuckerberg is the chairman of Facebook's board of directors. The board, in turn, formulates the operating policies for the company. The board also selects officers, such as a president and one or more vice presidents, to execute policy and to perform daily management functions. As a result of the Sarbanes-Oxley Act, the board is required to monitor management's actions closely. Many feel that the failures at Enron, WorldCom, and more recently MF Global could have been avoided by more diligent boards.

Illustration 11-1 depicts a typical organization chart showing the delegation of responsibility.

Illustration 11-1 Corporation organization chart

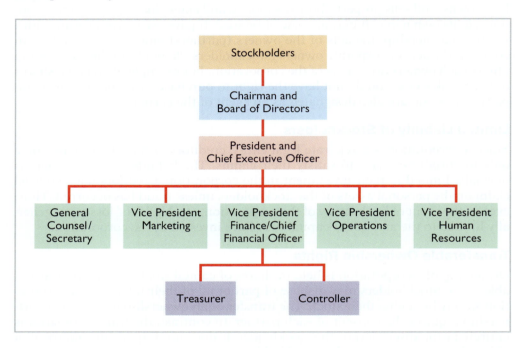

The chief executive officer (CEO) has overall responsibility for managing the business. As the organization chart shows, the CEO delegates responsibility to other officers. The chief accounting officer is the **controller**. The controller (1) maintains the accounting records, (2) maintains an adequate system of internal control, and (3) prepares financial statements, tax returns, and internal reports. The **treasurer** has custody of the corporation's funds and maintains the company's cash position.

The organizational structure of a corporation enables a company to hire professional managers to run the business. On the other hand, the separation of ownership and management often reduces an owner's ability to actively manage the company.

Government Regulations

A corporation is subject to numerous state and federal regulations. For example, state laws usually prescribe the requirements for issuing stock, the distributions of earnings permitted to stockholders, and acceptable methods for buying back and retiring stock. Federal securities laws govern the sale of capital stock to the general public. Also, publicly held corporations must disclose their financial affairs to the Securities and Exchange Commission (SEC) through quarterly and annual reports. The Sarbanes-Oxley Act increased the company's responsibility for the accuracy of these reports. In addition, when a corporate stock is listed and traded on organized securities exchanges, the corporation must comply with the reporting requirements of these exchanges.

People, Planet, and Profit Insight

The Impact of Corporate Social Responsibility

A recent survey conducted by Institutional Shareholder Services, a proxy advisory firm, shows that 83% of investors now believe environmental and social factors can significantly impact shareholder value over the long term. This belief is clearly visible in the rising level of support for shareholder proposals requesting action related to social and environmental issues.

The following table shows that the number of corporate social responsibility (CSR) related shareholder proposals rose from 150 in 2000 to 191 in 2010. Moreover, those proposals received average voting support of 18.4% of votes cast versus just 7.5% a decade earlier.

Trends in Shareholder Proposals on Corporate Responsibility

	2000	2005	2010
Number of proposals voted	150	155	191
Average voting support	7.5%	9.9%	18.4%
Percent proposals receiving >10% support	16.7%	31.2%	52.1%

Source: Investor Responsibility Research Center, Ernst & Young, *Seven Questions CEOs and Boards Should Ask About: "Triple Bottom Line" Reporting.*

? Why are CSR-related shareholder proposals increasing? (Answers in *Broadening Your Perspective.*)

Additional Taxes

Owners of proprietorships and partnerships report their share of earnings on their personal income tax returns. The individual owner then pays taxes on this amount. Corporations, on the other hand, must pay federal and state income taxes as a separate legal entity. These taxes can be substantial. They can amount to as much as 40% of taxable income.

In addition, stockholders are required to pay taxes on cash dividends. Thus, many argue that corporate income is **taxed twice (double taxation)**—once at the corporate level and again at the individual level.

Illustration 11-2 shows the advantages and disadvantages of a corporation compared to a sole proprietorship and partnership.

Additional taxes

Advantages	Disadvantages
• Separate legal existence • Limited liability of stockholders • Transferable ownership rights • Ability to acquire capital • Continuous life • Corporation management—professional managers	• Corporation management—separation of ownership and management • Government regulations • Additional taxes

Illustration 11-2 Advantages and disadvantages of a corporation

Other Forms of Business Organization

A variety of "hybrid" organizational forms—forms that combine different attributes of partnerships and corporations—now exist. For example, one type of corporate form, called an **S corporation**, allows for legal treatment as a corporation but tax treatment as a partnership—that is, no double taxation. Because of changes to the S corporation's rules, more small- and medium-sized businesses now may choose S corporation treatment. One of the primary criteria is that the company cannot have more than 75 shareholders. Other forms of organization include limited partnerships, limited liability partnerships (LLPs), and limited liability companies (LLCs).

DECISION TOOLKIT

DECISION CHECKPOINTS	INFO NEEDED FOR DECISION	TOOL TO USE FOR DECISION	HOW TO EVALUATE RESULTS
Should the company incorporate?	Capital needs, growth expectations, type of business, tax status	Corporations have limited liability, better capital-raising ability, and professional managers. But they suffer from additional taxes, government regulations, and separation of ownership from management.	Must carefully weigh the costs and benefits in light of the particular circumstances.

FORMING A CORPORATION

A corporation is formed by grant of a state charter. The charter is a document that describes the name and purpose of the corporation, the types and number of shares of stock that are authorized to be issued, the names of the individuals that formed the company, and the number of shares that these individuals agreed to purchase. Regardless of the number of states in which a corporation has operating divisions, it is incorporated in only one state. It is to the company's advantage to incorporate in a state whose laws are favorable to the corporate form of business organization. For example, although General Motors has its headquarters in Michigan, it is incorporated in New Jersey. In fact, more and more corporations have been incorporating in states with rules that favor existing management. For example, Gulf Oil changed its state of incorporation to Delaware to thwart possible unfriendly takeovers. There, certain defensive tactics against takeovers can be approved by the board of directors alone, without a vote by shareholders.

Upon receipt of its charter from the state of incorporation, the corporation establishes **by-laws**. The by-laws establish the internal rules and procedures for conducting the affairs of the corporation. Corporations engaged in interstate commerce must also obtain a **license** from each state in which they do business. The license subjects the corporation's operating activities to the general corporation laws of the state.

STOCKHOLDER RIGHTS

When chartered, the corporation begins selling shares of stock. When a corporation has only one class of stock, it is identified as **common stock**. Each share of common stock gives the stockholder the ownership rights pictured in Illustration 11-3. The articles of incorporation or the by-laws state the ownership rights of a share of stock.

Proof of stock ownership is evidenced by a printed or engraved form known as a **stock certificate**. As shown in Illustration 11-4, the face of the certificate shows the name of the corporation, the stockholder's name, the class and special features of the stock, the number of shares owned, and the signatures of authorized corporate officials. Certificates are prenumbered to ensure proper control over their use; they may be issued for any quantity of shares.

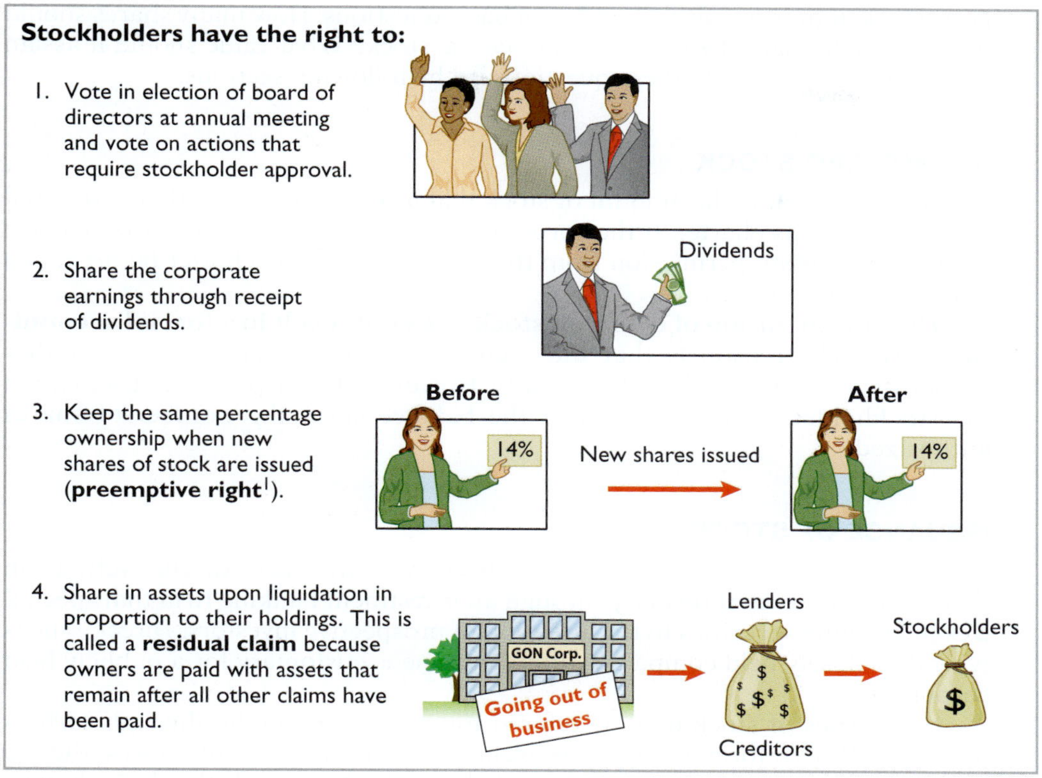

Stockholders have the right to:

1. Vote in election of board of directors at annual meeting and vote on actions that require stockholder approval.

2. Share the corporate earnings through receipt of dividends.

Dividends

3. Keep the same percentage ownership when new shares of stock are issued (**preemptive right**[1]).

Before
14%
New shares issued
After
14%

4. Share in assets upon liquidation in proportion to their holdings. This is called a **residual claim** because owners are paid with assets that remain after all other claims have been paid.

GON Corp.
Going out of business
Lenders
Stockholders
Creditors

Illustration 11-3
Ownership rights of stockholders

Illustration 11-4 A stock certificate

THE FRANKLIN LIFE INSURANCE COMPANY

9676   100

SPRINGFIELD, ILLINOIS
INCORPORATED UNDER THE LAWS OF THE STATE OF ILLINOIS

SEE REVERSE SIDE FOR CERTAIN DEFINITIONS

This Certifies that

Joann R. Rodriguez
188 So. Water Street
Galena, Illinois

is the owner of

ONE HUNDRED

FULL-PAID AND NON-ASSESSABLE SHARES OF THE PAR VALUE OF $2 EACH OF THE CAPITAL STOCK OF,
THE FRANKLIN LIFE INSURANCE COMPANY,

CORPORATE SEAL SPRINGFIELD, ILL.

Stock Issue Considerations

LEARNING OBJECTIVE 2
Record the issuance of common stock.

Although Facebook incorporated in 2004, it did not sell stock to the public until 2012. At that time, Facebook evidently decided it would benefit from the infusion of cash that a public sale of its shares would bring. When a corporation decides to

---

[1]A number of companies have eliminated the preemptive right because they believe it places an unnecessary and cumbersome demand on management. For example, IBM, by stockholder approval, has dropped its preemptive right for stockholders.

issue stock, it must resolve a number of basic questions: How many shares should it authorize for sale? How should it issue the stock? What value should it assign to the stock? We address these questions in the following sections.

AUTHORIZED STOCK

Authorized stock is the amount of stock that a corporation is authorized to sell as indicated in its charter. If the corporation has sold all of its authorized stock, then it must obtain permission from the state to change its charter before it can issue additional shares.

The authorization of common stock does not result in a formal accounting entry. The reason is that the event has no immediate effect on either corporate assets or stockholders' equity. However, the corporation discloses in the stockholders' equity section of the balance sheet the number of shares authorized.

ISSUANCE OF STOCK

A corporation can issue common stock **directly** to investors. Alternatively, it can issue common stock **indirectly** through an investment banking firm that specializes in bringing securities to the attention of prospective investors. Direct issue is typical in closely held companies. Indirect issue is customary for a publicly held corporation.

New issues of stock may be offered for sale to the public through various organized U.S. or foreign securities exchanges. Based on recent figures, the top five exchanges by value of shares traded are the New York Stock Exchange, Nasdaq stock market, London Stock Exchange, Tokyo Stock Exchange, and Euronext.

ANATOMY OF A FRAUD

The president, chief operating officer, and chief financial officer of SafeNet, a software encryption company, were each awarded employee stock options by the company's board of directors as part of their compensation package. Stock options enable an employee to buy a company's stock sometime in the future at the price that existed when the stock option was awarded. For example, suppose that you received stock options today, when the stock price of your company was $30. Three years later, if the stock price rose to $100, you could "exercise" your options and buy the stock for $30 per share, thereby making $70 per share. After being awarded their stock options, the three employees changed the award dates in the company's records to dates in the past, when the company's stock was trading at historical lows. For example, using the previous example, they would choose a past date when the stock was selling for $10 per share, rather than the $30 price on the actual award date. In our example, this would increase the profit from exercising the options to $90 per share.

Total take: $1.7 million

THE MISSING CONTROL

Independent internal verification. The company's board of directors should have ensured that the awards were properly administered. For example, the date on the minutes from the board meeting should be compared to the dates that were recorded for the awards. In addition, the dates should again be confirmed upon exercise.

PAR AND NO-PAR VALUE STOCKS

Par value stock is capital stock that has been assigned a value per share in the corporate charter. Years ago, par value determined the legal capital that must be retained in the business for the protection of corporate creditors. That amount is not available for withdrawal by stockholders. Thus, in the past, most states required the corporation to sell its shares at par or above.

However, the usefulness of par value as a device to protect creditors was limited because par value was often immaterial relative to the value of the company's stock in the securities markets—even at the time of issue. For example, Loews Corporation's par value is $0.01 per share, yet a new issue in a recent year would have sold at a **market price** in the $32 per share range. Thus, par has no relationship with market price. In the vast majority of cases, it is an immaterial amount. As a consequence, today many states do not require a par value. Instead, they use other means to protect creditors.

No-par value stock is capital stock that has not been assigned a value in the corporate charter. No-par value stock is fairly common today. For example, Nike and Procter & Gamble both have no-par stock. In many states, the board of directors assigns a stated value to the no-par shares.

ACCOUNTING FOR ISSUES OF COMMON STOCK

The stockholders' equity section of a corporation's balance sheet includes (1) **paid-in (contributed) capital** and (2) **retained earnings (earned capital)**. The distinction between paid-in capital and retained earnings is important from both a legal and an economic point of view. Paid-in capital is the amount stockholders paid to the corporation in exchange for shares of ownership. **Retained earnings** is earned capital held for future use in the business. In this section, we discuss the accounting for paid-in capital. In a later section, we discuss retained earnings.

Let's now look at how to account for new issues of common stock. The primary objectives in accounting for the issuance of common stock are (1) to identify the specific sources of paid-in capital and (2) to maintain the distinction between paid-in capital and retained earnings. As shown below, **the issuance of common stock affects only paid-in capital accounts**.

As discussed earlier, par value does not indicate a stock's market price. The cash proceeds from issuing par value stock may be equal to, greater than, or less than par value. When a company records the issuance of common stock for cash, it credits the par value of the shares to Common Stock and records in a separate paid-in capital account the portion of the proceeds that is above or below par value.

To illustrate, assume that Hydro-Slide, Inc. issues 1,000 shares of $1 par value common stock at par for cash. The entry to record this transaction is:

Cash	1,000	
Common Stock		1,000
(To record issuance of 1,000 shares of $1 par		
common stock at par)		

A = L + SE
+1,000
　　　　+1,000 CS

Cash Flows
+1,000

Now assume Hydro-Slide, Inc. issues an additional 1,000 shares of the $1 par value common stock for cash at $5 per share. The amount received above the par value, in this case $4 ($5 − $1), would be credited to Paid-in Capital in Excess of Par Value. The entry is:

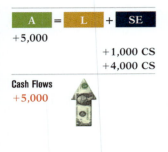

A	=	L	+	SE
+5,000				
				+1,000 CS
				+4,000 CS

Cash Flows
+5,000

Cash	5,000		
Common Stock (1,000 × $1)		1,000	
Paid-in Capital in Excess of Par Value		4,000	
(To record issuance of 1,000 shares of common			
stock in excess of par)			

The total paid-in capital from these two transactions is $6,000. If Hydro-Slide, Inc. has retained earnings of $27,000, the stockholders' equity section of the balance sheet is as shown in Illustration 11-5.

Illustration 11-5
Stockholders' equity—paid-in capital in excess of par value

HYDRO-SLIDE, INC.
Balance Sheet (partial)

Stockholders' equity	
Paid-in capital	
Common stock	$ 2,000
Paid-in capital in excess of par value	**4,000**
Total paid-in capital	6,000
Retained earnings	27,000
Total stockholders' equity	$33,000

Some companies issue no-par stock with a stated value. For accounting purposes, companies treat the stated value in the same way as the par value. For example, if in our Hydro-Slide example the stock was no-par stock with a stated value of $1, the entries would be the same as those presented for the par stock except the term "Par Value" would be replaced with "Stated Value." If a company issues no-par stock that does not have a stated value, then it credits to the Common Stock account the full amount received. In such a case, there is no need for the Paid-in Capital in Excess of Stated Value account.

Investor Insight

How to Read Stock Quotes

Organized exchanges trade the stock of publicly held companies at dollar prices per share established by the interaction between buyers and sellers. For each listed security, the financial press reports the high and low prices of the stock during the year, the total volume of stock traded on a given day, the high and low prices for the day, and the closing market price, with the net change for the day. Facebook is listed on the Nasdaq exchange. Here is a recent listing for Facebook:

	52 Weeks						
Stock	High	Low	Volume	High	Low	Close	Net Change
Facebook	45.00	25.52	30,129,088	32.08	29.41	30.01	−1.93

These numbers indicate the following. The high and low market prices for the last 52 weeks have been $45.00 and $25.52. The trading volume for the day was 30,129,088 shares. The high, low, and closing prices for that date were $32.08, $29.41, and $30.01, respectively. The net change for the day was a decrease of $1.93 per share.

? For stocks traded on organized exchanges, how are the dollar prices per share established? What factors might influence the price of shares in the marketplace? (Answers in *Broadening Your Perspective*.)

Accounting for Treasury Stock

Treasury stock is a corporation's own stock that has been reacquired by the corporation and is being held for future use. A corporation may acquire treasury stock for various reasons:

LEARNING OBJECTIVE 3
Explain the accounting for the purchase of treasury stock.

1. To reissue the shares to officers and employees under bonus and stock compensation plans.
2. To increase trading of the company's stock in the securities market. Companies expect that buying their own stock will signal that management believes the stock is underpriced, which they hope will enhance its market price.
3. To have additional shares available for use in acquiring other companies.
4. To reduce the number of shares outstanding and thereby increase earnings per share.

A less frequent reason for purchasing treasury shares is to eliminate hostile shareholders by buying them out.

Many corporations have treasury stock. For example, in the United States approximately 65% of companies have treasury stock.[2] In the first quarter of 2007, companies in the Standard & Poor's 500-stock index spent a record of about $118 billion to buy treasury stock. In a recent year, Nike purchased more than 6 million treasury shares. At one point, stock repurchases were so substantial that a study by two Federal Reserve economists suggested that a sharp reduction in corporate purchases of treasury shares might result in a sharp drop in the value of the U.S. stock market.

PURCHASE OF TREASURY STOCK

The purchase of treasury stock is generally accounted for by the **cost method**. This method derives its name from the fact that the Treasury Stock account is maintained at the cost of shares purchased. Under the cost method, **companies increase (debit) Treasury Stock by the price paid to reacquire the shares. Treasury Stock decreases by the same amount when the company later sells the shares**.

To illustrate, assume that on January 1, 2014, the stockholders' equity section for Mead, Inc. has 100,000 shares of $5 par value common stock outstanding (all issued at par value) and retained earnings of $200,000. Illustration 11-6 shows the stockholders' equity section of the balance sheet before purchase of treasury stock.

Illustration 11-6
Stockholders' equity with no treasury stock

MEAD, INC.
Balance Sheet (partial)

Stockholders' equity	
Paid-in capital	
Common stock, $5 par value, 400,000 shares authorized, 100,000 shares issued and outstanding	$500,000
Retained earnings	200,000
Total stockholders' equity	$700,000

[2]*Accounting Trends & Techniques—2011* (New York: American Institute of Certified Public Accountants).

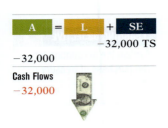

On February 1, 2014, Mead acquires 4,000 shares of its stock at $8 per share. The entry is:

Feb.	1	Treasury Stock	32,000	
		Cash		32,000
		(To record purchase of 4,000 shares of treasury stock at $8 per share)		

The Treasury Stock account would increase by the cost of the shares purchased ($32,000). The original paid-in capital account, Common Stock, would not be affected because **the number of issued shares does not change**.

Companies show treasury stock as a deduction from total paid-in capital and retained earnings in the stockholders' equity section of the balance sheet. Illustration 11-7 shows this presentation for Mead, Inc. Thus, the acquisition of treasury stock reduces stockholders' equity.

Illustration 11-7
Stockholders' equity with treasury stock

MEAD, INC.
Balance Sheet (partial)

Stockholders' equity	
Paid-in capital	
Common stock, $5 par value, 400,000 shares authorized,	
100,000 shares issued and 96,000 shares outstanding	$500,000
Retained earnings	200,000
Total paid-in capital and retained earnings	700,000
Less: Treasury stock (4,000 shares)	**32,000**
Total stockholders' equity	$668,000

Company balance sheets disclose both the number of shares issued (100,000) and the number in the treasury (4,000). The difference is the number of shares of stock outstanding (96,000). The term **outstanding stock** means the number of shares of issued stock that are being held by stockholders.

In a bold (and some would say risky) move, Reebok at one time bought back nearly a third of its shares. This repurchase of shares dramatically reduced Reebok's available cash. In fact, the company borrowed significant funds to accomplish the repurchase. In a press release, management stated that it was repurchasing the shares because it believed that the stock was severely underpriced. The repurchase of so many shares was meant to signal management's belief in good future earnings.

Skeptics, however, suggested that Reebok's management was repurchasing shares to make it less likely that the company would be acquired by another company (in which case Reebok's top managers would likely lose their jobs). Acquiring companies like to purchase companies with large cash reserves so they can pay off debt used in the acquisition. By depleting its cash, Reebok became a less likely acquisition target.

Preferred Stock

LEARNING OBJECTIVE 4
Differentiate preferred stock from common stock.

To appeal to a larger segment of potential investors, a corporation may issue an additional class of stock, called preferred stock. **Preferred stock** has contractual provisions that give it preference or priority over common stock in certain areas. Typically, preferred stockholders have a priority in relation to (1) dividends and (2) assets in the event of liquidation. However, they sometimes do not have voting rights. Facebook had 543 million preferred shares outstanding at the end of 2011, prior to going public. Approximately 6% of U.S. companies have one or more classes of preferred stock.[3]

Like common stock, companies issue preferred stock for cash or for noncash consideration. The entries for these transactions are similar to the entries for common stock. When a corporation has more than one class of stock, each paid-in capital account title should identify the stock to which it relates (e.g., Preferred Stock, Common Stock, Paid-in Capital in Excess of Par Value—Preferred Stock, and Paid-in Capital in Excess of Par Value—Common Stock).

Assume that Stine Corporation issues 10,000 shares of $10 par value preferred stock for $12 cash per share. The entry to record the issuance is:

Cash	120,000	
Preferred Stock		100,000
Paid-in Capital in Excess of Par Value—Preferred Stock		20,000
(To record the issuance of 10,000 shares of $10 par value preferred stock)		

A	=	L	+	SE
+120,000				
				+100,000 PS
				+20,000 PS

Cash Flows
+120,000

Preferred stock has either a par value or no-par value. In the stockholders' equity section of the balance sheet, companies show preferred stock first because of its dividend and liquidation preferences over common stock.

DIVIDEND PREFERENCES

As indicated above, **preferred stockholders have the right to share in the distribution of corporate income before common stockholders**. For example, if the dividend rate on preferred stock is $5 per share, common shareholders cannot receive any dividends in the current year until preferred stockholders have received $5 per share. The first claim to dividends does not, however, **guarantee** dividends. Dividends depend on many factors, such as adequate retained earnings and availability of cash.

For preferred stock, companies state the per share dividend amount as a percentage of the par value of the stock or as a specified amount. For example, EarthLink specifies a 3% dividend.

Cumulative Dividend

Preferred stock contracts often contain a **cumulative dividend** feature. This feature stipulates that preferred stockholders must be paid both current-year dividends and any unpaid prior-year dividends before common stockholders are paid dividends. When preferred stock is cumulative, preferred dividends not declared in a given period are called **dividends in arrears**.

To illustrate, assume that Scientific Leasing has 5,000 shares of 7%, $100 par value cumulative preferred stock outstanding. Each $100 share pays a $7 dividend (.07 × $100). The annual dividend is $35,000 (5,000 × $7 per share). If dividends are two years in arrears, preferred stockholders are entitled to receive in the current year the dividends as shown in Illustration 11-8.

Dividends in arrears ($35,000 × 2)	$ 70,000
Current-year dividends	35,000
Total preferred dividends	**$105,000**

Illustration 11-8 Computation of total dividends to preferred stock

[3]*Accounting Trends & Techniques—2011* (New York: American Institute of Certified Public Accountants).

No distribution can be made to common stockholders until Scientific Leasing pays this entire preferred dividend. In other words, companies cannot pay dividends to common stockholders while any preferred stock dividend is in arrears.

Dividends in arrears are not considered a liability. No obligation exists until the board of directors formally "declares" that the corporation will pay a dividend. However, companies should disclose in the notes to the financial statements the amount of dividends in arrears. Doing so enables investors to assess the potential impact of this obligation on the corporation's financial position.

The investment community does not look favorably upon companies that are unable to meet their dividend obligations. As a financial officer noted in discussing one company's failure to pay its cumulative preferred dividend for a period of time, "Not meeting your obligations on something like that is a major black mark on your record."

LIQUIDATION PREFERENCE

Most preferred stocks have a preference on corporate assets if the corporation fails. This feature provides security for the preferred stockholder. The preference to assets may be for the par value of the shares or for a specified liquidating value. For example, Commonwealth Edison issued preferred stock that entitled the holders to receive $31.80 per share, plus accrued and unpaid dividends, in the event of involuntary liquidation. The liquidation preference is used in litigation pertaining to bankruptcy lawsuits involving the respective claims of creditors and preferred stockholders.

Dividends

LEARNING OBJECTIVE 5

Prepare the entries for cash dividends and understand the effect of stock dividends and stock splits.

As noted earlier, a **dividend is a distribution by a corporation to its stockholders on a pro rata** (proportional to ownership) **basis**. Pro rata means that if you own, say, 10% of the common shares, you will receive 10% of the dividend. Dividends can take four forms: cash, property, scrip (promissory note to pay cash), or stock. Cash dividends, which predominate in practice, and stock dividends, which are declared with some frequency, are the focus of our discussion.

Investors are very interested in a company's dividend practices. In the financial press, **dividends are generally reported quarterly as a dollar amount per share**. (Sometimes they are reported on an annual basis.) For example, the **quarterly** dividend rate in the fourth quarter of 2011 was 36 cents per share for Nike, 15 cents per share for GE, and 24 cents per share for ConAgra Foods. Facebook does not pay dividends.

CASH DIVIDENDS

A **cash dividend** is a pro rata (proportional to ownership) distribution of cash to stockholders. Cash dividends are not paid on treasury shares. For a corporation to pay a cash dividend, it must have the following.

1. **Retained earnings.** Payment of dividends from retained earnings is legal in all states. In addition, loan agreements frequently constrain companies to pay dividends only from retained earnings. Many states prohibit payment of dividends from legal capital. However, payment of dividends from paid-in capital in excess of par value is legal in some states.

2. **Adequate cash.** Recently, Facebook had a balance in retained earnings of $1,606 million but a cash balance of only $1,512 million. If it had wanted to pay a dividend equal to its retained earnings, Facebook would have had to raise $94 million more in cash. It would have been unlikely to do this because it would not be able to pay this much in dividends in future years. In addition,

such a dividend would completely deplete Facebook's balance in retained earnings, so it would not be able to pay a dividend in the next year unless it had positive net income.

3. **Declared dividends.** The board of directors has full authority to determine the amount of income to distribute in the form of dividends. Dividends are not a liability until they are declared.

The amount and timing of a dividend are important issues for management to consider. The payment of a large cash dividend could lead to liquidity problems for the company. Conversely, a small dividend or a missed dividend may cause unhappiness among stockholders who expect to receive a reasonable cash payment from the company on a periodic basis. Many companies declare and pay cash dividends quarterly. On the other hand, a number of high-growth companies pay no dividends, preferring to conserve cash to finance future capital expenditures.

Investors monitor a company's dividend practices. For example, regular dividend boosts in the face of irregular earnings can be a warning signal. Companies with high dividends and rising debt may be borrowing money to pay shareholders. On the other hand, low dividends may not be a negative sign because it may mean the company is reinvesting in itself, which may result in high returns through increases in the stock price. Presumably, investors seeking regular dividends buy stock in companies that pay periodic dividends, and those seeking growth in the stock price (capital gains) buy stock in companies that retain their earnings rather than pay dividends.

Entries for Cash Dividends

Three dates are important in connection with dividends: (1) the declaration date, (2) the record date, and (3) the payment date. Companies make accounting entries on the declaration date and the payment date.

On the **declaration date**, the board of directors formally authorizes the cash dividend and announces it to stockholders. The declaration of a cash dividend **commits the corporation to a binding legal obligation**. Thus, the company must make an entry to recognize the increase in Cash Dividends and the increase in the liability Dividends Payable.

To illustrate, assume that on December 1, 2014, the directors of Media General declare a $0.50 per share cash dividend on 100,000 shares of $10 par value common stock. The dividend is $50,000 (100,000 × $0.50). The entry to record the declaration is:

Declaration Date

Dec. 1	Cash Dividends	50,000	
	Dividends Payable		50,000
	(To record declaration of cash dividend)		

A = L + SE
−50,000 Div
+50,000

Cash Flows
no effect

In Chapter 3, we used an account called Dividends to record a cash dividend. Here, we use the more specific title Cash Dividends to differentiate from other types of dividends, such as stock dividends. Dividends Payable is a current liability. It will normally be paid within the next several months.

At the **record date**, the company determines ownership of the outstanding shares for dividend purposes. The stockholders' records maintained by the corporation supply this information.

For Media General, the record date is December 22. No entry is required on the record date.

Record Date

Dec. 22 | No entry necessary

On the **payment date**, the company makes cash dividend payments to the stockholders on record as of December 22. It also records the payment of the dividend. If January 20 is the payment date for Media General, the entry on that date is:

−50,000

−50,000

Cash Flows
−50,000

Payment Date

Jan. 20	Dividends Payable		50,000	
	Cash			50,000
	(To record payment of cash dividend)			

Note that payment of the dividend on the payment date reduces both current assets and current liabilities, but it has no effect on stockholders' equity. The cumulative effect of the **declaration and payment** of a cash dividend on a company's financial statements is to **decrease both stockholders' equity and total assets**.

Accounting Across the Organization

Up, Down, and ??

The decision whether to pay a dividend, and how much to pay, is a very important management decision. As the chart below shows, from 2002 to 2007, many companies substantially increased their dividends, and total dividends paid by U.S. companies hit record levels. One reason for the increase is that Congress lowered, from 39% to 15%, the tax rate paid by investors on dividends received, making dividends more attractive to investors.

Then the financial crisis of 2008 occurred. As result, in 2009, 804 companies cut their dividends (see chart), the highest level since Standard & Poor's started collecting data in 1995. In 2010, more companies started to increase their dividends. However, potential higher taxes on dividends coming in the future and the possibility of a low-growth economy may stall any significant increase.

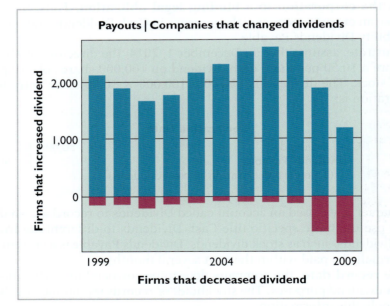

Source: Matt Phillips and Jay Miller, "Last Year's Dividend Slash Was $58 Billion," *Wall Street Journal* (January 8, 2010), p. C5.

? What factors must management consider in deciding how large a dividend to pay? (Answers in *Broadening Your Perspective*.)

STOCK DIVIDENDS

A **stock dividend** is a pro rata (proportional to ownership) distribution of the corporation's own stock to stockholders. Whereas a cash dividend is paid in cash, a stock dividend is paid in stock. **A stock dividend results in a decrease in retained earnings and an increase in paid-in capital.** Unlike a cash dividend, a stock dividend does not decrease total stockholders' equity or total assets.

Because a stock dividend does not result in a distribution of assets, some view it as nothing more than a publicity gesture. Stock dividends are often issued by companies that do not have adequate cash to issue a cash dividend. These companies may not want to announce that they are not going to be issuing a cash dividend at their normal time to do so. By issuing a stock dividend, they "save face" by giving the appearance of distributing a dividend. Note that since a stock dividend neither increases nor decreases the assets in the company, investors are not receiving anything they didn't already own. In a sense, it is like asking for two pieces of pie and having your host take one piece of pie and cut it into two smaller pieces. You are not better off, but you got your two pieces of pie.

To illustrate a stock dividend, assume that you have a 2% ownership interest in Cetus Inc.; you own 20 of its 1,000 shares of common stock. If Cetus declares a 10% stock dividend, it issues 100 shares (1,000 × 10%) of stock. You receive two shares (2% × 100), but your ownership interest remains at 2% (22 ÷ 1,100). **You now own more shares of stock, but your ownership interest has not changed.** Moreover, the company disburses no cash and assumes no liabilities.

What, then, are the purposes and benefits of a stock dividend? Corporations generally issue stock dividends for one of the following reasons.

1. To satisfy stockholders' dividend expectations without spending cash.
2. To increase the marketability of the stock by increasing the number of shares outstanding and thereby decreasing the market price per share. Decreasing the market price of the stock makes it easier for smaller investors to purchase the shares.
3. To emphasize that the company has permanently reinvested in the business a portion of stockholders' equity, which therefore is unavailable for cash dividends.

When the dividend is declared, the board of directors determines the size of the stock dividend and the value per share to use to record the transaction. In order to meet legal requirements, the per share amount must be at least equal to the par or stated value.

The accounting profession distinguishes between a **small stock dividend** (less than 20%–25% of the corporation's issued stock) and a **large stock dividend** (greater than 20%–25%). It recommends that the company use the **fair value per share** to record small stock dividends. The recommendation is based on the assumption that a small stock dividend will have little effect on the market price of the shares previously outstanding. Thus, many stockholders consider small stock dividends to be distributions of earnings equal to the fair value of the shares distributed. The accounting profession does not specify the value to use to record a large stock dividend. However, companies normally use **par or stated value per share**. Small stock dividends predominate in practice. In Appendix 11A at the end of the chapter, we illustrate the journal entries for small stock dividends.

Effects of Stock Dividends

How do stock dividends affect stockholders' equity? They **change the composition of stockholders' equity** because they result in a transfer of a portion of retained earnings to paid-in capital. However, **total stockholders' equity remains the same**. Stock dividends also have no effect on the par or stated value per share, but the number of shares outstanding increases.

Illustration 11-9 shows the effects that result when Medland Corp. declares a 10% stock dividend on its $10 par common stock when 50,000 shares were outstanding. The market price was $15 per share.

Illustration 11-9 Stock dividend effects

	Before Dividend	Change	After Dividend
Stockholders' equity			
Paid-in capital			
Common stock, $10 par	$ 500,000	$ 50,000	$ 550,000
Paid-in capital in excess of par value	—	25,000	25,000
Total paid-in capital	500,000	+75,000	**575,000**
Retained earnings	300,000	−75,000	**225,000**
Total stockholders' equity	**$800,000**	$ 0	**$800,000**
Outstanding shares	**50,000**	+ 5,000	**55,000**

In this example, total paid-in capital increased by $75,000 (50,000 shares × 10% × $15), and retained earnings decreased by the same amount. Note also that total stockholders' equity remains unchanged at $800,000. The number of shares increases by 5,000 (50,000 × 10%).

STOCK SPLITS

A **stock split**, like a stock dividend, involves the issuance of additional shares of stock to stockholders according to their percentage ownership. However, **a stock split results in a reduction in the par or stated value per share**. The purpose of a stock split is to increase the marketability of the stock by lowering its market price per share. This, in turn, makes it easier for the corporation to issue additional stock. After hitting a peak of 114 stock splits in 1986, the number of splits in the United States has fallen to about 30 per year. Google announced a 2-for-1 split in 2012 when its stock was selling for $650 per share.

Like a stock dividend, a stock split increases the number of shares owned by a shareholder, but it does not change the percentage of the total company that the shareholder owns. The effects of a 3-for-1 split are shown in Illustration 11-10.

Illustration 11-10 Effect of stock dividend or stock split for stockholders

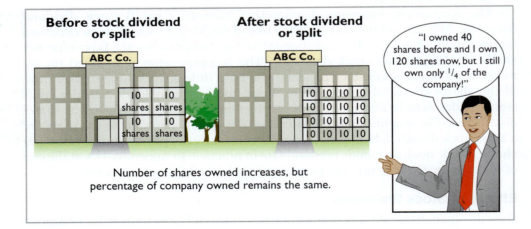

Number of shares owned increases, but percentage of company owned remains the same.

The effect of a split on market price is generally **inversely proportional** to the size of the split. For example, after a recent 2-for-1 stock split, the market price of Nike's stock fell from $111 to approximately $55.

Investor Insight
A No-Split Philosophy

Warren Buffett's company, Berkshire Hathaway, has two classes of shares. Until recently, the company had never split either class of stock. As a result, the class A stock had a market price of $97,000 and the class B sold for about $3,200 per share. Because the price per share is so high, the stock does not trade as frequently as the stock of other companies. Buffett has always opposed stock splits because he feels that a lower stock price attracts short-term investors. He appears to be correct. For example, while more than 6 million shares of IBM are exchanged on the average day, only about 1,000 class A shares of Berkshire are traded. Despite Buffett's aversion to splits, in order to accomplish a recent acquisition, Berkshire decided to split its class B shares 50 to 1.

Source: Scott Patterson, "Berkshire Nears Smaller Baby B's," *Wall Street Journal Online* (January 19, 2010).

? Why does Warren Buffett usually oppose stock splits? (Answers in *Broadening Your Perspective.*)

In a stock split, the company increases the number of shares in the same proportion that it decreases the par or stated value per share. For example, in a 2-for-1 split, the company exchanges one share of $10 par value stock for two shares of $5 par value stock. **A stock split does not have any effect on paid-in capital, retained earnings, and total stockholders' equity.** However, the number of shares outstanding increases. The effects of a 2-for-1 stock split of Medland Corporation's common stock are shown in Illustration 11-11.

	Before Stock Split	Change	After Stock Split
Stockholders' equity			
Paid-in capital			
Common stock			
(before: 50,000 $10 par shares; after: 100,000 $5 par shares)	$ 500,000		$ 500,000
Paid-in capital in excess of par value	0		0
Total paid-in capital	500,000	$ 0	500,000
Retained earnings	300,000	0	300,000
Total stockholders' equity	**$800,000**	$ 0	**$800,000**
Outstanding shares	**50,000**	**+ 50,000**	**100,000**

Illustration 11-11
Stock split effects

Because a stock split does not affect the balances in any stockholders' equity accounts, a company **does not need to journalize a stock split**. However, a memorandum entry explaining the effect of the split is typically made.

The differences between the effects of stock dividends and stock splits are shown in Illustration 11-12.

Item	Stock Dividend	Stock Split
Total paid-in capital	Increase	No change
Total retained earnings	Decrease	No change
Total par value (common stock)	Increase	No change
Par value per share	No change	Decrease
Shares outstanding	Increase	Increase

Illustration 11-12 Effects of stock splits and stock dividends differentiated

Retained Earnings

LEARNING OBJECTIVE 6
Identify the items that affect retained earnings.

Retained earnings is net income that a company retains in the business. The balance in retained earnings is part of the stockholders' claim on the total assets of the corporation. It does not, however, represent a claim on any specific asset. Nor can the amount of retained earnings be associated with the balance of any asset account. For example, a $100,000 balance in retained earnings does not mean that there should be $100,000 in cash. The reason is that the company may have used the cash resulting from the excess of revenues over expenses to purchase buildings, equipment, and other assets. Illustration 11-13 shows recent amounts of retained earnings and cash in selected companies.

Illustration 11-13 Retained earnings and cash balances

Company	Retained Earnings (in millions)	Cash (in millions)
Facebook	$ 1,606	$ 1,512
Google	20,082	10,198
Nike, Inc.	4,885	1,855
Starbucks Coffee Company	2,189	281
Amazon.com	(1,375)	2,539

When expenses exceed revenues, a **net loss** results. In contrast to net income, a net loss decreases retained earnings. In closing entries, a company debits a net loss to the Retained Earnings account. **It does not debit net losses to paid-in capital accounts.** To do so would destroy the distinction between paid-in and earned capital. If cumulative losses and dividends exceed cumulative income over a company's life, a debit balance in Retained Earnings results. A debit balance in Retained Earnings, such as that of Amazon.com in a recent year, is a **deficit**. A company reports a deficit as a deduction in the stockholders' equity section of the balance sheet, as shown in Illustration 11-14.

Illustration 11-14 Stockholders' equity with deficit

Real World

AMAZON.COM
Balance Sheet (partial)
(in millions)

Stockholders' equity	
Paid-in capital	
Common stock	$ 4
Paid-in capital in excess of par value	3,068
Total paid-in capital	3,072
Accumulated deficit	**(1,375)**
Total paid-in capital and retained earnings	1,697
Less: Treasury stock	500
Total stockholders' equity	$1,197

RETAINED EARNINGS RESTRICTIONS

The balance in retained earnings is generally available for dividend declarations. Some companies state this fact. In some circumstances, however, there may be **retained earnings restrictions**. These make a portion of the balance currently unavailable for dividends. Restrictions result from one or more of these causes: legal, contractual, or voluntary.

Companies generally disclose retained earnings restrictions in the notes to the financial statements. For example, Tektronix Inc., a manufacturer of electronic measurement devices, recently had total retained earnings of $774 million, but the unrestricted portion was only $223.8 million.

	TEKTRONIX INC.	
Real World	Notes to the Financial Statements	

Certain of the Company's debt agreements require compliance with debt covenants. The Company had unrestricted retained earnings of $223.8 million after meeting those requirements.

Illustration 11-15
Disclosure of unrestricted retained earnings

Financial Statement Presentation of Stockholders' Equity

BALANCE SHEET PRESENTATION

In the stockholders' equity section of the balance sheet, companies report paid-in capital and retained earnings and identify the specific sources of paid-in capital. Within paid-in capital, two classifications are recognized:

LEARNING OBJECTIVE 7
Prepare a comprehensive stockholders' equity section.

1. **Capital stock**, which consists of preferred and common stock. Companies show preferred stock before common stock because of its preferential rights. They report information about the par value, shares authorized, shares issued, and shares outstanding for each class of stock.

2. **Additional paid-in capital**, which includes the excess of amounts paid in over par or stated value.

Illustration 11-16 presents the stockholders' equity section of the balance sheet of Graber Inc. The company discloses a retained earnings restriction in the notes.

Illustration 11-16
Comprehensive stockholders' equity section

GRABER INC.
Balance Sheet (partial)

Stockholders' equity		
Paid-in capital		
Capital stock		
9% preferred stock, $100 par value, cumulative,		
10,000 shares authorized, 6,000 shares issued		
and outstanding		$ 600,000
Common stock, no par, $5 stated value,		
500,000 shares authorized, 400,000 shares		
issued, and 390,000 outstanding		2,000,000
Total capital stock		2,600,000
Additional paid-in capital		
Paid-in capital in excess of par value—preferred stock	$ 30,000	
Paid-in capital in excess of stated value—common stock	1,050,000	
Total additional paid-in capital		1,080,000
Total paid-in capital		3,680,000
Retained earnings (see Note R)		1,160,000
Total paid-in capital and retained earnings		4,840,000
Less: Treasury stock (10,000 common shares)		80,000
Total stockholders' equity		$4,760,000

Note R: Retained earnings is restricted for the cost of treasury stock, $80,000.

The stockholders' equity section for Graber Inc. includes most of the accounts discussed in this chapter. The disclosures pertaining to Graber's common stock indicate that 400,000 shares are issued; 100,000 shares are unissued (500,000 authorized less 400,000 issued); and 390,000 shares are outstanding (400,000 issued less 10,000 shares in treasury).

In published annual reports, companies seldom present subclassifications within the stockholders' equity section. Moreover, they often combine and report as a single amount the individual sources of additional paid-in capital. Notes often provide additional detail. Illustration 11-17 is an excerpt from Procter & Gamble Company's balance sheet in a recent year.

Illustration 11-17
Stockholders' equity section

Real World	**PROCTER & GAMBLE COMPANY**
	Balance Sheet (partial)
	(in millions)

Shareholders' equity	
Convertible Class A preferred stock, stated value	
$1 per share (600 shares authorized)	$ 1,406
Non-voting Class B preferred stock, stated value	
$1 per share (200 shares authorized)	—
Common stock, stated value $1 per share	
(10,000 shares authorized; issued: 3,989.7)	3,990
Additional paid-in capital	59,030
Total paid-in capital	64,426
Reserve for ESOP debt retirement	(1,308)
Retained earnings	41,797
Total paid-in capital and retained earnings	104,915
Accumulated other comprehensive income	617
Less: Treasury stock, at cost (shares held: 857.8)	38,772
Total shareholders' equity	$ 66,760

KEEPING AN EYE ON CASH

The balance sheet presents the balances of a company's stockholders' equity accounts at a point in time. Companies report in the "Financing Activities" section of the statement of cash flows information regarding cash inflows and outflows during the year that resulted from equity transactions. The excerpt below presents the cash flows from financing activities from the statement of cash flows of Sara Lee Corporation in a recent year. From this information, we learn that the company's purchases of treasury stock during the period far exceeded its issuances of new common stock, and its financing activities resulted in a net reduction in its cash balance.

Real World	**SARA LEE CORPORATION**
	Statement of Cash Flows (partial)
	(in millions)

Cash flows from financing activities	
Issuances of common stock	$ 38
Purchases of common stock	(686)
Payments of dividends	(374)
Borrowings of long-term debt	2,895
Repayments of long-term debt	(416)
Short-term (repayments) borrowings, net	(1,720)
Net cash used in financing activities	$ (263)

Measuring Corporate Performance

Investors are interested in both a company's dividend record and its earnings performance. Although those two measures are often parallel, that is not always the case. Thus, investors should investigate each one separately.

DIVIDEND RECORD

One way that companies reward stock investors for their investment is to pay them dividends. The **payout ratio** measures the percentage of earnings a company distributes in the form of cash dividends to common stockholders. It is computed by **dividing total cash dividends declared to common shareholders by net income**. Using the information shown below, the payout ratio for Nike in 2011 and 2010 is calculated in Illustration 11-18.

	2011	2010
Dividends (in millions)	$ 569	$ 515
Net income (in millions)	2,133	1,907

$$\text{Payout Ratio} = \frac{\text{Cash Dividends Declared on Common Stock}}{\text{Net Income}}$$

($ in millions)	2011	2010
Payout Ratio	$\frac{\$569}{\$2,133} = 26.7\%$	$\frac{\$515}{\$1,907} = 27.0\%$

Illustration 11-18 Nike's payout ratio

Nike's payout ratio was relatively constant at approximately 27%. Companies attempt to set their dividend rate at a level that will be sustainable.

Companies that have high growth rates are characterized by low payout ratios because they reinvest most of their net income in the business. Thus, a low payout ratio is not necessarily bad news. Companies that believe they have many good opportunities for growth, such as Facebook, will reinvest those funds in the company rather than pay dividends. However, low dividend payments, or a cut in dividend payments, might signal that a company has liquidity or solvency problems and is trying to conserve cash by not paying dividends. Thus, investors and analysts should investigate the reason for low dividend payments.

Illustration 11-19 lists recent payout ratios of four well-known companies.

Company	Payout Ratio
Microsoft	24.5%
Kellogg	43.3%
Facebook	0%
Wal-Mart	49.0%

Illustration 11-19 Payout ratios of companies

🧰 DECISION TOOLKIT

DECISION CHECKPOINTS	INFO NEEDED FOR DECISION	TOOL TO USE FOR DECISION	HOW TO EVALUATE RESULTS
What portion of its earnings does the company pay out in dividends?	Net income and total cash dividends on common stock	$\text{Payout ratio} = \frac{\text{Cash dividends declared on common stock}}{\text{Net income}}$	A low ratio may suggest that the company is retaining its earnings for investment in future growth.

EARNINGS PERFORMANCE

Another way to measure corporate performance is through profitability. A widely used ratio that measures profitability from the common stockholders' viewpoint is **return on common stockholders' equity (ROE)**. This ratio shows how many dollars of net income a company earned for each dollar of common stockholders' equity. It is computed by dividing net income available to common stockholders (Net income − Preferred dividends) by average common stockholders' equity. Common stockholders' equity is equal to total stockholders' equity minus any equity from preferred stock.

Using the information on the previous page and the additional information presented below, Illustration 11-20 shows Nike's return on common stockholders' equity.

(in millions)	2011	2010
Preferred dividends	$ −0−	$ −0−
Common stockholders' equity	9,843	9,754

$$\text{Return on Common Stockholders' Equity} = \frac{\text{Net Income} - \text{Preferred Dividends}}{\text{Average Common Stockholders' Equity}}$$			

($ in millions)	2011	2010
Return on Common Stockholders' Equity	$\dfrac{\$2{,}133 - \$0}{(\$9{,}843 + \$9{,}754)/2} = 21.8\%$	$\dfrac{\$1{,}907 - \$0}{(\$9{,}754 + \$8{,}693.1)/2} = 20.7\%$

Illustration 11-20 Nike's return on common stockholders' equity

From 2010 to 2011, Nike's return on common shareholders' equity increased. As a company grows larger, it becomes increasingly hard to sustain a high return. In Nike's case, since many believe the U.S. market for expensive sports shoes is saturated, it will need to grow either along new product lines, such as hiking shoes and golf equipment, or in new markets, such as Europe and Asia.

DEBT VERSUS EQUITY DECISION

When obtaining long-term capital, corporate managers must decide whether to issue bonds or to sell common stock. Bonds have three primary advantages relative to common stock, as shown in Illustration 11-21.

Illustration 11-21 Advantages of bond financing over common stock

Bond Financing	Advantages
	1. **Stockholder control is not affected.** Bondholders do not have voting rights, so current owners (stockholders) retain full control of the company.
	2. **Tax savings result.** Bond interest is deductible for tax purposes; dividends on stock are not.
	3. **Return on common stockholders' equity may be higher.** Although bond interest expense reduces net income, return on common stockholders' equity often is higher under bond financing because no additional shares of common stock are issued.

How does the debt versus equity decision affect the return on common stockholders' equity? Illustration 11-22 shows that the return on common stockholders' equity is affected by the return on assets and the amount of leverage a company uses—that is, by the company's reliance on debt (often measured by the debt to assets ratio). **If a company wants to increase its return on common stockholders' equity, it can either increase its return on assets or increase its reliance on debt financing.**

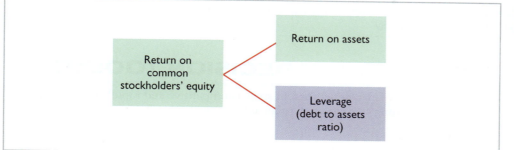

Illustration 11-22
Components of the return on common stockholders' equity

To illustrate the potential effect of debt financing on the return on common stockholders' equity, assume that Microsystems Inc. currently has 100,000 shares of common stock outstanding issued at $25 per share and no debt. It is considering two alternatives for raising an additional $5 million. Plan A involves issuing 200,000 shares of common stock at the current market price of $25 per share. Plan B involves issuing $5 million of 12% bonds at face value. Income before interest and taxes will be $1.5 million; income taxes are expected to be 30%. The alternative effects on the return on common stockholders' equity are shown in Illustration 11-23.

Illustration 11-23 Effects on return on common stockholders' equity of issuing debt

	Plan A: Issue stock	Plan B: Issue bonds
Income before interest and taxes	$1,500,000	$1,500,000
Interest (12% × $5,000,000)	—	600,000
Income before income taxes	1,500,000	900,000
Income tax expense (30%)	450,000	270,000
Net income	$1,050,000	$ 630,000
Common stockholders' equity	$7,500,000	$2,500,000
Return on common stockholders' equity	14%	25.2%

Note that with long-term debt financing (bonds), net income is $420,000 ($1,050,000 − $630,000) less. However, the return on common stockholders' equity increases from 14% to 25.2% with the use of debt financing because net income is spread over a smaller amount of common stockholders' equity. **In general, as long as the return on assets rate exceeds the rate paid on debt, a company will increase the return on common stockholders' equity by the use of debt.**

After seeing this illustration, you might ask, why don't companies rely almost exclusively on debt financing rather than equity? Debt has one major disadvantage: **Debt reduces solvency. The company locks in fixed payments that it must make in good times and bad. The company must pay interest on a periodic basis and must pay the principal (face value) of the bonds at maturity.** A company with fluctuating earnings and a relatively weak cash position may experience great difficulty in meeting interest requirements in periods of low earnings. In the extreme, this can result in bankruptcy. With common stock financing, on the other hand, the company can decide to pay low (or no) dividends if earnings are low.

DECISION TOOLKIT

DECISION CHECKPOINTS	INFO NEEDED FOR DECISION	TOOL TO USE FOR DECISION	HOW TO EVALUATE RESULTS
What is the company's return on common stockholders' investment?	Earnings available to common stockholders and average common stockholders' equity	Return on common stockholders' equity $= \dfrac{\text{Net income} - \text{Preferred dividends}}{\text{Average common stockholders' equity}}$	A high measure suggests strong earnings performance from common stockholders' perspective.

USING THE DECISION TOOLKIT

adidas is one of Nike's competitors. In such a competitive and rapidly changing environment, one wrong step can spell financial disaster.

Instructions

The following facts are available from adidas's annual report. As a German company, adidas reports under International Financial Reporting Standards (IFRS). Using this information, evaluate its (1) dividend record and (2) earnings performance, and contrast them with those for Nike for 2011 and 2010. Nike's earnings per share were $4.48 in 2011 and $3.93 in 2010.

(in millions)*	2010	2009	2008
Dividends declared	€73	€97	€99
Net income	€567	€245	€642
Preferred dividends	0	0	0
Shares outstanding at end of year	209	209	194
Common stockholders' equity	€4,616	€3,771	€3,386

*Nike has a year-end of May 31, 2011. For comparative purposes, we used adidas's December 31, 2010, data since that represents the closest year-end.

Solution

1. **Dividend record:** A measure to evaluate dividend record is the payout ratio. For adidas, this measure in 2010 and 2009 is calculated as shown below.

	2010	2009
Payout ratio	$\dfrac{€73}{€567} = 12.9\%$	$\dfrac{€97}{€245} = 39.6\%$

   Nike's payout ratio was 26.7%. adidas' payout ratio dramatically decreased from 2009 to 2010 and was significantly less than Nike's ratio in 2010.

2. **Earnings performance:** There are many measures of earnings performance. Some of those presented thus far in the textbook were earnings per share (chapter 2) and the return on common stockholders' equity (this chapter). These measures for adidas in 2010 and 2009 are calculated as shown here.

	2010	2009
Earnings per share	$\dfrac{€567 - 0}{(209 + 209)/2} = €2.71$	$\dfrac{€245 - 0}{(209 + 194)/2} = €1.22$
Return on common stockholders' equity	$\dfrac{€567 - 0}{(€4,616 + €3,771)/2} = 13.5\%$	$\dfrac{€245 - 0}{(€3,771 + €3,386)/2} = 6.8\%$

   From 2009 to 2010, adidas's net income improved 130% and its earnings per share increased 122%. Earnings per share should not be compared across companies because the number of shares varies considerably. Thus, we should not compare adidas's earnings per share with Nike's. adidas's return on common stockholders' equity increased from 6.8% to 13.5%.

Summary of Learning Objectives

1 Identify and discuss the major characteristics of a corporation. The major characteristics of a corporation are separate legal existence, limited liability of stockholders, transferable ownership rights, ability to acquire capital, continuous life, corporation management, government regulations, and additional taxes.

2 Record the issuance of common stock. When a company records issuance of common stock for cash, it credits the par value of the shares to Common Stock. It records in a separate paid-in capital account the portion of the proceeds that is above par value. When no-par common stock has a stated value, the entries are similar to those for par value stock. When no-par common stock does not have a stated value, the entire proceeds from the issue are credited to Common Stock.

3 Explain the accounting for the purchase of treasury stock. Companies generally use the cost method in accounting for treasury stock. Under this approach, a company debits Treasury Stock at the price paid to reacquire the shares.

4 Differentiate preferred stock from common stock. Preferred stock has contractual provisions that give it priority over common stock in certain areas. Typically, preferred stockholders have a preference as to (1) dividends and (2) assets in the event of liquidation. However, they sometimes do not have voting rights.

5 Prepare the entries for cash dividends and understand the effect of stock dividends and stock splits. Companies make entries for dividends at the declaration date and the payment date. At the declaration date, the entries for a cash dividend are debit Cash Dividends and credit Dividends Payable. The effects of stock dividends and splits are as follows. Small stock dividends transfer an amount equal to the fair value of the shares issued from retained earnings to the paid-in capital accounts. Stock splits reduce the par value per share of the common stock while increasing the number of shares so that the balance in the Common Stock account remains the same.

6 Identify the items that affect retained earnings. Additions to retained earnings consist of net income. Deductions consist of net loss and cash and stock dividends. In some instances, portions of retained earnings are restricted, making that portion unavailable for the payment of dividends.

7 Prepare a comprehensive stockholders' equity section. In the stockholders' equity section of the balance sheet, companies report paid-in capital and retained earnings and identify specific sources of paid-in capital. Within paid-in capital, companies show two classifications: capital stock and additional paid-in capital. If a corporation has treasury stock, it deducts the cost of treasury stock from total paid-in capital and retained earnings to determine total stockholders' equity.

8 Evaluate a corporation's dividend and earnings performance from a stockholder's perspective. A company's dividend record can be evaluated by looking at what percentage of net income it chooses to pay out in dividends, as measured by the dividend payout ratio (dividends divided by net income). Earnings performance is measured with the return on common stockholders' equity (income available to common stockholders divided by average common stockholders' equity).

🧰 DECISION TOOLKIT *A SUMMARY*

DECISION CHECKPOINTS	INFO NEEDED FOR DECISION	TOOL TO USE FOR DECISION	HOW TO EVALUATE RESULTS
Should the company incorporate?	Capital needs, growth expectations, type of business, tax status	Corporations have limited liability, better capital-raising ability, and professional managers. But they suffer from additional taxes, government regulations, and separation of ownership from management.	Must carefully weigh the costs and benefits in light of the particular circumstances.
What portion of its earnings does the company pay out in dividends?	Net income and total cash dividends on common stock	$$\text{Payout ratio} = \frac{\text{Cash dividends declared on common stock}}{\text{Net income}}$$	A low ratio may suggest that the company is retaining its earnings for investment in future growth.
What is the company's return on common stockholders' investment?	Earnings available to common stockholders and average common stockholders' equity	$$\text{Return on common stockholders' equity} = \frac{\text{Net income} - \text{Preferred dividends}}{\text{Average common stockholders' equity}}$$	A high measure suggests strong earnings performance from common stockholders' perspective.

Appendix 11A

Entries for Stock Dividends

To illustrate the accounting for stock dividends, assume that Medland Corporation has a balance of $300,000 in retained earnings and declares a 10% stock dividend on its 50,000 shares of $10 par value common stock. The current fair value of its stock is $15 per share. The number of shares to be issued is 5,000 (10% × 50,000), and the total amount to be debited to Retained Earnings is $75,000 (5,000 × $15). The entry to record this transaction at the declaration date is:

LEARNING OBJECTIVE 9
Prepare entries for stock dividends.

Stock Dividends	75,000	
Common Stock Dividends Distributable		50,000
Paid-in Capital in Excess of Par Value		25,000
(To record declaration of 10% stock dividend)		

A = L + SE
−75,000 Div
+50,000 CS
+25,000 CS

Cash Flows
no effect

At the declaration date, Medland increases (debits) Stock Dividends for the fair value of the stock issued, increases (credits) Common Stock Dividends Distributable for the par value of the dividend shares (5,000 × $10), and increases (credits) the excess over par (5,000 × $5) to an additional paid-in capital account.

Common Stock Dividends Distributable is a stockholders' equity account. It is not a liability because assets will not be used to pay the dividend. If Medland prepares a balance sheet before it issues the dividend shares, it reports the distributable account in paid-in capital as an addition to common stock issued, as shown in Illustration 11A-1.

MEDLAND CORPORATION
Balance Sheet (partial)

Paid-in capital		
Common stock	$500,000	
Common stock dividends distributable	**50,000**	**$550,000**

Illustration 11A-1 Statement presentation of common stock dividends distributable

When Medland issues the dividend shares, it decreases Common Stock Dividends Distributable and increases Common Stock as follows.

Common Stock Dividends Distributable	50,000	
Common Stock		50,000
(To record issuance of 5,000 shares in a stock dividend)		

A = L + SE
−50,000 CS
+50,000 CS

Cash Flows
no effect

Summary of Learning Objective for Appendix 11A

9 Prepare entries for stock dividends. To record the declaration of a small stock dividend (less than 20%), debit Stock Dividends for an amount equal to the fair value of the shares issued. Record a credit to a temporary stockholders' equity account—Common Stock Dividends Distributable—for the par value of the shares, and credit the balance to Paid-in Capital in Excess of Par Value. When the shares are issued, debit Common Stock Dividends Distributable and credit Common Stock.

Glossary

Terms are highlighted in **blue** throughout the chapter.

Authorized stock The amount of stock that a corporation is authorized to sell as indicated in its charter.

Cash dividend A pro rata (proportional to ownership) distribution of cash to stockholders.

Charter A document that describes a corporation's name and purpose, types of stock and number of shares authorized, names of individuals involved in the formation, and number of shares each individual has agreed to purchase.

Corporation A company organized as a separate legal entity, with most of the rights and privileges of a person.

Cumulative dividend A feature of preferred stock entitling the stockholder to receive current and unpaid prior-year dividends before common stockholders receive any dividends.

Declaration date The date the board of directors formally authorizes the dividend and announces it to stockholders.

Deficit A debit balance in Retained Earnings.

Dividend A distribution by a corporation to its stockholders on a pro rata (proportional to ownership) basis.

Dividends in arrears Preferred dividends that were supposed to be declared but were not declared during a given period.

Legal capital The amount of capital that must be retained in the business for the protection of corporate creditors.

No-par value stock Capital stock that has not been assigned a value in the corporate charter.

Outstanding stock Capital stock that has been issued and is being held by stockholders.

Paid-in capital The amount stockholders paid in to the corporation in exchange for shares of ownership.

Par value stock Capital stock that has been assigned a value per share in the corporate charter.

Payment date The date cash dividend payments are made to stockholders.

Payout ratio A measure of the percentage of earnings a company distributes in the form of cash dividends to common stockholders.

Preferred stock Capital stock that has contractual preferences over common stock in certain areas.

Privately held corporation A corporation that has only a few stockholders and whose stock is not available for sale to the general public.

Publicly held corporation A corporation that may have thousands of stockholders and whose stock is traded on a national securities market.

Record date The date when the company determines ownership of outstanding shares for dividend purposes.

Retained earnings Net income that a company retains in the business.

Retained earnings restrictions Circumstances that make a portion of retained earnings currently unavailable for dividends.

Return on common stockholders' equity (ROE) A measure of profitability from the stockholders' point of view; computed by dividing net income minus preferred dividends by average common stockholders' equity.

Stated value The amount per share assigned by the board of directors to no-par stock.

Stock dividend A pro rata (proportional to ownership) distribution of the corporation's own stock to stockholders.

Stock split The issuance of additional shares of stock to stockholders accompanied by a reduction in the par or stated value per share.

Treasury stock A corporation's own stock that has been reacquired by the corporation and is being held for future use.

PLUS **Self-Test, Brief Exercises, Exercises, Problem Set A, and many more resources are available for practice in WileyPLUS.**

Note: All Questions, Exercises, and Problems marked with an asterisk relate to material in the appendix to the chapter.

Self-Test Questions

(Answers in *Broadening Your Perspective*.)

(LO 1) **1.** Which of these is **not** a major advantage of a corporation?
   (a) Separate legal existence.
   (b) Continuous life.
   (c) Government regulations.
   (d) Transferable ownership rights.

(LO 1) **2.** A major **disadvantage** of a corporation is:
   (a) limited liability of stockholders.
   (b) additional taxes.

   (c) transferable ownership rights.
   (d) None of the above.

3. Which of these statements is **false**?   (LO 1)
   (a) Ownership of common stock gives the owner a voting right.
   (b) The stockholders' equity section begins with paid-in capital.
   (c) The authorization of capital stock does not result in a formal accounting entry.
   (d) Legal capital is intended to protect stockholders.

(LO 2) **4.** ABC Corp. issues 1,000 shares of $10 par value common stock at $12 per share. When the transaction is recorded, credits are made to:
(a) Common Stock $10,000 and Paid-in Capital in Excess of Stated Value $2,000.
(b) Common Stock $12,000.
(c) Common Stock $10,000 and Paid-in Capital in Excess of Par Value $2,000.
(d) Common Stock $10,000 and Retained Earnings $2,000.

(LO 3) **5.** Treasury stock may be repurchased:
(a) to reissue the shares to officers and employees under bonus and stock compensation plans.
(b) to signal to the stock market that management believes the stock is underpriced.
(c) to have additional shares available for use in the acquisition of other companies.
(d) More than one of the above.

(LO 4) **6.** Preferred stock may have which of the following features?
(a) Dividend preference.
(b) Preference to assets in the event of liquidation.
(c) Cumulative dividends.
(d) All of the above.

(LO 4) **7.** U-Bet Corporation has 10,000 shares of 8%, $100 par value, cumulative preferred stock outstanding at December 31, 2014. No dividends were declared in 2012 or 2013. If U-Bet wants to pay $375,000 of dividends in 2014, common stockholders will receive:
(a) $0.   (c) $215,000.
(b) $295,000. (d) $135,000.

(LO 5) **8.** Entries for cash dividends are required on the:
(a) declaration date and the record date.
(b) record date and the payment date.
(c) declaration date, record date, and payment date.
(d) declaration date and the payment date.

(LO 5) **9.** Which of these statements about stock dividends is **true**?
(a) Stock dividends reduce a company's cash balance.
(b) A stock dividend has no effect on total stockholders' equity.
(c) A stock dividend decreases total stockholders' equity.
(d) A stock dividend ordinarily will increase total stockholders' equity.

(LO 5) **10.** Zealot Inc. has retained earnings of $500,000 and total stockholders' equity of $2,000,000. It has 100,000 shares of $8 par value common stock outstanding, which is currently selling for $30 per share. If Zealot declares a 10% stock dividend on its common stock:
(a) net income will decrease by $80,000.
(b) retained earnings will decrease by $80,000 and total stockholders' equity will increase by $80,000.

(c) retained earnings will decrease by $300,000 and total stockholders' equity will increase by $300,000.
(d) retained earnings will decrease by $300,000 and total paid-in capital will increase by $300,000.

11. In the stockholders' equity section of the balance sheet, (LO 7) common stock:
(a) is listed before preferred stock.
(b) is listed after retained earnings.
(c) is part of paid-in capital.
(d) is subtracted from treasury stock.

12. In the stockholders' equity section, the cost of treasury (LO 7) stock is deducted from:
(a) total paid-in capital and retained earnings.
(b) retained earnings.
(c) total stockholders' equity.
(d) common stock in paid-in capital.

13. The return on common stockholders' (LO 8) equity is usually increased by all of the following, **except**:
(a) an increase in the return on assets ratio.
(b) an increase in the use of debt financing.
(c) an increase in the company's stock price.
(d) an increase in the company's net income.

14. Thomas is nearing retirement and would (LO 8) like to invest in a stock that will provide a good steady income. Thomas should choose a stock with a:
(a) high current ratio.
(b) high dividend payout.
(c) high earnings per share.
(d) high price-earnings ratio.

15. Jackson Inc. reported net income of $186,000 dur- (LO 8) ing 2014 and paid dividends of $26,000 on common stock. It also paid dividends on its 10,000 shares of 6%, $100 par value, noncumulative preferred stock. Common stockholders' equity was $1,200,000 on January 1, 2014, and $1,600,000 on December 31, 2014. The company's return on common stockholders' equity for 2014 is:
(a) 10.0%.   (c) 7.1%.
(b) 9.0%.   (d) 13.3%.

16. If everything else is held constant, earnings per share (LO 8) is increased by:
(a) the payment of a cash dividend to common shareholders.
(b) the payment of a cash dividend to preferred shareholders.
(c) the issuance of new shares of common stock.
(d) the purchase of treasury stock.

Go to the book's companion website, **www.wiley.com/college/kimmel**, to access additional Self-Test Questions.

Questions

1. Rob, a student, asks your help in understanding some characteristics of a corporation. Explain each of these to Rob.
   (a) Separate legal existence.
   (b) Limited liability of stockholders.
   (c) Transferable ownership rights.

2. (a) ⬅ Your friend C. J. Gibson cannot understand how the characteristic of corporate management is both an advantage and a disadvantage. Clarify this problem for C. J.
   (b) Identify and explain two other disadvantages of a corporation.

3. Janie Null believes a corporation must be incorporated in the state in which its headquarters office is located. Is Janie correct? Explain.

4. What are the basic ownership rights of common stockholders in the absence of restrictive provisions?

5. A corporation has been defined as an entity separate and distinct from its owners. In what ways is a corporation a separate legal entity?

6. What are the two principal components of stockholders' equity?

7. The corporate charter of Gagne Corporation allows the issuance of a maximum of 100,000 shares of common stock. During its first 2 years of operation, Gagne sold 70,000 shares to shareholders and reacquired 4,000 of these shares. After these transactions, how many shares are authorized, issued, and outstanding?

8. Which is the better investment—common stock with a par value of $5 per share or common stock with a par value of $20 per share?

9. ⬅ For what reasons might a company like IBM repurchase some of its stock (treasury stock)?

10. Diaz, Inc. purchases 1,000 shares of its own previously issued $5 par common stock for $11,000. Assuming the shares are held in the treasury, what effect does this transaction have on (a) net income, (b) total assets, (c) total paid-in capital, and (d) total stockholders' equity?

11. (a) What are the principal differences between common stock and preferred stock?
    (b) Preferred stock may be cumulative. Discuss this feature.
    (c) How are dividends in arrears presented in the financial statements?

12. Identify the events that result in credits and debits to retained earnings.

13. Indicate how each of these accounts should be classified in the stockholders' equity section of the balance sheet.
    (a) Common Stock.
    (b) Paid-in Capital in Excess of Par Value.
    (c) Retained Earnings.

(d) Treasury Stock.
(e) Paid-in Capital in Excess of Stated Value.
(f) Preferred Stock.

14. What three conditions must be met before a cash dividend is paid?

15. Three dates associated with Goff Company's cash dividend are May 1, May 15, and May 31. Discuss the significance of each date and give the entry at each date.

16. Contrast the effects of a cash dividend and a stock dividend on a corporation's balance sheet.

17. Angie Diltz asks, "Since stock dividends don't change anything, why declare them?" What is your answer to Angie?

18. Deane Corporation has 10,000 shares of $15 par value common stock outstanding when it announces a 3-for-1 split. Before the split, the stock had a market price of $120 per share. After the split, how many shares of stock will be outstanding, and what will be the approximate market price per share?

19. The board of directors is considering a stock split or a stock dividend. They understand that total stockholders' equity will remain the same under either action. However, they are not sure of the different effects of the two actions on other aspects of stockholders' equity. Explain the differences to the directors.

20. 🔲 What was the total cost of Tootsie Roll's treasury stock at December 31, 2011? What was the amount of the 2011 cash dividend? What was the total charge to Retained Earnings for the 2011 stock dividend?

21. (a) What is the purpose of a retained earnings restriction?
    (b) Identify the possible causes of retained earnings restrictions.

22. Hatch Inc.'s common stock has a par value of $1 and a current market price of $15. Explain why these amounts are different.

23. 🔧 What is the formula for the payout ratio? What does it indicate?

24. ⬅ 🔧 Explain the circumstances under which debt financing will increase the return on common stockholders' equity.

25. Under what circumstances will the return on assets and the return on common stockholders' equity be equal?

26. ⬅ Krause Corp. has a return on assets of 12%. It plans to issue bonds at 8% and use the cash to repurchase stock. What effect will this have on its debt to assets ratio and on its return on common stockholders' equity?

Brief Exercises

Cite advantages and disadvantages of a corporation.
(LO 1), **K**

BE11-1 Andrea Hanlin is planning to start a business. Identify for Andrea the advantages and disadvantages of the corporate form of business organization.

Journalize issuance of par value common stock.
(LO 2), **AP**

BE11-2 On May 10, Paige Corporation issues 2,500 shares of $5 par value common stock for cash at $13 per share. Journalize the issuance of the stock.

Journalize issuance of no-par common stock.
(LO 2), **AP**

BE11-3 On June 1, Tucker Inc. issues 3,000 shares of no-par common stock at a cash price of $7 per share. Journalize the issuance of the shares.

Journalize issuance of preferred stock.
(LO 4), **AP**

BE11-4 Pringle Inc. issues 8,000 shares of $100 par value preferred stock for cash at $106 per share. Journalize the issuance of the preferred stock.

Prepare entries for a cash dividend.
(LO 5), **AP**

BE11-5 Troutman Corporation has 7,000 shares of common stock outstanding. It declares a $1 per share cash dividend on November 1 to stockholders of record on December 1. The dividend is paid on December 31. Prepare the entries on the appropriate dates to record the declaration and payment of the cash dividend.

Show before-and-after effects of a stock dividend.
(LO 5), **AP**

BE11-6 The stockholders' equity section of Maley Corporation's balance sheet consists of common stock ($8 par) $1,000,000 and retained earnings $300,000. A 10% stock dividend (12,500 shares) is declared when the market price per share is $19. Show the before-and-after effects of the dividend on (a) the components of stockholders' equity and (b) the shares outstanding.

Compare impact of cash dividend, stock dividend, and stock split.
(LO 5), **K**

BE11-7 Indicate whether each of the following transactions would increase (+), decrease (−), or not affect (N/A) total assets, total liabilities, and total stockholders' equity.

Transaction	Assets	Liabilities	Stockholders' Equity
(a) Declared cash dividend.			
(b) Paid cash dividend declared in (a).			
(c) Declared stock dividend.			
(d) Distributed stock dividend declared in (c).			
(e) Split stock 3-for-1.			

Prepare a stockholders' equity section.
(LO 7), **AP**

BE11-8 Leiker Corporation has these accounts at December 31: Common Stock, $10 par, 5,000 shares issued, $50,000; Paid-in Capital in Excess of Par Value $22,000; Retained Earnings $42,000; and Treasury Stock, 500 shares, $11,000. Prepare the stockholders' equity section of the balance sheet.

Evaluate a company's dividend record.
(LO 8), **C**

BE11-9 Mike Haden, president of Haden Corporation, believes that it is a good practice for a company to maintain a constant payout of dividends relative to its earnings. Last year, net income was $600,000, and the corporation paid $120,000 in dividends. This year, due to some unusual circumstances, the corporation had income of $1,600,000. Mike expects next year's net income to be about $700,000. What was Haden Corporation's payout ratio last year? If it is to maintain the same payout ratio, what amount of dividends would it pay this year? Is this necessarily a good idea—that is, what are the pros and cons of maintaining a constant payout ratio in this scenario?

Calculate the return on stockholders' equity.
(LO 8), **AP**

BE11-10 SUPERVALU, one of the largest grocery retailers in the United States, is headquartered in Minneapolis. Suppose the following financial information (in millions) was taken from the company's 2014 annual report: net sales $44,597, net income $393, beginning stockholders' equity $2,581, and ending stockholders' equity $2,887. There were no dividends paid on preferred stock. Compute the return on common stockholders' equity. Provide a brief interpretation of your findings.

Compare bond financing to stock financing.
(LO 8), **AP**

BE11-11 Fugate Inc. is considering these two alternatives to finance its construction of a new $2 million plant:
1. Issuance of 200,000 shares of common stock at the market price of $10 per share.
2. Issuance of $2 million, 6% bonds at face value.
Complete the table and indicate which alternative is preferable.

	Issue Stock	Issue Bond
Income before interest and taxes	$1,500,000	$1,500,000
Interest expense from bonds	_____	_____
Income before income taxes		
Income tax expense (30%)	_____	_____
Net income	$ _____	$ _____
Outstanding shares	_____	700,000
Earnings per share	$ _____	$ _____

*BE11-12 Gast Corporation has 200,000 shares of $10 par value common stock outstanding. It declares a 12% stock dividend on December 1 when the market price per share is $17. The dividend shares are issued on December 31. Prepare the entries for the declaration and distribution of the stock dividend.

Prepare entries for a stock dividend.
(LO 9), AP

Exercises

E11-1 During its first year of operations, Rosa Corporation had these transactions pertaining to its common stock.

Journalize issuance of common stock.
(LO 2), AP

> Jan. 10   Issued 30,000 shares for cash at $5 per share.
> July 1   Issued 60,000 shares for cash at $7 per share.

Instructions
(a) Journalize the transactions, assuming that the common stock has a par value of $5 per share.
(b) Journalize the transactions, assuming that the common stock is no-par with a stated value of $1 per share.

E11-2 Fagan Co. had these transactions during the current period.

Journalize issuance of common stock and preferred stock and purchase of treasury stock.
(LO 2, 3, 4), AP

> June 12   Issued 80,000 shares of $1 par value common stock for cash of $300,000.
> July 11   Issued 3,000 shares of $100 par value preferred stock for cash at $106 per share.
> Nov. 28   Purchased 2,000 shares of treasury stock for $9,000.

Instructions
Prepare the journal entries for the Fagan Co. for these transactions.

E11-3 Meranda Corporation is authorized to issue both preferred and common stock. The par value of the preferred is $50. During the first year of operations, the company had the following events and transactions pertaining to its preferred stock.

Journalize preferred stock transactions and indicate statement presentation.
(LO 4, 7), AP

> Feb. 1   Issued 40,000 shares for cash at $51 per share.
> July 1   Issued 60,000 shares for cash at $56 per share.

Instructions
(a) Journalize the transactions.
(b) Post to the stockholders' equity accounts. (Use T-accounts.)
(c) Discuss the statement presentation of the accounts.

E11-4 The stockholders' equity section of Leyland Corporation's balance sheet at December 31 is presented here.

Answer questions about stockholders' equity section.
(LO 2, 3, 4, 7), C

LEYLAND CORPORATION
Balance Sheet (partial)

Stockholders' equity		
Paid-in capital		
Preferred stock, cumulative, 10,000 shares authorized,		
6,000 shares issued and outstanding		$ 600,000
Common stock, no par, 750,000 shares authorized,		
580,000 shares issued		2,900,000
Total paid-in capital		3,500,000
Retained earnings		1,158,000
Total paid-in capital and retained earnings		4,658,000
Less: Treasury stock (6,000 common shares)		32,000
Total stockholders' equity		$4,626,000

Instructions

From a review of the stockholders' equity section, answer the following questions.

(a) How many shares of common stock are outstanding?

(b) Assuming there is a stated value, what is the stated value of the common stock?

(c) What is the par value of the preferred stock?

(d) If the annual dividend on preferred stock is $36,000, what is the dividend rate on preferred stock?

(e) If dividends of $72,000 were in arrears on preferred stock, what would be the balance reported for retained earnings?

Prepare correct entries for capital stock transactions.

(LO 2, 3, 4), **AN**

E11-5 Garcia Corporation recently hired a new accountant with extensive experience in accounting for partnerships. Because of the pressure of the new job, the accountant was unable to review what he had learned earlier about corporation accounting. During the first month, he made the following entries for the corporation's capital stock.

May	2	Cash	104,000	
		Capital Stock		104,000
		(Issued 8,000 shares of $10 par value common stock at $13 per share)		
	10	Cash	530,000	
		Capital Stock		530,000
		(Issued 10,000 shares of $20 par value preferred stock at $53 per share)		
	15	Capital Stock	7,200	
		Cash		7,200
		(Purchased 600 shares of common stock for the treasury at $12 per share)		

Instructions

On the basis of the explanation for each entry, prepare the entries that should have been made for the capital stock transactions.

Journalize cash dividends and indicate statement presentation.

(LO 5), **AP**

E11-6 On January 1, Vanessa Corporation had 60,000 shares of no-par common stock issued and outstanding. The stock has a stated value of $4 per share. During the year, the following transactions occurred.

Apr.	1	Issued 9,000 additional shares of common stock for $11 per share.
June	15	Declared a cash dividend of $1.50 per share to stockholders of record on June 30.
July	10	Paid the $1.50 cash dividend.
Dec.	1	Issued 4,000 additional shares of common stock for $12 per share.
	15	Declared a cash dividend on outstanding shares of $1.60 per share to stockholders of record on December 31.

Instructions

(a) Prepare the entries, if any, on each of the three dates that involved dividends.

(b) How are dividends and dividends payable reported in the financial statements prepared at December 31?

Compare effects of a stock dividend and a stock split.

(LO 5), **AP**

E11-7 On October 31, the stockholders' equity section of Pele Company's balance sheet consists of common stock $648,000 and retained earnings $400,000. Pele is considering the following two courses of action: (1) declaring a 5% stock dividend on the 81,000 $8 par value shares outstanding or (2) effecting a 2-for-1 stock split that will reduce par value to $4 per share. The current market price is $17 per share.

Instructions

Prepare a tabular summary of the effects of the alternative actions on the company's stockholders' equity and outstanding shares. Use these column headings: **Before Action**, **After Stock Dividend**, and **After Stock Split**.

Prepare a stockholders' equity section.

(LO 7), **AP**

E11-8 Wells Fargo & Company, headquartered in San Francisco, is one of the nation's largest financial institutions. Suppose it reported the following selected accounts (in millions) as of December 31, 2014.

Retained earnings	$41,563
Preferred stock	8,485
Common stock—$1⅔ par value, authorized 6,000,000,000 shares; issued 5,245,971,422 shares	8,743
Treasury stock—67,346,829 common shares	(2,450)
Paid-in capital in excess of par value—common stock	52,878

Instructions

Prepare the stockholders' equity section of the balance sheet for Wells Fargo as of December 31, 2014.

E11-9 The following stockholders' equity accounts, arranged alphabetically, are in the ledger of Roder Corporation at December 31, 2014.

Prepare a stockholders' equity section.
(LO 7), AP

Common Stock ($2 stated value)	$1,600,000
Paid-in Capital in Excess of Par Value—Preferred Stock	45,000
Paid-in Capital in Excess of Stated Value—Common Stock	1,050,000
Preferred Stock (8%, $100 par, noncumulative)	600,000
Retained Earnings	1,334,000
Treasury Stock (12,000 common shares)	72,000

Instructions

Prepare the stockholders' equity section of the balance sheet at December 31, 2014.

E11-10 The following accounts appear in the ledger of Polzin Inc. after the books are closed at December 31, 2014.

Prepare a stockholders' equity section.
(LO 7), AP

Common Stock (no-par, $1 stated value, 400,000 shares authorized, 250,000 shares issued)	$ 250,000
Paid-in Capital in Excess of Stated Value—Common Stock	1,200,000
Preferred Stock ($50 par value, 8%, 40,000 shares authorized, 14,000 shares issued)	700,000
Retained Earnings	920,000
Treasury Stock (9,000 common shares)	64,000
Paid-in Capital in Excess of Par Value—Preferred Stock	24,000

Instructions

Prepare the stockholders' equity section at December 31, assuming $100,000 of retained earnings is restricted for plant expansion. (Use Note R.)

E11-11 The following financial information is available for Whitlock Corporation.

Calculate ratios to evaluate dividend and earnings performance.
(LO 8), AP

(in millions)	**2014**	**2013**
Average common stockholders' equity	$2,532	$2,591
Dividends declared for common stockholders	298	611
Dividends declared for preferred stockholders	40	40
Net income	504	555

Instructions

Calculate the payout ratio and return on common stockholders' equity for 2014 and 2013. Comment on your findings.

E11-12 Suppose the following financial information is available for Walgreen Company.

Calculate ratios to evaluate dividend and earnings performance.
(LO 8), AP

(in millions)	**2014**	**2013**
Average common stockholders' equity	$13,622.5	$11,986.5
Dividends declared for common stockholders	471	394
Dividends declared for preferred stockholders	0	0
Net income	2,006	2,157

Instructions

Calculate the payout ratio and return on common stockholders' equity for 2014 and 2013. Comment on your findings.

Calculate ratios to evaluate profitability and solvency.
(LO 8), **AN**

E11-13   Korsak Corporation decided to issue common stock and used the $300,000 proceeds to redeem all of its outstanding bonds on January 1, 2014. The following information is available for the company for 2013 and 2014.

	2014	2013
Net income	$ 182,000	$ 150,000
Dividends declared for preferred stockholders	8,000	8,000
Average common stockholders' equity	1,000,000	700,000
Total assets	1,200,000	1,200,000
Current liabilities	100,000	100,000
Total liabilities	200,000	500,000

Instructions
(a) Compute the return on common stockholders' equity for both years.
(b) Explain how it is possible that net income increased but the return on common stockholders' equity decreased.
(c) Compute the debt to assets ratio for both years, and comment on the implications of this change in the company's solvency.

Compare issuance of stock financing to issuance of bond financing.
(LO 8), **AN**

E11-14   Atlantic Airlines is considering these two alternatives for financing the purchase of a fleet of airplanes:

1. Issue 50,000 shares of common stock at $40 per share. (Cash dividends have not been paid nor is the payment of any contemplated.)
2. Issue 12%, 10-year bonds at face value for $2,000,000.

It is estimated that the company will earn $800,000 before interest and taxes as a result of this purchase. The company has an estimated tax rate of 30% and has 90,000 shares of common stock outstanding prior to the new financing.

Instructions
Determine the effect on net income and earnings per share for (a) issuing stock and (b) issuing bonds. Assume the new shares or new bonds will be outstanding for the entire year.

Compute ratios and interpret.
(LO 8), **AN**

E11-15   Sandberg Company has $1,000,000 in assets and $1,000,000 in stockholders' equity, with 40,000 shares outstanding the entire year. It has a return on assets of 10%. In the past year, it had net income of $100,000. On January 1, 2014, it issued $400,000 in debt at 4% and immediately repurchased 20,000 shares for $400,000. Management expected that, had it not issued the debt, it would have again had net income of $100,000.

Instructions
(a) Determine the company's net income and earnings per share for 2013 and 2014. (Ignore taxes in your computations.)
(b) Compute the company's return on common stockholders' equity for 2013 and 2014.
(c) Compute the company's debt to assets ratio for 2013 and 2014.
(d) Discuss the impact that the borrowing had on the company's profitability and solvency. Was it a good idea to borrow the money to buy the treasury stock?

Journalize stock dividends.
(LO 5, 9), **AP**

*E11-16   On January 1, 2014, Wilkens Corporation had $1,200,000 of common stock outstanding that was issued at par and retained earnings of $750,000. The company issued 30,000 shares of common stock at par on July 1 and earned net income of $400,000 for the year.

Instructions
Journalize the declaration of a 15% stock dividend on December 10, 2014, for the following two independent assumptions.
(a) Par value is $10 and market price is $15.
(b) Par value is $5 and market price is $8.

Challenge Exercises

Visit the book's companion website, at **www.wiley.com/college/kimmel**, and choose the Student Companion site to access Challenge Exercises.

Problems: Set A

P11-1A   Tidwell Corporation was organized on January 1, 2014. It is authorized to issue 20,000 shares of 6%, $50 par value preferred stock and 500,000 shares of no-par common stock with a stated value of $1 per share. The following stock transactions were completed during the first year.

Journalize stock transactions, post, and prepare paid-in capital section.

(LO 2, 4, 7), **AP**

Jan.	10	Issued 70,000 shares of common stock for cash at $4 per share.
Mar.	1	Issued 12,000 shares of preferred stock for cash at $53 per share.
May	1	Issued 120,000 shares of common stock for cash at $6 per share.
Sept.	1	Issued 5,000 shares of common stock for cash at $5 per share.
Nov.	1	Issued 3,000 shares of preferred stock for cash at $56 per share.

Instructions
(a) Journalize the transactions.
(b) Post to the stockholders' equity accounts. (Use T-accounts.)
(c) Prepare the paid-in capital portion of the stockholders' equity section at December 31, 2014.

(c) Tot. paid-in capital $1,829,000

P11-2A   The stockholders' equity accounts of Miley Corporation on January 1, 2014, were as follows.

Journalize transactions, post, and prepare a stockholders' equity section; calculate ratios.

(LO 2, 3, 5, 7, 8), **AP**

Preferred Stock (7%, $100 par noncumulative, 5,000 shares authorized)	$ 300,000
Common Stock ($4 stated value, 300,000 shares authorized)	1,000,000
Paid-in Capital in Excess of Par Value—Preferred Stock	15,000
Paid-in Capital in Excess of Stated Value—Common Stock	480,000
Retained Earnings	688,000
Treasury Stock (5,000 common shares)	40,000

During 2014, the corporation had the following transactions and events pertaining to its stockholders' equity.

Feb.	1	Issued 5,000 shares of common stock for $30,000.
Mar.	20	Purchased 1,000 additional shares of common treasury stock at $7 per share.
Oct.	1	Declared a 7% cash dividend on preferred stock, payable November 1.
Nov.	1	Paid the dividend declared on October 1.
Dec.	1	Declared a $0.50 per share cash dividend to common stockholders of record on December 15, payable December 31, 2014.
	31	Determined that net income for the year was $280,000. Paid the dividend declared on December 1.

Instructions
(a) Journalize the transactions. (Include entries to close net income and dividends to Retained Earnings.)
(b) Enter the beginning balances in the accounts and post the journal entries to the stockholders' equity accounts. (Use T-accounts.)
(c) Prepare the stockholders' equity section of the balance sheet at December 31, 2014.
(d) Calculate the payout ratio, earnings per share, and return on common stockholders' equity. (*Note:* Use the common shares outstanding on January 1 and December 31 to determine the average shares outstanding.)

(c) Tot. paid-in capital $1,825,000

P11-3A   On December 31, 2013, Paxson Company had 1,300,000 shares of $5 par common stock issued and outstanding. At December 31, 2013, stockholders' equity had the amounts listed here.

Prepare a stockholders' equity section.

(LO 7), **AP**

Common Stock	$6,500,000
Additional Paid-in Capital	1,800,000
Retained Earnings	1,200,000

Transactions during 2014 and other information related to stockholders' equity accounts were as follows.

1. On January 10, 2014, issued at $107 per share 120,000 shares of $100 par value, 9% cumulative preferred stock.
2. On February 8, 2014, reacquired 15,000 shares of its common stock for $11 per share.

3. On May 9, 2014, declared the yearly cash dividend on preferred stock, payable June 10, 2014, to stockholders of record on May 31, 2014.
4. On June 8, 2014, declared a cash dividend of $1.20 per share on the common stock outstanding, payable on July 10, 2014, to stockholders of record on July 1, 2014.
5. Net income for the year was $3,600,000.

Instructions

Tot. stockholders' equity $23,153,000

Prepare the stockholders' equity section of Paxson's balance sheet at December 31, 2014.

Reproduce retained earnings account, and prepare a stockholders' equity section.

(LO 5, 6, 7), AP

P11-4A The ledger of Wade Corporation at December 31, 2014, after the books have been closed, contains the following stockholders' equity accounts.

Preferred Stock (10,000 shares issued)	$1,000,000
Common Stock (300,000 shares issued)	1,500,000
Paid-in Capital in Excess of Par Value—Preferred Stock	200,000
Paid-in Capital in Excess of Stated Value—Common Stock	1,600,000
Retained Earnings	2,860,000

A review of the accounting records reveals this information:

1. Preferred stock is 8%, $100 par value, noncumulative. Since January 1, 2013, 10,000 shares have been outstanding; 20,000 shares are authorized.
2. Common stock is no-par with a stated value of $5 per share; 600,000 shares are authorized.
3. The January 1, 2014, balance in Retained Earnings was $2,380,000.
4. On October 1, 60,000 shares of common stock were sold for cash at $9 per share.
5. A cash dividend of $400,000 was declared and properly allocated to preferred and common stock on November 1. No dividends were paid to preferred stockholders in 2013.
6. Net income for the year was $880,000.
7. On December 31, 2014, the directors authorized disclosure of a $160,000 restriction of retained earnings for plant expansion. (Use Note A.)

Instructions

(a) Reproduce the Retained Earnings account (T-account) for the year.

(b) Tot. paid-in capital $4,300,000

(b) Prepare the stockholders' equity section of the balance sheet at December 31.

Prepare entries for stock transactions, and prepare a stockholders' equity section.

(LO 2, 3, 4, 7), AP

P11-5A Pringle Corporation has been authorized to issue 20,000 shares of $100 par value, 7%, noncumulative preferred stock and 1,000,000 shares of no-par common stock. The corporation assigned a $5 stated value to the common stock. At December 31, 2014, the ledger contained the following balances pertaining to stockholders' equity.

Preferred Stock	$ 150,000
Paid-in Capital in Excess of Par Value—Preferred Stock	20,000
Common Stock	2,000,000
Paid-in Capital in Excess of Stated Value—Common Stock	1,520,000
Treasury Stock (4,000 common shares)	36,000
Retained Earnings	82,000

The preferred stock was issued for $170,000 cash. All common stock issued was for cash. In November 4,000 shares of common stock were purchased for the treasury at a per share cost of $9. No dividends were declared in 2014.

Instructions

(a) Prepare the journal entries for the following.
(1) Issuance of preferred stock for cash.
(2) Issuance of common stock for cash.

(b) Tot. stockholders' equity

$3,736,000

(3) Purchase of common treasury stock for cash.
(b) Prepare the stockholders' equity section of the balance sheet at December 31, 2014.

Prepare a stockholders' equity section.

(LO 7), AP

P11-6A On January 1, 2014, Kessler Inc. had these stockholders' equity balances.

Common Stock, $1 par (2,000,000 shares authorized, 600,000 shares issued and outstanding)	$ 600,000
Paid-in Capital in Excess of Par Value	1,500,000
Retained Earnings	700,000

During 2014, the following transactions and events occurred.

1. Issued 50,000 shares of $1 par value common stock for $3 per share.
2. Issued 60,000 shares of common stock for cash at $4 per share.
3. Purchased 20,000 shares of common stock for the treasury at $3.80 per share.
4. Declared and paid a cash dividend of $207,000.
5. Earned net income of $410,000.

Instructions

Prepare the stockholders' equity section of the balance sheet at December 31, 2014.

Tot. stockholders' equity $3,317,000

P11-7A   Cepeda Company manufactures backpacks. During 2014, Cepeda issued bonds at 10% interest and used the cash proceeds to purchase treasury stock. The following financial information is available for Cepeda Company for the years 2014 and 2013.

Evaluate a company's profitability and solvency.
(LO 8), AP

	2014	2013
Sales revenue	$ 9,000,000	$ 9,000,000
Net income	2,240,000	2,500,000
Interest expense	500,000	140,000
Tax expense	670,000	750,000
Dividends paid on common stock	890,000	1,026,000
Dividends paid on preferred stock	300,000	300,000
Total assets (year-end)	14,500,000	16,875,000
Average total assets	15,687,500	17,763,000
Total liabilities (year-end)	6,000,000	3,000,000
Avg. total common stockholders' equity	9,400,000	14,100,000

Instructions

(a) Use the information above to calculate the following ratios for both years: (i) return on assets, (ii) return on common stockholders' equity, (iii) payout ratio, (iv) debt to assets ratio, and (v) times interest earned.

(b) Referring to your findings in part (a), discuss the changes in the company's profitability from 2013 to 2014.

(c) Referring to your findings in part (a), discuss the changes in the company's solvency from 2013 to 2014.

(d) Based on your findings in (b), was the decision to issue debt to purchase common stock a wise one?

*P11-8A   On January 1, 2014, Everett Corporation had these stockholders' equity accounts.

Prepare dividend entries, prepare a stockholders' equity section, and calculate ratios.
(LO 5, 7, 8, 9), AP

Common Stock ($10 par value, 70,000 shares issued and outstanding)	$700,000
Paid-in Capital in Excess of Par Value	500,000
Retained Earnings	620,000

During the year, the following transactions occurred.

Jan.	15	Declared a $0.50 cash dividend per share to stockholders of record on January 31, payable February 15.
Feb.	15	Paid the dividend declared in January.
Apr.	15	Declared a 10% stock dividend to stockholders of record on April 30, distributable May 15. On April 15, the market price of the stock was $14 per share.
May	15	Issued the shares for the stock dividend.
Dec.	1	Declared a $0.60 per share cash dividend to stockholders of record on December 15, payable January 10, 2015.
	31	Determined that net income for the year was $400,000.

Instructions

(a) Journalize the transactions. (Include entries to close net income and dividends to Retained Earnings.)

(b) Enter the beginning balances and post the entries to the stockholders' equity T-accounts. (*Note:* Open additional stockholders' equity accounts as needed.)

(c) Prepare the stockholders' equity section of the balance sheet at December 31.

(d) Calculate the payout ratio and return on common stockholders' equity.

(c) Tot. stockholders' equity
$2,138,800

Problems: Set B

Visit the book's companion website, at **www.wiley.com/college/kimmel**, and choose the Student Companion site to access Problem Set B.

Comprehensive Problem

CP11 Klinger Corporation's balance sheet at December 31, 2013, is presented below.

KLINGER CORPORATION
Balance Sheet
December 31, 2013

Cash	$ 24,600	Accounts payable	$ 25,600
Accounts receivable	45,500	Common stock ($10 par)	80,000
Allowance for doubtful		Retained earnings	127,400
accounts	(1,500)		$233,000
Supplies	4,400		
Land	40,000		
Buildings	142,000		
Accumulated depreciation—			
buildings	(22,000)		
	$233,000		

During 2014, the following transactions occurred.
1. On January 1, 2014, Klinger issued 1,200 shares of $40 par, 7% preferred stock for $49,200.
2. On January 1, 2014, Klinger also issued 900 shares of the $10 par value common stock for $21,000.
3. Klinger performed services for $320,000 on account.
4. On April 1, 2014, Klinger collected fees of $36,000 in advance for services to be performed from April 1, 2014, to March 31, 2015.
5. Klinger collected $276,000 from customers on account.
6. Klinger bought $35,100 of supplies on account.
7. Klinger paid $32,200 on accounts payable.
8. Klinger reacquired 400 shares of its common stock on June 1, 2014, for $28 per share.
9. Paid other operating expenses of $188,200.
10. On December 31, 2014, Klinger declared the annual preferred stock dividend and a $1.20 per share dividend on the outstanding common stock, all payable on January 15, 2015.
11. An account receivable of $1,700 which originated in 2013 is written off as uncollectible.

Adjustment data:
1. A count of supplies indicates that $5,900 of supplies remain unused at year-end.
2. Recorded revenue from item 4 above.
3. The allowance for doubtful accounts should have a balance of $3,500 at year end.
4. Depreciation is recorded on the building on a straight-line basis based on a 30-year life and a salvage value of $10,000.
5. The income tax rate is 30%. (*Hint:* Prepare the income statement up to income before taxes and multiply by 30% to compute the amount.)

Instructions
(You may want to set up T-accounts to determine ending balances.)
(a) Prepare journal entries for the transactions listed above and adjusting entries.
(b) Prepare an adjusted trial balance at December 31, 2014.
(c) Prepare an income statement and a retained earnings statement for the year ending December 31, 2014, and a classified balance sheet as of December 31, 2014.

(b) Totals $740,690
(c) Net income $81,970
  Tot. assets $421,000

Broadening Your Perspective

Financial Reporting and Analysis

FINANCIAL REPORTING PROBLEM: *Tootsie Roll Industries, Inc.*

BYP11-1 The stockholders' equity section of Tootsie Roll Industries' balance sheet is shown in the Consolidated Statement of Financial Position in Appendix A. You will also find data relative to this problem on other pages of Appendix A. **(Note that Tootsie Roll has two classes of common stock. To answer the following questions, add the two classes of stock together.)**

Instructions
Answer the following questions.
(a) What is the par or stated value per share of Tootsie Roll's common stock?
(b) What percentage of Tootsie Roll's authorized common stock was issued at December 31, 2011? (Round to the nearest full percent.)
(c) How many shares of common stock were outstanding at December 31, 2010, and at December 31, 2011?
(d) Calculate the payout ratio, earnings per share, and return on common stockholders' equity for 2011.

COMPARATIVE ANALYSIS PROBLEM: *Tootsie Roll vs. Hershey*

BYP11-2 The financial statements of The Hershey Company are presented in Appendix B, following the financial statements for Tootsie Roll in Appendix A.

Instructions
(a) Based on the information in these financial statements, compute the 2011 return on common stockholders' equity, debt to assets ratio, and return on assets for each company.
(b) What conclusions concerning the companies' profitability can be drawn from these ratios? Which company relies more on debt to boost its return to common shareholders?
(c) Compute the payout ratio for each company. Which pays out a higher percentage of its earnings?

RESEARCH CASES

BYP11-3 The March 15, 2010, edition of the *Wall Street Journal* includes an article by Martin Peers entitled "Media's Cash Focus Is Paying Dividends."

Instructions
Read the article and answer the following questions.
(a) What action did Viacom take with its excess cash before it decided to consider paying dividends or stock buybacks?
(b) What percentage of free cash flow does Time Warner pay out in dividends?
(c) Why might Viacom choose to pay a lower dividend and instead use its excess cash for a stock buyback program?
(d) How might the payment of a steady, significant dividend change the nature of shareholders that invest in media companies?
(e) What message might an increased dividend or stock buybacks send to shareholders regarding what the company will do with excess cash now, as opposed to what it used to do with excess cash?

BYP11-4 The November 10, 2011, edition of the *Financial Times* contains an article by Alan Rappeport entitled "McDonald's Looks to Buy More Property."

Instructions
Read the article and answer the following questions.
(a) Why is McDonald's shifting away from leasing its properties toward purchasing them?
(b) What percentage of the land that its stores sit on does McDonald's own? What percentage of its 30,000 restaurant buildings does it own?

(c) William Ackerman was a large McDonald's shareholder. Explain the proposal he had for the company.

(d) What impact would William Ackerman's proposal probably have had on the return on common stockholders' equity?

(e) Why did McDonald's probably choose to decline the Ackerman proposal?

INTERPRETING FINANCIAL STATEMENTS

BYP11-5 Marriott Corporation split into two companies: Host Marriott Corporation and Marriott International. Host Marriott retained ownership of the corporation's vast hotel and other properties, while Marriott International, rather than owning hotels, managed them. The purpose of this split was to free Marriott International from the "baggage" associated with Host Marriott, thus allowing it to be more aggressive in its pursuit of growth. The following information (in millions) is provided for each corporation for their first full year operating as independent companies.

	Host Marriott	**Marriott International**
Sales revenue	$1,501	$8,415
Net income	(25)	200
Total assets	3,822	3,207
Total liabilities	3,112	2,440
Common stockholders' equity	710	767

Instructions

(a) The two companies were split by the issuance of shares of Marriott International to all shareholders of the previous combined company. Discuss the nature of this transaction.

(b) Calculate the debt to assets ratio for each company.

(c) Calculate the return on assets and return on common stockholders' equity for each company.

(d) The company's debtholders were fiercely opposed to the original plan to split the two companies because the original plan had Host Marriott absorbing the majority of the company's debt. They relented only when Marriott International agreed to absorb a larger share of the debt. Discuss the possible reasons the debtholders were opposed to the plan to split the company.

REAL-WORLD FOCUS

BYP11-6 *Purpose:* Use the stockholders' equity section of an annual report and identify the major components.

Address: **www.annualreports.com**, or go to **www.wiley.com/college/kimmel**

Steps

1. Select a particular company.
2. Search by company name.
3. Follow instructions below.

Instructions

Answer the following questions.

(a) What is the company's name?

(b) What classes of capital stock has the company issued?

(c) For each class of stock:
   (1) How many shares are authorized, issued, and/or outstanding?
   (2) What is the par value?

(d) What are the company's retained earnings?

(e) Has the company acquired treasury stock? How many shares?

Critical Thinking

DECISION-MAKING ACROSS THE ORGANIZATION

BYP11-7 During a recent period, the fast-food chain Wendy's International purchased many treasury shares. This caused the number of shares outstanding to fall from 124 million to 105 million. The following information was drawn from the company's financial statements (in millions).

	Information for the Year after Purchase of Treasury Stock	Information for the Year before Purchase of Treasury Stock
Net income	$ 193.6	$ 123.4
Total assets	2,076.0	1,837.9
Average total assets	2,016.9	1,889.8
Total common stockholders' equity	1,029.8	1,068.1
Average common stockholders' equity	1,078.0	1,126.2
Total liabilities	1,046.3	769.9
Average total liabilities	939.0	763.7
Interest expense	30.2	19.8
Income taxes	113.7	84.3
Cash provided by operations	305.2	233.8
Cash dividends paid on common stock	26.8	31.0
Preferred stock dividends	0	0
Average number of common shares outstanding	109.7	119.9

Instructions

Use the information provided to answer the following questions.

(a) Compute earnings per share, return on common stockholders' equity, and return on assets for both years. Discuss the change in the company's profitability over this period.

(b) Compute the dividend payout ratio. Also compute the average cash dividend paid per share of common stock (dividends paid divided by the average number of common shares outstanding). Discuss any change in these ratios during this period and the implications for the company's dividend policy.

(c) Compute the debt to assets ratio and times interest earned. Discuss the change in the company's solvency.

(d) Based on your findings in (a) and (c), discuss to what extent any change in the return on common stockholders' equity was the result of increased reliance on debt.

(e) Does it appear that the purchase of treasury stock and the shift toward more reliance on debt were wise strategic moves?

COMMUNICATION ACTIVITY

BYP11-8   Ken Endicott, your uncle, is an inventor who has decided to incorporate. Uncle Ken knows that you are an accounting major at U.N.O. In a recent letter to you, he ends with the question, "I'm filling out a state incorporation application. Can you tell me the difference among the following terms: (1) authorized stock, (2) issued stock, (3) outstanding stock, and (4) preferred stock?"

Instructions

In a brief note, differentiate for Uncle Ken the four different stock terms. Write the letter to be friendly, yet professional.

ETHICS CASES

BYP11-9   The R&D division of Jobe Corp. has just developed a chemical for sterilizing the vicious Brazilian "killer bees" which are invading Mexico and the southern United States. The president of Jobe is anxious to get the chemical on the market because Jobe profits need a boost— and his job is in jeopardy because of decreasing sales and profits. Jobe has an opportunity to sell this chemical in Central American countries, where the laws are much more relaxed than in the United States.

The director of Jobe's R&D division strongly recommends further research in the laboratory to test the side effects of this chemical on other insects, birds, animals, plants, and even humans. He cautions the president, "We could be sued from all sides if the chemical has tragic side effects that we didn't even test for in the lab." The president answers, "We can't wait an additional year for your lab tests. We can avoid losses from such lawsuits by establishing a separate wholly owned corporation to shield Jobe Corp. from such lawsuits. We can't lose any more than our investment in the new corporation, and we'll invest just the patent covering this chemical. We'll reap the benefits if the chemical works and is safe, and avoid the losses from lawsuits if it's a disaster." The following week, Jobe creates a new wholly owned corporation called Windsor Inc., sells the chemical patent to it for $10, and watches the spraying begin.

Instructions
(a) Who are the stakeholders in this situation?
(b) Are the president's motives and actions ethical?
(c) Can Jobe shield itself against losses of Windsor Inc.?

BYP11-10 Osborn Corporation has paid 60 consecutive quarterly cash dividends (15 years). The last 6 months have been a real cash drain on the company, however, as profit margins have been greatly narrowed by increasing competition. With a cash balance sufficient to meet only day-to-day operating needs, the president, Barry Sigle, has decided that a stock dividend instead of a cash dividend should be declared. He tells Osborn's financial vice president, Mandy Drummond, to issue a press release stating that the company is extending its consecutive dividend record with the issuance of a 5% stock dividend. "Write the press release convincing the stockholders that the stock dividend is just as good as a cash dividend," he orders. "Just watch our stock rise when we announce the stock dividend; it must be a good thing if that happens."

Instructions
(a) Who are the stakeholders in this situation?
(b) Is there anything unethical about president Sigle's intentions or actions?
(c) What is the effect of a stock dividend on a corporation's stockholders' equity accounts? Which would you rather receive as a stockholder—a cash dividend or a stock dividend? Why?

ALL ABOUT YOU

BYP11-11 In response to the Sarbanes-Oxley Act, many companies have implemented formal ethics codes. Many other organizations also have ethics codes.

Instructions
Obtain the ethics code from an organization that you belong to (e.g., student organization, business school, employer, or a volunteer organization). Evaluate the ethics code based on how clearly it identifies proper and improper behavior. Discuss its strengths, and how it might be improved.

FASB CODIFICATION ACTIVITY

BYP11-12 If your school has a subscription to the FASB Codification, go to **http://aaahq.org/ascLogin.cfm** to log in and prepare responses to the following.
(a) What is the stock dividend?
(b) What is a stock split?
(c) At what percentage point does the issuance of additional shares qualify as a stock dividend, as opposed to a stock split?

CONSIDERING PEOPLE, PLANET, AND PROFIT

BYP11-13 The January 19, 2012, edition of the *Wall Street Journal* contains an article by Angus Loten entitled "With New Law, Profits Take a Back Seat."

Instructions
Read the article and answer the following questions.
(a) Summarize the nature of the new law that is discussed in the article.
(b) What do some proponents of the law say is the "biggest value" of the law? How does the article say that this would have impacted Ben & Jerry's?
(c) What are some criticisms of the law?
(d) How does incorporation as a benefit corporation differ from B Corp certification?
(e) What are some of the companies that the article cites as either having adopted benefit corporation standing or are considering it?

Answers to Insight and Accounting Across the Organization Questions

p. 497 The Impact of Corporate Social Responsibility Q: Why are CSR-related shareholder proposals increasing? **A:** The increase in shareholder proposals reflects a growing belief that a company's social and environmental policies correlate strongly with its risk-management strategy and ultimately its financial performance.

p. 502 How to Read Stock Quotes Q: For stocks traded on organized exchanges, how are the dollar prices per share established? What factors might influence the price of shares in the marketplace? **A:** The dollar prices per share are established by the interaction between buyers and sellers of the shares. The prices of shares are influenced by a company's earnings and dividends as well as by factors beyond a company's control, such as changes in interest rates, labor strikes, scarcity of supplies or resources, and politics. The number of willing buyers and sellers (demand and supply) also plays a part in the price of shares.

p. 508 Up, Down, and ?? Q: What factors must management consider in deciding how large a dividend to pay? **A:** Management must consider the size of the company's retained earnings balance, the amount of available cash, the company's expected near-term cash needs, the company's growth opportunities, and what level of dividend the company will be able to sustain based upon its expected future earnings.

p. 511 A No-Split Philosophy Q: Why does Warren Buffett usually oppose stock splits? **A:** Buffett prefers to attract shareholders that make a long-term commitment to his company, as opposed to traders that only hold their investment for a short period of time. He believes that a high stock price discourages short-term investment.

Answers to Self-Test Questions

1. c **2.** b **3.** d **4.** c **5.** d **6.** d **7.** d $375,000 - (\$100 \times 10,000 \times .08 \times 3)$ **8.** d **9.** b **10.** d $(100,000 \times \$30 \times .10)$ **11.** c **12.** a **13.** c **14.** b **15.** b $(\$186,000 - \$60,000) \div ((1,200,000 + \$1,600,000) \div 2)$ **16.** d

A Look at IFRS

The accounting for transactions related to stockholders' equity, such as issuance of shares, purchase of treasury stock, and declaration and payment of dividends, are similar under both IFRS and GAAP. Major differences relate to terminology used, introduction of items such as revaluation surplus, and presentation of stockholders' equity information.

> **LEARNING OBJECTIVE 10**
> Compare the accounting for transactions related to stockholders' equity under GAAP and IFRS.

KEY POINTS

- Under IFRS, the term **reserves** is used to describe all equity accounts other than those arising from contributed capital. This would include, for example, reserves related to retained earnings, asset revaluations, and fair value differences.

- Many countries have a different mix of investor groups than in the United States. For example, in Germany, financial institutions like banks are not only major creditors of corporations but often are the largest corporate stockholders as well. In the United States, Asia, and the United Kingdom, many companies rely on substantial investment from private investors.

- There are often terminology differences for equity accounts. The following summarizes some of the common differences in terminology.

GAAP	IFRS
Common stock	Share capital—ordinary
Stockholders	Shareholders
Par value	Nominal or face value
Authorized stock	Authorized share capital
Preferred stock	Share capital—preference
Paid-in capital	Issued/allocated share capital
Paid-in capital in excess of par value— common stock	Share premium—ordinary
Paid-in capital in excess of par value— preferred stock	Share premium—preference
Retained earnings	Retained earnings or Retained profits
Retained earnings deficit	Accumulated losses
Accumulated other comprehensive income	General reserve and other reserve accounts

As an example of how similar transactions use different terminology under IFRS, consider the accounting for the issuance of 1,000 shares of $1 par value stock for $5 per share. Under IFRS, the entry is as follows.

Cash	5,000	
Share Capital—Ordinary		1,000
Share Premium—Ordinary		4,000

- The accounting for treasury stock differs somewhat between IFRS and GAAP. (However, many of the differences are beyond the scope of this course.) Like GAAP, IFRS does not allow a company to record gains or losses on purchases of its own shares. One difference worth noting is that when a company purchases its own shares, IFRS treats it as a reduction of shareholders' equity but it does not specify which particular equity accounts are to be affected. Therefore, it could be shown as an increase to a contra equity account (Treasury Shares) or a decrease to retained earnings or share capital. IFRS requires that the number of treasury shares held be disclosed.

- A major difference between IFRS and GAAP relates to the account Revaluation Surplus. Revaluation surplus arises under IFRS because companies are permitted to revalue their property, plant, and equipment to fair value under certain circumstances. This account is part of general reserves under IFRS and is not considered contributed capital.

- As indicated earlier, the term **reserves** is used in IFRS to indicate all noncontributed (non–paid-in) capital. Reserves include retained earnings and other comprehensive income items, such as revaluation surplus and unrealized gains or losses on non-trading securities.

- IFRS often uses terms such as **retained profits** or **accumulated profit or loss** to describe retained earnings. The term **retained earnings** is also often used.

- The accounting related to prior period adjustments is essentially the same under IFRS and GAAP. IFRS addresses the accounting for errors in *IAS 8* ("Accounting Policies, Changes in Accounting Estimates, and Errors"). One area where IFRS and GAAP differ in reporting relates to error corrections in previously issued financial statements. While IFRS requires restatement with some exceptions, GAAP does not permit any exceptions.

- Equity is given various descriptions under IFRS, such as shareholders' equity, owners' equity, capital and reserves, and shareholders' funds.

LOOKING TO THE FUTURE

As indicated in earlier discussions, the IASB and the FASB are currently working on a project related to financial statement presentation. An important part of this study is to determine whether certain line items, subtotals, and totals should be clearly defined and required to be displayed in the financial statements. For example, it is likely that the statement of stockholders' equity and its presentation will be examined closely. In addition, the options of how to present other comprehensive income under GAAP will change in any converged standard.

IFRS PRACTICE

IFRS SELF-TEST QUESTIONS

1. Under IFRS, a purchase by a company of its own shares is recorded by:
   (a) an increase in Treasury Shares.
   (b) a decrease in contributed capital.
   (c) a decrease in share capital.
   (d) All of these are acceptable treatments.
2. The term **reserves** is used under IFRS with reference to all of the following **except**:
   (a) gains and losses on revaluation of property, plant, and equipment.
   (b) capital received in excess of the par value of issued shares.
   (c) retained earnings.
   (d) fair value differences.
3. Under IFRS, the amount of capital received in excess of par value on ordinary shares would be credited to:
   (a) Retained Earnings.
   (b) Contributed Capital.

(c) Share Premium—Ordinary.

(d) Par value is not used under IFRS.

4. Which of the following is **false**?

(a) Under GAAP, companies cannot record gains on transactions involving their own shares.

(b) Under IFRS, companies cannot record gains on transactions involving their own shares.

(c) Under IFRS, the statement of stockholders' equity is a required statement.

(d) Under IFRS, a company records a revaluation surplus when it experiences an increase in the price of its common stock.

5. Which of the following does **not** represent a pair of GAAP/IFRS-comparable terms?

(a) Additional paid-in capital/Share premium.

(b) Treasury stock/Repurchase reserve.

(c) Common stock/Share capital—ordinary.

(d) Preferred stock/Preference shares.

IFRS CONCEPTS AND APPLICATION

IFRS11-1   On May 10, Barone Corporation issues 1,000 shares of $10 par value ordinary shares for cash at $18 per share. Journalize the issuance of the shares.

IFRS11-2   Luther Corporation has the following accounts at December 31, 2014 (in euros): Share Capital—Ordinary, €10 par, 5,000 shares issued, €50,000; Share Premium—Ordinary €10,000; Retained Earnings €45,000; and Treasury Shares—Ordinary, 500 shares, €11,000. Prepare the equity section of the statement of financial position.

IFRS11-3   Vangundy Co. had the following transactions during the current period.

June 12   Issued 60,000 shares of $1 par value ordinary shares for cash of $375,000.
July 11   Issued 1,000 shares of $100 par value preference shares for cash at $110 per share.
Nov. 28   Purchased 2,000 treasury shares for $80,000.

Instructions

Journalize the above transactions.

IFRS11-4   The April 23, 2012, edition of the *Wall Street Journal Online* contains an article by Christopher Bjork entitled "Santander Prepares Record Mexico IPO."

Instructions

Read the article and answer the following questions.

(a) Why is the Spanish lender Santander issuing shares of its Mexican banking subsidiary to the public?

(b) The article suggests that Santander has previously issued shares of subsidiaries in other countries as well. Why does the bank like to do these so-called "local listings"?

(c) In what other countries has Santander done local listings? Why do regulators in those countries like the local listings?

(d) What advantage has Santander had over some of its European rivals in raising funds?

INTERNATIONAL FINANCIAL REPORTING PROBLEM: *Zetar plc*

IFRS11-5   The financial statements of Zetar plc are presented in Appendix C. The company's complete annual report, including the notes to its financial statements, is available in the Investors section at **www.zetarplc.com**.

Instructions

Use the company's annual report to answer the following questions.

(a) Using the information in the statement of changes in equity, prepare the journal entry to record the issuance of ordinary shares during the year ended April 30, 2010.

(b) Compute the company's return on ordinary shareholders' equity for the year ended April 30, 2011.

(c) Examine the equity section of the company's balance sheet. For each item in the equity section, provide the comparable label that would be used under GAAP.

Answers to IFRS Self-Test Questions

1. d   **2.** b   **3.** c   **4.** d   **5.** b

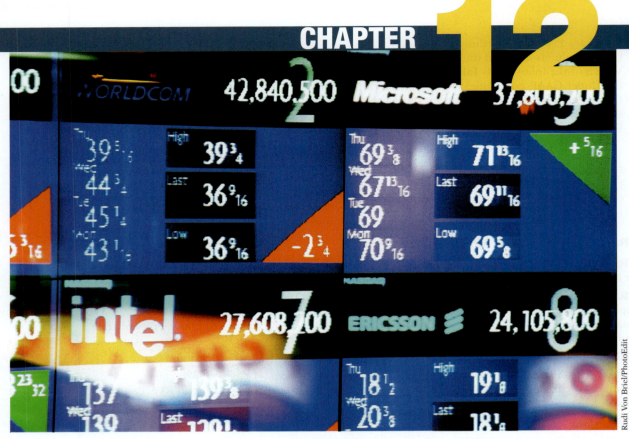

CHAPTER 12

Rudi Von Briel/PhotoEdit

STATEMENT OF CASH FLOWS

LEARNING OBJECTIVES

After studying this chapter, you should be able to:

1. Indicate the usefulness of the statement of cash flows.
2. Distinguish among operating, investing, and financing activities.
3. Explain the impact of the product life cycle on a company's cash flows.
4. Prepare a statement of cash flows using the indirect method.
5. Use the statement of cash flows to evaluate a company.

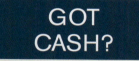

Companies must be ready to respond to changes quickly in order to survive and thrive. This requires careful management of cash. One company that managed cash successfully in its early years was Microsoft. During those years, the company paid much of its payroll with stock options (rights to purchase company stock in the future at a given price) instead of cash. This conserved cash and turned more than a thousand of its employees into millionaires.

In recent years, Microsoft has had a different kind of cash problem. Now that it has reached a more "mature" stage in life, it generates so much cash— roughly $1 billion per month—that it cannot always figure out what to do with it. At one time, Microsoft had accumulated $60 billion.

The company said it was accumulating cash to invest in new opportunities, buy other companies, and pay off pending lawsuits. Microsoft's stockholders complained that holding all this cash was putting a drag on the company's profitability. Why? Because Microsoft had the cash invested in very low-yielding government securities. Stockholders felt that the company either should find new investment projects that would bring higher returns, or return some of the cash to stockholders.

Finally, Microsoft announced a plan to return cash to stockholders by paying a special one-time $32 billion dividend. This special dividend was so large that, according to the U.S. Commerce Department, it caused total personal income in the United States to rise by 3.7% in one month—the largest increase ever recorded by the agency. (It also made the holiday season brighter, especially for retailers in the Seattle area.) Microsoft also doubled its regular annual dividend to $3.50 per share. Further, it announced that it would spend another $30 billion buying treasury stock.

In recent years, Apple also encountered this cash "problem." At the end of 2011, Apple had nearly $100 billion in liquid assets (cash, cash equivalents, and investment securities). At that time, it was generating $37 billion of cash per year from its operating activities but spending only about $7 billion on plant assets and purchases of patents. Shareholders pressured Apple to unload some of this cash. In response, Apple announced that it would begin to pay a quarterly dividend of $2.65 per share and it would buy back up to $10 billion of its stock. Analysts noted that the dividend consumes only $10 billion of cash per year. This leaves Apple wallowing in cash. The rest of us should have such problems.

Source: "Business: An End to Growth? Microsoft's Cash Bonanza," *The Economist* (July 23, 2005), p. 61.

GOT CASH?

INSIDE CHAPTER 12 . . .

- Net *What?*
- Operating with Negative Cash
- Burning Through Our Cash
- We Aren't Going to Fail—Really

The balance sheet, income statement, and retained earnings statement do not always show the whole picture of the financial condition of a company or institution. In fact, looking at the financial statements of some well-known companies, a thoughtful investor might ask questions like these: How did Eastman Kodak finance cash dividends of $649 million in a year in which it earned only $17 million? How could United Air Lines purchase new planes that cost $1.9 billion in a year in which it reported a net loss of over $2 billion? How did the companies that spent a combined fantastic $3.4 trillion on mergers and acquisitions in a recent year finance those deals? Answers to these and similar questions can be found in this chapter, which presents the statement of cash flows.

The content and organization of this chapter are as follows.

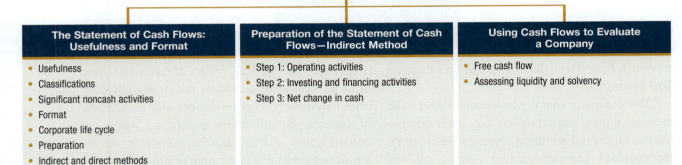

The Statement of Cash Flows: Usefulness and Format

LEARNING OBJECTIVE 1

Indicate the usefulness of the statement of cash flows.

The balance sheet, income statement, and retained earnings statement provide only limited information about a company's cash flows (cash receipts and cash payments). For example, comparative balance sheets show the increase in property, plant, and equipment during the year. But, they do not show how the additions were financed or paid for. The income statement shows net income. But, it does not indicate the amount of cash generated by operating activities. The retained earnings statement shows cash dividends declared but not the cash dividends paid during the year. None of these statements presents a detailed summary of where cash came from and how it was used.

USEFULNESS OF THE STATEMENT OF CASH FLOWS

The statement of cash flows reports the cash receipts and cash payments from operating, investing, and financing activities during a period, in a format that reconciles the beginning and ending cash balances. The information in a statement of cash flows helps investors, creditors, and others assess:

1. **The entity's ability to generate future cash flows.** By examining relationships between items in the statement of cash flows, investors make predictions

of the amounts, timing, and uncertainty of future cash flows better than they can from accrual-basis data.

2. **The entity's ability to pay dividends and meet obligations.** If a company does not have adequate cash, it cannot pay employees, settle debts, or pay dividends. Employees, creditors, and stockholders should be particularly interested in this statement because it alone shows the flows of cash in a business.

3. **The reasons for the difference between net income and net cash provided (used) by operating activities.** Net income provides information on the success or failure of a business enterprise. However, some financial statement users are critical of accrual-basis net income because it requires many estimates. As a result, users often challenge the reliability of the number. Such is not the case with cash. Many readers of the statement of cash flows want to know the reasons for the difference between net income and net cash provided by operating activities. Then they can assess for themselves the reliability of the income number.

4. **The cash investing and financing transactions during the period.** By examining a company's investing and financing transactions, a financial statement reader can better understand why assets and liabilities changed during the period.

CLASSIFICATION OF CASH FLOWS

The statement of cash flows classifies cash receipts and cash payments as operating, investing, and financing activities. Transactions and other events characteristic of each kind of activity are as follows.

> **LEARNING OBJECTIVE 2**
> Distinguish among operating, investing, and financing activities.

1. **Operating activities** include the cash effects of transactions that create revenues and expenses. They thus enter into the determination of net income.

2. **Investing activities** include (a) cash transactions that involve the purchase or disposal of investments and property, plant, and equipment, and (b) lending money and collecting the loans.

3. **Financing activities** include (a) obtaining cash from issuing debt and repaying the amounts borrowed, and (b) obtaining cash from stockholders, repurchasing shares, and paying dividends.

The operating activities category is the most important. It shows the cash provided by company operations. This source of cash is generally considered to be the best measure of a company's ability to generate sufficient cash to continue as a going concern.

Illustration 12-1 lists typical cash receipts and cash payments within each of the three classifications. **Study the list carefully.** It will be very useful in solving homework exercises and problems.

Note the following general guidelines:

1. Operating activities involve income statement items.

2. Investing activities involve cash flows resulting from changes in investments and long-term asset items.

3. Financing activities involve cash flows resulting from changes in long-term liability and stockholders' equity items.

Companies classify as operating activities some cash flows related to investing or financing activities. For example, receipts of investment revenue (interest and dividends) are classified as operating activities. So are payments of interest to lenders. Why are these considered operating activities? **Because companies report these items in the income statement, where results of operations are shown.**

Illustration 12-1 Typical receipt and payment classifications

Operating activities

Investing activities

Financing activities

Types of Cash Inflows and Outflows

Operating activities—Income statement items
    Cash inflows:
        From sale of goods or services.
        From interest received and dividends received.
    Cash outflows:
        To suppliers for inventory.
        To employees for wages.
        To government for taxes.
        To lenders for interest.
        To others for expenses.

Investing activities—Changes in investments and long-term assets
    Cash inflows:
        From sale of property, plant, and equipment.
        From sale of investments in debt or equity securities of other entities.
        From collection of principal on loans to other entities.
    Cash outflows:
        To purchase property, plant, and equipment.
        To purchase investments in debt or equity securities of other entities.
        To make loans to other entities.

Financing activities—Changes in long-term liabilities and stockholders' equity
    Cash inflows:
        From sale of common stock.
        From issuance of debt (bonds and notes).
    Cash outflows:
        To stockholders as dividends.
        To redeem long-term debt or reacquire capital stock (treasury stock).

SIGNIFICANT NONCASH ACTIVITIES

Not all of a company's significant activities involve cash. Examples of significant noncash activities are:

1. Direct issuance of common stock to purchase assets.
2. Conversion of bonds into common stock.
3. Direct issuance of debt to purchase assets.
4. Exchanges of plant assets.

    Companies do not report in the body of the statement of cash flows significant financing and investing activities that do not affect cash. Instead, they report these activities in either a **separate schedule** at the bottom of the statement of cash flows or in a **separate note or supplementary schedule** to the financial statements. The reporting of these noncash activities in a separate schedule satisfies the **full disclosure principle**.

    In solving homework assignments, you should present significant noncash investing and financing activities in a separate schedule at the bottom of the statement of cash flows. (See the last entry in Illustration 12-2 for an example.)

Accounting Across the Organization

Net *What?*

Net income is not the same as net cash provided by operating activities. The differences are illustrated by the following results from recent annual reports ($ in millions). Note the wide disparity among these companies that all engaged in retail merchandising.

Company	Net Income	Net Cash Provided by Operating Activities
Kohl's Corporation	$ 1,083	$ 1,234
Wal-Mart Stores, Inc.	11,284	20,169
JCPenney Company, Inc.	1,153	1,255
Costco Wholesale Corp.	1,082	2,076
Target Corporation	2,849	4,125

? In general, why do differences exist between net income and net cash provided by operating activities? (Answers in *Broadening Your Perspective*.)

FORMAT OF THE STATEMENT OF CASH FLOWS

The general format of the statement of cash flows presents the results of the three activities discussed previously—operating, investing, and financing—plus the significant noncash investing and financing activities. Illustration 12–2 shows a widely used form of the statement of cash flows.

COMPANY NAME
Statement of Cash Flows
Period Covered

Cash flows from operating activities		
(List of individual items)	XX	
Net cash provided (used) by operating activities		XXX
Cash flows from investing activities		
(List of individual inflows and outflows)	XX	
Net cash provided (used) by investing activities		XXX
Cash flows from financing activities		
(List of individual inflows and outflows)	XX	
Net cash provided (used) by financing activities		XXX
Net increase (decrease) in cash		XXX
Cash at beginning of period		XXX
Cash at end of period		XXX
Noncash investing and financing activities		
(List of individual noncash transactions)		XXX

Illustration 12-2 Format of statement of cash flows

The cash flows from operating activities section always appears first, followed by the investing activities section and then the financing activities section. The sum of the operating, investing, and financing activities sections equals the net increase or decrease in cash for the period. This amount is added to the beginning cash balance to arrive at the ending cash balance—the same amount reported on the balance sheet.

THE CORPORATE LIFE CYCLE

All products go through a series of phases called the **product life cycle**. The phases (in order of their occurrence) are **introductory phase**, **growth phase**, **maturity phase**, and **decline phase**. The introductory phase occurs at the beginning of a company's life, when it purchases fixed assets and begins to produce and sell products. During the growth phase, the company strives to expand its production and sales. In the maturity phase, sales and production level off. During the decline phase, sales of the product decline due to a weakening in consumer demand.

In the same way that products have life cycles, companies have life cycles as well. Companies generally have more than one product, and not all of a company's products are in the same phase of the product life cycle at the same time. This sometimes makes it difficult to classify a company's phase. Still, we can characterize a company as being in one of the four phases because the majority of its products are in a particular phase.

Illustration 12-3 shows that the phase a company is in affects its cash flows. In the **introductory phase**, we expect that the company will not generate positive cash from operations. That is, cash used in operations will exceed cash generated by operations in the introductory phase. Also, the company spends considerable amounts to purchase productive assets such as buildings and equipment. To support its asset purchases, the company issues stock or debt. Thus, during the introductory phase, we expect negative cash from operations, negative cash from investing, and positive cash from financing.

Illustration 12-3 Impact of product life cycle on cash flows

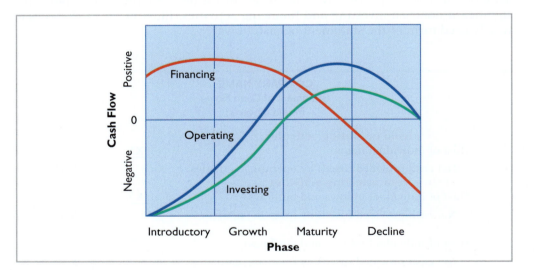

During the **growth phase**, we expect to see the company start to generate small amounts of cash from operations. During this phase, net cash provided by operating activities on the statement of cash flows is less than net income. One reason net income exceeds cash flow from operations during this period is explained by the difference between the cash paid for inventory and the amount expensed as cost of goods sold. Since the company projects increasing sales, the size of inventory purchases increases. Thus, in the growth phase, the company expenses less inventory on an accrual basis than it purchases on a cash basis. Also, collections on accounts receivable lag behind sales, and accrual sales during a period exceed cash collections during that period. Cash needed for asset acquisitions will continue to exceed net cash provided by operating activities. The company makes up the deficiency by issuing new stock or debt. Thus, in the growth phase, the company continues to show negative cash from investing and positive cash from financing activities.

During the **maturity phase**, net cash provided by operating activities and net income are approximately the same. Cash generated from operations exceeds investing needs. Thus, in the maturity phase, the company starts to pay dividends, retire debt, or buy back stock.

Investor Insight

Operating with Negative Cash

Listed here are recent amounts of net income and net cash provided (used) by operating, investing, and financing activities for a variety of companies. The final column suggests the companies' likely phase in the life cycle based on these figures.

Company ($ in millions)	Net Income	Net Cash Provided (Used) by Operating Activities	Net Cash Provided (Used) by Investing Activities	Net Cash Provided (Used) by Financing Activities	Likely Phase in Life Cycle
Amazon.com	$ 476	$1,405	$ (42)	$ (50)	Early maturity
LDK Solar	(144)	(81)	(329)	462	Introductory/ early growth
United States Steel	879	1,745	(4,675)	(1,891)	Maturity
Kellogg	1,103	1,503	(601)	(788)	Early decline
Southwest Airlines	645	2,845	(1,529)	493	Maturity
Starbucks	673	1,331	(1,202)	(172)	Maturity

? Why do companies have negative net cash provided by operating activities during the introductory phase? (Answers in *Broadening Your Perspective*.)

Finally, during the **decline phase**, net cash provided by operating activities decreases. Cash from investing activities might actually become positive as the company sells off excess assets. Cash from financing activities may be negative as the company buys back stock and redeems debt.

Consider Microsoft. During its early years, it had significant product development costs and little revenue. Microsoft was lucky in that its agreement with IBM to provide the operating system for IBM PCs gave it an early steady source of cash to support growth. As noted in the Feature Story, Microsoft conserved cash by paying employees with stock options rather than cash. Today, Microsoft could be characterized as being in the maturity phase. It continues to spend considerable amounts on research and development and investment in new assets. In recent years, though, its net cash provided by operating activities has exceeded its net income. Also, cash from operations over this period exceeded cash used for investing, and common stock repurchased exceeded common stock issued. For Microsoft, as for any large company, the challenge is to maintain its growth. In the software industry, where products become obsolete very quickly, the challenge is particularly great.

PREPARING THE STATEMENT OF CASH FLOWS

Companies prepare the statement of cash flows differently from the three other basic financial statements. First, it is not prepared from an adjusted trial balance. It requires detailed information concerning the changes in account balances that occurred between two points in time. An adjusted trial balance will not provide the necessary data. Second, the statement of cash flows deals with cash receipts and payments. As a result, the company **adjusts** the effects of the use of accrual accounting **to determine cash flows**.

The information to prepare this statement usually comes from three sources:

- **Comparative balance sheets.** Information in the comparative balance sheets indicates the amount of the changes in assets, liabilities, and stockholders' equities from the beginning to the end of the period.
- **Current income statement.** Information in this statement helps determine the amount of net cash provided or used by operating activities during the period.
- **Additional information.** Such information includes transaction data that are needed to determine how cash was provided or used during the period.

Preparing the statement of cash flows from these data sources involves three major steps, explained in Illustration 12-4.

INDIRECT AND DIRECT METHODS

In order to perform Step 1, a company **must convert net income from an accrual basis to a cash basis**. This conversion may be done by either of two methods: (1) the indirect method or (2) the direct method. **Both methods arrive at the same total amount** for "Net cash provided by operating activities." They differ in **how** they arrive at the amount.

The **indirect method** adjusts net income for items that do not affect cash to determine net cash provided by operating activities. A great majority of companies (98%) use this method, as shown in the chart on the left.[1] Companies favor the indirect method for two reasons. (1) It is easier and less costly to prepare, and

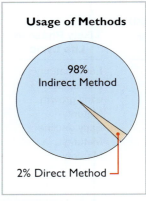

Usage of Methods

98% Indirect Method

2% Direct Method

Illustration 12-4 Three major steps in preparing the statement of cash flows

STEP 1: Determine net cash provided/used by operating activities by converting net income from an accrual basis to a cash basis.

This step involves analyzing not only the current year's income statement but also comparative balance sheets and selected additional data.

STEP 2: Analyze changes in noncurrent asset and liability accounts and record as investing and financing activities, or disclose as noncash transactions.

This step involves analyzing comparative balance sheet data and selected additional information for their effects on cash.

STEP 3: Compare the net change in cash on the statement of cash flows with the change in the cash account reported on the balance sheet to make sure the amounts agree.

The difference between the beginning and ending cash balances can be easily computed from comparative balance sheets.

[1]*Accounting Trends and Techniques—2011* (New York: American Institute of Certified Public Accountants, 2011).

(2) it focuses on the differences between net income and net cash flow from operating activities.

The **direct method** shows operating cash receipts and payments. It is prepared by adjusting each item in the income statement from the accrual basis to the cash basis. The FASB has expressed a preference for the direct method but allows the use of either method.

The next section illustrates the more popular indirect method. Appendix 12A illustrates the direct method. Appendix 12B demonstrates an approach that employs T-accounts to prepare the statement of cash flows. Many students find the T-account approach provides a useful structure. We encourage you to give it a try as you walk through the Computer Services example.

Preparation of the Statement of Cash Flows—Indirect Method

To explain how to prepare a statement of cash flows using the indirect method, we use financial information from Computer Services Company. Illustration 12-5 presents Computer Services' current and previous-year balance sheets, its current-year income statement, and related financial information.

LEARNING OBJECTIVE **4**

Prepare a statement of cash flows using the indirect method.

Illustration 12-5
Comparative balance sheets, income statement, and additional information for Computer Services Company

COMPUTER SERVICES COMPANY
Comparative Balance Sheets
December 31

Assets	2014	2013	Change in Account Balance Increase/Decrease
Current assets			
Cash	$ 55,000	$ 33,000	$ 22,000 Increase
Accounts receivable	20,000	30,000	10,000 Decrease
Inventory	15,000	10,000	5,000 Increase
Prepaid expenses	5,000	1,000	4,000 Increase
Property, plant, and equipment			
Land	130,000	20,000	110,000 Increase
Buildings	160,000	40,000	120,000 Increase
Accumulated depreciation—buildings	(11,000)	(5,000)	6,000 Increase
Equipment	27,000	10,000	17,000 Increase
Accumulated depreciation—equipment	(3,000)	(1,000)	2,000 Increase
Total assets	$398,000	$138,000	
Liabilities and Stockholders' Equity			
Current liabilities			
Accounts payable	$ 28,000	$ 12,000	$ 16,000 Increase
Income taxes payable	6,000	8,000	2,000 Decrease
Long-term liabilities			
Bonds payable	130,000	20,000	110,000 Increase
Stockholders' equity			
Common stock	70,000	50,000	20,000 Increase
Retained earnings	164,000	48,000	116,000 Increase
Total liabilities and stockholders' equity	$398,000	$138,000	

COMPUTER SERVICES COMPANY
Income Statement
For the Year Ended December 31, 2014

Sales revenue		$507,000
Cost of goods sold	$150,000	
Operating expenses (excluding depreciation)	111,000	
Depreciation expense	9,000	
Loss on disposal of plant assets	3,000	
Interest expense	42,000	315,000
Income before income tax		192,000
Income tax expense		47,000
Net income		$145,000

Additional information for 2014:
1. Depreciation expense was comprised of $6,000 for building and $3,000 for equipment.
2. The company sold equipment with a book value of $7,000 (cost $8,000, less accumulated depreciation $1,000) for $4,000 cash.
3. Issued $110,000 of long-term bonds in direct exchange for land.
4. A building costing $120,000 was purchased for cash. Equipment costing $25,000 was also purchased for cash.
5. Issued common stock for $20,000 cash.
6. The company declared and paid a $29,000 cash dividend.

We now apply the three steps to the information provided for Computer Services Company.

STEP 1: OPERATING ACTIVITIES

DETERMINE NET CASH PROVIDED/USED BY OPERATING ACTIVITIES BY CONVERTING NET INCOME FROM AN ACCRUAL BASIS TO A CASH BASIS

To determine net cash provided by operating activities under the indirect method, companies **adjust net income in numerous ways**. A useful starting point is to understand **why** net income must be converted to net cash provided by operating activities.

Under generally accepted accounting principles, most companies use the accrual basis of accounting. As you have learned, this basis requires that companies record revenue when the performance obligation is satisfied and record expenses when incurred. Revenues include credit sales for which the company has not yet collected cash. Expenses incurred include some items that it has not yet paid in cash. Thus, under the accrual basis of accounting, net income is not the same as net cash provided by operating activities.

Therefore, under the **indirect method**, companies must adjust net income to convert certain items to the cash basis. The indirect method (or reconciliation method) starts with net income and converts it to net cash provided by operating activities. Illustration 12-6 lists the three types of adjustments.

We explain the three types of adjustments in the next three sections.

Depreciation Expense

Computer Services' income statement reports depreciation expense of $9,000. Although depreciation expense reduces net income, it does not reduce cash. In other words, depreciation expense is a noncash charge. The company must add it back to net income to arrive at net cash provided by operating activities. Computer Services reports depreciation expense as follows in the statement of cash flows.

Net Income +/−	Adjustments	=	Net Cash Provided/ Used by Operating Activities
	• **Add back noncash expenses,** such as depreciation expense, amortization, or depletion.		
	• **Deduct gains and add losses** that resulted from investing and financing activities.		
	• **Analyze changes** to noncash current asset and current liability accounts.		

Illustration 12-6 Three types of adjustments to convert net income to net cash provided by operating activities

Cash flows from operating activities	
Net income	$145,000
Adjustments to reconcile net income to net cash provided by operating activities:	
Depreciation expense	**9,000**
Net cash provided by operating activities	$154,000

Illustration 12-7 Adjustment for depreciation

As the first adjustment to net income in the statement of cash flows, companies frequently list depreciation and similar noncash charges such as amortization of intangible assets, depletion expense, and bad debt expense.

Loss on Disposal of Plant Assets

Illustration 12-1 states that cash received from the sale of plant assets is reported in the investing activities section. Because of this, **companies eliminate from net income all gains and losses resulting from investing activities, to arrive at cash provided by operating activities**.

In our example, Computer Services' income statement reports a $3,000 loss on the disposal of plant assets (book value $7,000, less cash received from sale of equipment $4,000). The company's loss of $3,000 is eliminated in the operating activities section of the statement of cash flows. Illustration 12-8 shows that the $3,000 loss is eliminated by adding $3,000 back to net income to arrive at net cash provided by operating activities.

Cash flows from operating activities		
Net income		$145,000
Adjustments to reconcile net income to net cash provided by operating activities:		
Depreciation expense	$9,000	
Loss on disposal of plant assets	**3,000**	12,000
Net cash provided by operating activities		$157,000

Illustration 12-8 Adjustment for loss on disposal of plant assets

If a gain on sale occurs, the company deducts the gain from net income in order to determine net cash provided by operating activities. **In the case of either a gain or a loss, companies report the actual amount of cash received from the sale as a source of cash in the investing activities section of the statement of cash flows.**

Changes to Noncash Current Asset and Current Liability Accounts

A final adjustment in reconciling net income to net cash provided by operating activities involves examining all changes in current asset and current liability accounts. The accrual-accounting process records revenues in the period in which the performance obligation is satisfied and expenses in the period incurred. For example, Accounts Receivable reflects amounts owed to the company for sales that have been made but for which cash collections have not yet been received. Prepaid Insurance reflects insurance that has been paid for but which has not yet expired and therefore has not been expensed. Similarly, Salaries and Wages Payable reflects salaries expense that has been incurred but has not been paid.

As a result, we need to adjust net income for these accruals and prepayments to determine net cash provided by operating activities. Thus, we must analyze the change in each current asset and current liability account to determine its impact on net income and cash.

CHANGES IN NONCASH CURRENT ASSETS. The adjustments required for changes in noncash current asset accounts are as follows. **Deduct from net income increases in current asset accounts, and add to net income decreases in current asset accounts, to arrive at net cash provided by operating activities.** We observe these relationships by analyzing the accounts of Computer Services Company.

DECREASE IN ACCOUNTS RECEIVABLE. Computer Services Company's accounts receivable decreased by $10,000 (from $30,000 to $20,000) during the period. For Computer Services, this means that cash receipts were $10,000 higher than sales revenue. The Accounts Receivable account in Illustration 12-9 shows that Computer Services Company had $507,000 in sales revenue (as reported on the income statement), but it collected $517,000 in cash.

Illustration 12-9 Analysis of Accounts Receivable

Accounts Receivable				
1/1/12	Balance	30,000	**Receipts from customers**	**517,000**
	Sales revenue	**507,000**		
12/31/12	Balance	20,000		

As shown in Illustration 12-10, to adjust net income to net cash provided by operating activities, the company adds to net income the decrease of $10,000 in accounts receivable.

Illustration 12-10
Adjustments for changes in current asset accounts

Cash flows from operating activities		
Net income		$145,000
Adjustments to reconcile net income to net cash provided by operating activities:		
Depreciation expense	$ 9,000	
Loss on disposal of plant assets	3,000	
Decrease in accounts receivable	**10,000**	
Increase in inventory	**(5,000)**	
Increase in prepaid expenses	**(4,000)**	13,000
Net cash provided by operating activities		$158,000

When the Accounts Receivable balance increases, cash receipts are lower than revenue recorded under the accrual basis. Therefore, the company deducts from net income the amount of the increase in accounts receivable, to arrive at net cash provided by operating activities.

INCREASE IN INVENTORY. Computer Services Company's inventory increased $5,000 (from $10,000 to $15,000) during the period. The change in the Inventory account reflects the difference between the amount of inventory purchased and the amount sold. For Computer Services, this means that the cost of merchandise purchased exceeded the cost of goods sold by $5,000. As a result, cost of goods sold does not reflect $5,000 of cash payments made for merchandise. The company deducts from net income this inventory increase of $5,000 during the period, to arrive at net cash provided by operating activities (see Illustration 12-10). If inventory decreases, the company adds to net income the amount of the change, to arrive at net cash provided by operating activities.

INCREASE IN PREPAID EXPENSES. Computer Services' prepaid expenses increased during the period by $4,000. This means that cash paid for expenses is higher than expenses reported on an accrual basis. In other words, the company has made cash payments in the current period but will not charge expenses to income until future periods (as charges to the income statement). To adjust net income to net cash provided by operating activities, the company deducts from net income the $4,000 increase in prepaid expenses (see Illustration 12-10).

If prepaid expenses decrease, reported expenses are higher than the expenses paid. Therefore, the company adds to net income the decrease in prepaid expense, to arrive at net cash provided by operating activities.

CHANGES IN CURRENT LIABILITIES. The adjustments required for changes in current liability accounts are as follows. **Add to net income increases in current liability accounts, and deduct from net income decreases in current liability accounts, to arrive at net cash provided by operating activities.**

INCREASE IN ACCOUNTS PAYABLE. For Computer Services Company, accounts payable increased by $16,000 (from $12,000 to $28,000) during the period. That means the company received $16,000 more in goods than it actually paid for. As shown in Illustration 12-11 (below), to adjust net income to determine net cash provided by operating activities, the company adds to net income the $16,000 increase in the Accounts Payable account.

DECREASE IN INCOME TAXES PAYABLE. When a company incurs income tax expense but has not yet paid its taxes, it records income taxes payable. A change in the Income Taxes Payable account reflects the difference between income tax expense incurred and income tax actually paid. Computer Services' Income Taxes Payable account decreased by $2,000. That means the $47,000 of income tax expense reported on the income statement was $2,000 less than the amount of taxes paid during the period of $49,000. As shown in Illustration 12-11, to adjust net income to a cash basis, the company must reduce net income by $2,000.

Illustration 12-11 shows that after starting with net income of $145,000, the

Illustration 12-11
Adjustments for changes in current liability accounts

Cash flows from operating activities		
Net income		$145,000
Adjustments to reconcile net income to net cash provided by operating activities:		
Depreciation expense	$ 9,000	
Loss on disposal of plant assets	3,000	
Decrease in accounts receivable	10,000	
Increase in inventory	(5,000)	
Increase in prepaid expenses	(4,000)	
Increase in accounts payable	**16,000**	
Decrease in income taxes payable	**(2,000)**	27,000
Net cash provided by operating activities		$172,000

sum of all of the adjustments to net income was $27,000. This resulted in net cash provided by operating activities of $172,000.

SUMMARY OF CONVERSION TO NET CASH PROVIDED BY OPERATING ACTIVITIES—INDIRECT METHOD

As shown in the previous illustrations, the statement of cash flows prepared by the indirect method starts with net income. Items are then added or deducted to arrive at net cash provided by operating activities. The required adjustments are of three types:

1. Noncash charges such as depreciation, amortization, and depletion.
2. Gains and losses from investing and financing transactions, such as the sale of plant assets.
3. Changes in noncash current asset and current liability accounts.

Illustration 12-12 provides a summary of these changes.

Illustration 12-12
Adjustments required to convert net income to net cash provided by operating activities

		Adjustment Required to Convert Net Income to Net Cash Provided by Operating Activities
Noncash charges	Depreciation expense	Add
	Patent amortization expense	Add
Gains and losses	Loss on disposal of plant assets	Add
	Gain on disposal of plant assets	Deduct
Changes in current assets and current liabilities	Increase in current asset account	Deduct
	Decrease in current asset account	Add
	Increase in current liability account	Add
	Decrease in current liability account	Deduct

ANATOMY OF A FRAUD

For more than a decade, the top executives at the Italian dairy products company Parmalat engaged in multiple frauds that overstated cash and other assets by more than $1 billion while understating liabilities by between $8 and $12 billion. Much of the fraud involved creating fictitious sources and uses of cash. Some of these activities incorporated sophisticated financial transactions with subsidiaries created with the help of large international financial institutions. However, much of the fraud employed very basic, even sloppy, forgery of documents. For example, when outside auditors requested confirmation of bank accounts (such as a fake $4.8 billion account in the Cayman Islands), documents were created on scanners, with signatures that were cut and pasted from other documents. These were then passed through a fax machine numerous times to make them look real (if difficult to read). Similarly, fictitious bills were created in order to divert funds to other businesses owned by the Tanzi family (who controlled Parmalat).

Total take: Billions of dollars

THE MISSING CONTROL

Independent internal verification. Internal auditors at the company should have independently verified bank accounts and major transfers of cash to outside companies that were controlled by the Tanzi family.

STEP 2: INVESTING AND FINANCING ACTIVITIES

ANALYZE CHANGES IN NONCURRENT ASSET AND LIABILITY ACCOUNTS AND RECORD AS INVESTING AND FINANCING ACTIVITIES, OR DISCLOSE AS NONCASH TRANSACTIONS

INCREASE IN LAND. As indicated from the change in the Land account and the additional information, Computer Services Company purchased land of $110,000 by directly exchanging bonds for land. The exchange of bonds payable for land has no effect on cash. But, it is a significant noncash investing and financing activity that merits disclosure in a separate schedule. (See Illustration 12-14.)

INCREASE IN BUILDINGS. As the additional data indicate, Computer Services Company acquired an office building for $120,000 cash. This is a cash outflow reported in the investing activities section. (See Illustration 12-14.)

INCREASE IN EQUIPMENT. The Equipment account increased $17,000. The additional information explains that this was a net increase that resulted from two transactions: (1) a purchase of equipment of $25,000, and (2) the sale for $4,000 of equipment costing $8,000. These transactions are both investing activities. The company should report each transaction separately. Thus, it reports the purchase of equipment as an outflow of cash for $25,000. It reports the sale as an inflow of cash for $4,000. The T-account below shows the reasons for the change in this account during the year.

Illustration 12-13
Analysis of Equipment

Equipment			
1/1/14 Balance	10,000	Cost of equipment sold	8,000
Purchase of equipment	**25,000**		
12/31/14 Balance	27,000		

The following entry shows the details of the equipment sale transaction.

Cash	4,000	
Accumulated Depreciation	1,000	
Loss on Disposal of Plant Assets	3,000	
Equipment		8,000

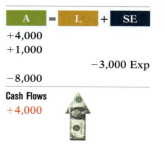

A	=	L	+	SE
+4,000				
+1,000				
				−3,000 Exp
−8,000				

Cash Flows
+4,000

INCREASE IN BONDS PAYABLE. The Bonds Payable account increased $110,000. As indicated in the additional information, the company acquired land by directly exchanging bonds for land. It reports this noncash transaction in a separate schedule at the bottom of the statement.

INCREASE IN COMMON STOCK. The balance sheet reports an increase in Common Stock of $20,000. The additional information section notes that this increase resulted from the issuance of new shares of stock. This is a cash inflow reported in the financing activities section.

INCREASE IN RETAINED EARNINGS. Retained earnings increased $116,000 during the year. This increase can be explained by two factors: (1) Net income of $145,000 increased retained earnings and (2) dividends of $29,000 decreased retained earnings. The company adjusts net income to net cash provided by operating activities in the operating activities section. Payment of the dividends (not the declaration) is a **cash outflow that the company reports as a financing activity**.

Statement of Cash Flows—2014

Using the previous information, we can now prepare a statement of cash flows for 2014 for Computer Services Company, as shown in Illustration 12-14.

STEP 3: NET CHANGE IN CASH

COMPARE THE NET CHANGE IN CASH ON THE STATEMENT OF CASH FLOWS WITH THE CHANGE IN THE CASH ACCOUNT REPORTED ON THE BALANCE SHEET TO MAKE SURE THE AMOUNTS AGREE

Illustration 12-14 indicates that the net change in cash during the period was an increase of $22,000. This agrees with the change in Cash account reported on the balance sheet in Illustration 12-5.

Illustration 12-14
Statement of cash flows, 2014—indirect method

COMPUTER SERVICES COMPANY
Statement of Cash Flows–Indirect Method
For the Year Ended December 31, 2014

Cash flows from operating activities		
Net income		$ 145,000
Adjustments to reconcile net income to net cash provided by operating activities:		
Depreciation expense	$ 9,000	
Loss on disposal of plant assets	3,000	
Decrease in accounts receivable	10,000	
Increase in inventory	(5,000)	
Increase in prepaid expenses	(4,000)	
Increase in accounts payable	16,000	
Decrease in income taxes payable	(2,000)	27,000
Net cash provided by operating activities		172,000
Cash flows from investing activities		
Sale of equipment	4,000	
Purchase of building	(120,000)	
Purchase of equipment	(25,000)	
Net cash used by investing activities		(141,000)
Cash flows from financing activities		
Issuance of common stock	20,000	
Payment of cash dividends	(29,000)	
Net cash used by financing activities		(9,000)
Net increase in cash		22,000
Cash at beginning of period		33,000
Cash at end of period		$ 55,000
Noncash investing and financing activities		
Issuance of bonds payable to purchase land		$ 110,000

Accounting Across the Organization

Burning Through Our Cash

Kodak used to dominate the market for photographic film—back when most cameras used film. But when digital cameras arrived, the company's cash flows steadily declined. Investors began to wonder whether Kodak's cash would run out before the company came up with an alternative source of income. Eventually, the company was forced to sell plant assets and intangibles such as patents in order to supplement its cash from operating activities. Finally, Kodak decided to borrow money against its line of credit. Investors in Kodak's stocks and bonds interpreted this as a desperate move (because it further increased the company's debt). The price of its stock and its bonds plummeted. Within months, Kodak had filed for bankruptcy.

Source: Dana Mattioli and Matt Marzemsky, "Clock Ticks as Kodak Burns Cash," *Wall Street Journal* (September 27, 2011).

? What impact did Kodak's sale of plant assets have on its net cash provided by investing activities? (Answers in *Broadening Your Perspective.*)

Using Cash Flows to Evaluate a Company

Traditionally, investors and creditors used ratios based on accrual accounting. These days, cash-based ratios are gaining increased acceptance among analysts. In this section, we review free cash flow and introduce two new measures.

LEARNING OBJECTIVE 5

Use the statement of cash flows to evaluate a company.

FREE CASH FLOW

In the statement of cash flows, net cash provided by operating activities is intended to indicate the cash-generating capability of the company. Analysts have noted, however, that **cash provided by operating activities fails to take into account that a company must invest in new fixed assets** just to maintain its current level of operations. Companies also must at least **maintain dividends at current levels** to satisfy investors. As we discussed in Chapter 2, the measurement of free cash flow provides additional insight regarding a company's cash-generating ability. **Free cash flow** describes the net cash provided by operating activities after adjustment for capital expenditures and dividends.

Consider the following example. Suppose that MPC produced and sold 10,000 personal computers this year. It reported $100,000 cash provided by operating activities. In order to maintain production at 10,000 computers, MPC invested $15,000 in equipment. It chose to pay $5,000 in dividends. Its free cash flow was $80,000 ($100,000 − $15,000 − $5,000). The company could use this $80,000 either to purchase new assets, pay off debt, or pay an $80,000 dividend. In practice, free cash flow is often calculated with the formula in Illustration 12-15. Alternative definitions also exist.

Free Cash Flow	=	Net Cash Provided by Operating Activities	−	Capital Expenditures	−	Cash Dividends

Illustration 12-15 Free cash flow

Illustration 12-16 provides basic information excerpted from the 2011 statement of cash flows of Apple (prior to the payment of its first dividends).

APPLE, INC.
Statement of Cash Flows Information (partial)
2011

Net cash provided by operating activities		$ 37,529
Cash flows from investing activities		
Additions to property and equipment and intangibles	$ (7,452)	
Purchases of investments	(102,576)	
Sales of investments	49,416	
Acquisitions of companies	(244)	
Maturities of investments	20,437	
Net cash used by investing activities		(40,419)
Cash paid for dividends		-0-

Illustration 12-16
Apple's cash flow information ($ in millions)

Apple's free cash flow is calculated as shown in Illustration 12-17 (in millions). Apple generated approximately $30 billion of free cash flow. This is a tremendous amount of cash generated in a single year. It is available for the acquisition of new assets, the buyback and retirement of stock or debt, or the payment of dividends.

Illustration 12-17 Calculation of Apple's free cash flow ($ in millions)

Net cash provided by operating activities	$37,529
Less: Expenditures on property, plant, and equipment and intangibles	7,452
Dividends paid	-0-
Free cash flow	$30,077

Also note that Apple's cash from operations of $37.5 billion exceeds its 2011 net income of $25.9 billion by $11 billion. This lends additional credibility to Apple's income number as an indicator of potential future performance. If anything, Apple's net income might understate its actual performance. Microsoft's free cash flow for 2011 was $19.5 billion, also an incredible amount of cash.

DECISION TOOLKIT

DECISION CHECKPOINTS	INFO NEEDED FOR DECISION	TOOL TO USE FOR DECISION	HOW TO EVALUATE RESULTS
How much cash did the company generate to either expand operations or pay dividends?	Net cash provided by operating activities, cash spent on fixed assets, and cash dividends	Free cash flow = Net cash provided by operating activities − Capital expenditures − Cash dividends	Significant free cash flow indicates greater potential to finance new investment and pay additional dividends.

KEEPING AN EYE ON CASH

Cash flow is closely monitored by analysts and investors for many reasons and in a variety of ways. One measure that is gaining increased attention is "price to cash flow." This is a variant of the price to earnings (P-E) ratio, which has been a staple of analysts for a long time. The difference is that rather than divide the company's stock price by its earnings per share (an accrual-accounting–based number), the price to cash flow ratio divides the company's stock price by its cash flow per share. A high measure suggests that the stock price is high relative to the company's ability to generate cash. A low measure indicates that the company's stock might be a bargain.

The average price to cash flow ratio for companies in the Standard and Poor's 500-stock index was recently 12.1, when the average price-earnings ratio was 19.9. The following table provides values for some well-known companies in a recent year. While you should not use this measure as the sole factor in choosing a stock, it can serve as a useful screen by which to identify companies that merit further investigation.

Company	Price/Cash Flow	Price/EPS
Microsoft	10.2	11.6
Apple	13.3	14.3
Nike	19.7	23.8
Wal-Mart	8.2	13.0
Ford	1.9	2.2
Jet Blue	3.7	13.6

ASSESSING LIQUIDITY AND SOLVENCY USING CASH FLOWS

Previous chapters have presented ratios used to analyze a company's liquidity and solvency. Many of those ratios used accrual-based numbers from the income statement and balance sheet. In this section, we focus on ratios that are **cash-based** rather than accrual-based. That is, instead of using numbers from the income statement, these ratios use numbers from the statement of cash flows.

As discussed earlier, many analysts are critical of accrual-based numbers because they feel that the adjustment process allows too much management discretion. These analysts like to supplement accrual-based analysis with measures that use the statement of cash flows. One disadvantage of these cash-based measures is that, unlike the more commonly employed accrual-based measures, there are no readily available industry averages for comparison. In the following discussion, we use cash flow-based ratios to analyze Apple. In addition to the cash flow information provided in Illustration 12-16, we need the following information related to Apple.

($ in millions)	2011	2010
Current liabilities	$27,970	$20,722
Total liabilities	39,756	27,392

Liquidity

Liquidity is the ability to pay obligations expected to become due within the next year. In Chapter 2, you learned that one measure of liquidity is the **current ratio**: current assets divided by current liabilities. A disadvantage of the current ratio is that it uses year-end balances of current asset and current liability accounts. These year-end balances may not be representative of the company's position during most of the year.

A ratio that partially corrects this problem is the **current cash debt coverage**. It is computed as net cash provided by operating activities divided by average current liabilities. Because net cash provided by operating activities involves the entire year rather than a balance at one point in time, this ratio is often considered a better representation of liquidity on the average day. In general, a value below .40 times is cause for additional investigation of a company's liquidity. Illustration 12-18 shows the current cash debt coverage for Apple, with comparative numbers for Microsoft. For comparative purposes, we have also provided each company's current ratio.

Illustration 12-18 Current cash debt coverage

($ in millions)	Current cash debt coverage	Current ratio
$$\text{Current Cash Debt Coverage} = \frac{\text{Net Cash Provided by Operating Activities}}{\text{Average Current Liabilities}}$$		
Apple	$\dfrac{\$37,529}{(\$27,970 + \$20,722)/2} = 1.54$ times	1.60:1
Microsoft	.98 times	2.60:1

Apple's net cash provided by operating activities is 1.54 times its average current liabilities. Microsoft's ratio of .98 times is lower than that of Apple. Both companies far exceed the threshold of .40 times. Keep in mind that both Apple and Microsoft have extraordinary cash positions. For example, many large companies now have current ratios in the range of 1.0. By this standard, Apple's current ratio of 1.60:1 and Microsoft's current ratio of 2.60:1 are both strong.

🧰 DECISION TOOLKIT

DECISION CHECKPOINTS	INFO NEEDED FOR DECISION	TOOL TO USE FOR DECISION	HOW TO EVALUATE RESULTS
Is the company generating sufficient net cash provided by operating activities to meet its current obligations?	Net cash provided by operating activities and average current liabilities	$$\text{Current cash debt coverage} = \frac{\text{Net cash provided by operating activities}}{\text{Average current liabilities}}$$	A high value suggests good liquidity. Since the numerator contains a "flow" measure, it provides a good supplement to the current ratio.

Solvency

Solvency is the ability of a company to survive over the long term. A measure of solvency that uses cash figures is the **cash debt coverage**. It is computed as the ratio of net cash provided by operating activities to total debt as represented by average total liabilities. This ratio indicates a company's ability to repay its liabilities from cash generated from operations—that is, without having to liquidate productive assets such as property, plant, and equipment. A general rule of thumb is that a cash debt coverage below .20 times is cause for additional investigation.

Illustration 12-19 shows the cash debt coverage for Apple and Microsoft for 2011. For comparative purposes, we have also provided the debt to assets ratios for each company.

Illustration 12-19 Cash debt coverage

$$\text{Cash Debt Coverage} = \frac{\text{Net Cash Provided by Operating Activities}}{\text{Average Total Liabilities}}$$

($ in millions)	Cash debt coverage	Debt to assets ratio
Apple	$\frac{\$37,529}{(\$39,756 + \$27,392)/2} = 1.12$ times	34%
Microsoft	.59 times	52%

Because Apple has long-term obligations, its cash debt coverage is lower than its current cash debt coverage. Obviously, Apple is very solvent. Microsoft's cash debt coverage of .59 times is not as strong as Apple's but still far exceeds the .20 threshold. Neither the cash nor accrual measures suggest any cause for concern regarding the solvency of either company.

🧰 DECISION TOOLKIT

DECISION CHECKPOINTS	INFO NEEDED FOR DECISION	TOOL TO USE FOR DECISION	HOW TO EVALUATE RESULTS
Is the company generating sufficient net cash provided by operating activities to meet its long-term obligations?	Net cash provided by operating activities and average total liabilities	$$\text{Cash debt coverage} = \frac{\text{Net cash provided by operating activities}}{\text{Average total liabilities}}$$	A high value suggests the company is solvent; that is, it will meet its obligations in the long term.

Investor Insight

We Aren't Going to Fail—Really

When an auditor determines that a company is at risk of failing, the auditor notes this concern about the company's ability to continue as a going concern in its audit opinion. Interestingly, during the first quarter of a recent year, 42% of the companies that filed to go public had such warnings in their audit opinions. At first glance, it would seem strange that a company that is at risk of failing would decide to issue shares to the public. Analysts explained that lenders were reluctant to grant loans due to a very low appetite for risk during and after the financial crisis. As a result, companies that might otherwise have borrowed money to supplement their net cash from operating activities were instead forced to try to raise money by issuing stock.

Source: Maxwell Murphy, "The Big Number: 42," *Wall Street Journal* (April 23, 2012).

? Do you think that issuing stock would be a cost-efficient way for these companies to raise funds? (Answers in *Broadening Your Perspective.*)

USING THE DECISION TOOLKIT

Intel Corporation is the leading producer of computer chips for personal computers. Its primary competitor is AMD. The two are vicious competitors, with frequent lawsuits filed between them. Financial statement data for Intel are provided below.

Instructions

Calculate the following cash-based measures for Intel and compare them with the comparative data for AMD which follows.

1. Free cash flow.
2. Current cash debt coverage.
3. Cash debt coverage.

Real World

INTEL CORPORATION
Balance Sheets
December 31, 2011 and 2010
(in millions)

Assets	2011	2010
Current assets	$25,872	$31,611
Noncurrent assets	45,247	31,575
Total assets	$71,119	$63,186
Liabilities and Stockholders' Equity		
Current liabilities	$12,028	$ 9,327
Long-term liabilities	13,180	4,429
Total liabilities	25,208	13,756
Stockholders' equity	45,911	49,430
Total liabilities and stockholders' equity	$71,119	$63,186

Real World

INTEL CORPORATION
Income Statements
For the Years Ended December 31, 2011 and 2010
(in millions)

	2011	2010
Net revenues	$53,999	$43,623
Expenses	41,057	32,159
Net income	$12,942	$11,464

Real World

INTEL CORPORATION
Statements of Cash Flows
For the Years Ended December 31, 2011 and 2010
(in millions)

	2011	2010
Net cash provided by operating activities	$ 20,963	$ 16,692
Net cash used for investing activities	(10,301)	(10,539)
Net cash used for financing activities	(11,100)	(4,642)
Net increase (decrease) in cash and cash equivalents	$ (438)	$ 1,511

Note. Cash spent on property, plant, and equipment in 2011 was $10,764. Cash paid for dividends was $4,127.

Comparative data for AMD:

1. Free cash flow $132 million
2. Current cash debt coverage   .22 times
3. Cash debt coverage   .11 times

Solution

1. Intel's free cash flow is $6,072 million ($20,963 − $10,764 − $4,127). AMD's is $132 million. This gives Intel an advantage in the ability to move quickly to invest in new projects.
2. The current cash debt coverage for Intel is calculated as follows.

$$\frac{\$20,963}{(\$12,028 + \$9,327)/2} = 1.96 \text{ times}$$

Compared to AMD's value of .22 times, Intel is significantly more liquid.
3. The cash debt coverage for Intel is calculated as follows.

$$\frac{\$20,963}{(\$25,208 + \$13,756)/2} = 1.08 \text{ times}$$

Compared to AMD's value of .11 times, Intel appears to be significantly more solvent.

Summary of Learning Objectives

1 Indicate the usefulness of the statement of cash flows. The statement of cash flows provides information about the cash receipts, cash payments, and net change in cash resulting from the operating, investing, and financing activities of a company during the period.

2 Distinguish among operating, investing, and financing activities. Operating activities include the cash effects of transactions that enter into the determination of net income. Investing activities involve cash flows resulting from changes in investments and long-term asset items. Financing activities involve cash flows resulting from changes in long-term liability and stockholders' equity items.

3 **Explain the impact of the product life cycle on a company's cash flows.** During the introductory stage, net cash provided by operating activities and net cash from investing activities are negative, and net cash from financing activities is positive. During the growth stage, net cash provided by operating activities becomes positive but is still not sufficient to meet investing needs. During the maturity stage, net cash provided by operating activities exceeds investing needs, so the company begins to retire debt. During the decline stage, net cash provided by operating activities is reduced, net cash from investing activities becomes positive (from selling off assets), and net cash from financing activities becomes more negative.

4 **Prepare a statement of cash flows using the indirect method.** The preparation of a statement of cash flows involves three major steps. (1) Determine net cash provided/used by operating activities by converting net income from an accrual basis to a cash basis. (2) Analyze changes in noncurrent asset and liability accounts and record as investing and financing activities, or disclose as noncash transactions. (3) Compare the net change in cash on the statement of cash flows with the change in the Cash account reported on the balance sheet to make sure the amounts agree.

5 **Use the statement of cash flows to evaluate a company.** A number of measures can be derived by using information from the statement of cash flows as well as the other required financial statements. Free cash flow indicates the amount of cash a company generated during the current year that is available for the payment of dividends or for expansion. Liquidity can be measured with the current cash debt coverage (net cash provided by operating activities divided by average current liabilities). Solvency can be measured by the cash debt coverage (net cash provided by operating activities divided by average total liabilities).

DECISION TOOLKIT *A SUMMARY*

DECISION CHECKPOINTS	INFO NEEDED FOR DECISION	TOOL TO USE FOR DECISION			HOW TO EVALUATE RESULTS
How much cash did the company generate to either expand operations or pay dividends?	Net cash provided by operating activities, cash spent on fixed assets, and cash dividends	$\text{Free cash flow} = \text{Net cash provided by operating activities}$	$- \text{Capital expenditures}$	$- \text{Cash dividends}$	Significant free cash flow indicates greater potential to finance new investment and pay additional dividends.
Is the company generating sufficient net cash provided by operating activities to meet its current obligations?	Net cash provided by operating activities and average current liabilities	$\text{Current cash debt coverage} = \dfrac{\text{Net cash provided by operating activities}}{\text{Average current liabilities}}$			A high value suggests good liquidity. Since the numerator contains a "flow" measure, it provides a good supplement to the current ratio.
Is the company generating sufficient net cash provided by operating activities to meet its long-term obligations?	Net cash provided by operating activities and average total liabilities	$\text{Cash debt coverage} = \dfrac{\text{Net cash provided by operating activities}}{\text{Average total liabilities}}$			A high value suggests the company is solvent; that is, it will meet its obligations in the long term.

Appendix 12A

Statement of Cash Flows—Direct Method

To explain and illustrate the direct method, we will use the transactions of Computer Services Company for 2014, to prepare a statement of cash flows. Illustration 12A-1 presents information related to 2014 for Computer Services Company.

LEARNING OBJECTIVE 6

Prepare a statement of cash flows using the direct method.

Illustration 12A-1
Comparative balance sheets, income statement, and additional information for Computer Services Company

COMPUTER SERVICES COMPANY
Comparative Balance Sheets
December 31

Assets	2014	2013	Change in Account Balance Increase/Decrease
Current assets			
Cash	$ 55,000	$ 33,000	$ 22,000 Increase
Accounts receivable	20,000	30,000	10,000 Decrease
Inventory	15,000	10,000	5,000 Increase
Prepaid expenses	5,000	1,000	4,000 Increase
Property, plant, and equipment			
Land	130,000	20,000	110,000 Increase
Buildings	160,000	40,000	120,000 Increase
Accumulated depreciation—buildings	(11,000)	(5,000)	6,000 Increase
Equipment	27,000	10,000	17,000 Increase
Accumulated depreciation—equipment	(3,000)	(1,000)	2,000 Increase
Total assets	$398,000	$138,000	

Liabilities and Stockholders' Equity			
Current liabilities			
Accounts payable	$ 28,000	$ 12,000	$ 16,000 Increase
Income taxes payable	6,000	8,000	2,000 Decrease
Long-term liabilities			
Bonds payable	130,000	20,000	110,000 Increase
Stockholders' equity			
Common stock	70,000	50,000	20,000 Increase
Retained earnings	164,000	48,000	116,000 Increase
Total liabilities and stockholders' equity	$398,000	$138,000	

COMPUTER SERVICES COMPANY
Income Statement
For the Year Ended December 31, 2014

Sales revenue		$507,000
Cost of goods sold	$150,000	
Operating expenses (excluding depreciation)	111,000	
Depreciation expense	9,000	
Loss on disposal of plant assets	3,000	
Interest expense	42,000	315,000
Income before income tax		192,000
Income tax expense		47,000
Net income		$145,000

Additional information for 2014:
1. Depreciation expense was comprised of $6,000 for building and $3,000 for equipment.
2. The company sold equipment with a book value of $7,000 (cost $8,000, less accumulated depreciation $1,000) for $4,000 cash.
3. Issued $110,000 of long-term bonds in direct exchange for land.
4. A building costing $120,000 was purchased for cash. Equipment costing $25,000 was also purchased for cash.
5. Issued common stock for $20,000 cash.
6. The company declared and paid a $29,000 cash dividend.

To prepare a statement of cash flows under the direct approach, we will apply the three steps outlined in Illustration 12-4.

STEP 1: OPERATING ACTIVITIES

DETERMINE NET CASH PROVIDED/USED BY OPERATING ACTIVITIES BY CONVERTING NET INCOME FROM AN ACCRUAL BASIS TO A CASH BASIS

Under the **direct method**, companies compute net cash provided by operating activities by **adjusting each item in the income statement** from the accrual basis to the cash basis. To simplify and condense the operating activities section, companies **report only major classes of operating cash receipts and cash payments**. For these major classes, the difference between cash receipts and cash payments is the net cash provided by operating activities. These relationships are as shown in Illustration 12A-2.

Illustration 12A-2 Major classes of cash receipts and payments

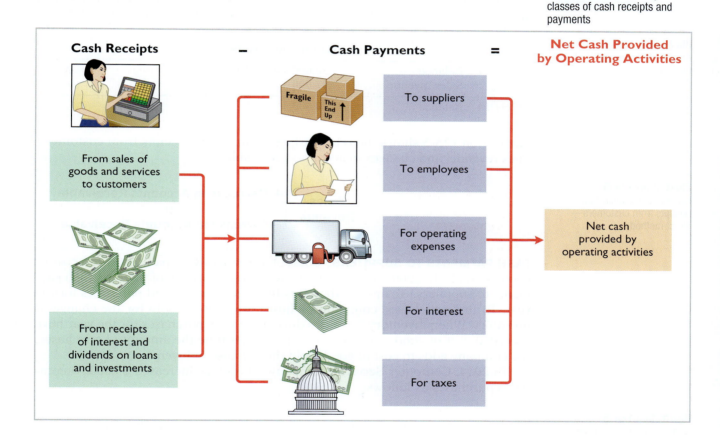

An **efficient way to apply the direct method is to analyze the items reported in the income statement in the order in which they are listed.** We then determine cash receipts and cash payments related to these revenues and expenses. The following pages present the adjustments required to prepare a statement of cash flows for Computer Services Company using the direct approach.

CASH RECEIPTS FROM CUSTOMERS. The income statement for Computer Services Company reported sales revenue from customers of $507,000. How much of that was cash receipts? To answer that, companies need to consider the change in accounts receivable during the year. When accounts receivable increase during the year, revenues on an accrual basis are higher than cash receipts from customers. Operations led to revenues, but not all of these revenues resulted in cash receipts.

To determine the amount of cash receipts, the company deducts from sales revenue the increase in accounts receivable. On the other hand, there may be a decrease in accounts receivable. That would occur if cash receipts from customers exceeded sales revenue. In that case, the company adds to sales revenue the decrease in accounts receivable. For Computer Services Company, accounts receivable decreased $10,000. Thus, cash receipts from customers were $517,000, computed as shown in Illustration 12A-3.

Illustration 12A-3
Computation of cash receipts from customers

Sales revenue	$ 507,000
Add: Decrease in accounts receivable	10,000
Cash receipts from customers	**$517,000**

Computer Services can also determine cash receipts from customers from an analysis of the Accounts Receivable account, as shown in Illustration 12A-4.

Illustration 12A-4
Analysis of Accounts Receivable

Accounts Receivable				
1/1/14	Balance	30,000	**Receipts from customers**	**517,000**
	Sales revenue	507,000		
12/31/14	Balance	20,000		

Illustration 12A-5 shows the relationships among cash receipts from customers, sales revenue, and changes in accounts receivable.

Illustration 12A-5
Formula to compute cash receipts from customers—direct method

Cash Receipts from Customers	=	**Sales Revenue**	**+ Decrease in Accounts Receivable** or **− Increase in Accounts Receivable**

CASH PAYMENTS TO SUPPLIERS. Computer Services Company reported cost of goods sold of $150,000 on its income statement. How much of that was cash payments to suppliers? To answer that, it is first necessary to find purchases for the year. To find purchases, companies adjust cost of goods sold for the change in inventory. When inventory increases during the year, purchases for the year have exceeded cost of goods sold. As a result, to determine the amount of purchases, the company adds to cost of goods sold the increase in inventory.

In 2014, Computer Services Company's inventory increased $5,000. It computes purchases as follows.

Illustration 12A-6
Computation of purchases

Cost of goods sold	$ 150,000
Add: Increase in inventory	5,000
Purchases	**$155,000**

After computing purchases, a company can determine cash payments to suppliers. This is done by adjusting purchases for the change in accounts payable. When accounts payable increase during the year, purchases on an accrual basis are higher than they are on a cash basis. As a result, to determine cash payments to suppliers, a company deducts from purchases the increase in accounts payable. On the other hand, if cash payments to suppliers exceed purchases, there may be a decrease in accounts payable. In that case, a company adds to purchases the decrease in accounts payable. For Computer Services Company, cash payments to suppliers were $139,000, computed as follows.

Purchases		$ 155,000
Deduct: Increase in accounts payable		16,000
Cash payments to suppliers		**$139,000**

Illustration 12A-7
Computation of cash payments to suppliers

Computer Services also can determine cash payments to suppliers from an analysis of the Accounts Payable account, as shown in Illustration 12A-8.

Accounts Payable				
Payments to suppliers	**139,000**	1/1/14	Balance	12,000
			Purchases	155,000
		12/31/14	Balance	28,000

Illustration 12A-8
Analysis of Accounts Payable

Illustration 12A-9 shows the relationships among cash payments to suppliers, cost of goods sold, changes in inventory, and changes in accounts payable.

Illustration 12A-9
Formula to compute cash payments to suppliers—direct method

CASH PAYMENTS FOR OPERATING EXPENSES. Computer Services reported on its income statement operating expenses of $111,000. How much of that amount was cash paid for operating expenses? To answer that, we need to adjust this amount for any changes in prepaid expenses and accrued expenses payable. For example, if prepaid expenses increased during the year, cash paid for operating expenses is higher than operating expenses reported on the income statement. To convert operating expenses to cash payments for operating expenses, a company adds the increase in prepaid expenses to operating expenses. On the other hand, if prepaid expenses decrease during the year, it deducts the decrease from operating expenses.

Companies must also adjust operating expenses for changes in accrued expenses payable. When accrued expenses payable increase during the year, operating expenses on an accrual basis are higher than they are in a cash basis. As a result, to determine cash payments for operating expenses, a company deducts from operating expenses an increase in accrued expenses payable. On the other hand, a company adds to operating expenses a decrease in accrued expenses payable because cash payments exceed operating expenses.

Computer Services Company's cash payments for operating expenses were $115,000, computed as follows.

Operating expenses		$ 111,000
Add: Increase in prepaid expenses		4,000
Cash payments for operating expenses		**$115,000**

Illustration 12A-10
Computation of cash payments for operating expenses

Illustration 12A-11 shows the relationships among cash payments for operating expenses, changes in prepaid expenses, and changes in accrued expenses payable.

DEPRECIATION EXPENSE AND LOSS ON DISPOSAL OF PLANT ASSETS. Computer Services' depreciation expense in 2014 was $9,000. Depreciation expense is not shown on a statement of cash flows under the direct method because it is a

Illustration 12A-11
Formula to compute cash payments for operating expenses—direct method

Cash Payments for Operating Expenses	=	Operating Expenses	+ Increase in Prepaid Expense or − Decrease in Prepaid Expense	+ Decrease in Accrued Expenses Payable or − Increase in Accrued Expenses Payable

noncash charge. If the amount for operating expenses includes depreciation expense, operating expenses must be reduced by the amount of depreciation to determine cash payments for operating expenses.

The loss on disposal of plant assets of $3,000 is also a noncash charge. The loss on disposal of plant assets reduces net income, but it does not reduce cash. Thus, the loss on disposal of plant assets is not shown on the statement of cash flows under the direct method.

Other charges to expense that do not require the use of cash, such as the amortization of intangible assets, depletion expense, and bad debt expense, are treated in the same manner as depreciation.

CASH PAYMENTS FOR INTEREST. Computer Services reported on the income statement interest expense of $42,000. Since the balance sheet did not include an accrual for interest payable for 2013 or 2014, the amount reported as expense is the same as the amount of interest paid.

CASH PAYMENTS FOR INCOME TAXES. Computer Services reported income tax expense of $47,000 on the income statement. Income taxes payable, however, decreased $2,000. This decrease means that income taxes paid were more than income taxes reported in the income statement. Cash payments for income taxes were, therefore, $49,000 as shown below.

Illustration 12A-12
Computation of cash payments for income taxes

Income tax expense	$ 47,000
Add: Decrease in income taxes payable	2,000
Cash payments for income taxes	**$49,000**

Illustration 12A-13 shows the relationships among cash payments for income taxes, income tax expense, and changes in income taxes payable.

Illustration 12A-13
Formula to compute cash payments for income taxes—direct method

Cash Payments for Income Taxes	=	Income Tax Expense	+ Decrease in Income Taxes Payable or − Increase in Income Taxes Payable

The operating activities section of the statement of cash flows of Computer Services Company is shown in Illustration 12A-14.

Illustration 12A-14
Operating activities section of the statement of cash flows

Cash flows from operating activities		
Cash receipts from customers		$517,000
Less: Cash payments:		
To suppliers	$139,000	
For operating expenses	115,000	
For interest expense	42,000	
For income taxes	49,000	345,000
Net cash provided by operating activities		$172,000

When a company uses the direct method, it must also provide in a **separate schedule** (not shown here) the net cash flows from operating activities as computed under the indirect method.

STEP 2: INVESTING AND FINANCING ACTIVITIES

ANALYZE CHANGES IN NONCURRENT ASSET AND LIABILITY ACCOUNTS AND RECORD AS INVESTING AND FINANCING ACTIVITIES, OR DISCLOSE AS NONCASH TRANSACTIONS

INCREASE IN LAND. As indicated from the change in the Land account and the additional information, Computer Services Company purchased land of $110,000 by directly exchanging bonds for land. The exchange of bonds payable for land has no effect on cash. But, it is a significant noncash investing and financing activity that merits disclosure in a separate schedule. (See Illustration 12A-16.)

INCREASE IN BUILDINGS. As the additional data indicate, Computer Services Company acquired an office building for $120,000 cash. This is a cash outflow reported in the investing activities section. (See Illustration 12A-16.)

INCREASE IN EQUIPMENT. The Equipment account increased $17,000. The additional information explains that this was a net increase that resulted from two transactions: (1) a purchase of equipment of $25,000, and (2) the sale for $4,000 of equipment costing $8,000. These transactions are investing activities. The company should report each transaction separately. The statement in Illustration 12A-16 reports the purchase of equipment as an outflow of cash for $25,000. It reports the sale as an inflow of cash for $4,000. The T-account below shows the reasons for the change in this account during the year.

Illustration 12A-15
Analysis of Equipment

Equipment			
1/1/14 Balance	10,000	Cost of equipment sold	8,000
Purchase of equipment	**25,000**		
12/31/14 Balance	27,000		

The following entry shows the details of the equipment sale transaction.

Cash	4,000	
Accumulated Depreciation	1,000	
Loss on Disposal of Plant Assets	3,000	
Equipment		8,000

A	=	L	+	SE
+4,000				
+1,000				
				−3,000 Exp
−8,000				

Cash Flows
+4,000

INCREASE IN BONDS PAYABLE. The Bonds Payable account increased $110,000. As indicated in the additional information, the company acquired land by directly exchanging bonds for land. Illustration 12A-16 reports this noncash transaction in a separate schedule at the bottom of the statement.

INCREASE IN COMMON STOCK. The balance sheet reports an increase in Common Stock of $20,000. The additional information section notes that this increase resulted from the issuance of new shares of stock. This is a cash inflow reported in the financing activities section in Illustration 12A-16.

INCREASE IN RETAINED EARNINGS. Retained earnings increased $116,000 during the year. This increase can be explained by two factors: (1) Net income of $145,000 increased retained earnings and (2) dividends of $29,000 decreased retained earnings. The company adjusts net income to net cash provided by operating activities in the operating activities section. **Payment** of the dividends (not the declaration) is a **cash outflow that the company reports as a financing activity in Illustration 12A-16**.

Statement of Cash Flows–2014

Illustration 12A-16 shows the statement of cash flows for Computer Services Company.

Illustration 12A-16
Statement of cash flows, 2014—direct method

COMPUTER SERVICES COMPANY
Statement of Cash Flows—Direct Method
For the Year Ended December 31, 2014

Cash flows from operating activities		
Cash receipts from customers		$ 517,000
Less: Cash payments:		
To suppliers	$ 139,000	
For operating expenses	115,000	
For income taxes	49,000	
For interest expense	42,000	345,000
Net cash provided by operating activities		172,000
Cash flows from investing activities		
Sale of equipment	4,000	
Purchase of building	(120,000)	
Purchase of equipment	(25,000)	
Net cash used by investing activities		(141,000)
Cash flows from financing activities		
Issuance of common stock	20,000	
Payment of cash dividends	(29,000)	
Net cash used by financing activities		(9,000)
Net increase in cash		22,000
Cash at beginning of period		33,000
Cash at end of period		$ 55,000
Noncash investing and financing activities		
Issuance of bonds payable to purchase land		$ 110,000

STEP 3: NET CHANGE IN CASH

COMPARE THE NET CHANGE IN CASH ON THE STATEMENT OF CASH FLOWS WITH THE CHANGE IN THE CASH ACCOUNT REPORTED ON THE BALANCE SHEET TO MAKE SURE THE AMOUNTS AGREE

Illustration 12A-16 indicates that the net change in cash during the period was an increase of $22,000. This agrees with the change in balances in the Cash account reported on the balance sheets in Illustration 12A-1.

Summary of Learning Objective for Appendix 12A

6 **Prepare a statement of cash flows using the direct method.** The preparation of the statement of cash flows involves three major steps: (1) Determine net cash provided/used by operating activities by converting net income from an accrual basis to a cash basis. (2) Analyze changes in noncurrent asset and liability accounts and record as investing and financing activities, or disclose as noncash transactions. (3) Compare the net change in cash on the statement of cash flows with the change in the Cash account reported on the balance sheet to make sure the amounts agree. The direct method reports cash receipts less cash payments to arrive at net cash provided by operating activities.

Appendix 12B

Statement of Cash Flows—T-Account Approach

LEARNING OBJECTIVE **7**

Use the T-account approach to prepare a statement of cash flows.

Many people like to use T-accounts to provide structure to the preparation of a statement of cash flows. The use of T-accounts is based on the accounting equation that you learned in Chapter 1. The basic equation is:

$$\text{Assets} = \text{Liabilities} + \text{Equity}$$

Now, let's rewrite the left-hand side as:

$$\textbf{Cash + Noncash Assets = Liabilities + Equity}$$

Next, rewrite the equation by subtracting Noncash Assets from each side to isolate Cash on the left-hand side:

$$\textbf{Cash = Liabilities + Equity − Noncash Assets}$$

Finally, if we insert the Δ symbol (which means "change in"), we have:

$$\textbf{Δ Cash = Δ Liabilities + Δ Equity − Δ Noncash Assets}$$

What this means is that the change in cash is equal to the change in all of the other balance sheet accounts. Another way to think about this is that if we analyze the changes in all of the noncash balance sheet accounts, we will explain the change in the Cash account. This, of course, is exactly what we are trying to do with the statement of cash flows.

To implement this approach, first prepare a large Cash T-account with sections for operating, investing, and financing activities. Then, prepare smaller T-accounts for all of the other noncash balance sheet accounts. Insert the beginning and ending balances for each of these accounts. Once you have done this, then walk through the steps outlined in Illustration 12-4. As you walk through the steps, enter debit and credit amounts into the affected accounts. When all of the changes in the T-accounts have been explained, you are done. To demonstrate, we will apply this approach to the example of Computer Services Company that is presented in the chapter. Each of the adjustments in Illustration 12B-1 is numbered so you can follow them through the T-accounts.

1. Post net income as a debit to the operating section of the Cash T-account and a credit to Retained Earnings. Make sure to label all adjustments to the Cash T-account. It also helps to number each adjustment so you can trace all of them if you make an error.

2. Post depreciation expense as a debit to the operating section of Cash and a credit to each of the appropriate accumulated depreciation accounts.

3. Post any gains or losses on the sale of property, plant, and equipment. To do this, it is best to first prepare the journal entry that was recorded at the time of the sale and then post each element of the journal entry. For example, for Computer Services the entry was:

Cash	4,000	
Accumulated Depreciation—Equipment	1,000	
Loss on Disposal of Plant Assets	3,000	
Equipment		8,000

The $4,000 cash entry is a source of cash in the investing section of the Cash account. Accumulated Depreciation—Equipment is debited for $1,000. The Loss on Disposal of Plant Assets is a debit to the operating section of the Cash T-account. Finally, Equipment is credited for $8,000.

4–8. Next, post each of the changes to the noncash current asset and current liability accounts. For example, to explain the $10,000 decline in Computer Services' accounts receivable, credit Accounts Receivable for $10,000 and debit the operating section of the Cash T-account for $10,000.

9. Analyze the changes in the noncurrent accounts. Land was purchased by issuing bonds payable. This requires a debit to Land for $110,000 and a credit to Bonds Payable for $110,000. Note that this is a significant noncash event that requires disclosure at the bottom of the statement of cash flows.

10. Buildings is debited for $120,000, and the investing section of the Cash T-account is credited for $120,000 as a use of cash from investing.

11. Equipment is debited for $25,000 and the investing section of the Cash T-account is credited for $25,000 as a use of cash from investing.

12. Common Stock is credited for $20,000 for the issuance of shares of stock, and the financing section of the Cash T-account is debited for $20,000.

13. Retained Earnings is debited to reflect the payment of the $29,000 dividend, and the financing section of the Cash T-account is credited to reflect the use of Cash.

Illustration 12B-1
T-account approach

Cash

Operating			
(1) Net income	145,000	5,000	Inventory (5)
(2) Depreciation expense	9,000	4,000	Prepaid expenses (6)
(3) Loss on equipment	3,000	2,000	Income taxes payable (8)
(4) Accounts receivable	10,000		
(7) Accounts payable	16,000		
Net cash provided by operating activities	172,000		
Investing			
(3) Sold equipment	4,000	120,000	Purchased building (10)
		25,000	Purchased equipment (11)
		141,000	Net cash used by investing activities
Financing			
(12) Issued common stock	20,000	29,000	Dividend paid (13)
		9,000	Net cash used by financing activities
	22,000		

Accounts Receivable		Inventory		Prepaid Expenses		Land	
30,000		10,000		1,000		20,000	
	10,000 (4)	(5) 5,000		(6) 4,000		(9) 110,000	
20,000		15,000		5,000		130,000	

Buildings		Accumulated Depreciation—Buildings		Equipment		Accumulated Depreciation—Equipment	
40,000			5,000	10,000			1,000
(10) 120,000			6,000 (2)	(11) 25,000	8,000 (3)	(3) 1,000	3,000 (2)
160,000			11,000	27,000			3,000

Accounts Payable		Income Taxes Payable		Bonds Payable		Common Stock		Retained Earnings	
	12,000		8,000		20,000		50,000		48,000
	16,000 (7)	(8) 2,000			110,000 (9)		20,000 (12)		145,000 (1)
	28,000		6,000		130,000		70,000	(13) 29,000	
									164,000

At this point, all of the changes in the noncash accounts have been explained. All that remains is to subtotal each section of the Cash T-account and compare the total change in cash with the change shown on the balance sheet. Once this is done, the information in the Cash T-account can be used to prepare a statement of cash flows.

Summary of Learning Objective for Appendix 12B

7 Use the T-account approach to prepare a statement of cash flows. To use T-accounts to prepare the statement of cash flows: (1) prepare a large Cash T-account with sections for operating, investing, and financing activities; (2) prepare smaller T-accounts for all other noncash accounts; (3) insert beginning and ending balances for all accounts; and (4) follows the steps in Illustration 12-4, entering debit and credit amounts as needed.

Glossary

Terms are highlighted in blue throughout the chapter.

Cash debt coverage A cash-based ratio used to evaluate solvency, calculated as net cash provided by operating activities divided by average total liabilities.

Current cash debt coverage A cash-based ratio used to evaluate liquidity, calculated as net cash provided by operating activities divided by average current liabilities.

Direct method A method of determining net cash provided by operating activities by adjusting each item in the income statement from the accrual basis to the cash basis. The direct method shows operating cash receipts and payments.

Financing activities Cash flow activities that include (a) obtaining cash from issuing debt and repaying the amounts borrowed and (b) obtaining cash from stockholders, repurchasing shares, and paying dividends.

Free cash flow Net cash provided by operating activities after adjusting for capital expenditures and dividends paid.

Indirect method A method of preparing a statement of cash flows in which net income is adjusted for items that do not affect cash, to determine net cash provided by operating activities.

Investing activities Cash flow activities that include (a) cash transactions that involve the purchase or disposal of investments and property, plant, and equipment using cash and (b) lending money and collecting the loans.

Operating activities Cash flow activities that include the cash effects of transactions that create revenues and expenses and thus enter into the determination of net income.

Product life cycle A series of phases in a product's sales and cash flows over time. These phases, in order of occurrence, are introductory, growth, maturity, and decline.

Statement of cash flows A basic financial statement that provides information about the cash receipts and cash payments of an entity during a period, classified as operating, investing, and financing activities, in a format that reconciles the beginning and ending cash balances.

WILEY PLUS Self-Test, Brief Exercises, Exercises, Problem Set A, and many more resources are available for practice in WileyPLUS.

Note: All Questions, Exercises, and Problems marked with an asterisk relate to material in the appendices to the chapter.

Self-Test Questions

(Answers in *Broadening Your Perspective.*)

(LO 1) **1.** Which of the following is **incorrect** about the statement of cash flows?
(a) It is a fourth basic financial statement.
(b) It provides information about cash receipts and cash payments of an entity during a period.
(c) It reconciles the ending cash account balance to the balance per the bank statement.
(d) It provides information about the operating, investing, and financing activities of the business.

(LO 1, 2) **2.** Which of the following will **not** be reported in the statement of cash flows?
(a) The net change in plant assets during the year.
(b) Cash payments for plant assets during the year.
(c) Cash receipts from sales of plant assets during the year.
(d) Sources of financing during the period.

(LO 2) **3.** The statement of cash flows classifies cash receipts and cash payments by these activities:
(a) operating and nonoperating.
(b) operating, investing, and financing.
(c) financing, operating, and nonoperating.
(d) investing, financing, and nonoperating.

(LO 2) **4.** Which is an example of a cash flow from an operating activity?
(a) Payment of cash to lenders for interest.
(b) Receipt of cash from the sale of capital stock.
(c) Payment of cash dividends to the company's stockholders.
(d) None of the above.

(LO 2) **5.** Which is an example of a cash flow from an investing activity?
(a) Receipt of cash from the issuance of bonds payable.
(b) Payment of cash to repurchase outstanding capital stock.

(c) Receipt of cash from the sale of equipment.
(d) Payment of cash to suppliers for inventory.

(LO 2) **6.** Cash dividends paid to stockholders are classified on the statement of cash flows as:
(a) operating activities.
(b) investing activities.
(c) a combination of (a) and (b).
(d) financing activities.

(LO 2) **7.** Which is an example of a cash flow from a financing activity?
(a) Receipt of cash from sale of land.
(b) Issuance of debt for cash.
(c) Purchase of equipment for cash.
(d) None of the above

(LO 2) **8.** Which of the following is **incorrect** about the statement of cash flows?
(a) The direct method may be used to report cash provided by operating activities.
(b) The statement shows the net cash provided (used) for three categories of activity.
(c) The operating activities section is the last section of the statement.
(d) The indirect method may be used to report net cash provided by operating activities.

(LO 3) **9.** During the introductory phase of a company's life cycle, one would normally expect to see:
(a) negative cash from operations, negative cash from investing, and positive cash from financing.
(b) negative cash from operations, positive cash from investing, and positive cash from financing.
(c) positive cash from operations, negative cash from investing, and negative cash from financing.
(d) positive cash from operations, negative cash from investing, and positive cash from financing.

Questions 10 through 12 apply only to the indirect method.

(LO 4) **10.** Net income is $132,000, accounts payable increased $10,000 during the year, inventory decreased $6,000 during the year, and accounts receivable increased $12,000 during the year. Under the indirect method, what is net cash provided by operating activities?
(a) $102,000.   (c) $124,000.
(b) $112,000.   (d) $136,000.

(LO 4) **11.** Items that are added back to net income in determining net cash provided by operating activities under the indirect method do **not** include:
(a) depreciation expense.
(b) an increase in inventory.
(c) amortization expense.
(d) loss on sale of equipment.

(LO 4) **12.** The following data are available for Bill Mack Corporation.

Net income	$200,000
Depreciation expense	40,000

Dividends paid	60,000
Gain on sale of land	10,000
Decrease in accounts receivable	20,000
Decrease in accounts payable	30,000

Net cash provided by operating activities is:
(a) $160,000.   (c) $240,000.
(b) $220,000.   (d) $280,000.

(LO 4, 6) **13.** The following are data concerning cash received or paid from various transactions for Orange Peels Corporation.

Sale of land	$100,000
Sale of equipment	50,000
Issuance of common stock	70,000
Purchase of equipment	30,000
Payment of cash dividends	60,000

Net cash provided by investing activities is:
(a) $120,000.   (c) $150,000.
(b) $130,000.   (d) $190,000.

(LO 4, 6) **14.** The following data are available for Retique!

Increase in bonds payable	$100,000
Sale of investment	50,000
Issuance of common stock	60,000
Payment of cash dividends	30,000

Net cash provided by financing activities is:
(a) $90,000.   (c) $160,000.
(b) $130,000.   (d) $170,000.

(LO 5) **15.** The cash debt coverage is:
(a) a measure of liquidity.
(b) a measure of profitability.
(c) net income divided by average total liabilities.
(d) a measure of solvency.

(LO 5) **16.** Free cash flow provides an indication of a company's ability to:
(a) generate net income.
(b) generate cash to pay dividends.
(c) generate cash to invest in new capital expenditures.
(d) Both (b) and (c).

Questions 17 and 18 apply only to the direct method.

(LO 6) *** 17.** The beginning balance in accounts receivable is $44,000, the ending balance is $42,000, and sales during the period are $129,000. What are cash receipts from customers?
(a) $127,000.   (c) $131,000.
(b) $129,000.   (d) $141,000.

(LO 6) *** 18.** Which of the following items is reported on a statement of cash flows prepared by the direct method?
(a) Loss on disposal of plant asset.
(b) Increase in accounts receivable.
(c) Depreciation expense.
(d) Cash payments to suppliers.

Go to the book's companion website, **www.wiley.com/college/kimmel**, to access additional Self-Test Questions.

Questions

1. (a) What is a statement of cash flows?
   (b) Mark Paxson maintains that the statement of cash flows is an optional financial statement. Do you agree? Explain.

2. What questions about cash are answered by the statement of cash flows?

3. Distinguish among the three activities reported in the statement of cash flows.

4. (a) What are the sources (inflows) of cash in a statement of cash flows?
   (b) What are the uses (outflows) of cash?

5. Why is it important to disclose certain noncash transactions? How should they be disclosed?

6. Diane Hollowell and Terry Parmenter were discussing the format of the statement of cash flows of Snowbarger Co. At the bottom of Snowbarger's statement of cash flows was a separate section entitled "Noncash investing and financing activities." Give three examples of significant noncash transactions that would be reported in this section.

7. Why is it necessary to use comparative balance sheets, a current income statement, and certain transaction data in preparing a statement of cash flows?

8. (a) What are the phases of the corporate life cycle?
   (b) What effect does each phase have on the numbers reported in a statement of cash flows?

9. Based on its statement of cash flows, in what stage of the product life cycle is Tootsie Roll Industries?

10. Contrast the advantages and disadvantages of the direct and indirect methods of preparing the statement of cash flows. Are both methods acceptable? Which method is preferred by the FASB? Which method is more popular?

11. When the total cash inflows exceed the total cash outflows in the statement of cash flows, how and where is this excess identified?

12. Describe the indirect method for determining net cash provided (used) by operating activities.

13. Why is it necessary to convert accrual-basis net income to cash-basis net income when preparing a statement of cash flows?

14. The president of Selby Company is puzzled. During the last year, the company experienced a net loss of $800,000, yet its cash increased $300,000 during the same period of time. Explain to the president how this could occur.

15. Identify five items that are adjustments to convert net income to net cash provided by operating activities under the indirect method.

16. Why and how is depreciation expense reported in a statement of cash flows prepared using the indirect method?

17. Why is the statement of cash flows useful?

18. During 2014, Markowitz Company exchanged $1,700,000 of its common stock for land. Indicate how the transaction would be reported on a statement of cash flows, if at all.

19. Give examples of accrual-based and cash-based ratios to measure each of these characteristics of a company:
    (a) Liquidity.   (b) Solvency.

*20. Describe the direct method for determining net cash provided by operating activities.

*21. Give the formulas under the direct method for computing (a) cash receipts from customers and (b) cash payments to suppliers.

*22. Detwiler Inc. reported sales of $2 million for 2014. Accounts receivable decreased $150,000 and accounts payable increased $300,000. Compute cash receipts from customers, assuming that the receivable and payable transactions are related to operations.

*23. In the direct method, why is depreciation expense not reported in the cash flows from operating activities section?

Brief Exercises

BE12-1   Each of these items must be considered in preparing a statement of cash flows for Irvin Co. for the year ended December 31, 2014. For each item, state how it should be shown in the statement of cash flows for 2014.
(a) Issued bonds for $200,000 cash.
(b) Purchased equipment for $180,000 cash.
(c) Sold land costing $20,000 for $20,000 cash.
(d) Declared and paid a $50,000 cash dividend.

Indicate statement presentation of selected transactions.
(LO 2), **K**

BE12-2   Classify each item as an operating, investing, or financing activity. Assume all items involve cash unless there is information to the contrary.
(a) Purchase of equipment.   (d) Depreciation.
(b) Sale of building.   (e) Payment of dividends.
(c) Redemption of bonds.   (f) Issuance of capital stock.

Classify items by activities.
(LO 2), **C**

Identify financing activity transactions.

(LO 2), **AP**

BE12-3 The following T-account is a summary of the cash account of Kemper Company.

Cash (Summary Form)

Balance, Jan. 1	8,000		
Receipts from customers	364,000	Payments for goods	200,000
Dividends on stock investments	6,000	Payments for operating expenses	140,000
Proceeds from sale of equipment	36,000	Interest paid	10,000
Proceeds from issuance of		Taxes paid	8,000
bonds payable	300,000	Dividends paid	40,000
Balance, Dec. 31	316,000		

What amount of net cash provided (used) by financing activities should be reported in the statement of cash flows?

Answer questions related to the phases of product life cycle.

(LO 3), **C**

BE12-4
(a) Why is net cash provided by operating activities likely to be lower than reported net income during the growth phase?
(b) Why is net cash from investing activities often positive during the late maturity phase and during the decline phase?

Compute net cash provided by operating activities—indirect method.

(LO 4), **AP**

BE12-5 Manuel, Inc. reported net income of $2.5 million in 2014. Depreciation for the year was $160,000, accounts receivable decreased $350,000, and accounts payable decreased $280,000. Compute net cash provided by operating activities using the indirect approach.

Compute net cash provided by operating activities—indirect method.

(LO 4), **AP**

BE12-6 The net income for Freeman Co. for 2014 was $280,000. For 2014, depreciation on plant assets was $70,000, and the company incurred a loss on disposal of plant assets of $28,000. Compute net cash provided by operating activities under the indirect method, assuming there were no other changes in the company's accounts.

Compute net cash provided by operating activities—indirect method.

(LO 4), **AP**

BE12-7 The comparative balance sheets for Lowery Company show these changes in noncash current asset accounts: accounts receivable decrease $80,000, prepaid expenses increase $28,000, and inventories increase $40,000. Compute net cash provided by operating activities using the indirect method, assuming that net income is $186,000.

Determine cash received from sale of equipment.

(LO 4), **AN**

BE12-8 The T-accounts for Equipment and the related Accumulated Depreciation—Equip. for Coldsmith Company at the end of 2014 are shown here.

Equipment					Accum. Depr.—Equip.			
Beg. bal.	80,000	Disposals	22,000	Disposals	5,100	Beg. bal.	44,500
Acquisitions	41,600					Depr. exp.	12,000
End. bal.	99,600					End. bal.	51,400

In addition, Coldsmith Company's income statement reported a loss on the disposal of plant assets of $3,500. What amount was reported on the statement of cash flows as "cash flow from sale of equipment"?

Calculate cash-based ratios.

(LO 5), **AP**

BE12-9 Suppose during 2014, Cypress Semiconductor Corporation reported net cash provided by operating activities of $89,303,000, cash used in investing of $43,126,000, and cash used in financing of $7,368,000. In addition, cash spent for fixed assets during the period was $25,823,000. Average current liabilities were $251,522,000, and average total liabilities were $286,214,500. No dividends were paid. Calculate these values:
(a) Free cash flow.
(b) Current cash debt coverage.
(c) Cash debt coverage.

Calculate cash-based ratios.

(LO 5), **AP**

BE12-10 Flowers Corporation reported net cash provided by operating activities of $412,000, net cash used by investing activities of $250,000, and net cash provided by financing activities of $70,000. In addition, cash spent for capital assets during the period was $200,000. Average current liabilities were $150,000, and average total liabilities were $225,000. No dividends were paid. Calculate these values:
(a) Free cash flow.
(b) Current cash debt coverage.
(c) Cash debt coverage.

BE12-11   Suppose Canwest Global Communications Corp. reported net cash used by operating activities of $104,539,000 and sales revenue of $2,867,459,000 during 2014. Cash spent on plant asset additions during the year was $79,330,000. Calculate free cash flow.

Calculate cash-based ratios.
(LO 5), **AP**

BE12-12   The management of Unruh Inc. is trying to decide whether it can increase its dividend. During the current year, it reported net income of $875,000. It had net cash provided by operating activities of $734,000, paid cash dividends of $92,000, and had capital expenditures of $310,000. Compute the company's free cash flow, and discuss whether an increase in the dividend appears warranted. What other factors should be considered?

Calculate and analyze free cash flow.
(LO 5), **AN**

***BE12-13**   Suppose Columbia Sportswear Company had accounts receivable of $299,585,000 at January 1, 2014, and $226,548,000 at December 31, 2014. Assume sales revenue was $1,244,023,000 for the year 2014. What is the amount of cash receipts from customers in 2014?

Compute receipts from customers—direct method.
(LO 6), **AP**

***BE12-14**   Kolmer Corporation reported income taxes of $370,000,000 on its 2014 income statement and income taxes payable of $277,000,000 at December 31, 2013, and $528,000,000 at December 31, 2014. What amount of cash payments were made for income taxes during 2014?

Compute cash payments for income taxes—direct method.
(LO 6), **AP**

***BE12-15**   Sellers Corporation reports operating expenses of $90,000, excluding depreciation expense of $15,000 for 2014. During the year, prepaid expenses decreased $7,200 and accrued expenses payable increased $4,400. Compute the cash payments for operating expenses in 2014.

Compute cash payments for operating expenses—direct method.
(LO 6), **AP**

Exercises

E12-1   Putnam Corporation had these transactions during 2014.
(a) Purchased a machine for $30,000, giving a long-term note in exchange.
(b) Issued $50,000 par value common stock for cash.
(c) Issued $200,000 par value common stock upon conversion of bonds having a face value of $200,000.
(d) Declared and paid a cash dividend of $13,000.
(e) Sold a long-term investment with a cost of $15,000 for $15,000 cash.
(f) Collected $16,000 of accounts receivable.
(g) Paid $18,000 on accounts payable.

Classify transactions by type of activity.
(LO 2), **C**

Instructions
Analyze the transactions and indicate whether each transaction resulted in a cash flow from operating activities, investing activities, financing activities, or noncash investing and financing activities.

E12-2   An analysis of comparative balance sheets, the current year's income statement, and the general ledger accounts of Judd Corp. uncovered the following items. Assume all items involve cash unless there is information to the contrary.

Classify transactions by type of activity.
(LO 2), **C**

(a) Payment of interest on notes payable.
(b) Exchange of land for patent.
(c) Sale of building at book value.
(d) Payment of dividends.
(e) Depreciation.
(f) Conversion of bonds into common stock.
(g) Receipt of interest on notes receivable.
(h) Issuance of capital stock.
(i) Amortization of patent.
(j) Issuance of bonds for land.
(k) Purchase of land.
(l) Receipt of dividends on investment in stock.
(m) Loss on disposal of plant assets.
(n) Retirement of bonds.

Instructions
Indicate how each item should be classified in the statement of cash flows using these four major classifications: operating activity (indirect method), investing activity, financing activity, and significant noncash investing and financing activity.

Identify phases of product life cycle.
(LO 3), C

E12-3 The information in the table is from the statement of cash flows for a company at four different points in time (A, B, C, and D). Negative values are presented in parentheses.

	Point in Time			
	A	**B**	**C**	**D**
Net cash provided by operating activities	$ (60,000)	$ 30,000	$120,000	$ (10,000)
Cash provided by investing activities	(100,000)	25,000	30,000	(40,000)
Cash provided by financing activities	70,000	(90,000)	(50,000)	120,000
Net income	(38,000)	10,000	100,000	(5,000)

Instructions
For each point in time, state whether the company is most likely in the introductory phase, growth phase, maturity phase, or decline phase. In each case, explain your choice.

Prepare the operating activities section—indirect method.
(LO 4), AP

E12-4 Cosi Company reported net income of $190,000 for 2014. Cosi also reported depreciation expense of $35,000 and a loss of $5,000 on the disposal of plant assets. The comparative balance sheet shows an increase in accounts receivable of $15,000 for the year, a $17,000 increase in accounts payable, and a $4,000 increase in prepaid expenses.

Instructions
Prepare the operating activities section of the statement of cash flows for 2014. Use the indirect method.

Prepare the operating activities section—indirect method.
(LO 4), AP

E12-5 The current sections of Sanford Inc.'s balance sheets at December 31, 2013 and 2014, are presented here. Sanford's net income for 2014 was $153,000. Depreciation expense was $27,000.

	2014	2013
Current assets		
Cash	$105,000	$ 99,000
Accounts receivable	80,000	89,000
Inventory	168,000	172,000
Prepaid expenses	27,000	22,000
Total current assets	$380,000	$382,000
Current liabilities		
Accrued expenses payable	$ 15,000	$ 5,000
Accounts payable	85,000	92,000
Total current liabilities	$100,000	$ 97,000

Instructions
Prepare the net cash provided by operating activities section of the company's statement of cash flows for the year ended December 31, 2014, using the indirect method.

Prepare statement of cash flows—indirect method.
(LO 4), AP

E12-6 The following information is available for Ramos Corporation for the year ended December 31, 2014.

Beginning cash balance	$ 45,000
Accounts payable decrease	3,700
Depreciation expense	162,000
Accounts receivable increase	8,200
Inventory increase	11,000
Net income	284,100
Cash received for sale of land at book value	35,000
Cash dividends paid	12,000
Income taxes payable increase	4,700
Cash used to purchase building	289,000
Cash used to purchase treasury stock	26,000
Cash received from issuing bonds	200,000

Instructions
Prepare a statement of cash flows using the indirect method.

E12-7 The three accounts shown below appear in the general ledger of Lauber Corp. during 2014.

Prepare partial statement of cash flows—indirect method. (LO 4), **AN**

Equipment

Date		Debit	Credit	Balance
Jan. 1	Balance			160,000
July 31	Purchase of equipment	70,000		230,000
Sept. 2	Cost of equipment constructed	53,000		283,000
Nov. 10	Cost of equipment sold		49,000	234,000

Accumulated Depreciation—Equipment

Date		Debit	Credit	Balance
Jan. 1	Balance			71,000
Nov. 10	Accumulated depreciation on equipment sold	16,000		55,000
Dec. 31	Depreciation for year		28,000	83,000

Retained Earnings

Date		Debit	Credit	Balance
Jan. 1	Balance			105,000
Aug. 23	Dividends (cash)	14,000		91,000
Dec. 31	Net income		72,000	163,000

Instructions
From the postings in the accounts, indicate how the information is reported on a statement of cash flows using the indirect method. The loss on disposal of plant assets was $8,000. (*Hint:* Cost of equipment constructed is reported in the investing activities section as a decrease in cash of $53,000.)

E12-8 Shown below are comparative balance sheets for Schmitt Company.

Prepare a statement of cash flows—indirect method, and compute cash-based ratios. (LO 4, 5), **AP**

SCHMITT COMPANY
Comparative Balance Sheets
December 31

Assets	2014	2013
Cash	$ 68,000	$ 22,000
Accounts receivable	88,000	76,000
Inventory	167,000	189,000
Land	80,000	100,000
Equipment	260,000	200,000
Accumulated depreciation—equipment	(66,000)	(32,000)
Total	$597,000	$555,000

Liabilities and Stockholders' Equity	2014	2013
Accounts payable	$ 39,000	$ 43,000
Bonds payable	150,000	200,000
Common stock ($1 par)	216,000	174,000
Retained earnings	192,000	138,000
Total	$597,000	$555,000

Additional information:
1. Net income for 2014 was $93,000.
2. Depreciation expense was $34,000.
3. Cash dividends of $39,000 were declared and paid.
4. Bonds payable amounting to $50,000 were redeemed for cash $50,000.
5. Common stock was issued for $42,000 cash.
6. No equipment was sold during 2014.
7. Land was sold for its book value.

Instructions

(a) Prepare a statement of cash flows for 2014 using the indirect method.

(b) Compute these cash-based ratios:
 (1) Current cash debt coverage.
 (2) Cash debt coverage.

Compare two companies by using cash-based ratios.

(LO 5), AN

E12-9 Suppose presented below is 2014 information for PepsiCo, Inc. and The Coca-Cola Company.

($ in millions)	PepsiCo	Coca-Cola
Net cash provided by operating activities	$ 6,796	$ 8,186
Average current liabilities	8,772	13,355
Average total liabilities	22,909	21,491
Net income	5,979	6,906
Sales revenue	43,232	30,990
Capital expenditures	2,128	1,993
Dividends paid	2,732	3,800

Instructions

Using the cash-based measures presented in this chapter, compare the (a) liquidity and (b) solvency of the two companies.

Compare two companies by using cash-based ratios.

(LO 5), AN

E12-10 Information for two companies in the same industry, Patton Corporation and Sager Corporation, is presented here.

	Patton Corporation	Sager Corporation
Net cash provided by operating activities	$ 80,000	$100,000
Average current liabilities	50,000	100,000
Average total liabilities	180,000	250,000
Net income	200,000	200,000
Capital expenditures	40,000	70,000
Dividends paid	5,000	10,000

Instructions

Using the cash-based measures presented in this chapter, compare the (a) liquidity and (b) solvency of the two companies.

Compute cash provided by operating activities—direct method.

(LO 6), AP

*E12-11 Metzger Company completed its first year of operations on December 31, 2014. Its initial income statement showed that Metzger had sales revenue of $198,000 and operating expenses of $83,000. Accounts receivable and accounts payable at year-end were $60,000 and $23,000, respectively. Assume that accounts payable related to operating expenses. Ignore income taxes.

Instructions

Compute net cash provided by operating activities using the direct method.

Compute cash payments— direct method.

(LO 6), AP

*E12-12 Suppose the 2014 income statement for McDonald's Corporation shows cost of goods sold $5,178.0 million and operating expenses (including depreciation expense of $1,216.2 million) $10,725.7 million. The comparative balance sheet for the year shows that inventory decreased $5.3 million, prepaid expenses increased $42.2 million, accounts payable (merchandise suppliers) increased $15.6 million, and accrued expenses payable increased $199.8 million.

Instructions

Using the direct method, compute (a) cash payments to suppliers and (b) cash payments for operating expenses.

*E12-13 The 2014 accounting records of Rogan Transport reveal these transactions and events.

Compute cash flow from operating activities—direct method.
(LO 6), **AP**

Payment of interest	$ 10,000	Payment of salaries and wages	$ 53,000
Cash sales	48,000	Depreciation expense	16,000
Receipt of dividend revenue	18,000	Proceeds from sale of vehicles	812,000
Payment of income taxes	12,000	Purchase of equipment for cash	22,000
Net income	38,000	Loss on sale of vehicles	3,000
Payment for merchandise	97,000	Payment of dividends	14,000
Payment for land	74,000	Payment of operating expenses	28,000
Collection of accounts receivable	195,000		

Instructions

Prepare the cash flows from operating activities section using the direct method.

*E12-14 The following information is available for Taliaferro Corp. for 2014.

Prepare statement of cash flows—direct method.
(LO 6), **AP**

Cash used to purchase treasury stock	$ 48,100
Cash dividends paid	21,800
Cash paid for interest	22,400
Net income	464,300
Sales revenue	802,000
Cash paid for taxes	99,000
Cash received from customers	566,100
Cash received from sale of building (at book value)	197,600
Cash paid for operating expenses	77,000
Beginning cash balance	11,000
Cash paid for goods and services	279,100
Cash received from issuing common stock	355,000
Cash paid to redeem bonds at maturity	200,000
Cash paid to purchase equipment	113,200

Instructions

Prepare a statement of cash flows using the direct method.

*E12-15 The following information is taken from the 2014 general ledger of Praeger Company.

Calculate cash flows—direct method.
(LO 6), **AN**

Rent	Rent expense	$ 30,000
	Prepaid rent, January 1	5,900
	Prepaid rent, December 31	7,400
Salaries	Salaries and wages expense	$ 54,000
	Salaries and wages payable, January 1	2,000
	Salaries and wages payable, December 31	8,000
Sales	Sales revenue	$160,000
	Accounts receivable, January 1	16,000
	Accounts receivable, December 31	7,000

Instructions

In each case, compute the amount that should be reported in the operating activities section of the statement of cash flows under the direct method.

Challenge Exercises

Visit the book's companion website, at **www.wiley.com/college/kimmel**, and choose the Student Companion site to access Challenge Exercises.

Problems: Set A

Distinguish among operating, investing, and financing activities.

(LO 2), C

P12-1A You are provided with the following transactions that took place during a recent fiscal year.

Transaction	Statement of Cash Flow Activity Affected	Cash Inflow, Outflow, or No Effect?
(a) Recorded depreciation expense on the plant assets.		
(b) Recorded and paid interest expense.		
(c) Recorded cash proceeds from a sale of plant assets.		
(d) Acquired land by issuing common stock.		
(e) Paid a cash dividend to preferred stockholders.		
(f) Paid a cash dividend to common stockholders.		
(g) Recorded cash sales.		
(h) Recorded sales on account.		
(i) Purchased inventory for cash.		
(j) Purchased inventory on account.		

Instructions

Complete the table, indicating whether each item (1) affects operating (O) activities, investing (I) activities, financing (F) activities, or is a noncash (NC) transaction reported in a separate schedule, and (2) represents a cash inflow or cash outflow or has no cash flow effect. Assume use of the indirect approach.

Determine cash flow effects of changes in equity accounts.

(LO 4), AN

P12-2A The following account balances relate to the stockholders' equity accounts of Smoltz Corp. at year-end.

	2014	2013
Common stock, 10,500 and 10,000 shares, respectively, for 2014 and 2013	$160,800	$140,000
Preferred stock, 5,000 shares	125,000	125,000
Retained earnings	300,000	270,000

A small stock dividend was declared and issued in 2014. The market price of the shares was $8,800. Cash dividends were $20,000 in both 2014 and 2013. The common stock has no par or stated value.

Instructions

(a) Net income $58,800

(a) What was the amount of net income reported by Smoltz Corp. in 2014?

(b) Determine the amounts of any cash inflows or outflows related to the common stock and dividend accounts in 2014.

(c) Indicate where each of the cash inflows or outflows identified in (b) would be classified on the statement of cash flows.

Prepare the operating activities section—indirect method.

(LO 4), AP

XLS

P12-3A The income statement of Paxson Company is presented here.

PAXSON COMPANY
Income Statement
For the Year Ended November 30, 2014

Sales revenue		$7,600,000
Cost of goods sold		
Beginning inventory	$1,900,000	
Purchases	4,400,000	
Goods available for sale	6,300,000	
Ending inventory	1,600,000	
Total cost of goods sold		4,700,000

Gross profit		2,900,000
Operating expenses		
Selling expenses	450,000	
Administrative expenses	700,000	1,150,000
Net income		$1,750,000

Additional information:

1. Accounts receivable decreased $380,000 during the year, and inventory decreased $300,000.
2. Prepaid expenses increased $150,000 during the year.
3. Accounts payable to suppliers of merchandise decreased $350,000 during the year.
4. Accrued expenses payable decreased $100,000 during the year.
5. Administrative expenses include depreciation expense of $110,000.

Instructions

Prepare the operating activities section of the statement of cash flows for the year ended November 30, 2014, for Paxson Company, using the indirect method.

P12-4A Data for Paxson Company are presented in P12-3A.

Instructions

Prepare the operating activities section of the statement of cash flows using the direct method.

P12-5A Thornton Company's income statement contained the condensed information below.

Net cash provided
$1,940,000

Prepare the operating activities section—direct method.
(LO 6), **AP**

Net cash provided–oper. act.
$1,940,000

Prepare the operating activities section—indirect method.
(LO 4), **AP**

THORNTON COMPANY
Income Statement
For the Year Ended December 31, 2014

Service revenue		$970,000
Operating expenses, excluding depreciation	$614,000	
Depreciation expense	55,000	
Loss on disposal of plant assets	16,000	685,000
Income before income taxes		285,000
Income tax expense		56,000
Net income		$229,000

Thornton's balance sheet contained the comparative data at December 31.

	2014	2013
Accounts receivable	$70,000	$60,000
Accounts payable	41,000	32,000
Income taxes payable	13,000	7,000

Accounts payable pertain to operating expenses.

Instructions

Prepare the operating activities section of the statement of cash flows using the indirect method.

P12-6A Data for Thornton Company are presented in P12-5A.

Instructions

Prepare the operating activities section of the statement of cash flows using the direct method.

P12-7A Presented below are the financial statements of Kurtzel Company.

Net cash provided
$305,000

Prepare the operating activities section—direct method.
(LO 6), **AP**

Net cash
provided
$305,000

KURTZEL COMPANY
Comparative Balance Sheets
December 31

Assets	2014	2013
Cash	$ 35,000	$ 20,000
Accounts receivable	20,000	14,000

Prepare a statement of cash flows—indirect method, and compute cash-based ratios.

(LO 4, 5), **AP**

Inventory	28,000	20,000
Property, plant, and equipment	60,000	78,000
Accumulated depreciation	(32,000)	(24,000)
Total	$111,000	$108,000

Liabilities and Stockholders' Equity

Accounts payable	$ 19,000	$ 15,000
Income taxes payable	7,000	8,000
Bonds payable	17,000	33,000
Common stock	18,000	14,000
Retained earnings	50,000	38,000
Total	$111,000	$108,000

KURTZEL COMPANY
Income Statement
For the Year Ended December 31, 2014

Sales revenue		$242,000
Cost of goods sold		175,000
Gross profit		67,000
Selling expenses	$18,000	
Administrative expenses	6,000	24,000
Income from operations		43,000
Interest expense		3,000
Income before income taxes		40,000
Income tax expense		8,000
Net income		$ 32,000

Additional data:
1. Depreciation expense was $17,500.
2. Dividends declared and paid were $20,000.
3. During the year equipment was sold for $8,500 cash. This equipment cost $18,000 originally and had accumulated depreciation of $9,500 at the time of sale.

Instructions

(a) Net cash provided–oper. act. $38,500

(a) Prepare a statement of cash flows using the indirect method.
(b) Compute these cash-based measures:
   (1) Current cash debt coverage.
   (2) Cash debt coverage.
   (3) Free cash flow.

Prepare a statement of cash flows—direct method, and compute cash-based ratios.

(LO 5, 6), **AP**

*P12-8A** Data for Kurtzel Company are presented in P12-7A. Further analysis reveals the following.
1. Accounts payable pertain to merchandise suppliers.
2. All operating expenses except for depreciation were paid in cash.
3. All depreciation expense is in the selling expense category.
4. All sales and purchases are on account.

Instructions

(a) Net cash provided–oper. act. $38,500

(a) Prepare a statement of cash flows for Kurtzel Company using the direct method.
(b) Compute these cash-based measures:
   (1) Current cash debt coverage.
   (2) Cash debt coverage.
   (3) Free cash flow.

P12-9A Condensed financial data of Odgers Inc. follow.

Prepare a statement of cash flows—indirect method.

(LO 4), **AP**

ODGERS INC.
Comparative Balance Sheets
December 31

Assets	2014	2013
Cash	$ 80,800	$ 48,400
Accounts receivable	87,800	38,000
Inventory	112,500	102,850
Prepaid expenses	28,400	26,000
Long-term investments	138,000	109,000
Plant assets	285,000	242,500
Accumulated depreciation	(50,000)	(52,000)
Total	$682,500	$514,750

Liabilities and Stockholders' Equity		
Accounts payable	$102,000	$ 67,300
Accrued expenses payable	16,500	21,000
Bonds payable	110,000	146,000
Common stock	220,000	175,000
Retained earnings	234,000	105,450
Total	$682,500	$514,750

ODGERS INC.
Income Statement Data
For the Year Ended December 31, 2014

Sales revenue		$388,460
Less:		
Cost of goods sold	$135,460	
Operating expenses, excluding depreciation	12,410	
Depreciation expense	46,500	
Income tax expense	27,280	
Interest expense	4,730	
Loss on disposal of plant assets	7,500	233,880
Net income		$154,580

Additional information:
1. New plant assets costing $100,000 were purchased for cash during the year.
2. Old plant assets having an original cost of $57,500 and accumulated depreciation of $48,500 were sold for $1,500 cash.
3. Bonds payable matured and were paid off at face value for cash.
4. A cash dividend of $26,030 was declared and paid during the year.

Net cash provided–oper. act.
$176,930

Instructions
Prepare a statement of cash flows using the indirect method.

*P12-10A Data for Odgers Inc. are presented in P12-9A. Further analysis reveals that accounts payable pertain to merchandise creditors.

Prepare a statement of cash flows—direct method.

(LO 6), **AP**

Net cash provided–oper. act.
$176,930

Instructions
Prepare a statement of cash flows for Odgers Inc. using the direct method.

P12-11A The comparative balance sheets for Yanik Company as of December 31 are presented below.

Prepare a statement of cash flows—indirect method.

(LO 4), **AP**

YANIK COMPANY
Comparative Balance Sheets
December 31

Assets	2014	2013
Cash	$ 68,000	$ 45,000
Accounts receivable	50,000	58,000

Inventory	151,450	142,000
Prepaid expenses	15,280	21,000
Land	145,000	130,000
Buildings	200,000	200,000
Accumulated depreciation—buildings	(60,000)	(40,000)
Equipment	225,000	155,000
Accumulated depreciation—equipment	(45,000)	(35,000)
Total	$749,730	$676,000

Liabilities and Stockholders' Equity

Accounts payable	$ 44,730	$ 36,000
Bonds payable	300,000	300,000
Common stock, $1 par	200,000	160,000
Retained earnings	205,000	180,000
Total	$749,730	$676,000

Additional information:
1. Operating expenses include depreciation expense of $42,000.
2. Land was sold for cash at book value.
3. Cash dividends of $12,000 were paid.
4. Net income for 2014 was $37,000.
5. Equipment was purchased for $92,000 cash. In addition, equipment costing $22,000 with a book value of $10,000 was sold for $8,000 cash.
6. 40,000 shares of $1 par value common stock were issued in exchange for land with a fair value of $40,000.

*Net cash provided–oper. act.
$94,000*

Identify the impact of transactions on ratios.

(LO 5), **C**

Instructions
Prepare a statement of cash flows for the year ended December 31, 2014, using the indirect method.

P12-12A You are provided with the following transactions that took place during the year.

Transactions	Free Cash Flow ($125,000)	Current Cash Debt Coverage (0.5 times)	Cash Debt Coverage (0.3 times)
(a) Recorded credit sales $2,500.			
(b) Collected $1,900 owed by customers.			
(c) Paid amount owed to suppliers $2,750.			
(d) Recorded sales returns of $500 and credited the customer's account.			
(e) Purchased new equipment $5,000; signed a long-term note payable for the cost of the equipment.			
(f) Purchased a patent and paid $65,000 cash for the asset.			

Instructions
For each transaction listed, indicate whether it will increase (I), decrease (D), or have no effect (NE) on the ratios.

Problems: Set B

Visit the book's companion website, at **www.wiley.com/college/kimmel**, and choose the Student Companion site to access Problem Set B.

Broadening Your Perspective

Financial Reporting and Analysis

FINANCIAL REPORTING PROBLEM: *Tootsie Roll Industries, Inc.*

BYP12-1 The financial statements of Tootsie Roll Industries are presented in Appendix A.

Instructions
Answer the following questions.
(a) What was the amount of net cash provided by operating activities for 2011? For 2010?
(b) What was the amount of increase or decrease in cash and cash equivalents for the year ended December 31, 2011?
(c) Which method of computing net cash provided by operating activities does Tootsie Roll use?
(d) From your analysis of the 2011 statement of cash flows, was the change in accounts receivable a decrease or an increase? Was the change in inventories a decrease or an increase? Was the change in accounts payable a decrease or an increase?
(e) What was the net cash used by investing activities for 2011?
(f) What was the amount of interest paid in 2011? What was the amount of income taxes paid in 2011?

COMPARATIVE ANALYSIS PROBLEM: *Tootsie Roll vs. Hershey*

BYP12-2 The financial statements of The Hershey Company are presented in Appendix B, following the financial statements for Tootsie Roll Industries in Appendix A.

Instructions
(a) Based on the information in these financial statements, compute these 2011 ratios for each company:
  (1) Current cash debt coverage.
  (2) Cash debt coverage.
(b) What conclusions about the management of cash can you draw from these data?

RESEARCH CASES

BYP12-3 The March 4, 2010, edition of the *Wall Street Journal Online* contains an article by Jeffrey McCracken and Tom McGinty entitled "With Fistfuls of Cash, Firms on Hunt."

Instructions
Read the article and answer the following questions.
(a) How much cash did the nonfinancial (that is, nonbank-like) firms in the Standard and Poor's 500 have at the end of 2009? How big an increase in cash did this represent over the prior year?
(b) What reasons are given in the article for why companies might not want to keep hoarding cash?
(c) What steps did Alcoa take to try to increase the company's cash? Were these efforts successful?
(d) Often, companies issue shares of stock to acquire other companies. This represents a significant noncash transaction. At the time the article was written, why were many companies using cash rather than stock to acquire other companies?
(e) In addition to acquisitions, what other steps can companies take to reduce their cash balances?

BYP12-4 The November 23, 2011, edition of the *Wall Street Journal Online* contains an article by John Jannarone entitled "Backlash from Netflix Buybacks."

Instructions
Read the article and answer the following questions.
(a) What was the stock price for the shares of common stock issued by Netflix in the article? What was the price of the stock a few months previously?
(b) Why did Netflix issue new shares at a time when its stock price was so depressed relative to previous valuations for its stock?
(c) What previous actions had Netflix taken to reduce its cash balance?
(d) What does the article say is the lesson that growth companies should learn from the Netflix example?

INTERPRETING FINANCIAL STATEMENTS

BYP12-5 The incredible growth of Amazon.com has put fear into the hearts of traditional retailers. Its stock price has soared to amazing levels. However, in 2001 many investors were very concerned about whether Amazon would survive since it had never earned a profit and it was burning through cash. Some investors sold, but others decided to hold on to their investment in the company's stock. The following information is taken from the 2001 and 2004 financial statements of Amazon.

($ in millions)	2001	2004
Current assets	$1,207.9	$2,539.4
Total assets	1,637.5	3,248.5
Current liabilities	921.4	1,620.4
Total liabilities	3,077.5	5,096.1
Cash provided by operations	(119.8)	566.6
Capital expenditures	50.3	89.1
Dividends paid	0	0
Net income (loss)	(567.3)	588.5
Average current liabilities	948.2	1,436.6
Average total liabilities	3,090.0	4,773.4

Instructions
(a) Calculate the current ratio and current cash debt coverage for Amazon for 2001 and 2004, and discuss its comparative liquidity.
(b) Calculate the cash debt coverage and the debt to assets ratio for Amazon for 2001 and 2004, and discuss its comparative solvency.
(c) Amazon has avoided purchasing large warehouses. Instead, it has used those of others. In order to increase customer satisfaction, Amazon may have to build its own warehouses. Calculate free cash flow for Amazon for 2001 and 2004, and discuss its ability to purchase warehouses and to finance expansion from internally generated cash.
(d) Based on your findings in parts (a) through (c), can you conclude whether or not Amazon's amazing stock price is justified?

REAL-WORLD FOCUS

BYP12-6 *Purpose:* Use the Internet to view SEC filings.

Address: **biz.yahoo.com/i**, or go to **www.wiley.com/college/kimmel**

Steps
1. Enter a company's name.
2. Choose **Quote**. Answer questions (a) and (b).
3. Choose **Profile**; then choose **SEC**. Answer questions (c) and (d).

Instructions
Answer the following questions.
(a) What company did you select?
(b) What is its stock symbol? What is its selling price?
(c) What recent SEC filings are available for your viewing?
(d) Which filing is the most recent? What is the date?

Critical Thinking

DECISION-MAKING ACROSS THE ORGANIZATION

BYP12-7 Ken Pember and Robyn Mays are examining the following statement of cash flows for Gilbert Company for the year ended January 31, 2014.

GILBERT COMPANY
Statement of Cash Flows
For the Year Ended January 31, 2014

Sources of cash	
From sales of merchandise	$385,000
From sale of capital stock	405,000

From sale of investment (purchased below)	80,000
From depreciation	55,000
From issuance of note for truck	20,000
From interest on investments	6,000
Total sources of cash	951,000
Uses of cash	
For purchase of fixtures and equipment	320,000
For merchandise purchased for resale	258,000
For operating expenses (including depreciation)	170,000
For purchase of investment	75,000
For purchase of truck by issuance of note	20,000
For purchase of treasury stock	10,000
For interest on note payable	3,000
Total uses of cash	856,000
Net increase in cash	$ 95,000

Ken claims that Gilbert's statement of cash flows is an excellent portrayal of a superb first year with cash increasing $95,000. Robyn replies that it was not a superb first year. Rather, she says, the year was an operating failure, that the statement is presented incorrectly, and that $95,000 is not the actual increase in cash. The cash balance at the beginning of the year was $140,000.

Instructions
With the class divided into groups, answer the following.
(a) Using the data provided, prepare a statement of cash flows in proper form using the indirect method. The only noncash items in the income statement are depreciation and the gain from the sale of the investment.
(b) With whom do you agree, Ken or Robyn? Explain your position.

COMMUNICATION ACTIVITY

BYP12-8 Jack Werth, the owner-president of Computer Services Company, is unfamiliar with the statement of cash flows that you, as his accountant, prepared. He asks for further explanation.

Instructions
Write him a brief memo explaining the form and content of the statement of cash flows as shown in Illustration 12-14.

ETHICS CASE

BYP12-9 Templeton Automotive Corp. is a medium-sized wholesaler of automotive parts. It has 10 stockholders who have been paid a total of $1 million in cash dividends for 8 consecutive years. The board's policy requires that, for this dividend to be declared, net cash provided by operating activities as reported in Templeton Automotive's current year's statement of cash flows must exceed $1 million. President and CEO Rick Hanigan's job is secure so long as he produces annual operating cash flows to support the usual dividend.

At the end of the current year, controller Nick Korte presents president Rick Hanigan with some disappointing news. The net cash provided by operating activities is calculated by the indirect method to be only $970,000. The president says to Nick, "We must get that amount above $1 million. Isn't there some way to increase operating cash flow by another $30,000?" Nick answers, "These figures were prepared by my assistant. I'll go back to my office and see what I can do." The president replies, "I know you won't let me down, Nick."

Upon close scrutiny of the statement of cash flows, Nick concludes that he can get the operating cash flows above $1 million by reclassifying a $60,000, 2-year note payable listed in the financing activities section as "Proceeds from bank loan—$60,000." He will report the note instead as "Increase in payables—$60,000" and treat it as an adjustment of net income in the operating activities section. He returns to the president, saying, "You can tell the board to declare their usual dividend. Our net cash flow provided by operating activities is $1,030,000." "Good man, Nick! I knew I could count on you," exults the president.

Instructions

(a) Who are the stakeholders in this situation?

(b) Was there anything unethical about the president's actions? Was there anything unethical about the controller's actions?

(c) Are the board members or anyone else likely to discover the misclassification?

ALL ABOUT YOU

BYP12-10 In this chapter, you learned that companies prepare a statement of cash flows in order to keep track of their sources and uses of cash and to help them plan for their future cash needs. Planning for your own short- and long-term cash needs is every bit as important as it is for a company.

Instructions

Read the article "Financial 'Uh-oh'? No Problem," at **www.fool.com/savings/shortterm/02.htm**, and answer the following questions.

(a) Describe the three factors that determine how much money you should set aside for short-term needs.

(b) How many months of living expenses does the article suggest to set aside?

(c) Estimate how much you should set aside based upon your current situation. Are you closer to Cliff's scenario or to Prudence's?

FASB CODIFICATION ACTIVITY

BYP12-11 If your school has a subscription to the FASB Codification, go to **http://aaahq.org/ ascLogin.cfm** to log in and prepare responses to the following. Use the Master Glossary to determine the proper definitions.

(a) What are cash equivalents?

(b) What are financing activities?

(c) What are investing activities?

(d) What are operating activities?

(e) What is the primary objective for the statement of cash flow? Is working capital the basis for meeting this objective?

(f) Do companies need to disclose information about investing and financing activities that do not affect cash receipts or cash payments? If so, how should such information be disclosed?

Answers to Insight and Accounting Across the Organization Questions

p. 545 Net *What?* Q: In general, why do differences exist between net income and net cash provided by operating activities? **A:** The differences are explained by differences in the timing of the reporting of revenues and expenses under accrual accounting versus cash. Under accrual accounting, companies report revenues when the performance obligation is satisfied, even if cash hasn't been received, and they report expenses when incurred, even if cash hasn't been paid.

p. 547 Operating with Negative Cash Q: Why do companies have negative net cash provided by operating activities during the introductory phase? **A:** During the introductory phase, companies usually spend more on inventory than the amount expensed for cost of goods sold because they are building up inventory and their cash collections frequently lag the amount reported for sales. Therefore, even if companies are reporting positive net income, they frequently report negative net cash provided by operating activities.

p. 556 Burning Through Our Cash Q: What impact did Kodak's sale of plant assets have on its net cash provided by investing activities? **A:** Kodak sold its plant assets to increase its net cash provided by investing activities. This net cash increase allowed Kodak to then invest in new product ideas.

p. 561 We Aren't Going to Fail—Really Q: Do you think that issuing stock would be a cost-efficient way for these companies to raise funds? **A:** When investors are exposed to more risk, they demand a higher return. In the case of stock investments, this means that the investors will pay a lower price in order to get a higher return. Since these companies are at risk of failing, this is a particularly risky investment. As a result, the cash received for new shares would be really low. Therefore, this would not be an efficient source of cash. However, the companies need cash to avoid failing, so they have no choice.

A Look at IFRS

> **LEARNING OBJECTIVE 8**
>
> Compare the accounting procedures for the statement of cash flows under GAAP and IFRS.

As in GAAP, the statement of cash flows is a required statement for IFRS. In addition, the content and presentation of an IFRS statement of cash flows is similar to the one used for GAAP. However, the disclosure requirements related to the statement of cash flows are more extensive under GAAP. *IAS 7* ("Cash Flow Statements") provides the overall IFRS requirements for cash flow information.

KEY POINTS

- Companies preparing financial statements under IFRS must prepare a statement of cash flows as an integral part of the financial statements.

- Both IFRS and GAAP require that the statement of cash flows should have three major sections—operating, investing, and financing activities—along with changes in cash and cash equivalents.

- Similar to GAAP, the statement of cash flows can be prepared using either the indirect or direct method under IFRS. In both U.S. and international settings, companies choose for the most part to use the indirect method for reporting net cash flows from operating activities.

- The definition of cash equivalents used in IFRS is similar to that used in GAAP. A major difference is that in certain situations, bank overdrafts are considered part of cash and cash equivalents under IFRS (which is not the case in GAAP). Under GAAP, bank overdrafts are classified as financing activities in the statement of cash flows and are reported as liabilities on the balance sheet.

- IFRS requires that noncash investing and financing activities be excluded from the statement of cash flows. Instead, these noncash activities should be reported elsewhere. This requirement is interpreted to mean that noncash investing and financing activities should be disclosed in the notes to the financial statements instead of in the financial statements. Under GAAP, companies may present this information on the face of the statement of cash flows.

- One area where there can be substantial differences between IFRS and GAAP relates to the classification of interest, dividends, and taxes. The following table indicates the differences between the two approaches.

Item	IFRS	GAAP
Interest paid	Operating or financing	Operating
Interest received	Operating or investing	Operating
Dividends paid	Operating or financing	Financing
Dividends received	Operating or investing	Operating
Taxes paid	Operating—unless specific identification with financing or investing activity	Operating

- Under IFRS, some companies present the operating section in a single line item, with a full reconciliation provided in the notes to the financial statements. This presentation is not seen under GAAP.

- Similar to GAAP, under IFRS companies must disclose the amount of taxes and interest paid. Under GAAP, companies disclose this in the notes to the financial statements. Under IFRS, some companies disclose this information in the notes, but others provide individual line items on the face of the statement. In order to provide this information on the face of the statement, companies first add back the amount of interest expense and tax expense (similar to adding back depreciation expense) and then further down the statement they subtract the cash amount paid for interest and taxes. This treatment can be seen in the statement of cash flows provided for Zetar in Appendix C.

LOOKING TO THE FUTURE

Presently, the FASB and the IASB are involved in a joint project on the presentation and organization of information in the financial statements. One interesting approach, revealed in a published proposal from that project, is that in the future the income statement and balance sheet would adopt headings similar to those of the statement of cash flows. That is, the income statement and balance sheet would be broken into operating, investing, and financing sections.

With respect to the statement of cash flows specifically, the notion of **cash equivalents** will probably not be retained. That is, cash equivalents will not be combined with cash but instead will be reported as a form of highly liquid, low-risk investment. The definition of cash in the existing literature would be retained, and the statement of cash flows would present information on changes in cash only. In addition, the FASB favors presentation of operating cash flows using the direct method only. However, the majority of IASB members express a preference for not requiring use of the direct method of reporting operating cash flows. The two Boards will have to resolve their differences in this area in order to issue a converged standard for the statement of cash flows.

IFRS PRACTICE

IFRS SELF-TEST QUESTIONS

1. Under IFRS, interest paid can be reported as:
   (a) only a financing activity.
   (b) a financing activity or an investing activity.
   (c) a financing activity or an operating activity.
   (d) only an operating activity.

2. IFRS requires that noncash items:
   (a) be reported in the section to which they relate, that is, a noncash investing activity would be reported in the investing section.
   (b) be disclosed in the notes to the financial statements.
   (c) do not need to be reported.
   (d) be treated in a fashion similar to cash equivalents.

3. In the future, it appears likely that:
   (a) the income statement and balance sheet will have headings of operating, investing, and financing, much like the statement of cash flows.
   (b) cash and cash equivalents will be combined in a single line item.
   (c) the IASB will not allow companies to use the direct approach to the statement of cash flows.
   (d) None of the above.

4. Under IFRS:
   (a) taxes are always treated as an operating activity.
   (b) the income statement uses the headings operating, investing, and financing.
   (c) dividends received can be either an operating or investing activity.
   (d) dividends paid can be either an operating or investing activity.

5. Which of the following is **correct**?
   (a) Under IFRS, the statement of cash flows is optional.
   (b) IFRS requires use of the direct approach in preparing the statement of cash flows.
   (c) The majority of companies following GAAP and the majority following IFRS employ the indirect approach to the statement of cash flows.
   (d) Cash and cash equivalents are reported as separate line items under IFRS.

IFRS CONCEPTS AND APPLICATION

IFRS 12-1   Discuss the differences that exist in the treatment of bank overdrafts under GAAP and IFRS.

IFRS 12-2   Describe the treatment of each of the following items under IFRS versus GAAP.
   (a) Interest paid.
   (b) Interest received.
   (c) Dividends paid.
   (d) Dividends received.

IFRS 12-3   Explain how the treatment of cash equivalents will probably change in the future.

INTERNATIONAL FINANCIAL REPORTING PROBLEM: *Zetar plc*

IFRS12-4   The financial statements of **Zetar plc** are presented in Appendix C. The company's complete annual report, including the notes to its financial statements, is available in the Investors section at **www.zetarplc.com**.

Instructions
Use the company's annual report to answer the following questions.

(a) In which section (operating, investing, or financing) does Zetar report interest paid?

(b) Explain why the amount that Zetar reports for cash and cash equivalents in its statement of cash flows is negative.

(c) If Zetar reported under GAAP rather than IFRS, how would its treatment of bank overdrafts differ?

(d) Zetar's statement of cash flows reports negative "net movement in working capital" in 2011 of £(6,040) (in thousands). According to the statement of cash flows, what were the components of this "net movement"?

Answers to IFRS Self-Test Questions

1. c **2.** b **3.** a **4.** c **5.** c

Daniel Acker/Bloomberg/Getty Images, Inc.

CHAPTER 13

FINANCIAL ANALYSIS: THE BIG PICTURE

LEARNING OBJECTIVES

After studying this chapter, you should be able to:

1 Understand the concept of sustainable income.

2 Indicate how irregular items are presented.

3 Explain the concept of comprehensive income.

4 Describe and apply horizontal analysis.

5 Describe and apply vertical analysis.

6 Identify and compute ratios used in analyzing a company's liquidity, solvency, and profitability.

7 Understand the concept of quality of earnings.

A recent issue of *Forbes* magazine listed Warren Buffett as the richest person in the world. His estimated wealth was $62 billion, give or take a few million. How much is $62 billion? If you invested $62 billion in an investment earning just 4%, you could spend $6.8 million per day—every day—forever.

So, how does Buffett spend his money? Basically, he doesn't! He still lives in the same house that he purchased in Omaha, Nebraska, in 1958 for $31,500. He still drives his own car (a Cadillac DTS). And, in case you were thinking that his kids are riding the road to Easy Street, think again. Buffett has committed to donate virtually all of his money to charity before he dies.

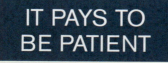

IT PAYS TO BE PATIENT

How did Buffett amass this wealth? Through careful investing. Buffett epitomizes a "value investor." He applies the basic techniques he learned in the 1950s from the great value investor Benjamin Graham. He looks for companies that have good long-term potential but are currently underpriced. He invests in companies that have low exposure to debt and that reinvest their earnings for future growth. He does not get caught up in fads or the latest trends.

Buffett sat out on the dot-com mania in the 1990s. When other investors put lots of money into fledgling high-tech firms, Buffett didn't bite because he did not find dot-com companies that met his criteria. He didn't get to enjoy the stock price boom on the way up, but on the other hand, he didn't have to ride the price back down to Earth. When the dot-com bubble burst, everyone else was suffering from investment shock. Buffett swooped in and scooped up deals on companies that he had been following for years.

In 2012, the stock market had again reached near record highs. Buffett's returns had been significantly lagging the market. Only 26% of his investments at that time were in stock, and he was sitting on $38 billion in cash. One commentator noted that "if the past is any guide, just when Buffett seems to look most like a loser, the party is about to end."

If you think you want to follow Buffett's example and transform your humble nest egg into a mountain of cash, be warned. His techniques have been widely circulated and emulated, but never practiced with the same degree of success. You should probably start by honing your financial analysis skills. A good way for you to begin your career as a successful investor is to master the fundamentals of financial analysis discussed in this chapter.

Source: Jason Zweig, "Buffett Is Out of Step," *Wall Street Journal* (May 7, 2012).

INSIDE CHAPTER 13 . . .

- **What Does "Non-Recurring" Really Mean?**
- **More Frequent Ups and Downs**
- **How to Manage the Current Ratio**
- **High Ratings Can Bring Low Returns**

We can all learn an important lesson from Warren Buffett: Study companies carefully if you wish to invest. Do not get caught up in fads but instead find companies that are financially healthy. Using some of the basic decision tools presented in this book, you can perform a rudimentary analysis on any company and draw basic conclusions about its financial health. Although it would not be wise for you to bet your life savings on a company's stock relying solely on your current level of knowledge, we strongly encourage you to practice your new skills wherever possible. Only with practice will you improve your ability to interpret financial numbers.

Before we unleash you on the world of high finance, we present a few more important concepts and techniques as well as one more comprehensive review of corporate financial statements. We use all of the decision tools presented in this textbook to analyze a single company, with comparisons to a competitor and industry averages.

The content and organization of Chapter 13 are as follows.

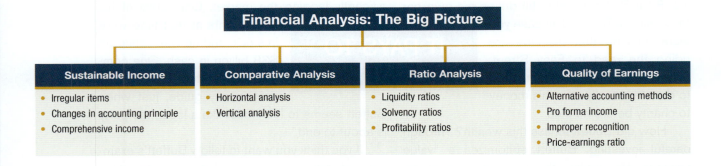

Sustainable Income

LEARNING OBJECTIVE 1

Understand the concept of sustainable income.

Ultimately, the value of a company is a function of its future cash flows. When analysts use this year's net income to estimate future cash flows, they must make sure that this year's net income does not include irregular (i.e., out of the ordinary) revenues, expenses, gains, or losses. Net income adjusted for irregular items is referred to as sustainable income. **Sustainable income is the most likely level of income to be obtained in the future.** Sustainable income differs from actual net income by the amount of irregular revenues, expenses, gains, and losses included in this year's net income.

Users are interested in sustainable income because it helps them derive an estimate of future earnings without the "noise" of irregular items. For example, suppose Rye Corporation reports that this year's net income is $500,000 but included in that amount is a once-in-a-lifetime gain of $400,000. In estimating next year's net income for Rye Corporation, we would likely ignore this $400,000 gain and estimate that next year's net income will be in the neighborhood of $100,000. That is, based on this year's results, the company's sustainable income is roughly $100,000. Therefore, identifying irregular items is important if you are going to use reported earnings to estimate a company's value.

In earlier chapters, you learned how to prepare and use a basic multiple-step income statement. In this chapter, we will explain additional components of the income statement as well as a broader measure of performance called

comprehensive income. Illustration 13-1 presents the components of the income statement and comprehensive income; new items are presented in red. When estimating future cash flows, analysts must consider the implications that each of these components has for future cash flows.

Income Statement	
Sales revenue	$XX
Cost of goods sold	XX
Gross profit	XX
Operating expenses	XX
Income from operations	XX
Other revenues (expenses) and gains (losses)	XX
Income before income taxes	XX
Income tax expense	XX
Income before irregular items	XX
Discontinued operations (net of tax)	XX
Extraordinary items (net of tax)	XX
Net income	XX
Other comprehensive income items (net of tax)	XX
Comprehensive income	$XX

Illustration 13-1
Components of the income statement

IRREGULAR ITEMS

To help determine sustainable income, we identify irregular items by type on the income statement. There, companies report two types of irregular items:

LEARNING OBJECTIVE 2
Indicate how irregular items are presented.

1. Discontinued operations
2. Extraordinary items

Irregular items are reported net of income taxes. That is, a company first calculates income tax expense for the income before irregular items. Then, it calculates income tax expense for each individual irregular item. The general concept is, "Let the tax follow the income or loss."

Discontinued Operations

To downsize its operations, General Dynamics Corp. sold its missile business to Hughes Aircraft Co. for $450 million. In its income statement, General Dynamics reported the sale in a separate section entitled "Discontinued operations." **Discontinued operations** refers to the disposal of a significant component of a business, such as the elimination of a major class of customers or an entire activity. When the disposal of a significant component occurs, the income statement should report the gain (or loss) from discontinued operations, net of tax.

To illustrate, assume that Rozek Inc. has revenues of $2.5 million and expenses of $1.7 million from continuing operations in 2014. The company has income before income taxes of $800,000. During 2014, the company discontinued and sold its unprofitable chemical division. The loss on disposal of the chemical division (net of $90,000 tax savings) was $210,000. Illustration 13-2 shows the income statement presentation, assuming a 30% tax rate on income before income taxes. This presentation clearly indicates the separate effects of continuing operations and discontinued operations on net income.

Illustration 13-2 Statement presentation of discontinued operations

ROZEK INC.
Income Statement (partial)
For the Year Ended December 31, 2014

Income before income taxes	$ 800,000
Income tax expense	240,000
Income before irregular items	560,000
Discontinued operations	
Loss from disposal of chemical division, net of	
$90,000 income tax savings	**(210,000)**
Net income	$ 350,000

DECISION TOOLKIT

DECISION CHECKPOINTS	INFO NEEDED FOR DECISION	TOOL TO USE FOR DECISION	HOW TO EVALUATE RESULTS
Has the company sold any major components of its business?	Discontinued operations section of income statement	Anything reported in this section indicates that the company has discontinued a major component of its business.	If a major component has been discontinued, its results during the current period should not be included in estimates of future net income.

Extraordinary Items

Extraordinary items are events and transactions that meet two conditions. They are **unusual in nature** and **infrequent in occurrence**. To be considered **unusual**, the item should be abnormal and only incidentally related to the customary activities of the entity. To be regarded as **infrequent**, the event or transaction should not be reasonably expected to recur in the foreseeable future.

A company must evaluate both criteria in terms of the environment in which it operates. Thus, Weyerhaeuser Co. reported the $36 million in damages to its timberland caused by the eruption of Mount St. Helens as an extraordinary item because the event was both unusual and infrequent. In contrast, Florida Citrus Company does not report frost damage to its citrus crop as an extraordinary item because frost damage is not viewed as infrequent.

Companies report extraordinary items net of taxes in a separate section of the income statement, immediately below discontinued operations. To illustrate, assume that in 2014 a revolutionary foreign government expropriated property held as an investment by Rozek Inc. If the loss is $70,000 before applicable income tax savings of $21,000, the income statement presentation will show a deduction of $49,000, as in Illustration 13-3.

Illustration 13-3 Statement presentation of extraordinary items

ROZEK INC.
Income Statement (partial)
For the Year Ended December 31, 2014

Income before income taxes	$ 800,000
Income tax expense	240,000
Income before irregular items	560,000
Discontinued operations: Loss from disposal of	
chemical division, net of $90,000 income tax savings	(210,000)
Extraordinary item: Expropriation of investment,	
net of $21,000 income tax savings	**(49,000)**
Net income	$ 301,000

If a transaction or event meets one but not both of the criteria for an extraordinary item, a company should report it as a separate line item in the upper portion of the income statement, rather than in the bottom portion as an extraordinary item. Usually, companies report these items under either "Other revenues and gains" or "Other expenses and losses" at their gross amount (not net of tax). This is true, for example, of gains (losses) resulting from the sale of property, plant, and equipment, as explained in Chapter 9. Illustration 13-4 shows the appropriate classification of extraordinary and ordinary items.

Illustration 13-4
Classification of extraordinary and ordinary items

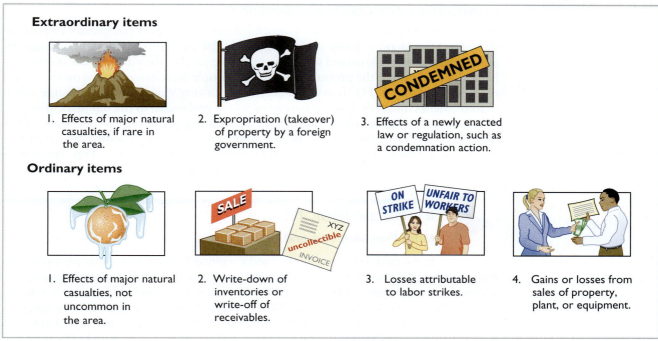

Extraordinary items

1. Effects of major natural casualties, if rare in the area.
2. Expropriation (takeover) of property by a foreign government.
3. Effects of a newly enacted law or regulation, such as a condemnation action.

Ordinary items

1. Effects of major natural casualties, not uncommon in the area.
2. Write-down of inventories or write-off of receivables.
3. Losses attributable to labor strikes.
4. Gains or losses from sales of property, plant, or equipment.

In summary, in evaluating a company, it generally makes sense to eliminate all irregular items in estimating future sustainable income.

Investor Insight

What Does "Non-Recurring" Really Mean?

Many companies incur restructuring charges as they attempt to reduce costs. They often label these items in the income statement as "non-recurring" charges, to suggest that they are isolated events, unlikely to occur in future periods. The question for analysts is, are these costs really one-time, "non-recurring events" or do they reflect problems that the company will be facing for many periods in the future? If they are one-time events, then they can be largely ignored when trying to predict future earnings.

But, some companies report "one-time" restructuring charges over and over again. For example, Procter & Gamble reported a restructuring charge in 12 consecutive quarters, and Motorola had "special" charges in 14 consecutive quarters. On the other hand, other companies have a restructuring charge only once in a 5- or 10-year period. There appears to be no substitute for careful analysis of the numbers that comprise net income.

? If a company takes a large restructuring charge, what is the effect on the company's current income statement versus future ones? (Answers in *Broadening Your Perspective*.)

DECISION TOOLKIT

DECISION CHECKPOINTS	INFO NEEDED FOR DECISION	TOOL TO USE FOR DECISION	HOW TO EVALUATE RESULTS
Has the company experienced any extraordinary events or transactions?	Extraordinary item section of income statement	Items reported in this section indicate that the company experienced an event that was both unusual and infrequent.	These items should usually be ignored in estimating future net income.

CHANGES IN ACCOUNTING PRINCIPLE

For ease of comparison, users of financial statements expect companies to prepare their statements on a basis **consistent** with the preceding period. A **change in accounting principle** occurs when the principle used in the current year is different from the one used in the preceding year. An example is a change in inventory costing methods (such as FIFO to average-cost). Accounting rules permit a change when management can show that the new principle is preferable to the old principle.

Companies report most changes in accounting principle retroactively.[1] That is, they report both the current period and previous periods using the new principle. As a result, the same principle applies in all periods. This treatment improves the ability to compare results across years.

Investor Insight

More Frequent Ups and Downs

In the past, U.S. companies used a method to account for their pension plans that smoothed out the gains and losses on their pension portfolios by spreading gains and losses over multiple years. Many felt that this approach was beneficial because it reduced the volatility of reported net income. However, recently some companies have opted to adopt a method approved by international accounting standard-setters. Under this approach, gains and losses on the pension portfolio affect net income in the period in which they occur. Some of the companies that have adopted this approach are United Parcel Service (UPS), Honeywell International, IBM, AT&T, and Verizon Communications. The CFO at UPS said he favored the new approach because "events that occurred in prior years will no longer distort current-year results. It will result in better transparency by eliminating the noise of past plan performance." When UPS switched, it resulted in a charge of $827 million from the change in accounting principle.

Source: Bob Sechler and Doug Cameron, "UPS Alters Pension-Plan Accounting," *Wall Street Journal* (January 30, 2012).

? When predicting future earnings, how should analysts treat the one-time charge that results from a switch to the different approach for accounting for pension plans? (Answers in *Broadening Your Perspective*.)

DECISION TOOLKIT

DECISION CHECKPOINTS	INFO NEEDED FOR DECISION	TOOL TO USE FOR DECISION	HOW TO EVALUATE RESULTS
Has the company changed any of its accounting principles?	Effect of change in accounting principle on current and prior periods.	Management indicates that the new principle is preferable to the old principle.	Examine current and prior years' reported income, using new-principle basis to assess trends for estimating future income.

---

[1]An exception to the general rule is a change in depreciation methods. The effects of this change are reported in current and future periods. Discussion of this approach is left for more advanced courses.

COMPREHENSIVE INCOME

Most revenues, expenses, gains, and losses are included in net income. However, certain gains and losses bypass net income. Instead, companies record these items as direct adjustments to stockholders' equity. Many analysts have expressed concern about this practice because they believe it reduces the usefulness of the income statement. To address this concern, the FASB requires companies to report not only net income but also comprehensive income. **Comprehensive income** includes all changes in stockholders' equity during a period except those changes resulting from investments by stockholders and distributions to stockholders.

LEARNING OBJECTIVE 3
Explain the concept of comprehensive income.

Illustration of Comprehensive Income

Accounting standards require that companies adjust most investments in stocks and bonds up or down to their market price at the end of each accounting period. For example, assume that during 2014 Stassi Company purchased IBM stock for $10,000 as an investment. At the end of 2014, Stassi was still holding the investment, but the stock's market price was now $8,000. In this case, Stassi is required to reduce the recorded value of its IBM investment by $2,000. The $2,000 difference is an unrealized loss.

Should Stassi include this $2,000 unrealized loss in net income? It depends on whether Stassi classifies the IBM stock as a trading security or an available-for-sale security. A **trading security** is bought and held primarily for sale in the near term to generate income on short-term price differences. Companies report unrealized losses on trading securities in the "Other expenses and losses" section of the income statement. The rationale: It is likely that the company will realize the unrealized loss (or an unrealized gain), so the company should report the loss (gain) as part of net income.

If Stassi did not purchase the investment for trading purposes, it is classified as available-for-sale. **Available-for-sale securities** are held with the intent of selling them sometime in the future. Companies do not include unrealized gains or losses on available-for-sale securities in net income. Instead, they report them as part of "Other comprehensive income." Other comprehensive income is not included in net income. It bypasses net income and is recorded as a direct adjustment to stockholders' equity.

Format

One format for reporting comprehensive income is to report a combined statement of income and comprehensive income.[2] For example, assuming that Stassi Company has a net income of $300,000, the unrealized loss would be reported below net income as follows.

STASSI CORPORATION Combined Statement of Income and Comprehensive Income (partial)	
Net income	$300,000
Unrealized loss on available-for-sale securities	2,000
Comprehensive income	$298,000

Illustration 13-5 Lower portion of combined statement of income and comprehensive income

Companies also report the unrealized loss on available-for-sale securities as a separate component of stockholders' equity. To illustrate, assume Stassi Corporation has common stock of $3,000,000, retained earnings of $1,500,000, and an unrealized loss on available-for-sale securities of $2,000. Illustration 13-6 shows the balance sheet presentation of the unrealized loss.

[2]Computation of comprehensive income is sometimes shown in a separate statement of comprehensive income or as a section in the stockholders' equity statement.

Illustration 13-6 Unrealized loss in stockholders' equity section

STASSI CORPORATION	
Balance Sheet (partial)	
Stockholders' equity	
Common stock	$3,000,000
Retained earnings	1,500,000
Total paid-in capital and retained earnings	4,500,000
Less: Unrealized loss on available-for-sale securities	(2,000)
Total stockholders' equity	$4,498,000

Note that the presentation of the loss is similar to the presentation of the cost of treasury stock in the stockholders' equity section. (An unrealized gain would be added in this section of the balance sheet.) Reporting the unrealized gain or loss in the stockholders' equity section serves two important purposes: (1) It reduces the volatility of net income due to fluctuations in fair value, and (2) it informs the financial statement user of the gain or loss that would occur if the company sold the securities at fair value.

Complete Income Statement

The income statement for Pace Corporation in Illustration 13-7 presents the types of items found on this statement, such as net sales, cost of goods sold, operating expenses, and income taxes. In addition, it shows how companies report irregular items and comprehensive income (highlighted in red).

Illustration 13-7 Complete income statement

PACE CORPORATION		
Income Statement and		
Statement of Comprehensive Income		
For the Year Ended December 31, 2014		
Net sales		$440,000
Cost of goods sold		260,000
Gross profit		180,000
Operating expenses		110,000
Income from operations		70,000
Other revenues and gains	$ 5,600	
Other expenses and losses	(9,600)	(4,000)
Income before income taxes		66,000
Income tax expense ($66,000 × 30%)		19,800
Income before irregular items		46,200
Discontinued operations: Gain on disposal of Plastics Division, net of $15,000 income taxes ($50,000 × 30%)		35,000
Extraordinary item: Tornado loss, net of income tax savings $18,000 ($60,000 × 30%)		(42,000)
Net income		39,200
Add: Unrealized gain on available-for-sale securities		10,000
Comprehensive income		$ 49,200

CONCLUDING REMARKS

We have shown that the computation of the correct net income number can be elusive. In assessing the future prospects of a company, some investors focus on income from operations and therefore ignore all irregular and other items. Others use measures such as net income, comprehensive income, or some modified version of one of these amounts.

Comparative Analysis

As indicated, in assessing the financial performance of a company, investors are interested in the core or sustainable earnings of a company. In addition, investors are interested in making comparisons from period to period. Throughout this textbook, we have relied on three types of comparisons to improve the decision-usefulness of financial information:

LEARNING OBJECTIVE **4**
Describe and apply horizontal analysis.

1. **Intracompany basis.** Comparisons within a company are often useful to detect changes in financial relationships and significant trends. For example, a comparison of Kellogg's current year's cash amount with the prior year's cash amount shows either an increase or a decrease. Likewise, a comparison of Kellogg's year-end cash amount with the amount of its total assets at year-end shows the proportion of total assets in the form of cash.

2. **Intercompany basis.** Comparisons with other companies provide insight into a company's competitive position. For example, investors can compare Kellogg's total sales for the year with the total sales of its competitors in the breakfast cereal area, such as General Mills.

3. **Industry averages.** Comparisons with industry averages provide information about a company's relative position within the industry. For example, financial statement readers can compare Kellogg's financial data with the averages for its industry compiled by financial rating organizations such as Dun & Bradstreet, Moody's, and Standard & Poor's, or with information provided on the Internet by organizations such as Yahoo! on its financial site.

We use three basic tools in financial statement analysis to highlight the significance of financial statement data:

1. Horizontal analysis
2. Vertical analysis
3. Ratio analysis

In previous chapters, we relied primarily on ratio analysis, supplemented with some basic horizontal and vertical analysis. In the remainder of this section, we introduce more formal forms of horizontal and vertical analysis. In the next section, we review ratio analysis in some detail.

HORIZONTAL ANALYSIS

Horizontal analysis, also known as trend analysis, is a technique for evaluating a series of financial statement data over a period of time. Its purpose is to determine the increase or decrease that has taken place, expressed as either an amount or a percentage. For example, here are recent net sales figures (in thousands) of Chicago Cereal Company:

2011	2010	2009	2008	2007
$11,776	$10,907	$10,177	$9,614	$8,812

If we assume that 2007 is the base year, we can measure all percentage increases or decreases relative to this base-period amount with the formula shown in Illustration 13-8.

$$\text{Change Since Base Period} = \frac{\text{Current-Year Amount} - \text{Base-Year Amount}}{\text{Base-Year Amount}}$$

Illustration 13-8 Horizontal analysis—computation of changes since base period

For example, we can determine that net sales for Chicago Cereal increased approximately 9.1% [($9,614 − $8,812) ÷ $8,812] from 2007 to 2008. Similarly, we can also determine that net sales increased by 33.6% [($11,776 − $8,812) ÷ $8,812] from 2007 to 2011.

Alternatively, we can express current-year sales as a percentage of the base period. To do so, we would divide the current-year amount by the base-year amount, as shown in Illustration 13-9.

Illustration 13-9 Horizontal analysis—computation of current year in relation to base year

$$\text{Current Results in Relation to Base Period} = \frac{\text{Current-Year Amount}}{\text{Base-Year Amount}}$$

Current-period sales expressed as a percentage of the base period for each of the five years, using 2007 as the base period, are shown in Illustration 13-10.

Illustration 13-10 Horizontal analysis of net sales

CHICAGO CEREAL COMPANY
Net Sales (in thousands)
Base Period 2007

2011	2010	2009	2008	2007
$11,776	$10,907	$10,177	$9,614	$8,812
133.6%	123.8%	115.5%	109.1%	100%

The large increase in net sales during 2008 would raise questions regarding possible reasons for such a significant change. Chicago Cereal's 2008 notes to the financial statements explain that the company completed an acquisition of Elf Foods Company during 2008. This major acquisition would help explain the increase in sales highlighted by horizontal analysis.

To further illustrate horizontal analysis, we use the financial statements of Chicago Cereal Company. Its two-year condensed balance sheets for 2011 and 2010, showing dollar and percentage changes, are presented in Illustration 13-11.

The comparative balance sheets show that a number of changes occurred in Chicago Cereal's financial position from 2010 to 2011. In the assets section,

Illustration 13-11 Horizontal analysis of balance sheets

CHICAGO CEREAL COMPANY
Condensed Balance Sheets
December 31 (in thousands)

Assets	2011	2010	Increase (Decrease) during 2011 Amount	Percent
Current assets	$ 2,717	$ 2,427	$ 290	11.9
Property assets (net)	2,990	2,816	174	6.2
Other assets	5,690	5,471	219	4.0
Total assets	$11,397	$10,714	$ 683	6.4
Liabilities and Stockholders' Equity				
Current liabilities	$ 4,044	$ 4,020	$ 24	0.6
Long-term liabilities	4,827	4,625	202	4.4
Total liabilities	8,871	8,645	226	2.6
Stockholders' equity				
Common stock	493	397	96	24.2
Retained earnings	3,390	2,584	806	31.2
Treasury stock (cost)	(1,357)	(912)	(445)	48.8
Total stockholders' equity	2,526	2,069	457	22.1
Total liabilities and stockholders' equity	$11,397	$10,714	$ 683	6.4

current assets increased $290,000, or 11.9% ($290 ÷ $2,427), and property assets (net) increased $174,000, or 6.2%. Other assets increased $219,000, or 4.0%. In the liabilities section, current liabilities increased $24,000, or 0.6%, while long-term liabilities increased $202,000, or 4.4%. In the stockholders' equity section, we find that retained earnings increased $806,000, or 31.2%.

Illustration 13-12 presents two-year comparative income statements of Chicago Cereal Company for 2011 and 2010, showing dollar and percentage changes.

Illustration 13-12 Horizontal analysis of income statements

CHICAGO CEREAL COMPANY
Condensed Income Statements
For the Years Ended December 31 (in thousands)

	2011	2010	Increase (Decrease) during 2011 Amount	Percent
Net sales	$11,776	$10,907	$869	8.0
Cost of goods sold	6,597	6,082	515	8.5
Gross profit	5,179	4,825	354	7.3
Selling and administrative expenses	3,311	3,059	252	8.2
Income from operations	1,868	1,766	102	5.8
Interest expense	319	307	12	3.9
Other income (expense), net	(2)	13	(15)	(115.4)
Income before income taxes	1,547	1,472	75	5.1
Income tax expense	444	468	(24)	(5.1)
Net income	$ 1,103	$ 1,004	$ 99	9.9

Horizontal analysis of the income statements shows the following changes. Net sales increased $869,000, or 8.0% ($869 ÷ $10,907). Cost of goods sold increased $515,000, or 8.5% ($515 ÷ $6,082). Selling and administrative expenses increased $252,000, or 8.2% ($252 ÷ $3,059). Overall, gross profit increased 7.3% and net income increased 9.9%. The increase in net income can be attributed to the increase in net sales and a decrease in income tax expense.

The measurement of changes from period to period in percentages is relatively straightforward and quite useful. However, complications can result in making the computations. If an item has no value in a base year or preceding year and a value in the next year, no percentage change can be computed. Likewise, no percentage change can be computed if a negative amount appears in the base or preceding period and a positive amount exists the following year.

DECISION TOOLKIT

DECISION CHECKPOINTS	INFO NEEDED FOR DECISION	TOOL TO USE FOR DECISION	HOW TO EVALUATE RESULTS
How do the company's financial position and operating results compare with those of the previous period?	Income statement and balance sheet	Comparative financial statements should be prepared over at least two years, with the first year reported being the base year. Changes in each line item relative to the base year should be presented both by amount and by percentage. This is called **horizontal analysis**.	Significant changes should be investigated to determine the reason for the change.

VERTICAL ANALYSIS

Vertical analysis, also called common-size analysis, is a technique for evaluating financial statement data that expresses each item in a financial statement as a **percentage of a base amount**. For example, on a balance sheet we might express current assets as 22% of total assets (total assets being the base amount). Or, on an income statement we might express selling expenses as 16% of net sales (net sales being the base amount).

Presented in Illustration 13-13 are the comparative balance sheets of Chicago Cereal for 2011 and 2010, analyzed vertically. The base for the asset items is **total assets**, and the base for the liability and stockholders' equity items is **total liabilities and stockholders' equity**.

Illustration 13-13 Vertical analysis of balance sheets

CHICAGO CEREAL COMPANY
Condensed Balance Sheets
December 31 (in thousands)

	2011		2010	
Assets	**Amount**	**Percent***	**Amount**	**Percent***
Current assets	$ 2,717	23.8	$ 2,427	22.6
Property assets (net)	2,990	26.2	2,816	26.3
Other assets	5,690	50.0	5,471	51.1
Total assets	$11,397	100.0	$10,714	100.0
Liabilities and Stockholders' Equity				
Current liabilities	$ 4,044	35.5	$ 4,020	37.5
Long-term liabilities	4,827	42.4	4,625	43.2
Total liabilities	8,871	77.9	8,645	80.7
Stockholders' equity				
Common stock	493	4.3	397	3.7
Retained earnings	3,390	29.7	2,584	24.1
Treasury stock (cost)	(1,357)	(11.9)	(912)	(8.5)
Total stockholders' equity	2,526	22.1	2,069	19.3
Total liabilities and stockholders' equity	$11,397	100.0	$10,714	100.0

*Numbers have been rounded to total 100%.

In addition to showing the relative size of each category on the balance sheets, vertical analysis can show the percentage change in the individual asset, liability, and stockholders' equity items. In this case, current assets increased $290,000 from 2010 to 2011, and they increased from 22.6% to 23.8% of total assets. Property assets (net) decreased from 26.3% to 26.2% of total assets. Other assets decreased from 51.1% to 50.0% of total assets. Also, retained earnings increased by $806,000 from 2010 to 2011, and total stockholders' equity increased from 19.3% to 22.1% of total liabilities and stockholders' equity. This switch to a higher percentage of equity financing has two causes: First, while total liabilities increased by $226,000, the percentage of liabilities declined from 80.7% to 77.9% of total liabilities and stockholders' equity. Second, retained earnings increased by $806,000, from 24.1% to 29.7% of total liabilities and stockholders' equity. Thus, the company shifted toward equity financing by relying less on debt and by increasing the amount of retained earnings.

Vertical analysis of the comparative income statements of Chicago Cereal, shown in Illustration 13-14, reveals that cost of goods sold **as a percentage of net sales** increased from 55.8% to 56.0%, and selling and administrative expenses increased from 28.0% to 28.1%. Net income as a percentage of net sales increased

CHICAGO CEREAL COMPANY
Condensed Income Statements
For the Years Ended December 31 (in thousands)

	2011 Amount	2011 Percent*	2010 Amount	2010 Percent*
Net sales	$11,776	100.0	$10,907	100.0
Cost of goods sold	6,597	56.0	6,082	55.8
Gross profit	5,179	44.0	4,825	44.2
Selling and administrative expenses	3,311	28.1	3,059	28.0
Income from operations	1,868	15.9	1,766	16.2
Interest expense	319	2.7	307	2.8
Other income (expense), net	(2)	.0	13	.0
Income before income taxes	1,547	13.2	1,472	13.4
Income tax expense	444	3.8	468	4.3
Net income	$ 1,103	9.4	$ 1,004	9.1

*Numbers have been rounded to total 100%.

Illustration 13-14 Vertical analysis of income statements

from 9.1% to 9.4%. Chicago Cereal's increase in net income as a percentage of sales is due primarily to the decrease in interest expense and income tax expense as a percentage of sales.

Vertical analysis also enables you to compare companies of different sizes. For example, one of Chicago Cereal's competitors is General Mills. General Mills' sales are 1,000 times larger than those of Chicago Cereal. Vertical analysis enables us to meaningfully compare the condensed income statements of Chicago Cereal and General Mills, as shown in Illustration 13-15.

CONDENSED INCOME STATEMENTS
For the Year Ended December 31, 2011

	Chicago Cereal (in thousands) Amount	Percent*	General Mills, Inc. (in millions) Amount	Percent*
Net sales	$11,776	100.0	$14,880	100.0
Cost of goods sold	6,597	56.0	8,927	60.0
Gross profit	5,179	44.0	5,953	40.0
Selling and administrative expenses	3,311	28.1	3,192	21.5
Non-recurring charges and (gains)	0	—	(13)	(0.1)
Income from operations	1,868	15.9	2,774	18.6
Other expenses and revenues (including income taxes)	765	6.5	976	6.5
Net income	$ 1,103	9.4	$ 1,798	12.1

*Numbers have been rounded to total 100%.

Illustration 13-15 Intercompany comparison by vertical analysis

Although Chicago Cereal's net sales are much less than those of General Mills, vertical analysis eliminates the impact of this size difference for our analysis. Chicago Cereal has a higher gross profit percentage 44.0%, compared to 40.0% for General Mills. But, Chicago Cereal's selling and administrative expenses are 28.1% of net sales, while those of General Mills are 21.5% of net sales. Looking at net income, we see that General Mills' percentage is higher. Chicago Cereal's net income as a percentage of net sales is 9.4%, compared to 12.1% for General Mills.

ANATOMY OF A FRAUD

This final *Anatomy of a Fraud* box demonstrates that sometimes relationships between numbers can be used by companies to detect fraud. Financial ratios that appear abnormal or statistical abnormalities in the numbers themselves can reveal fraud. For example, the fact that WorldCom's line costs, as a percentage of either total expenses or revenues, differed very significantly from its competitors should have alerted people to the possibility of fraud. Or, consider the case of a bank manager, who cooperated with a group of his friends to defraud the bank's credit card department. The manager's friends would apply for credit cards and then run up balances of slightly less than $5,000. The bank had a policy of allowing bank personnel to write-off balances of less than $5,000 without seeking supervisor approval. The fraud was detected by applying statistical analysis based on Benford's Law. Benford's Law states that in a random collection of numbers, the frequency of lower digits (e.g., 1, 2, or 3) should be much higher than higher digits (e.g., 7, 8, or 9). In this case, bank auditors analyzed the first two digits of amounts written off. There was a spike at 48 and 49, which was not consistent with what would be expected if the numbers were random.

Total take: Thousands of dollars

THE MISSING CONTROL

Independent internal verification. While it might be efficient to allow employees to write off accounts below a certain level, it is important that these write-offs be reviewed and verified periodically. Such a review would likely call attention to an employee with large amounts of write-offs, or in this case, write-offs that were frequently very close to the approval threshold.

Source: Mark J. Nigrini, "I've Got Your Number," *Journal of Accountancy Online* (May 1999).

DECISION TOOLKIT

DECISION CHECKPOINTS	INFO NEEDED FOR DECISION	TOOL TO USE FOR DECISION	HOW TO EVALUATE RESULTS
How do the relationships between items in this year's financial statements compare with those of last year or those of competitors?	Income statement and balance sheet	Each line item on the income statement should be presented as a percentage of net sales, and each line item on the balance sheet should be presented as a percentage of total assets or total liabilities and stockholders' equity. These percentages should be investigated for differences either across years in the same company or in the same year across different companies. This is called **vertical analysis**.	Any significant differences either across years or between companies should be investigated to determine the cause.

LEARNING OBJECTIVE 6

Identify and compute ratios used in analyzing a company's liquidity, solvency, and profitability.

Ratio Analysis

In previous chapters, we presented many ratios used for evaluating the financial health and performance of a company. Here, we provide a summary listing of those ratios. (Page references to prior discussions are provided if you feel you need to review any individual ratios.) Appendix 13A provides an example of a comprehensive financial analysis employing these ratios.

LIQUIDITY RATIOS

Liquidity ratios (Illustration 13-16) measure the short-term ability of the company to pay its maturing obligations and to meet unexpected needs for cash. Short-term creditors such as bankers and suppliers are particularly interested in assessing liquidity.

Illustration 13-16 Summary of liquidity ratios

Liquidity Ratios		
Working capital	Current assets − Current liabilities	p. 51
Current ratio	$\dfrac{\text{Current assets}}{\text{Current liabilities}}$	p. 52
Current cash debt coverage	$\dfrac{\text{Net cash provided by operating activities}}{\text{Average current liabilities}}$	p. 559
Inventory turnover	$\dfrac{\text{Cost of goods sold}}{\text{Average inventory}}$	p. 253
Days in inventory	$\dfrac{\text{365 days}}{\text{Inventory turnover}}$	p. 253
Accounts receivable turnover	$\dfrac{\text{Net credit sales}}{\text{Average net accounts receivable}}$	p. 357
Average collection period	$\dfrac{\text{365 days}}{\text{Accounts receivable turnover}}$	p. 357

Investor Insight

How to Manage the Current Ratio

The apparent simplicity of the current ratio can have real-world limitations because adding equal amounts to both the numerator and the denominator causes the ratio to decrease.

Assume, for example, that a company has $2,000,000 of current assets and $1,000,000 of current liabilities. Its current ratio is 2:1. If it purchases $1,000,000 of inventory on account, it will have $3,000,000 of current assets and $2,000,000 of current liabilities. Its current ratio decreases to 1.5:1. If, instead, the company pays off $500,000 of its current liabilities, it will have $1,500,000 of current assets and $500,000 of current liabilities. Its current ratio increases to 3:1. Thus, any trend analysis should be done with care because the ratio is susceptible to quick changes and is easily influenced by management.

? How might management influence a company's current ratio? (Answers in *Broadening Your Perspective*.)

SOLVENCY RATIOS

Solvency ratios (Illustration 13-17) measure the ability of the company to survive over a long period of time. Long-term creditors and stockholders are interested in a company's long-run solvency, particularly its ability to pay interest as it comes due and to repay the balance of debt at its maturity.

Illustration 13-17 Summary of solvency ratios

Solvency Ratios		
Debt to assets ratio	$\dfrac{\text{Total liabilities}}{\text{Total assets}}$	p. 53
Cash debt coverage	$\dfrac{\text{Net cash provided by operating activities}}{\text{Average total liabilities}}$	p. 560
Times interest earned	$\dfrac{\text{Net income + Interest expense + Tax expense}}{\text{Interest expense}}$	p. 453
Free cash flow	$\begin{array}{c}\text{Net cash provided}\\ \text{by operating activities}\end{array} - \begin{array}{c}\text{Capital}\\ \text{expenditures}\end{array} - \begin{array}{c}\text{Cash}\\ \text{dividends}\end{array}$	p. 55

PROFITABILITY RATIOS

Profitability ratios (Illustration 13-18) measure the income or operating success of a company for a given period of time. A company's income, or lack of it, affects its ability to obtain debt and equity financing, its liquidity position, and its ability to grow. As a consequence, creditors and investors alike are interested in evaluating profitability. Profitability is frequently used as the ultimate test of management's operating effectiveness.

Illustration 13-18 Summary of profitability ratios

Profitability Ratios		
Earnings per share	$\dfrac{\text{Net income} - \text{Preferred dividends}}{\text{Average common shares outstanding}}$	p. 48
Price-earnings ratio	$\dfrac{\text{Stock price per share}}{\text{Earnings per share}}$	p. 612
Gross profit rate	$\dfrac{\text{Gross profit}}{\text{Net sales}}$	p. 209
Profit margin	$\dfrac{\text{Net income}}{\text{Net sales}}$	p. 210
Return on assets	$\dfrac{\text{Net income}}{\text{Average total assets}}$	p. 399
Asset turnover	$\dfrac{\text{Net sales}}{\text{Average total assets}}$	p. 400
Payout ratio	$\dfrac{\text{Cash dividends declared on common stock}}{\text{Net income}}$	p. 515
Return on common stockholders' equity	$\dfrac{\text{Net income} - \text{Preferred dividends}}{\text{Average common stockholders' equity}}$	p. 516

Investor Insight

High Ratings Can Bring Low Returns

Moody's, Standard and Poor's, and Fitch are three big firms that perform financial analysis on publicly traded companies and then publish ratings of the companies' creditworthiness. Investors and lenders rely heavily on these ratings in making investment and lending decisions. Some people feel that the collapse of the financial markets was worsened by inadequate research reports and ratings provided by the financial rating agencies. Critics contend that the rating agencies were reluctant to give large companies low ratings because they feared that by offending them they would lose out on business opportunities. For example, the rating agencies gave many so-called mortgage-backed securities ratings that suggested that they were low risk. Later, many of these very securities became completely worthless. Steps have been taken to reduce the conflicts of interest that lead to these faulty ratings.

Source: Aaron Lucchetti and Judith Burns, "Moody's CEO Warned Profit Push Posed a Risk to Quality of Ratings," *Wall Street Journal Online* (October 23, 2008).

? Why are credit rating agencies important to the financial markets? (Answers in *Broadening Your Perspective.*)

LEARNING OBJECTIVE 7

Understand the concept of quality of earnings.

Quality of Earnings

The quality of a company's earnings is of extreme importance to analysts. A company that has a high **quality of earnings** provides full and transparent information that will not confuse or mislead users of the financial statements.

Recent accounting scandals suggest that some companies are spending too much time managing their income and not enough time managing their business. Here are some of the factors affecting quality of earnings.

ALTERNATIVE ACCOUNTING METHODS

Variations among companies in the application of generally accepted accounting principles may hamper comparability and reduce quality of earnings. For example, suppose one company uses the FIFO method of inventory costing, while another company in the same industry uses LIFO. If inventory is a significant asset to both companies, it is unlikely that their current ratios are comparable. For example, if General Motors Corporation used FIFO instead of LIFO for inventory valuation, its inventories in a recent year would have been 26% higher, which significantly affects the current ratio (and other ratios as well).

In addition to differences in inventory costing methods, differences also exist in reporting such items as depreciation and amortization. Although these differences in accounting methods might be detectable from reading the notes to the financial statements, adjusting the financial data to compensate for the different methods is often difficult, if not impossible.

PRO FORMA INCOME

Companies whose stock is publicly traded are required to present their income statement following generally accepted accounting principles (GAAP). In recent years, many companies have been also reporting a second measure of income, called pro forma income. **Pro forma income** usually excludes items that the company thinks are unusual or non-recurring. For example, in a recent year, Cisco Systems (a high-tech company) reported a quarterly net loss under GAAP of $2.7 billion. Cisco reported pro forma income for the same quarter as a profit of $230 million. This large difference in profits between GAAP income numbers and pro forma income is not unusual. For example, during one 9-month period, the 100 largest companies on the Nasdaq stock exchange reported a total pro forma income of $19.1 billion but a total loss as measured by GAAP of $82.3 billion—a difference of about $100 billion!

To compute pro forma income, companies generally exclude any items they deem inappropriate for measuring their performance. Many analysts and investors are critical of the practice of using pro forma income because these numbers often make companies look better than they really are. As the financial press noted, pro forma numbers might be called "earnings before bad stuff." Companies, on the other hand, argue that pro forma numbers more clearly indicate sustainable income because they exclude unusual and non-recurring expenses. "Cisco's technique gives readers of financial statements a clear picture of Cisco's normal business activities," the company said in a statement issued in response to questions about its pro forma income accounting.

Recently, the SEC provided some guidance on how companies should present pro forma information. Stay tuned: Everyone seems to agree that pro forma numbers can be useful if they provide insights into determining a company's sustainable income. However, many companies have abused the flexibility that pro forma numbers allow and have used the measure as a way to put their companies in a more favorable light.

IMPROPER RECOGNITION

Because some managers feel pressure from Wall Street to continually increase earnings, they manipulate earnings numbers to meet these expectations. The most common abuse is the improper recognition of revenue. One practice that some companies use is called **channel stuffing**. Offering deep discounts, companies encourage customers to buy early (stuff the channel) rather than later. This boosts earnings in the current period, but it often leads to a disaster in subsequent periods because customers have no need for additional goods. To illustrate, Bristol-Myers Squibb at one time indicated that it used sales incentives to encourage wholesalers to buy more drugs than they needed. As a result, the company had to issue revised financial statements showing corrected revenues and income.

Another practice is the improper capitalization of operating expenses. WorldCom capitalized over $7 billion of operating expenses in order to report positive net income. In other situations, companies fail to report all their liabilities. Enron promised to make payments on certain contracts if financial difficulty developed, but these guarantees were not reported as liabilities. In addition, disclosure was so lacking in transparency that it was impossible to understand what was happening at the company.

PRICE-EARNINGS RATIO

Earnings per share is net income available to common stockholders divided by the average number of common shares outstanding. The market price of a company's stock changes based on investors' expectations about a company's future earnings per share. To compare market prices and earnings across firms, investors calculate the **price-earnings (P-E) ratio**. The P-E ratio divides the market price of a share of common stock by earnings per share.

Illustration 13-19 Formula for price-earnings (P-E) ratio

$$\text{Price-Earnings (P-E) Ratio} = \frac{\text{Stock Price per Share}}{\text{Earnings per Share}}$$

The P-E ratio reflects investors' assessment of a company's future earnings. The ratio of price to earnings will be higher if investors think that earnings will increase substantially in the future and therefore are willing to pay more per share of stock. A low price-earnings ratio often signifies that investors think the company's future earnings will not be strong. In addition, sometimes a low P-E ratio reflects the market's belief that a company has poor-quality earnings.

To illustrate, assume that two identical companies each have earnings per share of $5. Suppose one of the companies manipulated its accounting numbers to achieve the $5 figure. If investors perceive that firm has lower-quality earnings, this perception will be reflected in a lower stock price and, consequently, a lower P-E.

Illustration 13-20 shows earnings per share and P-E ratios for five companies for a recent year. Note the difference in the P-E ratio of General Electric versus Google Inc.

Illustration 13-20 Earnings per share and P-E ratios of various companies

Company	Earnings per Share	Price-Earnings Ratio
Southwest Airlines	$ 0.44	18.6
Google Inc.	13.30	30.8
General Electric	2.17	13.2
Merck	1.49	14.6
Nike	3.70	15.9

USING THE **DECISION TOOLKIT**

In analyzing a company, you should always investigate an extended period of time in order to determine whether the condition and performance of the company are changing. The condensed financial statements of Kellogg Company for 2011 and 2010 are presented here.

Real World

KELLOGG COMPANY, INC.
Balance Sheets
December 31 (in millions)

Assets	2011	2010
Current assets		
Cash	$ 460	$ 444
Accounts receivable (net)	1,188	1,190
Inventories	1,132	1,056
Other current assets	247	225
Total current assets	3,027	2,915
Property (net)	3,281	3,128
Other assets	5,593	5,804
Total assets	$11,901	$11,847
Liabilities and Stockholders' Equity		
Current liabilities	$ 3,313	$ 3,184
Long-term liabilities	6,826	6,509
Stockholders' equity—common	1,762	2,154
Total liabilities and stockholders' equity	$11,901	$11,847

Real World

KELLOGG COMPANY, INC.
Condensed Income Statements
For the Years Ended December 31
(in millions)

	2011	2010
Net sales	$13,198	$12,397
Cost of goods sold	7,750	7,108
Gross profit	5,448	5,289
Selling and administrative expenses	3,472	3,299
Income from operations	1,976	1,990
Interest expense	233	248
Other (income) expense, net	11	–0–
Income before income taxes	1,732	1,742
Income tax expense	503	502
Net income	$ 1,229	$ 1,240

Instructions

Compute the following ratios for Kellogg for 2011 and discuss your findings (2010 values are provided for comparison).
1. Liquidity:
   (a) Current ratio (2010: .92:1).
   (b) Inventory turnover (2010: 7.2 times).
2. Solvency:
   (a) Debt to assets ratio (2010: 82%).
   (b) Times interest earned (2010: 8.0 times).

3. Profitability:
   (a) Return on assets (2010: 10.8%).
   (b) Profit margin (2010: 10.0%).
   (c) Return on common stockholders' equity (2010: 56%).

Solution

1. Liquidity
   (a) Current ratio:

   $$2011: \frac{\$3,027}{\$3,313} = .91{:}1 \qquad 2010: \quad .92{:}1$$

   (b) Inventory turnover:

   $$2011: \frac{\$7,750}{(\$1,132 + \$1,056)/2} = 7.1 \text{ times} \qquad 2010: \quad 7.2 \text{ times}$$

   We see that between 2010 and 2011, the current ratio declined slightly. The inventory turnover also decreased slightly. Combined these ratios suggest the company's liquidity was basically unchanged.

2. Solvency
   (a) Debt to assets ratio:

   $$2011: \frac{\$3,313 + \$6,826}{\$11,901} = 85\% \qquad 2010: \quad 82\%$$

   (b) Times interest earned:

   $$2011: \frac{\$1,229 + \$503 + \$233}{\$233} = 8.4 \text{ times} \qquad 2010: \quad 8.0 \text{ times}$$

   Kellogg's solvency as measured by the debt to assets ratio increased in 2011, suggesting its solvency declined. However, its times interest earned improved slightly, suggesting its solvency improved.

3. Profitability
   (a) Return on assets:

   $$2011: \frac{\$1,229}{(\$11,901 + \$11,847)/2} = 10.4\% \qquad 2010: \quad 10.8\%$$

   (b) Profit margin:

   $$2011: \frac{\$1,229}{\$13,198} = 9.3\% \qquad 2010: \quad 10.0\%$$

   (c) Return on common stockholders' equity:

   $$2011: \frac{\$1,229}{(\$1,762 + \$2,154)/2} = 63\% \qquad 2010: \quad 56\%$$

   Kellogg's return on assets declined. Its profit margin also declined, but its return on stockholders' equity increased.

Summary of Learning Objectives

1 **Understand the concept of sustainable income.** Sustainable income refers to a company's ability to sustain its profits from operations.

2 **Indicate how irregular items are presented.** Irregular items—discontinued operations and extraordinary items—are presented on the income statement net of tax below "Income before irregular items" to highlight their unusual nature. Changes in accounting principle are reported retroactively.

3 **Explain the concept of comprehensive income.** Comprehensive income includes all changes in stockholders' equity during a period except those resulting from investments by stockholders and distributions to stockholders. "Other comprehensive income" is added to or subtracted from net income to arrive at comprehensive income.

4 **Describe and apply horizontal analysis.** Horizontal analysis is a technique for evaluating a series of data over a period of time to determine the increase or decrease that has taken place, expressed as either an amount or a percentage.

5 Describe and apply vertical analysis. Vertical analysis is a technique that expresses each item in a financial statement as a percentage of a relevant total or a base amount.

6 Identify and compute ratios used in analyzing a company's liquidity, solvency, and profitability. Financial ratios are provided in Illustration 13-16 (liquidity),

Illustration 13-17 (solvency), and Illustration 13-18 (profitability).

7 Understand the concept of quality of earnings. A high quality of earnings provides full and transparent information that will not confuse or mislead users of the financial statements. Issues related to quality of earnings are (1) alternative accounting methods, (2) pro forma income, and (3) improper recognition. The price-earnings (P-E) ratio reflects investors' assessment of a company's future earnings potential.

🧰 DECISION TOOLKIT *A SUMMARY*

DECISION CHECKPOINTS	INFO NEEDED FOR DECISION	TOOL TO USE FOR DECISION	HOW TO EVALUATE RESULTS
Has the company sold any major components of its business?	Discontinued operations section of income statement	Anything reported in this section indicates that the company has discontinued a major component of its business.	If a major component has been discontinued, its results during the current period should not be included in estimates of future net income.
Has the company experienced any extraordinary events or transactions?	Extraordinary item section of income statement	Items reported in this section indicate that the company experienced an event that was both unusual and infrequent.	These items should usually be ignored in estimating future net income.
Has the company changed any of its accounting principles?	Effect of change in accounting principle on current and prior periods.	Management indicates that the new principle is preferable to the old principle.	Examine current and prior years' reported income, using new-principle basis to assess trends for estimating future income.
How do the company's financial position and operating results compare with those of the previous period?	Income statement and balance sheet	Comparative financial statements should be prepared over at least two years, with the first year reported being the base year. Changes in each line item relative to the base year should be presented both by amount and by percentage. This is called **horizontal analysis**.	Significant changes should be investigated to determine the reason for the change.
How do the relationships between items in this year's financial statements compare with those of last year or those of competitors?	Income statement and balance sheet	Each line item on the income statement should be presented as a percentage of net sales, and each line item on the balance sheet should be presented as a percentage of total assets or total liabilities and stockholders' equity. These percentages should be investigated for differences either across years in the same company or in the same year across different companies. This is called **vertical analysis**.	Any significant differences either across years or between companies should be investigated to determine the cause.

Appendix 13A

Comprehensive Illustration of Ratio Analysis

LEARNING OBJECTIVE 8

Evaluate a company comprehensively using ratio analysis.

In previous chapters, we presented many ratios used for evaluating the financial health and performance of a company. In this appendix, we provide a comprehensive review of those ratios and discuss some important relationships among them. Since earlier chapters demonstrated the calculation of each of these ratios, in this appendix we instead focus on their interpretation. Page references to prior discussions point you to any individual ratios you feel you need to review.

We used the financial information in Illustrations 13A-1 through 13A-4 to calculate Chicago Cereal Company's 2011 ratios. You can use these data to review the computations.

Illustration 13A-1 Chicago Cereal Company's balance sheets

CHICAGO CEREAL COMPANY
Balance Sheets
December 31 (in thousands)

Assets	2011	2010
Current assets		
Cash	$ 524	$ 411
Accounts receivable	1,026	945
Inventory	924	824
Prepaid expenses and other current assets	243	247
Total current assets	2,717	2,427
Property assets (net)	2,990	2,816
Intangibles and other assets	5,690	5,471
Total assets	$11,397	$10,714
Liabilities and Stockholders' Equity		
Current liabilities	$ 4,044	$ 4,020
Long-term liabilities	4,827	4,625
Stockholders' equity—common	2,526	2,069
Total liabilities and stockholders' equity	$11,397	$10,714

Illustration 13A-2 Chicago Cereal Company's income statements

CHICAGO CEREAL COMPANY
Condensed Income Statements
For the Years Ended December 31 (in thousands)

	2011	2010
Net sales	$11,776	$10,907
Cost of goods sold	6,597	6,082
Gross profit	5,179	4,825
Selling and administrative expenses	3,311	3,059
Income from operations	1,868	1,766
Interest expense	319	307
Other income (expense), net	(2)	13
Income before income taxes	1,547	1,472
Income tax expense	444	468
Net income	$ 1,103	$ 1,004

CHICAGO CEREAL COMPANY
Condensed Statements of Cash Flows
For the Years Ended December 31 (in thousands)

	2011	2010
Cash flows from operating activities		
Cash receipts from operating activities	$11,695	$10,841
Cash payments for operating activities	10,192	9,431
Net cash provided by operating activities	1,503	1,410
Cash flows from investing activities		
Purchases of property, plant, and equipment	(472)	(453)
Other investing activities	(129)	8
Net cash used in investing activities	(601)	(445)
Cash flows from financing activities		
Issuance of common stock	163	218
Issuance of debt	2,179	721
Reductions of debt	(2,011)	(650)
Payment of dividends	(475)	(450)
Repurchase of common stock and other items	(645)	(612)
Net cash provided (used) by financing activities	(789)	(773)
Increase (decrease) in cash and cash equivalents	113	192
Cash and cash equivalents at beginning of year	411	219
Cash and cash equivalents at end of year	$ 524	$ 411

Illustration 13A-3 Chicago Cereal Company's statements of cash flows

Additional information:

	2011	2010
Average number of shares (thousands)	418.7	418.5
Stock price at year-end	$52.92	$50.06

Illustration 13A-4 Additional information for Chicago Cereal Company

As indicated in the chapter, we can classify ratios into three types for analysis of the primary financial statements:

1. **Liquidity ratios.** Measures of the short-term ability of the company to pay its maturing obligations and to meet unexpected needs for cash.
2. **Solvency ratios.** Measures of the ability of the company to survive over a long period of time.
3. **Profitability ratios.** Measures of the income or operating success of a company for a given period of time.

As a tool of analysis, ratios can provide clues to underlying conditions that may not be apparent from an inspection of the individual components of a particular ratio. But, a single ratio by itself is not very meaningful. Accordingly, in this discussion we use the following three comparisons.

1. **Intracompany comparisons** covering two years for Chicago Cereal Company (using comparative financial information from Illustrations 13A-1 through 13A-4).
2. **Intercompany comparisons** using General Mills as one of Chicago Cereal's competitors.

3. **Industry average comparisons** based on MSN.com median ratios for manufacturers of flour and other grain mill products and comparisons with other sources. For some of the ratios that we use, industry comparisons are not available. (These are denoted "na.")

LIQUIDITY RATIOS

Liquidity ratios measure the short-term ability of the company to pay its maturing obligations and to meet unexpected needs for cash. Short-term creditors such as bankers and suppliers are particularly interested in assessing liquidity. The measures used to determine the company's short-term debt-paying ability are the current ratio, the current cash debt coverage, the accounts receivable turnover, the average collection period, the inventory turnover, and days in inventory.

1. **Current ratio.** The current ratio expresses the relationship of current assets to current liabilities, computed by dividing current assets by current liabilities. It is widely used for evaluating a company's liquidity and short-term debt-paying ability. The 2011 and 2010 current ratios for Chicago Cereal and comparative data are shown in Illustration 13A-5.

Illustration 13A-5
Current ratio

Ratio	Formula	Indicates	Chicago Cereal 2011	Chicago Cereal 2010	General Mills 2011	Industry 2011	Page in Textbook
Current ratio	Current assets / Current liabilities	Short-term debt-paying ability	.67	.60	1.00	1.20	52

What do the measures tell us? Chicago Cereal's 2011 current ratio of .67 means that for every dollar of current liabilities, it has $0.67 of current assets. We sometimes state such ratios as .67:1 to reinforce this interpretation. Its current ratio—and therefore its liquidity—increased significantly in 2011. It is well below the industry average and that of General Mills.

2. **Current cash debt coverage.** A disadvantage of the current ratio is that it uses year-end balances of current asset and current liability accounts. These year-end balances may not represent the company's current position during most of the year. The current cash debt coverage partially corrects for this problem. It is the ratio of net cash provided by operating activities to average current liabilities. Because it uses net cash provided by operating activities rather than a balance at one point in time, it may provide a better representation of liquidity. Chicago Cereal's current cash debt coverage is shown in Illustration 13A-6.

Illustration 13A-6
Current cash debt coverage

Ratio	Formula	Indicates	Chicago Cereal 2011	Chicago Cereal 2010	General Mills 2011	Industry 2011	Page in Textbook
Current cash debt coverage	Net cash provided by operating activities / Average current liabilities	Short-term debt-paying ability (cash basis)	.37	.39	.54	na	559

This ratio decreased slightly in 2011 for Chicago Cereal. Is the coverage adequate? Probably so. Its operating cash flow coverage of average current liabilities is less than that of General Mills, but it approximates a commonly accepted threshold of .40. No industry comparison is available.

3. **Accounts receivable turnover.** Analysts can measure liquidity by how quickly a company converts certain assets to cash. Low values of the previous ratios can sometimes be compensated for if some of the company's current assets are highly liquid.

How liquid, for example, are the receivables? The ratio used to assess the liquidity of the receivables is the **accounts receivable turnover**, which measures the number of times, on average, a company collects receivables during the period. The accounts receivable turnover is computed by dividing net credit sales (net sales less cash sales) by average net accounts receivable during the year. The accounts receivable turnover for Chicago Cereal is shown in Illustration 13A-7.

Illustration 13A-7
Accounts receivable turnover

Ratio	Formula	Indicates	Chicago Cereal 2011	Chicago Cereal 2010	General Mills 2011	Industry 2011	Page in Textbook
Accounts receivable turnover	$\dfrac{\text{Net credit sales}}{\text{Average net accounts receivable}}$	Liquidity of receivables	11.9	12.0	12.4	11.2	357

We have assumed that all Chicago Cereal's sales are credit sales. Its accounts receivable turnover declined slightly in 2011. The turnover of 11.9 times is higher than the industry average of 11.2 times, and slightly lower than General Mills' turnover of 12.4 times.

4. **Average collection period.** A popular variant of the accounts receivable turnover converts it into an **average collection period** in days. This is done by dividing the accounts receivable turnover into 365 days. The average collection period for Chicago Cereal is shown in Illustration 13A-8.

Illustration 13A-8
Average collection period

Ratio	Formula	Indicates	Chicago Cereal 2011	Chicago Cereal 2010	General Mills 2011	Industry 2011	Page in Textbook
Average collection period	$\dfrac{365 \text{ days}}{\text{Accounts receivable turnover}}$	Liquidity of receivables and collection success	30.7	30.4	29.4	32.6	357

Chicago Cereal's 2011 accounts receivable turnover of 11.9 times is divided into 365 days to obtain approximately 31 days. This means that the average collection period for receivables is about 31 days. Its average collection period is longer than that of General Mills and shorter than that of the industry.

Analysts frequently use the average collection period to assess the effectiveness of a company's credit and collection policies. The general rule is that the collection period should not greatly exceed the credit term period (i.e., the time allowed for payment).

5. **Inventory turnover.** The **inventory turnover** measures the number of times average inventory was sold during the period. Its purpose is to measure the liquidity of the inventory. A high measure indicates that inventory is being sold and replenished frequently. The inventory turnover is computed by dividing the cost of goods sold by the average inventory during the period. Unless seasonal factors are significant, average inventory can be computed

from the beginning and ending inventory balances. Chicago Cereal's inventory turnover is shown in Illustration 13A-9.

Illustration 13A-9
Inventory turnover

Ratio	Formula	Indicates	Chicago Cereal 2011	Chicago Cereal 2010	General Mills 2011	Industry 2011	Page in Textbook
Inventory turnover	Cost of goods sold / Average inventory	Liquidity of inventory	7.5	7.9	6.5	6.7	253

Chicago Cereal's inventory turnover decreased slightly in 2011. The turnover of 7.5 times is higher than the industry average of 6.7 times and better than General Mills' 6.5 times. Generally, the faster the inventory turnover, the less cash is tied up in inventory and the less the chance of inventory becoming obsolete. Of course, a downside of high inventory turnover is that it sometimes results in lost sales because if a company keeps less inventory on hand, it is more likely to run out of inventory when it is needed.

6. **Days in inventory.** A variant of the inventory turnover is the **days in inventory**, which measures the average number of days inventory is held. The days in inventory for Chicago Cereal is shown in Illustration 13A-10.

Illustration 13A-10
Days in inventory

Ratio	Formula	Indicates	Chicago Cereal 2011	Chicago Cereal 2010	General Mills 2011	Industry 2011	Page in Textbook
Days in inventory	365 days / Inventory turnover	Liquidity of inventory and inventory management	48.7	46.2	56.2	54.5	253

Chicago Cereal's 2011 inventory turnover of 7.5 divided into 365 is approximately 49 days. An average selling time of 49 days is faster than the industry average and faster than that of General Mills. Some of this difference might be explained by differences in product lines across the two companies, although in many ways the types of products of these two companies are quite similar.

Inventory turnovers vary considerably among industries. For example, grocery store chains have a turnover of 10 times and an average selling period of 37 days. In contrast, jewelry stores have an average turnover of 1.3 times and an average selling period of 281 days. Within a company, there may even be significant differences in inventory turnover among different types of products. Thus, in a grocery store the turnover of perishable items such as produce, meats, and dairy products is faster than the turnover of soaps and detergents.

To conclude, nearly all of these liquidity measures suggest that Chicago Cereal's liquidity changed little during 2011. Its liquidity appears acceptable when compared to the industry as a whole and when compared to General Mills.

SOLVENCY RATIOS

Solvency ratios measure the ability of the company to survive over a long period of time. Long-term creditors and stockholders are interested in a company's long-run solvency, particularly its ability to pay interest as it comes due and to repay the face value of debt at maturity. The debt to assets ratio, the times interest earned, and the cash debt coverage provide information about debt-paying ability. In addition, free cash flow provides information about the company's solvency and its ability to pay additional dividends or invest in new projects.

7. **Debt to assets ratio.** The debt to assets ratio measures the percentage of total financing provided by creditors. It is computed by dividing total liabilities (both current and long-term debt) by total assets. This ratio indicates the degree of financial leveraging. It also provides some indication of the company's ability to withstand losses without impairing the interests of its creditors. The higher the percentage of debt to assets, the greater the risk that the company may be unable to meet its maturing obligations. The lower the ratio, the more equity "buffer" is available to creditors if the company becomes insolvent. Thus, from the creditors' point of view, a low ratio of debt to assets is desirable. Chicago Cereal's debt to assets ratio is shown in Illustration 13A-11.

Illustration 13A-11
Debt to assets ratio

Ratio	Formula	Indicates	Chicago Cereal 2011	Chicago Cereal 2010	General Mills 2011	Industry 2011	Page in Textbook
Debt to assets ratio	Total liabilities / Total assets	Percentage of total assets provided by creditors	78%	81%	52%	49%	53

Chicago Cereal's 2011 ratio of 78% means that creditors have provided financing sufficient to cover 78% of the company's total assets. Alternatively, it says that it would have to liquidate 78% of its assets at their book value in order to pay off all of its debts. Its ratio is above the industry average of 49%, as well as that of General Mills. This suggests that it is less solvent than the industry average and General Mills. Chicago Cereal's solvency improved slightly during the year.

The adequacy of this ratio is often judged in light of the company's earnings. Generally, companies with relatively stable earnings, such as public utilities, have higher debt to assets ratios than cyclical companies with widely fluctuating earnings, such as many high-tech companies.

Another ratio with a similar meaning is the **debt to equity ratio**. It shows the relative use of borrowed funds (total liabilities) compared with resources invested by the owners. Because this ratio can be computed in several ways, be careful when making comparisons with it. Debt may be defined to include only the noncurrent portion of liabilities, and intangible assets may be excluded from stockholders' equity (which would equal tangible net worth). If debt and assets are defined as above (all liabilities and all assets), then when the debt to assets ratio equals 50%, the debt to equity ratio is 1:1.

8. **Times interest earned.** The times interest earned (also called interest coverage) indicates the company's ability to meet interest payments as they come due. It is computed by dividing income before interest expense and income taxes by interest expense. Note that this ratio uses income before interest expense and income taxes because this amount represents what is available to cover interest. Chicago Cereal's times interest earned is shown in Illustration 13A-12.

Illustration 13A-12
Times interest earned

Ratio	Formula	Indicates	Chicago Cereal 2011	Chicago Cereal 2010	General Mills 2011	Industry 2011	Page in Textbook
Times interest earned	(Net Income + Interest expense + Tax expense) / Interest expense	Ability to meet interest payments as they come due	5.8	5.8	7.2	19.6	453

For Chicago Cereal, the 2011 interest coverage was 5.8, which indicates that income before interest and taxes was 5.8 times the amount needed for interest expense. This is less than the rate for General Mills, and it is significantly less than the average rate for the industry. The debt to assets ratio decreased for Chicago Cereal during 2011, and its times interest earned held constant.

9. **Cash debt coverage.** The ratio of net cash provided by operating activities to average total liabilities, called the **cash debt coverage**, is a cash-basis measure of solvency. This ratio indicates a company's ability to repay its liabilities from net cash generated from operating activities without having to liquidate the assets used in its operations. Illustration 13A-13 shows Chicago Cereal's cash debt coverage.

Illustration 13A-13
Cash debt coverage

Ratio	Formula	Indicates	Chicago Cereal 2011	Chicago Cereal 2010	General Mills 2011	Industry 2011	Page in Textbook
Cash debt coverage	Net cash provided by operating activities / Average total liabilities	Long-term debt-paying ability (cash basis)	.17	.17	.13	na	560

An industry average for this measure is not available. Chicago Cereal's .17 is higher than General Mills' .13, and it remained unchanged from 2010. One way of interpreting this ratio is to say that net cash generated from one year of operations would be sufficient to pay off 17% of its total liabilities. If 17% of this year's liabilities were retired each year, it would take approximately 5.9 years to retire all of its debt. It would take General Mills approximately 7.7 years to do so. A general rule of thumb is that a cash debt coverage above .20 is acceptable.

10. **Free cash flow.** One indication of a company's solvency, as well as of its ability to pay dividends or expand operations, is the amount of excess cash it generated after investing in capital expenditures and paying dividends. This amount is referred to as **free cash flow**. For example, if you generate $100,000 of net cash provided by operating activities but you spend $30,000 on capital expenditures and pay $10,000 in dividends, you have $60,000 ($100,000 − $30,000 − $10,000) to use either to expand operations, pay additional dividends, or pay down debt. Chicago Cereal's free cash flow is shown in Illustration 13A-14.

Illustration 13A-14
Free cash flow

Ratio	Formula	Indicates	Chicago Cereal 2011	Chicago Cereal 2010	General Mills 2011	Industry 2011	Page in Textbook
Free cash flow	Net cash provided by operating activities − Capital expenditures − Cash dividends	Cash available for paying dividends or expanding operations	$556 (in thousands)	$507	$686 (in millions)	na	54

Chicago Cereal's free cash flow increased slightly from 2010 to 2011. During both years, the net cash provided by operating activities was more than enough to allow it to acquire additional productive assets and maintain dividend payments. It could have used the remaining cash to reduce debt if necessary. Given that Chicago Cereal is much smaller than General Mills, we would expect its free cash flow to be substantially smaller, which it is.

PROFITABILITY RATIOS

Profitability ratios measure the income or operating success of a company for a given period of time. A company's income, or the lack of it, affects its ability to obtain debt and equity financing, its liquidity position, and its ability to grow. As a consequence, creditors and investors alike are interested in evaluating profitability. Analysts frequently use profitability as the ultimate test of management's operating effectiveness.

Throughout this textbook, we have introduced numerous measures of profitability. The relationships among measures of profitability are very important. Understanding them can help management determine where to focus its efforts to improve profitability. Illustration 13A-15 diagrams these relationships. Our discussion of Chicago Cereal's profitability is structured around this diagram.

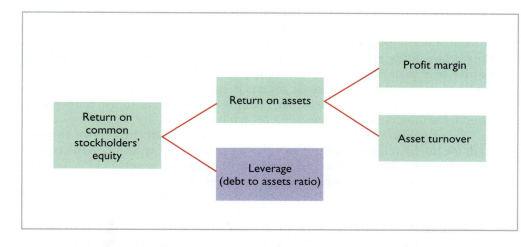

Illustration 13A-15
Relationships among profitability measures

11. **Return on common stockholders' equity (ROE).** A widely used measure of profitability from the common stockholder's viewpoint is the **return on common stockholders' equity (ROE).** This ratio shows how many dollars of net income the company earned for each dollar invested by the owners. It is computed by dividing net income minus any preferred dividends—that is, income available to common stockholders—by average common stockholders' equity. The return on common stockholders' equity for Chicago Cereal is shown in Illustration 13A-16.

Illustration 13A-16 Return on common stockholders' equity

Ratio	Formula	Indicates	Chicago Cereal 2011	Chicago Cereal 2010	General Mills 2011	Industry 2011	Page in Textbook
Return on common stockholders' equity	Net Income − Preferred dividends / Average common stockholders' equity	Profitability of common stockholders' investment	48%	46%	24%	24%	516

Chicago Cereal's 2011 rate of return on common stockholders' equity is unusually high at 48%. The industry average is 24% and General Mills' return is 24%. In the subsequent sections, we investigate the causes of this high return.

12. **Return on assets.** The return on common stockholders' equity is affected by two factors: the **return on assets** and the degree of leverage. The return on assets measures the overall profitability of assets in terms of the income

earned on each dollar invested in assets. It is computed by dividing net income by average total assets. Chicago Cereal's return on assets is shown in Illustration 13A-17.

Illustration 13A-17
Return on assets

Ratio	Formula	Indicates	Chicago Cereal 2011	Chicago Cereal 2010	General Mills 2011	Industry 2011	Page in Textbook
Return on assets	Net income / Average total assets	Overall profitability of assets	10.0%	9.4%	7.4%	8.7%	399

Chicago Cereal had a 10.0% return on assets in 2011. This rate is significantly higher than that of General Mills and the industry average.

Note that its rate of return on common stockholders' equity (48%) is substantially higher than its rate of return on assets (10%). The reason is that it has made effective use of **leverage**. **Leveraging** or **trading on the equity** at a gain means that the company has borrowed money at a lower rate of interest than the rate of return it earns on the assets it purchased with the borrowed funds. Leverage enables management to use money supplied by nonowners to increase the return to owners.

A comparison of the rate of return on assets with the rate of interest paid for borrowed money indicates the profitability of trading on the equity. If you borrow money at 8% and your rate of return on assets is 11%, you are trading on the equity at a gain. Note, however, that trading on the equity is a two-way street: For example, if you borrow money at 11% and earn only 8% on it, you are trading on the equity at a loss.

Chicago Cereal earns more on its borrowed funds than it has to pay in interest. Thus, the return to stockholders exceeds the return on assets because of the positive benefit of leverage. Recall from our earlier discussion that Chicago Cereal's percentage of debt financing, as measured by the ratio of debt to assets (or debt to equity), was higher than General Mills' and the industry average. It appears that Chicago Cereal's high return on common stockholders' equity is due in part to its use of leverage.

13. **Profit margin.** The return on assets is affected by two factors, the first of which is the profit margin. The **profit margin**, or rate of return on sales, is a measure of the percentage of each dollar of sales that results in net income. It is computed by dividing net income by net sales for the period. Chicago Cereal's profit margin is shown in Illustration 13A-18.

Illustration 13A-18
Profit margin

Ratio	Formula	Indicates	Chicago Cereal 2011	Chicago Cereal 2010	General Mills 2011	Industry 2011	Page in Textbook
Profit margin	Net income / Net sales	Net income generated by each dollar of sales	9.4%	9.2%	9.1%	8.8%	210

Chicago Cereal experienced a slight increase in its profit margin from 2010 to 2011 of 9.2% to 9.4%. Its profit margin was higher than the industry average and that of General Mills.

High-volume (high inventory turnover) businesses such as grocery stores and pharmacy chains generally have low profit margins. Low-volume businesses such as jewelry stores and airplane manufacturers have high profit margins.

14. **Asset turnover.** The other factor that affects the return on assets is the asset turnover. The **asset turnover** measures how efficiently a company uses its assets to generate sales. It is determined by dividing net sales by average total assets for the period. The resulting number shows the dollars of sales produced by each dollar invested in assets. Illustration 13A-19 shows the asset turnover for Chicago Cereal.

Illustration 13A-19
Asset turnover

Ratio	Formula	Indicates	Chicago Cereal 2011	Chicago Cereal 2010	General Mills 2011	Industry 2011	Page in Textbook
Asset turnover	Net sales / Average total assets	How efficiently assets are used to generate sales	1.07	1.02	.80	1.00	400

The asset turnover shows that in 2011, Chicago Cereal generated sales of $1.07 for each dollar it had invested in assets. The ratio rose from 2010 to 2011. Its asset turnover is above the industry average and that of General Mills.

Asset turnover varies considerably among industries. The average asset turnover for utility companies is .45, for example, while the grocery store industry has an average asset turnover of 3.49.

In summary, Chicago Cereal's return on assets increased from 9.4% in 2010 to 10.0% in 2011. Underlying this increase was an increased profitability on each dollar of sales (as measured by the profit margin) and a rise in the sales-generating efficiency of its assets (as measured by the asset turnover). We can analyze the combined effects of profit margin and asset turnover on return on assets for Chicago Cereal as shown in Illustration 13A-20.

Illustration 13A-20
Composition of return on assets

Ratios:	Profit Margin $\frac{\text{Net Income}}{\text{Net Sales}}$	×	Asset Turnover $\frac{\text{Net Sales}}{\text{Average Total Assets}}$	=	Return on Assets $\frac{\text{Net Income}}{\text{Average Total Assets}}$
Chicago Cereal					
2011	9.4%	×	1.07 times	=	10.1%*
2010	9.2%	×	1.02 times	=	9.4%

*Difference from value on page 624 due to rounding.

15. **Gross profit rate.** One factor that strongly influences the profit margin is the gross profit rate. The **gross profit rate** is determined by dividing gross profit (net sales less cost of goods sold) by net sales. This rate indicates a company's ability to maintain an adequate selling price above its cost of goods sold.

As an industry becomes more competitive, this ratio declines. For example, in the early years of the personal computer industry, gross profit rates were quite high. Today, because of increased competition and a belief that most brands of personal computers are similar in quality, gross profit rates

Illustration 13A-21
Gross profit rate

have become thin. Analysts should closely monitor gross profit rates over time. Illustration 13A-21 shows Chicago Cereal's gross profit rate.

Ratio	Formula	Indicates	Chicago Cereal 2011	Chicago Cereal 2010	General Mills 2011	Industry 2011	Page in Textbook
Gross profit rate	Gross profit / Net sales	Margin between selling price and cost of goods sold	44%	44%	36%	12%	209

Chicago Cereal's gross profit rate remained constant from 2010 to 2011.

16. **Earnings per share (EPS).** Stockholders usually think in terms of the number of shares they own or plan to buy or sell. Expressing net income earned on a per share basis provides a useful perspective for determining profitability. **Earnings per share** is a measure of the net income earned on each share of common stock. It is computed by dividing net income by the average number of common shares outstanding during the year.

The terms "net income per share" or "earnings per share" refer to the amount of net income applicable to each share of **common stock**. Therefore, when we compute earnings per share, if there are preferred dividends declared for the period, we must deduct them from net income to arrive at income available to the common stockholders. Chicago Cereal's earnings per share is shown in Illustration 13A-22.

Illustration 13A-22
Earnings per share

Ratio	Formula	Indicates	Chicago Cereal 2011	Chicago Cereal 2010	General Mills 2011	Industry 2011	Page in Textbook
Earnings per share (EPS)	Net income − Preferred dividends / Average common shares outstanding	Net income earned on each share of common stock	$2.63	$2.40	$2.35	na	48

Note that no industry average is presented in Illustration 13A-22. Industry data for earnings per share are not reported, and in fact the Chicago Cereal and General Mills ratios should not be compared. Such comparisons are not meaningful because of the wide variations in the number of shares of outstanding stock among companies. Chicago Cereal's earnings per share increased 23 cents per share in 2011. This represents a 9.6% increase from the 2010 EPS of $2.40.

17. **Price-earnings ratio.** The **price-earnings ratio** is an oft-quoted statistic that measures the ratio of the market price of each share of common stock to the earnings per share. The price-earnings (P-E) ratio reflects investors' assessments of a company's future earnings. It is computed by dividing the market price per share of the stock by earnings per share. Chicago Cereal's price-earnings ratio is shown in Illustration 13A-23.

Illustration 13A-23
Price-earnings ratio

Ratio	Formula	Indicates	Chicago Cereal 2011	Chicago Cereal 2010	General Mills 2011	Industry 2011	Page in Textbook
Price-earnings ratio	Stock price per share / Earnings per share	Relationship between market price per share and earnings per share	20.1	20.9	16.3	22.8	612

At the end of 2011 and 2010, the market price of Chicago Cereal's stock was $52.92 and $50.06, respectively.

In 2011, each share of Chicago Cereal's stock sold for 20.1 times the amount that was earned on each share. Chicago Cereal's price-earnings ratio is higher than General Mills' ratio of 16.3 and lower than the industry average of 22.8 times. Its higher P-E ratio suggests that the market is more optimistic about Chicago Cereal than about General Mills. However, it might also signal that Chicago Cereal's stock is overpriced. That is a matter for the analyst to determine.

18. **Payout ratio.** The payout ratio measures the percentage of earnings distributed in the form of cash dividends. It is computed by dividing cash dividends declared on common stock by net income. Companies that have high growth rates are characterized by low payout ratios because they reinvest most of their net income in the business. The payout ratio for Chicago Cereal is shown in Illustration 13A-24.

Illustration 13A-24
Payout ratio

Ratio	Formula	Indicates	Chicago Cereal 2011	Chicago Cereal 2010	General Mills 2011	Industry 2011	Page in Textbook
Payout ratio	Cash dividends declared on common stock / Net income	Percentage of earnings distributed in the form of cash dividends	43%	45%	50%	37%	515

The 2011 and 2010 payout ratios for Chicago Cereal are slightly lower than that of General Mills (50%) but higher than the industry average (37%).

Management has some control over the amount of dividends paid each year, and companies are generally reluctant to reduce a dividend below the amount paid in a previous year. Therefore, the payout ratio will actually increase if a company's net income declines but the company keeps its total dividend payment the same. Of course, unless the company returns to its previous level of profitability, maintaining this higher dividend payout ratio is probably not possible over the long run.

Before drawing any conclusions regarding Chicago Cereal's dividend payout ratio, we should calculate this ratio over a longer period of time to evaluate any trends and also try to find out whether management's philosophy regarding dividends has changed recently. The "Selected Financial Data" section of Chicago Cereal's Management Discussion and Analysis shows that over a 5-year period, earnings per share rose 45%, while dividends per share grew only 19%.

In terms of the types of financial information available and the ratios used by various industries, what can be practically covered in this textbook gives you only the "Titanic approach." That is, you are seeing only the tip of the iceberg compared to the vast databases and types of ratio analysis that are available on computers. The availability of information is not a problem. The real trick is to be discriminating enough to perform relevant analysis and select pertinent comparative data.

Summary of Learning Objective for Appendix 13A

8 **Evaluate a company comprehensively using ratio analysis.** To evaluate a company, ratios (liquidity, solvency, and profitability) provide clues to underlying conditions, but intracompany, intercompany, and industry average comparisons are also needed.

Glossary

Terms are highlighted in blue throughout the chapter.

Accounts receivable turnover A measure of the liquidity of receivables; computed as net credit sales divided by average net accounts receivable.

Asset turnover A measure of how efficiently a company uses its assets to generate sales; computed as net sales divided by average total assets.

Available-for-sale securities Securities that are held with the intent of selling them sometime in the future.

Average collection period The average number of days that receivables are outstanding; calculated as accounts receivable turnover divided into 365 days.

Cash debt coverage A cash-basis measure used to evaluate solvency, computed as net cash provided by operating activities divided by average total liabilities.

Change in accounting principle Use of an accounting principle in the current year different from the one used in the preceding year.

Comprehensive income A measure of income that includes all changes in stockholders' equity during a period except those resulting from investments by stockholders and distributions to stockholders.

Current cash debt coverage A cash-basis measure of liquidity; computed as net cash provided by operating activities divided by average current liabilities.

Current ratio A measure used to evaluate a company's liquidity and short-term debt-paying ability; calculated as current assets divided by current liabilities.

Days in inventory A measure of the average number of days inventory is held; computed as inventory turnover divided into 365 days.

Debt to assets ratio A measure of the percentage of total financing provided by creditors; computed as total liabilities divided by total assets.

Discontinued operations The disposal of a significant component of a business.

Earnings per share The net income earned by each share of common stock; computed as net income less preferred dividends divided by the average common shares outstanding.

Extraordinary items Events and transactions that meet two conditions: (1) unusual in nature and (2) infrequent in occurrence.

Free cash flow A measure of solvency. Cash remaining from operating activities after adjusting for capital expenditures and dividends paid.

Gross profit rate Gross profit expressed as a percentage of sales; computed as gross profit divided by net sales.

Horizontal analysis A technique for evaluating a series of financial statement data over a period of time to determine the increase (decrease) that has taken place, expressed as either an amount or a percentage.

Inventory turnover A measure of the liquidity of inventory. Measures the number of times average inventory was sold during the period; computed as cost of goods sold divided by average inventory.

Leveraging Borrowing money at a lower rate of interest than can be earned by using the borrowed money; also referred to as *trading on the equity*.

Liquidity ratios Measures of the short-term ability of the company to pay its maturing obligations and to meet unexpected needs for cash.

Payout ratio A measure of the percentage of earnings distributed in the form of cash dividends; calculated as cash dividends declared on common stock divided by net income.

Price-earnings (P-E) ratio A comparison of the market price of each share of common stock to the earnings per share; computed as the market price of the stock divided by earnings per share.

Profitability ratios Measures of the income or operating success of a company for a given period of time.

Profit margin A measure of the net income generated by each dollar of sales; computed as net income divided by net sales.

Pro forma income A measure of income that usually excludes items that a company thinks are unusual or non-recurring.

Quality of earnings Indicates the level of full and transparent information that is provided to users of the financial statements.

Return on assets A profitability measure that indicates the amount of net income generated by each dollar of assets; calculated as net income divided by average total assets.

Return on common stockholders' equity (ROE) A measure of the dollars of net income earned for each dollar invested by the owners; computed as income available to common stockholders divided by average common stockholders' equity.

Solvency ratios Measures of the ability of a company to survive over a long period of time, particularly to pay interest as it comes due and to repay the balance of debt at its maturity.

Sustainable income The most likely level of income to be obtained in the future; calculated as net income adjusted for irregular items.

Times interest earned A measure of a company's solvency and ability to meet interest payments as they come due; calculated as income before interest expense and income taxes divided by interest expense.

Trading on the equity See *leveraging*.

Trading securities Securities bought and held primarily for sale in the near term to generate income on short-term price differences.

Vertical analysis A technique for evaluating financial statement data that expresses each item in a financial statement as a percentage of a base amount.

WILEY PLUS Self-Test, Brief Exercises, Exercises, Problem Set A, and many more resources are available for practice in WileyPLUS.

Self-Test Questions

(Answers in *Broadening Your Perspective.*)

All of the Self-Test Questions in this chapter employ decision tools.

(LO 2) **1.** In reporting discontinued operations, the income statement should show in a special section:
(a) gains on the disposal of the discontinued component.
(b) losses on the disposal of the discontinued component.
(c) Neither (a) nor (b).
(d) Both (a) and (b).

(LO 2) **2.** Cool Stools Corporation has income before taxes of $400,000 and an extraordinary loss of $100,000. If the income tax rate is 25% on all items, the income statement should show income before irregular items and an extraordinary loss, respectively, of
(a) $325,000 and $100,000.
(b) $325,000 and $75,000.
(c) $300,000 and $100,000.
(d) $300,000 and $75,000.

(LO 3) **3.** Which of the following would be considered an "Other comprehensive income" item?
(a) Gain on disposal of discontinued operations.
(b) Unrealized loss on available-for-sale securities.
(c) Extraordinary loss related to flood.
(d) Net income.

(LO 4) **4.** In horizontal analysis, each item is expressed as a percentage of the:
(a) net income amount.
(b) stockholders' equity amount.
(c) total assets amount.
(d) base-year amount.

(LO 4) **5.** Adams Corporation reported net sales of $300,000, $330,000, and $360,000 in the years 2012, 2013, and 2014, respectively. If 2012 is the base year, what percentage do 2014 sales represent of the base?
(a) 77%.   (c) 120%.
(b) 108%.   (d) 130%.

(LO 5) **6.** The following schedule is a display of what type of analysis?

	Amount	Percent
Current assets	$200,000	25%
Property, plant, and equipment	600,000	75%
Total assets	$800,000	

(a) Horizontal analysis.   (c) Vertical analysis.
(b) Differential analysis.   (d) Ratio analysis.

(LO 5) **7.** In vertical analysis, the base amount for depreciation expense is generally:
(a) net sales.
(b) depreciation expense in a previous year.

(c) gross profit.
(d) fixed assets.

(LO 6) **8.** Which measure is an evaluation of a company's ability to pay current liabilities?
(a) Current cash debt coverage.
(b) Current ratio.
(c) Both (a) and (b).
(d) None of the above.

(LO 6) **9.** Which measure is useful in evaluating the efficiency in managing inventories?
(a) Inventory turnover.
(b) Days in inventory.
(c) Both (a) and (b).
(d) None of the above.

(LO 6) **10.** Which of these is **not** a liquidity ratio?
(a) Current ratio.
(b) Asset turnover.
(c) Inventory turnover.
(d) Accounts receivable turnover.

(LO 6) **11.** Plano Corporation reported net income $24,000; net sales $400,000; and average assets $600,000 for 2014. What is the 2014 profit margin?
(a) 6%.   (c) 40%.
(b) 12%.   (d) 200%.

Use the following financial statement information as of the end of each year to answer Self-Test Questions 12–16.

	2014	2013
Inventory	$ 54,000	$ 48,000
Current assets	81,000	106,000
Total assets	382,000	326,000
Current liabilities	27,000	36,000
Total liabilities	102,000	88,000
Common stockholders' equity	240,000	198,000
Net sales	784,000	697,000
Cost of goods sold	306,000	277,000
Net income	134,000	90,000
Tax expense	22,000	18,000
Interest expense	12,000	12,000
Dividends paid to preferred stockholders	4,000	4,000
Dividends paid to common stockholders	15,000	10,000

(LO 6) **12.** Compute the days in inventory for 2014.
(a) 64.4 days.   (c) 6 days.
(b) 60.8 days.   (d) 24 days.

(LO 6) **13.** Compute the current ratio for 2014.
(a) 1.26:1.   (c) 0.80:1.
(b) 3.0:1.   (d) 3.75:1.

(LO 6) **14.** Compute the profit margin for 2014.
(a) 17.1%.   (c) 37.9%.
(b) 18.1%.   (d) 5.9%.

(LO 6) **15.** Compute the return on common stockholders' equity for 2014.
  (a) 54.2%. (c) 61.2%.
  (b) 52.5%. (d) 59.4%.

(LO 6) **16.** Compute the times interest earned for 2014.
  (a) 11.2 times. (c) 14.0 times.
  (b) 65.3 times. (d) 13.0 times.

(LO 7) **17.** Which situation below might indicate a company has a low quality of earnings?
  (a) The same accounting principles are used each year.
  (b) Revenue is recognized when the performance obligation is satisfied.
  (c) Maintenance costs are capitalized and then depreciated.
  (d) The company's P-E ratio is high relative to competitors.

Go to the book's companion website, **www.wiley.com/ college/kimmel**, to access additional Self-Test Questions.

Questions

All of the Questions in this chapter employ decision tools.

1. Explain sustainable income. What relationship does this concept have to the treatment of irregular items on the income statement?

2. Indicate which of the following items would be reported as an extraordinary item on Pitchford Corporation's income statement.
  (a) Loss from damages caused by a volcano eruption in Iona.
  (b) Loss from the sale of short-term investments.
  (c) Loss attributable to a labor strike.
  (d) Loss of inventory from flood damage because a warehouse is located on a flood plain that floods every 5 to 10 years.
  (e) Loss on the write-down of outdated inventory.
  (f) Loss from a foreign government's expropriation of a production facility.
  (g) Loss from damage to a warehouse in southern California from a minor earthquake.

3. Garvey Inc. reported 2013 earnings per share of $3.26 and had no extraordinary items. In 2014, earnings per share on income before extraordinary items was $2.99, and earnings per share on net income was $3.49. Do you consider this trend to be favorable? Why or why not?

4. Hosemer Inc. has been in operation for 3 years and uses the FIFO method of pricing inventory. During the fourth year, Hosemer changes to the average-cost method for all its inventory. How will Hosemer report this change?

5. What amount did Tootsie Roll Industries report as "Other comprehensive earnings" in 2011? By what percentage did Tootsie Roll's "Comprehensive earnings" differ from its "Net earnings"?

6. (a) Jennifer Gorman believes that the analysis of financial statements is directed at two characteristics of a company: liquidity and profitability. Is Jennifer correct? Explain.
  (b) Are short-term creditors, long-term creditors, and stockholders interested in primarily the same characteristics of a company? Explain.

7. (a) Distinguish among the following bases of comparison: intracompany, intercompany and industry averages.
  (b) Give the principal value of using each of the three bases of comparison.

8. Two popular methods of financial statement analysis are horizontal analysis and vertical analysis. Explain the difference between these two methods.

9. (a) If Neer Company had net income of $300,000 in 2013 and it experienced a 24.5% increase in net income for 2014, what is its net income for 2014?
  (b) If 6 cents of every dollar of Neer's revenue is net income in 2013, what is the dollar amount of 2013 revenue?

10. Name the major ratios useful in assessing (a) liquidity and (b) solvency.

11. Tom Vernon is puzzled. His company had a profit margin of 10% in 2014. He feels that this is an indication that the company is doing well. Andrea Travis, his accountant, says that more information is needed to determine the company's financial well-being. Who is correct? Why?

12. What does each type of ratio measure?
  (a) Liquidity ratios.
  (b) Solvency ratios.
  (c) Profitability ratios.

13. What is the difference between the current ratio and working capital?

14. Quick Mart, a retail store, has an accounts receivable turnover of 4.5 times. The industry average is 12.5 times. Does Quick Mart have a collection problem with its receivables?

15. Which ratios should be used to help answer each of these questions?
  (a) How efficient is a company in using its assets to produce sales?

(b) How near to sale is the inventory on hand?

(c) How many dollars of net income were earned for each dollar invested by the owners?

(d) How able is a company to meet interest charges as they fall due?

16. At year-end, the price-earnings ratio of General Motors was 11.3, and the price-earnings ratio of Microsoft was 28.14. Which company did the stock market favor? Explain.

17. What is the formula for computing the payout ratio? Do you expect this ratio to be high or low for a growth company?

18. ⬅ Holding all other factors constant, indicate whether each of the following changes generally signals good or bad news about a company.

(a) Increase in profit margin.

(b) Decrease in inventory turnover.

(c) Increase in current ratio.

(d) Decrease in earnings per share.

(e) Increase in price-earnings ratio.

(f) Increase in debt to assets ratio.

(g) Decrease in times interest earned.

19. The return on assets for Espino Corporation is 7.6%. During the same year, Espino's return on common stockholders' equity is 12.8%. What is the explanation for the difference in the two rates?

20. Which two ratios do you think should be of greatest interest in each of the following cases?

(a) A pension fund considering the purchase of 20-year bonds.

(b) A bank contemplating a short-term loan.

(c) A common stockholder.

21. Kono Inc. has net income of $200,000, average shares of common stock outstanding of 40,000, and preferred dividends for the period of $20,000. What is Kono's earnings per share of common stock? Tim Frye, the president of Kono, believes that the computed EPS of the company is high. Comment.

22. Identify and explain factors that affect quality of earnings.

23. ⬅ Explain how the choice of one of the following accounting methods over the other raises or lowers a company's net income during a period of continuing inflation.

(a) Use of FIFO instead of LIFO for inventory costing.

(b) Use of a 6-year life for machinery instead of a 9-year life.

(c) Use of straight-line depreciation instead of declining-balance depreciation.

Brief Exercises

⚙━━ All of the Brief Exercises in this chapter employ decision tools.

BE13-1 On June 30, Reyes Corporation discontinued its operations in Mexico. On September 1, Reyes disposed of the Mexico facility at a pretax loss of $640,000. The applicable tax rate is 25%. Show the discontinued operations section of Reyes's income statement.

Prepare a discontinued operations section of an income statement.
(LO 2), AP

BE13-2 An inexperienced accountant for Fielder Corporation showed the following in Fielder's 2014 income statement: Income before income taxes $300,000; Income tax expense $72,000; Extraordinary loss from flood (before taxes) $80,000; and Net income $168,000. The extraordinary loss and taxable income are both subject to a 30% tax rate. Prepare a corrected income statement beginning with "Income before income taxes."

Prepare a corrected income statement with an extraordinary item.
(LO 2), AP

BE13-3 On January 1, 2014, Jenner Inc. changed from the LIFO method of inventory pricing to the FIFO method. Explain how this change in accounting principle should be treated in the company's financial statements.

Indicate how a change in accounting principle is reported.
(LO 2), C

BE13-4 Using these data from the comparative balance sheet of Ramirez Company, perform horizontal analysis.

Prepare horizontal analysis.
(LO 4), AP

	December 31, 2014	December 31, 2013
Accounts receivable	$ 460,000	$ 400,000
Inventory	780,000	650,000
Total assets	3,164,000	2,800,000

BE13-5 Using the data presented in BE13-4 for Ramirez Company, perform vertical analysis.

Prepare vertical analysis.
(LO 5), AP

BE13-6 Net income was $500,000 in 2012, $485,000 in 2013, and $518,400 in 2014. What is the percentage of change from (a) 2012 to 2013, and (b) from 2013 to 2014? Is the change an increase or a decrease?

Calculate percentage of change.
(LO 4), AP

BE13-7 If Francona Company had net income of $382,800 in 2014 and it experienced a 16% increase in net income over 2013, what was its 2013 net income?

Calculate net income.
(LO 4), AP

Analyze change in net income.

(LO 5), **AP**

BE13-8 Vertical analysis (common-size) percentages for Capuano Company's sales revenue, cost of goods sold, and expenses are listed here.

Vertical Analysis	2014	2013	2012
Sales revenue	100.0%	100.0%	100.0%
Cost of goods sold	60.5	62.9	64.8
Expenses	26.0	26.6	27.5

Did Capuano's net income as a percent of sales increase, decrease, or remain unchanged over the 3-year period? Provide numerical support for your answer.

Analyze change in net income.

(LO 4), **AP**

BE13-9 Horizontal analysis (trend analysis) percentages for Roswell Company's sales revenue, cost of goods sold, and expenses are listed here.

Horizontal Analysis	2014	2013	2012
Sales revenue	96.2%	104.8%	100.0%
Cost of goods sold	101.0	98.0	100.0
Expenses	105.6	95.4	100.0

Explain whether Roswell's net income increased, decreased, or remained unchanged over the 3-year period.

Calculate current ratio.

(LO 6), **AP**

BE13-10 Suppose these selected condensed data are taken from recent balance sheets of Bob Evans Farms (in thousands).

	2014	2013
Cash	$ 13,606	$ 7,669
Accounts receivable	23,045	19,951
Inventory	31,087	31,345
Other current assets	12,522	11,909
Total current assets	$ 80,260	$ 70,874
Total current liabilities	$245,805	$326,203

Compute the current ratio for each year and comment on your results.

Evaluate collection of accounts receivable.

(LO 6), **AN**

BE13-11 The following data are taken from the financial statements of Filbert Company.

	2014	2013
Accounts receivable (net), end of year	$ 550,000	$ 540,000
Net sales on account	4,300,000	4,000,000
Terms for all sales are 1/10, n/45		

Compute for each year (a) the accounts receivable turnover and (b) the average collection period. What conclusions about the management of accounts receivable can be drawn from these data? At the end of 2012, accounts receivable was $520,000.

Evaluate management of inventory.

(LO 6), **AN**

BE13-12 The following data were taken from the income statements of Imhoff Company.

	2014	2013
Sales revenue	$6,420,000	$6,240,000
Beginning inventory	960,000	840,000
Purchases	4,840,000	4,661,000
Ending inventory	1,020,000	960,000

Compute for each year (a) the inventory turnover and (b) days in inventory. What conclusions concerning the management of the inventory can be drawn from these data?

Calculate profitability ratios.

(LO 6), **AN**

BE13-13 Staples, Inc. is one of the largest suppliers of office products in the United States. Suppose it had net income of $738.7 million and sales of $24,275.5 million in 2014. Its total assets were $13,073.1 million at the beginning of the year and $13,717.3 million at the end of the year. What is Staples, Inc.'s (a) asset turnover and (b) profit margin? (Round to two decimals.) Provide a brief interpretation of your results.

BE13-14 Voorhees Company has stockholders' equity of $400,000 and net income of $72,000. It has a payout ratio of 18% and a return on assets of 20%. How much did Voorhees pay in cash dividends, and what were its average total assets?

Calculate profitability ratios.
(LO 6), **AN**

BE13-15 Selected data taken from a recent year's financial statements of trading card company Topps Company, Inc. are as follows (in millions).

Calculate cash-basis liquidity and solvency ratios.
(LO 6), **AN**

Net sales	$326.7
Current liabilities, beginning of year	41.1
Current liabilities, end of year	62.4
Net cash provided by operating activities	10.4
Total liabilities, beginning of year	65.2
Total liabilities, end of year	73.2
Capital expenditures	3.7
Cash dividends	6.2

Compute these ratios: (a) current cash debt coverage, (b) cash debt coverage, and (c) free cash flow. Provide a brief interpretation of your results.

Exercises

All of the Exercises in this chapter employ decision tools.

E13-1 Utech Company has income before irregular items of $310,000 for the year ended December 31, 2014. It also has the following items (before considering income taxes): (1) an extraordinary fire loss of $60,000 and (2) a gain of $30,000 from the disposal of a division. Assume all items are subject to income taxes at a 30% tax rate.

Prepare irregular items portion of an income statement.
(LO 2), **AP**

Instructions
Prepare Utech Company's income statement for 2014, beginning with "Income before irregular items."

E13-2 The *Wall Street Journal* routinely publishes summaries of corporate quarterly and annual earnings reports in a feature called the "Earnings Digest." A typical "digest" report takes the following form.

Evaluate the effects of unusual or irregular items.
(LO 1, 2, 6), **C**

ENERGY ENTERPRISES (A)

	Quarter ending July 31	
	2014	**2013**
Sales revenue	$2,049,000,000	$1,754,000,000
Net income	97,000,000	(a) 68,750,000
EPS: Net income	1.28	0.93

	12 months ending July 31	
	2014	**2013**
Sales revenue	$5,578,500,000	$5,065,300,000
Extraordinary item	(b) 1,900,000	
Net income	102,700,000	(a) 33,250,000
EPS: Net income	1.36	0.48

(a) Includes a net charge of $26,000,000 from loss on the sale of electrical equipment
(b) Extraordinary gain on Middle East property expropriation

The letter in parentheses following the company name indicates the exchange on which Energy Enterprises' stock is traded—in this case, the American Stock Exchange.

Instructions
Answer the following questions.
(a) How was the loss on the electrical equipment reported on the income statement? Was it reported in the fourth quarter of 2013? How can you tell?

(b) Why did the *Wall Street Journal* list the extraordinary item separately?

(c) What is the extraordinary item? Was it included in income for the fourth quarter? How can you tell?

(d) Did Energy Enterprises have an operating loss in any quarter of 2013? Of 2014? How do you know?

(e) Approximately how many shares of stock were outstanding in 2014? Did the number of outstanding shares change from July 31, 2013 to July 31, 2014?

(f) As an investor, what numbers should you use to determine Energy Enterprises' profit margin? Calculate the profit margin for 2013 and 2014 that you consider most useful. Explain your decision.

Prepare horizontal analysis.
(LO 4), **AP**

E13-3 Here is financial information for Spangles Inc.

	December 31, 2014	December 31, 2013
Current assets	$106,000	$ 90,000
Plant assets (net)	400,000	350,000
Current liabilities	99,000	65,000
Long-term liabilities	122,000	90,000
Common stock, $1 par	130,000	115,000
Retained earnings	155,000	170,000

Instructions
Prepare a schedule showing a horizontal analysis for 2014, using 2013 as the base year.

Prepare vertical analysis.
(LO 5), **AP**

E13-4 Operating data for Jacobs Corporation are presented below.

	2014	2013
Sales revenue	$800,000	$600,000
Cost of goods sold	520,000	408,000
Selling expenses	120,000	72,000
Administrative expenses	60,000	48,000
Income tax expense	30,000	24,000
Net income	70,000	48,000

Instructions
Prepare a schedule showing a vertical analysis for 2014 and 2013.

Prepare horizontal and vertical analyses.
(LO 4, 5), **AP**

E13-5 Suppose the comparative balance sheets of Nike, Inc. are presented here.

NIKE, INC.
Comparative Balance Sheets
May 31
($ in millions)

Assets	2014	2013
Current assets	$ 9,734	$ 8,839
Property, plant, and equipment (net)	1,958	1,891
Other assets	1,558	1,713
Total assets	$13,250	$12,443

Liabilities and Stockholders' Equity	2014	2013
Current liabilities	$ 3,277	$ 3,322
Long-term liabilities	1,280	1,296
Stockholders' equity	8,693	7,825
Total liabilities and stockholders' equity	$13,250	$12,443

Instructions
(a) Prepare a horizontal analysis of the balance sheet data for Nike, using 2013 as a base. (Show the amount of increase or decrease as well.)

Prepare horizontal and vertical analyses.
(LO 4, 5), **AP**

(b) Prepare a vertical analysis of the balance sheet data for Nike for 2014.

E13-6 Here are the comparative income statements of Eudaley Corporation.

EUDALEY CORPORATION
Comparative Income Statements
For the Years Ended December 31

	2014	2013
Net sales	$598,000	$500,000
Cost of goods sold	477,000	420,000
Gross profit	121,000	80,000
Operating expenses	80,000	44,000
Net income	$ 41,000	$ 36,000

Instructions
(a) Prepare a horizontal analysis of the income statement data for Eudaley Corporation, using 2013 as a base. (Show the amounts of increase or decrease.)
(b) Prepare a vertical analysis of the income statement data for Eudaley Corporation for both years.

E13-7 Nordstrom, Inc. operates department stores in numerous states. Suppose selected financial statement data (in millions) for 2014 are presented below.

Compute liquidity ratios.
(LO 6), AP

	End of Year	Beginning of Year
Cash and cash equivalents	$ 795	$ 72
Accounts receivable (net)	2,035	1,942
Inventory	898	900
Other current assets	326	303
Total current assets	$4,054	$3,217
Total current liabilities	$2,014	$1,601

For the year, net credit sales were $8,258 million, cost of goods sold was $5,328 million, and net cash provided by operating activities was $1,251 million.

Instructions
Compute the current ratio, current cash debt coverage, accounts receivable turnover, average collection period, inventory turnover, and days in inventory at the end of the current year.

E13-8 Wyne Incorporated had the following transactions involving current assets and current liabilities during February 2014.

Perform current ratio analysis.
(LO 6), AP

Feb.	3	Collected accounts receivable of $15,000.
	7	Purchased equipment for $23,000 cash.
	11	Paid $3,000 for a 1-year insurance policy.
	14	Paid accounts payable of $12,000.
	18	Declared cash dividends, $4,000.

Additional information:
As of February 1, 2014, current assets were $120,000 and current liabilities were $40,000.

Instructions
Compute the current ratio as of the beginning of the month and after each transaction.

E13-9 Kinder Company has these comparative balance sheet data:

Compute selected ratios.
(LO 6), AP

KINDER COMPANY
Balance Sheets
December 31

	2014	2013
Cash	$ 15,000	$ 30,000
Accounts receivable (net)	70,000	60,000
Inventory	60,000	50,000
Plant assets (net)	200,000	180,000
	$345,000	$320,000

Accounts payable	$ 50,000	$ 60,000
Mortgage payable (15%)	100,000	100,000
Common stock, $10 par	140,000	120,000
Retained earnings	55,000	40,000
	$345,000	$320,000

Additional information for 2014:
1. Net income was $25,000.
2. Sales on account were $375,000. Sales returns and allowances amounted to $25,000.
3. Cost of goods sold was $198,000.
4. Net cash provided by operating activities was $48,000.
5. Capital expenditures were $25,000, and cash dividends were $10,000.

Instructions
Compute the following ratios at December 31, 2014.
(a) Current ratio.   (e) Days in inventory.
(b) Accounts receivable turnover.   (f) Cash debt coverage.
(c) Average collection period.   (g) Current cash debt coverage.
(d) Inventory turnover.   (h) Free cash flow.

Compute selected ratios.
(LO 6), **AP**

E13-10 Suppose selected comparative statement data for the giant bookseller Barnes & Noble are presented here. All balance sheet data are as of the end of the fiscal year (in millions).

	2014	2013
Net sales	$5,121.8	$5,286.7
Cost of goods sold	3,540.6	3,679.8
Net income	75.9	135.8
Accounts receivable	81.0	107.1
Inventory	1,203.5	1,358.2
Total assets	2,993.9	3,249.8
Total common stockholders' equity	921.6	1,074.7

Instructions
Compute the following ratios for 2014.
(a) Profit margin.
(b) Asset turnover.
(c) Return on assets.
(d) Return on common stockholders' equity.
(e) Gross profit rate.

Compute selected ratios.
(LO 6), **AP**

E13-11 Here is the income statement for Eberle, Inc.

EBERLE, INC.
Income Statement
For the Year Ended December 31, 2014

Sales revenue	$400,000
Cost of goods sold	230,000
Gross profit	170,000
Expenses (including $16,000 interest and $24,000 income taxes)	98,000
Net income	$ 72,000

Additional information:
1. Common stock outstanding January 1, 2014, was 32,000 shares, and 40,000 shares were outstanding at December 31, 2014.
2. The market price of Eberle, Inc., stock was $14 in 2014.
3. Cash dividends of $21,000 were paid, $5,000 of which were to preferred stockholders.

Instructions
Compute the following measures for 2014.
(a) Earnings per share.   (c) Payout ratio.
(b) Price-earnings ratio.   (d) Times interest earned.

E13-12 Santo Corporation experienced a fire on December 31, 2014 in which its financial records were partially destroyed. It has been able to salvage some of the records and
has ascertained the following balances.

*Compute amounts from
ratios.*
(LO 6), **AP**

	December 31, 2014	December 31, 2013
Cash	$ 30,000	$ 10,000
Accounts receivable (net)	72,500	126,000
Inventory	200,000	180,000
Accounts payable	50,000	90,000
Notes payable	30,000	60,000
Common stock, $100 par	400,000	400,000
Retained earnings	113,500	101,000

Additional information:
1. The inventory turnover is 3.8 times.
2. The return on common stockholders' equity is 22%. The company had no additional
   paid-in capital.
3. The accounts receivable turnover is 11.2 times.
4. The return on assets is 18%.
5. Total assets at December 31, 2013, were $605,000.

Instructions
Compute the following for Santo Corporation.
(a) Cost of goods sold for 2014.
(b) Net credit sales for 2014.
(c) Net income for 2014.
(d) Total assets at December 31, 2014.

E13-13 The condensed financial statements of Elliott Company for the years 2013 and
2014 are presented below.

Compute ratios.
(LO 6), **AP**

ELLIOTT COMPANY
Balance Sheets
December 31 (in thousands)

	2014	2013
Current assets		
Cash and cash equivalents	$ 330	$ 360
Accounts receivable (net)	470	400
Inventory	460	390
Prepaid expenses	130	160
Total current assets	1,390	1,310
Property, plant, and equipment (net)	410	380
Investments	10	10
Intangibles and other assets	530	510
Total assets	$2,340	$2,210
Current liabilities	$ 820	$ 790
Long-term liabilities	480	380
Stockholders' equity—common	1,040	1,040
Total liabilities and stockholders' equity	$2,340	$2,210

ELLIOTT COMPANY
Income Statements
For the Year Ended December 31 (in thousands)

	2014	2013
Sales revenue	$3,800	$3,460
Costs and expenses		
Cost of goods sold	970	890
Selling & administrative expenses	2,400	2,330
Interest expense	10	20
Total costs and expenses	3,380	3,240

Income before income taxes	420	220
Income tax expense	168	88
Net income	$ 252	$ 132

Compute the following ratios for 2014 and 2013.
(a) Current ratio.
(b) Inventory turnover. (Inventory on December 31, 2012, was $340.)
(c) Profit margin.
(d) Return on assets. (Assets on December 31, 2012, were $1,900.)
(e) Return on common stockholders' equity. (Equity on December 31, 2012, was $900.)
(f) Debt to assets ratio.
(g) Times interest earned.

Challenge Exercises

Visit the book's companion website, at **www.wiley.com/college/kimmel**, and choose the Student Companion site to access Challenge Exercises.

Problems: Set A

⚙━━━━C All of the Problems in this chapter employ decision tools.

Prepare vertical analysis and comment on profitability.
(LO 5, 6), **AN**

P13-1A Here are comparative statement data for Prince Company and King Company, two competitors. All balance sheet data are as of December 31, 2014, and December 31, 2013.

	Prince Company		King Company	
	2014	**2013**	**2014**	**2013**
Net sales	$1,849,000		$546,000	
Cost of goods sold	1,063,200		289,000	
Operating expenses	240,000		82,000	
Interest expense	6,800		3,600	
Income tax expense	62,000		28,000	
Current assets	325,975	$312,410	83,336	$ 79,467
Plant assets (net)	526,800	500,000	139,728	125,812
Current liabilities	66,325	75,815	35,348	30,281
Long-term liabilities	113,990	90,000	29,620	25,000
Common stock, $10 par	500,000	500,000	120,000	120,000
Retained earnings	172,460	146,595	38,096	29,998

Instructions
(a) Prepare a vertical analysis of the 2014 income statement data for Prince Company and King Company.
(b) ✏━━━▶ Comment on the relative profitability of the companies by computing the 2014 return on assets and the return on common stockholders' equity for both companies.

Compute ratios from balance sheets and income statements.
(LO 6), **AP**

P13-2A The comparative statements of Osborne Company are presented here.

OSBORNE COMPANY
Income Statements
For the Years Ended December 31

	2014	**2013**
Net sales	$1,890,540	$1,750,500
Cost of goods sold	1,058,540	1,006,000
Gross profit	832,000	744,500
Selling and administrative expenses	500,000	479,000
Income from operations	332,000	265,500

Other expenses and losses		
Interest expense	22,000	20,000
Income before income taxes	310,000	245,500
Income tax expense	92,000	73,000
Net income	$ 218,000	$ 172,500

OSBORNE COMPANY
Balance Sheets
December 31

Assets	2014	2013
Current assets		
Cash	$ 60,100	$ 64,200
Debt investments (short-term)	74,000	50,000
Accounts receivable	117,800	102,800
Inventory	126,000	115,500
Total current assets	377,900	332,500
Plant assets (net)	649,000	520,300
Total assets	$1,026,900	$852,800
Liabilities and Stockholders' Equity		
Current liabilities		
Accounts payable	$ 160,000	$145,400
Income taxes payable	43,500	42,000
Total current liabilities	203,500	187,400
Bonds payable	220,000	200,000
Total liabilities	423,500	387,400
Stockholders' equity		
Common stock ($5 par)	290,000	300,000
Retained earnings	313,400	165,400
Total stockholders' equity	603,400	465,400
Total liabilities and stockholders' equity	$1,026,900	$852,800

All sales were on account. Net cash provided by operating activities for 2014 was $220,000. Capital expenditures were $136,000, and cash dividends were $70,000.

Instructions
Compute the following ratios for 2014.
(a) Earnings per share.
(b) Return on common stockholders' equity.
(c) Return on assets.
(d) Current ratio.
(e) Accounts receivable turnover.
(f) Average collection period.
(g) Inventory turnover.
(h) Days in inventory.
(i) Times interest earned.
(j) Asset turnover.
(k) Debt to assets.
(l) Current cash debt coverage.
(m) Cash debt coverage.
(n) Free cash flow.

P13-3A Condensed balance sheet and income statement data for Jernigan Corporation are presented here.

Perform ratio analysis, and discuss change in financial position and operating results.

(LO 6), **AN**

JERNIGAN CORPORATION
Balance Sheets
December 31

	2014	2013	2012
Cash	$ 30,000	$ 20,000	$ 18,000
Accounts receivable (net)	50,000	45,000	48,000
Other current assets	90,000	95,000	64,000
Investments	55,000	70,000	45,000
Plant and equipment (net)	500,000	370,000	358,000
	$725,000	$600,000	$533,000

Current liabilities	$ 85,000	$ 80,000	$ 70,000
Long-term debt	145,000	85,000	50,000
Common stock, $10 par	320,000	310,000	300,000
Retained earnings	175,000	125,000	113,000
	$725,000	$600,000	$533,000

JERNIGAN CORPORATION
Income Statements
For the Years Ended December 31

	2014	2013
Sales revenue	$740,000	$600,000
Less: Sales returns and allowances	40,000	30,000
Net sales	700,000	570,000
Cost of goods sold	425,000	350,000
Gross profit	275,000	220,000
Operating expenses (including income taxes)	180,000	150,000
Net income	$ 95,000	$ 70,000

Additional information:

1. The market price of Jernigan's common stock was $7.00, $7.50, and $8.50 for 2012, 2013, and 2014, respectively.
2. You must compute dividends paid. All dividends were paid in cash.

Instructions
(a) Compute the following ratios for 2013 and 2014.
   (1) Profit margin.
   (2) Gross profit rate.
   (3) Asset turnover.
   (4) Earnings per share.
   (5) Price-earnings ratio.
   (6) Payout ratio.
   (7) Debt to assets ratio.
(b) ✏️ Based on the ratios calculated, discuss briefly the improvement or lack thereof in the financial position and operating results from 2013 to 2014 of Jernigan Corporation.

Compute ratios; comment on overall liquidity and profitability.
(LO 6), AN

P13-4A The following financial information is for Frizell Company.

FRIZELL COMPANY
Balance Sheets
December 31

Assets	2014	2013
Cash	$ 70,000	$ 65,000
Debt investments (short-term)	55,000	40,000
Accounts receivable	104,000	90,000
Inventory	230,000	165,000
Prepaid expenses	25,000	23,000
Land	130,000	130,000
Building and equipment (net)	260,000	185,000
Total assets	$874,000	$698,000

Liabilities and Stockholders' Equity		
Notes payable	$170,000	$120,000
Accounts payable	65,000	52,000
Accrued liabilities	40,000	40,000
Bonds payable, due 2017	250,000	170,000
Common stock, $10 par	200,000	200,000
Retained earnings	149,000	116,000
Total liabilities and stockholders' equity	$874,000	$698,000

FRIZELL COMPANY
Income Statements
For the Years Ended December 31

	2014	2013
Sales revenue	$882,000	$790,000
Cost of goods sold	640,000	575,000
Gross profit	242,000	215,000
Operating expenses	190,000	167,000
Net income	$ 52,000	$ 48,000

Additional information:
1. Inventory at the beginning of 2013 was $115,000.
2. Accounts receivable (net) at the beginning of 2013 were $86,000.
3. Total assets at the beginning of 2013 were $660,000.
4. No common stock transactions occurred during 2013 or 2014.
5. All sales were on account.

Instructions
(a) Indicate, by using ratios, the change in liquidity and profitability of Frizell Company from 2013 to 2014. (*Note:* Not all profitability ratios can be computed nor can cash-basis ratios be computed.)
(b) Given below are three independent situations and a ratio that may be affected. For each situation, compute the affected ratio (1) as of December 31, 2014, and (2) as of December 31, 2015, after giving effect to the situation. Net income for 2015 was $54,000. Total assets on December 31, 2015, were $900,000.

Situation	Ratio
1. 18,000 shares of common stock were sold at par on July 1, 2015.	Return on common stockholders' equity
2. All of the notes payable were paid in 2015.	Debt to assets ratio
3. The market price of common stock was $9 and $12 on December 31, 2014 and 2015, respectively.	Price-earnings ratio

P13-5A Suppose selected financial data of Target and Wal-Mart for 2014 are presented here (in millions).

Compute selected ratios, and compare liquidity, profitability, and solvency for two companies.
(LO 6), **AN**

	Target Corporation	Wal-Mart Stores, Inc.
	Income Statement Data for Year	
Net sales	$65,357	$408,214
Cost of goods sold	45,583	304,657
Selling and administrative expenses	15,101	79,607
Interest expense	707	2,065
Other income (expense)	(94)	(411)
Income tax expense	1,384	7,139
Net income	$ 2,488	$ 14,335
	Balance Sheet Data (End of Year)	
Current assets	$18,424	$ 48,331
Noncurrent assets	26,109	122,375
Total assets	$44,533	$170,706
Current liabilities	$11,327	$ 55,561
Long-term debt	17,859	44,089
Total stockholders' equity	15,347	71,056
Total liabilities and stockholders' equity	$44,533	$170,706

	Beginning-of-Year Balances	
Total assets	$44,106	$163,429
Total stockholders' equity	13,712	65,682
Current liabilities	10,512	55,390
Total liabilities	30,394	97,747

	Other Data	
Average net accounts receivable	$ 7,525	$ 4,025
Average inventory	6,942	33,836
Net cash provided by operating activities	5,881	26,249
Capital expenditures	1,729	12,184
Dividends	496	4,217

Instructions
(a) For each company, compute the following ratios.

(1) Current ratio.	(8)	Return on assets.
(2) Accounts receivable turnover.	(9)	Return on common stockholders' equity.
(3) Average collection period.	(10)	Debt to assets ratio.
(4) Inventory turnover.	(11)	Times interest earned.
(5) Days in inventory.	(12)	Current cash debt coverage.
(6) Profit margin.	(13)	Cash debt coverage.
(7) Asset turnover.	(14)	Free cash flow.

(b) Compare the liquidity, solvency, and profitability of the two companies.

Problems: Set B

Visit the book's companion website, at **www.wiley.com/college/kimmel**, and choose the Student Companion site to access Problem Set B.

Broadening Your Perspective

Financial Reporting and Analysis

FINANCIAL REPORTING PROBLEM: *Tootsie Roll Industries, Inc.*

BYP13-1   Your parents are considering investing in Tootsie Roll Industries common stock. They ask you, as an accounting expert, to make an analysis of the company for them. Fortunately, excerpts from a recent annual report of Tootsie Roll are presented in Appendix A of this textbook.

Instructions
(a) Make a 5-year trend analysis, using 2007 as the base year, of (1) net sales and (2) net earnings. Comment on the significance of the trend results.
(b) Compute for 2011 and 2010 the (1) debt to assets ratio and (2) times interest earned. (See Note 6 for interest expense.) How would you evaluate Tootsie Roll's long-term solvency?
(c) Compute for 2011 and 2010 the (1) profit margin, (2) asset turnover, (3) return on assets, and (4) return on common stockholders' equity. How would you evaluate Tootsie Roll's profitability? Total assets at December 31, 2009, were $836,844,000, and total stockholders' equity at December 31, 2009, was $654,244,000.
(d) What information outside the annual report may also be useful to your parents in making a decision about Tootsie Roll?

COMPARATIVE ANALYSIS PROBLEM: *Tootsie Roll vs. Hershey*

BYP13-2   The financial statements of The Hershey Company are presented in Appendix B, following the financial statements for Tootsie Roll Industries in Appendix A.

Instructions

(a) Based on the information in the financial statements, determine each of the following for each company:
  (1) The percentage increase (i) in net sales and (ii) in net income from 2010 to 2011.
  (2) The percentage increase (i) in total assets and (ii) in total stockholders' equity from 2010 to 2011.
  (3) The earnings per share for 2011.
(b) What conclusions concerning the two companies can be drawn from these data?

RESEARCH CASES

BYP13-3   The April 21, 2008, issue of the *Wall Street Journal Online* included an article by David Reilly entitled "A Way Charges Stay off Bottom Line."

Instructions
Read the article and answer the following questions.
(a) According to the article, how do companies avoid reporting losses on certain types of investment securities in net income?
(b) At what point would these losses be reported in net income?
(c) At the time of the article, what was the total estimated amount of unrealized losses that companies in the Standard and Poor's 500 Stock Index were reporting in equity?
(d) Does the article suggest that these companies are violating accounting standards?
(e) What are the implications of this accounting practice for investors?

BYP13-4   The April 25, 2012, edition of the *Wall Street Journal* contains an article by Spencer Jakab entitled "Amazon's Valuation Is Hard to Justify."

Instructions
Read the article and answer the following questions.
(a) Explain what is meant by the statement that "On a split-adjusted basis, today's share price is the equivalent of $1,166."
(b) The article says that Amazon.com nearly doubled its capital spending on items such as fulfillment centers (sophisticated warehouses where it finds, packages, and ships goods to customers). Discuss the implications that this spending would have on the company's return on assets in the short-term and in the long-term.
(c) How does Amazon's P-E ratio compare to that of Apple, Netflix, and Wal-Mart? What does this suggest about investors' expectations about Amazon's future earnings?
(d) What factor does the article cite as a possible hurdle that might reduce Amazon's ability to raise its operating margin back to previous levels?

INTERPRETING FINANCIAL STATEMENTS

BYP13-5   The Coca-Cola Company and PepsiCo, Inc. provide refreshments to every corner of the world. Suppose selected data from the 2014 consolidated financial statements for The Coca-Cola Company and for PepsiCo, Inc. are presented here (in millions).

	Coca-Cola	PepsiCo
Total current assets	$17,551	$12,571
Total current liabilities	13,721	8,756
Net sales	30,990	43,232
Cost of goods sold	11,088	20,099
Net income	6,824	5,946
Average (net) accounts receivable for the year	3,424	4,654
Average inventories for the year	2,271	2,570
Average total assets	44,595	37,921
Average common stockholders' equity	22,636	14,556
Average current liabilities	13,355	8,772
Average total liabilities	21,960	23,466
Total assets	48,671	39,848
Total liabilities	23,872	23,044
Income taxes	2,040	2,100
Interest expense	355	397

Net cash provided by operating activities	8,186	6,796
Capital expenditures	1,993	2,128
Cash dividends	3,800	2,732

Instructions

(a) Compute the following liquidity ratios for 2014 for Coca-Cola and for PepsiCo and comment on the relative liquidity of the two competitors.

   (1) Current ratio.   (4) Inventory turnover.

   (2) Accounts receivable turnover.   (5) Days in inventory.

   (3) Average collection period.   (6) Current cash debt coverage.

(b) Compute the following solvency ratios for the two companies and comment on the relative solvency of the two competitors.

   (1) Debt to assets ratio.

   (2) Times interest earned.

   (3) Cash debt coverage.

   (4) Free cash flow.

(c) Compute the following profitability ratios for the two companies and comment on the relative profitability of the two competitors.

   (1) Profit margin.

   (2) Asset turnover.

   (3) Return on assets.

   (4) Return on common stockholders' equity.

REAL-WORLD FOCUS

BYP13-6 *Purpose:* To employ comparative data and industry data to evaluate a company's performance and financial position.

Address: **http://www.moneycentral.msn.com/investor/invsub/results/compare.asp**, or go to **www.wiley.com/college/kimmel**

Steps

(1) Identify two competing companies.

(2) Go to the above address.

(3) Type in the first company's stock symbol. (Use "symbol look-up.").

(4) Choose **Ratios**.

(5) Print out the results.

(6) Repeat steps 3–5 for the competitor.

Instructions

(a) Evaluate the company's liquidity relative to the industry averages and to the competitor that you chose.

(b) Evaluate the company's solvency relative to the industry averages and to the competitor that you chose.

(c) Evaluate the company's profitability relative to the industry averages and to the competitor that you chose.

Critical Thinking

DECISION-MAKING ACROSS THE ORGANIZATION

BYP13-7 You are a loan officer for Great Plains Bank of Davenport. Jason Putnam, president of J. Putnam Corporation, has just left your office. He is interested in an 8-year loan to expand the company's operations. The borrowed funds would be used to purchase new equipment. As evidence of the company's debt-worthiness, Putnam provided you with the following facts.

	2014	2013
Current ratio	3.1	2.1
Asset turnover	2.8	2.2
Cash debt coverage	.1	.2
Net income	Up 32%	Down 8%
Earnings per share	$3.30	$2.50

Putnam is a very insistent (some would say pushy) man. When you told him that you would need additional information before making your decision, he acted offended and said, "What more could you possibly want to know?" You responded that, at a minimum, you would need complete, audited financial statements.

Instructions
With the class divided into groups, answer the following.
(a) Explain why you would want the financial statements to be audited.
(b) Discuss the implications of the ratios provided for the lending decision you are to make. That is, does the information paint a favorable picture? Are these ratios relevant to the decision?
(c) List three other ratios that you would want to calculate for this company, and explain why you would use each.

COMMUNICATION ACTIVITY

BYP13-8 David Lemay is the chief executive officer of Brenna Electronics. Lemay is an expert engineer but a novice in accounting. Lemay asks you, as an accounting student, to explain (a) the bases for comparison in analyzing Brenna's financial statements and (b) the limitations, if any, in financial statement analysis.

Instructions
Write a memo to David Lemay that explains the basis for comparison and the factors affecting quality of earnings.

ETHICS CASE

BYP13-9 Kelli Rice, president of LR Industries, wishes to issue a press release to bolster her company's image and maybe even its stock price, which has been gradually falling. As controller, you have been asked to provide a list of 20 financial ratios and other operating statistics for LR Industries' first-quarter financials and operations.

Two days after you provide the data requested, Laurie Ellis, the public relations director of LR, asks you to prove the accuracy of the financial and operating data contained in the press release written by the president and edited by Laurie. In the news release, the president highlights the sales increase of 25% over last year's first quarter and the positive change in the current ratio from 1.5:1 last year to 3:1 this year. She also emphasizes that production was up 50% over the prior year's first quarter.

You note that the release contains only positive or improved ratios and none of the negative or deteriorated ratios. For instance, no mention is made that the debt to assets ratio has increased from 35% to 55%, that inventories are up 89%, and that although the current ratio improved, the current cash debt coverage fell from .15 to .05. Nor is there any mention that the reported profit for the quarter would have been a loss had not the estimated lives of LR plant and machinery been increased by 30%. Laurie emphasized, "The Pres wants this release by early this afternoon."

Instructions
(a) Who are the stakeholders in this situation?
(b) Is there anything unethical in the president's actions?
(c) Should you as controller remain silent? Does Laurie have any responsibility?

ALL ABOUT YOU

BYP13-10 In this chapter, you learned how to use many tools for performing a financial analysis of a company. When making personal investments, however, it is most likely that you won't be buying stocks and bonds in individual companies. Instead, when most people want to invest in stock, they buy mutual funds. By investing in a mutual fund, you reduce your risk because the fund diversifies by buying the stock of a variety of different companies, bonds, and other investments, depending on the stated goals of the fund.

Before you invest in a fund, you will need to decide what type of fund you want. For example, do you want a fund that has the potential of high growth (but also high risk), or are you looking for lower risk and a steady stream of income? Do you want a fund that invests only in U.S. companies, or do you want one that invests globally? Many resources are available to help you with these types of decisions.

Instructions

Go to **http://web.archive.org/web/20050210200843/http://www.cnb1.com/invallocmdl.htm** and complete the investment allocation questionnaire. Add up your total points to determine the type of investment fund that would be appropriate for you.

FASB CODIFICATION ACTIVITY

BYP13-11   If your school has a subscription to the FASB Codification, go to **http://aaahq.org/ascLogin.cfm** to log in and prepare responses to the following. Use the Master Glossary for determining the proper definitions.
(a) Discontinued operations.
(b) Extraordinary items.
(c) Comprehensive income.

Answers to Insight and Accounting Across the Organization Questions

p. 599 What Does "Non-Recurring" Really Mean? Q: If a company takes a large restructuring charge, what is the effect on the company's current income statement versus future ones? **A:** The current period's net income can be greatly diminished by a large restructuring charge. The net incomes in future periods can be enhanced because they are relieved of costs (i.e., depreciation and labor expenses) that would have been charged to them.

p. 600 More Frequent Ups and Downs Q: When predicting future earnings, how should analysts treat the one-time charge that results from a switch to the different approach for accounting for pension plans? **A:** Because the change in principle will only happen once, it should be ignored when predicting future earnings. That is, because it will not happen again in future periods, it would not be included in estimates of future results.

p. 609 How to Manage the Current Ratio Q: How might management influence a company's current ratio? **A:** Management can affect the current ratio by speeding up or withholding payments on accounts payable just before the balance sheet date. Management can alter the cash balance by increasing or decreasing long-term assets or long-term debt, or by issuing or purchasing common stock.

p. 610 High Ratings Can Bring Low Returns Q: Why are credit rating agencies important to the financial markets? **A:** Credit rating agencies perform financial analysis on publicly traded companies and then publish research reports and credit ratings. Investors and creditors rely on the information provided by credit rating agencies in making investment and lending decisions.

Answers to Self-Test Questions

1. d   **2.** d ($400,000 × .75); ($100,000 × .75)   **3.** b   **4.** d   **5.** c ($360,000 ÷ $300,000)   **6.** c   **7.** a
8. c   **9.** c   **10.** b   **11.** a ($24,000 ÷ $400,000)   **12.** b ($306,000 ÷ (($54,000 + $48,000)/2)) = 6; 365 ÷ 6   **13.** b ($81,000 ÷ $27,000)   **14.** a ($134,000 ÷ $784,000)   **15.** d ($134,000 − $4,000) ÷ (($240,000 + $198,000)/2))   **16.** c ($134,000 + $22,000 + $12,000) ÷ $12,000   **17.** c

A Look at IFRS

LEARNING OBJECTIVE 9

Compare the accounting for irregular items and the income statement format under GAAP and IFRS.

The first part of this chapter relates to the income statement and irregular items. As in GAAP, the income statement is a required statement under IFRS. In addition, the content and presentation of an IFRS income statement is similar to the one used for GAAP. *IAS 1* (revised), "Presentation of Financial Statements," provides general guidelines for the reporting of income statement information. In general, the differences in the presentation of financial statement information are relatively minor.

The latter sections of this chapter, dealing with the tools of financial analysis, are the same throughout the world. Techniques such as vertical and horizontal analysis, for example, are tools used by analysts regardless of whether GAAP- or IFRS-related financial statements are being evaluated. In addition, the ratios provided in the textbook are the same ones that are used internationally.

KEY POINTS

- The tools of financial statement analysis covered in this chapter are universal and therefore no significant differences exist in the analysis methods used.

- The basic objectives of the income statement are the same under both GAAP and IFRS. As indicated in the textbook, a very important objective is to ensure that users of the income statement can evaluate the earning power of the company. Earning power is the normal level of income to be obtained in the future. Thus, both the IASB and the FASB are interested in distinguishing normal levels of income from irregular items in order to better predict a company's future profitability.

- The basic accounting for discontinued operations is the same under IFRS and GAAP.

- Under IFRS, there is no classification for extraordinary items. In other words, extraordinary item treatment is prohibited under IFRS. All revenue and expense items are considered ordinary in nature. Disclosure, however, is extensive for items that are considered material to the financial results. Examples are write-downs of inventory or plant assets, or gains and losses on the disposal of plant assets.

- The accounting for changes in accounting principles and changes in accounting estimates are the same for both GAAP and IFRS.

- The income statement under IFRS is referred to as a **statement of comprehensive income**. The statement of comprehensive income can be prepared under the one-statement approach or the two-statement approach.

    Under the one-statement approach, all components of revenue and expense are reported in the income statement. This combined statement of comprehensive income first computes net income or loss, which is then followed by components of other comprehensive income or loss items to arrive at comprehensive income. An example appears below.

WALTER COMPANY
Statement of Comprehensive Income
For the Year Ended December 31, 2014

Sales revenue	$5,100,000
Cost of goods sold	3,800,000
Gross profit	1,300,000
Operating expenses	700,000
Net income	600,000
Other comprehensive income	
Unrealized gain on non-trading securities	75,000
Comprehensive income	$ 675,000

Under the two-statement approach, all the components of revenues and expenses are reported in a traditional income statement **except** for other comprehensive income or loss. In addition, a second statement (the statement of comprehensive income) is then prepared, starting with net income and followed by other comprehensive income or loss items to arrive at comprehensive income. An example of the two-statement approach, using the same data as that used above for Walter Company, appears below.

WALTER COMPANY
Income Statement
For the Year Ended December 31, 2014

Sales revenue	$5,100,000
Cost of goods sold	3,800,000
Gross profit	1,300,000
Operating expenses	700,000
Net income	$ 600,000

WALTER COMPANY
Statement of Comprehensive Income
For the Year Ended December 31, 2014

Net income	$600,000
Other comprehensive income	
Unrealized gain on non-trading securities	75,000
Comprehensive income	$675,000

- GAAP also permits the one-statement or two-statement approach. In addition, GAAP permits a third alternative, which is to show the computation of comprehensive income in the statement of stockholders' equity.
- The issues related to quality of earnings are the same under both GAAP and IFRS. It is hoped that by adopting a more principles-based approach, as found in IFRS, many of the earnings' quality issues will disappear.

LOOKING TO THE FUTURE

The FASB and the IASB are working on a project that would rework the structure of financial statements. Recently, the IASB decided to require a statement of comprehensive income, similar to what was required under GAAP. In addition, another part of this project addresses the issue of how to classify various items in the income statement. A main goal of this new approach is to provide information that better represents how businesses are run. In addition, the approach draws attention away from one number—net income.

IFRS PRACTICE

IFRS SELF-TEST QUESTIONS

1. The basic tools of financial analysis are the same under both GAAP and IFRS **except** that:
   (a) horizontal analysis cannot be done because the format of the statements is sometimes different.
   (b) analysis is different because vertical analysis cannot be done under IFRS.
   (c) the current ratio cannot be computed because current liabilities are often reported before current assets in IFRS statements of financial position.
   (d) None of the above.
2. Under IFRS:
   (a) the reporting of discontinued items is different than GAAP.
   (b) the reporting of extraordinary items is prohibited.
   (c) the reporting of changes in accounting principles is different than under GAAP.
   (d) None of the above.
3. Presentation of comprehensive income must be reported under IFRS in:
   (a) the statement of stockholders' equity.
   (b) the income statement ending with net income.
   (c) the notes to the financial statements.
   (d) a statement of comprehensive income.
4. Parmalane reports the following information:

Sales revenue	$500,000
Cost of goods sold	200,000
Operating expense	40,000
Unrealized loss on non-trading securities	10,000

Parmalane should report the following under the two-statement approach using IFRS:
   (a) net income of $260,000 and comprehensive income of $270,000.
   (b) net income of $270,000 and comprehensive income of $260,000.
   (c) other comprehensive income of $10,000 and comprehensive income of $270,000.
   (d) other comprehensive loss of $10,000 and comprehensive income of 250,000.

5. Assuming the same information as in Question 4, Parmalane should report the following using a one-statement approach under IFRS:
   (a) net income of $260,000 and comprehensive income of $270,000.
   (b) net income of $270,000 and comprehensive income of $260,000.
   (c) other comprehensive income of $10,000 and comprehensive income of $270,000.
   (d) other comprehensive loss of $10,000 and comprehensive income of $250,000.

IFRS CONCEPTS AND APPLICATION

IFRS13-1 Ling Company reports the following information for the year ended December 31, 2014: sales revenue $1,000,000, cost of goods sold $700,000, operating expenses $200,000, and an unrealized gain on non-trading securities of $75,000. Prepare a statement of comprehensive income using the one-statement approach.

IFRS13-2 Assume the same information for Ling Company as in IFRS13-1. Prepare the income statement using the two-statement approach.

INTERNATIONAL FINANCIAL REPORTING PROBLEM: *Zetar plc*

IFRS13-3 The financial statements of Zetar plc are presented in Appendix C. The company's complete annual report, including the notes to its financial statements, is available in the Investors section at **www.zetarplc.com**.

Instructions
Use the company's **2009 annual report** (not the 2011) to answer the following questions.
   (a) The company's income statement reports a loss on discontinued operations. What business did the company discontinue, and why did it choose to discontinue the business?
   (b) For the year ended April 30, 2009, what amount did the company lose on the operation of the discontinued business, and what amount did it lose on disposal?
   (c) What was the total recorded value of the net assets at the date of disposal, and what was the amount of costs incurred to dispose of the business?

Answers to IFRS Self-Test Questions
1. d **2.** b **3.** d **4.** d **5.** d

SPECIMEN FINANCIAL STATEMENTS: TOOTSIE ROLL INDUSTRIES, INC.

The Annual Report

Once each year, a corporation communicates to its stockholders and other interested parties by issuing a complete set of audited financial statements. The **annual report**, as this communication is called, summarizes the financial results of the company's operations for the year and its plans for the future. Many annual reports are attractive, multicolored, glossy public relations pieces, containing pictures of corporate officers and directors as well as photos and descriptions of new products and new buildings. Yet the basic function of every annual report is to report financial information, almost all of which is produced by the corporation's accounting system.

The content and organization of corporate annual reports have become fairly standardized. Excluding the public relations part of the report (pictures, products, and propaganda), the following items are the traditional financial portions of the annual report:

  Financial Highlights
  Letter to the Stockholders
  Management's Discussion and Analysis
  Financial Statements
  Notes to the Financial Statements
  Management's Report on Internal Control
  Management Certification of Financial Statements
  Auditor's Report
  Supplementary Financial Information

In this appendix, we illustrate current financial reporting with a comprehensive set of corporate financial statements that are prepared in accordance with generally accepted accounting principles and audited by an international independent certified public accounting firm. We are grateful for permission to use the actual financial statements and other accompanying financial information from the annual report of a large, publicly held company, Tootsie Roll Industries, Inc.

The financial information herein is reprinted with permission from the Tootsie Roll Industries, Inc. 2011 Annual Report. The complete financial statements for Tootsie Roll Industries are also available on the book's companion website at **www.wiley.com/college/kimmel**.

Corporate Profile

Tootsie Roll Industries, Inc. has been engaged in the manufacture and sale of confectionery products for 115 years. Our products are primarily sold under the familiar brand names: Tootsie Roll, Tootsie Roll Pops, Caramel Apple Pops, Child's Play, Charms, Blow Pop, Blue Razz, Cella's chocolate covered cherries, Tootsie Dots, Tootsie Crows, Junior Mints, Junior Caramels, Charleston Chew, Sugar Daddy, Sugar Babies, Andes, Fluffy Stuff cotton candy, Dubble Bubble, Razzles, Cry Baby, Nik-L-Nip and EI Bubble.

Melvin J. Gordon, Chairman and Chief Executive Officer
and Ellen R. Gordon, President and Chief Operating Officer.

Corporate Principles

We believe that the differences among companies are attributable to the caliber of their people, and therefore we strive to attract and retain superior people for each job.

We believe that an open family atmosphere at work combined with professional management fosters cooperation and enables each individual to maximize his or her contribution to the Company and realize the corresponding rewards.

We do not jeopardize long-term growth for immediate, short-term results.

We maintain a conservative financial posture in the deployment and management of our assets.

We run a trim operation and continually strive to eliminate waste, minimize cost and implement performance improvements.

We invest in the latest and most productive equipment to deliver the best quality product to our customers at the lowest cost.

We seek to outsource functions where appropriate and to vertically integrate operations where it is financially advantageous to do so.

We view our well known brands as prized assets to be aggressively advertised and promoted to each new generation of consumers.

We conduct business with the highest ethical standards and integrity which are codified in the Company's "Code of Business Conduct and Ethics."

Letter to the Stockholders

Nearly every annual report contains a letter to the stockholders from the chairman of the board or the president, or both. This letter typically discusses the company's accomplishments during the past year and highlights significant events such as mergers and acquisitions, new products, operating achievements, business philosophy, changes in officers or directors, financing commitments, expansion plans, and future prospects. The letter to the stockholders signed by Melvin J. Gordon, Chairman of the Board and Chief Executive Officer, and Ellen R. Gordon, President and Chief Operating Officer, of Tootsie Roll Industries is shown on the next pages.

To Our Shareholders

Net product sales in 2011 were a record $528 million, surpassing the previous record of $517 million set in 2010. The Company had another strong Halloween selling season and sales gains were achieved across many of our core brands. Sales benefited from successful promotional programs, new distribution and selected price increases.

Net earnings in 2011 were $44 million compared to $53 million in 2010. The decline in net earnings is primarily due to significantly higher raw material and packaging costs in 2011. While we endeavor to maintain the Company's profitability by adjusting prices in response to rising costs, we are mindful of the competitive value positioning of our products in the market place. We also remain true to the principles enumerated on the facing page, which have guided the Company for many years.

We focus in particular on the principles of taking a long-term perspective, reinvesting in our operations and our brands and maintaining a conservative financial posture. We believe that these principles have served the Company and its shareholders well over the years and we remain committed to them.

Financial Highlights

	December 31,	
	2011	**2010**
	(in thousands except per share data)	
Net Product Sales	$528,369	$517,149
Net Earnings	43,938	53,063
Working Capital	153,846	176,662
Net Property, Plant and Equipment	212,162	215,492
Shareholders' Equity	665,935	667,408
Average Shares Outstanding*	57,892	58,685
Per Share Items*		
Net Earnings	$ 0.76	$ 0.90
Cash Dividends Paid	.32	.32

*Adjusted for stock dividends.

Highlights in 2011 include:

- $16 million was invested in capital expenditures for property, plant and equipment.
- Cash dividends were paid for the sixty-ninth consecutive year.
- Our forty-seventh consecutive annual 3% stock dividend was distributed.
- 708,235 shares of our common stock were repurchased in the open market for an aggregate price of $18 million.
- The above actions were taken entirely with internally generated funds, and the Company remains essentially debt free.

As of December 31, 2011, the Company had $186 million in cash and investments. These financial resources enable us to continue distributing cash dividends to our shareholders, repurchasing our stock on the open market and reinvesting in operating assets and in our brands, including new products. We are also prepared to consider and respond to appropriate business acquisition opportunities as they may arise.

Sales and Marketing

Consumers have many tempting choices in the candy aisle and retailers are highly selective as to the products they stock. We have found that consumers respond well to the many high quality/high value brands in our portfolio. Additionally, the high percentage of sell-throughs and attractive margins of our items are appealing to the trade. This was evident once again in 2011. We used carefully targeted promotional initiatives to help move our products into distribution and to subsequently move them off the retail shelf. Our diverse portfolio of highly recognizable brands remains popular across all channels of trade.

Our broad range of offerings includes something for virtually every major consumer demographic, which we continue to refine and evolve to meet changing consumer preferences and the demands of the trade in today's fluctuating market place. We remain vigilant in keeping our products contemporary even as they retain their iconic character.

Halloween is a major selling season in our primary market, the United States, for a number of product categories including candy. It is a magical time of fun, family togetherness, gatherings and parties, evoking feelings of excitement and nostalgia. Our sales in the third quarter are centered on this popular holiday and are nearly double those of any other quarter during the year.

In 2011, we posted strong Halloween sales in the grocery, mass merchandiser, warehouse club, dollar store and drug store classes of trade. Our line of packaged goods, including straight goods as well as large bags of Child's Play and other mixed assortments, are offered in a number of merchandising presentations and are especially popular during this season. Other traditional merchandising presentations such as shippers, pallet packs and display ready cases contributed to Halloween sales.

Outside of Halloween, we continued our position of leadership in the theater box category. This category is no longer limited to the "big screen" venue and has developed into a major format for everyday candy purchases. Two new offerings in this important category were added to our line in 2011.

Blow Pop Minis, bite-sized candy tablets, each with a real Blow Pop bubble gum center, were extended into the theater box format. Popular and portable, this "Blow Pop with no stick!" includes four of the most popular Blow Pop flavors in each box, enveloped in a protective sealed pouch for added freshness. Blow Pop Minis continue to be a sales growth driver.

Blow Pop Minis' New Theater Box

Another winning addition to our theater box line was Tootsie Roll Raspberry Cremes. These delicious morsels feature a luscious, creamy raspberry center encased in a thin shell of pure dark chocolate. A perfect snacking indulgence for people on the go!

Raspberry Cremes

We also extended our market leadership position in the lollipop category with the introduction of Tear Jerkers Mini Pops. This exciting new addition to our bagged line packs a super sour punch into each pop! The assortment includes six tangy flavors in a laydown bag with eye catching graphics and great consumer appeal. Pucker up!

Tear Jerker Mini Pops

As big as we are in the lollipop category, in 2011 we introduced our biggest entry ever in the category—the Giant Sugar Daddy! This novelty item consists of a full pound of luscious caramel on a real wooden stick packaged in the familiar yellow and red Sugar Daddy wrapper and shape. The Giant Sugar Daddy makes a fun gift or an all-day good treat.

Giant Sugar Daddy

The Andes line was expanded with a delicious new seasonal offering. Andes Mint Truffles are beautifully packaged in a festive Christmas-themed red box highlighted with gold ornaments and featuring a decorative green foil tree topper. The individually wrapped treats feature a delicious truffle mint center that melts in your mouth. Perfect for holiday gift giving!

Andes Mint Truffles

The Dubble Bubble Nostalgic Big Bar was a new addition to the Dubble Bubble line in 2011. The wrapper features nostalgic graphics and is made of foil for lasting freshness. The Big Bar is a foot-long rope of bubble blowing fun.

Dubble Bubble Big Bar

Our popular line of novelty fun banks grew with the addition of two new items in 2011. The Dubble Bubble bank was launched in a patriotic red, white and blue motif and the Tootsie Roll bank took on a nostalgic tone with old-fashioned graphics at a price point that makes it an old-fashioned value. All of our banks feature a slotted lid so when the candy is gone you can begin to save for the next one. Fun you can bank on!

Advertising and Public Relations

Having been described as "elegant in its simplicity" for more than 40 years the Tootsie Pop "How Many Licks?" television ad has presented viewers with both an intriguing challenge and a clear concept of the product and its value proposition to several generations of consumers. In 2011, this ad was showcased in an exhibit at the Chicago Museum of Broadcast Communications.

The iconic ad, featuring the wise old Mr. Owl advising a young boy that indeed three licks was all it took before the inevitable crunch! when he bit his way to the middle of the Tootsie Pop, was culled from over 100,000 spots in the museum's archives and was selected as one of the 100 best commercials over the last six decades.

Dubble Bubble Patriotic and Tootsie Roll Nostalgic Banks

The ad has led to an inestimable number of experiments and trials, ranging from innovative licking machines built by physics students that counted strokes with scientific precision, to informal personal licking trials communicated to us in many thousands of consumer letters. Despite this massive amount of research, the provocative question posed by the announcer: "How many licks does it take to get to the Tootsie Roll center of a Tootsie Pop?" remains unanswered. So, as the commercial states, "the world may never know."

This message has been extended to social media, and in 2011 the Company continued to bring new users into the Tootsie Roll and Tootsie Pops franchises with a digital media campaign targeting moms with kids. Featuring our own "Mr. Owl" character, banner ads, online video ads, and search ads directed consumers to the brands' Facebook pages. There, consumers could send Halloween e-cards featuring our brands, play customized games and share photos and stories with their Facebook friends.

Additionally, several of our products were featured in special interest programs on the History Channel, the Travel Channel and the Food Channel. These programs are quite popular with viewing audiences and are often repeated, generating extensive recurring exposure and interest in the featured brands.

Purchasing

The markets for the majority of the Company's key ingredients, including corn syrup, edible oils, gum base, cocoa powder and sugar, rose sharply to record or near record levels in 2011. Likewise, the cost of many of our principle packaging materials, including corrugated, film and wax paper, increased over 2010. These input cost increases were well in excess of the price increases we implemented in 2011.

Competitive bidding, selective hedging and forward purchasing as well as leveraging our high volume of purchases are some of the means we use to manage costs to the greatest extent possible in an upward commodity and packaging materials price environment.

Operations and Supply Chain

We continue to invest capital and resources in projects that support evolving customer/consumer preferences and distribution patterns, promote growing product lines, improve quality and maximize efficiency across our operations. It is our goal to be the low cost producer in the categories in which we compete. As technology advances, we are constantly on the lookout for new cost saving process enhancements as they become feasible and financially justified.

We have also made a major commitment to information technology, and in 2011 the final phase of a comprehensive enterprise resource planning system was implemented. Investment in leading edge equipment and technology is one of our key corporate principles and we believe it has resulted in the Company's success and profitability over many years.

International

Sales in Mexico declined somewhat and operating income also declined, as price increases taken during the year were not sufficient to recover cost increases. Our export sales to the Canadian market decreased due to inventory reductions by a distributor.

Export sales to other countries were lower in 2011, though we continue to believe that the broad assortment of well-known brands that we offer will, over the long run, appeal to consumers in a variety of foreign markets and venues. Accordingly, we continue to actively cultivate these opportunities in over 40 foreign countries.

In Appreciation

We wish to express our appreciation to our many loyal employees, customers, suppliers, sales brokers and distributors throughout the world for their support during the past year. We also thank our fellow shareholders for their support in today's challenging business environment. We remain committed to the pursuit of excellence in every aspect of our business in order to ensure the Company's success both in the near term and far into the future.

Melvin J. Gordon
Chairman of the Board and
Chief Executive Officer

Ellen R. Gordon
President and
Chief Operating Officer

Management Discussion and Analysis

The management discussion and analysis (MD&A) section covers three financial aspects of a company: its results of operations, its ability to pay near-term obligations, and its ability to fund operations and expansion. Management must highlight favorable or unfavorable trends and identify significant events and uncertainties that affect these three factors. This discussion obviously involves a number of subjective estimates and opinions. The MD&A section of Tootsie Roll's annual report is presented below.

Management's Discussion and Analysis of Financial Condition and Results of Operations

(in thousands except per share, percentage and ratio figures)

FINANCIAL REVIEW

This financial review discusses the Company's financial condition, results of operations, liquidity and capital resources, significant accounting policies and estimates, new accounting pronouncements, market risks and other matters. It should be read in conjunction with the Consolidated Financial Statements and related footnotes that follow this discussion.

FINANCIAL CONDITION

The Company's overall financial position remains very strong as a result of its 2011 net product sales, net earnings and related cash flows provided by operating activities.

During 2011, the Company's net product sales increased from $517,149 in 2010 to $528,369 in 2011, an increase of $11,220 or 2.2%. Cash flows from operating activities totaled $50,390 in 2011 compared to $82,805 in 2010. The Company used its 2011 cash flows to pay cash dividends of $18,407, purchase and retire $18,190 of its outstanding shares, and make capital expenditures of $16,351.

The Company's net working capital was $153,846 at December 31, 2011 compared to $176,662 at December 31, 2010 reflecting a $37,364 decrease in cash and cash equivalents. As of December 31, 2011, the Company's aggregate cash, cash equivalents and investments, including all long-term investments in marketable securities, was $185,668 compared to $188,433 at December 31, 2010, a decrease of $2,765. The aforementioned includes $41,768 and $38,504 in trading securities as of December 31, 2011 and 2010, respectively. The Company invests in trading securities to provide an economic hedge for its deferred compensation liabilities, as further discussed herein and in Note 7 to the Consolidated Financial Statements.

Shareholders' equity decreased from $667,408 at December 31, 2010 to $665,935 as of December 31, 2011, principally reflecting 2011 net earnings of $43,938, less cash dividends and share repurchases of $18,407 and $18,190, respectively, and $8,740 of other comprehensive loss which is summarized in Note 12 to the Consolidated Financial Statements.

The Company has a relatively straight-forward financial structure and has historically maintained a conservative financial position. Except for an immaterial amount of operating leases, the Company has no special financing arrangements or "off-balance sheet" special purpose entities. Cash flows from operations plus maturities of short-term investments are expected to be adequate to meet the Company's overall financing needs, including capital expenditures, in 2012. Periodically, the Company considers possible acquisitions, and if the Company were to pursue and complete such an acquisition, that could result in bank borrowings or other financing.

Results of Operations

2011 vs. 2010

Net product sales were $528,369 in 2011 compared to $517,149 in 2010, an increase of $11,220 or 2.2%. This increase principally reflects sales price increases during 2011 which were required to recover some of our rising input costs as discussed below. Although price increases were made throughout 2011, most became effective during mid-fourth quarter 2011 after the Company's large pre-Halloween selling season, and therefore, a substantial portion of the benefits of such price increases will be realized in 2012.

Product cost of goods sold were $365,225 in 2011 compared to $349,334 in 2010, an increase of $15,891 or 4.5%. Product cost of goods sold includes $44 and $770 in certain deferred compensation expenses in 2011 and 2010, respectively. These deferred compensation expenses principally result from changes in the market value of investments and investment income from trading securities relating to compensation deferred in previous years and are not reflective of current operating results. Adjusting for the aforementioned, product cost of goods sold increased from $348,564 in 2010 to $365,181 in 2011, an increase of $16,617 or 4.8%. As a percent of net product sales, these adjusted costs increased from 67.4% in 2010 to 69.1% in 2011, an increase of 1.7% as a percent of net product sales. The Company was adversely affected by significantly higher input costs, including approximately $17,300 and $2,800 of unit cost increases in ingredients and packaging materials, respectively, in 2011 compared to 2010. The Company generally experienced significant cost increases in sugar, corn syrup, cocoa, edible oils, dairy and gum base inputs resulting in higher cost of goods sold as a percentage of sales.

Selling, marketing and administrative expenses were $108,276 in 2011 compared to $106,316 in 2010, an increase of $1,960 or 1.8%. Selling, marketing and administrative expenses reflect a $15 decrease and $2,594 increase in certain deferred compensation expenses in 2011 and 2010, respectively. These deferred compensation expenses principally result from changes in the market value of investments and investment income from trading securities relating to compensation deferred in previous years and are not reflective of current operating results. Adjusting for the aforementioned, selling, marketing and administrative expenses increased from $103,722 in 2010 to $108,291 in 2011, an increase of $4,569 or 4.4%. As a percent of net product sales, these adjusted expenses increased slightly from 20.1% of net product sales in 2010 to 20.5% of net product sales in 2011.

Selling, marketing and administrative expenses include $45,849 and $43,034 of freight, delivery and warehousing expenses in 2011 and 2010, respectively. These expenses increased from 8.3% of net product sales in 2010 to 8.7% of net product sales in 2011, principally reflecting an 8.7% increase in freight and delivery costs for trucking carriers including higher fuel surcharges for diesel fuel.

The Company believes that the carrying values of its trademarks and goodwill have indefinite lives as they are expected to generate cash flows indefinitely. In accordance with current accounting guidance, goodwill and indefinite-lived intangible assets are assessed at least annually for impairment as of December 31 or whenever events or circumstances indicate that the carrying values may not be recoverable from future cash flows. No impairments were recorded in 2011 or 2010.

The fair values of indefinite lived intangible assets are primarily assessed using the present value of estimated future cash flows. Management believes that all assumptions used for the impairment tests are consistent with those utilized by market participants performing similar valuations. The Company's fair value estimates based on these assumptions were used to prepare projected financial information which it believes to be reasonable. Actual future results may differ from those projections and the differences could be material. Holding all other assumptions constant at the test date, a 100 basis point increase in the discount rate or a 100 basis point decrease in the royalty rate would reduce the fair value of certain trademarks by approximately 16% and 11%, respectively. Individually, a 100 basis point increase in the discount rate would indicate a potential impairment of approximately $2,000 as of December 31, 2011; however, if the royalty rate were decreased by 100 basis points no potential impairment would be indicated as of December 31, 2011.

Earnings from operations were $57,966 in 2011 compared to $64,710 in 2010, a decrease of $6,744. Earnings from operations includes $29 and $3,364 in certain deferred compensation expenses in 2011 and 2010, respectively. As discussed above, these deferred compensation expenses relate to changes in deferred compensation liabilities resulting from corresponding changes in the market value of trading securities and related investment income that hedge these liabilities. Adjusting for these deferred compensation expenses, operating earnings were $57,995 and $68,074 in 2011 and 2010, respectively, a decrease of $10,079 or 14.8%. This decrease in earnings from operations principally reflects significantly higher ingredient costs and resulting lower gross profit margins, as well as higher freight and delivery expenses as discussed above.

Management believes the comparisons presented in the preceding paragraphs after adjusting for changes in deferred compensation are more reflective of the underlying operations of the Company.

Other income (expense), net was $2,946 in 2011 compared to $8,358 in 2010, a decrease of $5,412. This decrease principally reflects a $3,335 decrease in net gains and related investment income on trading securities of $29 and $3,364 in 2011 and 2010 which is discussed above. These trading securities were substantially offset by a like amount of expense in aggregate product cost of goods sold and selling, marketing, and administrative expenses in the respective years as discussed above. Foreign exchange gains in 2011 decreased $1,992 which includes a decrease in net realized gains on foreign currency hedging. Other income (expense), net also includes the operating losses of $194 and $342 for 2011 and 2010, respectively, relating to the Company's equity method investment in two 50% owned foreign companies.

As of December 31, 2011 and 2010, the Company's long-term investments include $7,453 and $6,775 ($13,550 original cost), respectively, of Jefferson County Alabama Sewer Revenue Refunding Warrants, originally purchased with an insurance-backed AAA rating. This is an auction rate security (ARS) that is classified as an available for sale security. Representatives of Jefferson County and the bond holders were unable to reach a settlement agreement, and therefore the County filed for bankruptcy in 2011. Due to adverse events related to Jefferson County and its bond insurance carrier, Financial Guaranty Insurance Company (FGIC), as well as events in the credit markets, the auctions for this ARS failed in 2008 through 2011 (and subsequent to December 31, 2011). As such, the Company estimated the fair value of this ARS as of December 31, 2011 and 2010 utilizing a valuation model with Level 3 inputs, as defined by guidance and discussed in Note 10 to the Consolidated Financial Statements. This valuation model considered, among others items, recent third-party trading and sales prices, the credit risk of the municipality and collateral underlying the ARS, the credit risk of the bond insurer, interest rates, and the amount and timing of expected future cash flows including assumptions about the market expectation of the next successful auction or a restructured security that is likely to be issued as a result of the municipality's bankruptcy.

During the fourth quarter of 2008, the Company determined that the market decline in fair value of its Jefferson County ARS became other-than-temporarily impaired, as defined, and recorded a pre-tax impairment of $5,140. During 2011 and 2010, the Company further evaluated this investment and concluded that additional increases and (declines) in the market value were temporary because it was not related to further credit impairment and recorded $678 and $(935), respectively, as adjustments to accumulated other comprehensive gain (loss). The Company has classified this ARS as non-current and has included it in long-term investments on the Consolidated Statements of Financial Position at December 31, 2011 and 2010 because the Company believes that the current financial conditions, including bankruptcy filing, of Jefferson County and the stressed financial condition of FGIC, as well as the conditions in the auction rate securities market, may take more than twelve months to resolve. Future evaluations of the fair value of this ARS could also result in additional other-than-temporary classification of declines in market value, and therefore result in additional charges to earnings. The Company continues to receive all contractual interest payments on this ARS on a timely basis, it is insured by FGIC and the Company has the intent and ability to hold this ARS until recovery of its amortized cost basis. The Company is not currently able to predict the outcome of this bankruptcy, or the amount and timing of net proceeds it may ultimately recover.

The consolidated effective tax rate was 27.9% and 27.4% in 2011 and 2010, respectively. At December 31, 2011, the Company has approximately $66,740 of foreign subsidiary tax loss carry-forwards expiring in future years 2014 through 2031. The Company has concluded that it is more-likely-than-not that it would realize the deferred tax assets relating to such tax operating loss carry-forwards because it is expected that sufficient levels of taxable income will be generated during the carry-forward periods.

Net earnings were $43,938 in 2011 compared to $53,063 in 2010, and earnings per share were $.76 and $.90 in 2011 and 2010, respectively, a decrease of $.14 or 15.6%. Earnings per share benefited from the reduction in average shares outstanding resulting from purchases of the Company's common stock (the "Common Stock") in the open market by the Company. Average shares outstanding decreased from 58,685 in 2010 to 57,892 in 2011.

2010 vs. 2009

Net product sales were $517,149 in 2010 compared to $495,592 in 2009, an increase of $21,557 or 4.3%. This increase principally reflects organic growth in volume, including product line extensions.

Product cost of goods sold were $349,334 in 2010 compared to $319,775 in 2009, an increase of $29,559 or 9.2%. Product cost of goods sold reflects a $228 decrease in certain deferred compensation expenses in 2010 compared to 2009. This decrease principally results from changes in the market value of investments in trading securities relating to compensation deferred in previous years and is not reflective of current operating results. Adjusting for the aforementioned, product cost of goods sold as a percentage of net product sales increased from 64.3% in 2009 to 67.4% in 2010, an increase of 3.1% as a percent of net product sales. The Company was adversely affected by significantly higher input costs, including approximately $16,600 of ingredient unit cost increases in 2010 compared to 2009. However, packaging material unit costs favorably decreased by approximately $800 in 2010. The Company generally experienced significant cost increases in sugar, cocoa, edible oils and dairy inputs, however, the Company experienced favorable declines in corn syrup.

Selling, marketing and administrative expenses were $106,316 in 2010 compared to $103,755 in 2009, an increase of $2,561 or 2.5%. Selling, marketing and administrative expenses reflect a $932 decrease in certain deferred compensation expense in 2010 compared to 2009. This decrease reflects changes in the market value of investments in trading securities and related investment income relating to compensation deferred in previous years and is not reflective of current operating results. Adjusting for the aforementioned, selling, marketing and administrative expenses increased from $100,230 in 2009 to $103,722 in 2010, an increase of $3,492 or 3.5%. As a percent of net product sales, these expenses decreased slightly from 20.2% of net product sales in 2009 to 20.1% of net product sales in 2010.

Selling, marketing and administrative expenses include $43,034 and $38,628 of freight, delivery and warehousing expenses in 2010 and 2009, respectively. These expenses increased from 7.8% of net product sales in 2009 to 8.3% of net product sales in 2010, primarily due to increases in warehousing expenses and an 11.3% increase in freight and delivery costs for trucking carriers including higher surcharges for diesel fuel.

Earnings from operations were $64,710 in 2010 compared to $60,949 in 2009, a decrease of $3,761. Earnings from operations reflect a $3,364 increase in certain deferred compensation expenses in 2010 compared to a $4,524 increase in 2009. As discussed above, these deferred compensation expenses relate to changes in deferred compensation liabilities resulting from corresponding changes in the market value of trading securities and related investment income that hedge these liabilities. Adjusting for these changes in deferred compensation, and excluding the non-recurring $14,000 non-cash impairment charge in 2009 relating to trademarks, operating earnings were $68,074 and $79,473 in 2010 and 2009, respectively, a decrease of $11,399 or 14.3%. This decrease in earnings from operations principally reflects significantly higher ingredient costs and resulting lower gross profit margins, as well as higher freight and delivery expenses as discussed above.

Management believes the comparisons presented in the preceding paragraphs after adjusting for changes in deferred compensation are more reflective of the underlying operations of the Company.

Other income (expense), net was $8,358 in 2010 compared to $2,100 in 2009, an increase of $6,258. This increase principally reflects a pre-tax impairment charge of $4,400 in 2009 to write down to market value the Company's equity method investment combined with a $3,139 increase in foreign exchange gains in 2010. The increase in foreign exchange gains consists primarily of net realized gains on foreign currency hedging. Other income (expense), net also includes gains on trading securities and related investment income of $3,364 and $4,524 in 2010 and 2009, respectively. These trading securities gains principally reflect market appreciation in the equity markets and related investment income in the respective years and were substantially offset by a like amount of expense in aggregate product cost of goods sold and selling, marketing, and administrative expenses in the respective years as discussed above. Other income (expense), net also includes the operating losses of $342 and $233 for 2010 and 2009, respectively, relating to the Company's equity method investment in two 50% owned foreign companies.

As of December 31, 2010 and 2009, the Company's long-term investments include $6,775 and $7,710 ($13,550 original cost), respectively, of Jefferson County Alabama Sewer Revenue Refunding Warrants. The Company estimated the fair value of this ARS as of December 31, 2010 and 2009 utilizing a valuation model with Level 3 inputs, as defined by guidance. During 2010 and 2009, the Company recorded $935 and $700, respectively, as a charge to accumulated other comprehensive loss.

The consolidated effective tax rate was 27.4% and 15.7% in 2010 and 2009, respectively. The increase in the effective income tax rate from the prior year reflects the release of Canadian income tax valuation allowances during 2009. Prior to fourth quarter 2009, Canadian income tax valuation allowances were recorded against Canadian deferred tax assets as a result of losses generated in 2009 and prior years. Because management determined that the Canadian net operating loss (NOL) carry-forward benefits were more-likely-than-not realizable as of December 31, 2009, the Company reversed approximately $10,700 of valuation allowances as a credit to income tax expense as of December 31, 2009.

Net earnings were $53,063 in 2010 compared to $53,157 in 2009, and earnings per share were $.90 and $.89 in 2010 and 2009, respectively, an increase of $.01 or 1%. Earnings per share benefited from the reduction in average shares outstanding resulting from Common Stock purchases in the open market by the Company. Average shares outstanding decreased from 59,425 in 2009 to 58,685 in 2010.

LIQUIDITY AND CAPITAL RESOURCES

Cash flows from operating activities were $50,390, $82,805 and $76,994 in 2011, 2010 and 2009, respectively. The $32,415 decrease in cash flows from operating activities from 2010 to 2011 primarily reflects the 2011 decrease in net earnings, increased accounts receivables and inventories, and decreases in income taxes payable and deferred.

During 2008 the Company contributed $16,050 to a VEBA trust to fund the estimated future costs of certain employee health, welfare and other benefits. The Company used the funds, as well as investment income in this VEBA trust, to pay the actual cost of such benefits during 2010, 2011 and will continue to do so through 2012. At December 31, 2011, the VEBA trust held $6,424 of aggregate cash, cash equivalents and investments; this asset value is included in prepaid expenses in the Company's current and other long-term assets.

Cash flows from investing activities reflect capital expenditures of $16,351, $12,813, and $20,831 in 2011, 2010 and 2009, respectively, including $3,025 related to the 2011 purchase of warehouse space and land planned for future use. The 2011, 2010 and 2009 capital additions include $727, $1,682 and $2,326, respectively, relating to computer systems and related implementation.

The Company had no bank borrowing or repayments in 2009, 2010, or 2011, and had no outstanding bank borrowings as of December 31, 2010 or 2011.

Financing activities include Common Stock purchases and retirements of $18,190, $22,881, and $20,723 in 2011, 2010 and 2009, respectively. Cash dividends of $18,407, $18,130, and $17,825 were paid in 2011, 2010 and 2009, respectively. The increase in cash dividends each year reflects the annual 3% stock dividend issued in each of these years less the effects of Common Stock purchases and retirements.

SIGNIFICANT ACCOUNTING POLICIES AND ESTIMATES

Preparation of the Company's financial statements involves judgments and estimates due to uncertainties affecting the application of accounting policies, and the likelihood that different amounts would be reported under different conditions or using different assumptions. The Company bases its estimates on historical experience and other assumptions, as discussed herein, that it believes are reasonable. If actual amounts are ultimately different from previous estimates, the revisions are included in the Company's results of operations for the period in which the actual amounts become known. The Company's significant accounting policies are discussed in Note 1 to the Consolidated Financial Statements.

Following is a summary and discussion of the more significant accounting policies which management believes to have a significant impact on the Company's operating results, financial position, cash flows and footnote disclosure.

Revenue recognition

Revenue, net of applicable provisions for discounts, returns, allowances and certain advertising and promotional costs, is recognized when products are delivered to customers based on a customer purchase order, and collectability is reasonably assured. The accounting for promotional costs is discussed under "Customer incentive programs, advertising and marketing" below.

Provisions for bad debts are recorded as selling, marketing and administrative expenses. Write-offs of bad debts did not exceed 0.1% of net product sales in each of 2011, 2010 and 2009, and accordingly, have not been significant to the Company's financial position or results of operations.

Intangible assets

The Company's intangible assets consist primarily of acquired trademarks and goodwill. In accordance with accounting guidance, goodwill and other indefinite-lived assets are not amortized, but are instead subjected to annual testing for impairment unless certain triggering events or circumstances are noted. The Company performs its annual impairment testing as of December 31. The Company may utilize third-party professional valuation firms to assist in the determination of valuation of certain intangibles.

The impairment test is performed by comparing the carrying value of the asset with its estimated fair value, which is calculated using estimates, including discounted projected future cash flows. If the carrying value exceeds the fair value, the second step of the process is necessary. The second step measures the difference between the carrying value and implied fair value of goodwill. These projected future cash flows are dependent on a number of factors including the execution of business plans, achievement of projected sales, including but not limited to future price increases, projected operating margins, and projected capital expenditures. Such operating results are also dependent upon future ingredient and packaging material costs, exchange rates for products manufactured or sold in foreign countries, operational efficiencies, cost savings initiatives, and competitive factors. Although the majority of the Company's trademarks relate to well established brands with a long history of consumer acceptance, projected cash flows are inherently uncertain. A change in the assumptions underlying the impairment analysis, including but not limited to a reduction in projected cash flows, the use of a different discount rate to discount future cash flows or a different royalty rate applied to the Company's trademarks, could cause impairment in the future.

Customer incentive programs, advertising and marketing

Advertising and marketing costs are recorded in the period to which such costs relate. The Company does not defer the recognition of any amounts on its consolidated balance sheet with respect to such costs. Customer incentives and other promotional costs are recorded at the time of sale based upon incentive program terms and historical utilization statistics, which are generally consistent from year to year.

The liabilities associated with these programs are reviewed quarterly and adjusted if utilization rates differ from management's original estimates. Such adjustments have not historically been material to the Company's operating results.

Split dollar officer life insurance

The Company provides split dollar life insurance benefits to certain executive officers and records an asset principally equal to the cumulative premiums paid. The Company will fully recover these premiums in future years under the terms of the plan. The Company retains a collateral assignment of the cash surrender values and policy death benefits payable to insure recovery of these premiums.

Valuation of long-lived assets

Long-lived assets, primarily property, plant and equipment are reviewed for impairment as events or changes in business circumstances occur indicating that the carrying value of the asset may not be recoverable. The estimated cash flows produced by assets or asset groups, are compared to the asset carrying value to determine whether impairment exists. Such estimates involve considerable management judgment and are based upon assumptions about expected future operating performance. As a result, actual cash flows could differ from management's estimates due to changes in business conditions, operating performance, and economic and competitive conditions.

Income taxes

Deferred income taxes are recognized for future tax effects of temporary differences between financial and income tax reporting using tax rates in effect for the years in which the differences are expected to reverse. The Company records valuation allowances in situations where the realization of deferred tax assets, including those relating to net operating tax losses, is not more-likely-than-not; and the Company adjusts and releases such valuation allowances when realization becomes more-likely-than-not as defined by accounting guidance. The Company periodically reviews assumptions and estimates of the Company's probable tax obligations and effects on its liability for uncertain tax positions, using informed judgment which may include the use of third-party consultants, advisors and legal counsel, and historical experience.

Valuation of investments

Investments, primarily municipal bonds, mutual funds and equity method investments are reviewed for impairment at each reporting period by comparing the carrying value or amortized cost to the fair market value. The Company may utilize third-party professional valuation firms as necessary to assist in the determination of the value of investments using a valuation model with Level 3 inputs as defined. In the event that an investment security's fair value is below carrying value or amortized cost, the Company will record an other-than-temporary impairment or a temporary impairment based on accounting guidance.

Other matters

In the opinion of management, other than contracts for foreign currency forwards and raw materials, including currency and commodity hedges and outstanding purchase orders for packaging, ingredients, supplies, and operational services, all entered into in the ordinary course of business, the Company does not have any significant contractual obligations or future commitments. The Company's outstanding contractual commitments as of December 31, 2011, all of which are generally normal and recurring in nature, are summarized in the chart on page 13.

RECENT ACCOUNTING PRONOUNCEMENTS

In May 2011, the Financial Accounting Standards Board (FASB) issued Accounting Standards Update (ASU) 2011-04, "Fair Value Measurement (Topic 820): Amendments to Achieve Common Fair Value Measurement and Disclosure Requirements in U.S. GAAP and International Financial Reporting Standards (IFRS)." ASU 2011-04 represents converged guidance between U.S. GAAP and IFRS resulting in common requirements for measuring fair value and for disclosing information about fair value measurements. This new guidance will be effective for fiscal years beginning after December 15, 2011 and subsequent interim periods. The Company is currently assessing the impact, if any, on the consolidated financial statements.

In June 2011, the FASB issued ASU 2011-05, "Presentation of Comprehensive Income." ASU 2011-05 requires us to present components of other comprehensive income and of net income in one continuous statement of comprehensive income or in two separate, but consecutive, statements. The option to report other comprehensive income within the statement of equity has been removed. This new presentation of comprehensive income will be effective for fiscal years beginning after December 15, 2011 and subsequent interim periods.

In September 2011, the FASB issued ASU 2011-08, "Testing Goodwill for Impairment". The revised standard is intended to simplify how entities test goodwill for impairment. Under certain circumstances, a two-step impairment test may be unnecessary. The revised standard is effective for annual and interim goodwill impairment tests performed for fiscal years beginning after December 15, 2011. The Company currently believes there will be no impact on its consolidated financial statements.

In September 2011, FASB issued ASU 2011-09, "Compensation-Retirement Benefits-Multiemployer Plans" which amends the guidance in ASC 715-80. The amendments in ASU 2011-09 provide additional disclosure requirements for entities which participate in multi-employer pension plans. The purpose of the new disclosures is to provide financial statement users with information about an employer's level of participation in and the financial health of significant plans. The new disclosures are effective for annual periods ending after December 15, 2011. There will be no impact on the Company's consolidated financial statements as the changes relate only to additional disclosures.

MARKET RISKS

The Company is exposed to market risks related to commodity prices, interest rates, investments in marketable securities, equity price and foreign exchange.

The Company's ability to forecast the direction and scope of changes to its major input costs is impacted by significant volatility in crude oil, sugar, corn, soybean and edible oils, cocoa and dairy products markets. The prices of these commodities are influenced by changes in global demand, changes in weather and crop yields, changes in governments' farm policies, including mandates for ethanol and bio-fuels, and environmental matters, including global warming, and fluctuations in the U.S. dollar relative to dollar-denominated commodities in world markets. The Company believes that its competitors face the same or similar challenges.

In order to address the impact of rising input and other costs, the Company periodically reviews each item in its product portfolio to ascertain if price increases, weight declines (indirect price increases) or other actions should be taken. These reviews include an evaluation of the risk factors relating to market place acceptance of such changes and their potential effect on future sales volumes. In addition, the estimated cost of packaging modifications associated with weight changes is evaluated. The Company also maintains ongoing cost reduction and productivity improvement programs under which cost savings initiatives are encouraged and progress monitored. The Company is not able to accurately predict the outcome of these cost savings initiatives and their effects on its future results.

Commodity future and foreign currency forward contracts

Commodity price risks relate to ingredients, primarily sugar, cocoa, chocolate, corn syrup, dextrose, soybean and edible oils, milk, whey and gum base ingredients. The Company believes its competitors face similar risks, and the industry has historically adjusted prices to compensate for adverse fluctuations in commodity costs. The Company, as well as competitors in the confectionery industry, have taken actions, including price increases and selective product weight declines (indirect price increases) to mitigate rising input costs for ingredients, energy, freight and delivery. Although management seeks to substantially recover cost increases over the long-term, there is risk that price increases and weight declines cannot be fully passed on to customers and, to the extent they are passed on, they could adversely affect customer and consumer acceptance and resulting sales volume.

The Company utilizes commodity futures contracts and commodity options contracts as well as annual supply agreements to hedge and plan for anticipated purchases of certain ingredients, including sugar, in order to mitigate commodity cost fluctuation. The Company also may purchase forward foreign exchange contracts to hedge its costs of manufacturing certain products in Canada for sale and distribution in the United States, and periodically does so for purchases of equipment or raw materials from foreign suppliers. Such commodity futures, commodity options and currency forward contracts are cash flow hedges and are effective as hedges as defined by accounting guidance. The unrealized gains and losses on such contracts are deferred as a component of accumulated other comprehensive loss and are recognized as a component of product cost of goods sold when the related inventory is sold.

The potential change in fair value of commodity and foreign currency derivative instruments held by the Company at December 31, 2011, assuming a 10% change in the underlying contract price, was $1,761. The analysis only includes commodity and foreign currency derivative instruments and, therefore, does not consider the offsetting effect of changes in the price of the underlying commodity or foreign currency. This amount is not significant compared with the net earnings and shareholders' equity of the Company.

Interest rates

Interest rate risks primarily relate to the Company's investments in tax exempt marketable securities, including ARS, with maturities or auction dates of generally up to three years.

The majority of the Company's investments, which are classified as available for sale, have historically been held until they mature, which limits the Company's exposure to interest rate fluctuations. The accompanying chart summarizes the maturities of the Company's investments in debt securities at December 31, 2011.

Less than 1 year	$10,854
1–2 years	17,753
2–3 years	29,133
Over 3 years	7,504
Total	$65,244

The Company's outstanding debt at December 31, 2011 and 2010 was $7,500 in an industrial revenue bond in which interest rates reset each week based on the current market rate. Therefore, the Company does not believe that it has significant interest rate risk with respect to its interest bearing debt.

Investment in marketable securities

As stated above, the Company invests primarily in tax exempt marketable securities, including ARS, with maturities or auction dates generally up to three years. The Company utilizes professional money managers and maintains investment policy guidelines which emphasize quality and liquidity in order to minimize the potential loss exposures that could result in the event of a default or other adverse event, including failed auctions.

However, given events in the municipal bond and ARS markets, including failed auctions, the Company continues to monitor these investments and markets, as well as its investment policies. Nonetheless, the financial markets have been experiencing unprecedented events in recent years, and future outcomes are less predictable than in the past.

Equity price

Equity price risk relates to the Company's investments in mutual funds which are principally used to fund and hedge the Company's deferred compensation liabilities. At December 31, 2011, the Company has investments in mutual funds, classified as trading securities, of $41,768. Any change in the fair value of these trading securities is completely offset by a corresponding change in the respective hedged deferred compensation liability.

Foreign currency

Foreign currency risk principally relates to the Company's foreign operations in Canada and Mexico, as well as periodic purchase commitments of machinery and equipment from foreign sources.

Certain of the Company's Canadian manufacturing costs, including local payroll and plant operations, and a portion of its packaging and ingredients are sourced in Canadian dollars. The Company may purchase Canadian forward contracts to receive Canadian dollars at a specified date in the future and uses its Canadian dollar collections on Canadian sales as a partial hedge of its overall Canadian manufacturing obligations sourced in Canadian dollars. The Company also periodically purchases and holds Canadian dollars to facilitate the risk management of these currency changes.

From time to time, the Company may use foreign exchange forward contracts and derivative instruments to mitigate its exposure to foreign exchange risks, as well as those related to firm commitments to purchase equipment from foreign vendors. As of December 31, 2011, the Company held foreign exchange forward contracts with a fair value of $205.

RISK FACTORS

The Company's operations and financial results are subject to a number of risks and uncertainties that could adversely affect the Company's operating results and financial condition. Significant risk factors, without limitations that could impact the Company, are the following: (i) significant competitive activity, including advertising, promotional and price competition, and changes in consumer demand for the Company's products; (ii) fluctuations in the cost and availability of commodities and ingredients, and packaging materials, and the ability to recover cost increases through product sales price increases; (iii) inherent risks in the marketplace, including uncertainties about trade and consumer acceptance of price increases and seasonal events such as Halloween; (iv) the effect of acquisitions on the Company's results of operations and financial condition; (v) the effect of changes in foreign currencies on the Company's foreign subsidiaries operating results, and the effect of the fluctuation of the Canadian dollar on products manufactured in Canada and marketed and sold in the United States in U.S. dollars; (vi) the Company's reliance on third party vendors for various goods and services, including commodities used for ingredients that are primarily grown or sourced from foreign locations; (vii) the Company's ability to successfully implement new production processes and lines, and new computer software systems; (viii) the effect of changes in assumptions, including discount rates, sales growth and profit margins and the capability to pass along higher ingredient and other input costs through price increases, relating to the Company's impairment testing and analysis of its goodwill and trademarks; (ix) changes in the confectionery marketplace including actions taken by major retailers and customers; (x) customer, consumer and competitor response to marketing programs and price and product weight adjustments, and new products; (xi) dependence on significant customers, including the volume and timing of their purchases, and availability of shelf space; (xii) increases in energy costs, including freight and delivery, that cannot be passed along to customers through increased prices due to competitive reasons; (xiii) any significant labor stoppages, strikes or production interruptions; (xiv) changes in governmental laws and regulations including taxes and tariffs; (xv) the adverse effects should the Company either voluntarily or involuntarily recall its product(s) from the marketplace; (xvi) the risk that the market value of Company's investments could decline including being classified as "other-than-temporary" as defined; (xvii) the Company's dependence on its enterprise resource planning computer system to manage its supply chain and customer deliveries, and the risk that the Company's information technology systems fail to perform adequately or the Company is unable to protect such information technology systems against data corruption, cyber-based attacks or network security breaches; and (xviii) the potential effects of current and future macroeconomic conditions and geopolitical events.

Forward-looking statements

This discussion and certain other sections contain forward-looking statements that are based largely on the Company's current expectations and are made pursuant to the safe harbor provision of the Private Securities Litigation Reform Act of 1995. Forward-looking statements can be identified by the use of words such as "anticipated," "believe," "expect," "intend," "estimate," "project," and other words of similar meaning in connection with a discussion of future operating or financial performance and are subject to certain factors, risks, trends and uncertainties that could cause actual results and achievements to differ materially from those expressed in the forward-looking statements. Such factors, risks, trends and uncertainties which in some instances are beyond the Company's control, include the overall competitive environment in the Company's industry, changes in assumptions and judgments discussed above under the heading "Significant Accounting Policies and Estimates", and factors identified and referred to above under the heading "Risk Factors."

The risk factors identified and referred to above are believed to be significant factors, but not necessarily all of the significant factors that could cause actual results to differ from those expressed in any forward-looking statement. Readers are cautioned not to place undue reliance on such forward-looking statements, which are made only as of the date of this report. The Company undertakes no obligation to update such forward-looking statements.

Open Contractual Commitments as of December 31, 2011

Payable in	Total	Less than 1 Year	1 to 3 Years	3 to 5 Years	More than 5 Years
Commodity hedges	$ 4,557	$ 4,538	$ 19	$ —	$ —
Foreign currency hedges	13,044	13,044	—	—	—
Purchase obligations	10,373	10,373	—	—	—
Interest bearing debt	7,500	—	—	—	7,500
Operating leases	3,926	1,047	1,836	1,043	—
Total	$39,400	$29,002	$1,855	$1,043	$7,500

Note: Commodity hedges and foreign currency hedges reflect the amounts at which the Company will settle the related contracts. The above amounts exclude deferred income tax liabilities of $43,521, liabilities for uncertain tax positions of $8,345, postretirement health care and life insurance benefits of $26,108 and deferred compensation and other liabilities of $48,092 because the timing of payments relating to these items cannot be reasonably determined.

Financial Statements and Accompanying Notes

The standard set of financial statements consists of (1) a comparative income statement for three years, (2) a comparative balance sheet for two years, (3) a comparative statement of cash flows for three years, (4) a statement of retained earnings (or stockholders' equity) for three years, and (5) a set of accompanying notes that are considered an integral part of the financial statements. The auditor's report, unless stated otherwise, covers the financial statements and the accompanying notes. The financial statements and accompanying notes plus some supplementary data and analyses for Tootsie Roll Industries follow.

CONSOLIDATED STATEMENTS OF

Earnings, Comprehensive Earnings and Retained Earnings

TOOTSIE ROLL INDUSTRIES, INC. AND SUBSIDIARIES (in thousands except per share data)

	For the year ended December 31,		
	2011	**2010**	**2009**
Net product sales	$528,369	$517,149	$495,592
Rental and royalty revenue	4,136	4,299	3,739
Total revenue	532,505	521,448	499,331
Product cost of goods sold	365,225	349,334	319,775
Rental and royalty cost	1,038	1,088	852
Total costs	366,263	350,422	320,627
Product gross margin	163,144	167,815	175,817
Rental and royalty gross margin	3,098	3,211	2,887
Total gross margin	166,242	171,026	178,704
Selling, marketing and administrative expenses	108,276	106,316	103,755
Impairment charges	—	—	14,000
Earnings from operations	57,966	64,710	60,949
Other income (expense), net	2,946	8,358	2,100
Earnings before income taxes	60,912	73,068	63,049
Provision for income taxes	16,974	20,005	9,892
Net earnings	$ 43,938	$ 53,063	$ 53,157
Net earnings	$ 43,938	$ 53,063	$ 53,157
Other comprehensive earnings (loss)	(8,740)	1,183	2,845
Comprehensive earnings	$ 35,198	$ 54,246	$ 56,002
Retained earnings at beginning of year	$135,866	$147,687	$144,949
Net earnings	43,938	53,063	53,157
Cash dividends	(18,360)	(18,078)	(17,790)
Stock dividends	(47,175)	(46,806)	(32,629)
Retained earnings at end of year	$114,269	$135,866	$147,687
Earnings per share	$ 0.76	$ 0.90	$ 0.89
Average Common and Class B Common shares outstanding	57,892	58,685	59,425

(The accompanying notes are an integral part of these statements.)

CONSOLIDATED STATEMENTS OF

Financial Position

TOOTSIE ROLL INDUSTRIES, INC. AND SUBSIDIARIES (in thousands except per share data)

Assets

	December 31, 2011	December 31, 2010
CURRENT ASSETS:		
Cash and cash equivalents	$ 78,612	$115,976
Investments	10,895	7,996
Accounts receivable trade, less allowances of $1,731 and $1,531	41,895	37,394
Other receivables	3,391	9,961
Inventories:		
Finished goods and work-in-process	42,676	35,416
Raw materials and supplies	29,084	21,236
Prepaid expenses	5,070	6,499
Deferred income taxes	578	689
Total current assets	212,201	235,167
PROPERTY, PLANT AND EQUIPMENT, at cost:		
Land	21,939	21,619
Buildings	107,567	102,934
Machinery and equipment	322,993	307,178
Construction in progress	2,598	9,243
	455,097	440,974
Less—Accumulated depreciation	242,935	225,482
Net property, plant and equipment	212,162	215,492
OTHER ASSETS:		
Goodwill	73,237	73,237
Trademarks	175,024	175,024
Investments	96,161	64,461
Split dollar officer life insurance	74,209	74,441
Prepaid expenses	3,212	6,680
Equity method investment	3,935	4,254
Deferred income taxes	7,715	9,203
Total other assets	433,493	407,300
Total assets	$857,856	$857,959

Liabilities and Shareholders' Equity

	December 31, 2011	December 31, 2010
CURRENT LIABILITIES:		
Accounts payable	$ 10,683	$ 9,791
Dividends payable	4,603	4,529
Accrued liabilities	43,069	44,185
Total current liabilities	58,355	58,505
NONCURRENT LIABILITES:		
Deferred income taxes	43,521	47,865
Postretirement health care and life insurance benefits	26,108	20,689
Industrial development bonds	7,500	7,500
Liability for uncertain tax positions	8,345	9,835
Deferred compensation and other liabilities	48,092	46,157
Total noncurrent liabilities	133,566	132,046
SHAREHOLDERS' EQUITY		
Common stock, $.69-4/9 par value— 120,000 shares authorized— 36,479 and 36,057, respectively, issued	25,333	25,040
Class B common stock, $.69-4/9 par value—40,000 shares authorized— 21,025 and 20,466, respectively, issued	14,601	14,212
Capital in excess of par value	533,677	505,495
Retained earnings, per accompanying statement	114,269	135,866
Accumulated other comprehensive loss	(19,953)	(11,213)
Treasury stock (at cost)—71 shares and 69 shares, respectively	(1,992)	(1,992)
Total shareholders' equity	665,935	667,408
Total liabilities and shareholders' equity	$857,856	$857,959

(The accompanying notes are an integral part of these statements.)

CONSOLIDATED STATEMENTS OF

Cash Flows

TOOTSIE ROLL INDUSTRIES, INC. AND SUBSIDIARIES (in thousands)

	For the year ended December 31,		
	2011	2010	2009
CASH FLOWS FROM OPERATING ACTIVITIES:			
Net earnings	$ 43,938	$ 53,063	$53,157
Adjustments to reconcile net earnings to net cash provided by operating activities:			
Depreciation	19,229	18,279	17,862
Impairment charges	—	—	14,000
Impairment of equity method investment	—	—	4,400
Loss from equity method investment	194	342	233
Amortization of marketable security premiums	1,267	522	320
Changes in operating assets and liabilities:			
Accounts receivable	(5,448)	717	(5,899)
Other receivables	3,963	(2,373)	(2,088)
Inventories	(15,631)	(1,447)	455
Prepaid expenses and other assets	5,106	4,936	5,203
Accounts payable and accrued liabilities	84	2,180	(2,755)
Income taxes payable and deferred	(5,772)	2,322	(12,543)
Postretirement health care and life insurance benefits	2,022	1,429	1,384
Deferred compensation and other liabilities	3,146	2,525	2,960
Other	(708)	310	305
Net cash provided by operating activities	50,390	82,805	76,994
CASH FLOWS FROM INVESTING ACTIVITIES:			
Capital expenditures	(16,351)	(12,813)	(20,831)
Net purchases of trading securities	(3,234)	(2,902)	(1,713)
Purchase of available for sale securities	(39,252)	(9,301)	(11,331)
Sale and maturity of available for sale securities	7,680	8,208	17,511
Net cash used in investing activities	(51,157)	(16,808)	(16,364)
CASH FLOWS FROM FINANCING ACTIVITIES:			
Shares purchased and retired	(18,190)	(22,881)	(20,723)
Dividends paid in cash	(18,407)	(18,130)	(17,825)
Net cash used in financing activities	(36,597)	(41,011)	(38,548)
Increase (decrease) in cash and cash equivalents	(37,364)	24,986	22,082
Cash and cash equivalents at beginning of year	115,976	90,990	68,908
Cash and cash equivalents at end of year	$ 78,612	$115,976	$90,990
Supplemental cash flow information:			
Income taxes paid	$ 16,906	$ 20,586	$22,364
Interest paid	$ 38	$ 49	$ 182
Stock dividend issued	$ 47,053	$ 46,683	$32,538

(The accompanying notes are an integral part of these statements.)

Notes to Consolidated Financial Statements ($ in thousands except per share data)

TOOTSIE ROLL INDUSTRIES, INC. AND SUBSIDIARIES

NOTE 1—SIGNIFICANT ACCOUNTING POLICIES:

Basis of consolidation:

The consolidated financial statements include the accounts of Tootsie Roll Industries, Inc. and its wholly-owned subsidiaries (the Company), which are primarily engaged in the manufacture and sales of candy products. All significant intercompany transactions have been eliminated.

The preparation of financial statements in conformity with generally accepted accounting principles in the United States of America requires management to make estimates and assumptions that affect the reported amounts of assets and liabilities and disclosure of contingent assets and liabilities at the date of the financial statements and the reported amounts of revenues and expenses during the reporting period. Actual results could differ from those estimates.

Revenue recognition:

Products are sold to customers based on accepted purchase orders which include quantity, sales price and other relevant terms of sale. Revenue, net of applicable provisions for discounts, returns, allowances and certain advertising and promotional costs, is recognized when products are delivered to customers and collectability is reasonably assured. Shipping and handling costs of $45,850, $43,034, and $38,628 in 2011, 2010 and 2009, respectively, are included in selling, marketing and administrative expenses. Accounts receivable are unsecured. Revenues from a major customer aggregated approximately 23.3%, 21.4% and 22.9% of net product sales during the years ended December 31, 2011, 2010 and 2009, respectively.

Cash and cash equivalents:

The Company considers temporary cash investments with an original maturity of three months or less to be cash equivalents.

Investments:

Investments consist of various marketable securities with maturities of generally up to three years. The Company classifies debt and equity securities as either available for sale or trading. Available for sale securities are not actively traded by the Company and are carried at fair value. The Company follows current fair value measurement guidance and unrealized gains and losses on these securities are excluded from earnings and are reported as a separate component of shareholders' equity, net of applicable taxes, until realized or other than temporarily impaired. Trading securities relate to deferred compensation arrangements and are carried at fair value with gains or losses included in other income (expense), net. The Company invests in trading securities to economically hedge changes in its deferred compensation liabilities.

The Company regularly reviews its investments to determine whether a decline in fair value below the cost basis is other than temporary. If the decline in fair value is judged to be other than temporary, the cost basis of the security is written down to fair value and the amount of the write-down is included in other income (expense), net. Further information regarding the fair value of the Company's investments is included in Note 10 to the Consolidated Financial Statements.

Derivative instruments and hedging activities:

Authoritative guidance requires qualitative disclosures about objectives and strategies for using derivatives, quantitative disclosures about fair value amounts of derivative instruments and related gains and losses, and disclosures about credit-risk-related contingent features in derivative agreements.

From time to time, the Company enters into commodity futures, commodity options contracts and foreign currency forward contracts. Commodity futures and options are intended and are effective as hedges of market price risks associated with the anticipated purchase of certain raw materials (primarily sugar). Foreign currency forward contracts are intended and are effective as hedges of the Company's exposure to the variability of cash flows, primarily related to the foreign exchange rate changes of products manufactured in Canada and sold in the United States, and periodic equipment purchases from foreign suppliers denominated in a foreign currency. The Company does not engage in trading or other speculative use of derivative instruments. Further information regarding derivative instruments and hedging activities is included in Note 11 to the Consolidated Financial Statements.

Inventories:

Inventories are stated at cost, not to exceed market. The cost of substantially all of the Company's inventories ($67,339 and $52,863 at December 31, 2011 and 2010, respectively) has been determined by the last-in, first-out (LIFO) method. The excess of current cost over LIFO cost of inventories approximates $24,043 and $19,379 at December 31, 2011 and 2010, respectively. The cost of certain foreign inventories ($4,421 and $3,789 at December 31, 2011 and 2010, respectively) has been determined by the first-in, first-out (FIFO) method. Rebates, discounts and other cash consideration received from vendors related to inventory purchases is reflected as a reduction in the cost of the related inventory item, and is therefore reflected in cost of sales when the related inventory item is sold.

Property, plant and equipment:

Depreciation is computed for financial reporting purposes by use of the straight-line method based on useful lives of 20 to 35 years for buildings and 5 to 20 years for machinery and equipment. Depreciation expense was $19,229, $18,279 and $17,862 in 2011, 2010 and 2009, respectively.

Carrying value of long-lived assets:

The Company reviews long-lived assets to determine if there are events or circumstances indicating that the amount of the asset reflected in the Company's balance sheet may not be recoverable. When such indicators are present, the Company compares the carrying value of the long-lived asset, or asset group, to the future undiscounted cash flows of the underlying assets to determine if an impairment exists. If applicable, an impairment charge would be recorded to write down the carrying value to its fair value. The determination of fair value involves the use of estimates of future cash flows that involve considerable management judgment and are based upon assumptions about expected future operating performance. The actual cash flows could differ from management's estimates due to changes in business conditions, operating performance, and economic conditions. No impairment charges of long-lived assets were recorded by the Company during 2011, 2010 and 2009.

Postretirement health care and life insurance benefits:

The Company provides certain postretirement health care and life insurance benefits. The cost of these postretirement benefits is accrued during employees' working careers. The Company also provides split dollar life benefits to certain executive officers. The Company records an asset equal to the cumulative insurance premiums paid that will be recovered upon the death of covered employees or earlier under the terms of the plan. No premiums were paid in 2011, 2010 and 2009.

Goodwill and intangible assets:

In accordance with authoritative guidance, goodwill and intangible assets with indefinite lives are not amortized, but rather tested for impairment at least annually unless certain interim triggering events or circumstances require more frequent testing. All trademarks have been assessed by management to have indefinite lives because they are expected to generate cash flows indefinitely. The Company has completed its annual impairment testing of its goodwill and trademarks at December 31 of each of the years presented. As of December 31, 2009, management ascertained that certain trademarks were impaired, and recorded a pre-tax charge of $14,000. No impairments of intangibles were recorded in 2011 and 2010.

This determination is made by comparing the carrying value of the asset with its estimated fair value, which is calculated using estimates including discounted projected future cash flows. If the carrying value of goodwill exceeds the fair value, a second step would measure the carrying value and implied fair value of goodwill. Management believes that all assumptions used for the impairment tests are consistent with those utilized by market participants performing similar valuations.

Income taxes:

Deferred income taxes are recorded and recognized for future tax effects of temporary differences between financial and income tax reporting. The Company records valuation allowances in situations where the realization of deferred tax assets is not more-likely-than-not. Federal income taxes are provided on the portion of income of foreign subsidiaries that is expected to be remitted to the U.S. and become taxable, but not on the portion that is considered to be permanently invested in the foreign subsidiary.

Foreign currency translation:

The U.S. dollar is used as the functional currency where a substantial portion of the subsidiary's business is indexed to the U.S. dollar or where its manufactured products are principally sold in the U.S. All other foreign subsidiaries use the local currency as their functional currency. Where the U.S. dollar is used as the functional currency, foreign currency remeasurements are recorded as a charge or credit to other income (expense), net in the statement of earnings. Where the foreign local currency is used as the functional currency, translation adjustments are recorded as a separate component of accumulated other comprehensive (loss).

Equity method investment:

The Company's 50% interest in two foreign companies is accounted for using the equity method. The Company records an increase in its investment to the extent of its share of earnings, and reduces its investment to the extent of losses and dividends received. No dividends were paid in 2011, 2010 and 2009.

As of December 31, 2009, management determined that the fair value of the asset was less than the carrying value. As a result, the Company recorded a pre-tax impairment charge of $4,400 in the fourth quarter 2009, resulting in an adjusted carrying value of $4,961 as of December 31, 2009. The fair value was primarily assessed using the present value of estimated future cash flows. No impairments were recorded in 2011 and 2010.

Comprehensive earnings:

Comprehensive earnings includes net earnings, foreign currency translation adjustments and unrealized gains/losses on commodity and/or foreign currency hedging contracts, available for sale securities and certain postretirement benefit obligations.

Earnings per share:

A dual presentation of basic and diluted earnings per share is not required due to the lack of potentially dilutive securities under the Company's simple capital structure. Therefore, all earnings per share amounts represent basic earnings per share.

The Class B Common Stock has essentially the same rights as Common Stock, except that each share of Class B Common Stock has ten votes per share (compared to one vote per share of Common Stock), is not traded on any exchange, is restricted as to transfer and is convertible on a share-for-share basis, at any time and at no cost to the holders, into shares of Common Stock which are traded on the New York Stock Exchange.

Use of estimates:

The preparation of consolidated financial statements in conformity with accounting principles generally accepted in the U.S. requires management to make estimates and assumptions that affect the amounts reported. Estimates are used when accounting for sales discounts, allowances and incentives, product liabilities, assets recorded at fair value, income taxes, depreciation, amortization, employee benefits, contingencies and intangible asset and liability valuations. For instance, in determining the annual post-employment benefit costs, the Company estimates the cost of future health care benefits. Actual results may or may not differ from those estimates.

Retrospective application of change in accounting principle:

During the fourth quarter of fiscal 2011, the Company changed the method used to compute the LIFO value of its domestic inventories. The change was largely driven by the fact that the Company has made changes in the business model over the last several years to achieve efficiencies in manufacturing, distribution and marketing processes and therefore combined multiple LIFO pools into a single LIFO pool to better reflect these changes. The Company has applied this change retrospectively, adjusting all prior periods presented. The cumulative effect of the change on retained earnings as of January 1, 2009, was a reduction of $174, with offsets to inventories and deferred taxes. For 2010, inventories and deferred income taxes reflect decreases of $2,424 and $878, respectively. For 2010 and 2009, product cost of goods sold increased $1,021 and $1,130, respectively; provision for income taxes decreased $370 and $409, respectively.

Recent accounting pronouncements:

In May 2011, the Financial Accounting Standards Board (FASB) issued Accounting Standards Update (ASU) 2011-04, "Fair Value Measurement (Topic 820): Amendments to Achieve Common Fair Value Measurement and Disclosure Requirements in U.S. GAAP and International Financial Reporting Standards (IFRS)." ASU 2011-04 represents converged guidance between U.S. GAAP and IFRS resulting in common requirements for measuring fair value and for disclosing information about fair value measurements. This new guidance will be effective for fiscal years beginning after December 15, 2011 and subsequent interim periods. The Company is currently assessing the impact, if any, on the consolidated financial statements.

In June 2011, the FASB issued ASU 2011-05, "Presentation of Comprehensive Income." ASU 2011-05 requires the Company to present components of other comprehensive income and of net income in one continuous statement of comprehensive income, or in two separate, but consecutive statements. The option to report other comprehensive income within the statement of equity has been removed. This new presentation of comprehensive income will be effective for fiscal years beginning after December 15, 2011 and subsequent interim periods.

In September 2011, the FASB issued ASU 2011-08, "Testing Goodwill for Impairment". The revised standard is intended to simplify how entities test goodwill for impairment. Under certain circumstances, a two-step impairment test may be unnecessary. The revised standard is effective for annual and interim goodwill impairment tests performed for fiscal years beginning after December 15, 2011. The Company currently believes there will be no impact on its consolidated financial statements.

In September 2011, FASB issued ASU 2011-09, "Compensation-Retirement Benefits-Multiemployer Plans" which amends the guidance in ASC 715-80. The amendments in ASU 2011-09 provide additional disclosure requirements for entities which participate in multi-employer pension plans. The purpose of the new disclosures is to provide financial statement users with information about an employer's level of participation in and the financial health of significant plans. The new disclosures are effective for annual periods ending after December 15, 2011. There will be no impact on the Company's consolidated financial statements as the changes relate only to additional disclosures.

NOTE 2—ACCRUED LIABILITIES:

Accrued liabilities are comprised of the following:

	December 31,	
	2011	**2010**
Compensation	$ 8,817	$ 9,750
Other employee benefits	2,004	2,030
Taxes, other than income	1,954	1,966
Advertising and promotions	20,568	20,775
Other	9,726	9,664
	$43,069	$44,185

NOTE 3—INDUSTRIAL DEVELOPMENT BONDS:

Industrial development bonds are due in 2027. The average floating interest rate was 0.3% and 0.4% in 2011 and 2010, respectively. See Note 10 to the Consolidated Financial Statements for fair value disclosures.

NOTE 4—INCOME TAXES:
The domestic and foreign components of pretax income are as follows:

	2011	**2010**	**2009**
Domestic	$56,651	$59,308	$68,649
Foreign	4,261	13,760	(5,600)
	$60,912	$73,068	$63,049

The provision for income taxes is comprised of the following:

	2011	**2010**	**2009**
Current:			
Federal	$15,568	$10,251	$21,836
Foreign	559	806	500
State	863	1,455	1,665
	16,990	12,512	24,001
Deferred:			
Federal	(1,230)	5,622	(432)
Foreign	1,221	2,518	(12,987)
State	(7)	(647)	(690)
	(16)	7,493	(14,109)
	$16,974	$20,005	$ 9,892

Significant components of the Company's net deferred tax liability at year end were as follows:

	December 31,	
	2011	**2010**
Deferred tax assets:		
Accrued customer promotions	$ 1,920	$ 1,634
Deferred compensation	15,593	11,602
Postretirement benefits	9,139	6,596
Other accrued expenses	6,347	5,475
Foreign subsidiary tax loss carry forward	16,406	16,582
Tax credit carry forward	841	978
Realized capital losses	1,349	—
Unrealized capital loss	6,401	6,566
	57,996	49,433
Valuation reserve	(2,190)	(686)
Total deferred tax assets	$55,806	$48,747
Deferred tax liabilities:		
Depreciation	$35,103	$32,376
Deductible goodwill and trademarks	38,635	35,790
Accrued export company commissions	4,649	4,532
Employee benefit plans	2,248	3,506
Inventory reserves	1,733	1,871
Prepaid insurance	289	377
Accounts receivable	733	624
Deferred gain on sale of real estate	7,644	7,644
Total deferred tax liabilities	$91,034	$86,720
Net deferred tax liability	$35,228	$37,973

At December 31, 2011, the Company recognized $3,854 of benefits related to capital loss carry forwards. The carry forward losses will begin to expire in 2013. A valuation allowance has been established for the carry forward losses to reduce the future income tax benefits to amounts expected to be realized.

At December 31, 2011 the Company recognized $841 of benefits related to foreign subsidiary tax credit carry forwards. The carry forward credits expire in 2017. A valuation allowance has been established for the carry forward losses to reduce the future income tax benefits to amounts expected to be realized.

At December 31, 2011, the tax benefits of foreign subsidiary tax loss carry forwards expiring by year are as follows: $697 in 2014, $2,672 in 2015, $366 in 2026, $640 in 2027, $6,578 in 2028, $4,681 in 2029 and $772 in 2031.

Certain out of period items have been included in the 2011 provision that are immaterial individually and in the aggregate. The effective income tax rate differs from the statutory rate as follows:

	2011	2010	2009
U.S. statutory rate	35.0%	35.0%	35.0%
State income taxes, net	1.2	1.1	1.7
Exempt municipal bond interest	(0.5)	(0.4)	(0.7)
Foreign tax rates	(0.4)	(2.0)	(4.9)
Release of prior period valuation allowances	—	—	(13.3)
Qualified domestic production activities deduction	(2.5)	(2.6)	(2.0)
Tax credits receivable	(0.4)	(0.2)	(0.4)
Adjustment of deferred tax balances	(1.7)	—	—
Reserve for uncertain tax benefits	(0.6)	(2.3)	1.3
Other, net	(2.2)	(1.2)	(1.0)
Effective income tax rate	27.9%	27.4%	15.7%

In connection with the acquisition in 2004 of Concord Confections, a Canadian subsidiary, the Company established an inter-company financing structure which included a loan from the U.S. parent to the Canadian subsidiary. By December of 2006, significant operating losses had accumulated in Canada and management determined that the realization of the net operating loss carry forward benefits was not more-likely-than-not, and provided a full tax valuation allowance. Consistent with relevant accounting guidance, these benefits continued to be reserved through 2008 and through the third quarter of 2009.

In December of 2008, a new U.S./Canada income tax treaty (Treaty) was ratified which effectively denies certain inter-company interest benefits to the U.S. shareholder of a Canadian company. Accordingly, in December of 2009, the Company decided to recapitalize its Canadian operations effective January 1, 2010. During the fourth quarter of 2009, the Company considered all of the evidence and relevant accounting guidance related to this recapitalization and based on reasonable assumptions, the Company concluded that it was more-likely-than-not that it would realize substantially all of the deferred tax assets related to the Canadian net operating loss carry forward benefits because it is expected that sufficient levels of income will be generated in the foreseeable future. As a result, the Company released $8.4 million of prior period valuation allowances and $2.3 million of allowances that were provided through the first nine months of 2009.

The Treaty also introduced a phase out of the withholding tax on payments from Canada to the U.S. allowing the Company to qualify for a zero percent withholding rate in 2010 if certain requirements of the Treaty were met. On January 4, 2010, the Canadian subsidiary repaid accrued interest to its U.S. parent in a manner consistent with these requirements. As a result, $1.5 million of withholding taxes accrued for 2007 and 2008 and through the third quarter of 2009 were released in the fourth quarter of 2009.

The Company has not provided for U.S. federal or foreign withholding taxes on $6,410 and $4,787 of foreign subsidiaries' undistributed earnings as of December 31, 2011 and December 31, 2010, respectively, because such earnings are considered to be permanently reinvested. It is not practicable to determine the amount of income taxes that would be payable upon remittance of the undistributed earnings.

The Company recognizes interest and penalties related to unrecognized tax benefits in the provision for income taxes on the Consolidated Statements of Earnings.

At December 31, 2011 and 2010, the Company had unrecognized tax benefits of $6,804 and $8,138, respectively. Included in this balance is $4,199 and $4,949, respectively, of unrecognized tax benefits that, if recognized, would favorably affect the annual effective income tax rate. As of December 31, 2011 and 2010, $1,541 and $1,697, respectively, of interest and penalties were included in the liability for uncertain tax positions.

A reconciliation of the beginning and ending balances of the total amounts of unrecognized tax benefits is as follows:

	2011	2010	2009
Unrecognized tax benefits at January 1	$8,138	$14,370	$13,069
Increases in tax positions for the current year	320	632	2,661
Reductions in tax positions for lapse of statute of limitations	(668)	(1,122)	(514)
Reductions in tax positions for withdrawal of positions previously taken	—	(5,256)	—
Reductions in tax positions for effective settlements	(986)	(486)	(846)
Unrecognized tax benefits at December 31	$6,804	$ 8,138	$14,370

The Company is subject to taxation in the U.S. and various state and foreign jurisdictions. The Company remains subject to examination by U.S. federal and state and foreign tax authorities for the years 2008 through 2010. With few exceptions, the Company is no longer subject to examinations by tax authorities for the year 2007 and prior.

The Company is currently subject to a U.S. federal examination for tax year 2009. The field work has not yet concluded and the Company is unable to determine the outcome at this time. The Company's Canadian subsidiary is currently subject to examination by the Canada Revenue Agency for tax years 2005 and 2006. The Company is unable to determine the outcome of the examination at this time. In addition, the Company is currently subject to various state tax examinations. One of the state examinations has been effectively settled and the corresponding liability for unrecognized tax benefits has been reduced. Although the Company is unable to determine the ultimate outcome of the ongoing examinations, the Company believes that its liability for uncertain tax positions relating to these jurisdictions for such years is adequate.

Beginning in 2008, statutory income tax rates in Canada will be reduced five percentage points with the final rate reduction coming in 2014. Accordingly in 2009, the Company's Canadian subsidiary has revalued its deferred tax assets and liabilities based on the rate in effect for the year the differences are expected to reverse.

NOTE 5—SHARE CAPITAL AND CAPITAL IN EXCESS OF PAR VALUE:

	Common Stock		Class B Common Stock		Treasury Stock		Capital in Excess of Par Value
	Shares (000's)	Amount	Shares (000's)	Amount	Shares (000's)	Amount	
Balance at January 1, 2009	35,658	$24,762	19,357	$13,442	(65)	$(1,992)	$470,927
Issuance of 3% stock dividend	1,064	739	580	403	(2)	—	31,396
Conversion of Class B common shares to common shares	18	12	(18)	(12)	—	—	—
Purchase and retirement of common shares	(938)	(651)	—	—	—	—	(20,073)
Balance at December 31, 2009	35,802	24,862	19,919	13,833	(67)	(1,992)	482,250
Issuance of 3% stock dividend	1,070	743	597	414	(2)	—	45,526
Conversion of Class B common shares to common shares	50	35	(50)	(35)	—	—	—
Purchase and retirement of common shares	(865)	(600)	—	—	—	—	(22,281)
Balance at December 31, 2010	36,057	25,040	20,466	14,212	(69)	(1,992)	505,495
Issuance of 3% stock dividend	1,077	748	612	426	(2)	—	45,880
Conversion of Class B common shares to common shares	53	37	(53)	(37)	—	—	—
Purchase and retirement of common shares	(708)	(492)	—	—	—	—	(17,698)
Balance at December 31, 2011	36,479	$25,333	21,025	$14,601	(71)	$(1,992)	$533,677

Average shares outstanding and all per share amounts included in the financial statements and notes thereto have been adjusted retroactively to reflect annual three percent stock dividends.

While the Company does not have a formal or publicly announced Company Common Stock purchase program, the Company's board of directors periodically authorizes a dollar amount for such share purchases.

Based upon this policy, shares were purchased and retired as follows:

Year	Total Number of Shares Purchased (000's)	Average Price Paid Per Share
2011	708	$25.64
2010	865	$26.41
2009	938	$22.05

NOTE 6—OTHER INCOME (EXPENSE), NET:

Other income (expense), net is comprised of the following:

	2011	2010	2009
Interest and dividend income	$1,087	$ 879	$1,439
Gains (losses) on trading securities relating to deferred compensation plans	29	3,364	4,524
Interest expense	(121)	(142)	(243)
Impairment of equity method investment	—	—	(4,400)
Equity method investment loss	(194)	(342)	(233)
Foreign exchange gains (losses)	2,098	4,090	951
Capital gains (losses)	(277)	(28)	(38)
Miscellaneous, net	274	537	100
	$2,946	$8,358	$2,100

As of December 31, 2009, management determined that the carrying value of an equity method investment was impaired as a result of accumulated losses from operations and review of future expectations. The Company recorded a pre-tax impairment charge of $4,400 resulting in an adjusted carrying value of $4,961 as of December 31, 2009. The fair value was primarily assessed using the present value of estimated future cash flows.

NOTE 7—EMPLOYEE BENEFIT PLANS:

Pension plans:

The Company sponsors defined contribution pension plans covering certain non-union employees with over one year of credited service. The Company's policy is to fund pension costs accrued based on compensation levels. Total pension expense for 2011, 2010 and 2009 approximated $4,011, $4,196 and $4,178, respectively. The Company also maintains certain profit sharing and retirement savings-investment plans. Company contributions in 2011, 2010 and 2009 to these plans were $1,024, $1,043 and $1,011, respectively.

The Company also contributes to multi-employer defined benefit pension plan for certain of its union employees under a collective bargaining agreement which expires on September 30, 2012, as follows:

Plan name: Bakery and Confectionery Union and Industry International Pension Fund

Employer Identification Number and plan number: 52-6118572, plan number 001

Funded Status as of the most recent year available: 86.51% funded as of January 1, 2010

The Company's contributions to such plan: $2,046, $1,923 and $1,633 in 2011, 2010 and 2009, respectively

Plan status: Not in reorganization and not insolvent as of December 31, 2010

Although the Company has been advised that the plan is currently in an underfunded status, the relative position of each employer associated with the multi-employer plan with respect to the actuarial present value of benefits and net plan assets is not determinable by the Company. The Company's annual contributions do not exceed 5% of total contributions to the Plan.

Deferred compensation:

The Company sponsors three deferred compensation plans for selected executives and other employees: (i) the Excess Benefit Plan, which restores retirement benefits lost due to IRS limitations on contributions to tax-qualified plans, (ii) the Supplemental Plan, which allows eligible employees to defer the receipt of eligible compensation until designated future dates and (iii) the Career Achievement Plan, which provides a deferred annual incentive award to selected executives. Participants in these plans earn a return on amounts due them based on several investment options, which mirror returns on underlying investments (primarily mutual funds). The Company economically hedges its obligations under the plans by investing in the actual underlying investments. These investments are classified as trading securities and are carried at fair value. At December 31, 2011 and 2010, these investments totaled $41,768 and $38,504, respectively. All gains and losses and related investment income in these investments, which are recorded in other income (expense), net, are equally offset by corresponding increases and decreases in the Company's deferred compensation liabilities.

Postretirement health care and life insurance benefit plans:

The Company provides certain postretirement health care and life insurance benefits for corporate office and management employees based upon their age, years of service, date of hire and if they agree to contribute a portion of the cost as determined by the Company. The Company has the right to modify or terminate these benefits and does not fund postretirement health care and life insurance benefits in advance of payments for benefit claims. The Company is currently contemplating changes to its postretirement health care and life insurance benefits with the intention of reducing the Company's cost of providing such benefits. These changes are likely to include increasing retiree premium contributions, reducing and eliminating certain benefits, and taking steps to ensure that the Company does not become subject to the excise tax on high value coverage instituted by the Patient Protection and Affordability Act. The Company is not presently able to determine the effects of such changes on its financial statements.

Amounts recognized in accumulated other comprehensive loss (pre-tax) at December 31, 2011 are as follows:

Prior service credit	$ (626)
Net actuarial loss	8,255
Net amount recognized in accumulated other comprehensive loss	$7,629

The estimated actuarial loss and prior service credit to be amortized from accumulated other comprehensive income into net periodic benefit cost during 2012 are $1,146 and $(125), respectively.

The changes in the accumulated postretirement benefit obligation at December 31, 2011 and 2010 consist of the following:

	December 31,	
	2011	**2010**
Benefit obligation, beginning of year	$20,689	$16,674
Service cost	831	696
Interest cost	1,117	958
Actuarial loss	3,898	2,714
Benefits paid	(427)	(353)
Benefit obligation, end of year	$26,108	$20,689

Net periodic postretirement benefit cost included the following components:

	2011	**2010**	**2009**
Service cost—benefits attributed to service during the period	$ 831	$ 696	$ 704
Interest cost on the accumulated postretirement benefit obligation	1,117	958	853
Net amortization	501	128	140
Net periodic postretirement benefit cost	$2,449	$1,782	$1,697

For measurement purposes, the 2012 annual rate of increase in the per capita cost of covered health care benefits was assumed to be 8.2% for pre-age 65 retirees, post 65 retirees and for prescription drugs; these rates were assumed to decrease gradually to 5.0% for 2019 and remain at that level thereafter. The health care cost trend rate assumption has a significant effect on the amounts reported. The weighted-average discount rate used in determining the accumulated postretirement benefit obligation was 4.31% and 5.47% at December 31, 2011 and 2010, respectively.

Increasing or decreasing the health care trend rates by one percentage point in each year would have the following effect:

	1% Increase	**1% Decrease**
Postretirement benefit obligation	$6,247	$(4,277)
Total of service and interest cost components	$ 484	$ (320)

The Company estimates future benefit payments will be $574, $710, $882, $993 and $1,095 in 2012 through 2016, respectively, and a total of $7,002 in 2017 through 2020. The future benefit payments are net of the annual Medicare Part D subsidy of approximately $1,094 beginning in 2012.

NOTE 8—COMMITMENTS:

Rental expense aggregated $1,042, $1,152 and $1,180 in 2011, 2010 and 2009, respectively.

Future operating lease commitments are not significant.

NOTE 9—SEGMENT AND GEOGRAPHIC INFORMATION:

The Company operates as a single reportable segment encompassing the manufacture and sale of confectionery products. Its principal manufacturing operations are located in the United States and Canada, and its principal market is the United States. The Company also manufactures and sells confectionery products in Mexico, and exports products to Canada and other countries worldwide.

The following geographic data includes net product sales summarized on the basis of the customer location and long-lived assets based on their physical location:

	2011	**2010**	**2009**
Net product sales:			
United States	$487,185	$471,714	$455,517
Foreign	41,184	45,435	40,075
	$528,369	$517,149	$495,592
Long-lived assets:			
United States	$170,173	$172,087	$176,044
Foreign	41,989	43,405	44,677
	$212,162	$215,492	$220,721

NOTE 10—FAIR VALUE MEASUREMENTS:

Current accounting guidance defines fair value as the price that would be received in the sale of an asset or paid to transfer a liability in an orderly transaction between market participants at the measurement date. Guidance requires disclosure of the extent to which fair value is used to measure financial assets and liabilities, the inputs utilized in calculating valuation measurements, and the effect of the measurement of significant unobservable inputs on earnings, or changes in net assets, as of the measurement date. Guidance establishes a three-level valuation hierarchy based upon the transparency of inputs utilized in the measurement and valuation of financial assets or liabilities as of the measurement date. Level 1 inputs include quoted prices for identical instruments and are the most observable. Level 2 inputs include quoted prices for similar assets and observable inputs such as interest rates, foreign currency exchange rates, commodity rates and yield curves. Level 3 inputs are not observable in the market and include management's own judgments about the assumptions market participants would use in pricing the asset or liability.

The use of observable and unobservable inputs is reflected in the hierarchy assessment disclosed in the table below.

As of December 31, 2011 and 2010, the Company held certain financial assets that are required to be measured at fair value on a recurring basis. These included derivative hedging instruments related to the foreign currency forward contracts and purchase of certain raw materials, investments in trading securities and available for sale securities, including an auction rate security (ARS). The Company's available for sale and trading securities principally consist of municipal bonds and mutual funds that are publicly traded.

The following tables present information about the Company's financial assets measured at fair value as of December 31, 2011 and 2010, and indicate the fair value hierarchy and the valuation techniques utilized by the Company to determine such fair value:

| | Estimated Fair Value December 31, 2011 | | | |
| | Total | Input Levels Used | | |
	Fair Value	Level 1	Level 2	Level 3
Cash and equivalents	$ 78,612	$ 78,612	$ —	$ —
Auction rate security	7,453	—	—	7,453
Available-for-sale securities, excluding the auction rate security	57,835	—	57,835	—
Foreign currency forward contracts	205	—	205	—
Commodity futures contracts	203	203	—	—
Commodity options contracts	—	—	—	—
Trading securities	41,768	41,768	—	—
Total assets measured at fair value	$186,076	$120,583	$58,040	$7,453

| | Estimated Fair Value December 31, 2010 | | | |
| | Total | Input Levels Used | | |
	Fair Value	Level 1	Level 2	Level 3
Cash and equivalents	$115,976	$115,976	$ —	$ —
Auction rate security	6,775	—	—	6,775
Available-for-sale securities, excluding the auction rate security	27,178	—	27,178	—
Foreign currency forward contracts	942	—	942	—
Commodity futures contracts	2,310	2,310	—	—
Commodity options contracts	5,369	5,369	—	—
Trading securities	38,504	38,504	—	—
Total assets measured at fair value	$197,054	$162,159	$28,120	$6,775

Available for sale securities which utilize level 2 inputs consist primarily of municipal bonds, which are valued based on quoted market prices or alternative pricing sources with reasonable level of price transparency.

A summary of the aggregate fair value, gross unrealized gains, gross unrealized losses, realized losses and amortized cost basis of the Company's investment portfolio by major security type is as follows:

| | December 31, 2011 | | | | |
| | Amortized | Fair | Unrealized | | Realized |
Available for Sale:	Cost	Value	Gains	Losses	Losses
Auction rate security	$ 8,410	$ 7,453	$ —	$ (957)	$ —
Municipal bonds	57,389	57,791	402	—	—
Mutual funds	45	44	—	(1)	—
	$65,844	$65,288	$402	$ (958)	$ —

| | December 31, 2010 | | | | |
| | Amortized | Fair | Unrealized | | Realized |
Available for Sale:	Cost	Value	Gains	Losses	Losses
Auction rate security	$ 8,410	$ 6,775	$ —	$(1,635)	$ —
Municipal bonds	27,073	27,122	49	—	—
Mutual funds	56	56	—	—	—
	$35,539	$33,953	$ 49	$(1,635)	$ —

As of December 31, 2011, the Company's long-term investments included an auction rate security, Jefferson County Alabama Sewer Revenue Refunding Warrants, reported at a fair value of $7,453, after reflecting a $5,140 other-than-temporary impairment and a $957 temporary, as defined, decline in market value against its $13,550 par value. This other-than-temporary impairment was recorded in other income (expense), net in 2008. In 2008, this auction rate security was determined to be other-than-temporarily impaired due to the duration and severity of the decline in fair value. The Company estimated the fair value of this auction rate security utilizing a valuation model with Level 3 inputs.

This valuation model considered, among other items, the credit risk of the collateral underlying the auction rate security, the credit risk of the bond insurer, interest rates, and the amount and timing of expected future cash flows including the Company's assumption about the market expectation of the next successful auction. See also the Management's Discussion and Analysis of Financial Condition and Results of Operations regarding Jefferson County auction rate security.

The Company classified this auction rate security as non-current and has included it in long-term investments on the Consolidated Statements of Financial Position at December 31, 2011 and 2010 because the Company believes that the current condition of the auction rate security market may take more than twelve months to improve.

The following table presents additional information about the Company's financial instruments (all ARS) measured at fair value on a recurring basis using Level 3 inputs at December 31, 2011 and 2010:

	2011	2010
Balance at January 1	$6,775	$7,710
Unrealized loss recognized in other comprehensive loss	678	(935)
Balance at December 31	$7,453	$6,775

The $7,500 carrying amount of the Company's industrial revenue development bonds at December 31, 2011 and 2010 approximates its estimated fair value as the bonds have a floating interest rate.

In addition to assets and liabilities that are recorded at fair value on a recurring basis, guidance requires the Company to record assets and liabilities at fair value on a nonrecurring basis generally as a result of impairment charges. Assets measured at fair value on a nonrecurring basis during 2009 are summarized below:

	Pre-Impairment Cost Basis	2009 Impairment Charge	New Cost Basis	Level 1	Level 2	Level 3
Equity method investment	$ 9,361	$ 4,400	$ 4,961	$ —	$ —	$ 4,961
Trademarks	189,024	14,000	175,024	—	—	175,024
Total	$198,385	$18,400	$179,985	$ —	$ —	$179,985

Twelve Months Ended December 31, 2009 / Level Used to Determine New Cost Basis

As discussed in Note 6, during the fourth quarter of 2009 the Company recognized an impairment of $4,400 in an equity method investment based on Level 3 inputs.

As discussed in Note 13, during the fourth quarter of 2009 the Company recognized a trademark impairment of $14,000 based on Level 3 inputs.

NOTE 11—DERIVATIVE INSTRUMENTS AND HEDGING ACTIVITIES:

From time to time, the Company uses derivative instruments, including foreign currency forward contracts, commodity futures contracts and commodity option contracts, to manage its exposures to foreign exchange and commodity prices. Commodity futures contracts and most commodity option contracts are intended and effective as hedges of market price risks associated with the anticipated purchase of certain raw materials (primarily sugar). Foreign currency forward contracts are intended and effective as hedges of the Company's exposure to the variability of cash flows, primarily related to the foreign exchange rate changes of products manufactured in Canada and sold in the United States, and periodic equipment purchases from foreign suppliers denominated in a foreign currency. The Company does not engage in trading or other speculative use of derivative instruments.

The Company recognizes all derivative instruments as either assets or liabilities at fair value in the Consolidated Statements of Financial Position. Derivative assets are recorded in other receivables and derivative liabilities are recorded in accrued liabilities. The Company uses either hedge accounting or mark-to-market accounting for its derivative instruments. Derivatives that qualify for hedge accounting are designated as cash flow hedges by formally documenting the hedge relationships, including identification of the hedging instruments, the hedged items and other critical terms, as well as the Company's risk management objectives and strategies for undertaking the hedge transaction.

Changes in the fair value of the Company's cash flow hedges are recorded in accumulated other comprehensive loss, net of tax, and are reclassified to earnings in the periods in which earnings are affected by the hedged item. Substantially all amounts reported in accumulated other comprehensive loss for commodity derivatives are expected to be reclassified to cost of goods sold. Substantially all amounts reported in accumulated other comprehensive loss for foreign currency derivatives are expected to be reclassified to other income (expense), net.

The following table summarizes the Company's outstanding derivative contracts and their effects on its Consolidated Statements of Financial Position at December 31, 2011 and 2010:

December 31, 2011

	Notional Amounts	Assets	Liabilities
Derivatives designated as hedging instruments:			
Foreign currency forward contracts	$13,044	$205	$ —
Commodity futures contracts	4,557	341	(138)
Commodity option contracts	—	—	—
Total derivatives		$546	$(138)

December 31, 2010

	Notional Amounts	Assets	Liabilities
Derivatives designated as hedging instruments:			
Foreign currency forward contracts	$ 3,572	$ 942	$ —
Commodity futures contracts	4,407	2,310	—
Commodity option contracts	10,344	5,481	(112)
Total derivatives		$8,733	$(112)

The effects of derivative instruments on the Company's Consolidated Statement of Earnings, Comprehensive Earnings and Retained Earnings for years ended December 31, 2011 and 2010 are as follows:

	For Year Ended December 31, 2011		
	Gain (Loss) Recognized in OCI	Gain (Loss) Reclassified from Accumulated OCI into Earnings	Gain (Loss) on Amount Excluded from Effectiveness Testing Recognized in Earnings
Foreign currency forward contracts	$ 317	$1,054	$ —
Commodity futures contracts	4,674	6,782	—
Commodity option contracts	(5,388)	(305)	—
Total	$ (397)	$7,531	$ —

	For Year Ended December 31, 2010		
	Gain (Loss) Recognized in OCI	Gain (Loss) Reclassified from Accumulated OCI into Earnings	Gain (Loss) on Amount Excluded from Effectiveness Testing Recognized in Earnings
Foreign currency forward contracts	$ 467	$3,199	$ —
Commodity futures contracts	2,120	(191)	—
Commodity option contracts	4,726	(357)	—
Total	$7,313	$2,651	$ —

For the years ended December 31, 2011 and 2010, the Company recognized a loss of $0 and $1,613 in earnings, respectively, related to mark-to-market accounting for certain commodity option contacts.

NOTE 12—COMPREHENSIVE EARNINGS (LOSS):

The following table sets forth information with respect to accumulated other comprehensive earnings (loss):

	Foreign Currency Translation Adjustment	Unrealized Gain (Loss) on		Postretirement and Pension Benefits	Accumulated Other Comprehensive Earning (Loss)
		Investments	Derivatives		
Balance at January 1, 2009	$(14,292)	$ 191	$ 220	$(1,360)	$(15,241)
Unrealized gains (losses)	1,183	(709)	4,341	109	4,924
(Gains) losses reclassified to net earnings	—	—	(1,015)	—	(1,015)
Tax effect	(118)	263	(1,232)	23	(1,064)
Net of tax amount	1,065	(446)	2,094	132	2,845
Balance at December 31, 2009	(13,227)	(255)	2,314	(1,228)	(12,396)
Unrealized gains (losses)	856	(1,179)	7,313	(3,007)	3,983
(Gains) losses reclassified to net earnings	—	—	(2,651)	—	(2,651)
Tax effect	135	435	(1,724)	1,005	(149)
Net of tax amount	991	(744)	2,938	(2,002)	1,183
Balance at December 31, 2010	(12,236)	(999)	5,252	(3,230)	(11,213)
Unrealized gains (losses)	(2,496)	1,030	(397)	(3,092)	(4,955)
(Gains) losses reclassified to net earnings	—	—	(7,531)	—	(7,531)
Tax effect	46	(382)	2,933	1,149	3,746
Net of tax amount	(2,450)	648	(4,995)	(1,943)	(8,740)
Balance at December 31, 2011	$(14,686)	$ (351)	$ 257	$(5,173)	$(19,953)

NOTE 13—GOODWILL AND INTANGIBLE ASSETS:

All of the Company's intangible indefinite-lived assets are trademarks.

The changes in the carrying amount of trademarks for 2011 and 2010 were as follows:

	2011	2010
Original cost	$193,767	$193,767
Accumulated impairment losses as of January 1	(18,743)	(18,743)
Balance at January 1	$175,024	$175,024
Current year impairment losses	—	—
Balance at December 31	$175,024	$175,024
Accumulated impairment losses as of December 31	$ (18,743)	$ (18,743)

As of December 31, 2009, management ascertained certain trademarks were impaired, and recorded a pre-tax charge of $14,000. The principal driver of this impairment charge was an increase in the discount rate required by market participants. The fair value of indefinite-lived intangible assets was primarily assessed using the present value of estimated future cash flows.

The Company has no accumulated impairment losses of goodwill.

Auditor's Report

All publicly held corporations, as well as many other businesses and organizations (both profit and not-for-profit, large and small), engage the services of independent certified public accountants (CPAs) for the purpose of obtaining an objective, expert report on their financial statements. Based on a comprehensive examination of the company's accounting system, accounting records, and the financial statements, the outside CPA issues the auditor's report.

The standard auditor's report should identify who and what was audited and indicate the responsibilities of management and the auditor relative to the financial statements. The report should clearly state that the audit was conducted in accordance with generally accepted auditing standards and discusses the nature and limitations of the audit. Finally, the report should express an informed opinion as to (1) the fairness of the financial statements and (2) their conformity with generally accepted accounting principles. The report of PricewaterhouseCoopers LLP appearing in Tootsie Roll's annual report is shown below.

Report of Independent Registered Public Accounting Firm

To the Board of Directors and Shareholders of Tootsie Roll Industries, Inc.:

In our opinion, the accompanying consolidated statements of financial position and the related consolidated statements of earnings, comprehensive earnings and retained earnings, and of cash flows present fairly, in all material respects, the financial position of Tootsie Roll Industries, Inc. and its subsidiaries at December 31, 2011 and December 31, 2010, and the results of their operations and their cash flows for each of the three years in the period ended December 31, 2011 in conformity with accounting principles generally accepted in the United States of America. Also in our opinion, the Company maintained, in all material respects, effective internal control over financial reporting as of December 31, 2011, based on criteria established in *Internal Control— Integrated Framework* issued by the Committee of Sponsoring Organizations of the Treadway Commission (COSO). The Company's management is responsible for these financial statements, for maintaining effective internal control over financial reporting and for its assessment of the effectiveness of internal control over financial reporting, included in Management's Report on Internal Control over Financial Reporting on page 27 of the 2011 Annual Report to Shareholders. Our responsibility is to express opinions on these financial statements and on the Company's internal control over financial reporting based on our integrated audits. We conducted our audits in accordance with the standards of the Public Company Accounting Oversight Board (United States). Those standards require that we plan and perform the audits to obtain reasonable assurance about whether the financial statements are free of material misstatement and whether effective internal control over financial reporting was maintained in all material respects. Our audits of the financial statements included examining, on a test basis, evidence supporting the amounts and disclosures in the financial statements, assessing the accounting principles used and significant estimates made by management, and evaluating the overall financial statement presentation. Our audit of internal control over financial reporting included obtaining an understanding of internal control over financial reporting, assessing the risk that a material weakness exists, and testing and evaluating the design and operating effectiveness of internal control based on the assessed risk. Our audits also included performing such other procedures as we considered necessary in the circumstances. We believe that our audits provide a reasonable basis for our opinions.

As discussed in Note 1 to the consolidated financial statements, the Company changed the manner in which it accounts for LIFO inventories in 2011.

A company's internal control over financial reporting is a process designed to provide reasonable assurance regarding the reliability of financial reporting and the preparation of financial statements for external purposes in accordance with generally accepted accounting principles. A company's internal control over financial reporting includes those policies and procedures that (i) pertain to the maintenance of records that, in reasonable detail, accurately and fairly reflect the transactions and dispositions of the assets of the company; (ii) provide reasonable assurance that transactions are recorded as necessary to permit preparation of financial statements in accordance with generally accepted accounting principles, and that receipts and expenditures of the company are being made only in accordance with authorizations of management and directors of the company; and (iii) provide reasonable assurance regarding prevention or timely detection of unauthorized acquisition, use, or disposition of the company's assets that could have a material effect on the financial statements.

Because of its inherent limitations, internal control over financial reporting may not prevent or detect misstatements. Also, projections of any evaluation of effectiveness to future periods are subject to the risk that controls may become inadequate because of changes in conditions, or that the degree of compliance with the policies or procedures may deteriorate.

PricewaterhouseCoopers LLP

Chicago, IL
February 29, 2012

Performance Graph

The following performance graph compares the cumulative total shareholder return on the Company's Common Stock for a five-year period (December 31, 2006 to December 31, 2011) with the cumulative total return of Standard & Poor's 500 Stock Index ("S&P 500") and the Dow Jones Industry Food Index ("Peer Group," which includes the Company), assuming (i) $100 invested on December 31 of the first year of the chart in each of the Company's Common Stock, S&P 500 and the Dow Jones Industry Food Index and (ii) the reinvestment of dividends.

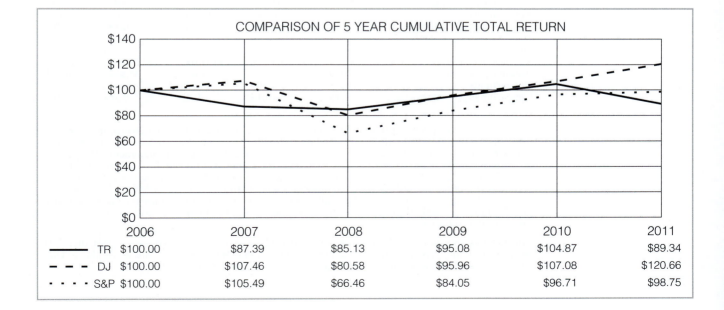

COMPARISON OF 5 YEAR CUMULATIVE TOTAL RETURN

	2006	2007	2008	2009	2010	2011
TR	$100.00	$87.39	$85.13	$95.08	$104.87	$89.34
DJ	$100.00	$107.46	$80.58	$95.96	$107.08	$120.66
S&P	$100.00	$105.49	$66.46	$84.05	$96.71	$98.75

Management's Report on Internal Control and Management Certifications of Financial Statements

The Sarbanes-Oxley Act requires managers of publicly traded companies to establish and maintain systems of internal control on the company's financial reporting processes. In addition, the act requires the company's top management to provide certifications regarding the accuracy of the financial statements. The reports of Tootsie Roll are shown below.

Management's Report on Internal Control Over Financial Reporting

The management of Tootsie Roll Industries, Inc. is responsible for establishing and maintaining adequate internal control over financial reporting, as such term is defined in the Securities Exchange Act of 1934 (SEC) Rule 13a-15(f). Our management conducted an evaluation of the effectiveness of the Company's internal control over financial reporting as of December 31, 2011 as required by SEC Rule 13a-15(c). In making this assessment, we used the criteria established in *Internal Control—Integrated Framework* issued by the Committee of Sponsoring Organizations of the Treadway Commission (the COSO criteria). Based on our evaluation under the COSO criteria, our management concluded that our internal control over financial reporting was effective as of December 31, 2011.

The effectiveness of the Company's internal control over financial reporting as of December 31, 2011 has been audited by PricewaterhouseCoopers LLP, an independent registered public accounting firm, as stated in their report which appears on page 26.

Tootsie Roll Industries, Inc.

Chicago, Illinois
February 29, 2012

Quarterly Financial Data (Unaudited)

TOOTSIE ROLL INDUSTRIES, INC. AND SUBSIDIARIES

	(Thousands of dollars except per share data)				
	First	Second	Third	Fourth	Year
2011					
Net product sales	$108,323	$104,884	$186,784	$128,378	$528,369
Product gross margin	34,799	33,898	54,554	39,893	163,144
Net earnings	8,330	6,486	18,855	10,267	43,938
Net earnings per share	0.14	0.11	0.33	0.18	0.76
2010					
Net product sales	$103,244	$105,026	$191,045	$117,834	$517,149
Product gross margin	34,909	35,450	61,649	35,807	167,815
Net earnings	9,068	8,309	26,245	9,441	53,063
Net earnings per share	0.15	0.14	0.45	0.16	0.90

The results for the quarters presented reflect the retrospective application of a change in accounting principle for inventory valuation and the related effects on product gross margin, net earnings and net earnings per share as discussed in Note 1 to the Consolidated Financial Statements. Product gross margin reflects increases (decreases) of $517, $504, and $811 for the three quarters of 2011 and $(212), $(216), $(375) and $(218) for the four quarters of 2010. Net earnings reflect increases (decreases) $330, $321, and $517 for the three quarters of 2011 and $(136), $(138), $(239) and $(138) for four quarters of 2010. Net earnings per share increased .01 per share for the third quarter of 2011 and decreased .01 per share for the first quarter of 2010. All other quarters remain unchanged as reported.

Net earnings per share is based upon average outstanding shares as adjusted for 3% stock dividends issued during the second quarter of each year and revision of net earnings as discussed above. The sum of the per share amounts may not equal annual amounts due to rounding.

2011-2010 QUARTERLY SUMMARY OF TOOTSIE ROLL INDUSTRIES, INC. STOCK PRICES AND DIVIDENDS PER SHARE

STOCK PRICES*

	2011		2010	
	High	**Low**	**High**	**Low**
1st Qtr	$29.45	$27.06	$28.24	$25.88
2nd Qtr	$29.68	$27.78	$28.04	$23.65
3rd Qtr	$29.80	$23.52	$25.95	$23.34
4th Qtr	$25.95	$22.85	$29.84	$24.64

*NYSE—Closing Price

Estimated Number of shareholders at February 2012:

Common Stock	18,000
Class B Common Stock	5,000

DIVIDENDS

	2011	**2010**
1st Qtr	$.08	$.08
2nd Qtr	$.08	$.08
3rd Qtr	$.08	$.08
4th Qtr	$.08	$.08

NOTE: In addition to the above cash dividends, a 3% stock dividend was issued on April 7, 2011 and April 8, 2010. Cash dividends are restated to reflect 3% stock dividends.

Financial Highlights

Companies often present the financial highlights section inside the front cover of the annual report or on its first two pages. This section generally reports the total or per share amounts for five to ten financial items for the current year and one or more previous years.

Five Year Summary of Earnings and Financial Highlights

TOOTSIE ROLL INDUSTRIES, INC. AND SUBSIDIARIES

(Thousands of dollars except per share, percentage and ratio figures)

(See management's comments starting on page 5)

	2011	2010	2009	2008	2007
Sales and Earnings Data (2)(3)(4)(5)					
Net product sales	$528,369	$517,149	$495,592	$492,051	$492,742
Product gross margin	163,144	167,815	175,817	158,055	165,456
Interest expense	121	142	243	378	53
Provision for income taxes	16,974	20,005	9,892	16,347	25,401
Net earnings	43,938	53,063	53,157	38,880	52,175
% of net product sales	8.3%	10.3%	10.7%	7.9%	10.6%
% of shareholders' equity	6.6%	8.0%	8.1%	6.1%	8.1%
Per Common Share Data (1)(3)(4)(5)					
Net earnings	$ 0.76	$ 0.90	$ 0.89	$ 0.65	$ 0.85
Cash dividends declared	0.32	0.32	0.32	0.32	0.32
Stock dividends	3%	3%	3%	3%	3%
Additional Financial data (1)(2)(3)(4)(5)					
Working capital	$153,846	$176,662	$154,409	$129,694	$142,163
Net cash provided by operating activities	50,390	82,805	76,994	57,533	90,148
Net cash provided by (used in) investing activities	(51,157)	(16,808)	(16,364)	(7,565)	(43,429)
Net cash used in financing activities	(36,597)	(41,011)	(38,548)	(38,666)	(44,842)
Property, plant & equipment additions	16,351	12,813	20,831	34,355	14,767
Net property, plant & equipment	212,162	215,492	220,721	217,628	201,401
Total assets	857,856	857,959	836,844	813,252	813,134
Long-term debt	7,500	7,500	7,500	7,500	7,500
Shareholders' equity	665,935	667,408	654,244	636,847	640,204
Average shares outstanding	57,892	58,685	59,425	60,152	61,580

(1) Per Common share data and average shares outstanding adjusted for annual 3% stock dividends.

(2) Certain reclassifications have been made to prior year numbers to conform to current year presentation.

(3) The 2009 data included the release of tax valuation allowances, charges related to the impairment of an equity method investment and impairment charges related to certain trademarks as discussed in Notes 4, 6 and 13 to the Consolidated Financial Statements, respectively.

(4) The 2008 data included a charge for the other-than-temporary impairment of an ARS. Further information is included in Note 10 to the Consolidated Financial Statements.

(5) Reflects the increase (decrease) retrospective application of a change in accounting principle for inventory valuation for the following:

	2010	2009	2008	2007
Product gross margin	$(1,021)	$(1,130)	$(682)	$409
Provision for income taxes	(370)	(409)	(247)	148
Net earnings	(651)	(721)	(435)	261
Net earnings per share	(0.02)	(0.02)	—	0.01
Working capital	(2,424)	(1,403)	(273)	409
Total assets	(2,424)	(1,403)	(273)	409
Shareholders' equity	(1,546)	(895)	(174)	261

APPENDIX B

SPECIMEN FINANCIAL STATEMENTS: THE HERSHEY COMPANY

THE HERSHEY COMPANY

CONSOLIDATED STATEMENTS OF INCOME

For the years ended December 31, In thousands of dollars except per share amounts	2011	2010	2009
Net Sales	$6,080,788	$5,671,009	$5,298,668
Costs and Expenses:			
Cost of sales	3,548,896	3,255,801	3,245,531
Selling, marketing and administrative	1,477,750	1,426,477	1,208,672
Business realignment and impairment (credits) charges, net	(886)	83,433	82,875
Total costs and expenses	5,025,760	4,765,711	4,537,078
Income before Interest and Income Taxes	1,055,028	905,298	761,590
Interest expense, net	92,183	96,434	90,459
Income before Income Taxes	962,845	808,864	671,131
Provision for income taxes	333,883	299,065	235,137
Net Income	$ 628,962	$ 509,799	$ 435,994
Net Income Per Share—Basic—Class B Common Stock	$ 2.58	$ 2.08	$ 1.77
Net Income Per Share—Diluted—Class B Common Stock	$ 2.56	$ 2.07	$ 1.77
Net Income Per Share—Basic—Common Stock	$ 2.85	$ 2.29	$ 1.97
Net Income Per Share—Diluted—Common Stock	$ 2.74	$ 2.21	$ 1.90
Cash Dividends Paid Per Share:			
Common Stock	$ 1.3800	$1.2800	$ 1.1900
Class B Common Stock	1.2500	1.1600	1.0712

The notes to consolidated financial statements are an integral part of these statements and are included in Hershey's 2011 Annual Report, available at **www.thehersheycompany.com**.

THE HERSHEY COMPANY

CONSOLIDATED BALANCE SHEETS

December 31,	2011	2010
In thousands of dollars		
ASSETS		
Current Assets:		
Cash and cash equivalents.	$ 693,686	$ 884,642
Accounts receivable—trade.	399,499	390,061
Inventories	648,953	533,622
Deferred income taxes.	136,861	55,760
Prepaid expenses and other.	167,559	141,132
Total current assets.	2,046,558	2,005,217
Property, Plant and Equipment, Net	1,559,717	1,437,702
Goodwill	516,745	524,134
Other Intangibles	111,913	123,080
Deferred Income Taxes	38,544	21,387
Other Assets	138,722	161,212
Total assets	$4,412,199	$4,272,732
LIABILITIES AND STOCKHOLDERS' EQUITY		
Current Liabilities:		
Accounts payable.	$ 420,017	$ 410,655
Accrued liabilities	612,186	593,308
Accrued income taxes	1,899	9,402
Short-term debt.	42,080	24,088
Current portion of long-term debt	97,593	261,392
Total current liabilities.	1,173,775	1,298,845
Long-term Debt.	1,748,500	1,541,825
Other Long-term Liabilities.	617,276	494,461
Total liabilities	3,539,551	3,335,131
Commitments and Contingencies	—	—
Stockholders' Equity:		
The Hershey Company Stockholders' Equity		
Preferred Stock, shares issued: none in 2011 and 2010.	—	—
Common Stock, shares issued: 299,269,702 in 2011 and 299,195,325 in 2010	299,269	299,195
Class B Common Stock, shares issued: 60,632,042 in 2011 and 60,706,419 in 2010	60,632	60,706
Additional paid-in capital.	490,817	434,865
Retained earnings.	4,699,597	4,374,718
Treasury—Common Stock shares, at cost: 134,695,826 in 2011 and 132,871,512 in 2010	(4,258,962)	(4,052,101)
Accumulated other comprehensive loss	(442,331)	(215,067)
The Hershey Company stockholders' equity	849,022	902,316
Noncontrolling interests in subsidiaries	23,626	35,285
Total stockholders' equity	872,648	937,601
Total liabilities and stockholders' equity	$4,412,199	$4,272,732

THE HERSHEY COMPANY

CONSOLIDATED STATEMENTS OF CASH FLOWS

For the years ended December 31, In thousands of dollars	2011	2010	2009
Cash Flows Provided from (Used by) Operating Activities			
Net income	$628,962	$509,799	$ 435,994
Adjustments to reconcile net income to net cash provided from operations:			
Depreciation and amortization	215,763	197,116	182,411
Stock-based compensation expense, net of tax of $15,127, $17,413 and $19,223, respectively	28,341	32,055	34,927
Excess tax benefits from stock-based compensation	(13,997)	(1,385)	(4,455)
Deferred income taxes	33,611	(18,654)	(40,578)
Gain on sale of trademark licensing rights, net of tax of $5,962	(11,072)	—	—
Business realignment and impairment charges, net of tax of $18,333, $20,635 and $38,308, respectively	30,838	77,935	60,823
Contributions to pension plans	(8,861)	(6,073)	(54,457)
Changes in assets and liabilities, net of effects from business acquisitions and divestitures:			
Accounts receivable—trade	(9,438)	20,329	46,584
Inventories	(115,331)	(13,910)	74,000
Accounts payable	7,860	90,434	37,228
Other assets and liabilities	(205,809)	13,777	293,272
Net Cash Provided from Operating Activities	580,867	901,423	1,065,749
Cash Flows Provided from (Used by) Investing Activities			
Capital additions	(323,961)	(179,538)	(126,324)
Capitalized software additions	(23,606)	(21,949)	(19,146)
Proceeds from sales of property, plant and equipment	312	2,201	10,364
Proceeds from sale of trademark licensing rights	20,000	—	—
Business acquisitions	(5,750)	—	(15,220)
Net Cash (Used by) Investing Activities	(333,005)	(199,286)	(150,326)
Cash Flows Provided from (Used by) Financing Activities			
Net change in short-term borrowings	10,834	1,156	(458,047)
Long-term borrowings	249,126	348,208	—
Repayment of long-term debt	(256,189)	(71,548)	(8,252)
Proceeds from lease financing agreement	47,601	—	—
Cash dividends paid	(304,083)	(283,434)	(263,403)
Exercise of stock options	184,411	92,033	28,318
Excess tax benefits from stock-based compensation	13,997	1,385	4,455
Contributions from noncontrolling interests in subsidiaries	—	10,199	7,322
Repurchase of Common Stock	(384,515)	(169,099)	(9,314)
Net Cash (Used by) Financing Activities	(438,818)	(71,100)	(698,921)
(Decrease) Increase in Cash and Cash Equivalents	(190,956)	631,037	216,502
Cash and Cash Equivalents as of January 1	884,642	253,605	37,103
Cash and Cash Equivalents as of December 31	$693,686	$884,642	$ 253,605
Interest Paid	$ 97,892	$ 97,932	$ 91,623
Income Taxes Paid	292,315	350,948	252,230

THE HERSHEY COMPANY
CONSOLIDATED STATEMENTS OF STOCKHOLDERS' EQUITY

In thousands of dollars

	Preferred Stock	Common Stock	Class B Common Stock	Additional Paid-in Capital	Retained Earnings	Treasury Common Stock	Accumulated Other Comprehensive Income (Loss)	Noncontrolling Interests in Subsidiaries	Total Stockholders' Equity
Balance as of January 1, 2009	$—	$299,190	$60,711	$352,375	$3,975,762	$(4,009,931)	$(359,908)	$31,745	$349,944
Net income					435,994				435,994
Other comprehensive income							157,064		157,064
Comprehensive income									593,058
Dividends:									
Common Stock, $1.19 per share					(198,371)				(198,371)
Class B Common Stock, $1.0712 per share					(65,032)				(65,032)
Conversion of Class B Common Stock into Common Stock		2	(2)						—
Incentive plan transactions				(355)		4,762			4,407
Stock-based compensation				44,704					44,704
Exercise of stock options				(2,046)		34,854			32,808
Repurchase of Common Stock						(9,314)			(9,314)
Noncontrolling interests in subsidiaries								8,135	8,135
Balance as of December 31, 2009	—	299,192	60,709	394,678	4,148,353	(3,979,629)	(202,844)	39,880	760,339
Net income					509,799				509,799
Other comprehensive loss							(12,223)		(12,223)
Comprehensive income									497,576
Dividends:									
Common Stock, $1.28 per share					(213,013)				(213,013)
Class B Common Stock, $1.16 per share					(70,421)				(70,421)
Conversion of Class B Common Stock into Common Stock		3	(3)						—
Incentive plan transactions				(7,453)		10,239			2,786
Stock-based compensation				40,630					40,630
Exercise of stock options				7,010		86,388			93,398
Repurchase of Common Stock						(169,099)			(169,099)
Noncontrolling interests in subsidiaries								(4,595)	(4,595)
Balance as of December 31, 2010	—	299,195	60,706	434,865	4,374,718	(4,052,101)	(215,067)	35,285	937,601
Net income					628,962				628,962
Other comprehensive loss							(227,264)		(227,264)
Comprehensive income									401,698
Dividends:									
Common Stock, $1.38 per share					(228,269)				(228,269)
Class B Common Stock, $1.25 per share					(75,814)				(75,814)
Conversion of Class B Common Stock into Common Stock		74	(74)						—
Incentive plan transactions				(15,844)		14,306			(1,538)
Stock-based compensation				40,439					40,439
Exercise of stock options				31,357		163,348			194,705
Repurchase of Common Stock						(384,515)			(384,515)
Noncontrolling interests in subsidiaries								(11,659)	(11,659)
Balance as of December 31, 2011	$—	$299,269	$60,632	$490,817	$4,699,597	$(4,258,962)	$(442,331)	$23,626	$872,648

SPECIMEN FINANCIAL STATEMENTS: ZETAR plc

Consolidated income statement

FOR THE YEAR ENDED 30 APRIL 2011

	Note	2011 Adjusted[1] results £'000	2011 Adjusting items £'000	2011 Total £'000	2010 Adjusted[1] results £'000	2010 Adjusting items £'000	2010 Total £'000
Revenue	5	**134,998**	**–**	**134,998**	131,922	–	131,922
Cost of sales		**(107,677)**	**–**	**(107,677)**	(105,112)	–	(105,112)
Gross profit		**27,321**	**–**	**27,321**	26,810	–	26,810
Distribution costs		**(5,550)**	**–**	**(5,550)**	(5,495)	–	(5,495)
Administrative expenses:							
– other administrative expenses		**(14,271)**	**(267)**	**(14,538)**	(14,003)	–	(14,003)
– amortisation of intangible assets	15	**–**	**(170)**	**(170)**	–	(299)	(299)
– share-based payments	10	**–**	**(330)**	**(330)**	–	(287)	(287)
Operating profit		**7,500**	**(767)**	**6,733**	7,312	(586)	6,726
Finance income	9	**3**	**–**	**3**	11	–	11
Finance costs	9	**(793)**	**(308)**	**(1,101)**	(968)	201	(767)
Profit from continuing operations before taxation		**6,710**	**(1,075)**	**5,635**	6,355	(385)	5,970
Tax on profit from continuing activities	11	**(1,764)**	**108**	**(1,656)**	(1,722)	20	(1,702)
Net result from continuing operations		**4,946**	**(967)**	**3,979**	4,633	(365)	4,268
Net result from discontinued operations	34	**–**	**503**	**503**	–	–	–
Profit for the year		**4,946**	**(464)**	**4,482**	4,633	(365)	4,268
Basic earnings per share (p)	13			**35.1**			32.6
Diluted earnings/per share (p)	13			**34.9**			32.6
Adjusted basic earnings per share (p)[1]	13	**38.7**			35.4		
Adjusted diluted earnings per share (p)[1]	13	**38.5**			35.4		

[1] Adjusted operating profit and adjusted earnings per share are stated before one-off items, amortisation of intangible assets, share-based payments and the fair value movement on financial instruments.

Consolidated statement of comprehensive income

FOR THE YEAR ENDED 30 APRIL 2011

	2011 Total £'000	2010 Total £'000
Profit for the year	**4,482**	4,268
Other comprehensive income:		
– currency translation differences	**245**	(917)
Other comprehensive income	**245**	(917)
Total comprehensive income for the year	**4,727**	3,351
Attributable to:		
– owners of the parent	**4,727**	3,351

The accompanying notes and accounting policies, which form an integral part of the financial statements, are included in Zetar's 2011 Annual Report, available at the company's website, **www.zetarplc.com**.

Consolidated balance sheet

AT 30 APRIL 2011

	Note	2011 £'000	2010 £'000
Non-current assets			
Goodwill	14	**30,520**	30,342
Other intangible assets	15	**140**	309
Property, plant and equipment	16	**16,583**	14,886
Deferred tax asset	22	**149**	213
		47,392	45,750
Current assets			
Inventories	17	**16,453**	16,039
Trade and other receivables	18	**24,935**	19,062
Cash at bank	27	**4,282**	4,257
		45,670	39,358
Total assets		**93,062**	85,108
Current liabilities			
Trade and other payables	19	**(25,075)**	(25,176)
Deferred consideration	12	**(38)**	–
Current tax liabilities		**(620)**	(524)
Obligations under finance leases	20	**(75)**	(90)
Derivative financial instruments	30	**(157)**	(406)
Borrowings and overdrafts	21	**(14,509)**	(12,885)
		(40,474)	(39,081)
Net current assets		**5,196**	277
Non-current liabilities			
Deferred consideration		**–**	(300)
Deferred tax liabilities	22	**(1,750)**	(1,605)
Obligations under finance leases	20	**(15)**	(77)
Borrowings and overdrafts	21	**(4,536)**	(2,290)
		(6,301)	(4,272)
Total liabilities		**(46,775)**	(43,353)
Net assets		**46,287**	41,755
Equity			
Share capital	23	**1,324**	1,324
Share premium account	24	**28,266**	28,266
Merger reserve		**3,411**	3,411
Equity reserve	25	**2,664**	2,089
Retained earnings	25	**10,622**	6,665
Total equity attributable to equity holders of the parent		**46,287**	41,755

The financial statements were approved by the Board for issue on 20 July 2011

IAN BLACKBURN
CHIEF EXECUTIVE

MARK STOTT
GROUP FINANCE DIRECTOR

Consolidated cash flow statement

FOR THE YEAR ENDED 30 APRIL 2011

	Note	2011 £'000	2010 £'000
Cash flow from operating activities			
Profit from continuing operations before taxation		5,635	5,970
Finance costs		1,101	767
Interest income		(3)	(11)
Share-based payments		330	287
Depreciation	6	2,267	2,337
Loss/(profit) on sale of plant and equipment	6	9	(113)
Amortisation of intangible assets	6	170	299
Net movement in working capital		(6,040)	(179)
Decrease/(increase) in inventories		72	(1,720)
(Increase)/decrease in receivables		(5,295)	128
(Decrease)/increase in payables		(817)	1,413
Total cash flow from operations		3,469	9,357
Net interest paid	9	(1,347)	(957)
Tax paid		(1,369)	(1,415)
Total cash flow from operating activities		753	6,985
Cash flow from investing activities			
Purchase of property, plant and equipment		(3,789)	(2,098)
Proceeds from sale of plant and equipment		45	259
Disposal of subsidiary		500	–
Total cash impact of acquisitions		(848)	(220)
Acquisition of business		(483)	(220)
Net borrowings assumed on acquisition		(365)	–
Net cash flow from investing activities		(4,092)	(2,059)
Cash flow from financing activities			
Net proceeds from issue of ordinary share capital		–	14
Purchase of own shares		(525)	(250)
Proceeds from new borrowings		7,000	–
Repayment of borrowings		(5,174)	(2,545)
Finance lease repayments		(91)	(214)
Net cash flow from financing activities		1,210	(2,995)
Net (decrease)/increase in cash and cash equivalents		(2,129)	1,931
Cash and cash equivalents at beginning of the year		(6,608)	(8,127)
Effect of foreign exchange rate movements		96	(412)
Cash and cash equivalents at the end of the year		(8,641)	(6,608)
Cash and cash equivalents comprise:			
– cash at bank	27	4,282	4,257
– bank overdraft	27	(12,923)	(10,865)
		(8,641)	(6,608)

Consolidated statement of changes in equity

FOR THE YEAR ENDED 30 APRIL 2011

	Attributable to equity holders of the parent					
	Share capital £'000	Share premium account £'000	Merger reserve £'000	Equity reserve £'000	Retained earnings £'000	Total £'000
Balance at 1 May 2009	1,324	28,252	3,411	2,719	2,647	38,353
Comprehensive income						
Profit for the year	–	–	–	–	4,268	4,268
Other comprehensive income						
Exchange (loss) on translation of foreign operations	–	–	–	(917)	–	(917)
Total other comprehensive income	–	–	–	(917)	–	(917)
Total comprehensive income	–	–	–	(917)	4,268	3,351
Transactions with owners:						
- issue of new ordinary shares	–	14	–	–	–	14
- purchase of own shares	–	–	–	–	(250)	(250)
- share-based payment charge	–	–	–	287	–	287
Total transactions with owners	–	14	–	287	(250)	51
Balance at 30 April 2010	1,324	28,266	3,411	2,089	6,665	41,755
Comprehensive income						
Profit for the year	–	–	–	–	4,482	4,482
Other comprehensive income						
Exchange gain on translation of foreign operations	–	–	–	245	–	245
Total other comprehensive income	–	–	–	245	–	245
Total comprehensive income	–	–	–	245	4,482	4,727
Transactions with owners:						
- purchase of own shares	–	–	–	–	(525)	(525)
- share-based payment charge	–	–	–	330	–	330
Total transactions with owners	–	–	–	330	(525)	(195)
Balance at 30 April 2011	**1,324**	**28,266**	**3,411**	**2,664**	**10,622**	**46,287**

APPENDIX D

TIME VALUE OF MONEY

LEARNING OBJECTIVES

After studying this appendix, you should be able to:

1 Distinguish between simple and compound interest.

2 Solve for future value of a single amount.

3 Solve for future value of an annuity.

4 Identify the variables fundamental to solving present value problems.

5 Solve for present value of a single amount.

6 Solve for present value of an annuity.

7 Compute the present value of notes and bonds.

8 Use a financial calculator to solve time value of money problems.

Nature of Interest

Would you rather receive $1,000 today or a year from now? You should prefer to receive the $1,000 today because you can invest the $1,000 and earn interest on it. As a result, you will have more than $1,000 a year from now. What this example illustrates is the concept of the **time value of money**. Everyone prefers to receive money today rather than the same amount in the future because of the interest factor.

LEARNING OBJECTIVE 1
Distinguish between simple and compound interest.

Interest is payment for the use of another person's money. It is the difference between the amount borrowed or invested (called the **principal**) and the amount repaid or collected. The amount of interest to be paid or collected is usually stated as a rate over a specific period of time. The rate of interest is generally stated as an annual rate.

The amount of interest involved in any financing transaction is based on three elements:

1. **Principal (p):** The original amount borrowed or invested.
2. **Interest Rate (i):** An annual percentage of the principal.
3. **Time (n):** The number of years that the principal is borrowed or invested.

SIMPLE INTEREST

Simple interest is computed on the principal amount only. It is the return on the principal for one period. Simple interest is usually expressed as shown in Illustration D-1.

Interest	=	Principal p	×	Rate i	×	Time n

Illustration D-1 Interest computation

For example, if you borrowed $5,000 for 2 years at a simple interest rate of 12% annually, you would pay $1,200 in total interest, computed as follows.

$$\text{Interest} = p \times i \times n$$
$$= \$5,000 \times .12 \times 2$$
$$= \$1,200$$

COMPOUND INTEREST

Compound interest is computed on principal **and** on any interest earned that has not been paid or withdrawn. It is the return on (or growth of) the principal for two or more time periods. Compounding computes interest not only on the principal but also on the interest earned to date on that principal, assuming the interest is left on deposit.

To illustrate the difference between simple and compound interest, assume that you deposit $1,000 in Bank Two, where it will earn simple interest of 9% per year, and you deposit another $1,000 in Citizens Bank, where it will earn compound interest of 9% per year compounded annually. Also assume that in both cases you will not withdraw any cash until three years from the date of deposit. Illustration D-2 shows the computation of interest to be received and the accumulated year-end balances.

Illustration D-2 Simple versus compound interest

Bank Two					Citizens Bank		
Simple Interest Calculation	Simple Interest	Accumulated Year-End Balance			Compound Interest Calculation	Compound Interest	Accumulated Year-End Balance
Year 1 $1,000.00 × 9%	$ 90.00	$1,090.00			Year 1 $1,000.00 × 9%	$ 90.00	$1,090.00
Year 2 $1,000.00 × 9%	90.00	$1,180.00			Year 2 $1,090.00 × 9%	98.10	$1,188.10
Year 3 $1,000.00 × 9%	90.00	$1,270.00			Year 3 $1,188.10 × 9%	106.93	$1,295.03
	$ 270.00		$25.03 Difference			$ 295.03	

Note in Illustration D-2 that simple interest uses the initial principal of $1,000 to compute the interest in all three years. Compound interest uses the accumulated balance (principal plus interest to date) at each year-end to compute interest in the succeeding year—which explains why your compound interest account is larger.

Obviously, if you had a choice between investing your money at simple interest or at compound interest, you would choose compound interest, all other things—especially risk—being equal. In the example, compounding provides $25.03 of additional interest income. For practical purposes, compounding assumes that unpaid interest earned becomes a part of the principal, and the accumulated balance at the end of each year becomes the new principal on which interest is earned during the next year.

Illustration D-2 indicates that you should invest your money at a bank that compounds interest. Most business situations use compound interest. Simple interest is generally applicable only to short-term situations of one year or less.

Future Value Concepts

LEARNING OBJECTIVE 2

Solve for future value of a single amount.

FUTURE VALUE OF A SINGLE AMOUNT

The **future value of a single amount** is the value at a future date of a given amount invested, assuming compound interest. For example, in Illustration D-2, $1,295.03 is the future value of the $1,000 investment earning 9% for three years. The $1,295.03 could be determined more easily by using the following formula.

$$FV = p \times (1 + i)^n$$

where:

FV = future value of a single amount
p = principal (or present value; the value today)
i = interest rate for one period
n = number of periods

The $1,295.03 is computed as follows.

$$
\begin{aligned}
FV &= \quad p \quad \times (1 + i)^n \\
&= \$1{,}000 \times (1 + .09)^3 \\
&= \$1{,}000 \times 1.29503 \\
&= \$1{,}295.03
\end{aligned}
$$

The 1.29503 is computed by multiplying (1.09 × 1.09 × 1.09). The amounts in this example can be depicted in the time diagram shown in Illustration D-4.

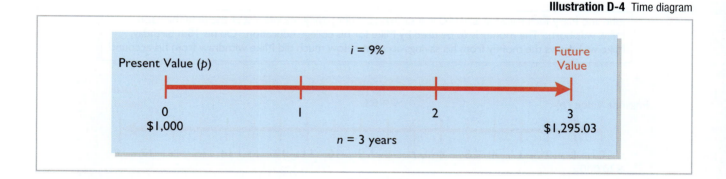

Another method used to compute the future value of a single amount involves a compound interest table. This table shows the future value of 1 for n periods. Table 1 on the next page is such a table.

In Table 1, n is the number of compounding periods, the percentages are the periodic interest rates, and the 5-digit decimal numbers in the respective columns are the future value of 1 factors. In using Table 1, you would multiply the principal amount by the future value factor for the specified number of periods and interest rate. For example, the future value factor for two periods at 9% is 1.18810. Multiplying this factor by $1,000 equals $1,188.10—which is the accumulated balance at the end of year 2 in the Citizens Bank example in Illustration D-2. The $1,295.03 accumulated balance at the end of the third year can be calculated from Table 1 by multiplying the future value factor for three periods (1.29503) by the $1,000.

The demonstration problem in Illustration D-5 (page D-4) shows how to use Table 1.

TABLE 1   Future Value of 1

(*n*) Periods	4%	5%	6%	7%	8%	9%	10%	11%	12%	15%
0	1.00000	1.00000	1.00000	1.00000	1.00000	1.00000	1.00000	1.00000	1.00000	1.00000
1	1.04000	1.05000	1.06000	1.07000	1.08000	1.09000	1.10000	1.11000	1.12000	1.15000
2	1.08160	1.10250	1.12360	1.14490	1.16640	1.18810	1.21000	1.23210	1.25440	1.32250
3	1.12486	1.15763	1.19102	1.22504	1.25971	1.29503	1.33100	1.36763	1.40493	1.52088
4	1.16986	1.21551	1.26248	1.31080	1.36049	1.41158	1.46410	1.51807	1.57352	1.74901
5	1.21665	1.27628	1.33823	1.40255	1.46933	1.53862	1.61051	1.68506	1.76234	2.01136
6	1.26532	1.34010	1.41852	1.50073	1.58687	1.67710	1.77156	1.87041	1.97382	2.31306
7	1.31593	1.40710	1.50363	1.60578	1.71382	1.82804	1.94872	2.07616	2.21068	2.66002
8	1.36857	1.47746	1.59385	1.71819	1.85093	1.99256	2.14359	2.30454	2.47596	3.05902
9	1.42331	1.55133	1.68948	1.83846	1.99900	2.17189	2.35795	2.55803	2.77308	3.51788
10	1.48024	1.62889	1.79085	1.96715	2.15892	2.36736	2.59374	2.83942	3.10585	4.04556
11	1.53945	1.71034	1.89830	2.10485	2.33164	2.58043	2.85312	3.15176	3.47855	4.65239
12	1.60103	1.79586	2.01220	2.25219	2.51817	2.81267	3.13843	3.49845	3.89598	5.35025
13	1.66507	1.88565	2.13293	2.40985	2.71962	3.06581	3.45227	3.88328	4.36349	6.15279
14	1.73168	1.97993	2.26090	2.57853	2.93719	3.34173	3.79750	4.31044	4.88711	7.07571
15	1.80094	2.07893	2.39656	2.75903	3.17217	3.64248	4.17725	4.78459	5.47357	8.13706
16	1.87298	2.18287	2.54035	2.95216	3.42594	3.97031	4.59497	5.31089	6.13039	9.35762
17	1.94790	2.29202	2.69277	3.15882	3.70002	4.32763	5.05447	5.89509	6.86604	10.76126
18	2.02582	2.40662	2.85434	3.37993	3.99602	4.71712	5.55992	6.54355	7.68997	12.37545
19	2.10685	2.52695	3.02560	3.61653	4.31570	5.14166	6.11591	7.26334	8.61276	14.23177
20	2.19112	2.65330	3.20714	3.86968	4.66096	5.60441	6.72750	8.06231	9.64629	16.36654

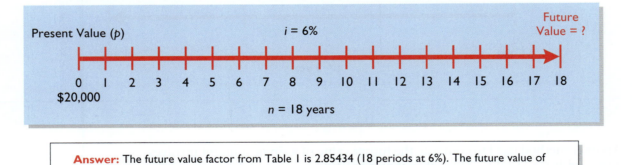

John and Mary Rich invested $20,000 in a savings account paying 6% interest at the time their son, Mike, was born. The money is to be used by Mike for his college education. On his 18th birthday, Mike withdraws the money from his savings account. How much did Mike withdraw from his account?

Present Value (*p*)   *i* = 6%   Future Value = ?

0 1 2 3 4 5 6 7 8 9 10 11 12 13 14 15 16 17 18

$20,000

n = 18 years

Answer: The future value factor from Table I is 2.85434 (18 periods at 6%). The future value of $20,000 earning 6% per year for 18 years is **$57,086.80** ($20,000 × 2.85434).

Illustration D-5
Demonstration problem—Using Table 1 for *FV* of 1

FUTURE VALUE OF AN ANNUITY

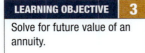

LEARNING OBJECTIVE 3

Solve for future value of an annuity.

The preceding discussion involved the accumulation of only a single principal sum. Individuals and businesses frequently encounter situations in which a **series** of equal dollar amounts are to be paid or received at evenly spaced time intervals (periodically), such as loans or lease (rental) contracts. Such payments or receipts of equal dollar amounts are referred to as **annuities**.

The **future value of an annuity** is the sum of all the payments (receipts) plus the accumulated compound interest on them. In computing the future value of an annuity, it is necessary to know (1) the interest rate, (2) the number of compounding periods, and (3) the amount of the periodic payments or receipts.

To illustrate the computation of the future value of an annuity, assume that you invest $2,000 at the end of each year for three years at 5% interest compounded annually. This situation is depicted in the time diagram in Illustration D-6.

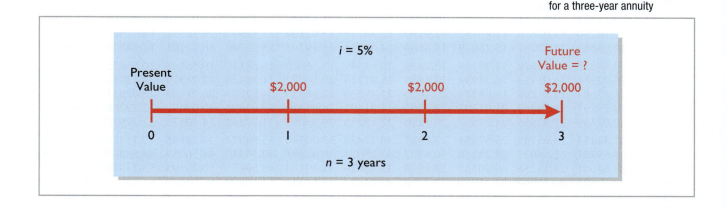

Illustration D-6 Time diagram for a three-year annuity

The $2,000 invested at the end of year 1 will earn interest for two years (years 2 and 3), and the $2,000 invested at the end of year 2 will earn interest for one year (year 3). However, the last $2,000 investment (made at the end of year 3) will not earn any interest. The future value of these periodic payments could be computed using the future value factors from Table 1, as shown in Illustration D-7.

Illustration D-7 Future value of periodic payment computation

Invested at End of Year	Number of Compounding Periods	Amount Invested	×	Future Value of 1 Factor at 5%	=	Future Value
1	2	$2,000	×	1.10250		$2,205
2	1	$2,000	×	1.05000		2,100
3	0	$2,000	×	1.00000		2,000
				3.15250		**$6,305**

The first $2,000 investment is multiplied by the future value factor for two periods (1.1025) because two years' interest will accumulate on it (in years 2 and 3). The second $2,000 investment will earn only one year's interest (in year 3) and therefore is multiplied by the future value factor for one year (1.0500). The final $2,000 investment is made at the end of the third year and will not earn any interest. Thus $n = 0$ and the future value factor is 1.00000. Consequently, the future value of the last $2,000 invested is only $2,000 since it does not accumulate any interest.

Calculating the future value of each individual cash flow is required when the periodic payments or receipts are not equal in each period. However, when the periodic payments (receipts) are **the same in each period**, the future value can be computed by using a future value of an annuity of 1 table. Table 2 (page D-6) is such a table.

TABLE 2 Future Value of an Annuity of 1

(n) Periods	4%	5%	6%	7%	8%	9%	10%	11%	12%	15%
1	1.00000	1.00000	1.00000	1.0000	1.00000	1.00000	1.00000	1.00000	1.00000	1.00000
2	2.04000	2.05000	2.06000	2.0700	2.08000	2.09000	2.10000	2.11000	2.12000	2.15000
3	3.12160	3.15250	3.18360	3.2149	3.24640	3.27810	3.31000	3.34210	3.37440	3.47250
4	4.24646	4.31013	4.37462	4.4399	4.50611	4.57313	4.64100	4.70973	4.77933	4.99338
5	5.41632	5.52563	5.63709	5.7507	5.86660	5.98471	6.10510	6.22780	6.35285	6.74238
6	6.63298	6.80191	6.97532	7.1533	7.33592	7.52334	7.71561	7.91286	8.11519	8.75374
7	7.89829	8.14201	8.39384	8.6540	8.92280	9.20044	9.48717	9.78327	10.08901	11.06680
8	9.21423	9.54911	9.89747	10.2598	10.63663	11.02847	11.43589	11.85943	12.29969	13.72682
9	10.58280	11.02656	11.49132	11.9780	12.48756	13.02104	13.57948	14.16397	14.77566	16.78584
10	12.00611	12.57789	13.18079	13.8164	14.48656	15.19293	15.93743	16.72201	17.54874	20.30372
11	13.48635	14.20679	14.97164	15.7836	16.64549	17.56029	18.53117	19.56143	20.65458	24.34928
12	15.02581	15.91713	16.86994	17.8885	18.97713	20.14072	21.38428	22.71319	24.13313	29.00167
13	16.62684	17.71298	18.88214	20.1406	21.49530	22.95339	24.52271	26.21164	28.02911	34.35192
14	18.29191	19.59863	21.01507	22.5505	24.21492	26.01919	27.97498	30.09492	32.39260	40.50471
15	20.02359	21.57856	23.27597	25.1290	27.15211	29.36092	31.77248	34.40536	37.27972	47.58041
16	21.82453	23.65749	25.67253	27.8881	30.32428	33.00340	35.94973	39.18995	42.75328	55.71747
17	23.69751	25.84037	28.21288	30.8402	33.75023	36.97351	40.54470	44.50084	48.88367	65.07509
18	25.64541	28.13238	30.90565	33.9990	37.45024	41.30134	45.59917	50.39593	55.74972	75.83636
19	27.67123	30.53900	33.75999	37.3790	41.44626	46.01846	51.15909	56.93949	63.43968	88.21181
20	29.77808	33.06595	36.78559	40.9955	45.76196	51.16012	57.27500	64.20283	72.05244	102.44358

Table 2 shows the future value of 1 to be received periodically for a given number of periods. It assumes that each payment is made at the **end** of each period. We can see from Table 2 that the future value of an annuity of 1 factor for three periods at 5% is 3.15250. The future value factor is the total of the three individual future value factors was shown in Illustration D-7. Multiplying this amount by the annual investment of $2,000 produces a future value of $6,305. The demonstration problem in Illustration D-8 shows how to use Table 2.

Illustration D-8
Demonstration problem—Using Table 2 for *FV* of an annuity of 1

John and Char Lewis' daughter, Debra, has just started high school. They decide to start a college fund for her and will invest $2,500 in a savings account at the end of each year she is in high school (4 payments total). The account will earn 6% interest compounded annually. How much will be in the college fund at the time Debra graduates from high school?

Answer: The future value factor from Table 2 is 4.37462 (4 periods at 6%). The future value of $2,500 invested each year for 4 years at 6% interest is **$10,936.55** ($2,500 × 4.37462).

Present Value Concepts

PRESENT VALUE VARIABLES

The **present value** is the value now of a given amount to be paid or received in the future, assuming compound interest. The present value, like the future value, is based on three variables: (1) the dollar amount to be received (future amount), (2) the length of time until the amount is received (number of periods), and (3) the interest rate (the discount rate). The process of determining the present value is referred to as **discounting the future amount**.

In this textbook, we use present value computations in measuring several items. For example, Chapter 10 computed the present value of the principal and interest payments to determine the market price of a bond. In addition, determining the amount to be reported for notes payable and lease liabilities involves present value computations.

> **LEARNING OBJECTIVE 4**
> Identify the variables fundamental to solving present value problems.

PRESENT VALUE OF A SINGLE AMOUNT

To illustrate present value, assume that you want to invest a sum of money today that will provide $1,000 at the end of one year. What amount would you need to invest today to have $1,000 one year from now? If you want a 10% rate of return, the investment or present value is $909.09 ($1,000 ÷ 1.10). The formula for calculating present value is shown in Illustration D-9.

> **LEARNING OBJECTIVE 5**
> Solve for present value of a single amount.

$$\text{Present Value} = \text{Future Value} \div (1 + i)^n$$

Illustration D-9 Formula for present value

The computation of $1,000 discounted at 10% for one year is as follows.

$$
\begin{aligned}
PV &= \quad FV \quad \div (1 + i)^n \\
&= \$1,000 \div (1 + .10)^1 \\
&= \$1,000 \div 1.10 \\
&= \$909.09
\end{aligned}
$$

The future amount ($1,000), the discount rate (10%), and the number of periods (1) are known. The variables in this situation can be depicted in the time diagram in Illustration D-10.

Illustration D-10 Finding present value if discounted for one period

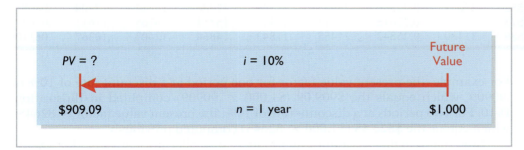

If the single amount of $1,000 is to be received **in two years** and discounted at 10% [$PV = \$1,000 \div (1 + .10)^2$], its present value is $826.45 [($1,000 ÷ 1.21), depicted as shown in Illustration D-11 on the next page.

Illustration D-11 Finding present value if discounted for two periods

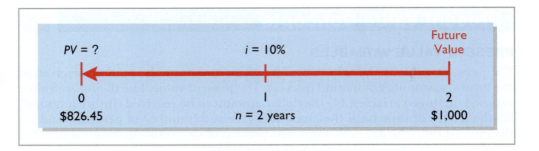

The present value of 1 may also be determined through tables that show the present value of 1 for n periods. In Table 3 below, n is the number of discounting periods involved. The percentages are the periodic interest rates or discount rates, and the 5-digit decimal numbers in the respective columns are the present value of 1 factors.

When using Table 3, the future value is multiplied by the present value factor specified at the intersection of the number of periods and the discount rate.

TABLE 3   Present Value of 1

(n) Periods	4%	5%	6%	7%	8%	9%	10%	11%	12%	15%
1	.96154	.95238	.94340	0.93458	.92593	.91743	.90909	.90090	.89286	.86957
2	.92456	.90703	.89000	0.87344	.85734	.84168	.82645	.81162	.79719	.75614
3	.88900	.86384	.83962	0.81630	.79383	.77218	.75132	.73119	.71178	.65752
4	.85480	.82270	.79209	0.76290	.73503	.70843	.68301	.65873	.63552	.57175
5	.82193	.78353	.74726	0.71299	.68058	.64993	.62092	.59345	.56743	.49718
6	.79031	.74622	.70496	0.66634	.63017	.59627	.56447	.53464	.50663	.43233
7	.75992	.71068	.66506	0.62275	.58349	.54703	.51316	.48166	.45235	.37594
8	.73069	.67684	.62741	0.58201	.54027	.50187	.46651	.43393	.40388	.32690
9	.70259	.64461	.59190	0.54393	.50025	.46043	.42410	.39092	.36061	.28426
10	.67556	.61391	.55839	0.50835	.46319	.42241	.38554	.35218	.32197	.24719
11	.64958	.58468	.52679	0.47509	.42888	.38753	.35049	.31728	.28748	.21494
12	.62460	.55684	.49697	0.44401	.39711	.35554	.31863	.28584	.25668	.18691
13	.60057	.53032	.46884	0.41496	.36770	.32618	.28966	.25751	.22917	.16253
14	.57748	.50507	.44230	0.38782	.34046	.29925	.26333	.23199	.20462	.14133
15	.55526	.48102	.41727	0.36245	.31524	.27454	.23939	.20900	.18270	.12289
16	.53391	.45811	.39365	0.33873	.29189	.25187	.21763	.18829	.16312	.10687
17	.51337	.43630	.37136	0.31657	.27027	.23107	.19785	.16963	.14564	.09293
18	.49363	.41552	.35034	0.29586	.25025	.21199	.17986	.15282	.13004	.08081
19	.47464	.39573	.33051	0.27615	.23171	.19449	.16351	.13768	.11611	.07027
20	.45639	.37689	.31180	0.25842	.21455	.17843	.14864	.12403	.10367	.06110

For example, the present value factor for one period at a discount rate of 10% is .90909, which equals the $909.09 ($1,000 × .90909) computed in Illustration D-10. For two periods at a discount rate of 10%, the present value factor is .82645, which equals the $826.45 ($1,000 × .82645) computed previously.

Note that a higher discount rate produces a smaller present value. For example, using a 15% discount rate, the present value of $1,000 due one year from now is $869.57 versus $909.09 at 10%. Also note that the further removed from the present the future value is, the smaller the present value. For example, using the same discount rate of 10%, the present value of $1,000 due in **five years** is $620.92. The present value of $1,000 due in **one year** is $909.09, a difference of $288.17.

The following two demonstration problems (Illustrations D-12 and D-13) illustrate how to use Table 3.

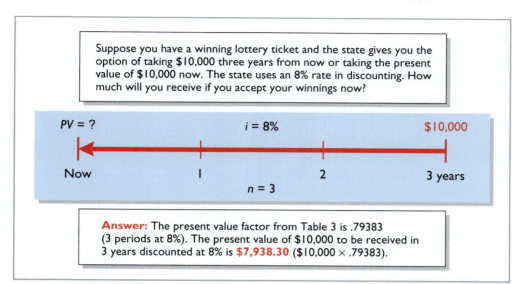

Illustration D-12
Demonstration problem—Using Table 3 for *PV* of 1

Suppose you have a winning lottery ticket and the state gives you the option of taking $10,000 three years from now or taking the present value of $10,000 now. The state uses an 8% rate in discounting. How much will you receive if you accept your winnings now?

PV = ?   i = 8% $10,000

Now   1   2   3 years

n = 3

Answer: The present value factor from Table 3 is .79383 (3 periods at 8%). The present value of $10,000 to be received in 3 years discounted at 8% is **$7,938.30** ($10,000 × .79383).

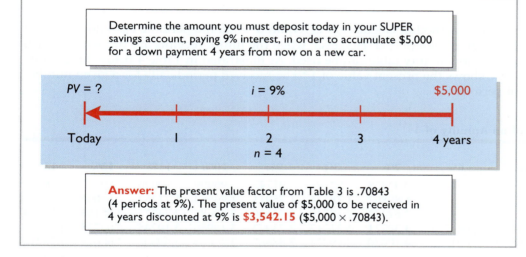

Illustration D-13
Demonstration problem—Using Table 3 for *PV* of 1

Determine the amount you must deposit today in your SUPER savings account, paying 9% interest, in order to accumulate $5,000 for a down payment 4 years from now on a new car.

PV = ?   i = 9% $5,000

Today   1   2   3   4 years

n = 4

Answer: The present value factor from Table 3 is .70843 (4 periods at 9%). The present value of $5,000 to be received in 4 years discounted at 9% is **$3,542.15** ($5,000 × .70843).

PRESENT VALUE OF AN ANNUITY

The preceding discussion involved the discounting of only a single future amount. Businesses and individuals frequently engage in transactions in which a series of equal dollar amounts are to be received or paid at evenly spaced time intervals (periodically). Examples of a series of periodic receipts or payments are loan agreements, installment sales, mortgage notes, lease (rental) contracts, and pension obligations. As discussed earlier, these periodic receipts or payments are **annuities**.

The **present value of an annuity** is the value now of a series of future receipts or payments, discounted assuming compound interest. In computing the present value of an annuity, it is necessary to know (1) the discount rate, (2) the number of discount periods, and (3) the amount of the periodic receipts or payments. To illustrate the computation of the present value of an annuity, assume that you

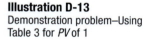

LEARNING OBJECTIVE 6

Solve for present value of an annuity.

will receive $1,000 cash annually for three years at a time when the discount rate is 10%. This situation is depicted in the time diagram in Illustration D-14. Illustration D-15 shows computation of the present value in this situation.

Illustration D-14 Time diagram for a three-year annuity

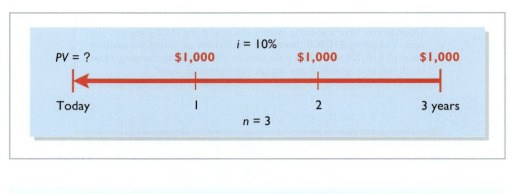

Illustration D-15 Present value of a series of future amounts computation

Future Amount	×	Present Value of 1 Factor at 10%	=	Present Value
$1,000 (one year away)		.90909		$ 909.09
1,000 (two years away)		.82645		826.45
1,000 (three years away)		.75132		751.32
		2.48686		**$2,486.86**

This method of calculation is required when the periodic cash flows are not uniform in each period. However, when the future receipts are the same in each period, an annuity table can be used. As illustrated in Table 4 below, an annuity table shows the present value of 1 to be received periodically for a given number of periods.

TABLE 4   Present Value of an Annuity of 1

(n) Periods	4%	5%	6%	7%	8%	9%	10%	11%	12%	15%
1	.96154	.95238	.94340	0.93458	.92593	.91743	.90909	.90090	.89286	.86957
2	1.88609	1.85941	1.83339	1.80802	1.78326	1.75911	1.73554	1.71252	1.69005	1.62571
3	2.77509	2.72325	2.67301	2.62432	2.57710	2.53130	2.48685	2.44371	2.40183	2.28323
4	3.62990	3.54595	3.46511	3.38721	3.31213	3.23972	3.16986	3.10245	3.03735	2.85498
5	4.45182	4.32948	4.21236	4.10020	3.99271	3.88965	3.79079	3.69590	3.60478	3.35216
6	5.24214	5.07569	4.91732	4.76654	4.62288	4.48592	4.35526	4.23054	4.11141	3.78448
7	6.00205	5.78637	5.58238	5.38989	5.20637	5.03295	4.86842	4.71220	4.56376	4.16042
8	6.73274	6.46321	6.20979	5.97130	5.74664	5.53482	5.33493	5.14612	4.96764	4.48732
9	7.43533	7.10782	6.80169	6.51523	6.24689	5.99525	5.75902	5.53705	5.32825	4.77158
10	8.11090	7.72173	7.36009	7.02358	6.71008	6.41766	6.14457	5.88923	5.65022	5.01877
11	8.76048	8.30641	7.88687	7.49867	7.13896	6.80519	6.49506	6.20652	5.93770	5.23371
12	9.38507	8.86325	8.38384	7.94269	7.53608	7.16073	6.81369	6.49236	6.19437	5.42062
13	9.98565	9.39357	8.85268	8.35765	7.90378	7.48690	7.10336	6.74987	6.42355	5.58315
14	10.56312	9.89864	9.29498	8.74547	8.24424	7.78615	7.36669	6.98187	6.62817	5.72448
15	11.11839	10.37966	9.71225	9.10791	8.55948	8.06069	7.60608	7.19087	6.81086	5.84737
16	11.65230	10.83777	10.10590	9.44665	8.85137	8.31256	7.82371	7.37916	6.97399	5.95424
17	12.16567	11.27407	10.47726	9.76322	9.12164	8.54363	8.02155	7.54879	7.11963	6.04716
18	12.65930	11.68959	10.82760	10.05909	9.37189	8.75563	8.20141	7.70162	7.24967	6.12797
19	13.13394	12.08532	11.15812	10.33560	9.60360	8.95012	8.36492	7.83929	7.36578	6.19823
20	13.59033	12.46221	11.46992	10.59401	9.81815	9.12855	8.51356	7.96333	7.46944	6.25933

Table 4 shows that the present value of an annuity of 1 factor for three periods at 10% is 2.48685.[1] This present value factor is the total of the three individual present value factors, as shown in Illustration D-15. Applying this amount to the annual cash flow of $1,000 produces a present value of $2,486.85.

The following demonstration problem (Illustration D-16) illustrates how to use Table 4.

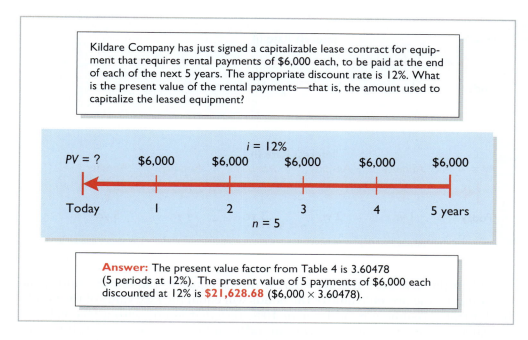

Illustration D-16
Demonstration problem—Using Table 4 for *PV* of an annuity of 1

Kildare Company has just signed a capitalizable lease contract for equipment that requires rental payments of $6,000 each, to be paid at the end of each of the next 5 years. The appropriate discount rate is 12%. What is the present value of the rental payments—that is, the amount used to capitalize the leased equipment?

$i = 12\%$

PV = ? $6,000 $6,000 $6,000 $6,000 $6,000

Today   1   2   3   4   5 years

$n = 5$

Answer: The present value factor from Table 4 is 3.60478 (5 periods at 12%). The present value of 5 payments of $6,000 each discounted at 12% is **$21,628.68** ($6,000 × 3.60478).

TIME PERIODS AND DISCOUNTING

In the preceding calculations, the discounting was done on an annual basis using an annual interest rate. Discounting may also be done over shorter periods of time such as monthly, quarterly, or semiannually.

When the time frame is less than one year, it is necessary to convert the annual interest rate to the applicable time frame. Assume, for example, that the investor in Illustration D-14 received $500 **semiannually** for three years instead of $1,000 annually. In this case, the number of periods becomes six (3 × 2), the discount rate is 5% (10% ÷ 2), the present value factor from Table 4 is 5.07569 (6 periods at 5%), and the present value of the future cash flows is $2,537.85 (5.07569 × $500). This amount is slightly higher than the $2,486.86 computed in Illustration D-15 because interest is computed twice during the same year. That is, during the second half of the year, interest is earned on the first half-year's interest.

COMPUTING THE PRESENT VALUE OF A LONG-TERM NOTE OR BOND

The present value (or market price) of a long-term note or bond is a function of three variables: (1) the payment amounts, (2) the length of time until the amounts are paid, and (3) the discount rate. Our illustration (on the next page) uses a five-year bond issue.

LEARNING OBJECTIVE   **7**

Compute the present value of notes and bonds.

---

[1]The difference of .00001 between 2.48686 and 2.48685 is due to rounding.

The first variable (dollars to be paid) is made up of two elements: (1) a series of interest payments (an annuity) and (2) the principal amount (a single sum). To compute the present value of the bond, both the interest payments and the principal amount must be discounted—two different computations. The time diagrams for a bond due in five years are shown in Illustration D-17.

Illustration D-17 Present value of a bond time diagram

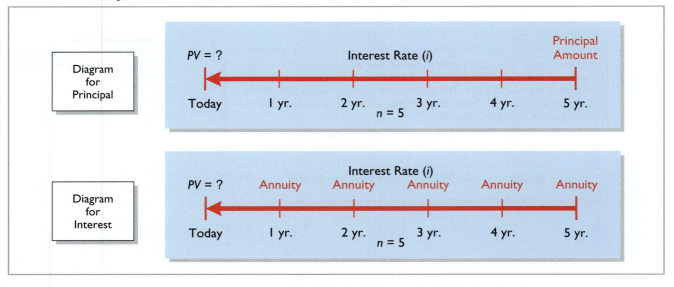

When the investor's market interest rate is equal to the bond's contractual interest rate, the present value of the bonds will equal the face value of the bonds. To illustrate, assume a bond issue of 10%, five-year bonds with a face value of $100,000 with interest payable **semiannually** on January 1 and July 1. If the discount rate is the same as the contractual rate, the bonds will sell at face value. In this case, the investor will receive (1) $100,000 at maturity and (2) a series of ten $5,000 interest payments [($100,000 × 10%) ÷ 2] over the term of the bonds. The length of time is expressed in terms of interest periods—in this case—10, and the discount rate per interest period, 5%. The following time diagram (Illustration D-18) depicts the variables involved in this discounting situation.

Illustration D-18 Time diagram for present value of a 10%, five-year bond paying interest semiannually

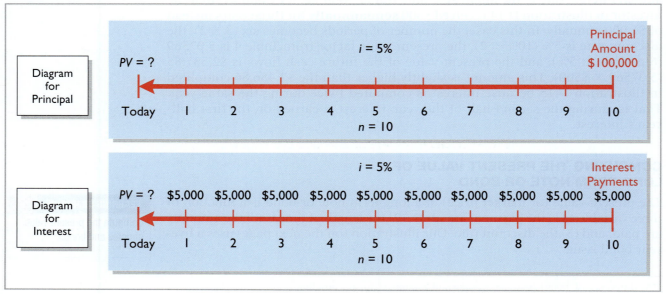

Illustration D-19 shows the computation of the present value of these bonds.

Illustration D-19 Present value of principal and interest– face value

<u>**10% Contractual Rate—10% Discount Rate**</u>

Present value of principal to be received at maturity
$100,000 × *PV* of 1 due in 10 periods at 5%
$100,000 × .61391 (Table 3) — $ 61,391
**Present value of interest to be received periodically
over the term of the bonds**
$5,000 × *PV* of 1 due periodically for 10 periods at 5%
$5,000 × 7.72173 (Table 4) — 38,609*
Present value of bonds — **$100,000**

*Rounded

Now assume that the investor's required rate of return is 12%, not 10%. The future amounts are again $100,000 and $5,000, respectively, but now a discount rate of 6% (12% ÷ 2) must be used. The present value of the bonds is $92,639, as computed in Illustration D-20.

Illustration D-20 Present value of principal and interest– discount

<u>**10% Contractual Rate—12% Discount Rate**</u>

Present value of principal to be received at maturity
$100,000 × .55839 (Table 3) — $ 55,839
**Present value of interest to be received periodically
over the term of the bonds**
$5,000 × 7.36009 (Table 4) — 36,800*
Present value of bonds — **$92,639**

*Rounded

Conversely, if the discount rate is 8% and the contractual rate is 10%, the present value of the bonds is $108,111, computed as shown in Illustration D-21.

Illustration D-21 Present value of principal and interest– premium

<u>**10% Contractual Rate—8% Discount Rate**</u>

Present value of principal to be received at maturity
$100,000 × .67556 (Table 3) — $ 67,556
**Present value of interest to be received periodically
over the term of the bonds**
$5,000 × 8.11090 (Table 4) — 40,555*
Present value of bonds — **$108,111**

*Rounded

The above discussion relied on present value tables in solving present value problems. Calculators may also be used to compute present values without the use of these tables. Many calculators, especially financial calculators, have present value (*PV*) functions that allow you to calculate present values by merely inputting the proper amount, discount rate, periods, and pressing the PV key. We discuss the use of financial calculators in the next section.

Using Financial Calculators

Business professionals, once they have mastered the underlying concepts in sections 1 and 2, often use a financial calculator to solve time value of money problems. In many cases, they must use calculators if interest rates or time periods do not correspond with the information provided in the compound interest tables.

To use financial calculators, you enter the time value of money variables into the calculator. Illustration D-22 shows the five most common keys used to solve time value of money problems.[2]

Illustration D-22 Financial calculator keys

where:

N = number of periods
I = interest rate per period (some calculators use I/YR or i)
PV = present value (occurs at the beginning of the first period)
PMT = payment (all payments are equal, and none are skipped)
FV = future value (occurs at the end of the last period)

In solving time value of money problems in this appendix, you will generally be given three of four variables and will have to solve for the remaining variable. The fifth key (the key not used) is given a value of zero to ensure that this variable is not used in the computation.

PRESENT VALUE OF A SINGLE SUM

To illustrate how to solve a present value problem using a financial calculator, assume that you want to know the present value of $84,253 to be received in five years, discounted at 11% compounded annually. Illustration D-23 depicts this problem.

Illustration D-23 Calculator solution for present value of a single sum

Illustration D-23 shows you the information (inputs) to enter into the calculator: N = 5, I = 11, PMT = 0, and FV = 84,253. You then press PV for the answer: −$50,000. As indicated, the PMT key was given a value of zero because a series of payments did not occur in this problem.

---

[2]On many calculators, these keys are actual buttons on the face of the calculator. On others, they appear on the display after the user accesses a present value menu.

Plus and Minus

The use of plus and minus signs in time value of money problems with a financial calculator can be confusing. Most financial calculators are programmed so that the positive and negative cash flows in any problem offset each other. In the present value problem above, we identified the $84,253 future value initial investment as a positive (inflow); the answer −$50,000 was shown as a negative amount, reflecting a cash outflow. If the 84,253 were entered as a negative, then the final answer would have been reported as a positive 50,000.

Hopefully, the sign convention will not cause confusion. If you understand what is required in a problem, you should be able to interpret a positive or negative amount in determining the solution to a problem.

Compounding Periods

In the problem above, we assumed that compounding occurs once a year. Some financial calculators have a default setting, which assumes that compounding occurs 12 times a year. You must determine what default period has been programmed into your calculator and change it as necessary to arrive at the proper compounding period.

Rounding

Most financial calculators store and calculate using 12 decimal places. As a result, because compound interest tables generally have factors only up to five decimal places, a slight difference in the final answer can result. In most time value of money problems, the final answer will not include more than two decimal places.

PRESENT VALUE OF AN ANNUITY

To illustrate how to solve a present value of an annuity problem using a financial calculator, assume that you are asked to determine the present value of rental receipts of $6,000 each to be received at the end of each of the next five years, when discounted at 12%, as pictured in Illustration D-24.

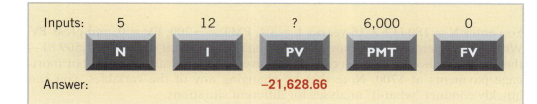

Illustration D-24 Calculator solution for present value of an annuity

In this case, you enter N = 5, I = 12, PMT = 6,000, FV = 0, and then press PV to arrive at the answer of −$21,628.66.

USEFUL APPLICATIONS OF THE FINANCIAL CALCULATOR

With a financial calculator, you can solve for any interest rate or for any number of periods in a time value of money problem. Here are some examples of these applications.

Auto Loan

Assume you are financing the purchase of a used car with a three-year loan. The loan has a 9.5% stated annual interest rate, compounded monthly. The price of the car is $6,000, and you want to determine the monthly payments, assuming that the payments start one month after the purchase. This problem is pictured in Illustration D-25.

Illustration D-25 Calculator solution for auto loan payments

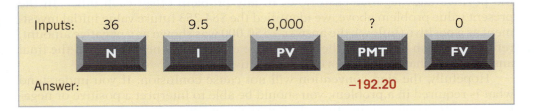

Inputs: 36   9.5   6,000   ?   0

N   I   PV   PMT   FV

Answer: −192.20

To solve this problem, you enter N = 36 (12 × 3), I = 9.5, PV = 6,000, FV = 0, and then press PMT. You will find that the monthly payments will be $192.20. Note that the payment key is usually programmed for 12 payments per year. Thus, you must change the default (compounding period) if the payments are other than monthly.

Mortgage Loan Amount

Let's say you are evaluating financing options for a loan on a house. You decide that the maximum mortgage payment you can afford is $700 per month. The annual interest rate is 8.4%. If you get a mortgage that requires you to make monthly payments over a 15-year period, what is the maximum home loan you can afford? Illustration D-26 depicts this problem.

Illustration D-26 Calculator solution for mortgage amount

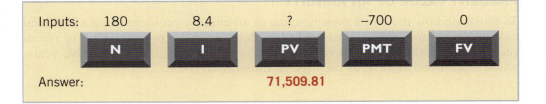

Inputs: 180   8.4   ?   −700   0

N   I   PV   PMT   FV

Answer: 71,509.81

You enter N = 180 (12 × 15 years), I = 8.4, PMT = −700, FV = 0, and press PV. With the payments-per-year key set at 12, you find a present value of $71,509.81— the maximum home loan you can afford, given that you want to keep your mortgage payments at $700. Note that by changing any of the variables, you can quickly conduct "what-if" analyses for different situations.

Summary of Learning Objectives

1 **Distinguish between simple and compound interest.** Simple interest is computed on the principal only, while compound interest is computed on the principal and any interest earned that has not been withdrawn.

2 **Solve for future value of a single amount.** Prepare a time diagram of the problem. Identify the principal amount, the number of compounding periods, and the interest rate. Using the future value of 1 table, multiply the principal amount by the future value factor specified at the intersection of the number of periods and the interest rate.

3 **Solve for future value of an annuity.** Prepare a time diagram of the problem. Identify the amount of the periodic payments, the number of compounding periods, and the interest rate. Using the future value of an annuity of 1 table, multiply the amount of the payments by the future value factor specified at the intersection of the number of periods and the interest rate.

4 **Identify the variables fundamental to solving present value problems.** The following three variables are fundamental to solving present value problems: (1) the future amount, (2) the number of periods, and (3) the interest rate (the discount rate).

5 **Solve for present value of a single amount.** Prepare a time diagram of the problem. Identify the future amount, the number of discounting periods, and the discount (interest) rate. Using the present value of a single amount table, multiply the future amount by the present value factor specified at the intersection of the number of periods and the discount rate.

6 **Solve for present value of an annuity.** Prepare a time diagram of the problem. Identify the amount of future periodic receipts or payment (annuities), the number of discounting periods, and the discount (interest) rate. Using the present value of an annuity of 1 table, multiply the amount of the annuity by the present value factor specified at the intersection of the number of periods and the interest rate.

7 **Compute the present value of notes and bonds.** Determine the present value of the principal amount: Multiply the principal amount (a single future amount) by the present value factor (from the present value of 1 table) intersecting at the number of periods

(number of interest payments) and the discount rate. Determine the present value of the series of interest payments: Multiply the amount of the interest payment by the present value factor (from the present value of an annuity of 1 table) intersecting at the number of periods (number of interest payments) and the discount rate. Add the present value of the principal amount to the present value of the interest payments to arrive at the present value of the note or bond.

8 **Use a financial calculator to solve time value of money problems.** Financial calculators can be used to solve the same and additional problems as those solved with time value of money tables. Enter into the financial calculator the amounts for all of the known elements of a time value of money problem (periods, interest rate, payments, future or present value), and it solves for the unknown element. Particularly useful situations involve interest rates and compounding periods not presented in the tables.

Glossary

Terms are highlighted in blue throughout the chapter.

Annuity A series of equal dollar amounts to be paid or received at evenly spaced time intervals (periodically).

Compound interest The interest computed on the principal and any interest earned that has not been paid or withdrawn.

Discounting the future amount(s) The process of determining present value.

Future value of a single amount The value at a future date of a given amount invested, assuming compound interest.

Future value of an annuity The sum of all the payments or receipts plus the accumulated compound interest on them.

Interest Payment for the use of another person's money.

Present value The value now of a given amount to be paid or received in the future assuming compound interest.

Present value of an annuity The value now of a series of future receipts or payments, discounted assuming compound interest.

Principal The amount borrowed or invested.

Simple interest The interest computed on the principal only.

WILEY PLUS Self-Test, Brief Exercises, Exercises, Problem Set A, and many more resources are available for practice in WileyPLUS.

Brief Exercises

(Use tables to solve exercises BED-1 to BED-23.)

Compute the future value of a single amount.
(LO 2), **AP**

BED-1 Jerry Rees invested $8,000 at 5% annual interest, and left the money invested without withdrawing any of the interest for 12 years. At the end of the 12 years, Jerry withdrew the accumulated amount of money. (a) What amount did Jerry withdraw, assuming the investment earns simple interest? (b) What amount did Jerry withdraw, assuming the investment earns interest compounded annually?

Use future value tables.
(LO 2, 3), C

BED-2 For each of the following cases, indicate (a) to what interest rate columns and (b) to what number of periods you would refer in looking up the future value factor.

(1) In Table 1 (future value of 1):

	Annual Rate	Number of Years Invested	Compounded
Case A	6%	3	Annually
Case B	8%	4	Semiannually

(2) In Table 2 (future value of an annuity of 1):

	Annual Rate	Number of Years Invested	Compounded
Case A	5%	8	Annually
Case B	6%	6	Semiannually

Compute the future value of a single amount.
(LO 2), AP

BED-3 Mayer Company signed a lease for an office building for a period of 12 years. Under the lease agreement, a security deposit of $9,200 is made. The deposit will be returned at the expiration of the lease with interest compounded at 4% per year. What amount will Mayer receive at the time the lease expires?

Compute the future value of an annuity.
(LO 3), AP

BED-4 Ekman Company issued $1,000,000, 10-year bonds and agreed to make annual sinking fund deposits of $78,000. The deposits are made at the end of each year into an account paying 5% annual interest. What amount will be in the sinking fund at the end of 10 years?

Compute the future value of a single amount and of an annuity.
(LO 2, 3), AP

BED-5 Terry and Jessica Benedict invested $6,000 in a savings account paying 4% annual interest when their daughter, Kristi, was born. They also deposited $1,000 on each of her birthdays until she was 18 (including her 18th birthday). How much was in the savings account on her 18th birthday (after the last deposit)?

Compute the future value of a single amount.
(LO 2), AP

BED-6 Jeff Farris borrowed $34,000 on July 1, 2014. This amount plus accrued interest at 9% compounded annually is to be repaid on July 1, 2019. How much will Jeff have to repay on July 1, 2019?

Use present value tables.
(LO 5, 6), C

BED-7 For each of the following cases, indicate (a) to what interest rate columns and (b) to what number of periods you would refer in looking up the discount rate.

(1) In Table 3 (present value of 1):

	Annual Rate	Number of Years Involved	Discounts per Year
Case A	12%	6	Annually
Case B	10%	11	Annually
Case C	6%	9	Semiannually

(2) In Table 4 (present value of an annuity of 1):

	Annual Rate	Number of Years Involved	Number of Payments Involved	Frequency of Payments
Case A	12%	20	20	Annually
Case B	10%	5	5	Annually
Case C	8%	4	8	Semiannually

Determine present values.
(LO 5, 6), AP

BED-8 (a) What is the present value of $28,000 due 9 periods from now, discounted at 10%?

(b) What is the present value of $28,000 to be received at the end of each of 6 periods, discounted at 9%?

Compute the present value of a single amount investment.
(LO 5), AP

BED-9 Elmdale Company is considering an investment that will return a lump sum of $750,000 five years from now. What amount should Elmdale Company pay for this investment to earn a 9% return?

BED-10   Orear Company earns 10% on an investment that will return $480,000 eight years from now. What is the amount Orear should invest now to earn this rate of return?

Compute the present value of a single amount investment.
(LO 5), **AP**

BED-11   Dayton Company is considering investing in an annuity contract that will return $45,000 annually at the end of each year for 15 years. What amount should Dayton Company pay for this investment if it earns a 5% return?

Compute the present value of an annuity investment.
(LO 6), **AP**

BED-12   Nolasko Enterprises earns 8% on an investment that pays back $90,000 at the end of each of the next 6 years. What is the amount Nolasko Enterprises invested to earn the 8% rate of return?

Compute the present value of an annuity investment.
(LO 6), **AP**

BED-13   Kirby Railroad Co. is about to issue $300,000 of 10-year bonds paying a 9% interest rate, with interest payable semiannually. The discount rate for such securities is 8%. How much can Kirby expect to receive for the sale of these bonds?

Compute the present value of bonds.
(LO 5, 6, 7), **AP**

BED-14   Assume the same information as BED-13 except that the discount rate was 10% instead of 8%. In this case, how much can Kirby expect to receive from the sale of these bonds?

Compute the present value of bonds.
(LO 5, 6, 7), **AP**

BED-15   Robertson Company receives a $64,000, 6-year note bearing interest of 6% (paid annually) from a customer at a time when the discount rate is 8%. What is the present value of the note received by Robertson?

Compute the present value of a note.
(LO 5, 6, 7), **AP**

BED-16   Jimenez Enterprises issued 9%, 8-year, $2,600,000 par value bonds that pay interest semiannually on October 1 and April 1. The bonds are dated April 1, 2014, and are issued on that date. The discount rate of interest for such bonds on April 1, 2014, is 10%. What cash proceeds did Jimenez receive from issuance of the bonds?

Compute the present value of bonds.
(LO 5, 6, 7), **AP**

BED-17   Phil Emley owns a garage and is contemplating purchasing a tire retreading machine for $18,000. After estimating costs and revenues, Phil projects a net cash flow from the retreading machine of $3,300 annually for 8 years. Phil hopes to earn a return of 10% on such investments. What is the present value of the retreading operation? Should Phil purchase the retreading machine?

Compute the present value of a machine for purposes of making a purchase decision.
(LO 6, 7), **AP**

BED-18   Jamison Company issues an 8%, 5-year mortgage note on January 1, 2014, to obtain financing for new equipment. Land is used as collateral for the note. The terms provide for semiannual installment payments of $46,850. What were the cash proceeds received from the issuance of the note?

Compute the present value of a note.
(LO 6), **AP**

BED-19   Pendley Company is considering purchasing equipment. The equipment will produce the following cash flows: Year 1, $38,000; Year 2, $40,000; and Year 3, $50,000. Pendley requires a minimum rate of return of 10%. What is the maximum price Pendley should pay for this equipment?

Compute the maximum price to pay for a machine.
(LO 6, 7), **AP**

BED-20   If Barbara Oxford invests $4,172.65 now and she will receive $10,000 at the end of 15 years, what annual rate of interest will Barbara earn on her investment? (*Hint:* Use Table 3.)

Compute the interest rate on a single amount.
(LO 5), **AN**

BED-21   Blake Mohr has been offered the opportunity of investing $25,490 now. The investment will earn 10% per year and at the end of that time will return Blake $80,000. How many years must Blake wait to receive $80,000? (*Hint:* Use Table 3.)

Compute the number of periods of a single amount.
(LO 5), **AN**

BED-22   Amanda Tevis made an investment of $9,128.55. From this investment, she will receive $1,000 annually for the next 20 years starting one year from now. What rate of interest will Amanda's investment be earning for her? (*Hint:* Use Table 4.)

Compute the interest rate on an annuity.
(LO 6), **AN**

BED-23   Kelly Reading invests $5,146.12 now for a series of $1,000 annual returns beginning one year from now. Kelly will earn a return of 11% on the initial investment. How many annual payments of $1,000 will Kelly receive? (*Hint:* Use Table 4.)

Compute the number of periods of an annuity.
(LO 6), **AN**

BED-24   Julie Vopat wishes to invest $18,000 on July 1, 2014, and have it accumulate to $50,000 by July 1, 2024. Use a financial calculator to determine at what exact annual rate of interest Julie must invest the $18,000.

Determine interest rate.
(LO 8), **AP**

BED-25   On July 17, 2014, Billy Prater borrowed $60,000 from his grandfather to open a clothing store. Starting July 17, 2020, Billy has to make 10 equal annual payments of $8,860 each to repay the loan. Use a financial calculator to determine what interest rate Billy is paying.

Determine interest rate.
(LO 8), **AP**

Determine interest rate.
(LO 8), **AP**

BED-26 As the purchaser of a new house, Manuel Rodriguez has signed a mortgage note to pay the Nashville National Bank and Trust Co. $8,400 every 6 months for 20 years, at the end of which time he will own the house. At the date the mortgage is signed, the purchase price was $198,000 and Rodriguez made a down payment of $20,000. The first payment will be made 6 months after the date the mortgage is signed. Using a financial calculator, compute the exact rate of interest earned on the mortgage by the bank.

Various time value of money situations.
(LO 8), **AP**

BED-27 Using a financial calculator, solve for the unknowns in each of the following situations.
(a) On June 1, 2014, Linda Cuningham purchases lakefront property from her neighbor, Donald Fancher, and agrees to pay the purchase price in seven payments of $16,000 each, the first payment to be payable June 1, 2015. (Assume that interest compounded at an annual rate of 6.9% is implicit in the payments.) What is the purchase price of the property?
(b) On January 1, 2014, Noonan Corporation purchased 200 of the $1,000 face value, 7% coupon, 10-year bonds of Lumley Inc. The bonds mature on January 1, 2022, and pay interest annually beginning January 1, 2015. Noonan purchased the bonds to yield 8.65%. How much did Noonan pay for the bonds?

Various time value of money situations.
(LO 8), **AP**

BED-28 Using a financial calculator, provide a solution to each of the following situations.
(a) Tina Deboer owes a debt of $42,000 from the purchase of her new sport utility vehicle. The debt bears annual interest of 7.8% compounded monthly. Tina wishes to pay the debt and interest in equal monthly payments over 8 years, beginning one month hence. What equal monthly payments will pay off the debt and interest?
(b) On January 1, 2014, Danny Herron offers to buy Mark Jacobs' used snowmobile for $8,000, payable in five equal annual installments, which are to include 7.25% interest on the unpaid balance and a portion of the principal. If the first payment is to be made on December 31, 2014, how much will each payment be?

REPORTING AND ANALYZING INVESTMENTS

LEARNING OBJECTIVES

After studying this appendix, you should be able to:

1 Identify the reasons corporations invest in stocks and debt securities.

2 Explain the accounting for debt investments.

3 Explain the accounting for stock investments.

4 Describe the purpose and usefulness of consolidated financial statements.

5 Indicate how debt and stock investments are valued and reported in the financial statements.

6 Distinguish between short-term and long-term investments.

Why Corporations Invest

Corporations purchase investments in debt or equity securities generally for one of three reasons. First, a corporation may **have excess cash** that it does not need for the immediate purchase of operating assets. For example, many companies experience seasonal fluctuations in sales. A Cape Cod marina has more sales in the spring and summer than in the fall and winter. The reverse is true for an Aspen ski shop. Thus, at the end of an operating cycle, many companies may have cash on hand that is temporarily idle until the start of another operating cycle. These companies may invest the excess funds to earn—through interest and dividends—a greater return than they would get by just holding the funds in the bank. Illustration E-1 shows the role that such temporary investments play in the operating cycle.

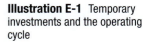

LEARNING OBJECTIVE **1**

Identify the reasons corporations invest in stocks and debt securities.

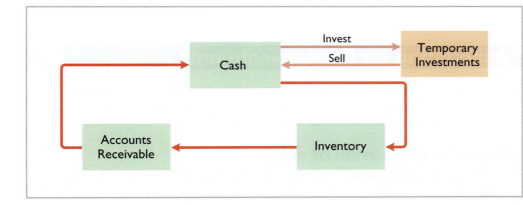

Illustration E-1 Temporary investments and the operating cycle

A second reason some companies such as banks purchase investments is to generate **earnings from investment income**. Although banks make most of their earnings by lending money, they also generate earnings by investing in debt and equity securities. Banks purchase investment securities because loan demand varies both seasonally and with changes in the economic climate. Thus, when loan demand is low, a bank must find other uses for its cash.

Some companies attempt to generate investment income through speculative investments. That is, they are speculating that the investment will increase in value and thus result in positive returns. Therefore, they invest primarily in the common stock of other corporations.

Third, companies also invest for **strategic reasons**. A company may purchase a noncontrolling interest in another company in a related industry in which it wishes to establish a presence. Alternatively, a company can exercise some influence over one of its customers or suppliers by purchasing a significant, but not controlling, interest in that company. Or, a corporation may choose to purchase a controlling interest in another company in order to enter a new industry without incurring the costs and risks associated with starting from scratch.

In summary, businesses invest in other companies for the reasons shown in Illustration E-2.

Illustration E-2 Why corporations invest

Reason	Typical Investment
To house excess cash until needed	Low-risk, highly liquid, short-term securities such as government-issued securities
To generate earnings	Banks and financial institutions often purchase debt securities, while mutual funds and index funds purchase both debt and stock securities
To meet strategic goals	Stocks of companies in a related industry or in an unrelated industry that the company wishes to enter

Accounting for Debt Investments

Debt investments are investments in government and corporation bonds. In accounting for debt investments, companies must make entries to record (1) the acquisition, (2) the interest revenue, and (3) the sale.

RECORDING ACQUISITION OF BONDS

At acquisition, debt investments are recorded at cost. Cost includes all expenditures necessary to acquire these investments, such as the price paid plus brokerage fees (commissions), if any.

For example, assume that Kuhl Corporation acquires 50 Doan Inc. 8%, 10-year, $1,000 bonds on January 1, 2014, at a cost of $50,000. Kuhl records the investment as:

Jan. 1	Debt Investments	50,000	
	Cash		50,000
	(To record purchase of 50 Doan Inc. bonds)		

RECORDING BOND INTEREST

The Doan Inc. bonds pay interest of $2,000 semiannually on July 1 and January 1 ($50,000 \times 8\% \times \frac{1}{2}$). The entry for the receipt of interest on July 1 is:

July 1	Cash	2,000	
	Interest Revenue		2,000
	(To record receipt of interest on Doan Inc. bonds)		

If Kuhl Corporation's fiscal year ends on December 31, it accrues the interest of $2,000 earned since July 1. The adjusting entry is:

Dec. 31	Interest Receivable	2,000	
	Interest Revenue		2,000
	(To accrue interest on Doan Inc. bonds)		

Kuhl reports Interest Receivable as a current asset in the balance sheet. It reports Interest Revenue under "Other revenues and gains" in the income statement.

Kuhl records receipt of the interest on January 1 as follows.

Jan. 1	Cash	2,000	
	Interest Receivable		2,000
	(To record receipt of accrued interest)		

A credit to Interest Revenue at this time would be incorrect. Why? Because the company earned and accrued the interest revenue in the preceding accounting period.

RECORDING SALE OF BONDS

When Kuhl sells the bond investments, it credits the investment account for the cost of the bonds. The company records as a gain or loss any difference between the net proceeds from the sale (sales price less brokerage fees) and the cost of the bonds.

Assume, for example, that Kuhl Corporation receives net proceeds of $54,000 on the sale of the Doan Inc. bonds on January 1, 2015, after receiving the interest due. Since the securities cost $50,000, Kuhl has realized a gain of $4,000. It records the sale as follows.

Helpful Hint The accounting for short-term debt investments and long-term debt investments is similar. Any exceptions are discussed in more advanced courses.

Jan. 1	Cash	54,000	
	Debt Investments		50,000
	Gain on Sale of Debt Investments		4,000
	(To record sale of Doan Inc. bonds)		

Kuhl reports the gain on the sale of debt investments under "Other revenues and gains" in the income statement and reports losses under "Other expenses and losses."

Accounting for Stock Investments

LEARNING OBJECTIVE 3
Explain the accounting for stock investments.

Stock investments are investments in the capital stock of corporations. When a company holds stock (and/or debt) of several different corporations, the group of securities is an **investment portfolio**.

The accounting for investments in common stock depends on the extent of the investor's influence over the operating and financial affairs of the issuing corporation (the **investee**). Illustration E-3 shows the general guidelines.

Illustration E-3 Accounting guidelines for stock investments

Investor's Ownership Interest in Investee's Common Stock	Presumed Influence on Investee	Accounting Guidelines
Less than 20%	Insignificant	Cost method
Between 20% and 50%	Significant	Equity method
More than 50%	Controlling	Consolidated financial statements

Companies are required to use judgment instead of blindly following the guidelines.[1] We explain and illustrate the application of each guideline next.

HOLDINGS OF LESS THAN 20%

In the accounting for stock investments of less than 20%, companies use the cost method. Under the **cost method**, companies record the investment at cost and recognize revenue only when cash dividends are received.

Recording Acquisition of Stock

At acquisition, stock investments are recorded at cost. Cost includes all expenditures necessary to acquire these investments, such as the price paid plus brokerage fees (commissions), if any.

Assume, for example, that on July 1, 2014, Sanchez Corporation acquires 1,000 shares (10% ownership) of Beal Corporation common stock at $40 per share. The entry for the purchase is:

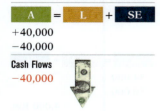

A = L + SE
+40,000
−40,000

Cash Flows
−40,000

July	1	Stock Investments	40,000	
		Cash		40,000
		(To record purchase of 1,000 shares of Beal common stock)		

[1]Among the factors that companies should consider in determining an investor's influence are whether (1) the investor has representation on the investee's board of directors, (2) the investor participates in the investee's policy-making process, (3) there are material transactions between the investor and the investee, and (4) the common stock held by other stockholders is concentrated or dispersed.

Recording Dividends

During the time the company holds the stock, it makes entries for any cash dividends received. Thus, if Sanchez Corporation receives a $2 per share dividend on December 31, the entry is:

Dec. 31	Cash (1,000 × $2)	2,000	
	Dividend Revenue		2,000
	(To record receipt of a cash dividend)		

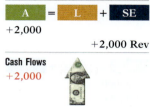

A = L + SE
+2,000
          +2,000 Rev

Cash Flows
+2,000

Sanchez reports Dividend Revenue under "Other revenues and gains" in the income statement.

Recording Sale of Stock

When a company sells a stock investment, it recognizes the difference between the net proceeds from the sale (sales price less brokerage fees) and the cost of the stock as a gain or a loss.

Assume, for instance, that Sanchez Corporation receives net proceeds of $39,500 on the sale of its Beal Corporation stock on February 10, 2015. Because the stock cost $40,000, Sanchez has incurred a loss of $500. It records the sale as:

Feb. 10	Cash	39,500	
	Loss on Sale of Stock Investments	500	
	Stock Investments		40,000
	(To record sale of Beal common stock)		

A = L + SE
+39,500
          −500 Exp
−40,000

Cash Flows
+39,500

Sanchez reports the loss account under "Other expenses and losses" in the income statement and shows a gain on sale under "Other revenues and gains."

HOLDINGS BETWEEN 20% AND 50%

When an investor company owns only a small portion of the shares of stock of another company, the investor cannot exercise control over the investee. But when an investor owns between 20% and 50% of the common stock of a corporation, it is presumed that the investor has significant influence over the financial and operating activities of the investee. The investor probably has a representative on the investee's board of directors. Through that representative, the investor begins to exercise some control over the investee—and the investee company in some sense becomes part of the investor company.

For example, even prior to purchasing all of Turner Broadcasting, Time Warner owned 20% of Turner. Because it exercised significant control over major decisions made by Turner, Time Warner used an approach called the equity method. Under the **equity method, the investor records its share of the net income of the investee in the year when it is earned**. An alternative might be to delay recognizing the investor's share of net income until a cash dividend is declared. But that approach would ignore the fact that the investor and investee are, in some sense, one company, making the investor better off by the investee's earned income.

Under the **equity method**, the company initially records the investment in common stock at cost. After that, it adjusts the investment account **annually** to show the investor's equity in the investee. Each year, the investor does the following. (1) It increases (debits) the investment account and increases (credits) revenue for its share of the investee's net income.[2] (2) The investor also decreases (credits) the investment account for the amount of dividends received. The investment account is reduced for dividends received because payment of a dividend decreases the net assets of the investee.

Recording Acquisition of Stock

Assume that Milar Corporation acquires 30% of the common stock of Beck Company for $120,000 on January 1, 2014. The entry to record this transaction is:

A	=	L	+	SE
+120,000				
−120,000				

Cash Flows
−120,000

Jan.	1	Stock Investments	120,000	
		Cash		120,000
		(To record purchase of Beck common stock)		

Recording Revenue and Dividends

For 2014, Beck reports net income of $100,000. It declares and pays a $40,000 cash dividend. Milar must record (1) its share of Beck's income, $30,000 (30% × $100,000), and (2) the reduction in the investment account for the dividends received, $12,000 (30% × $40,000). The entries are:

A	=	L	+	SE
+30,000				
				+30,000 Rev

Cash Flows
no effect

(1)

Dec.	31	Stock Investments	30,000	
		Revenue from Stock Investments		30,000
		(To record 30% equity in Beck's 2014 net income)		

A	=	L	+	SE
+12,000				
−12,000				

Cash Flows
+12,000

(2)

Dec.	31	Cash	12,000	
		Stock Investments		12,000
		(To record dividends received)		

After Milar posts the transactions for the year, the investment and revenue accounts are as shown in Illustration E-4.

Illustration E-4 Investment and revenue accounts after posting

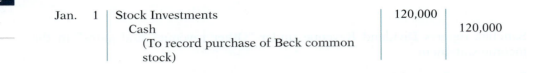

Stock Investments				Revenue from Stock Investments	
Jan. 1	120,000	Dec. 31	**12,000**		Dec. 31	**30,000**
Dec. 31	**30,000**				
Dec. 31 Bal.	138,000				

During the year, the investment account increased by $18,000. This $18,000 is Milar's 30% equity in the $60,000 increase in Beck's retained earnings ($100,000 − $40,000). In addition, Milar reports $30,000 of revenue from its investment, which is 30% of Beck's net income of $100,000.

---

[2]Conversely, the investor increases (debits) a loss account and decreases (credits) the investment account for its share of the investee's net loss.

Note that the difference between reported revenue under the cost method and reported revenue under the equity method can be significant. For example, Milar would report only $12,000 of dividend revenue (30% × $40,000) if it used the cost method.

HOLDINGS OF MORE THAN 50%

A company that owns more than 50% of the common stock of another entity is known as the **parent company**. The entity whose stock is owned by the parent company is called the **subsidiary (affiliated) company**. Because of its stock ownership, the parent company has a **controlling interest** in the subsidiary company.

When a company owns more than 50% of the common stock of another company, it usually prepares **consolidated financial statements**. Consolidated financial statements present the assets and liabilities controlled by the parent company. They also present the total revenues and expenses of the subsidiary companies. Companies prepare consolidated statements **in addition to** the financial statements for the individual parent and subsidiary companies.

As noted earlier, prior to acquiring all of Turner Broadcasting, Time Warner accounted for its investment in Turner using the equity method. Time Warner's net investment in Turner was reported in a single line item—Other investments. After the merger, Time Warner instead consolidated Turner's results with its own. Under this approach, Time Warner included the individual assets and liabilities of Turner with its own assets. That is, Turner's plant and equipment were added to Time Warner's plant and equipment, its receivables were added to Time Warner's receivables, and so on. A similar sort of consolidation went on when AOL merged with Time Warner.

Consolidated statements are useful to the stockholders, board of directors, and management of the parent company. Consolidated statements indicate to creditors, prospective investors, and regulatory agencies the magnitude and scope of operations of the companies under common control. For example, regulators and the courts undoubtedly used the consolidated statements of AT&T to determine whether a breakup of the company was in the public interest. Illustration E-5 lists three companies that prepare consolidated statements and some of the companies they have owned.

PepsiCo	Cendant	The Walt Disney Company
Frito-Lay	Howard Johnson	Capital Cities/ABC, Inc.
Tropicana	Ramada Inn	Disneyland, Disney World
Quaker Oats	Century 21	Mighty Ducks
Pepsi-Cola	Coldwell Banker	Anaheim Angels
Gatorade	Avis	ESPN

Illustration E-5 Examples of consolidated companies and their subsidiaries

LEARNING OBJECTIVE 4
Describe the purpose and usefulness of consolidated financial statements.

Valuing and Reporting Investments

The value of debt and stock investments may fluctuate greatly during the time they are held. For example, in a 12-month period, the stock of Time Warner hit a high of $58\frac{1}{2}$ and a low of 9. In light of such price fluctuations, how should companies value investments at the balance sheet date? Valuation could be at cost, at fair value, or at the lower-of-cost-or-market value.

LEARNING OBJECTIVE 5
Indicate how debt and stock investments are valued and reported in the financial statements.

Many people argue that fair value offers the best approach because it represents the expected cash realizable value of securities. **Fair value** is the amount for which a security could be sold in a normal market. Others counter that unless a security is going to be sold soon, the fair value is not relevant because the price of the security will likely change again.

CATEGORIES OF SECURITIES

For purposes of valuation and reporting at a financial statement date, debt and stock investments are classified into three categories of securities:

1. **Trading securities** are bought and held primarily for sale in the near term to generate income on short-term price differences.
2. **Available-for-sale securities** are held with the intent of selling them sometime in the future.
3. **Held-to-maturity securities** are debt securities that the investor has the intent and ability to hold to maturity.[3]

Illustration E-6 shows the valuation guidelines for these securities. **These guidelines apply to all debt securities and to those stock investments in which the holdings are less than 20%.**

Illustration E-6 Valuation guidelines

Trading	Available-for-sale	Held-to-maturity
"We'll sell within 10 days."	"We'll hold the stock for a while to see how it performs."	"We intend to hold until maturity."
At fair value with changes reported in net income	At fair value with changes reported in the stockholders' equity section	At amortized cost

Trading Securities

Trading securities are held with the intention of selling them in a short period of time (generally less than a month). **Trading** means frequent buying and selling. As indicated in Illustration E-6, companies adjust trading securities to fair value at the end of each period (an approach referred to as **mark-to-market** accounting). They report changes from cost **as part of net income**. The changes are reported as **unrealized gains or losses** because the securities have not been sold. The unrealized gain or loss is the difference between the **total cost** of trading securities and their **total fair value**. Companies classify trading securities as a current asset.

---

[3]This category is provided for completeness. The accounting and valuation issues related to held-to-maturity securities are discussed in more advanced accounting courses.

As an example, Illustration E-7 shows the costs and fair values for investments classified as trading securities for Pace Corporation on December 31, 2014. Pace Corporation has an unrealized gain of $7,000 because total fair value ($147,000) is $7,000 greater than total cost ($140,000).

Illustration E-7 Valuation of trading securities

Trading Securities, December 31, 2014

Investments	Cost	Fair Value	Unrealized Gain (Loss)
Yorkville Company bonds	$ 50,000	$ 48,000	$(2,000)
Kodak Company stock	90,000	99,000	9,000
Total	$140,000	$147,000	**$ 7,000**

The fact that trading securities are a short-term investment increases the likelihood that Pace will sell them at fair value for a gain. Pace records fair value and the unrealized gain through an adjusting entry at the time it prepares financial statements. In this entry, the company uses a valuation allowance account, Fair Value Adjustment—Trading, to record the difference between the total cost and the total fair value of the securities. The adjusting entry for Pace Corporation is:

Dec. 31	Fair Value Adjustment—Trading	7,000	
	Unrealized Gain—Income		7,000
	(To record unrealized gain on trading securities)		

A = L + SE
+7,000
+7,000 Rev

Cash Flows
no effect

The use of the Fair Value Adjustment—Trading account enables the company to maintain a record of the investment cost. Actual cost is needed to determine the gain or loss realized when the securities are sold. The company adds the debit balance (or subtracts a credit balance) of the Fair Value Adjustment—Trading account to the cost of the investments to arrive at a fair value for the trading securities.

The fair value of the securities is the amount companies report on the balance sheet. They report the unrealized gain on the income statement under "Other revenues and gains." The term **income** in the account title indicates that the gain affects net income. If the total cost of the trading securities is greater than total fair value, an unrealized loss has occurred. In such a case, the adjusting entry is a debit to Unrealized Loss—Income and a credit to Fair Value Adjustment—Trading. Companies report the unrealized loss under "Other expenses and losses" in the income statement.

The fair value adjustment account is carried forward into future accounting periods. No entries are made to this account during the period. At the end of each reporting period, a company adjusts the balance in the account to the difference between cost and fair value at that time. It closes the Unrealized Gain—Income account or Unrealized Loss—Income account at the end of the reporting period.

Available-for-Sale Securities

As indicated earlier, available-for-sale securities are held with the intent of selling them sometime in the future. If the intent is to sell the securities within the next year or operating cycle, a company classifies the securities as current assets in the balance sheet. Otherwise, it classifies them as long-term assets in the investments section of the balance sheet.

Companies also report available-for-sale securities at fair value. The procedure for determining fair value and unrealized gain or loss for these securities is the same as that for trading securities. To illustrate, assume that Elbert Corporation has two securities that are classified as available-for-sale. Illustration E-8 provides information on the cost, fair value, and amount of the unrealized gain or loss on December 31, 2014. There is an unrealized loss of $9,537 because total cost ($293,537) is $9,537 more than total fair value ($284,000).

Illustration E-8 Valuation of available-for-sale securities

	Available-for-Sale Securities, December 31, 2014		
Investments	**Cost**	**Fair Value**	**Unrealized Gain (Loss)**
Campbell Soup Corporation			
8% bonds	$ 93,537	$103,600	$10,063
Hershey Foods stock	200,000	180,400	(19,600)
Total	$293,537	$284,000	$(9,537)

BALANCE SHEET PRESENTATION

LEARNING OBJECTIVE 6
Distinguish between short-term and long-term investments.

For balance sheet presentation, companies must classify investments as either short-term or long-term.

Short-Term Investments

Short-term investments (also called **marketable securities**) are securities held by a company that are (1) **readily marketable** and (2) **intended to be converted into cash** within the next year or operating cycle, whichever is longer. Investments that do not meet **both criteria** are classified as **long-term investments**.

Both the adjusting entry and the reporting of the unrealized loss from Elbert's available-for-sale securities differ from those illustrated for trading securities. The differences result because these securities are not going to be sold in the near term. Thus, prior to actual sale it is much more likely that changes in fair value may reverse the unrealized loss. Therefore, Elbert does not report an unrealized loss in the income statement. Instead, the company reports it as a **separate component of stockholders' equity**. In the adjusting entry, Elbert identifies the fair value adjustment account with available-for-sale securities, and identifies the unrealized gain or loss account with stockholders' equity. The adjusting entry for Elbert Corporation to record the unrealized loss of $9,537 is:

−9,537 Eq

−9,537

Cash Flows

no effect

Margin Note Recently, the SEC accused investment bank Morgan Stanley of overstating the value of certain bond investments by $75 million. The SEC stated that, in applying fair value accounting, Morgan Stanley used its own more optimistic assumptions rather than relying on external pricing sources.

Dec. 31	Unrealized Gain or Loss—Equity	9,537	
	Fair Value Adjustment—Available-for-Sale		9,537
	(To record unrealized loss on available-for-sale securities)		

If total fair value exceeds total cost, Elbert would record the adjusting entry as an increase (debit) to Fair Value Adjustment—Available-for-Sale and a credit to Unrealized Gain or Loss—Equity.

For available-for-sale securities, the company carries forward the Unrealized Gain or Loss—Equity account to future periods. At each future balance sheet date, the account is adjusted with the fair value adjustment account to show the difference between cost and fair value at that time.

READILY MARKETABLE. An investment is readily marketable when it can be sold easily whenever the need for cash arises. Short-term paper[4] meets this criterion because a company can readily sell it to other investors. Stocks and bonds traded on organized securities markets, such as the New York Stock Exchange, are readily marketable because they can be bought and sold daily. In contrast, there may be only a limited market for the securities issued by small corporations and no market for the securities of a privately held company.

INTENT TO CONVERT. Intent to convert means that management intends to sell the investment within the next year or operating cycle, whichever is longer. Generally, this criterion is satisfied when the investment is considered a resource that the company will use whenever the need for cash arises. For example, a ski resort may invest idle cash during the summer months with the intent to sell the securities to buy supplies and equipment shortly before the next winter season. This investment is considered short-term even if lack of snow cancels the next ski season and eliminates the need to convert the securities into cash as intended.

Because of their high liquidity, companies list short-term investments immediately below Cash in the current assets section of the balance sheet. Short-term investments are reported at fair value. For example, Weber Corporation would report its trading securities as shown in Illustration E-9.

Illustration E-9 Balance sheet presentation of short-term investments

WEBER CORPORATION Balance Sheet (partial)	
Current assets	
Cash	$21,000
Short-term investments, at fair value	**60,000**

Long-Term Investments

Companies generally report long-term investments in a separate section of the balance sheet immediately below "Current assets," as shown in Illustration E-10. Long-term investments in available-for-sale securities are reported at fair value. Investments in common stock accounted for under the equity method are reported at equity.

Illustration E-10 Balance sheet presentation of long-term investments

WEBER CORPORATION Balance Sheet (partial)	
Investments	
Bond sinking fund	$100,000
Investments in stock of less than 20% owned companies, at fair value	**50,000**
Investment in stock of 20%–50% owned company, at equity	**150,000**
Total investments	$300,000

---

[4]Short-term paper includes (1) certificates of deposits (CDs) issued by banks, (2) money market certificates issued by banks and savings and loan associations, (3) Treasury bills issued by the U.S. government, and (4) commercial paper issued by corporations with good credit ratings.

PRESENTATION OF REALIZED AND UNREALIZED GAIN OR LOSS

Companies must present in the financial statements gains and losses on investments, whether realized or unrealized. In the income statement, companies report gains and losses, as well as interest and dividend revenue, in the nonoperating activities section under the categories listed in Illustration E-11.

Illustration E-11
Nonoperating items related to investments

Other Revenue and Gains	Other Expenses and Losses
Interest Revenue	Loss on Sale of Investments
Dividend Revenue	Unrealized Loss—Income
Gain on Sale of Investments	
Unrealized Gain—Income	

As indicated earlier, companies report an unrealized gain or loss on available-for-sale securities as a separate component of stockholders' equity. To illustrate, assume that Muzzillo Inc. has common stock of $3,000,000, retained earnings of $1,500,000, and an unrealized loss on available-for-sale securities of $100,000. Illustration E-12 shows the financial statement presentation of the unrealized loss.

Illustration E-12 Unrealized loss in stockholders' equity section

MUZZILLO INC. Balance Sheet (partial)	
Stockholders' equity	
Common stock	$3,000,000
Retained earnings	1,500,000
Total paid-in capital and retained earnings	4,500,000
Less: **Unrealized loss on available-for-sale securities**	**100,000**
Total stockholders' equity	$4,400,000

Note that the presentation of the loss is similar to the presentation of the cost of treasury stock in the stockholders' equity section. (It decreases stockholders' equity.) An unrealized gain would be added in this section. Reporting the unrealized gain or loss in the stockholders' equity section serves two important purposes. (1) It reduces the volatility of net income due to fluctuations in fair value. (2) It informs the financial statement user of the gain or loss that would occur if the company sold the securities at fair value.

Companies must report, as part of a more inclusive measure called **comprehensive income**, items such as unrealized gains and losses on available-for-sale securities, which affect stockholders' equity but are not included in the calculation of net income. For example, Tootsie Roll reported other comprehensive loss in 2011 of $8,740,000. Note 12 to Tootsie Roll's financial statements shows that one component of this amount was unrealized gains and losses on investment securities. Comprehensive income is discussed more fully in Chapter 13.

STATEMENT OF CASH FLOWS PRESENTATION

As shown previously in Illustrations E-9, E-10, and E-12, the balance sheet presents a company's investment accounts at a point in time. The "Investing activities" section of the statement of cash flows reports information on the cash inflows and outflows during the period that resulted from investment transactions.

Illustration E-13 presents the cash flows from investing activities from a recent statement of cash flows of The Walt Disney Company. From this information, we learn that Disney received $1,530 million from the sale or redemption of investments during the year.

Real World	THE WALT DISNEY COMPANY Statement of Cash Flows (partial) (in millions)	
Investing Activities		
Investments in parks, resorts and other property		$(1,566)
Acquisitions		(588)
Dispositions		—
Proceeds from sale of investments		**1,530**
Other		6
Cash used by investing activities		$ (618)

Illustration E-13 Statement of cash flows presentation of investment activities

Summary of Learning Objectives

1 **Identify the reasons corporations invest in stocks and debt securities.** Corporations invest for three common reasons. (a) They have excess cash. (b) They view investment income as a significant revenue source. (c) They have strategic goals such as gaining control of a competitor or supplier or moving into a new line of business.

2 **Explain the accounting for debt investments.** Entries for investments in debt securities are required when companies purchase bonds, receive or accrue interest, and sell bonds.

3 **Explain the accounting for stock investments.** Entries for investments in common stock are required when companies purchase stock, receive dividends, and sell stock. When ownership is less than 20%, the cost method is used—the investment is recorded at cost. When ownership is between 20% and 50%, the equity method should be used—the investor records its share of the net income of the investee in the year it is earned. When ownership is more than 50%, consolidated financial statements should be prepared.

4 **Describe the purpose and usefulness of consolidated financial statements.** When a company owns more than 50% of the common stock of another company, consolidated financial statements are usually prepared. These statements are especially useful to the stockholders, board of directors, and management of the parent company.

5 **Indicate how debt and stock investments are valued and reported in the financial statements.** Investments in debt and stock securities are classified as trading, available-for-sale, or held-to-maturity for valuation and reporting purposes. Trading securities are reported as current assets at fair value, with changes from cost reported in net income. Available-for-sale securities are also reported at fair value, with the changes from cost reported in stockholders' equity. Available-for-sale securities are classified as short-term or long-term depending on their expected realization.

6 **Distinguish between short-term and long-term investments.** Short-term investments are securities held by a company that are readily marketable and intended to be converted to cash within the next year or operating cycle, whichever is longer. Investments that do not meet both criteria are classified as long-term investments.

Glossary

Terms are highlighted in blue throughout the chapter.

Available-for-sale securities Securities that are held with the intent of selling them sometime in the future.

Consolidated financial statements Financial statements that present the assets and liabilities controlled by the parent company and the total revenues and expenses of the subsidiary companies.

Controlling interest Ownership of more than 50% of the common stock of another entity.

Cost method An accounting method in which the investment in common stock is recorded at cost and revenue is recognized only when cash dividends are received.

Debt investments Investments in government and corporation bonds.

Equity method An accounting method in which the investment in common stock is initially recorded at cost, and the investment account is then adjusted annually to show the investor's equity in the investee.

Fair value Amount for which a security could be sold in a normal market.

Held-to-maturity securities Debt securities that the investor has the intent and ability to hold to maturity.

Long-term investments Investments that are not readily marketable or that management does not intend to convert into cash within the next year or operating cycle, whichever is longer.

Mark-to-market A method of accounting for certain investments that requires that they be adjusted to their fair value at the end of each period.

Parent company A company that owns more than 50% of the common stock of another entity.

Short-term investments (marketable securities) Investments that are readily marketable and intended to be converted into cash within the next year or operating cycle, whichever is longer.

Stock investments Investments in the capital stock of corporations.

Subsidiary (affiliated) company A company in which more than 50% of its stock is owned by another company.

Trading securities Securities bought and held primarily for sale in the near term to generate income on short-term price differences.

Self-Test, Brief Exercises, Exercises, Problems, and many more resources are available for practice in WileyPLUS.

Self-Test Questions

Answers are at the end of the appendix.

(LO 1) **1.** Which of the following is **not** a primary reason why corporations invest in debt and equity securities?
 (a) They wish to gain control of a competitor.
 (b) They have excess cash.
 (c) They wish to move into a new line of business.
 (d) They are required to by law.

(LO 2) **2.** Debt investments are initially recorded at:
 (a) cost.
 (b) cost plus accrued interest.
 (c) book value.
 (d) None of the above

(LO 2) **3.** Stan Free Company sells debt investments costing $26,000 for $28,000 plus accrued interest that has been recorded. In journalizing the sale, credits are:
 (a) Debt Investments and Loss on Sale of Debt Investments.
 (b) Debt Investments, Gain on Sale of Debt Investments, and Bond Interest Receivable.
 (c) Stock Investments and Bond Interest Receivable.
 (d) The correct answer is not given.

(LO 3) **4.** Karen Duffy Company receives net proceeds of $42,000 on the sale of stock investments that cost $39,500. This transaction will result in reporting in the income statement a:
 (a) loss of $2,500 under "Other expenses and losses."
 (b) loss of $2,500 under "Operating expenses."
 (c) gain of $2,500 under "Other revenues and gains."
 (d) gain of $2,500 under "Operating revenues."

(LO 3) **5.** The equity method of accounting for long-term investments in stock should be used when the investor has significant influence over an investee and owns:

 (a) between 20% and 50% of the investee's common stock.
 (b) 20% or more of the investee's bonds.
 (c) more than 50% of the investee's common stock.
 (d) less than 20% of the investee's common stock.

6. Assume that Horicon Corp. acquired 25% of the com- (LO 3) mon stock of Sheboygan Corp. on January 1, 2014, for $300,000. During 2014, Sheboygan Corp. reported net income of $160,000 and paid total dividends of $60,000. If Horicon uses the equity method to account for its investment, the balance in the investment account on December 31, 2014, will be:
 (a) $300,000.   (c) $400,000.
 (b) $325,000.   (d) $340,000.

7. Using the information in Question 6, what entry would (LO 3) Horicon make to record the receipt of the dividend from Sheboygan?
 (a) Debit Cash and credit Revenue from Stock Investments.
 (b) Debit Dividends and credit Revenue from Stock Investments.
 (c) Debit Cash and credit Stock Investments.
 (d) Debit Cash and credit Dividend Revenue.

8. You have a controlling interest if: (LO 3)
 (a) you own more than 20% of a company's stock.
 (b) you are the president of the company.
 (c) you use the equity method.
 (d) you own more than 50% of a company's stock.

9. Which of these statements is **false**?   (LO 4)
 Consolidated financial statements are useful to:
 (a) determine the profitability of specific subsidiaries.
 (b) determine the aggregate profitability of companies under common control.

(c) determine the breadth of a parent company's operations.

(d) determine the full extent of aggregate obligations of companies under common control.

(LO 5) **10.** At the end of the first year of operations, the total cost of the trading securities portfolio is $120,000 and the total fair value is $115,000. What should the financial statements show?
(a) A reduction of an asset of $5,000 and a realized loss of $5,000.
(b) A reduction of an asset of $5,000 and an unrealized loss of $5,000 in the stockholders' equity section.
(c) A reduction of an asset of $5,000 in the current assets section and an unrealized loss of $5,000 under "Other expenses and losses."
(d) A reduction of an asset of $5,000 in the current assets section and a realized loss of $5,000 under "Other expenses and losses."

(LO 5) **11.** In the balance sheet, Unrealized Gain or Loss—Equity is reported as a:
(a) contra asset account.
(b) contra stockholders' equity account.
(c) loss in the income statement.
(d) loss in the retained earnings statement.

(LO 5) **12.** If a company wants to increase its reported income by manipulating its investment accounts, which should it do?
(a) Sell its "winner" trading securities and hold its "loser" trading securities.
(b) Hold its "winner" trading securities and sell its "loser" trading securities.

(c) Sell its "winner" available-for-sale securities and hold its "loser" available-for-sale securities.
(d) Hold its "winner" available-for-sale securities and sell its "loser" available-for-sale securities.

13. At December 31, 2014, the fair value of available-for- (LO 5) sale securities is $41,300 and the cost is $39,800. At January 1, 2014, there was a credit balance of $900 in the Fair Value Adjustment—Available-for-Sale account. The required adjusting entry would be:
(a) Debit Fair Value Adjustment—Available-for-Sale for $1,500, and credit Unrealized Gain or Loss—Equity for $1,500.
(b) Debit Fair Value Adjustment—Available-for-Sale for $600, and credit Unrealized Gain or Loss—Equity for $600.
(c) Debit Fair Value Adjustment—Available-for-Sale for $2,400, and credit Unrealized Gain or Loss—Equity for $2,400.
(d) Debit Unrealized Gain or Loss—Equity for $2,400, and credit Fair Value Adjustment—Available-for-Sale for $2,400.

14. To be classified as short-term investments, debt (LO 6) investments must be readily marketable and be expected to be sold within:
(a) 3 months from the date of purchase.
(b) the next year or operating cycle, whichever is shorter.
(c) the next year or operating cycle, whichever is longer.
(d) the operating cycle.

Questions

1. What are the reasons that companies invest in securities?

2. (a) What is the cost of an investment in bonds?
(b) When is interest on bonds recorded?

3. Jill Glendo is confused about losses and gains on the sale of debt investments. Explain these issues to Jill:
(a) How the gain or loss is computed.
(b) The statement presentation of gains and losses.

4. Townsend Company sells bonds that cost $40,000 for $45,000, including $1,000 of accrued interest. In recording the sale, Townsend books a $5,000 gain. Is this correct? Explain.

5. What is the cost of an investment in stock?

6. To acquire Engels Corporation stock, Kaiser Co. pays $61,500 in cash. What entry should be made for this investment, assuming the stock is readily marketable?

7. (a) When should a long-term investment in common stock be accounted for by the equity method?
(b) When is revenue recognized under the equity method?

8. Upson Corporation uses the equity method to account for its ownership of 30% of the common stock of Holland Packing. During 2014, Holland reported a net income of $80,000 and declares and pays cash dividends of $10,000. What recognition should Upson Corporation give to these events?

9. What constitutes "significant influence" when an investor's financial interest is less than 50%?

10. Distinguish between the cost and equity methods of accounting for investments in stocks.

11. What are consolidated financial statements?

12. What are the valuation guidelines for trading and available-for-sale investments at a balance sheet date?

13. Erica Pike is the controller of D-Products, Inc. At December 31, the company's investments in trading securities cost $74,000 and have a fair value of $70,000. Indicate how Erica would report these data in the financial statements prepared on December 31.

14. Using the data in Question 13, how would Erica report the data if the investments were long-term and the securities were classified as available-for-sale?

15. Napa Company's investments in available-for-sale securities at December 31 show total cost of $202,000 and total fair value of $210,000. Prepare the adjusting entry.

16. Using the data in Question 15, prepare the adjusting entry, assuming the securities are classified as trading securities.

17. ⚲══════C Where is Unrealized Gain or Loss—Equity reported on the balance sheet?

18. What purposes are served by reporting Unrealized Gains (Losses)—Equity in the stockholders' equity section?

19. Ginavan Wholesale Supply owns stock in Kriley Corporation, which it intends to hold indefinitely because of some negative tax consequences if sold. Should the investment in Kriley be classified as a short-term investment? Why?

Brief Exercises

Journalize entries for debt investments.
(LO 2), AP

BEE-1 Sprague Corporation purchased debt investments for $40,800 on January 1, 2014. On July 1, 2014, Sprague received cash interest of $1,660. Journalize the purchase and the receipt of interest. Assume no interest has been accrued.

Journalize entries for stock investments.
(LO 3), AP

BEE-2 On August 1, Frost Company buys 1,000 shares of ABC common stock for $35,600 cash. On December 1, the stock investments are sold for $38,000 in cash. Journalize the purchase and sale of the common stock.

Journalize transactions under the equity method.
(LO 3), AP

BEE-3 Bass Company owns 25% of Petit Company. For the current year, Petit reports net income of $150,000 and declares and pays a $60,000 cash dividend. Record Bass's equity in Petit's net income and the receipt of dividends from Petit.

Prepare adjusting entry using fair value.
(LO 5), AP

BEE-4 Cost and fair value data for the trading securities of Dobler Company at December 31, 2014, are $62,000 and $59,600, respectively. Prepare the adjusting entry to record the securities at fair value.

Indicate statement presentation using fair value.
(LO 6), AN

BEE-5 For the data presented in BEE-4, show the financial statement presentation of the trading securities and related accounts.

Prepare adjusting entry using fair value.
(LO 5), AP

BEE-6 In its first year of operations, Mallein Corporation purchased available-for-sale stock securities costing $72,000 as a long-term investment. At December 31, 2014, the fair value of the securities is $69,000. Prepare the adjusting entry to record the securities at fair value.

Indicate statement presentation using fair value.
(LO 6), AN

BEE-7 For the data presented in BEE-6, show the financial statement presentation of the securities and related accounts. Assume the securities are noncurrent.

Prepare investments section of balance sheet.
(LO 6), AP

BEE-8 Rhoads Corporation has these long-term investments: common stock of Wenn Co. (10% ownership) held as available-for-sale securities, cost $108,000, fair value $112,000; common stock of Thomas Inc. (30% ownership), cost $210,000, equity $230,000; and a bond sinking fund of $150,000. Prepare the investments section of the balance sheet.

Exercises

Journalize debt investment transactions, and accrue interest.
(LO 2), AP

EE-1 Maurer Corporation had these transactions pertaining to debt investments:

Jan. 1 Purchased 90 10%, $1,000 Landis Co. bonds for $90,000 cash. Interest is payable semiannually on July 1 and January 1.
July 1 Received semiannual interest on Landis Co. bonds.
July 1 Sold 30 Landis Co. bonds for $32,000.

Instructions
(a) Journalize the transactions.
(b) Prepare the adjusting entry for the accrual of interest at December 31.

Journalize stock investment transactions, and explain income statement presentation.
(LO 3), AN

EE-2 Soils Company had these transactions pertaining to stock investments:

Feb. 1 Purchased 1,200 shares of JB common stock (2% of outstanding shares) for $8,400.
July 1 Received cash dividends of $2 per share on JB common stock.
Sept. 1 Sold 500 shares of JB common stock for $5,400.
Dec. 1 Received cash dividends of $1 per share on JB common stock.

Instructions

(a) Journalize the transactions.
(b) Explain how dividend revenue and the gain (loss) on sale should be reported in the income statement.

EE-3 Kurzon Inc. had these transactions pertaining to investments in common stock:

Journalize transactions for investments in stock.
(LO 3), **AP**

Jan. 1 Purchased 1,200 shares of Fulten Corporation common stock (5% of outstanding shares) for $59,200 cash.
July 1 Received a cash dividend of $7 per share.
Dec. 1 Sold 900 shares of Fulten Corporation common stock for $47,200 cash.
     31 Received a cash dividend of $7 per share.

Instructions

Journalize the transactions.

EE-4 On January 1, Lambert Corporation purchased a 25% equity investment in Dougherty Corporation for $150,000. At December 31, Dougherty declared and paid a $80,000 cash dividend and reported net income of $380,000.

Journalize and post transactions under the equity method.
(LO 3), **AP**

Instructions

(a) Journalize the transactions.
(b) Determine the amount to be reported as an investment in Dougherty stock at December 31.

EE-5 These are two independent situations:

Journalize entries under cost and equity methods.
(LO 3), **AP**

1. Eusey Cosmetics acquired 12% of the 300,000 shares of common stock of High Fashion at a total cost of $14 per share on March 18, 2014. On June 30, High declared and paid a $75,000 dividend. On December 31, High reported net income of $244,000 for the year. At December 31, the market price of High Fashion was $16 per share. The stock is classified as available-for-sale.
2. Dickson Inc. obtained significant influence over Kiner Corporation by buying 25% of Kiner's 30,000 outstanding shares of common stock at a total cost of $11 per share on January 1, 2014. On June 15, Kiner declared and paid a cash dividend of $35,000. On December 31, Kiner reported a net income of $120,000 for the year.

Instructions

Prepare all the necessary journal entries for 2014 for (a) Eusey Cosmetics and (b) Dickson Inc.

EE-6 At December 31, 2014, the trading securities for Puckett, Inc. are as follows.

Prepare adjusting entry to record fair value, and indicate statement presentation.
(LO 5, 6), **AP**

Security	Cost	Fair Value
A	$18,100	$16,000
B	12,500	14,800
C	23,000	18,000
Total	$53,600	$48,800

Instructions

(a) Prepare the adjusting entry at December 31, 2014, to report the securities at fair value.
(b) Show the balance sheet and income statement presentation at December 31, 2014, after adjustment to fair value.

EE-7 Data for investments in stock classified as trading securities are presented in EE-6. Assume instead that the investments are classified as available-for-sale securities with the same cost and fair value data. The securities are considered to be a long-term investment.

Prepare adjusting entry to record fair value, and indicate statement presentation.
(LO 5, 6), **AN**

Instructions

(a) Prepare the adjusting entry at December 31, 2014, to report the securities at fair value.
(b) Show the statement presentation at December 31, 2014, after adjustment to fair value.
(c) ▬▬▶ Jayne Parks, a member of the board of directors, does not understand the reporting of the unrealized gains or losses on trading securities and available-for-sale securities. Write a letter to Ms. Parks explaining the reporting and the purposes it serves.

Prepare adjusting entries for fair value, and indicate statement presentation for two classes of securities.
(LO 5, 6), **AN**

EE-8 Swisher Company has these data at December 31, 2014:

Securities	Cost	Fair Value
Trading	$110,000	$122,000
Available-for-sale	100,000	96,000

The available-for-sale securities are held as a long-term investment.

Instructions
(a) Prepare the adjusting entries to report each class of securities at fair value.
(b) Indicate the statement presentation of each class of securities and the related unrealized gain (loss) accounts.

Problems

Journalize debt investment transactions.
(LO 2, 5, 6), **AN**

PE-1 Moore Farms is a grower of hybrid seed corn for DeKalb Genetics Corporation. It has had two exceptionally good years and has elected to invest its excess funds in bonds. The following selected transactions relate to bonds acquired as an investment by Moore Farms, whose fiscal year ends on December 31.

2014

Jan. 1 Purchased at par $600,000 of Vandiver Corporation 10-year, 7% bonds dated January 1, 2014, directly from the issuing corporation.
July 1 Received the semiannual interest on the Vandiver bonds.
Dec. 31 Accrual of interest at year-end on the Vandiver bonds.

Assume that all intervening transactions and adjustments have been properly recorded and the number of bonds owned has not changed from December 31, 2014, to December 31, 2016.

2017

Jan. 1 Received the semiannual interest on the Vandiver bonds.
Jan. 1 Sold $300,000 of Vandiver bonds at 110.
July 1 Received the semiannual interest on the Vandiver bonds.
Dec. 31 Accrual of interest at year-end on the Vandiver bonds.

Instructions
Journalize the listed transactions for the years 2014 and 2017.

Journalize investment transactions, prepare adjusting entry, and show financial statement presentation.
(LO 2, 3, 5, 6), **AN**

PE-2 In January 2014, the management of Weast Company concludes that it has sufficient cash to purchase some short-term investments in debt and stock securities. During the year, the following transactions occurred.

Feb. 1 Purchased 1,200 shares of ALF common stock for $51,600.
Mar. 1 Purchased 500 shares of LNC common stock for $18,500.
Apr. 1 Purchased 70 $1,000, 8% CRT bonds for $70,000. Interest is payable semiannually on April 1 and October 1.
July 1 Received a cash dividend of $0.80 per share on the ALF common stock.
Aug. 1 Sold 200 shares of ALF common stock at $42 per share.
Sept. 1 Received $2 per share cash dividend on the LNC common stock.
Oct. 1 Received the semiannual interest on the CRT bonds.
Oct. 1 Sold the CRT bonds for $75,700.

At December 31, the fair values of the ALF and LNC common stocks were $39 and $30 per share, respectively.

Instructions
(a) Journalize the transactions and post to the accounts Debt Investments and Stock Investments. (Use the T-account form.)
(b) Prepare the adjusting entry at December 31, 2014, to report the investments at fair value. All securities are considered to be trading securities.
(c) Show the balance sheet presentation of investment securities at December 31, 2014.
(d) Identify the income statement accounts and give the statement classification of each account.

PE-3   On December 31, 2013, Ogleby Associates owned the following securities that are held as long-term investments.

Journalize transactions, prepare adjusting entry for stock investments, and show balance sheet presentation.
(LO 3, 5, 6), **AN**

GLS

Common Stock	Shares	Cost
A Co.	1,000	$48,000
B Co.	5,000	36,000
C Co.	1,200	24,000

On this date, the total fair value of the securities was equal to its cost. The securities are not held for influence or control over the investees. In 2014, the following transactions occurred.

July   1   Received $2.00 per share semiannual cash dividend on B Co. common stock.
Aug.   1   Received $0.50 per share cash dividend on A Co. common stock.
Sept. 1   Sold 1,000 shares of B Co. common stock for cash at $9 per share.
Oct.   1   Sold 300 shares of A Co. common stock for cash at $53 per share.
Nov.   1   Received $1 per share cash dividend on C Co. common stock.
Dec. 15   Received $0.50 per share cash dividend on A Co. common stock.
       31   Received $2.20 per share semiannual cash dividend on B Co. common stock.

At December 31, the fair values per share of the common stocks were A Co. $47, B Co. $7, and C Co. $24.

Instructions
(a) Journalize the 2014 transactions and post to the account Stock Investments. (Use the T-account form.)
(b) Prepare the adjusting entry at December 31, 2014, to show the securities at fair value. The stock should be classified as available-for-sale securities.
(c) Show the balance sheet presentation of the investments and the unrealized gain (loss) at December 31, 2014. At this date, Ogleby Associates has common stock $2,000,000 and retained earnings $1,200,000.

PE-4   Farwell Company acquired 30% of the outstanding common stock of Ingold Inc. on January 1, 2014, by paying $1,800,000 for 60,000 shares. Ingold declared and paid a $0.50 per share cash dividend on June 30 and again on December 31, 2014. Ingold reported net income of $800,000 for the year.

Prepare entries under cost and equity methods, and prepare memorandum.
(LO 3), **AN**

Instructions
(a) Prepare the journal entries for Farwell Company for 2014, assuming Farwell cannot exercise significant influence over Ingold. (Use the cost method.)
(b) Prepare the journal entries for Farwell Company for 2014, assuming Farwell can exercise significant influence over Ingold. (Use the equity method.)
(c) The board of directors of Farwell Company is confused about the differences between the cost and equity methods. Prepare a memorandum for the board that explains each method and shows in tabular form the account balances under each method at December 31, 2014.

PE-5   Here is Kline Company's portfolio of long-term available-for-sale securities at December 31, 2013:

Journalize stock transactions, and show balance sheet presentation.
(LO 3, 5, 6), **AN**

	Cost
1,400 shares of Tabares Inc. common stock	$73,500
1,200 shares of Munoz Corporation common stock	84,000
800 shares of H. Hogan Corporation preferred stock	33,600

On December 31, the total cost of the portfolio equaled the total fair value. Kline had the following transactions related to the securities during 2014.

Jan. 20   Sold 1,400 shares of Tabares Inc. common stock at $55 per share.
      28   Purchased 400 shares of $10 par value common stock of M. Powell Corporation at $78 per share.
      30   Received a cash dividend of $1.25 per share on Munoz Corporation common stock.
Feb. 8   Received cash dividends of $0.40 per share on H. Hogan Corporation preferred stock.
      18   Sold all 800 shares of H. Hogan preferred stock at $35 per share.

July 30   Received a cash dividend of $1.10 per share on Munoz Corporation common stock.

Sept. 6   Purchased an additional 600 shares of the $10 par value common stock of M. Powell Corporation at $82 per share.

Dec. 1   Received a cash dividend of $1.50 per share on M. Powell Corporation common stock.

At December 31, 2014, the fair values of the securities were:

Munoz Corporation common stock	$65 per share
M. Powell Corporation common stock	$77 per share

Kline uses separate account titles for each investment, such as Investment in Munoz Corporation Common Stock.

Instructions
(a) Prepare journal entries to record the transactions.
(b) Post to the investment accounts. (Use separate T-accounts for each investment.)
(c) Prepare the adjusting entry at December 31, 2014, to report the portfolio at fair value.
(d) Show the balance sheet presentation at December 31, 2014.

Prepare a balance sheet.
(LO 6), **AP**

PE-6   The following data, presented in alphabetical order, are taken from the records of Wellman Corporation.

Accounts payable	$ 150,000
Accounts receivable	90,000
Accumulated depreciation—buildings	180,000
Accumulated depreciation—equipment	52,000
Allowance for doubtful accounts	6,000
Bonds payable (10%, due 2025)	350,000
Buildings	900,000
Cash	63,000
Common stock ($5 par value; 500,000 shares authorized, 240,000 shares issued)	$1,200,000
Debt investments	400,000
Discount on bonds payable	20,000
Dividends payable	50,000
Equipment	275,000
Goodwill	190,000
Income taxes payable	70,000
Inventory	170,000
Land	410,000
Notes payable (due 2015)	70,000
Paid-in capital in excess of par value	464,000
Prepaid insurance	16,000
Retained earnings	310,000
Stock investments (Lawton Inc. stock, 30% ownership, at equity)	240,000
Stock investments (short-term, at fair value)	128,000

Instructions
Prepare a balance sheet at December 31, 2014.

Answers to Self-Test Questions

1. d   **2.** a   **3.** b   **4.** c   **5.** a   **6.** b $300,000 + (($160,000 − $60,000) × .25)$ **7.** c   **8.** d
9. a   **10.** c   **11.** b   **12.** c   **13.** c $($41,300 − $39,800) + 900 **14.** c

COMPANY INDEX

A

Acer Inc., 251
Ag-Chem, 306
AIG, 7, 36
AirTran Airways, 395
Amazon.com, 12, 192, 195, 404, 512
AMD, 561–562
American Airlines, 383, 438
American Cancer Society, 494
American Express, 343, 358, 465
American Pharmaceutical Partners, 52
Anaheim Angels, E7
Apple, 138, 355, 401, 493, 541, 557–558, 559
AT&T, 600, E7
Avis, E7

B

Bank One Corporation, 91
Barnes & Noble, 404
Berkshire Hathaway, 511
Best Buy, 41, 42, 47–56, 58, 78, 146, 186, 402
BHP Billiton, 402
Blockbuster, Inc., 18
Boeing, 383, 385, 397
Boeing Capital Corporation, 388
Boise Cascade Corporation, 412
BP, 35, 249
Bristol-Myers Squibb, 157, 247, 612

C

Callaway Golf Company, 53
Campbell Soup Company, 247
Capital Cities/ABC, Inc., E7
Cargill Inc., 494
Caterpillar, 237–239, 249, 254, 255, 358, 385, 494

Caterpillar Financial Services, 358
CBS, 405
Cendant, E7
Century 21, E7
Chicago Cubs, 96
Chrysler, 36, 37, 435
Cisco Systems, 611
Citicorp, 7
Citigroup, 5, 51, 136
Clif Bar & Company, 3
CNH Global, 255
Coca-Cola, 5, 36, 405–407
Coldwell Banker, E7
Commonwealth Edison, 506
Computer Associates International, 157
ConAgra Foods, 156, 206, 506
ConocoPhilips, 402
Continental Bank, 388
Cooper Tire & Rubber Company, 45
Costco Wholesale Corp., 202, 545
Countrywide Financial Corporation, 354
Craig Consumer Electronics, 240
Credit Suisse Group, 102

D

Daimler-Benz, 435
DaimlerChrysler, 435
Dayton Hudson, 307
Deere & Company, 353
Dell, 239
Dell Financial Services, 388
Delta Air Lines, 56, 136, 306, 307, 397, 408
Dick's Sporting Goods, 209, 210
Discover, 358
Disney, 6, 396, 402
Disney World, E7

Disneyland, E7
Dow Chemical, 12
Duke Energy, 7
Dunkin' Donuts, Inc., 56
Dynegy, 6

E

EarthLink, 505
Eastman Kodak, 53, 542
eBay, 206, 339, 359, 379
Eli Lilly, 285
Enron, 6, 7, 36, 206, 450, 454, 496, 612
ESPN, E7
ExxonMobil, 5, 249, 299

F

Facebook, 12, 493–6, 499, 502, 505–507, 512, 515
Fannie Mae, 91, 148
Fitch, 610
Ford Motor Company (Ford), 57, 101, 194, 239, 251, 357, 340, 402, 435, 436, 452, 456–457, 558
Ford Motor Credit Corp., 358
Fox, 405
Frito-Lay, E7

G

Gatorade, E7
GE Capital, 358
General Dynamics Corp., 597
General Electric (GE), 6, 157, 200, 285, 340, 358, 494, 612
General Mills, 392, 603, 607, 617–619
General Motors (GM), 5, 6, 53, 78, 84, 85, 239, 435, 436, 439, 442, 450, 465, 494, 498, 611
Global Crossing, 450
Goldman Sachs, 7

Google, 12, 402, 403, 493, 494, 510, 512, 612
Green Bay Packers, 83
Groupon, 135, 136
Gulf Oil, 498

H
HealthSouth, 7
Hershey Company, 19, B1–B4
hhgregg, 47–48, 51–53
Hilton, 388
Home Depot, 240
Honeywell International, 600
Howard Johnson, E7
Hughes Aircraft Co., 597
Humana Corporation, 162–163

I
IBM, 42, 157, 206, 404, 494, 499, 511, 547, 600, 601
Institutional Shareholder Services, 497
Intel Corporation, 36, 212, 307, 340, 355, 403, 561–562
InterContinental, 388
International Outsourcing Services, LLC, 98

J
JCPenney, 342, 545
JetBlue Airways, 383–385, 387–388, 399–401
John Deere Capital Corporation, 388
J.P. Morgan Leasing, 388
JPMorgan Chase, 91

K
Kansas Farmers' Vertically Integrated Cooperative, Inc., 111–112
Kellogg Company (Kellogg), 515, 547, 603, 613–614
Kmart, 354
Kodak, 53, 542, 556, 590, E-9
Kohl's Corporation, 545
Kraft Foods, 98
Krispy Kreme, 157
Kroger Stores, 210, 247

L
LDK Solar Co., 251
Lease Finance Corporation, 388
Leslie Fay, 240

Linens'n Things, Inc., 354
Lockheed, 397
Loews Corporation, 501

M
Manitowoc Company, 255–256
Marcus Corporation, 47
Marriott, 157, 388, 392, 405
MasterCard, 358–359
Mattel Corporation, 311–312
Maxwell Car Company, 435
McDonald's Corporation, 7, 36, 465
McKesson Corp., 192, 307, 358
Merck, 210, 612
Merrill Lynch, 7
MF Global Holdings Ltd., 83, 93, 109, 496
Microsoft, 5, 53, 78, 83, 85, 100, 132, 200, 206, 212, 385, 402, 493, 515, 541, 547, 558–560
Mighty Ducks, E7
Moody's, 603, 610
Morgan Stanley, E10
Morrow Snowboards, Inc., 191, 195, 232
Motley Fool, 41
Motorola, 247, 599
Mountain Equipment Cooperative, 212–213

N
NBC, 405
New York Stock Exchange, 5, 494, 500, E11
Nike, 212, 308, 339, 340, 346, 358, 361–362, 374, 402, 495, 501, 503, 506, 510, 512, 515, 516, 518, 558, 612
Nortel Networks, 348
Novartis AG, 454

O
Office Depot, 192, 252
Office Max, 157

P
Packard Bell, 355
PairGain Technologies, 41
Parmalat, 36, 334, 554
PepsiCo, 5, 98, 211, 232, E7
Pilgrim's Pride, 157, 206
PricewaterhouseCoopers, 18

Procter & Gamble (P&G), 7, 46, 501, 514, 599
Prudential Real Estate, 7

Q
Quaker Oats, 251, E7

R
Radio Shack, 210
Ramada Inn, E7
Recreational Equipment Incorporated (REI), 191, 192, 196, 200, 203–205, 209–213
Reebok, 247, 504
REL Consultancy Group, 52
Rhino Foods, 6
Royal Dutch Shell, 249

S
SafeNet, 500
Safeway, 210, 287
Saks Fifth Avenue, 209
Salvation Army, 494
Sara Lee Corporation, 514
Sears, Roebuck & Co, 358
Sears Holdings Corporation, 53, 206, 358, 398
Skechers USA, 339, 348, 355–357, 361
Skype, 206
SkyTrax, 383
Softbank Corp., 406
Sony, 36, 253, 278
Southwest Airlines, 44, 383–385, 394–395, 399–401, 455, 547, 612
Sports Illustrated, 438
Sprint Nextel Corporation, 438
Standard & Poor's, 503, 508, 603
Standard Oil Company of California, 412
Stanley Black & Decker Manufacturing Company, 247
Starbucks, 247, 512, 547
Stephanie's Gourmet Coffee and More, 283, 284, 287, 289, 291, 295
Subway, 405

T
Target, 210, 240, 252–253, 299, 307, 545
Tektronix Inc., 513

The Receivables Exchange, 359
Tiffany and Co., 210
Time Warner, 45, E5, E7
Tootsie Roll, 3, 5, 8–10, 15–19, 84, A1–A32, E12
Toyota Motor Corporation, 36, 405, 451–453, 456
Trek, 7
Tropicana, E7
True Value Hardware, 240
Turner Broadcasting, E5, E7
Tweeter Home Entertainment, 58

U
United Airlines, 6, 439, 542
United Parcel Service (UPS), 600

United States Steel Corp., 442
United Stationers, 192
US Bancorp Equipment Finance, 388
USAir, 442

V
Valujet, 383
Verizon Communications, 600
Visa, 358, 359

W
Wachovia, 343
Walgreens, 192, 247
Wal-Mart, 191, 192, 209–212, 240, 252–253, 299, 385, 515, 545, 558

Walt Disney Company, E7, E13
Waste Management Company, 91
Wells Fargo, 284, 343
Wendy's International, 247
Weyerhaeuser Co., 598
WorldCom, 7, 36, 157, 292, 396, 450, 496, 608, 612

X
Xerox, 157

Y
Yahoo! Inc., 44, 603

Z
Zetar plc, C1–C4

The Receivable Exchange, 350

Tiffany and Co., 210

Time Warner, 15, E8, E7

Tootsie Roll, 5, 5, 8–10, 15–19, 84, A1–A3, B12

Toyota Motor Corporation, 36, 405, 451–453, 150

Trek, 7

Tropicana, E7

True Value Hardware, 240

Turner Broadcasting, E5, B7

Tweeter Home Entertainment, 58

U

United Airlines, 9, 439, 582

United Parcel Service (UPS), 600

United States Steel Corp., 449

United Stationers, 192

UPS Bancorp Equipment Finance, 248

USAir, 442

V

Valero, 583

Verizon Communications, 600

Visa, 378, 559

W

Wachovia, 343

Walgreens, 192, 247

Wal-Mart, 191, 193, 204–212, 210, 552–282, 290, 285, 574, 4545, 552

Walt Disney Company, B7, E11

Private Management

Company, 91

Wells Fargo, 286, 343

Wendy's International, 247

Weyerhaeuser Co., 508

WorldCom, 7, 30, 75, 192, 595, 450, 496, 603, 612

X

Xerox, 157

Y

Yahoo! Inc., 44, 603

Z

Zondervan, C1–C8

SUBJECT INDEX

A

Accelerated-depreciation methods, 411
Accounting cycle, 160–162
Accounting equation, 85–86
Accounting information system
the account, 92–98
accounting transactions and, 84–92
recording process steps and, 98–109
trial balance and, 109–112
Accounting principle changes, 600
Accounting transactions, 84–92
accuracy and, 91
balancing accounting equation, 85
expanded accounting equation, 86
investment of cash by stockholders, 86–87
new employee hiring, 91
note issued in exchange for cash, 87
payment of cash for employee salaries, 90–91
payment of dividends, 90
payment of rent, 89
purchase of insurance policy for cash, 89
purchase of office equipment for cash, 87
purchase of supplies on account, 90
receipt of cash in advance from customer, 87–88
services performed for cash, 88–89
summary of, 91–92
transaction analysis, 85–91

Accounts, 92–98
basic form of, 92
debit and credit procedures and, 93–96
debits and credits, 93–94
journalizing and, 98–100
Accounts payable
operating activities and, 10
statement of cash flows and, 11
Accounts receivable, 88–89, 341–348
aging the accounts receivable, 347
allowance method for uncollectible accounts, 344–348
bad debt expense and, 343
direct write-off method and, 343–344
estimating the allowance and, 346
percentage-of-receivables basis, 346
recognition of, 341–342
recording estimated uncollectibles and, 344–345
recording the write-off on an uncollectible account, 345
recovery of an uncollectible account, 346
statement of cash flows and, 552
turnover, 357, 609, 619
valuation of, 342–348
Accrual accounting concepts
accounting cycle summary and, 160–162
accrual vs. cash basis of accounting, 138–139

adjusted trial balance preparation, 154
automated world and, 165
basics of adjusting entries and, 139–153
closing the books, 158–160
expense recognition principle, 137
financial statement preparation, 155–156
international insight and, 138
quality of earnings and, 156–157
revenue recognition principle and, 136–137
timing issues and, 136–139
Accrual-based ratios, 559
Accruals, 147–151
accrued expenses and, 148–151
accrued revenues and, 147–148
categories and, 140
Accrued expenses
accrued interest, 148–150
accrued salaries, 150–151
adjusting entries for, 147–151
Accrued interest, 148–150
Accrued revenues, 147–148
Accrued salaries, 150–151
Accumulated depreciation, 45
Accuracy, importance of, 91
Actual losses, direct write-off method and, 343
Additional cost of borrowing, 445
Additions and improvements, 395
Adjusted cash balance, 304
Adjusted trial balance, 154–156

Adjustment entries, 139–153
  for accruals, 147–151
  basic relationships summary, 152–153
  categories of, 140
  for deferrals, 141–146
  trial balance and, 140
Administrative expenses, 10
Advance receipt of cash from customer, 87–88
Aging schedule, 355
Aging the accounts receivable, 347
Allowances
  for doubtful accounts, 344–348
  periodic inventory system and, 214–216
  purchases and, 197–198
  sales and, 215
  for uncollectible accounts, 344
Alternative accounting methods, quality of earnings and, 611
Amortization
  bonds at discount and, 447
  bonds at premium and, 447–449
  effective-interest method and, 461–465
  intangible assets and, 403
  quality of earnings and, 610–611
  straight-line method and, 459–461
Amount due at maturity, interest-bearing notes and, 351–352
Annual accounting period, 161
Annual rate, depreciation and, 391
Annual reports, 17–19, A1–A32
Annually recurring expenditures, equipment and, 387
Annuity
  future value of, D4–D6
  present value of, D9–D11
Assets. *See also* Plant assets
  debit and credit procedures for, 94
  reporting, leasing and, 388
  turnover and, 610, 625
Auditor's report, 18, A28–A29
Authorized stock, 500
Auto loans, D15–D16

Automated world, adjusting entries in, 165
Available-for-sale securities, 601, E8, E9–E10
Average collection period, 356–357, 609, 619
Average-cost method, 246–247, 259

B
Background checks, 292
Bad debt expense, 343, 344–348
Bad information, bad loans and, 353
Balance sheet, 13–14
  adjusted trial balance and, 155
  cost flow methods and, 249
  horizontal analysis of, 604
  inventory errors and, 261
  liabilities and, 450–451
  long-term investments and, E11
  short term investments and, E10–E11
  stockholders' equity and, 513–514
  user communication and, 10
  vertical analysis of, 606
Bank line of credit, 452
Bank reconciliation, 299–305
  bank memoranda and, 355
  bank service charges and, 304-305
  book error and, 304
  collection of note receivable and, 304
  deposits in transit and, 302
  electronic funds transfer system and, 305
  entries from, 304–305
  errors and, 302–303
  illustration of, 303
  NSF check and, 304
  outstanding checks and, 302
  procedures for, 301–303
  time lags and, 301
Bank statements, 302–303
Basic accounting equation, 13
Benford's Law, 608
Board of directors, 496
Bond financing, advantages over common stock and, 516–517

Bonding employees, handling cash and, 292
Bonds, 441–449
  accounting for redemptions and, 449
  additional cost of borrowing and, 446
  amortizing the discount and, 447
  amortizing the premium and, 448
  bond certificate, 442–443
  bond issues accounting, 444–449
  carrying (or book) value and, 446, 449
  contractual interest rate and, 442, 445–446
  convertible and callable bonds, 442
  discount or premium on bonds, 445–446
  discounting and, 443
  effective-interest amortization method and, 461–465
  face value and, 442
  interest expense and, 446
  interest payable as a current liability and, 445
  interest payments and, 444
  issuing at a discount, 446–447
  issuing at face value, 444–445
  issuing at premium, 447–449
  issuing procedures and, 442
  market interest rates and, 443, 445–446
  market price determination and, 443–444
  maturity date and, 442
  present value of, D11–D13
  principal and, 444
  recording acquisition of, E2–E3
  recording bond interest, E3
  recording sale of, E3
  redeeming at maturity, 449
  redeeming before maturity, 449
  secured and unsecured bonds, 442
  straight-line amortization method, 459–461
  types of, 442

Bonds payable
  debt securities and, 9
  statement of cash flows (direct method) and, 569–570
  statement of cash flows (indirect method) and, 555–556
Book error, bank reconciliation and, 304
Book (carrying) value
  bonds and, 446, 449
  declining-balance method and, 392
  depreciation and, 144, 389
Borrowing, additional cost of, 446
Buffett, Warren, 595
Buildings, 386–387
  construction of, 386
  depreciation and, 389
  interest costs and, 386–387
  purchasing of, 386
  statement of cash flows (direct method) and, 569
  statement of cash flows (indirect method) and, 555
Business activities, 8–10
  financing activities, 9
  investing activities, 9
  operating activities, 9–10
Business careers, 7
Business documents, recording sales and, 195
Business organizations forms, 4–5
Business size, internal controls and, 294
Buying or leasing, 388
By-laws, corporations and, 498

C

Calculators. *See* Financial calculators
Callable bonds, 442
Canceled checks, 301
Capital acquisition, corporations and, 495
Capital expenditures, 54, 395
Capital lease, 388
Capital stock, 46
Capitalized expenditures, improper, 385
Captive finance companies, 358
Carrying value. *See* Book (carrying) value

Cash
  adequacy, cash dividends and, 506–507
  advance receipt from customer, 87–88
  disbursements, 297–298
  equivalents, 306, 385
  handling, bonding employees and, 292
  increases and decreases in, 93
  insurance policy purchase with, 105
  investing activities and, 9
  investment by stockholders, 86–87, 102
  management of, 307–311
  (net) realizable value, 351
  note issued in exchange for, 87
  payment of employee salaries with, 90–91, 107
  payment of rent with, 89, 105
  purchase of insurance policy for, 89
  purchase of office equipment for, 87
  receipt in advance from customer, 104
  services performed for, 88–89, 104
Cash-based ratios, 558–559
Cash basis of accounting, accrual basis compared, 138–139
Cash controls, 294–299
  cash disbursements controls, 297–299
  cash receipt controls, 294–297
  mail receipts, 297
  over-the-counter receipts, 295–297
  petty cash fund, 298
  voucher system controls, 297–298
Cash debt coverage, 560, 609, 621
Cash disbursements controls, 297–299
  check register and, 297
  fraudulent disbursements and, 299
  internal control principles and, 298

  petty cash fund and, 298
  voucher system controls and, 297–298
Cash dividends, 506–508
  adequate cash and, 506–507
  declaration date and, 507
  declared dividends and, 507
  entries for, 507–508
  maintaining at current levels, 54
  payment date and, 508
  payout ratio and, 627
  record date and, 507
  retained earnings and, 506
Cash flows, 14–15. *See also* Statement of cash flows
  ability to generate future, 542–543
  classification of, 543
  financing activities and, 543
  inventory costing and, 249
  negative cash and, 546
  operating activities and, 543
  product life cycle and, 546–547
Cash fund, depreciation and, 390
Cash payments
  for income tax, 568
  for interest, 568
  major classes of, 565
  operating expenses and, 567
  statement of cash flows and, 566–567
Cash realizable value, 344
Cash receipts
  acceleration of, 358–361
  cash over and short, 297
  controls, 294–297
  internal control principles, 295
  mail receipts and, 297
  major classes of, 565
  over-the-counter receipts, 295–297
  statement of cash flows and, 565–566
Cash register documents, 199
Cash reporting, 306–307
  cash equivalents and, 306
  restricted cash and, 306–307
Cash sales, credit cards and, 359
Certified public accountant (CPA), 18

Change in accounting principle, 600
Channel stuffing, 612
Chart of accounts, 100–101
Check register, 297
Checks, outstanding, 302
Chief executive officer (CEO), 496
China, accrual accounting and, 139
Classified balance sheet, 42–46
  current assets and, 43–44
  current liabilities and, 46
  current ratio and, 51–52
  debt to assets ratio and, 52–53
  intangible assets and, 45
  liquidity and, 51–52
  long-term investments and, 44
  long-term liabilities and, 46
  property, plant, and equipment and, 45
  solvency and, 52–53
  stockholder's equity and, 46
  use of, 50–53
  working capital and, 51
Closing the books
  closing entries journalized, 159
  closing process, 159
  post-closing trial balance and, 159-160
  preparing closing entries, 158–159
  temporary vs. permanent accounts and, 158
Collection agent, 438
Collection monitoring, receivables and, 355
Collusion, 294
Combined statement of income and comprehensive income, 601
Commercial paper, 306
Common-size analysis, 606–608
Common stock
  accounting for issues of, 501–502
  bond financing advantages over, 516–517
  debit and credit procedures and, 94–95
  earnings per share and, 626
  financing activities and, 9

statement of cash flows (direct method) and, 568
statement of cash flows (indirect method) and, 555
stockholder rights and, 498
stockholders' equity and, 46
Company evaluation, statement of cash flows and, 557–560
Company officers, 5
Comparability, 56–57
Comparative analysis, 603–608
  horizontal analysis and, 603–605
  industry averages and, 603
  intercompany basis and, 603
  intracompany basis and, 603
  vertical analysis and, 606–608
Comparative balance sheets, statement of cash flows and, 548
Complete income statement, 602
Composition of current assets, 52
Compound interest, D2
Compound interest table, D3–D4
Compounding periods, financial calculators and, D15
Comprehensive income, 601–602, E12
  complete income statement and, 602
  components of, 597
  format and, 601–602
  illustration of, 601
Concentration of credit risk, 355
Confirmatory value, 56
Consigned goods, 241
Consistency, 57
Consolidated balance sheets, B2, C2
Consolidated cash flow statement, C3
Consolidated financial statements, stock holdings in another entity and, E7
Consolidated income statement, C1
Consolidated statement of changes in equity, C4
Consolidated statement of comprehensive income, C1
Consolidated statements of cash flows, B3

Consolidated statements of income, B1
Consolidated statements of stockholder's equity, B4
Construction, buildings and, 386
Contingencies, 454–455
Continuous life, corporations and, 495
Contra account, 201, 446
Contra stockholders' equity account, 503
Contractual interest rate, bonds and, 442, 445–446
Controller, 495
Controlling interest, E7
Convention of conservatism, 251
Convertible bonds, 442
Copyrights, 404
Corporate life cycle, 546–547
  decline phase, 547
  growth phase, 546
  introductory phase, 546
  maturity phase, 547
Corporations, 494–499
  ability to acquire capital and, 495
  additional taxes and, 497
  advantages and disadvantages of, 497
  characteristics of, 495–498
  classification by ownership, 494
  classification by purpose, 494
  common classifications of, 494
  continuous life and, 495
  controller and, 496
  description of, 4–5
  earnings from investment income and, E2
  establishing by-laws and, 498
  excess cash and, E1
  formation of, 498
  government regulations and, 496–497
  investing and, E1–E2
  limited liability of stockholders and, 495
  management and, 496
  obtaining license and, 498
  organization chart, 496
  S corporation, 497–498
  separate legal existence and, 495
  social responsibility and, 497

Corporations (*continued*)
  stock issue considerations
    and, 499–502
  stockholder rights and,
    498–499
  strategic reasons for
    investment, E2
  transferable ownership rights
    and, 495
  treasurer and, 496
Correct cash balance, 303
Cost constraint, 58
Cost factors, depreciation
  and, 390
Cost flow methods, 243–247
  average-cost method and,
    246–247
  balance sheet effects and, 249
  first-in, first-out method and,
    244–245
  income statement effects and,
    248–249
  last-in, first-out (LIFO)
    method and, 245–246
  tax effects and, 249
Cost method, stock holdings of
  less than 20% and,
  E4–E5
Cost of goods available for
  sale, 244
Cost of goods sold, 10, 192,
  204, 206–208
Covenant-lite debt, 456
Credit balance, 93
Credit card sales, 358, 359–360
Credit extension, receivables
  and, 354
Credit procedures, 93–96
Credit risk, concentration of,
  355–356
Credit terms, 198
Creditors, 6, 9
Current assets, 43–44
Current cash debt coverage,
  559, 609, 618
Current income statement, 548
Current liabilities, 436–441
  characteristics of, 436
  current maturities of
    long-term debt, 439
  examples of, 46
  interest payable as, 445
  notes payable, 437
  payroll and payroll taxes
    payable, 439–441

sales taxes payable,
    437–438
  statement of cash flows
    and, 553
  unearned revenues and,
    438–439
Current maturities of long-term
  debt, 439
Current-period sales, 604
Current ratio, 51–52, 452, 559,
  608, 618
Customers
  cash receipts from, 565–566
  receipt of cash in advance
    from, 87–88

D
Days in inventory, 341, 609, 619
Debit and credit procedures,
  93–96
  for assets and liabilities, 94
  for stockholders' equity, 94–96
  stockholders' equity
    relationships and, 97
  summary of, 97–98
Debit balance
  allowance account and, 348
  definition of, 93
Debit procedures, 93–96
Debt, economic downturns
  and, 452
Debt covenants, 456
Debt investments
  recording acquisitions for
    bonds, E2–E3
  recording bond interest, E3
  recording sale of bonds, E3
Debt masking, 454
Debt to assets ratio, 52–53,
  609, 621
Debt to equity ratio, 621
Debt *vs.* equity decisions,
  516–517
Declaration date, cash
  dividends and, 507
Declared dividends, 507
Decline phase, corporate life
  cycle and, 547
Declining-balance method,
  depreciation and,
  410–411
Declining book value, 410
Declining-value method,
  depreciation and, 392
Defaulted notes, 353

Deferrals, 141–146
  categories of, 140
  depreciation and, 143–144
  insurance and, 142–143
  prepaid expenses and,
    141–144
  supplies and, 141–142
  unearned revenues and,
    145–146
Delivery trucks, 386
Deposits in transit, 302
Depreciation, 389–398
  accelerated-depreciation
    methods, 410
  adjusting entries for,
    143–144
  as allocation concept, 143
  annual rate and, 391
  book value and, 144, 389
  cash fund and, 389
  cost factors and, 390
  declining-balance method
    and, 410–411
  declining-value method
    and, 392
  depreciable cost, 391
  depreciation schedule, 391
  disclosure in notes
    and, 394
  double-declining-balance
    method and, 392, 410
  fair value and, 389
  income taxes and, 394
  land and, 389
  manager's choice and, 393
  methods of, 390–394
  obsolescence and, 389
  patterns of, 393
  plant asset classes and, 389
  property, plant, and
    equipment and, 44
  proration and, 391
  quality of earnings and, 611
  revising periodic
    depreciation, 394–395
  salvage value and, 390
  statement of cash flows and,
    550–551, 567–568
  statement presentation and,
    143–144
  straight-line method and,
    390–392
  units-of-activity method and,
    392–393, 411–412
  useful life and, 390

Developing countries, notes receivable and, 351
Direct method (statement of cash flows), 548–549, 563–570
  cash payments for income taxes, 568
  cash payments for interest, 568
  cash payments for operating expenses, 567
  cash payments to suppliers, 566–567
  cash receipts from customers, 565–566
  depreciation expense, 567–568
  increase in bonds payable, 569
  increase in buildings, 569
  increase in common stock, 569
  increase in equipment, 569
  increase in land, 569
  increase in retained earnings, 569
  investing and financing activities and, 569–570
  loss on disposal of plant assets, 567–568
  net cash flows and, 568
  net change in cash, 570
  operating activities and, 565–568
Direct write-off method for uncollectible accounts, 343–344
Disbursements, cash, 297–299
Discontinued operations, sustainable income and, 597–598
Discounts
  amortization of, 447
  bonds and, 443, 445–447
  discount period, 198
  discounting the future amount, D7
  effective-interest amortization method and, 462–464
  periodic inventory system and, 215
  purchase, 198–199
  sales, 202
  straight-line amortization method and, 459–460
  time periods and, D11
Dishonor of notes receivable, 353

Disposals, plant assets, 397–398
Dividend record, measuring corporate performance and, 515
Dividends, 506–511
  in arrears, 505
  cash dividends, 506–508
  cumulative dividends, 505–506
  debit and credit procedures and, 95–96
  guarantee of, 505
  payment of, 90, 107
  preferred stocks and, 505–506
  reporting of, 506
  statement of cash flows and, 543
  stock dividends, 509–510
  stock investments between 20% and 50% and, E6–E7
  stock investments of less than 20% and, E5
Documentation procedures, 289–290, 396
Dollar-value last-in, first-out, 243
Double-declining-balance method, 392, 410
Double taxation, corporations and, 497
Down payments, leasing and, 388
Duties, segregation of, 287–289

E
Earnings, quality of, 156–157, 610–612
Earnings management, 156, 396
Earnings per share (EPS), 48–49, 610, 612, 626
Earnings performance, measuring corporate performance and, 516
Economic downturns, debt risks and, 452
Economic entity assumption, 57
Electronic data processing (EDP) systems, 84
Electronic funds transfer (ETF) system, 305
Employee salaries, payment of cash for, 90–91
Employees
  background checks and, 292

  bonding of, 292
  hiring of, 90
  requiring vacations and, 292
  rotating duties of, 292
Entry adjustments. See Adjustment entries
Equipment
  depreciation and, 389
  plant assets and, 387
  purchase of, 103
  statement of cash flows (direct method) and, 569
  statement of cash flows (indirect method) and, 555
Equity method, stock investments between 20% and 50% and, E5–E6
Equivalents, cash, 306
Errors, 109
Estimated uncollectibles, 344–345
Ethics
  bad debt expense and, 347
  convenient overstatement and, 102
  economic entity assumption and, 57
  employee theft, 299
  errors and irregularities, 110
  falsifying inventory, 240
  financial reporting and, 7–8
  fraudulent documents and, 98
  not-for-profit organizations and, 8
  overstating bond investment value, E10
  solving ethical dilemmas, 8
Euronext, 500
Exclusive rights, 45
Expense recognition principle, 137
Expenses
  accrued expenses, 147–151
  income statements and, 203
  operating activities and, 10
  stockholders' equity and, 96
External users, financial information and, 6–7
Extraordinary items, 598–599

F
Face value
  bonds and, 442, 444–445
  notes receivable and, 350–351

Factoring arrangements, 358–360

Factory machinery, 387

Fair value, depreciation and, 389

Fair value adjustment, E9

Fair value of securities, E8–E9

Fair value per share, 509

Fair value principle, 58

Faithful representation, 56

Federal Insurance Contribution Act (FICA), 439

Federal Trade Commission, 6

FIFO ending inventory, 244

Finance directors, 5

Financial Accounting Standards Board (FASB), 54, 331

Financial calculators, D14–D16
  auto loans, D15–D16
  compounding periods, D15
  mortgage loans, D16
  plus and minus, D15
  present value of annuity, D15
  present value of single sum and, D14
  rounding, D15

Financial highlights, A31–32

Financial information
  external users and, 6–7
  internal users and, 5–6

Financial reporting
  assumptions in, 57
  cost constraint and, 58
  economic entity assumption and, 57
  enhancing qualities and, 56–57
  ethics in, 7–8
  fair value principle and, 58
  faithful representation and, 56
  full disclosure principle and, 58
  going concern assumption and, 57
  historical cost principle and, 58
  measurement principles and, 58
  monetary unit assumption and, 57
  periodicity assumption and, 57
  relevance and, 56
  standard-setting environment and, 55

Financial statements, 10–18
  accompanying notes and, A14–A28
  adjusted trial balance and, 155–156
  balance sheet, 13–14
  classified balance sheet, 42–45, 50–53
  earnings per share and, 48–49
  income statement, 11–12, 47–48
  notes to, 17–18
  ratio analysis and, 47
  receivables and, 353
  retained earnings statement, 12
  statement interrelationships, 15–17
  statement of cash flows, 14–15
  statement of stockholders' equity, 49–50

Financing activities
  cash flows and, 14–15, 543
  corporations and, 9
  primary types of, 111
  statement of cash flows (direct method) and, 569–570
  statement of cash flows (indirect method) and, 555–556

Finished goods inventory, 238

First-in, first-out (FIFO) method, 244–245, 258, 611

Fiscal year, 56

Fixed assets, 45

Flow of costs, for merchandising company, 193–195

FOB destination, 196–197

FOB shipping point, 196–197

Franchises, 405

Fraud. *See also* Internal controls
  altered inventory figures and, 241
  definition and examples of, 284–285
  employee checks and, 441
  falsifying bank deposits and, 342
  financial pressure and, 285
  financial ratios and, 607
  fraud triangle, 284–285
  internal control systems and, 285–286

  net income and, 396
  opportunity and, 284–285
  overstated cash and, 554
  rationalization and, 285
  Sarbanes-Oxley Act and, 285
  stealing merchandise and, 201
  stock options and, 500

Free cash flow
  cash-generating abilities and, 53
  company's solvency and, 622
  solvency ratios and, 609
  statement of cash flows and, 557–558

Free on board (FOB), 196–197

Freight costs, 196–197
  incurred by buyer, 197
  incurred by seller, 197
  periodic inventory system and, 214

Full disclosure principle, 58, 543

Future value of a single amount, D2–D4

Future value of an annuity, D4–D6

G

Gain on sale, plant assets and, 397

General ledger, 100–101

Generally accepted accounting principles (GAAP), 55, 611

Gift cards, 146

Going concern assumption, 57

Goods in transit, 240–241

Goodwill, 45, 405–406

Government regulations, corporations and, 496–497

Graham, Benjamin, 595

Green marketing, 211

Gross margin, 204–205

Gross profit, multi-step income statement and, 203–204

Gross profit rate, 208–209
  decline in, 208–209
  expression by percentage and, 208
  by industry, 208
  industry competitiveness and, 625–626
  profitability ratios and, 610
  retailers and, 209

Growth phase, corporate life cycle and, 546

H

Held-to-maturity securities, E8
High-volume businesses, profit margin and, 624
Hiring of new employees, 90
Historical cost principle, 58, 385
Honor of notes receivable, 351–352
Horizontal analysis, 603–605
Human element, internal controls and, 294
Human resource controls
  background checks and, 292
  bonding employees and, 292
  employee hirings and, 441
  fraud and, 201
  limitations of, 293–294
  rotating employee duties and, 292

I

Idle cash, 308–309
Impairments, plant assets and, 396
Improper adjusting entries, 157
Improper recognition, quality of earnings and, 611–612
Improperly capitalized expenditures, 385
Improvements, plant assets and, 395
Income from operations, 203, 205
Income measurement process, merchandising company and, 192
Income statements
  adjusted trial balance and, 155
  complete income statement, 602
  components of, 597
  cost flow methods and, 248–249
  determining cost of good sold under periodic system, 206–208
  gross profit and, 203, 204
  horizontal analysis of, 605
  income from operations and, 203
  inventory efforts and, 260–261
  multiple-step income statements, 203–204

net income and, 11, 203
nonoperating activities and, 205–206
operating expenses and, 205
presentation, 203–208
revenues and expenses and, 203
sales revenues and, 204
single-step income statement, 203
specific time period and, 11
stock issues and, 11
user communication and, 10
uses of, 47–48
vertical analysis and, 606–607
Income summary, 158
Income taxes
  cash payments for, 568
  depreciation and, 394
  operating activities and, 10
  payable to government, 10
  statement of cash flows and, 553
Independent internal verification, fraud and, 241, 291–292, 342, 441, 500, 554, 608
Indirect method (statement of cash flows), 548–556
  changes in current liabilities, 553–554
  decrease in accounts receivable, 552
  decrease in income taxes payable, 553–554
  depreciation expense and, 550–551
  increase in accounts payable, 553
  increase in bonds payable, 555
  increase in buildings, 555
  increase in common stock, 555
  increase in equipment, 555
  increase in inventory, 552–553
  increase in land, 555
  increase in prepaid expenses, 553
  increase in retained earnings, 555
  investing and financing activities and, 555
  loss on disposal of plant assets, 551
  net change in cash and, 554

net income to net cash conversions, 550
noncash current assets and, 551–552
operating activities and, 550–554
Industries
  gross profit rate by, 208
  industry-average comparisons, 47, 603
  profit margins by, 210
Inflation, cost flow methods and, 248
Insurance, adjustment for, 142–143
Insurance policies, 89, 105
Intangible assets, 402–406
  accounting for, 403
  amortization of, 403
  copyrights, 404
  determining useful life and, 403
  franchises, 405
  goodwill, 405
  limited life and, 403
  patents, 404
  research and development costs, 404
  trademarks and tradenames, 405
  types of, 45, 404–406
Intent to convert, investments and, E11
Intercompany comparative analysis, 45, 603, 607
Interest
  accrued interest, 148–149
  bonds and, 442, 443, 445
  buildings and, 386–387
  cash payments for, 568
  compound interest, D2
  compound interest table, D3–D4
  coverage, 621
  expense, 10
  interest-bearing notes, 352
  interest rates, D1
  nature of, D1–D2
  notes receivable and, 350–351
  passing up discount and, 199
  payable, 10
  payable as a current liability, 445
  recording bond interest, E3

Interest (*continued*)
   revenue, 10
   simple interest, D1
Internal auditors, 292
Internal controls. *See also* Cash
      controls; Fraud
   bank reconciliations and,
      299–305
   bank statements and,
      300–301
   business size and, 294
   cash managing and
      monitoring, 307–311
   cash reporting, 306–307
   collusion and, 294
   control activities and, 286
   control environment and, 285
   documentation procedures
      and, 289–290
   human element and, 294
   human resource controls,
      292–293
   independent internal
      verification and, 291–292
   information and
      communication and, 286
   limitations of, 293–294
   monitoring and, 286
   petty cash funds, 314–315
   physical controls, 290–291
   principles of control
      activities, 286–293
   reasonable assurance and, 293
   responsibility establishment
      and, 287
   risk assessment and, 286
   segregation of duties and,
      287–289
   segregation of record-keeping
      from physical custody, 289
   segregation of related
      activities and, 288
   sustainability reporting and, 286
Internal users, financial
      information and, 5–6
Internal verification,
      independent, 291–292
International Accounting
      Standards Board (IASB),
      55, 351
International Financial
      Reporting Standards
      (IFRS), 36–37, 55, 78–80
Intracompany comparisons,
      47, 617

Introductory phase, corporate
      life cycle and, 546
Inventory
   analysis of, 252–255
   classifying, 238–239
   consigned goods and, 241
   conversion from LIFO to
      FIFO, 254
   costing of, 242–252
   determining ownership of
      goods and, 240–241
   determining quantities and,
      240–241
   errors in, 260–261
   falsifying of, 240
   finished goods inventory, 238
   goods in transit and, 240–241
   just-in-time inventory
      methods, 239
   manufacturing companies
      and, 238–239
   merchandise inventory, 238
   perpetual inventory systems,
      257–259
   raw materials and, 238
   statement of cash flows
      and, 552–553
   taking physical inventory, 240
   work in process, 238
Inventory analysis, 252–255
   computing days in
      inventory, 252
   inventory turnover and,
      252–253
   LIFO reserve and, 254–255
   recession and, 253
Inventory costing, 242–252. *See
      also* Cost flow methods
   average-cost method and,
      246–247
   balance sheet effects and, 249
   change in methods and, 600
   cost flow assumptions and,
      243–247
   first-in, first-out method and,
      244–245
   income statement effects and,
      248–249
   last-in, first-out method and,
      245–246
   lower-of-cost-or-market
      and, 251–252
   methods, 611
   specific identification and,
      242–243

tax effects and, 249
   using methods
      consistently, 251
   weighted-average unit cost
      and, 246
Inventory errors
   balance sheet effects and, 249
   income statement effects and,
      248–249
Inventory levels, cash
      management and, 308
Inventory turnover, 252–253,
      609, 619
Investment portfolios, E4
Investments
   available-for-sale securities, E8
   balance sheet presentation
      and, E10–E11
   cash flows and, 14–15, 543
   corporations and, E1–E2
   excess cash and, 9
   held-to-maturity securities, E8
   intent to convert and, E11
   nonoperating items related
      to, E12
   presentation of realized and
      unrealized gain or loss, E12
   readily marketable, E11
   security categories, E8
   statement of cash flows
      (direct method) and, 569
   statement of cash flows
      (indirect method) and, 555
   statement of cash flows
      presentation, E12–E13
   trading securities, E8–E9
   valuing and reporting of,
      E7–E13
Irregular items, sustainable
      income and, 597
Irregularity, 110
Issuing procedures, bonds
      and, 442–443

J
Journals, 98–100
Just-in-time inventory methods,
      239, 252

K
Korean discount, 55

L
Labor unions, 6
Land

Land (*continued*)
  costs related to, 385–386
  depreciation and, 389
  improvements and, 386
  statement of cash flows (direct method) and, 569
  statement of cash flows (indirect method) and, 555
Large stock dividends, 509
Last-in, first-out (LIFO) method, 245–246, 258–259, 611
Leasing, 388, 455
Ledger, 100
Legal capital, 501
Legal liability, organizational forms and, 5
Letter to stockholders, A2–A5
Leveraging, 624
Liabilities. *See also* Bonds
  analysis of, 451
  balance sheet presentation and, 13, 450
  bank line of credit and, 452
  bonds and, 441–449
  cash management and, 308
  contingencies and, 454–455
  credit balances and, 94
  current liabilities, 436–441
  debt covenants, 456
  debt masking and, 454
  leasing and, 388, 455
  liquidity ratios and, 451–452
  off-balance-sheet financing and, 454
  solvency ratios and, 452–453
  times interest earned and, 453
Licenses, corporations and, 498
LIFO ending inventory, 246
LIFO reserve, 254–255
Limited liability companies (LLCs), 5, 498
Limited liability of stockholders, corporations and, 495
Limited liability partnerships (LLPs), 498
Limited life, intangible assets and, 403
Limited partnerships, 498
Line of credit, liabilities and, 452
Liquid investments, 308–309
Liquidation preference, preferred stocks and, 506

Liquidity, 51–52
  excessive liquidity, 52
  receivables and, 356–357
  statement of cash flows and, 559
  working capital and, 51
Liquidity ratios, 618–620
  accounts receivable turnover, 357
  average collection period, 357, 619
  current cash debt coverage, 559, 618
  current ratio, 51–52, 618
  days in inventory, 253, 620
  inventory turnover, 253, 619–620
  liabilities and, 451–452
  role of, 47
  summary of, 609
  working capital, 51
London Stock Exchange, 500
Long-lived assets
  financial statement presentation of, 406–407
  intangible assets, 402–406
  plant assets, 384–402
Long-term debt, current maturities of, 439
Long-term investments
  balance sheet presentation and, E11
  characteristics of, 44
Long-term liabilities
  bonds, 441–449
  characteristics of, 46
  current liabilities and, 436
Long-term notes, present value of, D11–D13
Long-term notes payable, 465–466
Long-term notes receivable, 350–351
Loss on disposal of plant assets, 551
Loss on sale of plant assets, 398
Low-volume businesses, profit margin and, 624
Lower-of-cost-or-market (LCM), 251–252

M
Madoff, Bernard, 305
Madoff's ponzi scheme, 305
Mail receipts, 297

Major expenditures, cash management and, 308
Management, corporation, 496
Management certifications of financial statements, A30–A31
Management discussion and analysis, 17, A6–A13
Management's report on internal control, A30–A31
Market interest rates, bonds and, 443, 445–446
Market price, stock, 501
Market price determination, bonds and, 443–444
Market-to-market accounting, E8
Marketable securities, E10
Marketing expenses, 10
Marketing managers, 5
Marketing return on investment, 399
Matching principle, 137
Maturity date
  bonds and, 442
  notes receivable and, 350
  redeeming bonds at, 449
  redeeming bonds before, 461
Maturity phase, corporate life cycle and, 546–547
Maturity value, interest-bearing notes and, 352
Measurement principles, financial reporting and, 58
Memoranda, bank, 303
Merchandise inventory. *See* Inventory
Merchandise purchases, 195–199
  freight costs and, 196–197
  periodic inventory system and, 214
  purchase discounts and, 198–199
  purchase invoices and, 195–196
  purchase returns and allowances, 197–198
  transaction summary, 199
Merchandise sales, 199–202
  business documents and, 199
  cash register documents and, 199

Merchandise sales (*continued*)
 periodic inventory system
  and, 214
 sales accounts and, 200
 sales discounts, 202
 sales returns and allowances,
  200–202
Merchandise transactions,
 periodic inventory system
 and, 214
Merchandising operations,
 192–195
 flow of costs and, 193–195
 income measurement process
  for, 192
 operating cycles and, 193, 307
 periodic inventory system
  and, 194
 perpetual inventory system
  and, 194
Merchandising profit, 205
Modified accelerated cost
 recovery system
 (MARCS), 394
Monetary unit assumption, 57
Money market funds, 306
Mortgage loans, D16
Mortgage notes payable, 465
Moving-average method, 259
Multiple-step income
 statements, 203–204, 205

N
Nasdaq stock market, 500
National credit card sales,
 359–360
Negative cash, 546
Net 30, 198
Net cash, 161–162
Net cash flows, statement of
 cash flows and, 568
Net cash provided by
 operating activities,
 54, 543
Net change in cash
 statement of cash flows
  (direct method) and, 570
 statement of cash flows
  (indirect method) and, 556
Net income
 income statements and,
  11, 203
 net cash and, 161–162
 to net cash conversions, 551
 per share, 626

statement of cash flows
 and, 543
Net sales
 horizontal analysis of, 604
 income statement and, 204
New employee hiring, 106
New York Stock Exchange, 500
No-par stock, 502
Nominal accounts, 158
Non-recurring charges, 599
Noncash activities, statement of
 cash flows and, 544
Noncash current assets,
 statement of cash flows
 and, 552
Nonoperating items
 income statement
  presentation and, 205–206
 related to investments
  and, E12
Normal balances, 94
Not-for-profit organizations, 8
Note issued in exchange for
 cash, 87
Notes payable
 accounting for, 437
 financing activities and, 9
 issuance of, 103
 long-term, 465–466
Notes receivable, 349–353
 accrual of interest
  receivable, 352
 cash (net) realizable value
  and, 351
 collection of, 304
 computing interest and, 350
 determining maturity date
  and, 350
 dishonor of, 353
 disposing of, 351–352
 face value and, 351
 honor of, 351–352
 promissory notes and, 349
 recognizing notes
  receivable, 350–351
 valuing notes receivable, 351
Notes to financial
 statements, 18
NSF (not sufficient funds)
 checks, 301, 304

O
Obligations, statement of cash
 flows and, 547
Obsolescence

depreciation and, 389
 equipment and, 151
 leasing and, 388
Off-balance sheet financing,
 liabilities and, 454–455
Office equipment, purchase of
 for cash, 87
One-time items, 156–157
Operating activities, 9–10
 cash flows and, 14–15, 547
 classifying as, 110
 statement of cash flows
  (direct method) and,
  565–568
 statement of cash flows
  (indirect method) and,
  550–554
Operating cycles
 definition of, 44
 for merchandising
  company, 193
 for service company, 193
 temporary investments and, E1
Operating expenses
 cash payments for, 567
 improper capitalization of, 612
 income statement
  presentation and, 204
Operating leases, 455
Operations, income from, 203
Ordinary repairs, 395
Organization chart, corporations and, 496
Other expenses and losses, 205
Other revenues and gains, 205
Outstanding checks, 302
Over-the-counter receipts,
 295–297
Ownership of goods,
 determining, 240–241
Ownership rights, corporations
 and, 495

P
Paid-in capital
 stock dividends and, 509
 stock splits and, 511
 stockholders' equity and,
  501–502
Paper profit, 248
Par or stated value per share, 509
Par value stock, 501
Parent company, E7
Partnerships, 4
Patents, 404

Payment date, cash dividends and, 508
Payment period establishment, receivables and, 354
Payout ratio, 610, 627
Payroll, 439–441
Payroll taxes payable, 439–441
Pension portfolios, 600
Percentage, gross profit rate as, 208
Percentage of base amount, 606
Percentage of net sales, 606
Percentage-of-receivables basis, 340
Periodic inventory system, 214–216
    cost of goods sold under, 194, 207–208
    freight costs and, 214
    purchase discounts and, 215
    purchase returns and allowances, 215
    recording merchandise transactions and, 214
    recording purchases of merchandise, 214
    recording sales of merchandise, 215–216
    sales discounts and, 215
    sales returns and allowances and, 215
Periodicity assumption, 57
Permanent accounts, 158
Permanent decline in fair value, plant assets and, 396
Perpetual inventory systems
    advantages of, 194–195
    average-cost and, 259
    cost flow methods in, 257–259
    determining cost of goods sold under, 194
    first-in, first-out and, 258
    last-in, first-out and, 258–259
    periodic system compared, 207
Petty cash funds, 314–315
    establishment of, 314
    internal controls and, 298
    making payments from, 314
    replenishment of, 314–315
Phantom profit, 248
Physical controls, 201, 290–291
Physical custody, 289
Physical inventory, 240
Plant assets, 377–401. *See also* Depreciation

accounting for, 389–398
additions and improvements and, 395
analyzing, 398–400
asset turnover, 400
buildings, 386–387
buying or leasing, 388
capital expenditures and, 385
cash equivalent price and, 385
depreciation and, 45, 389–395
determining cost of, 385–387
disposals, 397–398
earnings management and, 396
equipment, 387
expenditures during useful life, 395
expense capitalization and, 385
gain on sale and, 397
historical cost principle and, 385
impairments and, 396
land, 385–386
land improvements, 386
loss on disposal of, 551, 567–568
loss on sale and, 398
ordinary repairs and, 395
profit margin and, 400–401
retirement of, 398
return on assets, 399–400
sale of, 398
Plus and minus, financial calculators and, D15
Ponzi schemes, 305
Post-closing trial balance, 159–160
Post-dated checks, 305
Posting, 101
Predictive value, 56
Preferred stock, 504–505
    cumulative dividends and, 505–506
    dividend preferences and, 505–506
    liquidation preference and, 506
Premiums
    bonds and, 444–445
    effective-interest amortization method and, 460–461
    issuing bonds at, 447–449
    straight-line amortization method and, 460–461
Prenumbered documents, 289
Prepaid expenses

accounting for, 144
adjusting entries for, 141–144
statement of cash flows and, 553–554
Prepaid insurance, 142–143
Present value of annuity, D9–D11, D15
Present value of long-term note or bond, D11–D13
Present value of single amount, D7–D9
Present value of single sum, D14
Present value variables, D7
Price-earnings (P-E) ratio, 610, 612, 626–627
Principal
    bonds and, 443
    interest rate and, D1
Pro forma income, 611
Production supervisors, 5
Profit margins, 209–211
    changes in, 210
    gross profit compared, 209
    plant assets and, 401
    profitability ratios and, 610, 623
    variation across industries and, 210
Profitability evaluation, 208–211
    gross profit rate, 208–209
    profit margin, 209–211
Profitability ratios, 610, 623–627
    asset turnover, 400, 625
    definition of, 47
    earnings per share, 48–49, 626
    gross profit rate, 208, 625–626
    payout ratio, 515, 627
    price-earnings ratio, 612, 626
    profit margin, 210, 624
    return on assets, 399, 623–624
    return on common stockholders' equity, 516, 623
Promissory notes, 349
Property taxes payable, 10
Proration, depreciation and, 391
Public Company Accounting Oversight Board (PCAOB), 55, 285
Purchase discounts, 198–199
    credit terms and, 198

Purchase discounts (*continued*)
discount period and, 198
inventory and, 198
paying interest and, 199
periodic inventory system
and, 214
Purchase invoices, 195–196
Purchase returns and
allowances, 197–198
Purchasing activities, internal
controls and, 288
Purchasing on account, 90

Q

Quality of earnings, 156–157, 611
alternative accounting
methods and, 611
cooking the books and, 157
earnings management and, 156
improper adjusting entries
and, 157
improper recognition
and, 611–612
indicators, 211
inflating revenue numbers
and, 157
inventory costing and, 251
one-time items and,
156–157
price-earnings ratio and, 612
pro forma income and, 611
Sarbanes-Oxley Act and, 157
Quarterly dividend rates, 506

R

Rating agencies, 610
Ratio analysis, 608–610
classifications, 47
comprehensive illustration of,
616–627
liquidity ratios and, 618,
714–716
profitability ratios and, 610,
623–627
solvency ratios and, 618,
620–622
Ratios, LIFO reserve and, 254
Raw materials, 238
Readily marketable
investments, E11
Real accounts, 158
Realized gain or loss,
investments and, E12
Reasonable assurance, internal
controls and, 293

Receivables
accounts receivable,
341–348
accounts receivable turnover,
356–357
average collection period and,
356–357
cash management and, 308
cash receipt acceleration and,
358–360
collection monitoring and,
355–356
concentration of credit risk
and, 356
extending credit and, 354
financial statement
presentation of, 353
liquidity evaluation and,
356–358
management of, 353–360
national credit card sales and,
359–360
notes receivable, 349–353
payment period establishment
and, 355
sale of, 358–359
sale of receivables to a
factor, 358–359
types of, 340–341
Recession, inventory
management and, 253
Reconciliation, bank accounts
and, 299–305
Record date, cash dividends
and, 507
Record keeping, segregation
from physical custody, 289
Recording estimated
uncollectibles, 344–345
Recording process, 98–109
chart of accounts and, 101
hiring of new employees, 106
illustrated, 102–107
investment of cash by
stockholders, 102
issue of note payable, 103
journal and, 98–100
ledger and, 100
payment of cash for employee
salaries, 107
payment of dividends, 107
payment of rent with
cash, 105
posting and, 101
purchase of equipment, 103

purchase of insurance policy
with cash, 105
purchase of supplies on
account, 106
receipt of cash in advance
from customer, 104
services performed for
cash, 104
source document and, 98
summary illustration and,
108–109
Recovery of uncollectible
account, 346
Redemptions, bonds and, 449
Regulatory agencies, 6
Related activities, segregation
of, 288
Relevance, information, 56
Rent, 89, 105
Research and development
costs (R&D), 404
Responsibility establishment,
internal controls and, 287
Restricted cash, 306–307
Restructuring charges, 599
Retailers, 192
Retained earnings, 512–513
adjusted trial balance
and, 155
cash dividends and, 506
common stock and, 501–502
debit and credit procedures
and, 94–96
net losses and, 512
preparing closing entries
and, 158
restrictions and, 512–513
statement of cash flows
(direct method) and, 569
statement of cash flows
(indirect method) and, 555
stock dividends and, 509
stock splits and, 510
stockholders' equity and, 46
Retirement of plant assets, 398
Return on assets, 399–400, 610,
623–624
Return on common stockholders'
equity, 516–517, 610, 623
Returns and allowances
periodic inventory system
and, 214–216
purchases and, 197–198
returns and, 215
Returns policy, 201

Revenues
accrued revenues, 147–148
income statements and, 203
inflating numbers and, 157
operating activities and, 9
revenue recognition principle, 136–137
stockholders' equity and, 95
unearned revenues, 145–146
Revised depreciation, 394–395
Risk-free investments, 308
Rounding, financial calculators and, D15

S

S corporation, 573–574
Salaries
accrued salaries, 150–151
payment of cash for, 90–91, 107
Sales
discounts and, 202
income statement presentation and, 203
internal controls and, 288
merchandising operations and, 192
periodic inventory system and, 216
plant assets and, 398–400
returns and allowances and, 200–202
revenue from, 10
sale of receivables to a factor, 358
Sales taxes payable, 10, 437–438
Salvage value, depreciation and, 390
Sarbanes-Oxley Act, 7, 91, 157, 285, 293, 496
Secured bonds, 442
Securities
available-for-sale securities, 601, E9–E10
categories of, E8
comprehensive income and, 601–602
trading of, E8–E9
trading securities, 601
Securities and Exchange Commission (SEC), 6, 55, 454, 496
Segregation of duties, 287–289, 386

Segregation of record-keeping from physical custody, 289
Segregation of related activities, 288
Selling expenses, 10
Separate legal existence, corporations and, 495
Service company, operating cycles for, 193
Service revenue, accounts after adjustment, 146
Services performed for cash, 88–89
Shoplifting losses, 293
Short-term investments, balance sheet presentation and, E10–E11
Signature requirements, documents and, 289
Simple interest, D1
Single-step income statement, 203
Small stock dividends, 509
Social responsibility, corporations and, 497
Social Security taxes, 441
Socially responsive business, 15
Sole proprietorships, 4–5
Solvency, 52–53, 452
Solvency assessment, statement of cash flows and, 560
Solvency ratios, 620–622
cash debt coverage, 560, 609, 621
debt to assets ratio, 53, 609, 621
definition of, 47
free cash flow, 54, 609, 622
summary of, 609
times interest earned, 453, 609, 621–622
Source document, recording process and, 98
Specific identification method of inventory costing, 242–243
Standard-setting environment, 55
Statement interrelationships, 15–17
Statement of cash flows, 14–15. *See also* Direct method; Indirect method
additional information and, 548

cash investing and financing transactions and, 543
classification of cash flows and, 543
company evaluation and, 557–558
comparative balance sheets and, 548
corporate life cycle and, 546–548
current income statement and, 548
direct method and, 548–549, 563–570
format of, 545
free cash flow and, 557–558
future cash flows and, 542–543
indirect method and, 548–555
investments and, E12–E13
liquidity assessment and, 558–559
major steps in, 548
net cash provided by operating activities and, 543
net income and, 543
paying dividends and meeting obligations and, 543
preparation of, 547–548
significant noncash activities and, 544
solvency assessment and, 560
T-account approach, 570–572
usefulness of, 542–543
user communication and, 10
Stock certificates, 498–499
Stock dividends, 509–510
effects of, 509–510
entries for, 520
fair value per share, 509
large stock dividend, 509
par or stated value per share, 509
purpose and benefits of, 509
small stock dividend, 509
stock splits differentiated, 510–511
stockholders' equity and, 509–510
Stock holdings of more than 50%, E7
Stock investments
accounting for, E4–E7

Stock investments (*continued*)
   holdings between 20% and
      50%, E5–E7
   holdings of less than 20%
      and, E4–E5
   holdings of more than 50%
      and, E7
Stock investments between 20%
      and 50%, E5–E7
   recording acquisition of
      stock, E6
   recording revenue and
      dividends, E6–E7
Stock investments of less than
      20%, E4–E5
   recording acquisition of
      stock, E4
   recording dividends, E5
   recording sale of stock, E5
Stock issue considerations,
      499–500
   authorized stock, 500
   market price and, 501
   par and no-par value
      stocks, 501
   stock issuance, 500
Stock quotes, reading, 502
Stock splits, 510–511
Stock value considerations, 501
Stockholders
   creditor claims *vs.*, 9
   investment of cash by,
      86–87, 102
   liability and, 495
   raising funds and, 5
   rights of, 498–499
Stockholders' equity
   accounting for treasury stock,
      503–504
   additional paid-in capital
      and, 513
   balance sheet presentation
      and, 13, 513–514
   capital stock and, 513
   common stock and, 94–95
   corporate form of
      organization and, 494–498
   debit and credit procedures
      for, 94–95
   debt *vs.* equity decision and,
      516–517
   dividend record and, 515
   dividends and, 95, 506–511
   earnings performance
      and, 516

   expenses and, 89
   financial statement
      presentation of, 513–514
   measuring corporate
      performance and, 515–517
   parts of, 46
   preferred stock and, 504–506
   relationships and, 97
   retained earnings and,
      95, 512–513
   return on common
      stockholders' equity (ROE),
      516–517
   revenue and, 88
   revenues and expenses
      and, 96
   stock issue considerations
      and, 499–502
   stock splits and, 510–511
   unrealized loss and, 602
   use of, 49–50
Straight-line amortization,
      459–461
   amortizing bond discount,
      459–460
   amortizing bond premium,
      460–461
Straight-line depreciation,
      390–391
Subchapter S corporations, 5
Subsidiary (affiliated)
      company, E7
Suppliers, cash payments to,
      566–567
Supplies
   adjusting entries for, 141–142
   operating activities and, 9
   purchase on account, 90, 106
Sustainability reports, 402
Sustainable income, 596–602
   change in accounting
      principle and, 600
   comprehensive income and,
      601–602
   discontinued operations and,
      597–598
   extraordinary items and,
      598–599
   irregular items and, 597

T

T-account approach, statement
      of cash flows and, 570–572
Tax advantages, leasing
      and, 388

Taxes. *See also* Income taxes
   corporations and, 497
   cost flow methods
      and, 249
   irregular items and, 597
   organizational forms and, 5
   taxing authorities, 6
Temporary accounts, 158
Temporary investments,
      operating cycle and, E1
Time periods
   discounting and, D11
   interest rates and, D1
Time value of money, 443
   computing present value of
      long-term note or bond,
      D11–D13
   future value of a single
      amount, D2–D4
   future value of an annuity,
      D4–D6
   nature of interest, D1–D2
   present value of annuity,
      D9–D11
   present value of single
      amount, D7–D9
   present value variables, D7
   time diagram, D3
   time periods and
      discounting, D11
   using financial calculators
      and, D14–D16
Timeliness, 56–57
Times interest earned, 453,
      609, 621
Timing issues, 136–137
   accrual *vs.* cash basis of
      accounting and,
      138–139
   expense recognition principle
      and, 137
   revenue recognition principle
      and, 136–137
Tokyo Stock Exchange, 500
Total cost of trading securities,
      E8
Total fair value of securities, E8
Trademarks, 405
Tradenames, 405
Trading on the equity, 624
Trading securities, 601, E8
Transferable ownership rights,
      corporations and, 495
Treasurer, 496
Treasury bills, 306

Treasury stock
  accounting for, 503–504
  purchase of, 503–504
Trial balance, 109–112
  example, 111–112
  limitations of, 110
  post-closing, 159–160
  types of adjusting entries
    and, 140–141
True cash balance, 303
Turnover, asset, 400

U

Uncollectible accounts
  allowance method for, 344
  direct write-off method for,
    343–344
  expense, 343
  recording estimated
    uncollectibles, 344–345
  recording the write-off of, 345
  recovery of, 346

Understandability, 56–57
Unearned revenues, 145–146,
  438–439
Units-of-activity method,
  depreciation and, 392–393,
  411–412
Units-of-production method.
  See Units-of-activity method
Unqualified opinions, 18
Unrealized gains or losses
  investments and, E12
  securities and, E8
  stockholders' equity and, 602
Unsecured bonds, 442
Useful life
  depreciation and, 390
  intangible assets and, 404

V

Vacations, requiring taking
  of, 292
Verifiability, 56–57

Verification, independent
  internal, 291–292
Vertical analysis, 606–607
Voucher register, 297
Voucher system controls,
  297–298

W

Wages payable, 10
Weighted-average unit
  cost, 246
Wholesalers, 192
Work in process, 238
Working capital, 51, 609
Worksheets, 165
Write-downs, 396
Write-off method, uncollectible
  accounts and, 343–344

RAPID REVIEW
Chapter Content

ACCOUNTING CONCEPTS (Chapters 2–4)

Fundamental Qualities	Enhancing Qualities	Assumptions	Principles	Constraint
Relevance	Comparability	Monetary unit	Historical cost	Materiality
Faithful representation	Consistency	Economic entity	Fair value	
	Verifiability	Periodicity	Full disclosure	
	Timeliness	Going concern	Revenue recognition	
	Understandability	Accrual basis	Expense recognition	

BASIC ACCOUNTING EQUATION (Chapter 3)

Basic Equation

Assets = Liabilities + Stockholders' Equity

Expanded Basic Equation

Assets = Liabilities + Common Stock + Retained Earnings + Revenues − Expenses − Dividends

Debit / Credit Rules

Assets		Liabilities		Common Stock		Retained Earnings		Revenues		Expenses		Dividends	
Dr. +	Cr. −	Dr. −	Cr. +	Dr. −	Cr. +	Dr. −	Cr. +	Dr. −	Cr. +	Dr. +	Cr. −	Dr. +	Cr. −

INVENTORY (Chapters 5 and 6)

Ownership

Freight Terms	Ownership of goods on public carrier resides with:
FOB Shipping point	Buyer
FOB Destination	Seller

ADJUSTING ENTRIES (Chapter 4)

	Type	Adjusting Entry	
Deferrals	1. Prepaid expenses	Dr. Expenses	Cr. Assets
	2. Unearned revenues	Dr. Liabilities	Cr. Revenues
Accruals	1. Accrued revenues	Dr. Assets	Cr. Revenues
	2. Accrued expenses	Dr. Expenses	Cr. Liabilities

Note: Each adjusting entry will affect one or more income statement accounts and one or more balance sheet accounts.

Interest Computation

Interest = Face value of note × Annual interest rate × Time in terms of one year

CLOSING ENTRIES (Chapter 4)

Purpose

1. Update the Retained Earnings account in the ledger by transferring net income (loss) and dividends to retained earnings.
2. Prepare the temporary accounts (revenue, expense, dividends) for the next period's postings by reducing their balances to zero.

ACCOUNTING CYCLE (Chapter 4)

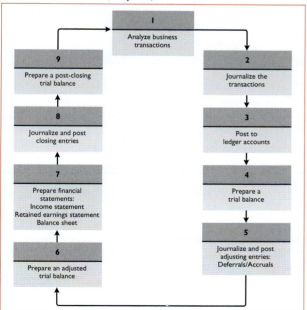

Perpetual vs. Periodic Journal Entries

Event	Perpetual	Periodic
Purchase of goods	Inventory 　Cash (A/P)	Purchases 　Cash (A/P)
Freight (shipping point)	Inventory 　Cash	Freight-In 　Cash
Return of goods	Cash (or A/P) 　Inventory	Cash (or A/P) 　Purchase Returns and Allowances
Sale of goods	Cash (or A/R) 　Sales Cost of Goods Sold 　Inventory	Cash (or A/R) 　Sales No entry
End of period	No entry	Closing or adjusting entry required

FRAUD, INTERNAL CONTROL, AND CASH (Chapter 7)

Principles of Internal Control

Establishment of responsibility
Segregation of duties
Documentation procedures
Physical controls
Independent internal verification
Human resource controls

The Fraud Triangle

Opportunity

Financial pressure — Rationalization

Bank Reconciliation

Bank	Books
Balance per bank statement Add: Deposits in transit	Balance per books Add: Unrecorded credit memoranda from bank statement
Deduct: Outstanding checks	Deduct: Unrecorded debit memoranda from bank statement
Adjusted cash balance	Adjusted cash balance

Note: 1. Errors should be offset (added or deducted) on the side that made the error.
2. Adjusting journal entries should only be made for items affecting books.

STOP AND CHECK: Does the adjusted cash balance in the Cash account equal the reconciled balance?

RAPID REVIEW
Chapter Content

RECEIVABLES (Chapter 8)

Two Methods to Account for Uncollectible Accounts

Direct write-off method	Record bad debt expense when the company determines a particular account to be uncollectible.
Allowance method	At the end of each period, estimate the amount of uncollectible receivables. Debit Bad Debt Expense and credit Allowance for Doubtful Accounts in an amount that results in a balance in the allowance account equal to the estimate of uncollectibles. As specific accounts become uncollectible, debit Allowance for Doubtful Accounts and credit Accounts Receivable.

Steps to Manage Accounts Receivable

1. Determine to whom to extend credit.
2. Establish a payment period.
3. Monitor collections.
4. Evaluate the receivables balance.
5. Accelerate cash receipts from receivables when necessary.

PLANT ASSETS (Chapter 9)

Computation of Annual Depreciation Expense

Straight-line	$\dfrac{\text{Cost} - \text{Salvage value}}{\text{Useful life (in years)}}$
*Declining-balance	Book value at beginning of year $\times$ Declining balance rate* *Declining-balance rate $= 1 \div$ Useful life (in years)
*Units-of-activity	$\dfrac{\text{Depreciable cost}}{\text{Useful life (in units)}} \times$ Units of activity during year

Note: If depreciation is calculated for partial periods, the straight-line and declining-balance methods must be adjusted for the relevant proportion of the year. Multiply the annual depreciation expense by the number of months expired in the year divided by 12 months.

BONDS (Chapter 10)

Premium	Market interest rate $<$ Contractual interest rate
Face Value	Market interest rate $=$ Contractual interest rate
Discount	Market interest rate $>$ Contractual interest rate

Computation of Annual Bond Interest Expense

Interest expense = Interest paid (payable) + Amortization of discount
(OR − Amortization of premium)

*Straight-line amortization	$\dfrac{\text{Bond discount (premium)}}{\text{Number of interest periods}}$	
*Effective-interest amortization (preferred method)	Bond interest expense	Bond interest paid
	Carrying value of bonds at beginning of period $\times$ Effective-interest rate	Face amount of bonds $\times$ Contractual interest rate

STOCKHOLDERS' EQUITY (Chapter 11)

No-Par Value vs. Par Value Stock Journal Entries

No-Par Value	Par Value

Cash
    Common Stock
	Cash
	    Common Stock (par value)
	    Paid-in Capital in Excess of Par Value

Comparison of Dividend Effects

	Cash	Common Stock	Retained Earnings
Cash dividend	↓	No effect	↓
Stock dividend	No effect	↑	↓
Stock split	No effect	No effect	No effect

STATEMENT OF CASH FLOWS (Chapter 12)

Cash flows from operating activities (**indirect method**)

Net income		
Add:	Amortization and depreciation	$ X
	Losses on disposals of assets	X
	Decreases in current assets	X
	Increases in current liabilities	X
Deduct:	Increases in current assets	(X)
	Decreases in current liabilities	(X)
	Gains on disposals of assets	(X)
Cash provided (used) by operating activities		$ X

Cash flows from operating activities (**direct method**)

Cash receipts
  (Examples: from sales of goods and services to customers, from receipts of interest and dividends) $ X
Cash payments
  (Examples: to suppliers, for operating expenses, for interest, for taxes)   (X)
Cash provided (used) by operating activities $ X

FINANCIAL STATEMENT ANALYSIS (Chapter 13)

Discontinued operations	Income statement (presented separately after "Income from continuing operations")
Extraordinary items	Income statement (presented separately after "Discontinued operations")
Changes in accounting principle	In most instances, use the new method in current period and restate previous years' results using new method. For changes in depreciation and amortization methods, use the new method in the current period, but do not restate previous periods.

Income Statement and Comprehensive Income

Sales	$ XX
Cost of goods sold	XX
Gross profit	XX
Operating expenses	XX
Income from operations	XX
Other revenues (expenses) and gains (losses)	XX
Income before income taxes	XX
Income tax expense	XX
Income before irregular items	XX
Irregular items (net of tax)	**XX**
Net income	**XX**
Other comprehensive income items (net of tax)	**XX**
Comprehensive income	**$ XX**

INVESTMENTS (Appendix E)

Comparison of Long-Term Bond Investment and Liability Journal Entries

Event	Investor	Investee

Purchase / issue of bonds	Debt Investments
	    Cash
		Cash
		    Bonds Payable

Interest receipt / payment	Cash
	    Interest Revenue
		Interest Expense
		    Cash

Comparison of Cost and Equity Methods of Accounting for Long-Term Stock Investments

Event	Cost	Equity

Acquisition	Stock Investments
	    Cash
		Stock Investments
		    Cash

Investee reports earnings	No entry	Stock Investments Investment Revenue

Investee pays dividends	Cash
	    Dividend Revenue
		Cash
		    Stock Investments

*Items with asterisk are covered in appendix.

Financial Statements

Order of Preparation	Date
1. Income statement	For the period ended
2. Retained earnings statement	For the period ended
3. Balance sheet	As of the end of the period
4. Statement of cash flows	For the period ended

Income Statement (perpetual inventory system)

Name of Company **Income Statement** **For the Period Ended**		
Sales revenues		
Sales	$ X	
Less: Sales returns and allowances	X	
Sales discounts	X	
Net sales		$ X
Cost of goods sold		X
Gross profit		X
Operating expenses		
(Examples: store salaries, advertising, delivery, rent, depreciation, utilities, insurance)		X
Income from operations		X
Other revenues and gains		
(Examples: interest, gains)	X	
Other expenses and losses		
(Examples: interest, losses)	X	X
Income before income taxes		X
Income tax expense		X
Net income		$ X

Income Statement (periodic inventory system)

Name of Company **Income Statement** **For the Period Ended**			
Sales revenues			
Sales		$ X	
Less: Sales returns and allowances		X	
Sales discounts		X	
Net sales			$ X
Cost of goods sold			
Beginning inventory		X	
Purchases	$ X		
Less: Purchase returns and allowances	X		
Net purchases	X		
Add: Freight in	X		
Cost of goods purchased		X	
Cost of goods available for sale		X	
Less: Ending inventory		X	
Cost of goods sold			X
Gross profit			X
Operating expenses			
(Examples: store salaries, advertising, delivery, rent, depreciation, utilities, insurance)			X
Income from operations			X
Other revenues and gains			
(Examples: interest, gains)		X	
Other expenses and losses			
(Examples: interest, losses)		X	X
Income before income taxes			X
Income tax expense			X
Net income			$ X

Retained Earnings Statement

Name of Company **Retained Earnings Statement** **For the Period Ended**	
Retained earnings, beginning of period	$ X
Add: Net income (or deduct net loss)	X
	X
Deduct: Dividends	X
Retained earnings, end of period	$ X

STOP AND CHECK: Net income (loss) presented on the retained earnings statement must equal the net income (loss) presented on the income statement.

Balance Sheet

Name of Company **Balance Sheet** **As of the End of the Period**			
Assets			
Current assets			
(Examples: cash, short-term investments, accounts receivable, inventory, prepaids)			$ X
Long-term investments			
(Examples: investments in bonds, investments in stocks)			X
Property, plant, and equipment			
Land		$ X	
Buildings and equipment	$ X		
Less: Accumulated depreciation	X	X	X
Intangible assets			X
Total assets			$ X
Liabilities and Stockholders' Equity			
Liabilities			
Current liabilities			
(Examples: notes payable, accounts payable, accruals, unearned revenues, current portion of notes payable)			$ X
Long-term liabilities			
(Examples: notes payable, bonds payable)			X
Total liabilities			X
Stockholders' equity			
Common stock			X
Retained earnings			X
Total liabilities and stockholders' equity			$ X

STOP AND CHECK: Total assets on the balance sheet must equal total liabilities plus stockholders' equity; and, ending retained earnings on the balance sheet must equal ending retained earnings on the retained earnings statement.

Statement of Cash Flows

Name of Company **Statement of Cash Flows** **For the Period Ended**	
Cash flows from operating activities	
Note: May be prepared using the direct or indirect method	
Cash provided (used) by operating activities	$ X
Cash flows from investing activities	
(Examples: purchase / sale of long-term assets)	
Cash provided (used) by investing activities	X
Cash flows from financing activities	
(Examples: issue / repayment of long-term liabilities, issue of stock, payment of dividends)	
Cash provided (used) by financing activities	X
Net increase (decrease) in cash	X
Cash, beginning of the period	X
Cash, end of the period	$ X

STOP AND CHECK: Cash, end of the period, on the statement of cash flows must equal cash presented on the balance sheet.

RAPID REVIEW
Tools for Analysis

Liquidity

Working capital	Current assets − Current liabilities	p. 51
Current ratio	$\dfrac{\text{Current assets}}{\text{Current liabilities}}$	p. 52
Current cash debt coverage	$\dfrac{\text{Cash provided by operations}}{\text{Average current liabilities}}$	p. 560
Inventory turnover	$\dfrac{\text{Cost of goods sold}}{\text{Average inventory}}$	p. 253
Days in inventory	$\dfrac{365 \text{ days}}{\text{Inventory turnover}}$	p. 253
Accounts receivable turnover	$\dfrac{\text{Net credit sales}}{\text{Average net accounts receivable}}$	p. 357
Average collection period	$\dfrac{365 \text{ days}}{\text{Accounts receivable turnover}}$	p. 357

Solvency

Debt to assets ratio	$\dfrac{\text{Total liabilities}}{\text{Total assets}}$	p. 53
Cash debt coverage	$\dfrac{\text{Net cash provided by operating activities}}{\text{Average total liabilities}}$	p. 559
Times interest earned	$\dfrac{\text{Net income + Interest expense + Tax expense}}{\text{Interest expense}}$	p. 453
Free cash flow	Net cash provided by operating activities − Capital expenditures − Cash dividends	p. 54

Profitability

Earnings per share	$\dfrac{\text{Net income − Preferred dividends}}{\text{Average common shares outstanding}}$	p. 49
Price-earnings ratio	$\dfrac{\text{Stock price per share}}{\text{Earnings per share}}$	p. 612
Gross profit rate	$\dfrac{\text{Gross profit}}{\text{Net sales}}$	p. 209
Profit margin	$\dfrac{\text{Net income}}{\text{Net sales}}$	p. 210
Return on assets	$\dfrac{\text{Net income}}{\text{Average total assets}}$	p. 399
Asset turnover	$\dfrac{\text{Net sales}}{\text{Average total assets}}$	p. 400
Payout ratio	$\dfrac{\text{Cash dividends declared on common stock}}{\text{Net income}}$	p. 515
Return on common stockholders' equity	$\dfrac{\text{Net income − Preferred dividends}}{\text{Average common stockholders' equity}}$	p. 516